# MODERN ADVANCED
# ACCOUNTING
## IN CANADA
### 8TH EDITION

**Darrell Herauf, CPA, CA, CGA**
Carleton University

**Murray W. Hilton, FCPA, FCA**
University of Manitoba

Mc
Graw
Hill
Education

**Modern Advanced Accounting in Canada**
**Eighth Edition**

The Internet addresses listed in the text were accurate at the time of publication. The inclusion of a web site does not indicate an endorsement by the authors or McGraw-Hill Ryerson, and McGraw-Hill Ryerson does not guarantee the accuracy of the information presented at these sites.

ISBN-13: 978-1-25-908755-4
ISBN-10: 1-25-908755-7

4 5 6 7 8 9 CTPS 1 9 8 7

Printed and bound in China.

Care has been taken to trace ownership of copyright material contained in this text; however, the publisher will welcome any information that enables them to rectify any reference or credit for subsequent editions.

Director of Product Management: *Rhondda McNabb*
Product Manager: *Keara Emmett*
Executive Marketing Manager: *Joy Armitage Taylor*
Product Developer: *Amy Rydzanicz*
Senior Product Team Associate: *Stephanie Giles*
Supervising Editor: *Jessica Barnoski*
Photo/Permissions Editor: *Nadine Bachan, MRM Associates*
Copy Editor: *Rodney Rawlings*
Plant Production Coordinator: *Sarah Strynatka*
Manufacturing Production Coordinator: *Sheryl MacAdam*
Cover Design: *Liz Harasymczuk*
Cover Image: *J.A. Kraulis/Masterfile*
Interior Design: *Liz Harasymczuk*
Page Layout: *SPi Global*
Printer: *China Translation & Printing Services Limited*

# About the Authors

### Darrell Herauf, CPA, CA, CGA

Darrell Herauf teaches graduate and undergraduate courses in financial accounting at the Eric Sprott School of Business, Carleton University. A Chartered Professional Accountant with a business degree from the University of Saskatchewan, this co-author of *Modern Advanced Accounting in Canada* has also been the author of test banks and reviewer for several financial accounting textbooks. He is the recipient of numerous teaching awards, and participates on many committees at the university. He has been active in faculty administration, having previously served as Accounting Area Coordinator and as Acting Director of the Master of Accounting Program. Darrell has been involved in professional accounting education at the Chartered Professional Accountants of Ontario for over 30 years in a variety of roles, including teaching, developing case/program material, and serving as a member of the Examinations subcommittee. For 28 years, he has been involved with the Certified General Accountants Association of Canada as national examiner, course author, and consultant. For relaxation, he enjoys cycling and skating.

### Murray W. Hilton, FCPA, FCA

Murray Hilton holds the rank of Senior Scholar at the University of Manitoba where he has continued to teach in the MBA programs since his retirement in 2002. For 35 years, he was Professor of Accounting at the university's Asper School of Business, teaching graduate and undergraduate courses in financial accounting. A Chartered Professional Accountant with business degrees from the University of Saskatchewan and Oregon State University, he has published five advanced accounting books. In addition, he has been active in university and faculty administration, having previously served as Head of the Department of Accounting and Finance and as Director of the Master of Accountancy Program. He is currently the Director of the Centre for Accounting Research and Education. Murray has also been very involved in the accounting profession, teaching CA and CMA courses for many years, and serving on numerous national and provincial committees of both accounting bodies. He has on two separate occasions been a member of the National Examination Board of the Society of Management Accountants of Canada. In 1991, he received the FCA designation from the Institute of Chartered Accountants of Manitoba, and in 1994 he was made an honorary member of the Society of Management Accountants of Manitoba. For relaxation, he enjoys reading, golfing, and fishing.

# Contents in Brief

# Contents

Contents

## CHAPTER 5
## Consolidation Subsequent to Acquisition Date 221

## CHAPTER 6
## Intercompany Inventory and Land Profits 319

Contents

# Preface

Welcome to the eighth edition of *Modern Advanced Accounting in Canada*. This book's reputation as the most current and technically accurate advanced accounting text on the market has been not only maintained but also improved upon in this new edition. This edition is 100% compliant with International Financial Reporting Standards (IFRSs), not only with regard to the typical advanced accounting topics of business combinations and foreign currency transactions, but also for the topics studied in intermediate accounting and other courses. It also contains the reporting requirements for private enterprises and not-for-profit organizations. All of the extracts from financial statements are taken from Canadian entities.

The book reflects standards expected to be in effect as of January 1, 2017, based on standards approved by the IASB or on exposure drafts that were outstanding as of December 31, 2015. We have made every effort to illustrate and explain the requirements of those standards current at the time of publication, anticipating how these might change, what the effects of the changes will be, and what they will mean to the industry, professionals, and students.

We have also continued the presentation of advanced accounting topics that has been so well received by so many instructors and students. Emphasis on the direct approach of preparing consolidated financial statements along with the "building block" development of the basics of consolidations has been maintained and strengthened. The working paper approach is illustrated in Chapters 3 through 5, in either the body or the appendices. Excel Worksheet Files are now available online to support the use of the working paper approach for 14 self-study problems.

Finally, as requested by instructors on behalf of their students, the following enhancements to problem material have been made in this edition:

- At least one new case has been added to each chapter to encourage critical thinking and classroom discussion. There are now five to seven cases in each chapter.
- The questions and/or solutions have been revised for approximately 58% of the end-of-chapter cases and problems.
- The number of algorithmic problems has increased from three to five per chapter to six to ten per chapter.
- Excel Worksheet Files are now available online to support the use of the working paper approach for 16 end-of-chapter problems.

## New Features

- A major section has been added in Chapter 1 on how to analyze a financial reporting case.
- Both the gross and net methods are now used to account for a forward contract in the first illustration in Chapter 9. All subsequent illustrations in the chapter and all solutions to end-of-chapter problems have been changed from the gross method to the net method.
- The learning objectives listed at the beginning of each chapter are now directly linked to the summary comments at end of each chapter.
- A major reorganization of topics has been made in Chapters 2, 11, and 12.
- There has been a substantial rewrite of certain topics in Chapters 4, 5, 6, and 8.

- Dated materials and/or methods have been removed in five chapters.
- Enhanced Connect technology (including new SmartBook adaptive reading and learning content) and new Connect Insight visual data analytics have been added.

# Organization

**Chapter 1** begins with an overview of the conceptual framework for financial reporting. The remainder of the chapter presents an overview of the different parts of the *CPA Canada Handbook*. Some of the major differences between IFRSs and ASPE are identified. A framework to solve an accounting and financial reporting case is added as an appendix.

**Chapter 2** commences with an overview of the different types of equity investments. The chapter continues with a comprehensive example to illustrate the fair value, cost, and equity methods of reporting investments in equity securities, and it concludes with two self-study problems that compare these different reporting methods. Coverage of the comprehensive example can be postponed until after Chapter 4 without breaking continuity, or omitted altogether if it is felt that adequate coverage has occurred in previous intermediate accounting courses. The new standard on financial instruments (IFRS 9) is briefly described.

**Chapter 3** describes three forms of business combinations. The definition of control is discussed and used as the criterion for preparation of consolidated financial statements. The direct and working paper methods are used to illustrate the acquisition method of accounting for a business combination. The new entity method is mentioned as an alternative method of accounting for business combinations for future consideration. Reverse takeovers are covered in an appendix.

**Chapter 4** examines the preparation of consolidated financial statements for non–wholly owned subsidiaries at the date of acquisition. The direct method is used in the body of the chapter and the working paper method is used in the appendix. Four theories of consolidation are mentioned, three of which are illustrated. All four are currently or have recently been required under Canadian GAAP. Accounting for contingent consideration and bargain purchases are also illustrated.

**Chapter 5** covers the preparation of consolidated financial statements subsequent to the date of acquisition when the parent uses the cost method in its internal records. The amortization and impairment of the acquisition differential is explained and illustrated, including an application of the effective interest method. Appendix A provides an enhanced discussion of goodwill impairment. The parent's journal entries under the equity method are summarized. Ten basic steps in the preparation of consolidated statements are introduced, forming the foundation for the consolidation topics in the chapters that follow. The direct approach is used in the body of the chapter. Appendix B illustrates the working paper approach for the same examples used throughout the chapter.

**Chapter 6** discusses and illustrates the accounting for intercompany revenues and expenses, as well as intercompany unrealized profits or losses in inventory and land. The revenue recognition, matching, and historical cost principles are used to explain the rationale for consolidation adjustments associated with the holdback and realization of intercompany profits. The consolidation adjustments when the entities use the revaluation model for reporting land are described in the appendix.

**Chapter 7** discusses the elimination of intercompany profits in depreciable assets, the recognition of gains or losses resulting from the elimination of intercompany bondholdings, and the related income tax adjustments required. Two self-study problems are presented using the direct approach and involving the effective interest method for bond amortization. The consolidation adjustments when an entity uses the revaluation model for reporting depreciable assets are described in the appendix.

**Chapter 8** discusses the preparation of the consolidated cash flow statement and such ownership issues as step purchases, reduction of parent's interest, subsidiaries with preferred shares, and indirect holdings. In all situations, the direct approach is used. The chapter concludes with two self-study problems involving changes in ownership and preferred shares.

**Chapter 9** examines other consolidation reporting issues, including special-purpose entities, deferred income taxes and business combinations, and segment disclosures. The accounting for joint arrangements is illustrated using the equity method or a form of proportionate consolidation. The chapter concludes with two self-study problems involving joint arrangements and deferred income taxes pertaining to business combinations.

**Chapter 10** introduces the topic of foreign currency and four different perspectives in which currencies can be viewed. Foreign currency transactions and the concepts of hedging and hedge accounting are discussed. The handling of foreign currency gains and losses is illustrated, as is the accounting for fair value and cash flow hedges. The appendix describes how discounting can be applied when determining the fair value of a forward contract.

**Chapter 11** concludes the foreign currency portion of the text by examining and illustrating the translation and subsequent consolidation of subsidiaries whose functional currencies are the same as the parent's and whose functional currencies are not the same as the parent's functional currency. The reporting of exchange gains and losses in other comprehensive income is also illustrated. The chapter concludes with two self-study problems on the translation of a foreign operation under the two translation methods and the preparation of consolidated financial statements after translating the foreign operations.

**Chapter 12** discusses in depth the 13 not-for-profit sections in the *CPA Canada Handbook*. The chapter concludes with a comprehensive illustration of the required journal entries and the preparation of financial statements using both the deferral method and the restricted fund method. Appendix A provides a real-life example of the deferral method by reproducing portions of the financial statements of the United Way/Centraide Ottawa. Appendix B illustrates the accounting for "net assets invested in capital assets" as a separate component of net assets. Appendix C provides a comprehensive outline of the PSAB reporting requirements for federal, provincial, and local governments.

## Market Leading Technology

### Learn without Limits

McGraw-Hill Connect® is an award-winning digital teaching and learning platform that gives students the means to better connect with their coursework, with their instructors, and with the important concepts they will need for success now and in the future. With Connect, instructors can take advantage of McGraw-Hill's trusted content to seamlessly deliver assignments, quizzes, and tests online. The platform continuously adapts to individual students, delivering precisely what they need when they need it, so class time is more engaging and effective. It makes teaching and learning personal, easy, and proven.

# Connect Key Features

## SmartBook®

As the first and only adaptive reading experience, SmartBook is changing the way students read and learn. It enables personalized reading by continuously adapting the reading experience, highlighting the most important concepts a student needs to learn at any given moment. This ensures that the student is focused on the content that closes his or her specific knowledge gaps—at the same time promoting long-term learning.

## Connect Insight®

Connect Insight is Connect's new, one-of-a-kind visual analytics dashboard—now available for instructors—that provides at-a-glance information regarding student performance that is immediately actionable. By presenting assignment, assessment, and topical performance results together with a time metric that is easily visible for aggregate or individual results, Connect Insight gives the instructor the ability to take a just-in-time approach to teaching and learning, something never before available. It presents data that helps instructors improve class performance efficiently and effectively.

## Simple Assignment Management

With Connect, creating assignments is easier than ever, so instructors spend more time teaching and less time managing. With it, one can

- assign SmartBook learning modules;
- edit existing questions and create new ones;
- draw on a variety of text-specific questions, resources, and test bank material to assign online;
- streamline lesson planning, student progress reporting, and assignment grading to make classroom management more efficient than ever.

## Smart Grading

When it comes to studying, time is precious. Connect helps students learn more efficiently by providing feedback and practice material when they need it, where they need it:

- automatically score assignments, giving students immediate feedback on their work and comparisons with correct answers;
- access and review each response;
- manually change grades or leave comments for students to review;
- track individual student performance—by question, by assignment, or in relation to the class overall—with detailed grade reports;
- reinforce classroom concepts with practice tests and instant quizzes;
- integrate grade reports easily with learning management systems such as Blackboard, D2L, and Moodle.

## Instructor Library

The Connect Instructor Library is a repository for additional resources to improve student engagement in and out of the class. It provides all the critical resources instructors need to build their course:

- access instructor resources;
- view assignments and resources created for past sections;
- post your own resources for students to use.

## Instructor Resources

The following instructor resources are available online on Connect:

- **Solutions Manual.** This manual, prepared by the author, contains complete solutions to all the text's end-of-chapter review questions, cases, problems, and web-based problems.
- **Computerized Test Bank.** This test bank contains over 1,000 multiple-choice, true/false, and problem questions. Each test item is coded for level of difficulty and learning objective.
- **Microsoft® PowerPoint® Presentations.** These slides cover key concepts found in each chapter using outlines, summaries, and visuals.

# Superior Learning Solutions and Support

The McGraw-Hill Education team is ready to help you assess and integrate any of our products, technology, and services into your course for optimal teaching and learning performance. Whether it's helping your students improve their grades or putting your entire course online, the team is here to help you do it. Contact your Learning Solutions Consultant today to learn how to maximize all of the resources!

For more information on the latest technology and Learning Solutions offered by McGraw-Hill Education and its partners, please visit us online at www.mheducation.ca/he/solutions.

# Acknowledgments

This text includes the thoughts and contributions of many individuals, and we wish to express our sincere appreciation to them. First and foremost, we thank all the students in our advanced accounting classes, from whom we have learned so much. In many respects, this text is an outcome of the learning experiences we have shared with our students. Second, we wish to thank the technical checkers, Ingrid McLeod-Dick and Stephen Spector. The accuracy of the text is due in large part to their efforts. We also wish to thank the following colleagues for their invaluable advice:

Talal Al-Hayale, *University of Windsor*
Pauline Downer, *Memorial University of Newfoundland*
Maureen Fizzell, *Simon Fraser University*
Stephen Hussey, *Algoma University*
Michelle Lum, *University of Waterloo*
Karen Matthews, *Okanagan College*
Carrie McMillan, *NAIT*
Akash Rattan, *Langara College*
Kevin Veenstra, *University of Toronto*
Barbara Wyntjes, *Kwantlen Polytechnic University*

Thanks also to the Chartered Professional Accountants of Canada for granting permission to reproduce material from the *CPA Canada Handbook* as well as questions from the Uniform Final Examinations (UFEs), and to the Certified General Accountants of Canada and the Certified Management Accountants for their permission to reproduce questions adapted from past examinations. Thank you to Peter Secord of St. Mary's University for all of his case contributions.

Thank you to Robert Ducharme of University of Waterloo for his work on the Test Bank, SmartBook, and Connect materials for this edition. Thanks also to Shannon Butler of Carleton University for her work on this edition's PowerPoint Presentations.

We are very grateful to the staff at McGraw-Hill Education: Director of Product Management Rhondda McNabb, Product Manager Keara Emmett, Product Developer Amy Rydzanicz, and Supervising Editor Jessica Barnoski, who applied pressure in a gentle but persistent manner when we strayed from the project's schedule. Thanks also to Copy Editor Rodney Rawlings, whose technical expertise was necessary to carry the project to its end.

And finally, we are grateful to our families for all of their support and encouragement. I, Darrell, want to especially thank my brother, Herb Herauf, who has been my mentor and strongest supporter over my entire academic career.

**Darrell Herauf**
*Sprott School of Business*
*Carleton University*

**Murray Hilton**
*Asper School of Business*
*University of Manitoba*

# CHAPTER 1

# Conceptual and Case Analysis Frameworks for Financial Reporting

## LEARNING OBJECTIVES

**After studying this chapter, you should be able to do the following:**

**LO1** Describe and apply the conceptual framework for financial reporting.

**LO2** Describe how accounting standards in Canada are tailored to different types of organizations.

**LO3** Identify some of the differences between IFRS and ASPE.

**LO4** Analyze and interpret financial statements to assess the impact of different accounting methods on key financial statement ratios.

**LO5** (Appendix 1A) Apply the case analysis framework to solve accounting and reporting issues.

## Introduction

Welcome to advanced accounting. We wish you a prosperous learning experience. We will study three major accounting topics: consolidations, foreign currency transactions and operations, and not-for-profit and government organizations. The topics are presented and illustrated in accordance with the generally accepted accounting principles (GAAP) that are expected to be in effect in Canada as of January 1, 2017. You may have had some exposure to these topics in your previous accounting courses. We will build on this prior knowledge while we develop a thorough understanding of these selected topics.

Prior to 2008, the study of accounting principles in Canada focused on made-in-Canada accounting standards and involved very little, if any, thought or discussion of accounting standards in other parts of the world. Since then, Canada has adopted International Financial Reporting Standards (IFRS) for public companies and has separate sections in the *CPA Canada Handbook* for public companies, private companies, not-for-profit organizations, and pension plans. The changes in reporting standards were due to the globalization of economic activity. Canadian companies now view the entire world as their marketplace. Not only are they exporting their products to more countries than ever before, but they are also establishing factories and offices in foreign locations. Companies that used to raise capital strictly in their home countries are now finding that capital markets are available to them around the world. Many accounting firms have offices throughout the world, and there are abundant opportunities for their Canadian staff members to transfer to these offices.

> *Canadian companies are now able to raise capital resources in the world's marketplace.*

In this chapter, we will begin by reviewing the conceptual framework for financial reporting. We will then describe and apply a framework for analyzing financial reporting cases. We will close by analyzing the impact of different financial reporting methods on key ratios in a company's financial statements.

## LO1 THE CONCEPTUAL FRAMEWORK FOR FINANCIAL REPORTING

Professional accountants provide a variety of services ranging from accounting to tax planning to assurance to business consulting. In this course, we will focus on financial accounting—that is, providing general-purpose financial information to external users such as investors and creditors. These users usually have limited financial resources to invest in an entity. Users wish to invest where they can earn the highest return with the lowest amount of risk. The general-purpose set of financial statements (balance sheet, income statement, statement of changes in equity, cash flow statement, and notes to the financial statements) will be used by the external users to help them make their resource allocation decisions and to assess the stewardship of management. The general-purpose reports are not the only source of information used for decision making but provide a good starting point.

> **Cautionary Note:** *The titles of the financial statements in International Accounting Standard (IAS) 1 are the recommended titles, but not mandatory. Many Canadian companies now use and will likely continue to use the titles* balance sheet *(rather than* statement of financial position*) and* income statement *(rather than* statement of profit or loss*). In this textbook, we will use both sets of titles. We will also vary the ordering of assets, liabilities, and shareholders' equity. In some cases, current assets will appear first and shareholders' equity will appear last. In other cases, long-term assets will be followed by current assets and shareholders' equity will precede liabilities on the credit side of the statement of financial position. Both formats are acceptable under IAS 1. In the problems and illustrations that do not involve other comprehensive income (OCI), we will focus only on the statement of profit or loss (i.e., the income statement) rather than the statement of comprehensive income, and on preparing a statement of retained earnings rather than preparing a complete statement of changes in equity.*

In most cases, users want to receive the general-purpose financial statements prepared in accordance with generally accepted accounting principles (GAAP) because by following these principles the information is made relevant, reliable, understandable, and comparable. However, there are times when users may want or require special-purpose financial reports that do not follow GAAP. For example, entities may need to prepare non-GAAP-based statements for legislative or regulatory purposes or for contract compliance. Or a prospective lender may want to receive a balance sheet with assets reported at fair value rather than historical cost. As accountants, we are able to provide financial information in a variety of formats or using a variety of accounting policies, because we have the skills and abilities to produce this information. If we do provide fair-value-based financial statements, we cannot say that the statements were prepared in accordance with GAAP. We would simply state that the statements were prepared in accordance with the policies described in the notes to the financial statements.

GAAP encompass broad principles and conventions of general application, as well as rules and procedures that determine accepted accounting practices at a particular time. The process of developing GAAP is political. Both preparers and users of financial statements have an opportunity to comment on a proposal for a new accounting standard before it becomes generally accepted. If a new requirement is preferred by the preparers but not accepted by users, it is unlikely to become part of GAAP. Therefore, as we study existing accounting practices and proposed changes, we need to continually evaluate whether information provided by a reporting entity will satisfy users' needs.

> *Financial statements should cater to the needs of the users.*

In most cases, the users of the financial statements have access to information about the entity in addition to that provided in the financial statements. For example, the owner of a private company may also be the manager and would have intimate knowledge of the company. In such cases, the owner/manager may place less reliance on the financial statements than outside investors in public companies do. In other situations, the owner may not understand the financial reporting for complex transactions such as business combinations. In both of these situations, the owners may feel that the costs of complying with some of the complex sections of the *Handbook* are not worth the benefit. They may prefer to issue more simplified statements. The Chartered Professional Accountants of Canada (CPA Canada) recognized this difference in users' needs. In 2011, the *Handbook* was reorganized and is now segregated into different parts for different types of organizations.

> *The* Handbook *is divided into different parts to cater to different types of reporting entities.*

The *CPA Canada Handbook* is an authoritative document in Canada because many legal statutes require its use. For example, companies incorporated under the *Canada Business Corporations Act* and certain provincial "Companies Acts" are required to prepare financial statements in accordance with the *CPA Canada Handbook*. Publicly traded companies are required to submit financial statements that comply with GAAP to the securities commissions under which they are registered.

The *CPA Canada Handbook* provides the accounting and reporting requirements as well as explanations and guidance for most transactions and events encountered by an entity. When an entity following IFRS encounters transactions or events not explicitly addressed by the standards, it should adopt accounting practices consistent with the spirit of the standards and consistent with financial statement concepts. These concepts are described in the "The Conceptual Framework for Financial Reporting," a document found just prior to IFRS in Part I of the *Handbook*. Entities reporting under Accounting Standards for Private Enterprises (ASPE) should adopt accounting practices consistent with Section 1000 *Financial Statement Concepts* in Part II of the *Handbook*.

The *financial statement concepts* describe the principles and assumptions underlying the preparation of financial statements. They are very important parts of GAAP, because they provide the framework for the development and issuance of other financial accounting standards. The main items included in this document are as follows:

- The objective of general-purpose financial reporting
- Qualitative characteristics of useful financial information
- Underlying assumptions
- Definition, recognition, and measurement of the elements of financial statements

You will probably recognize most of the concepts and remember studying them in your intermediate accounting courses. If you can explain the accounting practices learned there in terms of these basic concepts, you should have no trouble applying these concepts in the new situations we will encounter in this course. If you do not understand or cannot explain accounting requirements in terms of these basic concepts, it is never too late. As you study the accounting requirements in this course, try to understand them in terms of the basic concepts and principles the *Handbook* describes.

> *All accounting practices should be able to be traced back to and supported by the conceptual framework.*

By gaining a broad understanding of the logic and basic principles behind the accounting requirements, you will develop confidence and be able to apply these basic principles in a wide variety of situations. Rather than simply accepting accounting practices or memorizing specific requirements in the *Handbook*, you will begin to understand the logic of the requirements and evaluate whether these are consistent with the basic financial statement concepts. You will soon realize that most of the requirements in accounting can be understood, developed, and derived from these basic principles and concepts. Then, in turn, you will be able to use professional judgment to apply these principles to whatever situation you may encounter.

## Professional Judgment

Judgment is the ability to make a decision in situations in which the answer is not clear-cut. Professional judgment is the ability to make decisions for issues encountered by professionals in carrying out their day-to-day responsibilities. It is a skill developed over many years of studying and learning from one's experiences. It is not learned by memorization of requirements or answers to certain problems. It often involves choices between meaningful alternatives and the ability to understand the consequences of one's actions.

> *Lots of judgment is involved when preparing financial statements.*

In the preparation of financial statements, judgment needs to be applied in three main areas. First, accounting policies such as when to recognize revenue and whether to consolidate a special-purpose entity involve making a decision after considering various methods. The method adopted for a particular company must be appropriate for that company on the basis of its existing situation. For example, if Company A is selling to customers with poor credit histories and without obtaining security for the receivables from these customers, it is appropriate to recognize revenue when cash is received. If competitors are selling to customers with very high credit ratings, it is appropriate for them to recognize revenue when the goods are delivered. The professional judgment of an accountant will take these factors into consideration and recognize that although one method might be appropriate for the competitors, another might be more appropriate for Company A.

Second, judgment is involved in making accounting estimates of many kinds. What is the estimated useful life of property, plant, and equipment? What is the recoverable amount for goodwill? Will a forward contract be effective as a hedge of expected sales for the next three years? The answers to these questions are not clearly defined. In the classroom, we are usually provided with this information, but in the real world we must gather data and make our own assessment. Whether we feel that the company can continue as a going concern or not would likely have a material impact on the valuation of goodwill and the bottom line on the income statement.

> *Judgment is involved when adopting accounting policies, making estimates, and writing the notes to the financial statements.*

Third, judgment is involved in deciding what to disclose and how to disclose it in the notes to the financial statements. For example, in disclosing a contingent liability resulting from a lawsuit, the company might simply say that it has been sued but no provision is made in the financial statements because it feels that the lawsuit has no merit; or it might provide details of the lawsuit and give some probabilities of different outcomes in the note.

Is there too much latitude in accounting? Do the financial statements ever portray the complete facts? One could argue that there is no latitude because accountants are not free to randomly select any reporting method. They must represent faithfully what really happened and what really exists using the generally accepted conceptual framework. If the revenue has been earned, then the revenue should be recognized. If the expenditure will provide a future benefit, then the cost of the expenditure should be recognized as an asset. Latitude is necessary so that the accountant can choose the accounting treatment to reflect the real situation. If the requirements are written too rigidly, companies may be forced to use methods that do not reflect their own situations.

> *Financial statements should present what really happened during the period: that is, they should tell it how it is.*

If accountants take their jobs seriously and have high ethical standards, they will present the financial statements as reliably as possible by using appropriate accounting policies, by making the best estimates possible, and by making honest and forthright statements in the notes to the financial statements. They will use judgment to fairly present the financial position and financial performance of the entity. Otherwise, the individual accountants and the entire accounting profession will lose credibility.

In this course, we will have an opportunity to develop our judgment skills and to exercise judgment through the use of cases. The cases provide realistic scenarios where conflicts exist and choices must be made. As we have indicated, the answers are not usually clear-cut. In fact, different valid answers can be defended. For these cases, it is how you support your recommendation that is important, as opposed to what your final recommendation is. You will need to apply basic principles and use judgment to come up with an answer that "tells it how it is" as accurately as possible. In so doing, you will be developing the skills required of a professional accountant. See Appendix 1A for a discussion and illustration of a generic approach for analyzing and solving a case with issues in the domain of the aspiring accountant.

## LO2 ACCOUNTING STANDARDS IN CANADA

The *CPA Canada Handbook* contains five parts as follows:

| Part # | Applicable To: | Name for Standards |
|---|---|---|
| I | Publicly accountable entities | IFRS |
| II | Private enterprises | ASPE |
| III | Not-for-profit organizations | |
| IV | Pension plans | |
| V | All entities not yet using other parts | Pre-changeover GAAP |

The next few sections describe a bit of the history behind the development of different standards for different entities and the choices available for these entities in applying the different parts of the *CPA Canada Handbook.*

**GAAP FOR PUBLICLY ACCOUNTABLE ENTERPRISES**   Public companies seemed to be moving toward American accounting standards when in 1998 the CPA Canada announced that it would work with the Financial Accounting Standards Board (FASB) to harmonize the accounting standards of the United States and Canada, at the same time encouraging the International Accounting Standards Board (IASB) in its efforts to develop global accounting standards.

> *At one time, Canada intended to harmonize its standards with those of the United States.*

The concept of harmonization would probably have proven to be a fairly difficult one, because Canadian accounting standards tend to be broad-based while American standards tend to be based on detailed rules. This problem was alleviated when the CPA Canada's position changed in 2006 with the announcement of the adoption of a strategic plan that would see the harmonization of the *CPA Canada Handbook* with IFRS for *publicly accountable enterprises.* A publicly accountable enterprise (PAE) is defined as an entity other than a not-for-profit organization or a government or another entity in the public sector that

(i) has issued, or is in the process of issuing, debt or equity instruments that are, or will be, outstanding and traded in a public market (a domestic or foreign stock exchange or an over-the-counter market, including local and regional markets), or

(ii) holds assets in a fiduciary capacity for a broad group of outsiders as one of its primary businesses.

> *Canadian publicly accountable enterprises had to report under IFRS starting in 2011.*

Banks, credit unions, insurance companies, securities brokers or dealers, mutual funds, and investment banks typically meet the second of these criteria. Other entities may also hold assets in a fiduciary capacity for a broad group of outsiders, because they hold and manage financial resources entrusted to them by clients, customers, or members not involved in the management of the entity. However, if an entity does so for reasons incidental to one of its primary businesses (as, for example, may be the case for some travel or real estate agents, or cooperative enterprises requiring a nominal membership deposit), it is not considered publicly accountable.

Harmonization was chosen instead of the simple adoption of the international standards because security regulations and federal and provincial Companies Acts require financial reporting to be in accordance with Canadian GAAP. Because of this requirement, Part I of the *CPA Canada Handbook* now contains standards that are the same as IFRS. Rather than always referring to Part I of the *Handbook*, we will simply refer to IFRS. Commencing in 2011, Canadian publicly accountable enterprises had to report under IFRS.

> *Part I of the* CPA Canada Handbook *contains IFRS.*

The IFRSs were quite similar to Canadian standards prior to the adoption of the international standards, because they are based on similar conceptual frameworks and reach similar conclusions. However, there were many differences in the detailed requirements. IFRS often allow for optional treatments and in some instances allow or require the use of fair values in financial statement measurements, whereas Canadian standards did not often allow optional treatments and tended to require more historical cost measurements.

> *IFRS allows the use of fair values and optional treatments to a greater degree than pre-changeover Canadian GAAP (Part V of the CPA Canada Handbook).*

**GAAP FOR PRIVATE ENTERPRISES**   In the 1970s, there was considerable discussion in Canada of Big GAAP versus Little GAAP. The question was: Should there be different standards for big companies and little companies?

It was argued that accounting standards were becoming increasingly complex and that a small company's costs of preparing its financial statements in compliance with the standards were greater than the benefits received by the users of such statements. Hence, small companies should be granted some sort of relief from having to use complex and hard-to-understand standards. Counterarguments suggested that the concept of fair presentation and comparability could not be achieved with different sets of standards, and the dividing line between big and small would be too arbitrary to be useful. After much study and discussion, the concept of Big GAAP/Little GAAP was abandoned.

> *The cost-benefit constraint is used when determining whether a private enterprise can use simpler reporting methods.*

In the meantime, the issuance of new, complex financial reporting standards continued, and the last straw, so to speak, was the issuance of both the section on presentation and disclosure of financial instruments and the exposure draft on the related measurement issues in the early 1990s. The issue of different standards was revisited by a CPA Canada task force, but this time in relation to public versus non-public companies. The task force considered two basic approaches:

- A non-GAAP approach whereby non-public companies could use accounting policies completely separate from GAAP. An example is the use of cash-basis reporting instead of the required accrual basis. This approach was abandoned mainly because provincial and federal Companies Acts require companies to prepare financial statements in accordance with the *CPA Canada Handbook*.

- A GAAP approach. This was looked at from two perspectives: full differentiation and partial differentiation. Full differentiation would encompass two distinct sets of GAAP, somewhat similar to the accounting for non-profit organizations and governments (discussed in Chapter 12). Partial differentiation encompasses one set of accounting standards with different treatments. This latter approach was adopted in 2002 when Section 1300 *Differential Reporting* was issued and certain sections of the *CPA Canada Handbook* were amended to allow optional treatments.

> *Companies were following GAAP when they adopted differential reporting options.*

Section 1300 allowed a qualifying enterprise to select which reporting options it would apply when it prepared its financial statements. The differential reporting options allowed were contained in individual *Handbook* sections, and only a few sections contained such options.

Section 1300 was a part of the *Handbook* and was considered a primary source of GAAP. When a company adopted one or more of the differential reporting options, it was still considered to be following GAAP.

In 2006, when the decision was made by the Accounting Standards Board (AcSB) to adopt IFRS for publicly accountable enterprises commencing in 2011, a CPA Canada task force was established to revisit the question of what standards should be applied to private companies. The task force considered three different approaches:

- A non-GAAP approach, whereby private companies could use a more simplified method of reporting than what was presently required under differential reporting

- A GAAP approach based on requirements being developed by IASB for small and medium-sized enterprises

- A GAAP approach by developing a separate part of the *CPA Canada Handbook* dedicated solely to private enterprises

---

*Part II of the* CPA Canada Handbook *contains GAAP for private enterprises.*

---

After much discussion and input from interested stakeholders, in 2009, the Canadian AcSB chose the third approach. These standards are included in Part II of the *Handbook* and are referred to as Accounting Standards for Private Enterprises (ASPE). A private enterprise is defined as a profit-oriented enterprise that

(a) has not issued, and is not in the process of issuing, debt or equity instruments that are, or will be, outstanding and traded in a public market (a domestic or foreign stock exchange or an over-the-counter market, including local and regional markets), and

(b) does not hold assets in a fiduciary capacity for a broad group of outsiders as one of its primary businesses.

The standards are available to any private enterprise. No size threshold or other barriers such as unanimous consent by shareholders or other users is imposed. The standards stand alone (i.e., private enterprises applying them are not required to refer to standards applicable to publicly accountable enterprises).

---

*Private enterprises can report under either IFRS or ASPE.*

---

Private enterprises may adopt either ASPE (Part II) or IFRS (Part I). Whichever set of standards is adopted, it must be the whole package. It is not possible to apply certain standards from ASPE and others from IFRS.

Some private companies may choose to follow IFRS for the following reasons:

- The company may be of a similar size to certain public companies, and the users of its financial statements may insist on IFRS so that the company can be compared with other public companies.

- The company may be planning to go public in the near future.

- A parent company uses IFRS.

**LO3**

Exhibit 1.1 lists some of differences between IFRS and ASPE in topics discussed in intermediate accounting.

**EXHIBIT 1.1**

# Some Key Differences between IFRS and ASPE

| Accounting Item | IFRS | ASPE |
| --- | --- | --- |
| Disclosure | Very extensive for many items, especially financial instruments, post-employment benefits, and segment reporting | Moderate for financial instruments and post-employment benefits, and no disclosure for segments |
| Impaired loans | Discount future cash flows using original discount rate | Discount future cash flows using current rate of interest |
| Property, plant, and equipment | | |
| Revaluation option | Can be revalued to fair value with adjustment to OCI and with depreciation based on revalued amount | Must be measured at cost less accumulated depreciation |
| Asset impairment | | |
| Test for impairment if indicator requires | Asset's carrying amount exceeds the higher of its (1) value in use (discounted expected future cash flows) and (2) fair value less costs of disposal | Asset's carrying amount exceeds the undiscounted expected future cash flows from the asset. If so, write asset down to lower of carrying amount and fair value. |
| Subsequent reversal of impairment loss | Required if indicators change | Not allowed |
| Development costs | Capitalize if certain criteria are met | Choice between capitalize, if criteria met, or expense |
| Post-employment benefits | | |
| Actuarial gains/losses | Recognize immediately in OCI | Recognize immediately in net income |
| Income taxes | Set up deferred income taxes as applicable | Choice between taxes payable or future income tax methods |
| Interest capitalization | Capitalize if certain criteria are met | Choice between capitalize or expense |
| Compound financial instrument | Allocate between debt and equity | Can choose to allocate a nominal amount to equity |
| Preferred shares in tax planning arrangement | Assess whether debt or equity | Record as equity unless redemption demanded |
| Value of conversion option for convertible bonds | Record as equity | Choice between recognizing as debt or equity |

> *ASPE sometimes allow a choice between different reporting methods.*

For the next 10 chapters, we will concentrate on IFRS throughout the main body of each chapter. At the end of each chapter, we will summarize the main differences in the standards for private enterprises as compared with the standards for publicly accountable enterprises for the topics considered in that chapter.

**GAAP FOR NOT-FOR-PROFIT ORGANIZATIONS**  Prior to segmentation of the *CPA Canada Handbook* into five parts, the *Handbook* had a series of sections, the 4400 series, dedicated to not-for-profit organizations (NFPOs). Many of the other *Handbook* sections were also applicable to NFPOs. With the adoption of IFRS for public companies and ASPE for private enterprises, a decision had to be made on how to service the NFPOs.

In December 2008, the AcSB and the Public Sector Accounting Board (PSAB) jointly issued an Invitation to Comment, *Financial Reporting by Not-for-Profit Organizations.* In December 2010, the final standards for NFPOs were released. As part of this process, the not-for-profit (NFP) sector was divided into two sectors: the government NFP sector and the non-government NFP sector. The government NFP sector includes NFPOs that are controlled by the government. They have a choice to follow either the 4200 series of the CPA Canada *Public Sector Accounting (PSA) Handbook* or the *PSA Handbook* without the 4200 series. The non-government NFP sector includes NFPOs not controlled by the government. They have a choice to follow either IFRS (which do not currently contain any standards specifically tailored for NFPOs) or Part III of the *CPA Canada Handbook.* An NFPO applying Part III of the *Handbook* also applies the standards for private enterprises in Part II, to the extent that the Part II standards address topics not addressed in Part III.

---

*Non-government NFPOs can report under either IFRS or Part III of the* CPA Canada Handbook, *combined with relevant sections from Part II of the* Handbook.

---

Part III carries forward the 4400 series of sections from the pre-changeover *Handbook,* largely without change. Five new sections were added. They contain relevant material from Part II that the AcSB deemed necessary to clarify their applicability to NFPOs.

The accounting standards for NFPOs will be discussed and illustrated in Chapter 12.

**GAAP FOR GOVERNMENT AND OTHER GOVERNMENT ORGANIZATIONS** All levels of government should follow the *PSA Handbook.* Government business enterprises are expected to follow IFRS. Other government organizations can follow either IFRS or the *PSA Handbook.* The accounting standards for government entities are summarized in Appendix C for Chapter 12.

---

***Cautionary Note:*** *Unless otherwise stated, assume that IFRS should be applied when answering end-of-chapter material.*

---

The following table summarizes the standards required or allowed for different types of Canadian organizations:

| Type of Organization | Standards Required or Allowed |
|---|---|
| Publicly accountable organization | IFRS (Part I) |
| Private enterprise | IFRS (Part I) or ASPE (Part II) |
| Non-governmental NFPO | IFRS (Part I) or Standards for NFPOs (Part III) |
| Governmental NFPO | *PSA Handbook* with or without 4200 series |
| Government | *PSA Handbook* |
| Government business enterprise | IFRS (Part I) |
| Other government organization | IFRS (Part I) or *PSA Handbook* |
| Pension plan | Standards for Pension Plans (Part IV) |

By using the above-noted standards, the organization is considered to be following GAAP. In choosing between the various options, the organization would consider the needs of the users of their financial statements and the comparability of the organization with counterparts in the private or the public sector. In the notes to the financial statements, the set of standards being used should be explicitly stated.

> *The entity should specify in the notes to the financial statements the part of the* Handbook *being used for reporting purposes.*

## LO4 ANALYSIS AND INTERPRETATION OF FINANCIAL STATEMENTS

We have seen many examples in this chapter of differences in accounting and reporting practices. The CPA Canada *Public Sector Accounting (PSA) Handbook* is different from Parts I, II, or III of the *CPA Canada Handbook*. With all of these differences, is there an opportunity for a company to manipulate its financial statements by choosing policies to produce desirable results? Do financial analysts know that these choices exist in accounting? Do they understand the impact of the different accounting methods on the financial statements?

These questions point up the importance of disclosing accounting policies in the notes to the financial statements. This will allow users to determine whether the same policies are being used by different entities and whether adjustments must be made to make the statements comparable from one entity to the next.

> *Different accounting methods have different impacts on key financial statement ratios.*

At the end of every chapter, there is a section on analysis and interpretation of financial statements. It reminds the reader that different accounting methods will have an impact on the financial statements. In turn, the different methods will have an impact on the ratios used by analysts in evaluating an entity. As preparers and users of financial statements, we should understand the impact of accounting methods on the financial statements.

In this text, we will focus on the following key ratios:

| Ratio | Formula | What Is Measured |
|---|---|---|
| Current ratio | $\dfrac{\text{Current assets}}{\text{Current liabilities}}$ | Liquidity; i.e., ability to pay short-term obligations as they come due |
| Debt-to-equity ratio | $\dfrac{\text{Total debt}}{\text{Shareholders' equity}}$ | Solvency; i.e., ability to pay all debt as it comes due |
| Return on assets | $\dfrac{\text{Income before interest \& taxes}}{\text{Total assets}}$ | Profitability of assets |
| Return on equity | $\dfrac{\text{Net income}}{\text{Shareholders' equity}}$ | Profitability of owners' investment |

These ratios have been covered in previous courses in accounting. They are summarized above for ease of reference. When asked to indicate the impact on these ratios, be sure to always consider and/or comment on the impact on both the numerator and denominator. For the denominator for the return ratios, it is more appropriate to use average balances for the year because the assets or equity likely changed during the year. However, many analysts use balances at the end of the year because it is simpler. To make the expectations clear for the end-of-chapter problems, we will use average in the ratio—that is, return on average equity—when we want you to use average of opening and closing balances in your calculation. If we simply use return on equity, you should use the balance at the end of the year in your calculation of the ratio.

> *When determining the impact on ratios of changes in reporting methods, we must consider the impact on both the numerator and the denominator.*

See Self-Study Problem 1 for a good illustration of the impact of accounting policies on key financial ratios.

## SUMMARY

Financial statements are intended for users to help them assess the profitability and stability of the reporting entity. The conceptual framework has been established to provide guidance in preparing and understanding financial statements. Ideally, all present and future accounting standards should be consistent with the conceptual framework. Students should try to understand accounting practices, not as standards on their own, but as part of the concepts and principles of the conceptual framework. **(LO1)**

Accounting standards are continually changing to better reflect the profitability and financial position of the reporting entity and to respond to the needs of the users. Over the past decade, we have moved from one *Handbook* with differential reporting options to a *Handbook* with five distinct parts to satisfy the different needs of the users. With all the different reporting options available, it is important that the notes to the financial statements clearly describe the policies used in preparing the financial statements. **(LO2)**

ASPE is usually simpler and less costly to apply than IFRS. **(LO3)**

When reading and interpreting financial statements, users should pay close attention to the accounting policies used and should understand that different policies could have a significant impact on financial statement items. In this textbook, we will focus on four key ratios (current ratio, debt-to-equity ratio, return on assets, and return on equity) when analyzing and interpreting financial statements. **(LO4)**

## Self-Study Problem 1

LO2, 3, 4

Hyde Ltd. is a large, privately owned Canadian company that prepares its financial statements in accordance with ASPE. Its profit in Year 3 was $1,000,000, and shareholders' equity at December 31, Year 3, was $8,000,000.

Hyde plans to go public within the next five years and is wondering what the impact of converting to IFRS will have on its financial statements. Hyde has engaged you to reconcile profit and shareholders' equity under ASPE to IFRS for the Year 3 financial statements. You have identified the following five areas in which Hyde's accounting principles differ from IFRS:

1. Future income taxes
2. Property, plant, and equipment—measurement subsequent to initial recognition
3. Research and development costs—capitalization of development costs
4. Compound financial instrument
5. Property, plant, and equipment—impairment

Hyde provides the following information with respect to each of these accounting differences.

## Future Income Taxes

Hyde has been using the taxes payable method of reporting income taxes. Accordingly, it reported only the tax payable in the current year based on income tax laws and did not report any future income taxes assets or liabilities. Under IFRS, it would have reported deferred income tax liabilities of $190,000 at the end of Year 2 and $220,000 at the end of Year 3 along with a deferred income tax expense of $30,000 for Year 3.

## Property, Plant, and Equipment—Measurement Subsequent to Initial Recognition

Hyde acquired equipment at the beginning of Year 2 at a cost of $250,000. The equipment has an estimated useful life of 10 years and an estimated residual value of $50,000 and is being depreciated on a straight-line basis. At the end of Year 2 and end of Year 3, the equipment was appraised and determined to have a fair value of $320,000 and $330,000, respectively; it's estimated useful life and residual value did not change. When Hyde adopts IFRS, it would use the allowed alternative treatment in IAS 16 to periodically revalue the equipment at fair value subsequent to acquisition. The revaluation surplus goes through OCI.

## Research and Development Costs

Hyde incurred research and development costs of $100,000 in Year 3 and $250,000 prior to Year 3. Of these amounts, $60,000 in Year 3 and $41,000 prior to Year 3 related to development activities after the point in time when the criteria for capitalization of development costs had been met. At the end of Year 3, development of the new product had not been completed. Hyde has been expensing all research and development costs as incurred as allowed under ASPE.

## Compound Financial Instrument

On January 1, Year 3, Hyde issued convertible debt for proceeds of $310,000. The debt can be converted to common shares on or before December 31, Year 7. Otherwise, the principal amount of the debt, $300,000, is due on December 31, Year 8. Interest of $18,000 is due on December 31 each year. Hyde reported $300,000 of the proceeds as long-term debt and $10,000 as contributed surplus and expensed the interest payment when it was paid at the end of the year. Under IFRS, the proceeds should have been broken down to debt of $290,000 and contributed surplus of $20,000. The discount on the debt would be amortized using the effective interest method, which would have resulted in additional interest expense of $760 for Year 3.

### Property, Plant, and Equipment—Impairment

Hyde owns machinery on December 31, Year 3, with a carrying amount of $200,000, an estimated salvage value of $20,000, and an estimated remaining useful life of 10 years. On that date, there is an indication that the machinery may be impaired. The machinery is expected to generate future cash flows of $225,000 and has an estimated fair value, after deducting costs to sell, of $180,000. The present value of expected future cash flows is $186,000.

### Required

Prepare a schedule reconciling ASPE profit and ASPE shareholders' equity to an IFRS basis. Ignore income taxes on all items except for the future income tax item.

## Solution to Self-Study Problem 1

**Hyde Ltd. Reconciliation from ASPE to IFRS**

| | |
|---|---:|
| Profit for Year 3 under ASPE | $1,000,000 |
| Adjustments: | |
| Deferred tax expense (Note 1) | (30,000) |
| Additional depreciation on revalued equipment (Note 2) | (10,000) |
| Development costs capitalized (Note 3) | 60,000 |
| Additional interest expense for amortization of discount on bonds (Note 4) | (760) |
| Impairment loss (Note 5) | (14,000) |
| Profit for Year 3 under IFRS | $1,005,240 |
| | |
| Shareholders' equity at end of Year 3 under ASPE | $8,000,000 |
| Adjustments: | |
| Deferred tax liability (Note 1) | (220,000) |
| Revaluation surplus on equipment (Note 2) | 120,000 |
| Cumulative development costs capitalized (Note 3) | 101,000 |
| Decrease in debt portion of convertible debt (Note 4) | 9,240 |
| Write down equipment to recoverable amount (Note 5) | (14,000) |
| Shareholders' equity at end of Year 3 under IFRS | $7,996,240 |

### Notes:

1. **Future Income Taxes** Under IAS 12, deferred income taxes must be recognized on all temporary differences. Accordingly, a deferred tax liability of $220,000 must be recognized at the end of Year 3 and a deferred income tax expense of $30,000 reported in net income for Year 3. This will reduce shareholders' equity by $220,000 at the end of Year 3 and reduce net income by $30,000 for Year 3.

2. **Property, Plant, and Equipment** Under ASPE, depreciation expense on equipment would be $20,000 ([$250,000 − $50,000]/10 years), per year in Year 2 and Year 3. This would result in a carrying amount of $230,000 at the end of Year 2 and $210,000 at the end of Year 3.

    Under IAS 16, the revaluation surplus is reported in OCI each year and is accumulated as a separate component of shareholders' equity. Depreciation expense is based on the revalued asset. In Year 3, depreciation expense would be was $30,000 ([$320,000 − $50,000]/9 years). The additional depreciation expense under IFRS causes IFRS-based profit in Year 3 to be $10,000 lower than ASPE profit. The revaluation surplus cause IFRS-based shareholders' equity to be $120,000 ($330,000 − $210,000) higher than ASPE shareholders' equity at the end of Year 3.

3. **Research and Development Costs** Under ASPE, all of the research and development costs were expensed in the current and previous years. Under IAS 38, $60,000 in Year 3 and $41,000 prior to Year 3 of the research and development costs would have been capitalized as an intangible asset. Therefore, IFRS-based profit would be $60,000 higher in Year 3 and IFRS-based shareholders' equity would be $101,000 higher at the end of Year 3.

4. **Compound Financial Instrument** Under ASPE, a nominal amount of the proceeds on the issuance of the convertible debt can be allocated to shareholders' equity. Hyde reported only $10,000 of the proceeds in contributed surplus, which is a component of shareholders' equity. In turn, $300,000 was allocated to long-term debt; this amount was equal to the maturity value of the debt. IFRS 9 requires that the proceeds on the convertible debt be allocated to debt and equity on the basis of the relative value of each component. Since the debt has a maturity value of $300,000 and was initially assigned a value of $290,000, there is a $10,000 discount on the debt portion. The equity portion of the convertible bond must increase by $10,000. The discount would be amortized over the expected life of the debt using the effective interest method. In Year 3, the amortization of the discount resulted in an additional expense of $760. At the end of Year 3, the debt is $9,240 ([$300,000 − ($290,000 + $760)]) lower and the equity is $9,240 higher under IFRS than ASPE.

5. **Property, Plant, and Equipment** Since there is an indication that the asset may be impaired, an impairment test must be performed. Under IAS 36, an asset is impaired when its carrying amount exceeds its recoverable amount, which is the higher of (1) its value in use (present value of expected future cash flows) and (2) its fair value less costs of disposal. The machinery had a carrying amount of $200,000, and its value in use was $186,000, which is more than the fair value less cost to sell of $180,000. An impairment loss of $14,000 ($200,000 − $186,000) would have been recognized in determining Year 3 profit, with a corresponding reduction in retained earnings under IFRS.

Under ASPE, impairment occurs when an asset's carrying amount exceeds its undiscounted expected future cash flows. In this case, the expected future cash flows are $225,000, which is higher than the machinery's carrying amount, so no impairment occurred under ASPE.

# APPENDIX 1A

LO5

# A Generic Approach to Case Analysis[1]

Successful people usually have good judgment and are virtually always good decision makers. Decisions by these people may affect others, from as few as the members of their families to thousands of employees, investors and customers. Regardless of its impact on others though, every decision ever made affected the life of the person making that decision.

Those people who manage business concerns, especially smaller ones, rarely get the opportunity to study the techniques needed to ensure a thoroughly considered decision. As a result, managers often turn to professional accountants, not only for their technical knowledge, but also for their ability to logically analyze and solve a problem.

*Professional accountants are renowned for their problem-solving ability.*

For a person looking toward a career as an accountant, the ability to succeed in passing professional examinations requires the same skills necessary to serve employers or clients or society throughout a lifelong career. Professional accounting bodies judge the worthiness of its candidates through examinations, which stress the ability of providing decision-making information.

What abilities must be demonstrated to be successful as an accountant? Basically, people who hire accountants are looking for three major skills:

1. *Knowledge.* Not only technical comfort with accounting, auditing, finance and income tax rules, but also sufficient knowledge of ethical responsibilities to protect both the client's financial situation and reputation

2. *Creativity.* The talent to create a useful solution to the client's needs, within the ethical framework discussed above

3. *Organization.* The ability to make order out of a complex set of data

*Professional accountants are expected to be knowledgeable, creative, and organized.*

The purpose of this section is to provide a framework for making decisions. While the approach outlined in the notes details a method of answering professional accounting exams, its logic can be applied to any business decision-making situation.

Some decision settings are quite comprehensive in that they involve a relatively unstructured decision problem. The manager or report user is not really sure what the critical issues are, and leaves the diagnosis up to the professional accountant. In addition, resolving the critical issues may involve techniques that span several knowledge subject areas. Typically, there are several valid alternatives facing the decision maker, and the professional accountant must exercise professional judgment skills in deciding between alternatives and communication skills in recommending the alternative that best suits the objectives of the decision maker. In doing all this, the professional accountant must pay careful attention to his or her role, given the stated or implied expectations of the report user. Together, these skills constitute the essence of what we refer to as integration and analysis skills. Such skills are critical to a successful career as a professional accountant. Comprehensive cases seek to simulate such unstructured client situations.

Other decision settings are less comprehensive, yet may still require integration and analysis skills. For example, there may be relatively more direction as to what the critical issues are, so that diagnostic skills are not called upon to the same extent as above, yet issue ranking may still be important when writing the report. Fewer subject matter areas may be called upon, to resolve the critical issues, but some integration may still be important. Multi-subject cases seek to simulate client situations of this sort. When faced with such scenarios, the professional accountant must still identify the needs of the user of the report; there are often alternative valid approaches; professional judgment must again be exercised in deciding between alternatives; and, finally, good communication skills are again called upon in recommending the alternative that best suits the objectives of the decision maker. As with comprehensive situations, multi-subject client situations require careful attention to role.

## Generic Framework for Case Analysis

The generic approach that we recommend for integration and analysis cases is outlined in Exhibit 1A.1. The generic approach is ideally suited for shorter multi-competency questions on professional examinations, but, with flexibility, it can be applied to the longer comprehensive cases used in professional examinations. The integration and analysis cases used in this text are best characterized as shorter, multi-competency cases. Each of the items in the generic framework will be discussed in further detail in the next section and applied to Metal Caissons Limited, which is Self-Study Case at the end of this appendix. Before you attempt that case, however, let's look at a brief overview of the items suggested in our standard approach.

### EXHIBIT 1A.1

#### Generic Framework for Case Analysis

I Determine Your Role and Requirements
II Identify Users and Their Needs
III Identify and Rank Issues
IV Identify Viable Alternatives for Each Major Issue
V Analyze Alternatives Using Criteria for Resolving
VI Communicate Practical Recommendations/Conclusions

## I: Determine Your Role and Requirements

The first step is to determine who you are in the context of this case. The evaluation of your role will decide a number of factors important to your answer—your character's goals and constraints along with the level of technical knowledge and responsibility expected.

At the same time, you must decide what your character's task actually is in the case. In this earliest stage of the approach, your main job is to find the required. This usually means finding and reading the paragraph(s) which describe the case requirements. Look at the last two paragraphs at the end of the main body of the case first, before you begin a detailed reading, as most cases describe the task requirements near the end of the main body of the case, that is, just before the Exhibits.

> *The key requirements are often found in the last two paragraphs of the main body of the case.*

## II: Identify Users and Their Needs Given the Case Environment

After you decide on the role of your character in the case, the other characters must be defined. The other characters will undoubtedly be people seeking your expertise in financial matters. You need to determine who is asking for or who will benefit from the information you produce, what types of decisions they will be making, and how the information you provide will help them make that decision.

When focusing your task on the user's needs, always consider the environment in which you both operate. This could include any or all of the economic, legal, moral, and personal situations at play in the lives of the case participants.

## III: Identify and Rank Issues

Now that you know who you are and what must be done, you can finally settle down to the task of identifying the issues which must be addressed. Depending on the amount of direction in the case, the issues may or may not be clearly labelled. Read each paragraph of the case carefully. Few paragraphs in any multi-competency case are wasted with superfluous information. Most paragraphs will supply information either identifying issues to be dealt with or providing the data needed for analyzing the issue or environment.

Once issues are identified, two final steps are required before this initial planning stage of the case approach is complete: ranking the issues discovered and preparing your case plan.

To rank the issues, consider your users. Ideally, they want you to resolve and clarify all issues. But, if it is not possible to resolve all issues at this time, which issues are most important to them? The users probably want you to resolve the controversial items first—that is, the items with no clear-cut answer. The more controversial an issue, the more important it is and the more time you need to spend in explaining your answer. Second, users expect you to correct any errors. The bigger the dollar amount, the greater the need to correct it. Third, the complex items require clarification. Users want an explanation for the rationale for the policy or standard. Other factors that could be used to rank the issues are urgency of the matter, whether alternatives exist, and whether sufficient facts are available to be able to solve the issue.

---

*Issues are usually ranked based on controversy, errors, and complexity.*

---

When ranking the issues, be ruthless with yourself! Do not rank an item as important merely because you know a lot about the subject. Rank items solely on their importance to the other characters in the case.

After you decide on the ranking, begin to prepare your case plan by listing the issues in order of rank down the left side of a piece of paper. For each issue, in a middle column of the page, make a brief note of the type (qualitative and/or quantitative) and amount of analysis that you anticipate will be required. In other words, identify the decision criteria or criteria for resolving the issues. For example, for a revenue recognition issue, the analysis would be primarily qualitative and would likely involve assessing performance, collectability, etc. For a make-or-buy decision, the analysis would be primarily quantitative and would likely involve calculations of contribution margins under different scenarios. On the right side of the page, calculate a time budget that you will follow when identifying alternative responses and performing the expected analysis.

## IV: Identify Viable Alternatives for Each Major Issue

As in real life, very few case issues will have one correct answer. You will be expected to use your imagination to create various possible solutions to each case issue. A quick, black-and-white solution to an issue does not usually lend itself to the depth of analysis required to prepare a proper answer. Alternatives should be limited, through the demonstration of professional judgment, to those that may be practically supportable within the context of the scenario and constraints described in the case. After identifying the viable alternatives, you should identify the criteria to be used in deciding between the various alternatives.

> *The alternatives should be relevant and viable for the client's unique situation.*

## V: Analyze Alternatives Using Criteria for Resolving

For each issue listed on your case plan, an analysis of the previously identified alternatives should be performed. Depending on the type of issue, this may be in a quantitative and/or qualitative form. The analysis should use the decision criteria identified in IV. It should include an appropriate discussion of the technical aspects of the issue as they relate to the user's needs and should address the interrelationship of issues. This interrelationship is referred to in case circles as "integration."

Consideration of interrelationships should include: the combined impact of case facts on an issue ("fact integration"), the impact of an issue and its possible solutions in various technical areas ("subject area integration"), and, most difficult, the effect of one issue and its resolution on other case issues ("issue integration").

## VI: Communicate Practical Recommendations/Conclusions to Users

To conclude your solution to any case, refer back to the determinations made at the beginning of the case approach. Who is your character? What type of communication is expected from you? To whom are you writing? Your answer to the case should be in the form required by the question. It should provide clear, practical recommendations based on your detailed analysis above and should directly address the identified user's needs. Finally, your solution should demonstrate the organizational skills required of a professional person.

Your written report should provide recommendations and conclusions along with your supporting arguments. It need not describe everything you thought about as you analyzed the case, that is, it does not have to say something pertaining to all aspects of the case approach. Furthermore, it does not have to discuss all the alternatives you initially identified. It would only discuss alternatives for the very controversial issues—where the alternatives are fairly equal to each other.

Now that we have a basic understanding of the generic framework for analyzing a case, we will apply this framework to analyze and solve an accounting and financial reporting case.

## A Framework to Solve an Accounting and Financial Reporting Case

In this section, we will apply the framework for analyzing a case to the Metal Caissons Limited (MCL) case. We will use the framework to identify and solve the most significant issues of the case.

## I: Determine Your Role and Requirements

In this first step, before your detailed reading of the question, you should find your role in the case information. Often, this can be found in the first or second paragraph of the question. Sometimes, though, the case author will attempt to penalize poorly organized students by keeping your role hidden until the end of the narrative portion of the case. (The narration is the portion of the question that reads like a story. It is usually at the beginning of a case, before any Exhibits containing detailed information.)

Never read the entire question before knowing who your character is. If the role outline is not clearly indicated at either the beginning or end of the narrative portion of the case, take a few moments to scan the question to find the sentence in which your role is described. Knowing your situation in advance will colour your outlook on the facts provided in the case information.

Now read the narrative portion of the MCL case—that is, up to Exhibit A. What is your role and where did you find it?

As indicated in the last paragraph before the Exhibits, you are a CPA in charge of the audit of MCL. Your role is to deal with the accounting issues connected with this engagement.

Your role in almost all cases can be focused upon by looking at two basic classifications found in working life: the type of service your job is expected to provide and your level of responsibility in providing that service.

*Types of services.* Types of services expected from a character in a professional accounting engagement are usually restricted to a few job functions. A position in a public accounting firm and a controllership role are most common. While generally accepted accounting principles (GAAP) do require some knowledge in areas like government accounting and accounting for life insurance companies, cases rarely place you in jobs in those areas due to their high level of specialization.

However, some seemingly technical and specialized areas may arise in cases. Examples include controllership in the computer and natural resource industries. Questions that place you in a specialized role rarely expect you to know many of the detailed rules and regulations of that industry, but you are expected to know what basic GAAP apply to that industry. Such a question would also expect you to use your overall knowledge of accounting objectives and constraints to create a reasonable response to a user's request.

The type of service you provide determines the basic thrust of your analysis. A task assigned to a public accountant will demand a high level of knowledge and interest in auditing and taxation. A controller or financial vice-president would normally be most interested in management accounting, internal controls, and information systems. Both the financial accountant and the controller would be expected to deal with financial accounting issues. In MCL, your role as a CPA in charge requires the application of considerable technical knowledge to the significant accounting issues. As the case is written, you are not expected to deal with auditing, tax, or other issues.

> *The cases in this textbook will deal almost exclusively with financial accounting issues.*

*Level of responsibility.* Now that you have determined where you work, your level of responsibility must be decided. Your rank at your workplace provides much information regarding the quality of analysis and communication expected of you.

This case is an excellent example of how much can go wrong when the situation of your character is not adequately considered. In most academic situations, when you are asked a question, you are expected to produce an answer. For case questions, however, you must play your role. While the case could have asked you to discuss the accounting, auditing, and tax issues, it only asked about the accounting issues. It did not ask about auditing, tax, finance, or anything else.

What would it cost the respondent who also discussed auditing and/or tax issues? Plenty. The time spent on these issues would waste valuable minutes, which could have been used to address the accounting issues in more depth. Furthermore, no marks would have been awarded for the auditing or tax issues. Also, professional capabilities were not demonstrated if one did not recognize the professional responsibilities required in his or her role.

Rarely will you be offered a case character with absolutely unlimited responsibilities. In many public accounting firms, senior staff accountants in charge of fieldwork report to managers, who organize and check the technical accuracy of the work, who in turn report to partners who accept responsibility for the work. Even partners must answer to other partners concerning the marketing, profitability, and legal risk of engagements accepted or declined. In industry, controllers supervise the day-to-day accounting. They are overseen by financial vice-presidents and chief executives who themselves must report to directors and shareholders.

When you have found your role description in the preliminary stage of reading the case, always take a moment to imagine yourself in that job. Do not continue until you feel comfortable being that person, with his or her responsibilities and constraints.

In a case question, you are a character who must perform some task. The first part dealt with deciding who you are. Now you must determine what the expected task is to be. This function can be split into two parts: search and task identification.

*Search.*    As with finding your role, the search for the required must be done before the detailed reading of the case. This will enable you to identify important issues on only one read-through of the question. If the required were to be discovered only during your detailed reading of the question, you would likely have to read the question again to ensure that all important information was recognized. A second reading would waste valuable time.

Usually, though, this is not a difficult job. In many case questions, a paragraph of the narration contains the general task description. Often, this paragraph appears near the end of the main body of the case just before the Exhibits. It usually comes as a request from a partner, client, or executive asking for a report or memorandum concerning specific areas of interest. Other case questions are written in dialogue style, with you sitting in a meeting and conversing with others. In this sort of question, the task required will be in the lines of dialogue. If a brief look at the last two or three paragraphs of the question does not reveal the required task, quickly scan the question for key words such as prepare, draft, or analyze. This will lead you to your main requirement.

> *The earlier you determine the real required task, the more focused you can be in reading the case.*

You can see the above structure in MCL. While the last paragraph before the Exhibits did not identify the specific accounting issues to be analyzed, it clearly indicated that you were required to prepare a memo dealing with accounting issues for a partner in your firm.

*Task identification.*    A comment frequently made by evaluators at the conclusion of a professional examination is that the candidates did not adequately address the "required" of a question. If the equivalent of this happens with a client, you will likely have difficulty collecting your fee. Obviously, this can be a devastating problem. To avoid it, always consider what a proper result of your work should physically look like.

What is the user asking for? If a report is requested, a formal document must be prepared. If the user wants a memo, a more casual style may be used.

What does the user want in the communication? What topics concern them? Normally, these topics are set out in the sentence or paragraph containing the required. For example, in MCL, the last sentence of the narration asked you to "*prepare a memo for her dealing with the accounting issues*" (italics added). The topics outlined in the required not only provide a framework for listing issues found in the case information, but also give some indication of the amount of integration expected, if any.

## II: Identify Users and Their Needs Given the Case Environment

Now you know who you are and what communication is expected of you. You may now begin your detailed reading of the question. At this point, many students start listing technical issues. Not yet, please!

The time pressure and the desire to get words and numbers on paper often causes respondents to rush to an answer without considering both sides of the communication equation. As discussed in step I, you should have spent a significant effort in getting to know your character—the person writing the report or memorandum. No communication is useful, however, unless the writer considers the expected reader. This is especially relevant in a professional environment in which the reader (the partner, client, executive, or other user) is hiring the accountant to prepare the communication for some specific purpose. If the accountant does not address that purpose, collection of fees and repeat engagements may be difficult.

While it is hard to ignore the users of your service in real life (as they pay the bills), in an academic exercise such concerns can be easily forgotten. Too often the evaluator's comments on the professional examination indicate that candidates did not adequately consider the needs of the users of the information prepared. To ensure that you focus your attention on the user, before considering technical issues, we recommend that you begin a case plan with a small chart as shown in Exhibit 1A.2.

### EXHIBIT 1A.2

## User Needs Summary

|  | Report Recipient | Primary User #1 | Primary User #2 | Primary User #3 |
|---|---|---|---|---|
| Name |  |  |  |  |
| Goals |  |  |  |  |
| Key metric |  |  |  |  |
| Constraints |  |  |  |  |
| *Overall conclusions:* |  |  |  |  |

> *We need to distinguish between the person receiving the report and the end user(s) who will benefit from following the recommendations in the report.*

This chart allows you the opportunity to consider who the person receiving your report will be. We will refer to this person as the report recipient. Often, it will be a partner or executive at your character's workplace (as is seen in MCL, where partner Linda Presner is the person asking for the memo). In addition to the report recipient, there are usually one or more primary users affected by your recommendations. The primary users are the users who will be affected by the actions taken as a result of your recommendations. They will almost always include the client. If your recommendations deal with financial reporting issues, the primary users will be the people receiving the financial statements. Accordingly, other primary users often include a bank or other financing source, a regulatory agency or a potential purchaser. Usually, the sentence in which you found the required contains information as to who the report recipient will be. In addition, the first one or two paragraphs of the case normally contain background information that may indicate primary users. Professional judgment must be used to assign the proper amount of importance to the discovered primary users. Only those primary users who have a significant bearing on the report recipient should be listed in your planning chart.

> *For financial accounting cases, the primary users have to include users of the financial statements.*

Now reread the narrative portion of the MCL case and begin to fill out Exhibit 1A.2. Start by identifying the report recipient and primary users.

As indicated in the last paragraph before the required, you are a CPA in charge of the audit. The second-last paragraph explicitly identifies the main primary users. The earlier references to the DND and the bank loan, however, should have already alerted you to them as important primary users.

For the report recipient and each of the primary users, a space is provided in the planning chart to make a very brief summary of that person's main goal in reading your report. Examples could be:

- Partner—assess quality of financial reporting
- Client management—portray financial performance of entity
- Bank—assess ability to repay loan
- Potential purchaser—determine purchase price

The same goals cannot be plugged into similar users in all cases. For example, instead of the partner wanting to assess quality of financial reporting, his or her goal might be to minimize audit risk. Instead of wanting to accurately portray financial performance, client management may want to minimize income for tax purposes. Your approach to the case would likely be quite different if user goals were as diverse as those in the examples above. You must use facts provided in the case to form an opinion as to the primary users and their desires for this particular case.

Another space is provided in the planning chart for key metric. This space should be filled in for each of the primary users who will receive financial information. It should indicate the key financial item(s) that the user will focus on in assessing their ongoing relationship with the entity. Examples could be:

- Bank—debt-to-equity ratio and/or net income
- Shareholders—net income
- Canada Revenue Agency—income before taxes

> *Net income is the key metric for most external users of the financial statements.*

Finally, for each user, your plan should quickly describe factors that may limit or constrain the achievement of that user's goals. Without making this function into a major analysis in itself, you should consider the environment in which the users operate. Environmental categories that should be considered include:

- Economic—General economic factors and those specific to the industry in which the user operates

- Legal—Statutory restrictions such as income tax regulations, reporting requirements, and ecological responsibilities; political limitations often appear in situations concerning foreign subsidiaries and foreign exchange transactions

- Moral—Professional ethical responsibilities

- Personal—Interpersonal relationships (such as partnership and family relations or minority ownership interests) and personal religious or political beliefs

After completing this brief chart, you now have a frame of reference when analyzing issues and making recommendations. You can readily see if your analysis includes the factors important to the major users of your information. The chart also makes it easier to see the integration of your alternate solutions among the main characters in the case. Finally, recommendations made in the conclusion to your solution can be referenced to the need expressed by the report recipient in asking for your services.

If the case involves financial accounting issues, the following decisions should be made on the basis of an assessment and ranking of the primary users and their needs:

1. Should the entity provide general-purpose financial statements, that is, balance sheet, income statement, cash flow statement, statement of changes in equity, and notes to financial statements, or some sort of special-purpose financial statement(s)?

2. Should the financial statement(s) be prepared in accordance with GAAP or special (non-GAAP) policies? If GAAP are recommended, should it be IFRS (i.e., Part I) or Accounting Standards for Private Enterprises (i.e., ASPE)?

3. What is the most important financial statement item (i.e., key metric), and will management want to minimize or maximize this metric?

> *In most, but not all, situations, users expect to receive general-purpose financial statements in accordance with GAAP.*

A brief caution, though! The chart of user needs and constraints is a necessary step in producing a practical solution, not an end in itself. Do not spend a large amount of time fine-tuning all possible users, goals, and limitations. Fringe users and obscure limitations are not important to your solution. Do not dwell on them. Fill in the chart quickly and thoughtfully with only important users.

When first dealing with cases, you should prepare the chart in the detail provided in this section. As you get better at writing cases, you may be able to organize your thoughts without formally completing this chart. However, you would go through the same mental process. When you write your professional exams, write things down in your rough notes to the extent necessary to guide you through.

In most situations, this chart does not need to be formally incorporated in your final report. Rather, it is a part of your rough notes to ensure that you get on the right track. Only incorporate the conclusions from this analysis in your formal report. For example, you may conclude that the entity will prepare general-purpose financial statements in accordance with Part I of the *CPA Canada Handbook,* and management will want to maximize net income in order to attract potential investors and retain existing shareholders.

> *The user needs analysis helps you get on the right track; it usually is not formally incorporated in your final report.*

An example of a completed User Needs Summary is shown in Exhibit 1A.3 for the MCL case.

**EXHIBIT 1A.3**

## Completed User Needs Summary

|  | Report Recipient | Primary User #1 | Primary User #2 | Primary User #3 |
|---|---|---|---|---|
| Name | Audit partner | Bank | DND | |
| Goals | Assess quality of financial reporting | Assess ability to repay loan | Assess ability to produce and deliver caissons | |
| Key metric | | Net income Debt-to-equity | Current ratio Net income | |
| Constraints | Contract with DND has penalty clauses. Bank requires that ASPE be used. | | | |

*Overall Conclusion:* MCL will want to maximize net income and current ratio and minimize debt-to-equity ratio.

## III: Identify and Rank Issues

University examinations normally want a student to reach the answer to a question with a minimum of preamble. So far, though, we have seen that in a professional environment much more thought must go into a solution before tackling technical issues. The first two items in this section were devoted to beginning a case plan with an analysis of the characters of the case and their expectations. It's now time to complete the planning phase for your solution—identifying and ranking the important issues contained within the case.

At the completion of this part, you should have a comprehensive plan that you can use when preparing your formal analysis and recommendations. An example of the suggested format for the case plan is shown in Exhibit 1A.4.

**EXHIBIT 1A.4**

## Case Plan

| Competency Area and Issues | Rank | Anticipated Analysis | Time Budget |
|---|---|---|---|
| | | | |
| | | | |

As seen in Exhibit 1A.4, this final step in organizing your analysis can be divided into four key categories: identifying issues, ranking those issues in order of importance, anticipating the analysis that will be necessary in your solution, and, in an examination setting, the assignment of a time budget to each issue.

*Identifying issues.*    In step I, you found the sentences containing the required and determined the major competency areas that the report recipient wanted addressed. These areas can be shown as headings in the "Competency Area and Issues" column of your case plan. For example, in MCL, the only competency area to be addressed is financial reporting. Almost all issues found during your detailed reading of the question can then be immediately classified by competency area. When reading the case in detail, list the issues discovered in the question on your planning sheet under the appropriate area. Recognize that some issues could be listed under more than one heading if they require analysis from more than one competency area. In this textbook, most cases involve only the financial reporting competency area.

> *Issues should be organized by competency area: accounting, finance, auditing, etc.*

How will you recognize an issue to be addressed? You look for items that need to be resolved, corrected, or clarified. The case tells a story and often contains a plea for help. You have to listen to the story and determine how you can help. In the MCL case, you are only expected to discuss accounting issues. Therefore, you listen/read to determine the items to be resolved, corrected, or clarified. Look for items that the client explicitly asks for help with, that are done incorrectly, or that are crucial to the success of the entity.

> *Issues are items that need to be resolved, corrected, or clarified to put the end user in a better position.*

In most professional accounting cases, there are generally only two methods of presenting issues:

- *Bullet style.* This is the most direct method of outlining issues. It usually takes the form of a memo from a partner, notes from a client meeting, or excerpts from a previous working paper me. The name "bullet style" is taken from the way issues are distinguished by number or separate paragraph (often introduced with a dot, hyphen, or bullet). Metal Caissons Limited is an example of a bullet-style case. Your job in a bullet-style question centres on addressing the issues, not reading them. So, when such cases are encountered, do not waste time searching for hidden issues. If you discover a significant issue not included in one of the bullets, add it to your issue plan only after dealing with all of the obvious issues.

> *In a bullet-style case, each bullet usually contains a separate issue.*

- *Narrative style.* This style of question can often be recognized by its length and format. Narrative-style questions are generally much shorter than bullet-style ones. Rather than outline issues over a number of pages of fictional memos or discussion notes, narrative-style questions are truly short stories. Either through dialogue or straight narration, issues are blended in. This type of case puts much more emphasis on issue identification than that for bullet-style questions. A major task in a narrative-style case is to find the issues. This can only be done by reading every sentence carefully and thoughtfully. Fortunately, narrative-style questions are normally short (often only two or three pages), allowing the time necessary to search for issues while reading. Once you have read the case entirely, you should have a complete list on your planning sheet of the issues to be addressed.

These two types of cases represent the extreme styles. You will often find combinations of the two in a particular case. For example, in MCL, issues such as government grants, late-delivery penalties, and capitalized expenditures were readily identifiable and clearly set out in separate paragraphs (but without explicit "bullets"). But a very important issue, that of the going concern, was much less obvious. The identification of this issue required a clear assessment of the factors that might cause a going-concern problem. This may not have become apparent until the other issues have been analyzed.

Students frequently ask a question of planning style: Should marginal notes be made on the case question before transferring the issues to the planning sheet? It's a matter of personal preference. If you are able to list the discovered issues directly on the planning sheet (with any necessary reference of how to return quickly to important data in the question), you can save valuable time by not writing notes twice—once on the question and again on your planning sheet. If, however, you find that stopping your reading to list an issue on a separate sheet causes you to lose your place in reading the question, marginal notes may be the best way to organize yourself. When practising, consider trying both methods. Stay with the one that makes you feel most comfortable.

*Ranking issues.*    Those who neglect the first two parts in the overall case approach, considering their own role and the requirements of the information users, often find that their solutions begin to unravel at this point. The relative importance of issues to users is as vital in answering a case question as it is in real life.

For example, would you feel confident in a doctor who is obsessed with treating your rash when you are suffering a heart attack? Would you pay a lawyer hired to represent you in your murder trial if his or her efforts were concentrated on getting a few parking tickets cancelled?

It is human nature to prefer discussing in detail topics in which we have interest and confidence. You must suppress this trait, however, to be successful in professional examinations and as a professional accountant.

In the "Rank" column of your case plan, you should rank the issues 1, 2, 3, 4, etc., in order of importance to your users, keeping in mind any limitations caused by your own character's role. Do not rank an issue higher because you know a lot about it or can immediately imagine a clever analysis for that issue. When ranking issues, ask yourself: Would the users in this case pay me for dealing with this issue? If not, the issue is of little importance to either of you. Or: If I do not have enough time to answer all issues, which issues would the user want or expect me to answer with the time available? Are sufficient facts available in the case to be able to solve the issue?

> *When ranking issues, consider how to best serve the client.*

The biggest factor in ranking issues is the materiality of the item. If one problem involves a $10,000 item and another problem involves a $10 million item, then the $10 million item likely is the most important item. After that, issues are typically ranked in the following order of priority:

- Controversial or highly contentious items
- Items with errors
- Complex items

For example, a revenue recognition issue in which two alternatives can be almost equally supported is more contentious than a revenue recognition issue in which the correct method is much more obvious. The client would appreciate the help on the contentious item rather than the straightforward item. Errors always need to be identified and corrected. But errors are usually easier to identify and correct than the contentious items. Lastly, a client might know the right method to report revenue but not understand the reason. You earn your fee by explaining the rationale. In all these situations, you have helped the client resolve or clarify something.

Regardless of the style of question, after completing your list of issues and considering the user needs, a small number of issues will usually appear as most important. In many professional exams, you may only have time to answer the major issues and may only get marks on the major issues. It is better to get sufficient depth on the major issues than it is to scratch the surface on all issues.

*Anticipated analysis.* A separate column is provided in our case-planning sheet to allow you to plan the type of analysis that you think will be necessary to arrive at your recommendation. In this column, you should enter only a few words to remind you, during the analysis phase of the case, of what you feel is required.

Basically, there are only two broad categories of analysis seen in case solutions: qualitative and quantitative.

Qualitative analysis considers the intangible factors affecting the characters in the case. A simple way to organize these factors was shown in II as environmental considerations: economic, legal, moral, and personal factors. Most issues in a case require some thought as to the impact of these qualitative considerations on your recommendation.

Quantitative analysis deals with numbers. It is usually the type of analysis first considered by accounting students, as it relates most closely to the material studied at university. Some students are attracted to quantitative analysis because, in the end, you get what seems to be a concrete result. On the other hand, some students shy away from the numbers especially when they feel that there is not enough information to fully analyze the situation.

---

*A good solution will usually include a mix of quantitative and qualitative analysis.*

---

Rarely in a case question will you receive all of the numerical data that you would need for a complete quantitative analysis. Estimates and assumptions will have to be made that make the result less definitive than originally thought. In fact, important information like discount rates and asset lives may be based on qualitative factors such as the economy and environment.

A good solution will tailor the analysis to the particular question. Given the time constraints in answering a question, a technically perfect quantitative analysis is not expected. Unless clearly directed by the case information, a simple, technically reasonable calculation that leads to a consistent recommendation is all that is required. Assumptions should be clearly noted and, if possible, tied into the qualitative analysis that resulted in that assumption.

At this final stage of the planning process, though, only a few words should be written on your case plan. These words can lead you into your analysis later.

*Time budget.*    In the real world, time must be managed. This very difficult skill can be practised in a learning environment as well, especially when analyzing multi-competency and comprehensive cases. Every case differs slightly, but the reading and planning phase of approaching a case usually requires around 30% of the time assigned to the entire case. The report-writing phase may also require around 30% of the time. The remaining 40% of the available time is then devoted to the analysis phase.

> *The reading and planning phase is often underutilized because students are anxious to get started with the analysis and report writing phases.*

The last column in your case plan should be a budget of how much time you are able and willing to spend in the analysis phase for each issue. Having already completed the other columns of the planning sheet, you now know how many issues must be addressed, their relative importance and the work you expect of yourself. This should permit a quick allocation of the time to be used to prepare your analysis. Ensure that top-ranked issues are assigned enough time to do the detailed analysis they deserve. Allow sufficient time for writing the final report.

Time budgeting is a practised skill. When attempting practice cases, be very strict in keeping to your time budget. This will accomplish two things. First, you will be able to evaluate your time budgeting abilities and make any necessary adjustments to your thoughts. Second, you will become more comfortable in an environment in which you have only a fixed amount of time to perform a detailed task. This acclimatization is invaluable.

When first dealing with cases, you should take more than the allotted time to answer a case. Follow the guidance given here, work through the steps methodically, and see the benefits of doing so. As you get better at writing cases, you may be able to organize your thoughts without formally completing this chart. However, you would still go through the mental process. When you write your professional exams, write things down in your rough notes to the extent necessary to guide you through the process.

> *Not all cases should be written under tight time constraints. When first learning how to analyze a case, you should take much more than the allotted time so that you can practise each step and learn it properly.*

In most situations, this chart does not need to be formally incorporated in your final report. Rather, it is a part of your rough notes to ensure that you get on the right track. Only incorporate your analysis and conclusions from the analysis in your formal report.

Now read the rest of the MCL case and complete Exhibit 1A.4. An example of a completed Case Plan is shown in Exhibit 1A.5 for the MCL case.

## Completed Case Plan

| Competency Area and Issues | Rank | Anticipated Analysis | Time Budget |
|---|---|---|---|
| Financial reporting: | | | |
|    Government grants | 1 | Qualitative and impact on key metric | 8 |
|    Late fees | 5 | Qualitative and impact on key metric | 3 |
|    Useful lives of assets | 4 | Qualitative and impact on key metric | 3 |
|    Capitalized expenditures | 3 | Qualitative and impact on key metric | 5 |
|    Lawsuit | 2 | Qualitative and impact on key metric | 5 |

## IV: Identify Alternatives for Each Given Issue

A basic deficiency noted in a number of evaluators' reports on professional accounting exams concerns students' neglect of user needs and possible alternate solutions when preparing responses to case questions.

> *Why are these areas of disappointment to evaluators year after year? Both demand the use of imagination!*

The stereotypical accountant's life, to an outsider, seems bereft of variety and imagination. Normal university accounting courses do not encourage a broad-thinking attitude, as they concentrate on the coverage of a technical curriculum. As we have seen on a number of occasions in this section, though, professional examinations are quite different. Rather than merely expecting you to demonstrate technical knowledge, professional exams demand that you also show an ability to organize and think—the qualities that people hire you for in real life.

An important way to prove that you have those valuable qualities is by showing the maturity of knowing that, in many situations, more than one possible solution exists to solve the problem. In your heart, before any analysis begins, you may feel that you know the best solution to a problem. How better to prove yourself right, though, than by comparing your best answer to a number of reasonable alternatives?

> *Force yourself to consider at least two alternatives for every issue before coming to a conclusion.*

At the completion of this part, you should have an outline of the major issues. The outline will identify the viable alternatives and the criteria to be used in choosing between the viable alternatives. An example of the suggested format for the outline of issues is shown in Exhibit 1A.6.

*Identifying viable alternatives.* To begin, let's consider what makes a case statement an issue. An issue is created by disagreement. In your character's role, you may disagree with a technical approach proposed by a client user. Or case information may indicate a disagreement between a vendor and potential purchaser as to a company's value. Which side is right? In real life, jumping to a conclusion without considering all sides would insult those having a different point of view. In a case question, it would be a sure route to a poor response.

**EXHIBIT 1A.6**

## Outline of Issues

| Competency Area and Issues | Viable Alternatives | Criteria for Resolving/ Planned Analysis |
|---|---|---|
|  |  |  |
|  |  |  |

Thinking in terms of alternatives is another area in which practice, with honest feedback, is the best teacher. Sincerely attempting the remainder of the case in this section is a good start to that practice.

To get used to a broad-thinking approach when practising is not difficult. Assume the case information has a client proposing an accounting policy that you consider to be inappropriate. Your initial reaction is that a different policy would be most proper. There! You have two alternatives to discuss and compare already. Now, try to imagine a compromise position between yours and the client's. Another alternative! Finally, consider a possible solution outside the spectrum framed by the positions of you and the client. As you can see, an almost infinite number of alternatives could be invented if you had an unlimited amount of time.

In handling a case question, though, time is a very important factor. In the previous step to the overall approach, you assigned a limited amount of time to each issue based on its ranking. After all that planning, it would be foolish to waste time considering impractical alternatives. If you have identified more than three alternatives, narrow your list down to the two (or three at most) viable alternatives.

> In an exam situation, you usually only have time to analyze two (sometimes three) alternatives.

In many situations—both in real life and on professional examinations—the accountant is constrained by generally accepted accounting principles (GAAP). A good example of wasting time on impractical alternatives occurs when a student identifies theoretical accounting solutions when GAAP clearly recommend a specific solution—particularly when the user expects the financial statements to comply with GAAP. Take note, for example, in the MCL suggested approach, how the analysis of many of the accounting issues merely compares the non-GAAP approach used by MCL with the treatment recommended by ASPE. To illustrate, under the "Government grants" issue, the statements in the paragraph beginning with "The recording of the grants as revenue is inappropriate under ASPE" are mainly a summary of the ASPE requirements. When you are not constrained by GAAP, however, you can be much more imaginative in identifying alternative solutions.

When practising, get into the habit of debating with yourself. This ability will provide two tangible benefits. First, it will discourage you from straying and considering impractical alternatives. If your conscience says, "I couldn't realistically suggest that idea to anyone," then do not include it in the alternatives that you analyze. Second, debating with yourself will assist in doing the objective analysis required in part V of the overall approach.

This consideration of alternatives should be performed for each major issue in your case plan. Issues ranked as more minor often do not require the time-consuming quantitative analysis required for major issues. This makes them perfect for quick, qualitative analysis of alternative solutions.

The detailed analysis of issues is often done by means of preparing appendices that will be attached to the final recommendation summary. When beginning your analysis notes, always ensure, after describing the concern or disagreement behind the issue, that your limited list of alternative solutions is clearly shown. This will lead you into the detailed analysis discussed in part V.

## Identify Criteria for Resolving

After identifying the viable alternatives for a particular issue, identify the factors to be considered in choosing between the alternatives and coming up with a recommendation. Some people refer to these factors as the decision criteria. In this section, we refer to these factors as the criteria for resolving.

For example, the criteria for resolving a revenue recognition issue are performance, measurement and collectibility. The criteria for resolving a capital budgeting decision is present value of future cash flows. The criteria for resolving a make-or-buy decision is incremental contribution margin.

Rather than identifying a whole bunch of factors, identify the key factor for the fact situation given in the case. For example, the company may clearly meet the performance and collectibility criteria for revenue recognition but measurability is a big concern. Focus on measurability in the ensuing analysis.

> *The criteria for resolving are the benchmarks against which the alternatives will be evaluated.*

Now complete Exhibit 1A.6 for the MCL case. Then compare your outline to the completed outline of issues in Exhibit 1A.7.

When first dealing with cases, you should prepare this chart in the detail provided in this section. As you get better at writing cases, you may be able to organize your thoughts without formally completing this chart. However, you would still go through the mental process. When you

**EXHIBIT 1A.7**

## Completed Outline of Issues

| Competency Area and Issues | Viable Alternatives | Criteria for Resolving/Planned Analysis |
|---|---|---|
| Financial reporting: | | |
| Government grants | Contra to asset/expense account vs. deferred revenue vs. revenue | When is it earned? What best reflects purpose of grant, i.e., reduction of cost or future revenue? |
| Late fees | Accrue liability vs. disclose | Is future payment likely and measurable? |
| Useful lives of assets | Company's current # of years or a lesser # of years | What is the expected period and pattern of benefit? |
| Capitalized expenditures | Capitalize vs. expense Current classification vs. another account | Will there be any future benefits? What best reflects nature of asset? |
| Lawsuit | Accrue liability vs. disclose | Is future payment likely and measurable? |

write your professional exams, write things down in your rough notes to the extent necessary to guide you through the process.

In most situations, this chart does not need to be formally incorporated in your final report. Rather, it is a part of your rough notes to ensure that you get on the right track. Only incorporate your analysis and conclusions from the analysis in your formal report.

## V: Analyze Alternatives Using Criteria for Resolving

Up to this point in the overall case approach, the majority of the time has been spent planning and organizing information contained in the question. It has taken until this fifth of six parts to actually begin the detailed work that inexperienced students often want to begin as their first action.

Looking at what should be physically in front of us after completing the previous steps, we should see a sheet showing the user needs summary (Exhibit 1A.3), a case plan (Exhibit 1A.5), and an outline of issues (Exhibit 1A.7). Depending on your preference, you may also have already begun individual appendix sheets for each issue identified in your outline of issues. Each sheet would outline the concern caused by the issue and list a few practical alternative solutions. Some people find it easier to consider only one issue at a time through the analysis portion of this stage. They would combine the recognition of alternatives outlined in IV with the analysis portion of this phase and consider each issue separately. Either method is fine, provided that the integration portion of this stage discussed below is not neglected.

Now it's time to do the work that will lead to your final recommendations. As an exam candidate, your only responsibility is to prove to the evaluators that you have the abilities required to be a professional accountant. This phase of the overall approach stresses the evidence you can provide to prove those abilities—analysis and integration.

*Analysis.* In III, the two basic types of analysis were introduced. Qualitative analysis examines the environmental aspects of an issue. Quantitative analysis calculates the numerical data necessary to support or dispel a recommendation. In completing your case plan, you decided what combination of these two types of analysis would be most appropriate given the ranking of each issue. The type and amount of anticipated analysis was a major factor in determining the time budgeted to each issue. You should not deviate from your planned approach, except in extreme situations. Such a desperation change should only be considered when, in the course of your analysis, you discover that you have missed recognizing an important issue or seriously misjudged the ranking of an issue. Adjusting your plan during the analysis phase of the work may not have been expected but should be done when warranted. Hopefully, plenty of practice will make emergency plan adjustments unnecessary.

*Qualitative analysis.* University students do not generally receive much practice in considering accounting issues in a qualitative way. The concept of thinking about the effect of accounting issues on people's lives does not easily mesh with the learning of technical knowledge. As a result, when students take the large step from university to professional examinations, they are often disillusioned by evaluator comments claiming that the candidate's qualitative analysis was weak. How do you learn to perform a strong qualitative analysis when, by their nature, qualitative thoughts can be infinite?

An organized approach is a good place to start. A framework will limit the infinite possibilities to those that reasonably affect the characters in the question, while ensuring the depth of consideration expected. Also, an organized framework will discourage you from merely dumping into your answer all your technical knowledge about a subject, whether it is relevant or not.

The number of ways of organizing qualitative thoughts can be as endless as the number of thoughts themselves. Here, though, are three alternatives that you should consider as a beginning:

1. *Pro/con chart.* A chart can be arranged so that the advantages and disadvantages relative to the criteria for resolving of each alternate solution may be considered. If you find that a pro of one alternative is a con of another alternative, it may be more efficient to simply list pros of each alternative. While being very general, it allows a quick way to organize your thoughts. A pro/con chart is very useful when a fast, simple qualitative analysis is required and when there are few alternatives.

2. *Matrix.* When it is important to compare a number of alternatives at once, a matrix is often very useful. The matrix, which is really just a chart, could be arranged with the relevant alternatives in columns across the top. The important factors to be considered would then be shown in rows down the left side. This creates a number of boxes, which force you to address each of the factors for each of the alternatives. Enter your analysis in its respective box. When you think you are done, look at the matrix as a whole. Are there any empty boxes? If so, your analysis is incomplete and must be finished. Matrices are extremely useful when a number of factors must be considered in analyzing potential solutions.

3. *Checklist.* When in-depth qualitative analysis is needed, a checklist could be used that analyzes each alternative using the environmental categories outlined in the discussion of user needs in II:

   - Economic factors—What impact will this alternative have on the economic state of the user? What effect would changes in the general and industry economics have on this alternative?

   - Legal factors—Do any laws or regulations restrict the usefulness of this alternative?

   - Moral factors—Are there any professional, ethical, or other moral reasons why this alternative should not be chosen?

   - Personal factors—What impact do personal relationships and beliefs have on this alternative, and vice versa. In complex situations, it may be most useful to arrange the checklist in matrix form.

---

*Follow an organized approach to evaluate the alternatives against the criteria for resolving.*

---

Warning! Do not waste time merely repeating case facts. The evaluators, like any user, know what the situation is; otherwise, they would not have recognized the need for your services. Refer to case facts only as they relate to your criteria for resolving and restrict your analysis primarily to the case facts.

> *Explicitly state how the facts of the case meet or do not meet the criteria for resolving for each issue.*

The main goal in finding a method to organize your qualitative analysis is to ensure that sufficient thought is given to concerns that will affect the users of your recommendations. No one method is appropriate to all cases, but with experience you will become comfortable in assessing what form is required, or at least acceptable, in a given situation.

*Quantitative analysis.* Once you have decided what form your quantitative analysis should take, its actual performance is probably the only area of the question that compares to university examinations. Financial accounting calculations should be calculated from the technical knowledge gained during your previous studies. University exams expect you to clearly show your calculations and state any assumptions made. In both of these areas, however, you must go further in professional examinations.

It is imperative that your calculations not only be clear and well organized, but be as formal-looking as possible. Remember that the calculation is usually part of an appendix to a report or memo to a superior or bill-paying user. A messy, casual, technically correct answer will earn fewer marks than a technically correct answer that a little extra effort has made look formal.

Assumptions must not only be stated, they must relate to the users' needs and qualitative analysis performed for that issue. For example, it would be easy in a question to use the market value of equipment to assess whether the asset is impaired. However, the present value of future cash flows from continuing to use the asset may be a better way to assess the recoverable amount. The users want to know whether the asset is impaired. The value in use may be more complicated to calculate and may involve more assumptions, but it may also present a more realistic value for the equipment.

Ensure that assumptions are supported by the planning and analysis that you have done so far. In your work, clearly show the relationship of the assumptions to user needs and qualitative analysis. A general caution is in order. If you find yourself making many assumptions, you are probably straying too far from the case facts and marking key. This will result in attempting to perform an analysis that is too complicated.

> *Make assumptions as necessary to perform an appropriate amount of quantitative analysis.*

Keep quantitative calculations as simple as possible. Our natural inclination as accountants is to make numbers perfectly accurate. Exam case questions preclude detailed and perfectly accurate answers, however, by only offering a limited amount of time and information to perform the analysis. Make your calculation technically supportable without wasting time fine-tuning a particular answer. Remember, it's your recommendations that the user is paying for, not a masterpiece of calculation. Also, to save time, most professional examinations provide present value tables, income tax information, and a tax shield formula at the end of the exam. Be sure to use them instead of attempting detailed time-value calculations or assuming tax amounts yourself.

In spite of the typical accountant's well-earned reputation for being a "number cruncher," many professional examination reports lament the lack of quantitative analysis in candidates' responses.

For example, even though the suggested approach to MCL did not show much quantitative analysis, it was referred to a number of times in the evaluators' comments. For example, in the going concern issue, the evaluator commented, "The better responses presented some quantitative analysis." In discussing the late delivery penalties, "Most candidates did not quantify the amount of the possible penalty payment." Remember, in your case plan, to identify the necessity and type of quantitative analysis required. Then do it—as quickly, simply, and professionally as possible.

For financial accounting issues, the quantitative analysis should normally include an indication of the impact of your recommendation on the key metric. That is, how much will the key metric change if your recommendation is adopted? For example, assume that the key metric in a particular case is net income. What would be the change to net income if revenue were recognized on a percentage of completion (as per your recommendation) when the client's draft financial statements recognized revenue on signing of the contract.

*Integration.*   The performance of qualitative and quantitative analysis provides isolated information necessary to use in making your final recommendation. In real life, though, very few issues act in isolation. For example, a union safety grievance may result in a factory capital renovation requiring additional bank financing when credit limits are fully stretched.

While the case plan is very useful in breaking a complex case into bite-sized issues, it in itself, does not reflect the interrelationship of issues. To prepare a good solution, you must consider the integration, the bringing together, of factors within the case. Like qualitative analysis, this is an area in which it is easy to get bogged down with an unlimited number of thoughts if you are not strictly organized. To simplify the process, let's split the idea of integration down into its three basic components:

1. *Fact integration.* This relates to the combination of two or more case facts to create an issue. For example, in Metal Caissons Limited, the plant construction delays and contract delivery deadlines are two facts. Combined, however, they create the issue of unaccrued late payment penalties. A proper integration of case facts must be made during the issue identification step of the planning phase. Otherwise, complex and important issues will not be discovered until it is too late to deal with them. In MCL, note how the going concern issue is given its significance by integrating the implications of several facts. The going-concern issue was not mentioned (or even hinted at) in the question. Fact-integration skills can only become automatic by trying as many practice cases as possible.

> *The going-concern issue was identified in the analysis stage (rather than the planning stage) after integrating the various facts of the case.*

2. *Competency-area integration.* While all issues can be assigned to a technical area, many actually impact a number of different syllabus sections. Take, for example, a manufacturing company that does not provide an accrual for warranty expenses. The obvious category for such an issue is financial accounting. GAAP states that expenses should be matched to revenue. But any solution that suggests that a warranty provision be accrued must also consider the impact of that recommendation on: (a) auditing (How can the warranty accrual be audited? Will a specialist be required?); (b) income taxes (When will this warranty expense accrual be deductible for tax purposes?); and (c) other financial accounting issues. (If not tax-deductible now, does this accrual cause a timing difference creating deferred taxes?)

The last paragraph in the main body of the MCL case as it actually appeared on the CPA exam explicitly requested a memo dealing with the accounting, auditing, and tax issues in the engagement. Yet the evaluators commented in several sections that most candidates failed to address the audit implications of an issue. This deficiency was very likely caused by a failure to deliberately incorporate syllabus integration into the response.

3. *Issue integration.* What effect will your proposed recommendation have on other issues in the question? If, in the above example, your recommendation to accrue a warranty reserve changes working capital ratios to the point where financing cannot be obtained for a planned expansion, what changes, if any, in your recommendations will have to be made to usefully address both issues?

As you can see, once you get your imagination working, it's sometimes difficult to stop. How can you put enough depth into your answer while staying within your time budget? It is clear that the question of fact integration must mainly be addressed when issues are identified. This leaves syllabus and issue integration to be considered.

For this work, keep your case plan handy. After you have performed your analysis work on an issue, and have a proposed recommendation, do the following:

- *Look at the topic titles in your plan.* Imagine how, if at all, your recommendation might be discussed in the topics other than that in which it was assigned. This does not have to be onerous. If, for example, a financial accounting issue has been analyzed, you'll be asking yourself questions like: Does this recommendation cause an audit problem? What would the tax treatment of this solution be? How would this suggestion change the company's financing? By using the topic titles on your case plan as reminders, you will be sure to consider the effect of this issue on all relevant technical areas.

- *Now, look at each of the individual issues that you ranked as being major.* Consider what effect your proposed recommendation has on those other issues, and vice versa. If this thought process is performed for each major issue, you will ensure that all important interrelationships are considered and that all of your recommendations act consistently together.

The above two steps will accomplish the mental part of syllabus and issue integration. The portion of these thoughts that you will want to write in your appendix for each issue are those points in other topics and issues which either support or weaken your proposed recommendation. If the weakening points are minor, it indicates that your recommendation will be a compromise position in addressing the case issues. A compromise is not a bad thing, and usually very realistic. If the weakening points in your integration are major, however, other recommendations must be chosen which are more practical.

After the integration portion of this step is completed, for each issue on your case plan, you should now have a completed appendix outlining the concern caused by the issue and alternative solutions to that concern, along with details of the qualitative and quantitative analysis performed, the effect of this issue on other technical areas, the issue's interaction with other issues, and your recommendation.

Now perform the analysis phase for the MCL case. Your analysis will likely be a lot of thinking without too much writing. You should apply the *Handbook* rules and/or basic accounting principles to resolve the issues. Perhaps you can make rough notes to highlight what you want to say in your final report. You also want to calculate the impact of your recommendation on the key metric.

> *For financial accounting cases, the quantitative impact of the recommendation on the key metric should be determined and stated in the final report.*

You are now ready to write the final portion of your solution.

## VI: Communicate Practical Recommendations/Conclusions to Information Users

The amount of time spent in writing your final report or memorandum will vary from case to case. Some cases may require a lot of quantitative analysis, which is usually incorporated in appendices. Other reports may have few or no appendices. Appendices should be prepared in the analysis stage. The final report refers to and comments on the appendices and provides the recommendations.

> *Exhibits/appendices are prepared in the analysis phase, before the final report is written.*

After completing the five previous steps in this overall approach, you have done all of the necessary analysis and integration to produce a useful recommendation. The rest should be easy, right?

It should be, but candidates often fail to finish the job properly. Too often, students feel that once all of the work involved in preparing the appendices described in V is complete, the conclusion of the question is unimportant.

This would be similar to saying that it would be acceptable to prepare a technically perfect set of financial statement information, then writing those statements in crayon on the back of old grocery bags.

The product given to your client is the reason you get paid. Evaluators know that, too. They are testing not only your technical and analytical abilities in professional exams, but your communication skills as well.

You cannot expect to earn marks for pervasive skills such as problem solving and communicating effectively and efficiently if your technical work is weak. Poor candidates cannot earn marks merely by being able to write nice prose. Nevertheless, in a good technical answer, marks earned for communication sometimes mean the difference between deciles of candidate rankings. This in turn might mean the difference between passing and failing.

What do you have to do to earn these marks? By following the overall case approach to this point, you have prepared a number of appendices covering all of the issues identified in the question. You now have to write your final conclusion. Usually, you would expect this conclusion to be only a few pages long. It is intended to provide a summary of the work done in the first five steps of the approach. The conclusion must be in the form specified by the required—often a report or memorandum. It must be written by the character in the role assigned to you by the case. One method would be to prepare a brief summary of the users and their needs, followed by a short discussion of each of the identified issues, referenced to the detailed analysis and integration in the previously prepared appendices. Such a short discussion would then propose and support a clear recommendation for each issue. The implications of your recommendations on the key financial statements items should also be stated.

> *The main body of the final report contains your recommendations and conclusions along with supporting arguments and references to the analysis in the appendices.*

Let's look at some evaluators' comments that have been provided for pervasive skills on past professional exams:

- "Candidate recognized discussion/communication required between different users." In order to be assessed as competent, candidates were expected to play the assigned role and prepare the communication described by the required.

- "Communicated in a manner understandable by all parties." Part of properly playing a role is determining the type and level of communication relevant to the user. A report to a client filled with technical jargon and acronyms would not be acceptable in real life, as the client would not likely understand it. A memo to a partner in an accounting firm providing details of basic GAAP concepts might be considered insulting in real practice. Evaluators expect you to tailor your communication as you would in a practical situation. Have your character speak to the user in a way he or she can understand and use efficiently.

> *The report should be written at a level understandable by the primary recipient.*

- "Candidate tied analysis to objectives of users." All the effort spent planning your approach to the case was not merely to determine factors for the analysis phase. Your user needs summary allows you to show how you considered the user's goals and limitations in devising a solution to his or her problems. Ensure that your recommendations are practical given the needs and limitations you identified. Do not ignore all this planning work when writing your final conclusion.

- "Candidate presented analysis and recommendations clearly." In playing your role, a professional-looking, organized answer is vital. If, as suggested in V, the work done in the appendices has been prepared in a neat, organized manner, then that style should be carried through to the writing of the conclusion. Distinguish separate issues by use of headings or new paragraphs. Try to keep sentences short and to the point. Finally, in spite of the time pressure, try to make all your writing clearly legible. Your report will seem more professional, and marks will not be lost through a marker's inability to decipher your work.

- "Provided specific supported decision." Hard as it may be to imagine, even after all of the analysis work done by candidates in approaching a question, some students neglect to provide an answer to the important case issues. This is sometimes due to a lack of confidence in their conclusion. Please realize that, due to the nature of cases, no case answer is specifically correct. Any reasonably supported conclusion is far better than none at all. In all case questions, users are hiring you to provide a service. This service is demonstrated through your conclusions. Make those conclusions clear, as definite recommendations will inspire user confidence.

Once you have completed the final report or memorandum required by the question, the only thing left to do is to make certain that all appendices showing your detailed work are attached to the report and properly referenced in your solution. Also, you could include the Exhibits on users' needs, case summary, and outline of issues in your rough notes. These charts would usually not be referenced to your formal answer unless you ran out of time and did not have a chance to write about something outlined in one of these Exhibits.

Now write your final memo for the MCL case. It should contain your recommendations along with the analysis and arguments supporting your recommendations. It should also indicate the impact of your recommendations on the key metric. All work should be neat and professionally organized.

Your final memo does not need to discuss the alternatives for each issue unless the issue was very contentious. If in the analysis stage, you determined that there was clearly a right answer for a problem, then your report would provide your recommendation with the supporting arguments. It would be redundant at this stage to providing arguments for the alternatives that were dismissed. On the other hand, if you had a hard time deciding between alternatives because both alternatives had many benefits, then your final report could present the arguments for both alternatives along with your recommendation as to the best option in this contentious situation.

> *Only discuss alternatives in the final report when the alternatives were nearly equal in meeting the criteria for resolving. When one alternative is clearly better than the others, only that alternative would be discussed in your final report.*

Now compare your solution to the solution given below. You may be surprised to see that the going-concern issue is given significant attention even though it was not included on the outline of issues. After analyzing and resolving the issues on the outline, it should have become apparent that MCL would have to make significant reductions to net income. The company's financial situation would look a lot worse. This would raise questions about whether the company could continue as a going concern. Therefore, it would be appropriate to discuss the issue.

Having now read details of all six steps of our suggested case approach, you may feel that too much is expected of you. But consider the following. First, if you allow yourself plenty of time to practise, the steps will become automatic—something that you won't have to think about when attempting a real exam case. Second, few people need to start from scratch in developing skills in all steps. Before trying a real exam, you should write some practice exams and evaluate them using the suggested solutions or have them marked by someone else. Use their comments to determine what areas need improvement. Reread the relevant sections of this section and try another case.

Finally, realize that the skills you are learning in preparation for these examinations will not only allow you to become an accountant by passing professional exams, but also help you be a successful accountant and businessperson.

## Summary of Appendix 1A

The framework for case analysis involves identifying problems, analyzing alternatives, and making recommendations that solve the problems and respond to users' needs. **(LO5)**

## Self-Study Case 1

LO5

Metal Caissons Limited (MCL) was incorporated on December 15, Year 1, to build metal caissons, which are large containers used for transporting military equipment. John Ladd (president) and Paul Finch (vice-president) each own 50% of MCL's shares. Until September 30, Year 2, MCL's first fiscal year-end, they applied their energy to planning and organizing the business. John and Paul developed the product, sought government assistance, designed the plant, and negotiated a sales contract.

In October Year 2, MCL signed a $7.5 million contract with the Canadian Department of National Defence (DND). The contract stipulates that MCL must deliver one caisson to DND on the first business day of each month over a period of five years, commencing on April 1, Year 3. Any delay in delivery entails a $2,000 penalty per day, per caisson delivered late, up to a maximum of $50,000 per caisson. DND has the right to cancel its contract with MCL at any time if the company is unable to meet its commitments. The caissons must be manufactured according to DND's detailed plans and specifications. Any caisson not meeting the specifications will be rejected, thereby causing a delay in delivery.

During November Year 2, MCL obtained two government grants. Details of the grant agreements are as follows:

1. *A $1 million grant for the construction of a manufacturing plant.* The plant must be located in a designated area of the country and must be constructed primarily of Canadian-made components, failing which MCL must repay the grant in full.

2. *A $500,000 grant for job creation.* As a condition of the grant, MCL must employ at least 85% of its total workforce in the plant for a period of three years. If employment at the plant falls below this minimum level, MCL will have to repay the grant in full.

On December 1, Year 2, MCL borrowed $1 million from the bank to construct the plant in northern Quebec, one of the designated areas. Construction was scheduled to start immediately and to be completed by the end of February Year 3. Unfortunately, construction was delayed, and the manufacturing section of the plant was not fully operational until the beginning of May. As a result, the April, May, and June caissons were delivered 25, 18, and 12 days late, respectively. The inexperienced employees had to work quickly but met the delivery deadlines for the July and August caissons. The administrative section of the plant (supervisors' office, etc., representing 5% of the total area) is still under construction.

As a condition of a bank loan and the DND contract, the company must issue audited financial statements in accordance with ASPE commencing with the year ending September 30, Year 3.

It is now mid-September, Year 3. Linda Presner, a partner with Presner & Wolf, Chartered Accountants, and you, the CPA in charge of the audit, have just met with MCL's senior management to discuss MCL's accounting policies. During the meeting, you obtained the condensed internal financial statements of MCL for the 11 months ended August 31, Year 3 (Exhibit A) and other information on MCL (Exhibit B). After the meeting, Linda asks you to prepare a memo for her dealing with the accounting issues connected with this engagement.

*(CPA Canada adapted)*[2]

EXHIBIT A

## METAL CAISSONS LIMITED CONDENSED BALANCE SHEET
(in thousands of dollars, unaudited)

|  | Aug. 31 Year 3 | Sept. 30 Year 2 |
|---|---|---|
| Current assets | $2,388 | $242 |
| Property, plant, and equipment, net of amortization (Note 1) | 2,154 | |
| Capitalized expenditures, net of amortization (Note 1) | 109 | 120 |
| Investment in MSL, at cost | 240 | |
|  | $4,891 | $362 |
| Current liabilities | $2,489 | $120 |
| Long-term liabilities | 1,000 | |
| Shareholders' equity | 1,402 | 242 |
|  | $4,891 | $362 |

## METAL CAISSONS LIMITED CONDENSED INCOME STATEMENT
For the 11 months ended August 31, Year 3
(in thousands of dollars)

| | |
|---|---|
| Revenues | $2,125 |
| Cost of sales | 375 |
| Gross margin | 1,750 |
| Administrative expenses | 590 |
| Net income | $1,160 |

## METAL CAISSONS LIMITED
### EXTRACTS FROM NOTES TO CONDENSED FINANCIAL STATEMENTS
For the 11 months ended August 31, Year 3

1. Accounting policies

*Inventories.*   Inventories are valued at the lower of cost and net realizable value. Cost is determined on a first-in, first-out basis.

*Property, plant, and equipment.*   Property, plant, and equipment are recorded at cost. Depreciation is calculated on a straight-line basis over the following periods:

| | |
|---|---|
| Plant | 50 years |
| Production equipment | 15 years |
| Office equipment | 20 years |
| Computer equipment | 10 years |

*Capitalized expenditures.*   Capitalized expenditures consist of costs incurred during the start-up of the company. Amortization is calculated on a straight-line basis over a 10-year period.

*Capitalized interest.*   The company is capitalizing 100% of the interest on the long-term debt until construction of the plant is complete. This interest is included in the cost of the plant.

**EXHIBIT B**

## INFORMATION GATHERED BY CPA

The bank loan bears interest at 8% and is secured by a mortgage on the plant. The loan is repayable over 10 years, with monthly payments of interest and principal of $12,133.

The head office of MCL, located in Montreal, is strictly an administrative unit. Twenty-four people, including the president and the vice-president, work at head office. A bookkeeper who joined MCL in February Year 3 supervises the preparation of the various financial and administrative reports. The plant employs 90 people.

As at September 30, Year 2, capitalized expenditures included the following items:

| | |
|---|---:|
| Incorporation costs | $ 5,000 |
| Office equipment | 24,000 |
| Travel costs related to search for plant site | 16,000 |
| Costs of calls for tenders for manufacturing plant | 12,000 |
| Product development costs | 22,000 |
| Grant negotiation costs | 13,000 |
| Costs related to contract negotiations with DND | 10,000 |
| Miscellaneous administrative costs | 11,000 |
| Miscellaneous legal fees | 7,000 |
| | $120,000 |

The capitalized legal fees of $7,000 as at September 30, Year 2, include $2,000 in fees related to a $2.5 million lawsuit filed by Deutsch Production (a German company) against MCL for patent infringements. As at September 15, Year 3, John Ladd is unable to determine the outcome of the suit. In fiscal Year 3, $12,000 in legal fees has been incurred and expensed.

MCL reported no income or expenses in its Year 2 fiscal year.

DND did not take any action following the delays in delivery.

# SOLUTION TO SELF-STUDY CASE 1

Memo to: Linda Presner, Partner
From: CPA
Subject: Accounting issues regarding Metal Caissons Limited (MCL)

## Overview of the Engagement

The financial statements of MCL will be used by the two shareholders, the bank and the Department of National Defence (DND). All of these users' needs must be considered when assessing appropriate accounting policies and disclosures. John Ladd and Paul Finch wish to present financial statements conveying a picture of profitability and a strong financial position to the bank and the DND. However, it would be in their best interests to adopt policies that will also minimize corporate taxes. The bank and the DND would likely expect generally accepted accounting principles for private enterprises (ASPE) to be used in all instances.

## Going Concern

This issue must be assessed to determine whether the financial statements should be stated on the basis of historical costs or liquidation values. A potential going-concern problem is suggested by the following:

- By excluding the government grants from revenues, MCL would be in a loss position. If the year-to-date results are typical, the long-term profitability of MCL may be marginal. However, such losses may, however, be normal in a start-up situation.

- DND is the sole client and can cancel the contract if the terms of the contract are not met. Delivery dates have been missed; however, recent deliveries have been made on time.

- MCL's working-capital position indicates potential insolvency if government grants are not received. MCL has not met the terms of the job-creation grant, and this may explain why the grant has not yet been received.

- The working-capital position has deteriorated further because DND has not paid for the caissons received to date. The metal caissons must meet high standards of quality, and DND's inspection process may have slowed down approvals. Alternatively, the fact that DND has not paid may mean that there are problems that have not yet been disclosed to us.

- There is nothing to indicate that the contract with DND will be renewed at the end of five years or that the manufacturing process can be changed to another product at that time.

- The lawsuit pending against MCL, if successful, could drive the company into bankruptcy.

Although there are many factors that raise a concern about the ability of MCL to continue as a going concern, MCL continues to operate as a going concern. DND has not yet cancelled the contract and the bank has not called the loan. Therefore, MCL should continue to report on a going-concern basis. However, they should disclose their reliance on the DND contract and the significant risks that may bear on their ability to continue as a going concern.

## Government Grants

At present, 79% (90/[90 + 24]) of MCL's total workforce is employed in the plant, which is below the 85% specified in the job-creation grant. If the conditions cannot be met by their due date, the grant receivable will need to be written off.

The recording of the grants as revenue is inappropriate under ASPE since the grants pertain to the cost of the plant and cost of employees. The grants do not pertain to the sale of goods or provision of services. The building grant should be netted against the capitalized cost of the plant, or recorded as a deferred credit and amortized to income over the life of the plant. The job-creation grant should be deferred and amortized to income over the three-year period of the agreement and netted against the plant wages. It will be necessary to disclose the terms of the grants.

## Late Delivery Penalties

Further review of the contract with DND is required. It is apparent that the late delivery penalties ($110,000 for 55 days at $2,000 per day) for the first three caissons have not been accrued, and this issue must be discussed with management. DND should be contacted to find out whether the penalties will be enforced or waived and whether specifications have been met on all the caissons delivered to date. If the penalty is not waived, an accrual for the amount of the penalty will be required.

Clarification is needed on the procedures to be followed if a caisson proves unacceptable. To date no caissons have been returned; however, the amount of the penalties may increase with each day that the specifications continue not to be met. Related disclosures for the contracts, including the penalties, will be required.

## Capitalized Expenditures

Capitalizing costs is appropriate only if a future benefit is associated with the expenditure. The capitalized expenditures will likely be reclassified as follows:

| Expenditure | Accounting Treatment |
|---|---|
| Office furniture | Amounts spent on the purchase of office equipment should be added to the office equipment account and depreciated over the life of these assets. |
| Travel costs | Costs related to the search of the plant site should be included in the cost of land. |
| Calls for tender | The cost of calls for tender should be included in the cost of the plant and depreciated over the life of the plant. |
| Product development costs | These costs should be capitalized as development costs if the costs can be recovered through future sales of products or services. The costs should be amortized over the life of the related product. |
| Grant negotiations | These costs should be netted against the amount of the grants received and amortized on the same basis as the grants. |
| Contract negotiations | These costs should be capitalized as a cost of the DND contract and amortized over the life of the contract. |
| Administrative and legal costs | These costs and the incorporation costs should be expensed as incurred, since they do not provide any measurable future benefit |

## Miscellaneous Issues

The following issues must also be considered:

- We must discuss with management whether there are plans to manufacture products for customers other than the DND. MCL is economically dependent on the DND contract, and this relationship must be disclosed.

- After reviewing the government contract and after discussions with management and the DND, we should consider whether the present method of recording revenue at the time the product is shipped is appropriate. Perhaps, revenue should not be recognized until the client confirms that the detailed specifications have been met. Prior to this point, the performance criterion has not been met.

- MCL's lawyers will be contacted to assess the progress of the Deutsch Production lawsuit. Either the amount of the potential damages must be accrued or the appropriate disclosure made about the contingent liability depending on the certainty with respect to the outcome of the lawsuit. This is a critical issue considering the materiality of the amount and its impact on MCL as a going concern.

- We must find out why no principal payments of long-term debt have been recorded on the financial statements. If required payments have not been made, MCL could be in default, and this would be yet another consideration in the assessment of whether MCL is a going concern. Principal payments may also have been erroneously charged as interest expense.

- The current portion of the long-term debt should be classified separately and disclosure made of the debt agreement and the principal payments to be made over the next five years.

- Interest can be capitalized during the construction period only until production commences. It appears that interest has been capitalized beyond this period and an adjustment should be made. Once properly calculated, the amount should be disclosed in the notes to the financial statements.

- Depreciation has been calculated on plant equipment at what appears to be a low rate. The appropriateness of the rate will have to be assessed giving regard to the useful life of the related assets being depreciated.

## Review Questions

*Questions, cases, and problems that deal with the appendix material are denoted with an asterisk.*

LO1 **1.** Explain if and when it may be appropriate for an accountant to prepare financial statements for external users that are not in accordance with GAAP.

LO1 **2.** Identify three main areas where judgment needs to be applied when preparing financial statements.

LO1 **3.** Explain whether the needs of external users or management should take precedence in GAAP-based financial statements.

LO2 **4.** Briefly explain why the Canadian AcSB decided to create a separate section of the *CPA Canada Handbook* for private enterprises.

LO2 **5.** Briefly explain why a Canadian private company may decide to follow IFRS even though it could follow ASPE.

LO3 **6.** Identify some of the financial statement items for which ASPE is different from IFRS.

LO3 **7.** For the items listed in Exhibit 1.1, for which items would the debt-to-equity ratio not change when a company switched from ASPE to IFRS?

LO4 **8.** Identify the financial statement ratios typically used to assess profitability, liquidity and solvency, respectively.

LO4 **9.** In Year 1, XZY Co. expensed all development costs as incurred. How would the current ratio, debt-to-equity ratio and return on equity change if XZY Co. had capitalized the development costs?

LO5 *__10.__ List the six steps of the case framework.

LO5 *__11.__ Explain the difference between report recipient and primary users as they are described in the framework for analyzing a case and which users should be given priority in financial reporting.

LO5 *__12.__ Identify the main factors to be used when ranking the importance of issues to be resolved.

LO5 *__13.__ When writing the final case report, how much attention, if any, should be given to discussing alternatives?

# CASES

## Case 1-1

LO1, 3

In this era of rapidly changing technology, research and development (R&D) expenditures represent one of the most important factors in the future success of many companies. Organizations that spend too little on R&D risk being left behind by the competition. Conversely, companies that spend too much may waste money or not be able to make efficient use of the results.

IAS 38 *Intangible Assets* states that development costs can be capitalized as an intangible asset when a company can demonstrate

(a) the technical feasibility of completing the intangible asset so that it will be available for use or sale;

(b) its intention to complete the intangible asset and use or sell it;

(c) its ability to use or sell the intangible asset;

(d) how the intangible asset will generate probable future economic benefits—among other things, the entity can demonstrate the existence of a market for the output of the intangible asset or for the intangible asset itself or, if it is to be used internally, the usefulness of the intangible asset;

(e) the availability of adequate technical, financial, and other resources to complete the development and to use or sell the intangible asset; and

(f) its ability to measure reliably the expenditure attributable to the intangible asset during its development.

Under ASPE, a company can choose to capitalize or expense R&D expenditures even when the above conditions are met.

### Required

Using basic accounting principles as a guide, provide arguments to support

(a) the IASB approach for reporting R&D costs, and

(b) the ASPE approach for reporting R&D costs.

## Case 1-2

LO1, 3

You are examining the consolidated financial statements of a European company, which have been prepared in accordance with IFRS. You determine that property, plant, and equipment is revalued each year to its current fair value, income and equity are adjusted, and the notes to the financial statements include the following items as a part of the summary of significant accounting policies:

- Tangible fixed assets are measured at fair value, less accumulated depreciation. The fair value is based on valuations made by internal and external experts, taking technical and economic developments into account and supported by the experience gained in the construction of plant assets throughout the world.

- Valuation differences resulting from revaluation are credited or debited to equity, where it is applicable, after deduction of an amount for deferred tax liabilities.

- Depreciation based on fair value is applied on a straight-line basis in accordance with the estimated useful life of each asset.

The provisions of IFRS permit the use of alternatives to historical cost in the valuation of assets. IAS 16 specifically notes that as an allowed alternative treatment to historical cost:

> Subsequent to initial recognition as an asset, an item of property, plant, and equipment shall be carried at a revalued amount, being its fair value at the date of the revaluation less any subsequent accumulated depreciation and subsequent accumulated impairment losses. Revaluations should be made with sufficient regularity such that the carrying amount does not differ materially from that which would be determined using fair value at the balance sheet date.

The auditor of the company has expressed his opinion on the financial statements and concluded that they "present fairly" the financial position of the company.

The use of fair value accounting is a departure from the historical cost principle, which was required under Canadian GAAP prior to the adoption of IFRS and is still required under ASPE. The debate about the relative importance of relevance and reliability is one that surfaces often in the study of international accounting issues. Many countries are very strict as to the use of historical cost for all valuations and in the computation of income, and often allow reductions from historical cost (such as with the application of the lower of cost and market requirement), but not increases. Others are very flexible in the choice of permissible approaches, while still others are very strict in that particular alternatives to historical cost (such as fair value or general price-level-adjusted amounts) must be used.

**Required**

(a) Can any alternative to historical cost provide for fair presentation in financial reports, or are the risks too great? Discuss.

(b) Discuss the relative merits of historical cost accounting and fair value accounting. Consider the question of the achievement of a balance between relevance and reliability when trying to "present fairly" the financial position of the reporting entity.

(c) Financial statements are now beyond the comprehension of the average person. Many of the accounting terms and methods of accounting used are simply too complex to understand just from reading the financial statements. Additional explanations should be provided with, or in, the financial statements, to help investors understand the financial statements. Briefly discuss.

*(Adapted from a case developed by Peter Secord, St. Mary's University)*

## Case 1-3

LO1, 4, 5

John McCurdy has recently joined a consultant group that provides investment advice to the managers of a special investment fund. This investment fund was created by a group of NFPOs, all of which have endowment funds, and rather than investing their resources individually, they have instead chosen a pooled approach whereby a single fund invests their moneys and distributes the earnings back to them on an annual basis. The board of directors of the investment fund, made up of members from each of the NFPOs, meets periodically to review performance and to make investment decisions.

John has been following the fortunes of Ajax Communications Corporation for a number of years. Ajax is a Canadian company listed on the TSX. At the beginning of this past year, Ajax acquired 60% of the shares of Waqaas Inc., a U.S. company, which was and continues to be listed on the NYSE. Ajax must decide whether to prepare financial statements for Waqaas in accordance with IFRS or U.S. GAAP for reporting to the SEC.

As a starting point, John asked for and received the following comparison of financial statement information under U.S. GAAP and IFRS from the controller at Waqaas (in millions of dollars):

|  | U.S. GAAP (U.S. dollars) | IFRS (U.S. dollars) |
|---|---|---|
| **Income Statement** | | |
| Operating income | $ 89 | $ 329 |
| Income before extraordinary items | 14 | 199 |
| Net income | (66) | 199 |
| Comprehensive income | $ 158 | $ 545 |
| **Balance Sheet** | | |
| Total current assets | $1,262 | $1,360 |
| Investments | 233 | 59 |
| Property, plant, and equipment, net | 889 | 1,866 |
| Deferred income taxes | 50 | 47 |
| Intangibles, net | 3,016 | 5,473 |
| Other assets | 90 | 265 |
| Total assets | $5,540 | $9,070 |

Working with this list, John's next step will be to determine why there is such a difference in the numbers.

**Required**

(a) As John McCurdy, outline the initial approach that you will take in order to determine the reasons for the differences in the numbers.

(b) List some of the obvious items that need resolution, and indicate some of the possible causes of the discrepancies.

(c) In your opinion, which GAAP best reflects economic reality? Briefly explain.

*(Adapted from a case developed by Peter Secord, St. Mary's University)*

## Case 1-4

LO1, 2, 5

Roman Systems Inc. (RSI) is a Canadian private company. It was incorporated in Year 1 by its sole common shareholder, Marge Roman. RSI manufactures, installs, and provides product support for its line of surveillance cameras.

Marge started the company with a small investment. For Years 7 through 9, the company grew rapidly. Most of the expansion was funded through debt financing. The rapid growth is attributable to several large contracts signed with banks for the installation of security camera systems at their branches.

RSI has a June 30 year-end. You, the CPA, are with the firm of Sylvain and Charest, Chartered Professional Accountants (SC). Your firm has performed the audit of RSI since its incorporation and prepares RSI's corporate tax returns and those of Marge Roman and her family. RSI has been using IFRS for reporting purposes for the past few years.

Marge Roman called you in April Year 12 to inform you that she plans to take RSI public within the next year. Marge is negotiating with several underwriters, but no deal is in place yet. She plans to highlight the company's revenue growth in its annual press release publicizing its year-end results. Marge wants to show strong revenue growth to attract investors.

During the telephone conversation, Marge asked you and the partner on the audit to meet with her some time in early June to discuss and resolve potential issues related to the June 30 audit of RSI. In prior years, financial statements were issued in September, but this year the deadline for finalizing the financial statements will likely be in early August. Marge agreed that you would perform your interim audit procedures based on RSI's results as at April 30, Year 12.

It is now June Year 12. The planning and interim work for the fiscal Year 12 audit has been completed. A summary of items noted in the April 30, Year 12, interim financial statements as a result of work done to date is included in Exhibit I.

You are about to leave for the day when the partner in charge of the account comes into your office and announces that he has just received a call from Marge and she would like to meet with him within the next few days. He asks you to prepare a memo discussing the financial reporting issues arising from the interim audit work. Ignore any additional audit procedures that should be considered as a result of the issues raised during the interim audit.

---

**EXHIBIT I**

### NOTES FROM THE INTERIM AUDIT

**General**

Pre-tax earnings for the period ended April 30, Year 12, were $1,375,000. For the fiscal years Year 11 and Year 10, RSI recorded pre-tax earnings of $435,000 and $325,000, respectively.

Marge Roman has received a valuation report valuing the company at $12 million. Shareholders' equity as at April 30, Year 12, consisted of:

| | |
|---|---|
| 100 common shares (voting) | $100 |
| Retained earnings | $9,159,000 |

**New Software**

The company has been using a standard general ledger software package originally installed in Year 6 by a local computer consulting firm and upgraded annually.

In January Year 12, RSI hired BBC to oversee the implementation of a new third-party package. In March Year 12, RSI began converting its financial reporting system. The new general ledger software was installed in parallel with the old software and went live on April 1, Year 12.

The new general ledger software has been used to generate RSI's financial results since April 1, Year 12. Starting July 1, Year 12, the old system will no longer be used in parallel.

*(continued)*

To date, RSI has been invoiced $720,000 by BBC. These costs have all been capitalized in the April 30, Year 12, financial statements. The invoices show the following services and costs:

| | |
|---|---:|
| Initial review and recommendations | $110,000 |
| Cost of new software | 200,000 |
| Implementation work | 120,000 |
| Training work | 225,000 |
| Monthly support fee (April) | 25,000 |
| Other consulting (to April 30) | 40,000 |
| | $720,000 |

In addition, as at April 30, Year 12, RSI also capitalized $70,000 related to the salaries of four employees who have worked on the accounting software project since January 1, Year 12. As a result of these individuals being pulled out of their regular jobs to handle the problem, RSI had to hire two additional employees.

The costs will be amortized beginning on July 1, Year 12, on a straight-line basis over three years. RSI intends to treat approximately $135,000 of carrying amount for the old software as part of the cost of the new software by reallocating this balance.

## Revenues

During fiscal Year 11, total product revenue was $18.2 million and maintenance contract revenue was $5.6 million. For the period ended April Year 12, product revenue was $13.2 million, and maintenance contract revenue was $5.2 million.

RSI recognizes product revenue when shipment and installation take place. It is RSI's standard practice to request a customer sign-off for any installation work. The installation crew normally gets sign-off on the day of installation. During interim work for fiscal Year 12, it was noted in the audit file that approximately $640,000 of revenue recognized in April Year 12 related to work installed and invoiced in April, but customer sign-off was obtained only in early May. Such situations have not caught anyone's attention in previous years. RSI explained that it had recently hired new service technicians who were unfamiliar with the policy of customer sign-off, and accordingly had to send technicians back to the client days after the installation was completed to get the sign-offs.

Maintenance contract revenues relate to one-year agreements that RSI signs with customers wanting product support. During the year, the company changed its revenue recognition policy on maintenance contracts to recognize revenue based on estimated costs incurred on the contract. Revenue is recognized as follows: 25% in each of the first two months of the contract and 5% in each subsequent month. This allocation is based on a study done by RSI in Year 10, which showed that the costs incurred on the contracts are mostly incurred in the first two months, during which RSI sends out a technician to perform preventive maintenance. The preventive maintenance reduces the number of future service calls and, therefore, overall costs.

## ABM Business

As a result of RSI's strong relationship with its financial institution and Marge's desire to diversify RSI's product line, RSI began selling automated bank machines (ABMs) in fiscal Year 12. The machines are purchased from a large electronic equipment manufacturer responsible for ongoing maintenance of the ABMs. RSI sells the ABMs to restaurants, bars, and clubs at margins of 5%. The sales revenue is included as product revenue.

The standard ABM sales agreement states that for a three-year period from the date of sale, RSI receives 40% of the transaction fee charged to customers using the machine, in addition to the sales revenue. A further 40% of the fee is payable to the financial institution for managing the cash in the machines, and the remaining 20% is remitted to the machine owners. The transaction fee charged to customers using an ABM is normally $1.50, and is set by the financial institution. RSI is not responsible for stocking the ABM with cash or emptying the cash machine. The financial institution performs all cash management duties and remits to RSI, at month-end, a statement showing money owed to

**EXHIBIT I** *(continued)*

RSI for its share of the transaction fee. A day later, the funds are deposited directly into RSI's main bank account.

A total of 2,830,000 ABM transactions were processed in Year 12 for a total fee of $4,245,000. RSI has booked transaction-fee revenue of $4,245,000 and an expense of $2,547,000 related to the fees, attributable to the financial institution and the machine owners.

**Debentures**

In January Year 12, RSI needed long-term financing and issued to a third-party venture capitalist $2,500,000 of debentures maturing in 10 years, with interest at 7.35%. The debentures are included as long-term debt in the accounts. The debentures are convertible at the option of the holder, at a rate of one voting common share for every $5 of debenture, if RSI issues shares to the public. If RSI does not issue shares to the public before June 30, Year 13, the debentures are repayable upon demand.

**Accounts Receivable**

Review of the aging of accounts receivable at April 30, Year 12, showed an amount of $835,000 in the over-120-day category. According to RSI's collection department, the balance relates to payments withheld by one of RSI's largest customers, Mountain Bank. RSI had contracted to install security cameras at all of its branches. The work was performed in August Year 11, a customer sign-off was received at each branch, and invoices were sent in early September. Mountain Bank refused to pay individual invoices. It wants to pay the total of all invoices in one payment.

In October Year 11, a few branches of Mountain Bank contacted their head office and requested that no payment be made to RSI until certain corrections were made to the angles at which the cameras were installed. Although not required to do so under its agreement with Mountain Bank, RSI fixed the problems, as Mountain Bank is one of its largest customers.

On June 1, Year 12, $450,000 was received. Mountain Bank asserts that some work remains to be done at five to 10 sites and is withholding final payment until it is completely satisfied. All amounts related to the contract are recorded as revenues. Internal reports reveal that it takes a service person approximately one hour to fix the problems at each branch. No significant materials costs have been incurred for the follow-up visits.

*(CPA Canada adapted)*[3]

# Case 1-5

LO1, 2, 3, 5

Goal Products Limited (GPL) is the official manufacturer and distributor of soccer balls for the North American League Soccer (NALS), a professional soccer association. GPL is a private company. It has always prepared its financial statements in accordance with ASPE.

It is now October 20, Year 9. You, CPA, were recently hired as the manager of financial reporting for GPL. In your first week, you must review the first draft of the quarterly financial statements and provide comments to the financial reporting team on any issues you note. As you start your review you receive an email from the chief financial officer, Joey Donaducci (Exhibit II).

The quarterly financial statements, for the period ended September 30, Year 9, are still being finalized. So far you have received the balance sheet, statement of net income, and most of the planned note disclosures (Exhibit III) that will be provided to GPL's major lenders. You have received as well an internally prepared highlights summary (Exhibit IV) that will also be provided to GPL's major lenders. The statements of retained earnings and cash flows and the disclosures of changes in accounting policies are still being finalized.

**EXHIBIT II**

### EMAIL FROM JOEY BONADUCCI

Hi CPA,

As you may know, we are planning to transition for ASPE to IFRS in the near future. I've just returned from a conference on current issues facing private companies transitioning to IFRS. I don't think the transition will be difficult. The changes I've noted so far affect impairment of assets and extraordinary items. I'd like you to tell me how those IFRS would specifically apply to our most recent quarterly financial statements. You should also prepare a brief analysis that highlights any other major differences between ASPE policies and IFRS that are relevant for GPL.

JB

**EXHIBIT III**

### DRAFT INTERIM FINANCIAL STATEMENTS
### GOAL PRODUCTS LIMITED
### BALANCE SHEET
(in thousands of Canadian dollars)
(unaudited)
As at:

| | September 30, Year 9 | June 30, Year 9 |
|---|---|---|
| **Assets** | | |
| Current assets: | | |
| Cash and cash equivalents | $ 3,068 | $2,366 |
| Accounts receivable | 1,985 | 1,624 |
| Inventories (note 2) | 1,690 | 1,080 |
| Prepaid expenses | 548 | 438 |
| | 7,291 | 5,508 |
| Capital assets | 3,648 | 4,341 |
| Intangible assets | 680 | 688 |
| Other assets (note 3) | 68 | — |
| | $11,687 | $10,537 |
| Current liabilities: | | |
| Accounts payable and accrued liabilities | $ 2,578 | $2,300 |
| Income tax payable | 256 | 701 |
| | 2,834 | 3,001 |
| Long-term debt (note 3) | 1,000 | — |
| Future income tax liability | 124 | 103 |
| | 3,958 | 3,104 |
| Shareholders' equity: | | |
| Share capital | 2,872 | 2,872 |
| Retained earnings | 4,857 | 4,561 |
| | 7,729 | 7,433 |
| | $11,687 | $10,537 |

See accompanying notes to the consolidated financial statements.

*(continued)*

EXHIBIT III *(continued)*

**DRAFT INTERIM FINANCIAL STATEMENTS**
**GOAL PRODUCTS LIMITED**
**STATEMENT OF NET INCOME**
Three months ended September 30
(in thousands of Canadian dollars)

|  | Year 9 *(unaudited)* | Year 8 *(unaudited)* |
|---|---|---|
| Revenue | $16,000 | $15,180 |
| Cost of sales | 8,957 | 8,349 |
| Gross margin | 7,043 | 6,831 |
| Operating expenses: |  |  |
| General and administrative | 2,744 | 2,511 |
| Sales and marketing | 3,087 | 2,865 |
| Amortization of capital assets | 157 | 133 |
| Amortization of other assets (note 3) | 2 | — |
| Interest on long-term debt | 13 | — |
| Other interest expense | 4 | 3 |
| Income before income taxes and extraordinary item | 1,036 | 1,319 |
| Income tax expense: |  |  |
| Current | 329 | 430 |
| Future | 21 | 23 |
|  | 350 | 453 |
| Net income before extraordinary item | 686 | 866 |
| Extraordinary loss, net of tax of $219 (note 4) | (351) | — |
| Net income for the period | $ 335 | $ 866 |

See accompanying notes to the consolidated financial statements.

**GOAL PRODUCTS LIMITED**
**NOTES TO DRAFT INTERIM FINANCIAL STATEMENTS**
For the period ended September 30, Year 9
(unaudited)

### 1. Basis of Presentation

These interim financial statements were prepared using accounting policies and methods consistent with those used in the preparation of the Company's audited financial statements for the year ended June 30, Year 9. These interim financial statements conform in all respects to the requirements of Canadian generally accepted accounting principles for annual financial statements for private companies, with the exception of certain note disclosures, and should be read in conjunction with the Company's audited financial statements and notes for the year ended June 30, Year 9.

### 2. Inventories (in thousands)

|  | September 30, Year 9 | June 30, Year 9 |
|---|---|---|
| Raw materials | $ 146 | $ 124 |
| Finished goods | 1,544 | 956 |
|  | $1,690 | $1,080 |

### 3. Long-Term Debt

On July 1, Year 9, the Company entered into a $1 million, 10-year term loan bearing interest at 5%. Interest is payable quarterly. The principal of the debt can be converted, at the option of the lender, into 200,000 common shares of GPL at any time prior to maturity. The principal amount of the loan is due on July 1, 2019.

*(continued)*

Debt issue costs of $70,000 were incurred in relation to the loan agreement and have been capitalized to Other assets. The costs are being amortized over the term of the loan using the effective interest rate method.

**4. Extraordinary Item**

During the three months ended September 30, Year 9, the Company experienced a loss of $670,000 before tax as a result of a fire that burned a fleet of trucks containing several large shipments of soccer balls.

---

**EXHIBIT IV**

### INTERNALLY PREPARED HIGHLIGHTS SUMMARY

Revenue for Q1 (July to September Year 9) includes $900,000 booked for a special shipment of balls to the Pan-America Cup (PAC) at the end of the quarter. Title and risk of loss for the balls transferred once they were shipped, and we have invoiced the PAC committee for the full amount. The committee does not have to pay for the balls until they are sold at the PAC in November. They can return any unsold balls, but we are confident they will sell out.

General and administrative expenses increased because we hired three supervisors.

We discussed the treatment of the fleet truck fire as an extraordinary item with the external auditors, which they judged to be correct.

In July, we were sued by one of our suppliers for non-payment for a shipment of leather. After using the leather in the production process, we realized it was below our quality standards. The supplier is claiming for damages as well as loss of revenue in the amount of approximately $800,000. Legal counsel thinks the chance we will lose is just over 75%. If we lose, counsel believes we will have to pay the full claim. We think the court proceedings will be resolved by the end of our fiscal year. We are accruing $150,000 (25% of our probability estimate) so we will have $600,000 accrued by year-end.

The outlook for the rest of the year appears strong. We expect to operate the plant at capacity and produce approximately 2 million soccer balls. Consistent with other years, we expect Q1 and Q2 to have significantly higher sales and profits since these are our peak sale times (NALS pre-season and regular season).

During the year ended June 30, Year 9, we experienced a manufacturing equipment malfunction. Management determined the value of the equipment had permanently declined, and booked an impairment loss of $160,000 in the year. Recently, we think we located the critical part needed to make the equipment serviceable again, and will receive the part next month.

*(CPA Canada adapted)*[4]

---

# PROBLEMS

## Problem 1-1

LO2, 3, 4

IAS 16 *Property, Plant, and Equipment* requires assets to be initially measured at cost. Subsequently, assets may be carried at cost less accumulated depreciation, or they can be periodically revalued upward to current value and carried at the revalued amount less accumulated depreciation. If revalued, the adjustment is reported in other comprehensive income. Subsequent depreciation is based on the revalued amount. ASPE does not allow assets to be revalued at an amount exceeding historical cost less accumulated depreciation.

ABC Ltd., a private company, can report in accordance with either ASPE or IFRS. On January 1, Year 1, it acquired an asset at a cost of $10 million, which will be amortized on a straight-line basis over an estimated useful life of 20 years. On January 1, Year 3, the company hired an appraiser, who determined the fair value of the asset (net of accumulated depreciation) to be $12 million. The estimated useful life of the asset did not change.

**Required**

(a) Determine the depreciation expense recognized in Year 2, Year 3, and Year 4 under
   (i) the revaluation treatment allowed under IAS 16, and
   (ii) ASPE.
(b) Determine the carrying amount of the asset under the two different sets of accounting requirements at January 2, Year 3; December 31, Year 3; and December 31, Year 4.
(c) Summarize the differences in profit and shareholders' equity over the 20-year life of the asset using the two different sets of accounting requirements. Assume that future appraisals indicated that the fair value of the asset was equal to carrying amount.

## Problem 1-2

LO2, 3, 4

Fast Ltd. is a public company that prepares its consolidated financial statements in accordance with IFRS. Its net income in Year 2 was $200,000, and shareholders' equity at December 31, Year 2, was $1,800,000.

Mr. Lombardi, the major shareholder, has made an offer to buy out the other shareholders, delist the company and take it private. Thereafter, the company will report under ASPE. You have identified the following two areas in which Fast's accounting principles differ between IFRS and ASPE.

1. Fast incurred research and development costs of $500,000 in Year 1. Thirty percent of these costs were related to development activities that met the criteria for capitalization as an intangible asset. The newly developed product was brought to market in January Year 2 and is expected to generate sales revenue for 10 years.

2. Fast acquired equipment at the beginning of Year 1 at a cost of $100,000. The equipment has a five-year life with no expected residual value and is depreciated on a straight-line basis. At December 31, Year 1 Fast compiled the following information related to this equipment:

| | |
|---|---|
| Expected future cash flows from use of the equipment | $85,000 |
| Present value of expected future cash flows from use of the equipment | 75,000 |
| Net realizable value | 72,000 |

**Required**

(a) Determine the amount at which Fast should report each of the following on its balance sheet at December 31, Year 2, using (1) IFRS and (2) ASPE. Ignore the possibility of any additional impairment or reversal of impairment loss at the end of Year 2. Assume that Fast wants to minimize net income.
   (i) Research and development
   (ii) Equipment
(b) Prepare a reconciliation of net income for Year 2 and shareholders' equity at December 31, Year 2, under IFRS to an ASPE basis.

## Problem 1-3

LO2, 3, 4

Harmandeep Ltd. is a private company in the pharmaceutical industry. It has been preparing its financial statements in accordance with ASPE. Since it has plans to go public in the next three to five years, it is considering changing to IFRS for the current year. It wishes to adopt policies that will maximize the return on shareholders' equity. Based on the draft financial statements prepared in accordance with ASPE, its net income for Year 5 is $409,000, and its shareholders' equity at December 31, Year 5 is $3,590,000.

Harmandeep has engaged you to reconcile net income and shareholders' equity from ASPE to IFRS. You have identified the following five areas for which IFRS differs from ASPE:

1. Impaired loans—original versus market rate of interest

2. Interest costs—capitalize versus expense

3. Actuarial gains/losses—recognize immediately in net income versus recognize immediately in other comprehensive income

4. Compound financial instrument—debt versus equity components

5. Income taxes—future income tax method or taxes payable method

Harmandeep provides the following information with respect to each of these accounting differences.

### Impaired Loans

One of Harmandeep's debtors is in financial difficulty and defaulted on its loan payment during the year. The outstanding balance on this loan receivable at the end of Year 5 was $240,000. Harmandeep agreed to accept five annual payments of $59,000 with the first payment due at December 31, Year 6, as a full settlement of the loan. The original interest rate on the loan was 11%. The market rate of interest for this type of loan is 9%. No adjustment has been made for the impairment of the loan receivable.

### Interest Costs

Harmandeep arranged a loan of $980,000 to finance the construction of a warehouse. $490,000 was borrowed on March 1, Year 5, and another $490,000 was borrowed on October 1, Year 5. The loan is repayable over five years with an interest rate of 9%, with the first payment due on September 30, Year 6. The warehouse was nearly complete at the end of Year 5. No interest has been accrued on the loan at the end of Year 5.

### Actuarial Gains/Losses

Harmandeep instituted a defined benefit pension plan in Year 3. The first actuarial evaluation, which was done as at June 30, Year 5, indicated an actuarial gain of $163,500. The expected average remaining service life of the employee workforce was 15 years at the time of the actuarial evaluation. The actuarial gain has not yet been recognized in the preliminary financial statements.

### Compound Financial Instrument

Harmandeep issued bonds for proceeds of $1,180,000 on December 31, Year 5. The bonds are convertible into common shares at any time within the next five years. The bonds would have been worth only for $1,112,000 if they did not have the conversion feature. The proceeds on the bonds have been recognized as long-term debt in the preliminary financial statements.

### Income Tax

Harmandeep's income tax rate has been and is expected to continue at 40%. Assume that any adjustments to accounting income for the above items are fully deductible or taxable for tax purposes. The preliminary financial statements reflect the tax payable method of accounting for income taxes. If the future income tax method were adopted, future tax liabilities should be set up for $309,000 at the end of Year 4 and $358,000 at the end of Year 5.

### Required

Prepare a schedule to convert net income and total shareholders' equity from the preliminary financial statements amounts to amounts under ASPE and IFRS. Where accounting choices exist, choose policies that minimize return on total shareholders' equity under ASPE and maximize return on total shareholders' equity under IFRS.

## Problem 1-4

LO2, 3, 4

Andrew Ltd. is a large private company owned by the Andrew family. It operates a number of ski resorts in a very competitive industry. Its main competition comes from a couple of public companies. Andrew has been using ASPE in the past but has come under pressure from its bank to convert to IFRS. Its bank is particularly concerned with the debt to equity ratio and the return on total shareholders' equity.

Andrew reported the following on its preliminary Year 6 financial statements in compliance with ASPE:

| | | | |
|---|---|---|---|
| Net income | $5,600 | Total debt | $44,700 |
| | | Total shareholders' equity | 34,800 |

You have identified four areas in which Andrew's accounting policies could have differences between ASPE and IFRS. Where choices exist under ASPE, Andrew has adopted allowable policies that maximize net income and shareholders' equity.

The controller at Andrew provides the following information for the four areas:

### Intangible Assets

Andrew owns a number of intangible assets and depreciates them over their useful lives, ranging from three to seven years. The patents are checked for impairment when there is an indication that impairment may exist. Relevant values pertaining to these patents were as follows:

| | December 31, Year 5 | December 31, Year 6 |
|---|---|---|
| Carrying amount before impairment | $19,800 | $16,300 |
| Undiscounted future cash flows | 20,100 | 16,350 |
| Value in use | 16,900 | 12,000 |
| Fair value | 16,800 | 11,500 |

### Property, Plant, and Equipment

Andrew acquired equipment at the beginning of Year 4 at a cost of $2,550. The equipment has an estimated useful life of 10 years, an estimated residual value of $115, and is being depreciated on a straight-line basis. At the beginning of Year 6, the equipment was appraised and determined to have a fair value of $2,200; it's estimated useful life and residual value did not change. The company could adopt the revaluation option in IAS 16 to periodically revalue the equipment at fair value subsequent to acquisition.

### Research and Development Costs

Andrew incurred research and development costs of $200 in Year 6. Of this amount, 40% related to development activities subsequent to the point at which criteria indicating that the creation of an intangible asset had been met. As of year-end, development of the new product had not been completed.

### Redeemable Preferred Shares

In Year 4, Andrew issued redeemable preferred shares to the original founders of the company in exchange for their previously held common shares as part of a tax planning arrangement. The preferred shares were assigned a value of $750 and have been reported in shareholders' equity in the preliminary financial statements. The common shares, which had a carrying amount of $750, were cancelled. The preferred shares would be classified as long-term debt under IFRS and would need to be reported at their redemption value of $3,100.

The CEO is concerned about the impact of converting Andrew's financial statements from ASPE to IFRS.

### Required

(a) Calculate the two ratios first using ASPE and then using IFRS. Prepare a schedule showing any adjustments to the numerator and denominator for these ratios. Ignore income taxes.

(b) Explain whether Andrew's solvency and profitability look better or worse under IFRS after considering the combined impact of the four areas of difference.

## Problem 1-5

LO2, 3, 4

Becker Ltd. is a private Canadian company. It has been preparing its financial statements in accordance with ASPE but is now considering a change to IFRS. For its Year 4 financial statements, Becker reported the following in accordance with ASPE:

| | | | |
|---|---|---|---|
| Net income | $1,500,000 | Total debt | $12,600,000 |
| Current assets | 6,800,000 | Total shareholders' equity | 10,900,000 |
| Current liabilities | 5,400,000 | | |

You have identified the following three areas in which Becker's accounting policies have differences between ASPE and IFRS:

1. Impaired loans

2. Capitalization of interest

3. Actuarial gains/losses

The controller at Becker provides the following information with respect to each of these accounting differences and indicates that the Year 4 financial statements reflect the proper accounting for these items in accordance with ASPE:

### Impaired Loans

One of Becker's debtors is in financial difficulty and defaulted on its loan payment during the year. The outstanding balance on this loan receivable at the end of Year 4 was $480,000. Becker agreed to delay the annual payments for two years. The discounted present value of the delayed future payments as of December 31, Year 4 was $440,000 when discounted at the original interest rate on the loan of 6% or $452,000 when discounted at the market rate of interest for this type of loan of 5%.

### Interest Costs

Becker borrowed $500,000 on June 30, Year 3 to finance the construction of a storage facility. Interest only payments at the annual rate of 6% are payable every six months until the completion of the facility. Thereafter, principal and interest payments are payable every six months over a

10-year period to fully pay off the loan. The facility was completed in January Year 5. Becker has been expensing the interest costs as incurred.

**Actuarial Gains/Losses**

Becker instituted a defined benefit pension plan in Year 3. The first actuarial evaluation, which was done as at September 30, Year 4, indicated an actuarial loss of $115,000 and an overall pension fund deficit of $750,000.

The CEO is concerned about the impact of converting Becker's financial statements from ASPE to IFRS on the following metrics: current ratio, debt-to-equity ratio, and return on total shareholders' equity.

**Required**

(a) Calculate the three ratios first using ASPE and then using IFRS. Prepare a schedule showing any adjustments to the numerator and denominator for these ratios. Ignore income taxes.
(b) Explain whether Becker's liquidity, solvency and profitability look better or worse under IFRS after considering the combined impact of the three areas of difference.

## Problem 1-6

LO2, 3, 4

Maurice Ltd. is a private Canadian company. It has been preparing its financial statements in accordance with IFRS but is now considering a change to ASPE. For its Year 6 financial statements, Maurice reported the following in accordance with IFRS:

| | | | |
|---|---|---|---|
| Net income | $3,000 | Total debt | $25,200 |
| Current assets | 13,600 | Total shareholders' equity | 21,500 |
| Current liabilities | 10,700 | | |

You have identified the following three areas in which Maurice's accounting policies have differences between IFRS and ASPE:

1. Impairment losses

2. Convertible bonds

3. Income taxes

The controller at Maurice provides the following information with respect to each of these accounting differences and indicates that the Year 6 financial statements reflect the proper accounting for these items in accordance with IFRS:

**Impairment Losses**

Impairment tests were performed on the company's equipment for Years 5 and 6 with the following results:

| | December 31, Year 5 | December 31, Year 6 |
|---|---|---|
| Cost of equipment | $25,000 | $25,000 |
| Accumulated depreciation | 5,000 | 6,000 |
| Carrying amount before impairment | 20,000 | 19,000 |
| Undiscounted future cash flows | 19,500 | 18,000 |
| Value in use | 18,900 | 18,100 |
| Fair value | 17,700 | 18,200 |
| Depreciation expense for year | 1,000 | 1,000 |

At the end of Year 5, the equipment had an estimated remaining useful life of 20 years. There were no impairment losses prior to Year 5.

### Convertible Bonds

Maurice issued bonds for proceeds of $13,000 on January 1, Year 5. The bonds are convertible into common shares at any time within the next five years. The bonds would have been worth only $12,100 if they did not have the conversion feature. The amortization of the discount on bonds was $55,000 in Year 5 and $56,000 in Year 6.

### Income Taxes

Maurice's income tax rate has been and is expected to continue at 40%. The financial statements reflect the future taxes payable method of accounting for income taxes and contain the following amounts:

|  | December 31, Year 5 | December 31, Year 6 |
|---|---|---|
| Future income tax payable | $4,500 | $4,690 |
| Future income tax expense | 185 | 190 |

The CEO is concerned about the impact of converting Maurice's financial statements from IFRS to ASPE on the following metrics: current ratio, debt-to-equity ratio, and return on total shareholders' equity. Where ASPE provides an accounting policy choice, he wants to choose the method that is most simple and straightforward.

### Required

(a) Calculate the three ratios first using IFRS and then ASPE. Prepare a schedule showing any adjustments to the numerator and denominator for these ratios. Ignore income taxes on the impairment losses and convertible bonds.

(b) Explain whether Maurice's liquidity, solvency, and profitability look better or worse under ASPE after considering the combined impact of the three areas of difference.

## Endnotes

1   This material on case analysis was adapted with permission from a manuscript, *Integration and Analysis*, written by David A. Baker CPA, CA, B. Admin, Herbert M. Herauf, CPA, CA, MBA, and Gordon D. Richardson, Ph.D, MBA, FCPA, FCA, and published by the School of Accountancy, University of Waterloo. Any changes to the original manuscript are the sole responsibility of the author of this text, and have not been reviewed or endorsed by the original authors.

2   Adapted from *CICA UFE Report*, 1990-II-1, with permission. Chartered Professional Accountants of Canada, Toronto, Canada. Any changes to the original material are the sole responsibility of the author (and/or publisher) and have not been reviewed or endorsed by the Chartered Professional Accountants of Canada.

3   Adapted from *CICA UFE Report*, 2002-III-3, with permission. Chartered Professional Accountants of Canada, Toronto, Canada. Any changes to the original material are the sole responsibility of the author (and/or publisher) and have not been reviewed or endorsed by the Chartered Professional Accountants of Canada.

4   Adapted from *CICA UFE Report*, 2009-III-1, with permission. Chartered Professional Accountants of Canada, Toronto, Canada. Any changes to the original material are the sole responsibility of the author (and/or publisher) and have not been reviewed or endorsed by the Chartered Professional Accountants of Canada.

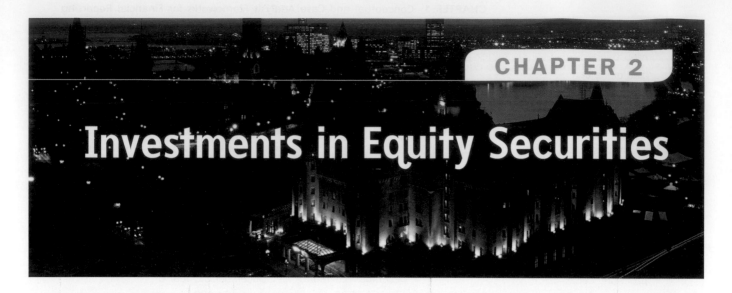

# CHAPTER 2

# Investments in Equity Securities

## LEARNING OBJECTIVES

**After studying this chapter, you should be able to do the following:**

**LO1** Describe the main changes in the reporting of equity investments over the past 12 years.

**LO2** Distinguish between the various types of equity investments measured at fair value.

**LO3** Prepare journal entries to account for investments under the cost and equity methods.

**LO4** Evaluate relevant factors to determine whether an investor has significant influence over an investee.

**LO5** Analyze and interpret financial statements involving investments in equity securities.

**LO6** Identify some of the differences between IFRS and ASPE for investments in equity securities.

# Introduction

Rogers Communications Inc. is a diversified public Canadian communications and media company with annual revenues in excess of $12 billion. It has operations in four segments—wireless, cable, business solutions, and media. The wireless segment includes 100% interests in Fido Solutions Inc. and Rogers Communications Partnership, which operates the wireless, cable, and business solutions businesses. The media segment includes the wholly owned subsidiary Rogers Media Inc. and its subsidiaries, including Rogers Broadcasting (which owns more than 50 radio stations), the CityTV television network, the Sportsnet channels, and Canadian specialty channels, including Outdoor Life Network and CityNews Channel; Digital Media, which provides digital advertising solutions to over 1,000 websites; Rogers Publishing, which produces more than 50 consumer, trade, and professional publications; and Rogers Sports Entertainment, which owns the Toronto Blue Jays Baseball Club and Rogers Centre. Media also holds ownership interests in entities involved in specialty television content, television production, and broadcast sales and has a 12-year exclusive broadcasting agreement with the National Hockey League.[1]

Such ownership structures are hardly uncommon in the business world; corporate as well as individual investors frequently acquire ownership shares of both domestic and foreign businesses. These investments can range from a few shares to the acquisition of 100% control. There are many different methods of reporting these investments, ranging from fair value to cost-based approaches. If fair value is used, unrealized gains can be recognized in net income or in other comprehensive income.

---

*There are many different methods for reporting investments in equity securities.*

---

Over the next eight chapters, we will examine various methods of reporting investments in equity securities. The focus is on investments in which one firm possesses either significant influence or control over another through ownership of voting shares. Transactions between these non-arm's-length entities require special scrutiny and special accounting procedures. We will begin our journey by reviewing the requirements for reporting equity investments in this chapter, and then spend considerable time in subsequent chapters preparing consolidated financial statements in increasingly complicated situations.

## LO1 EQUITY INVESTMENTS—THE BIG PICTURE

This is the first of eight chapters that make up a single accounting topic. This topic can be represented by the following question: How should a Canadian company report, in its financial statements, an investment in the shares of another company?

---

*Equity investments are investments in shares of another company.*

---

There are two main categories of equity investments: strategic and nonstrategic. For strategic investments, the investor intends to establish or maintain a long-term operating relationship with the entity in which the investment is made and has some level of influence over the strategic decisions of the investee company. The level of influence varies among full control, joint control, and significant influence. For nonstrategic investments, the investor is hoping for a reasonable rate of return without wanting or having the ability to play an active role in the strategic decisions of the investee company.

The methods of reporting equity investments have changed significantly over the past 12 years. Prior to 2005, these investments were typically reported at some cost-based amount. The investments were written down if there was impairment in value. However, the investments were not written up to reflect increases in value; gains were only reported when the investments were sold.

In 2005, IAS 39 *Financial Instruments—Recognition and Measurement* was introduced for the reporting of nonstrategic investments. For the first time, it was possible to report certain investments at fair value, regardless of whether fair value was higher or lower than the cost-based amounts. This was part of a trend to report more and more assets at fair value on the basis that fair value is more relevant information.

---

*There is a trend in financial reporting to measure more assets at fair value on an annual basis.*

---

The unrealized gains and losses were reported either in net income or in a new category of income called *other comprehensive income (OCI)*. When the investments were sold, the unrealized gains and losses were removed from OCI and reported in net income; that is, the unrealized gains were recycled through net income.

After a few years of reporting these nonstrategic investments at fair value with gains and losses reported either in net income or other comprehensive income, both preparers and users of the financial statements started to complain about the different reporting options under IAS 39. They felt that the financial statements were getting too complicated and that IAS 39 was difficult to understand, apply, and interpret. They urged the International Accounting Standards Board (IASB) to develop a new standard for the financial reporting of financial instruments that was principle-based and less complex. Although the Board amended IAS 39 several times to clarify requirements, add guidance, and eliminate internal inconsistencies, it had not previously undertaken a fundamental reconsideration of reporting for financial instruments.

In 2009, the IASB introduced a new accounting standard for nonstrategic investments, International Financial Reporting Standard (IFRS) 9 *Financial Instruments—Classification and Measurement*. IFRS 9 established principles for the financial reporting of financial assets and financial liabilities that will present relevant and useful information to users of financial statements for their assessment of the amounts, timing, and uncertainty of an entity's future cash flows. It has replaced and superseded the classification and measurement standards that were in IAS 39. IFRS 9 will be mandatorily effective for fiscal periods beginning on or after January 1, 2018, but early adoption is permitted. In this text, all illustrations will use the new standards in IFRS 9.

> *Starting in 2018, nonstrategic investments in private companies must be reported at fair value.*

IFRS 9 requires that all nonstrategic equity investments be measured at fair value, including investments in private companies. Under IAS 39, investments that did not have a quoted market price in an active market and whose fair value could not be reliably measured were reported at cost. This provision no longer exists under IFRS 9. However, in limited circumstances, cost may be an appropriate estimate of fair value. That may be the case if more recent information is insufficient to measure fair value, or if there is a wide range of possible fair value measurements and cost represents the best estimate of fair value within that range. Cost is never the best estimate of fair value for investments in quoted equity instruments.

The IASB recognizes that measuring all investments in equity instruments at fair value will impose additional costs on preparers. In the IASB's view, these costs are justified by improved and useful decision-making information about equity investments for users of financial statements. Measuring all investments in equity instruments in the same way also simplifies the accounting requirements and improves comparability.

IFRS 9 no longer refers to and does not have any specific provisions for available-for-sale (AFS) investments; in effect, the AFS investment disappears as a separate category of equity investments. However, on initial recognition, an entity can elect to present the fair value changes on an equity investment that is not held for trading in OCI. This concept is similar to that previously applied to AFS investments. One significant change is that the gains or losses are cleared out of accumulated OCI and transferred directly to retained earnings, and never recycled through net income.

> *Available-for-sale investments have been eliminated as a separate category of investments.*

In 2011, the IASB introduced a new accounting standard, IFRS 13 *Fair Value Measurement*. It replaced the fair value measurement guidance previously contained in individual IFRSs with a single, unified definition of fair value and a framework for measuring it. It also details the required disclosures about fair value measurements. Fair value is defined as the price that would be received to sell an asset or paid to transfer a liability in an orderly transaction between market participants at the measurement date (i.e., an exit price). It would reflect the highest and best use for a nonfinancial asset.

Exhibit 2.1 summarizes the reporting methods for equity investments. It would be easier if only one method was used for all investments, but such is not the case under current standards. The rationale for

**EXHIBIT 2.1**

## Reporting Methods for Investments in Equity Securities

| Type of Investment | Reporting Method | Reporting of Unrealized Gains/Losses |
| --- | --- | --- |
| Strategic investments: | | |
| Significant influence | Equity method | Not applicable |
| Control | Consolidation | Not applicable |
| Joint control | Equity method | Not applicable |
| Nonstrategic investments: | | |
| FVTPL (fair value through profit or loss) | Fair value method | In net income |
| Other – elect FVTOCI (fair value through OCI) | Fair value method | In other comprehensive income |

the different methods will be discussed as the methods are introduced throughout the text. It is important that you try to understand the rationale because that will make it easier to remember which method to apply to which situation.

> *Strategic investments are reported at values other than fair value.*
>
> *Non-strategic investments are reported at fair value.*

We will now illustrate the accounting and reporting of equity investments reported at fair value.

## LO2 INVESTMENTS MEASURED AT FAIR VALUE

IFRS 9 deals with two types of equity investments: fair value through profit or loss (FVTPL) and fair value through OCI (FVTOCI). FVTPL investments include investments held for short-term trading. These investments are classified as current assets on the basis that they are actively traded and intended by management to be sold within one year. FVTPL investments are initially measured at fair value and subsequently measured at fair value at each reporting date. The unrealized and realized gains and losses are reported in net income along with dividends received or receivable.

> *Unrealized gains and losses are reported in net income for FVTPL investments.*

FVTOCI investments are equity investments that are not held for short-term trading and those for which management, on initial acquisition, irrevocably elects to report all unrealized gains and losses in OCI. These investments are classified as current or noncurrent assets, depending on how long company managers intend to hold on to these shares. They are initially measured at fair value and subsequently remeasured at fair value at each reporting date. The unrealized and realized gains and losses are reported in OCI. Dividend income is reported in net income as the dividends are declared. The cumulative gains or losses are cleared out of accumulated OCI and transferred directly to retained earnings. The transfer to retained earnings would usually occur when the investment is sold or derecognized but could be transferred at any time.

> *Unrealized gains and losses are reported in OCI for FVTOCI investments.*

**ILLUSTRATION** On January 1, Year 5, Jenstar Corp. purchased 10% of the outstanding common shares of Safebuy Company at a cost of $95,000. Safebuy reported net income of $100,000 and paid dividends of $80,000 for the year ended December 31, Year 5. The fair value of Jenstar's 10% interest in Safebuy was $98,000 at December 31, Year 5. On January 10, Year 6, Jenstar sold its investment in Safebuy for $99,000. The following table presents Jenstar's journal entries for the above-noted transactions under FVTPL and the option under IFRS 9 to designate at FVTOCI. It ignores income tax and assumes that accumulated OCI for the FVTOCI investment is transferred to retained earnings when the investment is sold.

| | FVTPL | FVTOCI |
|---|---|---|
| *Jan. 1, Year 5* | | |
| Investment in Safebuy | 95,000 | 95,000 |
|     Cash | (95,000) | (95,000) |
| To record the acquisition of 10% of Safebuy's shares | | |
| *Dec. 31, Year 5* | | |
| Cash (10% × 80,000) | 8,000 | 8,000 |
|     Dividend income | (8,000) | (8,000) |
| Receipt of dividend from Safebuy | | |
| *Dec. 31, Year 5* | | |
| Investment in Safebuy (98,000–95,000) | 3,000 | 3,000 |
|     Unrealized gains (reported in net income) | (3,000) | |
|     OCI—unrealized gains | | (3,000) |
| To record investment at fair value | | |
| *Jan. 10, Year 6* | | |
| Cash | 99,000 | 99,000 |
|     Investment in Safebuy | (98,000) | (98,000) |
|     Gain on sale (reported in net income) | (1,000) | |
|     OCI—gain on sale | | (1,000) |
| Record sale of investment | | |
| *Jan. 10, Year 6* | | |
| Accumulated OCI—reclassification to retained earnings | | 4,000 |
|     Retained earnings—gain on sale of FVTOCI investments | | (4,000) |
| Clear accumulated OCI to retained earnings | | |

> *The investment is reported at fair value at each reporting date under both methods of reporting. The credit side of the entry is shown in brackets.*
>
> *Accumulated other comprehensive income is not included in retained earnings but is included as a separate component of shareholders' equity.*

# INVESTMENTS NOT MEASURED AT FAIR VALUE

When investments are not reported at fair value, they are usually reported using the cost method or the equity method. The next two subsections describe when these methods are used and illustrate how to apply them.

## LO3 Cost Method of Reporting an Equity Investment

The cost method is used under IFRS in the following situations:

- *For investments in controlled entities.* This is an option when the reporting entity prepares separate-entity financial statements in addition to or instead of consolidated financial statements. This situation will be discussed further in Chapter 3.

- *For available-for-sale investments that do not have a quoted market price in an active market and whose fair value cannot be reliably measured.* This requirement is specified in IAS 39 and is available until 2018, if the reporting entity does not adopt IFRS 9 early.

- *For a parent company's internal accounting records prior to preparing consolidated financial statements.* This situation will be discussed further in Chapter 5.

---

*The cost method is used for external reporting and internal recording purposes.*

---

The cost method is allowed under ASPE for equity investments that are not quoted in an active market. Under the cost method, the investment is initially recorded at cost. The investor's share of the dividends declared is reported in net income. The investment is reported at original cost at each reporting date unless the investment becomes impaired. Impairment losses are reported in net income. When the investment is sold, the realized gains or losses are reported in net income.

---

*The investment must be written down when there is impairment.*

---

Prior to 2009, a liquidating dividend was treated by the investor as a reduction in the investment account. A liquidating dividend occurred when the cumulative amount paid out as dividends was greater than the cumulative net incomes earned by the investee since the investment was acquired. Since dividends are a company's method of distributing earnings to its owners, it follows that a company cannot distribute as income more than it has earned. When it does so, it is really returning part of the original investment to its owners.

---

*A liquidating dividend is now reported as dividend income under the cost method.*

---

Even though it may be conceptually more appropriate to treat a liquidating dividend as a return of capital, the costs and complexities involved in determining whether the dividend is a liquidating dividend are often greater than the benefit. Accordingly, IAS 27 was changed in 2009 to require that all dividends be recognized in net income regardless of whether they were liquidating dividends.

Using the same data as in the previous illustration, Jenstar would make the following journal entries under the cost method:

| | | |
|---|---:|---:|
| *Jan. 1, Year 5* | | |
| Investment in Safebuy | 95,000 | |
|     Cash | | 95,000 |
| To record the acquisition of 10% of Safebuy's shares | | |
| | | |
| *Dec. 31, Year 5* | | |
| Cash | 8,000 | |
|     Dividend income | | 8,000 |
| Receipt of dividend from Safebuy | | |

| | | |
|---|---:|---:|
| *Jan. 10, Year 6* | | |
| Cash | 99,000 | |
|     Investment in Safebuy | | 95,000 |
|     Gain on sale (reported in net income) | | 4,000 |
| Record sale of investment | | |

> *Under the cost method, income is recognized when dividends are received or receivable.*

## LO4 Equity Method of Reporting an Investment in Associate

An investment in an associate is an investment in a corporation that permits the investor to exercise significant influence over the strategic operating and financing policies of the investee. Note that the criteria for this type of investment require only the *ability* to exercise significant influence; there is no requirement to show that such influence is actually being exercised in a particular situation.

> *An associate is an entity over which the investor has significant influence.*

The following conditions are possible indicators that significant influence is present and that the investee is an associate:

(a) Representation on the board of directors or equivalent governing body of the investee

(b) Participation in policy-making processes, including participation in decisions about dividends or other distributions

(c) Material transactions between the investor and the investee

(d) Interchange of managerial personnel

(e) Provision of essential technical information

IAS 28 suggests that holding 20–50% of voting shares may indicate the presence of significant influence, but it also states that a holding of this size does not necessarily mean that such influence exists. The following scenarios will illustrate this.

> *A guideline (not a rigid rule) in determining significant influence is holding 20–50% of voting shares.*

Given that A Company owns 60% of the voting shares of C Company (probably a control investment), does B Company's holding of 30% of C Company's shares indicate that B Company has a significant-influence investment? Not necessarily. If B Company were unable to obtain membership on the board of directors of C Company or participate in its strategic policy-making because of A Company's control, it would be difficult to conclude that B Company has significant influence. In such a situation, B Company's holding would be considered a nonstrategic investment. Would this situation be different if B Company were allowed membership on C Company's board of directors?

> *When one investor has control, other investors usually do not have significant influence.*

IAS 28 indicates that a substantial or majority ownership by another investor would not necessarily preclude an investor from exercising significant influence. In other words, another company's control investment in C Company does not mean that B Company's 30% investment in C Company can never be considered a significant influence. Determination of significant influence depends on the particular circumstances and the use of judgment.

On the other hand, is it possible to have significant influence with less than 20%? Normally, an investment of less than 20% would not allow the investor to elect any members to the board of directors of the investee corporation; because of this, it probably cannot exert any influence on the decision-making processes of that company. However, 20% is only a guideline, and an examination of the facts might suggest some other type of investment. For example, if the investee's shares are widely distributed, and all the other shareholders hold very small blocks of shares and display indifference as to the makeup of the board of directors, an investment of less than 20% may be considered a significant-influence investment. This could certainly be the case if some of the remaining shareholders gave the investor proxies to vote their shares.

> *When an investor has less than 20% of the voting shares, it usually does not have significant influence.*

From all these discussions and examples, it should be obvious that considerable professional judgment is required in determining whether an investor has significant influence. In later chapters, when we discuss the criteria used to determine whether a particular investment establishes control over an investee, we will also conclude that considerable professional judgment is required.

When an investor has significant influence, the investment should be reported by the equity method. The basic concept behind the equity method is that the investor records its proportionate share of the associate's income as its own income and reduces the investment account by its share of the associate's dividends declared.

## LO3 Illustration of Equity Method Basics

We return to the example of the Jenstar and Safebuy companies. All the facts remain the same, including the 10% ownership, except that we assume this is a significant-influence investment. Using the equity method, Jenstar's journal entries would be as follows:

| | | |
|---|---|---|
| *Jan. 1, Year 5* | | |
| Investment in Safebuy | 95,000 | |
|    Cash | | 95,000 |
| To record the acquisition of 10% of Safebuy's shares | | |
| *Dec. 31, Year 5* | | |
| Investment in Safebuy (10% × 100,000) | 10,000 | |
|    Equity method income | | 10,000 |
| 10% of Safebuy's Year 1 net income | | |
| Cash (10% × 80,000) | 8,000 | |
|    Investment in Safebuy | | 8,000 |
| Receipt of dividend from Safebuy | | |

> *Income is recognized based on the income reported by the associate, and dividends are reported as a reduction of the investment account.*

Under the equity method, the investor's investment account changes in direct relation to the changes taking place in the investee's equity accounts. The accounting objective is to reflect in the investor's financial statements the financial results arising from the close relationship between the companies.

The equity method is effective at achieving this. Because the investor is able to influence the associate's dividend policy, dividends could end up being paid in periods during which the investee was suffering considerable losses. The cost method of reporting would reflect the receipt of dividends as investment income, whereas the equity method would report investment losses during these periods and the investment account would be further reduced by the receipt of dividends.

> *The equity method picks up the investor's share of the changes in the associate's shareholders' equity.*

The equity method reflects the accrual method of income measurement. As the investee earns income, the investor accrues its share of this income. The associate is not obligated to pay out this income as a dividend on an annual basis. The investor can expect to get the dividend at a later date or to sell its shares at a higher value if the income is not paid out as a dividend. Therefore, the equity method does provide useful information about the future cash flow potential from the investment.

> *The equity method provides information on the potential for future cash flows.*

## Complexities Associated with the Equity Method

The previous example illustrated the basic concepts of the equity method. The following items add complexity to the equity method:

- The accounting for other changes in associate's equity
- Acquisition costs greater than carrying amount
- Unrealized intercompany profits
- Changes to and from the equity method
- Losses exceeding the balance in the investment account
- Impairment losses
- Gains or losses on sale of the investment
- Investment in associate held for sale
- Disclosure requirements

**OTHER CHANGES IN ASSOCIATE'S EQUITY**   In accounting for an investment by the equity method, IAS 28 requires that the investor's proportionate share of the associate's discontinued operations, other comprehensive income, changes in accounting policy, corrections of errors relating to prior-period financial statements, and capital transactions should be presented and disclosed in the investor's financial statements according to their nature.

> *The investor's statement of comprehensive income should reflect its share of the investee's income according to its nature and the different statement classifications.*

Companies report certain items separately on their statements of comprehensive income so that financial statement users can distinguish between the portion of comprehensive income that comes from continuing operations and the portion that comes from other sources such as discontinued operations and other comprehensive income. Retrospective adjustments of prior-period results and capital transactions are shown as separate components of retained earnings or are disclosed in the footnotes.

**EXAMPLE**   A Company owns 30% of B Company. The statement of comprehensive income for B Company for the current year is as follows:

**B COMPANY**
**STATEMENT OF COMPREHENSIVE INCOME**

| | |
|---|---:|
| Sales | $500,000 |
| Operating expenses | 200,000 |
| Operating income before income tax | 300,000 |
| Income tax | 120,000 |
| Net income from operations | 180,000 |
| Loss from discontinued operations (net of tax) | 40,000 |
| Net income | 140,000 |
| Other comprehensive income (net of tax) | 10,000 |
| Comprehensive income | $150,000 |

Upon receiving this statement of comprehensive income, A Company makes the following journal entry to apply the equity method:

| | | |
|---|---:|---:|
| Investment in B Company (30% × 150,000) | 45,000 | |
| Discontinued operations—investment loss (30% × 40,000) | 12,000 | |
|     Other comprehensive income—related to associate (30% × 10,000) | | 3,000 |
|     Equity method income (30% × 180,000) | | 54,000 |

> *The investor's shares of income from continuing operations, discontinued operations, and other comprehensive income are reported separately.*

All three income items, which total $45,000, will appear on A Company's statement of comprehensive income. The investment loss from discontinued operations and the other comprehensive income items require the same presentation as would be made if A Company had its own discontinued operations or other comprehensive income items. Full note disclosure is required to indicate that these particular items arise from an investment in associate accounted for by the equity method. Materiality has to be considered because these items do not require special treatment in A Company's statement of comprehensive income if they are not material from A Company's point of view, even though they are material from B Company's perspective.

Many of the accounting procedures for the application of the equity method are similar to the consolidation procedures for a parent and its subsidiary. Furthermore, the concepts underlying the procedures used in accounting for the acquisition of a subsidiary are also adopted in accounting for the acquisition of an investment in an associate. The next two sections briefly describe procedures required in applying the equity method that are equally applicable under the consolidation process. In this chapter, we will describe the procedures very generally. We will discuss these procedures in more detail in later chapters when we illustrate the consolidation of a parent and its subsidiary.

> *Many accounting procedures required for consolidated purposes are also required under the equity method.*

**ACQUISITION COSTS GREATER THAN CARRYING AMOUNTS**   In the previous examples, we recorded Jenstar's initial investment at its cost, but we did not consider the implications if this cost was different from the carrying amount of Safebuy's net assets[2] at the time of the acquisition. We now add a new feature to equity method reporting by considering the difference between the amount paid for the investment and the investor's share of the carrying amount of the associate's net assets.

Companies' shares often trade at prices that are different from their carrying amount. There are many reasons for this. The share price presumably reflects the fair value of the company as a whole. In effect, it reflects the fair value of the assets and liabilities of the company as a whole. However, many of the company's assets are reported at historical cost or cost less accumulated depreciation and amortization. For these assets, there will be a difference between the fair value and the carrying amount. Some of the company's value may be attributed to assets that are not even reported on the company's books. For example, the company may have expensed its research and development costs in the past but is now close to patenting a new technology. This technology could have considerable value to a prospective purchaser, even though there is no asset recorded in the company's books. Last but not least, the company's earnings potential may be so great that an investor is willing to pay an amount in excess of the fair value of the company's identifiable net assets. This excess payment is referred to as goodwill.

> *The investor's cost is usually greater than its share of the carrying amount of the associate's net assets.*

The difference between the investor's cost and the investor's percentage of the carrying amount of the associate's identifiable net assets is called the *acquisition differential*. The investor allocates this differential to specific assets and liabilities of the associate, and then either depreciates the allocated components over their useful lives or writes down the allocated component when there has been impairment in its value. This process of identifying, allocating, and amortizing the acquisition differential will be illustrated in later chapters.

**UNREALIZED PROFITS**   As we will see in later chapters, consolidated financial statements result from combining the financial statements of a parent company with the financial statements of its subsidiaries. The end result is the financial reporting of a single economic entity, made up of a number of separate legal entities. One of the major tasks in this process is to eliminate all intercompany transactions—especially intercompany "profits"—so that the consolidated statements reflect only transactions with outsiders. The basic premise behind the elimination is that, from the point of view of this single accounting entity, "you cannot make a profit selling to yourself." Any such "unrealized profits" from intercompany transfers of inventory (or other assets) must be held back until the specific assets involved are sold to outside entities or used in producing goods or providing services to outsiders.

> *Consolidated statements should reflect only the results of transactions with outsiders.*

In the case of a significant-influence investment, any transactions between the investor and the associate (they are related parties) must be scrutinized so that incomes are not overstated through the back-and-forth transfer of assets. From an accounting perspective, any transfer is acceptable provided that both parties record the transfer at the value at which it is being carried in the records of the selling company. However, if the transfer involves a profit, a portion of that profit must be held back on an after-tax basis in the investor's equity method journal entries. When the asset in question is sold outside or consumed by the purchaser, the after-tax profit is realized through an equity method journal entry, again made by the investor. The entries under the equity method to account for unrealized and realized profit from intercompany transactions will be discussed and illustrated in detail in Chapters 6 and 7.

> *Profits from intercompany transactions must be eliminated until the assets are sold to outsiders or used in producing goods or providing services to outsiders.*

**CHANGES TO AND FROM THE EQUITY METHOD**   The classification of investments will change as the particular facts change. An investment may initially be FVTPL and subsequently change to one of significant influence. This could happen if additional shares were acquired. Once significant influence has been achieved, a switch from the previous way of reporting is made on a prospective basis. The carrying amount of the FVTPL investment, which would be the fair value of the investment, becomes its new cost. If circumstances change, significant influence may also be achieved without additional shares being acquired, in which case the equity method would commence. For example, the holdings of a large block of investee shares by another company could prevent an investor from exercising significant influence. But if that other company sells its block on the market, the investor's previous FVTPL investment may now amount to significant influence. See part A of Self-Study Problem 1 for an example of changing from FVTPL to the equity method on a prospective basis.

> *Changes in reporting methods are accounted for prospectively if they are changed because of a change in circumstance.*

When an investment changes from significant influence to FVTPL, the equity method ceases to be appropriate and the fair value method takes its place, also on a prospective basis. On this date, the investor shall measure at fair value any investment the investor retains in the former associate. The investor shall recognize in net income any difference between

(a) the fair value of any retained investment and any proceeds from disposing of the part interest in the associate, and

(b) the carrying amount of the investment at the date when significant influence is lost.

If an investor loses significant influence over an associate, the investor must account for all amounts recognized in other comprehensive income in relation to that associate on the same basis as would be required if the associate had directly disposed of the related assets or liabilities. When the investor sells its investment in the associate, it is, in effect, selling its proportionate share of the assets and liabilities of the associate. Therefore, if a gain or loss previously recognized in other comprehensive income by an associate would be reclassified to net income on the disposal of the related assets or liabilities, the investor reclassifies the gain or loss from accumulated other comprehensive income to net income (as a reclassification adjustment) when it loses significant influence over the associate. For example, if an associate had reported other comprehensive income on a cash flow hedge and the investor loses significant influence over the associate, the investor must reclassify to net income the gain or loss previously recognized in OCI in relation to that hedge. If an investor's ownership interest in an associate is reduced, but the investment continues to be an associate, the investor must reclassify to net income only a proportionate amount of the gain or loss previously recognized in OCI.

When an investment changes from significant influence to control, the preparation of consolidated statements commences, again on a prospective basis. The concepts relating to this particular situation will be discussed at length in later chapters.

**LOSSES EXCEEDING THE BALANCE IN THE INVESTMENT ACCOUNT**   A question arises as to the appropriate accounting when an investor's share of an associate's losses exceeds the carrying amount of the investment. IAS 28 provides some guidance on this issue. After the investor's interest in the associate is reduced to zero, additional losses are provided for, and a liability is recognized, *only* to the extent that the investor has incurred legal or constructive obligations or made payments on behalf of the associate. The investor would have an obligation if it guaranteed certain liabilities of the associate or if it committed to provide additional financial support to the associate. In cases where the liability is not to be reported, the investor resumes recognizing its share of associate's profits only after its share of them equals the share of losses not recognized.

> *If an investor guaranteed an investee's obligations, the investor could end up reporting its investment as a liability rather than an asset.*

If the investor has other long-term interests in the associate over and above its equity investment, these other assets may also have to be written down. Such items may include preference shares and long-term receivables or loans but do not include trade receivables, trade payables, or any long-term receivables for which adequate collateral exists. Losses recognized under the equity method in excess of the investor's investment in ordinary shares are applied to the other components of the investor's interest in an associate in the reverse order of their seniority (i.e., priority in liquidation). Accordingly, an investment in preferred shares should be written down before a long-term note receivable because the preferred share becomes worthless before a note receivable. In other words, the note receivable has priority over the investment in preferred shares in the event that the associate is liquidated.

> *Other long-term interests in the associate may have to be written down when the associate is reporting losses.*

**IMPAIRMENT LOSSES**    If there is an indication that the investment may be impaired, the investment is tested for impairment in accordance with IAS 36, as a single asset, by comparing its recoverable amount (higher of value in use and fair value less costs of disposal) to its carrying amount. In determining the value in use of the investment, an entity estimates

(a) its share of the present value of the estimated future cash flows expected to be generated by the associate, including the cash flows from the operations of the associate and the proceeds on the ultimate disposal of the investment, or

(b) the present value of the estimated future cash flows expected to arise from dividends to be received from the investment and from its ultimate disposal.

If the recoverable amount is less than the carrying amount, the investment is written down to the recoverable amount. The impairment loss is not allocated to goodwill or any other assets underlying the carrying amount of the investment because these underlying assets were not separately recognized. If the recoverable amount increases in subsequent periods, the impairment loss can be reversed.

**GAINS AND LOSSES ON SALE OF INVESTMENTS**    When all the shares that make up a long-term investment are sold, the gain (loss) is shown on the income statement and is calculated as the difference between the sale proceeds and the carrying amount of the investment. When only some of the shares are sold, the gain is calculated using the average carrying amount of the investment. Formulas such as first in, first out (FIFO), last in, first out (LIFO), or specific identification are not permitted. If a portion of a significant influence or a control investment is sold, a reevaluation must be made to determine whether the previous classification is still valid.

> *Average cost should be used in determining any gain or loss when an investor sells part of its investment.*

**HELD FOR SALE**   Investments in associates that meet the criteria to be classified as held for sale should be measured at the lower of carrying amount and fair value less costs of disposal, and should be reported as current assets. An entity shall classify an investment in associate as held for sale if its carrying amount will be recovered principally through a sale transaction rather than through continuing use. For this to be the case, the asset must be available for immediate sale in its present condition, subject only to terms that are usual and customary for sales of such assets, and its sale must be highly probable. For the sale to be highly probable, the appropriate level of management must be committed to a plan to sell the asset, and an active program to locate a buyer and complete the plan must have been initiated. Further, the asset must be actively marketed for sale at a price that is reasonable in relation to its current fair value. In addition, the sale should be expected to qualify for recognition as a completed sale within one year from the date of classification, and actions required to complete the plan should indicate that it is unlikely that significant changes to the plan will be made or that the plan will be withdrawn.

**PRESENTATION AND DISCLOSURE REQUIREMENTS**   Investments in associates shall be classified as noncurrent assets. The investor's share of the profit or loss of such associates and the carrying amount of these investments must be separately disclosed. In addition, the following summarizes the main disclosures required in IFRS 12 for investments in associates:

(a) Nature of the entity's relationship with the associate and the proportion of ownership interest or participating share held by the entity

(b) Fair value of investments in associates for which there are published price quotations

(c) Summarized financial information of associates, including the aggregated amounts of assets, liabilities, revenues, and profit or loss

(d) Unrecognized share of losses of an associate, both for the period and cumulatively, if an investor has discontinued recognition of its share of losses of an associate

(e) Nature and extent of any significant restrictions on the ability of associates to transfer funds to the entity in the form of cash dividends, or to repay loans or advances made by the entity

(f) Contingent liabilities incurred relating to its interests in associates

> *The fair value of an investment in associate should be disclosed when it is readily available.*

Aecon Group Inc. is a publicly traded construction and infrastructure-development company incorporated in Canada. Aecon and its subsidiaries provide services to private and public sector clients throughout Canada and on a selected basis internationally. It reported numerous construction projects under the equity method in its 2014 financial statements. Excerpts from these statements are presented in Exhibit 2.2.

**EXHIBIT 2.2**

## EXTRACTS FROM AECON'S 2014 FINANCIAL STATEMENTS

*5. Summary of Significant Accounting Policies*

*5.14 Associates*

Entities in which the Company has significant influence and which are neither subsidiaries, nor joint arrangements, are accounted for using the equity method of accounting in accordance with IAS 28 *Investments in Associates and Joint Ventures*. Under the equity method of accounting, the Company's investments in associates are carried at cost and adjusted for post-acquisition changes in the net assets of the investment. Profit or loss reflects the Company's share of the results of these investments. Distributions received from an investee reduce the carrying amount of the investment. The consolidated statements of comprehensive income also include the Company's share of any amounts recognized by associates in OCI.

Where there has been a change recognized directly in the equity of the associate, the Company recognizes its share of that change in equity. The financial statements of the associates are generally prepared for the same reporting period as the Company, using consistent accounting policies. Adjustments are made to bring into line any dissimilar accounting policies that may exist in the underlying records of the associate. Adjustments are made in the consolidated financial statements to eliminate the Company's share of unrealized gains and losses on transactions between the Company and its associates.

The Company discontinues the use of the equity method from the date on which it ceases to have significant influence, and from that date accounts for the investment in accordance with IAS 39 *Financial Instruments: Recognition and Measurement* (its initial costs are the carrying amount of the associate on that date), provided the investment does not then qualify as a subsidiary or a joint arrangement.

## 11. PROJECTS ACCOUNTED FOR USING THE EQUITY METHOD

The Company performs some construction and concession related projects through non-consolidated entities. The Company's participation in these entities is conducted through joint ventures and associates and is accounted for using the equity method. The Company's joint ventures and associates are private entities and there is no quoted market price available for their shares.

The summarized financial information below reflects the Company's share of the amounts presented in the financial statements of joint ventures and associates:

| | December 31, 2014 | | | December 31, 2013 | | |
| --- | --- | --- | --- | --- | --- | --- |
| | Joint Ventures | Associates | Total | Joint Ventures | Associates | Total |
| | $ | $ | $ | $ | $ | $ |
| Cash and cash equivalents | 2,290 | 5,452 | 7,742 | 2,930 | 12,972 | 15,902 |
| Other current assets | 56,841 | 17,780 | 74,621 | 117,898 | 23,775 | 141,673 |
| Total current assets | 59,131 | 23,232 | 82,363 | 120,828 | 36,747 | 157,575 |
| Non-current assets | 418,294 | 1,248 | 419,542 | 386,899 | 1,247 | 388,146 |
| **Total assets** | 477,425 | 24,480 | 501,905 | 507,727 | 37,994 | 545,721 |
| Trade and other payables and provisions | 20,588 | 7,539 | 28,127 | 22,464 | 8,860 | 31,324 |
| Other current financial liabilities | 15,090 | 43 | 15,133 | 15,142 | 43 | 15,185 |
| Total current liabilities | 35,678 | 7,582 | 43,260 | 37,606 | 8,903 | 46,509 |
| Non-current financial liabilities | 134,571 | — | 134,571 | 193,847 | — | 193,847 |
| Other non-current liabilities | 78,347 | — | 78,347 | 72,898 | — | 72,898 |
| Total non-current liabilities | 212,918 | — | 212,918 | 266,745 | — | 266,745 |
| **Total liabilities** | 248,596 | 7,582 | 256,178 | 304,351 | 8,903 | 313,254 |
| **Net assets** | 228,829 | 16,898 | 245,727 | 203,376 | 29,091 | 232,467 |

**EXHIBIT 2.2**  *(continued)*

| | For the year ended | | | | | |
| | December 31, 2014 | | | December 31, 2013 | | |
| | Joint Ventures | Associates | Total | Joint Ventures | Associates | Total |
| | $ | $ | $ | $ | $ | $ |
| Revenue | 112,194 | 56,726 | 168,920 | 82,026 | 100,041 | 182,067 |
| Depreciation and amortization | (14,583) | — | (14,583) | (11,195) | — | (11,195) |
| Other costs | (57,285) | (48,920) | (106,205) | (34,469) | (86,319) | (120,788) |
| **Operating profit** | 40,326 | 7,806 | 48,132 | 36,362 | 13,722 | 50,084 |
| Finance costs | (13,416) | — | (13,416) | (10,150) | — | (10,150) |
| Income tax expense | (31) | — | (31) | (428) | — | (428) |
| Non-controlling interest | (1,690) | — | (1,690) | (1,654) | — | (1,654) |
| **Profit for the year** | 25,189 | 7,806 | 32,995 | 24,130 | 13,722 | 37,852 |
| Other comprehensive income | 19,437 | — | 19,437 | 11,406 | — | 11,406 |
| **Total comprehensive income** | 44,626 | 7,806 | 52,432 | 35,536 | 13,722 | 49,258 |

The movement in the investment in projects accounted for using the equity method is as follows:

| | December 31, 2014 | December 31, 2013 |
| | $ | $ |
| **Projects accounted for using the equity method—beginning of year** | 232,467 | 190,923 |
| Share of profit for the year | 32,995 | 37,852 |
| Share of other comprehensive income for the year | 19,437 | 11,406 |
| Distributions from projects accounted for using the equity method | (34,172) | (7,714) |
| **Projects accounted for using the equity method—end of year** | 245,727 | 232,467 |

Source: Aecon Group Inc., 2014 Annual Report. Page 62, Note 11. Used with the permission of Aecon Group Inc.

---

*Information on the income, assets, and liabilities of the associates and joint ventures must be disclosed.*

---

# LO5 ANALYSIS AND INTERPRETATION OF FINANCIAL STATEMENTS

In this chapter, we have used the Jenstar example to illustrate four different methods for reporting equity investments. Exhibit 2.3 presents financial data (ignoring income tax) for Jenstar for Year 5. The data for the investment in and investment income from Safebuy for each method below has been taken from the previous examples earlier in this chapter. All other data is now being given so that we can see the impact of the accounting policy choice on three key financial ratios.

The following observations are made on the data in Exhibit 2.3 when the fair value of the investments increased during the year:

- The current ratio is highest for the FVTPL method because the investment in Safebuy is shown as a current asset. Therefore, the FVTPL method shows the best liquidity.

- The last two methods show the lowest debt-to-equity ratio (and the best solvency) because equity is the highest under these two methods.

**EXHIBIT 2.3**

## Impact of Reporting Methods on Key Financial Ratios (in 000s)

| | Cost | Equity | FVTPL | FVTOCI |
|---|---|---|---|---|
| Dividend income | $ 8 | $ | $ 8 | $ 8 |
| Equity method income | | 10 | | |
| Unrealized gains | | | 3 | |
| Other income | 67 | 67 | 67 | 67 |
| Net income | 75 | 77 | 78 | 75 |
| OCI—unrealized gains | 0 | 0 | 0 | 3 |
| Comprehensive income | $ 75 | $ 77 | $ 78 | $ 78 |
| Investment in Safebuy | | | $ 98 | |
| Other current assets | $ 300 | $ 300 | 300 | $ 300 |
| Current assets | 300 | 300 | 398 | 300 |
| Investment in Safebuy | 95 | 97 | | 98 |
| Other noncurrent assets | 700 | 700 | 700 | 700 |
| Total assets | $1,095 | $1,097 | $1,098 | $1,098 |
| Current liabilities | $ 250 | $ 250 | $ 250 | $ 250 |
| Noncurrent liabilities | 400 | 400 | 400 | 400 |
| Total liabilities | 650 | 650 | 650 | 650 |
| Retained earnings | 75 | 77 | 78 | 75 |
| Accumulated OCI | | | | 3 |
| Other shareholders' equity | 370 | 370 | 370 | 370 |
| Total shareholders' equity | 445 | 447 | 448 | 448 |
| Liabilities and shareholders' equity | $1,095 | $1,097 | $1,098 | $1,098 |
| Current ratio | 1.20 | 1.20 | 1.59 | 1.20 |
| Debt-to-equity ratio | 1.461 | 1.454 | 1.451 | 1.451 |
| Return on equity | 16.85% | 17.23% | 17.41% | 16.74% |

> *The FVTPL investment must be shown as a current asset, whereas the other investments could be current or noncurrent, depending on management's intention.*
>
> *The FVTPL investment shows the best liquidity and profitability.*

- The return on equity is highest for the FVTPL ratio because net income, rather than comprehensive income, is typically used as the numerator for this equity. Therefore, the FVTPL method shows the best profitability even though FVTOCI shows the same comprehensive income as the FVTPL method.

Although the reporting methods show different values for liquidity, solvency, and profitability, the real economic situation is exactly the same for the four different methods. See Self-Study Problem 2 for another example, to compare the accounting for the different methods of reporting. This example shows that the timing of reporting income is different but the cumulative results are the same. If this is so, which method best represents the real economic situation? This is a question we should ask as we study different accounting and reporting methods throughout the course. Many of the end-of-chapter problems ask this question and give you an opportunity to express your own opinion.

## LO6 ASPE Differences

As mentioned in Chapter 1 and as we have seen in this chapter, most of the discussion in this textbook deals with IFRS. Starting in this chapter and in each subsequent chapter, we will have a section at the end of the chapter titled ASPE Differences, in which the differences in the reporting requirements for private entities for the topics discussed in the chapter will be summarized. Detailed illustrations will not be provided.

Section 3051 *Investments* of Part II of the *CPA Canada Handbook* has different standards for a private enterprise than for a publicly accountable enterprise. The following excerpts from Section 3051 outline the main requirements for significant-influence investments:

- An investor that is able to exercise significant influence over an investee should make an accounting policy choice to account for the investment using either the equity method or the cost method. An investor should account for all investments within the scope of this section using the same method.

- When an investee's equity securities are traded in an active market, the cost method cannot be used. Under such circumstances, the investment should be accounted for using the equity method or at fair value, with changes in fair value recorded in net income.

- The investments in and income from companies subject to significant influence, and other investments accounted for at cost, should be reported separately.

ASPE is also quite different for financial instruments. The following excerpts from Section 3856 *Financial Instruments* of Part II of the *CPA Canada Handbook* outline the main requirements for nonstrategic investments:

- Nonstrategic investments in equity instruments that are quoted in an active market are reported at fair value, and any changes in fair value are reported in net income.

- Nonstrategic investments in equity instruments that are not quoted in an active market should be reported at cost less any reduction for impairment, and the impairment losses should be reported in net income.

- An entity may irrevocably elect to measure any equity investment at fair value by designating that fair value measurement shall apply.

- Other comprehensive income does not exist under ASPE.

---

*Under ASPE, investments in associates can be reported using the cost method, equity method, or at fair value.*

*Under ASPE, nonstrategic equity investments should be reported at cost unless the value of the investment is quoted in an active market or the entity elects to report at fair value.*

---

**Cautionary Note:** *When answering the end-of-chapter material for Chapters 2 through 11, assume that IFRS is to be applied unless otherwise stated.*

# SUMMARY

Over the past 12 years, there has been a move from primarily using historical cost to using fair values for reporting investments in equity securities including investments in private companies. **(LO1)**

FVTPL, FVTOCI, and AFS investments are remeasured at fair value at each reporting date. Dividends from these investments are reported in income when declared. Unrealized gains and losses are initially reported in net income for FVTPL investments and in OCI for FVTOCI investments. When the investments are sold, the unrealized gains are recycled through net income for AFS investments and can be transferred to another category of shareholders' equity for FVTOCI investments. **(LO2)**

Under the cost method, investments are measured at cost at each reporting date unless there is a permanent impairment. Income is recognized as dividends are received or receivable. Under the equity method, the investments are initially reported at cost. Thereafter, they are adjusted for the investor's share of the change in investee's shareholders' equity adjusted for the amortization of the acquisition differential and the holdback and realization of profits from the intercompany sale of assets. Income is recognized as the income type reported by the investee. **(LO3)**

An investment in which the investor is able to significantly influence the operations of the investee is called an *investment in associate* and must be accounted for using the equity method. Significant influence can be achieved through representation on the board of directors, participation in policy-making processes, material transactions between the investor and the investee, and/or interchange of managerial personnel. **(LO4)**

The different methods for reporting equity investments will produce different values for net income, assets, and shareholders' equity. Users of the financial statements will need to be aware of these differences as they assess the profitability, liquidity, and solvency of the reporting entity. **(LO5)**

Under ASPE, nonstrategic equity investments are reported at fair value if the investment's share price is quoted in an active market or the entity elects to report at fair value. Under ASPE, investments in associates can be reported using the cost method, equity method, or at fair value. **(LO6)**

## Self-Study Problem 1

### Part A

LO2, 3

On January 1, Year 5, High Inc. purchased 10% of the outstanding common shares of Lowe Corp. for $192,000. From High's perspective, Lowe was a FVTPL investment. The fair value of High's investment was $200,000 at December 31, Year 5.

On January 1, Year 6, High purchased an additional 25% of Lowe's shares for $500,000. This second purchase allowed High to exert significant influence over Lowe. There was no acquisition differential on the date of the 25% acquisition.

During the two years, Lowe reported the following:

|  | Profit | Dividends |
|---|---|---|
| Year 5 | $200,000 | $120,000 |
| Year 6 | 270,000 | 130,000 |

### Required

Prepare High's journal entries with respect to this investment for both Year 5 and Year 6.

## Part B

The following are summarized income statements for the two companies for Year 7:

|  | High Inc. | Lowe Corp. |
| --- | --- | --- |
| Operating income before income taxes | $ 750,000 | $340,000 |
| Income tax expense | 300,000 | 140,000 |
| Net income before discontinued operations | 450,000 | 200,000 |
| Loss from discontinued operations (net of tax) | — | 20,000 |
| Net income | $ 450,000* | $180,000 |

*The net income of High does not include any investment income from its investment in Lowe.

Lowe paid no dividends in Year 7.

## Required

(a) Prepare the journal entries that High should make at the end of Year 7 with respect to its investment in Lowe.

(b) Prepare High's income statement for Year 7, taking into consideration the journal entries in part (a).

# Solution to Self-Study Problem 1

## Part A

The 10% purchase is accounted for under the FVTPL method. High's journal entries during Year 5 are as follows:

| | | |
| --- | --- | --- |
| Investment in Lowe | 192,000 | |
|     Cash | | 192,000 |
| Purchase of 10% of shares of Lowe | | |
| Cash (10% × 120,000) | 12,000 | |
|     Dividend income | | 12,000 |
| Investment in Lowe (200,000–192,000) | 8,000 | |
|     Unrealized gain on FVTPL investment | | 8,000 |

The 25% purchase in Year 6 changes the investment to one of significant influence, which is accounted for prospectively under the equity method.

The journal entries in Year 6 are as follows:

| | | |
| --- | --- | --- |
| Investment in Lowe | 500,000 | |
|     Cash | | 500,000 |
| Purchase of additional 25% of shares of Lowe | | |
| Investment in Lowe (35% × 270,000 profit) | 94,500 | |
|     Equity method income | | 94,500 |
| Cash (35% × 130,000 dividends) | 45,500 | |
|     Investment in Lowe | | 45,500 |

## Part B

(a) Applying the equity method, High makes the following journal entries in Year 7:

| | | |
| --- | --- | --- |
| Investment in Lowe (35% × 180,000) | 63,000 | |
| Discontinued operations—investment loss (35% × 20,000) | 7,000 | |
|     Equity method income (35% × 200,000) | | 70,000 |

(b)

**HIGH INC.**
**INCOME STATEMENT**
Year ended December 31, Year 7

| | |
|---|---:|
| Operating income | $750,000 |
| Equity method income* | 70,000 |
| Income before income taxes | 820,000 |
| Income tax expense | 300,000 |
| Net income before discontinued operations | 520,000 |
| Discontinued operations—investment loss (net of tax)* | 7,000 |
| Net income | $513,000 |

*A note would disclose that these items, in whole or in part, came from a 35% investment in Lowe, accounted for using the equity method.

## Self-Study Problem 2

LO2, 3, 5

On January 1, Year 7, Joshua Corp. purchased 20% of the outstanding ordinary shares of Deng Company at a cost of $950,000. Deng reported profit of $900,000 and paid dividends of $600,000 for the year ended December 31, Year 7. The market value of Joshua's 20% interest in Deng was $990,000 at December 31, Year 7. On June 30, Year 8, Deng paid dividends of $350,000. On July 2, Year 8 Joshua sold its investment in Deng for $1,005,000. Deng did not prepare financial statements for Year 8 until early in Year 9.

**Required**

(a) Prepare the journal entries for Joshua Corp. for Years 7 and 8 for the above-noted transactions under the following reporting methods: cost, equity, FVTPL, and FVTOCI.

(b) Prepare a schedule to show the profit, OCI, comprehensive income, and change in retained earnings for Joshua for Year 7, Year 8, and the total of the changes for Years 7 and 8 under the four methods.

(c) Prepare a schedule to compare the change in cash with change in profit, comprehensive income, and retained earnings for Joshua for the sum of the two years under the four methods.

(d) Comment on the similarities and differences in financial reporting for the four methods.

## Solution to Self-Study Problem 2

(a) Credit entries are noted in brackets.

| | Cost | Equity | FVTPL | FVTOCI |
|---|---|---|---|---|
| *Jan. 1, Year 7* | | | | |
| Investment in Deng | 950,000 | 950,000 | 950,000 | 950,000 |
| Cash | (950,000) | (950,000) | (950,000) | (950,000) |
| To record the acquisition of 20% of Deng's shares | | | | |
| *Dec. 31, Year 7* | | | | |
| Investment in Deng (20% × 900,000) | | 180,000 | | |
| Equity method income | | (180,000) | | |
| Accrue share of profit | | | | |
| Cash (20% × 600,000) | 120,000 | 120,000 | 120,000 | 120,000 |
| Dividend income | (120,000) | | (120,000) | (120,000) |
| Investment in Deng | | (120,000) | | |
| Receipt of dividend from Deng | | | | |
| Investment in Deng (990,000 – 950,000) | | | 40,000 | 40,000 |
| Unrealized gains (reported in profit) | | | (40,000) | |
| OCI | | | | (40,000) |
| To revalue investment at fair value | | | | |

| | Cost | Equity | FVTPL | FVTOCI |
|---|---|---|---|---|
| **June 30, Year 8** | | | | |
| Cash (20% × 350,000) | 70,000 | 70,000 | 70,000 | 70,000 |
|    Dividend income | (70,000) | | (70,000) | (70,000) |
|    Investment in Deng | | (70,000) | | |
| Receipt of dividend from Deng | | | | |
| **July 2, Year 8** | | | | |
| Cash | 1,005,000 | 1,005,000 | 1,005,000 | 1,005,000 |
|    Investment in Deng | (950,000) | (940,000) | (990,000) | (990,000) |
|    Gain on sale (reported in profit) | (55,000) | (65,000) | (15,000) | |
|    OCI—unrealized gains | | | | (15,000) |
| Record sale of investment | | | | |
| Accumulated OCI—reclassification to retained earnings | | | | 55,000 |
|    Retained earnings | | | | (55,000) |
| Clear accumulated OCI to retained earnings | | | | |

(b)

| (in $000s) | Cost | | | Equity | | | FVTPL | | | FVTOCI | | |
|---|---|---|---|---|---|---|---|---|---|---|---|---|
| | YR7 | YR8 | Total | YR7 | YR8 | Total | YR7 | YR8 | Total | YR7 | YR8 | Total |
| Profit | 120 | 125 | 245 | 180 | 65 | 245 | 160 | 85 | 245 | 120 | 70 | 190 |
| OCI | | | | | | | | | | 40 | 15 | 55 |
| Comprehensive income | 120 | 125 | 245 | 180 | 65 | 245 | 160 | 85 | 245 | 160 | 85 | 245 |
| Change in retained earnings | 120 | 125 | 245 | 180 | 65 | 245 | 160 | 85 | 245 | 120 | 125 | 245 |

(c)

| (in $000s) | Cost | Equity | FVTPL | FVTOCI |
|---|---|---|---|---|
| Cash received: | | | | |
|    Dividends in Year 1 | 120 | 120 | 120 | 120 |
|    Dividends in Year 2 | 70 | 70 | 70 | 70 |
|    Sales proceeds in Year 2 | 1,005 | 1,005 | 1,005 | 1,005 |
|    Total cash received | 1,195 | 1,195 | 1,195 | 1,195 |
| Cash paid for investment | 950 | 950 | 950 | 950 |
| Change in cash | 245 | 245 | 245 | 245 |
| Change in profit | 245 | 245 | 245 | 190 |
| Change in comprehensive income | 245 | 245 | 245 | 245 |
| Change in retained earnings | 245 | 245 | 245 | 245 |

(d)

**Similarities**

- Change in cash is the same for all methods.
- Profit for the two years in total is the same for the first three methods and comprehensive income is the same for all methods.
- Change in retained earnings for the two years in total is the same for all methods.
- Change in cash is equal to change in profit for the two years in total for the first three methods.
- Change in cash is equal to change in comprehensive income for the two years in total for all methods.
- Change in cash is equal to change in retained earnings for the two years in total for all methods.

**Differences**

- Timing of income recognition is different.
- Gains from appreciation go through profit for first three methods but never get reported in profit for the FVTOCI investment.

## Review Questions

LO1 **1.** Briefly describe the trend in reporting of investments in equity securities over the past 12 years.

LO2 **2.** Distinguish between the financial reporting for FVTPL investments and that for investments in associates.

LO2,4 **3.** What criteria would be used to determine whether the equity method should be used to account for a particular investment?

LO3 **4.** The equity method records dividends as a reduction in the investment account. Explain why.

LO4 **5.** The Ralston Company owns 35% of the outstanding voting shares of Purina Inc. Under what circumstances would Ralston determine that it is inappropriate to report this investment using the equity method?

LO3 **6.** Because of the acquisition of additional investee shares, an investor may need to change from the fair value method for a FVTPL investment to the equity method for a significant-influence investment. What procedures are applied to effect this accounting change?

LO3 **7.** An investor uses the equity method to report its investment in an investee. During the current year, the investee reports other comprehensive income on its statement of comprehensive income. How should this item be reflected in the investor's financial statements?

LO3 **8.** Ashton Inc. acquired a 40% interest in Villa Corp. for $200,000. In the first year after acquisition, Villa reported a loss of $700,000. Using the equity method, how should Ashton account for this loss assuming (a) Ashton has guaranteed the liabilities of Villa and (b) Ashton has not guaranteed the liabilities of Villa.

LO3 **9.** Able Company holds a 40% interest in Baker Corp. During the year, Able sold a portion of this investment. How should this investment be reported after the sale?

LO5 **10.** Which of the reporting methods described in this chapter would typically report the highest current ratio? Briefly explain.

LO6 **11.** How should a private company that has opted to follow ASPE report an investment in an associate?

LO2 **12.** How will the investment in a private company be reported under IFRS 9, and how does this differ from IAS 39?

# CASES

## Case 2-1

LO2, 4, 5

Hil Company purchased 10,000 common shares (10%) of Ton Inc. on January 1, Year 4, for $345,000, when Ton's shareholders' equity was $2,600,000, and it classified the investment as a FVTPL security. On January 1, Year 5, Hil acquired an additional 30,000 common shares (30%) of Ton for $1,050,000.

On both dates, any difference between the purchase price and the carrying amount of Ton's shareholders' equity was attributed to land. The market value of Ton's common shares was $35 per share on December 31, Year 4, and $37 per share on December 31, Year 5. Ton reported net income of $500,000 in Year 4 and $520,000 in Year 5, and paid dividends of $480,000 in both years.

The management of Hil is very excited about the increase in ownership interest in Ton because Ton has been very profitable. Hil pays a bonus to management based on its net income determined in accordance with GAAP.

The management of Hil is wondering how the increase in ownership will affect the reporting of the investment in Ton. Will Hil continue to classify the investment as FVTPL in Year 5? What factors will be considered in determining whether the equity method should now be used? If the equity method is now appropriate, will the change be made retroactively? They would like to see a comparison of income for Year 5 and the balance in the investment account at the end of Year 5 under the two options for reporting this investment. Last but not least, they would like to get your opinion on which method should be used to best reflect the performance of Hil for Year 5.

### Required

Respond to the questions raised and the requests made by management. Prepare schedules and/or financial statements to support your presentation.

## Case 2-2

LO2, 4, 6

Floyd's Specialty Foods Inc. (FSFI) operates over 60 shops throughout Ontario. The company was founded by George Floyd when he opened a single shop in the city of Cornwall. This store sold prepared dinners and directed its products at customers who were too busy to prepare meals after a long day at work. The concept proved to be very successful, and more stores were opened in Cornwall. Recently, new stores were opened in five other Ontario cities. Up to the current year, the shares of FSFI have been owned entirely by Floyd. However, during this year, the company suffered severe cash flow problems, due to too-rapid expansion exacerbated by a major decline in economic activity. Profitability suffered and creditors threatened to take legal action for long-overdue accounts. To avoid bankruptcy, Floyd sought additional financing from his old friend James Connelly, who is a majority shareholder of Cornwall Autobody Inc. (CAI), a public company. Subsequently, CAI paid $950,000 cash to FSFI to acquire enough newly issued shares of common stock for a one-third interest.

At the end of this year, CAI's accountants are discussing how they should properly report this investment in the company's financial statements.

One argues for maintaining the asset at original cost, saying, "What we have done is to advance money to bail out these stores. Floyd will continue to run the organization with little or no attention to us, so in effect we have lent him money. After all, what does anyone in our company know about the specialty food business? My guess is that as soon as the stores become solvent, Floyd will want to buy back our shares."

Another accountant disagrees, stating that the equity method is appropriate. "I realize that our company is not capable of running a specialty food company. But the requirements state that ownership of over 20% is evidence of significant influence."

A third accountant supports equity method reporting for a different reason. "If the investment gives us the ability to exert significant influence, that is all that is required. We don't have to actually exert it. One-third of the common shares certainly give us that ability."

## Required

How should CAI report its investment? Your answer should include a discussion of all three accountants' positions.

## Case 2-3

LO3, 6

It is January 20, Year 13. Mr. Neely, a partner in your office, wants to see you, CPA, about Bruin Car Parts Inc. (BCP), a client requiring assistance. BCP prepares its financial statements in accordance with ASPE. Richard (Rick) Bergeron, Lyle Chara, and Jean Perron each own 100 common shares of BCP. Jean wants BCP to buy him out. You made some notes on BCP during your discussion with Mr. Neely (Exhibit I).

Mr. Neely forwarded an email from Rick (Exhibit II) to you, along with excerpts from the Signed Shareholders' Agreement (SSA) (Exhibit III), the draft financial statements for BCP for the year ended November 30, Year 12 (Exhibit IV), and some additional information regarding the draft financial statements (Exhibit V).

Mr. Neely tells you, "CPA, we need to establish a buyout value. Our valuation must take into account any accounting adjustments required to comply with the SSA requirements. Please also consider any other issues that may be relevant to the other shareholders."

### EXHIBIT I

#### NOTES ON BRUIN CAR PARTS INC.

BCP was founded 30 years ago. It manufactures car parts for the North American automotive industry. All sales are made to Canadian-based companies.

All three shareholders have known each other for over 35 years and have different roles within BCP. Rick handles the financial and administrative duties, Lyle is in charge of product design and testing, and Jean is in charge of sales.

BCP's corporate tax rate is the small business rate of 12% for active business income. BCP applies the taxes payable method for accounting purposes. BCP incurred operating losses in the last few years and as a result has accumulated non-capital losses totalling $240,000, which can be applied against taxable income and thereby save taxes in future years.

BCP does research and development (R&D) every five years, on average. When it does, it is able to claim a 35% investment tax credit on its eligible R&D costs.

### EXHIBIT II

#### EMAIL FROM MR. BERGERON

Jean Perron told us on January 12 that he wants to be bought out of BCP. This request has shocked Lyle and me. He said that BCP must buy him out, as per the SSA. I knew Jean was having personal difficulties after his divorce, and he took time off, but he seemed better lately. He started asking for a repayment of his shareholder loan a few months ago to help with his cash flow, but we could not afford it. We were planning to repay him soon, since Year 12 was our best year in the past five years.

We need you to determine the impact of the buyout on BCP. I pulled out the SSA from our archived corporate files. It took me a while to find it, and I barely remembered what it said.

EXHIBIT III

*EXCERPTS FROM BCP'S SIGNED SHAREHOLDERS' AGREEMENT*

Between: Mr. Richard Bergeron, Mr. Lyle Chara, and Mr. Jean Perron ("the Shareholders") and Bruin Car Parts Inc. ("BCP")

**Clause 3:**

Any of the Shareholders may give notice, within 90 days after the end of the fiscal year, of the intent to sell their shares.

Effective the date the notice is given, the seller's shares will be exchanged for non-voting preferred shares, which BCP must then redeem. BCP shall redeem 10% of the shares within sixty (60) days of receiving notice. The rest of the shares will be redeemed over nine (9) years on an equal annual basis, with the first redemption one year after the initial payment.

To determine the value of the shares for redemption purposes, the starting point will be the shareholders' equity on BCP's balance sheet, prepared in accordance with Canadian generally accepted accounting principles, as at the latest fiscal year-end, with adjustments made to recognize the following factors:

- All capital assets and investments shall be at their fair market value.
- The value of the shares of BCP shall include a liability for current taxes for the latest fiscal year end.
- Any goodwill shall not have any value.
- Any non-capital losses shall be valued using the tax rate applicable at the date of the notice of redemption.
- Each share shall be valued at a pro rata portion of the total value of the company.

The following discount should be applied to the value of each share if the redemption occurs during the period referred to:

- Prior to the fifth anniversary of the SSA: 50%
- Prior to the tenth anniversary of the SSA: 25%
- After the tenth anniversary of the SSA: 10%

Upon notice of redemption, any balance due to the shareholder becomes payable on the same terms as for the redemption of the shares.

EXHIBIT IV

**BRUIN CAR PARTS INC.**
**DRAFT BALANCE SHEET**
As at November 30
(unaudited)

| | Year 12 | Year 11 |
|---|---|---|
| *Assets* | | |
| Cash | $ — | $ 110,000 |
| Accounts receivable | 2,800,000 | 2,020,000 |
| Inventories | 950,000 | 571,000 |
| Prepaids | 40,000 | 43,000 |
| Research and development | 200,000 | — |
| Investment | 90,000 | 90,000 |
| Property, plant, and equipment | 1,150,000 | 1,050,000 |
| | $ 5,230,000 | $ 3,884,000 |

*(continued)*

**EXHIBIT IV** *(continued)*

|  | Year 12 | Year 11 |
|---|---|---|
| *Liabilities* | | |
| Bank indebtedness | $    500,000 | $          — |
| Demand loan | 400,000 | 400,000 |
| Accounts payable | 400,000 | 250,000 |
| Shareholder loans | 600,000 | 600,000 |
|  | 1,900,000 | 1,250,000 |
| *Shareholders' equity* | | |
| Share capital | 300 | 300 |
| Retained earnings | 3,329,700 | 2,633,700 |
|  | 3,330,000 | 2,634,000 |
|  | $ 5,230,000 | $ 3,884,000 |

### BRUIN CAR PARTS INC.
### DRAFT INCOME STATEMENT
For the years ended November 30
(unaudited)

|  | Year 12 | Year 11 |
|---|---|---|
| Sales | $6,000,000 | $3,000,000 |
| Cost of goods sold | 4,700,000 | 2,700,000 |
| Gross margin | 1,300,000 | 300,000 |
| Expenses: | | |
|   Salaries | 250,000 | 250,000 |
|   Depreciation | 30,000 | 30,000 |
|   Interest | 100,000 | 75,000 |
|   General and administrative | 128,000 | 119,000 |
|   Professional fees | 15,000 | 14,000 |
|   Repairs and maintenance | 10,000 | 10,000 |
|   Research and development | — | — |
|   Travel | 71,000 | 25,000 |
|  | 604,000 | 523,000 |
| Income (loss) before tax | 696,000 | (223,000) |
| Current taxes | [to be determined] | — |
| Net income (loss) after tax | $    696,000 | $  (223,000) |

**EXHIBIT V**

*ADDITIONAL INFORMATION FROM RICK*
*REGARDING BCP'S DRAFT FINANCIAL STATEMENTS*

This year was much better due to advances in our product design and increased sales efforts. We gained efficiencies in our production processes, so our gross margins were also much better. The notes below explain some of the variances in the draft financials.

**EXHIBIT V** *(continued)*

### Accounts Receivable

Higher due to increased sales generated this year. Jean spent a lot more time travelling to conventions and made many visits to new and existing clients, all of which appears to have paid off based on the sales he generated. I wish we would get paid, though. Some of the sales Jean generated have been outstanding since the summer or earlier. A receivable of about $500,000 is due from one of the clients Jean brought in. Jean told us he visited their plant and they have a great operation. He figures it is a matter of time and cash flow management, but I am skeptical. The mailing address appears to be a warehouse in downtown Saskatoon. I phoned the number on file, and a recording said it was out of service. Jean is still confident they will pay us. Yesterday, he brought in a cheque from them for $100,000.

### Inventory

Inventory is carried at cost. However, due to recent legislative changes, about $200,000 of parts inventory may be obsolete. Jean has identified a client that is willing to buy the parts at cost, so we left the inventory on the books at year end. I am beginning to wonder about this deal, though. I have asked some of our other clients if they would purchase the parts, and they replied that they believed the new legislation would prohibit it. Besides these parts, the retail price of our inventory is about 20% higher than what we show on the books.

In June, a customer placed a special order that we stored off-site once completed. These parts were still in storage at year-end, and we therefore capitalized the $15,000 storage costs to inventory.

### Investment

The investment represents a 5% interest in shares of a company. The shares are not traded on the open market. There is a rumour that the company is once again involved in some lawsuits, and we are not sure if it is going to survive much longer. We have decided to sell our interest next week, based on an offer of $30,000 we received from a private investment firm. Gains or losses on investments are taxable/deductible for tax purposes in the year of the sale.

### Research and Development

Costs of $200,000 have been capitalized. We do R&D every five years, on average, since that is the average amount of time before a part becomes obsolete. This past year we were approached by an engineering firm that proposed a new design to us. Prior to purchasing this design we incurred costs, including some market research costs to ensure that it would generate additional sales. Subsequent to the purchase we asked our lawyers to patent the design so we could use it for the foreseeable future. All this work appears to be paying off as our sales have gone up. We expect to file an investment tax credit claim for the maximum amount of eligible expenditures.

Included in R&D costs are the following items:

| | |
|---|---:|
| Costs incurred to modify and improve manufacturing equipment to accommodate the design | $ 40,000 |
| Amount paid to engineering firm to acquire design | 125,000 |
| Legal fees for patent filings and registration (good for 17 years) | 10,000 |
| Market research costs related to the new design | 25,000 |

### Capital Assets

| Item | Carrying Amount at Nov. 30, Year 12 | Fair Market Value at Nov. 30, Year 12 |
|---|---:|---:|
| Land | $ 100,000 | $ 1,000,000 |
| Building | 100,000 | 350,000 |
| Power equipment | 350,000 | 400,000 |
| Computers | 40,000 | 35,000 |
| Other equipment | 560,000 | 600,000 |
| Total | $ 1,150,000 | $ 2,385,000 |

The original cost of the building was $200,000. The fair market value of all other depreciable property is less than the original cost. Only 50% of the excess of fair market value over original

*(continued)*

**EXHIBIT V** *(continued)*

cost is taxable for tax purposes in the year of the sale. The maximum capital cost allowance (CCA) that could be claimed for tax purposes in Year 12 is $201,268.

**Other**

Short-term liabilities increased to help finance production of inventories while waiting for payment from customers on account.

Shareholder loans are split equally between the three of us.

Interest expense includes late filing HST/GST interest and penalties of $1,500, which is not deductible for tax purposes.

*(CPA Canada adapted)*[3]

# Case 2-4

LO3

Canadian Computer Systems Limited (CCS) is a public company engaged in the development of computer software and the manufacturing of computer hardware. CCS is listed on a Canadian stock exchange and has a 40% non-controlling interest in Sandra Investments Limited (SIL), a U.S. public company that was de-listed by an American stock exchange due to financial difficulties. In addition, CCS has three wholly owned subsidiaries.

CCS is audited by Roth & Minch, a large public accounting firm. You, the CPA, are the audit manager responsible for the engagement.

CCS has a September 30 fiscal year-end. It is now mid-November, Year 11, and the year-end audit is nearing completion. CCS's draft financial statements are included in Exhibit VI. While reviewing the audit working papers (see Exhibit VII), you identify several issues that raise doubts about CCS's ability to realize its assets and discharge its liabilities in the normal course of business.

After you have reviewed the situation with the engagement partner, he asks you to prepare a memo for his use in discussing the going-concern problem with the president of CCS, and suggests that you look to IAS 1 for guidance. Your memo should include all factors necessary to assess CCS's ability to continue operations. You are also to comment on the accounting and disclosure implications.

**EXHIBIT VI**

**CANADIAN COMPUTER SYSTEMS LIMITED**
**EXTRACTS FROM CONSOLIDATED BALANCE SHEET**
As at September 30
(in thousands of dollars)

| | Year 11 | Year 10 |
|---|---|---|
| **Assets** | | |
| Current assets: | | |
| Cash | $ 190 | $ 170 |
| Accounts receivable | 2,540 | 1,600 |
| Inventories, at the lower of cost and net realizable value | 610 | 420 |
| | 3,340 | 2,190 |
| Plant assets (net of accumulated depreciation) | 33,930 | 34,970 |
| Property held for resale | 1,850 | 1,840 |
| Other assets | 410 | 420 |
| | $ 39,530 | $39,420 |

**EXHIBIT VI** *(continued)*

## Liabilities

Current liabilities:

| | | |
|---|---:|---:|
| Demand loans | $ 1,150 | $ 3,080 |
| Accrued interest payable | 11,510 | 10,480 |
| Accounts payable | 2,500 | 2,100 |
| Mortgages payable due currently because of loan defaults | 21,600 | 21,600 |
| Long-term debt due within one year | 290 | 1,780 |
| Debt obligation of Sandra Investments Limited | 50,000 | 55,420 |
| | 87,050 | 94,460 |
| Long-term debt | 26,830 | 21,330 |
| Other long-term liabilities | 250 | 330 |
| | 114,130 | 116,120 |

## Contributed Capital and Deficit

Contributed capital

Issued:

| | | | |
|---|---|---:|---:|
| 261 | 9% cumulative, convertible, preferred shares | 10 | 10 |
| 1,000,000 | Class B preferred shares | 250 | 250 |
| 10,243,019 | Common shares | 100,170 | 100,010 |
| | | 100,430 | 100,270 |
| Deficit | | (175,030) | (176,970) |
| | | (74,600) | (76,700) |
| | | $ 39,530 | $39,420 |

---

## CANADIAN COMPUTER SYSTEMS LIMITED
### EXTRACTS FROM CONSOLIDATED STATEMENT OF OPERATIONS AND DEFICIT
For the years ended September 30
(in thousands of dollars)

| | Year 11 | Year 10 |
|---|---:|---:|
| Sales: | | |
| Hardware | $ 12,430 | $ 19,960 |
| Software | 3,070 | 3,890 |
| | 15,500 | 23,850 |
| Other income | 1,120 | — |
| | 16,620 | 23,850 |
| Expenses: | | |
| Operating | 10,240 | 15,050 |
| Interest | 4,590 | 4,690 |
| General and administrative | 2,970 | 4,140 |
| Depreciation | 2,400 | 3,630 |
| Provision for impairment in plant assets | — | 2,220 |
| | 20,200 | 29,730 |
| Loss before the undernoted items | (3,580) | (5,880) |
| Loss from Sandra Investments Limited | (2,830) | (55,420) |
| Loss before discontinued operations | (6,410) | (61,300) |
| Gain (loss) from discontinued operations | 8,350 | (4,040) |
| Net income (loss) | 1,940 | (65,340) |
| Deficit, beginning of year | (176,970) | (111,630) |
| Deficit, end of year | $(175,030) | $(176,970) |

---

### EXHIBIT VII

#### EXTRACTS FROM AUDIT WORKING PAPERS

1. Cash receipts are collected by one of CCS's banks. This bank then releases funds to CCS based on operating budgets prepared by management. Demand loans bearing interest at 1% over the bank's prime rate are used to finance ongoing operations. The demand loans are secured by a general assignment of accounts receivable and a floating-charge debenture on all assets.

2. CCS accounts for its interest in SIL using the equity method. As a result of SIL's recurring losses in prior years, the investment account was written off in Year 9. In Year 10, CCS recorded in its accounts the amount of SIL's bank loan and accrued interest, as CCS guaranteed this amount. During Year 11, CCS made debt payments of $5.42 million and interest payments of $1.8 million on behalf of SIL. In October Year 11, SIL issued preferred shares in the amount of US$40 million, used the proceeds to pay down the bank loan, and was re-listed on the stock exchange. Interest expense on the debt obligation in Year 11 totalled $2.83 million and has been included in the income statement under "Loss from Sandra Investments Limited."

3. Current liabilities include mortgages payable of $21.6 million due currently. They have been reclassified from long-term debt because of CCS's failure to comply with operating covenants and restrictions. The prior year's financial statements have been restated for comparative purposes.

4. Long-term debt is repayable over varying periods of time. However, the banks reserve the right to declare the loans due and payable upon demand. The loan agreements require CCS to obtain advance approval in writing from the bank if it wishes to exceed certain limits on borrowing and capital expenditures. The agreements also prohibit the sale of certain plant assets, payment of dividends, and transfer of funds among related companies without prior written approval. One loan of $15 million was in default at September 30, Year 11.

5. During the year, CCS issued common shares to the directors and officers to satisfy amounts owing to them totalling $160,000. New equity issues are being considered for the Year 12 fiscal year.

6. On November 10, Year 11, a claim related to a breach of contract was filed against one of the company's subsidiaries in the amount of $3.7 million, plus interest and costs of the action. Management believes that this claim is without merit. However, if any amounts do have to be paid as a result of this action, management believes that the amounts would be covered by liability insurance.

7. In Year 11, operating expenses include $1 million in development costs relating to a computer software program. Sales of this software are expected to commence in Year 12.

*(CPA Canada adapted)*[4]

## Case 2-5

LO2, 4, 6

Michael Metals Limited (MML) has been a private company since it was incorporated under federal legislation over 40 years ago. At the present time (September, Year 45), ownership is divided among four cousins, each of whom holds 25% of the 100 outstanding common shares of MML. Each shareholder obtained the shares from his or her parents, who formed and operated the company for many years.

The owners have decided to offer the business for sale over a period of years. Laser Investments Limited (LIL), a public company holding shares of companies in a number of other businesses, has been given the opportunity to acquire 46.67% of MML immediately, and the balance over the next five years. The proposal is to purchase 70 shares now as follows:

|  |  | Percentage |
| --- | --- | --- |
| Obtain 33.33% by purchasing 50 new shares of MML | 50 | 33.33% |
| Acquire one-fifth of the shares held by each cousin, reducing their shares from 25 to 20 each | 20 | 13.34% |
|  | 70 | 46.67% |

The other 80 shares would be acquired at a rate of four per year from each cousin for five years. The purchase price of the 80 shares would be tied to MML's profitability as measured by accounting standards for private enterprises (ASPE).

The board of directors of LIL is interested in pursuing the investment in MML. The proposed purchase price of the initial 70 shares is to be partially based on the financial statements for fiscal Year 45 and for future years. The board of directors of LIL has asked its advisors, Bouchard and Co., Chartered Professional Accountants, to assist it in evaluating the proposed purchase. Jules Bouchard, the partner in charge of the engagement, has asked you, the CPA, to prepare a memo discussing (1) all relevant business considerations pertaining to the purchase so that he can discuss the issues with the board of directors and (2) how LIL should report its investment in MML if it were to proceed with the purchase of 70 shares.

MML has always been a scrap-metal dealer, primarily of iron and copper. In recent years, it has also dealt in lead, brass, aluminum, and other metals. Scrap iron is acquired from a variety of sources (e.g., old automobiles, appliances, and spoilage during manufacturing processes) and is sorted, compacted, and sold to steel mills. Much of the scrap copper is coated electrical wiring, which has to be stripped of the insulation coating and then chopped into pieces. The copper wire pieces are stored in barrels, which are about one metre high. In summary, a limited amount of processing is needed to convert the purchased scrap into saleable products.

Most of the scrap arrives at MML's storage yards on trucks, which are weighed both loaded and empty in order to determine the physical quantities of scrap on the truck. Some of the scrap is kept indoors, but most is kept outdoors in several large piles in different yard locations. MML's property is protected by tall wire fences and monitored by security cameras 24 hours a day.

To be successful in this industry, a scrap dealer has to buy at low prices and store the processed or unprocessed scrap until metal prices are high. Sometimes, quantities of some grades of metal have to be stored for several years. When selling prices are stable, the purchase price has to be sufficiently low that a profit can be made after processing costs have been incurred.

MML tends to operate at its maximum bank line of credit, as it is generally short of cash. MML's maximum line of credit is 70% of its receivables and 50% of its inventory.

Your client arranged for you to have access to all of MML's accounting records and the auditors' working papers. MML's fiscal year-end is June 30. From the accounting records and auditors' working papers, you and your staff have assembled the information provided in Exhibit VIII.

### EXHIBIT VIII

*INFORMATION GATHERED BY CPA FROM MML'S ACCOUNTING RECORDS AND AUDITORS' WORKING PAPERS*

1. From audit working paper reviews:
   a. Most of the processing equipment and the buildings are old and almost fully depreciated. The company's land was purchased many years ago. As a result, inventory often represents two-thirds of the balance sheet assets, and receivables are close to one-fifth of assets in most years. Total assets vary between $25 and $32 million from year to year. Accounts receivable turnover can be anywhere between 1.5 and 4 times per year.
   b. Perpetual records are limited to estimates of quantity because the quality of the scrap, the amount of insulation on wires, and a variety of other factors affect how much saleable metal will result from a bulk purchase of scrap.

*(continued)*

**EXHIBIT VIII** *(continued)*

c. A seller of scrap seldom knows how much it weighs. MML usually quotes a price per unit, but does not inform the seller of the weight until the delivery truck has been weighed at MML's yard. MML's auditors are suspicious that MML reduces weights before calculating the amount payable.

d. The auditors visit MML's yard and offices three times per year to conduct an interim audit, to attend the physical inventory count, and to carry out year-end substantive audit procedures.

2. MML owns 40% of a joint venture, Green Environmental Limited (GEL), a waste disposal company. The other 60% is owned by the spouses of the four cousins who own MML. All of MML's waste is handled by GEL, and MML purchases scrap iron and wire from GEL.

3. MML deals with a Japanese trading company that allows lengthy credit terms and uses letters of credit stating that MML does not have to pay for five or six months. A substantial amount of MML's metal purchases are from various sites that are owned by the Japanese company.

4. The truck weigh scales produce weigh tickets that can be attached to receivable and payable invoices. However, no numerical ticket sequence exists to account for all tickets that have been printed. Receiving records are handwritten in a looseleaf book.

5. Approximately 15% of sales invoices have to be adjusted for weight discrepancies between what was shipped and what the customer claims to have received. On average, the reductions are approximately 20% of the invoice amount.

6. The perpetual inventory weight records appear to have been adjusted each year to whatever the physical inventory count indicated.

7. In recent years, the after-tax profits of MML have ranged between $1.2 and $3 million, after management bonuses.

8. MML maintains two vacation homes, one in Florida and one in Barbados. These homes are usually occupied by suppliers and customers of MML, free of charge.

9. Accounts receivable and inventory are pledged as security to MML's bank. In addition, the bank has a general security agreement against all other assets, and has limited personal guarantees from the shareholders.

10. Revenue is usually recognized on shipment of the metal. Adjustments for weight discrepancies are made as they become known to MML.

11. MML's management has been considering expansion because one competitor is nearing retirement and wants to sell his company. In recent years, MML has purchased from, and sold to, this competitor. MML has also borrowed inventory from and loaned inventory to this competitor.

12. Some purchases of scrap are acquired on a conditional basis. MML pays the supplier only after it has determined the quality of metal that the scrap yielded when processed.

*(CPA Canada adapted)*[5]

# PROBLEMS

## Problem 2-1

LO2, 3

### Part A

On January 1, Year 5, Anderson Corporation paid $650,000 for 20,000 (20%) of the outstanding shares of Carter Inc. The investment was considered to be one of significant influence. In Year 5, Carter reported profit of $95,000; in Year 6, its profit was $105,000. Dividends paid were $60,000 in each of the two years.

### Required

Calculate the balance in Anderson's investment account as at December 31, Year 6.

**Part B**

Now assume that on December 31, Year 6, Anderson lost its ability to significantly influence the operating, investing, and financing decisions for Carter when another party obtained sufficient shares in the open market to obtain control over Carter. Accordingly, the investment in Carter was reclassified as a FVTPL investment. The fair value of the Carter shares was $35 per share on this date.

In Year 7, Carter reported profit of $115,000 and paid dividends of $50,000. On December 31, Year 7, Anderson sold its investment in Carter for $37 per share.

**Required**

(a) Prepare the journal entry at December 31, Year 6, to reclassify the investment from significant influence to FVTPL.

(b) Prepare all journal entries for Year 7 related to Anderson's investment in Carter.

## Problem 2-2

LO2, 3

Baskin purchased 20,000 common shares (20%) of Robbin on January 1, Year 5, for $275,000 and classified the investment as FVTPL. Robbin reported net income of $85,000 in Year 5 and $90,000 in Year 6, and paid dividends of $40,000 in each year. Robbin's shares were trading at $16 per share on December 31, Year 5, and January 1, Year 6. On January 1, Year 6, Baskin obtained significant influence over the operating, investing, and financing decisions of Robbin when the controlling shareholder sold some shares in the open market and lost control over Robbin. Accordingly, the investment in Robbin was reclassified to an investment in associate. On December 31, Year 6, Baskin sold its investment in Robbin for $17 per share.

**Required**

Prepare all journal entries for Years 5 and 6 related to Baskin's investment in Robbin.

## Problem 2-3

LO3, 5, 6

On January 1, Year 5, Blake Corporation purchased 25% of the outstanding common shares of Stergis Limited for $1,850,000.

The following relates to Stergis since the acquisition date:

| Year | Net Income | Other Comprehensive Income | Dividends Paid |
|------|-----------|---------------------------|----------------|
| Year 5 | $ 51,800 | $11,400 | $74,000 |
| Year 6 | 148,000 | 29,600 | 74,000 |

**Required**

(a) Assume that Blake is a public company and the number of shares held by Blake is enough to give it significant influence over Stergis. Prepare all the journal entries that Blake should make regarding this investment in Year 5 and Year 6. Also, state the disclosure requirements for Year 6 pertaining to Blake's investment in Stergis.

(b) Assume that Blake is a private company. Even though it has significant influence, it chose to use the cost method to account for its investment. Prepare all the journal entries that Blake should make regarding this investment in Year 5 and Year 6.

(c) If Blake wants to show the lowest debt-to-equity ratio at the end of Year 6, would it prefer to use the cost or equity method to report its investment in Stergis? Briefly explain.

## Problem 2-4

LO3, 5

Pender Corp. paid $285,000 for a 30% interest in Saltspring Limited on January 1, Year 6. During Year 6, Saltspring paid dividends of $110,000 and reported profit as follows:

| | |
|---|---|
| Profit before discontinued operations | $339,000 |
| Discontinued operations loss (net of tax) | (33,000) |
| Profit | $306,000 |

Pender's profit for Year 6 consisted of $990,000 in sales, expenses of $110,000, income tax expense of $352,000, and its investment income from Saltspring. Both companies have an income tax rate of 40%.

**Required**

(a) Assume that Pender reports its investment using the equity method.
   (i)  Prepare all journal entries necessary to account for Pender's investment for Year 6.
   (ii) Determine the correct balance in Pender's investment account at December 31, Year 6.
   (iii) Prepare an income statement for Pender for Year 6.

(b) Assume that Pender uses the cost method.
   (i)  Prepare all journal entries necessary to account for Pender's investment for Year 6.
   (ii) Determine the correct balance in Pender's investment account at December 31, Year 6.
   (iii) Prepare an income statement for Pender for Year 6.

(c) Which reporting method would Pender want to use if its bias is to report the highest possible return on investment to users of its financial statements? Briefly explain and show supporting calculations.

## Problem 2-5

LO2, 3, 5

Her Company purchased 22,000 common shares (20%) of Him Inc. on January 1, Year 4, for $374,000. Additional information on Him for the three years ending December 31, Year 6, is as follows:

| Year | Net Income | Dividends Paid | Market Value per Share at December 31 |
|---|---|---|---|
| Year 4 | $220,000 | $165,000 | $18 |
| Year 5 | 247,500 | 176,000 | 20 |
| Year 6 | 264,000 | 192,500 | 23 |

On December 31, Year 6, Her sold its investment in Him for $506,000.

**Required**

(a) Compute the balance in the investment account at the end of Year 5, assuming that the investment is classified as one of the following:
   (i)  FVTPL
   (ii) Investment in associate
   (iii) FVTOCI

(b) Calculate how much income will be reported in net income and other comprehensive income in each of Years 4, 5, and 6, and in total for the three years assuming that the investment is classified as one of the following:

  (i) FVTPL

  (ii) Investment in associate

  (iii) FVTOCI

(c) What are the similarities and differences in your answers for the three parts of (b)?

# Problem 2-6

**LO2,5**

On January 1, Year 2, Grow Corp. paid $200,000 to purchase 20,000 common shares of UP Inc., which represented an 8% interest in UP. On December 27, Year 2, UP declared and paid a dividend of $0.50 per common share. During Year 2, UP reported net income of $400,000. On December 31, Year 2, the market value of UP's common shares was $11.50 per share.

**Required**

(a) Indicate the amounts to be reported in the investment account on Grow's balance sheet at the end of Year 2 and the amounts to be reported in Grow's net income and other comprehensive income for Year 2 under two scenarios:

  (i) Grow designates its investment in UP as held for trading, that is, FVTPL.

  (ii) Grow designates its investment in UP as not held for trading, that is, FVTOCI.

(b) Which of the above reporting methods will report the most favourable current ratio, debt-to-equity ratio, and return on shareholders' equity on Grow's Year 2 financial statements? Briefly explain.

# Problem 2-7

**LO3**

Right Company purchased 25,000 common shares (25%) of ON Inc. on January 1, Year 11, for $250,000. Right uses the equity method to report its investment in ON because it has significant influence in the operating and investing decisions made by ON. Right has no legal obligation to pay any of ON's liabilities and has not committed to contribute any more funds to ON. Additional information for ON for the four years ending December 31, Year 14, is as follows:

| Year | Net Income | Dividends Paid | Market Value per Share at December 31 |
|------|-----------|----------------|----------------------------------------|
| Year 11 | $200,000 | $60,000 | $12 |
| Year 12 | (300,000) | 60,000 | 6 |
| Year 13 | (400,000) | 0 | 2 |
| Year 14 | (500,000) | 0 | 1 |

**Required**

(a) Calculate the balance in the investment account for each of the Years 11 through 14. Assume that the market value is used in determining whether the investment is impaired.

(b) Determine the total income to be reported by Right from its investment in ON for each of the Years 11 through 14.

## Problem 2-8

### LO1, 2, 3

COX Limited is a multinational telecommunication company owned by a Canadian businesswoman. It has numerous long-term investments in a wide variety of equity instruments.

Some investments have to be measured at fair value at each reporting date. In turn, the unrealized gains will be reported in either net income or other comprehensive income. Since COX has considerable external financing through a number of Canadian banks, it applies IFRS for public companies in its general-purpose financial statements.

The CFO of COX has heard about the new reporting standards for equity investments under IFRS 9 but has had limited time to study them in detail. He would like you to prepare a presentation on the reporting requirements. He wants to understand how equity investments should be reported. More specifically, he wants to know

- which investments must be measured at fair value and what the main rationale for this method of reporting is;
- how to determine whether the unrealized gains are to be reported in net income or other comprehensive income, and what the main rationale for the difference in reporting is; and
- which investments, if any, will still be reported using the cost method, using the equity method, or on a consolidated basis.

### Required

Prepare the slides for the presentation. Limit your presentation to six slides. Your presentation should cover the reporting of (1) FVTPL, (2) FVTOCI, (3) cost method, (4) investments in associates, and (5) investment in subsidiaries.

*(CGA Canada adapted)*[6]

## Problem 2-9

### LO1, 2, 3, 6

All facts are the same as in Problem 8 except that COX applies ASPE. Follow the same instructions as those given in the Required section of Problem 8.

## Endnotes

1   Rogers Communications Inc. 2014 Annual Report, https://netstorage-ion.rogers.com/downloads/IR/2014-annual-report/index.html, accessed June 30, 2015.

2   Net assets are equal to total assets less total liabilities. The dollar amount of shareholders' equity is equal to the dollar amount of net assets. Rather than calculating the difference between total assets and total liabilities, it is easier to simply use the dollar amount for shareholders' equity.

3   Adapted from *CICA UFE Report*, 2013-II-1, with permission. Chartered Professional Accountants of Canada, Toronto, Canada. Any changes to the original material are the sole responsibility of the author (and/or publisher) and have not been reviewed or endorsed by the Chartered Professional Accountants of Canada.

4   Adapted from *CICA UFE Report*, 1991-III-1, with permission. Chartered Professional Accountants of Canada, Toronto,

Canada. Any changes to the original material are the sole responsibility of the author (and/or publisher) and have not been reviewed or endorsed by the Chartered Professional Accountants of Canada.

5   Adapted from *CICA UFE Report*, 1995-III-5, with permission. Chartered Professional Accountants of Canada, Toronto, Canada. Any changes to the original material are the sole responsibility of the author (and/or publisher) and have not been reviewed or endorsed by the Chartered Professional Accountants of Canada.

6   Adapted from CGA Canada's FA4 Exam, March 2006, Q2, with permission Chartered Professional Accountants of Canada, Toronto, Canada. Any changes to the original material are the sole responsibility of the author (and/or publisher) and have not been reviewed or endorsed by the Chartered Professional Accountants of Canada.

# CHAPTER 3

# Business Combinations

## LEARNING OBJECTIVES

**After studying this chapter, you should be able to do the following:**

**LO1** Define a business combination and evaluate relevant factors to determine whether control exists in a business acquisition.

**LO2** Describe the basic forms for achieving a business combination.

**LO3** Apply the acquisition method to a purchase-of-net-assets business combination.

**LO4** Prepare consolidated financial statements for a purchase-of-shares business combination.

**LO5** Analyze and interpret financial statements involving business combinations.

**LO6** Identify some of the differences between IFRS and ASPE for business combinations.

**LO7** (Appendix 3A) Explain a reverse takeover and its reporting implications.

## Introduction

In Chapter 2, we illustrated the accounting for nonstrategic investments and significant influence investments. Chapters 3 to 8 are largely devoted to situations in which the investor has control of the investee. When one company obtains control of one or more businesses, a business combination has occurred.

Some of the reasons for business combinations are to[1]

- defend a competitive position within a market segment or with a particular customer;
- diversify into a new market and/or geographic region;
- gain access to new customers and/or partners;
- acquire new and/or complementary products or services;
- acquire new expertise or capabilities;
- accelerate time to market (for a product and/or service);
- improve the company's rate of innovation either by acquiring new technology and/or intellectual property;
- gain control over a supplier; and
- position the company to benefit from industry consolidation.

Business combinations are frequent events in Canada, the United States, and throughout the world. Hardly a week passes without some reference in the press to actual or proposed takeovers and mergers. Many people think that the typical takeover involves an American multinational swallowing up a smaller Canadian firm. But that is not always the case. In 2014, the biggest deals involving Canadian companies were as follows:

- Burger King Worldwide Inc.'s of the United States bought Tim Hortons Inc. of Canada for US$11.3 billion.
- Repsol S.A. of Spain bought Talisman Energy Inc. of Canada for US$13 billion.
- Caisse de dépôt et placement du Québec participation in the takeover of PetSmart Inc. of the United States was the biggest foreign takeover involving a Canadian acquirer in 2014 for US$8.6 billion.
- Encana Corporation of Canada's US$7.1 billion acquisition of Athlon Energy Inc. of the United States was the biggest purchase of a U.S. oil and gas producer by a Canadian company.
- Amaya Inc. of Canada purchased Oldford Group Limited of the Isle of Man for US$4.9 billion in June, making it the largest publicly held online gambling company in the world.
- BCE Inc. of Canada acquired the outstanding shares of Bell Aliant Inc. of Canada that it did not already own for CAD$4.5 billion.
- The Manufacturers Life Insurance Company of Canada bought Standard Life Financial Inc. and Standard Life Investments Inc. of the United Kingdom for CAD$4.0 billion.

> *Mergers and acquisitions occur regularly in Canada and throughout the world.*

Business combinations can be described as either friendly or hostile. Often a merger is initiated by one company submitting a formal tender offer to the shareholders of another company. In a friendly combination, the top management and the board of directors of the companies involved negotiate the terms of the combination and then submit the proposal to the shareholders of both companies along with a recommendation for approval. An unfriendly combination occurs when the board of directors of the target company recommends that its shareholders reject the tender offer. The management of the target company will often employ defences to resist the takeover. They include the following:

- *Poison pill.* This occurs when a company issues rights to its existing shareholders, exercisable only in the event of a potential takeover, to purchase additional shares at prices below market.
- *Pac-man defence.* This involves the target company making an unfriendly countervailing takeover offer to the shareholders of the company attempting to acquire it.
- *White knight.* In this case, the target company searches out another company that will come to its rescue with a more appealing offer for its shares.
- *Selling the crown jewels.* This involves selling certain desirable assets to other companies so that the would-be acquirer loses interest.

> *Business acquisitions can be friendly or hostile.*
>
> *There are many tactics to resist takeovers.*

In the next section of this chapter, we define a business combination. The discussion then proceeds to the accounting for business combinations in Canada.

# LO1 BUSINESS COMBINATIONS

A business combination is defined in International Financial Reporting Standard 3 (IFRS 3) as a transaction or other event in which an acquirer obtains control of one or more businesses. This definition has two key aspects: control and businesses. We will discuss each aspect in considerable depth, starting with businesses.

> *A business combination occurs when an acquirer obtains control of a business.*

A business is defined in IFRS 3, Appendix A as an integrated set of activities and assets that is capable of being conducted and managed for the purpose of providing a return in the form of dividends, lower costs, or other economic benefits directly to investors or other owners, members, or participants.

IFRS 3, Appendix B provides guidance to determine whether a business exists. A business consists of inputs and processes applied to those inputs that have the ability to create outputs. An input is any economic resource that creates, or has the ability to create, outputs when one or more processes are applied to it. Examples of inputs would include raw materials for a manufacturing company, intellectual property of a hi-tech company, and employees.

> *A business consists of inputs and processes applied to those inputs that have the ability to create outputs.*

A process is any system, standard, protocol, convention, or rule that, when applied to an input or inputs, creates or has the ability to create outputs. Examples include strategic management processes, operational processes, and resource management processes. A workforce with the necessary skills and experience following rules and conventions may provide the necessary processes capable, when applied to inputs, of creating outputs. An output is the result of inputs plus processes applied to those inputs, which then provide or have the ability to provide a return. Any product or service that is sold is obviously an example of an output.

The two essential elements of a business are inputs and processes applied to those inputs. Although businesses usually have outputs, outputs are not required for an integrated set of inputs and processes to qualify as a business. As long as the inputs and processes have the ability to produce outputs, the inputs and processes would qualify as a business. A company in the development stage may have materials and processes developed sufficiently that a prospective buyer could buy the company, complete the development, and begin producing outputs for sale to prospective customers. Alternatively, the buyer could integrate the seller's materials and processes with its own inputs and processes.

Determining whether a particular set of assets and activities is a business should be based on whether a potential buyer will be able to manage the integrated set as a business. In this evaluation, it is not relevant whether a seller operated the set as a business or whether the acquirer intends to operate the set as a business.

> *Buying a group of assets that do not constitute a business is a basket purchase, not a business combination.*

When a business combination does occur, the requirements of IFRS 3 must be applied. On the other hand, if an entity acquires all of the assets of another entity but they do not meet the definition of a business, IFRS 3 would not be applicable. Instead, the assets acquired would be treated as a basket purchase, and the total cost would be allocated to the individual assets in proportion to their fair market values. Basket purchases were studied in the property, plant, and equipment section of intermediate accounting.

Let us now turn our attention to the other key aspect of a business combination: control. Guidance for determining control is provided in IFRS 10.

Appendix A of IFRS 10 states that an investor controls an investee when it is exposed or has rights to variable returns from its involvement with the investee, and it has the ability to affect those returns through its power over the investee. This definition contains the following three elements:

(a) The investor has power over the investee.

(b) The investor has exposure, or rights, to variable returns from its involvement with the investee.

(c) The investor has the ability to use its power over the investee to affect the amount of the investor's returns.

All three elements must be met for the investor to have control. If the investor does have control over the investee, the investor is called the parent and the investee is called the *subsidiary*. Let us now discuss each element of control.

*Power.* An investor has power over an investee when the investor has existing rights giving it the current ability to direct relevant activities, that is, the activities that significantly affect the investee's returns. Sometimes, assessing power is straightforward, such as when power over an investee is obtained directly and solely from the voting rights granted by equity instruments such as shares and can be assessed by considering the voting rights from those shareholdings. In other cases, the assessment will be more complex and require consideration of more than one factor, for example, when power results from one or more contractual arrangements. An investor with the current ability to direct the relevant activities has power, even if its rights to direct have yet to be exercised. Evidence that the investor has been directing relevant activities can help determine whether the investor has power, but such evidence is not, in itself, conclusive in determining whether the investor has power over an investee. If two or more investors each have existing rights giving them unilateral ability to direct different relevant activities, the investor with the current ability that *most significantly* affects the returns of the investee has power over the investee.

> *Control is the power to direct the relevant activities of the investee.*

*Returns.* An investor is exposed or has rights to variable returns from its involvement with the investee when those returns from its involvement could vary as a result of the investee's performance; the investor's returns can be only positive, only negative, or both positive and negative. An investment in common shares is exposed to variable returns because the common shareholders receive the residual returns in the company. If the company is very profitable, the dividends to the shareholders or appreciation in the price of common shares will be positive and can be substantial. On the other hand, if the company is incurring losses, the prospects for dividends or appreciation in the share price is minimal or nonexistent.

> *The definition of control requires that the investor has exposure, or rights, to variable returns from its involvement with the investee.*

*Link between power and returns.* An investor controls an investee if the investor not only has power over the investee and exposure or rights to variable returns from its involvement with the investee, but the investor also has the ability to use its power to affect his or her returns from its involvement. A common shareholder usually has the power through voting rights and exposure to variable returns. A preferred shareholder may have exposure to a variable return. However, the preferred shareholder typically does not have voting rights and, therefore, does not have power over the relevant activities of the investee.

> *The definition of control requires that the investor has the ability to use its power over the investee to affect the amount of the investor's returns.*

Let us now apply the elements of control to some practical situations.

If the means of paying for the business is cash or a promise to pay cash in the future, the company making the payment is usually the one obtaining control. If shares were issued as a means of payment, relative holdings of voting shares of the combined company by shareholders of the combining companies is key. In a combination involving two companies, if one shareholder group holds more than 50% of the voting shares of the combined company, that company would usually have control. If more than two companies are involved, the shareholder group holding the largest number of voting shares would usually be identified as the company with control.

> *Owning more than 50% of the voting shares usually, but not always, indicates control.*

Since the board of directors establishes the strategic policies of a corporation, the ability to elect a majority of the members of the board would generally be evidence of control. Therefore, the first element of control is presumed to exist if the parent owns, directly or indirectly, enough voting shares to elect the majority of the board of directors of a subsidiary.

In most situations, more than 50% of the voting shares are required to elect the majority of the board, and so the first element of control is presumed to exist with greater than 50% ownership. However, we have to look at all factors. For example, if D Company owns 60% of the voting shares of E Company and F Company owns the other 40%, then we can presume that D Company has power over the activities of E Company. But if F Company owns convertible bonds of E Company or options or warrants to purchase E Company shares, which, if converted or exercised, would give F Company 62% of the outstanding shares of E Company, then F Company, not D Company, would have power over the activities of E Company.

There is also a general presumption that a holding of less than 50% of the voting shares does not constitute control. This presumption can be overcome if other factors clearly indicate control. For example, an irrevocable agreement with other shareholders to convey voting rights to the parent would constitute control, even if the parent owned less than 50% of the voting shares. A parent may also have power despite owning less than 50% of the voting shares if its holdings of rights, warrants, convertible debt, or convertible preferred shares would give it enough voting power to control the board of directors of the subsidiary. Exercise or conversion would not be necessary, only the right to exercise or convert is.

It is also possible for a parent to have power without a majority share ownership if it also has agreements in writing allowing it to dictate the operating policies of the subsidiary, resulting in it receiving fees, royalties, and profits from intercompany sales. For these situations, the parent makes the key decisions, receives the majority of the benefits, and absorbs most of the risk, even though the parent may own very few, if any, of the shares in the controlled company.

> *A company could have control with less than 50% of the voting shares when contractual agreements give it control.*

In another example, X Company owns 40% of Y Company, which is the largest single block of Y Company's outstanding shares. The other 60% is very widely held and only a very small proportion of the holders appear at the annual meeting of Y Company. As a result, X Company has had no trouble electing the majority of the board of directors. Thus, X Company could be deemed to have control in this situation as long as the other shareholders do not actively cooperate when they exercise their votes so as to have more voting power than X Company.

Temporary control of an entity does not of itself change the fact that control exists. During the time that control is held and until such time as control ceases, the reporting requirements for controlled entities should be applied.

The seizure of the company's assets by a trustee in a receivership or bankruptcy situation would be evidence that control has probably ceased, as would the imposition of governmental restrictions over a foreign company's ability to pay dividends to its Canadian investor. However, when a receiver seizes a specific asset in satisfaction of a default under a loan agreement but permits the company to continue in business under the direction of the parent, this is not a loss of control.

> *Normal business restrictions do not preclude control by the parent.*

A reporting entity can control another entity, even though other parties have protective rights relating to the activities of that other entity. Protective rights, which are discussed in IFRS 10, Appendix B, are designed to protect the interests of the party holding those rights, without giving that party control of the entity to which they relate. They include, for example, the following:

(a) Approval or veto rights granted to other parties that do not affect the strategic operating and financing policies of the entity. Protective rights often apply to fundamental changes in the activities of an entity, or apply only in exceptional circumstances. For example:

   (i) A lender might have rights that protect the lender from the risk that the entity will change its activities to the detriment of the lender, such as selling important assets or undertaking activities that change the credit risk of the entity.

   (ii) Non-controlling shareholders might have the right to approve capital expenditures greater than a particular amount, or the right to approve the issue of equity or debt instruments.

(b) The ability to remove the party that directs the activities of the entity in circumstances such as bankruptcy or on breach of contract by that party.

(c) Limitations on the operating activities of an entity. For example, a franchise agreement for which the entity is the franchisee might restrict the pricing, advertising, or other operating activities of the entity but would not give the franchisor control of the franchisee. Such rights usually protect the brand of the franchisor.

> *A parent can control a subsidiary, even though other parties have protective rights relating to the subsidiary.*

Appendix B of IFRS 10 provides extensive guidance to determine whether an entity has control. Paragraph B3 states that the following factors may assist in making the determination about control:

(a) The purpose and design of the investee

(b) What the relevant activities of the investee are and how decisions about those activities are made

(c) Whether the rights of the investor give it the current ability to direct the relevant activities

(d) Whether the investor is exposed, or has rights, to variable returns from its involvement with the investee

(e) Whether the investor has the ability to use its power over the investee to affect the amount of the investor's returns

The following is Example 1 from Appendix B of IFRS 10. It provides guidance in determining whether one of the two investors has control of the investee or whether the two investors each have joint control.

Two investors form an investee to develop and market a medical product. One investor is responsible for developing and obtaining regulatory approval of the medical product, a responsibility that includes having the unilateral ability to make all decisions relating to the development of the product and obtaining regulatory approval. Once the regulator has approved the product, the other investor will manufacture and market it. This investor has the unilateral ability to make all decisions about the manufacture and marketing of the project. If all the activities—developing and obtaining regulatory approval, as well as manufacturing and marketing of the medical product—are relevant activities, each investor needs to determine whether it is able to direct the activities that most significantly affect the investee's returns. Accordingly, each investor needs to consider which of developing and obtaining regulatory approval or manufacturing and marketing of the medical product is the activity that most significantly affects the investor's returns, and whether it is able to direct that activity. In determining which investor has power, the investors would consider the following:

(a) Purpose and design of the investee

(b) Factors that determine the profit margin, revenue, and value of the investee, as well as the value of the medical product

(c) Effect on the investee's returns resulting from each investor's decision-making authority, with respect to the factors in (b)

(d) Investors' exposure to variability of returns

In this particular example, the investors would also consider both of these:

(e) Uncertainty of, and effort required in, obtaining regulatory approval (considering the investor's record of successfully developing and obtaining regulatory approval of medical products)

(f) The investor who controls the medical product once the development phase is successful

*A key aspect of control is the ability to direct the activities that most significantly affect the investor's returns.*

Let us now discuss the common forms of business combinations and the reporting requirements for business combinations.

# LO2 FORMS OF BUSINESS COMBINATIONS

Essentially, there are three main forms of business combinations. One company can obtain control over the net assets of another company by (1) purchasing its net assets, (2) acquiring enough of its voting shares to control the use of its net assets, or (3) gaining control through a contractual arrangement.

**PURCHASE OF ASSETS OR NET ASSETS** An obvious way to obtain control over a business is by outright purchase of the assets that constitute a business. In this case, the selling company is left only with the cash or other consideration received as payment from the purchaser, and the liabilities present before the sale. In other cases, the acquirer purchases all the assets of the acquiree and assumes all its liabilities, which together are referred to as net assets. In either case, the shareholders of the selling company have to approve the sale, as well as decide whether their company should be wound up or continue operations after the sale.

*When purchasing assets or net assets, the transaction is carried out with the selling company.*

**PURCHASE OF SHARES**    As an alternative to the purchase of assets or net assets, the acquirer could purchase enough voting shares from the acquiree's shareholders to give it the power to determine the acquiree's strategic operating and financing policies. This is the most common form of combination, and it is often achieved through a tender offer made by the management of the acquirer to the shareholders of the acquiree. These shareholders are invited to exchange their shares for cash or for shares of the acquirer company.

> *When purchasing shares, the transaction is usually consummated with the shareholders of the selling company.*

The share-purchase form of combination is usually the least costly to the acquirer because control can be achieved by purchasing less than 100% of the outstanding voting shares. In addition, in Canada there can be important tax advantages to the vendor if shares rather than assets are sold. Because the transaction is between the acquirer and the acquiree's shareholders, the acquiree's accounting for its assets and liabilities is not affected,[2] and the company carries on as a subsidiary of the acquirer. The acquirer becomes a parent company and, therefore, must consolidate its subsidiary when it prepares its financial statements.

> *The acquired company makes no journal entries when the acquiring company purchases shares.*

**CONTROL THROUGH CONTRACTUAL ARRANGEMENT**    A company can get control of another company by signing an agreement with the acquiree's shareholders to give it control, without actually acquiring any shares of the other company. Nevertheless, the company with control will be deemed a parent and the controlled company will be a subsidiary. Since there were no actual transactions between the parent and the subsidiary for the transfer of control, there will be no entries made on the subsidiary's books to record this change in control. However, the parent would have to consolidate this subsidiary when it prepares its financial statements. We will discuss this type of arrangement in further detail in Chapter 9.

> *Control can be obtained through a contractual arrangement that does not involve buying assets or shares.*

All three forms of business combination result in the assets and liabilities of the two companies being combined. If control is achieved by purchasing net assets, the combining takes place in the accounting records of the acquirer. If control is achieved by purchasing shares or through contractual arrangement, the combining takes place when the consolidated financial statements are prepared.

**VARIATIONS**    One variation from the forms of business combinations described above occurs when the companies involved agree to create a new company, which either purchases the net assets of the combining companies or purchases enough shares from the shareholders of the combining companies to achieve control of these companies.

> *There are many different legal forms in which a business combination can be consummated.*

Another variation that can occur is a *statutory amalgamation,* whereby, under the provisions of federal or provincial law, two or more companies incorporated under the same Companies Act can combine and continue as a single entity. The shareholders of the combining companies become shareholders of the surviving company, and the non-surviving companies are wound up. The substance of a statutory amalgamation indicates that it is simply a variation of one of the basic forms. If only one of the companies survives, it is essentially a purchase of net assets, with the method of payment being shares of the surviving company.

> *A statutory amalgamation occurs when two or more companies combine to form a single legal entity.*

Exhibit 3.1 shows the intercompany shareholdings, both before and after a business combination, under a variety of forms. Intercompany shareholdings are often depicted in this manner. The arrow

EXHIBIT 3.1

## Different Forms of Business Combinations

Intercompany Shareholdings
before the Business Combination

Mr. A        Mr. X
100 |        10 |
A Co.        X Co.

Intercompany Shareholdings
after the Business Combination

**Consolidated Statements Not Required**

A Co. purchased net assets of X Co. with cash

Mr. A        Mr. X
100 |        10 |
A Co.        X Co.

A Co. purchased net assets of X Co. with 50 shares

Mr. A        Mr. X
100 |        10 |
A Co. ←—50— X Co.

New company purchased net assets of
both companies with cash

Mr. A          Mr. X
100 / \500   250/ \10
A Co.  New Co.    X Co.

A Co. purchased net assets of X Co.
with shares & X Co. is wound up
(Statutory amalgamation)

Mr. A        Mr. X
100 |     50 /
A Co. ←

Intercompany Shareholdings
after the Business Combination

**Consolidated Statements Are Required**

A Co. purchased shares of X Co. with cash

Mr. A        Mr. X
100 |
A Co. —10→ X Co.

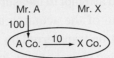

A Co. purchased shares of X Co. with 50 shares

Mr. A        Mr. X
100 |     50
A Co. —10→ X Co.

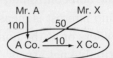

A Co. purchased shares of X Co. with 150 shares
(Reverse Takeover)

Mr. A        Mr. X
100 |     150
A Co. —10→ X Co.

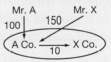

New company purchased shares of both
companies with shares

Mr. A        Mr. X
500 \      / 250
New Co.
100 /    \ 10
A Co.        X Co.

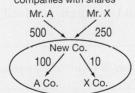

A Co. obtained control of X Co. through
contractual arrangement

Mr. A        Mr. X
100 |        10 |
A Co.        X Co.

---

*Stick diagrams can be an effective way to depict intercompany shareholdings.*

*Consolidated financial statements are not required when an acquirer directly purchases the net assets of a business.*

*Under a reverse takeover, the shareholders of the acquired company control the acquiring company.*

points from the investor to the investee company, with the number beside the arrow showing the number of shares owned by the investor. Mr. A and Mr. X were the sole shareholders in A Co. and X Co. prior to the business combination. We will be exposed to all of these different forms of business combinations as we proceed through the next few chapters.

# ACCOUNTING FOR BUSINESS COMBINATIONS UNDER ACQUISITION METHOD

IFRS 3 outlines the accounting requirements for business combinations. The main principles are as follows:

- All business combinations should be accounted for by applying the acquisition method.
- An acquirer should be identified for all business combinations.
- The acquisition date is the date the acquirer obtains control of the acquiree.
- The acquirer should attempt to measure the fair value of the acquiree, as a whole, as of the acquisition date. The fair value of the acquiree as a whole is usually determined by adding together the fair value of consideration transferred by the acquirer (i.e., the acquisition cost) plus the value assigned to the non-controlling shareholders. In this text, we will refer to the sum of the acquisition cost plus value assigned to the non-controlling shareholders as total consideration given. The value assigned to the non-controlling interest is measured as either the fair value of the shares owned by the non-controlling shareholders or as the non-controlling interest's proportionate share of the fair value of the acquiree's identifiable net assets. Business valuation techniques would be used to measure the fair value of the business acquired, especially if the parent acquired less than 100% of the shares, if control is obtained without transferring any consideration or if the consideration transferred does not represent the fair value of the business acquired. Certain business valuation techniques are referred to in IFRS 3 but are beyond the scope of this book.
- The acquirer should recognize and measure the identifiable assets acquired and the liabilities assumed at fair value and report them separately from goodwill.
- The acquirer should recognize goodwill, if any.

> *The acquisition method is required and an acquirer must be identified for all business combinations.*

**IDENTIFYING THE ACQUIRER AND DATE OF ACQUISITION**   The acquirer is the entity that obtains control of one or more businesses in a business combination. The concept of control and how to determine who has control was discussed earlier in this chapter. It is important to determine who has control because this determines whose net assets are reported at carrying amount and whose assets are reported at fair value at the date of acquisition. The date of acquisition is the date that one entity obtains control of one or more businesses.

**ACQUISITION COST**   The acquisition cost is made up of the following:

- Any cash paid
- Fair value of assets transferred by the acquirer

- Present value of any promises by the acquirer to pay cash in the future
- Fair value of any shares issued—the value of shares is based on the market price of the shares on the acquisition date
- Fair value of contingent consideration

> *The acquisition cost is measured as the fair value of consideration given to acquire the business.*

The acquisition cost does not include costs such as fees for consultants, accountants, and lawyers as these costs do not increase the fair value of the acquired company. These costs should be expensed in the period of acquisition.

Costs incurred in issuing debt or shares are also not considered part of the acquisition cost. These costs should be deducted from the amount recorded for the proceeds received for the debt or share issue; for example, deducted from loan payable or common shares as applicable. The deduction from loan payable would be treated like a discount on notes payable and would be amortized into income over the life of the loan using the effective interest method.

> *The acquisition cost does not include costs such as professional fees or costs of issuing shares.*

**RECOGNITION AND MEASUREMENT OF NET ASSETS ACQUIRED**   The acquirer should recognize and measure the identifiable assets acquired and the liabilities assumed at fair value and report them separately from goodwill. An identifiable asset is not necessarily one that is presently recognized in the records of the acquiree company. For example, the acquiree company may have patent rights that have a fair value but are not shown on its balance sheet because the rights had been developed internally.

> *Identifiable assets and liabilities should be recorded separately from goodwill.*

IAS 38 paragraph 12 defines an identifiable asset if it either

(a) is separable, that is, is capable of being separated or divided from the entity and sold, transferred, licensed, rented, or exchanged, either individually or together with a related contract, identifiable asset, or liability, regardless of whether the entity intends to do so; or

(b) arises from contractual or other legal rights, regardless of whether those rights are transferable or separable from the entity or from other rights and obligations.

To qualify for recognition, as part of applying the acquisition method, the identifiable assets acquired and liabilities assumed must meet the definitions of assets and liabilities in the IASB's *The Conceptual Framework for Financial Reporting* at the acquisition date. For example, costs that the acquirer expects but is not obliged to incur in the future to effect its plan to exit an activity of an acquiree or to terminate the employment of or to relocate an acquiree's employees do not meet the definition of a liability at the acquisition date. Therefore, the acquirer does not recognize those costs as a liability at the date of acquisition. Instead, the acquirer recognizes those costs in its post-combination financial statements in accordance with other IFRS.

Appendix B to IFRS 3 provides guidance in identifying assets to be recognized separately as part of a business combination.

There are some exceptions to the general principle in accounting for a business combination that all assets and liabilities of the acquired entity must be recognized and measured at fair value. One of the exceptions for recognition pertains to contingent liabilities. For the acquired company, following the usual standards in IAS 37 *Provisions, Contingent Liabilities and Contingent Assets*, the contingent liability would only be recognized in its separate entity financial statements if it were probable that an outflow of resources would be required to settle the obligation. Under IFRS 3 an exception is made, requiring the acquirer to recognize a contingent liability if it is a present obligation that arises from past events and its fair value can be measured reliably. Therefore, the acquirer recognizes the liability even if it is not probable that an outflow of resources embodying economic benefits will be required to settle the obligation.

Special requirements for recognition and measurement of financial statement items at the date of acquisition also apply to employee benefits, indemnification assets, reacquired rights, share-based payment awards, and assets held for sale. Deferred income tax assets and liabilities are not fair-valued and not carried forward. Instead, new amounts for deferred tax assets and liabilities are determined at the date of acquisition. Because of the complexity of accounting for deferred taxes, discussion and illustration of this topic is delayed until Chapter 9.

> *All of the acquiree's identifiable assets and liabilities must be recognized and most of these identifiable assets and liabilities would be measured at fair value at the date of acquisition.*

**RECOGNITION OF GOODWILL**    If the total consideration given by the controlling and non-controlling shareholders is greater than the fair value of identifiable assets and liabilities acquired, the excess is recorded in the acquirer's financial statements as goodwill. Goodwill represents the amount paid for excess earning power plus the value of other benefits that did not meet the criteria for recognition as an identifiable asset.

> *Goodwill is the excess of total consideration given over the fair value of identifiable assets and liabilities.*

If the total consideration given is less than the fair value of the identifiable net assets acquired, we have what used to be described as a "negative goodwill" situation. This negative goodwill is now recognized as a gain attributable to the acquirer on the acquisition date. We will illustrate the accounting for negative goodwill in Chapter 4.

> *Negative goodwill could result in the reporting of a gain on purchase by the acquiring company.*

To illustrate the accounting involved using the acquisition method, we will use the summarized balance sheets of two companies. Summarized statements are used here so that we can focus completely on the broad accounting concepts. In later examples, more detailed statements will be used. Exhibit 3.2 presents the December 31, Year 1, balance sheets of the two companies that are party to a business combination.

EXHIBIT 3.2

**A COMPANY LTD.**
**BALANCE SHEET**
At December 31, Year 1

| | |
|---|---:|
| Assets | $300,000 |
| Liabilities | $120,000 |
| Shareholders' equity: | |
| Common shares (Note 1) | 100,000 |
| Retained earnings | 80,000 |
| | $300,000 |

*Note 1*

The shareholders of the 5,000 common shares issued and outstanding are identified as Group X.

**B CORPORATION**
**BALANCE SHEET**
At December 31, Year 1

| | |
|---|---:|
| Assets | $ 88,000 |
| Liabilities | $ 30,000 |
| Shareholders' equity: | |
| Common shares (Note 2) | 25,000 |
| Retained earnings | 33,000 |
| | $ 88,000 |

The fair values of B Corporation's identifiable assets
and liabilities are as follows as at December 31, Year 1:

| | |
|---|---:|
| Fair value of assets | $109,000 |
| Fair value of liabilities | 29,000 |
| Fair value of net assets | $ 80,000 |

*Note 2*

The shareholders of the common shares of B Corporation are identified as Group Y.

The actual number of shares issued and outstanding has been purposely omitted because this number would have no bearing on the analysis required later.

*Company A and Company B are separate legal entities.*

Because the identification of an acquirer requires the analysis of shareholdings after the combination, Notes 1 and 2 are presented in the exhibit to identify the shareholders of each company as belonging to two distinct groups.

A Company Ltd. will initiate the takeover of B Corporation. The first two examples will involve the purchase of net assets with cash and the issuance of shares as the means of payment. Later examples will have A Company purchasing enough shares of B Corporation to obtain control over that company's net assets and will introduce the preparation of consolidated statements.

## LO3 Control through Purchase of Net Assets

In the following independent examples, A Company offers to buy all assets and assume all liabilities of B Corporation. The management of B Corporation accepts the offer.

**EXAMPLE 1**   Assume that on January 1, Year 2, A Company pays $95,000 in cash to B Corporation for all of the net assets of that company, and that no other direct costs are involved. Because cash is the means of payment, A Company is the acquirer. Goodwill is determined as follows:

| | |
|---|---:|
| Acquisition cost | $95,000 |
| Fair value of net assets acquired | 80,000 |
| Goodwill | $15,000 |

A Company would make the following journal entry to record the acquisition of B Corporation's net assets:

| | | |
|---|---:|---:|
| Assets (in detail) | 109,000 | |
| Goodwill | 15,000 | |
| Liabilities (in detail) | | 29,000 |
| Cash | | 95,000 |

The acquiring company records the net assets purchased on its own books at fair value.

A Company's balance sheet after the business combination would be as follows:

**A COMPANY LTD.**
**BALANCE SHEET**
At January 1, Year 2

| | |
|---|---:|
| Assets (300,000 − 95,000* + 109,000) | $314,000 |
| Goodwill | 15,000 |
| | $329,000 |
| Liabilities (120,000 + 29,000) | $149,000 |
| Shareholders' equity: | |
| Common shares | 100,000 |
| Retained earnings | 80,000 |
| | $329,000 |

*Cash paid by A Company to B Corporation.

> *The acquiring company's own assets and liabilities are not revalued when it purchases the net assets of the acquired company.*

While this example focuses on the balance sheet of A Company immediately after the business combination, it is also useful to look at B Corporation in order to see the effect of this economic event on that company. B Corporation would make the following journal entry to record the sale of its assets and liabilities to A Company:

| | | |
|---|---:|---:|
| Cash | 95,000 | |
| Liabilities (in detail) | 30,000 | |
| Assets (in detail) | | 88,000 |
| Gain on sale of assets and liabilities | | 37,000 |

> *The selling company records the sale of its net assets on its own books.*

The balance sheet of B Corporation immediately after the sale of all of its net assets follows:

**B CORPORATION**
**BALANCE SHEET**
At January 1, Year 2

| | |
|---|---:|
| Cash | $95,000 |
| Shareholders' equity: | |
| Common shares | $25,000 |
| Retained earnings (33,000 + 37,000*) | 70,000 |
| | $95,000 |

*The gain on sale of the net assets amounts to $37,000 (95,000 − [88,000 − 30,000].

The management of B Corporation must now decide the future of their company. They could decide to invest the company's cash in productive assets and carry on in some other line of business. Alternatively, they could decide to wind up the company and distribute the sole asset (cash) to the shareholders.

> *After the sale of net assets, B Corporation's sole asset is cash.*

**EXAMPLE 2**   Assume that on January 1, Year 2, A Company issues 4,000 common shares, with a market value of $23.75 per share, to B Corporation as payment for the company's net assets. B Corporation will be wound up after the sale of its net assets. Because the method of payment is shares, the following analysis is made to determine which company is the acquirer.

|  | Shares of A Company |
|---|---|
| Group X now holds | 5,000 |
| Group Y will hold (when B Corporation is wound up) | 4,000 |
|  | 9,000 |

Group X will hold 5/9 (56%) of the total shares of A Company after the combination, and Group Y will hold 4/9 (44%) of this total after the dissolution of B Corporation. Because one shareholder group holds more than 50% of the voting shares, that group will have power to make the key decisions for A Company. Accordingly, A Company is identified as the acquirer as Group X was the original shareholder of A Company.

> *The acquirer is determined based on which shareholder group controls A Company after B Corporation is wound up.*

Goodwill is determined as follows:

| | |
|---|---|
| Acquisition cost (4,000 shares @ 23.75) | $95,000 |
| Fair value of net assets acquired | 80,000 |
| Goodwill | $15,000 |

A Company would make the following journal entry to record the acquisition of B Corporation's net assets and the issuance of 4,000 common shares at fair value on January 1, Year 2:

| | | |
|---|---|---|
| Assets (in detail) | 109,000 | |
| Goodwill | 15,000 | |
| Liabilities (in detail) | | 29,000 |
| Common shares | | 95,000 |

A Company's balance sheet after the business combination would be as follows:

**A COMPANY LTD.**
**BALANCE SHEET**
At January 1, Year 2

| | |
|---|---|
| Assets (300,000 + 109,000) | $409,000 |
| Goodwill | 15,000 |
| | $424,000 |
| Liabilities (120,000 + 29,000) | $149,000 |
| Shareholders' equity: | |
| Common shares (100,000 + 95,000) | 195,000 |
| Retained earnings | 80,000 |
| | $424,000 |

This balance sheet was prepared by combining the carrying amounts of A Company's assets and liabilities with the fair values of those of B Corporation.

> *The recently purchased assets are recorded at fair value and A Company's old assets are retained at carrying amount.*

B Corporation would make the following journal entry to record the sale of its assets and liabilities to A Company:

| | | |
|---|---|---|
| Investment in shares of A Company | 95,000 | |
| Liabilities (in detail) | 30,000 | |
| Assets (in detail) | | 88,000 |
| Gain on sale of assets and liabilities | | 37,000 |

> *The selling company records the sale of its net assets in exchange for shares of the acquiring company.*

B Corporation's balance sheet immediately following the sale of its net assets is given below:

**B CORPORATION**
**BALANCE SHEET**
At January 1, Year 2

| | |
|---|---|
| Investment in shares of A Company | $95,000 |
| Shareholders' equity: | |
| Common shares | $25,000 |
| Retained earnings (33,000 + 37,000) | 70,000 |
| | $95,000 |

> *After the sale of net assets, B Corporation's sole asset is investment in shares of A Company.*

B Corporation's sole asset is 4,000 of the issued shares of A Company. This single block represents a voting threat to A Company's shareholders (Group X). A Company will likely insist that B Corporation be wound up and distribute these 4,000 shares to its shareholders (Group Y), who presumably will not get together to determine how to vote them.

## LO4 CONSOLIDATED FINANCIAL STATEMENTS

When an investor acquires sufficient voting shares to obtain control over the investee, a parent–subsidiary relationship is established. The investor is the parent, and the investee is the subsidiary. Usually, the two (or more) companies involved continue as separate legal entities, with each maintaining separate accounting records and producing separate financial statements. However, the two entities now operate as a family of companies. In effect, they operate or have the ability to operate as one economic entity. Users of the parent's financial statements would generally prefer to get one financial statement for the entire family rather than obtain separate statements for each company in the family. Therefore, it is not surprising that IFRS require the preparation of consolidated financial statements to present the financial position and financial performance for the family as a whole. The accounting principles involved in the preparation of consolidated financial statements are found in IFRS 10. In the material that follows in this and later chapters, the preparation of consolidated statements will follow this standard's requirements.

Consolidated statements consist of a balance sheet, a statement of comprehensive income, a statement of changes in equity, a cash flow statement, and the accompanying notes. In this chapter and in Chapter 4, we will illustrate the preparation of the consolidated balance sheet on the date that control is obtained by the parent company. Consolidation of other financial statements will be illustrated in later chapters.

---

*Distinguish between separate-entity financial statements and consolidated financial statements.*

---

The following definitions are provided in Appendix A of IFRS 10:

(a) *Consolidated financial statements.* The financial statements of a group in which the assets, liabilities, equity, income, expenses, and cash flows of the parent and its subsidiaries are presented as those of a single economic entity

(b) *Group.* A parent and its subsidiaries

(c) *Parent.* An entity that controls one or more entities

(d) *Subsidiary.* An entity that is controlled by another entity

(e) *Non-controlling interest.* Equity in a subsidiary not attributable, directly or indirectly, to a parent

When a parent company has control over one or more subsidiaries, it has the right to benefit economically from the subsidiaries' resources and, at the same time, is exposed to the related risks involved. Consolidated financial statements reflect a group of economic resources that are under the common control of the parent company, even though these resources are owned separately by the parent and the subsidiary companies. Note that the key concept is common control. This concept is reinforced in the IASB's *Conceptual Framework for Financial Reporting,* where the definition of an asset focuses on control rather than ownership.[3] When control over a subsidiary is present, the parent is required to consolidate its subsidiaries for external reporting purposes. In other words, the parent and subsidiary will each prepare their own financial statements (which we will refer to as separate-entity financial statements or financial statements for internal purposes). The consolidated financial statements are additional financial statements that combine the separate-entity financial statements of the parent and subsidiary under the hypothetical situation that these two legal entities were operating as one single entity. The consolidated financial statements are prepared by the parent company and are referred to in this text as the third set of financial statements.

---

*Consolidated financial statements combine the financial statements of the parent and its subsidiaries as if they were one entity.*

---

The following diagram shows the interrelationship of the two companies and the number of financial statements involved:

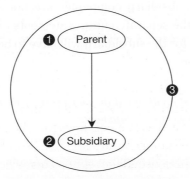

Financial statements 1 and 2 are the separate entity statements of the parent and subsidiary, respectively. Financial statements 3 are the consolidated financial statements. As we will soon see, consolidated financial statements are supported by working papers or worksheets that combine the accounts of the parent and subsidiaries. As we proceed through the next few chapters, it is important to understand in whose records or on which financial statements the journal entries or adjustments are being made. Consolidation adjustments are made to the consolidated financial statements (statements 3) and are not typically made to the separate entity records of the parent and subsidiary (statements 1 and 2).

> *Consolidated financial statements are a separate set of financial statements supported by a working paper that combines the separate-entity financial statements of the parent and subsidiaries.*

All intercompany transactions are eliminated in the preparation of the consolidated statements. As a result, these statements reflect only transactions of this single entity with those outside the entity. (The process required to eliminate these intercompany transactions will be discussed thoroughly in later chapters.)

> *Adjustments on consolidation are not typically recorded in the separate entity records for the parent or subsidiary.*

Consolidated statements are considered more useful to financial statement users than the separate financial statements of all of the companies that make up the group. Present and prospective shareholders of the parent company are interested in future profitability and cash flows. Creditors of the parent company want to be repaid and, accordingly, have information needs similar to those of the shareholders. The profitability and financial health of the parent are directly related to those of the companies it controls.

> *Consolidated financial statements are prepared primarily for the benefit of the shareholders and creditors of the parent company.*

While consolidated statements are considered the best vehicle to satisfy the needs of stakeholders in the parent, they also have limitations. A poor performance by certain subsidiaries can be hidden as a result of the aggregation process. In addition, many parent companies have subsidiaries in different industries in various countries throughout the world, and this can be hidden in a single set of statements. Note disclosures that present details about the companies' operating segments help to alleviate this problem. Segment reporting will be discussed in Chapter 9. Finally, the information needs of non-controlling shareholders and creditors of the subsidiary companies are not served by consolidated statements. These users are better served with the separate entity statements of the subsidiary by itself. Therefore, separate entity financial statements for the subsidiary will have to be prepared to satisfy the information needs of the subsidiary's stakeholders.

> *The non-controlling shareholders and creditors of the subsidiary find the separate-entity statements of the subsidiary more useful than the consolidated statements.*

IFRS 10 paragraph 4(a) states that a parent is not required to present consolidated financial statements for external reporting purposes if it meets all of the following conditions:

(a) It is a wholly owned subsidiary, or is a partially owned subsidiary, of another entity and its other owners, including those not otherwise entitled to vote, have been informed about, and do not object to, the parent not presenting consolidated financial statements.

(b) Its debt or equity instruments are not traded in a public market (a domestic or foreign stock exchange or an over-the-counter market, including local and regional markets).

(c) It did not file, nor is it in the process of filing, its financial statements with a securities commission or other regulatory organization for the purpose of issuing any class of instruments in a public market.

(d) Its ultimate or any intermediate parent produces financial statements available for public use and comply with IFRS.

> *A parent company does not have to issue consolidated financial statements if its parent issues consolidated financial statements.*

If the parent meets these conditions, it *can* (but is not required to) present *separate financial statements* in accordance with IFRS as its only financial statements to external users. When an entity prepares separate financial statements, it must follow IAS 27 *Separate Financial Statements*. Under IAS 27 paragraph 10, it should account for investments in subsidiaries

(a) at cost;

(b) in accordance with IFRS 9; or

(c) using the equity method as described in IAS 28.

> *In the parent's separate financial statements for external users, the investment in subsidiary would be reported at cost, at fair value or using the equity method.*

If a parent does not issue either consolidated or separate financial statements in accordance with IFRS to external users, it may still prepare financial statements for internal record-keeping purposes and/or for special external users with special needs. The accounting policies used for these special-purpose financial statements should be disclosed. Unless otherwise noted, our illustrations throughout the text will comply with IFRS and will produce general-purpose financial statements for use by external users.

Now that we have a better understanding of the concept of consolidated financial statements, we will turn our attention to business combinations resulting from the purchase of shares. We will continue to use the financial statements of the two companies from Exhibit 3.2.

## Control through Purchase of Shares

In the next two examples, A Company issues a tender offer to the shareholders of B Corporation (Group Y) for all of their shareholdings. Group Y accepts the offer.

**EXAMPLE 3**   Assume that on January 1, Year 2, A Company pays $95,000 in cash to the shareholders of B Corporation for all of their shares and that no other direct costs are involved. Because cash was the means of payment, A Company is the acquirer.

A Company's journal entry to record the acquisition of 100% of B Corporation's shares on January 1, Year 2, is as follows:

| | | |
|---|---|---|
| Investment in B Corporation | 95,000 | |
| Cash | | 95,000 |

The financial statements of B Corporation have not been affected by this transaction because the shareholders of B Corporation, not B Corporation itself, sold their shares. A Company is now a parent company and must prepare consolidated financial statements for external reporting purposes. We will now illustrate the preparation of the consolidated balance sheet as at January 1, Year 2, using a working paper approach.

> *With a purchase of shares, the transaction is with the shareholders of the acquired company, not with the acquired company itself.*

Before preparing the working paper, it is useful to calculate and allocate the acquisition differential. The acquisition differential is defined as the difference between the total consideration given and the carrying amount of the assets of the acquired company at the date of acquisition. The required calculation and allocation is shown in Exhibit 3.3.

## EXHIBIT 3.3

**CALCULATION AND ALLOCATION OF THE ACQUISITION DIFFERENTIAL**

| | | | | |
|---|---|---|---|---|
| Total consideration given | = cash paid by A Company | | | $ 95,000 |
| Less: Carrying amount of B Corporation's net assets: | | | | |
| Assets | | | $88,000 | |
| Liabilities | | | 30,000 | |
| | | | | 58,000 |
| Acquisition differential | | | | 37,000 |
| Allocated as follows: | | | | |
| Fair value excess | *Fair Value  −  Carrying Amount* | | | |
| Assets | 109,000  −  88,000 | = | $21,000 | |
| Liabilities | 29,000  −  30,000 | = | 1,000 | 22,000 |
| Balance—goodwill | | | | $ 15,000 |

Since A Company purchased all of the shares in an arm's length transaction, it is reasonable to conclude that the $95,000 cost of the investment represents the total fair value of the subsidiary on the date of acquisition. The $95,000 value can be segregated into three components as indicated in the following chart:

**Total Value of Subsidiary**

| |
|---|
| Carrying amount of identifiable assets and liabilities $58,000 |
| Excess of fair value over carrying amount of identifiable assets and liabilities $22,000 |
| Goodwill $15,000 |

> *The total value of the subsidiary can be segregated into three components.*

Since assets minus liabilities equals shareholders' equity, the top component of the bar chart could be described as either carrying amount of identifiable assets and liabilities or carrying amount of shareholders' equity. The carrying amount component is the amount reflected on the subsidiary's separate-entity balance sheet.

The sum of the top two components is equal to the fair value of identifiable assets and liabilities. The bottom component, goodwill, represents the additional value of the acquiree over and above the fair value of the identifiable net assets. When the parent acquires 100% of the subsidiary, goodwill can be calculated as follows:

| | | |
|---|---:|---:|
| Cost of A Company's investment | | $95,000 |
| Fair value of B Corporation's identifiable net assets: | | |
| Assets | 109,000 | |
| Liabilities | 29,000 | |
| | | 80,000 |
| Balance—goodwill | | $15,000 |

> *Goodwill is the difference between the total consideration given and the fair value of identifiable net assets.*

The fair value excess is added to the carrying amount of the subsidiary's assets on the consolidated balance sheet; it is not added to the tax basis of the assets for income tax purposes. The fair value excess meets the definition of a temporary difference. Accordingly, deferred taxes should be set up for the tax effect on these temporary differences. We will ignore the deferred tax implications for this example and for most examples in the text because they overly complicate the allocation of the acquisition differential. We will revisit this issue in Chapter 9.

Because consolidated working papers use the financial statements of the parent and its subsidiary as the starting point, the calculation and allocation of the acquisition differential is necessary because it provides the amounts needed to make the working paper eliminations and adjustments. The working paper for the preparation of the consolidated balance sheet on the date of acquisition is shown in Exhibit 3.4.

The following points should be noted regarding the preparation of this working paper:

1. A Company's asset "Investment in B Corporation" and B Corporation's common shares and retained earnings do not appear on the consolidated balance sheet. These items are eliminated because they are reciprocal in nature. The entry labelled **(1)** eliminates the parent's ownership percentage of the shareholders' equity of the subsidiary against the parent's investment account. These shareholders' equity accounts are separately shown in the working paper to facilitate this. The acquisition differential that results is the portion of the investment account not yet eliminated.

2. The acquisition differential line does not appear as a separate account on the consolidated balance sheet. With reference to the calculations of Exhibit 3.3, the acquisition differential is allocated to revalue the net assets of B Corporation for consolidation purposes. This is accomplished by the entry labelled **(2)**.

3. When we add the acquisition differential to the carrying amount of the net assets of B Corporation, the resulting amount used for the consolidation is the fair value of each individual asset and liability of B Corporation.

**EXHIBIT 3.4**

**A COMPANY LTD.**
**CONSOLIDATED BALANCE SHEET WORKING PAPER**
At January 1, Year 2

| | A Company | B Corp. | | Dr. | | Cr. | Consolidated Balance Sheet |
|---|---|---|---|---|---|---|---|
| | | | **Adjustments and Eliminations** | | | | |
| Assets | $205,000 | $88,000 | **(2)** | $ 21,000 | | | $314,000 |
| Investment in B Corporation | 95,000 | | | | **(1)** | $ 95,000 | |
| Acquisition differential | | | **(1)** | 37,000 | **(2)** | 37,000 | |
| Goodwill | | | **(2)** | 15,000 | | | 15,000 |
| | $300,000 | $88,000 | | | | | $329,000 |
| Liabilities | $120,000 | $30,000 | **(2)** | 1,000 | | | $149,000 |
| Common shares | 100,000 | | | | | | 100,000 |
| Retained earnings | 80,000 | | | | | | 80,000 |
| Common shares | | 25,000 | **(1)** | 25,000 | | | |
| Retained earnings | | 33,000 | **(1)** | 33,000 | | | |
| | $300,000 | $88,000 | | $132,000 | | $132,000 | $329,000 |

> *The consolidation entries are made on the consolidated working papers and not in the accounting records of the combining companies.*

4. The elimination entries are made on the working paper only. They are not entered in the accounting records of the parent or the subsidiary.

5. The consolidated balance sheet is prepared from the amounts shown in the last column of the working paper.

6. Under the acquisition method of accounting, consolidated shareholders' equity on acquisition date is that of the parent.

> *The consolidated balance sheet reflects the acquiring company's net assets at carrying amount and the acquired company's net assets at fair value.*

It is worth noting that the consolidated balance sheet for example 3 is exactly the same as A Company's balance sheet in example 1. This is not a coincidence. In both examples, the net assets of the two companies were combined and the amount paid for B Corporation was $95,000 in cash. In example 1, A Company acquired the net assets directly; in example 3, A Company acquired 100% of B Corporation's shares and thereby indirectly acquired B Corporation's net assets. As we proceed through more complicated examples of consolidation, it is important to remember that the consolidated financial statements should present the same results as if the parent had acquired the net assets directly.

> *The consolidated balance sheet produces the same financial position as when A Company purchased the net assets directly.*

**EXAMPLE 4**    Assume that on January 1, Year 2, A Company issues 4,000 common shares, with a fair value of $23.75 per share, to the shareholders of B Corporation (Group Y) for all of their shares and that there are no direct costs involved. The analysis made in Example 2 indicates that A Company is the acquirer.

A Company's January 1, Year 2, journal entry to record the issuance of 4,000 shares at market value in payment for the acquisition of 100% of B Corporation's shares is as follows:

| | | |
|---|---|---|
| Investment in B Corporation (4,000 shares × 23.75) | 95,000 | |
| Common shares | | 95,000 |

Once again, B Corporation would not make any journal entry because the transaction was with the shareholders of B Corporation and not with B Corporation itself.

The calculation and allocation of the acquisition differential is identical to the one used in the last example (see Exhibit 3.3). The working paper for the preparation of the consolidated balance sheet as at January 1, Year 2, is shown in Exhibit 3.5.

Once again, it is worth noting that the consolidated balance sheet for example 4 is exactly the same as A Company's balance sheet in Example 2. This is not a coincidence. In both examples, the net assets of the two companies were combined and the amount paid for B Corporation was $95,000 in the form of A Company shares.

**EXHIBIT 3.5**

**A COMPANY LTD.**
**CONSOLIDATED BALANCE SHEET WORKING PAPER**

At January 1, Year 2

| | A Company | B Corp. | Adjustments and Eliminations Dr. | | Adjustments and Eliminations Cr. | | Consolidated Balance Sheet |
|---|---|---|---|---|---|---|---|
| Assets | $300,000 | $88,000 | **(2)** | $ 21,000 | | | $409,000 |
| Investment in B Corporation | 95,000 | | | | **(1)** | $ 95,000 | |
| Acquisition differential | | | **(1)** | 37,000 | **(2)** | 37,000 | |
| Goodwill | | | **(2)** | 15,000 | | | 15,000 |
| | $395,000 | $88,000 | | | | | $424,000 |
| Liabilities | $120,000 | $30,000 | **(2)** | 1,000 | | | $149,000 |
| Common shares | 195,000 | | | | | | 195,000 |
| Retained earnings | 80,000 | | | | | | 80,000 |
| Common shares | | 25,000 | **(1)** | 25,000 | | | |
| Retained earnings | | 33,000 | **(1)** | 33,000 | | | |
| | $395,000 | $88,000 | | $132,000 | | $132,000 | $424,000 |

*The allocation of the acquisition differential is made on the consolidated worksheet and is not recorded in the accounting records of either of the combining companies.*

*Goodwill appears on the consolidated balance sheet—that is, on the third set of statements.*

**THE DIRECT APPROACH**   An alternative approach to the preparation of consolidated financial statements is to prepare the statements directly without the use of a working paper. We know from the working paper approach that the parent's investment account does not appear on the consolidated balance sheet because it is replaced with the underlying assets and liabilities of the subsidiary. The subsidiary's shareholders' equity accounts also do not appear on the consolidated balance sheet because they are not part of the consolidated entity's shareholders' equity. Therefore, we will never incorporate the investment account from the parent's balance sheet or the shareholders' equity accounts from the subsidiary's balance sheet when preparing the consolidated balance sheet at the date of acquisition.

We also know from the working paper approach that the allocation of the acquisition differential provides the amounts used to revalue the net assets of the subsidiary. By adding the acquisition differential to the carrying amount of the subsidiary's net assets on a line-by-line basis, we end up with the fair value of the subsidiary's assets and liabilities.

The direct approach achieves the same results as the working paper approach but with a slightly different format. The basic process involved in the direct approach is as follows:

| Carrying amount (parent) | $+$ | Carrying amount (subsidiary) | $+ (-)$ | Acquisition differential | $=$ | Consolidated amounts |
|---|---|---|---|---|---|---|

The preparation of the consolidated balance sheet using the direct approach for Example 4 is illustrated in Exhibit 3.6. The non-bolded amounts shown in brackets come from the separate-entity balance sheets of A Company and B Corporation. The bolded amounts in brackets are consolidation adjustments related to the allocation of the acquisition differential. Consolidated shareholders' equity on acquisition date is always that of the parent company.

> *On the date of acquisition, consolidated shareholders' equity = parent's shareholders' equity.*

**EXHIBIT 3.6**

## Illustration of the Direct Approach

**A COMPANY LTD.**
**CONSOLIDATED BALANCE SHEET**
At January 1, Year 2

| | |
|---|---|
| Assets (300,000 + 88,000 + **21,000**) | $409,000 |
| Goodwill (0 + 0 + **15,000**) | 15,000 |
| | $424,000 |
| Liabilities (120,000 + 30,000 − **1,000**) | $149,000 |
| Common shares | 195,000 |
| Retained earnings | 80,000 |
| | $424,000 |

> *Under the direct approach, the acquisition differential and other consolidation adjustments are added or subtracted to the appropriate line on the consolidated financial statements.*

The accounting for a business combination has been examined in four examples. The first two involved the acquisition of net assets directly, and the last two the acquisition of 100% of shareholdings. Because the amount paid was the same in each of these paired examples, the balance sheets prepared immediately after the combination are identical for each pair.

In the last two examples, it was quite clear that A Company was the acquirer. The former shareholders of A Company own 56% of the shares after the new 4,000 shares were issued to acquire B Corporation. If A Company had issued 6,000 rather than 4,000 new shares, the former shareholders of B Corporation would own 55% (6,000/11,000) of the outstanding shares of A Company and would control the combined company. This is an example of a reverse takeover where the shareholders of the company being acquired (in this case, B Corporation) own the majority of the shares of the acquirer (in this case, A Company). The legal parent, being A Company, is treated as the subsidiary and the legal subsidiary, being B Corporation, is treated as the parent for reporting purposes. Therefore, the consolidated balance sheet would incorporate B Corporation's net assets at carrying amounts and A Company's net assets at fair value. See Appendix 3A for a more detailed explanation and illustration of a reverse takeover situation.

> *In a reverse takeover, the consolidated balance sheet incorporates the carrying amount of the net assets of the deemed parent (the legal subsidiary) and the fair value of the deemed subsidiary (the legal parent).*

**REPORTING DEPRECIABLE ASSETS**　In the previous examples, we did not show the details for the subsidiary's assets because we wanted to illustrate the concepts in a simple scenario. We will now consider the complications when the subsidiary has a depreciable asset.

Assume the following data pertaining to a building for the parent and subsidiary at the date of acquisition:

|  | Parent | Subsidiary |
| --- | --- | --- |
| Cost | $500 | $200 |
| Accumulated depreciation | 180 | 50 |
| Carrying amount | 320 | 150 |
| Fair value | 375 | 210 |

The consolidated balance sheet should incorporate the carrying amount of $320 for the parent's building and the fair value of $210 for the subsidiary's building for a total value of $530. But, how much should be reported for cost and accumulated depreciation?

IFRS 10 does not give any guidance on how to report these two components. However, IAS 16 does give some guidance when using the revaluation model to report property, plant, and equipment at fair value on an annual basis. IAS 16 Paragraph 35 states that when an item of property, plant, and equipment is revalued, any accumulated depreciation at the date of the revaluation is treated in one of the following ways:

(a) Restated proportionately with the change in the gross carrying amount of the asset so that the carrying amount of the asset after revaluation equals its revalued amount. This method is similar to a depreciated replacement cost method because it shows the fair value of the asset as if it was new and then deducts accumulated depreciation to derive the fair value of the used asset. This method shows that the asset is used because it reports accumulated depreciation. (We will refer to this approach as the *proportionate method.*)

(b) Eliminated against the gross carrying amount of the asset and the net amount restated to the revalued amount of the asset. Under this method, it will appear as if the asset is new because it does not report any accumulated depreciation. (We will refer to this approach as the *net method.*)

> *Cautionary Note: In this textbook, we will use the net method unless otherwise indicated.*

Under the proportionate method, both the cost and accumulated depreciation of the subsidiary's building would be grossed up by a factor of 210/150 = 1.40 to produce a grossed-up cost of $280 ($200 × 1.4) and a grossed-up accumulated depreciation of $70 ($50 × 1.4). Under the net method, the accumulated depreciation will be reported at zero and the cost reported at $210. In both cases, the difference between cost and accumulated depreciation will be $210, which is the fair value of the building at that point in time.

The net method seems more appropriate because the parent is, in effect, acquiring the asset from the shareholders of the subsidiary at the date of acquisition. There should be no accumulated depreciation for a recently purchased asset.

The following presents the consolidated balance sheet amounts under the two different methods:

| | Parent | Subsidiary Proportionate Method | Consolidated Proportionate Method | Subsidiary Net Method | Consolidated Net Method |
|---|---|---|---|---|---|
| Cost | $500 | $280 | $780 | $210 | $710 |
| Accumulated depreciation | 180 | 70 | 250 | 0 | 180 |
| Carrying amount | 320 | 210 | 530 | 210 | 530 |

> *Both methods report the subsidiary's depreciable asset at fair value but report different amounts for cost and accumulated depreciation.*

See Self-Study Problem 2 for a further illustration and comparison of a purchase of net assets compared with a purchase of shares. This problem also incorporates the presentation of cost and accumulated depreciation on the consolidated balance sheet.

**OTHER CONSOLIDATED FINANCIAL STATEMENTS IN YEAR OF ACQUISITION** Consolidated financial statements must be prepared once an entity obtains control of the net assets of another entity. The assets and liabilities of the two entities are combined for reporting purposes as of the date that control has been obtained. Similarly, the revenues and expenses are combined starting on the date of acquisition; they are not combined on a retroactive basis. If a business combination occurs halfway through the year, the consolidated income statement for the year will incorporate only the income of the parent for the first half of the year and the income for both the parent and subsidiary for the second half of the year.[4] The column in the consolidated statements for last year (i.e., the comparative year) will only include the parent's income because the two companies were not one economic entity in the prior year. This treatment is consistent with what would be done if the parent had purchased the net assets directly from the subsidiary. That is, when a company acquires assets, it reports income from those assets starting on the date of purchase. It does not retroactively adjust to state what income would have been had these assets always belonged to the purchaser. The consolidated statements will combine the results of the parent and subsidiary for transactions occurring on and subsequent to the date of acquisition.

> *Consolidated net income, retained earnings, and cash flows include the subsidiary's income and cash flows only subsequent to the date of acquisition.*

To illustrate these financial reporting requirements, assume the following information for G Corporation and H Company for Years 1 and 2:

|  | Year 1 | Year 2 |
|---|---|---|
| **G Corporation:** |  |  |
| Separate income (excluding any income from H) | $30,000 | $30,000 |
| Common shares outstanding, December 31 | 10,000 | 14,000 |
| **H Company:** |  |  |
| Net income | $14,800 | $14,800 |

On January 1, Year 2, G Corporation issued 4,000 common shares to buy 100% of H Company's common shares. Assume that there was no acquisition differential on this business combination. The net income and earnings per share that G Corporation would present on its comparative consolidated financial statements at the end of Year 2 would be as follows:

|  | Year 1 | Year 2 |
|---|---|---|
| Net income (30,000 + 0; 30,000 + 14,800) | $30,000 | $44,800 |
| Earnings per share (30,000/10,000; 44,800/14,000) | $ 3.00 | $ 3.20 |

**DISCLOSURE REQUIREMENTS**  According to IFRS 12, the acquirer must disclose information that enables users of its financial statements to do the following:

> *The acquirer must disclose information that enables users of its financial statements to evaluate the nature of, and risks associated, with its interests in subsidiaries.*

(a) Evaluate the nature of, and risks associated with, its interests in subsidiaries

(b) Evaluate the effects of those interests on its financial position, financial performance, and cash flows

(c) Understand the significant judgments and assumptions it has made in determining that it has control of another entity

(d) Understand the composition of the group

(e) Evaluate the nature and extent of significant restrictions on its ability to access or use assets, and settle liabilities, of the group

Amaya Inc. is the largest publicly held online gambling company in the world. It purchased Oldford Group Limited, which owned the PokerStars and Full-Tilt brands. Excerpts from its 2014 financial statements are presented in Exhibit 3.7. Amaya set up a provision for further potential payments based on government regulations in Russia.

> *Amaya Inc. acquired the rights to PokerStars through its purchase of the shares of Oldford Group Ltd.*

EXHIBIT 3.7

## EXTRACTS FROM AMAYA INC.'S 2014 FINANCIAL STATEMENTS

Note 31. BUSINESS COMBINATIONS – Oldford Group Limited

The acquisition of 100% of the shares of Oldford Group Limited ("Oldford Group") has been accounted for using the acquisition method and the results of operations are included in the consolidated statements of earnings (loss) from the date of acquisition, which was August 1, 2014.

The following table summarizes the preliminary estimated fair value of the identifiable assets and liabilities acquired at the date of acquisition:

### FAIR VALUE ON ACQUISITION
### CAD$000s

| | |
|---|---:|
| Cash | 390,639 |
| Accounts receivable | 123,117 |
| Prepaid expenses and deposits | 38,599 |
| Investments | 373,692 |
| Property and equipment | 51,369 |
| Accounts payables and accrued liabilities | (111,818) |
| Other payables | (105,982) |
| Provisions | (21,844) |
| Customer deposits | (663,594) |
| Intangible assets | 2,213,606 |
| Goodwill | 3,055,410 |
| Deferred income tax liability | (22,820) |
| Other | (2,759) |
| Total consideration | 5,317,615 |
| Fair value of deferred payment | 391,000 |
| | 5,708,615 |

The main factors leading to the recognition of goodwill are the number of benefits to Amaya's shareholders the Corporation believes the acquisition will provide. These include the following:

- *Acquisition of Leading Brands:* The acquisition has resulted in a wholly owned subsidiary of Amaya owning two global leading brands in online poker, PokerStars and Full-Tilt.
- *Leading Liquidity:* PokerStars.com average cash game liquidity is approximately eight times larger than the next competitor, and PokerStars is a leader in almost every regulated market in which it operates.
- *New Verticals:* Introduction of online real money casino and/or online sportsbook in those markets where permitted, are new opportunities for cross selling to the existing poker player base and to acquire new customers.

If the acquisition had occurred on January 1, 2014, Oldford Group would have contributed CAD$1.26 billion and CAD$462 million to consolidated revenues and net earnings, respectively. Since the date of acquisition, Oldford Group has contributed CAD$547 million and CAD$230 million to consolidated revenues and net earnings, respectively.

Acquisition-related costs directly related to the Rational Group Acquisition were USD$17.81 million and were expensed in net earnings in the year ended December 31, 2014.

The Rational Group Acquisition includes a deferred payment of USD$400 million which shall be subject to adjustment, payable on February 1, 2017, based upon the regulatory status of online poker in Russia within 30 months of close. If Russia continues to operate under the status quo, the Corporation will owe USD$400 million. If Russia formally regulates online poker and the Corporation obtains a license in the newly regulated framework and there is evidence that the new tax rate would be "beneficial," as defined in the merger agreement, then the Corporation will owe up to USD$550 million. If Russia deems online poker illegal, the Corporation will owe USD$100 million.

The current fair value of the deferred payment of USD$ 346 million (CAD$ 391 million) is recorded in Provisions (see note 15) and was calculated using a 6% discount rate, equivalent to the discount rate negotiated by the parties in case of early payment of the deferred payment.

On March 11, 2015, the Corporation commented on a tax dispute between a subsidiary of Rational Group and Italian tax authorities related to operations of such subsidiary, particularly under the PokerStars brand, in Italy prior to the Rational Group Acquisition. The Corporation was aware of the dispute prior to Rational Group Acquisition, but believes Rational Group has operated in compliance with the applicable local tax regulations and has paid €120 million in local taxes during the period subject to the dispute.

Although management is currently assessing the potential exposure, if any, the Corporation believes that any tax liability as part of this matter are indemnifiable by the former owners of the Oldford Group under the agreement governing the transactions, subject to certain conditions. Pursuant to this agreement, the sellers have agreed to indemnify the Corporation for pre-closing tax liabilities including amounts held in an escrow account plus an additional amount not held in escrow and reserved solely for tax claims.

The purchase price allocation does not reflect the impact on any contingencies arising from circumstances that were present on the date of acquisition on August 1, 2014. In the event that a measurable outcome is ascertainable as a result of these contingencies during the reference period spanning one year from the date of acquisition, the impact will be recorded as an adjustment to purchase price allocation reflecting both the contingent liability and the offsetting indemnification asset. Any impact that becomes both measurable and more likely than not after the reference period will not be reflected as an adjustment to the purchase price allocation.

*Source: Amaya, Annual Financial Statements for the Year Ended December 31, 2014, Notes 1 and 31. Reproduced with permission from Amaya.*

---

> *Amaya set up a provision for further potential payments based on government regulations in Russia.*
>
> *The acquirer has up to one year from the date of acquisition to finalize the determination of fair value for the identifiable net assets.*

---

**PUSH-DOWN ACCOUNTING**   Under push-down accounting, the acquisition differential is "pushed down" to the actual accounting records of the subsidiary on the date of acquisition. The subsidiary revalues its assets and liabilities, including goodwill, to the same amount that is being used on the consolidated balance sheet. This practice became permissible under Canadian generally accepted accounting principles (GAAP) in 1992 with the issuance of Section 1625 *Comprehensive Revaluation of Assets and Liabilities*. Push-down accounting is not presently addressed and is, therefore, not allowed under IFRS. However, it is still permissible under Accounting Standards for Private Enterprises (ASPE). Since it may be incorporated in IFRS in the future, we will briefly describe how it works.

Push-down accounting is another instance in which GAAP allows a departure from historical cost accounting and allows the use of fair values in financial reporting. Even though the subsidiary was not involved in the transaction with the parent (the transaction involved the parent and the shareholders of the subsidiary), the subsidiary is allowed to revalue its identifiable assets and liabilities to fair value and its goodwill to the amount reported on the consolidated balance sheet. Since the parent and subsidiary were not related prior to the acquisition, the amount paid by the parent was probably equal to or fairly close to the fair value of these net assets. So, it is appropriate to use these values to provide more relevant, yet very reliable, information to the users of the subsidiary's financial statements.

---

> *Under push-down accounting, the subsidiary revalues its assets and liabilities, including goodwill, to the amounts included in the consolidated balance sheet.*

---

Section 1625 in Part II of the *Handbook* allows push-down accounting only when a subsidiary is at least 90% owned by a parent. Theoretically, a parent could demand a 95%-owned subsidiary to use it. Practically, it probably would not, because when a non-controlling interest is present, the consolidation becomes very complex and the benefits from its use disappear. We will not provide a detailed illustration of push-down accounting in this textbook; however, for those readers that wish to pursue this further, a full discussion and illustration of comprehensive revaluations can be found in the bonus chapters on Connect at www.mcgrawhillconnect.ca.

**SUBSIDIARY FORMED BY PARENT**   In some situations, a subsidiary is not acquired through a share purchase from an outside party. Rather, it is quite common in Canada and the United States for the parent company to set up the subsidiary company. The parent company purchases all of the initial share issue after the subsidiary is incorporated.[5] At this time, the carrying amounts and fair values of the subsidiary's net assets are obviously equal, and there is no goodwill. It should also be obvious that the subsidiary has no retained earnings at this time. The preparation of the consolidated balance sheet on the date of formation of the subsidiary is simplified, requiring only the elimination of the parent's investment account against the subsidiary's share capital.

> *When the parent establishes a new company as a subsidiary, there should be no acquisition differential.*

**NEW-ENTITY METHOD**   An alternative to the acquisition method, called the *new-entity method*, has been discussed in academic circles from time to time over the past 40 years. Under this method, the assets and liabilities of both the parent and the subsidiary are reported at fair value at the date of acquisition. It is another application of fair value accounting and is supported by people who believe that fair value information is more relevant and useful than historical cost information.

Proponents of this method suggest that a new entity has been created when two companies combine by the joining together of two ownership groups. As a result, the assets and liabilities contributed by the two combining companies should be reported by this new entity at their fair values. This would make the relevant contributions by the combining companies more comparable because the net assets are measured on the same basis.

This method has received virtually no support in the accounting profession because of the additional revaluation difficulties and costs that would result. Furthermore, it has been argued that if the owners were simply combining their interests, there would be no new invested capital and, therefore, no new entity has been created.

> *The net assets of both the acquiring company and acquired company are reported at their fair value under the new-entity method.*

See Self-Study Problem 1 for a simple example to compare the new entity and acquisition methods of reporting a business combination. It shows that the values can be quite different.

# LO5 ANALYSIS AND INTERPRETATION OF FINANCIAL STATEMENTS

Consolidated financial statements combine the financial statements of the separate entity financial statements of the parent and subsidiary. The separate entity financial statements of the parent present the investment in subsidiary as one line on the balance sheet. When the consolidated balance sheet is prepared, the investment account is replaced by the underlying assets and liabilities of the subsidiary. This gives the same result as if the investor had bought the subsidiary's assets and liabilities directly.

Exhibit 3.8 presents the separate-entity balance sheet of the parent and the parent's consolidated balance sheet. The values are taken directly from Exhibit 3.5. It also indicates the debt-to-equity ratio for each situation.

## Impact of Presentation Method on Debt-to-Equity Ratio

| | Separate Entity | Consolidated |
|---|---|---|
| Assets | $300,000 | $409,000 |
| Investment in B Corporation | 95,000 | |
| Goodwill | | 15,000 |
| | $395,000 | $424,000 |
| Liabilities | $120,000 | $149,000 |
| Shareholders' equity: | | |
| Common shares | 195,000 | 195,000 |
| Retained earnings | 80,000 | 80,000 |
| | $395,000 | $424,000 |
| Debt-to-equity ratio | 0.44 | 0.54 |

> *The debt-to-equity ratio is substantially higher for the consolidated balance sheet as compared with the separate-entity balance sheet.*

The separate-entity balance presents the legal situation for Company A in that Company A does, in fact, own an investment in shares of B Corporation. The consolidated balance sheet presents the combined financial position of the parent and subsidiary as if they were one economic entity. The debt-to-equity ratio is substantially higher for the consolidated balance sheet. This may better present the risk of insolvency to the parent's shareholders because it presents the total debt of the combined entity.

## LO6 ASPE Differences

The following paragraphs from Part II of the *CPA Canada Handbook* outline the main differences under ASPE in the accounting and reporting requirements for investments in subsidiaries:

- An enterprise shall make an accounting policy choice to either consolidate its subsidiaries or report its subsidiaries using either the equity method or the cost method. All subsidiaries should be reported using the same method. (Section 1590)

- When a subsidiary's equity securities are quoted in an active market and the parent would normally choose to use the cost method, the investment should not be reported at cost. Under such circumstances, the investment should be reported at fair value, with changes in fair value reported in net income. (Section 1590)

- Private companies can apply push-down accounting but must disclose the amount of the change in each major class of assets, liabilities, and shareholders' equity in the year that push-down accounting is first applied. (Section 1625)

> *A private entity can choose to report an investment in a subsidiary by preparing consolidated financial statements, by using the cost or equity methods or at fair value in limited situations.*

# SUMMARY

A *business combination* takes place when one company gains control over the net assets of a business. An investor controls an investee when it is exposed, or has rights, to variable returns from its involvement with the investee, and has the ability to affect those returns through its power over the investee. **(LO1)**

A business combination can be achieved by purchasing the net assets directly, by purchasing enough voting shares to gain control over the use of the net assets, or through contractual arrangements. The *acquisition method* must be used to report a business combination. The balance sheet for the combined entity at the date of acquisition includes the assets and liabilities of the acquirer at their carrying amounts and the identifiable assets and liabilities of the acquiree at their fair value. **(LO2)**

When a business combination is achieved by purchasing the net assets directly, the acquirer records the purchased assets and assumed liabilities in its own accounting records. Any excess of the total consideration given over the fair value of the subsidiary's identifiable assets and liabilities is recorded as goodwill. **(LO3)**

When a business combination is achieved by purchasing enough voting shares to gain control over the net assets of the acquired company, a parent–subsidiary relationship is created. The parent records the investment in subsidiary in its accounting records. Then, consolidated financial statements are prepared to capture the parent and subsidiary as if they were one economic entity. **(LO4)**

The parent's separate entity financial statements and the consolidated financial statements will present different values for net income, assets, liabilities and shareholder's equity. Users of the financial statements will need to be aware of these differences as they assess the profitability, liquidity and solvency of the reporting entity. **(LO5)**

Under ASPE, the parent can choose to report an investment in a subsidiary using the cost method, equity method, at fair value or by preparing consolidated financial statements. **(LO6)**

## Self-Study Problem 1

**LO4, 5**

On December 31, Year 1, P Company obtains control over the net assets of S Company by purchasing 100% of the ordinary shares of S Company. P Company paid for the purchase by issuing ordinary shares with a fair value of $44,000. In addition, P Company paid $1,000 for professional fees to facilitate the transaction. The following information has been assembled just prior to the acquisition date:

| | P Company Carrying Amount | P Company Fair Value | S Company Carrying Amount | S Company Fair Value |
|---|---|---|---|---|
| Goodwill | $      0 | $  38,000 | $      0 | $  22,000 |
| Plant assets (net) | 80,000 | 90,000 | 20,000 | 26,000 |
| Current assets | 50,000 | 55,000 | 15,000 | 14,000 |
| | $130,000 | $ 183,000 | $35,000 | $ 62,000 |
| Shareholders' equity | $ 75,000 | | $18,000 | |
| Long-term debt | 25,000 | $  29,000 | 7,000 | $  8,000 |
| Current liabilities | 30,000 | 30,000 | 10,000 | 10,000 |
| | $130,000 | | $35,000 | |

**Required**

(a) Prepare a consolidated statement of financial position for P Company and calculate the debt-to-equity ratio immediately after the combination under

  (i)  the acquisition method, and

  (ii) the new-entity method.

(b) Which method shows the better solvency position? Briefly explain.

(c) In your opinion, which method best reflects the true economic reality for the combined economic entity? Briefly explain.

## Solution to Self-Study Problem 1

(a)

**P COMPANY**
**CONSOLIDATED STATEMENT OF FINANCIAL POSITION**
At December 31, Year 1
(see notes)

| | (i) | (ii) |
|---|---|---|
| Goodwill | $ 22,000 | $ 60,000 |
| Plant assets (net) | 106,000 | 116,000 |
| Current assets | 63,000 | 68,000 |
| | $191,000 | $244,000 |
| | | |
| Shareholders' equity | $118,000 | $167,000 |
| Long-term debt | 33,000 | 37,000 |
| Current liabilities | 40,000 | 40,000 |
| | $191,000 | $244,000 |
| | | |
| Debt-to-equity ratio | 0.62:1 | 0.46:1 |

(b) The new-entity method shows the better solvency position because its debt-to-equity ratio is lower than the acquisition method. Both the debt and equity are higher under the new-entity method. However, the increase in equity is proportionately greater than the increase in debt.

(c) In the opinion of the author, fair values are better measures of the economic value of assets and liabilities than historical cost-based values. If so, the new-entity method would best reflect the true economic value of the combined economic entity. This method is not generally accepted at the present time, primarily because the cost of measuring the fair value of all of the parent's assets and liabilities, including goodwill, could be quite expensive and may not be worth the effort. If users continue to ask for more fair value information, and if the cost of measuring fair values of assets and liabilities decreases, the new-entity method could become generally accepted in the future.

**Notes:**

  1. The statement of financial position values for assets and liabilities are calculated as follows:

     (i)   Carrying amounts for P plus fair values for S

     (ii)  Fair values for P plus fair values for S

  2. The $1,000 paid for professional fees reduces cash (which is included in current assets) and increases expenses (which reduce retained earnings, a component of shareholders' equity).

3. Shareholders' equity is the amount required to balance the statement of financial position. Under the acquisition method, it is the parent's carrying amount for shareholders' equity plus the value of shares issued less the expense for the professional fees.

## Self-Study Problem 2

LO3, 4

On December 31, Year 1, the condensed balance sheets for ONT Limited and NB Inc. were as follows:

|  | ONT | NB |
|---|---|---|
| **Assets:** | | |
| Cash | $ 44,000 | $ 80,000 |
| Accounts receivable | 480,000 | 420,000 |
| Inventories | 650,000 | 540,000 |
| Property, plant, and equipment | 2,610,000 | 870,000 |
| Accumulated depreciation | (1,270,000) | (130,000) |
| | $2,514,000 | $1,780,000 |
| **Liabilities:** | | |
| Current liabilities | $ 660,000 | $ 560,000 |
| Bonds payable | 820,000 | 490,000 |
| | 1,480,000 | 1,050,000 |
| **Shareholders' equity:** | | |
| Common shares | 200,000 | 400,000 |
| Retained earnings | 834,000 | 330,000 |
| | 1,034,000 | 730,000 |
| | $2,514,000 | $1,780,000 |

The fair value of all of NB's assets and liabilities were equal to their carrying amounts except for the following:

| Asset | Carrying Amount | Fair Value |
|---|---|---|
| Inventories | $540,000 | $570,000 |
| Property, plant, and equipment | 740,000 | 790,000 |
| Bonds payable | 490,000 | 550,000 |

### Required

(a) Assume that on January 1, Year 2, ONT acquired all of NB's net assets by issuing new common shares with a fair value of $1,000,000. This was the only transaction on this day.

   (i)  Prepare the journal entry on ONT's book to record the purchase of NB's net assets.

   (ii) Prepare a balance sheet for ONT at January 1, Year 2, after recording the purchase of NB's net assets.

(b) Ignore part (a). Assume instead that on January 1, Year 2, ONT acquired all of NB's common shares by issuing new common shares with a fair value of $1,000,000. This was the only transaction on this day.

   (i)  Prepare the journal entry on ONT's book to record the purchase of NB's common shares.

   (ii) Prepare a schedule to calculate and allocate the acquisition differential.

   (iii) Prepare a consolidated balance sheet for ONT and its subsidiary at January 1, Year 2, after recording the purchase of NB's common shares.

(c) What are the similarities and differences between the balance sheets in parts (a) and (b)?

## Solution to Self-Study Problem 2

(a) (i)

| | | |
|---|---|---|
| Cash | 80,000 | |
| Accounts receivable | 420,000 | |
| Inventories | 570,000 | |
| Property, plant, and equipment | 790,000 | |
| Goodwill (see [b][ii]) | 250,000 | |
| Current liabilities | | 560,000 |
| Bonds payable | | 550,000 |
| Common shares | | 1,000,000 |

(ii)

**ONT LIMITED**
**BALANCE SHEET**
At January 1, Year 2

| | |
|---|---|
| Assets: | |
| Cash (44,000 + 80,000) | $ 124,000 |
| Accounts receivable (480,000 + 420,000) | 900,000 |
| Inventories (650,000 + 570,000) | 1,220,000 |
| Property, plant, and equipment (2,610,000 + 790,000) | 3,400,000 |
| Accumulated depreciation (1,270,000 + 0) | (1,270,000) |
| Goodwill | 250,000 |
| | $4,624,000 |
| Liabilities: | |
| Current liabilities (660,000 + 560,000) | $1,220,000 |
| Bonds payable (820,000 + 550,000) | 1,370,000 |
| | 2,590,000 |
| Shareholders' equity: | |
| Common shares (200,000 + 1,000,000) | 1,200,000 |
| Retained earnings | 834,000 |
| | 2,034,000 |
| | $4,624,000 |

(b) (i)

| | | |
|---|---|---|
| Investment in NB | 1,000,000 | |
| Common shares | | 1,000,000 |

(ii)

| | | |
|---|---|---|
| Cost of ONT's investment in NB | | $1,000,000 |
| Carrying amount of NB's net assets: | | |
| Assets | $1,780,000 | |
| Liabilities | (1,050,000) | 730,000 |
| Acquisition differential | | 270,000 |
| Allocated as follows: | | |
| Inventories (570,000 − 540,000) | $ 30,000 | |
| Property, plant, and equipment (790,000 − 740,000) | 50,000 | |
| Bonds payable (550,000 − 490,000) | (60,000) | 20,000 |
| Balance—goodwill | | $ 250,000 |

**ONT LIMITED**
**CONSOLIDATED BALANCE SHEET**
At January 1, Year 2

| | |
|---|---:|
| Cash (44,000 + 80,000) | $ 124,000 |
| Accounts receivable (480,000 + 420,000) | 900,000 |
| Inventories (650,000 + 540,000 + 30,000) | 1,220,000 |
| Property, plant, and equipment (2,610,000 + 870,000 − 130,000 + 50,000) | 3,400,000 |
| Accumulated depreciation (1,270,000 + 130,000 − 130,000) | (1,270,000) |
| Goodwill | 250,000 |
| | $ 4,624,000 |
| Liabilities: | |
| Current liabilities (660,000 + 560,000) | $ 1,220,000 |
| Bonds payable (820,000 + 490,000 + 60,000) | 1,370,000 |
| | 2,590,000 |
| Shareholders' equity: | |
| Common shares (200,000 + 1,000,000) | 1,200,000 |
| Retained earnings | 834,000 |
| | 2,034,000 |
| | $ 4,624,000 |

c. The balance sheets are exactly the same, except for the wording in the second line of the title. In part (a), it is ONT Limited's balance sheet for ONT by itself. In part (b), it is ONT Limited's consolidated balance sheet.

# APPENDIX 3A

..........

LO7

# Reverse Takeovers

A reverse takeover occurs when an enterprise obtains ownership of the shares of another enterprise but, as part of the transaction, issues enough voting shares as consideration that control of the combined enterprise passes to the shareholders of the acquired enterprise. Although, legally, the enterprise that issues the shares is regarded as the parent or continuing enterprise, the enterprise whose former shareholders now control the combined enterprise is treated as the acquirer for reporting purposes. As a result, the issuing enterprise (the legal parent) is deemed to be the acquiree and the company being acquired in appearance (the legal subsidiary) is deemed to have acquired control of the assets and business of the issuing enterprise.

> *For reporting purposes, the acquirer is identified based on which shareholder group has control over the combined entity.*

While it is not a common event, this form of business combination is often used by active non-public companies as a means to obtain a stock exchange listing without having to go through the listing procedures established by the exchange. A takeover of a public company that has a stock exchange listing is arranged in such a way that the public company emerges as the legal parent, but the former shareholders of the non-public company have control of the public company.

**REVERSE TAKEOVER ILLUSTRATION**   The balance sheets of Reverse Ltd. and Takeover Co. on the date of a reverse takeover business combination are shown in Exhibit 3A.1.

Reverse is a small public company engaged in business activity with a listing on a major stock exchange. Takeover is an active company not listed on any exchange. A business combination is initiated by Takeover whereby Reverse issues 240 shares to the shareholders of Takeover for 100% of their shareholdings. By structuring the combination in this manner, Reverse becomes the legal parent and Takeover the legal subsidiary.

> *In a reverse takeover, the legal parent is deemed to be the subsidiary for reporting purposes and the legal subsidiary is deemed to be the parent.*

An examination of the shares held by the two shareholder groups in the following manner clearly indicates that Takeover is identified as the acquirer:

|  | Shares of Reverse Ltd. | % |
|---|---|---|
| Former shareholders of Reverse Ltd. | 160 | 40% |
| Former shareholders of Takeover Co. | 240 | 60% |
|  | 400 | 100% |

Under the acquisition method of accounting for a business combination, the fair value of the net assets of the acquiree is combined with the carrying amount of the net assets of the acquirer. Because Takeover is the acquirer, the acquisition cost is determined *as if* Takeover had issued shares to the shareholders of Reverse. A calculation has to be made to determine the number of

**EXHIBIT 3A.1**

**BALANCE SHEETS**

|  | Reverse Ltd. | | Takeover Co. |
|---|---|---|---|
|  | Carrying Amount | Fair Value | Carrying Amount |
| Current assets | $  560 | $  700 | $1,560 |
| Plant assets | 1,600 | 1,650 | 5,100 |
|  | $2,160 | | $6,660 |
| Liabilities | $  720 | 720 | $3,060 |
| Common shares (160 shares) | 500 | | |
| Retained earnings | 940 | | |
| Common shares (96 shares)* | | | 1,080 |
| Retained earnings | | | 2,520 |
|  | $2,160 | | $6,660 |

*The shares of Takeover Co. have a fair value of $30 per share.

shares that Takeover would have issued to achieve the same result (i.e., so that its shareholders would end up holding 60% of Takeover's outstanding shares). The number of shares can be determined as follows:

1. Before the combination, the shareholders of Takeover hold 96 shares in that company.

2. Takeover would have to issue $X$ additional shares such that the 96 shares will represent 60% of the total shares outstanding.

3. After the share issue, the total shares outstanding will be $96 + X$ shares.

4. $96 = 0.6\,(96 + X)$. Therefore, $X = 64$ shares.

> *The acquisition cost for the deemed parent is determined based on a hypothetical situation that could have achieved the same percentage ownership in the combined entity.*

If Takeover had issued 64 shares, the holdings of the two groups of shareholders would have been as follows:

|  | Shares of Takeover Co. | % |
|---|---|---|
| Shareholders of Takeover | 96 | 60% |
| Shareholders of Reverse | 64 | 40% |
|  | 160 | 100% |

The acquisition cost is the number of shares that Takeover would have issued, measured at their fair value, and is allocated in the following manner:

| | |
|---|---|
| Acquisition cost—64 shares @ $30 | $1,920 |
| Fair value of identifiable net assets of Reverse Co. | 1,630 |
| Goodwill of Reverse Co. | $   290 |

> *Goodwill of the deemed subsidiary is based on the hypothetical acquisition cost.*

The balance sheet of the consolidated company immediately after the business combination is prepared by combining the fair value of the net assets of Reverse, including the goodwill from the combination, with the carrying amount of the net assets of Takeover. It should be noted that Takeover's shareholders' equity becomes the shareholders' equity of the combined company. The dollar amount shown for common shares is determined by summing the dollar amount of the common shares of Takeover before the combination and the deemed issue of 64 shares at fair value. However, the number of shares shown as issued is the number of outstanding shares of the legal parent Reverse. The consolidated balance sheet of Reverse immediately after the reverse takeover takes place is shown in Exhibit 3A.2.

> *Shareholders' equity should reflect the shareholders' equity of the deemed parent.*

The financial statements of Reverse would contain the following footnote to describe this event: During the year, Reverse Ltd. entered into a share exchange agreement with the shareholders of

**REVERSE LTD.**
**CONSOLIDATED BALANCE SHEET**

| | |
|---|---:|
| Current assets (700 + 1,560) | $2,260 |
| Plant assets (1,650 + 5,100) | 6,750 |
| Goodwill | 290 |
| | $9,300 |
| | |
| Liabilities (720 + 3,060) | $3,780 |
| Common shares* (1,080 + 1,920) | 3,000 |
| Retained earnings | 2,520 |
| | $9,300 |

*The number of shares issued and outstanding would be shown as 400 shares (160 + 240).*

> *The legal parent/deemed subsidiary's assets are brought in at fair value while the legal subsidiary/deemed parent's assets are brought in at carrying amount.*

Takeover Co. Under this agreement, Reverse exchanged 240 common shares for 100% of the issued and outstanding shares of Takeover. As a result of the share exchange, Takeover obtained control over Reverse.

> *Note disclosure is required to explain that the reporting follows the substance (rather than the legal form) of who has control.*

Legally, Reverse is the parent of Takeover; however, as a result of the share exchange, control of the combined companies passed to the shareholders of Takeover, which for reporting purposes is deemed to be the acquirer. For financial reporting purposes, this share exchange is considered to be a reverse takeover and Reverse is considered to be a continuation of Takeover. The net assets of Takeover are included in the balance sheet at carrying amounts, and the deemed acquisition of Reverse is accounted for by the acquisition method, with the net assets of Reverse recorded at fair values. The fair value of Reverse on the date of acquisition was as follows:

| | |
|---|---:|
| Current assets | $ 700 |
| Plant assets | 1,650 |
| Goodwill | 290 |
| Liabilities | (720) |
| | $1,920 |

In this example, the acquisition cost was determined by multiplying the number of shares that the legal subsidiary would have had to issue by the fair value of that company's shares. However, because the legal subsidiary is often a private company, the fair value of its shares may have to be determined using business valuation concepts. If a fair value cannot be determined for the shares of the legal subsidiary, the fair value of the net assets of the legal parent are used to determine acquisition cost.

Comparative amounts presented in the consolidated financial statements of the legal parent are those of the deemed parent. In the year of the reverse takeover, consolidated net income is made up of the income of the deemed parent *before* the takeover and the income of the combined company *after* the takeover.

> *The comparative amounts are those of the legal subsidiary/deemed parent.*

Because the outstanding shares shown on the consolidated balance sheet are those of the legal parent, the calculation of earnings per share is based on these shares; so is the calculation of the weighted average shares outstanding in the year of the takeover.

In the example of Reverse, assuming the combination date was July 31, the weighted average shares outstanding for the fiscal year December 31 is 307 shares, calculated as follows:

- 240 shares deemed outstanding for 7 months, and

- 400 shares outstanding for 5 months.

> *The consolidated financial statements use the name and shares outstanding of the legal parent.*

This calculation is in contrast to the normal calculation of weighted average shares outstanding, and requires further clarification. Remember that the consolidated statements of Reverse (the legal parent) are considered to be a continuation of those of Takeover (the deemed parent) and that the accounting assumes that the deemed parent (the legal subsidiary) acquired the legal parent. But the shares outstanding are those of the legal parent.

> *The consolidated financial statements use values consistent with whoever, in substance, is the parent and who, in substance, is the subsidiary.*

Consolidated net income for the year *does not* contain the income of Reverse prior to the takeover date because this income is considered to be pre-acquisition earnings. Reverse picked up the first seven months' income of Takeover with the issue of 240 shares. The last five months' income is that of Takeover and Reverse, during which time 400 shares (160 + 240) were outstanding.

The consolidated balance sheet of Reverse Ltd. (Exhibit 3A.2) was prepared using a non-working paper (or direct) approach. We will now illustrate the preparation of the consolidated balance sheet using a working paper (Exhibit 3A.3). On the date of the reverse takeover, Reverse (the legal parent) would make the following journal entry to record the acquisition of 100% of the outstanding shares of Takeover by the issuance of 240 common shares:

| | | |
|---|---|---|
| Investment in Takeover Co. | 1,920 | |
| Common shares (new) | | 1,920 |

These "new" shares are issued at the deemed acquisition cost and are shown separately on the working paper to simplify the consolidation process.

## EXHIBIT 3A.3

### REVERSE LTD.
### CONSOLIDATED BALANCE SHEET WORKING PAPER
(at date of acquisition)

| | Reverse Ltd. | Takeover Co. | | Adjustments and Eliminations Dr. | | Cr. | Consolidated Balance Sheet |
|---|---|---|---|---|---|---|---|
| Current assets | $ 560 | $1,560 | (2) | $ 140 | | | $2,260 |
| Plant assets | 1,600 | 5,100 | (2) | 50 | | | 6,750 |
| Investment in Takeover Co. | 1,920 | | | | (1) | $1,920 | |
| Acquisition differential | | | (1) | 480 | (2) | 480 | |
| Goodwill | | | (2) | 290 | | | 290 |
| | $4,080 | $6,660 | | | | | $9,300 |
| Liabilities | $ 720 | $3,060 | | | | | $3,780 |
| Common shares (old) | 500 | | (1) | 500 | | | |
| Retained earnings | 940 | | (1) | 940 | | | |
| Common shares | | 1,080 | | | | | 3,000 |
| Common shares (new) | 1,920 | | | | | | |
| Retained earnings | | 2,520 | | | | | 2,520 |
| | $4,080 | $6,660 | | $2,400 | | $2,400 | $9,300 |

> The assets reflect the fair values of the deemed subsidiary and the carrying amounts of the deemed parent.
>
> Retained earnings are the retained earnings of the deemed parent.

The calculation and allocation of the acquisition differential is as follows:

| | | | |
|---|---|---|---|
| Acquisition cost of Takeover Co. | | | $1,920 |
| Carrying amount of Reverse Ltd.'s net assets: | | | |
| Assets | | $2,160 | |
| Liabilities | | 720 | 1,440 |
| Acquisition differential | | | 480 |
| Allocated: | | | |
| Current assets (700 − 560) | | $ 140 | |
| Plant assets (1,650 − 1,600) | | 50 | 190 |
| Goodwill | | | $ 290 |

> The calculation of the acquisition differential uses the acquisition cost under the hypothetical situation.

Elimination entry (1) eliminates Reverse's investment in Takeover against Reverse's *precombination shareholders' equity,* with the acquisition differential the balancing amount.

Elimination (2) allocates the acquisition differential to revalue the net assets of Reverse.

The consolidated common shares are the common shares of Takeover (the deemed parent) before the takeover plus the new shares issued by Reverse, which are measured at Takeover's deemed acquisition cost of Reverse.

## Summary for Appendix 3A

A reverse takeover occurs when the former shareholders of the acquired company end up with control over the acquiring company. When the consolidated balance sheet is prepared at the date of acquisition, the legal acquiring company's assets and liabilities are reported at fair value wheras the legal acquired company's assets and liabilities are reported at carrying amount. **(LO7)**

## Review Questions

*Questions, cases, and problems that deal with the appendix material are denoted with an asterisk.*

LO1   **1.** What key element must be present in a business combination?

LO2   **2.** Can a statutory amalgamation be considered a form of business combination? Explain.

LO1   **3.** Explain how an acquirer is determined in a business combination for a 100%-owned subsidiary.

LO2   **4.** Outline the accounting involved with the acquisition method for a 100%-owned subsidiary.

LO4   **5.** Briefly describe the accounting involved with the new-entity method.

LO2   **6.** If one company issued shares as payment for the net assets of another company, it would probably insist that the other company be wound up after the sale. Explain why this condition would be part of the purchase agreement.

LO1   **7.** What criteria must be met for a subsidiary to be consolidated? Explain.

LO1   **8.** What part do irrevocable agreements, convertible securities, and warrants play in determining whether control exists? Explain.

LO4   **9.** What is an acquisition differential, and where does it appear on the consolidated balance sheet?

LO3 **10.** What are some reasons for the acquisition cost being in excess of the carrying amount of the acquiree's assets and liabilities? What does this say about the accuracy of the values used in the financial statements of the acquiree?

LO3 **11.** How is goodwill determined at the date of acquisition? Describe the nature of goodwill.

LO3 **12.** When must an intangible asset be shown separately from goodwill? What are the criteria for reporting these intangible assets separately from goodwill?

LO4 **13.** Does the historical cost principle or fair value reporting take precedence when preparing consolidated financial statements at the date of acquisition under the acquisition method? Explain.

LO4  **14.** What are separate financial statements, and when can they be presented to external users in accordance with IFRS?

LO1  **15.** What are protective rights, and how do they affect the decision of whether one entity has control over another entity?

LO4  **16.** In the preparation of a consolidated balance sheet, the differences between the fair value and the carrying amount of the subsidiary's net assets are used. Would these differences be used if the subsidiary applied push-down accounting? Explain.

LO6  **17.** What are some of the main differences between IFRS and ASPE for business combinations?

LO7 *18.** What is a reverse takeover, and why is such a transaction entered into?

LO7 *19.** Explain how the acquisition cost is determined for a reverse takeover.

# CASES

## Case 3-1

LO4

On December 30, Year 7, Pepper Company agreed to form a business combination with Salt Limited. Pepper issued 4,640 of its common shares for all (5,800) of the outstanding common shares of Salt. This transaction increased the number of the outstanding Pepper shares from 7,600 to 12,240. The market value of the shares was $50 per share for Pepper and $10 for Salt. The balance sheets for the two companies just prior to the acquisition were as follows (in 000s):

|  | Pepper | | Salt | |
| --- | --- | --- | --- | --- |
|  | Carrying Amount | Fair Value | Carrying Amount | Fair Value |
| Identifiable assets | $400 | $500 | $200 | $260 |
| Goodwill | 0 | 200 | 0 | 140 |
|  | $400 | $700 | $200 | $400 |
| Liabilities | $300 | $320 | $ 160 | $168 |
| Shareholders' equity | 100 | 380 | 40 | 232 |
|  | $400 | $700 | $200 | $400 |

Consolidated financial statements will be prepared to combine the financial statements for the two companies. The management of Pepper is concerned about not exceeding a debt-to-equity ratio of 3:1 because of a covenant in a borrowing agreement with its bank. It wants to see how these consolidated statements would differ under two different methods of reporting: acquisition and new-entity. Management also has the following questions when reporting this business combination:

- Why, under the acquisition method, is one set of assets and liabilities adjusted to fair value, whereas the other set is left at carrying amount?

- Given that under the acquisition method we can measure and report the net assets at fair values at the date of acquisition, why would we not report fair values at each subsequent reporting date?

- Which balance sheet best reflects the economic reality of the business combination?

**Required**

Prepare a consolidated balance sheet at the date of acquisition under the two methods and respond to the questions asked by management.

## Case 3-2

LO1

The directors of Atlas Inc. and Beta Corp. have reached an agreement in principle to merge the two companies and create a new company called AB Ltd. The basics of the agreement confirmed so far are outlined below:

- The new company will purchase all of the assets and assume all of the liabilities of Atlas and Beta by issuing shares. After the sale, the two companies will be wound up. Some but not all members of the top management of each company will be retained.

- The number of AB shares that will be issued has not yet been determined.

- The founding shareholders of Atlas Corp., who owned 60% of the voting shares of Atlas prior to the merger, have rights to veto any sale of patents, which they developed and registered. Some of the other shareholders of Atlas also owned non-voting preferred shares of Atlas. These preferred shares were convertible into common shares of Atlas on a one-for-one basis.

The chair of the merger committee has asked you to provide him with advice on the accounting implications that will result from this merger, even though many of the details have not yet been ironed out. He has requested that you submit to him a preliminary report.

**Required**

Prepare an outline of your report.

## Case 3-3

LO2, 4, 7

Manitoba Peat Moss (MPM) was the first Canadian company to provide a reliable supply of high-quality peat moss to be used for greenhouse operations. Owned by Paul Parker, the company's founder and president, MPM began operations approximately 30 years ago when demand for peat moss was high. It has shown consistently high profits and stable growth for over 20 years. Parker holds all of the 50,000 outstanding common shares in MPM.

Prairie Greenhouses (PG), a publicly traded company that purchases over 70% of MPM's output, provides tree seedlings to various government agencies and logging companies for reforestation projects. In Year 5, PG approached MPM with an offer to buy all of the company's outstanding shares in exchange for a part ownership in PG, with a view to integrating vertically. Parker was very interested in the offer, since he hoped to retire soon. PG currently has 100,000 shares outstanding, and they are widely distributed. It would issue 100,000 new common shares to Paul Parker in a two-for-one exchange for all of MPM's shares. PG's shares are currently trading on the TSX at $65 per share.

The board of directors of PG is uncertain of the accounting implications of the proposed share exchange. They believe that since they are purchasing all of the outstanding common shares of MPM, it is similar to buying the company outright. As a result, they want to report all of MPM's assets on PG's consolidated financial statements at fair value. This will be very advantageous to PG because the land carried on MPM's books was purchased 30 years ago and has appreciated substantially in value over the years.

The board has asked you, its accounting adviser, to prepare a report explaining how PG's purchase of shares should be reported. They are particularly interested in how the increase in the value of the land will be shown on the consolidated statements.

The condensed balance sheets of the two companies at the time of the offer are shown below:

|  | PG | MPM |
|---|---|---|
| Current assets | $ 870,000 | $ 450,000 |
| Property, plant, and equipment | 8,210,000 | 2,050,000 |
|  | $ 9,080,000 | $2,500,000 |
| Current liabilities | $ 525,000 | $ 200,000 |
| Long-term debt | 2,325,000 | 1,300,000 |
| Common shares | 4,000,000 | 500,000 |
| Retained earnings | 2,230,000 | 500,000 |
|  | $ 9,080,000 | $2,500,000 |

Note: Land held by MPM at a carrying amount of $1,000,000 has a fair value of $6,000,000. All other assets of both companies have carrying amounts approximately equal to their fair values.

**Required**

Prepare the report to the board of directors.

# Case 3-4

LO4

When Conoco Inc. of Houston, Texas announced the CAD$7 billion acquisition of Gulf Canada Resources Limited of Calgary, Alberta, a large segment of the press release was devoted to outlining all of the expected benefits to be received from the assets acquired. The acquisition price represented a 35% premium over Gulf's closing share price on the announcement date. Included in the assets of Gulf were the following:

- Proven reserves of over 1 billion barrels of oil

- Probable reserves of approximately 1.2 billion barrels of oil

- Proven reserves of 1.4 trillion cubic feet of natural gas

- Probable reserves of 2.9 trillion cubic feet of natural gas

- Four million acres of undeveloped land in western Canada

- A 72% interest in Gulf Indonesia Resources Limited; included in this company's assets were reserves of 180 million barrels of oil and 1.5 trillion cubic feet of gas

- A 9% interest in joint venture, Syncrude Canada Ltd., which is developing the heavy oil tar sands in northern Alberta

- Long-term contracts to deliver 3 trillion cubic feet of natural gas to Southeast Asia

- Recent exploration successes in Sumatra and offshore Java

**Required**

Many of the assets acquired in this business combination present particular valuation challenges. Provide guidance to the financial staff of Conoco on how the price should be allocated among various tangible and intangible assets (including goodwill) and how liabilities included in the portfolio of Gulf Canada Resources Limited should be measured. Explain your answer in terms of the provisions of IFRS.

*(Case prepared by Peter Secord, St. Mary's University)*

## Case 3-5

LO1, 3, 6

Regina Communications Ltd. develops and manufactures equipment for technology and communications enterprises. Since its incorporation, it has grown steadily through internal expansion. In the middle of Year 14, Arthur Lajord, the sole owner of Regina, met a couple of engineering students who were working on new technology to increase the efficiency of data transferred over cable lines. Arthur has provided moral support and some financial support to these students over the past few months. The company has developed some materials and processes sufficiently that a prospective buyer could buy the company, complete the development, and begin producing outputs for sale to prospective customers, or integrate the seller's materials and processes with its own inputs and processes.

At a lunch with the students last Friday, the students told Arthur that they had been able to register a patent to protect their technology. Furthermore, they were interested in selling their business, Davin Technologies Inc., which owns the patent and some other assets used in the development of this technology. After a week of negotiation, Arthur and the students agreed to the following:

- Rather than buying the shares of Davin, Regina would buy the assets and assume the liabilities of Davin effective January 1, Year 15.

- The purchase price would be payable as follows:

  - $400,000 on January 1, Year 15
  - $200,000 a year for three years commencing January 1, Year 16

- The students would commit to work for Regina as consultants over the next three years and would be paid $50 per hour for their services.

The condensed statement of financial position for Davin at January 1, Year 15, was as follows:

|  | Carrying Amount | Fair Value |
|---|---|---|
| Computer equipment | $ 60,000 | $70,000 |
| Patent registration costs | 50,000 | ? |
| Current assets | 100,000 | 100,000 |
|  | $210,000 | |
| Shareholders' equity | $190,000 | ? |
| Liabilities | 20,000 | 20,000 |
|  | $210,000 | |

Arthur was pleased and excited about the acquisition. He felt that it was a fair deal for both parties given that the business had not yet earned any revenue. He was particularly pleased that the students agreed to be paid over three years because he otherwise would have had to arrange a bank loan with an interest rate of 8%.

Arthur is now worried about the accounting for this acquisition because it is the first time that his company has purchased another business. Although Regina has always followed IFRS, he is wondering whether now is the time to opt for a simpler approach. In particular, he is wondering whether IFRS would allow the entire acquisition differential to be allocated to goodwill. This would keep it simple and would also avoid a charge to income over the first few years, since goodwill does not need to be amortized. If the acquisition differential is allocated to the patent, then Arthur would like to write off the patent over the maximum period of 17 years.

Arthur has asked you, a CGA, to prepare a presentation on the accounting implications for the proposed acquisition. He wants to understand how to determine the acquisition cost, how to measure the individual assets and liabilities, and how this measurement would affect profit in the first year after the date of acquisition.

### Required

Prepare the presentation slides and related speaker's notes for the presentation. Limit your presentation to five slides. Your presentation should provide recommendations related to the issues raised by Arthur. Use financial statement concepts to support your recommendations. Provide a detailed calculation to show the impact on profit for Year 15. State your assumptions.

*(CGA Canada adapted)*[6]

## Case 3-6

LO1, 2, 4

Planet Publishing Limited (Planet) is a medium-sized, privately owned Canadian company that holds exclusive Canadian distribution rights for the publications of Typset Daily Corporation (TDC). Space Communications Ltd. (Space), an unrelated privately owned Canadian company, held similar distribution rights for the publications of Worldwide Affairs Limited (WAL).

TDC and WAL were unrelated U.S. publishers of magazines and books. WAL went into receivership in early Year 3 and was then purchased by TDC. TDC did not want the exclusive rights for its publications split between two companies, and it did not believe that either Planet or Space, individually, could adequately distribute its products in Canada. In order to retain the distribution rights that otherwise would have been lost at the expiry of the contracts, Space merged with Planet on July 31, Year 3. Details regarding the merger and the restructuring that followed soon after the merger are provided in Exhibit I.

In September Year 3, the directors of Planet requested that your firm let its name be offered as auditor for the year ending February 28, Year 4. Your firm accepted the request. In prior years, two other firms audited Planet and Space. It is now October Year 3, and your firm was appointed as auditors at a shareholders' meeting. Subsequent to your appointment as auditors, the president requested a report on the following matters:

1. The accounting treatment that should be given to the merger and to the transactions that have arisen since February 28, Year 3, together with full reasons for all recommendations.

2. Any other issues (other than tax and assurance) that the president should be aware of, arising from the merger, or from recent events, together with recommendations.

The partner in charge of the engagement asked you, CPA, a manager in the firm, to prepare the draft report. You and your staff have gathered information on Planet. This information is contained in Exhibit II.

**EXHIBIT I**

*INFORMATION REGARDING THE MERGER*

1. The merger of Planet and Space took effect on July 31, Year 3, and involved these steps:

    a. Planet issued voting shares of the company to the shareholders of Space in exchange for all the outstanding shares of Space. Planet's original shareholders now own 75% of Planet's voting shares.

    b. Space was wound up.

    c. Space's offices were closed, and its operations were moved to Planet's offices. Space had a ten-year lease with four years remaining. All warehouses remained in operation.

    d. Several employees were terminated (and given two to six months' salary) or offered early retirement packages.

2. Planet retained the same year-end of February 28.

3. After the merger, Planet signed new exclusive distribution contracts with TDC and its wholly owned subsidiary, WAL. This gave Planet all the rights that had previously been assigned to Planet or to the former Space. The rights are for five years but are renewable for another five at the option of Planet. These rights include distribution of magazines, books, and videos that accompany books. TDC sells to Planet at a special discount that precludes Planet from returning any merchandise.

4. Before the merger Space had been in financial difficulty, incurring large losses over the past few years. During the merger negotiations Space and Planet approached Space's creditors with a plan to restructure Space's debt. In September Year 3, Planet had been able to finalize the restructuring of some of the debts of the former Space as follows:

    a. A trade account of US$320,000 due to TDC was converted into a two-year note payable, due in September Year 5. The note is non-interest-bearing and unsecured.

    b. Loans of $500,000 due to shareholders and accrued interest of $125,000 were converted in September Year 3 into convertible, preferred shares bearing an 8% non-cumulative dividend.

    c. One of the major shareholders forgave a loan of $110,000 in September, Year 3.

    d. Creditors who were owed $200,000 agreed to accept $0.80 on the dollar provided that they were paid before November 17, Year 3. Approximately 10% had been paid by the end of September, Year 3.

5. Under both the merger agreement and a separate contractual arrangement with Planet's banker, the shareholders of Planet were required to contribute $1.5 million of new equity into the company in August Year 3. After the funds had been deposited, the banker made the following loans:

    a. A $1 million demand loan to be secured by receivables, inventory, and a registered debenture on all unencumbered assets of Planet. In order to borrow the full $1 million, the company must maintain average balances of $1.2 million in receivables and $600,000 in inventory.

    b. A $2 million term loan on real property belonging to the original Planet, and chattels, for which the bank holds the first mortgage or a lien claim with priority over those of other creditors. The term loan is for up to two years and can be drawn upon as needed.

6. As part of the distribution agreement with TDC, Planet must provide financial statements to TDC for fiscal Year 4, Year 5, and Year 6.

7. The bank wants monthly listings of inventory, aged receivables, and cash flows. The bank loan agreement stipulates covenants that must be adhered to, including debt-to-equity ratios, no dividends on voting shares, maximum salary limits, and limits on bonuses.

**EXHIBIT II**

*INFORMATION ON PLANET*

1.  In August Year 3, Planet made the following transactions:

    a.  To diversify, Planet invested $800,000 cash in a Canadian specialist magazine. This magazine has been successful for several years, and it is expected to generate over $150,000 per year in cash flows after taxes. Planet acquired customer and advertiser lists, title to the magazine, some files, and many back issues. Six staff members from the magazine joined Planet, forming the core management and providing continuity.

    b.  Planet decided to invest about $350,000 in cash in an advertising program to attract new subscribers to the specialist magazine. The $350,000 is to be amortized over the expected subscription life of the group of new subscribers. The $350,000 was paid to an advertising agency in August Year 3. In addition, Planet and the agency have agreed that the agency will provide the equivalent of another $300,000 for a promotion campaign in exchange for free advertising space in Planet's specialist magazine. These free advertisements are expected to be published over the next six months.

        In recent years, the cost of preparing or producing a magazine published in Canada has tended to be three to four times the average subscription price. Throughout Year 3, subscriptions were offered at half price if subscribers paid in advance for three years.

2.  The sales of magazines published by TDC and other publishers account for most of Planet's (and the former Space's) business. Retail sales dollars and margins have remained constant over the past few years in this market. Retailers are generally permitted to return each month's unsold magazines to the distributor for credit against future sales.

3.  Arrangements with book stores allow them to return half of the books that they purchase, as long as the returns occur within six months of purchase. Over the past five to eight years, returns have varied considerably. Most book stores pay about 120 days after purchase.

4.  Several small book stores have gone bankrupt during the recent recession, and only some of the inventory was returned prior to bankruptcy. Minimal payments from trustees for these bankrupt stores are expected over the next three to five years.

5.  Over $400,000 had been withdrawn from Planet by the major shareholders in the two years leading to the merger. There are rumours that some minority shareholders may file a lawsuit against Planet.

6.  Before the merger, both Space and Planet engaged in various non-arm's-length transactions that were materially different from fair values. Notes to the respective financial statements mentioned that non-arm's-length transactions had occurred but did not provide any details.

7.  Planet's Year 4 financial statements will be included in documents designed to attract capital through an initial public offering in the near future. Planet wants to apply accounting standards for public enterprises.

8.  Considerable investment in subscription drives is expected over the next several months. Management wants to capitalize all expenditures and employ a 10-year amortization period.

9.  In the fiscal year ended in Year 3, about one-third of both Planet's and Space's sales came from Canadian published products and two-thirds from TDC and WAL products.

*(CPA Canada adapted)*[7]

# Case 3-7

LO1, 4

You, CPA, are employed at Beaulieu & Beauregard, Chartered Professional Accountants. On November 20, Year 3, Dominic Jones, a partner in your firm, sends you the following email:

Our firm has been reappointed auditors of Floral Impressions Ltd. (FIL) for the year ending December 31, Year 3. I met with the president and major shareholder of FIL, Liz Holtby, last week, and I toured the Vancouver warehouse and head office. I have prepared some background information on FIL for you to review, including the company's October 31, Year 3 internal non-consolidated balance sheet (Exhibit III). FIL is increasing the amount of business it does on the Internet, and Liz would like us to provide comments on the direction in which FIL is moving. I made notes on her plans for FIL's increasing use of the Internet (Exhibit IV). I also met with Craig Albertson, the controller, and I made notes from that meeting (Exhibit V).

Once you have reviewed the material, I would like you to draft a memo identifying the new accounting issues for the Year 3 audit. I would also like the memo to address Liz's specific requests.

## EXHIBIT III

### BACKGROUND INFORMATION

FIL, a small public company listed on a Canadian stock exchange, is a wholesaler of silk plants with three warehouses located in Ontario, Alberta, and British Columbia. It imports its inventory of silk flowers and accessories from Indonesia. FIL employees arrange bouquets, trees, wreaths, and decorative floral products for sale in Canada to flower shops, grocery stores, and other retailers.

The silk-plant concept was novel when FIL was incorporated 11 years ago. For the first three fiscal years, sales grew at approximately 40% per year, and FIL expanded to meet the demand. However, increased competition resulted in declining sales and operating losses over the next six years. Liz inherited the shares of the company in Year 1. She had just completed a marketing course and was very excited about becoming involved in the business and applying her new skills. The fiscal year ended December 31, Year 2, brought a return to higher sales levels and a modest net income. Liz's management contract, which was renegotiated in Year 2, provides for stock options to be granted to her each year based on the percentage increase of FIL's revenue from one year to the next. On October 31, Year 3, Liz was granted stock options for the first time. She received 4,500 stock options at $2.25 each, the market price on that date.

**FLORAL IMPRESSIONS LTD.**
**NON-CONSOLIDATED BALANCE SHEET**
(in thousands of dollars)
As at

|  | October 31, Year 3 (unaudited) | December 31, Year 2 (audited) |
|---|---|---|
| **Assets** | | |
| Current assets: | | |
| Accounts receivable | $ 2,003 | $ 1,610 |
| Inventory | 610 | 420 |
|  | 2,613 | 2,030 |
| Property, plant, and equipment | 216 | 239 |
| Computer development costs | 32 | 22 |
| Intangibles—customers list | 20 | — |
|  | $ 2,881 | $ 2,291 |
| **Liabilities** | | |
| Current liabilities: | | |
| Bank indebtedness | $ 1,850 | $ 1,520 |
| Accounts payable | 1,253 | 1,199 |
|  | 3,103 | 2,719 |

*(continued)*

### Shareholders' Equity (Deficit)

| | | |
|---|---:|---:|
| Common shares | | |
| (Year 3: 600,000; Year 2: 400,000) | 400 | 400 |
| Deficit, beginning | (828) | (417) |
| Net income | 206 | 89 |
| Deficit, end | (622) | (828) |
| | (222) | (428) |
| | $ 2,881 | $ 2,291 |

On January 15, Year 3, when shares were trading at $4 each, FIL announced an agreement with the shareholders of Rest-EZE Wreath Corporation (RWC) whereby FIL would acquire 100% of the voting shares of RWC by issuing 200,000 FIL common shares. The acquisition of RWC was completed on October 31, Year 3. The market value of FIL's shares has declined significantly since the announcement.

RWC, a small private Canadian corporation, sells funeral wreaths, made with fresh flowers, on the Internet. The suppliers, florists throughout Canada, advertise their wreath models on RWC's website, which is targeted at funeral homes and their customers. These clients order their flowers through RWC's website. RWC records 100% of the sale, invoices the clients for the same amount, and remits 85% of the proceeds to the supplier. RWC absorbs any bad debts. RWC's assets (mainly accounts receivable and office equipment) less the liabilities assumed have a fair value of $150,000, as established by an independent evaluator.

#### NOTES FROM DOMINIC JONES' CONVERSATION WITH LIZ HOLTBY

Liz believes the acquisition of RWC provides an opportunity to expand into a less cyclical market and to sell on the Internet. RWC has well-established relationships with two major funeral-home chains. Liz is excited about benefiting from RWC's website because the site fits perfectly with FIL's new direction and allows FIL to gain access to the Internet immediately. So far, the site has not generated significant new business for FIL, but Liz is confident that, with time, sales will increase. As soon as RWC's billing system allows payments by credit card, FIL also intends to link directly into RWC's accounting system to invoice its own clients. Liz anticipates that RWC will account for about 40% of FIL's consolidated revenue this year. Liz expects that the share price of FIL will increase substantially with the acquisition of RWC and plans to exercise her stock options and sell the shares acquired as soon as the share price reaches $9 or more.

To gain greater exposure on the Internet, FIL is also developing its own website. FIL will pay for the costs of running the site by selling advertising spots on the site to home decorating companies. Liz believes she can generate $80,000 in advertising revenue over a 12-month period once the site is up and running. So far, FIL has pre-sold 10 spots for $200 each. The advertisements are to run for one month. Unfortunately, the site delays have caused some advertisers to cancel their contracts. Others are threatening to cancel their contracts unless FIL gets the site up and running within the next month. The controller has recorded the advertising revenue as sales.

#### NOTES FROM DOMINIC JONES' CONVERSATION WITH CRAIG ALBERTSON

Craig Albertson was hired by FIL in September Year 3 as the controller. FIL's previous controller resigned in June Year 3 due to illness, and the position was temporarily filled by the accounts payable clerk. Craig anticipates that he will have all year-end information ready for our audit team by March 15, 2004.

Historically, FIL's sales are highest during February and March, and August to October. Accounts receivable consist of a large number of small-dollar-value accounts, with the exception of

*(continued)*

EXHIBIT V   *(continued)*

five large chain-store customers that account for approximately 40% of the total accounts receivable. The allowance for returns typically has been 1% of fourth quarter sales.

Management counts inventory at the end of each quarter and cost of goods sold is adjusted accordingly. At September 30, Year 3, inventories held at each location were as follows: 55% of the total dollar value in British Columbia, 35% in Alberta, and 10% in Ontario. By year end, Craig expects inventory at all sites to be at much lower levels. While visiting the warehouse, I observed that physical security over inventory was tight. Craig commented that FIL has never written down inventory in the past but that he estimates about 2% of the current inventory is obsolete because it is out of style.

During the year, management negotiated an operating line of credit with a new financial institution. The amount authorized is limited to 75% of accounts receivable under 90 days old and 50% of inventory, to a maximum of $2 million. The loan bears interest at prime plus 3%. Under this agreement, FIL is required to provide audited financial statements within 90 days of its fiscal year-end.

Craig did not record the investment in RWC, since the only change was in the number of common shares issued.

On October 1, Year 3, FIL purchased a customer list for $20,000 from a former competitor that was going out of business. FIL has not yet determined an amortization policy for this purchase.

Some employees and board members have questioned FIL's sudden focus on the Internet when other companies seem to be moving away from it and back to traditional sales methods. Craig raised the same concern. He doesn't understand why FIL is changing direction when the new management's marketing changes produced such good results in Year 2.

*(CPA Canada adapted)*[8]

# PROBLEMS

## Problem 3-1

LO3

The balance sheets of Abdul Co. and Lana Co. on June 30, Year 2, just before the transaction described below, were as follows:

|  | Abdul | Lana |
|---|---|---|
| Cash and receivables | $ 93,000 | $20,150 |
| Inventory | 60,500 | 8,150 |
| Plant assets (net) | 236,000 | 66,350 |
|  | $389,500 | $94,650 |
| Current liabilities | $ 65,500 | $27,600 |
| Long-term debt | 94,250 | 40,100 |
| Common shares | 140,500 | 40,050 |
| Retained earnings (deficit) | 89,250 | (13,100) |
|  | $389,500 | $94,650 |

On June 30, Year 2, Abdul Co. purchased all of Lana Co. assets and assumed all of Lana Co. liabilities for $58,000 in cash. The carrying amounts of Lana's net assets were equal to fair value except for the following:

|  | Fair Value |
|---|---|
| Inventory | $10,050 |
| Plant assets | 70,100 |
| Long-term debt | 33,800 |

**Required**

(a) Prepare the journal entries for Abdul Co. and for Lana Co. to record this transaction.

(b) Prepare the balance sheets for Abdul Co. and Lana Co. at June 30, Year 2 after recording the transaction noted above.

## Problem 3-2

LO4

The trial balances for Walla Corporation and Au Inc. at December 31, Year 4, just before the transaction described below, were as follows:

|  | Walla | Au Inc. |
|---|---|---|
| Current assets | $280,000 | $190,000 |
| Land | 600,000 | 450,000 |
| Other tangible assets | 500,000 | 270,000 |
| Liabilities | 400,000 | 310,000 |
| Common shares | 200,000 | 50,000 |
| Retained earnings, 1/1/Year 4 | 600,000 | 240,000 |
| Revenues | 800,000 | 640,000 |
| Expenses | 620,000 | 330,000 |

On December 31, Year 4, Walla purchased all of the outstanding shares of Au Inc. by issuing 20,000 common shares with a market value of $36 per share. The carrying amounts of Au Inc.'s assets and liabilities were equal to fair value except for the following:

|  | Fair Value |
|---|---|
| Land | $500,000 |
| Liabilities | 330,000 |

**Required**

What are the balances for the land, goodwill, investment in common shares, liabilities, common shares, and revenues after the transaction noted above on

(a) Walla's separate entity financial statements?

(b) Au Inc.'s separate entity financial statements?

(c) Walla's consolidated financial statements?

## Problem 3-3

**LO4, 5**

G Company is considering the takeover of K Company whereby it will issue 7,400 common shares for all of the outstanding shares of K Company. K Company will become a wholly owned subsidiary of G Company. Prior to the acquisition, G Company had 13,000 shares outstanding, which were trading at $8.00 per share. The following information has been assembled:

| | G Company | | K Company | |
|---|---|---|---|---|
| | *Carrying Amount* | *Fair Value* | *Carrying Amount* | *Fair Value* |
| Current assets | $ 47,000 | $54,500 | $ 24,000 | $16,200 |
| Plant assets (net) | 74,000 | 84,000 | 34,000 | 39,000 |
| | $121,000 | | $ 58,000 | |
| Current liabilities | $ 21,400 | 21,400 | $ 6,400 | 6,400 |
| Long-term debt | 22,000 | 26,000 | 3,900 | 4,600 |
| Common shares | 44,000 | | 24,000 | |
| Retained earnings | 33,600 | | 23,700 | |
| | $121,000 | | $ 58,000 | |

**Required**

(a) Prepare G Company's consolidated balance sheet immediately after the combination using the direct method and using
  (i) the acquisition method, and
  (ii) the new-entity method.

(b) Calculate the current ratio and debt-to-equity ratio for G Company under both methods. Explain which method shows the strongest liquidity and solvency position and which method best reflects the true financial condition of the company.

(c) Prepare G Company's consolidated balance sheet immediately after the combination using the worksheet approach and using the acquisition method.

## Problem 3-4

**LO2, 3**

Three companies, A, L, and M, whose December 31, Year 5, balance sheets appear below, have agreed to combine as at January 1, Year 6.

Each of the companies has a very small proportion of an intensely competitive market dominated by four much larger companies. In order to survive, they have decided to merge into one company. The merger agreement states that Company A will buy the assets and liabilities of each of the other two companies by issuing 27,000 common shares to Company L and 25,000 common shares to Company M, after which the two companies will be wound up.

Company A's shares are currently trading at $5 per share. Company A will incur the following costs:

| | |
|---|---|
| Costs of issuing shares | $ 8,000 |
| Professional fees | 20,000 |
| | $28,000 |

The following information has been assembled regarding the three companies:

**COMPANY A**

|  | Carrying Amount | Fair Value |
|---|---|---|
| Current assets | $ 44,400 | $102,000 |
| Plant and equipment (net) | 147,600 | 160,000 |
|  | $247,500 | |
| Liabilities | $ 80,000 | 75,000 |
| Common shares (50,000 shares) | 75,000 | |
| Retained earnings | 92,500 | |
|  | $247,500 | |

**COMPANY L**

|  | Carrying Amount | Fair Value |
|---|---|---|
| Current assets | $ 60,000 | $ 65,000 |
| Plant and equipment (net) | 93,000 | 98,000 |
|  | $153,000 | |
| Liabilities | $ 35,000 | 36,000 |
| Common shares (24,000 shares) | 48,000 | |
| Retained earnings | 70,000 | |
|  | $153,000 | |

**COMPANY M**

|  | Carrying Amount | Fair Value |
|---|---|---|
| Current assets | $ 52,000 | $ 68,000 |
| Plant and equipment (net) | 115,000 | 120,000 |
|  | $167,000 | |
| Liabilities | $ 72,000 | 70,000 |
| Common shares (33,000 shares) | 60,000 | |
| Retained earnings | 35,000 | |
|  | $167,000 | |

**Required**

Prepare the balance sheet of Company A on January 2, Year 6, after Company L and Company M have been wound up.

# Problem 3-5

LO3

The statement of financial position of Bagley Incorporated as at July 31, Year 4, is as follows:

**BAGLEY INCORPORATED**
**STATEMENT OF FINANCIAL POSITION**
At July 31, Year 4

|  | Carrying Amount | Fair Value |
|---|---|---|
| Plant and equipment—net | $ 913,000 | $1,056,000 |
| Patents | — | 81,000 |
| Current assets | 458,000 | 510,000 |
|  | $1,371,000 |  |
| Ordinary shares | $ 185,000 |  |
| Retained earnings | 517,000 |  |
| Long-term debt | 393,000 | 419,000 |
| Current liabilities | 276,000 | 276,000 |
|  | $1,371,000 |  |

On August 1, Year 4, the directors of Bagley considered a takeover offer from Davis Inc., whereby the corporation would sell all of its assets and liabilities. Davis's costs of investigation and drawing up the merger agreement would amount to $21,000.

**Required**

(a) Assume that Davis made a $1,090,600 cash payment to Bagley for its net assets. Prepare the journal entries in the accounting records of Davis to record the business combination.

(b) Assume that Davis issued 133,000 ordinary shares, with a market value of $8.20 per share, to Bagley for its net assets. Legal fees associated with issuing these shares amounted to $6,800 and were paid in cash. Davis had 153,000 shares outstanding prior to the takeover.
  (i)  Prepare the journal entries in the records of Davis to record the business combination.
  (ii) Prepare the statement of financial position of Bagley immediately after the sale.

# Problem 3-6

LO2, 4

The shareholders of Prong Company and Horn Company agreed to a statutory amalgamation under which a share exchange took place. On September 1, Year 5, Prong Company issued 60,000 ordinary shares for all of the ordinary shares of Horn Company, after which Horn Company was dissolved. The ordinary shares of Prong Company traded at $7 per share on this date. After the amalgamation, Prong Company changed its name to Pronghorn Corporation.

The statements of financial position of the two companies on August 31, Year 5, were as follows:

|  | Prong Company | Horn Company |
|---|---|---|
| Plant and equipment | $ 635,000 | $ 489,000 |
| Accumulated depreciation | (205,000) | (189,000) |
| Other assets | 41,000 | 20,000 |
| Current assets | 135,000 | 170,000 |
|  | $ 606,000 | $ 490,000 |

| | Prong Company | Horn Company |
|---|---|---|
| Ordinary shares (note 1) | $ 70,000 | $ 100,000 |
| Retained earnings | 260,000 | 200,000 |
| Long-term debt | 180,000 | 160,000 |
| Current liabilities | 96,000 | 30,000 |
| | $ 606,000 | $ 490,000 |
| Note 1: | | |
| Ordinary shares outstanding | 70,000 | 25,000 |

The carrying amounts of the net assets of both companies were equal to fair values except for plant and equipment. The fair values of plant and equipment were as follows:

| | |
|---|---|
| Prong Company | $500,000 |
| Horn Company | 280,000 |

Prong's other assets include patent registration costs with a carrying amount of $25,000. An independent appraiser placed a value of $100,000 on this patent.

**Required**

Prepare the statement of financial position of Pronghorn Corporation immediately after the statutory amalgamation.

## Problem 3-7

LO4, 5, 6

The balance sheet of Drake Enterprises as at December 31, Year 5, is as follows:

### Assets

| | |
|---|---|
| Cash | $ 99,000 |
| Accounts receivable | 143,000 |
| Inventory | 191,400 |
| Property, plant, and equipment | 1,692,000 |
| Accumulated depreciation | (900,000) |
| | $1,225,400 |

### Liabilities and Equity

| | |
|---|---|
| Current liabilities | $ 242,000 |
| Bonds payable | 352,000 |
| Common shares (100,000 shares) | 220,000 |
| Retained earnings | 411,400 |
| | $1,225,400 |

Effective January 1, Year 6, Drake proposes to issue 82,500 common shares (currently trading at $20 per share) for all of the common shares of Hanson Industries. In determining the acquisition price, the management of Drake noted that Hanson Industries has unrecorded customer service contracts and directed its accounting staff to reflect this when recording the acquisition. An independent appraiser placed a value of $150,000 on this unrecorded intangible asset. Direct costs associated with the acquisition were as follows:

| | |
|---|---|
| Costs of issuing shares | $44,000 |
| Professional fees | 38,500 |
| | $82,500 |

The balance sheet of Hanson Industries as at December 31, Year 5, is as follows:

|  | Carrying Amount | Fair Value |
|---|---|---|
| Cash | $ 55,000 | $ 55,000 |
| Accounts receivable | 275,000 | 280,500 |
| Inventory | 187,000 | 178,200 |
| Property, plant, and equipment | 1,169,000 | 1,017,500 |
| Accumulated depreciation | (300,000) | |
|  | $1,386,000 | |
|  |  |  |
| Current liabilities | $ 137,500 | 137,500 |
| Liability for warranties | 99,000 | 129,800 |
| Common shares | 660,000 | |
| Retained earnings | 489,500 | |
|  | $1,386,000 | |

Hanson Industries is to be wound up after the sale.

**Required**

(a) Assume that the shareholders of Hanson accept Drake's offer on the proposed date. Prepare Drake's January 1, Year 6, consolidated balance sheet after the proposed transaction occurred.

(b) Assume that Drake is a private entity, uses ASPE, and chooses to use the equity method to account for its investment in Hanson. Prepare Drake's January 1, Year 6, balance sheet after the proposed transaction occurred.

(c) Compare the balance sheets in parts (a) and (b). Which balance sheet shows the highest debt-to-equity ratio? Which balance sheet better reflects Drake's solvency risk? Briefly explain.

(d) Prepare Drake's consolidated balance sheet after the proposed transaction occurred using the worksheet approach.

# Problem 3-8

LO3

D Ltd. and H Corporation are both engaged in the manufacture of computers. On July 1, Year 5, they agree to a merger, whereby D will issue 300,000 shares with a current market value of $9 each for the net assets of H.

Summarized balance sheets of the two companies prior to the merger are presented below:

**BALANCE SHEET**
At June 30, Year 5

|  | D Ltd. | H Corporation | |
|---|---|---|---|
|  | Carrying Amount | Carrying Amount | Fair Value |
| Current assets | $ 450,000 | $ 500,000 | $ 510,000 |
| Non-current assets (net) | 4,950,000 | 3,200,000 | 3,500,000 |
|  | $5,400,000 | $3,700,000 | |
|  |  |  |  |
| Current liabilities | $ 600,000 | $ 800,000 | 800,000 |
| Long-term debt | 1,100,000 | 900,000 | 920,000 |
| Common shares | 2,500,000 | 500,000 | |
| Retained earnings | 1,200,000 | 1,500,000 | |
|  | $5,400,000 | $3,700,000 | |

In determining the purchase price, the management of D Ltd. noted that H Corporation leases a manufacturing facility under an operating lease that has terms that are favourable relative to market terms. However, the lease agreement explicitly prohibits transfer of the lease (through either sale or sublease). An independent appraiser placed a value of $60,000 on this favourable lease agreement.

**Required**

Prepare the July 1, Year 5, balance sheet of D, after the merger.

## Problem 3-9

LO4, 6

The July 31, Year 3, balance sheets of two companies that are parties to a business combination are as follows:

|  | Red Corp. | Sax Inc. | |
| --- | --- | --- | --- |
|  | Carrying Amount | Carrying Amount | Fair Value |
| Current assets | $1,600,000 | $ 420,000 | $468,000 |
| Property, plant, and equipment (net) | 1,080,000 | 840,000 | 972,000 |
| Patents | — | — | 72,000 |
|  | $2,680,000 | $1,260,000 | |
| Current liabilities | $1,360,000 | $ 252,000 | 252,000 |
| Long-term debt | 480,000 | 360,000 | 384,000 |
| Common shares | 720,000 | 168,000 | |
| Retained earnings | 120,000 | 480,000 | |
|  | $2,680,000 | $1,260,000 | |

In addition to the property, plant, and equipment identified above, Red Corp. attributed a value of $100,000 to Sax's assembled workforce. They have the knowledge and skill to operate Sax's manufacturing facility and are critical to the success of the operation. Although the eight manufacturing employees are not under any employment contracts, management of Red was willing to pay $100,000 as part of the purchase price on the belief that most or all of these employees would continue to work for the company.

Effective on August 1, Year 3, the shareholders of Sax accepted an offer from Red Corporation to purchase all of their common shares. Red's costs for investigating and drawing up the share purchase agreement amounted to $18,000.

**Required**

(a) Assume that Red made a $960,000 cash payment to the shareholders of Sax for 100% of their shares.
  (i) Prepare the journal entry in the records of Red to record the share acquisition.
  (ii) Prepare the consolidated balance sheet of Red Corp. as at August 1, Year 3. Explain the rationale for the accounting for the $100,000 value attributed to Sax's assembled workforce.

(b) Assume that Red issued 120,000 common shares, with a market value of $8 per share to the shareholders of Sax for 100% of their shares. Legal fees associated with issuing these shares amounted to $6,000 and were paid in cash. Red is identified as the acquirer.

(i) Prepare the journal entries in the records of Red to record the share acquisition and related fees.

(ii) Prepare the consolidated balance sheet of Red as at August 1, Year 3.

(c) Assume the same facts as part (b) expect that Red is a private company, uses ASPE, and chooses to use the cost method to account for its investment in Sax.

(i) Prepare the journal entries in the records of Red to record the share acquisition and related fees.

(ii) Prepare the balance sheet of Red as at August 1, Year 3.

## Problem 3-10

LO3

The following are summarized statements of financial position of three companies as at December 31, Year 3:

|  | Company X | Company Y | Company Z |
|---|---|---|---|
| Assets | $400,000 | $300,000 | $250,000 |
| Ordinary shares (note 1) | $ 75,000 | $ 48,000 | $ 60,000 |
| Retained earnings | 92,500 | 70,000 | 35,000 |
| Liabilities | 232,500 | 182,000 | 155,000 |
|  | $400,000 | $300,000 | $250,000 |
| Note 1: |  |  |  |
| Shares outstanding | 50,000 | 12,000 | 16,500 |

The fair values of the identifiable assets and liabilities of the three companies as at December 31, Year 3, were as follows:

|  | Company X | Company Y | Company Z |
|---|---|---|---|
| Assets | $420,000 | $350,000 | $265,000 |
| Liabilities | 233,000 | 180,000 | 162,000 |

On January 2, Year 4, Company X will purchase the assets and assume the liabilities of Company Y and Company Z. It has been agreed that Company X will issue common shares to each of the two companies as payment for their net assets as follows:

To Company Y—13,500 shares
To Company Z—12,000 shares

The shares of Company X traded at $15 on December 31, Year 3.

Company X will incur the following costs associated with this acquisition:

| Costs of registering and issuing shares | $12,000 |
|---|---|
| Other professional fees associated with the takeover | 30,000 |
|  | $42,000 |

Company Y and Company Z will be wound up after the sale.

### Required

(a) Prepare a summarized pro forma statement of financial position of Company X as at January 2, Year 4, after the purchase of net assets from Company Y and Company Z.

(b) Prepare the pro forma statements of financial position of Company Y and Company Z as at January 2, Year 4, after the sale of net assets to Company X and prior to being wound up.

## Problem 3-11

LO3

Myers Company Ltd. was formed 10 years ago by the issuance of 34,000 common shares to three shareholders. Four years later, the company went public and issued an additional 30,000 common shares.

The management of Myers is considering a takeover in which Myers would purchase all of the assets and assume all of the liabilities of Norris Inc. Two alternative proposals are being considered:

### PROPOSAL 1

Myers would offer to pay $446,400 cash for the Norris net assets, to be financed by a $446,400 bank loan due in five years. In addition, Myers would incur legal, appraisal, and finders' fees for a total cost of $6,200.

### PROPOSAL 2

Myers would issue 62,000 shares currently trading at $7.20 each for the Norris net assets. Other costs associated with the takeover would be as follows:

| | |
|---|---|
| Legal, appraisal, and finders' fees | $ 6,200 |
| Costs of issuing shares | 8,200 |
| | $14,400 |

Norris shareholders would be offered five seats on the 10-member board of directors of Myers, and the management of Norris would be absorbed into the surviving company.

Balance sheet data for the two companies prior to the combination are as follows:

| | Myers | Norris | Norris |
|---|---|---|---|
| | Carrying Amount | Carrying Amount | Fair Value |
| Cash | $ 152,000 | $ 64,500 | $ 64,500 |
| Accounts receivable | 179,200 | 73,450 | 68,200 |
| Inventory | 386,120 | 122,110 | 148,220 |
| Land | 437,000 | 87,000 | 222,000 |
| Buildings (net) | 262,505 | 33,020 | 36,020 |
| Equipment (net) | 90,945 | 29,705 | 27,945 |
| | $1,507,770 | $409,785 | |

(continued)

*(continued)*

| | Myers | Norris | Norris |
|---|---|---|---|
| | Carrying Amount | Carrying Amount | Fair Value |
| Current liabilities | $ 145,335 | $ 53,115 | 53,115 |
| Non-current liabilities | — | 162,000 | 167,000 |
| Common shares | 512,000 | 112,000 | |
| Retained earnings | 850,435 | 82,670 | |
| | $1,507,770 | $409,785 | |

## Required

(a) Prepare the journal entries of Myers for each of the two proposals being considered.

(b) Prepare the balance sheet of Myers after the takeover for each of the proposals being considered.

## Problem 3-12

### LO4

Refer to Problem 11. All of the facts and data are the same except that in the proposed takeover, Myers Company will purchase all of the outstanding common shares of Norris Inc.

## Required

(a) Prepare the journal entries of Myers for each of the two proposals being considered.

(b) Prepare the consolidated balance sheet of Myers after the takeover for each of the proposals being considered.

## Problem 3-13

### LO4

The financial statements for CAP Inc. and SAP Company for the year ended December 31, Year 5, follow:

| | CAP | SAP |
|---|---|---|
| Revenues | $ 928,000 | $ 328,000 |
| Expenses | 674,000 | 214,000 |
| Profit | $ 254,000 | $ 114,000 |
| Retained earnings, 1/1/Year 5 | $ 814,000 | $ 214,000 |
| Profit | 254,000 | 114,000 |
| Dividends paid | 104,000 | 0 |
| Retained earnings, 12/31/Year 5 | $ 964,000 | $ 328,000 |
| Equipment (net) | $ 714,000 | $ 614,000 |
| Patented technology (net) | 914,000 | 328,000 |
| Receivables and inventory | 414,000 | 184,000 |
| Cash | 94,000 | 124,000 |
| Total assets | $2,136,000 | $1,250,000 |

*(continued)*

| | CAP | SAP |
|---|---|---|
| Ordinary shares | $ 544,000 | $ 484,000 |
| Retained earnings | 978,000 | 342,000 |
| Liabilities | 614,000 | 424,000 |
| Total equities and liabilities | $2,136,000 | $1,250,000 |

On December 31, Year 5, after the above figures were prepared, CAP issued $314,000 in debt and 12,400 new shares to the owners of SAP to purchase all of the outstanding shares of that company. CAP shares had a fair value of $54 per share.

CAP also paid $37,000 to a broker for arranging the transaction. In addition, CAP paid $54,000 in stock issuance costs. SAP's equipment was actually worth $752,000 but its patented technology was valued at only $248,000.

**Required**

What are the balances for the following accounts on the Year 5 consolidated financial statements?

(a) Profit

(b) Retained earnings, 12/31/Year 5

(c) Equipment

(d) Patented technology

(e) Goodwill

(f) Ordinary shares

(g) Liabilities

## Problem 3-14

........

LO1

Z Ltd. is a public company with factories and distribution centres located throughout Canada. It has 100,000 common shares outstanding. In past years, it has reported high earnings, but in Year 5, its earnings declined substantially in part due to a loss of markets as a result of the North American Free Trade Agreement. In Year 6, it closed a large number of its manufacturing and distribution facilities and reported a substantial loss for the year.

Prior to Year 6, 70,000 of Z Ltd.'s shares were held by C Ltd., with the remaining shares being widely distributed in the hands of individual investors in Canada and the United States. On January 1, Year 6, C Ltd. sold 40,000 of its shares in Z Ltd. to W Corporation.

**Required**

(a) How should C Ltd. report its investment in Z Ltd., both before the sale of 40,000 shares and after the sale?

(b) How should W Corporation report its investment in Z Ltd.? Explain fully, and include in your answers a reference to Z Ltd.'s Year 6 loss.

# *Problem 3-15

LO7

The balance sheets of A Ltd. and B Ltd. on December 30, Year 6, are as follows:

| | A Ltd. | | B Ltd. | |
|---|---|---|---|---|
| | Carrying Amount | Fair Value | Carrying Amount | Fair Value |
| Current assets | $ 300 | $ 300 | $1,000 | $1,000 |
| Non-current assets | 1,500 | 1,700 | 2,700 | 2,800 |
| | $1,800 | | $3,700 | |
| Current liabilities | $ 400 | 400 | $ 900 | 900 |
| Long-term debt | 300 | 300 | 800 | 800 |
| Common shares—100 issued | 400 | | | |
| Common shares—60 issued | | | 600 | |
| Retained earnings | 700 | | 1,400 | |
| | $1,800 | | $3,700 | |

On December 31, Year 6, A issued 150 common shares for all 60 outstanding common shares of B. The fair value of each of B's common shares was $40 on this date.

**Required**

(a) Explain why this share issue most likely occurred.

(b) Prepare the consolidated balance sheet of A Ltd. on December 31, Year 6.

# Endnotes

1   Matt Davies, "CMA Management," *CMA Canada,* June/July 2010, pp. 14–15, with permission. Chartered Professional Accountants of Canada, Toronto, Canada. Any changes to the original material are the sole responsibility of the author (and/or publisher) and have not been reviewed or endorsed by the Chartered Professional Accountants of Canada.

2   An exception to this occurs when the acquiree applies "push-down accounting." This topic is discussed later in this chapter.

3   *Conceptual Framework for Financial Reporting,* paragraph 4.4.

4   The net income of the subsidiary earned after the acquisition date would be reduced by the amortization of the acquisition differential, because the asset values in the accounting records of the subsidiary are not the values used for consolidation. This concept will be discussed in Chapter 5.

5   It is also possible for a parent to form a less than 100%-owned subsidiary, or for a 100%-owned subsidiary to later issue shares that are not purchased by the parent. In either case, the observations made in this paragraph are basically the same.

6   Adapted from CGA Canada's FA4 Exam, September 2005, Q3, with permission. Chartered Professional Accountants of Canada, Toronto, Canada. Any changes to the original material are the sole responsibility of the author (and/or publisher) and have not been reviewed or endorsed by the Chartered Professional Accountants of Canada.

7   Adapted from *CICA UFE Report,* 1992-III-5, with permission. Chartered Professional Accountants of Canada, Toronto, Canada. Any changes to the original material are the sole responsibility of the author (and/or publisher) and have not been reviewed or endorsed by the Chartered Professional Accountants of Canada.

8   Adapted from *CICA UFE Report,* 2003-III-3, with permission. Chartered Professional Accountants of Canada, Toronto, Canada. Any changes to the original material are the sole responsibility of the author (and/or publisher) and have not been reviewed or endorsed by the Chartered Professional Accountants of Canada.

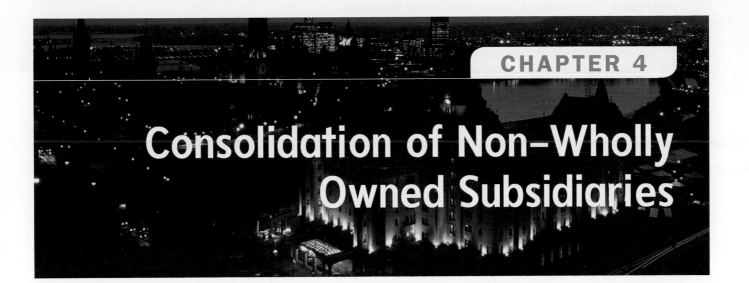

# Consolidation of Non-Wholly Owned Subsidiaries

## LEARNING OBJECTIVES

**After studying this chapter, you should be able to do the following for non–wholly owned subsidiaries at the date of acquisition:**

**LO1** Define non-controlling interest and explain how it is measured on the consolidated balance sheet.

**LO2** Prepare a consolidated balance sheet using the entity theory.

**LO3** Prepare a consolidated balance sheet using the parent company extension theory.

**LO4** Explain the concept of negative goodwill and describe how it should be treated when it arises in a business combination.

**LO5** Account for contingent consideration based on its classification as a liability or equity.

**LO6** Analyze and interpret financial statements involving consolidation of non–wholly owned subsidiaries.

**LO7** (Appendix 4A) Prepare a consolidated balance sheet using the working paper approach.

## Introduction

Financial statements published and distributed to owners, creditors, and other interested parties appear to report the operations and financial position of a single company. In reality, these statements frequently represent a number of separate organizations tied together through common control as a result of a business combination. Whenever financial statements represent more than one corporation, we refer to them as *consolidated financial statements.*

> *Consolidated financial statements report the combined results of the parent and all its subsidiaries.*

Consolidated financial statements are typical in today's business world. Most major organizations, and many smaller ones, have control over an array of organizations. For example, BMO Financial Group acquired or established 19 new subsidiaries in 2014 and owned a total of 62 subsidiaries at the end of 2014. With total assets of $589 billion and more than 46,000 employees at the end of 2014, BMO provides a broad range of retail banking, wealth management, and investment banking products and services to more than 12 million customers in Canada and around the world.[1] PepsiCo Inc., as another example, consolidates data from a multitude of companies into a single set of financial statements. By gaining control over these companies, which include, among others, Pepsi-Cola Company, Quaker Foods, and Frito-Lay, a single reporting entity is formed by PepsiCo.

The consolidation of financial information as exemplified by BMO and PepsiCo is one of the most complex procedures in all of accounting. To comprehend this process completely, the theoretical logic that underlies the creation of a business combination must be understood. Furthermore, a variety of procedural steps must be mastered to ensure that proper accounting is achieved for this single reporting entity. In Chapter 3, we introduced the preparation of a consolidated balance sheet at the date of acquisition using the acquisition method. Summarized financial statements were used to focus on the basic concepts involved. In this chapter, we elaborate on these concepts and use more detailed financial statements. We will now focus on the consolidation of non–wholly owned subsidiaries.

# LO1 NON–WHOLLY OWNED SUBSIDIARIES

In the illustrations in Chapter 3, the parent acquired 100% of the subsidiary. The parent's assets and liabilities were brought onto the consolidated balance sheet at carrying amount while the subsidiary's assets and liabilities were brought onto the consolidated balance sheet at fair value.[2] We will now consider situations where the parent acquires less than 100% of the shares. The parent's own assets and liabilities and the parent's share of the subsidiary's assets and liabilities will be measured at carrying value and fair value, respectively, on the consolidated balance sheet. Different theories will be discussed below on how to value the subsidiary's assets and liabilities.

The following example will form the basis of many of the illustrations that will be used in this chapter. We will call the two companies to be consolidated P Ltd. and S Ltd. Both companies have a June 30 fiscal year-end. The balance sheets of the two companies on June 29, Year 1, are shown in Exhibit 4.1.

**EXHIBIT 4.1**

**BALANCE SHEET**
At June 29, Year 1

|  | P Ltd. | S Ltd. | |
|---|---|---|---|
|  | **Carrying Amount** | **Carrying Amount** | **Fair Value** |
| Cash | $100,000 | $ 12,000 | $ 12,000 |
| Accounts receivable | 90,000 | 7,000 | 7,000 |
| Inventory | 130,000 | 20,000 | 22,000 |
| Plant | 280,000 | 50,000 | 59,000 |
| Patent | — | 11,000 | 10,000 |
| Total assets | $600,000 | $100,000 | $110,000 |
| Current liabilities | $ 60,000 | $ 8,000 | $ 8,000 |
| Long-term debt | 180,000 | 22,000 | 25,000 |
| Total liabilities | 240,000 | 30,000 | $ 33,000 |
| Common shares | 200,000 | 40,000 | |
| Retained earnings | 160,000 | 30,000 | |
| Total liabilities and shareholders' equity | $600,000 | $100,000 | |

*These balance sheets present the financial position just prior to the business combination.*

On June 30, Year 1, P Ltd. obtains control over S Ltd. by paying cash to the shareholders of S Ltd. for a portion of that company's outstanding common shares. No additional transactions take place on this date. Immediately after the share acquisition, P Ltd. prepares a consolidated balance sheet.

The shares not acquired by the parent are owned by other shareholders, who are referred to as the non-controlling shareholders. The value of the shares attributed to the non-controlling shareholders, when presented on the consolidated financial statements, is referred to as *non-controlling interest*, abbreviated as NCI. The non-controlling interest represents an additional set of owners who have legal claim to the subsidiary's net assets.

> *The part of the subsidiary not owned by the parent is called non-controlling interest (NCI).*

Three questions arise when preparing consolidated financial statements for less-than-100%-owned subsidiaries:

1. How should the portion of the subsidiary's assets and liabilities that was not acquired by the parent be measured on the consolidated financial statements?

2. How should NCI be measured on the consolidated financial statements?

3. How should NCI be presented on the consolidated financial statements?

The following theories have developed over time and have been proposed as solutions to preparing consolidated financial statements for non–wholly owned subsidiaries:

- Proprietary theory
- Parent company theory
- Parent company extension theory[3]
- Entity theory

> *There are many ways of measuring and presenting NCI on the consolidated financial statements.*

The entity theory is sometimes referred to as the *fair value of subsidiary as a whole method* or *full goodwill method*. The parent company extension theory is sometimes referred to as the *fair value of identifiable net assets method* or *partial goodwill method*. In this text, we will refer to the different theories by the names introduced in the previous paragraph.

Each of the theories has been or is currently required by generally accepted accounting principles (GAAP). The following table indicates the current status and effective usage dates for these four theories:

| Method | Status |
| --- | --- |
| Proprietary theory | Present GAAP for consolidating certain types of joint arrangements; was an option under GAAP prior to 2013 when consolidating joint ventures. |
| Parent company theory | Was GAAP for consolidating subsidiaries prior to January 1, 2011. |
| Parent company extension theory | An acceptable option for consolidating subsidiaries after January 1, 2011. |
| Entity theory | An acceptable option for consolidating subsidiaries after January 1, 2011. |

> *All four theories have been or now are required under Canadian GAAP under specified situations.*

The merits of these four theories are discussed in the following section.

# CONSOLIDATION THEORIES

These four theories differ in the valuation of the NCI and in how much of the subsidiary's value pertaining to the NCI is brought onto the consolidated financial statements. Exhibit 4.2 highlights the differences between the four theories. The left side for each theory shows the portion of the subsidiary owned by the parent while the right side shows the portion owned by the NCI. The shaded area represents the values brought onto the consolidated financial statements under the four different theories.

**EXHIBIT 4.2**

Consolidation Theories for Valuation of Subsidiary

| | Proprietary | | Parent Company | | Parent Company Extension | | Entity | |
|---|---|---|---|---|---|---|---|---|
| | Parent | NCI | Parent | NCI | Parent | NCI | Parent | NCI |
| Carrying amount of subsidiary's net assets | | | | | | | | |
| Fair value excess | | | | | | | | |
| Goodwill | | | | | | | | |

*The parent's portion of the subsidiary's value is fully represented under all theories. The NCI's share varies under the four theories.*

We will illustrate the preparation of consolidated financial statements under these theories using the following example. Assume that on June 30, Year 1, S Ltd. had 10,000 shares outstanding and P Ltd. purchases 8,000 shares (80%) of S Ltd. for a total cost of $72,000. P Ltd.'s journal entry to record this purchase is as follows:

| | | |
|---|---|---|
| Investment in S Ltd. | 72,000 | |
| Cash | | 72,000 |

The balance sheets of P Ltd. and S Ltd. just prior to this purchase on June 30, Year 1, were shown in Exhibit 4.1.

Proprietary theory views the consolidated entity from the standpoint of the shareholders of the parent company. The consolidated statements do not acknowledge or show the equity of the non-controlling shareholders. The consolidated balance sheet on the date of acquisition reflects only the parent's share of the assets and liabilities of the subsidiary, based on their fair values, and the resultant goodwill from the combination.

*Proprietary theory focuses solely on the parent's percentage interest in the subsidiary.*

The calculation and allocation of the acquisition differential is a useful first step in the preparation of the consolidated balance sheet. The information provided in this calculation forms the basis of the elimination and adjusting entries required. This calculation is shown in Exhibit 4.3. Goodwill is determined as part of this calculation.

**EXHIBIT 4.3**

### CALCULATION OF ACQUISITION DIFFERENTIAL
(proprietary theory)

| | | | |
|---|---|---|---|
| Cost of 80% investment in S Ltd. | | | $72,000 |
| Carrying amount of S Ltd.'s net assets: | | | |
| Assets | | 100,000 | |
| Liabilities | | (30,000) | |
| | | 70,000 | |
| P Ltd.'s ownership | | 80% | 56,000 |
| Acquisition differential | | | 16,000 |
| Allocated: | (FV − CA) × 80% | | |
| Inventory | + 2,000 × 80% = + 1,600 | | (a) |
| Plant | + 9,000 × 80% = + 7,200 | | (b) |
| Patent | − 1,000 × 80% = − 800 | | (c) |
| | | 8,000 | |
| Long-term debt | + 3,000 × 80% = +2,400 | 5,600 | (d) |
| Balance—goodwill | | $10,400 | (e) |

*The acquisition differential consists of 80% of the fair value excess plus the parent's share of the goodwill.*

Using the direct approach, the consolidated balance sheet is prepared by combining, on an item by-item basis, the carrying amounts of the parent with the *parent's share* of the fair values of the subsidiary, which is derived by using the parent's share of the carrying amount of the subsidiary plus the acquisition differential. This consolidation process is shown in Exhibit 4.4.

*Only the parent's share of the fair values of the subsidiary is brought onto the consolidated balance sheet.*

The consolidation process becomes increasingly more complex as we proceed from one chapter to the next. To make it easier to follow the consolidation adjustments, a referencing system will be adopted for Exhibit 4.4 and subsequent illustrations in the book. The references will be placed either after the account name or before the dollar figure to which they relate. The references will look something like this: (1b)—which means we are referring to item (b) in Exhibit 1 for this chapter.

Proprietary theory is not used in practice to consolidate a parent and its subsidiaries. However, it is used to report certain types of joint arrangements. This consolidation process is described as "proportionate consolidation" and will be illustrated again in Chapter 9.

Parent company theory is similar to proprietary theory in that the focus of the consolidated statements is directed toward the shareholders of the parent company. However, NCI is recognized and reflected as a liability in the consolidated balance sheet; its amount is based on the carrying amounts of the net assets of the subsidiary. Since the parent company theory is no longer used in practice, it will not be illustrated in this textbook.

*Parent company theory focuses on the parent company but gives some recognition to NCI.*

EXHIBIT 4.4

**ILLUSTRATION OF THE DIRECT APPROACH**
(proprietary theory)

**P LTD.**
**CONSOLIDATED BALANCE SHEET**
At June 30, Year 1

| | |
|---|---:|
| Cash (100,000 − 72,000* + 80% × 12,000) | $ 37,600 |
| Accounts receivable (90,000 + 80% × 7,000) | 95,600 |
| Inventory (130,000 + 80% × 20,000 + [3a] 1,600) | 147,600 |
| Plant (280,000 + 80% × 50,000 + [3b] 7,200) | 327,200 |
| Patent (0 + 80% × 11,000 − [3c] 800) | 8,000 |
| Goodwill (0 + 0 + [3e] 10,400) | 10,400 |
| | $626,400 |
| | |
| Current liabilities (60,000 + 80% × 8,000) | $ 66,400 |
| Long-term debt (180,000 + 80% × 22,000 + [3d] 2,400) | 200,000 |
| Total liabilities | 266,400 |

Shareholders' equity:

| | | |
|---|---:|---:|
| Common shares | 200,000 | |
| Retained earnings | 160,000 | 360,000 |
| | | $626,400 |

*Cash paid by P Ltd. to acquire S Ltd.

> *The consolidated amounts include 100% of the parent's carrying amount plus the parent's share of the fair value of the subsidiary's net assets.*
>
> *NCI is not recognized under the proprietary theory.*

## LO2 Entity Theory

Entity theory views the consolidated entity as having two distinct groups of shareholders—the controlling shareholders and the non-controlling shareholders. NCI is presented as a separate component of shareholders' equity on the consolidated balance sheet.

> *Entity theory gives equal attention to the controlling and non-controlling shareholders.*

In acquiring a controlling interest, a parent company becomes responsible for managing all the subsidiary's assets and liabilities, even though it may own only a partial interest. If a parent can control the business activities of its subsidiary, it directly follows that the parent is accountable to its investors and creditors for all of the subsidiary's assets, liabilities, and profits. To provide the users with a complete picture about the performance of the entity and the resources under its control, the consolidated statements should include 100% of the subsidiary's assets and liabilities. Furthermore, these assets and liabilities should be measured at full fair value at the date of acquisition, to enable users to better assess the cash-generating abilities of the identifiable net assets acquired in the business combination and the accountability of management for the resources entrusted to it.

The full fair value of the subsidiary is typically determined by combining the fair value of the controlling interest and the fair value of the NCI. Measurement of the controlling interest's fair value is straightforward in the vast majority of cases. The consideration paid by the parent typically provides the best evidence of fair value of the acquirer's interest. However, there is no parallel consideration transferred by the NCI to value the NCI. Therefore, the parent must employ other valuation techniques to estimate the fair value of the non-controlling interest at the acquisition date.

Usually, a parent can rely on readily available market trading activity to provide a fair valuation for its subsidiary's non-controlling interest. Market trading prices for the non-controlling interest's shares in the weeks before and after the acquisition provide an objective measure of their fair value. The fair value of these shares then becomes the initial basis for reporting the non-controlling interest in consolidated financial statements.

> *The trading price of the subsidiary's shares or shares of a comparable company in an active market is probably the most accurate reflection of the value of the NCI.*

Acquirers frequently must pay a premium price per share to garner sufficient shares to ensure a controlling interest. A control premium, however, typically is needed only to acquire sufficient shares to obtain a controlling interest. The remaining (non-controlling interest) shares provide no added benefit of transferring control to the new owner, and, therefore, may sell at a price less than that paid by the parent to obtain shares that provided control. Such control premiums are properly included in the fair value of the controlling interest but usually do not affect the fair values of the remaining subsidiary shares. Therefore, separate independent valuations for the controlling and non-controlling interests are typically best for measuring the total fair value of the subsidiary.

> *An investor typically pays a premium over the trading price of a company's shares when acquiring sufficient shares to obtain control of the company.*

In the absence of fair value evidence based on market trades, firms must turn to less objective measures for determining the fair value of the non-controlling interest. For example, comparable investments may be available to estimate fair value. Alternatively, valuation models based on subsidiary discounted cash flows or residual income projections can be employed to estimate the acquisition-date fair value of the non-controlling interest. Finally, if a control premium is unlikely, the consideration paid by the parent can be used to imply a fair value for the entire subsidiary. The non-controlling interest's fair value is then simply measured as its percentage of this implied subsidiary fair value. The following examples explain how NCI is measured under different scenarios under the entity theory.

> *Discounted cash flow analysis could be used to estimate the fair value of the subsidiary.*

### EXAMPLE 1    FAIR VALUE OF NON-CONTROLLING INTEREST AS EVIDENCED BY MARKET TRADES

In the majority of cases, direct evidence based on market activity in the outstanding subsidiary shares (not owned by the parent) will provide the best measure of acquisition-date fair value for the non-controlling interest. For example, assume that P Ltd. wished to acquire 8,000 of S Ltd.'s shares in order to obtain substantial synergies from the proposed acquisition. P Ltd. estimated that a 100% acquisition was not needed to extract these synergies. Also, P Ltd. projected that financing more than an 80% acquisition would be too costly.

P Ltd. then offered all of S Ltd.'s shareholders a premium price for up to 80% of the outstanding shares. To induce a sufficient number of shareholders to sell, P Ltd. needed to offer $9 per share, even though the shares had been trading in the $7.65 to $7.85 range. During the weeks following the acquisition, the 20% non-controlling interest shares in S Ltd. continued to trade in the $7.65 to $7.85 range.

In this case, the $9 per share paid by P Ltd. does not appear representative of the fair value of all the shares of S Ltd. The fact that the non-controlling interest shares continued to trade around $7.75 per share indicates a fair value for the 2,000 shares not owned by P Ltd of $15,500 ($7.75 × 2,000 shares). Therefore, the valuation of the non-controlling interest is best evidenced by the trading price of S Ltd.'s shares, not the price paid by P Ltd.

The $9 share price paid by P Ltd. nonetheless represents a negotiated value for the 8,000 shares. In the absence of any evidence to the contrary, P Ltd.'s shares have a fair value of $72,000 incorporating the additional value P Ltd. expects to extract from synergies with S Ltd. Thus, the fair value of S Ltd. as a whole is measured as the sum of the respective fair values of the controlling and non-controlling interests as follows:

| | |
|---|---|
| Fair value of controlling interest ($9 × 8,000 shares) | $72,000 |
| Fair value of non-controlling interest ($7.75 × 2,000 shares) | 15,500 |
| Total acquisition-date fair value of S Ltd. | $87,500 |

The calculation and allocation of the acquisition differential when the total fair value of the S Ltd. is $87,500 is shown in Exhibit 4.5. This schedule with separate columns for the parent and non-controlling interest should be used any time the value per share is different between the parent and non-controlling interest.

**EXHIBIT 4.5**

**CALCULATION OF ACQUISITION DIFFERENTIAL**
(entity theory—Example 1)

| | | Parent | NCI | Total |
|---|---|---|---|---|
| Percentage of S Ltd. | 80% | 20% | 100% | |
| Fair value at date of acquisition | | $ 72,000 | $15,500 | $87,500 |
| Carrying amount of S Ltd.'s net assets: | $100,000 | | | |
| Assets | (30,000) | | | |
| Liabilities | 70,000 | 56,000 | 14,000 | 70,000 |
| Acquisition differential | | 16,000 | 1,500 | 17,500 |
| Fair value excess: | FV − CA | | | |
| Inventory | 2,000 | | | |
| Plant | 9,000 | | | |
| Patent | (1,000) | | | |
| | 10,000 | | | |
| Long-term debt | 3,000 | | | |
| | 7,000 | 5,600 | 1,400 | 7,000 |
| Balance—goodwill | | $ 10,400 | $ 100 | $10,500 |

*The goodwill component as a percentage of total value is much higher for the controlling interest as compared with the non-controlling interest when a parent pays a premium to obtain control.*

**EXAMPLE 2   FAIR VALUE OF NON-CONTROLLING INTEREST IMPLIED BY PARENT'S CONSIDERATION PAID**   In some cases, the price paid by the parent on a per-share basis may reflect what would have been paid on a per-share basis for 100% of the subsidiary's shares. This is true in the following situations:

1. The parent acquired a large percentage of the acquiree's voting stock.

2. The parent's offer to buy shares was based on the value of the subsidiary as a whole.

3. The trading price of the acquiree's share just before and just after the business combination was similar to the price paid by the parent.

4. The non-controlling shareholders could use their minority shareholder rights to demand the same price per share that was paid to the other shareholders.

> *Sometimes, it is appropriate to measure NCI using the price per share paid by the parent to obtain control.*

Therefore, if there is compelling evidence that the $9 acquisition cost is representative of all of S Ltd.'s 10,000 shares, then it appears reasonable to estimate the fair value of the 20% non-controlling interest using the price paid by P Ltd. The total fair value of S Ltd. is then estimated at $90,000 and allocated as follows:

| | |
|---|---|
| Fair value of controlling interest ($9 × 8,000 shares) | $72,000 |
| Fair value of non-controlling interest ($9 × 2,000 shares) | 18,000 |
| Total acquisition-date fair value of S Ltd. | $90,000 |

Alternatively, the total fair value can be calculated using basic math by simply dividing the amount paid of $72,000 by the percentage ownership, 80% or 0.8, to get $90,000. Goodwill for the subsidiary as a whole would be valued at $13,000, as indicated in Exhibit 4.6. This schedule with only one column for the total value of the subsidiary can be used when the value per share is the same for both the parent's and non-controlling interest's investment in the subsidiary.

> *The implied value assumes that the parent's acquisition cost can be extrapolated linearly to determine the total value of the subsidiary.*

**EXHIBIT 4.6**

**CALCULATION OF ACQUISITION DIFFERENTIAL**
(entity theory—Example 2)

| | | | |
|---|---|---|---|
| Cost of 80% investment in S Ltd. | | | $72,000 |
| Implied value of 100% investment in S Ltd. ($72,000 ÷ 80%) | | | $90,000 |
| Carrying amount of S Ltd.'s net assets: | | | |
| Assets | | $100,000 | |
| Liabilities | | (30,000) | |
| | | | 70,000 |
| Implied acquisition differential | | | 20,000 |
| Allocated: | (FV − CA) × 100% | | |
| Inventory | + 2,000 × 100% = + 2,000 | | (a) |
| Plant | + 9,000 × 100% = + 9,000 | | (b) |
| Patent | − 1,000 × 100% = − 1,000 | | (c) |
| | 10,000 | | |
| Long-term debt | + 3,000 × 100% = + 3,000 | 7,000 | (d) |
| Balance—goodwill | | $13,000 | (e) |

*(continued)*

EXHIBIT 4.6   *(continued)*

| Calculation of NCI | |
| --- | --- |
| Implied value of 100% investment in S Ltd. | $90,000 |
| NCI ownership | 20% |
| | $18,000   (f) |

> *The acquisition differential consists of 100% of the fair value excess plus the implied value of total goodwill.*
>
> *NCI can be easily measured if we assume a linear relationship between percentage ownership and value of that ownership.*

A third approach for valuing the NCI is to perform an independent business valuation. This involves many assessments and assumptions relating to future cash flows, inflation rates, growth rates, discount rates, synergies between the parent and subsidiary, valuation of identifiable assets and liabilities, etc. Not only is a business valuation a very costly exercise, it also involves a lot of judgment. In some cases, the cost of determining the implied value of the subsidiary as a whole may not be worth the benefit of the information provided. If the reporting entity is unhappy or uncomfortable with the valuation of the non-controlling interest under any of the three approaches described above or any other method of valuation, it could choose to not use the entity theory.

> *NCI could be valued using business valuation techniques, but this is a costly exercise.*

We should note that the value assigned to the subsidiary as a whole will have a big impact on the value allocated to goodwill. The fair values of the identifiable assets and liabilities are usually readily available because these items (or similar items) are bought and sold quite often in the marketplace. However, goodwill is not traded in the marketplace by itself. Therefore, determining a value for goodwill is quite subjective and is directly tied to the overall value of the firm and the price paid by the parent.

Throughout this text, when the market price of the subsidiary's shares at the date of acquisition is not given, the implied value of the subsidiary as a whole will be calculated by dividing the price paid for the shares purchased by the percentage acquired. We recognize that this is an oversimplification; however, the material in this text is complex enough as is, and by keeping it simple in some cases, we may be able to see the forest rather than the multitude of trees. When the market price of the subsidiary's shares at the date of acquisition is given, we will use this price to value the NCI and then calculate the goodwill attributable to each of the controlling and non-controlling interests.

> *In this text, we will assume a linear relationship to calculate the value of NCI except when we are given the market price of the subsidiary's shares held by the non-controlling shareholders.*

Using the direct approach and the implied value of $90,000, the consolidated balance sheet is prepared by combining, on an item-by-item basis, the carrying amounts of P Ltd. with the fair values of S Ltd. The calculated goodwill is inserted as an asset, and the calculated NCI is shown in shareholders' equity. Exhibit 4.7 illustrates the preparation of the consolidated balance sheet using the direct approach.

**EXHIBIT 4.7**

### ILLUSTRATION OF THE DIRECT APPROACH
(entity theory)

**P LTD.**
**CONSOLIDATED BALANCE SHEET**
At June 30, Year 1

| | |
|---|---:|
| Cash (100,000 − 72,000* + 12,000) | $ 40,000 |
| Accounts receivable (90,000 + 7,000) | 97,000 |
| Inventory (130,000 + 20,000 + [6a] 2,000) | 152,000 |
| Plant (280,000 + 50,000 + [6b] 9,000) | 339,000 |
| Patent (0 + 11,000 − [6c] 1,000) | 10,000 |
| Goodwill (0 + 0 + [6e] 13,000) | 13,000 |
| | $651,000 |
| | |
| Current liabilities (60,000 + 8,000) | $ 68,000 |
| Long-term debt (180,000 + 22,000 + [6d] 3,000) | 205,000 |
| Total liabilities | 273,000 |
| Shareholders' equity: | |
| Controlling interest: | |
| Common shares | 200,000 |
| Retained earnings | 160,000 |
| | 360,000 |
| Non-controlling interest [6f] | 18,000 378,000 |
| | $651,000 |

*Cash paid by P Ltd. to acquire S Ltd.

> 100% of the subsidiary's fair values are brought on to the consolidated balance sheet.
>
> NCI is presented as a separate component in shareholders' equity.

The working paper used to prepare the consolidated balance sheet under the entity theory is shown in Exhibit 4A.1 in Appendix 4A.

> **Cautionary Note:** Unless otherwise noted, all of the illustrations throughout this text and in the end-of-chapter material will use the entity theory.

## LO3 PARENT COMPANY EXTENSION THEORY

Parent company extension theory was developed to address the concerns about goodwill valuation under entity theory. Given that many people feel that goodwill for the subsidiary, as a whole, is very difficult to measure when the parent does not purchase 100% of the subsidiary, they did not support the use of entity theory. However, there is much support for valuing the subsidiary's identifiable assets and liabilities at their full fair value on the consolidated statements at the time of acquisition. Parent company extension theory does just that—it values both the parent's share and the NCI's share of identifiable net assets at fair value. Only the parent's share of the subsidiary's goodwill is brought onto the consolidated statements at the value paid by the parent. Since the total value of the subsidiary's goodwill is not reasonably measurable, the NCI's portion of the subsidiary's goodwill is not measured and not brought onto the consolidated statements.

> *All of the subsidiary's value except for the NCI's share of goodwill is brought onto the consolidated balance sheet.*

Under parent company extension theory, NCI is recognized in shareholders' equity in the consolidated balance sheet, similar to entity theory. Its amount is based on the fair values of the identifiable net assets of the subsidiary; it excludes any value pertaining to the subsidiary's goodwill. NCI is calculated as follows:

| | |
|---|---:|
| Carrying amount of S Ltd.'s net assets: | |
|   Assets | $100,000 |
|   Liabilities | (30,000) |
| | 70,000 |
| Excess of fair value over carrying amount for identifiable net assets (see Exhibit 4.5) | 7,000 |
| Fair value of identifiable net assets | 77,000 |
| Non-controlling ownership percentage | 20% |
| Non-controlling interest | $ 15,400 |

> *NCI is based on the fair value of identifiable assets and liabilities.*

The consolidated balance sheet is prepared by combining, on an item-by-item basis, the carrying amount of the parent with the fair value of the subsidiary's identifiable net assets plus the parent's share of the subsidiary's goodwill. Exhibit 4.8 shows the preparation of the consolidated balance sheet under parent company extension theory. Notice that goodwill is $10,400, which is the same amount as under the proprietary theory. In both cases, it represents only the parent's portion of the subsidiary's goodwill. The non-controlling interest's share of goodwill is not reported under the parent company extension theory.

Either entity theory or parent company extension theory can be used under IFRS. It is an accounting policy choice. However, IFRS 3 does not use the term *parent company extension theory*. It simply states the following in paragraph 19:

> For each business combination, the acquirer shall measure any non-controlling interest in the acquiree either at fair value or at the non-controlling interest's proportionate share of the acquiree's identifiable net assets.

> *Either entity theory or parent company extension theory can be used under IFRS.*

See Self-Study Problem 1 for another example of preparing and comparing the consolidated balance sheet under these three theories. It shows that the values are quite different, and, in turn, the current ratio and debt-to-equity ratios are different. Also, see Self-Study Problem 2 for an illustration of the entity and parent company extension theories in a more complex situation. The problem also compares the consolidated balance sheet for a non–wholly owned subsidiary with the same data for a wholly owned subsidiary. There are a lot of similarities and only a few differences.

EXHIBIT 4.8

**ILLUSTRATION OF THE DIRECT APPROACH**
(parent company extension theory)
**P LTD.**
**CONSOLIDATED BALANCE SHEET**
At June 30, Year 1

| | |
|---|---:|
| Cash (100,000 − 72,000* + 12,000) | $ 40,000 |
| Accounts receivable (90,000 + 7,000) | 97,000 |
| Inventory (130,000 + 20,000 + **[6a] 2,000**) | 152,000 |
| Plant (280,000 + 50,000 + **[6b] 9,000**) | 339,000 |
| Patent (0 + 11,000 − **[6c] 1,000**) | 10,000 |
| Goodwill (0 + 0 + **[3e] 10,400**) | 10,400 |
| | $648,400 |
| | |
| Current liabilities (60,000 + 8,000) | $ 68,000 |
| Long-term debt (180,000 + 22,000 + **[6d] 3,000**) | 205,000 |
| Total liabilities | 273,000 |

Shareholders' equity:

| | | |
|---|---:|---:|
| Common shares | $200,000 | |
| Retained earnings | 160,000 | |
| Non-controlling interest | 15,400 | 375,400 |
| | | $648,400 |

*Cash paid by P Ltd. to acquire S Ltd.

> 100% of the subsidiary's fair values of identifiable assets and liabilities plus the parent's share of the subsidiary's goodwill are brought onto the consolidated balance sheet.
>
> NCI is presented in shareholders' equity at NCI's proportionate share of the subsidiary's fair values of the identifiable assets and liabilities.

## LO4 BARGAIN PURCHASES

In all of the business combinations in Chapter 3 and to this point in Chapter 4, the total consideration given by the controlling and non-controlling shareholders always exceeded the fair value of the identifiable net assets. Accordingly, goodwill appeared under a direct purchase of net assets on the balance sheet of the acquirer, or on the consolidated balance sheet when the parent acquired shares of the subsidiary. We will now consider situations where the total consideration given is less than the fair value of the subsidiary's identifiable net assets.

Assume that on June 30, Year 1, P Ltd. purchased 100% of the outstanding shares of S Ltd. at a total cost of $72,000. The calculation and allocation of the acquisition differential on this date is shown in Exhibit 4.9.

A business combination that results in negative goodwill is often described as a "bargain purchase." This means that the parent gained control over the subsidiary's assets and liabilities at a price that was less than the fair values of the identifiable assets and liabilities. This can occur when the subsidiary is an awkward situation and the shares are sold under conditions of a distressed sale. Or it could be that the fair value of the identifiable assets is overstated and/or the fair value of the liabilities is understated. Therefore, prior

EXHIBIT 4.9

**CALCULATION AND ALLOCATION OF ACQUISITION DIFFERENTIAL**
(negative goodwill, wholly owned subsidiary)

| | | | |
|---|---|---:|---:|
| Cost of investment in S Ltd. | | | $ 72,000 |
| Carrying amount of S Ltd.'s net assets: | | | |
| Assets | | 100,000 | |
| Liabilities | | (30,000) | 70,000 |
| Acquisition differential | | | 2,000 |
| Allocated: | | (FV − CA) | |
| Inventory | | + 2,000 | |
| Plant | | + 9,000 | |
| Patent | | − 1,000 | |
| | | 10,000 | |
| Long-term debt | | + 3,000 | 7,000 |
| Balance—"negative goodwill" (gain on bargain purchase) | | | $ (5,000) |

*Negative goodwill arises when the total consideration given is less than the fair value of identifiable net assets.*

*The negative goodwill is recognized as a gain on bargain purchase.*

to concluding that negative goodwill really does exist, IFRS 3 requires that all components of the negative goodwill calculation be reassessed to ensure that they are correct. After reassessment, if one still believes that the amount paid is less than the fair value of the identifiable net assets, a gain on purchase can be recognized. In our example, a gain of $5,000 would be recognized; it would be called a gain on bargain purchase.

*Since negative goodwill is very rare, the parent should check the valuations of the identifiable net assets before recording a gain on bargain purchase.*

To record a gain on a purchase of any asset may seem very strange. It goes against the long-standing tradition of recording assets at cost and recording gains only when realized. However, it is consistent with the general trend in financial reporting to use fair value more and more often to report assets and liabilities. Fair value is viewed as a relevant benchmark to help investors and creditors assess the success or failure of business activity. Fair value of the identifiable net assets is likely to be readily available since these assets and liabilities are usually traded on a regular basis. The cost involved in determining the fair value of the investee's assets and liabilities is more than offset by the benefits of the more relevant information. Therefore, when the acquirer pays less than the fair value of the identifiable net assets, it records a gain on purchase. It does not have to wait to sell the assets to recognize the gain. The gain is recorded on the consolidated income statement and ends up in consolidated retained earnings at the date of acquisition. If the parent company uses the equity method to account for its investment in the subsidiary, the following entry should be made in the parent's separate-entity records to record the $5,000 gain resulting from the bargain purchase:

| | | |
|---|---:|---:|
| Investment in S Ltd. | 5,000 | |
| Gain on bargain purchase of S Ltd. | | 5,000 |

This entry will result in the investment account being valued at the parent's share of the fair value of identifiable net assets of the subsidiary.

Let us now modify the situation by reducing the percentage of shares acquired in the business combination and changing the purchase price. Assume that on June 30, Year 1, P Ltd. purchased 80% of the outstanding shares of S Ltd. at a total cost of $60,000. If we used the implied value approach, the value of the subsidiary as a whole would be set at $75,000 ($60,000/0.8) and non-controlling interest would be valued at $15,000 ($75,000 − $60,000). This is less than the fair value of identifiable net assets of $77,000 and would imply negative goodwill of $2,000. Intuitively, the $2,000 gain would be split between the parent and non-controlling interest. However, IFRS 3 states that a gain on a bargain purchase can only be recognized by the acquirer. Any difference between the value assigned to the non-controlling interest and the non-controlling interest's share of the fair value of the subsidiary's identifiable net assets is attributed to the parent and is included in the overall gain on bargain purchase at the date of acquisition. The calculation and allocation of the acquisition differential on this date is shown in Exhibit 4.10.

Exhibit 4.11 illustrates the preparation of the consolidated balance sheet using the direct approach.

The working paper to prepare the consolidated balance sheet is shown in Exhibit 4A.2 in Appendix 4A.

### EXHIBIT 4.10

**CALCULATION AND ALLOCATION OF ACQUISITION DIFFERENTIAL**
(negative goodwill, non–wholly owned subsidiary)

|  |  | Parent 80% | NCI 20% | Total 100% |
|---|---|---|---|---|
| Cost of 80% investment in S Ltd. |  | $60,000 |  | $60,000 |
| Implied value of NCI (60,000/0.8 × 0.2) |  |  | $15,000 | 15,000 |
| Total implied value of subsidiary |  |  |  | 75,000 |
| Carrying amount of S Ltd.'s net assets: |  |  |  |  |
| Assets | $100,000 |  |  |  |
| Liabilities | (30,000) |  |  |  |
|  | $ 70,000 | 56,000 | 14,000 | 70,000 |
| Acquisition differential |  | 4,000 | 1,000 | 5,000 |
| Allocated: | (FV − CA) |  |  |  |
| Inventory | +$2,000 |  |  |  |
| Plant | + 9,000 |  |  |  |
| Patent | 1,000 |  |  |  |
|  | 10,000 |  |  |  |
| Long-term debt |  |  |  |  |
|  | + 3,000 |  |  |  |
|  | $7,000 | 5,600 | 1,400 | 7,000 |
| Negative goodwill before reallocation |  | 1,600 | 400 | 2,000 |
| Allocate NCI's gain to parent |  | 400 | (400) | 0 |
| Balance—"negative goodwill" (gain on bargain purchase) |  | $ 2,000 | $      0 | $ 2,000 (a) |

*Only the parent can recognize a gain on bargain purchase.*

**NEGATIVE ACQUISITION DIFFERENTIAL** It is possible for an acquisition differential to be negative. In this situation, the total consideration given would be less than the carrying amount of the subsidiary's net assets. A negative acquisition differential is not the same as negative goodwill, nor does it necessarily imply that there will be negative goodwill. If the fair values of the subsidiary's net assets are less than

EXHIBIT 4.11

**ILLUSTRATION OF THE DIRECT APPROACH**
(negative goodwill, non–wholly owned subsidiary)

**P LTD.**
**CONSOLIDATED BALANCE SHEET**
At June 30, Year 1

| | | |
|---|---|---|
| Cash (100,000 − 60,000* + 12,000) | | $ 52,000 |
| Accounts receivable (90,000 + 7,000) | | 97,000 |
| Inventory (130,000 + 20,000 + **[6a] 2,000**) | | 152,000 |
| Plant (280,000 + 50,000 + **[6b] 9,000**) | | 339,000 |
| Patent (0 + 11,000 − **[6c] 1,000**) | | 10,000 |
| | | $650,000 |
| | | |
| Current liabilities (60,000 + 8,000) | | $ 68,000 |
| Long-term debt (180,000 + 22,000 + **[6d] 3,000**) | | 205,000 |
|    Total liabilities | | 273,000 |
| Shareholders' equity: | | |
|    Common shares | $200,000 | |
|    Retained earnings (160,000 + **[10a] 2,000**) | 162,000 | |
|    Non-controlling interest | 15,000 | 377,000 |
| | | $650,000 |

*Cash paid by P Ltd. to acquire S Ltd.

> *The negative goodwill is not recognized as a separate item on the balance sheet.*
>
> *The gain on bargain purchase ends up in consolidated retained earnings.*

their carrying amounts, and if the total consideration given is greater than the fair value of the subsidiary's identifiable net assets, there will be positive goodwill.

> *A negative acquisition differential is not the same as negative goodwill.*

**SUBSIDIARY WITH GOODWILL**   The goodwill appearing on the balance sheet of a subsidiary on the date of a business combination is not carried forward when the consolidated balance sheet is prepared. At some date in the past, the subsidiary was the acquirer in a business combination and recorded the goodwill as the difference between the acquisition cost and the fair value of the identifiable net assets acquired. Now this company has itself become the acquiree. From the perspective of its new parent, the goodwill is not considered to be an identifiable asset at the time of the business combination. The acquisition differential is calculated as if the goodwill had been written off by the subsidiary, even though in fact this is not the case. The acquisition differential is allocated first to the fair value excess for identifiable net assets, and then the remaining balance goes to goodwill. In effect, the old goodwill is ignored and the acquisition cost determines the value, if any, of new goodwill at the date of acquisition. The following illustration will examine the consolidation process when the subsidiary has existing goodwill.

> *The subsidiary's goodwill arose in a previous business combination.*

Assume that on June 30, Year 1, P Ltd. purchased 80% of the outstanding shares of S Ltd. for a total cost of $62,000, paid in cash. Exhibit 4.12 shows the balance sheets of the two companies at this time.

**EXHIBIT 4.12**

**BALANCE SHEET**
At June 29, Year 1

|  | P Ltd. | S Ltd. | |
| --- | --- | --- | --- |
|  | Carrying Amount | Carrying Amount | Fair Value |
| Cash | $100,000 | $ 12,000 | $12,000 |
| Accounts receivable | 90,000 | 7,000 | 7,000 |
| Inventory | 130,000 | 20,000 | 22,000 |
| Plant | 280,000 | 50,000 | 59,000 |
| **Goodwill** | — | **11,000** | |
|  | $600,000 | $100,000 | |
| Current liabilities | $ 60,000 | $ 8,000 | 8,000 |
| Long-term debt | 180,000 | 22,000 | 25,000 |
| Common shares | 200,000 | 40,000 | |
| Retained earnings | 160,000 | 30,000 | |
|  | $600,000 | $100,000 | |

*The goodwill on the subsidiary's books (it is old goodwill) will be remeasured on the date of acquisition.*

Note that the goodwill (highlighted in boldface) of $11,000 was called a patent in Exhibit 4.1. When we calculate and allocate the acquisition differential in this illustration, the result is positive goodwill of $10,500, as shown in Exhibit 4.13.

**EXHIBIT 4.13**

**CALCULATION AND ALLOCATION OF ACQUISITION DIFFERENTIAL**
(subsidiary with goodwill)

| | | | | |
| --- | --- | --- | --- | --- |
| Cost of 80% investment in S Ltd. | | | $62,000 | |
| Implied value of 100% investment in S Ltd. | (62,000/0.80) | | $77,500 | |
| Carrying amount of S Ltd.'s net assets | | | | |
|   Assets | | $100,000 | | |
|   Liabilities | | (30,000) | | |
| | | 70,000 | | |
| Deduct old goodwill of S Ltd. | | 11,000 | | |
|   Adjusted net assets | | | 59,000 | |
| Acquisition differential | | | 18,500 | |
| Allocated: | (FV − CA) | | | |
|   Inventory | +$2,000 | | | **(b)** |
|   Plant | +9,000 | | | **(c)** |
| | 11,000 | | | |
|   Long-term debt | +3,000 | | 8,000 | **(d)** |
| Balance—goodwill | | | $10,500 | **(e)** |

*(continued)*

**EXHIBIT 4.13**  (continued)

<table>
<tr><td colspan="2" align="center">**Calculation of NCI**</td></tr>
<tr><td>Implied value of 100% investment in S Ltd.</td><td>$77,500</td></tr>
<tr><td>NCI ownership</td><td>20%</td></tr>
<tr><td></td><td>$15,500  **(f)**</td></tr>
</table>

> *The subsidiary's goodwill is now worth $10,500, based on the recent price paid by the parent.*
>
> *The subsidiary's goodwill was revalued at the date of acquisition. It is now worth $10,500, based on the recent price paid by the parent.*

The preparation of the June 30, Year 1, consolidated balance sheet using the direct approach is presented in Exhibit 4.14, and the working paper approach is presented in Exhibit A4.3 in Appendix 4A.

**EXHIBIT 4.14**

**ILLUSTRATION OF THE DIRECT APPROACH**
(subsidiary with goodwill)
**P LTD.**
**CONSOLIDATED BALANCE SHEET**
At June 30, Year 1

| | |
|---|---|
| Cash (100,000 − 62,000* + 12,000) | $ 50,000 |
| Accounts receivable (90,000 + 7,000) | 97,000 |
| Inventory (130,000 + 20,000 + **[13b] 2,000**) | 152,000 |
| Plant (280,000 + 50,000 + **[13c] 9,000**) | 339,000 |
| Goodwill (0 + 11,000 − **[13a] 11,000** + **[13e] 10,500**) | 10,500 |
| | $648,500 |
| | |
| Current liabilities (60,000 + 8,000) | $ 68,000 |
| Long-term debt (180,000 + 22,000 + **[13d] 3,000**) | 205,000 |
| Common shares | 200,000 |
| Retained earnings | 160,000 |
| Non-controlling interest **[13f]** | 15,500 |
| | $648,500 |

*Cash paid by P Ltd. to acquire S Ltd.

> *The direct approach produces the same results as the working paper approach but appears to be easier to perform.*

## LO5 CONTINGENT CONSIDERATION

The terms of a business combination may require an additional cash payment, or an additional share issue contingent on some specified future event. The accounting for contingent consideration is contained in IFRS 3. The material that follows illustrates the concepts involved.

Contingent consideration should be measured at fair value at the date of acquisition. To do so, the parent should assess the amount expected to be paid in the future under different scenarios, assign probabilities as to the likelihood of the scenarios occurring, derive an expected value of the likely amount to be paid, and use a discount rate to derive the value of the expected payment in today's dollars. This is all very subjective and involves a lot of judgment.

---

*Contingent consideration should be recorded at the date of acquisition at its expected value.*

---

The contingent consideration will be classified as either a liability or equity depending on its nature. If the contingent consideration will be paid in the form of cash, another asset or a variable number of shares to produce a fixed dollar amount, it will be classified as a liability. If issuing a fixed number of shares will satisfy the contingent consideration, it will be classified as equity. After the initial recognition, the contingent consideration classified as equity will not be remeasured.

After the acquisition date, the fair value of a contingent consideration classified as a liability may change due to changes in circumstances, such as meeting specified sales targets, fluctuations in share price, or subsequent events, such as receiving government approval on an in-process research and development project. Changes in the fair value of a contingent consideration classified as a liability due to changes in circumstances since the acquisition date should be recognized in earnings. Changes in the fair value of a contingent consideration due to gathering of new information about facts and circumstances that existed at the acquisition date and within a maximum of one year subsequent to the acquisition date would be considered as an adjustment of the acquisition cost.

Given the uncertainty involved, the following should be disclosed regarding contingent consideration:

- The amount of contingent consideration recognized on the acquisition date.

- A description of the arrangement and the basis for determining the amount of the payment.

- An estimate of the range of outcomes (undiscounted) or, if a range cannot be estimated, that fact and the reasons why a range cannot be estimated. If the maximum amount of the payment is unlimited, the acquirer shall disclose that fact.

---

*The range of potential payment for contingent consideration should be disclosed.*

---

The following discussions illustrate the two types of contingent consideration discussed above.

**CONTINGENT CONSIDERATION CLASSIFIED AS A LIABILITY**    If the contingency is classified as a liability, any consideration issued at some future date is recorded at fair value and the change in fair value is recognized in net income. The following example will illustrate this situation.

---

*Changes in contingent consideration classified as a liability are reported in net income.*

---

Able Corporation issues 500,000 common shares for all of the outstanding common shares of Baker Company on January 1, Year 4. The shares issued have a fair value of $10 at that time. The business combination agreement has an *earnout clause* that states the following: If the earnings of Baker Company exceed an average of $1.75 per share over the next two years, Able Corporation will make an additional cash payment of $600,000 to the former shareholders of Baker Company on January 1, Year 6. Able predicts that there is a 30% probability that Baker's average earnings over Years 4 and 5 will be less than $1.75 per share and a 70% probability that it will be greater than $1.75 per share. The probability-adjusted expected payment is $420,000 (30% × $0 + 70% × $600,000). Using a discount rate of 7%, the fair value of the contingent consideration at January 1, Year 1, is $366,844 ($420,000/1.07$^2$). Able's journal entry on January 1, Year 4, is as follows:

| | | |
|---|---|---|
| Investment in Baker Company | 5,366,844 | |
| Common shares | | 5,000,000 |
| Liability for contingent consideration | | 366,844 |

> *The expected value incorporates the probability of payments being made.*

The consolidated financial statements at January 1, Year 4 would be prepared using the $5,366,844 acquisition cost. This amount is allocated to the identifiable net assets of Baker Company in the usual manner and may result in goodwill, or "negative goodwill." If at the end of Year 4, the probability assessment has not changed, the undiscounted probability-adjusted expected payment remains at $420,000; but the present value is now $392,523 ($420,000/1.07), an increase of $25,679 since the beginning of the year. Able's journal entry at December 31, Year 4, is as follows:

| | | |
|---|---|---|
| Interest expense | 25,679 | |
| Liability for contingent consideration | | 25,679 |

> *The likelihood of having to make an additional payment should be reassessed and the liability remeasured, if necessary, at the end of each reporting period.*

If at the end of the two-year period it is determined that Baker's earnings exceeded the average of $1.75 per share, the change in contingent consideration will be recorded by Able on December 31, Year 5, as follows:

| | | |
|---|---|---|
| Liability for contingent consideration | 392,523 | |
| Interest expense (392,523 × 0.07) | 27,477 | |
| Loss from contingent consideration | 180,000 | |
| Liability for contingent consideration | | 600,000 |

If Baker did not exceed the earnings level and Able does not have to pay the contingent consideration, Able would make the following journal entry at December 31, Year 5:

| | | |
|---|---|---|
| Liability for contingent consideration | 392,523 | |
| Interest expense (392,523 × 0.07) | 27,477 | |
| Gain from contingent consideration | | 420,000 |

> *Each period, the liability is increased by the amount of interest accruing on the liability.*

Now assume that instead of the earnout clause described above, the purchase agreement states that if the market price of Able's shares is below $10 one year from the date of the agreement, Able will issue additional shares to the former shareholders of Baker in an amount that will compensate them for their loss in value. Able predicts that there is a 25% probability that Able's shares will be trading at $9 per share and a 75% probability that they will be trading at greater than $10 per share. If the shares are trading at $9 per share, Able will have to issue additional shares worth $500,000 (500,000 × [$10 − $9]). The probability-adjusted expected payment is $125,000 (25% × $500,000 + 75% × $0). Using a discount rate of 7%, the fair value of the contingent consideration at January 1, Year 4, is $116,822 ($125,000/1.07). The $116,822 would be added to the acquisition cost of the investment and the following entry would be made at the date of acquisition:

| | | |
|---|---|---|
| Investment in Baker Company | 5,116,822 | |
| Common shares | | 5,000,000 |
| Liability for contingent consideration | | 116,822 |

Any changes to the fair value of this contingent consideration would be recognized in net income in a similar fashion to the contingency for the earnout.

See the last half of Exhibit 3.7 for an interesting example of contingent consideration payable by Amaya Inc., the largest poker business in the world.

**CONTINGENT CONSIDERATION CLASSIFIED AS EQUITY**   If the contingency is classified as equity, any consideration issued at some future date will be recorded at fair value, but will not be considered an additional cost of the purchase. Instead, the consideration issued will be recognized but offset by a reduction in the amount recorded for the original share issue. Therefore, no amount will be set up for the contingent consideration at the date of acquisition. The following example illustrates this point.

Alpha Corporation issues 500,000 common shares for all the outstanding common shares of Beta Company on July 1, Year 1. If the shares issued have a fair market value of $5 per share, Alpha's journal entry is as follows:

| | | |
|---|---|---|
| Investment in Beta Company | 2,500,000 | |
| Common shares | | 2,500,000 |

The purchase agreement states that if the market price of Alpha's shares is below $5 one year from the date of the agreement, Alpha will issue 50,000 additional shares to the former shareholders of Beta as some compensation for their loss in value. What these additional shares will be worth at that time is unknown. Although there is some compensation for a loss in value, the exact amount of the compensation is unknown and will vary with the market value of the shares. On July 1, Year 2, the market price of Alpha's shares is $4.50. In accordance with the agreement, Alpha Corporation issues an additional 50,000 shares and records the transaction as follows:

| | | |
|---|---|---|
| Common shares—old shares | 225,000 | |
| Common shares—new shares (50,000 × 4.50) | | 225,000 |

> *The additional shares compensates for the loss in value for shares originally issued as consideration for the purchase.*

Alternatively, Alpha could simply make a memorandum entry to indicate that 50,000 additional shares were issued for no consideration. Footnote disclosure in the Year 2 statements will be made for the amount of and reasons for the consideration and the accounting treatment used.

**DISCLOSURE REQUIREMENTS**   IFRS 3 paragraph B64 requires that a reporting entity disclose the following for each business combination in which the acquirer holds less than 100% of the equity interests in the acquiree at the acquisition date:

(a) The amount of the NCI in the acquiree recognized at the acquisition date and the measurement basis for that amount.

(b) For each NCI in an acquiree measured at fair value, the valuation techniques and key model inputs used for determining that value.

> *Companies must disclose the value for NCI at the date of acquisition and how it was measured.*

Lundin Mining Corporation is a diversified Canadian base metals mining company. The company operates mines in Portugal, Sweden, Spain, and the United States. It has equity interests in mines and/or refineries in Chile, Congo, and Finland. The extracts in Exhibit 4.15 are taken from Lundin's 2014 consolidated financial statements.

**EXHIBIT 4.15**

# Extracts from Lundin Mining Corporation's 2014 Financial Statements

## 3. BUSINESS COMBINATIONS

### a) Candelaria acquisition

On November 3, 2014 the Company acquired 80% of Compañia Contractual Minera Candelaria S.A. and Compañia Contractual Minera Ojos del Salado S.A. copper mining operations and supporting infrastructure ("Candelaria Acquisition") from Freeport-McMoRan Inc. ("Freeport" or "FCX"). Total cash consideration paid was $1,852 million, consisting of a $1,800 million base purchase price plus $52 million for cash and non-cash working capital and other agreed adjustments. In addition, contingent consideration of up to $200 million is also payable and calculated as 5% of net copper revenue in any annual period over the next five years if the realized average copper price exceeds $4 per pound. The remaining 20% ownership stake continues to be held by Sumitomo Metal Mining Co., Ltd and Sumitomo Corporation. The Candelaria Acquisition was funded by a $1,000 million senior secured note financing, a US$601.5 million (C$674 million) subscription receipt equity financing and a $648 million upfront payment under the stream agreement with a subsidiary of Franco-Nevad Corporation ("Franco Nevada") (Note 14). The Company also repaid its existing $250 million term loan with the proceeds from the financings.

The purchase price is as follows:

| | |
|---|---:|
| Cash consideration | $1,851,759 |
| Cash acquired | (104,386) |
| Contingent consideration | 8,100 |
| Purchase price | $1,755,473 |

The fair value of the contingent consideration was calculated using a valuation method technique which involved determining probabilities for future copper prices. This liability has been recorded in other long-term liabilities.

| Assets acquired and liabilities assumed: | |
|---|---:|
| Trade and other receivables | $ 207,741 |
| Income taxes receivable | 8,549 |
| Inventories | 156,996 |
| Long-term inventory | 147,934 |
| Other assets | 6,485 |
| Deferred tax assets | 2,611 |
| Mineral properties, plant and equipment | 2,159,828 |
| Goodwill | 108,845 |
| Total assets | $2,798,989 |
| Trade and other payables | $117,633 |
| Current portion of reclamation and other closure provisions | 5,482 |
| Reclamation and other closure provisions | 94,629 |
| Deferred tax liabilities | 388,018 |
| Total liabilities | 605,762 |
| Non-controlling interests | 437,754 |
| Total assets acquired and liabilities assumed, net | $1,755,473 |

In accordance with the acquisition method of accounting, the purchase price has been allocated to the underlying assets acquired and liabilities assumed based primarily upon their estimated fair values at the date of acquisition. The purchase price allocation is preliminary subject to final tax analysis.

We primarily used a discounted cash flow model (net present value of expected future cash flows) to determine the fair value of the mineral interests and long-term inventory, and used a replacement cost approach in determining

*(continued)*

the fair values of real property, plant and equipment. Expected future cash flows are based on estimates of projected revenues, production costs, capital expenditures and expected conversions of resources to reserves based on the life of mine plan as at the acquisition date.

The excess of the purchase price over the net identifiable assets acquired represents goodwill. The goodwill recognized primarily represents future mineral resource development potential. The goodwill is not expected to be deductible for income tax purposes.

The Company used the proportionate method in measuring non-controlling interest at the acquisition date. Total proceeds received and funds used:

| | |
|---|---:|
| Common share issuance, net proceeds | $ 579,293 |
| Senior secured notes, net proceeds | 978,302 |
| Stream agreement, net proceeds | 632,064 |
| Total proceeds received | $2,189,659 |
| Purchase price | $1,851,759 |
| Term loan repayment, including accrued interest | 250,101 |
| Acquisition related fees | 25,706 |
| General corporate purposes | 62,093 |
| Total funds used | $2,189,659 |

Acquisition related fees are recorded in the consolidated statement of earnings as a business development cost (Note 20).

The revenue included in the consolidated statement of earnings since November 3, 2014 contributed by Candelaria was $215.2 million. The net earnings were $17.1 million for the same period.

If Candelaria had been consolidated from January 1, 2014, the consolidated statement of earnings would show pro forma sales of $1,767.5 million and net earnings of $235.6 million.

*Source: LUNDIN MINING, Management's Discussion and Analysis for the Year Ended December 31, 2014, pages 18–20. Reproduced with permission from Lundin Mining Corporation.*

---

*Lundin uses the parent company extension theory to account for its business combination.*

*Lundin expensed the acquisition related costs in the year of acquisition.*

---

## LO6 ANALYSIS AND INTERPRETATION OF FINANCIAL STATEMENTS

Exhibit 4.16 presents consolidated balance sheets, the current ratio, and the debt-to-equity ratio for the three theories illustrated in this chapter.

Note the following from Exhibit 4.16:

- Goodwill is the same under the proprietary theory and parent company extension theory.

- All accounts are the same under the entity theory and parent company extension theory except for goodwill and non-controlling interest. Under the parent company extension theory, the non-controlling interest's share of the subsidiary's goodwill is not included on the consolidated balance sheet.

- The current ratio is lowest and therefore the liquidity position looks the worst under the proprietary theory.

- The debt-to-equity ratio is lowest, and therefore the solvency position looks the best under entity theory. This could affect whether the company is in compliance with covenants for lending agreements.

- Financial analysts need to be aware of accounting policy choices and may need to make adjustments to companies' financial statements to make the financial statements truly comparable from one company to another.

**EXHIBIT 4.16**

## Impact of Consolidation Theories on Current and Debt-to-Equity Ratios

**P LTD.**
**CONSOLIDATED BALANCE SHEET**
At June 30, Year 1

|  | Proprietary (Exhibit 4.4) | Entity (Exhibit 4.7) | Parent Company Extension (Exhibit 4.8) |
|---|---|---|---|
| Cash | $ 37,600 | $ 40,000 | $ 40,000 |
| Accounts receivable | 95,600 | 97,000 | 97,000 |
| Inventory | 147,600 | 152,000 | 152,000 |
| Current assets | 280,800 | 289,000 | 289,000 |
| Plant | 327,200 | 339,000 | 339,000 |
| Patent | 8,000 | 10,000 | 10,000 |
| Goodwill | 10,400 | 13,000 | 10,400 |
|  | $626,400 | $651,000 | $648,400 |
| Current liabilities | $ 66,400 | $ 68,000 | $ 68,000 |
| Long-term debt | 200,000 | 205,000 | 205,000 |
| Total liabilities | 266,400 | 273,000 | 273,000 |
| Common shares | 200,000 | 200,000 | 200,000 |
| Retained earnings | 160,000 | 160,000 | 160,000 |
| Non-controlling interest |  | 18,000 | 15,400 |
| Shareholders' equity | 360,000 | 378,000 | 375,400 |
|  | $626,400 | $651,000 | $648,400 |
| Current ratio | 4.23 | 4.25 | 4.25 |
| Debt-to-equity ratio | 0.74 | 0.72 | 0.73 |

> *The key ratios are different under the different reporting methods.*
>
> *The value and classification of NCI is significantly different under the three theories.*
>
> *The classification of non-controlling interest has a big impact on the debt-to-equity ratio.*

## ASPE Differences

As mentioned in Chapter 3, private companies can either consolidate their subsidiaries or report their investments in subsidiaries under the cost method or the equity method, or at fair value if they would otherwise have chosen the cost method and the equity securities of the investee are quoted in an active market.

# SUMMARY

A consolidated balance sheet presents the combined financial position of the parent and subsidiaries. The portion of the subsidiary not owned by the parent is called the non-controlling interest. It is measured at the non-controlling interest's proportionate share of the fair value of the subsidiary's assets and liabilities at the date of acquisition and is presented as a separate component of shareholders' equity. **(LO1)**

Under the entity theory, all of the subsidiary's assets and liabilities including goodwill are fully included on the consolidated balance sheet and measured at fair value. **(LO2)** Under the parent company extension theory, only the parent's share of the subsidiary's goodwill is reported on the consolidated balance sheet. Non-controlling interest is measured at the non-controlling interest's proportionate share of the fair value of the subsidiary's *identifiable* net assets, which excludes goodwill. **(LO3)**

When the total consideration given is less than the fair value of the subsidiary's identifiable net assets, a gain on bargain purchase is reported on the consolidated income statement. When a subsidiary has goodwill on its separate-entity balance sheet, this goodwill is eliminated on consolidation and replaced by the goodwill inherent in the parent's purchase of the subsidiary. **(LO4)**

When the terms of a business combination require an additional payment contingent on some specified future event, the fair value of the contingent consideration should be estimated and recorded as part of the acquisition cost at the date of acquisition. **(LO5)**

The values reported on the consolidated financial statements for assets, liabilities, and shareholder's equity will differ depending on the consolidation theory used to prepare the statements. Either the entity theory or the parent company extension theory must be used under IFRS. Users of the financial statements will need to be aware of the different consolidation policies as they assess the profitability, liquidity, and solvency of the reporting entity. **(LO6)**

## Self-Study Problem 1

LO1, 6

On December 31, Year 1, CAN Company (CAN) takes control over the net assets of UKS Company (UKS) by purchasing 80% of the ordinary shares of UKS. CAN paid for the purchase by issuing ordinary shares with a market value of $35,200. The following information has been assembled:

|  | **CAN Company** | **UKS Company** | |
|---|---|---|---|
|  | Carrying Amount | Carrying Amount | Fair Value |
| Plant assets | $ 80,000 | $20,000 | $26,000 |
| Goodwill | 0 | 0 | 22,000 |
| Current assets | 50,000 | 15,000 | 14,000 |
|  | $130,000 | $35,000 | $62,000 |
|  |  |  |  |
| Shareholders' equity | $ 75,000 | $18,000 |  |
| Long-term debt | 25,000 | 7,000 | $ 8,000 |
| Current liabilities | 30,000 | 10,000 | 10,000 |
|  | $130,000 | $35,000 |  |

**Required**

(a) Prepare a consolidated statement of financial position for CAN and calculate the current and debt-to-equity ratios immediately after the combination under

   (i) proprietary theory,

   (ii) parent company extension theory, and

   (iii) entity theory.

(b) Which theory shows the better liquidity position, and which theory shows the best solvency position? Briefly explain.

(c) Which theory best portrays the economic value of the subsidiary? Briefly explain.

## Solution to Self-Study Problem 1

(a)

**CAN COMPANY**
**CONSOLIDATED BALANCE SHEET**
At December 31, Year 1

|  | Proprietary | Parent Company Extension | Entity |
|---|---|---|---|
| **See notes below:** | (a.i) | (a.ii) | (a.iii) |
| Plant assets | $100,800 | $106,000 | $106,000 |
| Goodwill | 17,600 | 17,600 | 22,000 |
| Current assets | 61,200 | 64,000 | 64,000 |
|  | $179,600 | $187,600 | $192,000 |
| Shareholders' equity: |  |  |  |
|   Controlling interest | $110,200 | $110,200 | $110,200 |
|   Non-controlling interest |  | 4,400 | 8,800 |
| Long-term debt | 31,400 | 33,000 | 33,000 |
| Current liabilities | 38,000 | 40,000 | 40,000 |
|  | $179,600 | $187,600 | $192,000 |
| Current ratio | 1.611 | 1.600 | 1.600 |
| Debt-to-equity ratio | 0.63 | 0.64 | 0.61 |

(b) Proprietary theory shows the best liquidity position because its current ratio is higher than the other theories. Entity theory shows the best solvency position because its debt-to-equity ratio is lower than the other theories. Both the debt and equity are higher under entity theory. However, the increase in equity is proportionately greater than the increase in debt.

(c) In the opinion of the author of this text, fair values are better measures of the economic value of assets and liabilities than historical cost-based values. If so, entity theory best reflects the true economic value of the subsidiary. All of the subsidiaries' identifiable assets and liabilities are reported at fair value, and the full value of the subsidiary's goodwill is included in the consolidated financial statements.

**Notes:**

  1. The assets and liabilities are calculated as follows:

    (a.i) Carrying amounts for CAN and 80% of fair values for UKS

    (a.ii) Carrying amounts for CAN and carrying amounts for UKS plus 100% of fair value excess for UKS's identifiable assets and liabilities plus 80% of the value of UKS's goodwill

(a.iii) Carrying amounts for CAN and carrying amounts for UKS plus 100% of fair value excess for UKS's identifiable assets and liabilities plus 100% of the value of UKS's goodwill

2. The non-controlling interest is calculated as follows:

(a.ii)  20% × fair value of UKS's identifiable assets and liabilities

(a.iii) 20% × **fair value** of UKS's identifiable assets, identifiable liabilities, and goodwill

## Self-Study Problem 2

LO4, 5

On December 31, Year 1, the condensed balance sheets for ONT Limited and NB Inc. were as follows:

|  | ONT | NB |
|---|---|---|
| **Assets:** | | |
| Cash | $ 44,000 | $ 80,000 |
| Accounts receivable | 480,000 | 420,000 |
| Inventories | 650,000 | 540,000 |
| Property, plant, and equipment | 2,610,000 | 870,000 |
| Accumulated depreciation | (1,270,000) | (130,000) |
| | $2,514,000 | $1,780,000 |
| | | |
| **Liabilities:** | | |
| Current liabilities | $ 660,000 | $ 560,000 |
| Bonds payable | 820,000 | 490,000 |
| | 1,480,000 | 1,050,000 |
| | | |
| **Shareholders' equity:** | | |
| Ordinary shares | 200,000 | 400,000 |
| Retained earnings | 834,000 | 330,000 |
| | 1,034,000 | 730,000 |
| | $2,514,000 | $1,780,000 |

The fair value of all of NB's assets and liabilities were equal to their carrying amounts except for the following:

| Asset | Carrying Amount | Fair Value |
|---|---|---|
| Inventories | $540,000 | $570,000 |
| Property, plant, and equipment | 740,000 | 790,000 |
| Bonds payable | 490,000 | 550,000 |

## Required

(a) Assume that on January 1, Year 2, ONT acquired 70% of NB's ordinary shares by issuing new ordinary shares with a fair value of $700,000. This was the only transaction on this day.

  (i) Prepare the journal entry on ONT's book to record the purchase of NB's ordinary shares.

  (ii) Prepare a schedule to calculate and allocate the acquisition differential.

  (iii) Prepare a consolidated balance sheet for ONT and its subsidiary at January 1, Year 2, after recording the purchase of NB's ordinary shares.

(b) In Self-Study Problem 2 in Chapter 3, the same set of data was presented except that ONT acquired 100% of NB's ordinary shares for $1,000,000. What are the similarities and differences between the balance sheet above and the balance from part (b) in Self-Study Problem 2 in Chapter 3?

(c) Calculate goodwill and non-controlling interest on the consolidated balance sheet on January 1, Year 2, under the parent company extension theory.

## Solution to Self-Study Problem 2

(a) (i)

| | | |
|---|---:|---:|
| Investment in NB | 700,000 | |
| Common shares | | 700,000 (a) |

(ii)

| | | |
|---|---:|---:|
| Cost of ONT's 70% investment in NB | | $ 700,000 |
| Implied value of 100% investment in NB (700,000/0.70) | | $1,000,000 (b) |
| Carrying amount of NB's net assets: | | |
| Assets | $1,780,000 | |
| Liabilities | (1,050,000) | 730,000 |
| Acquisition differential | | 270,000 |
| Allocated as follows: | | |
| Inventories (570,000 − 540,000) | $ 30,000 | (c) |
| Property, plant, and equipment (790,000 − 740,000) | 50,000 | (d) |
| Bonds payable (550,000 − 490,000) | (60,000) (e) | 20,000 |
| Balance—goodwill | | $ 250,000 (f) |
| Non-controlling interest (30% × [b] 1,000,000) | | $ 300,000 (g) |

(iii)

**ONT LIMITED**
Consolidated Balance Sheet
January 1, Year 2

| | |
|---|---:|
| Assets: | |
| Cash (44,000 + 80,000) | $ 124,000 |
| Accounts receivable (480,000 + 420,000) | 900,000 |
| Inventories (650,000 + 540,000 + [c] 30,000) | 1,220,000 |
| Property, plant, and equipment (2,610,000 + 870,000 − 130,000* + [d] 50,000) | 3,400,000 |
| Accumulated depreciation (1,270,000 + 130,000 − 130,000*) | (1,270,000) |
| Goodwill [f] | 250,000 |
| | $4,624,000 |
| Liabilities: | |
| Current liabilities (660,000 + 560,000) | $1,220,000 |
| Bonds payable (820,000 + 490,000 + [e] 60,000) | 1,370,000 |
| | 2,590,000 |
| Shareholders' equity: | |
| Common shares (200,000 + [a] 700,000) | 900,000 |
| Retained earnings | 834,000 |
| Non-controlling interest [g] | 300,000 |
| | 2,034,000 |
| | $4,624,000 |

*Eliminates NB's accumulated depreciation.

(b) The balance sheets are exactly the same except for shareholders' equity. The assets and liabilities are exactly the same because the implied value of the subsidiary as a whole is $1,000,000 in both cases. In Chapter 3, the purchase price was $1,000,000 for 100% of the subsidiary. In

Chapter 4, the parent paid $700,000 for 70%, which produces an implied value of $1,000,000 for the subsidiary as a whole. The difference between the total value of $1,000,000 and the purchase price of $700,000 for 70% is attributed to non-controlling interest. Therefore, consolidated common shares are $300,000 less and NCI is $300,000 more when the parent only acquired 70% of the subsidiary

| (c) | Goodwill under entity theory | $250,000 |
| | Less: NCI's share (30%) | 75,000 |
| | Goodwill under parent company extension theory | $175,000 |
| | | |
| | NCI under entity theory | $300,000 |
| | Less: NCI's share of goodwill (30%) | 75,000 |
| | NCI under parent company extension theory | $225,000 |

# APPENDIX 4A

## Working Paper Approach for Consolidation of Non–Wholly Owned Subsidiaries

**LO7**

In this chapter, we illustrated the direct approach for preparing a consolidated balance sheet for non–wholly owned subsidiaries at the date of acquisition. We considered three different theories of consolidations, bargain purchases, and subsidiaries with goodwill on their own balance sheet. We will now illustrate the working paper approach using the same examples.

A number of methods can be used to prepare consolidation working papers at the date of acquisition. All methods must result in identical consolidated amounts. Our approach is to prepare adjusting entries to eliminate the investment account, establish non-controlling interest, and allocate the acquisition differential to appropriate accounts. The entries are supported by the same calculations and schedules used under the direct approach.

### Entity Theory

Exhibit 4A.1 shows the preparation of the consolidated balance sheet when P Ltd. acquires 80% of the common shares of S Ltd. for $72,000. P Ltd. uses the entity theory and thereby reports 100% of the fair value of the S Ltd.'s goodwill on the consolidated balance sheet. To compare it with the direct approach, see Exhibit 4.7.

Three working paper entries are used. Entry **(1)** establishes the NCI on the consolidated balance sheet and adds this additional value to the investment account, which would then include both the parent's and NCI proportionate interest in the subsidiary. Entry **(2)** eliminates the investment account and the subsidiary's shareholders' equity accounts with the difference established as the acquisition differential. Entry **(3)** allocates the acquisition differential to revalue the identifiable net assets of the subsidiary to fair value, and establishes the resulting goodwill.

EXHIBIT 4A.1

**P LTD.**
**CONSOLIDATED BALANCE SHEET WORKING PAPER**
(entity theory)

| | P Ltd. | S Ltd. | Adjustments and Eliminations Dr. | Cr. | Consolidated Balance Sheet |
|---|---|---|---|---|---|
| Cash | $ 28,000 | $ 12,000 | | | $ 40,000 |
| Accounts receivable | 90,000 | 7,000 | | | 97,000 |
| Inventory | 130,000 | 20,000 | (3) $ 2,000 | | 152,000 |
| Plant | 280,000 | 50,000 | (3) 9,000 | | 339,000 |
| Patent | | 11,000 | | (3) $ 1,000 | 10,000 |
| Investment in S Ltd. | 72,000 | | (1) 18,000 | (2) 90,000 | |
| Acquisition differential | | | (2) 20,000 | (3) 20,000 | |
| Goodwill | | | (3) 13,000 | | 13,000 |
| | $600,000 | $100,000 | | | $651,000 |
| Current liabilities | $ 60,000 | $ 8,000 | | | $ 68,000 |
| Long-term debt | 180,000 | 22,000 | | (3) 3,000 | 205,000 |
| Common shares | 200,000 | | | | 200,000 |
| Retained earnings | 160,000 | | | | 160,000 |
| Common shares | | 40,000 | (2) 40,000 | | |
| Retained earnings | | 30,000 | (2) 30,000 | | |
| Non-controlling interest | | | | (1) 18,000 | 18,000 |
| | $600,000 | $100,000 | $132,000 | $132,000 | $651,000 |

> *The subsidiary's assets and liabilities are brought onto the consolidated balance sheet at 100% of their fair values.*
>
> *NCI is presented as a component of shareholders' equity on the consolidated balance sheet.*

The three working paper elimination entries are as follows:

| (1) Investment in S Ltd. | 18,000 | |
|---|---|---|
| Non-controlling interest | | 18,000 |
| (2) Common shares—S Ltd. | 40,000 | |
| Retained earnings—S Ltd. | 30,000 | |
| Acquisition differential | 20,000 | |
| Investment in S Ltd. | | 90,000 |
| (3) Inventory—S Ltd. | 2,000 | |
| Plant—S Ltd. | 9,000 | |
| Goodwill—S Ltd. | 13,000 | |
| Patent—S Ltd. | | 1,000 |
| Long-term debt—S Ltd. | | 3,000 |
| Acquisition differential | | 20,000 |

> *The first two entries establish NCI and the acquisition differential.*
>
> *The implied acquisition differential is allocated to identifiable assets and liabilities and goodwill.*

It must be emphasized again that these worksheet entries are made only in the working paper; they are *not* entered in the accounting records of either P Ltd. or S Ltd.

## Bargain Purchase

Exhibit 4A.2 shows the preparation of the consolidated balance sheet when P Ltd. acquires 80% of the common shares of S Ltd. for $60,000. This results in negative goodwill, which is reported as a gain on bargain purchase. To compare it with the direct approach, see Exhibit 4.11.

Three working paper entries are used. Entry **(1)** establishes the NCI on the consolidated balance sheet and adds this additional value to the investment account, which would then include both the parent's and NCI proportionate interest in the subsidiary. Entry **(2)** eliminates the investment account and the subsidiary's shareholders' equity accounts with the difference established as the acquisition differential. Entry **(3)** allocates the acquisition differential to revalue the identifiable net assets of the subsidiary to fair value, and establishes the resulting gain on purchase.

**EXHIBIT 4A.2**

**P LTD.**
**CONSOLIDATED BALANCE SHEET WORKING PAPER**
(bargain purchase, non–wholly owned subsidiary)

| | P Ltd. | S Ltd. | Adjustments and Eliminations Dr. | Adjustments and Eliminations Cr. | Consolidated Balance Sheet |
|---|---|---|---|---|---|
| Cash | $ 40,000 | $12,000 | | | $ 52,000 |
| Accounts receivable | 90,000 | 7,000 | | | 97,000 |
| Inventory | 130,000 | 20,000 | **(3)** 2,000 | | 152,000 |
| Plant | 280,000 | 50,000 | **(3)** 9,000 | | 339,000 |
| Patent | | 11,000 | | **(3)** $ 1,000 | 10,000 |
| Investment in S Ltd. | 60,000 | | **(1)** 15,000 | **(2)** 75,000 | |
| Acquisition differential | — | — | **(2)** 5,000 | **(3)** 5,000 | — |
| | $600,000 | $100,000 | | | $650,000 |
| Current liabilities | $ 60,000 | $ 8,000 | | | $ 68,000 |
| Long-term debt | 180,000 | 22,000 | | **(3)** 3,000 | 205,000 |
| Common shares | 200,000 | | | | 200,000 |
| Retained earnings | 160,000 | | | **(3)** 2,000 | 162,000 |
| Common shares | | 40,000 | **(2)** 40,000 | | |
| Retained earnings | | 30,000 | **(2)** 30,000 | | |
| Non-controlling interest | | | | **(1)** 15,000 | 15,000 |
| | $600,000 | $100,000 | $101,000 | $101,000 | $650,000 |

> The subsidiary's identifiable assets and liabilities are measured at fair value on the consolidated balance sheet.
>
> The gain from the bargain purchase is recorded in income and ends up in consolidated retained earnings on the date of acquisition.

The three working paper elimination entries are as follows:

| | | | |
|---|---|---|---|
| (1) | Investment in S Ltd. | 15,000 | |
| | Non-controlling interest | | 15,000 |
| (2) | Common shares—S Ltd. | 40,000 | |
| | Retained earnings—S Ltd. | 30,000 | |
| | Acquisition differential | 5,000 | |
| | Investment in S Ltd. | | 75,000 |
| (3) | Inventory—S Ltd. | 2,000 | |
| | Plant—S Ltd. | 9,000 | |
| | Patent—S Ltd. | | 1,000 |
| | Long-term debt—S Ltd. | | 3,000 |
| | Retained earnings (gain on bargain purchase) | | 2,000 |
| | Acquisition differential | | 5,000 |

**SUBSIDIARY WITH GOODWILL**    Exhibit 4A.3 shows the preparation of the consolidated balance sheet when S Ltd. had goodwill on its own balance sheet. P Ltd. pays $62,000 for 80% of the common shares of S Ltd. This results in goodwill of $10,500 on the consolidated balance sheet. To compare it with the direct approach, see Exhibit 4.14.

Four working paper entries are required. Entry **(1)** writes off the previous goodwill (labelled "old" goodwill in the working paper) to S Ltd.'s retained earnings for purposes of consolidation. Entry **(2)** establishes the NCI on the consolidated balance sheet with the offsetting amount going to Investment in S Ltd. Entry **(3)** eliminates the subsidiary's common shares and adjusted retained earnings and the parent's investment account, and establishes the difference as the acquisition differential. Entry **(4)** allocates the acquisition differential to revalue the net assets of the subsidiary, and establishes the new goodwill from the business combination.

The four working paper elimination entries are shown below:

| | | | |
|---|---|---|---|
| (1) | Retained earnings—S Ltd. | 11,000 | |
| | Goodwill—old: S Ltd. | | 11,000 |
| (2) | Investment in S Ltd. | 15,500 | |
| | NCI | | 15,500 |
| (3) | Common shares—S Ltd. | 40,000 | |
| | Retained earnings—S Ltd. (30,000 − 11,000) | 19,000 | |
| | Acquisition differential | 18,500 | |
| | Investment in S Ltd. | | 77,500 |
| (4) | Inventory—S Ltd. | 2,000 | |
| | Plant—S Ltd. | 9,000 | |
| | Goodwill—S Ltd. | 10,500 | |
| | Long-term debt—S Ltd. | | 3,000 |
| | Acquisition differential | | 18,500 |

> *These worksheet entries establish the appropriate account balances for the consolidated balance sheet.*

**EXHIBIT 4A.3**

**P LTD.**
**CONSOLIDATED BALANCE SHEET WORKING PAPER**
At June 30, Year 1

| | P Ltd. | S Ltd. | Adjustments and Eliminations Dr. | | Adjustments and Eliminations Cr. | | Consolidated Balance Sheet |
|---|---|---|---|---|---|---|---|
| Cash | $ 38,000 | $ 12,000 | | | | | $ 50,000 |
| Accounts receivable | 90,000 | 7,000 | | | | | 97,000 |
| Inventory | 130,000 | 20,000 | **(4)** $ | 2,000 | | | 152,000 |
| Plant | 280,000 | 50,000 | **(4)** | 9,000 | | | 339,000 |
| Goodwill—old | | 11,000 | | | **(1)** $ | 11,000 | |
| Investment in S Ltd. | 62,000 | | **(2)** | 15,500 | **(3)** | 77,500 | |
| Acquisition differential | | | **(3)** | 18,500 | **(4)** | 18,500 | |
| Goodwill | | | **(4)** | 10,500 | | | 10,500 |
| | $600,000 | $100,000 | | | | | $648,500 |
| | | | | | | | |
| Current liabilities | $ 60,000 | $ 8,000 | | | | | $ 68,000 |
| Long-term debt | 180,000 | 22,000 | | | **(4)** | 3,000 | 205,000 |
| Common shares | 200,000 | | | | | | 200,000 |
| Retained earnings | 160,000 | | | | | | 160,000 |
| Common shares | | 40,000 | **(3)** | 40,000 | | | |
| Retained earnings | | 30,000 | **(1)** | 11,000 | | | |
| | | | **(3)** | 19,000 | | | |
| NCI | | | | | **(2)** | 15,500 | 15,500 |
| | $600,000 | $100,000 | $ | 125,500 | $ | 125,500 | $648,500 |

*The revalued goodwill appears on the consolidated balance sheet.*

*The working paper approach produces the same results as the direct approach.*

All entries were working paper entries and were not recorded in the records of S Ltd. Since S Ltd. does not write off its goodwill in its separate-entity records, the preparation of consolidated statements in Year 2 and all future years will require working paper entries to write off any goodwill that still exists in S Ltd.'s records, and to reverse goodwill impairment that has been recorded.

# SUMMARY OF APPENDIX 4A

A working paper can be used to help prepare the consolidated statements, and is necessary if there are a large number of subsidiaries to consolidate. The preparation of the consolidated worksheet at the date of acquisition involves establishing the non-controlling interest (NCI), eliminating the parent's investment account, eliminating the subsidiary's shareholders' equity accounts, and allocating the acquisition differential. **(LO7)**

## Review Questions

*Questions, cases, and problems that deal with the appendix material are denoted with an asterisk.*

LO4    **1.** Is a negative acquisition differential the same as negative goodwill? Explain.

LO1,    **2.** With respect to the valuation of non-controlling interest, what are the major differences
2, 3        among proprietary, parent company extension, and entity theories?

LO4    **3.** How is the goodwill appearing on the statement of financial position of a subsidiary prior
to a business combination treated in the subsequent preparation of consolidated statements? Explain.

LO2    **4.** Under the entity theory and when using the implied value approach, consolidated goodwill is determined by inference. Describe how this is achieved, and comment on its shortcomings.

LO1,    **5.** What is non-controlling interest, and where is it reported in the consolidated balance sheet
2, 3        under the parent company extension and entity theories?

LO3    **6.** What accounts on the consolidated balance sheet differ in value between entity theory and parent company extension theory? Briefly explain why they differ.

LO5    **7.** What is contingent consideration, and how is it measured at the date of acquisition?

LO5    **8.** Explain how changes in the fair value of contingent consideration should be reported, assuming that the contingent consideration will be paid in the form of cash.

LO6    **9.** What reporting options related to business combinations are available to private companies?

LO4    **10.** What is negative goodwill, and how is it accounted for?

LO4    **11.** Explain whether the historical cost principle is applied when accounting for negative goodwill.

LO2    **12.** How is the net income earned by a subsidiary in the year of acquisition incorporated in the consolidated income statement?

LO7* **13.** In whose accounting records are the consolidation elimination entries recorded? Explain.

LO2    **14.** Don Ltd. purchased 80% of the outstanding shares of Gunn Ltd. Before the purchase, Gunn had a deferred charge of $10.5 million on its balance sheet. This item consisted of organization costs that were being amortized over a 20-year period. What amount should be reported in Don's consolidated statements with respect to this deferred charge? Explain briefly.

LO2    **15.** How would the consolidation of a parent-founded subsidiary differ from the consolidation of a purchased subsidiary?

# CASES

## Case 4-1

LO1, 2, 3

On December 31, Year 7, Maple Company issued preferred shares with a fair value of $1,200,000 to acquire 24,000 (60%) of the common shares of Leafs Limited. The Leafs shares were trading in the market at around $40 per share just days prior to and just after the purchase by Maple. Maple had to and was willing to pay a premium of $10 per share, or $240,000 in total, in order to gain control over Leafs. The balance sheets for the two companies just prior to acquisition were as follows (in 000s):

| | Maple | | Leafs | |
|---|---|---|---|---|
| | Carrying Amount | Fair Value | Carrying Amount | Fair Value |
| Identifiable assets | $4,000 | $5,000 | $2,000 | $2,000 |
| Goodwill | 0 | ?? | 0 | ?? |
| | $4,000 | | $2,000 | |
| Liabilities | $3,000 | 3,200 | $1,600 | 1,680 |
| Shareholders' equity | 1,000 | ?? | 400 | ?? |
| | $4,000 | | $2,000 | |

Consolidated financial statements will be prepared to combine the financial statements for the two companies. The management of Maple is concerned about the valuation of goodwill on the consolidated financial statements. It was willing to pay a premium of $240,000 to gain control of Leafs. It maintains that it would have paid the same premium in total whether it acquired 60% or 100% of the shares of Leafs.

Given that the return on assets is a closely monitored ratio by the shareholders, the management of Maple would like to minimize the value assigned to goodwill on consolidation. Management wants to see how the consolidated balance sheet would differ under three different theories of reporting: proprietary, parent company extension, and entity. Management also has the following questions when reporting this business combination:

- How will we determine the value of the goodwill for the subsidiary?

- How will this affect the valuation of NCI?

- Will we have to revalue the subsidiary's assets and liabilities every year when we prepare the consolidated financial statements?

- Which consolidation theory best reflects the economic reality of the business combination?

**Required**

Prepare a consolidated balance sheet at the date of acquisition under the three theories, and respond to the questions asked by management.

## Case 4-2

.........

LO2

Eternal Rest Limited (ERL) is a public company; its shares are traded on a stock exchange in Canada. ERL operates both funeral homes and cemeteries in Canada. Funeral services (casket, flowers, cemetery stone, prayer service) are sold on an "as needed" basis and also "in advance" (prepaid). ERL recognizes revenue only as the funeral services are performed.

Cemetery land is purchased years in advance, and carrying costs (e.g., interest and property taxes) are capitalized. The company sells burial plots or gravesites in advance, or on an "as needed" basis. Revenues from plots sold in advance are recognized upon signing a contract, regardless of the timing of receipt of cash. The cost of maintenance for 100 years is recognized as an expense of earning revenue. By law, funds for maintenance are sent to a trustee, for investment. Funds are allowed to be withdrawn annually for current maintenance costs. The cost of the cemetery land and land improvements (including trees, fencing, and pathways) is allocated to cost of sales.

As a result of acquisitions, ERL tripled its assets in fiscal Year 5. Effective September 1, Year 4, ERL acquired the assets and liabilities of Tranquil Cemeteries Limited (Tranquil) by issuing common shares and debt. ERL also acquired, effective November 1, Year 4, 70% of the voting common shares of Peaceful Cemeteries Limited (Peaceful) in exchange for $1 million cash (borrowed from ERL's banker) plus common shares of ERL. Peaceful was privately owned by a single shareholder before the purchase of its shares by ERL. The common shares of ERL that were issued with respect to the acquisitions have been escrowed and may not be sold for one year from their issuance date.

You, a CPA, are a new manager with a CPA firm. Your firm was appointed as the auditor of ERL in September Year 4, for the year ending June 30, Year 5. Your firm was also appointed as the auditor of Peaceful.

It is now September Year 5. Your firm has experienced severe staffing shortages. The partner has advised you that because of the recent departure of another manager, you have been assigned to the ERL and Peaceful engagements. The audit fieldwork has been completed, but the file review has not taken place. The partner has asked you to review the audit files and notes prepared by the senior in charge of the engagements and to prepare a memo that provides your analysis and disposition of the accounting issues.

The following information was assembled from your review of the working papers of ERL and Peaceful.

1. The acquisition of Tranquil's net assets resulted in the following additions to ERL's balance sheet as at September 1, Year 4 (in thousands of dollars):

| | |
|---|---:|
| Working capital | $ 850 |
| Land | 1,400 |
| Buildings and equipment, net | 3,700 |
| Non-competition agreements | 3,000 |
| Goodwill | 11,250 |
| Total net assets of Tranquil | $20,200 |

The $20.2 million was paid as follows:

| | |
|---|---:|
| 5-year non-interest-bearing first mortgage bonds of ERL | $18,150 |
| Common shares of ERL, escrowed for one year | 2,050 |
| | $20,200 |

The auditors read the purchase and sale agreement and noted that $820,000 of the working capital represented funds that were being held in trust for future maintenance of the cemetery lands. The new common shares issued by ERL were measured at the market price on the day prior to the signing of the agreement.

The $3 million paid for non-competition agreements represents a payment to the sellers of Tranquil in exchange for their commitment not to engage in the same type of business for five years. The $3 million represents the otherwise expected earnings of the sellers, discounted at the 9% market rate of interest that prevailed at the time. The $1.4 million and $3.7 million assigned to land, buildings, and equipment represent management's estimates of the fair values of these assets and coincide with carrying amounts on Tranquil's books.

2. The shares of Peaceful were acquired primarily because the company had non-capital loss carry-forwards for income tax purposes. The purchase price for the acquisition was a $1 million cash payment by ERL plus the issuance of $24 million of ERL shares for the 70% ownership. The acquisition cost was allocated to assets and liabilities in a manner similar to the allocation for the Tranquil acquisition. The auditors did not request that the estimated value of the loss carry-forward be recorded. ERL attributed $4 million to non-competition agreements (to be amortized over five years) and $14 million to goodwill.

3. After the acquisition of Peaceful by ERL, sufficient business was directed to Peaceful to commence the process of utilizing the tax loss carry-forwards. During fiscal Year 5, the benefit realized from the utilization of the loss carry-forwards amounted to $2.36 million and was recognized as a gain on the income statement.

4. Excess cemetery land (acquired in the purchase of Tranquil) was sold in December Year 4 at a gain of $1.2 million. The proceeds were reported as "other revenue."

5. One working paper entitled "Land" contains the following note: "Land recorded on the books at $2,305,600 and called 'Sunset Hill' is undeveloped and is not scheduled for use until Year 8 or Year 9. It is subject to a Year 5 government order requiring that ERL clear up environmental concerns on the site. I asked one employee what the cost would be and was told 'half a million dollars.' No amount was accrued because of uncertainty."

6. A working paper entitled "Management Compensation" shows that senior management shares in what is called a "Bonus Pool." The bonus is 15% of income before income taxes.

*(CPA Canada adapted)*[4]

# Case 4-3

..........

## LO2

Factory Optical Distributors (FOD) is a publicly held manufacturer and distributor of high-quality eyeglass lenses located in Burnaby, British Columbia. For the past 10 years, the company has sold its lenses on a wholesale basis to optical shops across Canada. Beginning in Year 3, the company began to offer franchise opportunities to opticians wanting to sell only FOD lenses.

The franchise agreements contain the following stipulations:

- Each franchise must be a corporation. FOD (Burnaby) will purchase 35% of the corporation's outstanding common shares and the franchisee will hold the remaining 65%. No other equity instruments can be issued.

- Franchises can be established in new locations or in existing locations under the name Factory Optical Distributors. If a new building is required, FOD (Burnaby) will guarantee the mortgage to ensure that the best interest rates can be obtained. If an existing location is used, it must be renovated to meet company specifications, and again FOD (Burnaby) will guarantee any required financing.

- To qualify as a franchisee, an individual must be a licensed optician and must commit to 40 hours a week in the franchise location, managing the day-to-day activities.

- Franchisees are to be paid a salary that does not exceed 1.5 times the industry average for opticians with equivalent experience.

- The franchise agreement specifies that only FOD lenses can be sold in franchise locations. FOD lenses can be purchased by franchisees at 20% below normal selling price for the first $500,000 of purchases and at 25% below normal selling price if purchases exceed $500,000 on an annual basis.

- The agreement also requires that frames sold by the franchisee be purchased from designated suppliers, to ensure the best quality and fit to FOD lenses.

- All franchise advertising must be approved by FOD (Burnaby). Franchisees must allocate 1% of revenue to advertising each month.

- The franchisee is required to participate in special promotions and seasonal sales as determined by FOD (Burnaby).

- A franchise fee of 2% of sales is payable monthly to FOD (Burnaby).

- Other products and services can be sold from the franchise location provided that they do not negatively impact the sale of FOD lenses.

During Year 5, eight franchise agreements were signed in locations across Canada. At December 31, Year 5, the company's year-end, five of these locations were open for business.

It is now January Year 6. You are the senior auditor on the FOD (Burnaby) account. The company's corporate controller has come to you with the franchise agreement to discuss how FOD must report its share ownership in the five operating franchises. She has heard that the definition of control in IFRS 10 encompasses some situations where 50% share ownership does not exist.

### Required

Examine the details of the franchise agreement. Do you think FOD controls the franchise operations? Would consolidation be required? Explain.

*(Adapted from a case prepared by J.C. Thatcher, Lakehead University, and Margaret Forbes, University of Saskatchewan)*

## Case 4-4

........

LO2

When Valero Energy Corp. acquired Ultramar Diamond Shamrock Corp. (UDS) for US$6 billion, it created the second-largest refiner of petroleum products in North America, with over 23,000 employees in the United States and Canada, total assets of $10 billion, and combined revenues of $32 billion. Combined, it had 13 refineries with a total throughput capacity of just under 2 million barrels per day (BPD); it also became one of the continent's largest retailers, with more than 5,000 retail outlets in the United States and Canada. The Canadian operations of UDS continued to operate under the Ultramar brand.

It was announced that the combination of Valero's complex refining system and an extensive UDS refining, logistics, and retail network created synergies and strategic benefits that would result in cost savings of approximately $200 million per year and the enhanced ability to compete effectively in a rapidly consolidating industry.

The retail assets included in the acquisition were the brands Ultramar, Diamond Shamrock, Beacon, and Total. UDS had more than 2,500 company-owned sites in the United States and Canada, and also supplied 2,500 dealer, truck stop, and cardlock sites. The company-owned stores had extensive brand support programs such as proprietary consumer and fleet credit cards, radio and television brand support, and strong in-store marketing programs, to which Valero was able to add its 350-store retail network in California. In addition, UDS operated one of the largest home heating oil businesses in North America, selling heating oil to approximately 250,000 households.

The acquisition clearly included more than the physical assets of Ultramar Diamond Shamrock. A variety of unrecorded intangible assets were represented in the portfolio of assets held by UDS, and these are the matters that require your attention at this time.

### Required

With reference to IFRS 3, prepare a memorandum including the following items to the chief financial officer of Valero:

- Discuss the valuation of the various intangible assets included in this acquisition.

- Indicate which items should be included in the amount assigned to goodwill in the acquisition.

- Indicate which items should be separately identified as intangible assets.

- Discuss how you would measure the various items identified and what amortization policy (if any) is appropriate.

*(Case prepared by Peter Secord, St. Mary's University)*

## Case 4-5

LO2

Lauder Adventures Limited (LAL) was incorporated over 40 years ago as an amusement park and golf course. Over time, a nearby city has grown to the point where it borders on LAL's properties. In recent years LAL's owners, who are all members of one family, have seen LAL's land values increase significantly. LAL's majority shareholder, Hassan Poosti, owns 55% of the outstanding shares and is not active in LAL's day-to-day activities.

Last year, Hassan hired a new chief executive officer, Leo Titan. Leo has a reputation for being an aggressive risk taker. Hassan is committed, and has the personal financial resources required, to support Leo's plans.

Eight months ago, LAL became the successful bidder for a new sports franchise, in conjunction with a minority partner. Under the terms of the franchise agreement, LAL is required to build a sports arena, which is currently being constructed. The arena is being built on a section of the amusement park. Another section of the amusement park is being relocated to ensure that the entrances to the arena are close to public transportation and parking. Consequently, some of the rides will be relocated. LAL is the sole owner of the arena at present.

The sports franchise is separately incorporated as Northern Sports Limited (NSL); LAL holds 75% of the shares in the company. Another bid is being prepared by NSL to obtain a second sports franchise so that the arena can be used more often. NSL will be required to lease space from LAL when the arena is completed, in about 22 months.

For the first two sports seasons, NSL will have to lease arena space from Aggressive Limited (AL). During this time, NSL does not expect to be profitable because

- it may take time to build a competitive team;

- AL is charging a high rent, and it is not giving NSL a share of concession (hot dogs, drinks) revenue;

- AL cannot make the better dates (e.g., Saturday night) available to NSL to attract sports fans; and

- as a newcomer to the league, NSL is restricted with regard to the players who are available to it and the days of the week it can play in its home city.

Consequently, NSL has arranged to borrow funds from LAL and from others to finance costs and losses.

Your employer, Fabio & Fox, Chartered Professional Accountants, has conducted the audit of LAL for several years. LAL has tended to be marginally profitable one year and then have losses the next year. The company has continued to operate because the directors know that the real estate holdings were becoming increasingly valuable.

Leo is expected to oversee the expanded accounting and finance functions in the company. He has met with you and the partner in charge of the LAL audit and discussed various issues related to the year ending September 30, Year 8. His comments are provided in Exhibit I.

It is September 5, Year 8. You have been asked by the partner to prepare a report for him, which will be used for the next meeting with Leo. He would like you to discuss the accounting issues related to your discussion with Leo. The partner wants a thorough analysis of all important issues as well as support for your position. LAL has been and wishes to continue using IFRS.

In your review of documents, and as a result of various conversations, you have learned the following:

1. The arena will be mortgaged, but only for about 50% of its expected cost. Lenders are concerned about the special-use nature of the arena and whether it will be successfully rented for other events such as concerts.

2. The mortgage lenders to LAL and the non-controlling shareholders in NSL are both expected to want to see appraisals and financial statements before deciding whether to invest. Covenants will be required by the lenders to ensure that excessive expenditures are not undertaken and that cash is preserved.

3. Leo does not intend to consolidate NSL until it is profitable. The investment in NSL will be reported on LAL's financial statements at cost. Thus, LAL's financial statements will also be used for income tax purposes.

4. LAL's non-controlling shareholders are not active in the business and want quarterly financial statements in order to monitor progress and assess Leo's performance. The non-controlling shareholders have all expressed concern over Leo's growth strategy over the past year. Most are relying on LAL to supplement their income.

**EXHIBIT I**

## Notes from Discussion with Leo Titan

1. In order to build a road to the arena's parking lot, two holes of the 18-hole golf course will be relocated next spring. Costs of $140,000 are expected to be incurred this year in design, tree planting, ground preparation, and grass seeding in order to ready the area for next spring. These costs are to be capitalized as part of the golf course lands, along with related property taxes of $13,000 and interest of $15,000.

2. In May Year 8, LAL acquired, for $4.25 million, all of the shares of an amusement park in a different city when its land lease expired. The amusement park company was wound up and the equipment, rides, concessions, and other assets are being transported to LAL at a cost of $350,000. The estimated fair value of the assets and liabilities (according to Leo) is as follows:

*(continued)*

**EXHIBIT I**

| | |
|---|---:|
| Concession prizes (e.g., stuffed animals) | $ 22,500 |
| Rides and games | 4,200,000 |
| Equipment and parts | 1,650,000 |
| Electrical supplies | 75,000 |
| Lighting and signs | 100,000 |
| Estimated present value of tax loss carry-forward | 700,000 |
| | 6,747,500 |
| Liabilities | 1,200,000 |
| Net assets | $5,547,500 |

LAL expects to spend approximately $400,000 in getting the assets in operating order and $500,000 on foundations and site preparations for the rides. Leo wants to "capitalize as much as possible."

3. Approximately $600,000 will be required to relocate the rides that are currently on land that is needed for the arena. This amount is to be capitalized, net of scrap recovery of $60,000 on dismantled and redundant equipment. Virtually all the rides were fully depreciated years ago.

4. To assist in financing the new ventures, LAL sold excess land to developers who intend to construct a shopping centre, office buildings, and expensive homes adjacent to the golf course and away from the amusement park.

The developers and LAL agreed to these terms:

| | |
|---|---:|
| Paid to LAL on May 1, Year 8 | $ 6,000,000 |
| To be paid to LAL on March 1, Year 9 | 10,000,000 |
| To be paid to LAL on March 1, Year 10 | 8,000,000 |
| | $24,000,000 |

The land is to be turned over to the developers on or about February 1, Year 9, but the sale is to be reported in fiscal Year 8.

5. An additional "contingent profit" will accrue to LAL if the developers earn a return on investment of more than 25% when they resell the newly constructed buildings. Leo wants a note to the Year 8 financial statements that describes the probability of a contingent gain.

6. The excess land that was sold to developers was carried on LAL's books at $1.35 million, on a pro rata cost basis. Leo would like to revalue the remaining land from $5.4 million to about $100 million in the Year 8 financial statements.

7. The golf course has been unprofitable in recent years. However, green fees are to be raised and specific tee-off times will be allotted to a private club, which is currently being organized. Members of the private club will pay a non-refundable entrance fee of $2,000 per member plus $100 per month for five years. The $2,000 is to be recorded as revenue on receipt. Approximately $350,000 is to be spent to upgrade the club facilities.

8. Leo wants to capitalize all costs of NSL on NSL's books until it has completed its first year of operations. In addition to the franchise fee, $20 million will have to be spent on the following:

| | |
|---|---:|
| Acquisition of player contracts | $12,000,000 |
| Advertising and promotion | 1,500,000 |
| Equipment | 3,200,000 |
| Wages, benefits, and bonuses | 6,800,000 |
| Other operating costs | 3,300,000 |
| | 26,800,000 |
| Less: | |
| Revenue: | |
| Ticket sales | (6,000,000) |
| Other | (800,000) |
| | $20,000,000 |

*(continued)*

---

**EXHIBIT I** *(continued)*

The value of players can change quickly, depending upon their performance, injuries, and other factors.

9. The new sports arena will have private boxes in which a company can entertain groups of clients. The boxes are leased on a five-year contract basis, and they must be occupied for a fixed number of nights at a minimum price per night. To date, 12 boxes have been leased for $15,000 per box for a five-year period, exclusive of nightly charges. A down payment of $3,000 was required; the payments have been recorded as revenue.

10. Three senior officers of LAL, including Leo, receive bonuses based on income before income taxes. The three have agreed to have their fiscal Year 8 bonuses accrued in fiscal Year 9 along with their fiscal Year 9 bonuses. Actual payments to them are scheduled for January Year 10.

11. Insurance premiums on the construction activity that is taking place total $1.4 million in fiscal Year 8, and to date they have been capitalized.

12. A $500,000 fee was paid to a mortgage broker to arrange financing for LAL. This amount has been recorded as "Other assets." No financing has been arranged to date.

*(CPA Canada adapted)*[5]

---

## Case 4-6

LO2

It is September 15, Year 8. The partner has called you, CPA, into his office to discuss a special engagement related to a purchase agreement. John Toffler, a successful entrepreneur with several different businesses in the automotive sector, is finalizing the acquisition of Super Sports Limited (SSL). The seller, Carl Thomas, founded SSL over 20 years ago, and has decided to retire and sell his business. He has agreed to manage the business until the shares are transferred.

SSL, a wholesale distributor of sports equipment and related products, is very profitable. The company originally sold summer sports items, such as jet skis and canoes, and recently acquired a wholesaler of winter sports items such as snowmobiles. SSL has loyal customers and good relationships with its suppliers.

Excerpts from the purchase agreement are provided in Exhibit II. The purchase price for the SSL shares is the carrying amount of net assets, according to the approved audited financial statements as at August 10, Year 8, plus any increase in the fair value of the land and building. See Exhibit III for excerpts from the August 10, Year 8, statements submitted to Toffler for his approval.

Toffler asked Jill Savage, who works for one of his companies, to review SSL's financial statements and the audit working papers provided by SSL's auditor. Jill raised several concerns as part of her review (see Exhibit IV). In the spirit of fairness, Thomas and Toffler have requested your firm's views on the accounting issues noted by Jill before continuing with the approval of the financial statements as per clause 29.1. The partner has asked you to draft a memo to his attention, supporting your views.

## Excerpts from Purchase Agreement (dated August 1, Year 8)

2.1 The effective date of the sale of SSL is August 10, Year 8.

10.2 The purchaser reviewed the inventory balance as at July 31, Year 8, and noted a general obsolescence provision of $75,000, which the seller will update at the effective date.

13.1 Based on a review of the accounts receivable performed on July 31, both parties agree that $90,000 is a reasonable allowance for doubtful accounts to be booked in the August 10 financial statements.

15.1 All amounts due to the shareholder will be paid before August 10.

29.1 As part of the final acceptance of this agreement, both the purchaser and the seller must approve the August 10 audited financial statements.

35.1 Both parties accept that unforeseen circumstances related to the agreement might arise that require an adjustment to the purchase price, and will work in good faith to arrive at a fair settlement.

**SUPER SPORTS LIMITED**
**EXCERPTS FROM AUDITED BALANCE SHEET**
(in thousands of dollars)

| | As At: | |
| --- | --- | --- |
| | Aug. 10, Year 8 | Oct. 31, Year 7 (year-end) |
| **Assets** | | |
| Current assets: | | |
| Accounts receivable | $1,459 | $ 996 |
| Inventory | 2,475 | 2,098 |
| | 3,934 | 3,094 |
| Property, plant, and equipment, net | 451 | 504 |
| Goodwill and intangibles | 60 | 80 |
| | $4,445 | $3,678 |
| **Liabilities** | | |
| Current liabilities: | | |
| Bank overdraft | $ 821 | $ 9 |
| Accounts payable | 2,004 | 1,547 |
| Salaries and bonuses payable | 40 | 231 |
| Income tax payable | 63 | 17 |
| | 2,928 | 1,804 |
| Due to shareholder | — | 750 |
| | 2,928 | 2,554 |
| **Shareholders' Equity** | | |
| Common shares | 100 | 100 |
| Retained earnings | 1,417 | 1,024 |
| | 1,517 | 1,124 |
| | $4,445 | $3,678 |

INVENTORY   The audit working papers include the following (in $000s):

## List of Concerns Prepared by Jill Savage (including excerpts from audit working papers)

**Summary of Writedowns**

| Category | August 10, Year 8 | | | October 31, Year 7 | | |
| --- | --- | --- | --- | --- | --- | --- |
| | Cost | Net Realizable Value | Write-down | Cost | Net Realizable Value | Write-down |
| Snowmobiles (stock and customized) | $ 876 | $ 865 | $11 | $ 449 | $ 404 | $ 45 |
| Winter parts and accessories | 387 | 450 | – | 229 | 265 | – |
| Subtotal | 1,263 | 1,315 | 11 | 678 | 669 | 45 |
| Jet skis | 420 | 386 | 34 | 499 | 474 | 25 |
| Motorboats | 478 | 466 | 12 | 539 | 531 | 8 |
| Canoes and kayaks | 263 | 325 | – | 280 | 345 | – |
| Summer parts and accessories | 126 | 101 | 25 | 202 | 180 | 22 |
| Subtotal | 1,287 | 1,278 | 71 | 1,520 | 1,530 | 55 |
| Total | $2,550 | $2,593 | $82 | $2,198 | $2,199 | $100 |
| Days' sales in inventory | 60 days | | | 63 days | | |

SSL applied the lower of cost and market using net realizable value as the definition of market value, in accordance with its accounting policy. I do not agree with the method used. GAAP requires conservatism, and using net realizable value less normal profit margin is more conservative and would ensure historic profit margins are maintained. A further writedown of the inventory and a reduction in purchase price are necessary.

The file noted that except for the custom snowmobile inventory, which SSL accounts for on an item-by-item basis, SSL applies the lower of cost and market by product line using a weighted average. As a result, increases in the value of some items offset declines in the value of others. The last shipment of snowmobiles received had a lower unit price than the units still in inventory purchased earlier in the season. I believe the snowmobile inventory, excluding the customized items, should be valued at the lower unit price based on a first-in-first-out cost formula. Applying the lower of cost or market in this way is in accordance with GAAP.

The auditor tested the valuation of inventory by referencing purchase invoices to subsequent selling prices, reviewing sales margins after the cut-off date, and reviewing for obsolete or slow-moving items while attending the physical count. The auditor also tested the inventory tracking system and noted no errors or problems. I believe the auditor did not do enough work on inventory, and did not realize that the amount booked should have been increased from $75,000, as stated in Clause 10.2, to $82,000, as calculated by the auditor (see summary of unadjusted misstatements), plus the normal profit margin on an item-by-item basis.

The audit working papers noted that a jet ski and accessories that were sitting in a separate area of the warehouse were included in the count. SSL received a layaway payment for the items from the customer on the day of the count and recorded a liability as of August 10. The audit file noted that the repeat customer picked up the items, worth $30,000, two weeks later. This is an obvious cut-off error. There should not be a liability. Since the items were sold the day of the count, the inventory on the August 10 statements should have been reduced and a receivable recorded.

**ACCOUNTS RECEIVABLE AND BAD DEBT EXPENSE**  The following is the schedule prepared by the auditor to calculate the required allowance for doubtful accounts (in $000s):

| Accounts Receivable Aging | August 10, Year 8 | | | October 31, Year 7 | | |
|---|---|---|---|---|---|---|
| | $ Accounts Receivable | % | $ Allowance | $ Accounts Receivable | % | $ Allowance |
| Current | 503 | 1.6 | 8 | 300 | 1.7 | 5 |
| 30–60 days | 626 | 2.1 | 13 | 442 | 2.0 | 9 |
| 61–90 days | 200 | 8.0 | 16 | 162 | 8.0 | 13 |
| Over 90 days | 220 | 15.0 | 33 | 140 | 15.0 | 21 |
| Total | 1,549 | | 70 | 1,044 | | 48 |

The audit files indicate that the aging was tested and large accounts were reviewed. Accounts were confirmed on a test basis, and no significant errors were found. Subsequent payments were also reviewed.

On September 4, Year 8, I read in the newspaper that Fast and Furious (FF), a customer of SSL, declared bankruptcy due to a fire. The balance in FF's account on August 10 was $145,000, of which $50,000 remained unpaid when it declared bankruptcy. Since the account will probably not be collected, SSL should increase the $90,000 allowance at the purchase date to include the loss of $50,000 because the sale to FF was made before our purchase of SSL.

**ACCOUNTS PAYABLE**  Accounts payable for previous periods included an accrual of $180,000 related to a disputed payable to a supplier. The supplier initially sued SSL for payment, and SSL responded with a countersuit. The audit file indicates that the dispute has been ongoing for about three years, and SSL came close to going to court on a few occasions but the date was delayed by procedural details. Carl Thomas had worked diligently to reach a settlement. On the August 10 statements, SSL reduced the accrual to $80,000, representing the settlement amount and the related legal costs. The $100,000 difference was taken into income. The file includes documents, signed by Carl Thomas on behalf of SSL, indicating that he finally settled the matter out of court on August 25, Year 8.

Carl did not tell you he had reached a settlement, nor did he get your approval before signing off on it. Given that the settlement was a management decision, not the result of a court order, and that it was reached after the purchase date, the full $180,000 accrual should have been left on the August 10 balance sheet. The treatment is not in accordance with GAAP.

**GOODWILL AND INTANGIBLES**  The auditor assessed $80,000 of goodwill and intangibles, and made a $20,000 writedown due to impairment, as SSL is no longer the exclusive distributor of Polaris snowmobiles in the region. The file indicated that Polaris is changing its distribution strategy. If SSL lost exclusivity of the Polaris line, in my mind they are also likely to lose the Ski-Doo and Yamaha lines. Therefore, the intangibles have no value. No amount should be paid for goodwill either, as Carl is not staying. The auditor should have written off the entire balance.

*(CPA Canada adapted)*[6]

# PROBLEMS

## Problem 4-1

LO2, 3

The statements of financial position of Pork Co. and Barrel Ltd. on December 31, Year 2, are shown next:

|  | Pork Co. | Barrel Ltd. |
|---|---|---|
| Plant and equipment (net) | $400,000 | $270,000 |
| Investment in Barrel Ltd. | 329,000 | — |
| Inventory | 120,000 | 102,000 |
| Accounts receivable | 45,000 | 48,000 |
| Cash | 22,000 | 60,000 |
|  | $916,000 | $480,000 |
|  |  |  |
| Ordinary shares | $260,000 | $120,000 |
| Retained earnings | 200,000 | 180,000 |
| Long-term debt | 240,000 | 108,000 |
| Current liabilities | 216,000 | 72,000 |
|  | $916,000 | $480,000 |

Pork acquired 70% of the outstanding shares of Barrel on December 30, Year 2, for $329,000. Direct costs of the acquisition amounted to $12,000. The carrying amounts of the net assets of Barrel approximated fair values except for plant and equipment, which had a fair value of $320,000.

**Required**

(a) Prepare a consolidated statement of financial position at December 31, Year 2, under entity theory.

(b) Calculate goodwill and non-controlling interest on the consolidated statement of financial position at December 31, Year 2, under parent company extension theory.

## Problem 4-2

LO2, 4

The balance sheets of Par Ltd. and Sub Ltd. on December 31, Year 1, are as follows:

|  | Par Ltd. | Sub Ltd. |
|---|---|---|
| Cash | $100,000 | $ 2,000 |
| Accounts receivable | 25,000 | 7,000 |
| Inventory | 30,000 | 21,000 |
| Plant | 175,000 | 51,000 |
| Trademarks | — | 7,000 |
|  | $330,000 | $88,000 |
|  |  |  |
| Current liabilities | $ 50,000 | $10,000 |
| Long-term debt | 80,000 | 20,000 |
| Common shares | 110,000 | 30,000 |
| Retained earnings | 90,000 | 28,000 |
|  | $330,000 | $88,000 |

The fair values of the identifiable net assets of Sub on December 31, Year 1, are as follows:

| | | |
|---|---:|---:|
| Cash | | $ 2,000 |
| Accounts receivable | | 7,000 |
| Inventory | | 26,000 |
| Plant | | 60,000 |
| Trademarks | | 14,000 |
| | | 109,000 |
| Current liabilities | $10,000 | |
| Long-term debt | 19,000 | 29,000 |
| Net assets | | $ 80,000 |

Assume that the following took place on January 1, Year 2. (Par acquired the shares with a cash payment to the shareholders of Sub.)

*Case 1.* Par paid $95,000 to acquire all of the common shares of Sub.

*Case 2.* Par paid $76,000 to acquire 80% of the common shares of Sub.

*Case 3.* Par paid $80,000 to acquire all of the common shares of Sub.

*Case 4.* Par paid $70,000 to acquire all of the common shares of Sub.

*Case 5.* Par paid $63,000 to acquire 90% of the common shares of Sub.

**Required**

For each of the five cases, prepare a consolidated balance sheet as at January 1, Year 2.

## Problem 4-3

LO2, 4

The balance sheets of Petron Co. and Seeview Co. on June 29, Year 2, were as follows:

| | Petron | Seeview |
|---|---:|---:|
| Cash and receivables | $ 93,000 | $20,150 |
| Inventory | 60,500 | 8,150 |
| Plant assets (net) | 203,000 | 60,050 |
| Intangible assets | 33,000 | 6,300 |
| | $389,500 | $94,650 |
| | | |
| Current liabilities | $ 65,500 | $27,600 |
| Long-term debt | 94,250 | 40,100 |
| Common shares | 140,500 | 40,050 |
| Retained earnings (deficit) | 89,250 | (13,100) |
| | $389,500 | $94,650 |

On June 30, Year 2, Petron Co. purchased 90% of the outstanding shares of Seeview Co. for $52,200 cash. Legal fees involved with the acquisition were an additional $2,300. These two transactions were the only transactions on this date. The carrying amounts of Seeview's net assets were equal to fair value except for the following:

| | Fair Value |
|---|---:|
| Inventory | $10,050 |
| Plant assets | 70,100 |
| Intangible assets | 10,100 |
| Long-term debt | 33,800 |

Seeview has a five-year agreement to supply goods to Bardier. Both Petron and Seeview believe that Bardier will renew the agreement at the end of the current contract. The agreement is between Seeview and Bardier; it cannot be transferred to another company without Seeview's consent. Seeview does not report any value with respect to this contract on its balance sheet. However, an independent appraiser feels that this contract is worth $23,000.

**Required**

(a) Assume that Petron Co. is a public entity. Prepare the consolidated balance sheet of Petron Co. on June 30, Year 2. (Round all calculations to the nearest dollar.)

(b) Assume that Petron is a private entity, uses ASPE, and chooses to use the equity method to account for its investment in Seeview. Prepare Petron's June 30, Year 2, separate-entity balance sheet after the business combination.

 *(c) Prepare Petron Co.'s consolidated balance sheet using the worksheet approach.

# Problem 4-4

LO2, 5

The balance sheets of Hill Corp. and McGraw Ltd. on December 31, Year 4, were as follows:

|  | Hill Corp. | McGraw Ltd. |
|---|---|---|
| Cash | $ 13,000 | $ 6,500 |
| Accounts receivable | 181,300 | 45,500 |
| Inventory | 117,000 | 208,000 |
| Land | 91,000 | 52,000 |
| Plant and equipment | 468,000 | 377,000 |
| Investment in McGraw Ltd. | 288,000 | — |
| Goodwill | 117,000 | 39,000 |
|  | $1,275,300 | $728,000 |
|  |  |  |
| Current liabilities | $ 156,000 | $104,000 |
| Long-term debt | 416,000 | 286,000 |
| Common shares | 520,000 | 390,000 |
| Retained earnings (deficit) | 183,300 | (52,000) |
|  | $1,275,300 | $728,000 |

On December 31, Year 4, Hill purchased 80% of the common shares of McGraw for $288,000 plus a commitment to pay an additional $100,000 in two years if sales grow by more than 30% over the next two years. An independent business valuator stated that Hill could have paid an extra $40,000 at the date of acquisition instead of agreeing to a potential payment of $100,000 in two years. On this date, the inventory of McGraw had a fair value of $214,500, its land had a fair value of $91,000, and its plant and equipment had a fair value of $364,000.

**Required**

Prepare a consolidated balance sheet as at December 31, Year 4.

# Problem 4-5

LO2

On December 31, Year 2, Blue purchased a percentage of the outstanding ordinary shares of Joy. On this date all but two categories of Joy's identifiable assets and liabilities had fair values equal to carrying amounts.

Following are the statements of financial position of Blue Ltd. and Joy Corp. on December 31, Year 2 subsequent to the acquisition.

| | Blue Ltd. | Joy Corp. |
|---|---|---|
| Plant and equipment | $ 648,000 | $434,000 |
| Accumulated amortization | (204,000) | (114,000) |
| Investment in Joy Corp. | 456,000 | — |
| Inventory | 109,000 | 224,000 |
| Accounts receivable | 82,000 | 39,000 |
| Cash | 21,000 | 8,000 |
| | $1,112,000 | $591,000 |
| | | |
| Ordinary shares | $ 426,000 | $304,000 |
| Retained earnings | 260,000 | (41,000) |
| Long-term debt | 254,000 | 244,000 |
| Current liabilities | 172,000 | 84,000 |
| | $1,112,000 | $591,000 |

Below is the consolidated statement of financial position for Blue at December 31, Year 2.

**BLUE LTD.**
**CONSOLIDATED STATEMENT OF FINANCIAL POSITION**
December 31, Year 2

| | |
|---|---|
| Plant and equipment | $1,072,000 |
| Accumulated amortization | (204,000) |
| Goodwill | 183,000 |
| Inventory | 353,000 |
| Accounts receivable | 121,000 |
| Cash | 29,000 |
| | $1,554,000 |
| | |
| Ordinary shares | $ 426,000 |
| Retained earnings | 260,000 |
| Non-controlling interest | 114,000 |
| Long-term debt | 498,000 |
| Current liabilities | 256,000 |
| | $1,554,000 |

## Required

(a) From the information provided, determine the percentage of Joy's ordinary shares purchased by Blue on December 31, Year 2.

(b) Which of Joy's assets or liabilities had fair values that were not equal to their carrying amounts at acquisition? Calculate the fair value of each of these assets at December 31, Year 2.

## Problem 4-6

LO2, 3, 4

The balance sheets of E Ltd. and J Ltd. on December 30, Year 6, were as follows:

|  | E Ltd. | J Ltd. |
|---|---|---|
| Cash and receivables | $ 96,000 | $ 19,500 |
| Inventory | 57,000 | 9,000 |
| Plant assets (net) | 228,000 | 70,500 |
| Intangible assets | 24,000 | 6,000 |
|  | $405,000 | $105,000 |
| Current liabilities | $ 63,000 | $ 30,000 |
| Long-term debt | 97,500 | 45,000 |
| Common shares | 153,000 | 46,500 |
| Retained earnings (deficit) | 91,500 | (16,500) |
|  | $405,000 | $105,000 |

On December 31, Year 6, E Ltd. issued 350 shares, with a fair value of $40 each, for 70% of the outstanding shares of J Ltd. Costs involved in the acquisition, paid in cash, were as follows:

| Costs of arranging the acquisition | $2,500 |
|---|---|
| Costs of issuing shares | 1,600 |
|  | $4,100 |

The carrying amounts of J Ltd.'s net assets were equal to fair values on this date except for the following:

|  | Fair Value |
|---|---|
| Plant assets | $65,000 |
| Long-term debt | 40,000 |

E Ltd. was identified as the acquirer in the combination.

**Required**

(a) Prepare the consolidated balance sheet of E Ltd. on December 31, Year 6, under the parent company extension theory.
(b) Prepare the consolidated balance sheet of E Ltd. on December 31, Year 6, under the entity theory.

## Problem 4-7

LO1, 2, 3, 6

On December 31, Year 1, P Company purchased 80% of the outstanding shares of S Company for $7,900 cash.

The statements of financial position of the two companies immediately after the acquisition transaction appear below.

| | P Company | S Company | |
| --- | --- | --- | --- |
| | Carrying Amount | Carrying Amount | Fair Value |
| Plant and equipment (net) | $ 9,600 | $ 8,300 | $7,000 |
| Investment in S Company | 7,900 | — | |
| Inventory | 6,660 | 5,300 | 5,500 |
| Accounts receivable | 6,150 | 3,300 | 3,300 |
| Cash | 4,500 | 2,550 | 2,550 |
| | $34,810 | $19,450 | |
| | | | |
| Ordinary shares | $12,000 | $ 4,500 | |
| Retained earnings | 15,410 | 5,950 | |
| Long-term liabilities | 4,500 | 3,500 | 3,500 |
| Other current liabilities | 1,500 | 3,300 | 3,300 |
| Accounts payable | 1,400 | 2,200 | 2,200 |
| | $34,810 | $19,450 | |

**Required**

(a) Calculate consolidated goodwill at the date of acquisition under the proprietary theory.

(b) Prepare a consolidated statement of financial position at the date of acquisition under each of the following:

 (i)  Parent company extension theory

 (ii)  Entity theory

(c) Calculate the current ratio and debt-to-equity ratio for P Company under the two theories. Explain which theory shows the strongest liquidity and solvency position and which method best reflects the true financial condition of the company.

# Problem 4-8

...........

LO2

On January 1, Year 5, Black Corp. purchased 90% of the common shares of Whyte Inc. On this date, the following differences were observed with regard to specific net assets of Whyte:

|  | Fair Value—Carrying Amount Differences |
| --- | --- |
| Land | + 50,000 |
| Buildings (net) | + 20,000 |
| Equipment (net) | − 10,000 |
| Notes payable | + 5,000 |

The non-consolidated and consolidated balance sheets of Black Corp. on January 1, Year 5, are presented below. Whyte's retained earnings were $140,000 on this date.

|  | Non-consolidated | Consolidated |
|---|---|---|
| Cash | $    36,000 | $    52,000 |
| Accounts receivable | 116,000 | 168,000 |
| Inventory | 144,000 | 234,000 |
| Investment in Whyte | 292,500 | — |
| Land | 210,000 | 280,000 |
| Buildings (net) | 640,000 | 720,000 |
| Equipment (net) | 308,000 | 338,000 |
| Goodwill | — | 50,000 |
|  | $1,746,500 | $1,842,000 |
|  |  |  |
| Accounts payable | $    88,000 | $    96,000 |
| Notes payable | 507,500 | 562,500 |
| Common shares | 380,000 | 380,000 |
| Retained earnings | 771,000 | 771,000 |
| Non-controlling interest | — | 32,500 |
|  | $1,746,500 | $1,842,000 |

**Required**

Prepare the January 1, Year 5, balance sheet of Whyte Inc.


# Problem 4-9

LO2

The balance sheets of Percy Corp. and Saltz Ltd. on December 31, Year 10, are shown below:

|  | Percy | Saltz |
|---|---|---|
| Cash | $ 200,000 | $    4,000 |
| Accounts receivable | 50,000 | 14,000 |
| Inventory | 60,000 | 42,000 |
| Plant | 475,000 | 192,000 |
| Accumulated amortization | (125,000) | (90,000) |
| Trademarks—net | — | 14,000 |
|  | $660,000 | $176,000 |
|  |  |  |
| Current liabilities | $100,000 | $  20,000 |
| Long-term debt | 160,000 | 40,000 |
| Common shares | 220,000 | 60,000 |
| Retained earnings | 180,000 | 56,000 |
|  | $660,000 | $176,000 |

The fair values of the identifiable net assets of Saltz Ltd. on December 31, Year 10, were as follows:

| | | |
|---|---|---:|
| Cash | | $ 4,000 |
| Accounts receivable | | 14,000 |
| Inventory | | 52,000 |
| Plant | | 120,000 |
| Trademarks | | 28,000 |
| | | 218,000 |
| Current liabilities | $20,000 | |
| Long-term debt | 38,000 | 58,000 |
| Net assets | | $160,000 |

In addition to the assets identified above, Saltz owned a taxi licence in the City of Moose Jaw. This licence expires in nine years. These licences are selling in the open market at approximately $40,000. On January 1, Year 11, Percy Corp paid $175,000 in cash to acquire 7,000 (70%) of the common shares of Saltz Ltd. Saltz's shares were trading for $20 per share just after the acquisition by Percy.

**Required**
Prepare the consolidated balance sheet on January 1, Year 11.

# Problem 4-10

LO2, 3

The balance sheets of Prima Ltd. and Donna Corp. on December 31, Year 5, are shown below:

| | Prima | Donna |
|---|---:|---:|
| Cash | $ 374,000 | $ 10,400 |
| Accounts receivable | 84,000 | 26,400 |
| Inventory | 100,000 | 69,200 |
| Plant | 514,000 | 165,200 |
| Patents | 104,000 | 26,400 |
| | $1,176,000 | $297,600 |
| | | |
| Current liabilities | $ 164,000 | $ 36,000 |
| Long-term debt | 260,000 | 66,000 |
| Common shares | 356,000 | 100,000 |
| Retained earnings | 396,000 | 95,600 |
| | $1,176,000 | $297,600 |

The fair values of the identifiable net assets of Donna Corp. on this date are as follows:

| | |
|---|---:|
| Cash | $ 10,400 |
| Accounts receivable | 22,000 |
| Inventory | 89,000 |
| Plant | 196,000 |
| Trademarks | 34,000 |
| Patents | 62,000 |
| Current liabilities | 36,000 |
| Long-term debt | 74,000 |

In addition to the assets identified above, Donna owned a significant number of Internet domain names, which are unique alphanumeric names that are used to identify a particular numeric Internet address. These domain names can be sold separately and are estimated to be worth $54,000.

On January 1, Year 6, Prima Ltd. paid $328,000 in cash to acquire 80% of the common shares of Donna Corp.

**Required**

(a) Prepare the consolidated balance sheet on January 1, Year 6, under entity theory.
(b) Now assume that an independent business valuator valued the NCI at $76,000 at the date of acquisition. What accounts on the consolidated balance would change, and at what amount would they be reported?
(c) Assume that Prima is a private entity, uses ASPE, and chooses to use the cost method to account for its investment in Donna. Prepare Prima's January 1, Year 6, separate-entity balance sheet after the business combination.

 *(d) Prepare the consolidated balance sheet using the worksheet approach.

# Problem 4-11

LO2, 3

On January 1, Year 5, FLA Company issued 6,300 ordinary shares to purchase 9,000 ordinary shares of MES Company. Prior to the acquisition, FLA had 180,000 and MES had 10,000 ordinary shares outstanding, which were trading at $5 and $3 per share, respectively. The following information has been assembled for these two companies just prior to the acquisition:

|  | **FLA Company** | | **MES Company** | |
|---|---|---|---|---|
|  | Carrying Amount | Fair Value | Carrying Amount | Fair Value |
| Plant assets | $ 60,000 | $70,000 | $20,000 | $25,000 |
| Current assets | 40,000 | 47,500 | 10,000 | 11,200 |
|  | $100,000 | | $30,000 | |
|  |  |  |  |  |
| Ordinary shares | $ 30,000 | | $10,000 | |
| Retained earnings | 35,000 | | 12,500 | |
| Long-term debt | 15,000 | 19,000 | 2,500 | 3,200 |
| Current liabilities | 20,000 | 20,000 | 5,000 | 5,000 |
|  | $100,000 | | $30,000 | |

**Required**

(a) Prepare a consolidated statement of financial position for FLA Company and its non–wholly owned subsidiary at January 1, Year 5, under each of the following:
  (i)  Parent company extension theory
  (ii) Entity theory
(b) Which of the above theories is required under IFRS 3?

# Problem 4-12

.........

LO2

The condensed financial statements for OIL Inc. and ERS Company for the year ended December 31, Year 5, follow:

|  | OIL | ERS |
|---|---|---|
| Revenues | $ 924,000 | $ 316,000 |
| Expenses | 668,000 | 208,000 |
| Net income | $ 256,000 | $ 108,000 |
|  |  |  |
| Retained earnings, 1/1/Year 5 | $ 808,000 | $ 208,000 |
| Net income | 256,000 | 108,000 |
| Dividends paid | 98,000 | 0 |
| Retained earnings, 12/31/Year 5 | $ 966,000 | $ 316,000 |
|  |  |  |
| Cash | $ 88,000 | $ 118,000 |
| Receivables and inventory | 408,000 | 178,000 |
| Patented technology (net) | 908,000 | 312,000 |
| Equipment (net) | 708,000 | 608,000 |
| Total assets | $2,112,000 | $1,216,000 |
|  |  |  |
| Liabilities | $ 608,000 | $ 422,000 |
| Common shares | 538,000 | 478,000 |
| Retained earnings | 966,000 | 316,000 |
| Total liabilities and equities | $2,112,000 | $1,216,000 |

On December 31, Year 5, after the above figures were prepared, OIL issued $252,000 in debt and 12,000 new shares to the owners of ERS for 90% of the outstanding shares of that company. OIL shares had a fair value of $48 per share.

OIL also paid $38,000 to a broker for arranging the transaction. In addition, OIL paid $40,000 in stock issuance costs. ERS's equipment was actually worth $706,000, but its patented technology was appraised at only $288,000.

## Required

What are the consolidated balances for the year ended/at December 31, Year 5, for the following accounts?

(a) Net income
(b) Retained earnings, 1/1/Year 5
(c) Equipment
(d) Patented technology
(e) Goodwill
(f) Liabilities
(g) Common shares
(h) Non-controlling interest

# Problem 4-13

LO2

The July 31, Year 3, balance sheets of two companies that are parties to a business combination are as follows:

|  | Ravinder Corp. | Robin Inc. | |
|---|---|---|---|
|  | Carrying Amount | Carrying Amount | Fair Value |
| Current assets | $1,600,000 | $ 420,000 | $468,000 |
| Plant and equipment | 1,330,000 | 1,340,000 | 972,000 |
| Accumulated depreciation | (250,000) | (500,000) | |
| Patents—net | — | — | 72,000 |
|  | $2,680,000 | $1,260,000 | |
| Current liabilities | $1,360,000 | $ 252,000 | 252,000 |
| Long-term debt | 480,000 | 360,000 | 384,000 |
| Common shares | 720,000 | 168,000 | |
| Retained earnings | 120,000 | 480,000 | |
|  | $2,680,000 | $1,260,000 | |

In addition to the assets identified above, Ravinder Corp. attributed a value of $100,000 to a major research project that Robin Inc. was working on. Robin Inc. feels that it is within a year of developing a prototype for a state-of-the-art bio-medical device. If this device can ever be patented, it could be worth hundreds of thousands of dollars.

Effective on August 1, Year 3, the shareholders of Robin Inc. accepted an offer from Ravinder Corp. to purchase 80% of their common shares for $1,040,000 in cash. Ravinder Corp.'s legal fees for investigating and drawing up the share purchase agreement amounted to $25,000.

**Required**

(a) Prepare the journal entries in the records of Ravinder Corp. to record the share acquisition and cost of legal fees.

(b) Prepare a schedule to calculate and allocate the acquisition differential. Explain the rationale for the accounting treatment of the $100,000 attributed to the research project.

(c) Prepare Ravinder Corp.'s consolidated balance sheet as at August 1, Year 3. Assume there were no transactions on this date other than the transactions described above.

# Problem 4-14

LO2, 3

The balance sheets of Bates Co. and Casey Co. on June 30, Year 2 just before the transaction described below, were as follows:

|  | Bates | Casey |
|---|---|---|
| Cash and receivables | $ 93,000 | $20,150 |
| Inventory | 60,500 | 8,150 |
| Plant assets (net) | 236,000 | 66,350 |
|  | $389,500 | $94,650 |

*(continued)*

|                              | Bates     | Casey    |
|------------------------------|-----------|----------|
| Current liabilities          | $ 65,500  | $27,600  |
| Long-term debt               | 94,250    | 40,100   |
| Common shares                | 140,500   | 40,050   |
| Retained earnings (deficit)  | 89,250    | (13,100) |
|                              | $389,500  | $94,650  |

On June 30, Year 2, Bates Co. purchased 2,400 (80%) of Casey Co.'s common shares for $48,000 in cash. On that date, Casey's shares were trading at $17 per share in the open market. The carrying amounts of Casey's net assets were equal to fair value except for the following:

| Inventory      | $10,050 |
|----------------|---------|
| Plant assets   | 70,100  |
| Long-term debt | 33,800  |

**Required**

(a) Calculate consolidated goodwill at the date of acquisition under the proprietary theory.
(b) Prepare the consolidated balance sheet of Bates Co. on June 30, Year 2, under each of the following:
  (i) Entity theory
  (ii) Parent company extension theory

# Problem 4-15

..........

LO5

Calof Inc. acquires 100% of the common shares of Xiyu Company on January 1, Year 4, for the following consideration:

- $275,000 market value of 5,000 shares of its common shares.

- A contingent payment of $40,000 cash on January 1, Year 5 if Xiyu generates cash flows from operations of $10,000 or more in Year 4.

- A payment of sufficient shares of Calof common shares to ensure a total value of $275,000 if the price per share is less than $55 on January 1, Year 5.

For the cash contingency, Calof estimates that there is a 30% chance that the $40,000 payment will be required. For the share contingency, Calof estimates that there is a 20% probability that the 5,000 shares issued will have a market value of $270,000 on January 1, Year 5, and an 80% probability that the market value of the 5,000 shares will exceed $275,000. Calof uses an interest rate of 4% to incorporate the time value of money.

In Year 4, Xiyu exceeds the cash flow from operations threshold of $10,000, thus requiring an additional payment of $40,000. Also, Calof's stock price had fallen to $54.46 at January 1, Year 5. Because the acquisition agreement called for a $275,000 total value at January 1, Year 5, Calof must issue an additional 50 shares ($2,700 shortfall/$54.46 per share) to the former owners of Xiyu.

**Required**

(a) Prepare Calof's journal entry at January 1, Year 4 to record the investment in Xiyu including any contingent consideration.

(b) Prepare adjusting entries relating to the contingent consideration at December 31, Year 4.

(c) Indicate what amounts relating to the contingent consideration will appear on the balance sheet at December 31, Year 4 and how they will be presented.

# Endnotes

1  "Who We Are," BMO Financial Group, www.bmo.com/home/about/banking/investor-relations/who-we-are.

2  Carrying amount + (Fair value - Carrying amount) = Fair value

3  The parent company extension method emerged as an articulated set of practices with the 1973 release of an exposure draft by CPA Canada's Accounting Research Committee, "Consolidated Financial Statements and the Equity Method of Accounting."

4  Adapted from *CICA UFE Report*, 1995-II-6, with permission. Chartered Professional Accountants of Canada, Toronto, Canada. Any changes to the original material are the sole responsibility of the author (and/or publisher) and have not been reviewed or endorsed by the Chartered Professional Accountants of Canada.

5  Adapted from *CICA UFE Report*, 1998-III-2, with permission. Chartered Professional Accountants of Canada, Toronto, Canada. Any changes to the original material are the sole responsibility of the author (and/or publisher) and have not been reviewed or endorsed by the Chartered Professional Accountants of Canada.

6  Adapted from *CICA UFE Report*, 2008-III-s, with permission. Chartered Professional Accountants of Canada, Toronto, Canada. Any changes to the original material are the sole responsibility of the author (and/or publisher) and have not been reviewed or endorsed by the Chartered Professional Accountants of Canada.

# CHAPTER 5

# Consolidation Subsequent to Acquisition Date

## LEARNING OBJECTIVES

**After studying this chapter, you should be able to do the following for consolidations subsequent to the date of acquisition:**

**LO1** Perform impairment tests on property, plant, equipment, intangible assets, and goodwill.

**LO2** Prepare schedules to allocate and amortize the acquisition differential on both an annual and a cumulative basis.

**LO3** Prepare consolidated financial statements using the entity theory subsequent to the date of acquisition.

**LO4** Prepare consolidated financial statements using parent company extension theory subsequent to the date of acquisition.

**LO5** Prepare journal entries and calculate balance in the investment account under the equity method.

**LO6** Analyze and interpret financial statements involving consolidations subsequent to the date of acquisition.

**LO7** (Appendix 5A) Perform impairment test for goodwill in complex situations.

**LO8** (Appendix 5B) Prepare consolidated financial statements subsequent to date of acquisition using the working paper approach.

## Introduction

In Chapters 3 and 4, we discussed and illustrated the preparation of a consolidated balance sheet immediately after a parent company gained control over a subsidiary. We saw that the acquisition differential was allocated to identifiable assets and liabilities when the fair values were different than carrying amounts, and the excess was recognized as goodwill. In this chapter, we will see that the acquisition differential must be amortized and tested for impairment when preparing consolidated financial statements subsequent to the date of acquisition. The impairment testing can result in huge impairment losses. Some of the more significant losses reported in 2014 were as follows:

- Barrick Gold Corporation, the largest gold mining company in the world, cited $1.4 billion of goodwill impairment loss and $2.7 billion of impairment losses on other non-current assets largely related to significant decreases in estimated fair values of several of its copper and gold mines.[1]

- CIBC, a major financial institution in Canada, reported a $420 million goodwill impairment loss due to challenging economic conditions in the Caribbean unit environment.[2]
- GLENTEL Inc. reported $15.5 million of impairment losses relating to intangible assets due to impairment of brand, vendor contracts and franchise agreements, and $9.5 million of goodwill impairment losses.[3]

> *Some Canadian companies have reported substantial impairment losses on goodwill and other intangible assets.*

In this chapter, we will prepare the consolidated income statement, retained earnings statement, and balance sheet at fiscal year-ends after the date of acquisition. The consolidated cash flow statement will be discussed in a later chapter. We will start by looking at how the parent accounts for its investment in its own internal records.

# METHODS OF ACCOUNTING FOR AN INVESTMENT IN A SUBSIDIARY

For a parent company, two methods are available to account for an investment in a subsidiary in its own internal accounting records in periods subsequent to the date of acquisition: the *cost method* and the *equity method*. The cost and equity methods of accounting for various types of equity investments were discussed in Chapter 2. While this chapter is concerned with control investments (requiring consolidation), the accounting concepts involved with the cost and equity methods are identical to those presented in Chapter 2. These concepts will be applied in this chapter and in the ones that follow. The key difference is that here they are discussed in relation to the preparation of consolidated financial statements, whereas earlier the emphasis was on the presentation in an investor's unconsolidated financial statements for external users.

> *The cost and equity methods are used in the parent's own internal records for accounting for investments in subsidiaries.*

The cost method is a method of accounting for investments whereby the investment is initially recorded at cost; income from the subsidiary is recognized in net income when the investor's right to receive a dividend is established. This usually occurs when the dividend is declared.

> *The cost method records income when the investor's right to receive a dividend is established.*

IAS 28 defines the equity method as a method of accounting whereby the investment is initially recognized at cost and adjusted thereafter for the post-acquisition change in the investor's share of net assets of the investee. The profit or loss of the investor includes the investor's share of the profit or loss of the investee. Distributions received from an investee reduce the carrying amount of the investment. Adjustments to the carrying amount may also be necessary for changes in the investor's proportionate interest in the investee's other comprehensive income. Such changes include those arising from the revaluation of property, plant, and equipment and from foreign-exchange translation differences. The investor's share of those changes is recognized in other comprehensive income.

> *The equity method captures the investor's share of any changes to the investee's shareholders' equity.*

The cost method is the simpler of the two methods because, typically, the only entry made by the parent each year is to record, as income, its pro rata share of dividends declared by the subsidiary. Occasionally, there may be an entry to record an impairment loss on the investment.

IAS 28 states that the concepts underlying the procedures used in accounting for the acquisition of a subsidiary are also adopted in accounting for the acquisition of an investment in an associate, which is reported using the equity method. This means that the types of adjustments made for consolidation purposes will also be made under the equity method. If used fully and correctly for an investment in a subsidiary, the net income, other comprehensive income, and retained earnings under the equity method in the internal records of the parent will be equal to net income, other comprehensive income, and retained earnings attributable to the parent's shareholders on the parent's consolidated financial statements. The only difference is that the consolidated financial statements incorporate the subsidiary's values on a line-by-line basis, whereas the equity method incorporates the net amount of the subsidiary's values on one line (investment in the subsidiary) on the balance sheet and, typically, on one line (equity method income from the subsidiary) on the income statement.

> *The equity method captures the net effect of any adjustments that would be made on the consolidated financial statements.*

As we will see later in this chapter, the acquisition differential must be amortized or written off over the useful lives of the related assets. The consolidated financial statements must be adjusted to reflect the amortization and/or impairment. In Chapters 6 and 7, we will make consolidation adjustments to eliminate unrealized profits from intercompany transactions. When the parent uses the equity method to account for its investment in the subsidiary, the net effect of the aforementioned consolidation adjustments must be processed through the investment and equity method accounts in the parent's internal records.

It is very important that we differentiate between the internal accounting records and the financial statements for external users. Each entity maintains its own internal accounting records—that is, a general ledger supported by various subledgers. In the internal records for the parent, there will be an investment in subsidiary account, which will be accounted for using the cost, equity, or fair value method. Since the parent controls the subsidiary, it will prepare consolidated financial statements for distribution to its external users. The consolidated financial statements will be supported by a worksheet or set of working papers.

> *We must differentiate between accounting in the internal records and reporting in the external financial statements.*

In addition to the consolidated financial statements, the parent could also prepare non-consolidated financial statements for its external users. In this text, we will refer to these non-consolidated financial statements as separate-entity financial statements, which may or may not be prepared in accordance with IFRS. Since income tax is assessed in Canada at a separate-entity level, a Canadian company must prepare non-consolidated statements for the Canada Revenue Agency.[4] Since dividends received and equity method income pertaining to a subsidiary are not usually taxable for income tax purposes, this income will have to be reversed when calculating taxable income. Accordingly, the income tax authorities are indifferent as to whether the parent uses the cost method or the equity method on its separate-entity financial statements. In fact, the statements given to the tax authorities may be prepared using tax laws rather than IFRS.

---

*An entity could issue non-consolidated financial statements to external users in addition to consolidated financial statements.*

*Dividend income and equity method income from a subsidiary are usually not taxable.*

---

When a bank or other external user wants to receive non-consolidated statements, it may insist that they be prepared in accordance with IFRS. If so, IAS 27 requires that the investment in subsidiary on the separate-entity financial statements be reported at cost, equity method or in accordance with IFRS 9.

The following diagram shows the interrelationships between the various records and financial statements:

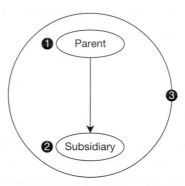

Each circle represents a different set of records/financial statements. The triangle indicates the number given to the set of records/financial statements—the parent's set is number 1, the subsidiary's set is number 2, and the consolidated set is number 3. In the first part of this chapter, the parent will be using the cost method on set number 1.

At the end of this chapter, we will show the entries if the parent had used the equity method in its internal records. The adjustments on consolidation will be different, depending on whether the parent uses the cost method or the equity method on set 1. However, the consolidated financial statements will look exactly the same regardless of whether the parent used the cost method or the equity method in its internal records.

---

*Consolidated net income will be the same regardless of whether the parent used the cost method or the equity method for its internal accounting records.*

---

The parent can choose any method to account for its investment for internal purposes. In most cases, it will use the cost method because it is simple and involves little effort. However, if the entity wants to capture its share of the income earned by the subsidiary without having to prepare consolidated financial statements, the equity method should be used. Since comprehensive income under the equity method should be equal to consolidated comprehensive income attributable to the parent's shareholders, the results from the equity method should be compared with the consolidated financial statements to ensure that no errors have been made. In the end, it is a cost-benefit decision. The equity method should be used for internal purposes only if the benefits derived from the information provided exceed the extra cost involved in using this method.

# CONSOLIDATED INCOME AND RETAINED EARNINGS STATEMENTS

Before examining the details for preparing consolidated income and retained earnings statements,[5] it is useful to outline the overall consolidation process. Just as a consolidated balance sheet is prepared basically by combining, on an item-by-item basis, the assets and liabilities of the parent and the subsidiary, the consolidated statement of comprehensive income is prepared by combining, on an item-by-item basis, the revenues, expenses, and other comprehensive income of the two companies. The parent's investment does not appear on the consolidated balance sheet, and some of the subsidiary's assets and liabilities are remeasured to reflect the fair values used in the consolidation process. In a similar manner, the parent's investment income from its subsidiary does not appear on the consolidated statement of comprehensive income, and some of the revenues and expenses of the subsidiary are remeasured to reflect the amortizations and impairments of the fair values being used in the consolidated balance sheet. Except for the eliminations and adjustments that are required, the whole consolidation process is basically one of combining the components of financial statements. No preparation is required for the consolidated retained earnings statement when the parent has used the equity method because, as previously mentioned, the parent's retained earnings reported in its internal records under the equity method should be equal to consolidated retained earnings.

> *The investment income from subsidiary is replaced by the subsidiary's revenues and expenses on a line-by-line basis.*

We commence our discussion of the preparation of the consolidated income statement by describing the make-up of the bottom line, consolidated net income. Consolidated net income for any fiscal period is made up of the following:

| | |
|---|---|
| The net income of the parent from its own operations (i.e., excluding any income resulting from its investment in the subsidiary) | $ XXX |
| Plus: The net income of the subsidiary | XXX |
| Less: The amortization and impairment of the acquisition differential | (XXX) |
| Equals: Consolidated net income | $ XXX |
| Attributable to: | |
| Shareholders of parent company | $ XXX |
| Non-controlling interest | XXX |

> *The amortization of the acquisition differential is reflected on the consolidated financial statements—not on the subsidiary's financial statements.*

It is important to note the distinction between consolidated net income and consolidated net income attributable to the shareholders of the parent company. Consolidated net income includes the combined income of the parent and subsidiary, plus or minus consolidation adjustments. Consolidated net income attributable to the shareholders of the parent company is the parent's shareholders' share of consolidated net income. It is the latter amount that is recorded by the parent when the parent uses the equity method for its own internal records.

Assume that a 100%-owned subsidiary was purchased at carrying amount (i.e., no acquisition differential and no fair value–carrying amount differences). Consolidated net income will be made up of the sum of the parent's and the subsidiary's net incomes. If the subsidiary was purchased at a price greater than carrying amount, the subsidiary's net income from its separate-entity financial statements will not be correct from a consolidated point of view because the subsidiary's expenses have not been measured using amortizations of the fair values being used in the consolidated balance sheet. Therefore, the third component—the amortization and impairment of the acquisition differential—must be deducted in determining consolidated net income.

The acquisition differential is allocated to remeasure the assets and liabilities of the subsidiary at fair value for consolidation purposes. It must be amortized or written off for consolidation purposes to reflect the use, impairment, or sale of the underlying net assets. The amount amortized or written off is calculated in the same way as if these items were owned directly by the parent. The acquisition differential related to long-term assets with definite useful lives (such as buildings, equipment, and patents) is amortized over the useful lives of these assets. Inventory is not amortized but is reflected on the income statement as cost of goods sold expense when it is sold. The amount allocated to land is not amortized; it is incorporated in the calculation of the gain or loss and recognized on the income statement only when it is sold or impaired. Goodwill and certain other intangible assets are also not amortized, but, instead, a loss is reflected on the income statement when a test indicates that they are impaired. Testing for impairment is explained in more detail in the following section.

> *The acquisition differential is amortized or written off on consolidation as if the parent had purchased these net assets directly.*

Consolidated retained earnings on the date of acquisition are the parent's retained earnings only. Subsequent to acquisition, consolidated retained earnings reflect the parent's shareholders' share of the combined operations. The NCI's share of the combined operations is reflected in the NCI account, which is a separate account within the shareholders' equity section of the consolidated balance sheet. The changes in consolidated retained earnings subsequent to acquisition consist of the yearly consolidated net incomes attributable to the parent, less the yearly dividends declared by the parent. The changes in NCI subsequent to acquisition consist of the yearly consolidated net incomes attributable to the NCI, less the dividends paid by the subsidiary to the NCI. Dividends paid or declared by a subsidiary company to the parent do not appear on the consolidated statements because they do not change the financial position of the combined entity. This is an example of an intercompany transaction that must be eliminated when preparing consolidated financial statements. Intercompany transactions are discussed and illustrated in much more detail in Chapter 6.

> *The parent's separate-entity retained earnings accounted for under the equity method should always be equal to consolidated retained earnings.*

# LO1 TESTING GOODWILL AND OTHER ASSETS FOR IMPAIRMENT

In 2011, the impairment test for long-term tangible and intangible assets changed with the adoption of IFRS. Now, IAS 36 *Impairment of Assets* applies to all assets, unless they are specifically excluded because of a requirement in another standard. IAS 36 prescribes the procedures that an entity applies to ensure that its assets are carried at no more than their recoverable amount. It indicates that an asset, a group of assets, or a cash-generating unit should be written down if its carrying amount exceeds the amount to be recovered through use or sale of the asset. The write-down is called an *impairment loss* and is reported in net income, unless the asset is carried at a revalued amount in accordance with another standard such as the revaluation model in IAS 16. In certain cases, the revaluation loss would be reported in other comprehensive income.

> *An asset is impaired if its carrying amount exceeds its recoverable amount.*

*Recoverable amount* is defined as the higher of fair value less costs of disposal and value in use. *Fair value* is defined as the price that would be received to sell an asset or paid to transfer a liability in an orderly transaction between market participants at the measurement date (i.e., an exit price). It would reflect the highest and best use for nonfinancial assets. It can be determined by using quoted market prices, if available, or by making comparisons with the prices of other similar assets. *Value in use* is the present value of the future cash flows expected to be derived from the asset or group of assets.

> *Recoverable amount is the higher of fair value less costs of disposal and value in use.*

It may not be necessary to measure both fair value less costs of disposal and value in use when testing for impairment. If it is determined that one of these values is higher than the carrying amount, then the asset is not impaired and the other value need not be determined. Sometimes, it will not be possible to determine fair value less costs of disposal because there is no basis for making a reliable estimate of the amount obtainable from the sale of the asset in an orderly transaction. In this case, the entity may use the asset's value in use as its recoverable amount. When an asset is being held for disposal, most of its value in use will consist of the net disposal proceeds to be received in the near term, and future cash flows from continuing use of the asset until its disposal are likely to be negligible. In this situation, the fair value less costs of disposal would be very similar to value in use, and it would be unnecessary to explicitly determine a value in use.

Impairment testing requires the estimation of future net cash flows (cash inflows less cash outflows) associated with an individual asset. In many instances, it is impossible to associate cash flows with a single asset, and so the standard suggests that it should be accomplished with a cash-generating unit, which is defined as the smallest identifiable group of assets that generates cash inflows that are largely independent of the cash inflows from other assets or groups of assets. In the ensuing discussion on impairment testing, any reference to an individual asset is equally applicable to an individual asset or a cash-generating unit.

In this chapter, we will discuss impairment at the level of the consolidated financial statements. Although the principles of impairment testing are the same whether applied at the consolidated or the separate-entity level, the results might be different. For example, a subsidiary might determine there is no impairment of its assets based on the carrying amounts used in its separate-entity statements. Since the values used on the consolidated statements are often reported at a higher amount than the separate-entity statements because of the acquisition differential, there might be impairment at the consolidated level.

> *It is possible for an asset not to be impaired at the subsidiary level but to be impaired at the consolidated level.*

IAS 36 has different requirements for impairment testing for the following types of assets:

- Property, plant, equipment, and intangible assets with definite useful lives
- Intangible assets with indefinite useful lives or not yet available for use
- Cash-generating units and goodwill

We will discuss these three different groups separately in the following sections.

## Property, Plant, Equipment, and Intangible Assets with Definite Useful Lives

Property (except for land with an unlimited useful life), plant, equipment, and intangible assets with definite useful lives should be amortized over their useful lives. At the end of each reporting period, there is a two-step approach to determining whether an impairment loss should be reported. In step 1, the entity assesses whether indicators exist that an asset may be impaired. If, in the preparer's judgment, any such indicators exist, then step 2 must be performed and the recoverable amount determined. If no indicators exist, then it is not necessary to perform step 2.

> *The recoverable amount needs to be determined only if indicators exist that the asset may be impaired.*

In step 2, the recoverable amount is determined and compared with the asset's carrying amount. If the recoverable amount is greater than the carrying amount, no impairment exists and the asset is reported at the carrying amount. If the recoverable amount is less than the carrying amount, impairment exists and the asset is written down to its recoverable amount.

The following factors should be considered at a minimum when assessing whether there is an indication of impairment:

| External Factors | Internal Factors |
|---|---|
| An asset's market value has declined significantly. | There is evidence of obsolescence or physical damage of an asset. |
| Significant adverse changes in the technological, market, economic, or legal environment of the entity have occurred. | There have been significant adverse changes in how an asset is used or expected to be used. |
| A significant increase in market rates of return has occurred that will cause a reduction to value in use. | Evidence has arisen that the economic performance of an asset is, or will be, worse than expected. |
| The carrying amount of the net assets of the entity is more than its market capitalization. | The carrying amount of the investment in subsidiary in the separate-entity financial statements exceeds the carrying amounts in the consolidated financial statements of the investee's net assets, including associated goodwill. |
| | The dividend from the subsidiary exceeds the total comprehensive income of the subsidiary. |

> *Internal and external factors are considered when assessing if there is an indication that the asset may be impaired.*

## Intangible Assets with Indefinite Useful Lives

Intangible assets with indefinite[6] useful lives are not amortized but must be assessed for impairment on an annual basis, regardless of whether there is any indication that it may be impaired. In other words, step 1 as mentioned in the previous section is ignored and step 2 must be performed. This same requirement is applied to an intangible asset that is not yet available for use.

> *An intangible asset that is not subject to amortization is tested for impairment annually (step 2).*

This impairment test may be performed at any time during an annual period, provided it is performed at the same time every year. Different intangible assets may be tested for impairment at different times. However, if such an intangible asset was initially recognized during the current annual period, that intangible asset must be tested for impairment before the end of the current annual period.

In exceptional circumstances, the entity can use the recoverable amount from a preceding period rather than determine a new recoverable amount this period. This cost-saving measure may be used, provided all of the following criteria (as specified in IAS 36 paragraph 24) are met:

(a) If the intangible asset does not generate cash inflows from continuing use that are largely independent of those from other assets or groups of assets, and is therefore tested for impairment as part of the cash-generating unit to which it belongs, the assets and liabilities making up that unit have not changed significantly since the most recent recoverable amount calculation.

(b) The most recent recoverable amount calculation resulted in an amount that exceeded the asset's carrying amount by a substantial margin.

(c) Based on an analysis of events that have occurred and circumstances that have changed since the most recent recoverable amount calculation, the likelihood that a current recoverable amount determination would be less than the asset's carrying amount is remote.

> *When certain criteria are met, the recoverable amount from a preceding period can be used rather than determining a new recoverable amount for the current year.*

## Cash-Generating Units and Goodwill

Cash-generating units that have goodwill assigned to them must be assessed for impairment on an annual basis, and more frequently if there is an indication that the unit may be impaired. In identifying individual cash-generating units, the entity must consider whether the cash inflows from an asset (or group of assets) are largely independent of the cash inflows from other assets (or groups of assets). Various factors should be considered, such as how management monitors the entity's operations—by product line, business, individual location, district, or regional area—or how management makes decisions about continuing or disposing of the entity's assets and operations. Each unit or group of units to which the goodwill is so allocated must

(a) represent the lowest level within the entity at which the goodwill is monitored for internal management purposes; and

(b) not be larger than an operating segment determined in accordance with IFRS 8 *Operating Segments.*[7]

> *Goodwill is tested for impairment annually at the cash-generating unit level.*

The following example from IAS 36 illustrates the application of this requirement.

A bus company provides services under contract with a municipality that requires minimum service on each of five separate routes. Assets devoted to each route and the cash flows from each route can be identified separately. One of the routes operates at a significant loss. Because the entity does not have the option to curtail any one bus route, the lowest level of identifiable cash inflows that are largely independent of the cash inflows from other assets or groups of assets is the cash inflows generated by the five routes together. Therefore, the individual bus routes cannot be identified as cash-generating units. The company as a whole is identified as the cash-generating unit.

> **Cautionary Note:** *Unless otherwise noted, the examples used in the body of the text and in the end-of-chapter material will assume that goodwill is assessed for impairment at the level of the entity as a whole. When information is available to test for impairment at lower levels, then the tests should be performed at the lower level.*

To test goodwill for impairment, the recoverable amount for the subsidiary as a whole is compared with the carrying amount of the subsidiary's assets and liabilities, including goodwill. If the recoverable amount exceeds the carrying amount, goodwill is not impaired. If the recoverable amount is less than the carrying amount, an impairment loss should be recognized and should be allocated to reduce the carrying amount of the assets in the following order:

(a) First, to reduce the carrying amount of any goodwill

(b) Then, to the other assets of the unit pro rata on the basis of the carrying amount of each asset

> *Any impairment loss for a CGU is applied first to goodwill and then to other assets.*

The following example illustrates the goodwill impairment test when the subsidiary as a whole is identified as the cash-generating unit: On January 1, Year 5, P Co. acquired 100% of S Co. for $1,000. At the date of acquisition, $900 was assigned to identifiable net assets and $100 was recognized as goodwill. At the end of Year 5, the carrying amount of S Co.'s net assets was $950, including the goodwill of $100. Since S Co is now wholly owned by P Co., the shares of S are not being traded and a market value is not readily available. Therefore, the recoverable amount for S Co. at the end of Year 5 is based on the present value of future cash flows.

The following table shows the goodwill impairment test under three different scenarios:

|  | #1 | #2 | #3 |
|---|---|---|---|
| Recoverable amount | 995 | 945 | 840 |
| Carrying amount | 950 | 950 | 950 |
| Total impairment | n/a | 5 | 110 |
| Goodwill impairment loss | n/a | 5 | 100 |
| Impairment of other assets | n/a | n/a | 10 |
| Goodwill before impairment | 100 | 100 | 100 |
| Goodwill after impairment | 100 | 95 | 0 |

Appendix 5A provides further details of the tests for goodwill impairment and illustrations of goodwill impairment in more complex situations.

## Reversing an Impairment Loss

An impairment loss recognized in a prior period for an asset or cash-generating unit can be reversed under certain conditions. However, an impairment loss recognized for goodwill cannot be reversed in a subsequent period. A two-step process for reversing an impairment loss is followed, similar to the process followed for the initial recognition of impairment losses. In step 1, an entity assesses whether there is any indication that an impairment loss may no longer exist or may have decreased. If any such indication exists, then step 2 must be performed and the recoverable amount determined. If no such indication exists, it is not necessary to perform step 2.

---

*Impairment losses on assets other than goodwill can be reversed.*

---

Indications of a potential decrease in an impairment loss are basically the same as those of a potential impairment loss, which were described earlier. If there is an indication that an impairment loss may no longer exist or may have decreased, this may signal that the remaining useful life, the depreciation method, or the residual value may need to be reviewed and adjusted in accordance with the IFRS applicable to the asset, even if no impairment loss is reversed for the asset.

An impairment loss shall be reversed if, and only if, there has been a change in the estimates used to determine the asset's recoverable amount. An impairment loss is not reversed when the recoverable amount increases strictly due to the passage of time; that is, the present value of future cash inflows increases as they become closer to occurring.

The reversal of an impairment loss is reported in net income unless the asset is carried at a revalued amount in accordance with another standard (e.g., in accordance with the revaluation model in IAS 16). The assets should not be written up to an amount exceeding the carrying amount that would have been determined had no impairment loss been recognized for the asset in prior years.

---

*The asset cannot be written up to an amount higher than it would have been if impairment losses had not been recognized.*

---

A reversal of an impairment loss for a cash-generating unit must be allocated to the assets of the unit pro rata with the carrying amount of those assets. However, an asset should never be reduced to less than its recoverable amount. An impairment loss relating to goodwill must not be reversed. Any increase in the recoverable amount of goodwill is likely to be an increase in internally generated goodwill, rather than a reversal of the impairment loss recognized for the acquired goodwill. IAS 38 prohibits the recognition of internally generated goodwill.

## Disclosure Requirements

The disclosure requirements related to impairment of assets are quite extensive and are stated in paragraphs 126 to 134 of IAS 36. The following summarizes the main requirements:

- For each class of assets—the amount of impairment losses and reversals of impairment losses segregated by what amounts are recognized in net income versus other comprehensive income

- For each major impairment loss recognized or reversed related to individual assets—the events and circumstances that led to the recognition or reversal, whether the recoverable amount is its fair value less costs of disposal or value in use; the basis used to determine fair value less costs of disposal; and the discount rate(s) used in determining value in use

- For cash-generating units or intangible assets with indefinite lives—the carrying amount of goodwill and of intangible assets with indefinite useful lives allocated to the unit, the basis used in determining recoverable amount, a description of key assumptions on which management has based its cash flow projections, and the methodology used to determine fair value less costs of disposal

> *Substantial information relating to impairment losses and reversals of impairment losses must be disclosed.*

Canadian Imperial Bank of Commerce (CIBC) is a diversified financial institution with three main business units: Retail and Business Banking, Wealth Management and Wholesale Banking. CIBC provides a full range of financial services and products to 11 million individual, small business, commercial, corporate and institutional clients in Canada and around the world. It reported goodwill impairment losses of $420 million in its 2014 income statement. Excerpts from these statements are presented in Exhibit 5.1.

### EXHIBIT 5.1

## Extracts from CIBC'S 2014 Financial Statements

**NOTE 1: BASIS OF PREPARATION AND SUMMARY OF SIGNIFICANT ACCOUNTING POLICIES**
**GOODWILL, SOFTWARE AND OTHER INTANGIBLE ASSETS**

Goodwill represents the excess of the purchase price over the fair value of the net identifiable assets, liabilities and contingent liabilities acquired in business combinations. Identifiable intangible assets are recognized separately from goodwill when they are separable or arise from contractual or other legal rights, and have fair values that can be reliably measured.

Goodwill is not amortized, but is subject to impairment review at least annually or more frequently if there is indication that the goodwill may be impaired. Refer to the "Impairment of non-financial assets" policy below.

**IMPAIRMENT OF NON-FINANCIAL ASSETS**

The carrying value of non-financial assets with definite useful lives, including buildings and equipment, investment property, and intangible assets with definite useful lives are reviewed to determine whether there is any indication of impairment. Goodwill and intangible assets with indefinite useful lives are tested for impairment at least annually, and whenever there is an indication that the asset may be impaired. If any such indication of impairment exists, the recoverable amount of the asset is estimated in order to determine the extent of the impairment loss, if any.

*(continued)*

Goodwill is assessed for impairment based on the group of CGUs expected to benefit from the synergies of the business combination, and the lowest level at which management monitors the goodwill. Any potential goodwill impairment is identified by comparing the recoverable amount of the CGU grouping to which the goodwill is allocated to its carrying value including the allocated goodwill. If the recoverable amount is less than its carrying value, an impairment loss is recognized in the consolidated statement of income in the period in which it occurs. Impairment losses on goodwill are not subsequently reversed if conditions change.

### NOTE 8: GOODWILL, SOFTWARE AND OTHER INTANGIBLE ASSETS

### GOODWILL

The carrying amount of goodwill is reviewed for impairment annually as at August 1 and whenever there are events or changes in circumstances which indicate that the carrying amount may not be recoverable. Goodwill is allocated to CGUs for the purposes of impairment testing based on the lowest level for which identifiable cash inflows are largely independent of cash inflows of other assets or groups of assets. The goodwill impairment test is performed by comparing the recoverable amount of the CGU to which goodwill has been allocated, with the carrying amount of the CGU including goodwill, with any deficiency recognized as impairment to goodwill. The recoverable amount of a CGU is defined as the higher of its estimated fair value less cost to sell and value in use.

> *Goodwill is tested for impairment annually and whenever there is an indication of impairment.*

We have three significant CGUs to which goodwill has been allocated. The changes in the carrying amount of goodwill are allocated to each CGU as follows:

**CGUs**

**$ MILLIONS, FOR THE YEAR ENDED OCTOBER 31**

|  | CIBC FirstCaribbean | Canadian Wealth Management | Atlantic Trust | Other | Total |
|---|---|---|---|---|---|
| 2014 Balance at beginning of year | $727 | $884 | $ — | $122 | $1,733 |
| Acquisitions | — | — | 84 | — | 84 |
| Impairment | (420) | — | — | — | (420) |
| Adjustments (1) | 46 | — | 5 | 2 | 53 |
| Balance at end of year | $353 | $884 | $89 | $124 | $1,450 |
| 2013 Balance at beginning of year | $696 | $884 | $ — | $121 | $1,701 |
| Adjustments (1) | 31 | — | — | 1 | 32 |
| Balance at end of year | $727 | $884 | $ — | $122 | $1,733 |

(1) Includes foreign currency translation adjustments.

### IMPAIRMENT TESTING OF GOODWILL AND KEY ASSUMPTIONS

### CIBC FirstCaribbean

CIBC became the majority shareholder of CIBC FirstCaribbean in December 2006 and now holds 91.7% of its shares. CIBC FirstCaribbean is a major Caribbean bank offering a full range of financial services in corporate banking, retail banking, wealth management, credit cards, treasury sales and trading, and investment banking. CIBC FirstCaribbean, which has assets of over US$11 billion, operates in the Caribbean and is traded on the stock exchanges of Barbados, Trinidad, Bahamas and Eastern Caribbean. The results of CIBC FirstCaribbean are included in Corporate and Other.

The recoverable amount of the CIBC FirstCaribbean CGU is based on a value in use calculation that is estimated using a five-year cash flow projection approved by management of CIBC FirstCaribbean and an estimate of the capital required to be maintained in the region to support ongoing operations.

> *The recoverable amount of the FirstCaribbean CGU is based on a value in use calculation.*

(continued)

**EXHIBIT 5.1** *(continued)*

During the second quarter of 2014, we revised our expectations concerning the extent and timing of the recovery of economic conditions in the Caribbean region. We identified this change in expectation as an indicator of impairment and therefore estimated the recoverable amount of CIBC FirstCaribbean as at April 30, 2014 based on forecasts adjusted to reflect management's belief that the economic recovery expected in the Caribbean region would occur over a longer period of time than previously forecasted, and that estimated realizable values of underlying collateral for non-performing loans would be lower than previously expected. We determined that the carrying amount of the CIBC FirstCaribbean CGU exceeded our estimate of its recoverable amount as at April 30, 2014. As a result, we recognized a goodwill impairment charge in other non-interest expense of $420 million during the three months ended April 30, 2014. This charge is reflected in the results of the Corporate and Other reporting segment.

We also performed our annual impairment test as of August 1, 2014 based on an updated five-year forecast prepared by management of CIBC FirstCaribbean during the fourth quarter of 2014. The forecast continues to reflect the currently challenging economic conditions and an expected, but delayed, recovery in those conditions within the Caribbean region. For the impairment test performed as at August 1, 2014, we determined that the recoverable amount of the CIBC FirstCaribbean CGU approximated its carrying value. As a result, no additional impairment loss has been recognized.

A terminal growth rate of 2.5% as at August 1, 2014 (April 30, 2014: 2.5%; August 1, 2013: 2.5%) was applied to the years after the five-year forecast. All of the forecast cash flows were discounted at an after-tax rate of 13% as at August 1, 2014 (13.73% pre-tax) which we believe to be a risk adjusted interest rate appropriate to CIBC FirstCaribbean (we used an identical after-tax rate of 13% as at April 30, 2014 and as at August 1, 2013). The determination of a discount rate and a terminal growth rate require the exercise of judgment. The discount rate was determined based on the following primary factors: (i) the risk-free rate, (ii) an equity risk premium, (iii) beta adjustment to the equity risk premium based on a review of betas of comparable publicly traded financial institutions in the region, and (iv) a country risk premium. The terminal growth rate was based on management's expectations of real growth and forecast inflation rates.

> *CIBC used an after-tax risk adjusted discount rate of 13% to determine the value in use.*

Estimation of the recoverable amount is an area of significant judgment. Reductions in the estimated recoverable amount could arise from various factors, such as, reductions in forecasted cash flows, an increase in the assumed level of required capital, and any adverse changes to the discount rate or the terminal growth rate either in isolation or in any combination thereof. We estimated that a 10% decrease in each of the terminal year's and subsequent years' forecasted cash flows would result in a reduction in the estimated recoverable amount of the CIBC FirstCaribbean CGU of approximately $130 million as at August 1, 2014. We also estimated that a 50 basis point increase in the after-tax discount rate would result in a reduction in the estimated recoverable amount of the CIBC FirstCaribbean CGU of approximately $75 million as at August 1, 2014. These sensitivities are indicative only and should be considered with caution, as the effect of the variation in each assumption on the estimated recoverable amount is calculated in isolation without changing any other assumptions. In practice, changes in one factor may result in changes in another, which may magnify, counteract or obfuscate the disclosed sensitivities.

*Source: CIBC, 2014 Annual Report. Pages 102 & 126. Reproduced with permission from CIBC.*

Now that we have seen how to test for impairment, we will illustrate the preparation of consolidated financial statements subsequent to the date of acquisition. The first illustrations assume that the subsidiary is 100% owned. Later illustrations will assume a less than 100%-owned subsidiary.

## LO2 CONSOLIDATION OF A 100%-OWNED SUBSIDIARY

Company P purchased 100% of the outstanding common shares of Company S on January 1, Year 5, for $19,000. On that date, Company S's common shares had a carrying amount of $10,000 and its retained earnings balance was $6,000. The inventory of Company S had a fair value that was $2,000 greater than carrying amount, and the carrying amounts of all other assets and liabilities of Company S were equal to fair values. Any goodwill will be tested yearly for impairment. Both companies have a December 31 year-end. The journal entry made by Company P to record the acquisition of 100% of Company S was as follows:

| | | |
|---|---|---|
| Investment in S | 19,000 | |
| Cash | | 19,000 |

There is no compelling reason for Company P to prepare a consolidated balance sheet on acquisition date; however, it is useful to illustrate its preparation as the starting point for the preparation of consolidated statements in subsequent years. The calculation and allocation of the acquisition differential is shown in Exhibit 5.2.

**EXHIBIT 5.2**

### CALCULATION OF ACQUISITION DIFFERENTIAL
#### January 1, Year 5

| | | |
|---|---|---|
| Cost of 100% of Company S | | $19,000 |
| Carrying amount of Company S's net assets: | | |
| Assets | $27,000 | |
| Liabilities | (11,000) | |
| | | 16,000 |
| Acquisition differential | | 3,000 |
| Allocated: | FV – CA | |
| Inventory | 2,000 | 2,000 **(a)** |
| Balance—goodwill | | $ 1,000 **(b)** |

Below are the individual balance sheets of Company P and Company S on January 1, Year 5, along with Company P's consolidated balance sheet prepared using the *direct approach*.

### BALANCE SHEETS
#### At January 1, Year 5

| | Company P | Company S | Consolidated |
|---|---|---|---|
| Miscellaneous assets | $139,000 | $17,000 | $156,000 |
| Inventory | 22,000 | 10,000 | 34,000 |
| Investment in S | 19,000 | — | — |
| Goodwill | — | — | 1,000 |
| | $180,000 | $27,000 | $191,000 |
| Liabilities | $45,000 | $11,000 | $56,000 |
| Common shares | 50,000 | 10,000 | 50,000 |
| Retained earnings | 85,000 | 6,000 | 85,000 |
| | $180,000 | $27,000 | $191,000 |

> *The investment account is replaced by the carrying amount of the subsidiary's assets and liabilities plus the acquisition differential.*

The consolidated balance sheet was prepared by eliminating the shareholders' equity of Company S ($16,000) against Company P's investment account ($19,000) and then by allocating the resultant acquisition differential ($3,000) to the inventory of Company S ($2,000), with the unallocated balance recognized as goodwill ($1,000).

## Consolidated Statements, End of Year 5

In Year 5, Company S reported net income of $7,300 and paid a cash dividend of $2,500. Company P's net income for the year was $18,300 (not including income from its investment in Company S). Using the cost method to account for its investment, Company P makes a single entry to record the dividend received from Company S on December 31, Year 5, as follows:

| | | |
|---|---|---|
| Cash | 2,500 | |
|     Dividend income | | 2,500 |
| Dividend received from Company S | | |

---

*The cost method records income when dividends are received or receivable.*

---

Company P adds the dividend income ($2,500) to its earnings from its own operations ($18,300) and reports a final net income for Year 5 of $20,800. An impairment test on goodwill conducted on December 31, Year 5, indicated that a $50 loss had occurred.

The financial statements of Company P and Company S as at December 31, Year 5, are presented in Exhibit 5.3.

**EXHIBIT 5.3**

### YEAR 5 INCOME STATEMENTS

| | Company P | Company S |
|---|---|---|
| Sales | $ 50,000 | $30,000 |
| Dividend income | 2,500 | — |
|     Total revenue | 52,500 | 30,000 |
| Cost of sales | 26,500 | 14,700 |
| Expenses (miscellaneous) | 5,200 | 8,000 |
|     Total expenses | 31,700 | 22,700 |
|       Net income | $ 20,800 | $ 7,300 |

---

*The parent's income from its own operations is $20,800 − $2,500 = $18,300.*

---

### YEAR 5 RETAINED EARNINGS STATEMENTS

| | Company P | Company S |
|---|---|---|
| Balance, January 1 | $ 85,000 | $ 6,000 |
| Net income | 20,800 | 7,300 |
| | 105,800 | 13,300 |
| Dividends | 6,000 | 2,500 |
| Balance, December 31 | $ 99,800 | $10,800 |

*(continued)*

**BALANCE SHEETS**

At December 31, Year 5

| | Company P | Company S |
|---|---|---|
| Miscellaneous assets | $147,800 | $18,300 |
| Inventory | 30,000 | 14,000 |
| Investment in S (cost method) | 19,000 | — |
| | $196,800 | $32,300 |
| Liabilities | $ 47,000 | $11,500 |
| Common shares | 50,000 | 10,000 |
| Retained earnings | 99,800 | 10,800 |
| | $196,800 | $32,300 |

> *The investment account remains at the original cost in the parent's separate-entity balance sheet.*

Before beginning to prepare the consolidated financial statements, Company P prepares Exhibit 5.4, which shows the amortization of the acquisition differential for Year 5. This schedule and the financial statements of the two companies shown in Exhibit 5.3 form the basis for the preparation of Company P's Year 5 consolidated statements, shown in Exhibit 5.5.

**EXHIBIT 5.4**

**ACQUISITION DIFFERENTIAL AMORTIZATION AND IMPAIRMENT SCHEDULE**

| | Balance Jan. 1, Year 5 | Amortization and Impairment Year 5 | Balance Dec. 31, Year 5 | |
|---|---|---|---|---|
| Inventory **(2a)** | $2,000 | $2,000 | $ — | **(a)** |
| Goodwill **(2b)** | 1,000 | 50 | 950 | **(b)** |
| | $3,000 | $2,050 | $950 | **(c)** |

> *The amortization and impairment of the acquisition differential will be reflected on the consolidated financial statements.*

**EXHIBIT 5.5**

**YEAR 5 CONSOLIDATED FINANCIAL STATEMENTS**

(direct approach)

**COMPANY P**

**CONSOLIDATED INCOME STATEMENT**

For the year ended December 31, Year 5

| | |
|---|---|
| Sales (50,000 + 30,000) | $ 80,000 |
| Cost of sales (26,500 + 14,700 + **[4a] 2,000**) | 43,200 |
| Goodwill impairment loss (0 + 0 + **[4b] 50**) | 50 |
| Expenses (misc.) (5,200 + 8,000) | 13,200 |
| | 56,450 |
| Net income | $ 23,550 |

*(continued)*

**EXHIBIT 5.5** *(continued)*

> *Consolidated net income is the same regardless of whether the parent used the cost method or the equity method in its internal records.*

**COMPANY P**
**CONSOLIDATED STATEMENT OF RETAINED EARNINGS**
For the year ended December 31, Year 5

| | |
|---|---:|
| Balance, January 1 | $ 85,000 |
| Net income | 23,550 |
| | 108,550 |
| Dividends | 6,000 |
| Balance, December 31 | $102,550 |

> *Dividends on the consolidated statement of retained earnings are the dividends of the parent.*

**COMPANY P**
**CONSOLIDATED BALANCE SHEET**
At December 31, Year 5

| | |
|---|---:|
| Miscellaneous assets (147,800 + 18,300) | $166,100 |
| Inventory (30,000 + 14,000 + **[4a] 0**) | 44,000 |
| Goodwill (0 + 0 + **[4b] 950**) | 950 |
| | $211,050 |
| Liabilities (47,000 + 11,500) | $ 58,500 |
| Common shares | 50,000 |
| Retained earnings | 102,550 |
| | $211,050 |

The details of the Year 5 amortizations are explained as follows:

1. The inventory of Company S was remeasured for consolidated purposes on January 1, Year 5, to reflect its fair value. If we assume that Company S uses a FIFO cost flow,[8] it would be safe to assume that this inventory was sold during Year 5. Since the cost of sales of Company S does not reflect the $2,000 additional cost, cost of sales on the Year 5 consolidated income statement will be increased by $2,000 to reflect the additional cost of Company S.

2. An impairment test on goodwill conducted on December 31, Year 5, indicated that a $50 loss had occurred.

3. The $1,000 goodwill is not reflected in the financial statements of Company S, nor is the impairment loss. The consolidated income statement will have to reflect this loss, and at December 31, Year 5, the consolidated balance sheet will have to show the goodwill at cost less accumulated impairment losses.

> *The acquisition differential related to inventory is expensed when the inventory is sold.*

Using the schedule we introduced in the Consolidated Income and Retained Earnings Statements section earlier in this chapter, we make the following calculation:

### CALCULATION OF CONSOLIDATED NET INCOME
Year 5

| | | |
|---|---:|---:|
| Company P net income—cost method | | $20,800 |
| Less dividend income from Company S | | 2,500 |
| Company P net income, own operations | | 18,300 |
| Company S net income | 7,300 | |
| Acquisition differential amortization and impairment **(4c)** | (2,050) | 5,250 |
| Consolidated net income | | $23,550 |

*This calculation starts with income under the cost method and converts it to consolidated net income.*

Since Company P owns 100% of Company S, all of the consolidated net income is attributable to the shareholders of Company P.

Note that dividend income from Company S is not included in consolidated net income because this income was not received from an external party. The consolidated income statement is prepared by excluding the dividend income and adding the revenues and expenses of the two companies.

The preparation of the Year 5 consolidated financial statements is shown in Exhibit 5.5. The consolidated amounts were determined by adding the amounts shown in brackets. These amounts came from the financial statements of Company P and Company S and from the acquisition differential amortization and impairment schedule. Note the bracketed amounts shown for goodwill impairment loss and for goodwill on the balance sheet. The two zero amounts indicate that these items do not appear in the separate-entity financial statements of Company P and Company S.

*The amortization/impairment of the various components of the acquisition differential is reflected on the consolidated financial statements.*

The Year 5 consolidated retained earnings statement is prepared using the January 1 retained earnings of Company P, consolidated net income attributable to Company P, and Company P's dividends. Only Company P's retained earnings are included on January 1 because, as we learned in Chapter 3, consolidated retained earnings at the date of acquisition consist only of the parent's retained earnings. Only the parent's dividends are included on the consolidated statement of retained earnings, because only the parent's dividends were paid to shareholders outside of the consolidated entity. The subsidiary's dividends were received by the parent and were not paid to anyone outside of the consolidated entity, and they are therefore eliminated when preparing the consolidated financial statements.

The parent's investment account does not appear on the consolidated balance sheet. Consolidated shareholders' equity contains the common shares of the parent and retained earnings from the consolidated retained earnings statement. The net assets of the parent are combined with the net assets of the subsidiary after they have been remeasured with the unamortized acquisition differential.

*The underlying assets and liabilities of the subsidiary plus the unamortized acquisition differential replace the investment account.*

If the parent had used the equity method in its internal records, the entries made during the year would have been different than under the cost method. When preparing the consolidated net income at the end of the year, the subsidiary's assets, liabilities, revenues, and expenses replace the investment account and equity method income account. After making the adjustments for the amortization of the acquisition differential, the consolidated financial statements will look exactly the same as the statements above. Further explanation and illustration of the consolidation process when the parent used the equity method is provided later in this chapter.

## Consolidated Statements, End of Year 6

In Year 6, Company S reported net income of $10,000 and paid a cash dividend of $3,000. Company P's net income for the year was $19,000 (not including income from its investment in Company S). An impairment test conducted on December 31, Year 6, indicated that the goodwill had a recoverable amount of $870. As a result, a loss of $80 has occurred.

On December 31, Year 6, Company P makes the following cost-method journal entry:

| | | |
|---|---|---|
| Cash | 3,000 | |
| Dividend income | | 3,000 |
| Dividend received by Company S | | |

The dividend income ($3,000) combined with the previous operating earnings ($19,000) gives Company P a final net income for Year 6 of $22,000.

The financial statements of the two companies as at December 31, Year 6, are presented in Exhibit 5.6, and the acquisition differential amortization and impairment schedule at the end of Year 6 follow, in Exhibit 5.7.

**EXHIBIT 5.6**

### YEAR 6 INCOME STATEMENTS

| | Company P | Company S |
|---|---|---|
| Sales | $ 60,000 | $40,000 |
| Dividend income | 3,000 | — |
| Total revenue | 63,000 | 40,000 |
| Cost of sales | 32,000 | 18,000 |
| Expenses (misc.) | 9,000 | 12,000 |
| Total expenses | 41,000 | 30,000 |
| Net income | $ 22,000 | $10,000 |

> *The parent's income includes dividend income from the subsidiary, which can be reconciled to dividends paid by the subsidiary.*

### YEAR 6 RETAINED EARNINGS STATEMENTS

| | Company P | Company S |
|---|---|---|
| Balance, January 1 | $ 99,800 | $10,800 |
| Net income | 22,000 | 10,000 |
| | 121,800 | 20,800 |
| Dividends | 8,000 | 3,000 |
| Balance, December 31 | $113,800 | $17,800 |

*(continued)*

**BALANCE SHEETS**

At December 31, Year 6

|  | Company P | Company S |
|---|---|---|
| Miscellaneous assets | $131,800 | $21,000 |
| Inventory | 35,000 | 16,000 |
| Investment in S (cost method) | 19,000 | — |
|  | $185,800 | $37,000 |
| Liabilities | $ 22,000 | $ 9,200 |
| Common shares | 50,000 | 10,000 |
| Retained earnings | 113,800 | 17,800 |
|  | $185,800 | $37,000 |

*The investment account still remains at the original cost.*

**EXHIBIT 5.7**

**ACQUISITION DIFFERENTIAL AMORTIZATION AND IMPAIRMENT SCHEDULE**

|  | Balance Jan. 1, Year 5 | Amort. & Impair. to End of Year 5 | Balance Dec. 31, Year 5 | Amort. & Impair. Year 6 | Balance Dec. 31, Year 6 |  |
|---|---|---|---|---|---|---|
| Inventory **(2a)** | $2,000 | $2,000 | $ — | $ — | $ — | **(a)** |
| Goodwill **(2b)** | 1,000 | 50 | 950 | 80 | 870 | **(b)** |
|  | $3,000 | $2,050 | $950 | $80 | $870 | **(c)** |

*The amortization of the acquisition differential is not reflected in the investment account when the parent uses the cost method.*

Because Company P has used the cost method, it is necessary to make two preliminary calculations before preparing the consolidated income statement and retained earnings statement. We first calculate consolidated net income for Year 6, as follows:

| | | |
|---|---|---|
| Company P net income—cost method | | $22,000 |
| Less: dividend income from Company S | | 3,000 |
| Company P net income, own operations | | 19,000 |
| Company S net income | 10,000 | |
| Acquisition differential amortization and impairment **(7c)** | (80) | 9,920 |
| Consolidated net income | | $28,920 |

*Only the Year 6 amortization of the acquisition differential is deducted when calculating consolidated net income for Year 6.*

Because we are consolidating more than one year after the date of acquisition, an additional calculation is required. Company P's separate-entity retained earnings on January 1, Year 6, are not equal to consolidated retained earnings. The calculation of consolidated retained earnings as at January 1, Year 6, is as follows:

| | | |
|---|---:|---:|
| Company P retained earnings, Jan. 1, Year 6 (cost method) | | $ 99,800 |
| Company S retained earnings, Jan. 1, Year 6 | 10,800 | |
| Company S retained earnings, acquisition date | 6,000 | |
| Increase since acquisition | 4,800 | |
| Acquisition differential amortization and impairment to end of Year 5 **(7c)** | (2,050) | |
| | 2,750 | |
| Company P ownership | 100% | 2,750 |
| Consolidated retained earnings, Jan. 1, Year 6 | | $102,550 |

---

*This calculation converts retained earnings from the cost method to the equity method at a point in time.*

*Retained earnings reflect the cumulative effect of all adjustments to a point in time.*

---

The points that follow are presented as further explanation of why a calculation of this nature adjusts a parent's retained earnings under the cost method to retained earnings under the equity method. These points require careful reading because it is very important that you understand fully why this particular process actually works.

1. Consolidated retained earnings at the acquisition date consist only of the retained earnings of the parent company. Consolidated retained earnings subsequent to the date of acquisition represent only the parent's portion of retained earnings of the combined entities. The non-controlling interest's portion of retained earnings is incorporated in non-controlling interest, which is reported in a separate line in shareholders' equity.

2. Consolidated net income attributable to the parent company in any single year since the acquisition date consists of the net income of the parent company (from its own operations), plus the parent's share of the net income of the subsidiary, less the parent's share of the acquisition-differential amortization for that year.

3. It should logically follow that the consolidated retained earnings balance at any time subsequent to the acquisition date must contain the parent's share of the subsidiary's net incomes earned since the acquisition date, less the total of the amortization of the acquisition differential to that date.

4. Since the parent has used the cost method for internal record keeping, the parent's retained earnings contain only the parent's share of the dividends that the subsidiary has declared since the acquisition date.

---

*The parent's retained earnings under the cost method include dividend income from the subsidiary since the date of acquisition.*

---

5. The sum of net incomes less the sum of dividends, both measured from the acquisition date, equals the change (increase or decrease) in retained earnings measured from the same date.

6. When we add the parent's share of the change in the retained earnings of the subsidiary to the retained earnings of the parent (which contain the parent's share of the subsidiary's dividends under the cost method), the resulting calculated amount now contains the parent's share of the subsidiary's net income earned since the date of acquisition. By deducting the parent's share of the total amortization of the acquisition differential to date from this amount, we arrive at a retained earnings number that represents the retained earnings of the parent under the equity method, which of course is equal to consolidated retained earnings.

---

*The change in retained earnings plus cumulative dividends paid is equal to cumulative net income.*

---

The consolidated income statement is prepared—using the income statements of the two companies (see Exhibit 5.6), the Year 6 acquisition differential amortization and impairment schedule, and the calculation of consolidated net income for Year 6—by adding the revenues and expenses of the two companies, adjusting the expenses for the Year 6 amortization, excluding the dividend income, and verifying that the net income on the statement equals the calculated net income.

The consolidated retained earnings statement for Year 6 is prepared using the calculated amount for consolidated retained earnings for January 1, adding consolidated net income, and deducting the dividends of Company P.

The consolidated balance sheet is prepared in the usual manner, except that the amount for retained earnings is taken from the consolidated retained earnings statement.

---

*The consolidated financial statements present the combined position of the parent and the subsidiary as if the parent had acquired the subsidiary's assets and liabilities directly.*

---

Exhibit 5.8 shows the preparation of the Year 6 consolidated financial statements using the direct approach.

**EXHIBIT 5.8**

### YEAR 6 CONSOLIDATED FINANCIAL STATEMENTS
(direct approach)
### COMPANY P
### CONSOLIDATED INCOME STATEMENT
For the year ended December 31, Year 6

| | |
|---|---:|
| Sales (60,000 + 40,000) | $100,000 |
| Cost of sales (32,000 + 18,000) | 50,000 |
| Goodwill impairment loss (0 + 0 + **(7b) 80**) | 80 |
| Expenses (misc.) (9,000 + 12,000) | 21,000 |
| | 71,080 |
| Net income | $ 28,920 |

*(continued)*

**EXHIBIT 5.8** *(continued)*

### COMPANY P
### CONSOLIDATED STATEMENT OF RETAINED EARNINGS
For the year ended December 31, Year 6

| | |
|---|---|
| Balance, January 1 | $102,550 |
| Net income | 28,920 |
| | 131,470 |
| Dividends | 8,000 |
| Balance, December 31 | $123,470 |

> *Consolidated retained earnings are the same regardless of whether the parent used the cost method or the equity method in its internal records.*

### COMPANY P
### CONSOLIDATED BALANCE SHEET
At December 31, Year 6

| | |
|---|---|
| Miscellaneous assets (131,800 + 21,000) | $152,800 |
| Inventory (35,000 + 16,000) | 51,000 |
| Goodwill (0 + 0 + **(7b) 870**) | 870 |
| | $204,670 |
| | |
| Liabilities (22,000 + 9,200) | $ 31,200 |
| Common shares | 50,000 |
| Retained earnings | 123,470 |
| | $204,670 |

> *The unamortized acquisition differential related to goodwill is reported on the consolidated balance sheet and is the same amount regardless of whether the parent used the cost method or the equity method in its internal records.*

## LO3 CONSOLIDATION OF AN 80%-OWNED SUBSIDIARY—DIRECT APPROACH

We now illustrate the consolidation of Company P and its 80%-owned subsidiary, Company S, over a two-year period when the cost method has been used to account for the investment.

Assume that on January 1, Year 5, instead of purchasing 100% of Company S for $19,000, Company P purchased 80% for $15,200. Non-controlling interest is measured using the fair value enterprise approach; that is, entity theory. All other facts about the two companies are the same as in the previous example. The journal entry of Company P on January 1, Year 5, is as follows:

| | | |
|---|---|---|
| Investment in S | 15,200 | |
| Cash | | 15,200 |

The calculation and allocation of the acquisition differential and the calculation of the non-controlling interest on January 1, Year 5, are shown in Exhibit 5.9. The following are the individual balance sheets of Company P and Company S, as well as Company P's consolidated balance sheet on January 1, Year 5, prepared using the direct approach:

**BALANCE SHEETS**

At January 1, Year 5

|  | Company P | Company S | Consolidated |
|---|---|---|---|
| Miscellaneous assets | $142,800 | $17,000 | $159,800 |
| Inventory | 22,000 | 10,000 | 34,000 |
| Investment in S | 15,200 | — | — |
| Goodwill | — | — | 1,000 |
|  | $180,000 | $27,000 | $194,800 |
| Liabilities | $ 45,000 | $11,000 | $ 56,000 |
| Common shares | 50,000 | 10,000 | 50,000 |
| Retained earnings | 85,000 | 6,000 | 85,000 |
| Non-controlling interest | — | — | 3,800 |
|  | $180,000 | $27,000 | $194,800 |

*The subsidiary's assets and liabilities are brought onto the consolidated financial statements at 100% of their fair values.*

**EXHIBIT 5.9**

**COMPANY P**

**CALCULATION AND ALLOCATION OF ACQUISITION DIFFERENTIAL**

January 1, Year 5

| | | |
|---|---|---|
| Cost of 80% of Company S | | $15,200 |
| Implied value of 100% of Company S | | $19,000 |
| Carrying amount of Company S's net assets: | | |
| Assets | $27,000 | |
| Liabilities | (11,000) | |
| | | 16,000 |
| Acquisition differential | | 3,000 |
| Allocated: | (FV – CA) | |
| Inventory | 2,000 | 2,000 (a) |
| Balance—goodwill | | $ 1,000 (b) |

*The implied value of the subsidiary is derived by taking the purchase price and dividing by the percentage ownership acquired by the parent.*

**CALCULATION OF NON-CONTROLLING INTEREST**

January 1, Year 5

| | |
|---|---|
| Implied fair value, Company S (above) | $19,000 |
| Non-controlling interest's percentage ownership | 20% |
| Non-controlling interest | $ 3,800 (c) |

*NCI is based on the implied value of the subsidiary as a whole.*

The consolidated balance sheet was prepared as follows:

1. Eliminate the investment account and Company S's shareholders' equity.

2. Add the implied acquisition differential to Company S's assets and liabilities in order to use 100% of the fair values for Company S's assets and liabilities.

3. Report non-controlling interest as a component of shareholders' equity at a value representing the non-controlling interest's share of Company S's implied value.

## Consolidated Statements, End of Year 5

In Year 5, Company S reported net income of $7,300 and paid a cash dividend of $2,500. Company P's net income for the year was $18,300 (not including income from its investment in Company S).

The cost method journal entry of Company P on December 31, Year 5, is as follows:

| | | |
|---|---|---|
| Cash | 2,000 | |
| Dividend income | | 2,000 |
| 80% of the dividend received from Company S | | |

---

*Company P's dividend income is 80% of dividends paid by the subsidiary.*

---

Company P's net income for Year 5 is reported as $20,300 after the receipt of the dividend from Company S. An impairment test on goodwill conducted on December 31, Year 5, indicated that a $50 loss had occurred. The financial statements of Company P and Company S as at December 31, Year 5, are shown in Exhibit 5.10.

### EXHIBIT 5.10

#### YEAR 5 INCOME STATEMENTS

| | Company P | Company S | |
|---|---|---|---|
| Sales | $ 50,000 | $30,000 | |
| Dividend income | 2,000 | — | (a) |
| Total revenue | 52,000 | 30,000 | |
| Cost of sales | 26,500 | 14,700 | |
| Expenses (miscellaneous) | 5,200 | 8,000 | |
| Total expenses | 31,700 | 22,700 | |
| Net income | $ 20,300 | $ 7,300 | (b) |

---

*The parent's income includes dividend income from the subsidiary, which can be reconciled to dividends paid by the subsidiary.*

---

#### YEAR 5 RETAINED EARNINGS STATEMENTS

| | Company P | Company S | |
|---|---|---|---|
| Balance, January 1 | $ 85,000 | $ 6,000 | (c) |
| Net income | 20,300 | 7,300 | |
| | 105,300 | 13,300 | |
| Dividends | 6,000 | 2,500 | |
| Balance, December 31 | $ 99,300 | $10,800 | |

*(continued)*

> *The parent's retained earnings include the parent's income under the cost method, which includes dividend income from the subsidiary.*

**BALANCE SHEETS**

At December 31, Year 5

|  | Company P | Company S | |
|---|---|---|---|
| Miscellaneous assets | $151,100 | $18,300 | |
| Inventory | 30,000 | 14,000 | |
| Investment in S (cost method) | 15,200 | — | |
|  | $196,300 | $32,300 | |
| Liabilities | $ 47,000 | $11,500 | |
| Common shares | 50,000 | 10,000 | **(d)** |
| Retained earnings | 99,300 | 10,800 | **(e)** |
|  | $196,300 | $32,300 | |

> *These are the separate-entity balance sheets of the two legal entities.*

The Year 5 amortizations of the acquisition differential and consolidated net income must be calculated before the consolidated financial statements can be prepared. These calculations are as shown in Exhibit 5.11.

**EXHIBIT 5.11**

**ACQUISITION DIFFERENTIAL AMORTIZATION AND IMPAIRMENT SCHEDULE**

|  | Balance Jan. 1, Year 5 | Amortization and Impairment Year 5 | Balance Dec. 31, Year 5 | |
|---|---|---|---|---|
| Inventory **(9a)** | $2,000 | $2,000 | $ — | **(a)** |
| Goodwill **(9b)** | 1,000 | 50 | 950 | **(b)** |
|  | $3,000 | $2,050 | $ 950 | **(c)** |

> *This schedule reflects 100% of the acquisition differential, which will be attributed to the shareholders of the parent and the non-controlling interest.*

**CALCULATION OF CONSOLIDATED NET INCOME**

Year 5

| | | |
|---|---|---|
| Company P net income—cost method **(10b)** | | $20,300 |
| Less: dividend income from Company S **(10a)** | | 2,000 |
| Company P net income, own operations | | 18,300 |
| Company S net income **(10b)** | $7,300 | |
| Less: Acquisition differential amortization and impairment | (2,050) | |
| | | 5,250 **(d)** |
| Consolidated net income | | $23,550 **(e)** |
| Attributable to: | | |
| Shareholders of Company P | | $22,500 **(f)** |
| Non-controlling interest (20% × **[d] 5,250**) | | 1,050 **(g)** |

These calculations form the basis for preparing the Year 5 consolidated financial statements for both the direct and the working paper approaches (see Appendix 5B for the latter).

Exhibit 5.12 shows the preparation of the consolidated financial statements when the direct approach is used. The consolidated income statement is prepared by combining the revenues and expenses of the two companies, adjusted for the Year 5 amortization of the acquisition differential. Company P's dividend income is excluded. The bottom portion of the consolidated income statement attributes the consolidated net income between the shareholders of the parent company and the non-controlling interest. First, the portion attributable to the non-controlling interest is calculated by multiplying the non-controlling interest's percentage ownership times the subsidiary's net income less the amortization of the acquisition differential. The portion attributable to the parent is equal to consolidated net income less the portion attributable to the non-controlling interest.

> *The consolidated income statement combines the income statements of the separate legal entities and incorporates consolidation adjustments for the amortization of the acquisition differential.*

Alternatively, consolidated net income attributable to the parent's shareholders could be calculated directly as follows:

| | |
|---|---:|
| Company P net income, own operations | $18,300 |
| Share of Company S net income after consolidation adjustments (80% × **[d] 5,250**) | 4,200 |
| | $22,500 |

The consolidated retained earnings statement contains the retained earnings of Company P at the beginning of the year, consolidated net income attributable to Company P, and the dividends paid by Company P.

The consolidated balance sheet is prepared by combining the assets and liabilities of the two companies, adjusted for the unamortized acquisition differential. The parent's investment account is excluded, and the non-controlling interest in the net assets of the subsidiary is shown as a component of shareholders' equity. The non-controlling interest is 20% of the December 31 shareholders' equity of Company S plus 20% of the unamortized acquisition differential.

The changes in non-controlling interest would be presented in the column for non-controlling interest in the statement of changes in equity as follows:

### CHANGES IN NON-CONTROLLING INTEREST

| | |
|---|---:|
| Balance, January 1 **(9c)** | $3,800 |
| Allocated income of entity **(11g)** | 1,050 |
| | 4,850 |
| Dividends to non-controlling shareholders | 500* |
| Balance, December 31 | $4,350 |

*$2,500 × 20% = $500.

> *Non-controlling interest on the balance sheet increases when the subsidiary earns income and decreases when the subsidiary pays a dividend.*

It is often useful to prepare this reconciliation when preparing a solution to consolidation problems because it helps show where the allocated income of this single entity and the dividends of the subsidiary end up in the consolidated financial statements. The consolidated retained earnings statement does not contain the dividends of the subsidiary. In this example, Company S paid $2,500 in dividends. Eighty percent of this amount ($2,000) was paid to Company P and therefore did not leave the consolidated entity. The other 20% ($500) was paid to the non-controlling shareholders and reduced the equity of that group, as shown above in the statement of changes in non-controlling interest.

**EXHIBIT 5.12**

## YEAR 5 CONSOLIDATED FINANCIAL STATEMENTS
(direct approach)
### COMPANY P
### CONSOLIDATED INCOME STATEMENTS
For the year ended December 31, Year 5

| | |
|---|---:|
| Sales (50,000 + 30,000) | $ 80,000 |
| Cost of sales (26,500 + 14,700 + **[11a] 2,000**) | 43,200 |
| Goodwill impairment loss (0 + 0 + **[11b] 50**) | 50 |
| Expenses (miscellaneous) (5,200 + 8,000) | 13,200 |
| | 56,450 |
| Net income | $ 23,550 |
| Attributable to: | |
| Shareholders of Company P **(11f)** | $ 22,500 |
| Non-controlling interest **(11g)** | 1,050 |

> *Consolidated net income is attributed to the controlling shareholders and non-controlling interest.*

### COMPANY P
### CONSOLIDATED STATEMENT OF RETAINED EARNINGS
For the year ended December 31, Year 5

| | |
|---|---:|
| Balance, January 1 | $ 85,000 |
| Net income | 22,500 |
| | 107,500 |
| Dividends | 6,000 |
| Balance, December 31 | $101,500 |

### COMPANY P
### CONSOLIDATED BALANCE SHEET
At December 31, Year 5

| | |
|---|---:|
| Miscellaneous assets (151,100 + 18,300) | $169,400 |
| Inventory (30,000 + 14,000) | 44,000 |
| Goodwill (0 + 0 + **(11b) 950**) | 950 |
| | $214,350 |
| Liabilities (47,000 + 11,500) | $ 58,500 |
| Common shares | 50,000 |
| Retained earnings | 101,500 |
| Non-controlling interest (20% × [**(10d) 10,000** + **(10e) 10,800** + **(11c) 950**]) | 4,350 |
| | $214,350 |

> *Non-controlling interest is shown as a component of shareholders' equity.*

The consolidation of the 80%-owned subsidiary for Year 5 financial statements using the working paper approach is illustrated in Appendix 5B.

## Consolidated Statements, End of Year 6

In Year 6, Company S reported earnings of $10,000 and paid a cash dividend of $3,000. Company P's earnings for the year were $19,000 (excluding any income from its investment in Company S). Company P's journal entry to record the dividend received from Company S is as follows:

| | | |
|---|---|---|
| Cash | 2,400 | |
|     Dividend income (80% × 3,000) | | 2,400 |
|   80% of the dividend paid by Company S | | |

> *Under the cost method, investment income is reported when dividends are received or receivable from the investee company.*

Company P reports earnings of $21,400 in Year 6. That amount includes this dividend income. An impairment test conducted on December 31, Year 6, indicated that the goodwill had a recoverable amount of $870, and therefore an $80 impairment loss had occurred. The financial statements of the two companies as at December 31, Year 6, are shown in Exhibit 5.13.

**EXHIBIT 5.13**

### YEAR 2 INCOME STATEMENTS

| | Company P | Company S | |
|---|---|---|---|
| Sales | $ 60,000 | $40,000 | |
| Dividend income | 2,400 | — | (a) |
|     Total revenue | 62,400 | 40,000 | |
| Cost of sales | 32,000 | 18,000 | |
| Expenses (misc.) | 9,000 | 12,000 | |
|     Total expenses | 41,000 | 30,000 | |
|       Net income | $ 21,400 | $10,000 | (b) |

> *These statements are the separate-entity statements of the parent and the subsidiary.*

### YEAR 2 RETAINED EARNINGS STATEMENTS

| | Company P | Company S | |
|---|---|---|---|
| Balance, Jan. 1 | $ 99,300 | $10,800 | (c) |
| Net income | 21,400 | 10,000 | |
| | 120,700 | 20,800 | |
| Dividends | 8,000 | 3,000 | |
| Balance, Dec. 31 | $112,700 | $17,800 | (d) |

> *The parent's retained earnings include dividend income received from the subsidiary since the date of acquisition.*

*(continued)*

### BALANCE SHEETS—AT DECEMBER 31, YEAR 6

| | Company P | Company S | |
|---|---|---|---|
| Miscellaneous assets | $134,500 | $21,000 | |
| Inventory | 35,000 | 16,000 | |
| Investment in S (cost method) | 15,200 | — | |
| | $184,700 | $37,000 | |
| Liabilities | $ 22,000 | $ 9,200 | |
| Common shares | 50,000 | 10,000 | **(e)** |
| Retained earnings | 112,700 | 17,800 | **(f)** |
| | $184,700 | $37,000 | |

*The parent has used the cost method on its separate-entity financial statements.*

Regardless of the approach to be used (direct or working paper), the four calculations shown in Exhibit 5.14 must be made before the consolidated financial statements are prepared. These four calculations are the starting point for the preparation of the consolidated financial statements whether the direct or the working paper approach is used.

**EXHIBIT 5.14**

### ACQUISITION DIFFERENTIAL IMPAIRMENT SCHEDULE

| | Balance Jan. 1, Year 6 | Impairment Year 6 | Balance Dec. 31, Year 6 | |
|---|---|---|---|---|
| Inventory **(11a)** | $ — | $ — | $ — | |
| Goodwill **(11b)** | 950 | 80 | 870 | |
| | $950 | $80 | $870 | **(a)** |

*This schedule is used to support adjustments made when preparing consolidated financial statements.*

### CALCULATION OF CONSOLIDATED NET INCOME—YEAR 6

| | | | |
|---|---|---|---|
| Company P net income—cost method **(13b)** | | $ 21,400 | |
| Less: Dividend income from Company S **(13a)** | | 2,400 | |
| Company P net income, own operations | | 19,000 | |
| Company S net income **(13b)** | 10,000 | | |
| Less: Acquisition differential impairment **(14a)** | (80) | | |
| | | 9,920 | **(b)** |
| Consolidated net income | | $ 28,920 | **(c)** |
| Attributable to: | | | |
| Shareholders of Company P | | $ 26,936 | **(d)** |
| Non-controlling interest (20% × **[14b]** 9,920) | | 1,984 | **(e)** |

*This schedule calculates the bottom line for the consolidated income statement.*

*(continued)*

**EXHIBIT 5.14**   *(continued)*

### CALCULATION OF CONSOLIDATED RETAINED EARNINGS
As at January 1, Year 6

| | | |
|---|---:|---|
| Company P retained earnings, Jan. 1, Year 6 (cost method) **(13c)** | | $ 99,300 |
| Company S retained earnings, Jan. 1, Year 6 **(13c)** | 10,800 | |
| Company S retained earnings, acquisition date **(10c)** | 6,000 | |
| Increase since acquisition | 4,800 | |
| Less: Acquisition differential amortization and impairment | | |
| to end of Year 5 **(11c)** | (2,050) | |
| | 2,750 | **(f)** |
| Company P's ownership percentage | 80% | |
| | 2,200 | |
| Consolidated retained earnings (which is equal to Company P's | | |
| retained earnings—equity method) | $101,500 | **(g)** |

*This schedule incorporates cumulative adjustments to a point in time.*

### CALCULATION OF NON-CONTROLLING INTEREST
December 31, Year 6

| | |
|---|---:|
| Shareholders' equity—Company S: | |
| Common shares **(13e)** | $10,000 |
| Retained earnings **(13f)** | 17,800 |
| Unamortized acquisition differential **(14a)** | 870 |
| | 28,670 |
| Non-controlling interest's ownership | 20% |
| | $ 5,734   **(h)** |

*This schedule calculates non-controlling interest on the balance sheet at a point in time.*

Exhibit 5.15 shows the consolidated financial statements prepared using the direct approach. The concepts involved are the same as were outlined earlier for a 100%-owned subsidiary. The only difference here is that the non-controlling interest is reflected in the consolidated income statement and balance sheet.

**EXHIBIT 5.15**

### YEAR 6 CONSOLIDATED FINANCIAL STATEMENTS
(direct approach)

**COMPANY P**
**CONSOLIDATED INCOME STATEMENT**
For the year ended December 31, Year 6

| | |
|---|---:|
| Sales (60,000 + 40,000) | $100,000 |
| Cost of sales (32,000 + 18,000) | 50,000 |
| Goodwill impairment loss (0 + 0 + **[14a] 80**) | 80 |
| Expenses (misc.) (9,000 + 12,000) | 21,000 |
| | 71,080 |
| Net income | $ 28,920 |
| Attributable to: | |
| Shareholders of Company P **(14d)** | $ 26,936 |
| Non-controlling interest **(14e)** | 1,984 |

*(continued)*

> *The income statement includes adjustments for only one year and non-controlling interest's share of income for only one year.*

### COMPANY P
### CONSOLIDATED STATEMENT OF RETAINED EARNINGS
For the year ended December 31, Year 6

| | |
|---|---:|
| Balance, January 1 (14g) | $101,500 |
| Net income | 26,936 |
| | 128,436 |
| Dividends | 8,000 |
| Balance, December 31 | $120,436 |

### COMPANY P
### CONSOLIDATED BALANCE SHEET
At December 31, Year 6

| | |
|---|---:|
| Miscellaneous assets (134,500 + 21,000) | $155,500 |
| Inventory (35,000 + 16,000) | 51,000 |
| Goodwill (0 + 0 + [14a] 870) | 870 |
| | $207,370 |
| | |
| Liabilities (22,000 + 9,200) | $ 31,200 |
| Common shares | 50,000 |
| Retained earnings | 120,436 |
| Non-controlling interest (14h) | 5,734 |
| | $207,370 |

> *The balance sheet reflects adjustments at the end of the year and non-controlling interest's share of net assets at the end of the year.*

The consolidation of the 80%-owned subsidiary for Year 6 financial statements using the working paper approach is illustrated in Appendix 5B.

**ADDITIONAL CALCULATIONS** The preparation of the consolidated financial statements of companies P and S for Year 6 has been illustrated. Because the parent, Company P, used the cost method, additional calculations had to be made to determine certain consolidated amounts. An additional calculation can be made to verify the consolidated retained earnings shown on the balance sheet. This calculation is shown below:

### CALCULATION OF CONSOLIDATED RETAINED EARNINGS
At December 31, Year 6

| | | | |
|---|---:|---:|---:|
| Company P retained earnings, Dec. 31, Year 6—cost method (13d) | | | $112,700 |
| Company S retained earnings, Dec. 31, Year 6 (13d) | 17,800 | | |
| Company S retained earnings, acquisition date (10c) | 6,000 | | |
| Increase since acquisition | 11,800 | | |
| Less acquisition differential amortization and impairment to the | | | |
| end of Year 6 ([11c] 2,050 + [14a] 80) | (2,130) | | |
| | 9,670 | | (a) |
| Company P's ownership | 80% | 7,736 | |
| Consolidated retained earnings | | $120,436 | |

> *This schedule incorporates cumulative adjustments to the end of Year 6 and is used to verify retained earnings at the end of Year 6.*

An alternative way to calculate NCI at the end of Year 6 under the entity theory is as follows:

| | | |
|---|---|---|
| NCI at date of acquisition **(9c)** | | $3,800 |
| Increase is Company S retained earnings, since acquisition | | |
| net of consolidation adjustments (as per **(a)** above) | 9,670 | |
| Non-controlling interest's ownership | 20% | 1,934 |
| NCI, end of year 2 | | $5,734 |

## LO4 Parent Company Extension Theory

If the non-controlling interest was measured using the fair value of identifiable net assets approach—that is, parent company extension theory—only the parent's share of the subsidiary's goodwill would be included on the consolidated financial statements. The NCI's share of the subsidiary's goodwill would be excluded. Once goodwill and NCI have been calculated under the entity theory, we can simply back out the NCI's share of goodwill to determine these two accounts under parent company extension theory. The following shows these calculations at the end of Year 6:

| | |
|---|---|
| Goodwill under entity theory **(14a)** | $ 870 |
| Less: NCI's share of goodwill (× 20%) | 174 |
| Goodwill under parent company extension theory | $696 |
| NCI under entity theory **(14h)** | $5,734 |
| Less: NCI's share of goodwill | 174 |
| NCI under parent company extension theory | $5,560 |

> *Goodwill and NCI are the only two accounts on the consolidated balance sheet that would be different under parent company extension theory compared with entity theory.*

Self-Study Problem 2 involves the parent company extension theory throughout the problem and solutions. All of the schedules and financial statements are prepared using this theory. The problem also involves amortization and impairment of the acquisition differential pertaining to depreciable assets.

## Acquisition Differential Assigned to Liabilities

With the considerable swings in interest rates over the past decade, companies often find that liabilities assumed in a business combination have fair values different from their carrying amounts. As with assets acquired, liabilities assumed in a business combination must be measured at their fair values. The difference between fair value and carrying amount for these liabilities is similar to a bond premium or discount that must be amortized over its remaining life.

Prior to 2006, Canadian GAAP was silent on the amortization method to be used in amortizing any premium or discount on a bond payable or investment in bonds. Companies could use either the straight-line method or the effective interest method. Most companies used the straight-line method because it is simpler to use. IFRS 9 requires the use of the effective interest method. Some companies may continue to use the straight-line method where the difference between the two methods is not material. In this text, we will use both the straight-line and the effective interest methods.

> *The effective interest method should be used to account for financial assets and liabilities.*

For situation A, assume that Pubco acquires 100% of the common shares of Subco on December 31, Year 2. On that date, Pubco had no bonds payable outstanding and Subco had bonds payable with a carrying amount of $100,000 and a fair value of $105,154. These bonds were issued on January 1, Year 1, at their par value of $100,000, and mature on December 31, Year 9. The bonds pay interest on December 31 each year at a stated rate of 10%. The market rate of interest was 8% on December 31, Year 2. Given that the stated rate of interest was higher than the market rate, the bonds were trading at a premium. The fair value of the bonds can be determined by taking the present value of future cash flows for the three years to maturity using a discount rate of 8% as follows:

| | |
|---|---:|
| Principal $100,000 × (P/F, 8%, 3 years) (0.79383) | $ 79,383 |
| Interest $10,000 × (P/A, 8%, 3 years) (2.57710) | 25,771 |
| | $105,154 |

> *Bonds trade at a premium when the stated rate is greater than the market rate of interest.*

The acquisition differential of $5,154 is considered a premium on the bonds from a consolidated viewpoint. On the date of acquisition, the entire $5,154 is assigned to the bonds payable, and bonds payable will be reported at $105,154 on the consolidated balance sheet. The following schedule shows the amortization of this premium using the effective interest method as if Pubco had actually issued these bonds at $105,154 on December 31, Year 2:

| Period | Interest Paid | Interest Expense | Amortization of Bond Premium | Amortized Cost of Bonds |
|---|---|---|---|---|
| Year 2 | | | | $105,154 |
| Year 3 | $10,000[1] | $8,412[2] | $1,588[3] | $103,566[4] |
| Year 4 | 10,000 | 8,285 | 1,715 | 101,851 |
| Year 5 | 10,000 | 8,149 | 1,851 | 100,000 |

[1] $100,000 × 10% = $10,000  [3] $10,000 − $8,412 = $1,588
[2] $105,154 × 8% = $8,412  [4] $105,154 − $1,588 = $103,566

In preparing consolidated financial statements subsequent to the date of acquisition, interest expense and bonds payable must be adjusted as follows to obtain the same results as if the parent had issued the bonds itself:

| Period | Subco's Interest Expense | Adjustment on Consolidation | Consolidated Interest Expense | Subco's Bond Payable | Adjustment on Consolidation | Consolidated Bond Payable |
|---|---|---|---|---|---|---|
| Year 2 | | | | $100,000 | $5,154 | $105,154 |
| Year 3 | $10,000 | $1,588 | $8,412 | 100,000 | 3,566 | 103,566 |
| Year 4 | 10,000 | 1,715 | 8,285 | 100,000 | 1,851 | 101,851 |
| Year 5 | 10,000 | 1,851 | 8,149 | 100,000 | 0 | 100,000 |

> *Under IFRS, the acquisition differential related to bonds payable should, theoretically, be amortized using the effective interest method.*

Subco's interest expense is equal to the interest paid because the bonds were issued at par; that is, there is no premium or discount on the bonds.

For situation B, assume that Subco had issued the bonds on January 1, Year 1, at $92,791 when the market rate of interest was 12% and everything else was the same as in situation A. Given that the stated rate of interest was lower than the market rate, the bonds were issued at a discount. The following schedule shows how Subco would amortize this discount on its separate-entity financial statements:

| Period | Interest Paid | Interest Expense | Amortization of Bond Discount | Amortized Cost of Bonds |
|---|---|---|---|---|
| Year 0 | | | | $ 92,791 |
| Year 1 | $10,000[1] | $11,135[2] | $1,135[3] | 93,926[4] |
| Year 2 | 10,000 | 11,271 | 1,271 | 95,197 |
| Year 3 | 10,000 | 11,424 | 1,424 | 96,621 |
| Year 4 | 10,000 | 11,594 | 1,594 | 98,215 |
| Year 5 | 10,000 | 11,785 | 1,785 | 100,000 |

[1] $100,000 × 10% = $10,000  [3] $10,000 − $11,135 = −$1,135
[2] $92,791 × 12% = $11,135  [4] $92,791 + $1,135 = $93,926

*The subsidiary amortizes the bond discount for its separate-entity financial statements.*

The acquisition differential on December 31, Year 2, the date of acquisition, would now be $9,957 ($105,154 − $95,197) and is considered a premium on the bonds from a consolidated viewpoint. The entire $9,957 is assigned to the bonds payable, and bonds payable will be reported at $105,154 (same amount as in situation A) on the consolidated balance sheet. In preparing consolidated financial statements subsequent to the date of acquisition, interest expense and bonds payable must be adjusted as follows to obtain the same results as in situation A:

| Period | Subco's Interest Expense | Adjustment on Consolidation | Consolidated Interest Expense | Subco's Bond Payable | Adjustment on Consolidation | Consolidated Bond Payable |
|---|---|---|---|---|---|---|
| Year 2 | | | | $ 95,197 | $9,957 | $105,154 |
| Year 3 | $11,424 | $3,012 | $8,412 | 96,621 | 6,945 | 103,566 |
| Year 4 | 11,594 | 3,309 | 8,285 | 98,215 | 3,636 | 101,851 |
| Year 5 | 11,785 | 3,636 | 8,149 | 100,000 | 0 | 100,000 |

In both situations, the acquisition differential was amortized over the three-year term to maturity of the bonds. Under the effective interest method, the annual amortization changes over time. If the straight-line method were used, the annual amortization would be the same each year. The following schedule summarizes the amortization of the acquisition differential under the effective interest and straight-line methods:

| | Acquisition Differential at Acquisition | Amortization of Acquisition Differential Effective Interest Method | | | Straight-Line per Year |
|---|---|---|---|---|---|
| | | Year 3 | Year 4 | Year 5 | |
| A | $5,154 | $1,588 | $1,715 | $1,851 | $1,718 |
| B | 9,957 | 3,012 | 3,309 | 3,636 | 3,319 |

*The straight-line and effective interest methods produce the same results in total over the life of the bond.*

If Pubco acquired less than 100% of Subco, the non-controlling interest would absorb their share of the acquisition differential and amortization of the acquisition differential.

See Self-Study Problem 1 for a comprehensive example of consolidating a non–wholly owned subsidiary subsequent to the date of acquisition. It includes most of the issues we have covered in this chapter and includes a bond amortization schedule using the effective interest method.

## Intercompany Receivables and Payables

Consolidated financial statements are designed to reflect the results of transactions between the single consolidated entity and those outside the entity. All transactions between the parent and its subsidiaries, or between the subsidiaries of a parent, must be eliminated in the consolidation process to reflect this single-entity concept. While many of these intercompany eliminations are discussed in later chapters, we will introduce the topic now by discussing the elimination of intercompany receivables and payables. If the parent's accounts receivable contain a receivable of $5,000 from its subsidiary, then the accounts payable of the subsidiary must contain a $5,000 payable to the parent. If these intercompany receivables and payables were not eliminated in the consolidation process, both the accounts receivable and the accounts payable on the consolidated balance sheet would be overstated from a single-entity point of view. The entry to eliminate these intercompany balances on the consolidated worksheet or working papers is as follows:

| | | |
|---|---|---|
| Accounts payable—subsidiary | 5,000 | |
| Accounts receivable—parent | | 5,000 |

> *The consolidated financial statements should reflect only the result of transactions with outsiders.*

Because the net assets (assets less liabilities) are unchanged after this elimination, the equities of the non-controlling and controlling interests are not affected.

## Subsidiary Acquired during the Year

In all of our examples to date, we have assumed that the parent acquired the subsidiary on the first day of the fiscal year. As a result, when we prepared the first consolidated income statement at the end of the first fiscal year, it contained all of the subsidiary's revenue and expenses for that year. We will now describe the consolidation process if the acquisition took place *during* the year.

Assume that Parent Inc. (which has a December 31 year-end) acquired 80% of Subsidiary Ltd. on September 30, Year 2. The Year 2 operations of Subsidiary would impact the December 31, Year 2, consolidated income statement in the following manner:

*Revenues.* Subsidiary's revenues October 1 to December 31

*Expenses.* Subsidiary's expenses plus amortization and impairment of acquisition differential October 1 to December 31

*Net impact on consolidated net income attributable to shareholders of Parent Inc.* Increased by 80% of Subsidiary's net income adjusted for amortization and impairment of acquisition differential for period October 1 to December 31.

*Net impact on consolidated net income attributable to non-controlling interest.* 20% × Subsidiary's net income adjusted for amortization and impairment of acquisition differential for period October 1 to December 31.

> *The consolidated financial statements should include the subsidiary's income only from the date of acquisition.*

This form of presentation makes subsequent-year comparisons difficult for readers. To assist users, IFRS 3 requires disclosure of what the revenue and profit or loss of the combined entity for the current reporting period would have been if the acquisition date for all business combinations that occurred during the year had been as of the beginning of the annual reporting period. Alternatively, a pro forma consolidated income statement could be prepared as if the subsidiary had been acquired at the beginning of the fiscal year. This pro forma consolidated income statement could be presented in summary form in the notes to the financial statements.

## LO5 EQUITY METHOD OF RECORDING

The illustrations throughout this chapter have assumed that the parent used the cost method of recording its investment for its internal records. We will use the same example for an 80%-owned subsidiary to illustrate the use of the equity method. The key events of the example are repeated here for ease of use.

> *The parent can use the cost method or equity method in its general ledger to account for an investment in a subsidiary.*

On January 1, Year 5, Company P purchased 80% of Company S for $15,200. In Year 5, Company S reported net income of $7,300 and paid a cash dividend of $2,500. Company P's net income for the year was $18,300 (not including income from its investment in Company S).

Company P would make the following journal entries in Year 5 under the equity method:

| | | |
|---|---:|---:|
| *January 1, Year 5* | | |
| Investment in S | 15,200 | |
|    Cash | | 15,200 |
| Purchased 80% of Company S | | |
| | | |
| *December 31, Year 5* | | |
| Investment in S (7,300 × 80%) | 5,840 | |
|    Equity method income | | 5,840 |
| 80% of Company S Year 5 net income | | |
| | | |
| Cash (2,500 × 80%) | 2,000 | |
|    Investment in S | | 2,000 |
| 80% of the dividend received from Company S | | |
| | | |
| Equity method income (2,050 × 80%) | 1,640 | |
|    Investment in S | | 1,640 |
| 80% of acquisition differential amortization and impairment for Year 5 | | |

> *Only the investor's share of the investee's income, dividends, and amortization of acquisition differential are recorded in the investor's records.*

After these journal entries are posted, the two related accounts in the records of Company P will show the following changes and balances under the equity method:

| | Investment in S | Equity Method Income |
|---|---:|---:|
| January 1, Year 5 | $15,200 | |
| Changes during Year 5: | | |
| Income from S | 5,840 | $5,840 |
| Dividends from S | (2,000) | — |
| Acquisition differential amortization and impairment | (1,640) | (1,640) |
| Balance, December 31, Year 5 | $17,400 | $4,200 |

Company P's net income for Year 5 would now be $22,500 ($18,300 + $4,200). It is not a coincidence that P's net income is now equal to P's share of consolidated net income. In fact, it should be equal to the consolidated net income attributable to the shareholders of Company P, as reported on the consolidated income statement. That is why the equity method is sometimes referred to as *one-line consolidation*. The "one line" on Company P's non-consolidated income statement is "Equity method income"; it captures the net effect of all entries related to the subsidiary such that net income from the separate-entity books for Company P equals the consolidated net income attributable to the shareholders of Company P.

> *The parent's separate-entity net income should be equal to consolidated net income attributable to shareholders of the parent.*

Even though Company P has used the equity method for its internal record keeping, the amounts reported on the consolidated financial statements would be exactly the same as in our previous illustration when P used the cost method. What differs is what is recorded in Company P's general ledger. This does not change what is reported on the consolidated financial statements.

At this point, it is useful to discuss a further relationship that results from the use of the equity method of accounting. The balance in the investment account at any point in time can be broken down into two components—the carrying amount of the subsidiary's shareholders' equity and the unamortized acquisition differential. The following illustrates this point at December 31, Year 5:

| | Total 100% | P's Share 80% | NCI's Share 20% |
|---|---:|---:|---:|
| Shareholders' equity, Company S: | | | |
| Common shares | $10,000 | | |
| Retained earnings | 10,800 | | |
| | 20,800 | $16,640 | $4,160 |
| Unamortized acquisition differential | 950 | 760 | 190 |
| | $21,750 | | |
| Balance in the investment account | | $17,400 | |
| Non-controlling interest | | | $4,350 |

> *The investment account can be reconciled to the carrying amount of the subsidiary's shareholders' equity and the unamortized acquisition differential.*

Let us now look at what happens in Year 6.

In Year 6, Company S reported earnings of $10,000 and paid a cash dividend of $3,000. Company P's earnings for the year were $19,000 (excluding any income from its investment in Company S).

On December 31, Year 6, Company P would make the following journal entries under the equity method:

| | | |
|---|---|---|
| Investment in S (10,000 × 80%) | 8,000 | |
|     Equity method income | | 8,000 |
| 80% of Company S, Year 6, net income | | |
| | | |
| Cash (3,000 × 80%) | 2,400 | |
|     Investment in S | | 2,400 |
| Dividends received from Company S | | |
| | | |
| Equity method income (80 × 80%) | 64 | |
|     Investment in S | | 64 |
| 80% of acquisition differential amortization and impairment for Year 6 | | |

After these journal entries are posted, the investment in S account and the equity method income account in the records of P Company will show the following changes and balances:

| | Investment in S | Equity Method Income |
|---|---|---|
| December 31, Year 5 | $17,400 | |
| Changes during Year 6 | | |
|   Income from S | 8,000 | $8,000 |
|   Dividends from S | (2,400) | |
|   Acquisition differential amortization and impairment | (64) | (64) |
|     Balance, December 31, Year 6 | $22,936 | $7,936 |

> *The investment account captures all adjustments since the date of acquisition, whereas equity method income captures adjustments for the current period.*

Company P combines its Year 6 equity method income ($7,936) with the earnings from its own operations ($19,000) and reports a final net income of $26,936. Once again, it is not a coincidence that P's net income is now equal to P's share of consolidated net income.

The parent's use of the equity method should always produce the following results:

- The parent's net income reported in its internal records in any one year will always be equal to consolidated net income attributable to the shareholders of the parent for that year.

- The parent's retained earnings in its internal records are always equal to consolidated retained earnings.

> *The parent's retained earnings under the equity method should be equal to consolidated retained earnings.*

The equity method captures the parent's share of the net effect of any adjustments made on consolidation. When the cost method is used, the consolidated net income attributable to the parent and consolidated retained earnings *do not* equal the parent's net income and retained earnings recorded in its internal records. However, one of the consolidation procedures involved when using the working paper approach is to adjust the parent's accounts from the cost method to the balances that would have resulted if the equity method had been used instead.

The following schedule converts the investment account from the cost method to the equity method:

| | | |
|---|---:|---:|
| Investment in Company S, Dec. 31, Year 6—cost method | | $15,200 |
| Company S retained earnings, Dec. 31, Year 6 **(13d)** | 17,800 | |
| Company S retained earnings, acquisition date **(10c)** | 6,000 | |
| Increase since acquisition | 11,800 | |
| Less acquisition differential amortization and impairment to the end of Year 6 (**[11c]** 2,050 + **[14a]** 80) | (2,130) | |
| | 9,670 **(a)** | |
| Company P's ownership | 80% | 7,736 |
| Investment in Company S, Dec. 31, Year 6—equity method | | $22,936 |

Compare the calculation above to the calculation of consolidated retained earnings found after Exhibit 5.15. The adjustments are exactly the same. When you adjust the investment account, something else must change on the balance sheet. The other change is to retained earnings.

A thorough understanding of the equity method and the financial statement numbers that it produces will help you to understand the consolidation process. See Self-Study Problem 2 for a comprehensive example of consolidating a non–wholly owned subsidiary when the parent uses the equity method for its internal records.

> *Investment in subsidiary and retained earnings are the only two accounts on the parent's separate-entity balance sheet that would be different under the equity method as compared with the cost method.*

## LO6 ANALYSIS AND INTERPRETATION OF FINANCIAL STATEMENTS

The parent company can use the cost or equity method to account for the investment in subsidiary for its internal records. The separate-entity financial statements of the parent present the investment in subsidiary as one line on the balance sheet and investment income from the subsidiary as one line on the income statement. When the consolidated financial statements are prepared, the investment in subsidiary line on the balance sheet and the investment income from subsidiary line on the income statement are eliminated and replaced by the underlying assets, liabilities, revenues, and expenses of the subsidiary, plus or minus the acquisition differential. The consolidated financial statements are not affected by the method used by the parent to account for its investment in the subsidiary. The adjustments to get from the separate-entity statements to the consolidated statements may be different, depending on the method used by the parent. But the end result is the exact same set of consolidated financial statements.

Exhibit 5.16 presents the income statements and balance sheets for the parent's separate-entity statements under two scenarios: first, when the parent uses the cost method and, second, when the parent uses the equity method. The last column presents the consolidated financial statements. The values for the cost method are taken directly from Exhibit 5.13. The values for the equity method are the same as the cost method, except for the investment account and equity method income (which are taken from the previous section) and retained earnings (which is taken from the consolidated balance sheet in Exhibit 5.15). The consolidated statements are taken from Exhibit 5.15. The exhibit also indicates the debt-to-equity ratio and return-on-equity ratio for each set of financial statements. The return on equity for all shareholders uses consolidated net income and total shareholders' equity, including the non-controlling interest. The return on equity for shareholders of Company P uses consolidated net income attributable to the shareholders of Company P and total shareholders' equity, excluding the non-controlling interest.

EXHIBIT 5.16

# Impact of Presentation Method on Debt-to-Equity and Return-on-Equity Ratios

## INCOME STATEMENTS
### For the year ended December 31, Year 6

| | Company P—Separate Entity | | Consolidated |
|---|---|---|---|
| | Cost | Equity | |
| Sales | $ 60,000 | $ 60,000 | $100,000 |
| Income from Company S | 2,400 | 7,936 | — |
| Total revenue | 62,400 | 67,936 | 100,000 |
| Cost of sales | 32,000 | 32,000 | 50,000 |
| Goodwill impairment loss | | | 80 |
| Expenses (misc.) | 9,000 | 9,000 | 21,000 |
| Total expenses | 41,000 | 41,000 | 71,080 |
| Net income | $ 21,400 | $ 26,936 | $ 28,920 |
| Attributable to: | | | |
| Shareholders of Company P | | | $ 26,936 |
| Non-controlling interest | | | 1,984 |

> *Net income on the parent's separate-entity income statement under the equity method should always be equal to net income attributable to the shareholders of the parent on the consolidated income statement.*

## BALANCE SHEETS
### At December 31, Year 6

| | Company P—Separate Entity | | Consolidated |
|---|---|---|---|
| | Cost | Equity | |
| Miscellaneous assets | $134,500 | $134,500 | $155,500 |
| Inventory | 35,000 | 35,000 | 51,000 |
| Goodwill | | | 870 |
| Investment in S | 15,200 | 22,936 | |
| | $184,700 | $192,436 | $207,370 |
| Liabilities | $ 22,000 | $ 22,000 | $ 31,200 |
| Common shares | 50,000 | 50,000 | 50,000 |
| Retained earnings | 112,700 | 120,436 | 120,436 |
| Non-controlling interest | | | 5,734 |
| | $184,700 | $192,436 | $207,370 |
| Debt-to-equity | 0.14 | 0.13 | 0.18 |
| Return on equity: | | | |
| For all shareholders (28,920/(50,000 + 120,436 + 5,734) | n/a | n/a | 16.4% |
| For shareholders of Company P | 13.2% | 15.8% | 15.8% |

> *Retained earnings on the parent's separate-entity balance sheet under the equity method should always be equal to consolidated retained earnings.*

> *Consolidated financial statements are exactly the same and do not depend on whether the parent uses the cost method or equity method for internal record keeping.*

Note the following regarding the cost and equity columns from Exhibit 5.16:

- All of the income statement accounts are the same except for dividend income under the cost method and equity income under the equity method.

- If the dividend income or equity income had not yet been recorded by the parent, the parent's net income would have been $19,000 in both cases. This $19,000 is often referred to as the parent's income from its own operations.

- All of the balance sheet accounts are the same except for Investment in Company S and retained earnings.

- The difference in the investment account between the cost and equity method is $7,736. The difference in retained earnings between the cost and equity method is $7,736. This is not a coincidence. This should always be the case because these are the only two balance sheet accounts that are different between the two methods.

Now, look at the consolidated income statement and consolidated balance sheet. These consolidated statements no longer contain the investment account or investment income from Company S. These are the combined statements of the parent and subsidiary as if they were one. These statements would not change regardless of the method of accounting used by the parent on its separate-entity financial statements.

Now, notice the following for the three columns:

- Consolidated net income attributable to the parent on the consolidated income statement is $26,936, which is equal to the parent's net income on the parent's separate-entity income statement under the equity method.

- Consolidated retained earnings on the consolidated balance sheet is exactly the same as the parent's retained earnings on the parent's separate-entity balance sheet under the equity method.

Finally, notice the following about the ratios:

- The separate-entity net income and return-on-equity ratio under the cost and equity methods are different.

- The separate-entity return on equity under the equity method is equal to the consolidated return on equity for the shareholders of Company P.

- The solvency position looks worst on the consolidated financial statements because the subsidiary's debt is included on the consolidated financial statements. This increases the debt-to-equity ratio.

> *Return on equity for the parent's separate-entity financial statements under the equity method should always be equal to the return on equity for the shareholders of Company P on the consolidated financial statements.*

The above illustration indicates that the cost and equity methods apply only to the parent's separate-entity statements. The consolidated statements have nothing to do with the cost or equity methods. They reflect the combined operations and position of the parent and subsidiary as if they were one entity. Goodwill, retained earnings, and non-controlling interest would be the same amount on consolidation regardless of the method used by the parent to account for its investment for internal purposes.

## ASPE Differences

- As mentioned in Chapter 3, private companies could either consolidate their subsidiaries or report their investments in subsidiaries under the cost method, under the equity method, or at fair value if the market value is quoted in an active market.

- The investments in and income from non-consolidated subsidiaries should be presented separately from other investments.

- All intangible assets with indefinite useful lives and goodwill should be tested for impairment whenever events or changes in circumstances indicate that the carrying amount may exceed the fair value.

- The impairment test for property, plant, and equipment and for intangible assets with definite useful lives has three steps. In step 1, consider whether there are any events or circumstances indicating that the asset may be impaired. If not, no further testing is required. In step 2, determine whether the carrying amount exceeds its recoverable amount (i.e., the sum of the undiscounted cash flows expected to result from its use and eventual disposition). If not, no further testing is required. In step 3, determine whether the carrying amount of the asset exceeds its fair value. If so, an impairment loss should be recognized. If not, there is no impairment.

- For intangible assets with indefinite useful lives and goodwill, an impairment loss should be recognized when the carrying amount exceeds its fair value.

- In all cases, the impairment loss is equal to the excess of carrying amount over the fair value, and impairment losses cannot be reversed.

> *Undiscounted cash flows are considered in step 2.*
>
> *The impairment loss is equal to the excess of carrying amount over the fair value.*

## SUMMARY

According to the matching principle, the cost of using assets to earn income should be expensed in the same period as the related revenue is recognized. Accordingly, inventory is expensed when the goods are sold and equipment is depreciated over its useful life. Impairment tests require that assets be written down when the carrying amount exceeds the future benefits to be received from either selling the asset (fair value) or continuing to use it (value in use). **(LO1)**

The acquisition differential must be amortized, written off, or otherwise brought into income just as though these assets and liabilities were purchased or assumed directly. A schedule is prepared for consolidation purposes to indicate the amount and timing for the amortization and impairment of the acquisition differential. **(LO2)**

In periods subsequent to acquisition, we will have to prepare schedules to allocate consolidated net income between the parent and non-controlling interest for a period of time and to calculate consolidated retained earnings and non-controlling interest at a point in time. Under the entity theory, the full amount of the subsidiary's goodwill and goodwill impairment loss are reflected in the consolidated statements. **(LO3)** Under the parent company extension theory, only the parent's share of the subsidiary's goodwill and goodwill impairment loss is reported in the consolidated statements. Non-controlling interest would not be affected by a goodwill impairment loss. **(LO4)**

The consolidated statements are the same regardless of whether the parent used the cost or the equity method for its separate entity financial statements. However, the number of schedules required to prepare the consolidated statements are quite different because the starting point is quite different. Under the equity method, the parent's books already reflect its share of the subsidiary's net income and amortization and impairment of the acquisition differential. Accordingly, the equity method is sometimes referred to as *one-line consolidation.* The income and retained earnings reported by the parent on its separate-entity financial statements will be equal to the consolidated net income attributable to shareholders of the parent and consolidated retained earnings, respectively. **(LO5)** When analyzing financial statements, it is important to note what accounting policies have been used in preparing the statements and how they will impact the amounts reported in the financial statements. **(LO6)**

The basic steps in the consolidation process when the parent has used the equity and cost methods are outlined in Exhibit 5.17. It is important to have a good grasp of the procedures under both methods, because these procedures are the foundation for the consolidation issues we will introduce in the chapters that follow.

**EXHIBIT 5.17**

### PREPARATION OF CONSOLIDATED FINANCIAL STATEMENTS
Basic Steps

| | Parent Company Uses: | |
| --- | :---: | :---: |
| | *Cost Method* | *Equity Method* |
| 1. Calculate and allocate the acquisition differential at the date of acquisition. | Yes | Yes |
| 2. Prepare an acquisition differential amortization and impairment schedule (date of acquisition to present date). | Yes | Yes |
| 3. Calculate consolidated net income—current year. | Yes | No* |
| 4. Prepare the consolidated income statement. | Yes | Yes |
| 5. Calculate the start-of-year balance of consolidated retained earnings.** | Yes | No* |
| 6. Prepare the consolidated retained earnings statement.*** | Yes | Yes |
| 7. Calculate the end-of-year balance of consolidated retained earnings. | Yes | No* |
| 8. Calculate non-controlling interest at the end of the year (for the consolidated balance sheet). | Yes | Yes |
| 9. Prepare a statement of changes in non-controlling interest (optional). | Yes | Yes |
| 10. Prepare a consolidated balance sheet. | Yes | Yes |

*If the parent company uses the equity method of accounting, the parent's net income equals consolidated net income attributable to the shareholders of the parent, and the parent's retained earnings always equal consolidated retained earnings. Therefore, the calculations in steps 3, 5, and 7 are not necessary.

**Only do so if preparing a statement of retained earnings.

***Not required in all problems.

## Self-Study Problem 1

LO1, 2, 3, 5, 6

On January 1, Year 11, Allen Company acquired 7,000 (70%) of the outstanding common shares of Bell Company for $87,500 in cash. On that date, Bell had common shares of $50,000 and retained earnings of $45,000. The Bell shares were trading for $11 per share just after the date of acquisition. At acquisition, the identifiable assets and liabilities of Bell had fair values that were equal to carrying amounts, except for equipment, which had a fair value of $150,000, a cost of $200,000, and accumulated depreciation of $80,000; inventory, which had a fair value $8,000 less than carrying amount; and bonds payable, which had a fair value $12,420 greater than carrying amount. The equipment had a remaining useful life of eight years on January 1, Year 11, and is amortized on a straight-line basis. The bonds payable mature on December 31, Year 18; pay interest annually; and are amortized using the effective interest method. The market rate of interest for similar bonds is 6%.

Financial statements for the Year 16 fiscal year are as follows:

|  | Allen | Bell |
|---|---|---|
| *Income Statements* | | |
| Sales | $ 400,000 | $250,000 |
| Rent revenue | 15,000 | — |
| Dividend revenue | 3,500 | — |
|  | 418,500 | 250,000 |
| Cost of sales | 200,000 | 160,000 |
| Depreciation | 55,000 | 20,000 |
| Interest expense | 32,000 | 8,000 |
| Other expenses | 28,000 | 42,000 |
|  | 315,000 | 230,000 |
| Profit | $ 103,500 | $ 20,000 |
| *Retained Earnings Statements* | | |
| Balance, January 1 | $400,000 | $ 65,000 |
| Profit | 103,500 | 20,000 |
|  | 503,500 | 85,000 |
| Dividends | 30,000 | 5,000 |
| Balance, December 31 | $ 473,500 | $ 80,000 |
| *Statement of Financial Position* | | |
| Property, plant, and equipment | $1,200,000 | $400,000 |
| Accumulated depreciation | (300,000) | (210,000) |
| Investment in Bell—cost method | 87,500 | — |
| Inventory | 200,000 | 40,000 |
| Accounts receivable | 60,000 | 25,000 |
| Cash | 12,500 | 10,000 |
|  | $1,260,000 | $265,000 |
| Ordinary shares | $ 300,000 | $ 50,000 |
| Retained earnings | 473,500 | 80,000 |
| Bonds payable, 8% | 400,000 | 100,000 |
| Accounts payable | 86,500 | 35,000 |
|  | $1,260,000 | $265,000 |

## Additional Information

In Year 12, a goodwill impairment loss of $7,000 was recorded ($6,300 pertained to Allen's 70% interest). Subsequent goodwill testing yielded no further evidence of impairment until Year 16, when a decline in the recoverable amount of Bell Company occurred and management decided to reflect an impairment loss of $6,000 in the year's consolidated statements ($5,400 pertained to Allen's 70% interest).

On December 31, Year 16, Bell Company owes Allen Company $9,000.

## Required

(a) Using the direct approach, prepare the following Year 16 consolidated financial statements:

    (i) Income statement

    (ii) Retained earnings statement

    (iii) Statement of financial position

(b) Prepare a schedule of the Year 16 changes in non-controlling interest.

(c) Now assume that Allen had used the equity method to account for its investment in Bell. What line items (other than totals and subtotals) on the income statement and statement of financial position would be different on the

    (i) parent's separate entity statements?

    (ii) subsidiary's separate entity statements?

    (iii) consolidated statements?

*e**X**cel*

## Solution to Self-Study Problem 1

### CALCULATION OF ACQUISITION DIFFERENTIAL

|  | Parent's 70% | Non-controlling Interest's 30% | Total 100% |
|---|---|---|---|
| Cost of 70% of Bell | $87,500 | | |
| Value of 30% of Bell (3,000 shares × $11) | | $33,000 | |
| Implied value of 100% of Bell | | | $120,500 |
| Carrying amount of Bell's net assets = Carrying amount of shareholders' equity | | | |
| Ordinary shares | 50,000 | | |
| Retained earnings | 45,000 | | |
| | 95,000 | 66,500 | 28,500 | 95,000 |
| Acquisition differential | | 21,000 | 4,500 | 25,500 |
| Allocated: | FV − CA | | | |
| Equipment (150,000 − [200,000 − 80,000]) | 30,000 | | | **(a)** |
| Inventory | −8,000 | | | **(b)** |
| Bonds payable | −12,420 | | | **(c)** |
| | 9,580 | 6,706 | 2,874 | 9,580 |
| Goodwill (approximately 90% of total) | $14,294 **(d)** | | |
| Goodwill (approximately 10% of total) | | $ 1,626 **(e)** | |
| Total goodwill | | | $ 15,920 |

## BOND AMORTIZATION SCHEDULE

| Date | Cash Paid | Interest Expense | Bond Premium Amortization | Amortized Cost of Bonds |
|---|---|---|---|---|
| Jan. 1/Year 11 | | | | $112,420 |
| Dec. 31/Year 11 | $ 8,000 | $ 6,745 | $ 1,255 | 111,165 |
| Dec. 31/Year 12 | 8,000 | 6,670 | 1,330 | 109,835 |
| Dec. 31/Year 13 | 8,000 | 6,590 | 1,410 | 108,425 |
| Dec. 31/Year 14 | 8,000 | 6,506 | 1,494 | 106,931 |
| Dec. 31/Year 15 | 8,000 | 6,416 | 1,584 | 105,347 |
| | 40,000 | 32,927 | 7,073 | |
| Dec. 31/Year 16 | 8,000 | 6,321 | 1,679 | 103,668 (f) |
| Dec. 31/Year 17 | 8,000 | 6,220 | 1,780 | 101,888 |
| Dec. 31/Year 18 | 8,000 | 6,112 | 1,888 | 100,000 |
| | $64,000 | $51,580 | $12,420 | |

## ACQUISITION DIFFERENTIAL AMORTIZATION AND IMPAIRMENT

| | Balance Jan. 1/ Year 11 | Amortization and Impairment To End of Year 15 | Year 16 | Balance Dec. 31/ Year 16 |
|---|---|---|---|---|
| Equipment (a) | $30,000 | $18,750 | $ 3,750 | $   7,500 (g) |
| Inventory (b) | −8,000 | −8,000 | — | — (h) |
| Bonds payable (c) | −12,420 | −7,073 | −1,679 | −3,668 (i) |
| | 9,580 | 3,677 | 2,071 | 3,832 (j) |
| Goodwill—parent (d) | 14,294 | 6,300 | 5,400 | 2,594 (k) |
| Goodwill—NCI (e) | 1,626 | 700 | 600 | 326 (l) |
| Goodwill—total | 15,920 | 7,000 | 6,000 | 2,920 (m) |
| | $25,500 | $10,677 | $ 8,071 | $   6,752 |

## CALCULATION OF CONSOLIDATED NET INCOME ATTRIBUTABLE TO PARENT
### Year 16

| | | |
|---|---|---|
| Profit—Allen | | $103,500 |
| Less dividend from Bell | | 3,500 (n) |
| | | 100,000 |
| Profit—Bell | 20,000 | (o) |
| Allen's ownership | 70% | 14,000 |
| Parent's share of acquisition differential amortization and impairment: | | |
| (70% × [j] 2,071 + [k] 5,400) | | −6,850 (p) |
| | | $107,150 (q) |

## CALCULATION OF CONSOLIDATED NET INCOME ATTRIBUTABLE TO NCI

| | | |
|---|---|---|
| Net income—Bell | | $ 20,000 |
| NCI's ownership | | 30% |
| | | 6,000 |
| NCI's share of acquisition differential amortization and impairment: | | |
| (30% × [j] 2,071 + [l] 600) | | −1,221 |
| | | $   4,779 (r) |

## CALCULATION OF CONSOLIDATED RETAINED EARNINGS
### January 1, Year 16

| | | |
|---|---|---|
| Retained earnings—Allen | | $ 400,000 |
| Retained earnings—Bell | 65,000 | |
| Retained earnings—Bell, acquisition date | 45,000 | |
| Increase since acquisition | 20,000 | |
| Allen's ownership | 70% | |
| | | 14,000 |
| Parent's share of acquisition differential amortization and impairment: | | |
| (70% × [j] **3,677** + [k] **6,300**) | | −8,874 (s) |
| | | $ 405,126 (t) |

## CALCULATION OF CONSOLIDATED RETAINED EARNINGS
### December 31, Year 16

| | | |
|---|---|---|
| Retained earnings—Allen | | $ 473,500 |
| Retained earnings—Bell | 80,000 | |
| Retained earnings—Bell, acquisition date | 45,000 | |
| Increase since acquisition | 35,000 | |
| Allen's ownership | 70% | 24,500 |
| Parent's share of acquisition differential amortization and impairment: | | |
| ([p] **6,850** + [s] **8,874**) | | −15,724 (u) |
| | | $ 482,276 (v) |

## CALCULATION OF NON-CONTROLLING INTEREST (Method 1)
### At December 31, Year 16

| | | |
|---|---|---|
| Ordinary shares—Bell | | $ 50,000 |
| Retained earnings—Bell | | 80,000 |
| | | 130,000 |
| NCI's ownership | | 30% |
| | | 39,000 |
| NCI's share of unamortized acquisition differential: | | |
| (30% × [j] **3,832** + [l] **326**) | | 1,476 |
| | | $ 40,476 (w) |

## CALCULATION OF NON-CONTROLLING INTEREST (Method 2)

| | | |
|---|---|---|
| Non-controlling interest at acquisition (3,000 shares × $11) | | $ 33,000 |
| Increase in Bell's retained earnings since acquisition | 35,000 | |
| NCI's share @ 30% | | 10,500 |
| NCI's share of amortization of acquisition differential: | | |
| ([[(j) **3,677** + (j) **2,071**] × 30% + [l] **700** + [l] **600**) | | (3,024) |
| | | $ 40,476 (w) |

Accumulated depreciation and equipment need to be reduced by $80,000 so that equipment held by subsidiary is reported at a cost of $150,000 with no accumulated depreciation at date of acquisition.

$ 80,000 (x)

(a) (i)

## ALLEN COMPANY
## CONSOLIDATED INCOME STATEMENT
For the year ended December 31, Year 16

| | |
|---|---:|
| Sales (400,000 + 250,000) | $ 650,000 |
| Rent revenue | 15,000 |
| Dividend revenue (3,500 + 0 − **[n] 3,500**) | — |
| | 665,000 |
| Cost of sales (200,000 + 160,000) | 360,000 |
| Depreciation (55,000 + 20,000 + **[g] 3,750**) | 78,750 |
| Interest expense (32,000 + 8,000 − **[i] 1,679**) | 38,321 |
| Other expenses (28,000 + 42,000) | 70,000 |
| Goodwill impairment loss **(m)** | 6,000 |
| | 553,071 |
| Profit | $ 111,929 |
| Attributable to: | |
| Shareholders of Allen **(q)** | $ 107,150 |
| Non-controlling interest **(r)** | 4,779 |

(ii)

## ALLEN COMPANY
## CONSOLIDATED RETAINED EARNINGS STATEMENT
For the year ended December 31, Year 16

| | |
|---|---:|
| Balance, January 1 **(t)** | $ 405,126 |
| Profit | 107,150 |
| | 512,276 |
| Dividends | 30,000 |
| Balance, December 31 **(v)** | $ 482,276 |

(iii)

## ALLEN COMPANY
## CONSOLIDATED STATEMENT OF FINANCIAL POSITION
December 31, Year 16

| | |
|---|---:|
| Plant and equipment (1,200,000 + 400,000 + **[a] 30,000** − **[x] 80,000**) | $1,550,000 |
| Accumulated depreciation | |
| (300,000 + 210,000 + **[g] 18,750** + **[g] 3,750** − **[x]) 80,000**) | (452,500) |
| Goodwill **(m)** | 2,920 |
| Inventory (200,000 + 40,000) | 240,000 |
| Accounts receivable (60,000 + 25,000 − **9,000***) | 76,000 |
| Cash (12,500 + 10,000) | 22,500 |
| | $1,438,920 |
| Ordinary shares | $ 300,000 |
| Retained earnings **(v)** | 482,276 |
| Non-controlling interest **(w)** | 40,476 |
| | 822,752 |
| Bonds payable (400,000 + 100,000 + **[i] 3,668**) | 503,668 |
| Accounts payable (86,500 + 35,000 − **9,000***) | 112,500 |
| | $1,438,920 |

*Intercompany receivable/payable.*

(b)

### YEAR 16 CHANGES IN NON-CONTROLLING INTEREST

| | | |
|---|---|---|
| Balance, January 1* | | $37,197 |
| Allocation of entity net income **(r)** | | 4,779 |
| | | 41,976 |
| Dividends (30% × 5,000) | | 1,500 |
| Balance, December 31 **(w)** | | $40,476 |
| *Ordinary shares | $50,000 | |
| Retained earnings, January 1 | 65,000 | |
| | 115,000 | |
| NCI's ownership | 30% | |
| | 34,500 | |
| NCI's share of unamortized acquisition differential | | |
| (30% × **[j]** **[9,580 − 3,677]** + **[l]** **[1,626 − 700]**) | 2,697 | |
| | $37,197 | |

(c)

(i) Dividend revenue would disappear from the income statement. Equity method income of $7,150 would appear. Allen's profit would now be $107,150, which is equal to consolidated profit attributable to the shareholders of Allen. On the statement of financial position, the investment in Bell and retained earnings would increase by $8,776 to $96,276 and $482,276, respectively. Bell's retained earnings would be equal to consolidated retained earnings.

(ii) None of the line items would change on the subsidiary's separate-entity financial statements.

(iii) None of the line items would change on the consolidated financial statements.

The above analysis indicates that the cost and equity methods apply only to the parent's separate-entity statements. The consolidated statements have nothing to do with the cost or equity methods. They reflect the combined operations and position of the parent and subsidiary. All of the financial statement items would be the same amount on consolidation regardless of the method used by the parent to account for its investment for internal purposes. However, the consolidating entries would change because the starting position on the parent's separate-entity statements is different.

## Self-Study Problem 2

LO1, 2, 4, 5

On December 31, Year 2, Pat Inc. purchased 80% of the outstanding common shares of Sam Company for $620,000. At that date, Sam had common shares of $400,000 and retained earnings of $125,000. In negotiating the purchase price, it was agreed that the assets on Sam's balance sheet were fairly valued, except for plant assets, which had an $80,000 excess of fair value over carrying amount. It was also agreed that Sam had unrecognized intangible assets consisting of trademarks that had an estimated value of $50,000. The plant assets had a remaining useful life of eight years at the acquisition date, and the trademarks would be amortized over a 10-year period. Any goodwill arising from this business combination would be tested periodically for impairment. Pat accounts for its investment using the equity method and prepares consolidated statements using the parent company extension theory.

## Additional Information

- Impairment tests performed at the end of Year 6 indicated that Pat's portion of the goodwill had a recoverable amount of $85,000 and the trademarks had a recoverable amount of $29,000. The impairment loss on these assets occurred entirely in Year 6.
- On December 26, Year 6, Pat declared dividends of $72,000 while Sam declared dividends of $40,000.
- Amortization expense is reported in selling expenses, while impairment losses are reported in other expenses.

Condensed financial statements for Pat and Sam for the year ended December 31, Year 6, were as follows:

### STATEMENTS OF FINANCIAL POSITION
December 31, Year 6

|  | Pat | Sam |
|---|---|---|
| Plant assets—net | $ 460,000 | $ 320,000 |
| Investment in Sam Company | 700,200 | — |
| Other assets | 580,000 | 804,000 |
|  | $1,740,200 | $1,124,000 |
| Common shares | $1,000,000 | $ 400,000 |
| Retained earnings | 300,200 | 300,000 |
| Liabilities | 440,000 | 424,000 |
|  | $1,740,200 | $1,124,000 |

### INCOME STATEMENTS
For the year ended December 31, Year 6

|  | Pat | Sam |
|---|---|---|
| Sales | $1,740,000 | $1,030,000 |
| Cost of goods sold | (1,276,000) | (720,000) |
| Gross profit | 464,000 | 310,000 |
| Selling expenses | (44,000) | (70,000) |
| Other expenses | (296,000) | (144,000) |
| Interest and investment income | 92,200 | 4,000 |
| Profit | $ 216,200 | $ 100,000 |

## Required

(a) Prepare a schedule to allocate the acquisition differential at the date of acquisition and a schedule to amortize the acquisition differential from the date of acquisition to the end of Year 6.

(b) Prepare the journal entries for Pat's separate-entity books to account for the investment in Sam for Year 6, and determine the investment income from Sam for Year 6 under
  (i) the equity method, and
  (ii) the cost method.

 (c) Prepare consolidated financial statements for Year 6.

## Solution to Self-Study Problem 2

**(a)**

### CALCULATION OF ACQUISITION DIFFERENTIAL

| | | | |
|---|---|---:|---:|
| Cost of 80% of Sam | | | $620,000 |
| Implied value of 100% (620,000/0.8) | | | $775,000 |
| Carrying amount of Sam's net assets = Carrying amount of Sam's shareholders' equity | | | |
| Common shares | | 400,000 | |
| Retained earnings | | 125,000 | 525,000 **(a)** |
| Acquisition differential | | | 250,000 |
| Allocated: | | FV − CA | |
| Plant assets | | 80,000 | |
| Trademarks | | 50,000 | 130,000 **(b)** |
| Goodwill for 100% | | | 120,000 |
| Less: NCI's share at 20% | | | 24,000 |
| Goodwill for Sam's 80% | | | $ 96,000 |
| NCI at date of acquisition (20% × [**(a) 525,000** + **(b) 130,000**]) | | | $131,000 **(c)** |

| | Bal. Dec. 31/Yr2 | Amortization to Dec.31/Yr5 | Yr6 | Loss Yr6 | Bal. Dec. 31/Yr6 | |
|---|---:|---:|---:|---:|---:|---|
| Plant assets (8 years) | $ 80,000 | $30,000 | $10,000 | | $ 40,000 | **(d)** |
| Trademarks (10 years) | 50,000 | 15,000 | 5,000 | $ 1,000 | 29,000 | **(e)** |
| Subtotal | 130,000 | 45,000 | 15,000 | 1,000 | 69,000 | **(f)** |
| Goodwill for Sam's 80% | 96,000 | ---------- | ---------- | 11,000 | 85,000 | **(g)** |
| Total | $226,000 | $45,000 | $15,000 | $12,000 | $154,000 | **(h)** |
| NCI's share [20% × **(f)**] | $ 26,000 | $ 9,000 | $ 3,000 | $ 200 | $ 13,800 | **(i)** |
| Pat's share | 200,000 | 36,000 | 12,000 | 11,800 | 140,200 | **(j)** |

**(b)**

| | (i) Equity Method | | (ii) Cost Method | |
|---|---:|---:|---:|---:|
| Investment in Sam (80% × 100,000) | 80,000 | | | |
| Equity method income | | 80,000 | | |
| To record Pat's share of Sam's income | | | | |
| Cash (80% × 40,000) | 32,000 | | 32,000 | |
| Investment in Sam | | 32,000 | | |
| Investment income | | | | 32,000 |
| To record Pat's share of Sam's dividend | | | | |
| Equity method income [**(j)** (**12,000** + **(j) 11,800**)] | 23,800 | | | |
| Investment in Sam | | 23,800 | | |
| To record Pat's share of amortization and impairment of acquisition differential | | | | |

Investment income for Year 6 under the equity method is $56,200 **(k)**
($80,000 − $23,800) and $32,000 under the cost method.

**(c)**

### CALCULATION OF CONSOLIDATED PROFIT ATTRIBUTABLE TO NCI

| | |
|---|---:|
| Sam's profit | 100,000 |
| NCI's share @ 20% | 20,000 |
| Acquisition differential amortization [**(i)** (**3,000** + **(i) 200**)] | (3,200) |
| | 16,800 **(l)** |

## PAT INC.
### CONSOLIDATED INCOME STATEMENT
For the year ended December 31, Year 6

| | |
|---|---:|
| Sales (1,740,000 + 1,030,000) | $2,770,000 |
| Interest and investment income (92,200 + 4,000 − **[k] 56,200**) | 40,000 |
| | 2,810,000 |
| Cost of sales (1,276,000 + 720,000) | 1,996,000 |
| Selling expenses (44,000 + 70,000 + **[h] 15,000**) | 129,000 |
| Other expenses (296,000 + 144,000 + **[h] 12,000**) | 452,000 |
| | 2,577,000 |
| Profit | $  233,000 |
| Attributable to: | |
| Pat's shareholders (= income under equity method) | $  216,200 |
| Non-controlling interest **(l)** | 16,800 |
| | $  233,000 |

### CALCULATION OF NCI AT DECEMBER 31, YEAR 6

| | | |
|---|---:|---:|
| NCI at acquisition **(c)** | | 131,000 |
| Sam's retained earnings Dec. 31, Year 6 | 300,000 | |
| Sam's retained earnings at acquisition | 125,000 | |
| Increase | 175,000 | |
| NCI's share | × 20% | 35,000 |
| Less: Acquisition differential amortization (**(i) 9,000** + 3,000 + 200) | | (12,200) |
| | | 153,800  **(m)** |

## PAT INC.
### CONSOLIDATED BALANCE SHEET
At December 31, Year 6

| | |
|---|---:|
| Plant assets (460,000 + 320,000 + **[d] 40,000**) | $  820,000 |
| Trademarks (0 + 0 + **[e] 29,000**) | 29,000 |
| Goodwill (0 + 0 + **[g] 85,000**) | 85,000 |
| Other assets (580,000 + 804,000) | 1,384,000 |
| | $2,318,000 |
| Common shares | $1,000,000 |
| Retained earnings (= retained earnings under equity method) | 300,200 |
| Non-controlling interest **(m)** | 153,800 |
| Liabilities (440,000 + 424,000) | 864,000 |
| | $2,318,000 |

# APPENDIX 5A

## Goodwill Impairment

LO7

Goodwill is recorded only when it is purchased as part of a business combination. When the subsidiary is made up of more than one cash-generating unit (CGU), these CGUs must be identified at the date of acquisition. The assets and liabilities (including goodwill) acquired in a business combination are then assigned to these identified CGUs. The assignment should consider where the acquired assets and liabilities will be employed. The goodwill should be assigned to those units that are expected to benefit from the synergies of the combination. Overall, the objective of the assignment of acquired assets and liabilities to CGUs is to facilitate the required fair value/carrying amount comparisons for periodic impairment testing.

> *At the date of acquisition, the total value of the subsidiary is segregated into cash-generating units.*

Each year, starting with the year of acquisition, goodwill in each cash-generating unit is tested for impairment. At the time of impairment testing of a cash-generating unit to which goodwill has been allocated, there may be an indication of an impairment of an asset within the unit containing the goodwill. In such circumstances, the entity tests the individual asset for impairment first and recognizes any impairment loss for that asset before testing for impairment of the CGU containing the goodwill. In other words, the impairment procedures are applied at the single-asset level first and the CGU levels last.

> *Individual assets should be tested for impairment before each cash-generating unit is tested for impairment.*

To test goodwill for impairment, the recoverable amount of each CGU is compared with its carrying amount, including goodwill. If the recoverable amount exceeds the carrying amount, goodwill is not impaired. If the recoverable amount is less than the carrying amount, an impairment loss should be recognized and allocated to reduce the carrying amount of the assets of the unit (group of units) in the following order:

(a) First, to reduce the carrying amount of any goodwill allocated to the cash-generating unit

(b) Then, to the other assets of the unit, pro rata on the basis of the carrying amount of each asset in the unit

> *The recoverable amount is compared with the carrying amount of net assets for each cash-generating unit.*

However, an entity must not reduce the carrying amount of an individual asset below the higher of its recoverable amount and zero. The amount of the impairment loss that could not be allocated to an individual asset because of this limitation must be allocated pro rata to the other assets of the unit (group of units).

Several alternative methods exist for determining the recoverable amount of the cash-generating units that compose a consolidated entity. First, any quoted market prices that exist can provide a basis for assessing fair value, especially for subsidiaries with actively traded non-controlling interests. Second, comparable businesses may exist that can help indicate market values. Third, present value of future cash flow streams or profit projections can be calculated to determine the value in use. The discount rate used in the present value calculations should consider the riskiness of the future flows.

The following example[9] illustrates impairment testing for a subsidiary with more than one CGU. At the end of Year 1, T Company acquires 100% of the common shares of M Limited for $10,000. M has manufacturing plants in three countries. Each country is deemed to be a separate cash-generating unit because activities in each country represent the lowest level at which the goodwill is monitored for internal management purposes. The acquisition cost was allocated to the CGUs as follows at the date of acquisition:

| CGU | Allocation of Acquisition Cost | Fair Value of Identifiable Assets | Goodwill |
|---|---|---|---|
| Activities in Country A | $ 3,000 | $2,000 | $1,000 |
| Activities in Country B | 2,000 | 1,500 | 500 |
| Activities in Country C | 5,000 | 3,500 | 1,500 |
| Total | $10,000 | $7,000 | $3,000 |

*CGUs are identified based on the lowest level at which the goodwill is monitored for internal management purposes.*

Because goodwill has been allocated to the activities in each country, each of those activities must be tested for impairment annually, or more frequently if there is any indication that it may be impaired. The recoverable amounts of the cash-generating units are determined on the basis of value in use calculations. At the end of Year 1 and Year 2, the value in use of each cash-generating unit exceeds its carrying amount. Therefore, the activities in each country and the goodwill allocated to those activities are regarded as not impaired.

At the beginning of Year 3, a new government is elected in Country A. It passes legislation significantly restricting exports of M's main product. As a result, and for the foreseeable future, M's production in Country A will be cut by 40%. The significant export restriction and the resulting production decrease require M also to estimate the recoverable amount of the Country A operations at the beginning of Year 3.

*The new legislation in Country A is an example of an indicator that goodwill may be impaired.*

To determine the value in use for the Country A cash-generating unit, M does the following:

(a) Prepares cash flow forecasts derived from the most recent financial budgets/forecasts for the next five years (Years 3–7) approved by management

(b) Estimates subsequent cash flows (Years 8–13) based on declining growth rates. The growth rate for Year 8 is estimated to be 3%. This rate is lower than the average long-term growth rate for the market in Country A

(c) Selects a 15% discount rate, which represents a pre-tax rate that reflects current market assessments of the time value of money and the risks specific to the Country A cash-generating unit

*The value in use is determined by calculating the present value of future cash flows.*

Exhibit 5A.1 shows the calculation of the value in use of the Country A cash-generating unit at the beginning of Year 3.

**EXHIBIT 5A.1**

### VALUE IN USE OF COUNTRY A CASH-GENERATING UNIT

| Year | Long-Term Growth Rates | Future Cash Flows | Present Value at 15% Discount Rate | Discounted Future Cash Flows |
|------|------------------------|-------------------|-----------------------------------|------------------------------|
| Year 3 ($n = 1$) | | $230 | 0.86957 | $  200 |
| Year 4 | | 253 | 0.75614 | 191 |
| Year 5 | | 273 | 0.65752 | 180 |
| Year 6 | | 290 | 0.57175 | 166 |
| Year 7 | | 304 | 0.49718 | 151 |
| Year 8 | 3% | 313 | 0.43233 | 135 |
| Year 9 | −2% | 307 | 0.37594 | 115 |
| Year 10 | −6% | 289 | 0.32690 | 94 |
| Year 11 | −15% | 245 | 0.28426 | 70 |
| Year 12 | −25% | 184 | 0.24719 | 45 |
| Year 13 | −67% | 61 | 0.21494 | 13 |
| Value in use | | | | $1,360 |

*Future cash flows are discounted using a pre-tax rate that reflects current market assessments of the time value of money and the risks specific to the cash-generating unit.*

Based on the calculation in Exhibit 5A.1, the recoverable amount of the Country A cash-generating unit is $1,360. Assuming that the carrying amount of Country A's identifiable net assets is $1,833 at the beginning of Year 3, there would be an impairment loss of $1,473 calculated as follows:

| | |
|---|---|
| Carrying amount of Country A's: | |
| Identifiable net assets | $1,833 |
| Goodwill | 1,000 |
| Total carrying amount | 2,833 |
| Recoverable amount | 1,360 |
| Total impairment loss | $1,473 |

The impairment loss is applied first to goodwill to reduce it to zero and then to identifiable assets as indicated by the following:

| | Goodwill | Identifiable Assets | Total |
|---|---------|---------------------|-------|
| Carrying amount | 1,000 | 1,833 | 2,833 |
| Impairment loss | (1,000) | (473) | (1,473) |
| Carrying amount after impairment loss | 0 | 1,360 | 1,360 |

*The impairment loss is allocated to goodwill first and then to other identifiable net assets.*

In the example above, the subsidiary is wholly owned by the parent. The value in use was calculated for the CGU as a whole and compared to the carrying amount of goodwill and identifiable net assets for the unit as a whole. When the subsidiary is non–wholly owned, certain adjustments may be required when making this comparison. This is especially important when parent company extension theory is used to account for NCI. In this situation, the carrying amount of goodwill allocated to the unit will have to be grossed up to include the goodwill attributable to the non-controlling interest. This adjusted carrying amount is then compared with the recoverable amount of the unit to determine whether the cash-generating unit is impaired. The following example[10] illustrates impairment testing for a non-wholly subsidiary accounted for using parent company extension theory.

Parent acquired an 80% ownership interest in Subsidiary for $2,200 on January 1, Year 3. At that date, Subsidiary's net identifiable assets had a fair value of $1,500. Parent chooses to measure the non-controlling interest as the proportionate interest of Subsidiary's identifiable net assets of $300 (20% × $1,500). Goodwill of $1,000 is the difference between the total consideration given, $2,500 ($2,200 + $300) and the fair value of the identifiable net assets, $1,500.

The assets of Subsidiary together are the smallest group of assets that generate cash inflows that are largely independent of the cash inflows from other assets or groups of assets. Therefore, Subsidiary is a cash-generating unit. Because other cash-generating units of Parent are expected to benefit from the synergies of the combination, goodwill of $600 related to those synergies has been allocated to other cash-generating units within Parent. Therefore, only $400 of goodwill is allocated to Subsidiary. Because the cash-generating unit Subsidiary is made up of includes goodwill within its carrying amount, it must be tested for impairment annually, or more frequently if there is an indication that it may be impaired.

---

*Goodwill at the date of acquisition is allocated to the CGUs that benefit from the synergies of the business combination.*

---

At the end of Year 3, Parent determines that the recoverable amount of cash-generating unit Subsidiary is $1,200. The carrying amount of the net assets of Subsidiary, excluding goodwill, is $1,350.

Goodwill attributable to non-controlling interest is included in Subsidiary's recoverable amount of $1,200 but has not been recognized in Parent's consolidated financial statements. Therefore, the carrying amount of Subsidiary is grossed up to include goodwill attributable to the non-controlling interest, before being compared with the recoverable amount of $1,200. Goodwill attributable to Parent's 80% interest in Subsidiary at the acquisition date is $400 after allocating $600 to other cash-generating units within Parent. The goodwill attributable to the 20% non-controlling interest in Subsidiary at the acquisition date is $100 ($400 × 20/80). The adjusted carrying amount of goodwill is $500 ($400 pertaining to parent's 80% interest plus $100 pertaining to the NCI's unrecognized interest). The impairment loss is $650 calculated as follows:

| | |
|---|---|
| Carrying amount of Subsidiary's: | |
| Identifiable net assets | $1,350 |
| Goodwill | 500 |
| Total carrying amount | 1,850 |
| Recoverable amount | 1,200 |
| Total impairment loss | $ 650 |

> *The carrying amount of the subsidiary must be grossed up for the unrecognized portion of its goodwill (i.e., the NCI's portion) to make it comparable to the recoverable amount for the subsidiary as a whole.*

The impairment loss is applied first to goodwill to reduce it to zero and then to identifiable assets. Since the calculation of impairment loss included a value for the NCI's unrecognized share of goodwill, part of the impairment loss should be allocated to the NCI as follows:

|  | Parent's Goodwill | NCI's Goodwill | Identifiable assets | Total |
|---|---|---|---|---|
| Carrying amount | $400 | $100 | $1,350 | $1,850 |
| Impairment loss | (400) | (100) | (150) | (650) |
| Carrying amount after impairment loss | 0 | 0 | $1,200 | $1,200 |

The previous examples have shown that the impairment testing for goodwill has added a new and complex valuation exercise to the consolidation process. The determination of recoverable amounts will be a costly one for many companies and will likely require the yearly services of business valuation specialists.

> *The impairment tests are complex and often require considerable professional judgment.*

Although impairment testing for goodwill and intangible assets with indefinite lives is required on an annual basis, a detailed evaluation of the recoverable amount may not be required annually. IAS 36 paragraph 24 states that the most recent detailed calculation made in a preceding period of the recoverable amount of a CGU to which goodwill has been allocated may be used in the impairment test of that unit in the current period given the following:

(a) There is very little change in the make-up of the assets and liabilities of the CGU since the most recent recoverable amount determination.

(b) The most recent recoverable amount determination yielded an amount that substantially exceeded the carrying amount of the unit.

(c) Based on analyzing events since the most recent recoverable amount determination, the likelihood that a current recoverable amount determination would be less than the carrying amount of the unit is remote.

## Summary of Appendix 5A

Goodwill is impaired when the recoverable amount of the cash-generating unit as a whole exceeds the carrying amount of the net assets of the cash-generating unit as a whole. Recoverable amount is the greater of fair value from selling the unit today and value in use, which is the present value of future cash flows from continuing to operate the unit. (LO7)

## APPENDIX 5B

## Working Paper Approach for Consolidations Subsequent to Acquisition

LO8

In this chapter, we illustrated the direct approach for preparing consolidated financial statements when the parent used the cost method to account for its investment. In the examples used, we first examined the situation where the subsidiary was 100% owned, and then the situation where the parent's ownership was 80%. We will now illustrate the working paper approach using the same examples.

## Year 5 Consolidated Financial Statement Working Paper

A number of methods can be used to prepare consolidated financial statement working papers when the parent has used the cost method. All methods used must result in identical consolidated amounts. The approach that we will illustrate adjusts the parent's retained earnings account on the working paper to what they would have been if the equity method had been used to account for the investment. Since retained earnings under the equity method are equal to consolidated retained earnings, we are, in effect, adjusting the parent's cost-method retained earnings to consolidated retained earnings. The adjustment is made as of the earliest date that retained earnings are needed for the current year's financial statements. If a statement of retained earnings or a statement of changes in shareholders' equity is prepared, the balance for retained earnings is needed as of the beginning of the reporting period.

> There are many different ways of using a working paper to support the preparation of consolidated financial statements.

The working paper approach requires the same additional calculations used in the direct approach. Then, we make "adjustments and eliminations" similar to Chapters 3 and 4. In this chapter, we have shortened the description to "eliminations." Exhibit 5B.1 shows the preparation of the consolidated financial statements for Year 5 using a working paper, assuming Company S is a 100%-owned subsidiary of Company P. To compare it with the direct approach, see Exhibit 5.5. Before explaining the various entries, a few comments about the overall format would be useful.[11]

1. In observing the effect of the elimination entries, the reader must take into account the debit and credit balances of the financial statement items. Revenues, net income, retained earnings, liabilities, and share capital accounts have credit balances, while expenses, dividends, and assets have debit balances. The debit and credit elimination entries are either increasing or decreasing these financial statement items, depending on their nature.

2. Some elimination entries affect two or more of the financial statements, but the total debits and credits for each entry are equal.

3. The totals from the net income line from the income statement, including the totals of the elimination entries made there, are carried down to the net income line in the retained earnings statement. In a similar manner, the end-of-year retained earnings totals are carried down to the

retained earnings on the balance sheet. Because the cumulative effect of the elimination entries from each statement has been carried down to the balance sheet, the total elimination debits and credits on that statement are equal.

---

*Total debits must equal total credits on the consolidated worksheet.*

---

**EXHIBIT 5B.1**

### CONSOLIDATED FINANCIAL STATEMENT WORKING PAPER
#### December 31, Year 5 (cost method)

| | P | S | Eliminations Dr. | Cr. | Consolidated |
|---|---|---|---|---|---|
| Sales | $ 50,000 | $30,000 | | | $ 80,000 |
| Dividend income | 2,500 | | **(1)** $ 2,500 | | |
| | 52,500 | 30,000 | | | 80,000 |
| Cost of sales | 26,500 | 14,700 | **(3)** 2,000 | | 43,200 |
| Goodwill impairment loss | | | **(3)** 50 | | 50 |
| Misc. expenses | 5,200 | 8,000 | | | 13,200 |
| | 31,700 | 22,700 | | | 56,450 |
| Net income | $ 20,800 | $ 7,300 | $ 4,550 | $ 0 | $ 23,550* |
| Retained earnings, Jan. 1 | $ 85,000 | $ 6,000 | **(2)** $ 6,000 | | $ 85,000 |
| Net income | 20,800 | 7,300 | 4,550 | $ 0 | 23,550 |
| | 105,800 | 13,300 | | | 108,550 |
| Dividends | 6,000 | 2,500 | | **(1)** 2,500 | 6,000 |
| Retained earnings: | | | | | |
| Dec. 31 | $ 99,800 | $10,800 | $10,550 | $ 2,500 | $102,550 |
| Assets, misc. | $147,800 | $18,300 | | | $166,100 |
| Inventory | 30,000 | 14,000 | | | 44,000 |
| Investment in S | 19,000 | | | **(2)** 19,000 | |
| Acquisition differential | | | **(2)** 3,000 | **(3)** 3,000 | |
| Goodwill | | | **(3)** 950 | | 950 |
| | $196,800 | $32,300 | | | $211,050 |
| Liabilities | $ 47,000 | $11,500 | | | $ 58,500 |
| Common shares | 50,000 | 10,000 | **(2)** 10,000 | | 50,000 |
| Retained earnings | 99,800 | 10,800 | 10,550 | 2,500 | 102,550 |
| | $196,800 | $32,300 | $24,500 | $24,500 | $211,050 |

*Attributable to shareholders of Company P.

---

*The consolidated balances are derived by combining the carrying amount from the parent's and subsidiary's separate-entity financial statements, plus or minus consolidation adjustments.*

*The investment account is replaced by the carrying amount of the subsidiary's assets and liabilities plus the unamortized acquisition differential.*

Since Year 5 is the first period since the date of acquisition, the retained earnings at the beginning of Year 5 would be the same amount under both the cost and equity methods. Therefore, no adjustment is necessary to convert retained earnings at the beginning of this reporting period to the equity method.

The working paper elimination entries are reproduced below, with an explanation of each.

| | | | |
|---|---|---|---|
| **(1)** | Dividend income—Company P | 2,500 | |
| | Dividends—Company S | | 2,500 |

> *Dividend income is eliminated against the dividends paid by the subsidiary.*

The parent's dividend income does not appear in the consolidated income statement, and the subsidiary's dividends do not appear in the consolidated retained earnings statement. Therefore, these accounts need to be eliminated. Now, the revenue and expenses of the parent and subsidiary can be combined, plus or minus adjustments for amortization of the acquisition differential, to determine consolidated revenues and expenses.

| | | | |
|---|---|---|---|
| **(2)** | Retained earnings Jan. 1—Company S | 6,000 | |
| | Common shares—Company S | 10,000 | |
| | Acquisition differential | 3,000 | |
| | Investment in S—Company P | | 19,000 |

> *The investment account is eliminated since it will be replaced by the carrying amount of the subsidiary's assets and liabilities plus the unamortized acquisition differential.*

This entry eliminates the parent's share of the start-of-year retained earnings and common shares of Company S, and the investment in S account of Company P, and establishes the acquisition differential at the beginning of the year. (In Year 5, this is the acquisition differential on the date of acquisition.)

| | | | |
|---|---|---|---|
| **(3)** | Cost of sales—Company S | 2,000 | |
| | Goodwill impairment loss | 50 | |
| | Goodwill | 950 | |
| | Acquisition differential | | 3,000 |

This entry eliminates the acquisition differential established by entry (2), and allocates it in accordance with the acquisition differential amortization schedule by (a) adjusting the expenses of Company S and (b) reflecting the unamortized balance at the end of the year on the consolidated balance sheet.

## Year 6 Consolidated Financial Statement Working Paper

The working papers for the preparation of the Year 6 consolidated financial statements are presented in Exhibit 5B.2. See Exhibit 5.8 to compare with the direct approach.

**EXHIBIT 5B.2**

### CONSOLIDATED FINANCIAL STATEMENT WORKING PAPER
December 31, Year 6 (cost method)

| | P | S | Eliminations Dr. | Eliminations Cr. | Consolidated |
|---|---|---|---|---|---|
| Sales | $ 60,000 | $40,000 | | | $100,000 |
| Dividend income | 3,000 | | **(1)** $ 3,000 | | |
| | 63,000 | 40,000 | | | 100,000 |
| Cost of sales | 32,000 | 18,000 | | | 50,000 |
| Goodwill impairment loss | | | **(3)** 80 | | 80 |
| Expenses, misc. | 9,000 | 12,000 | | | 21,000 |
| | 41,000 | 30,000 | | | 71,080 |
| Net income | $ 22,000 | $10,000 | $ 3,080 | $ 0 | $ 28,920* |
| Retained earnings, Jan. 1 | $ 99,800 | $10,800 | **(2)** $10,800 | **(a)** $2,750 | $102,550 |
| Net income | 22,000 | 10,000 | 3,080 | 0 | 28,920 |
| | 121,800 | 20,800 | | | 131,470 |
| Dividends | 8,000 | 3,000 | | **(1)** 3,000 | 8,000 |
| Retained earnings, Dec. 31 | $113,800 | $17,800 | $13,880 | $ 5,750 | $123,470 |
| Assets, misc. | $131,800 | $21,000 | | | $152,800 |
| Inventory | 35,000 | 16,000 | | | 51,000 |
| Investment in S | 19,000 | | **(a)** $ 2,750 | **(2)** 21,750 | |
| Acquisition differential | | | **(2)** 950 | **(3)** 950 | |
| Goodwill | | | **(3)** 870 | | 870 |
| | $185,800 | $37,000 | | | $204,670 |
| Liabilities | $ 22,000 | $ 9,200 | | | $ 31,200 |
| Common shares | 50,000 | 10,000 | **(2)** 10,000 | | 50,000 |
| Retained earnings | 113,800 | 17,800 | 13,880 | 5,750 | 123,470 |
| | $185,800 | $37,000 | $28,450 | $28,450 | $204,670 |

*Attributable to shareholders of Company P.

> *The entries on the income statement are adjustments for one period to bring the accounts to the desired balance for one period of time, that is, for one year.*
>
> *The entries on the balance sheet are cumulative adjustments to bring the accounts to the desired balance at the end of the period, that is, at a point in time.*

Elimination entry (a) adjusts Company P's retained earnings to the balance under the equity method as at the beginning of Year 6, which is the same balance as at the end of Year 5. Retained earnings under the equity method are equal to consolidated retained earnings. Therefore, retained earnings at the beginning of Year 6 have to be adjusted from $99,800 under the cost method to $102,550 under the equity method.

| (a) | Investment in S—Company P | 2,750 | |
| | Retained earnings, Jan. 1—Company P (102,550 – 99,800) | | 2,750 |

> *First, convert the parent's beginning retained earnings from the cost method to the equity method.*

This entry adjusts the investment in S account and the January 1 retained earnings of Company P to the equity method balances at the beginning of the year. The calculation of consolidated retained earnings as at January 1, Year 6, following Exhibit 5.7 provides the amounts for this entry.

The working paper elimination entries are reproduced below, with an explanation of each.

| (1) | Dividend income—Company P | 3,000 | |
| | Dividends—Company S | | 3,000 |

This entry eliminates Company P's dividend income account and the dividend account of Company S. Now, the revenue and expenses of the parent and subsidiary can be combined, plus or minus adjustments for amortization of the acquisition differential, to determine consolidated revenues and expenses.

| (2) | Retained earnings Jan. 1—Company S | 10,800 | |
| | Common shares—Company S | 10,000 | |
| | Acquisition differential | 950 | |
| | Investment in S | | 21,750 |

This entry eliminates the common shares and retained earnings of Company S on January 1, Year 6, against the January 1, Year 6, balance of Company P's investment account; it also establishes the difference as the *unamortized* acquisition differential on that date.

| (3) | Goodwill impairment loss | 80 | |
| | Goodwill | 870 | |
| | Acquisition differential | | 950 |

This entry eliminates the unamortized acquisition differential at the end of Year 5 and allocates it in accordance with the Year 6 acquisition differential amortization schedule.

> *These entries bring the consolidated account balances to the desired amounts.*

## 80%-Owned Subsidiary—Year 5

Exhibit 5B.3 shows the preparation of the consolidated financial statements as at December 31, Year 5, using a working paper. See Exhibit 5.12 to compare with the direct approach.

The working paper entries are produced and explained below. The only new items here are the entries required to establish the non-controlling interest.

| (1) | Dividend income—Company P | 2,000 | |
| | Dividends—Company S | | 2,000 |

**EXHIBIT 5B.3**

### CONSOLIDATED FINANCIAL STATEMENT WORKING PAPER
December 31, Year 5 (cost method)

|  | P | S | Eliminations Dr. | Cr. | Consolidated |
|---|---|---|---|---|---|
| Sales | $ 50,000 | $30,000 |  |  | $ 80,000 |
| Dividend income | 2,000 |  | (1) $ 2,000 |  |  |
|  | 52,000 | 30,000 |  |  | 80,000 |
| Cost of sales | 26,500 | 14,700 | (4) 2,000 |  | 43,200 |
| Goodwill impairment loss |  |  | (4) 50 |  | 50 |
| Misc. expenses | 5,200 | 8,000 |  |  | 13,200 |
|  | 31,700 | 22,700 |  |  | 56,450 |
| Net income | $ 20,300 | $ 7,300 |  |  | $ 23,550 |
| Attributable to: |  |  |  |  |  |
| Non-controlling interest |  |  | (5) 1,050 |  | $ 1,050 |
| Company P's shareholders |  |  |  |  | 22,500 |
|  |  |  | $ 5,100 | $ 0 | 23,550 |
| Retained earnings, |  |  |  |  |  |
| Jan. 1 | $ 85,000 | $ 6,000 | (3) $ 6,000 |  | $ 85,000 |
| Net income | 20,300 | 7,300 | 5,100 | $ 0 | 22,500 |
|  | 105,300 | 13,300 |  |  | 107,500 |
| Dividends | 6,000 | 2,500 |  | (1) 2,000 | 6,000 |
|  |  |  |  | (6) 500 |  |
| Retained earnings, |  |  |  |  |  |
| Dec. 31 | $ 99,300 | $10,800 | $11,100 | $ 2,500 | $101,500 |
| Assets, misc. | $151,100 | $18,300 |  |  | $169,400 |
| Equipment (net) | 30,000 | 14,000 |  |  | 44,000 |
| Investment in S | 15,200 |  | (2) 3,800 | (3) 19,000 |  |
| Acquisition differential |  |  | (3) 3,000 | (4) 3,000 |  |
| Goodwill |  |  | (4) 950 |  | 950 |
|  | $196,300 | $32,300 |  |  | $214,350 |
| Liabilities | $ 47,000 | $11,500 |  |  | $ 58,500 |
| Common shares | 50,000 | 10,000 | (3) 10,000 |  | 50,000 |
| Retained earnings | 99,300 | 10,800 | 11,100 | 2,500 | 101,500 |
| Non-controlling interest |  |  |  | (2) 3,800 |  |
|  |  |  | (6) 500 | (5) 1,050 | 4,350 |
|  | $196,300 | $32,300 | $29,350 | $29,350 | $214,350 |

---

*The entries on the worksheet are recorded only on the worksheet and not in the separate-entity books of the parent or the subsidiary.*

*Non-controlling interest appears both on the income statement (for a period of time) and on the balance sheet (at a point in time).*

This entry eliminates the dividend income against Company P's share of the dividends of Company S.

| **(2)** | Investment in S | 3,800 | |
| | Non-controlling interest (balance sheet) | | 3,800 |

This entry establishes non-controlling interest at the beginning of the year. Note that there is no separate section of the working paper for changes in non-controlling interest. Instead, the establishment of non-controlling interest at the beginning of the year is recorded directly to non-controlling interest in the balance sheet section of the working paper.

| **(3)** | Retained earnings, Jan. 1—Company S | 6,000 | |
| | Common shares—Company S | 10,000 | |
| | Acquisition differential | 3,000 | |
| | Investment in S | | 19,000 |

> *The investment account is eliminated, since it will be replaced by the carrying value of the subsidiary's assets and liabilities, the unamortized acquisition differential, and non-controlling interest.*

This entry eliminates 100% of the start-of-year shareholders' equity of Company S and the investment account, and establishes the acquisition differential. Entries (5) and (6) below record the changes to non-controlling interest during the year. They are also recorded directly to non-controlling interest in the balance sheet section of the working paper. These entries to non-controlling interest will be needed to prepare the non-controlling interest column in the statement of changes in equity during the year.

| **(4)** | Cost of sales—Company S | 2,000 | |
| | Goodwill impairment loss | 50 | |
| | Goodwill | 950 | |
| | Acquisition differential | | 3,000 |

In accordance with the Year 5 amortization schedule, this entry reflects the acquisition differential amortization on the consolidated income statement and the unamortized balance of the acquisition differential on the consolidated balance sheet.

| **(5)** | Non-controlling interest (income statement) | 1,050 | |
| | Non-controlling interest (balance sheet) | | 1,050 |

This entry establishes the net income attributable to the non-controlling interest on both the consolidated income statement and consolidated balance sheet.

| **(6)** | Non-controlling interest (balance sheet) | 500 | |
| | Dividends—Company S | | 500 |

This final entry eliminates 20% of the dividends of Company S that were paid to the non-controlling interest shareholders and reduces the equity of that group on the consolidated balance sheet.

## 80%-Owned Subsidiary—Year 6

Exhibit 5B.4 shows the working paper approach to the preparation of the Year 6 consolidated financial statements. See Exhibit 5.15 to compare with the direct approach.

**EXHIBIT 5B.4**

## CONSOLIDATED FINANCIAL STATEMENT WORKING PAPER
### December 31, Year 6 (cost method)

| | P | S | Eliminations Dr. | | Eliminations Cr. | | Consolidated |
|---|---|---|---|---|---|---|---|
| Sales | $ 60,000 | $40,000 | | | | | $100,000 |
| Dividend income | 2,400 | | **(1)** | $ 2,400 | | | |
| | 62,400 | 40,000 | | | | | 100,000 |
| Cost of sales | 32,000 | 18,000 | | | | | 50,000 |
| Goodwill impairment loss | | | **(4)** | 80 | | | 80 |
| Expenses, misc. | 9,000 | 12,000 | | | | | 21,000 |
| | 41,000 | 30,000 | | | | | 71,080 |
| Net income | $ 21,400 | $10,000 | | | | | $ 28,920 |
| Attributable to: | | | | | | | |
| Non-controlling interest | | | **(5)** | 1,984 | | | $ 1,984 |
| Company P's shareholders | | | | | | | 26,936 |
| | | | | $ 4,464 | $ | 0 | $ 28,920 |
| | | | | | | | |
| Retained earnings: | | | | | | | |
| Jan. 1 | $ 99,300 | $10,800 | **(3)** | $10,800 | **(a)** | $ 2,200 | $101,500 |
| Net income | 21,400 | 10,000 | **(above)** 4,464 | | **(above)** 0 | | 26,936 |
| | 120,700 | 20,800 | | | | | 128,436 |
| Dividends | 8,000 | 3,000 | | | **(1)** | 2,400 | 8,000 |
| | | | | | **(6)** | 600 | |
| Retained earnings: | | | | | | | |
| Dec. 31 | $112,700 | $17,800 | | $15,264 | | $ 5,200 | $120,436 |
| Assets, misc. | $134,500 | $21,000 | | | | | $155,500 |
| Inventory | 35,000 | 16,000 | | | | | 51,000 |
| Investment in S | 15,200 | | **(a)** | $ 2,200 | **(3)** | 21,750 | |
| | | | **(2)** | $ 4,350 | | | |
| Acquisition differential | | | **(3)** | 950 | **(4)** | 950 | |
| Goodwill | | | **(4)** | 870 | | | 870 |
| | $184,700 | $37,000 | | | | | $207,370 |
| Liabilities | $ 22,000 | $ 9,200 | | | | | $ 31,200 |
| Common shares | 50,000 | 10,000 | **(3)** | 10,000 | | | 50,000 |
| Retained earnings | 112,700 | 17,800 | **(above)** 15,264 | | **(above)** 5,200 | | 120,436 |
| Non-controlling interest | | | | | **(2)** | 4,350 | 5,734 |
| | | | **(6)** | 600 | **(5)** | 1,984 | |
| | $184,700 | $37,000 | | $34,234 | | $34,234 | $207,370 |

> *Consolidated net income attributable to parent's shareholders is equal to the parent's separate-entity income under the equity method.*
>
> *Consolidated retained earnings are equal to the parent's separate-entity retained earnings under the equity method.*

Elimination entry (a) adjusts the accounts of Company P to equity method balances at the beginning of Year 6, which is the same balance as at the end of Year 5. Retained earnings under the equity method are equal to consolidated retained earnings. Therefore, retained earnings at the beginning of Year 6 have to be adjusted from $99,300 under the cost method to $101,500 under the equity method.

| | | | |
|---|---|---|---|
| **(a)** | Investment in S—Company P | 2,200 | |
| | Retained earnings, Jan. 1—Company P (101,500 − 99,300) | | 2,200 |

> *Adjust the investment in subsidiary at the beginning of the current period from the balance under the cost method to the balance under the equity method.*

The remaining elimination entries are produced and explained below.

| | | | |
|---|---|---|---|
| **(1)** | Dividend income—Company P | 2,400 | |
| | Dividends—Company S | | 2,400 |

This entry eliminates Company P's dividend income account against 80% of the dividends of Company S. The remaining 20% of the dividends of Company S are eliminated in entry (6).

| | | | |
|---|---|---|---|
| **(2)** | Investment in S | 4,350 | |
| | Non-controlling interest | | 4,350 |

This entry establishes non-controlling interest at the beginning of the year. It represents 20% of the start-of-year common shares and retained earnings accounts of Company S, plus 20% of the unamortized acquisition differential.

| | | | |
|---|---|---|---|
| **(3)** | Retained earnings, January 1—Company S | 10,800 | |
| | Common shares—Company S | 10,000 | |
| | Acquisition differential | 950 | |
| | Investment in S—Company P | | 21,750 |

This entry eliminates 100% of the start-of-year retained earnings and common share accounts of Company S against the start-of-year balance in Company P's investment account and it establishes the unamortized acquisition differential at the beginning of Year 6.

| | | | |
|---|---|---|---|
| **(4)** | Goodwill impairment loss | 80 | |
| | Goodwill | 870 | |
| | Acquisition differential | | 950 |

Entry (4) allocates the unamortized acquisition differential in accordance with the Year 6 amortization schedule.

| | | | |
|---|---|---|---|
| **(5)** | Non-controlling interest (income statement) | 1,984 | |
| | Non-controlling interest (balance sheet) | | 1,984 |

Entry (5) allocates the net income attributable to the non-controlling interest for Year 6 to the equity of the non-controlling interest on the balance sheet.

| | | |
|---|---|---|
| **(6)** Non-controlling interest (balance sheet) | 600 | |
| Dividends—Company S | | 600 |

The final entry (6) eliminates the remaining 20% of the dividends of Company S and reduces the equity of the non-controlling interest on the balance sheet by this amount.

> *These journal entries appear only on the consolidated worksheet and are not posted to the separate-entity accounting records.*

In this appendix, we have illustrated the working paper approach, which allows the reader to see where all of the eliminations end up. However, as we proceed with some of the more difficult aspects of consolidated statement preparation, the number of elimination entries used becomes overwhelming. Additionally, there is no set standard working paper approach. This appendix presented elimination entries associated with a financial statement working paper. Other approaches could use a different set of entries and still arrive at the same consolidated amounts. If a trial balance working paper approach had been used instead, the entries would have been different. In practice, a computerized spreadsheet or a specialized software program would probably be used in the majority of cases. The working paper entries required by these programs would no doubt be different from those illustrated here.

As you will see, working papers are not used in the chapters that follow because the major focus of this text is the direct approach, which stresses understanding of relationships rather than memorization of working paper entries. If a thorough understanding of the consolidation process is present, it can then be applied to any computerized working paper program that may be seen in practice. When consolidation questions appear on professional accounting examinations in Canada, a direct approach is invariably expected to be used when formulating an answer.

> *The direct approach will be used exclusively in subsequent chapters of this text.*

## Summary of Appendix 5B

The preparation of the consolidated worksheet subsequent to the date of acquisition starts with bringing the investment in subsidiary account to its position at the beginning of the year and establishing the non-controlling interest at the beginning of the year. Then, entries are made to eliminate the parent's investment account and the subsidiary's shareholders' equity accounts and allocate the acquisition differential at the beginning of the year. The subsidiary's own income statement picks up the subsidiary's income for the year. Adjusting entries are required to amortize the acquisition differential for the year and split the subsidiary's income and dividend paid between the parent and non-controlling interest. **(LO8)**

## Review Questions

*Questions, cases, and problems that deal with the appendix material are denoted with an asterisk.*

LO1   **1.** Briefly outline the process for determining if goodwill is impaired and how to allocate any impairment loss.

LO1   **2.** Is the impairment test for intangibles other than goodwill the same as the one used for goodwill? Briefly explain.

**LO**
**3, 4**

**3.** When the parent has used the equity method, its net income equals consolidated net income attributable to its shareholders, and its retained earnings equal consolidated retained earnings. However, the parent's financial statements are not the same as consolidated statements. On consolidated statements, which assets and income are replaced from the parent's statements, and what are they replaced with?

**LO5**

**4.** A parent company's 75%-owned subsidiary declared and paid a dividend totalling $10,000. How would the parent company record this dividend under the equity method? Under the cost method?

**LO5**

**5.** By which method, cost or equity, does IFRS require a parent company to record its investment in a subsidiary? Why?

**LO**
**3,4**

**6.** The retained earnings column in the consolidated statement of changes in equity shows dividends declared during the year. Do these dividends consist of the parent's, the subsidiary's, or both? Explain.

**LO2**

**7.** "An acquisition differential allocated to revalue the land of a subsidiary on acquisition date will always appear on subsequent consolidated balance sheets." Do you agree? Explain.

**LO5**

**8.** "Under the equity method, the investment account is adjusted for the investor's share of post-acquisition earnings computed by the consolidation method." Explain this statement.

**LO5**

**9.** At the end of the year, the parent's investment account had an equity method balance of $120,000. At this time, its 75%-owned subsidiary had shareholders' equity totalling $125,000. How much was the unamortized acquisition differential at the end of the year?

**LO**
**3, 4**

**10.** On the consolidated balance sheet, what effect does the elimination of intercompany receivables and payables have on shareholders' equity and non-controlling interest?

**LO2**

**11.** Explain how the matching principle is applied when amortizing the acquisition differential.

**LO5**

**12.** What accounts in the financial statements of the parent company have balances that differ depending on whether the cost or the equity method has been used?

**LO**
**3, 4**

**13.** Why does adding the parent's share of the increase in retained earnings of the subsidiary and the parent's retained earnings under the cost method result in consolidated retained earnings? Assume that there is no acquisition differential.

**LO**
**3, 4**

**14.** A subsidiary was acquired in the middle of the fiscal year of the parent. Describe the preparation of the consolidated income statement for the year.

**LO**
**5, 8**

**\*15.** What are the initial entries on the working paper when the parent has used the cost method to account for its investment?

**LO**
**3, 4, 5**

**\*16.** When the parent company uses the cost method, an adjustment must be made to its retained earnings on consolidation in every year after the year of acquisition. Why is this entry necessary? Why is a similar entry not required when the parent utilized the equity method?

# CASES

## Case 5-1

LO1

BIO Company is a private company. It employs 30 engineers and scientists who are involved with research and development of various biomedical devices. All of the engineers and scientists are highly regarded and highly paid in the field of biomedical research. BIO is 50% owned by Rod Smart, who started the company in Year 3, and 50% owned by a group of venture capitalists who contributed $10 million of equity capital in Year 4 to fund the R&D activity of the group.

On January 1, Year 6, REX Ltd., a public company listed on the TSX Venture Exchange, acquired 100% of the shares of BIO by issuing 5 million of its own shares. Its shares were trading at $4 per share on the date of this transaction.

The balance sheet for BIO on January 1, Year 6, was as follows:

| | |
|---|---|
| Cash and marketable securities | $ 2,500,000 |
| Property, plant, and equipment—net | 800,000 |
| Development costs | 3,000,000 |
| | $ 6,300,000 |
| Liabilities | $ 900,000 |
| Common shares | 10,100,000 |
| Deficit | (4,700,000) |
| | $ 6,300,000 |

The cash, marketable securities, property, plant, and equipment, and liabilities have fair values equal to carrying amounts. Prior to Year 5, all of the research and development costs were expensed. Starting in Year 5, the developments costs were capitalized because the management of BIO felt that they were getting close to patenting some of their products.

The management of REX is aware that BIO will need to be included in REX's consolidated financial statements. The questions below were asked by management concerning these consolidated financial statements.

**Required**

(a) Will any part of the acquisition cost be allocated to BIO's skilled workers? If so, how will this asset be measured, and how will it be amortized or checked for impairment on an annual basis?

(b) Will any part of the acquisition cost be allocated to identifiable intangible assets? If so, how will this asset be measured, and how will it be amortized or checked for impairment on an annual basis?

(c) How much of the purchase price will be recognized as goodwill, and how will goodwill be evaluated for impairment on an annual basis?

## Case 5-2

LO1

It is now mid-September Year 3. Growth Investments Limited (GIL) has been owned by Sam and Ida Growth since its incorporation under the *Canada Business Corporations Act* many years ago. The owners, both 55 years of age, have decided to effect a corporate reorganization of capital in the form of an estate freeze. Sam and Ida will maintain control by holding voting preferred shares that carry a fixed dividend. New common shares will be issued to the three Growth children and to Mario Thibeault, a GIL manager who has been with the company since its inception.

GIL operates primarily in the real estate industry. It holds raw land, which will be subdivided and sold in the future, and it owns a variety of revenue-producing properties. The land and the properties are owned either directly or through wholly owned subsidiaries. A valuation of GIL's net assets will be done as of November 30, Year 3, the date of the proposed corporate reorganization.

Innes & Panners has audited GIL's financial statements for the past several years. The financial statements are used by the owners and the company's banker as well as for tax purposes. One of the rights of the preferred shareholders (Sam and Ida) will be to have audited financial statements for GIL's year-end, which has always been November 30.

You, the CPA, have been hired as a consultant to GIL for the year ending November 30, Year 3. The board of directors of GIL has engaged your firm, at the request of Mario Thibeault, to advise on alternatives available with respect to accounting and reporting policies for the company for Year 3 and subsequent years. This engagement is separate from the audit engagement. They are hoping that the financial statement for Year 3 could reflect the fair values of all identifiable assets and liabilities.

You will prepare a report that should be addressed to the board of directors of GIL. It should outline the feasible accounting and reporting alternatives that exist in preparing audited, comparative financial statements for Year 3 and subsequent years.

You and your staff have learned the following about GIL's activities during the current fiscal year:

1. Under the plan for reorganizing capital, Sam and Ida are to be issued preferred shares on November 30, Year 3 in exchange for all their common shares. The preferred shares will be redeemable at the fair value of the company as determined at November 30, Year 3. Each of the four new shareholders will pay $100 for 25% of the new voting common shares of GIL. The valuation of GIL's net assets is nearly complete.

2. Except for one parcel of raw land, all of GIL's real estate assets have an appraisal value that exceeds cost, or cost less capital cost allowance to date. (GIL has always used income tax methods and rates for depreciation purposes.) Each asset's fair value is based on an estimated net selling price as at November 30, Year 3. For the one parcel of raw land, fair value is expected to be approximately 70% of cost.

3. Current five-year mortgage interest rates on properties similar to GIL's range between 10% and $10\frac{1}{2}$% per annum. GIL's debt, as of November 30, Year 3, will consist of:

| | |
|---|---|
| $2,200,000 | 14% rate; due in 3 years |
| 1,600,000 | 8% rate; due in 4 years |
| 1,300,000 | $10\frac{1}{2}$% rate; due to bank on demand |

4. In December Year 2, GIL sold an apartment building for $2,500,000 in a province that is subject to rent controls and took back a non-interest-bearing note. Payments of $500,000 per year are due on December 15 for each of the next five years, commencing in Year 3. GIL's financial statements at August 31, Year 3, show the $2,500,000 as a current asset.

5. In all years to November 30, Year 2, GIL had expensed real estate taxes and interest on debt incurred to finance raw land purchases. The new shareholders have asked whether these sums ought to be capitalized retroactively for all raw land held at November 29, Year 3.

6. An application is pending to have one of GIL's apartment buildings converted to condominium status. Several levels of government have to approve the conversion, but ultimate approval is expected in Year 4 because other buildings in the vicinity have already been accepted as condominiums. When approval is received, the fair value of this building will increase from $4,300,000 to about $5,700,000. Each condominium apartment unit will be offered for sale to its occupants, or to others.

7. GIL leases its head office building space on a 20-year lease; 14 years are left in the lease. GIL pays $100,000 per year plus all occupancy costs such as light, heat, insurance, and cleaning. Current leasing costs have increased, and GIL would have to pay $220,000 per year for equivalent space in the same building if it were to sign a lease in Year 3. The financial statements at November 30, Year 2 treat the head office situation as an operating lease. They contain a short note on lease obligations.

8. Construction of a shopping centre is in progress for GIL. A fixed-price contract for $8 million has been signed with a construction company, which has undertaken to complete the centre by August Year 4. Financing for 10 years at 12% interest per annum on a $6 million mortgage has been approved. GIL purchased the land on which the centre is being located several years ago. It paid $750,000 for the land and sold one-half interest to the 50% partner for $1,800,000 in December Year 2. Approximately one-half of the shopping centre space has been leased for five or ten years commencing August Year 4. Several of the leases contain escalation-of-rent clauses tied to store sales. GIL paid a demolition company $120,000 in December Year 2 to clear old farm buildings and fences and ready the site for construction. It also paid $110,000 in July Year 3 to the agent who arranged the leases.

9. In December Year 2, GIL sold a small office building for $4,200,000 cash, and paid off the $2 million mortgage on the property plus a penalty of $82,000. The purchase/sale agreement contains a clause that enables GIL to receive sums additional to the $4,200,000 if rental receipts for the next four years exceed an average of $700,000 per year. On the basis of new leases signed by the purchaser in Year 3, GIL ought to be receiving some additional compensation each year.

10. Traditionally, the senior management of GIL has received a bonus based on audited net income.

*(CPA Canada adapted)*[12]

## Case 5-3

**LO2**

Total Protection Limited (TPL) was incorporated on January 1, Year 1, by five homebuilders in central Canada to provide warranty protection for new-home buyers. Each shareholder owns a 20% interest in TPL. While most homebuilders provide one-year warranties, TPL offers 10-year warranties and includes protection for a number of items not usually covered. For example, if a problem arose as a result of faulty construction or construction materials, TPL would protect its customers against any resulting decline in the market value of their property and would provide for the costs of restoring the property. TPL does not, however, cover general declines in market value.

The five shareholders believe TPL will increase their home sales and at the same time minimize their individual risks. The idea for TPL originated with Safe-Way Builders and, therefore, this shareholder will receive a royalty payment of 5% of income before income taxes. The shareholders have engaged your firm to prepare a report that will assist them in managing TPL in order to maximize its long-term profitability. In particular, they are wondering whether TPL is pricing its services appropriately and adequately controlling its costs. In addition, as a separate report, the shareholders would like your firm to recommend appropriate financial accounting policies for TPL.

It is mid-December Year 1. You, the CPA, and the partner on the engagement, meet with Gina Filmore, president of Safe-Way Builders. Filmore is currently operating TPL from the offices of Safe-Way Builders, for which TPL will be charged rent. Filmore provides you with the following information on TPL's operations.

"TPL's revenues consist of an initial fee paid at the time of purchase of the warranty and an annual maintenance fee paid over the term of the warranty. Currently, the initial fee and annual maintenance fee depend on a number of factors, including the cost of the home, reputation of the builder, construction design of the home (for example, brick versus aluminum siding), and the home's location. The warranties are sold through each builder, who can adjust the initial fee and the annual maintenance fee if it is considered necessary to make the sale. The builder receives a commission of 10% of the total warranty revenue, which should ensure that the builder would try to maximize the initial fee and the annual maintenance fee. Typically, a buyer of a brick house worth $250,000 that was constructed by a good-quality builder should expect to pay an initial fee of $2,000 plus an annual maintenance fee of $250.

"To date, TPL has been doing very well, primarily as a result of two factors: central Canada has been experiencing a boom in the residential construction industry, and TPL has expanded to offer coverage for homes built by builders other than the shareholders. Quite frankly, an increasing share of our business is from these outside builders, many of which have entered the industry just to try to capitalize on the demand. We don't think that permitting these homebuilders to sell coverage will hurt our home sales, since most of them are in the low-price segment of the market, keeping costs down by employing new, less expensive construction methods and materials. We require that their initial fee be at least $1,500 per home to ensure that they don't lower the price just to make a sale.

"Our real problem is keeping up with the paperwork. I have my own business to run and cannot devote much time to TPL. We haven't even had time to get organized or set up any system for TPL. Lately, I must admit that I've lost track of what's going on. All I know is that we're making money. In just 11 months, TPL has collected about $1.6 million while paying out only $224,000 in repair costs. Keep in mind, however, that I've been able to keep these repair costs down by having Safe-Way Builders do the repairs. Business will only get better when we expand within the next month to offer coverage in western Canada and the southwestern United States.

"Since we have accumulated a lot of cash, we recently decided, in a 3 to 2 vote among the shareholders, to buy 100% of the shares of Gainery Construction Ltd., a local construction company. Mr. Gainery, the owner of the company, had a heart attack about six months ago and wanted to get out of the business. Details of the purchase agreement are provided in Exhibit I."

Just before you leave the client's premises, you manage to collect some additional information on the operations of TPL (see Exhibit II).

When you return to the office, the partner reminds you that he will be meeting with TPL shareholders in one week and asks you to prepare the reports requested by the shareholders.

---

**EXHIBIT I**

## Information Gathered from Purchase Agreement

1. Closing date will be December 31, Year 1.
2. TPL will purchase 100% of the shares of Gainery Construction Ltd. for $500,000 in cash on closing, plus $500,000 per year for the next two years.
3. Mr. Gainery will provide, without additional consideration, a minimum of 300 hours of consulting services in the first year and a minimum of 150 hours in the second year, to ensure a smooth transition of the business.
4. The carrying amount and estimated fair value of identifiable assets and liabilities were as follows on the date of acquisition:

|  | Carrying Value | Fair Value |
|---|---|---|
| Cash | $ 100,000 | $ 100,000 |
| Accounts receivable | 200,000 | 200,000 |
| Homes under construction | 1,300,000 | 1,500,000 |
| Undeveloped land | 1,000,000 | 1,600,000 |
| Equipment, net | 700,000 | 650,000 |
| Other assets | 70,000 | 70,000 |
|  | $3,370,000 | $4,120,000 |
| Liabilities | $2,470,000 | $2,470,000 |
| Common shares | 100,000 |  |
| Retained earnings | 800,000 |  |
|  | $3,370,000 |  |

---

**EXHIBIT II**

### INFORMATION GATHERED FROM CLIENT'S RECORDS

#### TPL Shareholders

|  | Larkview Estates | Towne Homes | Granite Homes | Kings Road | Safe-Way Builders | Other Builders | Total |
|---|---|---|---|---|---|---|---|
| Number of warranties sold | 50 | 85 | 190 | 250 | 175 | 465 | 1,215 |
| Warranty revenue (000s) | $120 | $165 | $395 | $ 90 | $160 | $705 | $1,635 |
| Repair costs incurred (000s) | $ 6 | $ 9 | $ 21 | $ 42 | $ 39 | $107 | $ 224 |

*(CPA Canada adapted)*[13]

# Case 5-4

LO3, 4, 6

Beaver Ridge Oilers' Players Association and Mr. Slim, the CEO of the Beaver Ridge Oilers Hockey Club (Club), ask for your help in resolving a salary dispute. Mr. Slim presents the following income statement to the player representatives:

**BEAVER RIDGE OILERS HOCKEY CLUB**
**INCOME STATEMENT**

| | | |
|---|---|---|
| Ticket revenues | | $6,000,000 |
| Player salaries | $1,200,000 | |
| Stadium rent | 4,200,000 | |
| Staff salaries | 1,000,000 | |
| Advertising | 400,000 | 6,800,000 |
| Net Income (loss) | | $ (800,000) |

Mr. Slim argues that the Club loses money and cannot afford a salary increase. After further investigation, you determine that the Club owns 90% of the voting shares of Oilers Stadium Inc. (Stadium), which is used primarily by the Oilers. The Club accounts for its investment in the Stadium under the cost method. The Stadium has not declared any dividends since its inception three years ago. As such, the Club has never reported any income on its investment in the Stadium.

Mr. Slim insists that the income for the Stadium should not be a factor in the negotiation of the players' salaries since the Stadium is a separate legal entity and is taxed as a separate legal entity. The income statement for the Stadium is as follows:

**OILERS STADIUM INC.**
**INCOME STATEMENT**

| | | |
|---|---:|---:|
| Stadium rent revenue | $4,200,000 | |
| Concession revenue | 2,400,000 | |
| Parking revenue | 200,000 | $6,800,000 |
| Cost of concessions | 800,000 | |
| Depreciation of stadium | 1,000,000 | |
| Staff salaries | 1,400,000 | 3,200,000 |
| Net income | | $3,600,000 |

### Required

(a) What advice would you give the negotiating parties regarding the issue of whether to consider the Stadium's income in the salary negotiations? Give supporting arguments. Indicate what other pertinent information you would need to provide specific recommendations.

(b) How would your advice change if the Stadium were 90% owned by Mr. Slim directly rather than by the Club? Explain.

## Case 5-5

LO1, 5, 6

Gerry's Fabrics Ltd. (GFL), a private company, manufactures a variety of clothing for women and children and sells it to retailers across Canada. Until recently, the company has operated from the same plant since its incorporation under federal legislation 40 years ago. Over the years, the profits of the company have varied widely, and there have been periods of losses.

In the year ended March 31, Year 41, the company entered into an arrangement whereby it issued common shares from treasury to a group of new shareholders. At the same time, the existing shareholders were given the option of exchanging their common shares for preferred shares, which are redeemable at the option of the company and retractable at the option of the shareholder. One shareholder, who had held 25 percent of the common shares, elected to accept the preferred shares, while the other shareholders elected to retain their common shares.

A "Preferred Share Agreement" (the Agreement), was signed by the shareholder who had accepted the preferred shares (the "preferred shareholder"). Under the Agreement, the preferred shareholder can require GFL to redeem all of his shares in any year, after giving at least 90 days' notice prior to the fiscal year-end. The Agreement does not provide for partial redemptions. The total redemption price for all shares is 1.25 times "income before taxes" for that year. The term *income before taxes* is defined in the Agreement as follows:

1. Income before taxes for the year of redemption must be calculated
   - in accordance with the accounting policies set forth in this Agreement, or
   - where no accounting policy has been clearly specified, in accordance with policies consistent in intent with the policies contained in this Agreement.

2. Income before taxes for the year of redemption need not, for the purposes of the Agreement, be the same as that reported to shareholders or that used for calculating income taxes payable.

The Agreement specifies the applicable accounting policies as follows:

## A. Revenue Recognition

1. In cases in which a deposit of 10% or more of the sales price has been received from the customer, revenue shall be recognized on completion of the manufacturing of the goods ordered.

2. In all other cases, revenue shall be recognized upon shipment to the customer, and no allowance shall be made for returned merchandise or adjustments.

## B. Cost of Goods Sold and Inventory

1. All inventory on hand at the end of a fiscal year (excluding raw materials) shall be costed at actual production costs, including its full share of all overhead expenditures.

2. Raw materials inventory shall include all expenditures that were needed to make the inventory available for use, including unpacking and storing costs.

## C. Amortization

1. All applicable amortization shall be computed on a straight-line basis using realistic residual values.

2. Amortization shall be recorded over the physical life of the assets, regardless of their useful life to the company.

3. No amortization shall be recorded on assets that are increasing in value.

## D. Capitalization

1. All expenditures shall be capitalized as assets unless their life is limited to the current financial period. All maintenance and repair costs that extend an asset's useful life shall be capitalized.

2. Assets shall be recorded at cost and amortized in accordance with C above.

## E. Liabilities

1. Each liability shall be recorded at the amount required to settle the obligation. A debt-to-equity ratio of 1:1 is assumed to exist. Interest incurred on debt in excess of this ratio will not be deductible in computing income before taxes.

## F. Errors and Adjustments

1. All errors, adjustments, and changes in value shall be attributed to the year to which the error or adjustment or change relates.

### G. Compensation and Related Transactions

1. Average compensation per employee shall be in accordance with levels used in fiscal Year 41 adjusted by the consumer price index.

2. All related-party transactions must be measured at fair value or values established in the marketplace for transactions between GFL and unrelated third parties.

The Agreement also contains a separate clause that deals with "arbitration procedures." These procedures allow an independent arbitrator to calculate the share redemption price after having obtained full access to the books and records of GFL.

The preferred shareholder has advised GFL of his intention to have GFL redeem his preferred shares and has provided GFL with the required 90 days' notice. The redemption price, calculated by GFL, was based on the March 31, Year 45, financial statements. However, the preferred shareholder disagrees with GFL's figure for income before taxes.

Since the price is being disputed, the matter is to be resolved by an independent arbitrator. Both parties have agreed to engage Cook & Co., Chartered Professional Accountants, to make a binding decision. You, CPA, are employed by Cook & Co. The engagement partner has asked you to prepare a memo providing complete analyses required for and recommendations to be considered in the calculation of the share-redemption price. Your notes from your investigations are contained in Exhibit III.

### EXHIBIT III

## Notes from Investigation of GFL

1. The disputed share-redemption price calculation was prepared by the vice-president of finance of GFL and is 1.25 times the company's unaudited income before taxes of $895,420 for the year ended March 31, Year 45.

2. The unaudited financial statements for the year ended March 31, Year 45, reflect the following transactions and accounting policies:

   - During fiscal Year 44, GFL acquired all the shares of a competing company (J Ltd.) for $8 million. Most of the amount by which the purchase price exceeded the carrying amount of the assets and liabilities acquired was recorded as goodwill and is being amortized over ten years. The purchase was financed almost entirely by debt at 10% interest for five years.

   - On January 1, Year 45, a volume discount policy was introduced. At March 31, Year 45, an estimated liability of $95,500 was provided for volume discounts that may become due.

   - In fiscal Year 44, the manufacturing processes were altered to introduce more mechanization, and standard costing was adopted. All variances from standard costs are being expensed.

   - In order to reduce taxable income and save cash, all employee incentives are being accrued at year-end and paid five months later.

   - In Year 43, GFL decided to account for one of its successful investments on the equity basis. During fiscal Year 45, the directors of GFL chose to revert to the cost basis for the investment.

   - In fiscal Year 45, GFL commenced construction of another manufacturing facility at a cost of $1.8 million, including equipment. Some manufacturing occurred in a part of the new facility before the whole facility was ready for use. To be conservative, any costs that were incurred after manufacturing had commenced were expensed, except for new equipment installations.

   - Land that has been held for several years for future expansion of the company was recorded at cost plus carrying costs (property taxes, maintenance, and similar) until fiscal Year 45. The land was reclassified in late fiscal Year 5 as inventory and was written down to the lower of cost and net realizable value.

*(continued)*

- In March Year 45, GFL sold some of its capital assets under a deferred payment arrangement. Gains on sale will be recorded as payment is received, on a proportional basis.
- In April Year 45, an enhanced executive pension plan was introduced. The March 31, Year 45, financial statements include pension expenses that reflect the additional costs resulting from the new pension plan enhancements.

3. Notes to the financial statements for fiscal Year 45 disclose the following:

- During the year, GFL sold $4 million worth of goods to DGR Ltd. DGR is owned by several of the common shareholders of GFL. DGR purchased goods at a special price that was about $380,000 lower than the price paid by other retailers.
- A $200,000 liability has been recorded for legal costs pertaining to a patent infringement case that is before the courts.

*(CPA Canada adapted)*[14]

# Case 5-6

LO3, 4

Digital Future Technologies (DFT) is a public technology company. It has a September 30 year-end, and last year it adopted IFRS. Kin Lo is a partner with Hi & Lo, the accounting firm that was newly appointed as DFT's auditor in July for the year ending September 30, Year 12. Kin met with the CFO, Anne Rather, to gather information on the business.

It is now September 12, Year 12. You, CPA, work for Hi & Lo. Last week, Kin provided you with the notes that he took in his initial meeting with Anne (Exhibit IV). You met with Anne a couple of days ago to find out what has happened at DFT since Kin's meeting, and have summarized your discussion in Exhibit V. Anne gave you updated projected results for September 30, Year 12 (Exhibit VI).

Kin asks you to prepare a memo summarizing the accounting issues of significance. He is particularly concerned about issues that affect earnings because management is anticipating a more profitable year than previous years. Management is now part of a new bonus program that is based on earnings before interest, income taxes, depreciation, and amortization (EBITDA). The bonus begins to accumulate once EBITDA exceeds $14 million.

---

**EXHIBIT IV**

## Notes from Kin's Initial Meeting with Anne—July Year 12

### Knowledge of the Business

DFT manufactures electronic components for telephone and cable in both the wired and wireless markets. While quarterly sales can be quite variable due to inconsistent demand, the company has grown significantly over the past few years. It must constantly reinvest in research and development to ensure that its products remain relevant and can integrate with the latest technology.

A new growth market in the industry is the development of equipment that can convert transmissions from analog to digital signals. The equipment allows companies to maximize their transmissions through the bandwidth of existing infrastructure. DFT is anticipating completion of Zeus, a new product that is targeted to this growth market and is expected to be the first of its kind on the market, by mid-August, Year 12.

A new bonus program was instituted at the beginning of fiscal Year 12 with the objective of motivating management to contribute to profitability by being innovative and developing new products.

*(continued)*

**EXHIBIT IV** *(continued)*

### Revenue Recognition

- *Product.* Most revenue relates to product sales. Revenue is recognized once the products are shipped, assuming collection is reasonably assured. DFT targets an average margin of 40%.
- *Service.* DFT also has non-recurring engineering (NRE) revenue, which it expects to be $1.5 million by year-end. Customers pay DFT to research and develop add-on components for existing DFT products. In most cases, DFT is not required to do anything beyond the initial engineering phase. NRE revenue is therefore recognized as soon as the work for the specific component is complete. DFT targets a margin of 60%.

**EXHIBIT V**

## Notes from CPA's Meeting with Anne—September 10, Year 12

A number of events have occurred since July that gave rise to revisions to the projected results for the year ending September 30, Year 12.

### Indo-Tech

DFT had been negotiating since early in Year 12 with Indo-Tech (Indo), a major customer based in India. The deal described below was signed.

DFT and Indo have contracted with Safe Storage, an unrelated third-party warehouse in India. Indo provided DFT with its forecasted production needs by component and the dates the components are required to be at the warehouse. DFT must ensure that the components arrive at the warehouse in time. Inventory stored at the warehouse is owned by DFT. Safe Storage must notify DFT when Indo takes components from the warehouse, and ownership of the inventory transfers to Indo once it is taken. At no time shall inventory remain in the warehouse for more than 60 days. Any inventory not taken within 60 days of arrival is considered sold to Indo and shall be segregated for removal by Indo as soon as possible.

A minimum of $1.5 million in components inventory had to be at the warehouse by June 30, but nothing was taken by Indo from the warehouse until August 2. DFT could only recognize the $1.5 million in revenue at that time. Because DFT had not included the sale in the projection done on July 8, the sale was picked up in the revised projection. Since August 2, DFT has sold another $1.85 million in components and shipped them to the warehouse. Based on Indo's forecasted needs, DFT will not be shipping any more components prior to year-end. Indo has not taken out any of the $1.85 million in inventory that is in the warehouse, but DFT is confident it will do so and has recorded the revenue.

### Non-Recurring Engineering (NRE) Contract

DFT has booked a total of $2.5 million in NRE revenue. The amount exceeds expectations because DFT had additional NRE revenue in July that was worth $1 million.

The customer only accepted our normal price on the NRE portion because DFT agreed to provide a discount in fiscal Year 13 of $225,000 on product sales with a usual selling price of $750,000. Of the total contract, the $1 million NRE revenue portion was recorded in the current year's projection as the work was completed before the September 15, Year 12 deadline.

### Zeus

Due in part to the focus on the above NRE project, as well as unanticipated technical difficulties, development of the new product, Zeus, was delayed. DFT will likely only realize total sales of $200,000 for Zeus by year-end. It will also likely have $400,000 of units in inventory at year-end. However, production has just begun. Also, due to the delay, a competitor was able to place a similar product on the market first. As a result, DFT isn't sure it can sell Zeus at the planned price.

### Research and Development

DFT defers and amortizes eligible development costs. Deferral ceases once a product is ready for market, and the costs are amortized over the estimated life of the product, generally three years or less. DFT successfully

*(continued)*

pursued government funding for research and development. The funds received from the grants, totaling $800,000, were not anticipated in the July projection, and have now been included in revenue. Approximately 75% of the related development costs remain in deferred development costs.

DFT has now abandoned development of one of its products, Ares, which still had approximately $450,000 in deferred development costs. However, DFT's R&D manager believes that the development can be leveraged for a new product, Hades, so it continues to defer the development costs.

## Business Acquisition

Crolla purchased 70% of the outstanding common shares of Dao on August 31, Year 12, at a cost of $5,600,000. On that date, Dao had common shares of $1,000,000 and retained earnings of $4,000,000, and fair values were equal to carrying amounts for all its recognized net assets.

In determining the purchase price, the management of Crolla noted that Dao had a five-year agreement to supply goods to Customer Co. Both Crolla and Dao believe that Customer will renew the agreement at the end of the current contract. Neither party to the agreement can transfer, assign or sell their rights or obligation under the agreement to any other party. Management of Crolla would prefer to assign any acquisition differential on the acquisition of Crolla to goodwill for three reasons: the agreement between Dao and Customer is not separable; it would be impracticable to determine the fair value of the agreement; and there would be no annual amortization expense if the entire acquisition differential is assigned to goodwill.

## Other

A HST audit was finally completed in late August Year 12. It resulted in a reassessment of $125,000. DFT paid the amount immediately to prevent incurring any penalties, but has recorded it as a prepaid expense. It is appealing the reassessment, based on the belief that it is incorrect.

DFT has incurred an impairment loss of $100,000 on production equipment that is becoming obsolete. The impairment loss has been included in amortization of capital assets.

Based on the revised projection for September, Anne believes that everyone in the program will receive a bonus. Therefore, she will accrue an estimate of $300,000 before year-end and needs to adjust the projection.

---

**EXHIBIT VI**

### PROJECTED NET INCOME FOR THE YEAR ENDING SEPTEMBER 30, YEAR 12

(in thousands of Canadian dollars)

| | Sept. 30, Year 12 Original Projection (prepared on July 8, Year 12) | Note | DFT Adjustments | Note | Sept. 30, Year 12 Adjusted Projection (prepared on Sept. 10, Year 12) |
|---|---|---|---|---|---|
| Revenue | $55,374 | 1 | $3,850 | 5 | $59,224 |
| Cost of sales | 31,942 | 2 | 1,930 | 5 | 33,872 |
| Gross margin | 23,432 | | 1,920 | | 25,352 |
| Operating expenses: | | | | | |
| Research and development | 3,991 | 3 | | | 3,991 |
| Sales and marketing | 2,622 | | | | 2,622 |
| General and administrative | 7,824 | 4 | 100 | 6 | 7,924 |
| Interest | 314 | | | | 314 |
| Total operating expenses | 14,751 | | 100 | | 14,851 |
| Income before taxes | 8,681 | | 1,820 | | 10,501 |
| Income taxes (30%) | 2,604 | | 546 | 7 | 3,150 |
| Net income | $ 6,077 | | $1,274 | | $7,351 |

EBITDA (for bonus calculation) to be determined.

*Notes (also in thousands of Canadian dollars):*

*(continued)*

**EXHIBIT VI** *(continued)*

Initial Projection Notes (as of July 8)

1. Revenue includes anticipated sales of $1,500 for the new Zeus product. The related costs are reflected in cost of sales.
2. Cost of sales includes cost of Zeus product and projected amortization of $430 for production-related assets.
3. Research and development expenses include projected amortization of $1,620 related to deferred development costs.
4. General and administrative expenses include projected amortization of $2,995 related to capital assets.

Revisions to Projection (as of September 10)

5. Revenue and cost of sales

   - For Indo, sales have been increased by $3,350 ($1,500 + $1,850), and cost of sales has been increased by $2,010 ($900 + $1,110) (based on 40% gross margin). For new NRE revenue, sales have been increased by $1,000, and cost of sales has been increased by $400 (based on 60% gross margin). Nothing was booked for the product sales since they only occur in Year 13.
   - Government grants of $800 were recorded in revenue.
   - For Zeus, sales have been decreased by $1,300 and cost of sales has been decreased by $480 (based on 40% gross margin) due to lower than projected sales.
6. Impairment loss related to production equipment is $100.
7. Tax provision has been adjusted by $546.

*(CPA Canada adapted)*[15]

# PROBLEMS

## Problem 5-1

LO1, 2, 3

The following information is available for the assets of Saman Ltd. at December 31, Year 5:

|  | Carrying Amount | Fair Value |
| --- | --- | --- |
| Tangible assets, net | $1,164 | $1,174 |
| Recognized intangible assets, net | 510 | 520 |
| Internally developed patent | 0 | 60 |
| Goodwill | 420 | |
| Total | $2,094 | |

**Required**

(The following 3 parts are independent situations.)

*Part A.* Assume that the total fair value for all of Saman's assets as a group is $1,860.

(a) Calculate the total impairment loss for Year 5.

(b) After recognizing any impairment loss in (a), what are the reported carrying amounts for assets listed above?

*Part B.* Assume that the total fair value for all of Saman's assets as a group is $1,450.

(a) Calculate the total impairment loss for Year 5.

(b) After recognizing any impairment loss in (a), what are the reported carrying amounts for assets listed above?

*Part C.* Assume that Cyrus acquired all of Saman's assets for $1,860 as a business acquisition.

(a) Determine the amount to allocate to each of the assets listed above on the date of acquisition.

(b) Briefly explain why there is a difference in the amount of goodwill between Part A and Part C.

## Problem 5-2

LO2, 3, 5

Large Ltd. purchased 70% of Small Company on January 1, Year 6, for $770,000, when the statement of financial position for Small showed common shares of $560,000 and retained earnings of $260,000. On that date, the inventory of Small was undervalued by $71,000, and a patent with an estimated remaining life of five years was overvalued by $90,000.

Small reported the following subsequent to January 1, Year 6:

|  | Profit (Loss) | Dividends |
|---|---|---|
| Year 6 | $144,000 | $41,000 |
| Year 7 | (51,000) | 26,000 |
| Year 8 | 106,000 | 56,000 |

A test for goodwill impairment on December 31, Year 8, indicated a loss of $20,900 should be reported for Year 8 on the consolidated income statement. Large uses the cost method to account for its investment in Small and reported the following for Year 8 for its separate-entity statement of changes in equity:

| | |
|---|---|
| Retained earnings, beginning | $660,000 |
| Profit | 360,000 |
| Dividends | (54,000) |
| Retained earnings, end | $966,000 |

## Required

(a) Prepare the cost method journal entries of Large for each year.

(b) Compute the following on the consolidated financial statements for the year ended December 31, Year 8:

   (i) Goodwill

   (ii) Non-controlling interest on the statement of financial position

   (iii) Retained earnings, beginning of year

   (iv) Profit attributable to Large's shareholders

   (v) Profit attributable to non-controlling interest

(c) Now assume that Large is a private entity, uses ASPE, and chooses to use the equity method to report its investment in Small.

   (i) Prepare Large's journal entries for each year related to its investment in Small.

   (ii) Determine the investment in Small at December 31, Year 8.

## Problem 5-3

LO1, 2, 3

On January 1, Year 2, Gros Corporation acquired 70% of the outstanding common shares of Petite Company for a total cost of $84,000. On that date, Petite had $35,000 of common shares and $25,000 of retained earnings. The carrying amounts of each of Petite's identifiable assets and liabilities were equal to their fair values except for the following:

|  | Carrying Amount | Fair Value |
|---|---|---|
| Inventory | $45,000 | $55,000 |
| Equipment | 70,000 | 90,000 |

The equipment had an estimated useful life of ten years as at January 1, Year 2, and the entire inventory was sold during Year 2.

Selected account balances from the records of Gros and Petite for the year ended December 31, Year 6, were as follows:

|  | Gros | Petite |
|---|---|---|
| Inventory | $150,000 | $ 80,000 |
| Equipment, net | 326,000 | 160,000 |
| Goodwill |  |  |
| Retained earnings, end of year | 270,000 | 50,000 |
| Non-controlling interest on balance sheet |  |  |
| Cost of goods purchased | 500,000 | 450,000 |
| Change in inventory | 20,000 | 12,000 |
| Amortization expense | 35,000 | 20,000 |
| Non-controlling interest on income statement |  |  |
| Net income | 90,000 | 48,000 |
| Dividends paid | 30,000 | 10,000 |

### Additional Information

- Gros uses the cost method to account for its investment in Petite.
- An independent valuator has estimated that the goodwill associated with Gros's acquisition of Petite had a recoverable amount of $28,000 as of December 31, Year 6. (*Note:* No impairment losses have been recognized in all years prior to Year 6.)

### Required

(a) Determine the amounts on the Year 6 consolidated financial statements for the selected accounts noted above.

(b) If the independent appraisal of the recoverable amount for goodwill as at December 31, Year 6, showed an amount of $8,000 instead of the $28,000 indicated above, what would be the impact on the following?
  (i) Consolidated net income attributable to Gros's shareholders
  (ii) Consolidated retained earnings
  (iii) Consolidated net income attributable to non-controlling interest

# Problem 5-4

### LO3, 5

Summarized balance sheets of Corner Company and its subsidiary Brook Corporation on December 31, Year 4, were as follows:

|  | Corner | Brook | Consolidated |
|---|---|---|---|
| Current assets | $ 160,000 | $ 700,000 | $ 860,000 |
| Investment in Brook (cost) | 640,000 |  |  |
| Other assets | 600,000 | 900,000 | 1,500,000 |
|  | $1,400,000 | $1,600,000 | $2,360,000 |
| Liabilities | $ 800,000 | $ 200,000 | $1,000,000 |
| Common shares | 900,000 | 600,000 | 900,000 |
| Retained earnings | (300,000) | 800,000 | 180,000 |
| Non-controlling interest | — | — | 280,000 |
|  | $1,400,000 | $1,600,000 | $2,360,000 |

On the date that Corner acquired its interest in Brook, there was no acquisition differential and the carrying amounts of Brook's net assets were equal to fair values. During Year 4, Corner reported a net loss of $60,000, while Brook reported a net income of $140,000. No dividends were declared by either company during Year 4. Corner uses the cost method to account for its investment.

**Required**

Compute the following:

(a) The percentage of Brook's shares owned by Corner

(b) Consolidated net income attributable to Corner's shareholders for Year 4

(c) Corner's December 31, Year 3, retained earnings if it had used the equity method to account for its investment

(d) The retained earnings of Brook on the date that Corner acquired its interest in Brook

# Problem 5-5

### LO2, 3, 5

Pen Ltd. acquired an 85% interest in Silk Corp. on December 31, Year 1, for $646,000. On that date, Silk had common shares of $500,000 and retained earnings of $100,000. The imputed acquisition differential was allocated $70,000 to inventory, with the balance to patents being amortized over ten years. Silk reported profit of $30,000 in Year 2 and $52,000 in Year 3. While no dividends were declared in Year 2, Silk declared a dividend of $15,000 in Year 3.

Pen, which uses the cost method, reported a profit of $28,000 in Year 2 and a loss of $45,000 in Year 3. Pen's retained earnings on December 31, Year 3, were $91,000.

**Required**

Compute the following:

(a) Non-controlling interest in profit for Year 2 and Year 3

(b) Consolidated profit attributable to Pen's shareholders for Year 2 and Year 3

(c) Consolidated retained earnings at December 31, Year 3
(d) Non-controlling interest at December 31, Year 3
(e) Investment in Silk at December 31, Year 3, if Pen had used the equity method
(f) Consolidated patents at December 31, Year 3

## Problem 5-6

LO2, 3, 5

Peach Ltd. acquired 80% of the common shares of Cherry Company on January 1, Year 4. On that date, Cherry had common shares of $710,000 and retained earnings of $410,000.

The following is a summary of the changes in Peach's investment account from January 1, Year 4, to December 31, Year 6:

### INVESTMENT IN CHERRY

| | | |
|---|---|---:|
| January 1, Year 4 | Cost | $ 935,000 |
| December 31, Year 4 | Equity method income | 68,300 |
| | Dividends | (39,000) |
| December 31, Year 5 | Equity method income | 80,200 |
| | Dividends | (46,000) |
| December 31, Year 6 | Equity method income | 94,900 |
| | Dividends | (53,000) |
| | Balance | $1,040,400 |

### Additional Information

- Dividends declared by Cherry each year were equal to 50% of Cherry's reported profit each year.
- On January 1, Year 4, the carrying amounts of the identifiable net assets of Cherry were equal to fair values.
- There was a goodwill impairment loss each year since the date of acquisition.

### Required

Calculate the following:

(a) The amount of dividends declared by Cherry in Year 4
(b) The reported profit of Cherry for Year 5
(c) The amount for non-controlling interest that would appear in the Year 6 consolidated income statement and statement of financial position
(d) The amount of goodwill that would appear on the December 31, Year 6, consolidated statement of financial position

## Problem 5-7

LO1, 2, 3

On January 1, Year 4, Grant Corporation bought 8,000 (80%) of the outstanding common shares of Lee Company for $70,000 cash. Lee's shares were trading for $7 per share on the date of acquisition. On that date, Lee had $25,000 of common shares outstanding and $30,000 retained earnings. Also on that date, the carrying amount of each of Lee's identifiable assets and liabilities was equal to its fair value except for the following:

|  | Carrying Amount | Fair Value |
|---|---|---|
| Inventory | $50,000 | $55,000 |
| Patent | 10,000 | 20,000 |

The patent had an estimated useful life of five years at January 1, Year 4, and the entire inventory was sold during Year 4. Grant uses the cost method to account for its investment.

## Additional Information

- The recoverable amount for goodwill was determined to be $10,000 on December 31, Year 7. The goodwill impairment loss occurred in Year 7.
- Grant's accounts receivable contains $30,000 owing from Lee.
- Amortization expense is grouped with distribution expenses and impairment losses are grouped with other expenses.

The following are the separate-entity financial statements of Grant and Lee as at December 31, Year 7:

### BALANCE SHEETS
At December 31, Year 7

|  | Grant | Lee |
|---|---|---|
| *Assets* | | |
| Cash | $ 5,000 | $ 18,000 |
| Accounts receivable | 185,000 | 82,000 |
| Inventory | 310,000 | 100,000 |
| Investment in Lee | 70,000 | — |
| Equipment, net | 230,000 | 205,000 |
| Patent, net | — | 2,000 |
|  | $800,000 | $407,000 |
| | | |
| *Liabilities and Shareholders' Equity* | | |
| Accounts payable | $190,000 | $195,000 |
| Other accrued liabilities | 60,000 | 50,000 |
| Income taxes payable | 80,000 | 72,000 |
| Common shares | 170,000 | 25,000 |
| Retained earnings | 300,000 | 65,000 |
|  | $800,000 | $407,000 |

### INCOME STATEMENT
Year ended December 31, Year 7

|  | Grant | Lee |
|---|---|---|
| Sales | $900,000 | $360,000 |
| Cost of goods sold | (340,000) | (240,000) |
| Gross margin | 560,000 | 120,000 |
| Distribution expense | (30,000) | (25,000) |
| Other expenses | (180,000) | (56,000) |
| Income tax expense | (120,000) | (16,000) |
| Net income | $230,000 | $ 23,000 |

**Required**

(a) Calculate consolidated retained earnings at December 31, Year 7.

(b) Prepare consolidated financial statements for Year 7.

## Problem 5-8

LO2, 3, 5

On January 1, Year 4, Cyrus Inc. paid $914,000 in cash to acquire all of the ordinary shares of Fazli Company. On that date, Fazli's retained earnings were $200,000. All of Fazli's assets and liabilities had fair values equal to carrying amounts except for equipment, which was worth $50,000 more than carrying amount and had a remaining useful life of five years.

In Year 4, Cyrus reported net income from its own operations (exclusive of any income from Fazli) of $125,000 and declared no dividends. In Year 4, Fazli reported net income of $90,000 and paid a $40,000 cash dividend. Cyrus uses the cost method to report its investment in Fazli.

The financial statements for Cyrus and Fazli for the year ended December 31, Year 5, were as follows:

|  | Cyrus | Fazli |
|---|---|---|
| Revenues and investment income | $  928,000 | $  844,000 |
| Expenses | 674,000 | 710,000 |
| Profit | $  254,000 | $  134,000 |
| Retained earnings, 1/1/Year 5 | $  814,000 | $  250,000 |
| Profit | 254,000 | 134,000 |
| Dividends paid | (104,000) | (42,000) |
| Retained earnings, 12/31/Year 5 | $  964,000 | $  342,000 |
| Equipment (net) | $  714,000 | $  614,000 |
| Investment in Fazli | 914,000 | 0 |
| Receivables and inventory | 414,000 | 484,000 |
| Cash | 94,000 | 152,000 |
| Total assets | $2,136,000 | $1,250,000 |
| Ordinary shares | $  558,000 | $  484,000 |
| Retained earnings | 964,000 | 342,000 |
| Liabilities | 614,000 | 424,000 |
| Total equities and liabilities | $2,136,000 | $1,250,000 |

**Required**

(a) Prepare a schedule to allocate and amortize the acquisition differential for Years 4 and 5.

(b) Calculate equipment and goodwill for the consolidated balance sheet at the end of Year 5.

(c) Calculate investment income from Fazli and investment in Fazli account balances for Cyrus's separate entity financial statements for Year 5, assuming Cyrus uses the

   (i)  Cost method

   (ii) Equity method

(d) How does the parent's method of accounting for its investment affect the amount reported for expenses in its December 31, Year 5, consolidated income statement?

(e) How does the parent's method of accounting for its investment affect the amount reported for equipment in its December 31, Year 5, consolidated balance sheet?

(f) What is Cyrus's January 1, Year 5, retained earnings account balance assuming Cyrus accounts for its investment in Fazli using the
  (i) cost method?
  (ii) equity method?

(g) What is consolidated retained earnings at January 1, Year 5 assuming Cyrus accounts for its investment in Fazli using the
  (i) cost method?
  (ii) equity method?

## Problem 5-9

LO1, 2, 3

On July 1, Year 5, Big purchased 80% of the outstanding common shares of Little for $122,080. On that date, Little's equipment had a fair value that was $21,600 less than carrying amount. The equipment had accumulated depreciation of $20,000 and an estimated remaining useful life of 8 years. Also, at the date of acquisition, Little had an exclusive contract with the provincial government to perform periodic environmental audits of selected mining companies for the next five years. An independent business valuator indicated that a third party might pay up to $50,000 to take over this contract. All other assets and liabilities had carrying amounts equal to fair values. On June 30, Year 6, goodwill had a recoverable amount of $20,000.

On June 30, Year 6, the following financial statements were prepared. Big uses the cost method to account for its investment.

### INCOME STATEMENTS

|  | Big | Little |
|---|---|---|
| Sales | $ 270,000 | $162,000 |
| Investment income | 10,800 | — |
|  | 280,800 | 162,000 |
| Cost of sales | 140,100 | 94,380 |
| Expenses (misc.) | 31,080 | 28,200 |
|  | 171,180 | 122,580 |
| Net income | $ 109,620 | $ 39,420 |

### RETAINED EARNINGS STATEMENTS

|  | Big | Little |
|---|---|---|
| Balance, July 1 | $ 459,000 | $ 32,400 |
| Net income | 109,620 | 39,420 |
|  | 568,620 | 71,820 |
| Dividends | 32,400 | 13,500 |
| Balance, June 30 | $ 536,220 | $ 58,320 |

### BALANCE SHEETS
At June 30, Year 6

|  | Big | Little |
|---|---|---|
| Miscellaneous assets | $ 835,940 | $128,820 |
| Equipment | 162,000 | 95,600 |
| Accumulated depreciation | (60,000) | (50,000) |
| Investment in Little | 122,080 | — |
|  | $1,060,020 | $174,420 |
| Liabilities | $ 253,800 | $ 62,100 |
| Common shares | 270,000 | 54,000 |
| Retained earnings | 536,220 | 58,320 |
|  | $1,060,020 | $174,420 |

**Required**

(a) Prepare a schedule to calculate and allocate the acquisition differential. Explain the rationale for the accounting treatment of the $50,000 attributed to the government contract.

(b) Prepare the consolidated financial statements of Big as at June 30, Year 6.

(c) Prepare a schedule showing the changes in non-controlling interest during the year.

(d) Now assume that the market value of the shares held by the non-controlling interest at the date of acquisition was $25,000. Recalculate consolidated goodwill at the end of Year 6 and goodwill impairment loss for Year 6.

## Problem 5-10

LO1, 2, 3, 6

On December 31, Year 2, Palm Inc. purchased 80% of the outstanding ordinary shares of Storm Company for $350,000. At that date, Storm had ordinary shares of $240,000 and retained earnings of $64,000. In negotiating the purchase price, it was agreed that the assets on Storm's statement of financial position were fairly valued except for plant assets, which had a $44,000 excess of fair value over carrying amount. It was also agreed that Storm had unrecognized intangible assets consisting of trademarks that had an estimated value of $36,000. The plant assets had a remaining useful life of eight years at the acquisition date and the trademarks would be amortized over a 12-year period. Any goodwill arising from this business combination would be tested periodically for impairment. Palm accounts for its investment using the cost method.

Financial statements for Palm and Storm for the year ended December 31, Year 6, were as follows:

### STATEMENTS OF FINANCIAL POSITION
December 31, Year 6

|  | Palm | Storm |
|---|---|---|
| *Assets* | | |
| Plant assets—net | $270,000 | $200,000 |
| Investment in Storm | 350,000 | — |
| Other investments | 86,000 | 26,000 |
| Notes receivable | — | 14,000 |
| Inventory | 140,000 | 220,000 |
| Accounts receivable | 92,000 | 180,000 |
| Cash | 24,000 | 34,000 |
|  | $962,000 | $674,000 |
| *Shareholders' Equity and Liabilities* | | |
| Ordinary shares | $540,000 | $240,000 |
| Retained earnings | 150,000 | 190,000 |
| Notes payable | 150,000 | 120,000 |
| Other current liabilities | 14,000 | 54,000 |
| Accounts payable | 108,000 | 70,000 |
|  | $962,000 | $674,000 |

### INCOME STATEMENTS
For the year ended December 31, Year 6

|  | Palm | Storm |
|---|---|---|
| Sales | $910,000 | $555,000 |
| Cost of goods sold | (658,000) | (380,000) |
| Gross profit | 252,000 | 175,000 |
| Selling expenses | (26,000) | (39,000) |
| Other expenses | (156,000) | (80,000) |
| Interest and dividend income | 38,000 | 6,000 |
| Profit | $108,000 | $ 62,000 |

## Additional Information

- At December 31, Year 6, an impairment test of Storm's goodwill revealed the following:

| | |
|---|---|
| Fair value less disposal costs based on recent offer from prospective purchaser | $50,000 |
| Value in use based on undiscounted future net cash flows | 69,000 |
| Value in use based on discounted future net cash flows using a discount rate of: | |
| 8%, which is Storm's incremental borrowing rate | 42,000 |
| 2%, which is the risk-free rate on government bonds | 47,000 |

- An impairment test indicated that the trademarks had a recoverable amount of $14,350. The impairment loss on these assets occurred entirely in Year 6.

- On December 26, Year 6, Palm declared dividends of $40,000, while Storm declared dividends of $24,000.

- Amortization expense is reported in selling expenses, while impairment losses are reported in other expenses.

## Required

(a) Prepare consolidated financial statements.

(b) If none of the acquisition differential had been allocated to trademarks at the date of acquisition, how would this affect
  (i)  the return on total shareholders' equity for Year 6?
  (ii) the debt-to-equity ratio at the end of Year 6?

# Problem 5-11

LO2, 3, 4

On July 1, Year 4, Aaron Co. purchased 80% of the voting shares of Bondi Ltd. for $543,840. The statement of financial position of Bondi on that date follows. The accounts receivable of Bondi were collected in October Year 4, and the inventory was completely sold by May Year 5. Bondi's fixed assets had a remaining life of 15 years on July 1, Year 4, and the bonds payable mature on June 30, Year 8. The bonds were issued on July 1, Year 1. The stated rate of interest on the bonds is 6% payable semi-annually. The market rate of interest was 8% on July 1, Year 4. Tests for impairment of goodwill indicated a loss of $8,329 in Year 5 and $5,553 in Year 6.

**BONDI LTD.**
**STATEMENT OF FINANCIAL POSITION**
As at July 1, Year 4

| | Carrying Amount | Fair Value |
|---|---|---|
| Plant assets (net) | $540,000 | $450,000 |
| Inventory | 180,000 | 228,000 |
| Accounts receivable | 120,000 | 144,004 |
| Cash | 96,000 | 96,000 |
| | $936,000 | |
| | | |
| Ordinary shares | $120,000 | |
| Retained earnings | 508,800 | |
| Bonds payable | 200,000 | 186,534 |
| Current liabilities | 107,200 | 107,200 |
| | $936,000 | |

The financial statements for Aaron and Bondi at December 31, Year 6, are presented below. Aaron has used the equity method to account for its investment in Bondi.

## STATEMENTS OF FINANCIAL POSITION

| | Aaron | Bondi |
|---|---|---|
| Plant assets (net) | $ 720,000 | $ 540,000 |
| Investment in Bondi | 520,319 | — |
| Other investments | 250,666 | — |
| Inventory | 300,000 | 276,000 |
| Accounts receivable | 180,000 | 114,000 |
| Cash | 120,000 | 84,000 |
| | $2,090,985 | $1,014,000 |
| Ordinary shares | $ 300,600 | $ 120,000 |
| Retained earnings | 1,295,185 | 558,200 |
| Bonds payable | 315,000 | 200,000 |
| Current liabilities | 180,200 | 135,800 |
| | $2,090,985 | $1,014,000 |

## INCOME STATEMENTS

| | Aaron | Bondi |
|---|---|---|
| Sales | $1,261,000 | $1,200,000 |
| Equity method income from Bondi | 4,394 | — |
| Income from other investments | 25,000 | — |
| | 1,290,394 | 1,200,000 |
| Raw materials used | 880,000 | 1,005,000 |
| Change in inventory | (40,000) | 15,000 |
| Depreciation | 60,000 | 54,000 |
| Interest expense | 37,000 | 26,400 |
| Other expenses | 227,000 | 91,200 |
| | 1,164,000 | 1,191,600 |
| Profit | $ 126,394 | $ 8,400 |

## Required

(a) Prepare the consolidated financial statements for the year ended December 31, Year 6.

(b) Calculate goodwill impairment loss and non-controlling interest on the consolidated income statement for the year ended December 31, Year 6, under parent company extension theory.

(c) Calculate goodwill and non-controlling interest on the consolidated statement of financial position at December 31, Year 6, under the parent company extension theory.

# Problem 5-12

LO1, 2, 3, 4

Foxx Corp. purchased 75% of the outstanding shares of Rabb Ltd. on January 1, Year 3, at a cost of $117,000. Non-controlling interest was valued at $35,000 by an independent business valuator at the date of acquisition. On that date, Rabb had common shares of $50,000 and retained earnings of $30,000. Fair values were equal to carrying amounts for all the net assets except the following:

| | Carrying Amount | Fair Value |
|---|---|---|
| Inventory | $30,000 | $19,000 |
| Equipment | 45,000 | 69,000 |
| Software | — | 15,000 |

The equipment had an estimated remaining useful life of six years on January 1, Year 3, and the software was to be amortized over ten years. Foxx uses the cost method to account for its investment. The testing for impairment at December 31, Year 6, yielded the following fair values:

| | |
|---|---|
| Software | $ 8,000 |
| Goodwill | 20,000 |

The impairment loss on these assets occurred entirely in Year 6. Amortization expense is grouped with administrative expenses, and impairment losses are grouped with miscellaneous expenses. The parent's share of the goodwill noted above is $16,364.

The following are the financial statements of Foxx Corp. and its subsidiary Rabb Ltd. for Year 6:

### BALANCE SHEETS
At December 31, Year 6

| | Foxx Corp. | Rabb Ltd. |
|---|---|---|
| Cash | $ — | $ 10,000 |
| Accounts receivable | 40,000 | 30,000 |
| Note receivable | — | 40,000 |
| Inventory | 66,000 | 44,000 |
| Equipment, net | 220,000 | 76,000 |
| Land | 150,000 | 30,000 |
| Investment in Rabb | 117,000 | — |
| | $593,000 | $230,000 |
| Bank indebtedness | $ 90,000 | $ — |
| Accounts payable | 70,000 | 60,000 |
| Notes payable | 40,000 | — |
| Common shares | 150,000 | 50,000 |
| Retained earnings | 243,000 | 120,000 |
| | $593,000 | $230,000 |

### STATEMENTS OF RETAINED EARNINGS
Year ended December 31, Year 6

| | | |
|---|---|---|
| Retained earnings, January 1, Year 6 | $153,000 | $ 92,000 |
| Net income | 120,000 | 48,000 |
| Dividends | (30,000) | (20,000) |
| Retained earnings, December 31, Year 6 | $243,000 | $120,000 |

### INCOME STATEMENTS
For the year ended December 31, Year 6

| | | |
|---|---|---|
| Sales | $821,000 | $320,000 |
| Investment income | 15,000 | 3,600 |
| | 836,000 | 323,600 |
| Cost of sales | 480,000 | 200,000 |
| Administrative expenses | 40,000 | 12,000 |
| Miscellaneous expenses | 116,000 | 31,600 |
| Income taxes | 80,000 | 32,000 |
| | 716,000 | 275,600 |
| Net income | $120,000 | $ 48,000 |

**Additional Information**

The notes payable are intercompany.

**Required**

(a) Prepare the Year 6 consolidated financial statements.

(b) Calculate goodwill impairment loss and non-controlling interest on the consolidated income statement for the year ended December 31, Year 6, under parent company extension theory.

(c) If Foxx used parent company extension theory rather than entity theory, how would this affect the debt-to-equity ratio at the end of Year 6?

# Problem 5-13

LO2, 3, 4, 8

The following financial statements were prepared on December 31, Year 6.

## BALANCE SHEET

|  | Pearl | Silver |
|---|---|---|
| Cash | $ 390,000 | $ 190,000 |
| Accounts receivable | 290,000 | — |
| Inventory | 2,450,000 | 510,000 |
| Plant and equipment | 3,450,000 | 3,590,000 |
| Accumulated depreciation | (840,000) | (400,000) |
| Investment in Silver Company—at cost | 3,300,000 | — |
|  | $9,040,000 | $3,890,000 |
| Liabilities | $ 737,000 | $ 543,000 |
| Common shares | 3,750,000 | 2,050,000 |
| Retained earnings | 4,553,000 | 1,297,000 |
|  | $9,040,000 | $3,890,000 |

## INCOME STATEMENT

|  | Pearl | Silver |
|---|---|---|
| Sales | $4,450,000 | $1,450,000 |
| Dividend income | 232,000 | — |
|  | 4,682,000 | 1,450,000 |
| Cost of sales | 2,590,000 | 490,000 |
| Miscellaneous expenses | 365,000 | 79,000 |
| Administrative expense | 89,000 | 19,000 |
| Income tax expense | 295,000 | 165,000 |
|  | 3,339,000 | 753,000 |
| Net income | $1,343,000 | $ 697,000 |

## RETAINED EARNINGS STATEMENT

|  | Pearl | Silver |
|---|---|---|
| Balance, January 1 | $3,800,000 | $ 890,000 |
| Net income | 1,343,000 | 697,000 |
|  | 5,143,000 | 1,587,000 |
| Dividends | 590,000 | 290,000 |
| Balance, December 31 | $4,553,000 | $1,297,000 |

## Additional Information

Pearl purchased 80% of the outstanding voting shares of Silver for $3,300,000 on July 1, Year 2, at which time Silver's retained earnings were $445,000, and accumulated depreciation was $69,000. The acquisition differential on this date was allocated as follows:

- 20% to undervalued inventory
- 40% to equipment—remaining useful life eight years
- Balance to goodwill

During Year 3, a goodwill impairment loss of $79,000 was recognized, and an impairment test conducted as at December 31, Year 6, indicated that a further loss of $29,000 had occurred.

Amortization expense is grouped with cost of goods sold and impairment losses are grouped with administrative expenses.

Silver owes Pearl $84,000 on December 31, Year 6.

## Required

(a) Prepare consolidated financial statements on December 31, Year 6.
(b) Calculate goodwill impairment loss and non-controlling interest on the consolidated income statement for the year ended December 31, Year 6, under parent company extension theory.
(c) Calculate goodwill and non-controlling interest on the consolidated balance sheet at December 31, Year 6, under parent company extension theory.
*(d) Prepare the consolidated financial statements using the worksheet approach.

*eXcel*

## Problem 5-14

LO2, 3

Balance sheet and income statement data for two affiliated companies for the current year appear on the next page.

## Additional Information

- Albeniz acquired an 80% interest in Bach on January 1, Year 3, for $272,000. On that date, the following information was noted about specific net assets of Bach:

|  | Carrying Amount | Fair Value |
|---|---|---|
| Inventory | $20,000 | $50,000 |
| Land | 25,000 | 45,000 |
| Equipment (estimated useful life 15 years) | 60,000 | 78,000 |
| Misc. intangibles (estimated useful life 20 years) | — | 42,000 |

Amortization expense is grouped with distribution expenses. Albeniz's accumulated depreciation was $240,000 at the date of acquisition.

- On January 1, Year 3, Bach had a retained earnings balance of $30,000.
- Albeniz carries its investment at cost.

## BALANCE SHEET
### As at December 31, Year 6

|  | Albeniz | Bach |
|---|---|---|
| Cash | $ 40,000 | $ 21,000 |
| Receivables | 92,000 | 84,000 |
| Inventories | 56,000 | 45,000 |
| Land | 20,000 | 60,000 |
| Plant and equipment | 200,000 | 700,000 |
| Accumulated depreciation | (80,000) | (350,000) |
| Investment in Bach Company (cost) | 272,000 | — |
| Advances to Bach Company | 100,000 | — |
| Total assets | $700,000 | $560,000 |
| Accounts payable | $130,000 | $ 96,500 |
| Advances payable | — | 100,000 |
| Common shares | 400,000 | 200,000 |
| Retained earnings | 170,000 | 163,500 |
| Total liabilities and shareholders' equity | $700,000 | $560,000 |

## INCOME STATEMENT
### For the year ended December 31, Year 6

|  | Albeniz | Bach |
|---|---|---|
| Sales revenues | $600,000 | $400,000 |
| Interest income | 6,700 | — |
| Dividend income from Bach | 6,400 | — |
| Total revenues | 613,100 | 400,000 |
| Cost of goods sold | 334,000 | 225,000 |
| Distribution expense | 20,000 | 70,000 |
| Selling and administrative expense | 207,000 | 74,000 |
| Financing expense | 1,700 | 6,000 |
| Income taxes expense | 20,700 | 7,500 |
| Total expenses | 583,400 | 382,500 |
| Net income | $ 29,700 | $ 17,500 |

### Required

Prepare the following:

(a) Consolidated income statement

(b) Consolidated balance sheet

# Problem 5-15

LO2, 3, 5, 6, 8

On January 2, Year 4, Brady Ltd. purchased 80% of the outstanding shares of Partridge Ltd. for $4,320,000. Partridge's statement of financial position and the fair values of its identifiable assets and liabilities for that date were as follows:

| | Carrying Amount | Fair Value |
|---|---|---|
| Plant and equipment (net) | $4,600,000 | $4,600,000 |
| Patents (net) | 1,100,000 | 1,620,000 |
| Inventory | 2,100,000 | 2,320,000 |
| Accounts receivable | 1,600,000 | 1,600,000 |
| Cash | 520,000 | 520,000 |
| | $9,920,000 | |
| Ordinary shares | $2,021,000 | |
| Retained earnings | 2,620,000 | |
| 10% bonds payable | 3,100,000 | 3,420,000 |
| Accounts payable | 2,179,000 | 2,179,000 |
| | $9,920,000 | |

The patents had a remaining useful life of ten years on the acquisition date. The bonds were issued on January 1, Year 4, and mature on December 31, Year 13. Goodwill impairment losses were recorded as follows:

- Year 4: $31,000
- Year 6: $18,000

Partridge declared and paid dividends of $110,000 in Year 6.

On December 31, Year 6, the financial statements of the two companies were as follows:

### STATEMENT OF FINANCIAL POSITION

| | Brady | Partridge |
|---|---|---|
| Plant and equipment (net) | $ 8,200,000 | $5,200,000 |
| Patents (net) | — | 720,000 |
| Investment in Partridge Ltd. (equity method) | 4,584,000 | — |
| Inventory | 4,800,000 | 2,000,000 |
| Accounts receivable | 1,100,000 | 1,400,000 |
| Cash | 420,000 | 620,000 |
| | $19,104,000 | $9,940,000 |
| Ordinary shares | $ 5,100,000 | $2,021,000 |
| Retained earnings | 6,382,000 | 3,279,000 |
| Bonds payable | 4,100,000 | 3,100,000 |
| Accounts payable | 3,522,000 | 1,540,000 |
| | $19,104,000 | $9,940,000 |

### INCOME STATEMENTS

| | Brady | Partridge |
|---|---|---|
| Sales | $10,100,000 | $5,100,000 |
| Equity method income | 136,000 | — |
| | 10,236,000 | 5,100,000 |
| Cost of goods purchased | 6,950,000 | 2,910,000 |
| Change in inventory | 72,000 | 120,000 |
| Depreciation expense | 920,000 | 402,000 |
| Patent amortization expense | — | 120,000 |
| Interest expense | 490,000 | 310,000 |
| Other expenses | 700,000 | 870,000 |
| Income taxes | 620,000 | 160,000 |
| | 9,752,000 | 4,892,000 |
| Profit | $ 484,000 | $ 208,000 |

**Required**

(a) Prepare consolidated financial statements on December 31, Year 6.

(b) Assume that Brady is a private entity, uses ASPE, and chooses to use the cost method to account for its investment in Partridge. Which items on Brady's separate-entity financial statements would have amounts different from those shown? Compute the cost method balances of these items.

(c) Calculate the current ratio, debt-to-equity ratio, and return on total shareholders' equity for Brady's Year 6 financial statements assuming that the

   (i)   equity method was used to report its investment in Partridge;

   (ii)  cost method was used to report its investment in Partridge; and

   (iii) consolidated statements were used to report the business combination with Partridge.

   Round percentages to one decimal point and other ratios to two decimal points.

(d) Briefly explain which of the different reporting methods in (c) report the highest

   (i)   Liquidity

   (ii)  Risk of insolvency

   (iii) Profitability

 *(e) Prepare the consolidated financial statements using the worksheet approach.

# Endnotes

1   SEDAR Filings, http://sedar.com/GetFile.do?lang=EN& docClass=5&issuerNo=00000923&fileName=/csfsprod/ data150/filings/02309791/00000001/z%3A%5CBarrickGol d%5CAFS%5C2014%5C2014-AFS.pdf, p. 141.

2   SEDAR Filings, http://sedar.com/GetFile.do?lang=EN& docClass=5&issuerNo=00028227&fileName=/csfsprod/ data150/filings/02290393/00000001/e%3A%5CCCIBC_ SEDAR%5CCIBC_FINS_2014_ENG.pdf, p. 126.

3   SEDAR Filings, http://sedar.com/GetFile.do?lang=EN& docClass=5&issuerNo=00003131&fileName=/csfsprod/ data150/filings/02275072/00000001/k%3A%5Cfilings%5Cl ivework%5Cwkout%5C43540%5CGlentel_Q3.pdf, p. 25.

4   Some foreign jurisdictions assess tax at the corporate group level.

5   IAS 1 *Presentation of Financial Statements* requires a statement of changes in equity as part of the complete set of financial statements. It does not require a separate statement of retained earnings. However, the statement of changes in equity does provide reconciliation between the carrying amount of each component of equity at the beginning and the end of the period. Retained earnings are one of those components. In this textbook, we will use the statement of retained earnings as a surrogate for the retained earnings component of the statement of changes in equity.

6   *Indefinite* does not necessarily mean infinite, but rather extending beyond the foreseeable future.

7   IFRS 8 *Operating Segments* is discussed in more detail in Chapter 9.

8   LIFO is not acceptable under IFRS. Unless otherwise noted, we will assume a FIFO cost flow in all examples in the text.

9   This example is adapted from Example 2 of IAS 36 *Illustrative Examples*.

10  This example is adapted from Example 7a of IAS 36 *Illustrative Examples*.

11  It should be emphasized again that the elimination entries shown in the working paper are not recorded in the accounting records of either the parent or the subsidiary.

12  Adapted from *CICA UFE Report*, 1988-II-6, with permission. Chartered Professional Accountants of Canada, Toronto, Canada. Any changes to the original material are the sole responsibility of the author (and/or publisher) and have not been reviewed or endorsed by the Chartered Professional Accountants of Canada.

13  Adapted from *CICA UFE Report*, 1990-III-2, with permission. Chartered Professional Accountants of Canada, Toronto, Canada. Any changes to the original material are the sole responsibility of the author (and/or publisher) and have not been reviewed or endorsed by the Chartered Professional Accountants of Canada.

14  Adapted from *CICA UFE Report*, 1994-IV-4, with permission. Chartered Professional Accountants of Canada, Toronto, Canada. Any changes to the original material are the sole responsibility of the author (and/or publisher) and have not been reviewed or endorsed by the Chartered Professional Accountants of Canada.

15  Adapted from *CICA UFE Report*, 2012-II-2, with permission. Chartered Professional Accountants of Canada, Toronto, Canada. Any changes to the original material are the sole responsibility of the author (and/or publisher) and have not been reviewed or endorsed by the Chartered Professional Accountants of Canada.

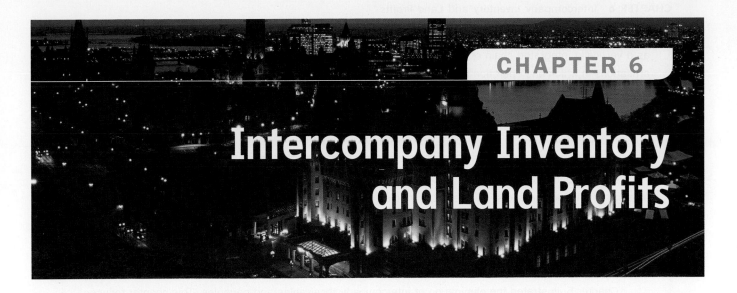

# CHAPTER 6

# Intercompany Inventory and Land Profits

## LEARNING OBJECTIVES

**After studying this chapter, you should be able to do the following:**

**LO1** Describe the effect on consolidated profit of the elimination of intercompany revenues and expenses.

**LO2** Prepare consolidated financial statements that reflect the elimination and subsequent realization of upstream and downstream intercompany profits in inventory.

**LO3** Explain how the cost, revenue recognition, and matching principles are used to support adjustments for intercompany transactions when preparing consolidated financial statements.

**LO4** Prepare consolidated financial statements that reflect the elimination and subsequent realization of upstream and downstream intercompany profits in land.

**LO5** Prepare the journal entries under the equity method to reflect the elimination and subsequent realization of intercompany profits in inventory and land.

**LO6** Analyze and interpret financial statements involving intercompany transactions.

**LO7** (Appendix 6A) Prepare consolidated financial statements when land is remeasured to fair value each reporting period.

## Introduction

In previous discussions, we stressed that consolidated financial statements report the activities of a group of affiliated companies as if they constitute a single company. While these companies may transact business with one another as well as with non-affiliated companies, all intercompany transactions are eliminated so that the final consolidated statements reflect only the result of transactions with entities outside the group. The elimination of intercompany transactions and unrealized profit is one of the most complex topics encountered in the consolidation process. The volume of transfers within most large enterprises can be quite large. For example, CIBC, one of Canada's largest financial institutions, reported intersegment revenue of $933 million in 2014.[1] Such transactions are especially common in companies that have been constructed as a vertically integrated chain of organizations. These entities reduce their costs and risks by developing affiliations in which one operation furnishes products to another.

> *Consolidated financial statements should reflect only transactions with entities outside of the consolidated entity.*

Intercompany transactions are also used to shift income from one jurisdiction to another to minimize or avoid paying income taxes. As a result, Canadian legislation prevents Canadian companies from trying to avoid paying income tax by using offshore tax havens such as non-resident trusts and foreign investment entities. The legislation was enacted because the government felt that multinational companies operating in Canada had avoided "hundreds of millions" of dollars in taxes over the previous decade through the use of tax havens.

Chapter 5 illustrated the elimination of intercompany receivables and payables. This chapter focuses on the elimination of other transactions that occur between a parent and its subsidiaries or between two or more subsidiaries that have a common parent.

## LO1 INTERCOMPANY REVENUE AND EXPENSES

### Intercompany Sales and Purchases

The following simple example will be used to illustrate the basic idea behind the elimination of intercompany sales and purchases in the preparation of a consolidated income statement.

Let your imagination stray a bit, and suppose that when you went shopping for groceries, the change you received from the cashier included some dollar coins. When you got home you noticed that the loon on one of these coins was upside down. You took the coin to a dealer and learned that some coins with this flaw had been accidentally released into circulation by the Royal Canadian Mint and as a result were worth substantially more than their face value. The dealer offered you $41 for this dollar coin, which you accepted. It is obvious that you made a profit of $40 on this transaction. An income statement showing only this transaction would appear as follows:

**INCOME STATEMENT—COIN TRANSACTION**

| | |
|---|---|
| Sales | $41 |
| Cost of goods sold | 1 |
| Net income | $40 |

> *The transaction with the coin dealer is an arm's-length transaction (i.e., with an outsider).*

Now let your imagination stray even further, and assume that the following events took place between the time you received the coin from the supermarket and the time you sold it to the coin dealer. Your pants have four pockets. Let us call them pocket 1, pocket 2, pocket 3, and pocket 4. Pocket 1 received the coin from the supermarket and sold it to pocket 2 for $10. Pocket 2 sold the coin to pocket 3 for $15. Pocket 3 sold the coin to pocket 4 for $25, and then pocket 4 sold the coin to the dealer for $41. Has any part of the transaction changed as far as you (as an entity) are concerned? The answer is, of course, no. You still had sales of $41, cost of goods sold of $1, and a net income of $40. But assume that each of your pockets recorded its part in the transaction and prepared an income statement:

### INCOME STATEMENTS OF FOUR POCKETS

|  | Pocket 1 | Pocket 2 | Pocket 3 | Pocket 4 |
|---|---|---|---|---|
| Sales | $10 | $15 | $25 | $41 |
| Cost of goods sold | 1 | 10 | 15 | 25 |
| Net income | $ 9 | $ 5 | $10 | $16 |

---

*Income was recorded when the coin was moved from one pocket to another.*

---

The arrows indicate the interpocket transactions that took place. Also, the sum of the net incomes of your four pockets is equal to your net income of $40. We should therefore be able to prepare an income statement for you (as an entity) by combining the components of the income statements of your four pockets as follows:

### COMBINED INCOME STATEMENT FOR FOUR POCKETS

| | |
|---|---|
| Sales (10 + 15 + 25 + 41) | $91 |
| Cost of goods sold (1 + 10 + 15 + 25) | 51 |
| Net income | $40 |

However, sales and cost of goods sold are not the correct amounts because they contain the interpocket sales and purchases. Both items should reflect only sales to and purchases from *outside* the entity. If we eliminate the interpocket sales and purchases, we will have an income statement that reflects only transactions that you as an entity incurred with others outside the entity. This statement can be prepared as follows:

### COMBINED INCOME STATEMENT—ENTITY

|  | Total of Four Pockets | Interpocket Sales and Purchases | Total |
|---|---|---|---|
| Sales | $91 | $50 | $41 |
| Cost of goods sold | 51 | 50 | 1 |
| Net income | $40 | $ 0 | $40 |

---

*Revenue is recognized when it is earned in a transaction with an outsider in accordance with the revenue recognition principle.*

*The cost of the coin is expensed in the same period as the revenue in accordance with the matching principle.*

---

Note that if we eliminate an equal amount of revenue and expense from an income statement, the resultant net income remains unchanged.

Your four pockets in this example are similar in all respects to a parent company and its subsidiary companies. Let us assume that a parent company (P) has holdings in three subsidiaries as follows: P owns 80% of S1, 90% of S2, and 75% of S3. The coin transactions previously illustrated were carried out by P and its three subsidiaries. These were the only transactions that took place during the current year. At year-end, the parent and its subsidiaries prepared the following income statements:

### INCOME STATEMENTS—PARENT AND SUBSIDIARIES

|  | P | S1 | S2 | S3 |
|---|---|---|---|---|
| Sales | $10 | $15 | $25 | $41 |
| Cost of goods sold | 1 | 10 | 15 | 25 |
| Net income | $ 9 | $ 5 | $10 | $16 |

---

*Only S3 had a transaction with an outsider.*

---

We are assuming that P uses the equity method but has made no entries during the current year and that all acquisition differentials have been fully amortized in prior years.

Before preparing a consolidated income statement, we can calculate consolidated net income attributable to P as follows:

| | S1 | S2 | S3 | Total | |
|---|---|---|---|---|---|
| P's net income | | | | | $ 9 |
| Subsidiary net income | $ 5 | $10 | $16 | $31 | |
| P's ownership | 80% | 90% | 75% | | |
| Share of subsidiary's net income | $ 4 | $ 9 | $12 | | 25 |
| Consolidated net income attributable to P | | | | | $34 |

Suppose we prepare a consolidated income statement without eliminating intercompany sales and purchases, in the following manner:

### P AND SUBSIDIARIES
### CONSOLIDATED INCOME STATEMENT
For current year

| | |
|---|---|
| Sales (10 + 15 + 25 + 41) | $91 |
| Cost of goods sold (1 + 10 + 15 + 25) | 51 |
| Net income | $40 |
| Attributable to: | |
| Shareholders of parent | $34 |
| Non-controlling interest | 6 |

### CALCULATION OF NET INCOME
### ATTRIBUTABLE TO NON-CONTROLLING INTEREST

| | |
|---|---|
| S1 (20% × 5) | $ 1 |
| S2 (10% × 10) | 1 |
| S3 (25% × 16) | 4 |
| | $ 6 |

---

*Sales and cost of sales are overstated because intercompany sales and purchases have not yet been eliminated.*

---

Note that the net income of the consolidated entity is made up of the net incomes of the parent and its three subsidiaries. But we have not eliminated the intercompany sales and purchases that took place during the year. If we eliminate these intercompany transactions, the bottom-line net income earned by the consolidated entity will not change. Non-controlling interest and consolidated net income are only *allocations* of the entity's net income, so they also will not be affected by the elimination of these intercompany sales and purchases. The consolidated income statement after the elimination of intercompany sales and purchases is as follows:

**CONSOLIDATED INCOME STATEMENT**
(after elimination of intercompany items)

| | |
|---|---|
| Sales (91 − 50) | $41 |
| Cost of goods sold (51 − 50) | 1 |
| Net income | $40 |
| Attributable to: | |
| Shareholders of parent | $34 |
| Non-controlling interest | 6 |

---

*The consolidated income statement now reflects only the transactions with outsiders.*

---

## Other Examples of Intercompany Revenue and Expenses

Suppose the parent company lends $100,000 to the subsidiary company and receives a note payable on demand with interest at 10% paid annually. The transactions would be recorded as follows:

| *Parent Company* | | | *Subsidiary Company* | | |
|---|---|---|---|---|---|
| Note receivable | 100,000 | | Cash | 100,000 | |
|   Cash | | 100,000 |   Note payable | | 100,000 |

To record intercompany borrowings on January 1 of the current year

| | | | | | |
|---|---|---|---|---|---|
| Cash | 10,000 | | Interest expense | 10,000 | |
|   Interest revenue | | 10,000 |   Cash | | 10,000 |

To record the intercompany payment of interest on December 31 of the current year

---

*These transactions are recorded on the separate-entity books of the parent and the subsidiary.*

---

From the consolidated entity's point of view, all that has happened is that cash has been transferred from one bank account to another. No revenue has been earned, no expense has been incurred, and there are no receivables or payables with parties outside the consolidated entity. The elimination of $10,000 interest revenue and interest expense on the consolidated income statement does not change the net income of the consolidated entity. If total net income is not affected, then the amount allocated to the non-controlling and controlling interest is also not affected. On the consolidated balance sheet, we eliminate $100,000 from notes receivable and notes payable. An equal elimination of assets and liabilities on the balance sheet leaves the amounts of the two equities (non-controlling interest and controlling interest) unchanged.

---

*Consolidated net income does not change when we eliminate an equal amount of revenue and expense.*

---

Note also that if the roles are reversed and the *subsidiary* lends $100,000 to the *parent*, the eliminations on the consolidated income statement and balance sheet are the same and have no effect on the amount of the non-controlling interest appearing on each statement.

**INTERCOMPANY MANAGEMENT FEES**   Often the parent will charge its subsidiary companies a yearly management fee as a means of allocating head office costs to all the companies within the group. (We will not discuss the pros and cons of this procedure here. Readers who are interested in the reasons for, and effectiveness of, allocations of this nature are advised to consult a management accounting textbook.) From an external reporting point of view, we have intercompany revenues and expenses that must be eliminated on the consolidated income statement.

**INTERCOMPANY RENTALS**   Occasionally, buildings or equipment owned by one company are used by another company within the group. Rather than transfer legal title, the companies agree on a yearly rental to be charged. In such cases, intercompany rental revenues and expenses must be eliminated from the consolidated income statement.

The four examples mentioned above and any other intercompany revenues and expenses are eliminated to ensure that revenue is recognized only when it is earned with a party outside of the consolidated entity and to stop the double-counting of revenues and expenses. This has no effect on the calculation of the non-controlling interest in the net income of the subsidiary companies, since there is no change to consolidated net income.

# INTERCOMPANY PROFITS IN ASSETS

When one affiliated company sells assets to another affiliated company, it is possible that the profit or loss recorded on the transaction has not been realized from the point of view of the consolidated entity. If the purchasing affiliate has sold these assets outside the group, all profits (losses) recorded are realized. If, however, all or a portion of these assets have not been sold outside the group, we must eliminate the remaining intercompany profit and may need to eliminate the intercompany loss[2] from the consolidated statements. The intercompany profit (loss) will be realized for consolidation purposes during the accounting period in which the particular asset is sold to outsiders. The sale to outsiders may also result in an additional profit (loss) that is not adjusted in the consolidation process. Three types of unrealized intercompany profits (losses) are eliminated:

- Profits in inventory
- Profits in nondepreciable assets
- Profits in depreciable assets

The examples that follow illustrate the holdback of unrealized intercompany profits in one accounting period and the realization of the profit in a subsequent period.

**UPSTREAM VERSUS DOWNSTREAM TRANSACTIONS**   When we talk about intercompany transactions, it is important to distinguish between downstream and upstream transactions. When the parent sells to the subsidiary, the transaction is referred to as a downstream transaction. When the subsidiary sells to the parent, it is referred to as an upstream transaction. The name of the method is consistent with the common perception that the parent is the head of the family and the subsidiary is the child of the parent. From a physical height perspective, the parent looks down to the child, while the child looks up to the parent.

The company doing the selling is the company recognizing the profit on the sale. When we eliminate the profit from intercompany transactions, we should take it away from the selling company, that is, from the company that recognized the profit in the first place. On downstream transactions, we will eliminate the profit that the parent had recognized. On upstream transactions, we will eliminate the profit that the subsidiary had recognized.

> *In a downstream transaction, the parent sells to a subsidiary. In an upstream transaction, the subsidiary sells to the parent or another subsidiary of the parent.*

The name of the method is also based on which company was the selling company. When one subsidiary sells to another subsidiary, the profit must also be eliminated because it is not realized with an outside party. Since a subsidiary was the selling company, this lateral type of transaction is also referred to as an upstream transaction.

> *Downstream and upstream transactions are defined by who the seller is.*

To illustrate the concepts involved in the elimination of intercompany profits, we will use as a simple example the financial statements of a parent and its 90%-owned subsidiary one year after the acquisition date.

On January 1, Year 4, Parent Company acquired 90% of the common shares of Sub Incorporated for $11,250. On that date, Sub had common shares of $8,000 and retained earnings of $4,500, and there were no differences between the fair values and the carrying amounts of its identifiable net assets. The acquisition differential was calculated as follows:

| | | |
|---|---|---|
| Cost of 90% of Sub | | $11,250 |
| Implied value of 100% of Sub | | $12,500 |
| Carrying amount of Sub's net assets (equals Sub's shareholders' equity): | | |
| Common shares | 8,000 | |
| Retained earnings | 4,500 | |
| | | 12,500 |
| Acquisition differential | | $ 0 |

The financial statements of Parent and Sub as at December 31, Year 4, are presented in Exhibit 6.1. Parent accounts for its investment using the cost method, and because there were no dividends declared by Sub, no entry was made on December 31, Year 4.

## Intercompany Inventory Profits: Subsidiary Selling (Upstream Transactions)

The following intercompany transactions occurred during Year 4:

1. During Year 4, Sub made sales to Parent amounting to $5,000 at a gross profit rate of 30%. Sub had purchased these goods from outsiders for $3,500.

2. Later in Year 4, Parent sold 80% of these goods to outsiders for $6,150. At the end of Year 4, Parent's inventory contained the remaining goods purchased from Sub for $1,000.

3. Both companies paid (or accrued) income tax on its taxable income at a rate of 40%.

> *From Sub's separate-entity perspective, it earned the income on the sale to the Parent.*

**EXHIBIT 6.1**

**YEAR 4 INCOME STATEMENTS**

|  | Parent | Sub |
|---|---|---|
| Sales | $20,000 | $ 8,000 |
| Cost of sales | 13,000 | 4,300 |
| Miscellaneous expenses | 1,400 | 900 |
| Income tax expense | 2,200 | 1,100 |
|  | 16,600 | 6,300 |
| Net income | $ 3,400 | $ 1,700 |

> *These are the separate-entity statements of the parent and the subsidiary.*

**BALANCE SHEETS**
At December 31, Year 4

|  | Parent | Sub |
|---|---|---|
| Inventory | $ 7,500 | $ 4,000 |
| Miscellaneous assets | 21,650 | 19,200 |
| Investment in Sub Inc. | 11,250 | — |
|  | $40,400 | $23,200 |
| Liabilities | $12,000 | $ 9,000 |
| Common shares | 15,000 | 8,000 |
| Retained earnings | 13,400 | 6,200 |
|  | $40,400 | $23,200 |

> *The parent uses the cost method in its separate-entity records.*

Exhibit 6.2 summarizes the results of these intercompany transactions in isolation. It shows the adjustments required to derive the correct balances for the consolidated income statement. Notice the following for this exhibit:

- Cost of sales is broken down into its three components, that is, beginning inventory, purchases, and ending inventory. Every time one of these three items is adjusted, the cost of sales will change.

- The column "Consolidated" only shows the results of transactions with outsiders.

- The adjustments to get to the desired consolidated balances are shown in the adjust column. Entry (a) eliminates the intercompany sale/purchase. Entry (b) brings the inventory down to the original cost when the Sub purchased the inventory from outsiders. Entry (c) brings the tax expense down to the level required for the income presented in the consolidated column.

- The ending inventory amounts within the cost of sales would be the same amounts for inventory on the balance sheet at the end of the period.

Further explanation of the consolidation adjustments is provided below.

**HOLDBACK OF INVENTORY PROFITS—YEAR 4**  It should be noted that the subsidiary recorded a gross profit of $1,500 (30% × $5,000) on its sales to the parent during the year and paid income tax of $600 (40% × $1,500) on this profit. If the parent had sold all of its intercompany purchases to customers

## EXHIBIT 6.2

### YEAR 4 INCOME STATEMENTS
#### Related to intercompany sales

|  | Parent | Sub | Adjust | Consolidated |
|---|---|---|---|---|
| Sales | $6,150 | $5,000 | (a) −5,000 | $6,150 |
| Cost of sales: |  |  |  |  |
| Beginning inventory | 0 | 0 |  | 0 |
| Purchases | 5,000 | 3,500 | (a) −5,000 | 3,500 |
| Goods available | 5,000 | 3,500 |  | 3,500 |
| Ending inventory | 1,000 | 0 | (b) −300 | 700 |
| Cost of sales | 4,000 | 3,500 |  | 2,800 |
| Gross margin | 2,150 | 1,500 |  | 3,350 |
| Income tax expense (40%) | 860 | 600 | (c) −120 | 1,340 |
| Net income | $1,290 | $ 900 |  | $2,010 |

> When the purchases component of cost of sales is reduced, overall cost of sales will decrease.
>
> When the ending inventory component of cost of sales is reduced, overall cost of sales will increase and net income will decrease.

outside the entity, this $1,500 gross profit would be considered realized from the point of view of this consolidated single entity. But the parent's inventory contains items purchased from the subsidiary for $1,000. There is an unrealized intercompany profit of $300 (30% × $1,000) in this inventory, which must be held back from consolidated income in Year 4 and realized in the period in which it is sold to outsiders. In addition, the $120 tax expense relating to this profit must also be held back from the Year 4 consolidated income statement. When this $300 gross profit is realized on a future consolidated income statement, the income tax expense will be matched on that statement with the profit realized.

> From the consolidated perspective, some of Sub's income was not realized with an outsider.

Not only do we have to hold back an unrealized profit for consolidation purposes, but also we must make an adjustment for the income taxes relating to that profit. Since income taxes are computed at the individual company level rather than at the consolidated-entity level, the company that recorded the profit also paid (or accrued) income taxes on that profit, and the income tax expense on its income statement reflects this. The matching of expenses with revenues is a basic accounting concept; the adjustment made for income taxes on intercompany profits is a perfect example of this matching process.

> Income tax should be expensed in the same period as profit.

The difference between the buyer's tax basis and the cost of transferred assets as reported in the consolidated financial statements meets the definition of a temporary difference and will give rise to deferred income taxes. While IAS 27 explicitly states that profits and losses resulting from intragroup transactions should be eliminated in full, it does not explicitly state how the eliminated amount should be allocated between the controlling and non-controlling interests. Because the amount attributed to non-controlling interest will affect the amount attributed to the shareholders of the parent, the handling of this issue can affect the reported profitability of a business combination.

> *From a consolidated perspective, some of the tax paid by the subsidiary was prepaid, since the income was not yet earned.*

To determine an appropriate allocation, the relationship between an intercompany transaction and the non-controlling shareholders must be analyzed. If a transfer were downstream, a logical view would be that the unrealized gross profit belongs to the parent company. The parent made the original sale; therefore, the gross profit is included in its financial records. Since the non-controlling shareholders do not have any interest in the parent company, it seems appropriate that they should not be affected by the elimination of the profit on downstream transactions.

> *Non-controlling interest is not affected by intercompany profits made on downstream transactions.*

In contrast, if the subsidiary sells inventory to the parent, the subsidiary's financial records recognize the gross profit. If this profit is eliminated when preparing the consolidated financial statements, the parties having an interest in the subsidiary's profit are affected by the elimination of the profit. Since the non-controlling shareholders do have an interest in the subsidiary, it seems appropriate that they should be affected by the elimination of the profit on upstream transactions. Throughout this textbook, the non-controlling interest's share of profit and retained earnings will be computed based on the reported profit and retained earnings of the subsidiary after they have been adjusted for any unrealized profits on upstream transactions.

> *Non-controlling interest is affected and will share in intercompany profits made on upstream transactions.*

**LO2** Using the direct approach, we will now prepare the Year 4 consolidated statements after making the consolidation adjustments shown in Exhibit 6.3.

Remember that the purpose of the calculation of consolidated net income is to adjust the parent's cost method net income to what it would have been under the equity method. Note that the after-tax profit is deducted from the net income of Sub because the subsidiary was the selling company and its net income contains this profit being held back for consolidation purposes. Note also that the non-controlling interest's share of the Year 4 income is based on the *adjusted income* of Sub.

---

**EXHIBIT 6.3**

### INTERCOMPANY TRANSACTIONS

| | |
|---|---|
| Intercompany sales and purchases | $ 5,000 **(a)** |
| Intercompany inventory profits: | |
| Unrealized profit in ending inventory—Sub selling (upstream) | $    300 **(b)** |
| Income tax (40%) | 120 **(c)** |
| Unrealized after-tax profit in ending inventory | $    180 **(d)** |

*(continued)*

## CALCULATION OF CONSOLIDATED NET INCOME
### Year 4

| | | |
|---|---|---|
| Net income—Parent Co. | | $ 3,400 |
| Net income—Sub Inc. | 1,700 | |
| Less: After-tax profit in ending inventory **(d)** | 180 | |
| Adjusted net income—Sub Inc. | | 1,520 |
| Net income | | $ 4,920 |
| Attributable to: | | |
| Shareholders of parent | | $ 4,768 **(e)** |
| Non-controlling interest (10% × 1,520) | | 152 **(f)** |

> *The unrealized profit is always deducted from the selling company's income.*

## CALCULATION OF CONSOLIDATED RETAINED EARNINGS
### At December 31, Year 4

| | | |
|---|---|---|
| Retained earnings—Parent Co. | | $13,400 |
| Retained earnings—Sub Inc. | 6,200 | |
| Acquisition retained earnings | 4,500 | |
| Increase since acquisition | 1,700 | |
| Less: After-tax profit in ending inventory **(d)** | 180 | |
| Adjusted increase since acquisition | 1,520 | **(g)** |
| Parent Co.'s share | 90% | 1,368 |
| Consolidated retained earnings | | $14,768 **(h)** |

> *The unrealized profit at the end of Year 4 must be eliminated when calculating consolidated retained earnings at the end of Year 4.*

## CALCULATION OF NON-CONTROLLING INTEREST
### (method 1)
### At December 31, Year 4

| | |
|---|---|
| Shareholders' equity—Sub Inc. | |
| Common shares | $ 8,000 |
| Retained earnings | 6,200 |
| | 14,200 |
| Less: After-tax profit in ending inventory **(d)** | 180 |
| Adjusted shareholders' equity | 14,020 |
| Non-controlling interest's share | 10% |
| | $ 1,402 **(i)** |

> *Non-controlling interest is affected when there are unrealized profits on upstream transactions.*

*(continued)*

**EXHIBIT 6.3** *(continued)*

### CALCULATION OF NON-CONTROLLING INTEREST
(method 2)

| | | |
|---|---:|---:|
| Non-controlling interest at date of acquisition (10% × [11,250/0.9]) | | $ 1,250 |
| Sub's adjusted increase in retained earnings **(g)** | 1,520 | |
| NCI's share @ 10% | | 152 |
| Non-controlling interest, December 31, Year 3 | | $ 1,402 **(i)** |

Exhibit 6.4 illustrates the preparation of the Year 4 consolidated financial statements.

**EXHIBIT 6.4**

### YEAR 4 CONSOLIDATED STATEMENTS
### ELIMINATION OF INTERCOMPANY PROFITS IN INVENTORY
(direct approach)
### PARENT COMPANY
### CONSOLIDATED INCOME STATEMENT
For the year ended December 31, Year 4

| | |
|---|---:|
| Sales (20,000 + 8,000 − **[3a] 5,000**) | $23,000 |
| Cost of sales (13,000 + 4,300 − **[3a] 5,000** + **[3b] 300**) | 12,600 |
| Miscellaneous expenses (1,400 + 900) | 2,300 |
| Income tax expense (2,200 + 1,100 − **[3c] 120**) | 3,180 |
| | 18,080 |
| Net income | $ 4,920 |
| Attributable to: | |
| Shareholders of parent **(3e)** | $ 4,768 |
| Non-controlling interest **(3f)** | 152 |

> *The unrealized profits are eliminated on the consolidated financial statements.*

### PARENT COMPANY
### CONSOLIDATED BALANCE SHEET
At December 31, Year 4

| | |
|---|---:|
| Inventory (7,500 + 4,000 − **[3b] 300**) | $11,200 |
| Miscellaneous assets (21,650 + 19,200) | 40,850 |
| Deferred income taxes (0 + 0 + **[3c] 120**) | 120 |
| | $52,170 |
| Liabilities (12,000 + 9,000) | $21,000 |
| Common shares | 15,000 |
| Retained earnings **(3h)** | 14,768 |
| Non-controlling interest **(3i)** | 1,402 |
| | $52,170 |

> *By eliminating the unrealized profit, inventory is now stated at cost to the consolidated entity.*

The first two numbers in brackets are from the statements of Parent and Sub. Any additional numbers, which are in boldface and labelled, are adjustments made to eliminate the intercompany transactions. The eliminations made on the income statement require further elaboration:

1. The eliminations of intercompany sales and purchases are equal reductions of revenues and expenses that do not change the net income of the consolidated entity or the amount allocated to the non-controlling and controlling equities.

2. To hold back the gross profit of $300 from the consolidated entity's net income, we increase cost of goods sold by $300. The reasoning is as follows:

    (a) Cost of goods sold is made up of opening inventory, plus purchases, less ending inventory.
    (b) The ending inventory contains the $300 gross profit.
    (c) If we subtract the $300 profit from the ending inventory on the balance sheet, the ending inventory is now stated at cost to the consolidated entity.
    (d) A reduction of $300 from ending inventory in the cost of goods sold calculation increases cost of goods sold by $300.
    (e) This increase to cost of goods sold reduces the before-tax net income earned by the entity by $300.

3. Because the entity's before-tax net income has been reduced by $300, it is necessary to reduce the income tax expense (the tax paid on the profit held back) by $120.

4. A reduction of income tax expense increases the net income of the consolidated entity.

5. A $300 increase in cost of goods sold, together with a $120 reduction in income tax expense, results in the after-tax profit of $180 being removed from consolidated net income.

> *When ending inventory is overstated, cost of sales is understated.*
>
> *When cost of sales is increased, income decreases and income tax expense should decrease.*

The $300 adjustment to inventory and cost of goods sold is similar to the adjustment we studied in intermediate accounting to correct errors in inventory. If you have difficulty understanding the adjustments for unrealized profits in inventory, you may want to go back to your intermediate accounting text to review the adjustment for errors in inventory.

**LO3** As a result of the adjustments above, the following accounting principles have been properly applied:

- *Cost principle.* Inventory is reported at $11,200, which is the original cost to the consolidated entity when the inventory was purchased from outsiders.

- *Revenue recognition principle.* Sales are reported at $23,000, which is the amount earned on sales to outsiders.

- *Matching principle.* Cost of goods sold is recognized as an expense in the same period as the related revenue, and therefore is matched to the revenue. The amount of $12,600 is the inventory actually sold to outsiders at the amount paid when the goods were originally purchased from outsiders. Similarly, income tax is expensed in the same period as the related income and in proportion to the income earned.

> *The adjustments to eliminate the unrealized profits are needed in order to properly apply the cost, revenue recognition, and matching principles.*

It is important to realize that all of the above adjustments are being made on the consolidated working papers and not on the separate-entity financial statements. What was recorded on the subsidiary's own books was legitimate from its own perspective. But from the consolidated perspective, some of the profit was not yet realized. It must be held back from the consolidated financial statements.

> *The unrealized profits are not eliminated on the separate-entity financial statements.*

Again it is important to note the following components of the entity's net income:

| | |
|---|---|
| Net income—Parent Co. | $3,400 |
| Adjusted net income—Sub Inc. | 1,520 |
| Consolidated net income | $4,920 |

The only new concepts relating to the preparation of the consolidated balance sheet involve the adjustments made on the asset side (a) to eliminate the unrealized profit in inventory and (b) to set up the deferred income taxes on this profit. These adjustments are shown in boldface in Exhibit 6.4 and are labelled to correspond with the calculations in Exhibit 6.3. The reasons for these adjustments can be further explained as follows:

1. The holdback of the $300 gross profit on the consolidated income statement was accomplished by reducing the amount of ending inventory in calculating the cost of goods sold. (A reduction in ending inventory increases cost of goods sold.) The ending inventory in the cost of goods sold calculation is the inventory balance on the consolidated balance sheet. Removing the $300 gross profit from the asset will result in the consolidated inventory being reflected at cost to the entity.

> *The unrealized profit is deducted from the inventory to bring inventory back to its original cost in accordance with the historical cost principle.*

2. On the consolidated income statement, we reduced income tax expense by $120, representing the tax paid on the gross profit. As far as the consolidated entity is concerned, this tax of $120 was paid prematurely because the income was not yet earned. The tax will become an expense when the inventory is sold to outsiders. This results in a temporary difference for the consolidated entity. The resultant deferred income taxes are "added into" the assets on the consolidated balance sheet. (The illustration assumes that neither the parent nor the subsidiary had deferred income taxes on their individual balance sheets.)

3. A reduction of $300 from inventory and a $120 increase in deferred income taxes results in a net reduction to consolidated assets of $180, which equals the $180 reduction that has been made on the equity side.

> *Income tax will be expensed when the profit is realized in accordance with the matching principle.*

**LO5 EQUITY METHOD JOURNAL ENTRIES** While our example has assumed that Parent uses the cost method to account for its investment, it is useful to see where the differences would lie if the equity method was used. If Parent was using the equity method, the following journal entries would be made on December 31, Year 4:

| | | |
|---|---|---|
| Investment in Sub Inc. | 1,530 | |
| Equity method income | | 1,530 |
| 90% of the net income of Sub Inc. (90% × 1,700 = 1,530) | | |
| Equity method income | 162 | |
| Investment in Sub Inc. | | 162 |
| To hold back 90% of the after-tax inventory profit recorded by Sub Inc. (90% × 180 = 162) | | |

---

*The equity method captures the net effect of all consolidation entries.*

---

After these entries were posted, the two related equity method accounts of Parent would show the following changes and balances:

| | Investment in Sub Inc. | Equity Method Income |
|---|---|---|
| January 1, Year 4 | $11,250 | $ — |
| *December 31, Year 4* | | |
| Income from Sub Inc. | 1,530 | 1,530 |
| Unrealized after-tax inventory profit | (162) | (162) |
| Balance, December 31, Year 4 | $12,618 | $1,368 |

Parent's total income under the equity method would be $4,768, consisting of $3,400 from its own operations as reported in Exhibit 6.1, plus equity method income of $1,368, as reported above. This income of $4,768 should be and is equal to consolidated net income attributable to Parent's shareholders.

---

*The parent's income under the equity method should be equal to consolidated net income attributable to Parent's shareholders.*

---

**REALIZATION OF INVENTORY PROFITS—YEAR 5** The previous example illustrated the holdback of an unrealized intercompany inventory profit in Year 4. We will continue our example of Parent Company and Sub Inc. by looking at the events of Year 5. On December 31, Year 5, Parent reported earnings from its own operations of $4,050 and declared dividends of $2,500. Sub reported a net income of $3,100 and, again, did not declare a dividend. Using the cost method, Parent made no journal entries with respect to the operations of Sub. During Year 5, there were no new intercompany transactions. However, Parent did sell the remaining goods it had purchased from Sub in Year 4 to outsiders for $1,550. At year-end, the inventory of Parent contained no items purchased from Sub. The unrealized profit that was held back for consolidated purposes in Year 4 will have to be released into income in Year 5. Exhibit 6.5 shows the impact of the sale of the goods to outsiders on the income statements for the separate entities and consolidated entity. It shows the adjustments required to derive the correct balances for the consolidated income statement. Notice the following for this exhibit:

- The column "Consolidated" only shows the results of transactions with outsiders.

- The adjustments to get to the desired consolidated balances are shown in the adjust column. Entry (a) brings the beginning inventory down to the original cost when the Sub purchased the inventory from outsiders. Entry (b) brings the tax expense up to the level required for the income presented in the consolidated column.

> *In Year 5, the parent sold its Year 4 inventory to outsiders.*

**EXHIBIT 6.5**

### YEAR 5 INCOME STATEMENTS
#### Related to intercompany sales

| | Parent | Sub | Adjust | Consolidated |
|---|---|---|---|---|
| Sales | $1,550 | $0 | | $1,550 |
| Cost of sales: | | | | |
| Beginning inventory | 1,000 | 0 | **(a)** −300 | 700 |
| Purchases | 0 | 0 | | 0 |
| Goods available | 1,000 | 0 | | 700 |
| Ending inventory | 0 | 0 | | 0 |
| Cost of sales | 1,000 | 0 | | 700 |
| Gross margin | 550 | 0 | | 850 |
| Income tax expense (40%) | 220 | 0 | **(b)** +120 | 340 |
| Net income | $ 330 | $0 | | $ 510 |

> *When the beginning inventory component of cost of sales is decreased, overall cost of sales will decrease and income will increase.*

The financial statements of Parent and Sub are presented in Exhibit 6.6. Before we prepare the Year 5 consolidated income statement, we must carry out the calculations shown in Exhibit 6.7.

The after-tax inventory profit of $180 that was held back in Year 4 is being realized in Year 5 and is added to the net income of Sub, because the subsidiary was the company that originally recorded the profit. Note that the non-controlling interest's share of the Year 5 net income of Sub is based on the *adjusted net income* of that company.

**EXHIBIT 6.6**

### YEAR 5 INCOME STATEMENTS

| | Parent | Sub |
|---|---|---|
| Sales | $25,000 | $12,000 |
| Cost of sales | 16,000 | 5,500 |
| Miscellaneous expenses | 2,350 | 1,400 |
| Income tax expense | 2,600 | 2,000 |
| | 20,950 | 8,900 |
| Net income | $ 4,050 | $ 3,100 |

> *Cost of sales for the parent includes the overstated inventory value at the beginning of the year.*

*(continued)*

## BALANCE SHEETS
### At December 31, Year 5

| | Parent | Sub |
|---|---|---|
| Inventory | $ 9,900 | $ 7,500 |
| Miscellaneous assets | 22,800 | 20,800 |
| Investment in Sub Inc. | 11,250 | — |
| | $43,950 | $28,300 |
| Liabilities | $14,000 | $11,000 |
| Common shares | 15,000 | 8,000 |
| Retained earnings | 14,950 | 9,300 |
| | $43,950 | $28,300 |

> *Inventory at the end of Year 5 does not include any unrealized profit.*

---

**EXHIBIT 6.7**

## INTERCOMPANY INVENTORY PROFITS
### Year 5

Intercompany inventory profits:

| | | |
|---|---|---|
| Realized profit in opening inventory—Sub selling (upstream) | $   300 | **(a)** |
| Income tax (40%) | 120 | **(b)** |
| Realized after-tax profit in opening inventory | $   180 | **(c)** |

## CALCULATION OF CONSOLIDATED NET INCOME
### Year 5

| | | |
|---|---|---|
| Net income—Parent Co. | | $ 4,050 |
| Net income—Sub Inc. | 3,100 | |
| Add after-tax profit in opening inventory **(c)** | 180 | |
| Adjusted net income—Sub Inc. | | 3,280 |
| Net income | | $ 7,330 |
| Attributable to: | | |
| Shareholders of parent | | $ 7,002  **(d)** |
| Non-controlling interest (10% × 3,280) | | 328  **(e)** |

> *When the profits are realized, they are credited to the income of the original seller.*

## CALCULATION OF CONSOLIDATED RETAINED EARNINGS
### December 31, Year 5

| | | |
|---|---|---|
| Retained earnings—Parent Co. | | $14,950 |
| Retained earnings—Sub Inc. | 9,300 | |
| Acquisition retained earnings | 4,500 | |
| Increase since acquisition | 4,800 | **(f)** |
| Parent Co.'s share | 90% | 4,320 |
| Consolidated retained earnings | | $19,270  **(g)** |

*(continued)*

**EXHIBIT 6.7**  *(continued)*

### CALCULATION OF NON-CONTROLLING INTEREST (METHOD 1)
December 31, Year 5

| | |
|---|---:|
| Common shares—Sub Inc. | $ 8,000 |
| Retained earnings—Sub Inc. | 9,300 |
| | 17,300 |
| Non-controlling interest's share | 10% |
| Non-controlling interest, December 31, Year 5 | $ 1,730  **(h)** |

> *There are no unrealized profits in the subsidiary's shareholders' equity from a consolidated perspective at the end of Year 5.*

### CALCULATION OF NON-CONTROLLING INTEREST (METHOD 2)

| | | |
|---|---:|---:|
| Non-controlling interest at date of acquisition (10% × [11,250/0.9]) | | $ 1,250 |
| Sub's adjusted increase in retained earnings **(f)** | 4,800 | |
| Non-controlling interest's share @ 10% | | 480 |
| Non-controlling interest, December 31, Year 5 | | $ 1,730  **(i)** |

The calculation of consolidated retained earnings at December 31, Year 5, does not require any adjustments for unrealized profits because there are no unrealized profits at the end of Year 5. The subsidiary had reported profits in Year 4 on an intercompany sale to the parent. The unrealized profits were eliminated when calculating consolidated retained earnings at the end of Year 4. When the parent sold the inventory to outsiders, the previous unrealized profit was realized from a consolidated perspective. Since neither the parent nor the subsidiary had any inventory at the end of Year 5 that had been purchased through an intercompany sale, there was no unrealized profit in ending inventory. Consequently, there is no unrealized profit in retained earnings at the end of Year 5.

Exhibit 6.8 illustrates the preparation of the Year 5 consolidated financial statements using the *direct* approach.

In preparing the Year 5 consolidated income statement, we make consolidation adjustments that bring the original before-tax profit into the income statement and increase income tax expense for the tax on this profit. The eliminations (i.e., adjustments) made are shown in boldface and are labelled. The elimination entries are explained as follows:

1. There were no intercompany sales or purchases in Year 5, and therefore no elimination is required on the income statement.

2. To realize the gross profit of $300 in Year 5, we decrease cost of goods sold by $300. The reasoning behind this is as follows:

   (a) Cost of goods sold is made up of opening inventory, plus purchases, less ending inventory.

   (b) Parent's opening inventory contains the $300 gross profit. After we reduce it by $300, the opening inventory is at cost to the entity.

   (c) A reduction of $300 from opening inventory decreases cost of goods sold by $300.

   (d) This decrease in cost of goods sold increases the before-tax net income earned by the entity by $300.

3. Using the concepts of matching, we increase income tax expense by $120 in order to match it with the $300 gross profit being realized. Note that the deferred income tax on the December 31, Year 4, consolidated balance sheet (see Exhibit 6.4) becomes an expense on the Year 5 consolidated income statement, because the December 31, Year 4, inventory was sold in Year 5.

4. A $300 decrease in cost of goods sold, together with a $120 increase in income tax expense, results in the after-tax intercompany Year 4 profit of $180 being realized for consolidation purposes in Year 5.

> *Since beginning inventory was overstated, cost of sales for Year 5 was overstated.*
>
> *When cost of sales is decreased, income increases, and tax expense should increase.*

**EXHIBIT 6.8**

### YEAR 5 CONSOLIDATED STATEMENTS
(direct approach)
#### PARENT COMPANY
#### CONSOLIDATED INCOME STATEMENT
For the year ended December 31, Year 5

| | |
|---|---:|
| Sales (25,000 + 12,000) | $37,000 |
| Cost of sales (16,000 + 5,500 − **[7a] 300**) | 21,200 |
| Miscellaneous expenses (2,350 + 1,400) | 3,750 |
| Income tax expense (2,600 + 2,000 + **[7b] 120**) | 4,720 |
| | 29,670 |
| Net income | $ 7,330 |
| Attributable to: | |
| Shareholders of parent **(7d)** | $ 7,002 |
| Non-controlling interest **(7e)** | 328 |

> *The unrealized profits from the end of Year 4 are released into consolidated income in Year 5.*

#### PARENT COMPANY
#### CONSOLIDATED BALANCE SHEET
At December 31, Year 5

| | |
|---|---:|
| Inventory (9,900 + 7,500) | $17,400 |
| Miscellaneous assets (22,800 + 20,800) | 43,600 |
| | $61,000 |
| | |
| Liabilities (14,000 + 11,000) | $25,000 |
| Common shares | 15,000 |
| Retained earnings **(7g)** | 19,270 |
| Non-controlling interest **(7h)** | 1,730 |
| | $61,000 |

> *There are no unrealized profits at the end of Year 5.*

Before the consolidated balance sheet is prepared, we must calculate non-controlling interest at December 31, Year 5. This calculation was shown in Exhibit 6.7.

The preparation of the consolidated balance sheet on December 31, Year 5, is straightforward because no inventory profit eliminations are required. The inventory of Parent does not contain any unrealized profit, and there are no related deferred income taxes on the balance sheet. All previous unrealized inventory profits have now been realized for consolidation purposes.

When you view the adjustments that were made to prepare the Year 5 consolidated statements (see Exhibit 6.8), it may strike you that the adjustments made on the income statement have not been reflected in the rest of the consolidated statements, and that, as a result, the statements should not balance. But they *do* balance, so the $180 increase in the after-tax net income of the entity must have been offset by a $180 change in the retained earnings statement and balance sheet. To see where this $180 difference ended up, it is useful to prepare a calculation that shows the changes in non-controlling interest during Year 5. This calculation is shown below.

### CHANGES IN NON-CONTROLLING INTEREST
Year 5

| | | |
|---|---:|---:|
| Sub Inc.: | | |
| Common shares | $ 8,000 | |
| Retained earnings—January 1, Year 5 | 6,200 | |
| | 14,200 | |
| Less unrealized after-tax inventory profit, end of Year 4 | 180 | |
| Adjusted | $14,020 | |
| | 10% | |
| Non-controlling interest, January 1, Year 5 | | $1,402 |
| Allocation of Year 5 consolidated net income (7e) | | 328 |
| Non-controlling interest, December 31, Year 5 | | $1,730 |

> *Non-controlling interest is based on Sub's shareholders' equity after it has been adjusted for unrealized profit on upstream transactions.*

In examining this calculation and the calculation of consolidated retained earnings on December 31, Year 4, in Exhibit 6.3, we see that the $180 increase in the entity's Year 5 consolidated net income was offset by a $180 *decrease* in the December 31, Year 4, balances of non-controlling interest and retained earnings, allocated as follows:

| | |
|---|---:|
| To non-controlling interest (10% × 180) | $ 18 |
| To controlling interest (90% × 180) | 162 |
| | $180 |

> *The intercompany profit of $180 was recorded in Sub's separate-entity income in Year 4 but reported in consolidated income in Year 5.*

**LO5 EQUITY METHOD JOURNAL ENTRIES**   If Parent had used the equity method, the following journal entries would have been made on December 31, Year 5:

| | | |
|---|---|---|
| Investment in Sub Inc. | 2,790 | |
|     Equity method income | | 2,790 |
| To record 90% of the reported income of Sub Inc. (90% × 3,100) | | |
| Investment in Sub Inc. | 162 | |
|     Equity method income | | 162 |
| To release in Year 5 the after-tax inventory profit held back in Year 4 (90% × 180) | | |

> *The equity method captures the net effect of all consolidation entries, including the adjustment for realized profits.*

After these entries are posted, the two related equity method accounts of Parent show the following changes and balances:

| | *Investment in Sub Inc.* | *Equity Method Income* |
|---|---|---|
| January 1, Year 5 | $12,618 | $ — |
| Changes during Year 5: | | |
|   Income from Sub Inc. | 2,790 | 2,790 |
|   After-tax inventory profit (realized) | 162 | 162 |
|   Balance, Dec. 31, Year 5 | $15,570 | $2,952 |

Note that the January 1 balance ($12,618) included the $162 holdback and that this amount was realized during the year with a journal entry. It should be obvious that the December 31 balance ($15,570) does not contain any holdback.

## Intercompany Inventory Profits: Parent Selling (Downstream Transactions)

In our previous example, the subsidiary was the selling company in the intercompany profit transaction (an upstream transaction). This resulted in the $180 after-tax profit elimination being allocated to the controlling and non-controlling equities.

Suppose it was the parent company that sold the inventory to the subsidiary (a downstream transaction). The calculation of consolidated net income for each of the two years should indicate where the differences lie.

### CALCULATION OF CONSOLIDATED NET INCOME
#### Year 4

| | |
|---|---|
| Net income—Parent Co. | $3,400 |
| Less unrealized after-tax profit in ending inventory—Parent selling (downstream) | 180 |
|   Adjusted net income—Parent Co. | 3,220 |
| Net income—Sub Inc. | 1,700 |
| Consolidated net income | $4,920 |
| Attributable to: | |
|   Shareholders of parent | $4,750 |
|   Non-controlling interest (10% × 1,700) | 170 |

Note that the after-tax profit is deducted from the net income of Parent because it was the selling company, and that Parent's net income contains this profit being held back for consolidation purposes.

> *Unrealized profits on downstream transactions are deducted from the parent's separate-entity income.*

The eliminations on the consolidated income statement for intercompany sales and purchases and for unrealized profit in inventory, and the related adjustment to income tax expense would not change. But the split of the consolidated net income between the shareholders of the parent and the non-controlling interest is different, as indicated in the previous calculation. Because Parent was the selling company, all of the $180 holdback was allocated to the parent and none was allocated to the non-controlling interest.

> *Non-controlling interest is not affected by the elimination of unrealized profits on downstream transactions.*

On the December 31, Year 4, consolidated balance sheet, the elimination entries to adjust inventory and deferred income taxes would be the same as before. However, the non-controlling interest on the consolidated balance sheet is based on the December 31, Year 4, balances of the common shares and retained earnings of Sub. The after-tax inventory holdback is *not* allocated to non-controlling interest; because Parent was the selling company, it has been allocated entirely to consolidated retained earnings.

Year 5 consolidated net income is calculated as follows:

| | |
|---|---:|
| Net income—Parent Co. | $4,050 |
| Add: Unrealized after-tax profit in opening inventory | 180 |
| Adjusted net income—Parent Co. | 4,230 |
| Net income—Sub Inc. | 3,100 |
| Consolidated net income | $7,330 |
| Attributable to: | |
| Shareholders of parent | $7,020 |
| Non-controlling interest (10% × 3,100) | 310 |

> *When unrealized profits on downstream transactions are realized, they are added to the parent's separate-entity income.*

The elimination entries on the Year 5 consolidated income statement would be the same as in the previous illustration (see Exhibit 6.8), but because the amount for non-controlling interest is $310, the consolidated net income attributable to Parent's shareholders is a higher amount, as indicated in the previous calculations.

To summarize, the holdback and subsequent realization of intercompany profits in assets is allocated to the non-controlling and controlling equities *only if* the subsidiary was the original seller in the intercompany transaction. If the parent was the original seller, the allocation is entirely to the controlling equity.

.........

LO5 **EQUITY METHOD JOURNAL ENTRIES** If Parent used the equity method to account for its investment, it would make the following entries as at December 31, Year 4:

| | | |
|---|---|---|
| Investment in Sub Inc. | 1,530 | |
| Equity method income | | 1,530 |

To record 90% of the reported Year 4, net income of Sub Inc. (90% × 1,700)

| | | |
|---|---|---|
| Equity method income | 180 | |
| Investment in Sub Inc. | | 180 |

To hold back the after-tax inventory profit recorded by Parent Co. in Year 4

---

*The parent absorbs the full charge for unrealized profits on downstream transactions in Year 4.*

---

An astute reader will notice that because the parent was the selling company, the second entry is removing the profit from accounts that did not contain it in the first place. This is, of course, quite true. However, it is the equity method income account that establishes the equality between Parent's net income (under the equity method) and consolidated net income attributable to Parent's shareholders. In the same manner, the investment in Sub on the balance sheet of Parent establishes the equality between Parent's retained earnings (under the equity method) and consolidated retained earnings. This means that all adjustments that affect consolidated net income are reflected in these two accounts.

---

*The equity method is referred to as the one-line consolidation.*

---

Rather than preparing two separate entries, the following entry could be made to capture the overall impact of the two separate entries:

| | | |
|---|---|---|
| Investment in Sub Inc. | 1,350 | |
| Equity method income | | 1,350 |

To record equity method income from Sub Inc. net of adjustment for unrealized profit in ending inventory (90% × 1,700 − 100% × 180)

On December 31, Year 5, Parent would make the following journal entries if it used the equity method:

| | | |
|---|---|---|
| Investment in Sub Inc. | 2,790 | |
| Equity method Income | | 2,790 |

To record 90% of the reported net income of Sub Inc. (90% × 3,100)

| | | |
|---|---|---|
| Investment in Sub Inc. | 180 | |
| Equity method income | | 180 |

To release in Year 5 the after-tax inventory profit held back in Year 4

---

*The parent receives the full benefit when unrealized profits on downstream transactions are realized in Year 5.*

---

Alternatively, the following entry could be made to capture the overall impact of the two separate entries:

| | | |
|---|---|---|
| Investment in Sub Inc. | 2,970 | |
| Equity method income | | 2,970 |

To record equity method income from Sub Inc. net of adjustment for realized profit in beginning Inventory (90% × 3,100 + 100% × 180)

**UNREALIZED PROFITS WITH ASSOCIATES** When the investor only has significant influence in an associate, it cannot control the decisions made by the associate. As such, transactions with the associate are similar to transactions with outsiders. Therefore, the accounting for unrealized profits on downstream transactions is a bit different for an investment in an associate. Rather than eliminating all of the profit, only the investor's percentage ownership of the associate times the profit earned on the transaction with the associate is eliminated. For example, if X Co. had a 40% interest in Y Co. and made a profit of $100 on a transaction with Y Co., only $40 (40% × $100) of the profit would be eliminated as part of the entries under the equity method. The $100 of profit would be recorded in the sales and cost of sales accounts, and the $40 would be eliminated through the investment account. That leaves $60 of profit remaining in income. This $60 is deemed to be a transaction with outsiders.

> *Only the investor's share of profit on intercompany transactions with associates is eliminated.*

Self-Study Problem 1 illustrates the preparation of consolidated financial statements when there are intercompany sales of inventory. It also shows the accounting for unrealized profits with an associate.

**INCOME STATEMENT WITH EXPENSES CLASSIFIED BY NATURE** The previous illustrations in this chapter presented cost of goods sold as a separate line on the income statement. This would typically occur under two scenarios:

1. When expenses are classified according to their function and cost of goods sold represents the expenses of the production function

2. When expenses are classified by nature and the reporting entity is a merchandising company—that is, it buys and sells finished goods

When a manufacturing company presents its expenses according to their nature, a cost-of-goods-sold line typically does not exist. Instead, raw materials consumed, labour costs, depreciation of factory equipment, and other conversion costs are shown separately. In addition, there is a separate line for changes in inventories of work in progress and finished goods.

The adjustments on consolidation to eliminate the intercompany transactions and any unrealized profits are slightly different when expenses are classified according to their nature. If the intercompany transaction involves raw materials, all consolidation adjustments are put through the raw materials account on the balance sheet and the raw materials consumed account on the income statement. If the intercompany transaction involves work in progress or finished goods, the intercompany purchase is eliminated from the purchases of work in progress and finished goods accounts on the income statement; the unrealized profits are eliminated from work in progress and finished goods inventory on the balance sheet, and from the changes in inventories of work in progress and finished goods account on the income statement.

> *Consolidation adjustments for unrealized profits in inventory will likely be made to the changes in inventory account rather than cost of goods sold.*

## Losses on Intercompany Transactions

When one affiliated company sells inventory to another affiliated company at a loss, the intercompany transaction and any unrealized losses should normally be eliminated on consolidation in a similar fashion to the previous discussion for unrealized profits. However, selling inventory at a loss raises a red flag that it may be impaired. If the inventory is impaired, it should be written down to its net realizable value. Ideally, the impairment should be reported on the separate-entity statements. If not, the impairment will have to be reported on the consolidated statements. The following example illustrates these issues.

Sub has inventory with an original cost of $5,500 and a net realizable value of $4,800. If Sub were to value its inventory at net realizable value at this point, it would recognize a loss of $700.

In Year 4, Sub sells this inventory to Parent for $5,000. It had not written down the inventory to its net realizable value prior to the sale to Parent. Before the end of Year 4, Parent sells 80% of these goods to outsiders for $3,840, which equals their net realizable value. It has the remaining inventory purchased from Sub on its books at $1,000 at the end of Year 4. The net realizable value of this inventory is $960, which is the same net realizable value prior to the sale by Sub.

---

*Impairment tests for inventory are usually performed at the end of the fiscal period.*

---

Based solely on the above information, selected accounts from the financial statements for Parent and Sub for Year 4 are as follows:

|  | Parent | Sub |
|---|---|---|
| Inventory on balance sheet | $1,000 |  |
| Sales | $3,840 | $5,000 |
| Cost of sales | 4,000 | 5,500 |
| Gross profit | $ −160 | $ −500 |

The following adjustments would normally be made on consolidation:

**(a)** Sales and cost of goods sold should be reduced by $5,000, being the amount of the intercompany sale.

**(b)** Unrealized loss in ending inventory of $100 (500/5,000 × $1,000) should be eliminated.

---

*When intercompany losses are eliminated, the inventory is brought back to the original cost to the selling entity.*

---

The consolidated financial statements show the following amounts for the selected accounts:

| | |
|---|---|
| Inventory on balance sheet (1,000 + 0 + **[b] 100**) | $1,100 |
| Sales (3,840 + 5,000 − **[a] 5,000**) | $3,840 |
| Cost of sales (4,000 + 5,500 − **[a] 5,000** − **[b] 100**) | 4,400 |
| Gross profit | $−560 |

By eliminating the unrealized loss and not making any adjustment for impairment of the inventory, the inventory is measured at $1,100, which is 20% of the original cost to Sub. This is consistent with the historical cost principle. However, this inventory is stated above its net realizable value of $960. It should be written down from $1,100 to $960, a write-down of $140. If the write-down were made as adjustment (c) on consolidation, the consolidated financial statements would show the following amounts for the selected accounts:

| | |
|---|---|
| Inventory on balance sheet (1,000 + 0 + **[b] 100** − **[c] 140**) | $ 960 |
| Sales (3,840 + 5,000 − **[a] 5,000**) | $3,840 |
| Cost of sales (4,000 + 5,500 − **[a] 5,000** − **[b] 100**) | 4,400 |
| Gross profit | −560 |
| Loss in value of inventory (0 + 0 + **[c] 140**) | −140 |
| Profit before tax on the above items | $−700 |

> *Inventory on the consolidated balance sheet should be reported at the lower of cost and net realizable value.*

Now the consolidated balance sheet reports inventory at the lower of cost and net realizable value, and the consolidated income statement reports a loss of $700, being the total impairment loss on the inventory. This more faithfully represents the situation for the consolidated entity.

It might seem strange to adjust the inventory upward by $100 in (b), and then to adjust it downward by $140 in (c). The same result could have been achieved by not eliminating the unrealized loss in (b) and then writing down the inventory from $1,000 to $960 for a $40 adjustment in (c). For this reason, some people believe that unrealized losses should not be eliminated on consolidation, but the losses should be a warning sign for possible impairment.

If the subsidiary had not sold any of the inventory to the parent or to outsiders, it should have tested the inventory for impairment at the end of Year 4. In so doing, it would have determined that inventory was impaired and that an impairment loss of $700 would need to be reported.

In some cases, the exchange price on intercompany transactions between the parent and the subsidiary does not reflect the true value of the inventory. Even though the net realizable value of the inventory in the above example was $4,800, the subsidiary could have sold the inventory to the parent for $4,000. If so, the inventory would be reported by the parent at less than net realizable value on its separate-entity balance sheet. If the unrealized loss is not eliminated, the inventory and net income of the consolidated entity will be understated. For this reason, IFRS suggest that the intercompany loss be eliminated on consolidation. Then, the reporting entity should perform an impairment test to determine if the inventory is impaired from the perspective of the consolidated entity.

> *Intercompany transactions are not always consummated at market value.*

## LO4 Intercompany Land Profit Holdback

The holdback and realization of an intercompany profit in land is accomplished in a more straightforward manner on the consolidated income statement. Suppose that in Year 4 there was an intercompany sale of land for $2,300 on which a before-tax profit of $300 was recorded, that $120 tax was accrued, and that on December 31, Year 4, the land was still held by the purchasing company. (Throughout the text and end-of-chapter material, we assume that these gains are not capital gains.) The selling company would make the following entry to record the intercompany transaction:

| | | |
|---|---|---|
| Cash | 2,300 | |
| Land | | 2,000 |
| Gain on sale of land | | 300 |

The purchasing company would record the intercompany transaction as follows:

| | | |
|---|---|---|
| Land | 2,300 | |
|    Cash | | 2,300 |

---

*The purchasing company's cost is $300 higher than the selling company's cost.*

---

When consolidated financial statements are prepared, the profit elimination and the related income tax adjustment will take place as follows:

**PARENT COMPANY**
**CONSOLIDATED INCOME STATEMENT**
Year 4

| | |
|---|---|
| Gain on sale of land (300 − **300**) | $ 0 |
| Income tax expense (P + S − **120**) | XXX |
|   Net income | $XXX |
| Attributable to: | |
|   Shareholders of parent | $XXX |
|   Non-controlling interest | XXX |

It should be obvious that the holdback of the gain, along with the reduction of the income tax expense, has reduced the consolidated entity's net income by $180. If the subsidiary is the selling company, the $180 after-tax profit held back will be used to calculate non-controlling interest in the consolidated income statement; in this manner, it will be allocated to the two equities. If the parent is the selling company, non-controlling interest will not be affected and the entire after-tax holdback will be allocated to the controlling entity.

---

*On consolidation, the after-tax profit is deducted from the selling company's separate-entity income.*

---

The following shows the eliminations required in the preparation of the assets section of the Year 4 balance sheet:

**PARENT COMPANY**
**CONSOLIDATED BALANCE SHEET**
At December 31,
Year 4

| | |
|---|---|
| Land (2,300 − **300**) | $2,000 |
| Deferred income taxes (P + S + **120**) | 120 |
|   Total assets | $ XXX |

---

*After eliminating the profit, the land is stated at the original cost to the consolidated entity.*

---

The balance sheet eliminations for a land profit are very similar to those for an inventory profit. The before-tax profit is deducted from land rather than from inventory. The tax asset is added into the consolidated balance sheet. We will refer to this tax asset as deferred income taxes.

The equity side of the balance sheet is not presented. If the subsidiary is the selling company, the calculation of non-controlling interest on December 31, Year 4, will have to reflect this fact. If the parent is the selling company, the entire $180 after-tax profit holdback is attributed to the parent company's shareholders and is reflected in the retained earnings shown on the balance sheet.

## Realization of Intercompany Land Profits

An unrealized intercompany inventory profit held back for consolidation purposes in Year 4 is considered realized in Year 5 because any inventory on hand at the beginning of a year has usually been sold by the end of that year.

When are intercompany land profits considered realized for consolidation purposes? The answer: when the land is sold to outsiders, which may be many years later. At the end of each successive year prior to the sale to outsiders, the preparation of the consolidated balance sheet requires the same adjustments as those of Year 4. Consolidated income statements require no adjustment until the year of the sale to outsiders because in each year prior to that event, the income statements of both affiliates will not contain any transactions with regard to the land.

However, assuming that Parent Company uses the cost method, the calculation of beginning consolidated retained earnings each year will have to include an adjustment to hold back the $180 unrealized land profit. The calculation would be identical to that shown in Exhibit 6.7, except that it would be described as land profit rather than profit in opening inventory. (This particular calculation is based on the assumption that Sub Inc. was the selling company.) Each successive year would require the same adjustment, until the land is sold to outsiders.

> *The unrealized profits will be eliminated from retained earnings of the selling company on the consolidated working papers each year until the land is sold to outsiders.*

In this case, let us assume that the land was sold to outsiders during Year 8 at a profit of $1,300. The company making the sale in Year 8 would record the following journal entry:

| | | |
|---|---|---|
| Cash | 3,600 | |
| Land | | 2,300 |
| Gain on sale of land | | 1,300 |

> *The gain on the separate-entity income statement is $1,300.*

While the selling company recorded a gain of $1,300, the gain to the entity is $1,600 ($1,300 + $300). On the Year 8 consolidated income statement, the gain held back in Year 4 is realized and the income tax expense is adjusted as follows:

**PARENT COMPANY**
**CONSOLIDATED INCOME STATEMENT**
Year 8

| | |
|---|---|
| Gain on sale of land (1,300 + **300**) | $1,600 |
| Income tax expense (P + S + **120**) | XXX |
| Net income | $ XXX |
| Attributable to: | |
|    Shareholders of parent | $ XXX |
|    Non-controlling interest | XXX |

> *The gain on the consolidated income statement is $1,600 ($1,300 + $300 previously held back).*

The entity's consolidated net income is increased by $180 ($300 − $120). If the subsidiary was the original selling company, the net income of the non-controlling interest is affected in Year 8; the entire $180 is attributed to the controlling interest if the parent was the original seller.

Appendix 6A of this chapter illustrates the consolidation adjustments relating to an intercompany sale of land when the parent company uses the revaluation model under IAS 16 and periodically revalues its land to fair value.

**LO5 EQUITY METHOD JOURNAL ENTRIES** Parent Co.'s equity journal entries for the land gain in Years 1 and 8 would be identical to the entries illustrated previously for inventory in Years 1 and 2, depending of course on which company was the original seller in the intercompany profit transaction.

> *The equity method reports only the investor's share of the subsidiary's profit that has been realized from a consolidated viewpoint.*

The examples in this chapter regarding the elimination of unrealized intercompany profits follow the dictates of entity theory, which requires the same accounting treatment for measuring the controlling and non-controlling shareholders' interest in the subsidiary. Entity theory is also required when measuring the subsidiary's assets and liabilities at fair value at the date of acquisition, as we learned in Chapter 4. Therefore, the standard-setters are consistent in requiring the use of entity theory in many different aspects of preparing consolidated financial statements.

See Self-Study Problem 6-2 for a comprehensive problem that includes acquisition differential and intercompany sales of inventory and land.

## Intercompany Transfer Pricing

In our coin example at the beginning of this chapter, we saw a loonie sold for a gross profit of $40, which was allocated to the four related companies as follows:

| | |
|---|---:|
| Parent | $ 9 |
| Sub 1 | 5 |
| Sub 2 | 10 |
| Sub 3 | 16 |
| Total | $40 |

From a financial reporting point of view, we are not concerned with the amount of profit earned by each company, but only with eliminating intercompany transactions and profits that are unrealized because they have not been sold outside the consolidated entity. From a Canadian taxation point of view, the consolidated entity is not subject to tax; rather each company pays tax on its taxable income. It should seem obvious that the management of the parent company would be interested in maximizing the after-tax profit of this single entity, if possible. If all of the companies are in one taxation jurisdiction, there is nothing that management can do to increase the after-tax profit. However, if some of the companies are in jurisdictions with low rates of corporate income tax while others are in high-tax-rate jurisdictions, management may try to structure each company's transfer price so that the majority (or all) of the $40 profit is earned in low-tax-rate jurisdictions. This will often bring companies into conflict with the governments of the high-tax-rate jurisdictions.

> *Intercompany transactions are sometimes undertaken to transfer profit from high-tax to low-tax jurisdictions.*

**DISCLOSURE REQUIREMENTS**  The disclosure requirements for consolidated financial statements were summarized in Chapters 3 and 4. In addition to those requirements, the entity would normally indicate that intercompany transactions have been eliminated. The excerpt in Exhibit 6.9 below is taken from the 2014 financial statements of Eastern Platinum Limited, Canada's leading platinum group metals producer.

**EXHIBIT 6.9**

### EXTRACTS FROM EASTERN PLATINUM'S 2014 FINANCIAL STATEMENTS

**4. Summary of significant accounting policies**

*(a) Basis of consolidation*

These consolidated financial statements incorporate the financial statements of the Company and the entities controlled by the Company. Control exists when the Company has (i) power over the investee, (ii) exposure, or rights, to variable returns from its involvement with the investee, and (iii) the ability to use its power over the investee to affect the amount of the investor's returns. The financial statements of subsidiaries are included in the consolidated financial statements from the date that control commences until the date that control ceases. All significant intercompany transactions, balances, revenues and expenses have been eliminated.

*Source: Eastern Platinum Limited. Consolidated financial statements of Eastern Platinum Limited: December 31, 2014 and 2013. Page 10. Reproduced with permission from Eastern Platinum Limited.*

> *Companies typically disclose that all significant intercompany transactions and balances have been eliminated.*

## LO6 ANALYSIS AND INTERPRETATION OF FINANCIAL STATEMENTS

In this chapter, we prepared consolidated financial statements under two scenarios: first, for upstream transactions and, second, for downstream transactions. In both cases, the unrealized profits from the intercompany transactions had to be eliminated. The elimination entries were made on the consolidated financial statements. The net effect of the consolidation adjustments was captured in the parent's internal records when the parent used the equity method.

Exhibit 6.10 presents the Year 4 separate entity and consolidated financial statements that were developed for the intercompany transactions involving inventory. The first three columns present the statements when the intercompany transactions were upstream. In the last three columns, the intercompany transactions were downstream.

**EXHIBIT 6.10**

## Impact of Presentation Method on Debt-to-Equity and Return-on-Equity Ratios

**INCOME STATEMENTS**

For the year ended December 31, Year 4

| | Upstream Transaction | | | Downstream Transaction | | |
|---|---|---|---|---|---|---|
| | Parent Cost | Parent Equity | Consol. | Parent Cost | Parent Equity | Consol. |
| Sales | $20,000 | $20,000 | $23,000 | $20,000 | $20,000 | $23,000 |
| Equity method income | 0 | 1,368 | 0 | 0 | 1,350 | 0 |
| Total income | 20,000 | 21,368 | 23,000 | 20,000 | 21,350 | 23,000 |
| Cost of sales | 13,000 | 13,000 | 12,600 | 13,000 | 13,000 | 12,600 |
| Miscellaneous expenses | 1,400 | 1,400 | 2,300 | 1,400 | 1,400 | 2,300 |
| Income tax expense | 2,200 | 2,200 | 3,180 | 2,200 | 2,200 | 3,180 |
| | 16,600 | 16,600 | 18,080 | 16,600 | 16,600 | 18,080 |
| Net income | $ 3,400 | $ 4,768 | $ 4,920 | $ 3,400 | $ 4,750 | $ 4,920 |
| Attributable to: | | | | | | |
| Shareholders of Parent | | | $4,768 | | | $ 4,750 |
| Non-controlling interest | | | 152 | | | 170 |

**BALANCE SHEETS**

At December 31, Year 4

| | | | | | | |
|---|---|---|---|---|---|---|
| Inventory | $7,500 | $ 7,500 | $11,200 | $ 7,500 | $ 7,500 | $11,200 |
| Miscellaneous assets | 21,650 | 21,650 | 40,850 | 21,650 | 21,650 | 40,850 |
| Deferred income tax | | | 120 | | | 120 |
| Investment in Sub Inc. | 11,250 | 12,618 | 0 | 11,250 | 12,600 | 0 |
| | $40,400 | $41,768 | $52,170 | $40,400 | $41,750 | $52,170 |
| Liabilities | $12,000 | $12,000 | $21,000 | $12,000 | $12,000 | $21,000 |
| Common shares | 15,000 | 15,000 | 15,000 | 15,000 | 15,000 | 15,000 |
| Retained earnings | 13,400 | 14,768 | 14,768 | 13,400 | 14,750 | 14,750 |
| Non-controlling interest | 0 | 0 | 1,402 | 0 | 0 | 1,420 |
| | $40,400 | $41,768 | $52,170 | $40,400 | $41,750 | $52,170 |
| Debt-to-equity | 0.42 | 0.40 | 0.67 | 0.42 | 0.40 | 0.67 |
| Return on equity: | | | | | | |
| For all shareholders | n/a | n/a | 15.78% | n/a | n/a | 15.78% |
| For shareholders of Parent | 11.97% | 16.02% | 16.02% | 11.97% | 15.97% | 15.97% |

> *The parent's separate-entity income statement reports the parent's revenues and expenses, whereas the consolidated income statement reports the combined revenues and expenses of the parent and its subsidiaries.*
>
> *The parent's separate-entity balance sheet reports the parent's assets and liabilities, whereas the consolidated balance sheet reports the combined assets and liabilities of the parent and its subsidiaries.*

The exhibit also indicates the debt-to-equity and return-on-equity ratios for each set of financial statements. The return on equity for all shareholders uses consolidated net income and total shareholders' equity including the non-controlling interest. The return on equity for shareholders of Parent uses consolidated net income attributable to the shareholders of Parent and total shareholders' equity excluding the non-controlling interest.

Note the following from Exhibit 6.10:

- The separate-entity statements under the cost method are the same for upstream and downstream transactions because the cost method does not record anything pertaining to the subsidiary's income or unrealized profits from intercompany transactions.

- The separate-entity statements under the cost method are the same as the statements under the equity method except for the investment account, retained earnings, and equity method income.

- Consolidated net income is the same regardless of whether the transactions were upstream or downstream. However, the split of the consolidated net income between the shareholders of the parent and the non-controlling interest is different. In turn, consolidated retained earnings and non-controlling interest are different, depending on whether the transactions were upstream or downstream. The separate-entity net income and retained earnings under the equity method are equal to consolidated net income attributable to the shareholders of Parent and consolidated retained earnings, respectively.

- The return on equity for the separate-entity statements under the equity method is equal to the consolidated return on equity for the shareholders of Parent.

- The return on equity for the downstream scenario is lower than the upstream scenario because the shareholders of Parent absorb the full charge when the unrealized profits are eliminated.

- The solvency position looks worst on the consolidated financial statements, because the subsidiary's debt is included on the consolidated financial statements. This increases the debt-to-equity ratio.

> *The return on equity for the separate-entity statements under the equity method is equal to the consolidated return on equity for the shareholders of Parent.*
>
> *The return on equity for shareholders of Parent for the downstream scenario is lower than the upstream scenario because the shareholders of Parent absorb the full charge when the unrealized profits are eliminated.*

## ASPE Differences

As mentioned in Chapter 3, private companies can either consolidate their subsidiaries or report their investments in subsidiaries under the cost method, under the equity method, or at fair value.

# SUMMARY

To ensure that consolidated financial statements reflect only transactions between the combined entity and those outside the entity, all intercompany transactions are eliminated. The elimination of intercompany revenues and expenses does not affect the net income of this combined entity; therefore, it cannot affect the amounts allocated to the two equities in the balance sheet. **(LO1)**

The elimination of unrealized intercompany profits in inventory reduces the net income of the consolidated entity. The income tax recorded on the unrealized profit is also removed from the consolidated income statement and is shown as a deferred income tax asset or liability until a sale to outsiders takes place. When the assets that contain the intercompany profit are sold outside the entity, the profit is considered realized and is reflected in the consolidated income statement. The appropriate income tax is removed from the consolidated balance sheet and reflected as an expense in the income statement. **(LO2)**

The cost principle requires that inventory be reported at cost, i.e., the amount paid when purchased from an outsider. The revenue recognition principle supports the recognition of profits only when realized with outsiders. The matching principle requires that cost of sales and income tax expense are recognized in the same period as the revenue. **(LO3)**

The principles described above also apply when eliminating profits pertaining to intercompany profits in land. The subsequent realization of the profits may not occur for many years because the land may not be sold to outsiders for many years. **(LO4)**

The equity method captures the parent's share of all changes to the subsidiary's shareholders' equity plus its share of adjustments made on consolidation for amortization of acquisition differential and elimination and subsequent realization of profits from intercompany transactions. When the equity method is properly applied, the retained earnings on the parent's separate entity balance sheet should be equal to consolidated retained earnings. **(LO5)**

When the subsidiary is the seller, the intercompany transactions are called upstream transactions. When the parent is the seller, the intercompany transactions are called downstream transactions. When profits are eliminated, the parent absorbs the entire amount on downstream transactions but only absorbs its proportionate interest on upstream transactions. Therefore, consolidated net income attributable to the parent and non-controlling interest will differ depending on whether the intercompany transactions are upstream or downstream. This will affect the ratios typically used when analyzing financial statements. **(LO6)**

## Self-Study Problem 1

LO2, 3, 4, 5

On December 31, Year 5, the EL Company purchased 70% of the outstanding common shares of the BOW Company for $5.6 million in cash when BOW's shareholders' equity consisted of $2,000,000 of common shares and $6,000,000 of retained earnings. There was no acquisition differential. For the year ending December 31, Year 10, the income statements for EL and BOW were as follows:

| | EL | BOW |
|---|---|---|
| Sales and other income | $28,800,000 | $13,000,000 |
| Cost of goods sold | 18,000,000 | 8,200,000 |
| Depreciation expense | 3,400,000 | 1,800,000 |
| Income tax and other expenses | 4,200,000 | 1,600,000 |
| Total expenses | 25,600,000 | 11,600,000 |
| Net income | $ 3,200,000 | $ 1,400,000 |

At December 31, Year 10, the condensed balance sheets for the two companies were as follows:

| | EL | BOW |
|---|---|---|
| Current assets | $15,000,000 | $8,800,000 |
| Investment in BOW | 5,600,000 | |
| Other noncurrent assets | 23,000,000 | 17,400,000 |
| Total assets | $43,600,000 | $26,200,000 |
| Liabilities | $26,400,000 | $13,800,000 |
| Common shares | 4,000,000 | 2,000,000 |
| Retained earnings | 13,200,000 | 10,400,000 |
| Total | $43,600,000 | $26,200,000 |

## Other Information

1. During Year 10, EL sold merchandise to BOW for $600,000. Seventy-five percent of this merchandise remains in BOW's inventory at December 31, Year 10. On December 31, Year 9, the inventory of BOW contained $100,000 of merchandise purchased from EL. EL earns a gross margin of 30% on its intercompany sales.

2. On January 2, Year 8, BOW sold land to EL for $1,200,000. BOW purchased the land on January 1, Year 6, for $1,100,000. EL still owns this land at December 31, Year 10.

3. During Year 10, EL declared and paid dividends of $2,600,000, while BOW declared and paid dividends of $800,000.

4. EL accounts for its investment in BOW using the cost method.

5. Both companies pay income tax at the rate of 40%.

## Required

(a) Prepare a consolidated income statement for the year ended December 31, Year 10. Show supporting calculations.

(b) Calculate consolidated retained earnings at December 31, Year 10. Show supporting calculations.

(c) Assume that BOW is a subsidiary and EL is a private entity. EL uses ASPE and chooses to use the equity method to account for its investment in BOW. Prepare EL's separate entity balance sheet at December 31, Year 10.

(d) Assume that BOW is an associate rather than a subsidiary and that EL uses IFRS. Calculate the balance in the investment in BOW account under the equity method at December 31, Year 10.

# Solution to Self-Study Problem 1

## (a) Supporting schedules:

### INTERCOMPANY TRANSACTIONS

| | | |
|---|---|---|
| Intercompany sales and cost of goods sold | $600,000 | **(a)** |
| Intercompany dividend (800,000 × 70%) | 560,000 | **(b)** |

Intercompany inventory profits—EL selling (downstream)

| | Before Tax | 40% Tax | After Tax | |
|---|---|---|---|---|
| Realized from beginning inventory (100,000 × 30%) | $30,000 | $12,000 | $18,000 | **(c)** |
| Unrealized in ending inventory (600,000 × 75% × 30%) | 135,000 | 54,000 | 81,000 | **(d)** |
| Unrealized gain on sale of land in Year 6 | 100,000 | 40,000 | 60,000 | **(e)** |
| (1,200,000 − 1,100,000)—Bow selling (upstream) | | | | |

### EL COMPANY
### CONSOLIDATED STATEMENT OF INCOME
For year ended December 31, Year 10

| | |
|---|---|
| Sales and other income | |
| [28,800,000 + 13,000,000 − **(a)** 600,000 − **(b)** 560,000] | $40,640,000 |
| Cost of goods sold | |
| [18,000,000 + 8,200,000 − **(a)** 600,000 − **(c)** 30,000 + **(d)** 135,000] | 25,705,000 |
| Depreciation expense [3,400,000 + 1,800,000] | 5,200,000 |
| Income tax and other expenses | |
| [4,200,000 + 1,600,000 + **(c)** 12,000 − **(d)** 54,000] | 5,758,000 |
| Total expenses | 36,663,000 |
| Net income | $ 3,977,000 |
| Attributable to: | |
| Shareholders of EL | |
| (3,200,000 − **(b)** 560,000 + **(c)** 18,000 − **(d)** 81,000 + 70% × 1,400,00) | $ 3,557,000 |
| Non-controlling interests (30% × 1,400,000) | 420,000 |

## (b)

| | | |
|---|---|---|
| EL's retained earnings, Dec. 31, Year 10 | | $13,200,000 |
| Unrealized after-tax profit in ending inventory (downstream) **(d)** | | (81,000) |
| BOW's retained earnings, Dec. 31, Year 10 | 10,400,000 | |
| BOW's retained earnings, at acquisition | 6,000,000 | |
| Change in retained earnings since acquisition | 4,400,000 | |
| Unrealized after-tax gain on land (upstream) **(e)** | (60,000) | |
| | 4,340,000 | |
| EL's share @ 70% | | 3,038,000 |
| Consolidated retained earnings, Dec. 31, Year 10 | | $16,157,000 |

## (c) Supporting schedules

| | | |
|---|---|---|
| Investment in BOW, cost method | | $ 5,600,000 |
| Unrealized after-tax profit in ending inventory (downstream) **(d)** | | (81,000) |
| BOW's retained earnings, Dec. 31, Year 10 | 10,400,000 | |
| BOW's retained earnings, at acquisition | 6,000,000 | |
| Change in retained earnings since acquisition | 4,400,000 | |
| Unrealized after-tax gain on land (upstream) **(e)** | (60,000) | |
| | 4,340,000 | |

| | | |
|---|---|---:|
| EL's share @ 70% | | 3,038,000 |
| Investment in BOW, equity method | | $ 8,557,000 |

OR:

| | |
|---|---:|
| Consolidated retained earnings, Dec. 31, Year 10 | $16,157,000 |
| EL's retained earnings, cost method, Dec. 31, Year 10 | 13,200,000 |
| Change from cost to consolidation | 2,957,000 |
| Investment in BOW, cost method | 5,600,000 |
| Investment in BOW, equity method | $ 8,557,000 |

**EL COMPANY**
**BALANCE SHEET**
At December 31, Year 10

| | |
|---|---:|
| Current assets | $ 15,000,000 |
| Investment in BOW | 8,557,000 |
| Other noncurrent assets | 23,000,000 |
| Total assets | $ 46,557,000 |
| Liabilities | $ 26,400,000 |
| Common shares | 4,000,000 |
| Retained earnings (same as consolidation) | 16,157,000 |
| Total | $ 46,557,000 |

(d) For a downstream transaction with an associate, only the investor's share of the profit in ending inventory is considered unrealized.

| | | |
|---|---:|---:|
| Investment in BOW, cost method | | $5,600,000 |
| Unrealized after-tax profit in ending inventory (downstream) (81,000 × 70%) | | (56,700) |
| BOW's retained earnings, Dec. 31, Year 10 | 10,400,000 | |
| BOW's retained earnings, at acquisition | 6,000,000 | |
| Change in retained earnings since acquisition | 4,400,000 | |
| Unrealized after-tax gain on land (upstream) **(e)** | (60,000) | |
| | 4,340,000 | |
| EL's share @ 70% | | 3,038,000 |
| Investment in BOW, equity method | | $8,581,300 |

# Self-Study Problem 2

LO1, 2, 4, 5

The following are the Year 5 financial statements of Peter Corporation and its subsidiary, Salt Company:

| | Peter | Salt |
|---|---:|---:|
| **YEAR 5 INCOME STATEMENTS** | | |
| Sales | $900,000 | $250,000 |
| Management fees | 25,000 | — |
| Interest | — | 3,600 |
| Gain on land sale | — | 20,000 |
| Dividend income | 12,000 | — |
| | 937,000 | 273,600 |

|  | Peter | Salt |
|---|---|---|
| **YEAR 5 INCOME STATEMENTS** | | |
| Cost of sales | 540,000 | 162,000 |
| Interest expense | 3,600 | — |
| Other expenses | 196,400 | 71,600 |
| Income tax expense | 80,000 | 16,000 |
|  | 820,000 | 249,600 |
| Profit | $117,000 | $ 24,000 |
| **YEAR 5 STATEMENTS OF RETAINED EARNINGS** | | |
| Balance, January 1 | $153,000 | $ 72,000 |
| Profit | 117,000 | 24,000 |
|  | 270,000 | 96,000 |
| Dividends | 50,000 | 15,000 |
| Balance, December 31 | $220,000 | $ 81,000 |
| **STATEMENTS OF FINANCIAL POSITION** December 31, Year 5 | | |
| Land | $175,000 | $ 19,000 |
| Plant and equipment, net | 238,000 | 47,000 |
| Investment in Salt Co. | 65,000 | — |
| Inventory | 32,000 | 27,000 |
| Notes receivable | — | 60,000 |
| Accounts receivable | 70,000 | 10,000 |
| Cash | 12,000 | 8,000 |
|  | $592,000 | $171,000 |
| Ordinary shares | $100,000 | $ 50,000 |
| Retained earnings | 220,000 | 81,000 |
| Notes payable | 60,000 | — |
| Other liabilities | 212,000 | 40,000 |
|  | $592,000 | $171,000 |

## Additional Information

- On January 1, Year 3, Peter purchased 80% of the ordinary shares of Salt for $65,000. On that date, Salt had retained earnings of $10,000, and the carrying amounts of its identifiable net assets were equal to fair values.
- The companies sell merchandise to each other. Peter sells to Salt at a gross profit rate of 35%; Salt earns a gross profit of 40% from its sales to Peter.
- The December 31, Year 4, inventory of Peter contained purchases made from Salt amounting to $7,000. There were no intercompany purchases in the inventory of Salt on this date.
- During Year 5, the following intercompany transactions took place:
  - (a) Salt made a $25,000 payment to Peter for management fees, which was recorded as "other expenses."
  - (b) Salt made sales of $75,000 to Peter. The December 31, Year 5, inventory of Peter contained merchandise purchased from Salt amounting to $16,500.
  - (c) Peter made sales of $100,000 to Salt. The December 31, Year 5, inventory of Salt contained merchandise purchased from Peter amounting to $15,000.

(d) On July 1, Year 5, Peter borrowed $60,000 from Salt and signed a note bearing interest at 12% per annum. Interest on this note was paid on December 31, Year 5.

(e) In Year 5, Salt sold land to Peter, recording a gain of $20,000. This land is being held by Peter on December 31, Year 5.

- Goodwill impairment tests have been conducted yearly since the date of acquisition. Losses due to impairment were as follows: Year 3, $2,600; Year 4, $800; Year 5, $1,700.
- Peter accounts for its investment using the cost method.
- Both companies pay income tax at a rate of 40%.

## Required

*eXcel*

(a) Prepare the Year 5 consolidated financial statements.

(b) Prepare the following:

   (i)   A calculation of consolidated retained earnings as at December 31, Year 5

   (ii)  A calculation of non-controlling interest at December 31, Year 5

   (iii) A statement of changes in deferred income taxes for Year 5

(c) Assume that Peter changes from the cost method to the equity method for its internal records.

   (i)   Calculate the balance in the investment account under the equity method as at December 31, Year 4.

   (ii)  Prepare Peter's equity method journal entries for Year 5.

## Solution to Self-Study Problem 2

(a) Supporting schedules

### CALCULATION AND IMPAIRMENT OF THE ACQUISITION DIFFERENTIAL

| | | | |
|---|---:|---:|---|
| Cost of 80% of Salt, Jan. 1, Year 3 | | $ 65,000 | |
| Implied value of 100% of Salt | | $ 81,250 | |
| Carrying amount of Salt, Jan. 1, Year 3: | | | |
|    Ordinary shares | 50,000 | | |
|    Retained earnings | 10,000 | | |
| | | 60,000 | |
| Acquisition differential | | 21,250 | |
| Allocated to revalue the net assets of Salt | | 0 | |
| Goodwill, Jan. 1, Year 3 | | 21,250 | |
| Impairment losses: | | | |
|    Year 3—Year 4 | 3,400 | | **(a)** |
|    Year 5 | 1,700 | 5,100 | **(b)** |
|      Goodwill, Dec. 31, Year 5 | | $ 16,150 | **(c)** |
| Non-controlling interest at date of acquisition (20% × 81,250) | | $ 16,250 | **(d)** |

### INTERCOMPANY ITEMS

| | | |
|---|---:|---|
| Notes receivable and payable | $ 60,000 | **(e)** |
| Management fee revenue and expense | $ 25,000 | **(f)** |
| Sales and purchases (100,000 + 75,000) | $175,000 | **(g)** |
| Interest revenue and expense (12% × 60,000 × ½ year) | $ 3,600 | **(h)** |
| Dividend from Salt (80% × 15,000) | $ 12,000 | **(i)** |

## UNREALIZED PROFITS

| | Before Tax | 40% Tax | After Tax | |
|---|---|---|---|---|
| Inventory: | | | | |
| Opening (7,000 × 40%)—Salt selling (upstream) | $ 2,800 | $1,120 | $ 1,680 | **(j)** |
| Ending: | | | | |
| Salt selling (upstream) (16,500 × 40%) | $ 6,600 | $2,640 | $ 3,960 | **(k)** |
| Peter selling (downstream) (15,000 × 35%) | 5,250 | 2,100 | 3,150 | **(l)** |
| | $11,850 | $4,740 | $ 7,110 | **(m)** |
| Land—Salt selling (upstream) | $20,000 | $8,000 | $ 12,000 | **(n)** |

## CALCULATION OF CONSOLIDATED PROFIT
### Year 5

| | | | |
|---|---|---|---|
| Profit of Peter | | | $117,000 |
| Less: | | | |
| Dividends from Salt **(i)** | | 12,000 | |
| Unrealized after-tax profit in ending inventory profit **(l)** (downstream) | | 3,150 | 15,150 |
| Adjusted profit | | | 101,850 |
| Profit of Salt | | 24,000 | |
| Less: | | | |
| Unrealized after-tax profit in ending inventory profit **(k)** (upstream) | 3,960 | | |
| Unrealized after-tax gain in land gain (upstream) **(n)** | 12,000 | | |
| Impairment of acquisition differential **(b)** | 1,700 | 17,660 | |
| | | 6,340 | |
| Add: | | | |
| Realized after-tax profit in opening inventory (upstream) **(j)** | | 1,680 | |
| Adjusted profit | | | 8,020 |
| Profit | | | $109,870 |
| Attributable to: | | | |
| Shareholders of parent | | | $108,266 **(o)** |
| Non-controlling interest (20% × 8,020) | | | 1,604 **(p)** |

## CALCULATION OF CONSOLIDATED RETAINED EARNINGS
### January 1, Year 5

| | | |
|---|---|---|
| Retained earnings—Peter | | $153,000 |
| Retained earnings—Salt | 72,000 | |
| Acquisition retained earnings | 10,000 | |
| Increase | 62,000 | |
| Less: Unrealized after-tax profit in opening inventory profit (upstream) **(j)** | 1,680 | |
| Less: Acquisition-differential impairment Year 3—Year 4 **(a)** | 3,400 | |
| Adjusted increase | 56,920 | |
| Peter's share | 80% | 45,536 **(q)** |
| Consolidated retained earnings, Jan. 1, Year 5 | | $198,536 **(r)** |

## CALCULATION OF DEFERRED INCOME TAXES
### December 31, Year 5

| | |
|---|---|
| Ending inventory **(m)** | $ 4,740 |
| Land **(n)** | 8,000 |
| | $12,740 **(s)** |

## CALCULATION OF NON-CONTROLLING INTEREST
### December 31, Year 5

| | | |
|---|---:|---:|
| Ordinary shares—Salt | | $50,000 |
| Retained earnings—Salt | | 81,000 |
| | | 131,000 |
| Add: Unamortized acquisition differential **(c)** | | 16,150 |
| Less: Unrealized after-tax profit in ending inventory profit (upstream) **(k)** | 3,960 | |
| Unrealized after-tax gain in land (upstream) **(n)** | 12,000 | (15,960) |
| Adjusted | | 131,190 |
| Non-controlling interest's share | | 20% |
| | | $26,238   **(t)** |

## PETER CORPORATION
## CONSOLIDATED INCOME STATEMENT
### Year 5

| | |
|---|---:|
| Sales (900,000 + 250,000 − **[g] 175,000**) | $975,000 |
| Management fees (25,000 + 0 − **[f] 25,000**) | 0 |
| Interest (0 + 3,600 − **[h] 3,600**) | 0 |
| Gain on land sale (0 + 20,000 − **[n] 20,000**) | 0 |
| Dividend income (12,000 + 0 − **[i] 12,000**) | 0 |
| Cost of sales (540,000 + 162,000 − **[g] 175,000** − **[j] 2,800** + **[m] 11,850**) | 536,050 |
| Interest expense (3,600 + 0 − **[h] 3,600**) | 0 |
| Other expenses (196,400 + 71,600 + **[b] 1,700** − **[f] 25,000**) | 244,700 |
| Income tax (80,000 + 16,000 − **[n] 8,000** + **[j] 1,120** − **[m] 4,740**) | 84,380 |
| Total expense | 865,130 |
| Net income | $109,870 |
| Attributable to: | |
| Shareholders of parent **(o)** | $108,266 |
| Non-controlling interest **(p)** | 1,604 |

## PETER CORPORATION
## CONSOLIDATED RETAINED EARNINGS STATEMENT
### Year 5

| | |
|---|---:|
| Balance, January 1 **(r)** | $198,536 |
| Profit | 108,266 |
| | 306,802 |
| Dividends | 50,000 |
| Balance, December 31 | $256,802 |

## PETER CORPORATION
## CONSOLIDATED STATEMENT OF FINANCIAL POSITION
### December 31, Year 5

| | |
|---|---:|
| Land (175,000 + 19,000 − **[n] 20,000**) | $174,000 |
| Plant and equipment, net (238,000 + 47,000) | 285,000 |
| Goodwill **(c)** | 16,150 |
| Deferred tax asset **(s)** | 12,740 |
| Inventory (32,000 + 27,000 − **[m] 11,850**) | 47,150 |
| Accounts receivable (70,000 + 10,000) | 80,000 |
| Cash (12,000 + 8,000) | 20,000 |
| | $635,040 |

| Ordinary shares | | $100,000 |
| Retained earnings | | 256,802 |
| Non-controlling interest (t) | | 26,238 |
| Other liabilities (212,000 + 40,000) | | 252,000 |
| | | $635,040 |

## (b) (i) CALCULATION OF CONSOLIDATED RETAINED EARNINGS
### December 31, Year 5

| | | | |
|---|---|---|---|
| Retained earnings, Dec. 31, Year 5—Peter | | | $220,000 |
| Less: Unrealized after-tax profit in ending inventory | | | |
|     (downstream) (l) | | | 3,150 |
|  Adjusted | | | 216,850 |
| Retained earnings, Dec. 31, Year 5—Salt | | 81,000 | |
| Acquisition retained earnings | | 10,000 | |
| Increase | | 71,000 | |
| Less: Acquisition-differential impairment (a) + (b) | 5,100 | | |
|     Unrealized after-tax profit in ending inventory | | | |
|     (upstream) (k) | 3,960 | | |
|     Unrealized after-tax gain in land (upstream) (n) | 12,000 | 21,060 | |
| Adjusted increase | | 49,940 | (u) |
| Peter's share | | 80% | 39,952 |
|     Consolidated retained earnings, December 31, Year 5 | | | $256,802 |

## (ii) CALCULATION OF NON-CONTROLLING INTEREST
### Dec. 31 Year 5

| | | |
|---|---|---|
| Non-controlling interest at date of acquisition (d) | | $16,250 |
| Increase in Company S retained earnings, since acquisition net | | |
| of consolidation adjustments (u) | 49,940 | |
| Non-controlling interest's ownership | 20% | 9,988 |
| NCI, end of Year 5 | | $26,238 |

## (iii) CHANGES IN DEFERRED TAX ASSETS
### Year 5

| | | |
|---|---|---|
| Balance, Jan. 1, Year 5 (inventory) (j) | | $ 1,120 |
| Taxes paid in Year 5 but deferred | | |
|     Inventory (m) | 4,740 | |
|     Land (n) | 8,000 | 12,740 |
| | | 13,860 |
| Expensed Year 5 (j) | | 1,120 |
| Balance, Dec. 31, Year 5 | | $12,740 |

| | | | |
|---|---|---|---|
| (c) (i) Investment in Salt, Dec. 31, Year 4 (cost method) | | | $ 65,000 |
| Retained earnings, Dec. 31, Year 4—Salt | | 72,000 | |
| Acquisition retained earnings | | 10,000 | |
| Increase | | 62,000 | |
| Less: Unrealized after-tax profit in inventory (upstream) (j) | 1,680 | | |
|     Amort. of acquisition differential (a) | 3,400 | 5,080 | |
| Adjusted increase | | 56,920 | |
| Peter's share | | 80% | 45,536 |
| Investment in Salt, Dec. 31, Year 4 (equity method) | | | $110,536 |

| EQUITY METHOD JOURNAL ENTRIES | | |
|---|---|---|
| (ii) Year 5 | | |
| (see calculation of consolidated profit) | | |
| Investment in Salt Co. | 6,416 | |
| Equity method income | | 6,416 |
| 80% of adjusted profit of Salt Co. (80% × 8,020) | | |
| Cash | 12,000 | |
| Investment in Salt Co. | | 12,000 |
| Dividends from Salt Co. **(i)** | | |
| Equity method income | 3,150 | |
| Investment in Salt Co. | | 3,150 |
| Unrealized after-tax profit in ending inventory—Peter selling (downstream) **(l)** | | |

# APPENDIX 6A

## Reporting Land under Revaluation Model

LO7

IAS 16 *Property, Plant and Equipment* allows a reporting entity the option to periodically revalue its property, plant, and equipment to fair value. Any increase in the fair value of the asset over the carrying amount without the revaluation is reported in other comprehensive income. Any decrease in the fair value below the carrying amount without the revaluation is an impairment loss and is reported in net income. The reversal of an impairment loss is also reported in net income. Any balance in accumulated other comprehensive income relating to the revaluation surplus is transferred directly to retained earnings, either when the asset is sold or as the asset is being depreciated over its useful life.

In the example found in the sections "Intercompany Land Profit Holdback" and "Realization of Intercompany Land Profits" earlier in this chapter, the companies used the cost model to account for land. We will use the same figures from that example to illustrate the accounting when the company periodically revalues land to fair value under the revaluation model. At the end of Year 0, selected account balances from the separate-entity balance sheet for the company holding the land were as follows:

| | |
|---|---|
| Land at cost | $2,000 |
| Fair value excess for land | 250 |
| Deferred income tax liability (40% × 250) | 100 |
| Accumulated revaluation surplus, net of tax (250 − 100) | 150 |

> *An entity can report its property, plant, and equipment at fair value on an annual basis.*

The fair value excess for land is a contra account[3] to the land account. When added to the land account, land will be reported at fair value. The accumulated revaluation surplus account is reported separately as a component of shareholders' equity. It is also referred to as accumulated other comprehensive income.

The selling company would make the following entries pertaining to the sale of the land in Year 1:

| | | |
|---|---|---|
| Cash | 2,300 | |
| Land | | 2,000 |
| Fair value excess for land | | 250 |
| Gain on sale of land | | 50 |
| To record sale of land | | |

---

*The revaluation surplus is transferred to retained earnings when the property is sold.*

---

| | | |
|---|---|---|
| Accumulated revaluation surplus | 150 | |
| Retained earnings | | 150 |
| To transfer revaluation surplus to retained earnings on sale of land | | |
| Income tax expense | 20 | |
| Deferred income tax liability | 100 | |
| Income tax payable | | 120 |
| To record tax on sale and transfer deferred income tax liability to current income taxes payable | | |

Assuming that the fair value of the land is $2,325 at the end of Year 1, the purchasing company would make the following entries pertaining to the land in Year 1:

| | | |
|---|---|---|
| Land | 2,300 | |
| Cash | | 2,300 |
| To record purchase of land | | |
| Fair value excess for land | 25 | |
| Other comprehensive income—revaluation surplus for land | | 25 |
| To revalue land to fair value | | |
| Other comprehensive income—income tax on revaluation surplus for land | 10 | |
| Deferred income tax liability | | 10 |
| To record income tax on revaluation surplus | | |

---

*The revaluation surplus is reported through other comprehensive income on an after-tax basis.*

---

The following summarizes what would be reported on the separate-entity statements and what should be reported on the consolidated statements for Year 1:

| | Selling Co. | Buying Co. | Consolidated |
|---|---|---|---|
| Land | | $2,300 | $2,000 |
| Fair value excess for land | | 25 | 325 |
| Income tax payable | $120 | | |
| Deferred income tax liability | | 10 | 130 |
| Accumulated revaluation surplus | | 15 | 195 |
| Gain on sale of land | 50 | | |
| Income tax expense | 20 | | |
| Other comprehensive income—revaluation surplus for land, net of tax (2,325 − 2,250) × (1 − 40%) | | 15 | 45 |

The consolidated statements present what would have been reported on the selling company's statements had the intercompany transaction not taken place.

> *The consolidated statements should report amounts that would have existed had the intercompany transaction not occurred.*

## SUMMARY OF APPENDIX 6A

Under the revaluation model, land is reported at fair value at each reporting date on both the separate entity and consolidated balance sheet. Unrealized profits from intercompany transactions are moved from net income on the separate entity financial statements to other comprehensive income on the consolidated financial statements. **(LO7)**

## Review Questions

LO1 **1.** In what way are an individual's pants with four pockets similar to a parent company with three subsidiaries? Explain, with reference to intercompany revenues and expenses.

LO1, 2 **2.** List the types of intercompany revenue and expenses that are eliminated in the preparation of a consolidated income statement, and indicate the effect that each elimination has on the amount of net income attributable to non-controlling interest.

LO1 **3.** "From a consolidated-entity point of view, intercompany revenue and expenses and intercompany borrowings do nothing more than transfer cash from one bank account to another." Explain.

LO2, 3 **4.** If an intercompany profit is recorded on the sale of an asset to an affiliate within the consolidated entity in Period 1, when should this profit be considered realized? Explain.

LO3 **5.** Explain how the revenue recognition principle supports the elimination of intercompany transactions when preparing consolidated financial statements.

LO2 **6.** "The reduction of a $1,000 intercompany gross profit from ending inventory should be accompanied by a $400 increase to deferred income taxes in consolidated assets." Do you agree? Explain.

LO3 **7.** Explain how the matching principle supports adjustments to income tax expense when eliminating intercompany profits from consolidated financial statements.

LO1 **8.** A parent company rents a sales office to its wholly owned subsidiary under an operating lease requiring rent of $2,000 a month. What adjustments to consolidated income tax expense should accompany the elimination of the parent's $24,000 rent revenue and the subsidiary's $24,000 rent expense when a consolidated income statement is being prepared? Explain.

LO2 **9.** "Intercompany losses recorded on the sale of assets to an affiliate within the consolidated entity should always be eliminated when consolidated financial statements are prepared." Do you agree with this statement? Explain.

**LO1, 2** **10.** Describe the effects that the elimination of intercompany sales and intercompany profits in ending inventory will have on the various elements of the consolidated financial statements.

**LO4** **11.** What difference does it make on the consolidated financial statements if there are unrealized profits in land resulting from a downstream transaction as compared with an upstream transaction?

**LO2** **12.** When there are unrealized profits in inventory at the end of Year 1, consolidated profit would normally be affected for Years 1 and 2. Explain.

**LO4** **13.** An intercompany gain on the sale of land is eliminated in the preparation of the consolidated statements in the year that the gain was recorded. Will this gain be eliminated in the preparation of subsequent consolidated statements? Explain.

**LO4 \*14.** A subsidiary periodically revalues its land to fair value under the revaluation option for property, plant, and equipment. Explain the adjustments required to the consolidated financial statements if the subsidiary sells this land to the parent at an amount in excess of its carrying amount.

**LO5** **15.** Describe the journal entry on the parent's books under the equity method to adjust for unrealized profits in ending inventory for upstream transactions.

# CASES

## Case 6-1

**LO2, 3**

You, the controller, recently had the following discussion with the president:

**President:** I just don't understand why we can't recognize the revenue from the intercompany sale of inventory on the consolidated financial statements. The subsidiary company sold the goods to the parent at fair value and received the cash for the sale. We need to record the profit on this sale in order to maintain a steady earnings growth for our company. Otherwise, the bank will be concerned about our ability to repay the loan.

**Controller:** You are right that the subsidiary has received the cash, but that is not the main criterion for determining when to recognize the revenue. Furthermore, you need to understand that the consolidated financial statements are different from the individual financial statements for the parent and the subsidiary.

**President:** I have never understood why we need to prepare consolidated financial statements. It is just extra work. Who uses these statements? Furthermore, the profit on the intercompany transaction should be reported on the income statement because tax had to be paid on this profit. Surely, if tax is paid, the profit is legitimate.

**Controller:** Once again, cash payments do not determine when we report income tax expense on the income statement. How about we get together for lunch tomorrow? I will prepare a brief presentation to illustrate the difference between the income for the parent and subsidiary and the income for the consolidated entity and will explain how all of these statements properly apply generally accepted accounting principles for revenue and expense recognition.

As part of the presentation, you decided to prepare monthly income statements for the parent, subsidiary, and consolidated entity for the following situation:

- Parent owns 100% of the subsidiary.
- Subsidiary buys goods from outsiders for $400 in July and sells them to Parent in August at a markup of 20% of cost.
- In September, Parent sells these goods to an outsider at a markup of 20% of selling price.
- Both companies pay income tax at the rate of 40%.

**Required**

Prepare notes for your presentation to the president.

## Case 6-2

LO2

In early September Year 1, your firm's audit client, D Ltd. (D) acquired in separate transactions an 80% interest in N Ltd. (N) and a 40% interest in K Ltd. (K). All three companies are federally incorporated Canadian companies and have August 31 year-ends. They all manufacture small appliances, but they do not compete with each other.

You are the senior on the audit of D. The partner has just received the preliminary consolidated financial statements from the controller of D along with unconsolidated statements for the three separate companies. Extracts from these statements are summarized in Exhibit I. The partner has requested that you provide him with a memorandum discussing the important financial accounting issues of D. Account balances for the consolidated financial statements should be recalculated to the extent that information is available.

**EXHIBIT I**

**EXTRACTS FROM FINANCIAL STATEMENTS**
At August 31, Year 2
(in thousands)

|  | Unconsolidated | | | Consolidated |
|  | D | N | K | D |
|---|---|---|---|---|
| Investment in N Ltd., at cost | $4,000 | | | |
| Investment in K Ltd., at cost | 2,100 | | | $2,100 |
| Deferred development costs | | $ 90 | | |
| Goodwill | | 60 | | |
| Non-controlling interest | | | | 590 |
| Common shares | 6,000 | 1,000 | $2,000 | 6,000 |
| Retained earnings, beginning | 618 | 1,850 | 1,760 | 618 |
| Profit | 600 | 300 | 100 | 660 |
| Dividends | (400) | (200) | (150) | (400) |
| Retained earnings, end of year | $ 818 | $1,950 | $1,710 | $ 878 |

D acquired the 80% interest in N for $4,000,000 paid as follows:

(1) $2,000,000 in cash, and
(2) 160,000 common shares of D recorded in the books of D at $2,000,000.

*(continued)*

D acquired its 40% interest in K at a cost of $2,100,000 paid as follows:

(1)  $100,000 in cash, and

(2)  160,000 common shares of D recorded in the books of D at $2,000,000.

During the course of the audit, the following information was obtained:

1.  The carrying amount of 80% of N's net assets at the date of acquisition was $2,280,000. The acquisition differential consisted of the following:

| | |
|---|---:|
| The excess of fair value of land over carrying amount | $ 800,000 |
| The excess of fair value of plant and equipment over carrying amount | 700,000 |
| 20% non-controlling interest's share of excess of fair value over carrying amount | (300,000) |
| Goodwill of N written off | (48,000) |
| Deferred research and development expenditures written off | (72,000) |
| Unallocated excess | 640,000 |
| | $1,720,000 |

The plant and equipment had a remaining useful life of ten years when D acquired N.

2.  The price paid by D for its investment in K was 10% lower than 40% of the fair value of K's identifiable net assets.

3.  During August Year 2, K sold goods to D as follows:

| | |
|---|---:|
| Cost to K | $1,000,000 |
| Normal selling price | 1,250,000 |
| Price paid by D | 1,200,000 |

D had not sold these goods as of August 31, Year 2.
N also sold goods to D in August Year 2 and D had not sold them by August 31, Year 2.

| | |
|---|---:|
| Cost to N | $630,000 |
| Normal selling price | 750,000 |
| Price paid by D | 850,000 |

4.  For the year ended August 31, Year 2, D's sales were $8,423,300 and N's sales were $6,144,500.

5.  The companies pay income tax at the rate of 40%.

*(CPA Canada adapted)*[4]

# Case 6-3

LO2, 6

Good Quality Auto Parts Limited (GQ) is a medium-sized, privately owned producer of auto parts, which are sold to car manufacturers, repair shops, and retail outlets. In March Year 10, the union negotiated a new three-year contract with the company for the 200 shop-floor employees. At the time, GQ was in financial difficulty and management felt unable to meet the contract demands of the union. Management also believed that a strike of any length would force the company into bankruptcy.

The company proposed that in exchange for wage concessions, the company would implement a profit-sharing plan whereby the shop floor employees would receive 10% of the company's annual after-tax profit as a bonus in each year of the contract. Although the union generally finds this type of contract undesirable, it believed that insisting on the prevailing industry settlement would jeopardize GQ's survival. As a result, the contract terms were accepted.

The contract specifies that no major changes in accounting policies may be made without the change being approved by GQ's auditor. Another clause in the contract allows the union to engage a chartered professional accountant accountant to examine the books of the company and meet with GQ's management and auditor to discuss any issues. Under the terms of the contract, any controversial accounting issues are to be negotiated by the union and management to arrive at a mutual agreement. If the parties cannot agree, the positions of the parties are to be presented to an independent arbitrator for resolution.

GQ presented to the union its annual financial statements and the unqualified audit report, for the year ended February 28, Year 11, the first year during which the profit-sharing plan was in effect. The union engaged you, CPA, to analyze these financial statements and determine whether there are any controversial accounting issues. As a result of your examination, you identified a number of issues that are of concern to you. You met with the controller of the company and obtained the following information:

1. GQ wrote off $250,000 of inventory manufactured between Year 4 and Year 7. There have been no sales from this inventory in over two years. The controller explained that up until this year she had some hope that the inventory could be sold as replacement parts. However, she now believes that the parts cannot be sold.

2. The contracts GQ has with the large auto manufacturers allow the purchaser to return items for any reason. The company has increased the allowance for returned items by 10% in the year just ended. The controller contends that because of the weak economy and stiff competition faced by the auto manufacturers with whom GQ does business, there will likely be a significant increase in the parts returned.

3. In April Year 10, GQ purchased $500,000 of new manufacturing equipment. To reduce the financial strain of the acquisition, the company negotiated a six-year payment schedule. Management believed that the company would be at a serious competitive disadvantage if it did not emerge from the current downturn with updated equipment. GQ decided to use accelerated depreciation at a rate of 40% for the new equipment. The controller argued that because of the rapid technological changes occurring in the industry, equipment purchased now is more likely to become technologically, rather than operationally, obsolete. The straight-line depreciation method applied to the existing equipment has not been changed.

4. In Year 5, GQ purchased 100% of the shares of Brake Inc., a manufacturer of car brakes. At the time of acquisition, $35,000 of goodwill was reported on GQ's consolidated financial statements and was being amortized over 35 years. The company has written off the goodwill in the year just ended. The controller explained that the poor performance of the auto parts industry, and of GQ in particular, has made the goodwill worthless.

5. During Year 11, Brake Inc. sold brakes to GQ for $800,000. Ten percent of this merchandise remains in GQ's inventory at February 28, Year 11. On February 28, Year 10, the inventory of GQ contained $200,000 of merchandise purchased from Brake. Brake earns a gross margin of 35% on its intercompany sales. GQ has not made any adjustments for the intercompany transactions for Year 11.

6. In February Year 11, the president and the chairman of the board, who between them own 75% of the voting shares of the company, received bonuses of $250,000 each. GQ did not pay any

dividends during the current year. In the prior year, dividends amounting to $650,000 were paid. The controller said that the board of directors justified the bonuses as a reward for keeping the company afloat despite extremely difficult economic times.

7. Until this year, GQ used the taxes-payable method for accounting purposes. This year, the company has used the liability method of accounting for income taxes. The change has been made retroactively. The effect of the change has been to reduce net income for fiscal Year 11. The controller argued that, because the company is likely to need significant external financing from new sources in the upcoming year, the company should adopt policies under ASPE that are the same as IFRS.

The union has asked you to prepare a report on the position it should take on the issues identified when discussing them with management. The union also wants to know what additional information you require in order to support this position.

*(CPA Canada adapted)*[5]

## Case 6-4

### LO3

You, the CPA, an audit senior at Grey & Co., Chartered Professional Accountants, are in charge of this year's audit of Plex-Fame Corporation (PFC). PFC is a rapidly expanding, diversified, and publicly owned entertainment company with operations throughout Canada and the United States. PFC's operations include movie theatres, live theatre production, and television production. It is June 22, Year 7, the week before PFC's year-end. You meet with the chief financial officer of PFC to get an update on current developments and learn the following.

PFC acquires real estate in prime locations where an existing theatre chain does not adequately serve the market. After acquiring a theatre site, the company engages a contractor to construct the theatre complex. During the year, the company received a $2 million payment from one such contractor who had built a ten-theatre complex for PFC in Montreal. This payment represents a penalty for not completing the theatre complex on time. Construction began in June Year 6 and was to have been completed by December Year 6. Instead, the complex was not completed until the end of May Year 7.

The company is staging a Canadian version of "Rue St. Jacques," which is to open in November Year 7. The smash-hit musical has been running in Paris for three years and is still playing to sold-out audiences. PFC started receiving advance bookings in November Year 6, and the first 40 weeks of the show's run are completely sold out. As at June 22, Year 7, PFC has already collected $22 million from the advance bookings and invested the cash in interest-bearing securities. It included in revenue $1.7 million of interest collected on the funds received from advance ticket sales. In addition to the substantial investment in advertising for this production ($4 million), the company will have invested $15 million in pre-production costs by November Year 7 and will incur weekly production costs of $250,000 once the show opens.

PFC has retained Media Inc. (Media), a company that specializes in entertainment-related advertising and promotion, to promote PFC's activities. Media bills PFC's corporate office for all advertising and promotion related to PFC's activities. Advertising and promotions have significantly increased this year, in part due to large costs associated with the forthcoming opening of "Rue St. Jacques." Media has billed PFC $12 million this year for advertising and promotion, an increase of $7 million over the preceding year.

PFC has $43 million invested in Government of Canada treasury bills. During the past year, $30 million of these treasury bills were set aside to cover interest and principal obligations on the company's syndicated loan of US$25 million. At the time the loan agreement was signed, PFC entered into a forward contract to buy U.S. dollars for the same amounts as the obligations under the syndicated loan and for the same dates as the obligations came due. PFC considers that in substance the debt has been settled, and as a result, both the treasury bills and the syndicated loan have been removed from the company's balance sheet.

PFC started selling movie theatres a couple of years ago. Each theatre's contribution to long-run operating cash flow is assessed and, if the value of the real estate is greater than the present value of future theatre operating profits, the theatre is sold. In the past, revenue from these sales has been relatively minor, but this year 25% of net income (i.e., $6 million) came from the sale of theatres. Since these sales are considered an ongoing part of the company's operations, proceeds from the sale of theatres are recorded as revenue in the income statement.

On May 31, Year 7, PFC and an unrelated company, Odyssey Inc. (Odyssey), formed a partnership, Phantom. Odyssey contributed $40 million in cash. PFC contributed the assets of its TV production company, which had a carrying amount of $65 million. The $90 million value assigned to PFC's contribution may be adjusted if the net income of Phantom earned between July 1, Year 7, and June 30, Year 8, does not meet expectations. PFC has recorded a gain of $25 million. The partnership agreement states that PFC is permitted to withdraw the $40 million for its own use, and it has done so. As a result, Odyssey has a 45% interest in the partnership and PFC has the remaining 55% interest. The profits are split according to the ownership interests. Although all major operating and financing decisions are discussed by both parties, PFC has the final say in any contentious issues.

PFC's bank operating loan in the amount of $200 million is well within its maximum of $240 million. The loan agreement calls for a maximum debt-to-equity ratio of 2:1, where debt is defined as monetary liabilities. Failure to meet the loan covenant would cause the operating loan to become payable within 30 days. On the May 31, Year 7, interim financial statements, PFC meets the restriction because its debt is $1,490 million while its shareholders' equity is $780 million.

PFC's consolidated income before tax was $147 million for the 11 months ended May 31, Year 7. PFC hopes to maintain its recent trend of reporting a minimum before-tax return on shareholders' equity of 20%.

When you return to the office, you discuss the aforementioned issues with the partner in charge of the PFC audit. She asks you to prepare a report on the accounting implications of the issues you have identified as a result of your meeting. When the accounting for an individual transaction has not been specified, you should indicate how it should be accounted for and the impact that the accounting would have had on the key metric(s).

*(CPA Canada adapted)*[6]

# Case 6-5

............
LO1, 3

Wedding Planners Limited (WP), owned by Anne and François Tremblay, provides wedding planning and related services. WP owns a building (the Pavilion) that has been custom-made for hosting weddings. Usually, WP plans a wedding from start to finish and hosts the wedding day events—photos, ceremony, reception, and dance—in the Pavilion. Anne also owns a janitorial company that is involved in the wedding day events. In addition, François is the majority owner of a disc jockey company that provides music to weddings and receptions. Selected financial information and details on the ownership of the companies are provided in Exhibit II.

You, CPA, work at Olivier & Myriam Chartered Professional Accountants (OM). The Tremblays have come to you because of events that occurred early in Year 6. While at a wedding at the Pavilion, a negligent act by a guest resulted in a lawsuit by other guests. There was no damage to the Pavilion or any WP property. However, since the incident occurred at a WP event, WP was named as one of several defendants in the lawsuit. Anne and François, busy organizing more weddings, were not too concerned. The lawsuit went to court and the judge ruled in favour of the plaintiffs. WP was told to pay $800,000. Somewhat in shock, WP immediately made the payment on September 30, Year 6, and expensed it on the financial statements.

The large cash outflow and financial statement loss eroded WP's financial position to the point that its bank loan was called. WP now has until January 31, Year 7, to repay its $700,000 loan in full to the bank. So far, no other bank approached by WP is willing to loan it money because WP has no collateral to offer beyond the building. However, WP has found a financing company that is willing to provide a short-term loan equivalent to WP's estimated tax refund as well as a three-year term loan.

It is January 15, Year 7. You have been assigned to a team of specialists for this special engagement. A tax specialist will calculate WP's tax refund. A finance specialist will calculate the amount of the term loan WP might require in the next few years as a result of the lawsuit. As you begin your work, the partner on the review engagement of WP provides you with a list of the outstanding accounting issues related to the review engagement (see Exhibit III) and asks you to address them while working on your assignment.

**EXHIBIT II**

### SELECTED FINANCIAL AND OWNERSHIP INFORMATION
### INCOME STATEMENT
For the year ended December 31, Year 6

| | Wedding Planners Ltd. (WP) | J's Janitorial Co. (JJ) | DJ Music Co. (DJ) |
|---|---|---|---|
| Gross margin | $ 707,147 | $ 193,331 | $ 95,525 |
| Selected expenses: | | | |
| Selling and administrative (note 1) | 207,004 | 10,755 | 11,095 |
| Amortization (note 2) | 69,134 | 1,533 | 3,887 |
| Lawsuit judgment | 800,000 | — | — |
| Preliminary net income (loss) | (335,996) | 144,378 | 63,505 |

*(continued)*

**EXHIBIT II** *(continued)*

Notes:

1. All employees are paid through WP. JJ and DJ have no payroll expense.
2. All companies use tax capital cost allowance (CCA) for accounting amortization purposes.
3. WP collects deposits from potential wedding customers. These deposits are recorded in revenue when received. At December 31, Year 5 and Year 6, there was $130,000 and $155,000, respectively, in deposits.

Organizational structure:

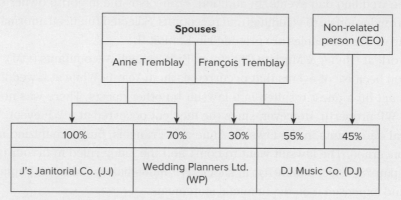

Dividends: During Year 6, JJ paid $70,000 in dividends.

**EXHIBIT III**

### OUTSTANDING ACCOUNTING ISSUES RELATED TO THE REVIEW ENGAGEMENT

#### Champagne

One of the most popular wedding alcohols is champagne. In January Year 4, Anne entered into a five-year fixed-price contract at $360 per case to protect WP against market fluctuations. The champagne bought under the contract is recorded at the fixed price in the financial statements. During Year 6, Anne's decision appeared to be a good one, as the price of champagne continued to go up, hitting a high of $400 per case. However, at December 31, Year 6, the market price of one case of champagne is now down to $336. Anne heard that the price per case is expected to remain at this level or drop a bit more over the next two years. On December 31, Anne triggered the cancellation clause that allows WP to get out of the contract for $60,000. The payment was made January 2, Year 7. WP still has 60 cases on hand that were bought at $360.

As part of WP's efforts to retain good employees, Anne and François started giving deserving employees a case of champagne as a reward for their hard work. Thus far, WP has given away 50 cases. The feedback from the employees has been extremely positive, so Anne and François are planning to formalize the program and give away 10 cases a month. The cost of the champagne given away thus far has been absorbed in cost of sales.

#### Lawsuit Judgment Appeal

WP's lawyer was unhappy with Anne and François for paying the lawsuit without consulting her, and she immediately launched an appeal. She recently sent a letter to WP stating she is positive that the $800,000 judgment against WP will be refunded, with interest, within two to three years, for the following reasons:

- Several breaches of protocol by both the plaintiffs' lawyer and the judge in the original court case have been identified.
- The guest who committed the negligent act, and who had originally left Canada to avoid charges, has returned to Canada.
- There has just been a similar case settled through appeal in a higher Canadian court where the defendant was refunded all of the original damages.

Anne and François have not had the opportunity to think about the repercussions of the letter.

**Intercompany Transactions**

During Year 6, the following transactions occurred between the companies:

- WP sold one of its vehicles, a van, to JJ. The van had a carrying amount of $55,000 and was sold to JJ for its market value of $25,000. The loss on sale has been included in the gross margin of WP.
- JJ provides janitorial services to WP and DJ at its estimated cost. All of JJ's other customers are external and pay full market value for janitorial services. Had WP paid market value for JJ's services in Year 6, its costs would have increased by $50,000.
- Occasionally, DJ requires alcohol for its own events and purchases it from WP at WP's cost. DJ pays around $15,000 per year for the alcohol from WP. This alcohol has a sale value at wedding receptions of $40,000.
- Anne Tremblay is the CEO of WP and JJ. Her salary is paid by WP.
- DJ has a shareholder agreement that states that no cash can be removed from the company without the written consent of all shareholders. The CEO of DJ has stated that he does not want to remove the cash from the company, so François has never broached the matter.

*(CPA Canada adapted)*[7]

# PROBLEMS

## Problem 6-1

LO2

On January 1, Year 2, PAT Ltd. acquired 90% of SAT Inc. when SAT's retained earnings were $1,000,000. There was no acquisition differential. PAT accounts for its investment under the cost method. SAT sells inventory to PAT on a regular basis at a markup of 30% of selling price. The intercompany sales were $160,000 in Year 2 and $190,000 in Year 3. The total amount owing by PAT related to these intercompany sales was $60,000 at the end of Year 2 and $50,000 at the end of Year 3. On January 1, Year 3, the inventory of PAT contained goods purchased from SAT amounting to $70,000, while the December 31, Year 3, inventory contained goods purchased from SAT amounting to $80,000. Both companies pay income tax at the rate of 40%.

Selected account balances from the records of PAT and SAT for the year ended December 31, Year 3, were as follows:

|  | PAT | SAT |
|---|---|---|
| Inventory | $ 510,000 | $ 400,000 |
| Accounts payable | 700,000 | 420,000 |
| Retained earnings, beginning of year | 2,500,000 | 1,200,000 |
| Sales | 4,100,000 | 2,600,000 |
| Cost of sales | 3,200,000 | 1,800,000 |
| Income tax expense | 180,000 | 150,000 |

**Required**

(a) Determine the amount to report on the Year 3 consolidated financial statements for the selected accounts noted above.

(b) Indicate how non-controlling interest on the Year 3 consolidated income statement and Year 3 consolidated balance sheet will be affected by the intercompany transactions noted above.

## Problem 6-2

LO1, 2, 3

The consolidated income statement of a parent and its 90%-owned subsidiary appears below. It was prepared by an accounting student before reading this chapter.

### CONSOLIDATED INCOME STATEMENT

| | |
|---|---:|
| Sales | $500,000 |
| Rental revenue | 24,000 |
| Interest revenue | 50,000 |
| Total revenue | 574,000 |
| Cost of goods sold | 350,000 |
| Rent expense | 24,000 |
| Interest expense | 35,000 |
| Administration expenses | 45,000 |
| Income tax expense | 42,000 |
| Non-controlling interest in profit | 9,000 |
| Total costs and expenses | 505,000 |
| Profit | $ 69,000 |

The following items were overlooked when the statement was prepared:

- The opening inventory of the parent contained an intercompany profit of $5,000. This inventory was sold by the parent during the current year.
- During the year, intercompany sales (at a 30% gross profit rate) were made as follows:

| | |
|---|---:|
| By the parent to the subsidiary | $100,000 |
| By the subsidiary to the parent | 80,000 |

- At the end of the year, half of the items purchased from the parent remained in the inventory of the subsidiary and none of the inventory purchased from the subsidiary remained in the parent's inventory.
- All of the rental revenue and 70% of the interest revenue were intercompany and appeared on the income statement of the parent.
- Assume a 40% rate for income tax.

**Required**

(a) Prepare a correct consolidated income statement.
(b) Use the matching principle to explain the adjustments for unrealized profits on intercompany sales when preparing consolidated financial statements.

## Problem 6-3

LO4

On January 1, Year 1, Spike Ltd. purchased land from outsiders for $200,000. On December 31, Year 1, Pike Co. acquired all of the common shares of Spike. The fair value of Spike's land on this date was $230,000.

On December 31, Year 2, Spike sold its land to Pike for $256,000. On December 31, Year 3, Pike sold the land to an arm's-length party for $280,000.

Both companies use the cost model for valuing their land and pay income tax at the rate of 40%. Assume that any gain on sale of land is fully taxable. The only land owned by these two companies is the land purchased by Spike in Year 1.

**Required**

Determine the account balances for land, gain on sale of land, and income tax on gain for Years 1, 2, and 3 for three sets of financial statements (i.e., separate-entity statements for Pike and Spike and consolidated statements) by completing the following table:

|  | Pike | Spike | Consolidated |
|---|---|---|---|
| December 31, Year 1: | | | |
| Land | | | |
| Gain on sale | | | |
| Income tax on gain | | | |
| December 31, Year 2: | | | |
| Land | | | |
| Gain on sale | | | |
| Income tax on gain | | | |
| December 31, Year 3: | | | |
| Land | | | |
| Gain on sale | | | |
| Income tax on gain | | | |

# Problem 6-4

**LO1, 2, 3, 5**

The income statements for Paste Company and its subsidiaries, Waste Company, and Baste Company were prepared for the year ended December 31, Year 9, and are shown below:

|  | Paste | Waste | Baste |
|---|---|---|---|
| Income | | | |
| Sales | $450,000 | $270,000 | $190,000 |
| Dividend | 43,750 | — | — |
| Rent | — | 130,000 | — |
| Interest | 10,000 | — | — |
| Total income | 503,750 | 400,000 | 190,000 |
| Expenses | | | |
| Cost of sales | 300,000 | 163,000 | 145,000 |
| General and administrative | 93,000 | 48,000 | 29,000 |
| Interest | — | 10,000 | — |
| Income tax | 27,000 | 75,000 | 7,000 |
| Total expenses | 420,000 | 296,000 | 181,000 |
| Profit | $ 83,750 | $104,000 | $ 9,000 |

**Additional Information**

- Paste purchased its 80% interest in Waste on January 1, Year 4. On this date, Waste had a retained earnings balance of $40,000, and the acquisition differential amounting to $15,000 was allocated entirely to plant, with an estimated remaining life of eight years. The plant is used exclusively for manufacturing goods for resale.

- Paste purchased its 75% interest in Baste on December 31, Year 6. On this date, Baste had a retained earnings balance of $80,000. The acquisition differential amounting to $19,000 was allocated to goodwill; however, because Baste had failed to report adequate profits, the goodwill was entirely written off for consolidated purposes by the end of Year 8.
- Paste has established a policy that any intercompany sales will be made at a gross profit rate of 30%.
- On January 1, Year 9, the inventory of Paste contained goods purchased from Waste for $15,000.
- During Year 9, the following intercompany sales took place:

| | |
|---|---|
| Paste to Waste | $ 90,000 |
| Waste to Baste | 170,000 |
| Baste to Paste | 150,000 |

- On December 31, Year 9, the inventories of each of the three companies contained items purchased on an intercompany basis in the following amounts:

| | |
|---|---|
| Paste from Baste | $60,000 |
| Waste from Paste | 22,000 |
| Baste from Waste | 60,000 |

- In addition to its merchandising activities, Waste is in the office equipment rental business. Both Paste and Baste rent office equipment from Waste. General and administrative expenses for Paste and Baste include rent expense of $25,000 and $14,000, respectively.
- During Year 6, Waste paid $10,000 interest to Paste for intercompany advances.
- All of Paste's dividend revenue pertains to its investments in Waste and Baste.
- Retained earnings at December 31, Year 9, for Paste, Waste, and Baste were $703,750, $146,000, and $79,000, respectively.
- Paste Company uses the cost method to account for its investments, and uses tax allocation at a rate of 40% when it prepares consolidated financial statements.

**Required**

(a) Prepare a consolidated income statement for Year 9.

(b) Calculate consolidated retained earnings at December 31, Year 9.

(c) Now assume that Paste is a private company, uses ASPE, and chooses to use the equity method. Calculate its income from investments for Year 9.

(d) Use the criteria for revenue recognition to explain the adjustments for unrealized profits on intercompany sales when preparing consolidated financial statements.

# Problem 6-5

LO2, 4, 5, 6

X Co. acquired 75% of Y Co. on January 1, Year 3, when Y Co. had common shares of $100,000 and retained earnings of $70,000. The acquisition differential was allocated as follows on this date:

| | |
|---|---|
| Inventory | $ 60,000 |
| Equipment (15-year life) | 45,000 |
| Total acquisition differential | $105,000 |

Since this date the following events have occurred:

## Year 3

- Y Co. reported a net income of $130,000 and paid dividends of $25,000.
- On July 3, X Co. sold land to Y Co. for $112,000. This land was carried in the records of X Co. at $75,000.
- On December 31, Year 3, the inventory of X Co. contained an intercompany profit of $30,000.
- X Co. reported a net income of $400,000 from its own operations.

## Year 4

- Y Co. reported a net loss of $16,000 and paid dividends of $5,000.
- Y Co. sold the land that it purchased from X Co. to an unrelated company for $130,000.
- On December 31, Year 4, the inventory of Y Co. contained an intercompany profit of $12,000.
- X Co. reported a net income from its own operations of $72,000.

## Required

Assume a 40% tax rate.

(a) Prepare X Co.'s equity method journal entries subsequent to the date of acquisition for each of Years 3 and 4.
(b) Calculate consolidated net income attributable to X Co.'s shareholders for each of Years 3 and 4.
(c) Prepare a statement showing the changes in non-controlling interest in each of Years 3 and 4.
(d) Now assume that X Co. is a private company, uses ASPE, and chooses to use the equity method. Calculate the balance in the Investment in Y Co. account as at December 31, Year 4.

# Problem 6-6

LO2

L Co. owns a controlling interest in M Co. and Q Co. L Co. purchased an 80% interest in M Co. at a time when M Co. reported retained earnings of $500,000. L Co. purchased a 70% interest in Q Co. at a time when Q Co. reported retained earnings of $50,000. There was no acquisition differential for either of these acquisitions.

An analysis of the changes in retained earnings of the three companies during the current year appears below:

|  | L Co. | M Co. | Q Co. |
|---|---|---|---|
| Retained earnings, beginning of current year | $ 976,000 | $ 843,000 | $682,000 |
| Profit | 580,000 | 360,000 | 240,000 |
| Dividends paid or declared | (250,000) | (200,000) | (150,000) |
| Retained earnings, end of current year | $1,306,000 | $1,003,000 | $772,000 |

Q Co. sells parts to L Co., which after further processing and assembly, are sold by L Co. to M Co., where they become a part of the finished product sold by M Co. Intercompany profits included in raw materials inventories at the beginning and end of the current year are estimated as follows:

|  | Beginning Inventory | Ending Inventory |
|---|---|---|
| On sales from Q to L | $80,000 | $ 35,000 |
| On sales from L to M | 52,000 | 118,000 |

L Co. uses the cost method to account for its investments and income tax allocation at a 40% rate when it prepares consolidated financial statements.

**Required**

(a) Calculate consolidated profit attributable to M Co.'s shareholders for the current year.

(b) Calculate consolidated retained earnings at the beginning of the current year.

# Problem 6-7

LO2, 3, 4, 6

On January 1, Year 3, the Most Company purchased 80% of the outstanding voting shares of the Least Company for $1.6 million in cash. On that date, Least's balance sheet and the fair values of its identifiable assets and liabilities were as follows:

|  | Carrying Value | Fair Value |
|---|---|---|
| Cash | $ 25,000 | $ 25,000 |
| Accounts receivable | 310,000 | 290,000 |
| Inventories | 650,000 | 600,000 |
| Plant and equipment (net) | 2,015,000 | 2,050,000 |
| Total assets | $3,000,000 | |
| Current liabilities | $ 300,000 | 300,000 |
| Long-term liabilities | 1,200,000 | 1,100,000 |
| Common shares | 500,000 | |
| Retained earnings | 1,000,000 | |
| Total liabilities and shareholders' equity | $3,000,000 | |

On January 1, Year 3, Least's plant and equipment had a remaining useful life of 8 years. Its long-term liabilities matured on January 1, Year 7. Goodwill, if any, is to be tested yearly for impairment. The balance sheets as at December 31, Year 9, for the two companies were as follows:

**BALANCE SHEETS**

At December 31, Year 9

|  | Most | Least |
|---|---|---|
| Cash | $ 500,000 | $ 40,000 |
| Accounts receivable | 1,700,000 | 500,000 |
| Inventories | 2,300,000 | 1,200,000 |
| Plant and equipment, net | 8,200,000 | 4,000,000 |
| Investment in Least, at cost | 1,600,000 | — |
| Land | 700,000 | 260,000 |
| Total assets | $15,000,000 | $6,000,000 |
| Current liabilities | $ 600,000 | $ 200,000 |
| Long-term liabilities | 3,000,000 | 3,000,000 |
| Common shares | 1,000,000 | 500,000 |
| Retained earnings | 10,400,000 | 2,300,000 |
| Total liabilities and shareholders' equity | $15,000,000 | $6,000,000 |

**Additional Information**

- The inventories of both companies have a maximum turnover period of one year. Receivables have a maximum turnover period of 62 days.

- On July 1, Year 7, Most sold a parcel of land to Least for $100,000. Most had purchased this land in Year 4 for $150,000. On September 30, Year 9, Least sold the property to another company for $190,000.
- During Year 9, $2 million of Most's sales were to Least. Of these sales, $500,000 remains in the December 31, Year 9, inventories of Least. The December 31, Year 8, inventories of Least contained $312,500 of merchandise purchased from Most. Most's sales to Least are priced to provide it with a gross profit of 20%.
- Most and Least reported net income of $1,000,000 and $400,000, respectively, for Year 9.
- During Year 9, $1.5 million of Least's sales were to Most. Of these sales, $714,280 remains in the December 31, Year 9, inventories of Most. The December 31, Year 8, inventories of Most contained $857,140 of merchandise purchased from Least. Least's sales to Most are priced to provide it with a gross profit of 30%.
- Dividends declared on December 31, Year 9, were as follows:

| | |
|---|---|
| Most | $350,000 |
| Least | 100,000 |

- Goodwill impairment tests resulted in losses of $52,200 in Year 4 and $8,700 in Year 9.
- Assume a 40% tax rate for both companies and that dividends have not yet been paid.

**Required**

(a) Prepare the consolidated statement of changes in equity for Year 9.
(b) Prepare the consolidated balance sheet.
(c) Explain how the cost principle supports the adjustments to inventory when eliminating unrealized profits from intercompany sales from the consolidated financial statements.
(d) If Most had used the parent company extension theory rather than the entity theory, how would this affect the debt-to-equity ratio at the end of Year 9? Briefly explain.

## Problem 6-8

LO2, 5, 6

On January 1, Year 8, Fazli Co. acquired all of the common shares of Gervais. The following transactions occurred in January and February, Year 8:

- On January 10, Gervais purchased $10,000 of inventory from outsiders.
- On January 20, Gervais sold $6,000 of this inventory to Fazli for $7,200, which represents a markup of 20% over cost.
- On January 30, Fazli sold $5,000 of the inventory purchased from Gervais to outsiders for $6,250, which represents a markup of 25% over cost.
- On February 10, Gervais purchased $12,000 of inventory from outsiders.
- On February 20, Gervais sold $9,000 of inventory to Fazli for $10,800, which represents a markup of 20% over cost.
- On February 30, Fazli sold $8,500 of inventory purchased from Gervais to outsiders for $10,625, which represents a markup of 25% over cost.

Fazli uses the cost method to account for its investment in Gervais. Both companies pay income tax at the rate of 40%. Gervais did not pay any dividends in Year 8.

**Required**

(a) Prepare income statements for January and February for Fazli, Gervais, and Consolidation. Break down cost of sales into its three components.

(b) Now assume that Fazli uses the equity method to account for its investment in Gervais. What accounts would change on the three statements in January and what would be the account balance?

(c) Now assume that Fazli only owns 80% of the common shares of Gervais and uses the cost method to account for its investment in Gervais. What accounts would change (as compared to part (a)) on the three statements in January and what would be the account balance?

(d) Now assume that Gervais was the parent, Fazli was the subsidiary, and Gervais owned 80% of Fazli. How would this change the allocation of consolidated net income for January?

## Problem 6-9

LO2, 6

Yosef Corporation acquired 90% of the outstanding voting stock of Randeep Inc. on January 1, Year 6. During Year 6, intercompany sales of inventory of $45,000 (original cost of $27,000) were made. Only 20% of this inventory was still held within the consolidated entity at the end of Year 6 and was sold in Year 7. Intercompany sales of inventory of $60,000 (original cost of $33,000) occurred in Year 7. Of this merchandise, 30% had not been resold to outside parties by the end of the year.

At the end of Year 7, selected figures from the two companies' financial statements were as follows:

|  | Yosef | Randeep |
|---|---|---|
| Inventory | $ 70,000 | $ 45,000 |
| Retained earnings, beginning of year | 500,000 | 300,000 |
| Net income | 150,000 | 55,000 |
| Dividends declared | 50,000 | 20,000 |
| Retained earnings, end of year | 600,000 | 335,000 |

Yosef uses the cost method to account for its investment in Randeep. Both companies pay income tax at the rate of 40%.

**Required**

(a) Assume that all intercompany sales were upstream. Calculate the amount to be reported on the Year 7 consolidated financial statements for the following accounts/items:

(i) Consolidated net income

(ii) Consolidated net income attributable to the controlling and non-controlling interest

(iii) Deferred income tax asset

(iv) Inventory

(v) Net adjustment to retained earnings at beginning of year pertaining to intercompany sales

(vi) Net adjustment to retained earnings at end of year pertaining to intercompany sales

(b) Now, assume that all intercompany sales were downstream. Calculate the amount to be reported on the Year 7 consolidated financial statements for the accounts/items listed in part (a).

# Problem 6-10

LO1, 2

The income statements of Evans Company and Falcon Company for the current year are shown below:

|  | Evans | Falcon |
|---|---|---|
| Sales revenues | $450,000 | $600,000 |
| Dividend revenues | 32,000 | — |
| Rental revenues | 33,600 | — |
| Interest revenues | — | 18,000 |
|  | 515,600 | 618,000 |
| Raw materials and finished goods purchased | 268,000 | 328,000 |
| Changes in inventory | 20,000 | 25,000 |
| Other expenses | 104,000 | 146,000 |
| Interest expense | 30,000 | — |
| Income taxes | 31,700 | 43,500 |
|  | 453,700 | 542,500 |
| Profit | $ 61,900 | $ 75,500 |

The following amounts were taken from the statement of changes in equity for the two companies:

|  | Evans | Falcon |
|---|---|---|
| Retained earnings, beginning of year | $632,000 | $348,000 |
| Dividends declared | 30,000 | 10,000 |

Evans owns 80% of the outstanding common shares of Falcon, purchased at the time the latter company was organized.

Evans sells parts to Falcon at a price that is 25% above cost. Total sales from Evans to Falcon during the year were $90,000. Included in Falcon's inventories were parts purchased from Evans amounting to $21,250 in beginning inventory and $28,750 in the ending inventory.

Falcon sells back to Evans certain finished goods, at a price that gives Falcon an average gross profit of 30% on these intercompany sales. Total sales from Falcon to Evans during the year were $177,000. Included in the inventories of Evans were finished goods acquired from Falcon amounting to $11,000 in beginning inventory and $3,000 in ending inventory.

Falcon rents an office building from Evans and pays $2,800 per month in rent. Evans has borrowed $600,000 through a series of 5% notes, of which Falcon holds $360,000 as notes receivable. Use income tax allocation at a 40% rate.

## Required

(a) Prepare a consolidated income statement with expenses classified by nature.
(b) Calculate retained earnings, beginning of year, and dividends declared for the consolidated statement of changes in equity for the current year.

## Problem 6-11

LO2

The partial trial balances of P Co. and S Co. at December 31, Year 10, were as follows:

|  | P Co. | | S Co. | |
|---|---|---|---|---|
|  | Dr. | Cr. | Dr. | Cr. |
| Investment in S. Co. | 90,000 | | | |
| Common shares | | 150,000 | | 60,000 |
| Retained earnings (charged with dividends, no other changes during the year) | | 101,000 | | 34,000 |

### Additional Information

- The investment in the shares of S Co. (a 90% interest) was acquired January 2, Year 6, for $90,000. At that time, the shareholders' equity of S Co. was common shares of $60,000 and retained earnings of $20,000 and the common shares for P Co. of $150,000.
- Net incomes of the two companies for the year were as follows:

| P Co. | $60,000 |
|---|---|
| S Co. | 48,000 |

- During Year 10, sales of P Co. to S Co. were $10,000, and sales of S Co. to P Co. were $50,000. Rates of gross profit on intercompany sales in Years 9 and 10 were 40% of sales.
- On December 31, Year 9, the inventory of P Co. included $7,000 of merchandise purchased from S Co., and the inventory of S Co. included $3,000 of merchandise purchased from P Co. On December 31, Year 10, the inventory of P Co. included $20,000 of merchandise purchased from S Co. and the inventory of S Co. included $5,000 of merchandise purchased from P Co.
- During the year ended December 31, Year 10, P Co. paid dividends of $12,000 and S Co. paid dividends of $10,000.
- At the time that P Co. purchased the shares of S Co., the acquisition differential was allocated to patents of S Co. These patents are being amortized for consolidation purposes over a period of five years.
- In Year 8, land that originally cost $40,000 was sold by S Co. to P Co. for $50,000. The land is still owned by P Co.
- Assume a corporate tax rate of 40%.

### Required

Prepare a consolidated statement of changes in equity for the year ended December 31, Year 10.

## Problem 6-12

LO1, 2, 5, 6

On January 2, Year 5, Road Ltd. acquired 70% of the outstanding voting shares of Runner Ltd. The acquisition differential of $520,000 on that date was allocated in the following manner:

| Inventory | $160,000 | |
|---|---|---|
| Land | 110,000 | |
| Plant and equipment | 120,000 | Estimated life 5 years |
| Patent | 40,000 | Estimated life 8 years |
| Goodwill | 90,000 | |
| | $520,000 | |

The Year 9 income statements for the two companies were as follows:

| | Road | Runner |
|---|---|---|
| Sales | $4,600,000 | $2,160,000 |
| Intercompany investment income | 206,500 | — |
| Rental revenue | — | 190,000 |
| Total income | 4,806,500 | 2,350,000 |
| Materials used in manufacturing | 2,300,000 | 860,000 |
| Changes in work-in-progress and finished goods inventory | 105,000 | (10,000) |
| Employee benefits | 610,000 | 540,000 |
| Interest expense | 310,000 | 200,000 |
| Depreciation | 465,000 | 275,000 |
| Patent amortization | — | 55,000 |
| Rental expense | 95,000 | — |
| Income tax | 360,000 | 191,200 |
| Total expenses | 4,205,000 | 2,111,200 |
| Profit | $ 561,500 | $ 238,800 |

### Additional Information

- Runner regularly sells raw materials to Road. Intercompany sales in Year 9 totalled $480,000.
- Intercompany profits in the inventories of Road were as follows:

| | |
|---|---|
| January 1, Year 9 | $247,000 |
| December 31, Year 9 | 100,000 |

- Road's entire rental expense relates to equipment rented from Runner.
- A goodwill impairment loss of $3,000 occurred in Year 9.
- Retained earnings at December 31, Year 9, for Road and Runner were $2,523,300 and $1,210,000, respectively.
- Road uses the equity method to account for its investment, and uses income tax allocation at the rate of 40% when it prepares consolidated statements.

### Required

(a) Prepare a consolidated income statement for Year 9 with expenses classified by nature.
(b) Calculate consolidated retained earnings at December 31, Year 9.
(c) If Road had used parent company extension theory rather than entity theory, how would this affect the return on equity attributable to shareholders of Road for Year 9? Briefly explain.

## Problem 6-13

LO1, 2, 4, 6

The financial statements of Post Corporation and its subsidiary, Sage Company, as at December 31, Year 6 are presented on the next page.

### Additional Information

- Post purchased 70% of the outstanding shares of Sage on January 1, Year 4, at a cost of $84,000. On that date, Sage had accumulated depreciation of $13,000, retained earnings of $18,000, and fair values were equal to carrying amounts for all its net assets, except inventory (overvalued by $15,000).

## STATEMENTS OF FINANCIAL POSITION
### December 31, Year 6

| | Post | Sage |
|---|---|---|
| Land | $178,000 | $ 22,000 |
| Plant and equipment | 529,000 | 64,000 |
| Accumulated depreciation | (233,000) | (20,000) |
| Investment in Sage | 129,227 | — |
| Inventory | 34,000 | 30,000 |
| Notes receivable | — | 54,000 |
| Accounts receivable | 17,500 | 10,200 |
| Cash | 12,500 | 13,200 |
| | $667,227 | $173,400 |
| Ordinary shares | $100,000 | $ 50,000 |
| Retained earnings | 266,200 | 89,000 |
| Notes payable | 54,000 | — |
| Accounts payable | 247,027 | 34,400 |
| | $667,227 | $173,400 |

## STATEMENTS OF PROFIT—YEAR 6

| | Post | Sage |
|---|---|---|
| Sales | $930,000 | $259,000 |
| Management fee revenue | 27,000 | — |
| Interest revenue | — | 7,100 |
| Equity method income from Sage | 2,100 | — |
| Gain on sale of land | — | 34,000 |
| | 959,100 | 300,100 |
| Cost of goods sold | 570,000 | 182,000 |
| Interest expense | 20,300 | — |
| Other expenses | 183,000 | 75,100 |
| Income tax expense | 83,000 | 16,000 |
| | 856,300 | 273,100 |
| Profit | $102,800 | $ 27,000 |

## Additional Information (continued)

- In determining the purchase price, the management of Post noted that Sage, as lessee, leases a warehouse under an operating lease that has terms that are unfavourable relative to market terms. However, t he lease agreement explicitly prohibits transfer of the lease (through either sale or sublease). An independent appraiser indicated that the fair value of this unfavourable lease agreement is $21,000. There were five years remaining on this lease on the date of acquisition.
- The companies sell merchandise to each other at a gross profit rate of 25%.
- The December 31, Year 5, inventory of Post contained purchases made from Sage amounting to $17,000. There were no intercompany purchases in the inventory of Sage on this date.
- During Year 6 the following intercompany transactions took place:
  - Sage made a payment of $27,000 to Post for management fees, which was recorded under the category "other expenses."

- Sage made sales of $102,000 to Post. The December 31, Year 6, inventory of Post contained goods purchased from Sage amounting to $30,000. ✗
- Post made sales of $130,000 to Sage. The December 31, Year 6, inventory of Sage contained goods purchased from Post amounting to $21,000. ✗
- On July 1, Year 6, Post borrowed $54,000 from Sage and signed a note bearing interest at 12% per annum. The interest on this note was paid on December 31, Year 6.
- During the year, Sage sold land to Post and recorded a gain of $34,000 on the transaction. This land is being held by Post on December 31, Year 6. ✗
- Goodwill impairment losses occurred as follows: Year 4, $2,700; Year 5, $540; Year 6, $1,350. ✗
- Neither Post nor Sage paid any dividends during the year. ✗ − Post paid 15,000
- Post uses the equity method to account for its investment in Sage.
- Both companies pay income tax at 40% on their taxable incomes.

**Required**

(a) Prepare the following consolidated financial statements for Year 6:
  (i) Income statement
  (ii) Statement of financial position
(b) Calculate goodwill impairment loss and profit attributable to non-controlling interest for the year ended December 31, Year 6, under parent company extension theory.
(c) Calculate goodwill and non-controlling interest on the consolidated statement of financial position at December 31, Year 6, under parent company extension theory.
(d) Prepare the consolidated financial statements using the worksheet approach.

*eXcel*

## Problem 6-14

LO1, 2, 4, 6

On January 1, Year 7, the Vine Company purchased 60,000 of the 80,000 ordinary shares of the Devine Company for $80 per share. On that date, Devine had ordinary shares of $3,440,000, and retained earnings of $2,170,000. When acquired, Devine had inventories with fair values $300,000 less than carrying amount, a parcel of land with a fair value $270,000 greater than the carrying amount, and equipment with a fair value $270,000 less than carrying amount. There were also internally generated patents with an estimated market value of $470,000 and a five-year remaining life. A long-term liability had a market value $170,000 greater than carrying amount; this liability was paid off December 31, Year 10. All other identifiable assets and liabilities of Devine had fair values equal to their carrying amounts. Devine's accumulated depreciation on the plant and equipment was $570,000 at the date of acquisition.

At the acquisition date, the equipment had an expected remaining useful life of ten years. Both companies use the straight-line method for all depreciation and amortization calculations and the FIFO inventory cost flow assumption. Assume a 40% income tax rate on all applicable items and that there were no impairment losses for goodwill.

On September 1, Year 11, Devine sold a parcel of land to Vine and recorded a total non-operating gain of $470,000.

Sales of finished goods from Vine to Devine totalled $1,070,000 in Year 10 and $2,070,000 in Year 11. These sales were priced to provide a gross profit margin on selling price of 33⅓% to the Vine

Company. Devine's December 31, Year 10, inventory contained $321,000 of these sales; December 31, Year 11, inventory contained $621,000 of these sales.

Sales of finished goods from Devine to Vine were $870,000 in Year 10 and $1,270,000 in Year 11. These sales were priced to provide a gross profit margin on selling price of 40% to the Devine Company. Vine's December 31, Year 10, inventory contained $170,000 of these sales; the December 31, Year 11, inventory contained $570,000 of these sales.

Vine's investment in Devine's account is carried in accordance with the cost method and includes advances to Devine of $270,000, which are also included in current liabilities.

There are no intercompany amounts other than those noted, except for the dividends of $500,000 (total amount) declared and paid by Devine.

## INCOME STATEMENTS
### For year ending December 31, Year 11
(in thousands of dollars)

|  | Vine | Devine |
|---|---|---|
| Sales | $13,000 | $4,400 |
| Dividends, investment income, and gains | 1,800 | 2,400 |
| Total income | 14,800 | 6,800 |
| Cost of goods sold | 10,100 | 2,900 |
| Other expenses | 500 | 500 |
| Income taxes | 200 | 200 |
| Total expenses | 10,800 | 3,600 |
| Profit | $ 4,000 | $3,200 |

## STATEMENTS OF FINANCIAL POSITION
### December 31, Year 11
(in thousands of dollars)

|  | Vine | Devine |
|---|---|---|
| Land | $ 6,000 | $ 2,500 |
| Plant and equipment | 20,200 | 13,200 |
| Accumulated depreciation | (4,400) | (3,600) |
| Investment in Devine, cost | 5,070 |  |
| Inventories | 6,000 | 3,800 |
| Cash and current receivables | 2,360 | 1,700 |
| Total assets | $35,230 | $17,600 |
| Ordinary shares | $10,000 | $ 3,440 |
| Retained earnings | 10,600 | 5,600 |
| Long-term liabilities | 8,000 | 2,500 |
| Deferred income taxes | 1,600 | 100 |
| Current liabilities | 5,030 | 5,960 |
| Total equity and liabilities | $35,230 | $17,600 |

## Required

(a) Show the allocation of the acquisition cost at acquisition and the related amortization schedule. Show and label all calculations.

(b) Prepare a consolidated income statement with expenses classified by function.

(c) Calculate consolidated retained earnings at December 31, Year 11.

(d) Prepare a consolidated statement of financial position for Vine Company at December 31, Year 11.

(e) Assume that Devine's shares were trading at $75 per share shortly before and after the date of acquisition, and that this data was used to value non-controlling interest at the date of acquisition. Calculate goodwill and non-controlling interest at December 31, Year 11.

(f) Prepare the consolidated financial statements using the worksheet approach.

*eXcel*

*(Adapted from a problem prepared by Peter Secord, St. Mary's University)*

## Problem 6-15

LO1, 2, 4, 5, 6

Paper Corp. purchased 70% of the outstanding shares of Sand Ltd. on January 1, Year 2, at a cost of $84,000. Paper has always used the equity method to account for its investments. On January 1, Year 2, Sand had common shares of $50,000 and retained earnings of $30,000, and fair values were equal to carrying amounts for all its net assets, except inventory (fair value was $9,000 less than carrying amount) and equipment (fair value was $24,000 greater than carrying amount). The equipment, which is used for research, had an estimated remaining life of six years on January 1, Year 2.

The following are the financial statements of Paper Corp. and its subsidiary Sand Ltd. as at December 31, Year 5:

**BALANCE SHEETS**

At December 31, Year 5

|  | Paper | Sand |
|---|---|---|
| Cash | $ — | $ 10,000 |
| Accounts receivable | 36,000 | 30,000 |
| Note receivable | — | 40,000 |
| Inventory | 66,000 | 44,000 |
| Equipment, net | 220,000 | 76,000 |
| Land | 155,000 | 30,000 |
| Investment in Sand | 112,350 | — |
|  | $589,350 | $230,000 |
| Bank indebtedness | $ 90,000 | $ — |
| Accounts payable | 50,000 | 60,000 |
| Notes payable | 45,000 | — |
| Common shares | 150,000 | 50,000 |
| Retained earnings | 254,350 | 120,000 |
|  | $589,350 | $230,000 |

*(continued)*

*(continued)*

**INCOME STATEMENTS**

For the year ended December 31, Year 5

|  | Paper | Sand |
|---|---|---|
| Sales | $798,000 | $300,000 |
| Management fee revenue | 24,000 | — |
| Equity method income from Sand | 1,050 | — |
| Interest income | — | 3,600 |
| Gain on sale of land | — | 20,000 |
|  | 823,050 | 323,600 |
| Cost of sales | 480,000 | 200,000 |
| Research and development expenses | 40,000 | 12,000 |
| Interest expense | 10,000 | — |
| Miscellaneous expenses | 106,000 | 31,600 |
| Income taxes | 80,000 | 32,000 |
|  | 716,000 | 275,600 |
| Net income | $107,050 | $ 48,000 |

## Additional Information

- During Year 5, Sand made a cash payment of $2,000 per month to Paper for management fees, which is included in Sand's "Miscellaneous expenses."

- During Year 5, Paper made intercompany sales of $100,000 to Sand. The December 31, Year 5, inventory of Sand contained goods purchased from Paper amounting to $30,000. These sales had a gross profit of 35%.

- On April 1, Year 5, Paper acquired land from Sand for $45,000. This land had been recorded on Sand's books at a carrying amount of $20,000. Paper paid for the land by signing a $45,000 note payable to Sand, bearing yearly interest at 8%. Interest for Year 5 was paid by Paper in cash on December 31, Year 5. This land was still being held by Paper on December 31, Year 5.

- The fair value of consolidated goodwill remained unchanged from January 1, Year 5 to July Year 5. On July 1, Year 5, a valuation was performed, indicating that the recoverable amount of consolidated goodwill was $3,500.

- During the year ended December 31, Year 5, Paper paid dividends of $80,000 and Sand paid dividends of $20,000.

- Sand and Paper pay taxes at a 40% rate. Assume that none of the gains or losses were capital gains or losses.

## Required

(a) Prepare, in good form, a calculation of goodwill and any unamortized acquisition differential as of December 31, Year 5.

(b) Prepare Paper's consolidated income statement for the year ended December 31, Year 5, with expenses classified by function.

(c) Calculate the following balances that would appear on Paper's consolidated balance sheet as at December 31, Year 5:

   (i) Inventory

   (ii) Land

   (iii) Notes payable

(iv) Non-controlling interest

(v) Common shares

(d) Assume that an independent business valuator valued the non-controlling interest at $30,000 at the date of acquisition. Calculate goodwill impairment loss and profit attributable to non-controlling interest for the year ended December 31, Year 5.

*(CGA Canada adapted)*[8]

# Endnotes

1   SEDAR Filings, http://sedar.com/GetFile.do?lang=EN& docClass=5&issuerNo=00000326&fileName=/csfsprod/ data150/filings/02318340/00000001/x%3A%5CASedar% 5C2015%5CBCE%5CAFS%5CAnnFinStatEng.pdf, p. 129.

2   Intercompany losses are not eliminated when the assets are impaired. This situation will be discussed later in this chapter.

3   The use of a contra account is optional. Companies could record the adjustment to fair value directly in the land account. If so, they would lose track of the original cost in the general ledger. The company could use a property, plant, and equipment subledger to track the necessary information.

4   Adapted from *CICA UFE Report*, 1990-II-1, with permission. Chartered Professional Accountants of Canada, Toronto, Canada. Any changes to the original material are the sole responsibility of the author (and/or publisher) and have not been reviewed or endorsed by the Chartered Professional Accountants of Canada.

5   Adapted from *CICA UFE Report*, 1991-II-2, with permission. Chartered Professional Accountants of Canada, Toronto, Canada. Any changes to the original material are the sole

responsibility of the author (and/or publisher) and have not been reviewed or endorsed by the Chartered Professional Accountants of Canada.

6   Adapted from *CICA UFE Report*, 1997-III-4, with permission. Chartered Professional Accountants of Canada, Toronto, Canada. Any changes to the original material are the sole responsibility of the author (and/or publisher) and have not been reviewed or endorsed by the Chartered Professional Accountants of Canada.

7   Adapted from *CICA UFE Report*, 1997-II-1, with permission. Chartered Professional Accountants of Canada, Toronto, Canada. Any changes to the original material are the sole responsibility of the author (and/or publisher) and have not been reviewed or endorsed by the Chartered Professional Accountants of Canada.

8   Adapted from CGA Canada's FA4 Exam, June 2003, Q5, with permission Chartered Professional Accountants of Canada, Toronto, Canada. Any changes to the original material are the sole responsibility of the author (and/or publisher) and have not been reviewed or endorsed by the Chartered Professional Accountants of Canada.

# CHAPTER 7

# (A) Intercompany Profits in Depreciable Assets (B) Intercompany Bondholdings

## LEARNING OBJECTIVES

**After studying this chapter, you should be able to do the following:**

**LO1** Prepare consolidated financial statements that reflect the elimination and subsequent realization of upstream and downstream intercompany profits in depreciable assets.

**LO2** Explain how the historical cost principle supports the elimination of unrealized profits resulting from intercompany transactions when preparing consolidated financial statements.

**LO3** Prepare the journal entries under the equity method to reflect the elimination and subsequent realization of intercompany profits in depreciable assets.

**LO4** Analyze and interpret financial statements with intercompany transactions involving depreciable assets.

**LO5** Calculate the gain or loss that results from the elimination of intercompany bondholdings and the allocation of such gain or loss to the equities of the controlling and non-controlling interests.

**LO6** Explain how the recognition of gains on the elimination of intercompany bondholdings is consistent with the principle of recording gains only when they are realized.

**LO7** Prepare consolidated financial statements that reflect the gains or losses that are the result of intercompany bondholdings.

**LO8** (Appendix 7A) Prepare consolidated financial statements when depreciable assets are remeasured to fair value each period.

# Introduction

The elimination of intercompany transactions and unrealized profit is one of the most significant problems encountered in the consolidation process. The volume of transfers within most large enterprises can be quite large. For example, Suncor Energy Inc., Canada's largest integrated energy company, reported intersegment revenue of $4,473 million in 2014,[1] which represented 11.2% of total revenues.

In this chapter, we complete our examination of intercompany profits in assets. We also examine the consolidation issues that arise from intercompany bondholdings. Because these transactions are so distinctly different in their impact on the consolidated statements, this chapter is divided into two parts.

**Part (A)** looks at the elimination and realization of intercompany profits (losses) in depreciable assets. The concepts involved in the holdback of profits (losses) are similar to those examined previously with regard to intercompany land profits (losses), but the realization concepts are different because they are based on consumption rather than a sale.

**Part (B)** examines the gains (losses) that are created in the consolidated financial statements when intercompany bondholdings are eliminated.

# LO1 (A) INTERCOMPANY PROFITS IN DEPRECIABLE ASSETS

## Holdback and Realization—Year 4

In Chapter 6, we illustrated the holdback of an intercompany profit in inventory and land. In both cases, the before-tax profit of $300 and the corresponding income tax of $120 were held back in the year of the intercompany transaction and realized in the year that the asset was sold to outsiders. In both cases, the profit was eventually recognized in both the financial statements of the individual companies and the consolidated financial statements. Only the timing of the recognition was different. We will now examine the holdback and the realization in the consolidated statements of an intercompany profit in a depreciable asset.

---

*Profit is recognized when the goods are sold to outsiders.*

---

We return to the Chapter 6 example of Parent Company and its 90%-owned subsidiary, Sub Inc. The Year 4 financial statements of the two companies are shown in Exhibit 7.1. Parent has used the cost method to account for its investment.

**EXHIBIT 7.1**

**INCOME STATEMENTS**
For Year 4

| | Parent | Sub |
|---|---|---|
| Sales | $20,000 | $7,700 |
| Gain on sale of equipment | — | 300 |
| | 20,000 | 8,000 |
| Depreciation expense | 600 | — |
| Miscellaneous expenses | 13,800 | 5,200 |
| Income tax expense | 2,200 | 1,100 |
| | 16,600 | 6,300 |
| Net income | $ 3,400 | $1,700 |

*The gain on sale is recorded on the separate-entity books of Sub.*

*(continued)*

**EXHIBIT 7.1**   *(continued)*

### RETAINED EARNINGS STATEMENTS
For Year 4

|  | Parent | Sub |
|---|---|---|
| Balance, January 1 | $12,000 | $ 4,500 |
| Net income | 3,400 | 1,700 |
|  | 15,400 | 6,200 |
| Dividends | 2,000 | — |
| Balance, December 31 | $13,400 | $ 6,200 |

### BALANCE SHEETS
At December 31, Year 4

|  | Parent | Sub |
|---|---|---|
| Miscellaneous assets | $27,950 | $23,200 |
| Equipment | 1,800 | — |
| Accumulated depreciation | (600) | — |
| Investment in Sub Inc. | 11,250 | — |
|  | $40,400 | $23,200 |
| Liabilities | $12,000 | $ 9,000 |
| Common shares | 15,000 | 8,000 |
| Retained earnings | 13,400 | 6,200 |
|  | $40,400 | $23,200 |

> *The equipment is recorded at the parent's cost on the separate-entity books of Parent.*

Note that although the net incomes and total assets of the two companies are unchanged from the Chapter 6 example, the details on each statement have been changed so that we can focus on the following intercompany transaction involving equipment that occurred during the year. On January 1, Year 4, Sub sold highly specialized equipment with a very short useful life to Parent and recorded a profit of $300 on the transaction. We are assuming that Sub purchased this equipment for $1,500 on this date with the intention of using it, but instead immediately sold it to Parent for $1,800. The two companies recorded this intercompany transaction in the following manner:

| Parent Company | | | Sub Inc. | | |
|---|---|---|---|---|---|
| Equipment | 1,800 | | Cash | 1,800 | |
| Cash | | 1,800 | Equipment | | 1,500 |
| | | | Gain on sale of equipment | | 300 |

It is also assumed that this transaction was not a capital gain for tax purposes, and that Sub's tax rate is 40%. This means that Sub paid $120 (40% × $300) income tax on this profit. We further assume that this is the only depreciable asset held by either company and that the equipment is expected to have a remaining useful life of three years. On December 31, Year 4, Parent recorded depreciation expense on this equipment in the following manner:

| Depreciation expense | 600 | |
|---|---|---|
| Accumulated depreciation | | 600 |
| To record depreciation for the year (1,800 ÷ 3 = 600) | | |

> *The parent's depreciation expense is based on the parent's cost of the equipment.*

**LO2** It should be noted that if Sub had sold the equipment at its cost, Parent's Year 4 depreciation expense would have been $500 ($1,500 ÷ 3). This is the amount of depreciation expense that should appear in the income statement of the consolidated entity (i.e., in the consolidated income statement) for Year 4 in that it represents depreciation based on the historical cost of the equipment to the consolidated entity.

---

*The cost of the equipment to the combined economic entity was $1,500.*

---

When we examine the separate income statements of the two companies (see Exhibit 7.1), it should be obvious that the $300 gain is not a gain from a combined entity point of view and that the $600 depreciation expense does not represent historical cost depreciation to the entity. Two adjustments need to be made when the Year 4 consolidated income statement is prepared; these have opposite effects on the before-tax income of the entity. The first adjustment eliminates the gain on sale of equipment recorded on January 1, Year 4, because as of that date the gain is unrealized from the combined entity point of view. This adjustment reduces before-tax income by $300 and holds back this profit for consolidation purposes. A corresponding reduction of $120 should be made to income tax expense so that a net after-tax gain of $180 is held back. This concept is similar in all respects to the holdback of the land gain that was illustrated in Chapter 6.

The second adjustment reduces depreciation expense by $100 ($300 ÷ 3). The amount of the reduction represents the depreciation taken in Year 4 on this $300 gain and results in a consolidated depreciation expense of $500 based on historical cost, as required. This reduction of depreciation expense increases the before-tax income of the entity by $100. In other words, the parent uses the equipment to carry out its business of selling goods or providing services to its customers. Even though the equipment is not sold to outsiders, the products or services are sold to outsiders. Therefore, the gain from the intercompany sale of the equipment is realized over the remaining life of the equipment as the parent uses it to produce goods or provide services for outsiders. This concept bases the realization of the gain on the consumption (by depreciation) of the asset containing the unrealized gain. A corresponding increase of $40 should be made to income tax expense, to match the tax with the portion of the gain realized. The result will be a net after-tax realization of $60 for consolidation purposes.

---

*The depreciation expense for the combined economic entity was $500.*

---

The net effect of the two after-tax adjustments results in the entity's Year 4 net income being reduced by $120 ($180 − $60). Because Sub was the selling company, this $120 reduction is allocated to the noncontrolling and controlling interests in the same manner as was illustrated in Chapter 6.

The preceding paragraphs have briefly outlined the concepts involved in the holdback and realization of an intercompany gain in a depreciable fixed asset. We will now apply these concepts by preparing the Year 4 consolidated financial statements of Parent using the direct approach. It is useful to start by preparing the three calculations shown in Exhibit 7.2.

It should be noted that the calculation of consolidated net income attributable to the parent is made to adjust the net income of the parent from the cost method to the equity method. If the parent had used the equity method, we would still have to adjust for unrealized profits from intercompany transactions.

**EXHIBIT 7.2**

### EQUIPMENT GAIN—SUB INC. SELLING[2]

| | Before Tax | 40% Tax | After Tax | |
|---|---|---|---|---|
| Unrealized gain, January 1, Year 4 | $300 | $120 | $ 180 | (a) |
| Less realized by depreciation for Year 4 | 100 | 40 | 60 | (b) |
| Balance, unrealized at Dec. 31, Year 4 | $200 | $ 80 | $ 120 | (c) |

> *This is an upstream transaction, since Sub sold to Parent.*

### CALCULATION OF CONSOLIDATED NET INCOME
#### For Year 4

| | | |
|---|---|---|
| Net income—Parent Co. | | $ 3,400 |
| Net income—Sub Inc. | 1,700 | |
| Less unrealized gain on sale of equipment[3] (2a) | 180 | |
| | 1,520 | |
| Add realized gain through use of equipment (2b) | 60 | |
| Adjusted net income—Sub Inc. | | 1,580 |
| Consolidated net income | | $ 4,980 |
| Attributable to: | | |
| Shareholders of Parent | | $ 4,822 (d) |
| Non-controlling interest (10% × 1,580) | | 158 (e) |

> *Sub's income is adjusted for both the unrealized gain and the realization of the gain through use by Parent.*

### CALCULATION OF NON-CONTROLLING INTEREST
#### At December 31, Year 4

| | |
|---|---|
| Shareholders' equity—Sub Inc. | |
| Common shares | $ 8,000 |
| Retained earnings | 6,200 |
| | 14,200 |
| Less unrealized gain on sale of equipment (2c) | 120 |
| Adjusted shareholders' equity | 14,080 |
| Non-controlling interest's share | 10% |
| | $ 1,408 (f) |

> *Non-controlling interest is affected by unrealized and realized profits on upstream transactions.*

Exhibit 7.3 illustrates the preparation of the consolidated financial statements using the direct approach. The consolidated income statement was prepared by combining, line by line, the revenues and expenses of the two companies. The amount for non-controlling interest is based on the *adjusted income* of Sub. The intercompany eliminations are shown in the exhibit in boldface and are summarized as follows:

**EXHIBIT 7.3**

### YEAR 4 CONSOLIDATED STATEMENTS
### ADJUSTED FOR INTERCOMPANY EQUIPMENT PROFIT
(direct approach)
### PARENT COMPANY
### CONSOLIDATED INCOME STATEMENT
For the year ended December 31, Year 4

| | |
|---|---:|
| Sales (20,000 + 7,700) | $27,700 |
| Gain on sale of equipment (0 + 300 − **[2a] 300**) | –0– |
| | 27,700 |
| | |
| Depreciation expense (600 + 0 − **[2b] 100**) | 500 |
| Miscellaneous expenses (13,800 + 5,200) | 19,000 |
| Income tax expense (2,200 + 1,100 − **[2a] 120** + **[2b] 40**) | 3,220 |
| | 22,720 |
| | |
| Net income | $ 4,980 |
| Attributable to: | |
| Shareholders of Parent **(2d)** | $ 4,822 |
| Non-controlling interest **(2e)** | 158 |

> *Income tax expense is matched to the income of the consolidated entity.*

### PARENT COMPANY
### CONSOLIDATED RETAINED EARNINGS STATEMENT
For the year ended December 31, Year 4

| | |
|---|---:|
| Balance, January 1 | $12,000 |
| Net income | 4,822 |
| | 16,822 |
| Dividends | 2,000 |
| Balance, December 31 | $14,822 |

### PARENT COMPANY
### CONSOLIDATED BALANCE SHEET
At December 31, Year 4

| | |
|---|---:|
| Miscellaneous assets (27,950 + 23,200) | $51,150 |
| Equipment (1,800 + 0 − **[2a] 300**) | 1,500 |
| Accumulated depreciation (600 + 0 − **[2b] 100**) | (500) |
| Deferred income taxes (0 + 0 + **[2a] 120** − **[2b] 40**) | 80 |
| | $52,230 |
| | |
| Liabilities (12,000 + 9,000) | $21,000 |
| Common shares | 15,000 |
| Retained earnings | 14,822 |
| Non-controlling interest **(2f)** | 1,408 |
| | $52,230 |

> *The equipment is reported at its cost when it was purchased from outsiders.*

(i) The $300 gain on sale of the equipment and the income tax expense for the tax on this gain are eliminated. The net effect is to reduce the after-tax income of the entity by $180.

(ii) The excess depreciation to the consolidated entity in Year 4 is eliminated. Consolidated depreciation is now based on historical cost. Because this elimination results in a realization of $100 of the original gain, income tax expense is increased by $40 to match the tax with the gain realized. The net result is an after-tax realization of $60.

The two eliminations decreased the entity's net income by $120, which was allocated to the two equities as follows:

| | |
|---|---|
| To non-controlling interest (10% × 120) | $ 12 |
| To controlling interest (90% × 120) | 108 |
| | $120 |

The consolidated retained earnings statement has been prepared in the normal manner. Because we are consolidating one year after acquisition, consolidated retained earnings at the beginning of the year are equal to the parent's retained earnings on that date.

The consolidated balance sheet was prepared by combining the assets and liabilities of the two companies and by making the following adjustments (shown in Exhibit 7.3 in boldface) for the equipment gain:

(i) When the before-tax gain of $300 is removed from the equipment, the resulting balance of $1,500 represents the original cost to the entity. The $120 increase to deferred income taxes represents the tax on this gain and corresponds to the reduction of tax expense in the income statement.

(ii) The excess depreciation taken by the parent is removed from accumulated depreciation. The resulting amount ($500) is the accumulated depreciation on the original cost. The $40 decrease to deferred income taxes corresponds to the increase in income tax expense made in the income statement.

---

*The tax paid on the unrealized profits represents a prepayment from a consolidated viewpoint.*

*Accumulated depreciation is based on the original cost to the consolidated entity.*

---

Note that the $200 reduction of the carrying amount of the equipment ($300 − $100), together with an increase in deferred income taxes of $80 (40% × $200), results in total consolidated assets being reduced by $120, which corresponds to the reduction made to the entity's net income in the consolidated income statement. The fact that this reduction was allocated to the two equities was noted above.

## LO3 Equity Method Journal Entries

Our example has assumed that Parent uses the cost method to account for its investment. If Parent were using the equity method, the following journal entries would be made on December 31, Year 4:

| | | |
|---|---|---|
| Investment in Sub Inc. | 1,530 | |
| Equity method income | | 1,530 |

90% of the net income of Sub Inc. (90% × 1,700 = 1,530)

| | | |
|---|---|---|
| Equity method income | 162 | |
| Investment in Sub Inc. | | 162 |

To hold back 90% of the after-tax equipment profit recorded by Sub
(90% × 180 = 162)

| | | |
|---|---|---|
| Investment in Sub Inc. | 54 | |
| Equity method income | | 54 |

To realize 90% of the after-tax profit realized by depreciation (90% × 60 = 54)

---

*The equity method captures the net effect of all consolidation entries.*

---

After these entries are posted, the two related equity method accounts of Parent would show the following changes and balances:

| | Investment in Sub Inc. | Equity Method Income |
|---|---|---|
| Balance, January 1, Year 4 | $11,250 | |
| Income from Sub Inc. | 1,530 | $1,530 |
| Equipment profit held back | (162) | (162) |
| Equipment profit realized | 54 | 54 |
| Balance, December 31, Year 4 | $12,672 | $1,422 |

---

*The investment account is a balance sheet account at the end of the year, whereas equity method income is an income statement account for one period of time.*

---

Parent's total income under the equity method would be $4,822, consisting of $3,400 from its own operations as reported in Exhibit 7.1 plus equity method income of $1,422 as reported above. This income of $4,822 should be and is equal to consolidated net income attributable to the parent.

---

*The parent's income under the equity method should be equal to consolidated net income attributable to the parent.*

---

**DOWNSTREAM TRANSACTION** If the sale of equipment had been from the parent to the subsidiary—a downstream transaction—the consolidated net income would be the same as before. The elimination of after-tax unrealized profits of $180 and subsequent realization of after-tax profit of $60 would be charged and credited, respectively, entirely to the parent. The non-controlling interest would not have been charged anything for the consolidation adjustments. Therefore, consolidated net income attributable to non-controlling interest would increase by $12 from $158 to $170. The consolidated net income attributable to the parent's shareholders and the parent's net income under the equity method would decrease by $12 (from $4,822 to $4,810) to offset the increase to the non-controlling interest.

## LO4 ANALYSIS AND INTERPRETATION OF FINANCIAL STATEMENTS

In this chapter, we prepared consolidated financial statements where there were unrealized profits from the intercompany sale of depreciable assets. The elimination entries were made on the consolidated financial statements. The net effect of the consolidation adjustments was captured in the parent's internal records when the parent used the equity method.

Exhibit 7.4 presents selected accounts from the Year 4 separate entity and consolidated financial statements that were developed for the intercompany transactions involving equipment. The first three columns present the statements when the intercompany transactions were upstream. In the last three columns, the intercompany transactions were downstream.

### EXHIBIT 7.4

## Impact of Presentation Method on Debt-to-Equity and Return-on-Equity Ratios

### INCOME STATEMENTS, SELECTED ACCOUNTS
For the year ended December 31, Year 4

|  | Upstream Transaction | | | Downstream Transaction | | |
|---|---|---|---|---|---|---|
|  | Parent Cost | Parent Equity | Consol. | Parent Cost | Parent Equity | Consol. |
| Equity method income | $    0 | $ 1,422 | $    0 | $    0 | $ 1,410 | $    0 |
| Net income | 3,400 | 4,822 | 4,980 | 3,400 | 4,810 | 4,980 |
| Attributable to: |  |  |  |  |  |  |
| Shareholders of Parent |  |  | $ 4,822 |  |  | $ 4,810 |
| Non-controlling interest |  |  | 158 |  |  | 170 |

> *The net income for the parent's separate-entity income statement under the equity method is equal to consolidated net income attributable to the shareholders of the parent.*

### BALANCE SHEETS, SELECTED ACCOUNTS
At December 31, Year 4

| | | | | | | |
|---|---|---|---|---|---|---|
| Equipment | $ 1,800 | $ 1,800 | $ 1,500 | $ 1,800 | $ 1,800 | $ 1,500 |
| Accumulated depreciation | (600) | (600) | (500) | (600) | (600) | (500) |
| Investment in Sub Inc. | 11,250 | 12,672 | 0 | 11,250 | 12,660 | 0 |
| Liabilities | 12,000 | 12,000 | 21,000 | 12,000 | 12,000 | 21,000 |
| Common shares | 15,000 | 15,000 | 15,000 | 15,000 | 15,000 | 15,000 |
| Retained earnings | 13,400 | 14,822 | 14,822 | 13,400 | 14,810 | 11,010 |
| Non-controlling interest | 0 | 0 | 1,408 | 0 | 0 | 1,420 |
| Debt-to-equity | 0.42 | 0.40 | 0.67 | 0.42 | 0.40 | 0.67 |
| Return on equity: |  |  |  |  |  |  |
| For all shareholders | n/a | n/a | 15.94% | n/a | n/a | 15.95% |
| For shareholders of Parent | 12.0% | 16.2% | 16.2% | 12.0% | 16.14% | 16.14% |

The exhibit also indicates the debt-to-equity and return-on-equity ratios for each set of financial statements. The return on equity for all shareholders uses consolidated net income and total shareholders' equity, including the non-controlling interest. The return on equity for shareholders of Parent uses consolidated net income attributable to the shareholders of Parent, and total shareholders' equity excluding the non-controlling interest.

Note the following from Exhibit 7.4:

- The separate-entity statements under the cost method are the same for upstream and downstream transactions because the cost method does not record any adjustments pertaining to the subsidiary's income or unrealized profits from intercompany transactions.

- The separate-entity statements under the cost method are the same as the statements under the equity method except for the investment account, equity method income, and retained earnings.

- Consolidated net income is the same regardless of whether the transactions where upstream or downstream. However, the split of the consolidated net income between the shareholders of the parent and the non-controlling interest is different. In turn, consolidated retained earnings and non-controlling interest are different, depending on whether the transactions were upstream or downstream. The separate-entity net income and retained earnings under the equity method are equal to consolidated net income attributable to the shareholders of Parent and consolidated retained earnings, respectively.

- The return on equity for the separate-entity statements under the equity method is equal to the consolidated return on equity for the shareholders of Parent.

- The return on equity for the downstream scenario is lower than the upstream scenario because the shareholders of Parent absorb the full charge when the unrealized profits are eliminated.

- The solvency position looks worst on the consolidated financial statements because the subsidiary's debt is included on the consolidated financial statements. This increases the debt-to-equity ratio.

---

*Retained earnings for the parent's separate-entity balance sheet under the equity method are equal to consolidated retained earnings.*

*The return on equity for the parent's separate-entity statements under the equity method is equal to the consolidated return on equity for the shareholders of Parent.*

*The parent's return on equity for the downstream scenario is lower than the upstream scenario because the shareholders of Parent absorb the full charge when the unrealized profits are eliminated.*

---

## Realization of Remaining Gain—Years 5 and 6

The equipment sold to the parent on January 1, Year 4, had a remaining life of 3 years on that date. When the Year 4 consolidated income statement was prepared, both the holdback of the total gain and the realization of one-third of the gain took place. When the consolidated income statement is prepared for each of Years 5 and 6, adjustments will be made to realize the remaining two-thirds of the gain. This intercompany gain will be fully realized for consolidation purposes at the end of Year 6, only because the equipment had a short life of three years on the date of the intercompany sale. The Year 6 financial statements for the two companies are shown in Exhibit 7.5. The Year 5 financial statements are not shown. Coincidentally, the Parent's and the Sub's net income and dividends paid in Year 5 were the same as their net income and dividends paid in Year 6.

**EXHIBIT 7.5**

### INCOME STATEMENTS
#### For Year 6

| | Parent | Sub |
|---|---|---|
| Sales | $ 25,000 | $ 12,000 |
| Depreciation expense | 600 | — |
| Miscellaneous expenses | 17,150 | 6,900 |
| Income tax expense | 2,600 | 2,000 |
| | 20,350 | 8,900 |
| Net income | $ 4,650 | $ 3,100 |

> *The parent reports depreciation expense for one full year on its separate-entity income statement.*

### RETAINED EARNINGS STATEMENTS
#### For Year 6

| | Parent | Sub |
|---|---|---|
| Balance, January 1 | $ 15,550 | $ 9,300 |
| Net income | 4,650 | 3,100 |
| | 20,200 | 12,400 |
| Dividends | 2,500 | — |
| Balance, December 31 | $ 17,700 | $ 12,400 |

### BALANCE SHEETS
#### At December 31, Year 6

| | Parent | Sub |
|---|---|---|
| Miscellaneous assets | $ 35,450 | $ 31,400 |
| Equipment | 1,800 | — |
| Accumulated depreciation | (1,800) | — |
| Investment in Sub Inc. | 11,250 | — |
| | $ 46,700 | $ 31,400 |
| | | |
| Liabilities | $ 14,000 | $ 11,000 |
| Common shares | 15,000 | 8,000 |
| Retained earnings | 17,700 | 12,400 |
| | $ 46,700 | $ 31,400 |

> *The parent reports accumulated depreciation for three years on its separate-entity balance sheet.*

Before the consolidated financial statements are prepared, we must make the four calculations shown in Exhibit 7.6. In the first table in Exhibit 7.6, you should note that the $300 gain on sale in Year 4 is fully realized from a consolidated perspective by the end of Year 6. From a consolidated perspective, the $300 gain was eliminated in Year 4 but was realized by adjusting depreciation expense over the remaining life of the equipment. Since the remaining life of the equipment was only 3 years at the date of the intercompany sale, the $300 gain was brought into consolidated income over three years. If the remaining useful life were five years, the $300 gain would be brought into consolidated income over five years.

**EXHIBIT 7.6**

### EQUIPMENT GAIN—SUB INC. SELLING

|  | Before Tax | 40% Tax | After Tax | |
|---|---|---|---|---|
| Unrealized gain, January 1, Year 4 | $300 | $ 120 | $   180 | **(a)** |
| Less realized through usage for Years 4 and 5 | 200 | 80 | 120 | **(b)** |
| Balance unrealized at Dec. 31, Year 5 | 100 | 40 | 60 | **(c)** |
| Less realized through usage for Year 6 | 100 | 40 | 60 | **(d)** |
| Balance unrealized at Dec. 31, Year 6 | $–0– | $ –0– | $    –0– | |

> *Differentiate between adjustments for a period of time (i.e., for Year 6) versus a point in time (i.e., at the end of Year 6).*

### CALCULATION OF CONSOLIDATED NET INCOME
#### For Year 6

| | | |
|---|---|---|
| Net income—Parent Co. | | $ 4,650 |
| Net Income—Sub Inc. | 3,100 | |
| Add realized gain on equipment **(d)** | 60 | |
| Adjusted net income—Sub Inc. | | 3,160 |
| Consolidated net income | | $ 7,810 |
| Attributable to: | | |
| Shareholders of Parent | | $ 7,494   **(e)** |
| Non-controlling interest (10% × 3,160) | | 316   **(f)** |

> *This schedule shows the calculation for a period of time, that is, for Year 6.*

### CALCULATION OF CONSOLIDATED RETAINED EARNINGS
#### At January 1, Year 6

| | | |
|---|---|---|
| Retained earnings—Parent Co. | | $15,550 |
| Retained earnings—Sub Inc. | 9,300 | |
| Acquisition retained earnings | 4,500 | |
| Increase since acquisition | 4,800 | |
| Less unrealized gain on equipment, Jan. 1 **(c)** | 60 | |
| Adjusted increase since acquisition | 4,740 | |
| Parent Co.'s share | 90% | 4,266 |
| Consolidated retained earnings | | $19,816   **(g)** |

> *This schedule shows the calculation at a point in time, that is, at the beginning of Year 6, which is the same as the end of Year 5.*

### CALCULATION OF NON-CONTROLLING INTEREST
#### At December 31, Year 6

| | |
|---|---|
| Common shares—Sub Inc. | $ 8,000 |
| Retained earnings—Sub Inc. | 12,400 |
| | 20,400 |
| Non-controlling interest's share | 10% |
| | $ 2,040   **(h)** |

> *At the end of Year 6, the intercompany gain has been fully realized and no adjustment is necessary on the Year 6 consolidated balance sheet.*

The Year 6 consolidated financial statements prepared using the direct approach are shown in Exhibit 7.7. Eliminations required for the intercompany equipment gain are shown in boldface.

**EXHIBIT 7.7**

**YEAR 6 CONSOLIDATED STATEMENTS**
**ADJUSTED FOR INTERCOMPANY EQUIPMENT PROFIT**
(direct approach)

**PARENT COMPANY**
**CONSOLIDATED INCOME STATEMENT**
For the year ended December 31, Year 6

| | |
|---|---|
| Sales (25,000 + 12,000) | $37,000 |
| Depreciation expense (600 + 0 − **[6d] 100**) | 500 |
| Miscellaneous expenses (17,150 + 6,900) | 24,050 |
| Income tax expense (2,600 + 2,000 + **[6d] 40**) | 4,640 |
| | 29,190 |
| Net income | $ 7,810 |
| Attributable to: | |
| Shareholders of Parent **(6e)** | $ 7,494 |
| Non-controlling interest **(6f)** | 316 |

*Depreciation expense for one year is based on the original cost to the consolidated entity.*

**PARENT COMPANY**
**CONSOLIDATED RETAINED EARNINGS STATEMENT**
For the year ended December 31, Year 6

| | |
|---|---|
| Balance, January 1 **(6g)** | $19,816 |
| Net income | 7,494 |
| | 27,310 |
| Dividends | 2,500 |
| Balance, December 31 | $24,810 |

**PARENT COMPANY**
**CONSOLIDATED BALANCE SHEET**
At December 31, Year 6

| | |
|---|---|
| Miscellaneous assets (35,450 + 31,400) | $66,850 |
| Equipment (1,800 + 0 − **[6a] 300**) | 1,500 |
| Accumulated depreciation (1,800 + 0 − **[6b + 6d] 300**) | (1,500) |
| | $66,850 |
| | |
| Liabilities (14,000 + 11,000) | $25,000 |
| Common shares | 15,000 |
| Retained earnings | 24,810 |
| Non-controlling interest **(6h)** | 2,040 |
| | $66,850 |

*Accumulated depreciation is total depreciation taken to the end of Year 6, based on the original cost to the consolidated entity.*

When the consolidated income statement is prepared, the depreciation expense is reduced by $100. The result is a consolidated depreciation expense of $500 based on the consolidated entity's cost. This adjustment realizes $100 of the equipment gain for consolidation purposes. Income tax expense is increased by $40 to match expense with the gain realized. The net effect of the two adjustments in the income statement is to increase the consolidated entity's net income by an after-tax realization amounting to $60.

The Year 6 consolidated retained earnings statement is prepared using the calculated January 1 balance, consolidated net income attributable to the parent, and the dividends of Parent Company.

Two adjustments are required in the preparation of the consolidated balance sheet. A reduction of $300 in equipment removes the gain and restates the equipment to the $1,500 historical cost to the entity. This equipment is fully depreciated on December 31, Year 6; therefore, accumulated depreciation should be equal to the historical cost of $1,500. When the accumulated depreciation is reduced by $300, the resulting balance ($1,500) is equal to the entity's historical cost.

> *At the end of Year 6, the equipment's carrying amount is zero on Parent's separate-entity balance sheet and on the consolidated balance sheet.*

Note that when both the equipment and the accumulated depreciation are reduced by $300, total consolidated assets are not changed. The net gain held back on the Year 4 consolidated balance sheet has been realized as at the end of Year 6. If no unrealized gains are being held back, there will be no deferred income tax adjustments made in the consolidated balance sheet. The deferred charge of $80 that appeared in the December 31, Year 4, consolidated balance sheet became an expense in the consolidated income statements for Years 5 and 6.

> *The unrealized profit at the end of Year 4 was realized in income for Years 5 and 6.*

As discussed above, the adjustments made in the consolidated income statement increased the entity's net income by $60, while the adjustments made in the asset side of the consolidated balance sheet did not change total assets. In order for this to balance out, there must have been both an increase and a decrease of $60 on the credit side of the consolidated balance sheet. The $60 increase occurred in the income statement and was allocated to the two equities. The $60 decrease occurred in Sub's retained earnings at the beginning of the year and was allocated to the two equities. In the calculation of consolidated retained earnings in Exhibit 7.6, Parent absorbs $54 (90% × $60). In the schedule below, which shows the changes in non-controlling interest for the year, we see that the remaining $6 (10% × $60) decreases non-controlling interest.

#### CHANGES IN NON-CONTROLLING INTEREST
##### For Year 6

| | |
|---|---|
| Sub Inc.: | |
| Common shares | $8,000 |
| Retained earnings, Jan. 1 | 9,300 |
| | 17,300 |
| Less unrealized gain on equipment **(6c)** | 60 |
| Adjusted | 17,240 |
| | 10% |
| Non-controlling interest Jan. 1 | 1,724 |
| Year 5 entity net income allocated **(6f)** | 316 |
| Non-controlling interest, Dec. 31 **(6h)** | $2,040 |

> *NCI is affected by the realization of the gain in Year 6, even though Parent recorded the excess depreciation.*

**EQUITY METHOD JOURNAL ENTRIES**  If Parent had been using the equity method, the following journal entries would have been made on December 31, Year 6:

| | | |
|---|---|---|
| Investment in Sub Inc. | 2,790 | |
| Equity method income | | 2,790 |

90% of Sub Inc.'s Year 6 net income (90% × 3,100 = 2,790)

| | | |
|---|---|---|
| Investment in Sub Inc. | 54 | |
| Equity method income | | 54 |

90% of the portion of the after-tax equipment gain realized through usage in Year 6 (90% × 60 = 54)

After these entries are posted for each of Year 5 and Year 6, the two related equity method accounts of Parent show the following changes and balances:

| | Investment in Sub Inc. | Equity Method Income |
|---|---|---|
| Balance, January 1, Year 5 | $12,672 | |
| Income from Sub Inc. for Year 5 | 2,790 | $2,790 |
| Equipment gain realized in Year 5 | 54 | 54 |
| Balance, December 31, Year 5 | 15,516 | $2,844 |
| Income from Sub Inc. for Year 6 | 2,790 | $2,790 |
| Equipment gain realized in Year 6 | 54 | 54 |
| Balance, December 31, Year 6 | $18,360 | $2,844 |

> *The investment account contains all adjustments to the end of the period, whereas the equity method income account contains adjustments for only one period.*

**INTERCOMPANY SALE OF A USED DEPRECIABLE ASSET**  In the preceding illustration, the equipment sold by Sub was a new asset. As such, Sub had not yet recorded any accumulated depreciation, and the cost to Sub was the same as the carrying amount on the date of the intercompany sale. Let us now consider the sale of a used depreciable asset, that is, an asset with accumulated depreciation.

Assume that Sub had acquired the equipment for $5,000 seven years prior to the intercompany sale, and had been depreciating it over an estimated useful life of ten years. The accumulated depreciation on January 1, Year 4, would have been $3,500 and the carrying amount would have been $1,500. Sub would have made the following entry when it sold the equipment to Parent for $1,800:

| | | |
|---|---|---|
| Cash | 1,800 | |
| Accumulated depreciation | 3,500 | |
| Equipment | | 5,000 |
| Gain on sale of equipment | | 300 |

All of the previous calculations of unrealized gains and excess depreciation would be the same for this situation. However, the consolidated balance sheet at the end of Year 4 should reflect the equipment at $5,000, the original cost to the consolidated entity, and accumulated depreciation at $4,000, the amount that would have appeared on Sub's books had the intercompany transaction not occurred. Therefore, the following journal entry should be made in the consolidation working papers at the end of Year 4 to gross up the equipment and accumulated depreciation:

| | | |
|---|---|---|
| Equipment | 3,500 | |
| Accumulated depreciation | | 3,500 |

This entry does not change the carrying amount of the equipment but does change the cost and accumulated depreciation on the consolidated balance sheet. This entry should be made on the consolidation working papers year after year as long as Parent has this equipment on its separate-entity books.

> *Equipment and accumulated depreciation need to be grossed up to the original cost to the consolidated entity.*

Appendix 7A of this chapter illustrates the consolidation adjustments relating to an intercompany sale of a depreciable asset when the parent company periodically revalues its equipment to fair value under IAS 16.

## Comparison of Realization of Inventory and Equipment Profits over a Three-Year Period

In Chapter 6, the holdback and realization of an intercompany profit in inventory was illustrated. In this chapter, we have illustrated the holdback and realization of an intercompany gain in equipment. In both cases, the after-tax profit (gain) was $180 (60% × $300), and the subsidiary was the selling company. The following summarizes the effect on the entity's net income over a three-year period:

### INTERCOMPANY INVENTORY PROFIT

|  | Year 4 | Year 5 | Year 6 | Total |
|---|---|---|---|---|
| Parent Co., net income | $3,400 | $4,050 | $4,050 | $11,500 |
| Sub Inc., net income | 1,700 | 3,100 | 3,100 | 7,900 |
|  | 5,100 | 7,150 | 7,150 | 19,400 |
| After-tax profit (held back) realized | (180) | 180 | –0– | –0– |
| Net income—consolidated entity | $4,920 | $7,330 | $7,150 | $19,400 |
| Allocated to the two equities: |  |  |  |  |
| Non-controlling interest | $ 152 | $ 328 | $ 310 | $ 790 |
| Shareholders of parent | 4,768 | 7,002 | 6,840 | 18,610 |
|  | $4,920 | $7,330 | $7,150 | $19,400 |

> *The intercompany profits are eventually realized from a consolidated viewpoint.*

### INTERCOMPANY EQUIPMENT GAIN

|  | Year 4 | Year 5 | Year 6 | Total |
|---|---|---|---|---|
| Parent Co., net income | $3,400 | $4,050 | $4,050 | $11,500 |
| Sub Inc., net income | 1,700 | 3,100 | 3,100 | 7,900 |
|  | 5,100 | 7,150 | 7,150 | 19,400 |
| Unrealized gain | (180) | –0– | –0– | (180) |
| Realized gain | 60 | 60 | 60 | 180 |
| Net income—consolidated entity | $4,980 | $7,210 | $7,210 | $19,400 |
| Allocated as follows: |  |  |  |  |
| Non-controlling interest | $ 158 | $ 316 | $ 316 | $ 790 |
| Shareholders of parent | 4,822 | 6,894 | 6,894 | 18,610 |
|  | $4,980 | $7,210 | $7,210 | $19,400 |

> *Intercompany profits on depreciable assets are realized as the assets are used over their useful lives.*

The three-year summaries just shown help illustrate a number of significant points in relation to consolidated financial statements:

1. The consolidated entity's net income is measured for periods of time that are usually one year in length.

2. During this measurement process, the holdback and subsequent realization of profits (losses) resulting from intercompany transactions takes place.

3. The realization of previously held back profits (losses) occurs during the period in which the acquiring company either sells the asset containing the profit (loss) to outsiders or depreciates the asset, thereby consuming the asset while it produces other products or services for outsiders.

4. If we examine a time period longer than one year, and if, at the end of that period, the assets of the constituent companies do not contain intercompany profits, the following becomes evident. The consolidated entity's net income for this longer period consists of

   (a) the reported net income of the parent company, exclusive of intercompany investment or dividend income,

   (b) *plus* the reported net income of the subsidiary company (or companies),

   (c) *minus* the acquisition-differential amortization.

   In the illustration above, we assumed that the acquisition differential was zero.

5. The entity's net income measurement for this longer time period is not affected by the fact that assets were sold at intercompany profits (losses) during the period. (See the three-year total column.) The same is true of the allocation to the two equities.

6. When consolidated statements are prepared at the end of an intervening time period (e.g., Year 4, Year 5, Year 6) we have to determine whether there were profits (losses) recorded by any of the constituent companies that were not realized by the end of the period.

7. The profit holdbacks and realizations are used in the measurement of the consolidated entity's net income and are adjustments to the reported net income of the selling constituent in the allocation of that net income.

---

*Differentiate between point-in-time (balance sheet) and period-of-time (income statement) adjustments.*

*Adjustments for unrealized and realized profits from intercompany transactions are always charged or credited to the original seller.*

---

In Chapter 6, we also illustrated the holdback and realization of a $180 after-tax intercompany gain in land. In that case, the realization process took place in Year 8; however, the overall concepts discussed above remain the same.

See Self-Study Problem 1 for a comprehensive consolidation problem involving intercompany profits in depreciable assets. It includes most of the issues we have covered so far in this chapter. Also, see the Summary for a description of how the learning objectives were applied when accounting for intercompany sales of depreciable assets.

**DISCLOSURE REQUIREMENTS**   The disclosure requirements for consolidated financial statements were summarized in Chapters 3 and 4. In addition to those requirements, the entity would normally indicate that intercompany transactions have been eliminated. The excerpt below is taken from the 2014 financial statements of Bell Canada Enterprises Inc., Canada's largest telecommunications company.

**BASIS OF CONSOLIDATION**   We consolidate the financial statements of all our subsidiaries. Subsidiaries are entities we control, where control is achieved when the company is exposed or has the right to variable returns from its involvement with the investee and has the current ability to direct the activities of the investee that significantly affect the investee's returns. The results of subsidiaries acquired (sold) during the year are (de-)consolidated from the date of acquisition (disposal). Where necessary, adjustments are made to the financial statements of acquired subsidiaries to conform their accounting policies to ours. All intercompany transactions, balances, income and expenses are eliminated on consolidation.[4]

# LO5 (B) INTERCOMPANY BONDHOLDINGS

Our discussions so far have focused on gains (losses) resulting from the intercompany sale of inventory, land, and depreciable assets. The treatment of these gains (losses) in the preparation of consolidated financial statements can be summarized as follows: Gains (losses) resulting from the intercompany sale of assets are realized subsequent to the recording of the intercompany transaction by the selling affiliate.

Occasionally, one affiliate will purchase all or a portion of the bonds issued by another affiliate. When consolidated financial statements are being prepared, the elimination of the intercompany accounts (investment in bonds and bonds payable, interest revenue and interest expense) may result in a gain (loss) being reflected in those statements. The treatment of this type of gain (loss) can be summarized in the following manner: Gains (losses) arising because of the elimination of intercompany bondholding accounts are realized and recognized on the consolidated statements prior to the recording of these gains (losses) by the affiliates on their separate-entity statements. Before we examine how these gains and losses occur in the elimination of the intercompany accounts, let us look at intercompany bondholding situations that do not result in gains or losses.

---

*Gains or losses on intercompany bondholdings are reported on consolidated statements prior to recording them on the separate-entity statements.*

---

## Intercompany Bondholdings—No Gain or Loss

Not all intercompany bondholdings result in gains or losses being reflected in the consolidated statements. For example, let us assume that one affiliate issued $10,000 in bonds and that another affiliate acquired the whole issue. (The amounts used are unrealistically low for a bond issue but are realistic in relation to the size of Parent Company and Sub Inc., the two companies that we have been using in our illustrations. In any case, the concepts are the same regardless of the amounts used.) Immediately after the issue, the records of the two companies would show the following accounts:

| *Acquiring Affiliate's Records* | | *Issuing Affiliate's Records* | |
|---|---|---|---|
| Investment in bonds | 10,000 | Bonds payable | 10,000 |

---

*The asset and liability appear on the separate-entity financial statements.*

---

From the combined entity's point of view, the two accounts are similar to intercompany receivables and payables and would be eliminated by the following working paper entry when the consolidated balance sheet is being prepared:

| | | |
|---|---|---|
| Bonds payable | 10,000 | |
| Investment in bonds | | 10,000 |

---

*This entry is made on the consolidation working papers.*

---

It is important to note that the eliminations are equal, and because of this, there is no gain or loss resulting from the working paper elimination of these two intercompany accounts. At the end of each succeeding year, this working paper elimination is repeated until the bonds mature. After that date, the two accounts no longer exist in the affiliates' records and further working paper eliminations are not required.

The consolidated balance sheet is not the only statement requiring working paper eliminations. If we assume that the bonds pay interest at the rate of 10%, the income statement of the issuing affiliate will show interest expense of $1,000, while the income statement of the acquiring affiliate will show interest revenue of $1,000. These intercompany revenue and expense accounts are eliminated by the following working paper entry when the consolidated income statement is being prepared:

| | | |
|---|---|---|
| Interest revenue | 1,000 | |
| Interest expense | | 1,000 |

---

*This entry does not change the net income of the consolidated entity.*

---

Again, it is important to note that the amounts are equal and that because of this, there is no gain or loss resulting from this working paper elimination. The consolidated income statement working paper elimination is repeated each year until the bonds mature.

Our example has assumed that the bonds were issued at par. Suppose, now, that the bonds were issued to the purchasing affiliate at a premium or a discount. Provided that both affiliates use the same methods to amortize the issue premium or discount and the purchase premium or discount, the amounts in the intercompany accounts on all successive balance sheets and income statements will be equal. The important concept of equal eliminations on both statements would still be true.

## Intercompany Bondholdings—with Gain or Loss

When the market rate is different from the coupon rate on the date of a bond issue, the bonds will be issued at a price that is different from the par or face value. If the market interest rates are higher (lower) than the coupon rate, the bonds will be issued at a discount (premium). Subsequent to the issue, bond market prices will rise (fall) if the market interest rate falls (rises). It is the market price differential on the date of an intercompany purchase, combined with any unamortized issue discount or premium, that causes the consolidated gains or losses that result from the elimination of intercompany bondholdings. Let us change our example slightly to illustrate this.

---

*The market price of bonds moves inversely with changes in interest rates.*

---

Parent Co. has a $10,000 bond issue outstanding that pays 10% interest annually on December 31. The bonds were originally issued at a premium, which is being amortized by the company on a straight-line basis at the rate of $25 per year.[5] On December 31, Year 4, the unamortized issue premium amounts to $100. The bonds mature on December 31, Year 5.

On December 31, Year 4, Sub purchases all of the outstanding bonds of Parent on the open market at a cost of $9,800. Immediately after Sub acquires these bonds, the records of the two companies would show the following accounts:

| *Sub Inc.'s Records* | | *Parent Co.'s Records* | |
|---|---|---|---|
| Investment in bonds of | | Bonds payable | $10,000 |
| Parent Co. | $10,000 | Add unamortized issue | |
| Less discount on purchase | 200 | premium | 100 |
| Net | $ 9,800 | Net | $10,100 |

> *Sub purchased the bonds in the market for $9,800, which is $300 less than the carrying amount of these bonds on Parent's books.*

The net amounts reflect how the asset and the liability would be presented on the respective balance sheets of the two companies on December 31, Year 4. The preparation of the consolidated balance sheet on this date would require the elimination of the two intercompany amounts by the following working paper entry:

| | | |
|---|---|---|
| Bonds Payable—Parent Co. | 10,100 | |
| Investment in bonds of Parent Co.—Sub. Inc. | | 9,800 |
| Gain on bond retirement | | 300 |

To eliminate the intercompany bond accounts and recognize the resulting gain on the retirement of bonds

> *A gain of $300 is recorded on the consolidation working papers.*

**LO6** The eliminations of the asset and the liability would appear in the consolidated balance sheet working paper. The balancing amount of the elimination entry "Gain on bond retirement" appears in the consolidated income statement working paper. From the consolidated entity's point of view, the bonds of the entity have been purchased on the open market and retired. The retirement gain can be calculated in the following manner:

| | |
|---|---|
| Carrying amount of the bond liability | $10,100 |
| Cost of purchasing bonds in the open market | 9,800 |
| Gain on bond retirement | $ 300 |

> *From the consolidated perspective, Parent's bonds have been retired; Parent no longer has a bond payable to outsiders.*

The gain should be recognized because the benefits and risks of the consolidated entity have substantially changed in a transaction with outsiders. From a consolidated perspective, the entity has retired a liability of $10,100 by paying $9,800 to external investors. Its financial position has improved; the gain has been realized and should be recognized.

> *The gain on bond retirement was realized on a transaction with outsiders.*

Note that if Parent had acquired and retired its own bonds in the same manner, it would have recorded a gain on bond retirement of the same amount. This gain would appear on Parent's income statement and would also appear on the consolidated income statement. The actual event was different (Sub purchased the bonds), but because the two companies are a single economic entity, the gain will still appear on the consolidated income statement. The only difference is that the gain on the consolidated income statement does not appear on the income statement of the parent. Instead, it appears on the consolidated income statement as a result of the unequal elimination of the intercompany asset and liability accounts in the preparation of the consolidated balance sheet.

> *The gain is reported on the consolidated statements, not on the single-entity statements.*

An examination of the makeup of the asset and liability accounts will indicate why there is a gain of $300. If the bonds had originally been issued at par (face value), and if they had been acquired on the open market at a price equal to par, there would be no gain on retirement. It is the unamortized premium on the issued bonds and the discount on the bond purchase that cause the gain. This premium and discount will be amortized by the two companies in Years 5 to 8, and thus will be reflected in the individual income statements of the two companies in those future periods. This will become clearer when we examine the consolidation procedures in Year 5. The important point to note at this stage is that the constituent companies will pay tax on this gain in future periods when the actual recording of the gain takes place. The consolidated entity is realizing the gain in Year 4; therefore, this timing difference requires income tax allocation if a proper matching is to take place. Assuming a 40% tax rate, the following additional working paper elimination entry is required:

| | | |
|---|---|---|
| Income tax expense | 120 | |
|     Deferred income tax liability | | 120 |
| To record the deferred income tax liability and expense on the Year 4 intercompany bond gain | | |
| (40% × 300 = 120) | | |

> *Income tax expense is reported on the consolidated statements in accordance with the matching principle.*

The effect of the two eliminating entries on the Year 4 consolidated income is to increase the net income of the entity by $180 ($300 − $120). The entity's net income consists of the net income of the parent plus the net income of the subsidiary; therefore, the after-tax increase must affect one or the other, or perhaps both.

Four possible approaches could be taken:

1. Allocate the gain to the issuing company because the company purchasing the bonds is acting as an agent for the issuing company. (This approach is commonly referred to as the *agency approach*.)

2. Allocate the gain to the purchasing company because its investment led to the retirement of the bonds for consolidation purposes.

3. Allocate the gain to the parent company because its management controls the actions of all the affiliated companies in the group. This would only be a separate alternative if both parties to the transaction were subsidiaries of that parent.

4. Allocate the gain between the issuing and purchasing companies based on the premium or discount on the respective company's books.

> *There are various approaches to allocate the gain between the two companies.*

An allocation of the gain would not be required in the case of 100%-owned subsidiaries, because there would be no non-controlling interest in the consolidated financial statements. The approach adopted is very important when the subsidiaries are less than 100% owned, because approaches 1, 2, and 4 could result in all or a portion of the gain being allocated to the subsidiary company, and this would affect non-controlling interest. IFRS is silent regarding the approach to be taken. In the illustrations that follow, any gains (losses) from the elimination of intercompany bondholding will be allocated to the purchasing and issuing affiliates (approach 4), because it reflects how each company will actually record the transaction in future years.

> *We will use approach 4, because it is consistent with the income measurement by the separate entities in future years.*

## LO7 Calculation of the Portion of the Gain Allocated to the Affiliates

From the point of view of the purchasing affiliate, the cost of the acquisition is compared with the par value of the bonds acquired, the difference being a gain or loss. From the point of view of the issuing affiliate, the cost to retire the bonds is compared with the par value of the bonds; the difference between the par value and the carrying amount is the gain or loss. The gain and its allocation can be calculated in the following manner:

| | |
|---|---:|
| Par (face) value of bond liability | $10,000 |
| Cost of investment in bonds | 9,800 |
| Gain allocated to purchasing affiliate—before tax | $ 200 |
| | |
| Carrying amount of bond liability | $10,100 |
| Par (face) value of bond liability | 10,000 |
| Gain allocated to issuing affiliate—before tax | $ 100 |

Note that the gain to the consolidated entity of $300 is made up of the two gains allocated to the affiliates ($200 + $100). The gain allocated to the purchasing affiliate is equal to the discount on the purchase affiliate's books, and the gain allocated to the issuing affiliate is equal to the premium on the issuing affiliate's books. Both the entity's gain and the amounts allocated are expressed in before-tax dollars. The chart in Exhibit 7.8 is useful in calculating the after-tax amounts required when the entity's after-tax net income is being allocated to the two equities.

> *The $300 gain is allocated to the affiliates based on the premium or discount on their separate-entity books.*

**EXHIBIT 7.8**

### ALLOCATION OF GAIN ON BOND

| | Entity | | | Parent Co. | | | Sub Inc. | | |
|---|---|---|---|---|---|---|---|---|---|
| | Before Tax | 40% Tax | After Tax | Before Tax | 40% Tax | After Tax | Before Tax | 40% Tax | After Tax |
| Gain on bond retirement— Dec. 31, Year 4 | $300 | $120 | $180 | $100 | $40 | $60 | $200 | $80 | $120 |
| | (a) | (b) | (c) | (d) | (e) | (f) | (g) | (h) | (i) |

> *This chart shows how the after-tax gains are allocated for consolidation purposes.*

The Year 4 financial statements of the two companies are shown in Exhibit 7.9. Parent Co. has used the cost method to account for its investment.

**EXHIBIT 7.9**

### INCOME STATEMENTS
For Year 4

| | Parent | Sub |
|---|---|---|
| Sales | $ 20,000 | $ 8,000 |
| Interest expense | 975 | — |
| Miscellaneous expenses | 13,425 | 5,200 |
| Income tax expense | 2,200 | 1,100 |
| | 16,600 | 6,300 |
| Net income | $ 3,400 | $ 1,700 |

> *Sub has no interest revenue because it purchased the bonds on the last day of the year.*

### RETAINED EARNINGS STATEMENTS
For Year 4

| | Parent | Sub |
|---|---|---|
| Balance, January 1 | $ 12,000 | $ 4,500 |
| Net income | 3,400 | 1,700 |
| | 15,400 | 6,200 |
| Dividends | 2,000 | — |
| Balance, December 31 | $ 13,400 | $ 6,200 |

*(continued)*

**BALANCE SHEETS**

At December 31, Year 4

|  | Parent | Sub |
|---|---|---|
| Miscellaneous assets | $29,150 | $13,400 |
| Investment in Parent Co. bonds | — | 9,800 |
| Investment in Sub Inc. | 11,250 | — |
|  | $40,400 | $23,200 |
| Miscellaneous liabilities | $ 1,900 | $ 9,000 |
| Bonds payable | 10,100 | — |
| Common shares | 15,000 | 8,000 |
| Retained earnings | 13,400 | 6,200 |
|  | $40,400 | $23,200 |

*The investment in bonds and bonds payable are reported on the separate-entity balance sheets.*

The net incomes and total assets of the two companies are unchanged from previous examples. However, the details on each statement have been changed to reflect the intercompany bond transaction that occurred on December 31, Year 4. Remember that the intercompany bond purchase occurred on December 31, Year 4 and therefore the interest expense of Parent for Year 4 relates to bonds held by bondholders outside the consolidated entity. The amount of expense ($975) is made up of the $1,000 interest paid, less the $25 amortization of the issue premium.

*Parent has interest expense of $975 on its separate-entity books.*

Before the Year 4 consolidated financial statements are prepared, the three calculations in Exhibit 7.10 are made. Exhibit 7.11 illustrates the direct approach to the preparation of the Year 4 consolidated financial statements.

**EXHIBIT 7.10**

**CALCULATION OF CONSOLIDATED NET INCOME**

For Year 4

| | | |
|---|---|---|
| Net income—Parent Co. | | $3,400 |
| Add realized bond gain allocated **(8f)** | | 60 |
| Adjusted | | 3,460 |
| Net income—Sub Inc. | 1,700 | |
| Add realized bond gain allocated **(8i)** | 120 | |
| Adjusted | | 1,820 |
| Consolidated net income | | $5,280 |
| Attributable to: | | |
| Shareholders of Parent | | $5,098 **(a)** |
| Non-controlling interest (10% × 1,820) | | 182 **(b)** |

*The gain on bond retirement is allocated to the two affiliates as a consolidation adjustment.*

**EXHIBIT 7.10**   *(continued)*

### CALCULATION OF NON-CONTROLLING INTEREST
At December 31, Year 4

| | | |
|---|---|---|
| Sub Inc.: | | |
| Common shares | | $8,000 |
| Retained earnings | | 6,200 |
| | | 14,200 |
| Add realized bond gain allocated **(8i)** | | 120 |
| Adjusted | | 14,320 |
| Non-controlling interest's ownership | | 10% |
| | | $1,432   **(c)** |

*The gain allocated to Sub affects non-controlling interest at the end of the year.*

### CALCULATION OF CONSOLIDATED RETAINED EARNINGS
At December 31, Year 4

| | | |
|---|---|---|
| Retained earnings—Parent Co. | | $13,400 |
| Add realized bond gain allocated **(8f)** | | 60 |
| Adjusted | | 13,460 |
| Retained earnings—Sub Inc. | 6,200 | |
| Acquisition retained earnings | 4,500 | |
| Increase since acquisition | 1,700 | |
| Add realized bond gain allocated **(8i)** | 120 | |
| Adjusted | 1,820 | |
| Parent's ownership | 90% | 1,638 |
| | | $15,098   **(d)** |

*This schedule shows the calculation at a point in time, that is, at the end of Year 4.*

**EXHIBIT 7.11**

### YEAR 4 CONSOLIDATED STATEMENTS
### ADJUSTED FOR INTERCOMPANY BONDHOLDINGS
(direct approach)
### PARENT COMPANY
### CONSOLIDATED INCOME STATEMENT
For the year ended December 31, Year 4

| | |
|---|---|
| Sales (20,000 + 8,000) | $28,000 |
| Gain on bond retirement (0 + 0 + **[8a] 300**) | 300 |
| | 28,300 |
| Interest expense (975 + 0) | 975 |
| Miscellaneous expenses (13,425 + 5,200) | 18,625 |
| Income tax expense (2,200 + 1,100 + **[8b] 120**) | 3,420 |
| | 23,020 |
| Net income | $ 5,280 |
| Attributable to: | |
| Shareholders of Parent **(10a)** | $ 5,098 |
| Non-controlling interest **(10b)** | 182 |

*The gain on bond retirement appears on the consolidated income statement because the gain was realized when the subsidiary purchased the parent's bonds from outsiders.*

**PARENT COMPANY**
**CONSOLIDATED RETAINED EARNINGS STATEMENT**
For the year ended December 31, Year 4

| | |
|---|---:|
| Balance, January 1 | $12,000 |
| Net income | 5,098 |
| | 17,098 |
| Dividends | 2,000 |
| Balance, December 31 | $15,098 |

**PARENT COMPANY**
**CONSOLIDATED BALANCE SHEET**
At December 31, Year 4

| | |
|---|---:|
| Miscellaneous assets (29,150 + 13,400) | $42,550 |
| Investment in Parent Co. bonds (0 + 9,800 − **9,800**) | –0– |
| | $42,550 |
| Miscellaneous liabilities (1,900 + 9,000) | $10,900 |
| Bonds payable (10,100 + 0 − **10,100**) | –0– |
| Deferred income tax liability (0 + 0 + **[8b] 120**) | 120 |
| Total liabilities | 11,020 |
| Common shares | 15,000 |
| Retained earnings | 15,098 |
| Non-controlling interest **(10o)** | 1,432 |
| | $42,550 |

> *The bonds payable are zero on the consolidated balance sheet because outsiders no longer hold them.*

Exhibit 7.8, which was prepared to allocate the gain in both before-tax and after-tax dollars, was used in preparing the consolidated income statement and in calculating consolidated net income and retained earnings, as follows:

1. The entity column reflects the amounts used in preparing the consolidated income statement. Note that the after-tax column is not used because the before tax amount and the tax amount are adjusted separately.

2. Both of the allocation columns (Parent Co. and Sub Inc.) were used to calculate consolidated net income attributable to the parent and non-controlling interest for the year, and to calculate non-controlling interest and consolidated retained earnings at the end of the year, but only using after-tax amounts. This is because they are used to adjust the after-tax net incomes and equities of the two companies. The before-tax and tax columns are presented only to show that the columns cross-add.

In summary, the eliminations made for the intercompany bondholdings had the following effect on the consolidated statements:

1. The elimination of $9,800 in assets and $10,100 in liabilities resulted in a $300 before-tax gain, which was reflected in the income statement.

2. An increase of $120 (40% × $300) to income tax expense and to a deferred tax liability reflected the tax effects of the gain.

3. The two adjustments in the income statement increased the net income of the entity by $180; this was allocated to the two equities in the balance sheet, as follows:

|  | Total | Non-controlling Interest | Controlling Interest |
|---|---|---|---|
| Gain allocated to Parent Co. | $ 60 | $— | $ 60 |
| Gain allocated to Sub Inc. | 120 | 12 | 108 |
|  | $180 | $12 | $168 |

---

*Income tax is accrued on the consolidated financial statements to match the gain on bond retirement.*

---

4. The adjustments made in preparing the consolidated balance sheet can be summarized conceptually as follows:

*Debit Side*

| Investment in bonds | − 9,800 |
|---|---|

*Credit Side*

| Bonds payable | −10,100 |
|---|---|
| Deferred income tax liability | + 120 |
| Non-controlling interest | + 12 |
| Retained earnings | + 168 |
|  | − 9,800 |

---

*The after-tax gain is allocated to non-controlling and controlling interests.*

---

## EQUITY METHOD JOURNAL ENTRIES   If Parent used the equity method, the following entries would be made on December 31, Year 4:

| Investment in Sub Inc. | 1,530 | |
|---|---|---|
| Equity method income | | 1,530 |

90% of the Year 4 net income of Sub Inc. (90% × 1,700 = 1,530)

| Investment in Sub Inc. | 60 | |
|---|---|---|
| Equity method income | | 60 |

Bond gain allocated to Parent Co.

| Investment in Sub Inc. | 108 | |
|---|---|---|
| Equity method income | | 108 |

90% of bond gain allocated to Sub Inc. (90% × 120 = 108)

---

*These entries capture the net effect of all consolidation adjustments.*

---

The related equity method accounts of Parent will show the following changes and balances in Year 4:

|  | Investment in Sub Inc. | Equity Method Income |
|---|---|---|
| January 1, Year 4 | $11,250 | |
| Changes during Year 4: | | |
| Income from Sub Inc. | 1,530 | $1,530 |
| Bond gain to parent | 60 | 60 |
| 90% of bond gain to subsidiary | 108 | 108 |
| Balance, December 31, Year 4 | $12,948 | $1,698 |

*The investment account contains cumulative adjustments to the end of the period, whereas the equity method income account contains adjustments for only one period.*

## Accounting for Gain in Subsequent Years

We will now focus on Year 5 so that we can illustrate the consolidation eliminations that must be made in years subsequent to the original intercompany bond purchase.

At the end of Year 5, the two companies prepared the financial statements shown in Exhibit 7.12.

**EXHIBIT 7.12**

**INCOME STATEMENTS**
For Year 5

|  | Parent | Sub |
|---|---|---|
| Sales | $25,000 | $10,950 |
| Interest revenue | — | 1,050 |
|  | 25,000 | 12,000 |
| Interest expense | 975 | — |
| Miscellaneous expenses | 17,375 | 6,900 |
| Income tax expense | 2,600 | 2,000 |
|  | 20,950 | 8,900 |
| Net income | $ 4,050 | $ 3,100 |

*The separate-entity income statements show interest revenue and expense for bonds that were retired from a consolidated viewpoint.*

**RETAINED EARNINGS STATEMENTS**
For Year 5

|  | Parent | Sub |
|---|---|---|
| Balance, January 1 | $13,400 | $ 6,200 |
| Net income | 4,050 | 3,100 |
|  | 17,450 | 9,300 |
| Dividends | 2,500 | — |
| Balance, December 31 | $14,950 | $ 9,300 |

*(continued)*

**EXHIBIT 7.12** *(continued)*

**BALANCE SHEETS**

At December 31, Year 5

| | Parent | Sub |
|---|---|---|
| Miscellaneous assets | $ 32,700 | $18,450 |
| Investment in Parent Co. bonds | — | 9,850 |
| Investment in Sub Inc. | 11,250 | — |
| | $43,950 | $28,300 |
| | | |
| Miscellaneous liabilities | $ 3,925 | $11,000 |
| Bonds payable | 10,075 | — |
| Common shares | 15,000 | 8,000 |
| Retained earnings | 14,950 | 9,300 |
| | $43,950 | $28,300 |

*The separate-entity balance sheets show investment and bonds payable for bonds that were retired from a consolidated viewpoint.*

Focus initially on the items "interest revenue"[6] and "interest expense," which each company recorded in the following manner:

| Parent Company | | | Sub Inc. | | |
|---|---|---|---|---|---|
| Interest expense | 1,000 | | Cash | 1,000 | |
| Cash | | 1,000 | Interest revenue | | 1,000 |
| To record payment of Year 5 interest | | | To record receipt of Year 5 interest | | |
| Bonds payable | 25 | | Investment in bonds of | | |
| Interest expense | | 25 | Parent Co. | 50 | |
| To amortize issue premium (100 ÷ 4 = 25) | | | Interest revenue | | 50 |
| | | | To amortize discount on the purchase of bonds (200 ÷ 4 = 50) | | |

*These entries are made on the separate-entity books of Parent and Sub.*

Note that the entries recording the amortization of the issue premium and the purchase discount increased the respective net incomes of the two companies. The $25 of income reported by Parent is equal to one-quarter of the gain that was attributed to Parent from a consolidated point of view on December 31, Year 4, from the deemed retirement of the bonds. In the same manner, the $50 of income reported by Sub is equal to one-quarter of the gain that was attributed to Sub from a consolidated point of view on December 31, Year 4, from the deemed retirement of the bonds. Because the bonds mature four years after the date of the intercompany purchase and because the original gain on bond retirement was created due to the existence of the unamortized issue premium and the discount on the intercompany purchase of bonds ($100 + $200 = $300), the concept that the gain is realized on the consolidated financial statements before it is recorded by the constituent companies becomes evident.

*The income resulting from the premium and discount amortization, which is being reported by the separate entities, has already been reported on the consolidated financial statements.*

Both Sub's interest revenue of $1,050 ($1,000 + $50) and Parent's interest expense of $975 ($1,000 − $25) represent intercompany revenues and expenses that are eliminated on the Year 5 consolidated income statement with the following incomplete working paper entry:

| | | |
|---|---|---|
| Interest revenue | 1,050 | |
| Interest expense | | 975 |
| To eliminate Year 5 intercompany interest revenue and expense | | |

> *The difference between interest revenue and interest expense is due to the difference in amortization of the bond premium and discount.*

In past examples, the elimination of intercompany revenues and expenses (sales and purchases, rental revenue and expense, etc.) had no effect on the net income of the entity because the amounts eliminated were always equal. Referring back to the journal entries made by both companies, you will see that this equal component is still present. We are still eliminating $1,000 in interest revenue and expense in the working paper elimination. However, we are also eliminating the portions of the gain on bond retirement that were recorded by both companies as a result of the amortization of the premium and discount in Year 5. Failure to do this would result in the gain on bond retirement being recorded twice over the life of the bonds. It is because we do not allow this portion of the gain to be reflected in the Year 5 consolidated income statement that we have an unequal elimination of intercompany revenue and expense on the working paper elimination entry. The elimination of $1,050 intercompany interest revenue and $975 intercompany interest expense decreases the before-tax net income of the entity by $75. We will describe this reduction of the entity's before-tax net income as the "interest elimination loss."

> *The intercompany interest must be eliminated on consolidation to avoid double counting of income pertaining to the bonds.*

The realization of a gain on bond retirement on the consolidated income statement in the year of acquisition of intercompany bonds will always result in an interest elimination loss affecting the entity's before-tax net income in all subsequent consolidated income statements until the bonds mature. This interest elimination loss does not appear as such in the consolidated income statement, because it results from eliminating an amount of intercompany interest revenue that is larger than the amount of intercompany interest expense eliminated. Conversely, the realization of a loss on bond retirement in the year of acquisition of intercompany bonds will always result in an "interest elimination gain" in all subsequent consolidated income statements because the amount of interest expense eliminated will always be larger than the amount of interest revenue eliminated.

> *Income tax expense must be eliminated on consolidation to match with the elimination of the interest revenue and interest expense.*

As stated previously, the entity's Year 5 before-tax net income has been decreased by $75. This results from eliminating the portion of the gain on bond retirement recorded by the constituent companies in Year 5. Recall that the entire before-tax gain was realized for consolidated purposes in Year 4; also recall that to satisfy the matching principle an income tax expense was recorded and a deferred tax liability was set up on the consolidated balance sheet. Both companies paid (or accrued) income tax on a portion of this gain in Year 5—a total of $30 ($75 × 40%). These companies also recorded the income tax paid (or accrued) as an expense, but from a consolidated point of view, the payment was a reduction of the deferred tax liability previously set up. We must therefore decrease income tax expense when preparing the consolidated income statement because it is not a consolidated expense.[7] The *incomplete* income statement working paper elimination entry is as follows:

| | | |
|---|---:|---:|
| Interest revenue | 1,050 | |
|    Interest expense | | 975 |
|    Income tax expense | | 30 |
| To eliminate Year 5 intercompany interest revenue and expense and to adjust for the income tax effect of the elimination | | |

The addition of the income tax expense entry still leaves us with an unequal elimination on the consolidated income statement. However, this interest elimination loss is now in after-tax dollars and amounts to $45 ($1,050 − $975 − $30). A reconstruction of the intercompany bond chart for the life of the bonds as shown in Exhibit 7.13 will illustrate how this loss is allocated to the two constituents each year.

**EXHIBIT 7.13**

**ALLOCATION OF GAIN ON BOND**

| | Entity | | | Parent Co. | | | Sub Inc. | | | |
|---|---|---|---|---|---|---|---|---|---|---|
| | Before Tax | 40% Tax | After Tax | Before Tax | 40% Tax | After Tax | Before Tax | 40% Tax | After Tax | |
| Gain on bond, Dec. 31, Year 4 | $300 | $120 | $180 | $100 | $ 40 | $ 60 | $200 | $ 80 | $120 | **(a)** |
| Interest elimination loss—Year 5 | 75 | 30 | 45 | 25 | 10 | 15 | 50 | 20 | 30 | **(b)** |
| Balance—gain— Dec. 31, Year 5 | 225 | 90 | 135 | 75 | 30 | 45 | 150 | 60 | 90 | **(c)** |
| Interest elimination loss—Year 6 | 75 | 30 | 45 | 25 | 10 | 15 | 50 | 20 | 30 | |
| Balance—gain— Dec. 31, Year 6 | 150 | 60 | 90 | 50 | 20 | 30 | 100 | 40 | 60 | |
| Interest elimination loss—Year 7 | 75 | 30 | 45 | 25 | 10 | 15 | 50 | 20 | 30 | |
| Balance—gain— Dec. 31, Year 7 | 75 | 30 | 45 | 25 | 10 | 15 | 50 | 20 | 30 | |
| Interest elimination loss—Year 8 | 75 | 30 | 45 | 25 | 10 | 15 | 50 | 20 | 30 | |
| Balance, Dec. 31, Year 8 | $–0– | $–0– | $–0– | $–0– | $–0– | $–0– | $–0– | $–0– | $–0– | |

> *The interest elimination loss for each year is equal to the amortization of the bond premium and bond discount on the separate-entity books.*

To further illustrate this, examine the interest accounts of the two companies from the date of the intercompany purchase to the date of maturity of the bonds.

| Year Ended Dec. 31 | Parent's Interest Expense | Sub's Interest Revenue | Difference |
|---|---:|---:|---:|
| Year 5 | $  975 | $1,050 | $ 75 |
| Year 6 | 975 | 1,050 | 75 |
| Year 7 | 975 | 1,050 | 75 |
| Year 8 | 975 | 1,050 | 75 |
| | $3,900 | $4,200 | $300 |

> *By the end of Year 8, the cumulative income recorded on the separate-entity books of Parent and Sub is equal to the $300 gain on bond retirement that was reported in the Year 4 consolidated income statement.*

The preparation of a bond chart would be the first step in the preparation of the Year 5 consolidated statements. This chart would have the same format as the one shown above but would comprise only the first three lines from that particular chart. Before the Year 5 consolidated financial statements are prepared, the three calculations in Exhibit 7.14 are made. The Year 5 consolidated financial statements prepared using the direct approach are shown in Exhibit 7.15.

**EXHIBIT 7.14**

## CALCULATION OF CONSOLIDATED NET INCOME
### For Year 5

| | | |
|---|---:|---:|
| Net income—Parent Co. | | $ 4,050 |
| Less interest elimination loss allocated **(13b)** | | 15 |
| Adjusted | | 4,035 |
| Net income—Sub Inc. | 3,100 | |
| Less interest elimination loss allocated **(13b)** | 30 | |
| Adjusted | | 3,070 |
| Consolidated net income | | $ 7,105 |
| Attributable to: | | |
| Shareholders of Parent | | $ 6,798 **(a)** |
| Non-controlling interest (10% × 3,070) | | 307 **(b)** |

*The interest elimination loss is allocated to Parent and Sub based on Exhibit 7.13.*

## CALCULATION OF CONSOLIDATED RETAINED EARNINGS
### At January 1, Year 5

| | | |
|---|---:|---:|
| Retained earnings—Parent Co. | | $13,400 |
| Add realized bond gain allocated **(13a)** | | 60 |
| Adjusted | | 13,460 |
| Retained earnings—Sub Inc. | 6,200 | |
| Acquisition retained earnings | 4,500 | |
| Increase since acquisition | 1,700 | |
| Add realized bond gain allocated **(13a)** | 120 | |
| Adjusted | 1,820 | |
| Parent Co. ownership | 90% | 1,638 |
| Consolidated retained earnings | | $15,098 **(c)** |

*This schedule shows the calculation at a point in time, that is, at the beginning of Year 5, which is the same as at the end of Year 4.*

## CALCULATION OF NON-CONTROLLING INTEREST
### at December 31, Year 5

| | |
|---|---:|
| Sub Inc.: | |
| Common shares | $ 8,000 |
| Retained earnings | 9,300 |
| | 17,300 |
| Add realized bond gain allocated as at Dec. 31, Year 5 **(13c)** | 90 |
| Adjusted shareholders' equity | 17,390 |
| Non-controlling interest's ownership | 10% |
| | $ 1,739 **(d)** |

*Only the portion of the gain on bond retirement allocated to Sub affects non-controlling interest.*

EXHIBIT 7.15

**YEAR 5 CONSOLIDATED STATEMENTS**
**ADJUSTED FOR INTERCOMPANY BONDHOLDINGS**
(direct approach)

**PARENT COMPANY**
**CONSOLIDATED INCOME STATEMENT**
For the year ended December 31, Year 5

| | |
|---|---:|
| Sales (25,000 + 10,950) | $35,950 |
| Interest revenue (0 + 1,050 − **1,050**) | –0– |
| | 35,950 |
| Interest expense (975 + 0 − **975**) | –0– |
| Miscellaneous expenses (17,375 + 6,900) | 24,275 |
| Income tax expense (2,600 + 2,000 − **[13b] 30**) | 4,570 |
| | 28,845 |
| Net income | $ 7,105 |
| Attributable to: | |
| Shareholders of Parent **(14a)** | $ 6,798 |
| Non-controlling interest **(14b)** | 307 |

> *There was no interest revenue earned from outsiders and no interest expense paid to outsiders* during the year.

**PARENT COMPANY**
**CONSOLIDATED RETAINED EARNINGS STATEMENT**
For the year ended December 31, Year 5

| | |
|---|---:|
| Balance, January 1 **(14c)** | $15,098 |
| Net income | 6,798 |
| | 21,896 |
| Dividends | 2,500 |
| Balance, December 31 | $19,396 |

**PARENT COMPANY**
**CONSOLIDATED BALANCE SHEET**
At December 31, Year 5

| | |
|---|---:|
| Miscellaneous assets (32,700 + 18,450) | $51,150 |
| Investment in Parent Co. bonds (0 + 9,850 − **9,850**) | –0– |
| | $51,150 |
| Miscellaneous liabilities (3,925 + 11,000) | $14,925 |
| Bonds payable (10,075 + 0 − **10,075**) | –0– |
| Deferred income tax liability (0 + 0 + **[13c] 90**) | 90 |
| Total liabilities | 15,015 |
| Common shares | 15,000 |
| Retained earnings | 19,396 |
| Non-controlling interest **(14d)** | 1,739 |
| | $51,150 |

> *There is no bond payable to outsiders and no investment in bonds of outsiders* at the end of the year.

The unequal elimination of the intercompany interest revenue and expense and the income tax adjustment made in the preparation of the consolidated income statement were explained earlier. This created the "hidden" after-tax interest elimination loss of $45 in this statement. This loss is depicted and allocated in the chart contained in Exhibit 7.13.

The eliminations made in the preparation of the Year 5 consolidated balance sheet require elaboration. The item "Investment in Parent Co. bonds" in the balance sheet of Sub has a balance of $9,850 after the Year 5 amortization of the discount on purchase ($9,800 + $50). Bonds payable in the balance sheet of Parent Co. has a balance of $10,075 after the Year 5 amortization on the issue premium ($10,100 − $25). When the consolidated balance sheet is being prepared, these two intercompany accounts are eliminated by the following *incomplete* entry:

| | | |
|---|---|---|
| Bonds payable | 10,075 | |
| Investment in Parent Co. bonds | | 9,850 |
| To eliminate the intercompany bonds on December 31, Year 5 | | |

*This entry eliminates the bonds payable and investment in bonds but is not yet complete.*

This entry is somewhat similar to the entry made on December 31, Year 4 (see under the section "Intercompany Bondholdings—with Gain or Loss") except that the before-tax amount needed to balance at this time is a gain of $225 instead of the $300 gain that was required a year ago. Furthermore, the $225 gain does not appear as such in the consolidated income statement in Year 5. Recall that the $300 gain appeared on the Year 4 consolidated income statement. A gain on bond retirement appears as such only once in the year of the intercompany purchase. Recall also that a portion of the gain was recorded in Year 5 by Parent and Sub, was eliminated in preparing the Year 5 consolidated income statement and is not reflected again. The $225 needed to balance this journal entry is, therefore, a credit of $300 to retained earnings at the beginning of Year 5 and the combined effect of $75 from eliminating the intercompany interest revenue and interest expense pertaining to the bonds. The bond chart (see Exhibit 7.13) indicates that the entity's deferred income tax liability with respect to this gain is $90 as at December 31, Year 5. We can now extend the working paper entry by including the deferred tax component as follows:

| | | |
|---|---|---|
| Bonds payable | 10,075 | |
| Investment in Parent Co. bonds | | 9,850 |
| Deferred income tax liability | | 90 |
| To eliminate the intercompany bond accounts and set up the deferred tax liability as at December 31, Year 5 | | |

*At the end of Year 5, the deferred tax liability is the 40% tax on the difference between income recognized for consolidation purposes ($300) and income recognized by the separate entities ($75).*

The after-tax gain needed to balance is now $135. The bond chart (see Exhibit 7.13) shows this gain as allocated $45 to Parent and $90 to Sub.

To summarize, the Year 5 elimination entries made for the intercompany bondholdings had the following effect on the consolidated statements:

1. The adjustments made in the income statement created an after-tax interest elimination loss of $45, which decreased the entity's net income and was allocated to the two equities as follows:

|  | Total | Non-controlling Interest | Controlling Interest |
|---|---|---|---|
| Loss allocated to Parent Co. | $15 | $— | $15 |
| Loss allocated to Sub Inc. | 30 | 3 | 27 |
|  | $45 | $ 3 | $42 |

> *The interest elimination loss for the year is first allocated to Parent and Sub and then to non-controlling and controlling interests for the year.*

2. The elimination of $9,850 in assets and $10,075 in bond liabilities, together with the adjustment to reflect the $90 deferred tax liability, resulted in an after-tax increase of $135 in the equity side of the balance sheet. This was allocated to the two equities, at December 31, Year 5, as follows:

|  | Total | Non-controlling interest | Controlling interest |
|---|---|---|---|
| Gain allocated to Parent Co. | $ 45 | $— | $ 45 |
| Gain allocated to Sub Inc. | 90 | 9 | 81 |
|  | $135 | $ 9 | $126 |

> *The difference between gain on bond retirement and interest elimination loss for all years to date is first allocated to Parent and Sub and then to non-controlling and controlling interests at the end of the year.*

Remember that the original $300 gain in Year 4 was allocated to the two equities in the consolidated balance sheet as at December 31, Year 4 (see Exhibit 7.11).

3. The adjustments made in the preparation of both the December 31, Year 5, balance sheet and the Year 5 income statement can be summarized conceptually with respect to their effect on the consolidated balance sheet as follows:

| | | |
|---|---|---|
| *Asset side:* Investment in bonds | | − 9,850 |
| *Liability side:* | | |
|     Bonds payable | | − 10,075 |
|     Deferred income tax liability | | + 90 |
| Non-controlling interest: | | |
|     Balance, Dec. 31, Year 4 | + 12 | |
|     Year 5 entity net income | − 3 | + 9 |
| Consolidated retained earnings: | | |
|     Balance, Dec. 31, Year 4 | +168 | |
|     Year 5 entity net income | − 42 | + 126 |
| | | − 9,850 |

> *This chart shows the adjustments to the consolidated balance sheet at the end of Year 5.*

The $126 increase in consolidated retained earnings is automatically reflected when the consolidated income and retained earnings statements are prepared. The $9 increase in non-controlling interest is captured in the calculation of the amount of this equity.

**EQUITY METHOD JOURNAL ENTRIES**  If Parent has used the equity method, the following entries will be made on December 31, Year 5:

| | | |
|---|---|---|
| Investment in Sub Inc. | 2,790 | |
| Equity method income | | 2,790 |

90% of the Year 5 net income of Sub Inc. (90% × 3,100 = 2,790)

| | | |
|---|---|---|
| Equity method income | 15 | |
| Investment in Sub Inc. | | 15 |

Interest elimination loss allocated to Parent Co.

| | | |
|---|---|---|
| Equity method income | 27 | |
| Investment in Sub Inc. | | 27 |

90% of interest elimination loss allocated to Sub Inc. (90% × 30 = 27)

> *These entries should cause Parent's separate-entity income under the equity method to be equal to consolidated net income attributable to Parent's shareholders.*

The related equity method accounts of Parent will show the following changes and balances in Year 5:

| | Investment in Sub Inc. | Equity Method Income |
|---|---|---|
| December 31, Year 4 | $12,948 | |
| Change during Year 5: | | |
| Income from Sub Inc. | 2,790 | $2,790 |
| Interest loss to parent | (15) | (15) |
| 90% of interest loss to subsidiary | (27) | (27) |
| Balance, December 31, Year 5 | $15,696 | $2,748 |

> *The investment account under the equity method ($15,696) is different from the investment account under the cost method ($11,250 as per Exhibit 7.9).*

## Less Than 100% Purchase of Affiliate's Bonds

Our example assumed that Sub purchased 100% of Parent's bonds for $9,800 on December 31, Year 4. Suppose we changed the assumption so that only 40% of Parent's bonds were purchased, for $3,920. The elimination needed to prepare the Year 4 consolidated statements would be as follows:

| | | |
|---|---|---|
| Bonds payable (40% × 10,100) | 4,040 | |
| Investment in bonds of Parent Co. | | 3,920 |
| Gain on bond retirement | | 120 |

> *A gain on bond retirement is recognized only on the portion of the bonds being retired from a consolidated perspective.*

If only 40% of the bond liability has been eliminated, the consolidated balance sheet will show bonds payable amounting to $6,060, representing the 60% that is not intercompany and is payable to bondholders outside the entity. When consolidated income statements are later prepared, only 40% of the interest expense will be eliminated; the remaining 60% will be left as consolidated interest expense.

## Effective-Yield Method of Amortization

Our previous examples have assumed that both companies use the straight-line method to amortize the premiums and discounts. All of the end-of-chapter problems assume the straight-line method, unless stated otherwise. This method leads to fairly easy calculations because the yearly amortizations are equal. If one or both companies use the effective-interest method of amortization, the calculations become more complex, but the concepts remain the same. The following examples illustrate the effective- interest method.

On December 31, Year 0, Subco issued $100,000 face value bonds for a price of $92,791. The bonds pay interest on December 31 each year at a stated rate of 10%, and mature on December 31, Year 5. The market rate of interest was 12% on December 31, Year 0. Given that the stated rate of interest was lower than the market rate, the bonds were issued at a discount. The issue price of the bonds can be determined by taking the present value of future cash flows using a discount rate of 12% as follows:

| | |
|---|---:|
| Principal $100,000 × (P/F, 12%, 5 years) (0.56743) | $56,743 |
| Interest 10,000 × (P/A, 12%, 5 years) (3.60478) | 36,048 |
| | $92,791 |

> *The effective rate used in the present value calculations and bond amortization tables is the market rate of 12%.*

The following schedule shows how Subco would amortize the discount for its separate-entity financial statements and that the amortization of the bond discount increases interest expense (decreases income) each year over the term of the bonds:

| Period | Interest Paid | Interest Expense | Amortization of Bond Discount | Amortized Cost of Bonds |
|---|---|---|---|---|
| Year 0 | | | | $92,791 |
| Year 1 | $10,000[1] | $11,135[2] | $1,135[3] | 93,926[4] |
| Year 2 | 10,000 | 11,271 | 1,271 | 95,197 |
| Year 3 | 10,000 | 11,424 | 1,424 | 96,621 |
| Year 4 | 10,000 | 11,594 | 1,594 | 98,215 |
| Year 5 | 10,000 | 11,785 | 1,785 | 100,000 |

[1]$100,000 × 10% = $10,000     [2]$92,791 × 12% = $11,135
[3]$10,000 − $11,135 = − $1,135     [4]$92,791 + $1,135 = $93,926

> *The bond discount is amortized on Subco's separate-entity books over the remaining term of the bonds using the effective rate of 12%.*

The market rate of interest for these bonds decreased to 8%, and these bonds were trading at a price of $105,154 on December 31, Year 2. If Subco redeems the bonds on this date, it will prepare the following journal entry:

| | | |
|---|---|---|
| Loss on bond redemption | 9,957 | |
| Bonds payable | 95,197 | |
| Cash | | 105,154 |

---

*The market value of the bonds will increase when the market rate decreases.*

---

Now assume that Subco did not redeem its own bonds but Pubco purchased them in the open market on December 31, Year 2, for $105,154. The following schedule shows the amortization of this premium by Pubco using the effective-interest method and shows that the amortization of the bond premium decreases interest revenue (decreases income) each year over the remaining term of the bonds:

| Period | Interest Received | Interest Revenue | Amortization of Bond Premium | Amortized Cost of Bonds |
|---|---|---|---|---|
| Year 2 | | | | $105,154 |
| Year 3 | $10,000[1] | $8,412[2] | $1,588[3] | 103,566[4] |
| Year 4 | 10,000 | 8,285 | 1,715 | 101,851 |
| Year 5 | 10,000 | 8,149 | 1,851 | 100,000 |

[1]$100,000 × 10% = $10,000  
[3]$10,000 − $8,412 = $1,588  
[2]$105,154 × 8% = $8,412  
[4]$105,154 − $1,588 = $103,566

---

*Pubco amortizes its bond premium on its separate-entity books using its effective rate of 8%.*

---

From a separate legal entity perspective, Subco has bonds payable on its balance sheet, while Pubco has an investment in bonds on its balance sheet. From a consolidated perspective, these bonds were redeemed when Pubco purchased them on the open market. A loss on redemption of $9,957 ($105,154 − $95,197) should be recorded on the consolidated income statement. In subsequent years, Subco and Pubco will amortize the bond discount and premium on their separate-entity books. From a consolidated perspective, the amortization of the bond discount and premium should be eliminated because the bonds no longer exist. The following bond chart shows how the loss on bond redemption and the elimination of bond amortization is allocated to Pubco and Subco each year over the remaining life of the bonds:

| | Entity | Pubco | Subco |
|---|---|---|---|
| Loss on bond, Dec. 31, Year 2 | $9,957 | $5,154 | $4,803 |
| Interest elimination gain—Year 3 | 3,012 | 1,588 | 1,424 |
| Balance—loss, Dec. 31, Year 3 | 6,945 | 3,566 | 3,379 |
| Interest elimination gain—Year 4 | 3,309 | 1,715 | 1,594 |
| Balance—loss, Dec. 31, Year 4 | 3,636 | 1,851 | 1,785 |
| Interest elimination gain—Year 5 | 3,636 | 1,851 | 1,785 |
| Balance—loss, Dec. 31, Year 5 | $ –0– | $ –0– | $ –0– |

---

*From a consolidated perspective, the bonds were redeemed at a loss of $9,957.*

---

To further illustrate, examine the interest accounts of the two companies from the date of the intercompany purchase to the date of maturity of the bonds:

| Year Ended Dec. 31 | Pubco's Interest Revenue | Subco's Interest Expense | Difference |
|---|---|---|---|
| Year 3 | $ 8,412 | $11,424 | $3,012 |
| Year 4 | 8,285 | 11,594 | 3,309 |
| Year 5 | 8,149 | 11,785 | 3,636 |
| | $24,846 | $34,803 | $9,957 |

---

*From the separate-entity perspective, Pubco and Subco continue to amortize the bond discount or premium using their effective rates.*

*The loss on redemption was recognized in Year 2 from a consolidated perspective and over the three-year period ending in Year 5 from a single-entity perspective.*

---

Under the effective-interest method, the difference between interest revenue and interest expense changes over time. Under the straight-line method, the difference would be $3,319 ($9,957/3) each year for three years. Under both methods, a loss on bond redemption of $9,957 is recorded on the consolidated income statement in Year 2. In turn, consolidated income is increased by a total of $9,957 over the three-year remaining term of the bonds as the amortization of the bond premium and discount is eliminated.

See Self-Study Problem 2 for a comprehensive consolidation problem involving intercompany bondholdings. It includes most of the issues we have covered in Part B of this chapter.

## ASPE Differences

- As mentioned in Chapter 3, private companies can either consolidate their subsidiaries or report their investments in subsidiaries under the cost method, equity method, or fair value method.

- Whereas public companies can adopt the revaluation model or the cost model to value property, plant, and equipment, private companies using ASPE must use the cost model.

- Whereas impairment losses for property, plant, and equipment and intangible assets other than goodwill can be reversed under IFRS, they cannot be reversed under ASPE.

## SUMMARY

This chapter completed the illustrations of the holdback and realization of intercompany profits and gains in assets by examining the consolidation procedures involved when the profit relates to an asset subject to depreciation. The gain is held back because it has not been realized with a sale to an outside entity. The intercompany profit is subsequently realized as the assets are used or consumed in generating revenues over its remaining life. **(LO1)** By holding back the gain, the depreciable asset is reported at its historical cost less accumulated depreciation from a consolidated perspective as if the asset had not been sold. **(LO2)** The equity method captures the parent's share of all changes to the subsidiary's shareholders' equity and all consolidation adjustments. When the equity method is properly applied, the parent's net income on the parent's separate entity financial statements will be equal to consolidated net income attributable to the parent's shareholders' on the consolidated financial statements. **(LO3)** However, the account balances for individual lines on the two financial statements will be very different and will produce significantly different financial ratios. **(LO4)**

The second part of the chapter examined the gains and losses that are created in the consolidated statements by the elimination of intercompany bondholdings. The difference between the price paid to retire the bonds and the carrying amount of the bonds is a gain or a loss. These gains and losses can occur only if there were premiums or discounts involved in the issue or purchase of these bonds. **(LO5)** When the investing company purchases the bonds from outsiders, the bonds are effectively retired from a consolidated perspective and risk of holding bonds has been eliminated. Therefore, any gains or losses on the retirement are considered realized and can be recognized on the consolidated financial statements. **(LO6)** In the case of intercompany bondholdings, the gains or losses are recognized in the consolidated statements before they are recorded by the affiliated companies, whereas intercompany asset gains are recorded by the affiliated companies before they are recognized in the consolidated statements. **(LO7)**

## Self-Study Problem 1

### LO1, 3

The following are the Year 15 financial statements of Penn Company and its subsidiary Sill Corp.

| | Penn | Sill |
|---|---|---|
| **Year 15 Income Statements** | | |
| Miscellaneous revenues | $500,000 | $300,000 |
| Equity method income | 9,194 | — |
| Gain on sale of equipment | 14,000 | — |
| Gain on sale of patent | — | 7,500 |
| | 523,194 | 307,500 |
| Miscellaneous expenses | 309,600 | 186,500 |
| Depreciation expense | 120,000 | 80,000 |
| Patent amortization expense | 800 | — |
| Income tax expense | 33,000 | 16,000 |
| | 463,400 | 282,500 |
| Profit | $ 59,794 | $ 25,000 |
| **Year 15 Retained Earnings Statements** | | |
| Balance, January 1 | $162,000 | $154,000 |
| Profit | 59,794 | 25,000 |
| | 221,794 | 179,000 |
| Dividends | 25,000 | 8,000 |
| Balance, December 31 | $196,794 | $171,000 |

*(continued)*

*(continued)*

|  | Penn | Sill |
|---|---|---|
| *Statement of Financial Position* | | |
| *December 31, Year 15* | | |
| Miscellaneous assets | $271,600 | $131,000 |
| Land and buildings | 200,000 | 656,000 |
| Equipment | — | 44,000* |
| Accumulated depreciation | (80,000) | (250,000) |
| Patent (net) | 19,200 | — |
| Investment in Sill Corp. | 285,994 | — |
|  | $696,794 | $581,000 |
| Ordinary shares | $400,000 | $200,000 |
| Retained earnings | 196,794 | 171,000 |
| Miscellaneous liabilities | 100,000 | 210,000 |
|  | $696,794 | $581,000 |

*For illustrative purposes, we are assuming that this is the only equipment owned by either company.*

## Additional Information

Penn owns 80% of Sill and has used the equity method to account for its investment. The acquisition differential on acquisition date has been fully amortized for consolidation purposes prior to Year 15, and there were no unrealized intercompany profits or losses in the assets of the companies on December 31, Year 14. During Year 15, the following intercompany transactions took place:

- On January 1, Year 15, Penn sold used equipment to Sill and recorded a $14,000 gain on the transaction as follows:

| | | |
|---|---|---|
| Selling price of equipment | | $44,000 |
| Carrying amount of equipment sold: | | |
|   Cost | 70,000 | |
|   Accumulated depreciation—Dec. 31, Year 14 | 40,000 | 30,000 |
| Gain on sale of equipment | | $14,000 |

This equipment had an estimated remaining life of eight years on this date.

- On January 1, Year 5, Sill developed a patent at a cost of $34,000. It has been amortizing this patent over 17 years. On October 1, Year 15, Sill sold the patent to Penn and recorded a $7,500 gain, calculated as follows:

| | | | |
|---|---|---|---|
| Selling price of patent | | | $20,000 |
| Carrying amount of patent sold | | | |
|   Cost | | 34,000 | |
|   Amortization: | | | |
|     To December 31, Year 14 (10 × 2,000) | 20,000 | | |
|     Year 15 (¾ × 2,000) | 1,500 | 21,500 | 12,500 |
| Gain on sale of patent | | | $ 7,500 |

Penn is amortizing this patent over its remaining legal life of 6¼ years.

- Both gains were assessed income tax at a rate of 40%.

## Required

(a) Using the reported profits of both companies, prepare a calculation which shows that Penn's separate-entity profit is equal to consolidated profit attributable to Penn's shareholders.

(b) Using Penn's investment account, prepare a calculation which shows that the acquisition differential is fully amortized.

(c) Prepare the following Year 15 consolidated financial statements:

*eXcel*

   (i) Income statement

   (ii) Retained earnings statement

   (iii) Statement of financial position

## Solution to Self-Study Problem 1

### UNREALIZED PROFITS

| | Before Tax | 40% Tax | After Tax | |
|---|---|---|---|---|
| Equipment (Penn selling): | | | | |
| Gain recorded, Jan. 1, Year 15 | $14,000 | $5,600 | $ 8,400 | **(a)** |
| Depreciation, Year 15 (14,000 ÷ 8) | 1,750 | 700 | 1,050 | **(b)** |
| Balance unrealized, Dec. 31, Year 15 | $12,250 | $4,900 | $ 7,350 | **(c)** |
| | | | | |
| Patent (Sill selling): | | | | |
| Gain recorded, Oct. 1, Year 15 | $ 7,500 | $3,000 | $ 4,500 | **(d)** |
| Amortization, Year 15 (7,500 ÷ 6¼ × ¼) | 300 | 120 | 180 | **(e)** |
| Balance unrealized Dec. 31, Year 15 | $ 7,200 | $2,880 | $ 4,320 | **(f)** |
| Deferred income tax asset—December 31, Year 15: | | | | |
| Equipment profit | | | $ 4,900 | **(g)** |
| Patent profit | | | 2,880 | **(h)** |
| | | | $ 7,780 | **(i)** |

| | | |
|---|---|---|
| **(a)** Profit Penn Co. | | $ 59,794 |
| Less: Equity method income | | 9,194 |
| Profit Penn—own operations | | 50,600 |
| Less: Unrealized equipment gain **(a)** | | 8,400 |
| | | 42,200 |
| Add: Realized equipment gain in Year 15 **(b)** | | 1,050 |
| Adjusted profit | | 43,250 |
| Profit Sill Corp. | 25,000 | |
| Less: Unrealized patent gain **(d)** | 4,500 | |
| | 20,500 | |
| Add: Patent gain realized in Year 15 **(e)** | 180 | |
| Adjusted profit | | 20,680 |
| Consolidated profit | | $ 63,930 |
| Attributable to: | | |
| Shareholders of Penn | | $ 59,794 **(j)** |
| Non-controlling interest (20% × 20,680) | | 4,136 **(k)** |

| | | |
|---|---|---|
| **(b)** Investment in Sill Corp. (equity method): | | |
| Balance, Dec. 31, Year 15 | | $285,994 |
| Add: Unrealized equipment gain, Dec. 31, Year 15 **(c)** | | 7,350 |
| | | 293,344 |
| Sill Corp., Dec. 31, Year 15: | | |
| Ordinary shares | 200,000 | |
| Retained earnings | 171,000 | |
| | 371,000 | |
| Less: Unrealized patent gain, Dec. 31, Year 15 **(f)** | 4,320 | |
| Adjusted shareholders' equity | 366,680 | |
| Penn's ownership | 80% | 293,344 |
| Unamortized acquisition differential | | $ –0– |

**(c) (i)**

### CONSOLIDATED INCOME STATEMENT
#### For Year 15

| | |
|---|---:|
| Miscellaneous revenues (500,000 + 300,000) | $800,000 |
| Gain on sale of equipment (14,000 + 0 − **[a] 14,000**) | –0– |
| Gain on sale of patents (0 + 7,500 − **[d] 7,500**) | –0– |
| Miscellaneous expenses (309,600 + 186,500) | 496,100 |
| Depreciation expense (120,000 + 80,000 − **[b] 1,750**) | 198,250 |
| Patent amortization expense (800 − **[e] 300**) | 500 |
| Income tax expense (33,000 + 16,000 − **[a] 5,600** + **[b] 700** − **[d] 3,000** + **[e] 120**) | 41,220 |
| | 736,070 |
| Profit | $ 63,930 |
| Attributable to: | |
| Shareholders of Parent **(j)** | $ 59,794 |
| Non-controlling interest **(k)** | 4,136 |

**(ii)**

### CONSOLIDATED RETAINED EARNINGS STATEMENT
#### For Year 15

| | |
|---|---:|
| Balance, January 1 | $ 162,000 |
| Profit | 59,794 |
| | 221,794 |
| Dividends | 25,000 |
| Balance, December 31 | $ 196,794 |

**(iii)**

### CONSOLIDATED STATEMENT OF FINANCIAL POSITION
#### At December 31, Year 15

| | |
|---|---:|
| Miscellaneous assets (271,600 + 131,000) | $ 402,600 |
| Land and buildings (200,000 + 656,000) | 856,000 |
| Equipment (0 + 44,000 − **[a] 14,000** + **40,000***) | 70,000 |
| Accumulated depreciation (80,000 + 250,000 − **[b] 1,750** + **40,000***) | (368,250) |
| Patent (19,200 + 0 − **[f] 7,200**) | 12,000 |
| Deferred income taxes (0 + 0 + **[i] 7,780**) | 7,780 |
| | $ 980,130 |
| Ordinary shares | $400,000 |
| Retained earnings | 196,794 |
| Non-controlling interest** | 73,336 |
| Miscellaneous liabilities (100,000 + 210,000) | 310,000 |
| | $980,130 |

*It is necessary to increase equipment and accumulated depreciation by $40,000 in order to reestablish the original historical cost of the equipment and the accumulated depreciation as at the date of the intercompany sale.

**Sill Corp.—Adjusted shareholders' equity (see part [b])

| | |
|---|---:|
| | $366,680 |
| | 20% |
| Non-controlling interest | $ 73,336 |

# Self-Study Problem 2

The financial statements of Parson Corp. and Sloan Inc. for the year ended December 31, Year 8, are as follows:

## INCOME STATEMENTS
### For Year 8

| | Parson | Sloan |
|---|---|---|
| Miscellaneous revenues | $650,000 | $200,000 |
| Interest revenue | 5,662 | — |
| Dividend revenue | 7,500 | — |
| | 663,162 | 200,000 |
| Miscellaneous expenses | 432,000 | 129,600 |
| Interest expense | — | 9,723 |
| Income tax expense | 92,000 | 24,000 |
| | 524,000 | 163,323 |
| Profit | $139,162 | $ 36,677 |

## RETAINED EARNINGS STATEMENTS
### For Year 8

| | Parson | Sloan |
|---|---|---|
| Balance, January 1 | $245,000 | $ 90,000 |
| Profit | 139,162 | 36,677 |
| | 384,162 | 126,677 |
| Dividends | 70,000 | 10,000 |
| Balance, December 31 | $314,162 | $116,677 |

## STATEMENTS OF FINANCIAL POSITION
### At December 31, Year 8

| | Parson | Sloan |
|---|---|---|
| Investment in Sloan shares | $ 96,000 | $ |
| Investment in Sloan bonds | 61,210 | — |
| Miscellaneous assets | 607,000 | 372,600 |
| | $764,210 | $372,600 |
| Ordinary shares | $150,000 | $ 80,000 |
| Retained earnings | 314,162 | 116,677 |
| Bonds payable | — | 101,002 |
| Miscellaneous liabilities | 300,048 | 74,921 |
| | $764,210 | $372,600 |

## Additional Information

- Parson acquired 75% of Sloan on January 1, Year 4, at a cost of $96,000. On this date, Sloan's ordinary shares and retained earnings were $80,000 and $40,000, respectively, and the acquisition differential was allocated entirely to goodwill. Impairment tests conducted yearly since acquisition yielded a loss of $3,200 in Year 5 and a further loss of $800 in Year 8. Parson uses the cost method to account for the investment.
- Sloan has a 10%, $100,000 bond issue outstanding. These bonds were originally issued at a premium to reduce the effective interest cost to 9.6%, and mature on December 31, Year 11. On January 1, Year 8, the unamortized issue premium amounted to $1,279. Sloan uses the effective interest method to amortize the premium.
- On January 1, Year 8, Parson acquired $60,000 face value of Sloan's bonds at a cost of $61,548, which generates an effective rate of return of 9.2%. The purchase premium is being amortized by Parson using the effective interest method.

- Both companies pay income tax at a rate of 40%.
- Gains and losses from intercompany bondholdings are to be allocated to the two companies when consolidated statements are prepared.

**Required**

eXcel

(a) Prepare the following Year 8 consolidated financial statements:

   (i) Income statement

   (ii) Retained earnings statement

   (iii) Statement of financial position

(b) Prepare a calculation of consolidated retained earnings at December 31, Year 8.

(c) Prepare the Year 8 journal entries that would be made by Parson if the equity method was used to account for the investment in Sloan's shares.

(d) Calculate the balance in the "Investment in Sloan shares" account as at December 31, Year 8, if Parson had used the equity method.

## Solution to Self-Study Problem 2

| | | |
|---|---:|---:|
| Cost of 75% of Sloan | | $ 96,000 |
| Implied value of 100% of Sloan | | $128,000 |
| Carrying amount of Sloan, January 1, Year 4: | | |
|   Ordinary shares | 80,000 | |
|   Retained earnings | 40,000 | |
| | | 120,000 |
| Acquisition differential—January 1, Year 4 | | 8,000 |
| Allocated to revalue Sloan's identifiable net assets | | –0– |
| Balance—goodwill | | 8,000 |
| Impairment losses: | | |
|   Year 4 to Year 7 | | 3,200 **(a)** |
|   Year 8 | | 800 **(b)** |
| Balance—goodwill, December 31, Year 8 | | $ 4,000 **(c)** |
| Non-controlling interest, January 1, Year 4 (25% × 128,000) | | $ 32,000 **(d)** |

**INTERCOMPANY TRANSACTIONS**

Year 5 Before-Tax Bond Loss

| | | |
|---|---:|---:|
| Cost of 60% of Sloan's bonds acquired Jan. 1, Year 8 | | $61,548 |
| Carrying amount of liability: | | |
|   Bonds payable | 100,000 | |
|   Bond premium | 1,279 | |
| | 101,279 | |
| Amount acquired by Parson | 60% | 60,767 |
|   Bond loss to be reflected in the Year 8 consolidated income statement | | $ 781 **(e)** |
| Allocated as follows: | | |
|   Cost of bonds | | $61,548 |
|   Face value of bonds (intercompany portion) | | 60,000 |
|     Before-tax loss—Parson | | $ 1,548 **(f)** |
| Face value of bonds | | $60,000 |
| Carrying amount of bonds (intercompany portion) | | 60,767 |
|   Before-tax gain—Sloan | | $ 767 **(g)** |

## BOND AMORTIZATION SCHEDULE—SLOAN

| Period | Interest Paid | Interest Expense | Amortization of Bond Premium | Amortized Cost of Bonds |
|---|---|---|---|---|
| Jan. 1, Year 8 | | | | $101,279 |
| Year 8 | $10,000[1] | $9,723[2] | $277[3] | 101,002[4] |

[1]$100,000 × 10% = $10,000
[3]$10,000 − $9,723 = $277

[2]$101,279 × 9.6% = $9,723
[4]$101,279 − $277 = $101,002

## BOND AMORTIZATION SCHEDULE—PARSON

| Period | Interest Received | Interest Revenue | Amortization of Bond Premium | Amortized Cost of Bonds |
|---|---|---|---|---|
| Jan. 1, Year 8 | | | | $61,548 |
| Year 8 | $6,000[1] | $5,662[2] | $338[3] | 61,210[4] |

[1]$60,000 × 10% = $6,000
[2]$61,548 × 9.2% = $5,662

[3]$6,000 − $5,662 = $338
[4]$61,548 − $338 = $61,210

## INTERCOMPANY INTEREST REVENUE AND EXPENSE

| | | | |
|---|---|---|---|
| Interest paid by Sloan: | | | |
| 10% × 100,000 | 10,000 | | |
| Premium amortization | 277 | | |
| Total expense | 9,723 | | |
| Intercompany portion | 60% | $5,834 | **(h)** |
| Interest received by Parson: | | | |
| 10% × 60,000 | 6,000 | | |
| Premium amortization | 338 | 5,662 | **(i)** |
| Before-tax interest elimination gain to entity | | $   172 | **(j)** |
| Allocated: | | | |
| Before-tax loss to Sloan (277 × 60%) | | $  (166) | **(k)** |
| Before-tax gain to Parson | | 338 | **(l)** |
| Total gain allocated (before-tax dollars) | | $   172 | **(m)** |

## SUMMARY

| | Entity | | | Parson Co. | | | Sloan Inc. | | | |
|---|---|---|---|---|---|---|---|---|---|---|
| | Before Tax | 40% Tax | After Tax | Before Tax | 40% Tax | After Tax | Before Tax | 40% Tax | After Tax | |
| Jan. 1, Year 8, bond loss (gain) | $781 | $312 | $469 | $1,548 | $619 | $929 | $(767) | $(307) | $(460) | **(n)** |
| Int. elim. gain (loss) Year 8 | 172 | 69 | 103 | 338 | 135 | 203 | (166) | ( 66) | (100) | **(o)** |
| Dec. 31, Year 8, balance, loss (gain) | $609 | $243 | $366 | $1,210 | $484 | $726 | $(601) | $(241) | $(360) | **(p)** |

## CALCULATION OF CONSOLIDATED NET INCOME

(a) (i)                                    For Year 8

| | | |
|---|---:|---:|
| Profit—Parson | | $139,162 |
| Less: Dividend from Sloan | 7,500 | |
| January 1 bond loss allocated **(n)** | 929 | 8,429 |
| | | 130,733 |
| Add: Year 8 interest elimination gain allocated **(o)** | | 203 |
| Adjusted profit—Parson | | 130,936 |
| Profit—Sloan | 36,677 | |
| Add: January 1 bond gain allocated **(n)** | 460 | |
| Less: Year 8 interest elimination loss allocated **(o)** | (100) | |
| Acquisition-differential amortization **(b)** | (800) | |
| Adjusted profit—Sloan | | 36,237 |
| Consolidated profit | | $167,173 |
| Attributable to: | | |
| Shareholders of Parson | | $158,114  **(q)** |
| Non-controlling interest (25% × 36,267) | | 9,059  **(r)** |

## CONSOLIDATED INCOME STATEMENT
### For Year 8

| | |
|---|---:|
| Miscellaneous revenues (650,000 + 200,000) | $850,000 |
| Interest revenue (5,662 + 0 − **[i] 5,662**) | — |
| Dividend revenue (7,500 + 0 − **7,500**) | — |
| Miscellaneous expenses (432,000 + 129,600) | 561,600 |
| Loss on bond retirement **(n)** | 781 |
| Interest expense (9,723 − **[h] 5,834**) | 3,889 |
| Goodwill impairment loss **(b)** | 800 |
| Income tax expense (92,000 + 24,000 − **[n] 312** + **[o] 69**) | 115,757 |
| | 682,827 |
| Profit | $167,173 |
| Attributable to: | |
| Shareholders of Parson **(q)** | $158,114 |
| Non-controlling interest **(r)** | 9,059 |

(ii)      ## CALCULATION OF CONSOLIDATED RETAINED EARNINGS
### at January 1, Year 8

| | | |
|---|---:|---:|
| Retained earnings—Parson | | $245,000 |
| Retained earnings—Sloan | 90,000 | |
| Acquisition retained earnings | 40,000 | |
| Increase since acquisition | 50,000 | |
| Less: Goodwill impairment loss **(a)** | 3,200 | |
| | 46,800  **(s)** | |
| Parson's ownership | 75% | 35,100 |
| Consolidated retained earnings, Jan. 1, Year 8 | | $280,100  **(t)** |

## CONSOLIDATED RETAINED EARNINGS STATEMENT
### For Year 8

| | |
|---|---:|
| Balance, January 1 **(t)** | $280,100 |
| Profit | 158,114 |
| | 438,214 |
| Dividends | 70,000 |
| Balance, December 31 | $368,214 |

(iii)
## CALCULATION OF NON-CONTROLLING INTEREST
### At December 31, Year 8

| | |
|---|---:|
| Shareholders' equity—Sloan: | |
| Ordinary shares | $ 80,000 |
| Retained earnings | 116,677 |
| | 196,677 |
| Add: Net Year 8 bond gain allocated **(p)** | 360 |
| Add: Unimpaired goodwill **(c)** | 4,000 |
| Adjusted shareholders' equity | 201,037 |
| | 25% |
| | $ 50,259 **(u)** |

## ALTERNATIVE FORMAT

| | |
|---|---:|
| Non-controlling interest, date of acquisition **(d)** | $ 32,000 |
| Adjusted increase in Sloan's retained earnings since acquisition (25% × **[v]** 73,037) | 18,259 |
| | $ 50,259 |

## CONSOLIDATED STATEMENT OF FINANCIAL POSITION
### At December 31, Year 8

| | |
|---|---:|
| Goodwill **(c)** | $ 4,000 |
| Deferred income tax asset **(p)** | 243 |
| Investment in Sloan bonds (61,210 + 0 − 61,210) | — |
| Miscellaneous assets (607,000 + 372,600) | 979,600 |
| | $983,843 |
| Ordinary shares | $150,000 |
| Retained earnings | 368,214 |
| Non-controlling Interest **(u)** | 50,259 |
| Bonds payable (101,002 − 60,000 − **[p] 601**) | 40,401 |
| Miscellaneous liabilities (300,048 + 74,921) | 374,969 |
| | $983,843 |

(b)
## PROOF—CONSOLIDATED RETAINED EARNINGS
### At December 31, Year 8

| | | |
|---|---:|---:|
| Retained earnings—Parson | | $314,162 |
| Less: Net Year 8 bond loss allocated **(p)** | | 726 |
| Adjusted retained earnings | | 313,436 |
| Retained earnings—Sloan | 116,677 | |
| Acquisition retained earnings | 40,000 | |
| Increase since acquisition | 76,677 | |
| Less: Goodwill impairment losses ( **[a] 3,200** + **[b] 800**) | (4,000) | |
| Add: Net Year 8 bond gain allocated **(p)** | 360 | |
| Adjusted increase | 73,037 | **(v)** |
| Parsons' ownership | 75% | 54,778 |
| Consolidated retained earnings | | $368,214 |

(c)                    **EQUITY METHOD JOURNAL ENTRIES**

| | | |
|---|---|---|
| Investment in Sloan | 27,508 | |
|    Equity method income | | 27,508 |
| 75% of Sloan's Year 8 profit (75% × 36,677) | | |
| Investment in Sloan | 270 | |
|    Equity method income | | 270 |
| 75% of the net Year 8 bond gain allocated to Sloan (75% × 360) | | |
| Cash | 7,500 | |
|    Investment in Sloan | | 7,500 |
| Dividends received from Sloan | | |
| Equity method income | 600 | |
|    Investment in Sloan | | 600 |
| Year 8 goodwill impairment loss (75% × 800) | | |
| Equity method income | 726 | |
|    Investment in Sloan | | 726 |
| Year 8 net bond loss allocated to Parson | | |

| (d) | Investment in Sloan Shares |
|---|---|
| Balance, December 31, Year 7—cost method | $ 96,000 |
| Increase in retained earnings to Jan. 1, Year 8 ([s] **46,800** × 75%) | 35,100 |
| Balance, December 31, Year 7—equity method | 131,100 |
| Equity method income, Year 8 (see equity method journal entries) | 26,452 |
| Dividends from Sloan | (7,500) |
|    Balance, December 31, Year 8—equity method | $150,052 |

# APPENDIX 7A

## Depreciable Assets under Revaluation Model

.........

### LO8

IAS 16 *Property, Plant and Equipment* allows a reporting entity to use either the revaluation method or the cost method to measure its property, plant, and equipment. The same method must be used for each class of property, plant, and equipment. The revaluation adjustment is reported in other comprehensive income if it is reporting or reversing a revaluation surplus. It is reported in net income if it is reporting or reversing an impairment loss. Depreciation expense is based on the revalued amount. The revaluation surplus is transferred directly to retained earnings, either as the asset is depreciated or when the asset is sold.

We will illustrate the preparation of consolidated financial statements when there has been an intercompany sale of equipment, which had been remeasured under the revaluation model allowed in IAS 16.

*An entity can choose to revalue its property, plant, and equipment to fair value on an annual basis.*

Sub acquired equipment for $5,000 on January 1, Year 6 and was depreciating the equipment over an estimated useful life of five years. After two years, the accumulated depreciation was $2,000 and the carrying amount was $3,000. Let us now assume that on December 31, Year 7, Sub remeasured its equipment to $3,300, the fair value of the equipment, and that both the original cost and the accumulated depreciation were to be grossed up using the proportional method for the increase in value. Sub had not revalued the equipment since it was acquired. Sub would make the following entry on its separate-entity books:

| | | |
|---|---|---|
| Equipment [(3,300/3,000 × 5,000) − 5,000] | 500 | |
| Accumulated depreciation [(3,300/3,000 × 2,000) − 2,000] | | 200 |
| Other comprehensive income—revaluation surplus | | 300 |

> *The revaluation surplus is reported through other comprehensive income.*

Depreciation expense for Year 8 would have been $1,100 ($3,300/3 years) on Sub's books. Now assume that Sub sold the equipment to Parent for $2,600 on January 1, Year 9. It would make the following entries on its separate-entity books:

| | | |
|---|---|---|
| Cash | 2,600 | |
| Accumulated depreciation (2,000 + 200 + 1,100) | 3,300 | |
| Equipment (5,000 + 500) | | 5,500 |
| Gain on sale of equipment[8] | | 400 |
| To record sale of equipment | | |
| Accumulated other comprehensive income—revaluation surplus | 300 | |
| Retained earnings | | 300 |
| To transfer revaluation surplus to retained earnings | | |

> *The revaluation surplus is transferred to retained earnings when the property is sold.*

Given that the parent controls the subsidiary, the parent could have imposed the sale price for the equipment. It does not necessarily reflect the fair value of the equipment. The parent would make the following entries related to the equipment in Year 9:

| | | |
|---|---|---|
| Equipment | 2,600 | |
| Cash | | 2,600 |
| To purchase equipment | | |
| Depreciation expense | 1,300 | |
| Accumulated depreciation | | 1,300 |
| Depreciation expense for Year 9 | | |

When preparing the consolidated financial statements at the end of Year 9, the following entries would have to be made in the consolidated working papers to report the amounts that would have appeared had the intercompany transaction not occurred:

| | | |
|---|---|---|
| Gain on sale of equipment | 400 | |
| Equipment | | 400 |
| To reverse gain on sale | | |

| Equipment | 3,300 | |
| Accumulated depreciation (2,000 + 200 + 1,100) | | 3,300 |
| To reinstate accumulated depreciation at date of intercompany sale | | |
| Accumulated depreciation | 200 | |
| Depreciation expense (1,300 − 1,100) | | 200 |
| To recognize gain through usage of equipment by reversing excess depreciation | | |
| Retained earnings | 300 | |
| Accumulated other comprehensive income—revaluation surplus | | 300 |
| To reinstate revaluation surplus | | |

The following table summarizes what would have appeared on the three sets of financial statements for Year 9 after processing the journal entries indicated above:

| | Parent | Sub | Consolidated |
|---|---|---|---|
| Equipment | 2,600 | | 5,500 |
| Accumulated depreciation | 1,300 | | 4,400 |
| Equipment—net | 1,300 | | 1,100 |
| Accumulated other comprehensive income | | | 300 |
| Gain on sale | | 400 | |
| Depreciation expense | 1,300 | 200 | 1,100 |

---

*The consolidated statements should report amounts that would have existed had the intercompany transaction not occurred.*

---

The consolidated amounts reflect what would have been on Sub's separate-entity financial statements and on the consolidated financial statements had the intercompany transaction not occurred.

## Summary of Appendix 7A

Under the revaluation model, depreciable assets are reported at fair value at each revaluation date on both the separate entity and consolidated balance sheets. Unrealized profits from intercompany transactions are removed on the consolidated financial statements and the account balances reflect what would have been reported had the intercompany sale not occurred. **(LO8)**

## Review Questions

*Questions, cases, and problems that deal with the appendix material are denoted with an asterisk.*

LO1, 2    **1.** Explain how an intercompany gain of $2,700 on the sale of a depreciable asset is held back on the consolidated income statement in the year of sale and realized on subsequent consolidated income statements. What income tax adjustments should be made in each instance?

**LO1**   **2.** "The realization of intercompany inventory and depreciable asset profits is really an adjustment made in the preparation of consolidated income statements to arrive at historical cost numbers." Explain.

**LO2**   **3.** An intercompany inventory profit is realized when the inventory is sold outside the entity. Is this also the case with respect to an intercompany profit in a depreciable asset? Explain.

**LO1, 2**   **4.** An intercompany gain on a depreciable asset resulting from a sale by the parent company is subsequently realized by an adjustment to the subsidiary's depreciation expense in the preparation of consolidated income statements. Should this adjustment be taken into account in the calculation of net income attributable to non-controlling interest? Explain.

**LO1, 2**   **5.** Why does an intercompany sale of a depreciable asset (such as equipment or a building) require subsequent adjustments to depreciation expense within the consolidation process?

**LO1, 2**   **6.** If an intercompany sale of a depreciable asset has been made at a price above carrying amount, the beginning retained earnings of the seller are reduced when preparing each subsequent consolidation. Why does the amount of the adjustment change from year to year?

**LO1, 2**   **7.** When there has been an intercompany sale of a used depreciable asset (i.e., accumulated depreciation has been recorded for this asset), it is necessary to gross up the asset and accumulated depreciation when preparing the consolidated financial statement. Explain what is meant by grossing up the asset and accumulated depreciation and why this action is necessary.

**LO8**   *****8.** When a company sells equipment that had previously been remeasured to fair value under the revaluation model of IAS 16, it transfers the revaluation surplus from accumulated other comprehensive income directly to retained earnings. What adjustments must be made to accumulated other comprehensive income when preparing consolidated financial statements if the sale is from the parent to the subsidiary?

**LO8**   *****9.** "There should never be a gain on an intercompany sale of equipment when the selling company uses the revaluation model under IAS 16 and the equipment is sold at fair value." Is this statement true or false? Explain.

**LO5**   **10.** Four approaches could be used to allocate gains (losses) on the elimination of intercompany bondholdings in the preparation of consolidated financial statements. Outline these four approaches. Which approach is conceptually superior? Explain.

**LO5**   **11.** An interest elimination gain (loss) does not appear as a distinguishable item on a consolidated income statement. Explain.

**LO1, 5**   **12.** The adjustment for the holdback of an intercompany gain in assets requires a corresponding adjustment to a consolidated deferred tax asset. The adjustment for a gain from intercompany bondholdings requires a corresponding adjustment to a consolidated deferred tax liability. In both cases, the tax adjustment is made because of a gain. Why is the tax adjustment different? Explain.

**LO1, 5**   **13.** "Some intercompany gains (losses) are realized for consolidation purposes subsequent to their actual recording by the affiliates, while others are recorded by the affiliates subsequent to their realization for consolidation purposes." Explain and refer to the type of gains (losses) that apply in each case.

LO6 **14.** Explain how the recognition of gains on the elimination of intercompany bondholdings is consistent with the principle of recording gains only when they are realized.

LO6 **15.** Explain how the matching principle supports the recognition of deferred income tax expense when a gain is recognized on the elimination of intercompany bondholdings.

# CASES

## Case 7-1

LO1, 3

Enron Corporation's 2000 financial statements disclosed the following transaction with LIM2, a non-consolidated special purpose entity (SPE) that was formed by Enron:

> In June 2000, LIM2 purchased dark fibre optic cable from Enron for a purchase price of $100 million. LIM2 paid Enron $30 million in cash and the balance in an interest-bearing note for $70 million. Enron recognized $67 million in pre-tax earnings in 2000 related to the asset sale.

Investigators later discovered that LIM2 was in many ways controlled by Enron. In the wake of the bankruptcy of Enron, both American and Canadian standard-setters introduced accounting standards that require the consolidation of SPEs that are essentially controlled by their sponsor firm.

By selling goods to SPEs that it controlled but did not consolidate, did Enron overstate its earnings?

**Required**

Determine how this transaction should have been accounted for assuming that

(a) Enron controlled LIM2 and used consolidated financial statements to report its investment in LIM2;

(b) Enron had significant influence over LIM2 and used the equity method to report its investment; and

(c) Enron did not have control or significant influence over LIM2 but LIM2 was considered a related party and Enron had to apply IAS 24 *Related Party Disclosures*.

## Case 7-2

LO5

Several years ago, the Penston Company purchased 90% of the outstanding shares of Swansan Corporation. The acquisition was made because Swansan produced a vital component used in Penston's manufacturing process. Penston wanted to ensure an adequate supply of this item at a reasonable price. The former owner, James Swansan, who agreed to continue managing this organization, retained the remaining 10% of Swansan's shares. He was given responsibility over the subsidiary's daily manufacturing operations but not for any of the financial decisions.

At a recent meeting, the president of Penston and the company's chief financial officer began discussing Swansan's debt position. The subsidiary had a debt-to-equity ratio that seemed unreasonably high considering the significant amount of cash flows being generated by both companies. Payment of the interest expense, especially on the subsidiary's outstanding bonds, was a major cost, one that the corporate officials hoped to reduce. However, the bond indenture specified that Swansan could retire this debt prior to maturity only by paying 107% of face value.

This premium was considered prohibitive. Thus, to avoid contractual problems, Penston acquired a large portion of Swansan's liability on the open market for 101% of face value. Penston's purchase created an effective loss on the debt of $300,000: the excess of the price over the carrying amount of the debt as reported on Swansan's books.

Company accountants are currently computing the non-controlling interest's share of consolidated net income to be reported for the current year. They are unsure about the impact of this $300,000 loss. The subsidiary's debt was retired, but officials of the parent company made the decision.

**Required**

(a) Determine who lost the $300,000.

(b) Explain, in qualitative terms, how the loss should be allocated on the consolidated financial statements.

## Case 7-3

LO1, 2

On January 1, Year 4, Plum purchased 100% of the common shares of Slum. On December 31, Year 5, Slum purchased a machine for $168,000 from an external supplier. The machine had an estimated useful life of six years with no residual value. On December 31, Year 7, Plum purchased the machine from Slum for $200,000. The estimated remaining life at the time of the intercompany sale was four years. Plum pays income tax at the rate of 40%, whereas Slum is taxed at a rate of 30%.

When preparing the consolidated statements for Year 8, the controller and manager of accounting at Plum got into a heated debate as to the proper tax rate to use when eliminating the tax on the excess depreciation being taken by Plum. The controller thought that Slum's tax rate should be used since Slum was the owner of this machine before the intercompany sale. The manager of accounting thought that Plum's tax rate should be used since Plum was the actual company saving the tax at the rate of 40%.

In Year 9, the Canada Revenue Agency (CRA) audited Plum. It questioned the legitimacy of the intercompany transaction for the following reasons:

1. Was the selling price of $200,000 a fair reflection of market value?

2. Was Plum trying to gain a tax advantage by saving tax at a rate of 40% rather than the 30% saving that Slum used to realize?

Plum argued that, under the terms of the sale, CRA was better off because it received tax in Year 7 from the gain on the intercompany sale. Had the intercompany sale not occurred, it would not have received this tax.

**Required**

(a) Determine the economic benefits, if any, to the consolidated entity from tax savings as a result of this intercompany transaction. Was it a good financial decision to undertake this transaction? Explain.

(b) Would your answer to (a) be any different if Plum owned only 60% of the common shares of Slum? Explain.

(c) Indicate what amount of tax savings related to depreciation expense would be reflected on the consolidated income statement under the alternatives suggested by the controller and manager, or other options you could suggest. Which method would you recommend? Explain your answer using basic accounting principles.

## Case 7-4

LO1, 2

Stephanie Baker is an audit senior with the public accounting firm of Wilson & Lang. It is February Year 9, and the audit of Canadian Development Limited (CDL) for the year ended December 31, Year 8, is proceeding. Stephanie has identified several transactions that occurred in the Year 8 fiscal year that have major accounting implications. The engagement partner has asked Stephanie to draft a memo addressing the accounting implications, financial statement disclosure issues, and any other important matters regarding these transactions.

CDL is an important player in many sectors of the economy. The company has both debt and equity securities that trade on a Canadian stock exchange. Except for a controlling interest (53%) owned by the Robichaud family, CDL's shares are widely held. The company has interests in the natural resources, commercial and residential real estate, construction, transportation, and technology development sectors, among others.

### Changes in Capital Structure

During Year 8, CDL's underwriters recommended some changes to the company's capital structure. As a result, the company raised $250 million by issuing one million convertible, redeemable debentures at $250 each. Each debenture is convertible into one common share at any time. CDL's controlling shareholders acquired a sizeable block of the one million debentures issued; a few large institutional investors took up the remainder.

The company proposes to partition the balance sheet in a manner that will include a section titled "Shareholders' Equity and Convertible Debentures." The company views this classification as appropriate because the convertible debt, being much more akin to equity than debt, represents a part of the company's permanent capital. Maurice Richard, the controller of CDL, has emphasized that the interest rate on the debentures is considerably lower than on normal convertible issues and that it is expected that the majority of investors will exercise their conversion privilege. The company has the option of repaying the debt at maturity in 20 years' time, through the issuance of common shares. The option will be lost if the company is unable to meet certain solvency tests at the maturity date. The company's intention was to raise additional permanent capital, and convertible debt was chosen because of the attractive tax savings. The debentures are redeemable by the investors at $250 from January 1, Year 15, to January 1, Year 18.

At the same time as the company issued the convertible debentures, two million common shares were converted into two million preferred, redeemable shares. The carrying amount of the two million common shares was $20 million. The preferred shares do not bear dividends and are mandatorily redeemable in five years at $20 per share. They have been recorded at their redemption value of $40 million, and the difference between this redemption value and the carrying amount of the common shares ($20 million) has been charged against retained earnings.

### Disposal of Residential Real Estate Segment

Intercity Real Estate Corporation (IRE) is a wholly owned subsidiary of CDL and has two operating divisions: a money-losing residential real estate division and a highly profitable commercial real estate division. The two divisions had been combined into one legal entity for tax purposes as the losses arising from the residential real estate division have more than offset the profits from the commercial real estate division.

During Year 8, CDL decided to dispose of its shares of IRE. However, CDL wished to retain the commercial real estate division and decided to transfer the division's assets to another corporation prior to selling the shares of IRE. As part of the sale agreement, just before the closing, the commercial real estate assets were transferred out of IRC to CDL, which then transferred the assets to a newly created subsidiary, Real Property Inc. (RPI). In order to maximize the asset base of RPI, the commercial real estate assets were transferred at fair values, which greatly increased their tax base and created considerable income for tax purposes.

Maurice has explained to Stephanie that since the transfer would create income for tax purposes, it was necessary for both CDL and the purchaser to agree on the fair value of the commercial real estate assets, even though they were not part of the IRC sale. IRC's purchaser agreed to the values used because the loss carry-forwards, which would otherwise have expired, offset the income for tax purposes.

CDL is planning to take RPI public sometime this year. The commercial real estate assets of RPI have been recorded at the values established in the sale of IRC, because management believes that this amount represents the cost of acquiring the business from IRC. Maurice has stressed that the transfer between IRC and RPI is very different from the majority of transactions between companies under common control. He argues that the transfer of the commercial real estate assets to RPI represents a bona fide business combination, since there is a change of substance and not just of form. CDL maintains a policy of granting subsidiaries a high degree of autonomy and, in substance, they do not function "under common control." Maurice indicated that the real estate assets are worth more to CDL as a result of this transaction because of the increase in the tax values of the assets. Finally, an unrelated party was involved in the transaction and in the determination of the fair value of the assets.

Stephanie noted that after the transfer the real estate business changed. RPI has undertaken a major refurbishing program and has just bought a large chain of shopping centres that has doubled the company's asset base.

*(CPA Canada adapted)*[9]

## Case 7-5

**LO1, 8**

It is Monday, September 13, Year 10. You, CPA, work at Fife & Richardson LLP, a CPA firm. Ken Simpson, one of the partners, approaches you mid-morning regarding Brennan & Sons Limited (BSL), a private company client for which you performed the August 31, Year 9, year-end audit.

"It seems there have been substantial changes at BSL this year," Ken explains. "I'm going there tomorrow, and since you will be on the audit again this year, it would be beneficial for you to come. I took the liberty of retrieving information from last year's files so you can refresh your memory about this client" (see Exhibit I).

The next day, you and Ken meet with Jack Wright, the accounting manager at BSL. Jack gives you the internally prepared financial statements (Exhibit II). To your surprise, there are also financial statements for two new companies. Jack quickly explains that BSL incorporated two subsidiaries in January Year 10, each with the same year-end as BSL:

- Brennan Transport Ltd. (Transport)—100% owned by BSL

- Brennan Fuel Tank Installations Inc. (Tanks)—75% owned by BSL

You diligently take notes during the meeting (Exhibit III). Jack states that BSL will follow ASPE and will prepare consolidated financial statements to satisfy the bank's request.

## EXHIBIT I

Information from Last Year's Audit Files—Excerpt from Permanent File

| | |
|---|---|
| Date of incorporation: | 21 years ago |
| Year-end: | August 31 |
| Ownership: | 50 common shares Harold Thomas |
| | 50 common shares Kyle Stanton |

Nature of the business: BSL operates as a scrap metal dealer and processor. It buys used scrap metal from individuals and businesses, then bundles the different metals and sells them in larger quantities at a higher price to bigger recycling businesses. BSL's revenue fluctuates significantly because of the volatility in the market rates for steel and non-ferrous metals. To help control costs, BSL uses its own trucks and trailers to do the pickups. BSL earns additional revenue by providing transportation services to other businesses and by renting out the trucks during slower periods.

## EXHIBIT II

## Internal Financial Statements

**BRENNAN & SONS LIMITED**
**BALANCE SHEET**
As at August 31
(thousands of dollars)

| | Year 9 (audited) | Year 10 (unaudited) | | |
|---|---|---|---|---|
| | BSL | BSL | Transport | Tanks |
| **Assets** | | | | |
| Cash | $ 467 | $ 75 | $ 67 | $ 82 |
| Accounts receivable | 970 | 603 | 119 | — |
| Inventory | 10 | 500 | — | 15 |
| | 1,447 | 1,178 | 186 | 97 |
| Note receivable (note 1) | — | 431 | — | — |
| Property, plant, and equipment | 4,768 | 13,400 | 400 | 80 |
| Investment in subsidiaries | — | 2 | — | — |
| Intangible asset (note 2) | — | — | — | 20 |
| | $6,215 | $15,011 | $586 | $197 |

*(continued)*

**BRENNAN & SONS LIMITED**
**BALANCE SHEET**
As at August 31
(thousands of dollars)

| | Year 9 (audited) | Year 10 (unaudited) | | |
|---|---|---|---|---|
| | BSL | BSL | Transport | Tanks |
| **Liabilities** | | | | |
| Accounts payable | $ 315 | $ 813 | $128 | $166 |
| Note payable (note 1) | — | — | 431 | — |
| Mortgage payable | 100 | 6,500 | — | — |
| | 415 | 7,313 | 559 | 166 |
| **Shareholders' Equity** | | | | |
| Common stock (note 3) | 1 | 1 | 1 | 1 |
| Retained earnings | 5,799 | 7,697 | 26 | 30 |
| | 5,800 | 7,698 | 27 | 31 |
| | $6,215 | $15,011 | $586 | $197 |

**Notes:**

1. Note receivable/payable for sale of trucks and trailers from BSL to Transport, interest at 8%.

2. Training costs for Sean Piper, owner/installer.

3. Includes Sean's equity interest.

**INCOME STATEMENT**
For the year ended August 31
(in thousands of dollars)

| | Year 9 (audited) | Year 10 (unaudited) | | |
|---|---|---|---|---|
| | BSL (12 months) | BSL (12 months) | Transport (8 months) | Tanks (8 months) |
| Revenue: | | | | |
| Scrap metal | $11,000 | $10,003 | $ — | $ — |
| Transportation services (note 4) | 900 | 300 | 700 | — |
| Fuel tank installations | — | — | — | 320 |
| | 11,900 | 10,303 | 700 | 320 |
| Cost of sales: | | | | |
| Scrap metal | 1,600 | 1,440 | — | — |
| Transportation services | 700 | 340 | 550 | — |
| Fuel tank installations | — | — | — | 220 |
| Gross margin | 9,600 | 8,523 | 150 | 100 |

*(continued)*

**EXHIBIT II** (continued)

| | Year 9 (audited) | Year 10 (unaudited) | | |
| --- | --- | --- | --- | --- |
| | BSL (12 months) | BSL (12 months) | Transport (8 months) | Tanks (8 months) |
| General and administration (note 5) | 8,491 | 7,930 | 90 | 50 |
| Interest expense | 9 | 120 | 16 | — |
| Income before other income | 1,100 | 473 | 44 | 50 |
| Other income: | | | | |
| Gain on sale of equipment | — | 84 | — | — |
| Gain on sale of property | — | 2,500 | — | — |
| Interest income | — | 16 | — | — |
| Property rental (note 6) | — | 90 | — | — |
| Income before income tax | 1,100 | 3,163 | 44 | 50 |
| Income tax | 440 | 1,265 | 18 | 20 |
| Net income | $ 660 | $1,898 | $26 | $30 |

**Notes:**

4. Transport took over transportation services in January.

5. Year 10 General and administration includes amortization.

6. $10,000 per month from Transport and $5,000 per month from Tanks for six months.

**EXHIBIT III**

## Notes from Your Meeting with Jack Wright

BSL continues to operate the scrap metal business. BSL's management thinks the price of metal is going to go up in the near future, and has therefore started stockpiling for the first time. Unfortunately, BSL doesn't really have an inventory tracking system in place. If in fact it turns out stockpiling is a good way for BSL to make money, it will install a better system. The company did its best to log each of the amounts going into the stockpile as it was added, knowing that an amount for its year-end inventory balance would need to be determined. BSL also used a known engineering formula to come up with an estimate for year-end inventory and tried to measure the different piles of metal as a way of counting what was on hand at August 31, Year 10. The different methods came up with different amounts, so management went with the initial amount based on the log. Jack noted that we would have had a good laugh at the different ways they tried to measure the piles if we'd been there to see it.

As soon as it was incorporated on January 1, Year 10, Transport took over BSL's transportation operations. Transport provides transportation services to BSL and external customers, the same as BSL did. BSL sold the trucks to Transport in late January at fair market value; however, Transport didn't have the funds to buy the equipment, so BSL issued a note receivable at what Jack believed to be the market interest rate.

*(continued)*

**EXHIBIT III**

Tanks installs and maintains pre-engineered, above-ground fuel storage tank systems, a new line of business for BSL. Sean Piper, a good friend of one of BSL's owners, approached BSL last fall with the idea. Sean was willing to take the necessary training to become a certified fuel tank installer, and he wanted 50% ownership in Tanks. The owners of BSL agreed it was a great opportunity but wanted more control. The parties settled on Sean's receiving 25% ownership of Tanks.

As part of the agreement, BSL was required to provide a guarantee pertaining to Tanks' licensing application to the environmental authority since Tanks was a newly formed corporation. Although other vendors sell the same tanks and installation services separately, Tanks only sells the tank combined with installation and service. The tank is marked up by 20% on the price paid and is sold including installation and a five-year maintenance package for a total of $40,000. One hundred percent of the revenue is recognized when the sales agreement is signed by the client. The tank is then delivered and installed at the client's site within two to three weeks of signing. The fuel tanks need to be pressure-tested every year and the measurement gauge needs to be checked. Tanks will perform the maintenance services for clients for the first five years. Thereafter, Tanks will offer to continue to perform the maintenance for a contract price of $5,000 a year.

BSL's owners decided it was time to move to a bigger location, so in March Year 10 the company sold its land and building on Frank St. and bought land and a building in the Johnson Industrial Park. The new building is large enough to accommodate all the companies' operations, and more. BSL's owners are thinking of renting some of the extra space to other businesses and have already been approached by a few interested parties. All tenants, including BSL's subsidiaries, will be charged the same rent per square foot, based on current market rates.

*(CPA Canada adapted)*[10]

# Case 7-6

**LO1, 8**

Enviro Facilities Inc. (EFI) is a large, diversified Canadian-controlled private company with several Canadian and U.S. subsidiaries, operating mainly in the waste management and disposal industry. EFI was incorporated more than 50 years ago, and has grown to become one of the top four waste management firms in Canada. The Glass family started the business, but currently no family members are actively involved in the management. The shares are owned by family members, family trusts, and a limited number of friends. In Year 4, the Glass family decided to sell the company to a third party within the next two or three years, to realize the value of their shareholdings. EFI has an August 31 year-end. The company has elected to report using IFRS.

Up until the Year 4 fiscal year-end, a national firm of chartered professional accountants had audited EFI. In early Year 5, the company put the audit up for tender and replaced the incumbent firm with Bevan & Bevan (BB), a regional firm.

It is now October 18, Year 6. Three days ago, BB resigned from the engagement because of a conflict of interest, although the audit was reportedly 60% complete. Chu and Partners (Chu), Chartered Professional Accountants, was the runner-up firm in the Year 5 audit tender. EFI offered the engagement to Chu. After speaking with the BB partner in charge of the audit, Chu accepted the audit engagement on condition that BB provides all the audit documentation prepared to date. Chu was formally appointed auditors, and an engagement letter has been signed. Materiality has been set by Chu at $6 million, based on income and balance sheet trends.

You, CPA, work for Chu. BB's audit files have now arrived, and you and your staff have prepared the following notes:

1. A team of provincial sales tax auditors has been auditing EFI for nearly six months, but the audit is still not complete. The auditors are disputing the exemption claimed by EFI from the 7% tax on purchases of certain waste processing supplies and equipment. About 20% of total purchases of $451 million fell into this category during the four-year audit period, according to EFI.

2. On June 23, Year 6, EFI received a wire transfer of 10 million Hong Kong dollars to its general Canadian dollar bank account, in payment of an outstanding customer invoice. EFI's bank converted the funds to $9.0 million Canadian, incorrectly assuming that the transfer was for Singapore dollars. On that day, 6.49 Hong Kong dollars would buy a Canadian dollar. EFI has not informed the bank of the error and has taken the difference into income.

3. During Year 6, EFI lost a decision in the Federal Court of Appeal in a lawsuit brought by Waste Systems Integrated Limited for patent infringement. In an unusual award, the court ordered EFI to pay $20 million for shares of Waste Systems Integrated Limited, a private company, which had been in some financial difficulty. EFI has decided not to appeal the decision to the Supreme Court, and the shares were purchased before year-end.

4. EFI issues debt for long-term financing purposes through three major investment dealers. In July Year 6, Moody's, the credit rating agency, put EFI's credit rating on alert for downgrade due to the potential negative effects of progressive toughening of environmental legislation applying to waste disposal sites.

5. EFI bids on various municipal waste pickup and disposal contracts. EFI buys waste-disposal sites to dump the waste collected and defers and amortizes the cost of the sites over the expected useful lives, stated in tonnes of capacity, years of remaining usage, or cubic metres of waste capacity. Amortization of the cost of these sites represents 41% of EFI's operating expenses. Of EFI's assets, 64% are waste disposal sites. Provisions for cleanup and site-sealing costs are accrued on the same basis as the amortization of the sites.

6. EFI defers and amortizes over five years the costs of locating new waste disposal sites and negotiating agreements with municipalities.

7. During Year 6, EFI was awarded a contract to collect and dispose of all the waste for the Regional Municipality of Onkon-Lakerton for five years, commencing in Year 7. The contract requires the municipality to pay EFI $9.50 per tonne of waste collected. Because of aggressive recycling, composting, and waste reduction programs being carried out by the municipality, EFI negotiated a clause in the agreement that states that the company will be paid a minimum of $3.4 million per annum, regardless of the collection volume. EFI has recorded $17 million ($3.4 million × 5 years) as revenue in Year 6.

8. In July Year 6, two U.S. subsidiaries of the company were notified that they are potentially responsible for violations of U.S. law. The legal proceedings have commenced, on the basis

of allegations that prior to being acquired by EFI, these subsidiaries improperly disposed of hazardous waste. The sale-purchase agreement under which the subsidiaries were acquired contains price-adjustment clauses to protect EFI against pre-purchase liabilities.

9. In October Year 6, EFI sold trucks and other garbage collection equipment to a U.S. subsidiary for $20 million, and reported a gain of $9 million. The terms of the sale required a cash payment of $12 million on delivery, with the balance due in annual installments of $4 million, plus interest over a two-year period.

10. Every year, EFI updates the estimates of the remaining useful lives of waste disposal sites, using the services of a consulting engineering firm. In the past, EFI used Folk & Co., Environmental Engineers, for these reviews. Folk & Co. did no other work for EFI. Starting in Year 6, EFI used Cajanza Consulting Engineers for the reviews. Based on the new consultants' report, the useful lives of all waste-disposal sites have been increased between 4% and 26%, and the sealing/cleanup provision reduced by $13.6 million.

11. In light of the planned sale of EFI, the board of directors has decided to stop buying waste-disposal sites and to sell two sites where the cleanup provisions exceed the sites' carrying amounts. EFI plans to sell the two sites to Enviro (Bermuda) Inc. for a dollar. The controlling shareholders of Enviro (Bermuda) Inc. are the same as the controlling shareholders of EFI. EFI plans to dump waste in these sites. Chu's audit personnel heard a rumour that Enviro (Bermuda) Inc. does not plan to comply with environmental legislation.

12. During the year, EFI implemented a new cost accounting system for the production of composting material. Organic material is extracted from residential garbage collected, and then processed, composted, bagged, and sold for use by gardeners. In the past, no cost has been assigned to the raw material inputs. The new system allocates a portion of total collection costs to these raw material inputs at standard cost.

*(CPA Canada adapted)*[11]

# PROBLEMS

## Problem 7-1

**LO3**

X Company owns 80% of Y Company and uses the equity method to account for its investment. On January 1, Year 2, the investment in Y Company account had a balance of $86,900, and Y Company's common shares and retained earnings totalled $100,000. The unamortized acquisition differential had an estimated remaining life of six years at this time. The following intercompany asset transfers took place in Years 2 and 3: January 1, Year 2, sale of asset to X at a profit of $45,000; and April 30, Year 3, sale of asset to Y at a profit of $60,000. Both assets purchased are being depreciated over five years. In Year 2, Y reported a net income of $125,000 and dividends paid of $70,000, while in Year 3 its net income and dividends were $104,000 and $70,000, respectively.

**Required**

Calculate the December 31, Year 3, balance in the account "Investment in Y." (Assume a 40% tax rate.)

## Problem 7-2

LO1

Peggy Company owns 75% of Sally Inc. and uses the cost method to account for its investment. The following data were taken from the Year 4 income statements of the two companies:

|  | Peggy | Sally |
|---|---|---|
| Revenues | $580,000 | $270,000 |
| Miscellaneous expenses | 110,000 | 85,000 |
| Depreciation expense | 162,000 | 97,000 |
| Income tax expense | 123,000 | 35,000 |
| Total expenses | 395,000 | 217,000 |
| Profit | $185,000 | $ 53,000 |

On January 1, Year 2, Sally sold equipment to Peggy at a gain of $15,000. Peggy has been depreciating this equipment over a five-year period. Sally did not pay any dividends in Year 4. Use income tax allocation at a rate of 40%.

### Required

(a) Calculate consolidated profit attributable to Peggy's shareholders for Year 4.
(b) Prepare a consolidated income statement for Year 4.
(c) Calculate the deferred income tax asset that would appear on the Year 4 consolidated statement of financial position.

## Problem 7-3

LO1

The comparative consolidated income statements of a parent and its 75%-owned subsidiary were prepared incorrectly as at December 31 and are shown in the following table. The following items were overlooked when the statements were prepared:

- The Year 5 gain on sale of assets resulted from the subsidiary selling equipment to the parent on September 30. The parent immediately leased the equipment back to the subsidiary at an annual rental of $42,000. This was the only intercompany rent transaction that occurred each year. The equipment had a remaining life of five years on the date of the intercompany sale.
- The Year 6 gain on sale of assets resulted from the January 1 sale of a building, with a remaining life of seven years, by the subsidiary to the parent.
- Both gains were taxed at a rate of 40%.

**CONSOLIDATED INCOME STATEMENTS**

|  | Year 5 | Year 6 |
|---|---|---|
| Miscellaneous revenues | $875,000 | $ 950,000 |
| Gain on sale of assets | 28,000 | 59,500 |
| Rental revenue | 10,500 | 42,000 |
|  | 913,500 | 1,051,500 |
| Miscellaneous expenses | 419,800 | 497,340 |
| Rental expense | 70,200 | 71,800 |
| Depreciation expense | 100,000 | 98,200 |
| Income tax expense | 93,500 | 107,000 |
| Non-controlling interest | 45,000 | 8,160 |
|  | 728,500 | 782,500 |
| Net income | $185,000 | $ 269,000 |

**Required**

Prepare correct consolidated income statements for Years 5 and 6.

## Problem 7-4

LO1

Hanna Corporation owns 80% of the outstanding voting stock of Fellow Inc. At the date of acquisition, Fellow's retained earnings were $2,100,000. On December 31, Year 2, Hanna Inc. sold equipment to Fellow at its fair value of $2,000,000 and recorded a gain of $500,000. The equipment had a remaining useful life of five years on the date of the intercompany transaction. This equipment was still held within the consolidated entity at the end of Year 4.

At the end of Year 4, selected figures from the two companies' financial statements were as follows:

|  | Hanna | Fellow |
|---|---|---|
| Equipment | $7,000,000 | $4,000,000 |
| Accumulated depreciation | 2,700,000 | 1,450,000 |
| Retained earnings, beginning of year | 5,000,000 | 3,000,000 |
| Depreciation expense | 800,000 | 610,000 |
| Net income | 1,500,000 | 550,000 |
| Dividends declared | 500,000 | 200,000 |

Hanna uses the cost method to account for its investment in Fellow. Both companies pay income tax at the rate of 40%.

**Required**

(a) Calculate the amount to be reported on the Year 4 consolidated financial statements for the accounts/items listed above.

(b) Now, assume that the Year 2 intercompany sale was upstream, that is, Fellow sold to Hanna. Calculate the amount to be reported on the Year 4 consolidated financial statements for the accounts/items listed above.

## Problem 7-5

LO1, 3, 4

On December 31, Year 2, HABS Inc. sold equipment to NORD at its fair value of $2,000,000 and recorded a gain of $500,000. This was HABS's only income (other than any investment income from NORD) during the year. NORD reported income (other than any investment income from HABS) of $200,000 for Year 2. Both companies paid dividends of $100,000 during Year 2.

**Required**

(a) Calculate NORD's income before taxes for Year 2 assuming that
   (i) HABS and NORD are not related;
   (ii) NORD owns 75% of HABS and reports its investment in HABS on a consolidated basis;
   (iii) NORD owns 75% of HABS and reports its investment in HABS using the equity method; and
   (iv) NORD owns 75% of HABS and reports its investment in HABS using the cost method.

(b) Calculate HABS's income before taxes for Year 2 assuming that
   (i) NORD and HABS are not related;
   (ii) HABS owns 75% of NORD and reports its investment in NORD on a consolidated basis;

(iii) HABS owns 75% of NORD and reports its investment in NORD using the equity method; and

(iv) HABS owns 75% of NORD and reports its investment in NORD using the cost method.

(c) Compare and contrast the income reported under the reporting methods (ii), (iii), and (iv) above. Which method best reflects the economic reality of the business transaction?

## Problem 7-6

LO4, 5, 7

The balance sheets of Forest Company and Garden Company are presented below as at December 31, Year 8.

### BALANCE SHEETS

At December 31, Year 8

|  | Forest | Garden |
|---|---|---|
| Cash | $ 13,000 | $ 48,800 |
| Receivables | 25,000 | 86,674 |
| Inventories | 80,000 | 62,000 |
| Investment in shares of Garden | 207,900 | — |
| Plant and equipment | 740,000 | 460,000 |
| Accumulated depreciation | (625,900) | (348,400) |
| Patents | — | 4,500 |
| Investment in bonds of Forest | — | 58,426 |
|  | $440,000 | $372,000 |
| Current liabilities | $ 59,154 | $ 53,000 |
| Dividends payable | 6,000 | 30,000 |
| Bonds payable 6% | 94,846 | — |
| Common shares | 200,000 | 150,000 |
| Retained earnings | 80,000 | 139,000 |
|  | $440,000 | $372,000 |

### Additional Information

- Forest acquired 90% of Garden for $207,900 on July 1, Year 1, and accounts for its investment under the cost method. At that time, the shareholders' equity of Garden amounted to $175,000, the accumulated amortization was $95,000, and the assets of Garden were undervalued by the following amounts:

| Inventory | $12,000 | |
| Buildings | $10,000 | Remaining life, 10 years |
| Patents | $16,000 | Remaining life, 8 years |

- During Year 8, Forest reported net income of $41,000 and declared dividends of $25,000, whereas Garden reported net income of $63,000 and declared dividends of $50,000.
- During Years 2 to 7, goodwill impairment losses totalled $1,950. An impairment test conducted in Year 8 indicated a further loss of $7,150.
- Forest sells goods to Garden on a regular basis at a gross profit of 30%. During Year 8, these sales totalled $150,000. On January 1, Year 8, the inventory of Garden contained goods purchased from Forest amounting to $18,000, while the December 31, Year 8, inventory contained goods purchased from Forest amounting to $22,000.

- On August 1, Year 6, Garden sold land to Forest at a profit of $18,000. During Year 8, Forest sold one-quarter of the land to an unrelated company.
- Forest's bonds have a par value of $100,000, pay interest annually on December 31 at a stated rate of 6%, and mature on December 31, Year 11. Forest incurs an effective interest cost of 8% on these bonds. They had a carrying amount of $93,376 on January 1, Year 8. On that date, Garden acquired $60,000 of these bonds on the open market at a cost of $57,968. Garden will earn an effective rate of return of 7% on them. Both companies use the effective-interest method to account for their bonds.

  The Year 8 income statements of the two companies show the following with respect to bond interest.

|  | Forest | Garden |
|---|---|---|
| Interest expense | $7,470 | |
| Interest revenue | | $4,058 |

- Garden owes Forest $22,000 on open account on December 31, Year 8.
- Assume a 40% corporate tax rate and allocate bond gains (losses) between the two companies.

**Required**

(a) Prepare the following statements:
  (i) Consolidated balance sheet
  (ii) Consolidated retained earnings statement
(b) Prepare the Year 8 journal entries that would be made on the books of Forest if the equity method was used to account for the investment.
(c) Explain how a loss on the elimination of intercompany bondholdings is viewed as a temporary difference and gives rise to a deferred income tax asset.
(d) If Forest had used parent company extension theory rather than entity theory, how would this affect the debt-to-equity ratio at the end of Year 9? Briefly explain.

# Problem 7-7

LO1, 3, 4

On January 1, Year 4, Goodkey Co. acquired all of the common shares of Jingya. The condensed income statements for the two companies for January Year 5, were as follows:

|  | Goodkey | Jingya |
|---|---|---|
| Sales | $10,000,000 | $6,000,000 |
| Gain on sale of equipment | | 240,000 |
| Other income | 800,000 | 50,000 |
|  | 10,800,000 | 6,290,000 |
| Depreciation expense | 450,000 | 180,000 |
| Other expenses | 6,600,000 | 4,300,000 |
| Income tax expense | 1,220,000 | 719,000 |
|  | 8,270,000 | 5,199,000 |
| Net income | $ 2,530,000 | $1,091,000 |

The following transactions occurred in January, Year 5, and are properly reflected in the income statements above:

- On January 1, Year 5, Jingya sold equipment to Goodkey for $1,000,000 and reported a gain of $240,000. On this date, the equipment had a remaining useful life of four years.
- On January 31, Year 5, Jingya paid a dividend of $600,000.

  Goodkey uses the cost method to account for its investment in Jingya. Both companies pay income tax at the rate of 40%.

### Required

(a) Prepare a consolidated income statement for January Year 5.

(b) Now assume that Goodkey uses the equity method to account for its investment in Jingya. What accounts would change on the three income statements (Goodkey, Jingya, and consolidated) in January Year 5, and what would be the account balances?

(c) Now assume that Goodkey only owns 80% of the common shares of Jingya and uses the cost method to account for its investment in Jingya. What accounts would change (as compared to part (a)) on the three income statements (Goodkey, Jingya, and consolidated) in January Year 5, and what would be the account balances?

## Problem 7-8

LO1, 3

Income statements of M Cop. and K Co. for the year ended December 31, Year 9, are presented below:

|  | M Co. | K Co. |
| --- | --- | --- |
| Sales | $600,000 | $350,000 |
| Rent revenue | — | 50,000 |
| Interest revenue | 6,700 | — |
| Income from subsidiary | 30,320 | — |
| Gain on land sale | — | 8,000 |
|  | 637,020 | 408,000 |
| Cost of goods sold | 334,000 | 225,000 |
| Distribution expense | 80,000 | 70,000 |
| Administrative expense | 147,000 | 74,000 |
| Interest expense | 1,700 | 6,000 |
| Income tax expense | 20,700 | 7,500 |
|  | 583,400 | 382,500 |
| Profit | $ 53,620 | $ 25,500 |

### Additional Information

- M Co. uses the equity method to account for its investment in K Co.
- M Co. acquired its 80% interest in K Co. on January 1, Year 4. On that date, the acquisition differential of $25,000 was allocated entirely to buildings; it is being amortized over a 20-year period.
- Amortization expense is grouped with distribution expenses, and impairment losses, if any, are grouped with other expenses.
- M Co. made an advance of $100,000 to K Co. on July 1, Year 9. This loan is due on demand and requires the payment of interest at 12% per year.
- M Co. rents marine equipment from K Co. During Year 6, $50,000 rent was paid and was charged to administrative expense.

- In Year 7, M Co. sold land to K Co. and recorded a profit of $10,000 on the sale. K Co. held the land until October, Year 9, when it was sold to an unrelated company.
- During Year 9, K Co. made sales to M Co. totalling $90,000. The December 31, Year 9, inventories of M Co. contain an unrealized profit of $5,000. The January 1, Year 9, inventories of M Co. contained an unrealized profit of $12,000.
- On January 1, Year 7, M Co. sold machinery to K Co. and recorded a profit of $13,000. The remaining useful life on that date was five years. Assume straight-line depreciation.
- K Co. paid dividends of $20,000 during Year 9.
- Tax allocation is to be used, assuming a 40% average corporate tax rate for this purpose.

**Required**

(a) Prepare a consolidated income statement for Year 9.
(b) Now assume that M Co. is a private company, uses ASPE, and chooses to use the cost method to report its investment in K Co. Prepare M Co.'s income statement for Year 9 under the cost method.

## Problem 7-9

LO1, 5

Pure Company purchased 70% of the ordinary shares of Gold Company on January 1, Year 6, for $483,000 when the latter company's accumulated depreciation, ordinary shares and retained earnings were $75,000, $500,000 and $40,000, respectively. Non-controlling interest was valued at $195,000 by an independent business valuator at the date of acquisition. On this date, an appraisal of the assets of Gold disclosed the following differences:

|  | Carrying Amount | Fair Value |
| --- | --- | --- |
| Land | $ 150,000 | $ 200,000 |
| Plant and equipment | 700,000 | 770,000 |
| Inventory | 120,000 | 108,000 |

The plant and equipment had an estimated life of 20 years on this date.

The statements of financial position of Pure and Gold, prepared on December 31, Year 11, follow:

|  | Pure | Gold |
| --- | --- | --- |
| Land | $ 100,000 | $ 150,000 |
| Plant and equipment | 625,000 | 940,000 |
| Less accumulated depreciation | (183,000) | (220,000) |
| Patent (net of amortization) | 31,500 | — |
| Investment in Gold Co. shares (equity method) | 546,670 | — |
| Investment in Gold Co. bonds | 227,000 | — |
| Inventory | 225,000 | 180,000 |
| Accounts receivable | 212,150 | 170,000 |
| Cash | 41,670 | 57,500 |
|  | $1,825,990 | $1,277,500 |
| Ordinary shares | $ 750,000 | $ 500,000 |
| Retained earnings | 1,019,960 | 200,000 |
| Bonds payable (due Year 20) | — | 477,500 |
| Accounts payable | 56,030 | 100,000 |
|  | $ 1,825,990 | $1,277,500 |

## Additional Information

- Goodwill impairment tests have resulted in impairment losses totalling $18,000.
- On January 1, Year 1, Gold issued $500,000 of 8 1/2% bonds at 90, maturing in 20 years (on December 31, Year 20).
- On January 1, Year 11, Pure acquired $200,000 of Gold's bonds on the open market at a cost of $230,000.
- On July 1, Year 8, Gold sold a patent to Pure for $63,000. The patent had a carrying amount on Gold's books of $42,000 on this date and an estimated remaining life of seven years.
- Pure uses tax allocation (40% rate) and allocates bond gains between affiliates when it consolidates Gold.
- Pure uses the equity method to account for its investment.

## Required

Prepare a consolidated statement of financial position as at December 31, Year 11.

# Problem 7-10

LO1, 3, 5, 6, 7

On January 2, Year 4, Poplar Ltd. purchased 80% of the outstanding shares of Spruce Ltd. for $2,000,000. At that date, Spruce had common shares of $500,000 and retained earnings of $1,250,000 and accumulated depreciation of $600,000. Poplar acquired the Spruce shares to obtain control of mineral rights owned by Spruce. At the date of acquisition, these mineral rights were valued at $750,000, were not recognized on Spruce's separate-entity balance sheet, and had an indefinite useful life. Except for the mineral rights, the carrying amount of the recorded assets and liabilities of Spruce were equal to their fair values. On December 31, Year 7, the trial balances of the two companies were as follows:

|  | Poplar | Spruce |
|---|---|---|
| Cash | $ 1,000,000 | $   500,000 |
| Accounts receivable | 2,000,000 | 356,000 |
| Inventory | 3,000,000 | 2,006,000 |
| Plant and equipment | 14,000,000 | 2,900,000 |
| Investment in Spruce (cost) | 2,000,000 | — |
| Investment in bonds | — | 488,000 |
| Cost of goods sold | 2,400,000 | 850,000 |
| Other expenses | 962,000 | 300,000 |
| Interest expense | 38,000 | — |
| Income tax expense | 600,000 | 350,000 |
| Dividends | 600,000 | 250,000 |
|  | $26,600,000 | $8,000,000 |
| Accounts payable | $ 2,492,000 | $2,478,500 |
| Accumulated depreciation: plant and equipment | 4,000,000 | 1,000,000 |
| Bonds payable | 500,000 | — |
| Premium on bonds payable | 8,000 | — |
| Common shares | 4,500,000 | 500,000 |
| Retained earnings, January 1 | 10,000,000 | 2,000,000 |
| Sales | 4,900,000 | 2,000,000 |
| Dividend revenue | 200,000 | — |
| Interest revenue | — | 21,500 |
|  | $26,600,000 | $8,000,000 |

## Additional Information

- The Year 7 net incomes of the two companies are as follows:

| | |
|---|---|
| Poplar Ltd. | $1,100,000 |
| Spruce Ltd. | 521,500 |

- The mineral rights owned by Spruce have increased in value since the date of acquisition and were worth $925,000 at December 31, Year 7.
- On January 2, Year 5, Spruce sold equipment to Poplar for $500,000. The equipment had a carrying amount of $400,000 at the time of the sale. The remaining useful life of the equipment was five years.
- The Year 7 opening inventories of Poplar contained $500,000 of merchandise purchased from Spruce during Year 6. Spruce had recorded a gross profit of $200,000 on this merchandise.
- During Year 7, Spruce's sales to Poplar totalled $1,000,000. These sales were made at a gross profit rate of 40%.
- Poplar's ending inventory contains $300,000 of merchandise purchased from Spruce.
- Other expenses include depreciation expense and copyright amortization expense.
- Tax allocation will be at a rate of 40%.

## Required

(a) Prepare the following consolidated financial statements for Year 7:
   (i)  Income statement
   (ii) Retained earnings statement
   (iii) Balance sheet
(b) Calculate the December 31, Year 7, balance in the account "Investment in Spruce" if Poplar had used the equity method to account for its investment.
(c) Explain how the recognition of gains on the elimination of intercompany bondholdings is consistent with the principle of recording gains only when they are realized.

# Problem 7-11

LO5, 7

Alpha Corporation owns 90% of the ordinary shares of Beta Corporation and uses the equity method to account for its investment.

On January 1, Year 4, Alpha purchased $160,000 of Beta's 10% bonds for $150,064. Beta's bond liability on this date consisted of $800,000 par 10% bonds due January 1, Year 8, and unamortized discount of $73,065. Interest payment dates are June 30 and December 31. The effective rate of interest is 6% every six months on Alpha's bond investment and 6.5% every six months for Beta's bond liability.

Both companies have a December 31 year-end and use the effective-interest method to account for bonds. Alpha uses income tax allocation at a 40% tax rate when it prepares its consolidated financial statements.

Beta reported a profit of $114,000 in Year 4 and declared a dividend of $30,000 on December 31.

## Required

(a) Calculate the amount of the gain or the loss that will appear as a separate item on the Year 4 consolidated income statement as a result of the bond transaction that occurred during the year.

(b) Prepare the equity method journal entries that Alpha would make on December 31, Year 4.

(c) Calculate the amount of the bond liability that will appear on the December 31, Year 4, consolidated statement of financial position.

## Problem 7-12

LO5, 7

Parent Co. owns 75% of Sub Co. and uses the cost method to account for its investment. The following are summarized income statements for the year ended December 31, Year 7.

### INCOME STATEMENTS
#### For Year 7

|  | Parent | Sub |
|---|---|---|
| Interest revenue | $ 21,875 | $  — |
| Other misc. revenues | 900,000 | 500,000 |
|  | 921,875 | 500,000 |
| Interest expense | — | 44,000 |
| Other misc. expenses | 600,000 | 350,000 |
| Income tax expense | 124,000 | 42,000 |
|  | 724,000 | 436,000 |
| Net income | $197,875 | $ 64,000 |

### Additional Information

- On July 1, Year 7, Parent purchased all of the outstanding bonds of Sub for $381,250. On that date, Sub had $400,000 of 10% bonds payable outstanding, which mature in five years. The bond discount on the books of Sub on July 1, Year 7, amounted to $20,000. Interest is payable January 1 and July 1. Any gains (losses) are to be allocated to each company. Both companies use the straight-line method to account for bonds.

- Sub Co. did not declare or pay dividends in Year 7.

### Required

Prepare a consolidated income statement for Year 7 using a 40% tax rate.

## Problem 7-13

LO5, 7

Palmer Corporation owns 70% of the ordinary shares of Scott Corporation and uses the equity method to account for its investment.

Scott purchased $80,000 par of Palmer's 10% bonds from outsiders on October 1, Year 5, for $72,000. Palmer's bond liability on October 1, Year 5, consisted of $400,000 par of 10% bonds due on October 1, Year 9, with unamortized discount of $16,000. Interest payment dates are April 1 and October 1 of each year, and straight-line amortization is used. Intercompany bond gains (losses) are to be allocated to each affiliate.

Both companies have a December 31 year-end. Scott's financial statements for Year 5 indicate that it earned profit of $60,000 and that on December 31, Year 5, it declared a dividend of $13,000.

**Required**

(a) Prepare the journal entries under the equity method that Palmer would make in Year 5. (Assume a 40% tax rate.)

(b) Compute the amount of the bond liability that will appear on the December 31, Year 5, consolidated statement of financial position.

## Problem 7-14

LO1, 4

On December 31, Year 4, RAV Company purchased 60% of the outstanding common shares of ENS Company for $1,260,000. On that date, ENS had common shares of $500,000 and retained earnings of $130,000. In negotiating the purchase price, it was agreed that recorded assets and liabilities were fairly valued except for equipment, which had a $24,000 excess of carrying amount over fair value, and land, which had a $150,000 excess of fair value over carrying amount. The equipment had a remaining useful life of six years at the acquisition date and no salvage value. ENS did not record the fair value deficiency on the equipment because ENS felt that it would recover the carrying amount of this equipment through future cash flows. In addition, ENS registered and owns a number of Internet domain names, which are estimated to be worth $100,000. The right to the names expires in 12 years but the registration can be renewed for 20 years every 20 years, for a nominal fee.

The adjusted trial balances for RAV and ENS for the year ended December 31, Year 8, were as follows:

|  | RAV | ENS |
|---|---|---|
| Cash | $ 175,000 | $ 91,000 |
| Accounts receivable | 261,000 | 242,000 |
| Inventory | 626,000 | 305,000 |
| Land | 700,000 | 330,000 |
| Building—net | 870,000 | 665,000 |
| Equipment—net | 722,000 | 397,000 |
| Investment in ENS | 654,600 | |
| Cost of goods purchased | 2,388,000 | 2,377,000 |
| Change in inventory | 92,000 | (46,000) |
| Amortization expense | 208,000 | 104,000 |
| Income taxes and other expenses | 912,000 | 448,000 |
| Dividends paid | 416,400 | 256,000 |
| Total debits | $8,025,000 | $5,169,000 |
| Accounts payable | $ 481,000 | $ 328,000 |
| Long-term debt | 349,200 | 732,000 |
| Common shares | 1,200,000 | 500,000 |
| Retained earnings, beginning | 615,000 | 279,000 |
| Sales | 5,020,000 | 3,330,000 |
| Other revenues | 109,000 | |
| Equity method income from ENS | 250,800 | |
| Total credits | $8,025,000 | $5,169,000 |

### Additional Information

- Every year, goodwill is evaluated to determine if there has been a loss. The recoverable amount for ENS's goodwill was valued at $100,000 at the end of Year 7 and $75,000 at the end of Year 8.

- RAV's inventories contained $450,000 of merchandise purchased from ENS at December 31, Year 8, and $350,000 at December 31, Year 7. During Year 8, sales from ENS to RAV were $650,000. Merchandise was priced at the same profit margin as applicable to other customers. RAV owed $182,000 to ENS at December 31, Year 8, and $190,000 at December 31, Year 7.

- On July 1, Year 5, ENS purchased a building from RAV for $782,000. The building had an original cost of $832,000 and a carrying amount of $632,000 on RAV's books on July 1, Year 5. ENS estimated the remaining life of the building was 15 years at the time of the purchase from RAV.

- ENS rented another building from RAV throughout the year for $6,000 per month.

- RAV uses the equity method of accounting for its long-term investments.

- Both companies pay tax at the rate of 40%. Ignore deferred income taxes when allocating and amortizing the acquisition differential.

### Required

(a) Prepare a consolidated income statement for the year ended December 31, Year 8.

(b) Prepare the current assets, property, plant, and equipment, and intangible assets sections of the consolidated balance sheet at December 31, Year 8.

(c) Calculate non-controlling interest on the consolidated balance sheet at December 31, Year 7.

(d) If RAV had used the cost method instead of the equity method of accounting for its investment in ENS, would RAV's net income for Year 8 increase, decrease, or remain the same on

(i) its separate-entity income statement?

(ii) the consolidated income statement?

Briefly explain.

*(e) Prepare the consolidated financial statements using the worksheet approach.

*(CGA Canada adapted)*[12]

## Problem 7-15

LO5, 7

Shown below are selected ledger accounts from the trial balance of a parent and its subsidiary as of December 31, Year 10.

|  | P Co. | S Co. |
|---|---|---|
| Investment in bonds of P | $ — | $38,000 |
| Investment in shares of S (equity method) | 158,899 | — |
| Sales | 687,000 | 416,000 |
| Interest income | — | 2,000 |
| Equity method income | 125,763 | — |
| Gain on sale of land | 7,000 | — |
| Common shares | 300,000 | 100,000 |
| Retained earnings, beginning of year | 78,000 | 48,000 |

| | P Co. | S Co. |
|---|---|---|
| Bonds payable 8% | 199,000 | — |
| Cost of sales | 412,200 | 249,600 |
| Interest expense | 16,500 | — |
| Selling and administrative expense | 48,000 | 24,000 |
| Income tax expense | 15,000 | 9,690 |
| Dividends | 10,000 | 8,000 |

## Additional Information

- P Company purchased its 90% interest in S Company in Year 2, on the date that S Company was incorporated, and has followed the equity method to account for its investment since that date.
- On April 1, Year 6, land that had originally cost $21,000 was sold by S Company to P Company for $28,000. P purchased the land with the intention of developing it, but in Year 10 it decided that the location was not suitable and the land was sold to a chain of drug stores.
- On January 1, Year 3, P Company issued $200,000 face value bonds due in 10 years. The proceeds from the bond issue amounted to $195,000.
- On July 1, Year 10, S Company purchased $40,000 of these bonds on the open market at a cost of $38,000. Intercompany bondholding gains (losses) are allocated between the two affiliates.
- S Company had $76,000 in sales to P Company during Year 10.
- Use income tax allocation at a 40% tax rate.

## Required

(a) Prepare a consolidated income statement for Year 10.
(b) Prepare a consolidated statement of retained earnings for Year 10.

# Problem 7-16

LO1, 2, 4

Financial statements of Champlain Ltd. and its 80%-owned subsidiary Samuel Ltd. as at December 31, Year 8, are presented below.

### STATEMENTS OF FINANCIAL POSITION
#### at December 31, Year 8

| | Champlain | Samuel |
|---|---|---|
| Property, plant, and equipment | $198,000 | $104,000 |
| Accumulated depreciation | (86,000) | (30,000) |
| Investment in Samuel—at cost | 129,200 | — |
| Inventories | 35,000 | 46,000 |
| Accounts receivable | 60,000 | 55,000 |
| Cash | 18,100 | 20,600 |
| | $354,300 | $195,600 |
| Ordinary shares | $225,000 | $50,000 |
| Retained earnings | 68,300 | 70,000 |
| Dividends payable | 5,000 | 5,500 |
| Accounts payable | 56,000 | 70,100 |
| | $354,300 | $195,600 |

### STATEMENTS OF INCOME AND RETAINED EARNINGS
For the year ended December 31, Year 8

| | Champlain | Samuel |
|---|---|---|
| Sales | $535,400 | $270,000 |
| Dividend and miscellaneous income | 9,900 | — |
| | 545,300 | 270,000 |
| Cost of sales | 364,000 | 206,000 |
| Selling expense | 78,400 | 24,100 |
| Administrative expense (including depreciation and goodwill impairment) | 46,300 | 20,700 |
| Income taxes | 13,800 | 6,200 |
| | 502,500 | 257,000 |
| Profit | 42,800 | 13,000 |
| Retained earnings, January 1 | 45,500 | 68,000 |
| Dividends paid | (20,000) | (11,000) |
| Retained earnings, December 31 | $ 68,300 | $ 70,000 |

## Additional Information

- Champlain acquired 8,000 ordinary shares of Samuel on January 1, Year 4, for $129,200. Samuel's shares were trading for $14 per share on the date of acquisition. The retained earnings and accumulated depreciation of Samuel were $12,000 and $17,000, respectively, on that date, and there have been no subsequent changes in the ordinary shares account. On January 1, Year 4, fair values were equal to carrying amounts except for the following:

| | Carrying Value | Fair Value |
|---|---|---|
| Inventory | $50,000 | $32,000 |
| Patent | –0– | 14,000 |

- The patent of Samuel had a remaining legal life of eight years on January 1, Year 4, and any goodwill was to be tested annually for impairment. As a result, impairment losses occurred as follows:

| Pertaining To: | Year 5 | Year 7 | Year 8 |
|---|---|---|---|
| Champlain's purchase | $21,000 | $13,800 | $19,200 |
| Non-controlling interest's share | 4,000 | 2,600 | 3,600 |
| | $25,000 | $16,400 | $22,800 |

- On January 1, Year 8, the inventories of Champlain contained items purchased from Samuel on which Samuel had made a profit of $1,900. During Year 8, Samuel sold goods to Champlain for $92,000, of which $21,000 remained unpaid at the end of the year. Samuel made a profit of $3,300 on goods remaining in Champlain's inventory at December 31, Year 8.

- On January 1, Year 6, Samuel sold equipment to Champlain at a price that was $21,000 in excess of its carrying amount. The equipment had an estimated remaining life of six years on that date.

- Champlain sold a tract of land to Samuel in Year 5 at a profit of $7,000. This land is still held by Samuel at the end of Year 8.

- Assume a corporate tax rate of 40%.

## Required

(a) Prepare the following consolidated financial statements:
- (i) Income statement
- (ii) Retained earnings statement
- (iii) Statement of financial position

(b) Explain how the historical cost principle supports the elimination of the profit on the sale of the equipment from Samuel to Champlain when preparing Samuel's consolidated financial statements.

(c) Calculate goodwill and non-controlling interest on the consolidated statement of financial position at December 31, Year 8, under the parent company extension theory.

(d) If Champlain had used the parent company extension theory rather than the entity theory, how would this affect the return on equity attributable to shareholders of Champlain for Year 8?

(e) Prepare the consolidated financial statements using the worksheet approach.

*eXcel*

## Problem 7-17

LO1, 2, 4

On January 1, Year 4, Handy Company (Handy) purchased 70% of the outstanding common shares of Dandy Limited (Dandy) for $13,300. On that date, Dandy's shareholders' equity consisted of common shares of $1,250 and retained earnings of $6,500.

The financial statements for Handy and Dandy for Year 9 were as follows:

### BALANCE SHEETS
At December 31, Year 9

| | Handy | Dandy |
|---|---|---|
| Cash | $ 1,540 | $ 980 |
| Accounts receivable | 3,000 | 1,250 |
| Inventory | 3,600 | 4,250 |
| Property, plant, and equipment—net | 4,540 | 3,210 |
| Investment in Dandy | 7,000 | — |
| Total | $19,680 | $ 9,690 |
| Current liabilities | $ 4,560 | $ 680 |
| Long-term liabilities | 3,300 | 1,430 |
| Common shares | 1,200 | 450 |
| Retained earnings | 10,620 | 7,130 |
| Total | $19,680 | $ 9,690 |

### STATEMENTS OF INCOME AND RETAINED EARNINGS
For year ended December 31, Year 9

| | Handy | Dandy |
|---|---|---|
| Sales | $22,900 | $8,440 |
| Cost of sales | 15,200 | 3,680 |
| Gross profit | 7,700 | 4,760 |
| Other revenue | 1,820 | — |
| Selling and administrative expense | (1,040) | (620) |
| Other expenses | (5,520) | (2,240) |
| Income before income taxes | 2,960 | 1,900 |
| Income tax expense | 1,000 | 840 |
| Net income | 1,960 | 1,060 |
| Retained earnings, beginning of year | 10,620 | 7,050 |
| Dividends paid | (1,960) | (980) |
| Retained earnings, end of year | $10,620 | $7,130 |

## Additional Information

- In negotiating the purchase price at the date of acquisition, it was agreed that the fair values of all of Dandy's assets and liabilities were equal to their carrying amounts, except for the following:

| | Carrying Amount | Fair Value |
|---|---|---|
| Inventory | $2,300 | $2,400 |
| Equipment | 2,700 | 3,200 |

- Both companies use FIFO to account for their inventory and the straight-line method for amortizing their property, plant, and equipment. Dandy's equipment had a remaining useful life of 10 years at the acquisition date.
- Goodwill is not amortized on a systematic basis. However, each year, goodwill is evaluated to determine if there has been a permanent impairment. It was determined that goodwill on the consolidated balance sheet should be reported at its recoverable amount of $1,300 on December 31, Year 8, and $1,110 on December 31, Year 9.
- During Year 9, inventory sales from Dandy to Handy were $5,900. Handy's inventories contained merchandise purchased from Dandy for $3,400 at December 31, Year 8, and $4,500 at December 31, Year 9. Dandy earns a gross margin of 50% on its intercompany sales.
- On January 1, Year 5, Handy sold some equipment to Dandy for $3,000 and recorded a gain of $360 before taxes. This equipment had a remaining useful life of eight years at the time of the purchase by Dandy.
- Handy charges $50 per month to Dandy for consulting services and has been doing so throughout Years 8 and 9.
- Handy uses the cost method of accounting for its long-term investment.
- Both companies pay taxes at the rate of 40%.
- Amortization expense is grouped with production expenses, and impairment losses are grouped with other expenses.

## Required

(a) Prepare a consolidated statement of income for the year ended December 31, Year 9. Show supporting calculations.

(b) Calculate consolidated retained earnings at January 1, Year 9, and then prepare a consolidated statement of retained earnings for the year ended December 31, Year 9. Show supporting calculations.

(c) Explain how the historical cost principle supports the adjustments made on consolidation when there has been an intercompany sale of equipment.

(d) Calculate goodwill impairment loss and non-controlling interest on the consolidated income statement for the year ended December 31, Year 9, under the parent company extension theory.

(e) Prepare the consolidated financial statements using the worksheet approach.

*(CGA Canada adapted)*[13]

## *Problem 7-18

LO5, 7

SENS Ltd. acquired equipment on January 1, Year 1, for $500,000. The equipment was depreciated on a straight-line basis over an estimated useful life of 10 years.

On January 1, Year 3, SENS sold this equipment to MEL Corp., its parent company, for $420,000. MEL is depreciating this equipment on a straight-line basis over an estimated useful life of eight years.

MEL and SENS revalue their property, plant, and equipment to fair value each year under IAS 16 and transfer the revaluation surplus to retained earnings over the useful life of the asset or upon sale of the asset. The fair value of this equipment was $460,000 at the end of Year 1, $416,000 at the end of Year 2, and $370,000 at the end of Year 3. When the equipment is remeasured to fair value, both the original cost and accumulated depreciation are grossed up for the increase in value.

**Required**

Assume that this is the only equipment owned by the two companies and ignore income tax. Compute the balances that would appear in MEL's separate-entity statements, SENS's separate-entity statements, and MEL's consolidated statements for Years 1, 2, and 3 for each of the following:

(a) Equipment
(b) Accumulated depreciation
(c) Accumulated other comprehensive income—revaluation surplus
(d) Gain on sale of equipment
(e) Depreciation expense

## Endnotes

1. Suncor Energy Inc., "Annual Report 2014," www.suncor.com/pdf/Annual_Report_2014.pdf.

2. In Chapter 6, we used the following description for this schedule: Equipment Gain—Sub Inc. selling (upstream). From now on, we will not specify "upstream" or "downstream" in the line description. When the subsidiary is selling, it is upstream; when the parent is selling, it is downstream. If you need clarification for the missing words, review Chapter 6.

3. In Chapter 6, we used the following description for this adjustment: Unrealized after-tax gain on equipment (upstream). From now on, we will continue to make after-tax adjustments but will omit "after-tax" to shorten the description. Similarly, we will not specify "upstream" or "downstream" in the line description; it should be obvious on the basis of whether the adjustments are made against the parent (downstream) or the subsidiary (upstream). If you need clarification for the missing words, review Chapter 6.

4. BCE Inc., "2014 Annual Report," www.bce.ca/assets/investors/AR_2014/BCE_2014_Annual_Report.pdf.

5. We will use the straight-line method in the first few illustrations, because it is easier to understand. Later in the chapter, we will illustrate the effective-interest method, which is required by IFRS.

6. The entry for interest revenue or interest expense is usually one entry that incorporates the amortization of the premium or discount on the bonds. In this example, we are showing two separate entries so that it is easier to see that the cash amounts are equal and offsetting.

7. We must also reduce the amount of the deferred tax liability that was set up in Year 1 by $30.

8. One could argue that the gain on sale should also be reported in other comprehensive income, since it is similar to revaluing

the asset to its fair value. However, IAS 16 explicitly states that the gain or loss on derecognition of property, plant, and equipment should be reported in net income.

9. Adapted from *CICA UFE Report*, 2010-II-1, with permission. Chartered Professional Accountants of Canada, Toronto, Canada. Any changes to the original material are the sole responsibility of the author (and/or publisher) and have not been reviewed or endorsed by the Chartered Professional Accountants of Canada.

10. Adapted from *CICA UFE Report*, 1989-IV-1, with permission. Chartered Professional Accountants of Canada, Toronto, Canada. Any changes to the original material are the sole responsibility of the author (and/or publisher) and have not been reviewed or endorsed by the Chartered Professional Accountants of Canada.

11. Adapted from *CICA UFE Report*, 1996-II-3, with permission. Chartered Professional Accountants of Canada, Toronto, Canada. Any changes to the original material are the sole responsibility of the author (and/or publisher) and have not been reviewed or endorsed by the Chartered Professional Accountants of Canada.

12. Adapted from CGA Canada's FA4 Exam, December 2006, Q3, with permission Chartered Professional Accountants of Canada, Toronto, Canada. Any changes to the original material are the sole responsibility of the author (and/or publisher) and have not been reviewed or endorsed by the Chartered Professional Accountants of Canada.

13. Adapted from CGA Canada's FA4 Exam, March 2003, Q2, with permission Chartered Professional Accountants of Canada, Toronto, Canada. Any changes to the original material are the sole responsibility of the author (and/or publisher) and have not been reviewed or endorsed by the Chartered Professional Accountants of Canada.

# CHAPTER 8

# Consolidated Cash Flows and Changes in Ownership

## LEARNING OBJECTIVES

**After studying this chapter, you should be able to do the following:**

**LO1** Prepare a consolidated cash flow statement by applying concepts learned in prior courses and unique consolidation concepts discussed here.

**LO2** Prepare consolidated financial statements in situations where the parent's ownership has increased (step purchase).

**LO3** Prepare consolidated financial statements after the parent's ownership has decreased.

**LO4** Prepare consolidated financial statements in situations where the subsidiary has preferred shares in its capital structure.

**LO5** Calculate consolidated net income attributable to the shareholders of the parent and non-controlling interest in situations where a parent has direct and indirect control over a number of subsidiary companies.

**LO6** Analyze and interpret financial statements involving ownership changes.

## Introduction

While it is still the norm in Canada for the capital structure of a company to consist of common and/or preferred shares, some companies no longer use the terms *common shares* and *preferred shares* to describe their shares. Instead, they may use terms such as *Class A* and *Class B* shares and then describe the essential features of them. In other parts of the world, common shares are often referred to as *ordinary shares*.

Celestica Inc., a world leader in the delivery of innovative supply chain solutions, refers to its two classes of shares as *subordinate voting shares* and *multiple voting shares*. The subordinate shares entitle the holder to one vote per share, whereas the multiple voting shares entitle the holder to 25 votes per share. The holders of the subordinate voting shares and multiple voting shares are entitled to share ratably in any dividends of the company. Onex Corporation, one of Canada's largest corporations, with global operations in the services, manufacturing, and technology industries, owns the multiple voting shares of Celestica, while the non-controlling shareholders own most of the subordinated voting shares. This share distribution gives Onex Corporation 75% of the votes but only 11% of the dividends. The non-controlling interest gets 25% of the votes but 89% of the dividends.[1]

> *Different classes of shares typically have different voting and/or different dividend rights.*

Up to now in this text, the companies involved in the business combination had only common shares outstanding, and the parent obtained control over the subsidiary in one purchase. In this chapter, we will consider situations where the subsidiary also has preferred shares outstanding and those where the parent's ownership interest changes. We commence the chapter with a discussion of certain factors that are unique to the overall consolidation process and that must be considered when the consolidated cash flow statement is prepared.

# LO1 CONSOLIDATED CASH FLOW STATEMENT

In the previous chapters, we illustrated the direct approach to preparing the consolidated balance sheet and the consolidated income and retained earnings statements. In this approach, the individual statements of the parent and its subsidiaries are combined. We will now focus on the preparation of the final consolidated statement—the cash flow statement. While this statement could be prepared by combining the separate cash flow statements of the parent and its subsidiaries, this would involve eliminating all intercompany transactions, including intercompany transfers of cash. It is much easier to prepare the cash flow statement using comparative consolidated balance sheets and the consolidated income statement because these statements do not contain any intercompany transactions. In all of the illustrations in this chapter, we will assume that cash flows from operations are presented using the indirect method, whereby net income is adjusted for the effects of non-cash items such as depreciation, amortization, and changes in working capital items and for gains and losses associated with investing and financing cash flows. If the direct method were used, only the items affecting cash would be presented in the first place. Therefore, we would not need to adjust for non-cash items.

> *Under the indirect method, we start with net income and show the adjustments to convert it to a cash basis.*

The preparation of the cash flow statement for a single unconsolidated company is well covered in introductory and intermediate accounting texts. The basic process used to determine the reasons for the change in cash or cash equivalents is one of analyzing the changes that have occurred in all non-cash items on the balance sheet. The procedures used to carry out this analysis (a working paper or a series of T-accounts) will not be repeated here. Instead, we will describe items that are unique to consolidated statements and that must be taken into account in the analysis. The major items that require special attention are summarized below:

> *The change in cash can be determined by analyzing the change in non-cash items during the period.*

1. Acquisition-date fair value differences are depreciated in the consolidated income statement. While some of the amortizations may be obvious from their descriptions in the income statement, others may be buried in expense accounts. Because amortizations have no effect on cash flows, we must adjust the year's net income for them in order to arrive at cash flow from operations.

> *The consolidated cash flow statement contains adjustments for items that are unique to consolidated financial statements, such as amortization of the acquisition differential.*

2. Dividends paid by subsidiaries to the parent company do not change the consolidated entity's cash. Dividends paid by the parent to its shareholders, and dividends paid by the subsidiaries to non-controlling shareholders, reduce the cash of the consolidated entity. These dividends can be presented as either operating or financing activities. The dividends paid to non-controlling shareholders should be disclosed or presented separately.

3. A change in the parent's ownership percentage during the year requires a careful analysis to determine its effect on consolidated assets, liabilities, and equities. This will be illustrated in a later section of this chapter (on ownership changes).

4. In the year that a subsidiary is acquired, special disclosures are required in the cash flow statement. The following example illustrates this.

The consolidated balance sheet of Parent Company and its five subsidiaries as at December 31, Year 1, is shown below:

**PARENT COMPANY**
**CONSOLIDATED BALANCE SHEET**
At December 31, Year 1

| | |
|---|---:|
| Cash | $  500,000 |
| Other assets | 900,000 |
| Goodwill | 120,000 |
| | $1,520,000 |
| | |
| Liabilities | $  500,000 |
| Common shares | 200,000 |
| Retained earnings | 720,000 |
| Non-controlling interests | 100,000 |
| | $1,520,000 |

On January 1, Year 2, Parent acquired 80% of the outstanding common shares of its sixth subsidiary, Sable Ltd., for a total cost of $140,000. The shareholders of Sable received cash of $90,000 and common shares of Parent with a market value of $50,000 in this transaction. The management of Parent determined that the other assets of Sable had a fair value of $205,000 on this date. The balance sheet of Sable on December 31, Year 1, is shown below:

**SABLE LTD.**
**BALANCE SHEET**
At December 31, Year 1

| | |
|---|---:|
| Cash | $  30,000 |
| Other assets | 200,000 |
| | $230,000 |
| | |
| Liabilities | $  70,000 |
| Common shares | 100,000 |
| Retained earnings | 60,000 |
| | $230,000 |

> *This is the separate-entity balance sheet of Sable.*

Parent's journal entry to record the acquisition of 80% of the common shares of Sable would be as follows on January 1, Year 2:

| | | |
|---|---|---|
| Investment in Sable Ltd. | 140,000 | |
| Common shares | | 50,000 |
| Cash | | 90,000 |

> *This entry is recorded on the separate-entity records for Parent.*

We will now prepare the consolidated balance sheet of Parent on January 1, Year 2, incorporating the latest acquisition and assuming that this acquisition was the only transaction that occurred on January 1, Year 2, for the parent and all of its subsidiaries.

The calculation and allocation of the acquisition differential for the Sable investment is shown:

| | |
|---|---|
| Cost of 80% investment in Sable | $140,000 |
| Implied value of 100% of Sable | $175,000 |
| Carrying amount of Sable | 160,000 |
| Acquisition differential | 15,000 |
| Allocated: | |
| Other assets | 5,000 |
| Goodwill | $ 10,000 |
| Non-controlling interest (175,000 × 20%) | $ 35,000 |

> *The components of the acquisition differential are reported on the consolidated balance sheet.*

The consolidated balance sheet appears below:

**PARENT COMPANY**
**CONSOLIDATED BALANCE SHEET**
At January 1, Year 2

| | |
|---|---|
| Cash (500,000 + 30,000 − 90,000) | $ 440,000 |
| Other assets (900,000 + 200,000 + 5,000) | 1,105,000 |
| Goodwill (120,000 + 10,000) | 130,000 |
| | $1,675,000 |
| | |
| Liabilities (500,000 + 70,000) | $ 570,000 |
| Common shares (200,000 + 50,000) | 250,000 |
| Retained earnings | 720,000 |
| Non-controlling interests (100,000 + 35,000) | 135,000 |
| | $1,675,000 |

> *The assets and liabilities of the subsidiary are added to the consolidated balance sheet.*

## Preparing the Consolidated Cash Flow Statement

We can now prepare the consolidated cash flow statement for the day that has elapsed by analyzing the changes in the two consolidated balance sheets. We know that the only transaction that has taken place is Parent's acquisition of 80% of Sable. The journal entry of Parent to record the acquisition was illustrated earlier. If we were preparing the cash flow statement of the parent company, we would use our knowledge of this entry in our analysis. But we are preparing the consolidated cash flow statement, and the account "Investment in Sable" does not appear in the consolidated balance sheet. In order to do the proper analysis we need to visualize the effect of this new acquisition on the consolidated balance sheet. We can depict this effect in the form of a "consolidating entry" in the following manner:

| | | |
|---|---|---|
| **Cash** | **30,000** | |
| **Other assets (200,000 + 5,000)** | **205,000** | |
| **Goodwill** | **10,000** | |
| **Liabilities** | | **70,000** |
| **Non-controlling interest** | | **35,000** |
| Cash | | 90,000 |
| Common shares | | 50,000 |

> *This entry shows the incremental effect of purchasing the subsidiary.*
>
> *The investment account is replaced by the underlying assets and liabilities in the consolidation process.*

Note that the portion of the entry shown in boldface is the amount of the account "Investment in Sable" that made up the parent's acquisition journal entry. Using this analysis, we would normally show the purchase of other assets and goodwill as cash outflows from investing activities and the increase in liabilities, non-controlling interest, and common shares as cash inflows from financing activities. However, IAS 7 requires that only the net cash outflow from a business combination be presented on the cash flow statement, and the details of the changes in non-cash accounts arising from the business combination be disclosed in the notes to financial statements.[2] Therefore, the consolidated cash flow statement for Parent Company would be presented as follows:

**PARENT COMPANY**
**CONSOLIDATED CASH FLOW STATEMENT**
For the day ended January 1, Year 2

| | |
|---|---|
| Operating cash flow | $      nil |
| Investing cash flow: | |
|    Acquisition of Sable, less cash acquired in acquisition $30,000 (note 1) | (60,000) |
| Financing cash flow | nil |
| Net change in cash for the two-day period | (60,000) |
| Cash, December 31, Year 1 | 500,000 |
| Cash, January 1, Year 2 | $440,000 |

> *Only the net change in cash is presented on the consolidated cash flow statement.*

*Note 1:* Effective January 1, Year 2, the company acquired 80% of the common shares of Sable for a total consideration of $140,000. The acquisition, which was accounted for by the acquisition method, is summarized as follows:

| | |
|---|---:|
| Net assets acquired: | |
| Other assets | $205,000 |
| Goodwill | 10,000 |
| Liabilities | (70,000) |
| Non-controlling interest | (35,000) |
| | $110,000 |
| Consideration given: | |
| Common shares | $ 50,000 |
| Cash | 90,000 |
| | 140,000 |
| Less cash acquired on acquisition | 30,000 |
| | $110,000 |

> *The details of the changes in non-cash items are disclosed in the notes to the consolidated cash flow statement.*

Note that the only item appearing on the cash flow statement is a $60,000 cash outflow under investing activities. The $60,000 is the difference between the cash paid for the shares of the subsidiary ($90,000) and the cash held by the subsidiary on the date of acquisition ($30,000). The other assets acquired and liabilities assumed in the business acquisition are not shown on the face of the cash flow statement as investing and financing activities but are disclosed in the notes to the financial statements. Therefore, when we prepare a cash flow statement, we must differentiate between those changes in non-cash items arising from a business combination and those arising from other activities. Those changes arising from the business combination are netted and given one line on the cash flow statement, with the details disclosed in the notes to the financial statements. The other changes are presented on the face of the cash flow statement, according to normal practices.

In our discussion of the consolidated cash flow statement, we have focused entirely on items unique to consolidated statements, on the assumption that the overall process for preparing such statements has been covered in earlier financial accounting courses. The next major topic in this chapter, *ownership changes,* also presents items that require analysis as to their effects on consolidated cash flows. The cash flow effects for these ownership changes will be discussed in the appropriate sections.

# CHANGES IN PARENT'S OWNERSHIP INTEREST

A parent's ownership interest will change for any of the following:

(a) The parent purchases additional holdings in its subsidiary (block acquisitions).

(b) The parent sells some of its holdings in its subsidiary.

(c) The subsidiary issues additional common shares to the public, and the parent does not maintain its previous ownership percentage.

(d) The subsidiary repurchases some of its common shares from the non-controlling interest.

> *The parent's percentage of ownership can change when the parent buys or sells shares of the subsidiary or when the subsidiary issues or repurchases shares.*

When the parent's ownership changes, the percentage of subsidiary common shares held by the non-controlling interest also changes. The major consolidation problem involved with ownership change is the effect such changes have on the valuation of subsidiary net assets and non-controlling interest in the consolidated statements. When the parent's ownership percentage *increases*, a portion of the unamortized acquisition differential will be transferred from the non-controlling interest to the parent. When the parent's ownership *decreases*, a portion of the unamortized acquisition differential will be transferred from the parent to the non-controlling interest. We will use a comprehensive example to illustrate various changes in a parent's ownership interest. We will begin with step-by-step acquisitions.

> *Any time the parent's percentage of ownership increases, we will account for the transaction as a purchase.*
> *Any time the parent's percentage decreases, we will account for the transaction as a sale.*

## LO2 Block Acquisitions of Subsidiary (Step Purchases)

The consolidation illustrations that we have used in previous chapters have assumed that the parent company achieved its control in a subsidiary by making a single purchase of the subsidiary's common shares. On the date of acquisition, the fair values of the subsidiary's assets (including goodwill) and liabilities were determined and then brought onto the consolidated balance sheet along with the carrying amounts of the parent's assets and liabilities. The non-controlling interest at the date of acquisition was also measured at fair value. In periods subsequent to the date of acquisition, the subsidiary's net assets were accounted for based on the values determined at the date of acquisition. They were not remeasured to fair value at each reporting date.

> *The subsidiary is measured at fair value on the consolidated balance sheet on the date the parent obtains control.*

We will now consider a situation where the parent achieves its control position through a series of block acquisitions (sometimes described as "step purchases").

**PURCHASE OF FIRST BLOCK OF SHARES**   On November 1, Year 1, Par Company acquires 1,000 common shares (10% of the outstanding shares) of Star Company for $21,000. The 10% voting interest does not give Par control or significant influence. The investment is classified as fair value through profit or loss (FVTPL). On this date, the shareholders' equity of Star consists of common shares of $100,000 and retained earnings of $70,000. During Year 1, Star reported net income of $10,000 and did not declare any dividends. At the end of Year 1, the fair value of Star's shares was $22 per share. Par's journal entries for Year 1 for the FVTPL investment follow:

| | | |
|---|---|---|
| Investment in Star | 21,000 | |
| Cash | | 21,000 |
| To record purchase of 1,000 shares of Star for $21 per share | | |
| Investment in Star | 1,000 | |
| Gain on Star | | 1,000 |
| To record unrealized gain on FVTPL investment in Star | | |

> *FVTPL investments are reported at fair value at each reporting date.*

Under the FVTPL method, the acquisition differential at the date of acquisition is ignored. Par's share of Star's income for the year is also ignored because only dividend income and unrealized gains are reported under the FVTPL method.

**PURCHASE OF SECOND BLOCK OF SHARES**   On January 1, Year 2, Par acquires another 2,000 common shares of Star for $44,000. The carrying amounts of Star's net assets are equal to fair values except for specialized equipment, which is undervalued by $10,000. The equipment has an estimated remaining useful life of five years. During Year 2, Star reported a net income of $30,000 and paid dividends of $20,000. At December 31, Year 2, the fair value of Star's shares was $25 per share.

Par now owns 30% of Star and, presuming no other factors to the contrary, has obtained significant influence in the key decisions for Star. As a result, Star is now an associate and Par will now adopt the equity method of accounting for its 30% interest. The change in reporting method will be accounted for prospectively as a change in estimate because the circumstances changed from not having significant influence to having significant influence.[3] In our current example, the investment in Star will reflect the fair value of Star's share at January 1, Year 2. Par paid fair value for the 2,000 shares it just purchased. The carrying amount of the previous investment also reflects its fair value because as a FVTPL investment it must be reported at fair value.

> *The equity method is used once the investor obtains significant influence.*

If the previous investment had been reported at cost, it would be revalued to fair value when the equity method was first adopted, and a gain or loss on revaluation would be reported in net income. The carrying amount of the investment in Star after the new investment would be equal to the fair value of the shares in Star at this date. Support for revaluing to fair value can be found in paragraph 26 of IAS 28, which states that the concepts underlying the procedures used in accounting for the acquisition of a subsidiary are also adopted in accounting for the acquisition of an investment in an associate. As we will see later, the revaluation of a previous investment to fair value is consistent with the requirements when an investor first obtains control of a subsidiary. Revaluing to fair value can also be supported by the use of the equity method, which requires that an investment in an associate must initially be recorded at cost. The cost of the asset 30% interest in Star is the fair value of the 10% investment in Star plus the $44,000 in cash.

> *The investment account is adjusted to fair value when the investor obtains significant influence over the investee.*

Under the equity method, an acquisition differential is calculated and subsequently amortized, similar to the process used for consolidation. The acquisition differential is first calculated when the equity method first becomes applicable and is calculated as if the entire 30% were purchased on this date. The acquisition cost incorporates the cost of the current purchase plus the fair value of the prior investments.

The calculation and allocation of the acquisition differential as at January 1, Year 2, is as follows:

| | | |
|---|---:|---:|
| Acquisition cost for 30% of Star (44,000 + 20,000 + 2,000) | | $66,000 |
| Carrying amount of Star's net assets: | | |
|    Common shares | 100,000 | |
|    Retained earnings (70,000 + 10,000) | 80,000 | |
| Total shareholders' equity | 180,000 | |
| Par's ownership interest | 30% | 54,000 |
| Acquisition differential | | 12,000 |
| Allocated: | | |
|    Equipment (10,000 × 30%) | | 3,000 |
| Goodwill | | $ 9,000 |

> *The acquisition differential must be identified and amortized under the equity method.*

The investment in Star is reported as a separate line on Par's balance sheet and is accounted for using the equity method. Consolidated financial statements are not appropriate, since Par only has significant influence and does not have control over Star. The acquisition differential, which includes the fair value excess pertaining to the equipment and the goodwill, is retained as a component of the investment account and not reported separately on Par's balance sheet. Since the fair value of Star's shares went up during Year 2, there appears to be no impairment in the investment in Star or the underlying goodwill. The fair value excess component pertaining to the equipment must be depreciated over its useful life of five years. Par's journal entries for Year 2 for the significant-influence investment would be as follows:

| | | |
|---|---|---|
| Investment in Star | 44,000 | |
|     Cash | | 44,000 |
| To record purchase of 2,000 shares of Star for $22 per share | | |
| Investment in Star | 9,000 | |
|     Investment income | | 9,000 |
| To record 30% of reported income for the year (30% × 30,000) | | |
| Investment income | 600 | |
|     Investment in Star | | 600 |
| To record amortization of acquisition differential related to equipment (3,000/5 years) | | |
| Cash | 6,000 | |
|     Investment in Star | | 6,000 |
| To record dividends received during the year (30% × 20,000) | | |

---

*The investment is not reported at fair value under the equity method.*

---

The balance in the investment account at the end of Year 2 is $68,400 ($22,000 + $44,000 + $9,000 − $600 − $6,000). The fair value of the investment is $75,000 (3,000 shares × $25 per share) but is ignored under the equity method, since it exceeds the carrying amount of the investment.

**PURCHASE OF THIRD BLOCK OF SHARES**    On January 1, Year 3, Par acquires another 1,000 common shares of Star for $25,000. The carrying amounts of Star's net assets are equal to fair values except for specialized equipment, which is undervalued by $10,000. The equipment has an estimated remaining useful life of four years. During Year 3, Star reported a net income of $40,000 and paid dividends of $20,000. At December 31, Year 3, the fair value of Star's shares was $29 per share.

Par now owns 40% of Star, still has significant influence in the key decisions for Star, and will continue using the equity method. An acquisition differential for this 10% step is calculated and allocated as follows:

| | | | |
|---|---|---|---|
| Cost of 10% of Star | | | $25,000 |
| Carrying amount of Star's net assets: | | | |
|     Common shares | | 100,000 | |
|     Retained earnings (80,000 + 30,000 − 20,000) | | 90,000 | |
|     Total shareholders' equity | | 190,000 | |
|     Par's ownership interest | 10% | | 19,000 |
| Acquisition differential | | | 6,000 |
| Allocated: | | | |
|     Equipment (10,000 × 10%) | | | 1,000 |
| Goodwill | | | $ 5,000 |

---

*A separate allocation of the acquisition differential should be prepared for each incremental investment.*

---

There are now two separate and incremental calculations and allocations of acquisition differential based on the purchase price for each step. The allocation for the 30% step is carried forward with its previous values and is not revalued to fair value on the date of the third step. The following acquisition-differential amortization schedule is prepared to keep track of the allocation and amortization of the acquisition differentials for each step:

| | Second Step | | Third Step | | |
|---|---|---|---|---|---|
| **ACQUISITION-DIFFERENTIAL AMORTIZATION SCHEDULE** | | | | | |
| | *Equip.* | *Goodwill* | *Equip.* | *Goodwill* | *Total* |
| Jan 1, Year 2, purchase | $3,000 | $9,000 | | | $12,000 |
| Amortization for Year 2 | (600) | | | | (600) |
| Balance, December 31, Year 2 | 2,400 | 9,000 | | | 11,400 |
| Jan 1, Year 3, purchase | | | $1,000 | $5,000 | 6,000 |
| Amortization for Year 3 | (600) | | (250) | | (850) |
| Balance, December 31, Year 3 | $1,800 | $9,000 | $ 750 | $5,000 | $16,550 |

> *The previous block acquisitions are not normally revalued when there is a new acquisition.*

Since the fair value of Star's shares went up during Year 3, there appears to be no impairment in the investment in Star or the underlying goodwill. The fair value excess component of the investment account is being depreciated over its useful life.

Par's journal entries for Year 3 for the investment in Star, an associate, would be as follows:

| | | |
|---|---|---|
| Investment in Star | 25,000 | |
| Cash | | 25,000 |
| To record purchase of 1,000 shares of Star for $25 per share | | |
| Investment in Star | 16,000 | |
| Investment income | | 16,000 |
| To record 40% of reported income for the year (40% × 40,000) | | |
| Investment income | 850 | |
| Investment in Star | | 850 |
| To record amortization of acquisition differential related to equipment | | |
| Cash | 8,000 | |
| Investment in Star | | 8,000 |
| To record dividends received during the year (40% × 20,000) | | |

> *The amortization of the acquisition differential is recorded in the investment account under the equity method.*

The balance in the investment account at the end of Year 3 is $100,550 ($68,400 + $25,000 + $16,000 − $850 − $8,000). The fair value of the investment is $116,000 (4,000 shares × $29 per share) but is ignored under the equity method, since it exceeds the carrying amount of the investment.

**PURCHASE OF FOURTH BLOCK OF SHARES**   On January 1, Year 4, Par acquires another 3,000 common shares of Star for $87,000. The carrying amounts of Star's net assets are equal to fair values except for specialized equipment, which is undervalued by $7,500. The equipment has an estimated remaining useful life of three years. During Year 4, Star reported a net income of $50,000 and paid dividends of $20,000. At December 31, Year 4, the fair value of Star's shares was $34 per share.

> *The investment account is adjusted to fair value when the investor first obtains control of the investee.*

Par now owns 70% and has control over Star. The business combination should be reported on a consolidated basis. The change in reporting method will be accounted for prospectively as a change in estimate because the circumstances changed from not having control to having control. Paragraph 42 of IFRS 3 states that the previously held equity interest should be revalued at fair value with the revaluation adjustment reported in net income. If, before the business combination, the acquirer recognized changes in the value of its non-controlling equity investment in other comprehensive income, the amount that was recognized in other comprehensive income is reclassified and included in the calculation of any gain or loss as of the acquisition date. Therefore, Par will make the following entries on January 1, Year 4:

| | | |
|---|---|---|
| Investment in Star | 15,450 | |
|     Unrealized gain on investment | | 15,450 |
| To adjust investment in Star to fair value (116,000 − 100,550) | | |
| Investment in Star | 87,000 | |
|     Cash | | 87,000 |
| To record purchase of 3,000 shares at $29 per share | | |

> *Any previous acquisition cost allocations are replaced by a new acquisition cost allocation on the date of a business combination.*

The investment in Star now contains a balance of $203,000 ($100,550 + $15,450 + $87,000), which is equal to the fair value of the 7,000 shares. When the parent first obtains control of the subsidiary, we must prepare a new calculation and allocation of the acquisition differential for the percentage ownership at the time of the purchase, to reflect the revaluation of the entire subsidiary to fair value. In so doing, we will ignore the acquisition differentials and amortizations from the previous steps. The acquisition-differential calculation and amortization for the 70% interest as at January 1, Year 4, is as follows:

| | | |
|---|---|---|
| Value of 70% of Star | | $203,000 |
| Implied value of 100% of Star | | $290,000 |
| Carrying amount of Star's net assets: | | |
|     Common shares | 100,000 | |
|     Retained earnings (90,000 + 40,000 − 20,000) | 110,000 | |
| Total shareholders' equity | | 210,000 |
| Acquisition differential | | 80,000 |
| Allocated: | | |
|     Equipment | | 7,500 |
| Goodwill | | $ 72,500 |

> *The acquisition differential is calculated and allocated to value the subsidiary at 100% of its fair value.*

Since the fair value of Star's shares went up during Year 4, there appears to be no impairment in Star's goodwill. The fair value excess attributed to the equipment must be depreciated over its useful life of three years. The following acquisition-differential amortization schedule is prepared to keep track of the allocation and amortization of the acquisition differential.

## ACQUISITION DIFFERENTIAL AMORTIZATION SCHEDULE

|  | Balance Jan. 1, Year 4 | Amortization Year 4 | Balance Dec. 31, Year 4 |
|---|---|---|---|
| Equipment | $ 7,500 | $2,500 | $ 5,000 |
| Goodwill | 72,500 |  | 72,500 |
|  | $80,000 | $2,500 | $77,500 |

Assuming that Par continues to use the equity method on its separate-entity books, the journal entries for Year 4 would be as follows:

| | | |
|---|---|---|
| Investment in Star | 35,000 | |
|    Investment income | | 35,000 |
| To record 70% of reported income for the year (70% × 50,000) | | |
| Investment income | 1,750 | |
|    Investment in Star | | 1,750 |
| To record Par's share of amortization of acquisition differential related to equipment (70% × 2,500) | | |
| Cash | 14,000 | |
|    Investment in Star | | 14,000 |
| To record dividends received during the year (70% × 20,000) | | |

> *Only the parent's share of the amortization of the acquisition differential is recorded in the parent's books.*

The balance in the investment account at the end of Year 4 is $222,250 ($203,000 + $35,000 − $1,750 − $14,000). The fair value of the investment is $238,000 (7,000 shares × $34 per share) but is ignored under the equity method and under consolidation, since it exceeds the carrying amount of the investment.

The investment account is not adjusted to fair value subsequent to the date of acquisition.

**PURCHASE OF FIFTH BLOCK OF SHARES**   On January 1, Year 5, Par acquires another 2,000 common shares of Star for $68,000. The carrying amounts of Star's net assets are equal to fair values except for specialized equipment, which is undervalued by $6,000. The equipment has an estimated remaining useful life of two years. During Year 5, Star reported a net income of $60,000 and paid dividends of $20,000. At December 31, Year 5, the fair value of Star's shares was $38 per share.

Par now owns 90% of Star, continues to have control over Star, and continues to report its investment on a consolidated basis. However, it does not treat this additional purchase like the other step purchases because there is no change in control; that is, it does not calculate an acquisition differential for this purchase and does not revalue the existing acquisition differential. The transaction is treated as an equity transaction; that is, a transaction with owners in their capacity as owners. Simply put, the parent is acquiring an additional 20% of Star from the non-controlling interest. In such circumstances, the carrying amount of the portion of the non-controlling interest sold to the parent will be allocated to the parent. Any difference between the amounts by which the non-controlling interest is adjusted and the fair value of the consideration paid or received by the parent must be recognized as a direct charge or credit to owners' equity, and attributed to the owners of the parent.

> *The subsidiary's net assets are not revalued on the consolidated financial statements when the parent's percentage ownership increases.*

The carrying amount of the non-controlling interest sold to the parent was $63,500, calculated as follows:

| | |
|---|---:|
| Star's common shares | $100,000 |
| Star's retained earnings (110,000 + 50,000 − 20,000) | 140,000 |
| | 240,000 |
| Unamortized acquisition differential | 77,500 |
| | 317,500 |
| Non-controlling interest's percentage ownership | 30% |
| Non-controlling interest at December 31, Year 4 | $ 95,250 |
| Portion sold to controlling interest (2,000/3,000) | $ 63,500 |

> *Any difference between the amount paid and the carrying amount of net assets being purchased from the non-controlling interest is recognized as a direct charge or credit to owner's equity.*

Since Par paid $68,000 for the shares, it paid $4,500 more than the carrying amount previously attributed to these shares on the consolidated balance sheet. This $4,500 would be recognized as a direct charge to Par's retained earnings on the date of the purchase and is akin to a dividend paid to shareholders.

Since the fair value of Star's shares went up during the year, there appears to be no impairment in Star's goodwill. The acquisition differential amortization schedule for Year 5 is as follows:

| | Balance Jan. 1, Year 5 | Amortization Year 5 | Balance Dec. 31, Year 5 |
|---|---:|---:|---:|
| Equipment | $ 5,000 | $2,500 | $ 2,500 |
| Goodwill | 72,500 | | 72,500 |
| | $77,500 | $2,500 | $75,000 |

Assuming that Par continues to use the equity method on its separate-entity books, the journal entries for Year 5 would be as follows:

| | | |
|---|---:|---:|
| Investment in Star | 63,500 | |
| Retained earnings | 4,500 | |
|    Cash | | 68,000 |
| To record purchase of 2,000 shares at $34 per share | | |
| Investment in Star | 54,000 | |
|    Investment income | | 54,000 |
| To record 90% of reported income for the year (90% × 60,000) | | |
| Investment income | 2,250 | |
|    Investment in Star | | 2,250 |
| To record Par's share of amortization of acquisition differential related to equipment (90% × 2,500) | | |
| Cash | 18,000 | |
|    Investment in Star | | 18,000 |
| To record dividends received during the year (90% × 20,000) | | |

> *These entries are recorded on the separate-entity books of the parent.*

The balance in the investment account at the end of Year 5 is $319,500 ($222,250 + $63,500 + $54,000 − $2,250 − $18,000). The investment account can be segregated as follows:

| | |
|---|---:|
| Carrying amount of Star's net assets: | |
| Common shares | $100,000 |
| Retained earnings (140,000 + 60,000 − 20,000) | 180,000 |
| Total shareholders' equity | 280,000 |
| Unamortized acquisition differential | 75,000 |
| | 355,000 |
| Par's ownership interest | 90% |
| Total | $319,500 |

---

*The investment account can be reconciled to the subsidiary's equity at any point in time when the parent uses the equity method.*

---

Similarly, the non-controlling interest can be calculated using these same components as follows:

| | |
|---|---:|
| Carrying amount of Star's net assets | $280,000 |
| Unamortized acquisition differential | 75,000 |
| | 355,000 |
| Non-controlling interest's ownership interest | 10% |
| | $ 35,500 |

---

*Non-controlling interest on the balance sheet comprises the non-controlling interest's share of the subsidiary's equity and the unamortized acquisition differential at the balance sheet date.*

---

We will now illustrate the consolidation process by using the following condensed balance sheets for Par and Star at the end of Year 5:

| | Par | Star |
|---|---:|---:|
| Investment in Star (equity method) | $ 319,500 | |
| Equipment—net | 500,000 | $140,000 |
| Other assets | 700,000 | 490,000 |
| | $1,519,500 | $630,000 |
| Liabilities | $450,000 | $350,000 |
| Common shares | 500,000 | 100,000 |
| Retained earnings | 569,500 | 180,000 |
| | $1,519,500 | $630,000 |

---

*The parent's retained earnings under the equity method are equal to consolidated retained earnings.*

---

The consolidated balance sheet at December 31, Year 5, is as follows:

**PAR COMPANY**
**CONSOLIDATED BALANCE SHEET**
At December 31, Year 5

| | |
|---|---:|
| Equipment—net (500,000 + 140,000 + 2,500) | $ 642,500 |
| Other assets (700,000 + 490,000) | 1,190,000 |
| Goodwill (0 + 0 + 72,500) | 72,500 |
| | $1,905,000 |
| Liabilities (450,000 + 350,000) | $ 800,000 |
| Common shares | 500,000 |
| Retained earnings | 569,500 |
| Non-controlling interest | 35,500 |
| | $1,905,000 |

---

*Both the parent's and the non-controlling interest's shares of the unamortized acquisition differential appear on the consolidated balance sheet.*

---

**NUMEROUS SMALL PURCHASES**   Assume that Par attempts to purchase the remaining outstanding shares of Star by making daily open-market purchases of the subsidiary's shares. At the end of two months, it abandons the idea. During this period, it has made 35 separate share purchases, which, in total, represent 4% of the subsidiary's outstanding shares. Since it would be impractical to calculate 35 acquisition differentials, these purchases can be combined and treated as a single block purchase of 4%.

---

*Numerous small purchases can be grouped into one block purchase when calculating and allocating the acquisition differential.*

---

**REPURCHASE OF SHARES BY SUBSIDIARY**   When the subsidiary repurchases and cancels some or all of the common shares being held by the non-controlling shareholders, the parent's percentage ownership in the common shares will increase. The increase in ownership will be accounted for as an equity transaction similar to the purchase of the fifth block of shares.

**CONSOLIDATED RETAINED EARNINGS—COST METHOD**   The examples used to illustrate block purchases have assumed that the parent company uses the equity method to account for its investment. If the parent had used the cost method, schedules would have to be prepared to derive account balances such as retained earnings for the consolidated financial statements. These schedules have been extensively illustrated in earlier chapters and require only slight modification when block acquisitions have been made.

In our comprehensive example, Par used the equity method during the period it had control of Star. If Par had used the cost method for internal record keeping, it likely would have adopted the cost method when it first obtained control of Star on January 1, Year 4. It would simply have added the $87,000 cost of the fourth purchase to the carrying amount of the investment at that point, which was $100,550 as per our earlier discussion. It would not likely have made any adjustment to value the investment at fair value as required for consolidation purposes. If so, the balance in the investment account at January 1, Year 4, would have been $187,550 ($100,550 + $87,000). The $68,000 cost of the fifth purchase would be added on January 1, Year 5, to bring the investment account to $255,550 ($187,550 + $68,000) at that date and at December 31, Year 5. This compares to a balance of $319,500 under the equity method at the end of Year 5. The difference of $63,950 ($319,500 − $255,550) for the investment account would be same difference for retained earnings. Therefore, retained earnings for Par under the cost method would have been $505,550 ($569,500 under equity method minus $63,950) at December 31, Year 5. Consolidated retained earnings would be calculated as follows:

### CALCULATION OF CONSOLIDATED RETAINED EARNINGS
at December 31, Year 5

| | | |
|---|---:|---:|
| Retained earnings of parent—cost method | | $505,550 |
| Adjust investment account to fair value at date of business combination | | 15,450 |
| Less: Parent's share of acquisition differential amortizations: | | |
| Year 4 purchase | 1,750 | |
| Year 5 purchase | 2,250 | (4,000) |
| Retained earnings of subsidiary at the time of Year 5 purchase | 140,000 | |
| Retained earnings of subsidiary at the time of Year 4 purchase | 110,000 | |
| Increase since Year 4 purchase | 30,000 | |
| Parent's ownership percentage | 70% | 21,000 |
| Retained earnings of subsidiary—Dec. 31, Year 5 | 180,000 | |
| Retained earnings of subsidiary at the time of Year 5 purchase | 140,000 | |
| Increase since Year 5 purchase | 40,000 | |
| Parent's ownership percentage | 90% | 36,000 |
| Loss on purchase of shares from non-controlling interest, Jan. 1, Year 5 | | (4,500) |
| Consolidated retained earnings | | $569,500 |

> *The only two balance sheet accounts on the parent's separate entity books that are different between the cost and equity methods are the investment account and the retained earnings account.*
>
> *Consolidated retained earnings should recognize the parent's percentage interest in the change in the subsidiary's retained earnings for each step of the step-by-step acquisitions.*

**CONSOLIDATED CASH FLOW ANALYSIS**   Par Company's fifth block purchase of shares (on January 1, Year 5, for $68,000) requires further analysis to determine the effect on the Year 5 consolidated balance sheet. This cash has left the consolidated entity, so the effect of the transaction must appear on the Year 5 consolidated cash flow statement. We can depict the effect of the fifth purchase on the consolidated balance sheet with the following entry:

| | | |
|---|---:|---:|
| Retained earnings | 4,500 | |
| Non-controlling interest | 63,500 | |
| Cash | | 68,000 |

This transaction simply moved cash and reallocated shareholders' equity between the controlling and non-controlling interests. No new assets were acquired. The $68,000 cash outflow should appear in the financing activities section of the cash flow statement, since it is similar to purchasing shares from a shareholder. It would be described as "Purchase of additional shares in subsidiary from non-controlling interest."

> *The cost of purchasing additional shares in the subsidiary should be reported in financing activities on the consolidated cash flow statement.*

## LO3 Parent Sells Some of Its Holdings in Subsidiary

Let us continue with the previous illustration involving Par and Star. Assume that on January 1, Year 6, Par sold 900 shares in Star Company on the open market for $34,200. Note that after the sale, Par's ownership percentage is 81% (8,100 ÷ 10,000). Note also that Par has disposed of 10% of its investment in Star (900 ÷ 9,000). Another way of calculating the percentage of investment disposed is as follows:

| | |
|---|---:|
| Ownership before sale | 90% |
| Ownership after sale | 81% |
| Change | 9% |
| Percentage of investment sold: 9 ÷ 90 = 10% | |

Since Par still has control of Star, consolidated financial statements will continue to be prepared. This transaction is, once again, treated as an equity transaction; that is, a transaction between shareholders of the consolidated entity. The parent is selling part of its interest in Star to the non-controlling interest. The carrying amount of the portion sold is $31,950 (10% × $319,500 as determined under the equity method); it will be allocated from the parent to the non-controlling interest. Since the amount received was $34,200, the owners of the parent are better off by $2,250 as a result of this transaction. This benefit is not reported in net income since this transaction between owners has not resulted in a change in control. The gain will be recognized as a direct increase to consolidated contributed surplus.

> *Gains (losses) on transactions with shareholders are credited (charged) directly to shareholders' equity.*

Since the equity method should produce the same results as the consolidated financial statements, Par would make the following entry to record the sale of 900 shares:

| | | |
|---|---:|---:|
| Cash | 34,200 | |
|     Investment in Star (10% × 319,500) | | 31,950 |
|     Contributed surplus | | 2,250 |

The total unamortized acquisition differential to be reported on the consolidated financial statements would remain the same in total. However, the portion belonging to the non-controlling interest would increase because the non-controlling interest now owns 19% of the subsidiary. The portion belonging to the controlling interest would decrease because the parent has sold 10% of its interest.

> *Non-controlling interest is increased by the carrying amount of the shares sold by the parent.*

The following schedule shows the change in values for the controlling and non-controlling interests as a result of Par's sale of 900 shares:

| | Controlling Interest | | | Non-controlling Interest | | | |
|---|---|---|---|---|---|---|---|
| | Before | Sold | After | Before | Bought | After | |
| Percentage ownership | 90% | 9% | 81% | 10% | 9% | 19% | |
| Share of Star's shareholders' equity | $252,000 | $25,200 | $226,800 | $28,000 | $25,200 | $53,200 | |
| Unamortized acquisition differential: | | | | | | | |
| Equipment | 2,250 | 225 | 2,025 | 250 | 225 | 475 | (a) |
| Goodwill | 65,250 | 6,525 | 58,725 | 7,250 | 6,525 | 13,775 | (b) |
| Total | $319,500 | $31,950 | $287,550 | $35,500 | $31,950 | $67,450 | |

> *The total acquisition differential remains the same but the split between the parent and non-controlling interest does change.*

We will now illustrate the consolidation process by using the following condensed balance sheets for Par and Star at January 1, Year 6. The previous balance sheets have been updated for the entry to record the sale of 900 shares by Par.

| | Par | Star |
|---|---|---|
| Investment in Star (319,500 − 31,950) | $ 287,550 | |
| Equipment—net | 500,000 | $140,000 |
| Other assets (700,000 + 34,200) | 734,200 | 490,000 |
| | $1,521,750 | $630,000 |
| | | |
| Liabilities | $ 450,000 | $350,000 |
| Common shares | 500,000 | 100,000 |
| Retained earnings | 569,500 | 180,000 |
| Contributed surplus | 2,250 | |
| | $1,521,750 | $630,000 |

The consolidated balance sheet at January 1, Year 6, is as follows:

**PAR COMPANY**
**CONSOLIDATED BALANCE SHEET**
At January 1, Year 6

| | |
|---|---|
| Equipment—net (500,000 + 140,000 + **(a) 2,025 + 475**) | $ 642,500 |
| Other assets (734,200 + 490,000) | 1,224,200 |
| Goodwill (**(b) 58,725 + 13,775**) | 72,500 |
| | $1,939,200 |
| | |
| Liabilities (450,000 + 350,000) | $ 800,000 |
| Common shares | 500,000 |
| Retained earnings | 569,500 |
| Contributed surplus | 2,250 |
| Non-controlling interest | 67,450 |
| | $1,939,200 |

> *The subsidiary's net assets are not revalued when the parent sells a portion of its investment in the subsidiary.*

The sale of the shares to the non-controlling interest increased the entity's cash by $34,200. This cash inflow must appear on the consolidated cash flow statement. We can depict the effect of the sale on the consolidated balance sheet with the following entry:

| | | |
|---|---|---|
| Cash | 34,200 | |
|     Non-controlling interest | | 31,950 |
|     Contributed surplus | | 2,250 |

This transaction simply reallocated shareholders' equity between the controlling and non-controlling interests. The $34,200 cash inflow should appear in the financing activities section of the cash flow statement and would be described as "Sale of shares in subsidiary to non-controlling interest."

> *The proceeds from selling shares in the subsidiary should be reported in financing activities on the consolidated cash flow statement.*

## Income Statement Analysis

On December 31, Year 6, Star reported a net income of $40,000 and paid dividends amounting to $15,000. A goodwill impairment test conducted on December 31, Year 6, indicated that an impairment loss of $6,000 had occurred. The following acquisition differential amortization schedule would be made on December 31, Year 6:

**ACQUISITION DIFFERENTIAL AMORTIZATION AND IMPAIRMENT SCHEDULE**

| | Balance Jan. 1, Year 6 | Amortization/Impairment Year 6 | Balance Dec. 31, Year 6 |
|---|---|---|---|
| Equipment | $ 2,500 | $2,500 | $ 0 |
| Goodwill | 72,500 | 6,000 | 66,500 |
| | $75,000 | $8,500 | $66,500 |

Note that the Year 6 amortization completely eliminates the acquisition differential related to the equipment because this is the last year of the equipment's useful life.

Par's equity method journal entries for Year 6 would be as follows:

| | | |
|---|---|---|
| Investment in Star | 32,400 | |
|     Investment income | | 32,400 |
| To record 81% of Star's net income for Year 6 (40,000 × 81%) | | |
| Cash | 12,150 | |
|     Investment in Star | | 12,150 |
| To record dividends received from Star in Year 6 (15,000 × 81%) | | |
| Investment income | 6,885 | |
|     Investment in Star | | 6,885 |
| To record Par's share of amortization of the acquisition differential for Year 6 (8,500 × 81%) | | |

> *Dividends received from the subsidiary are recorded as a reduction in the investment account under the equity method.*

The following are the Year 6 income statements of Par and Star:

|  | Par | Star |
|---|---|---|
| Miscellaneous revenue | $200,000 | $150,000 |
| Investment income | 25,515 | — |
|  | 225,515 | 150,000 |
| Miscellaneous expenses | 130,000 | 90,000 |
| Equipment depreciation expense | — | 20,000 |
|  | 130,000 | 110,000 |
| Net income | $ 95,515 | $ 40,000 |

Investment income is replaced with the revenues and expenses of Star, the amortization of the acquisition differentials, and the non-controlling interest. The Year 6 consolidated income statement prepared using the direct approach appears below:

**PAR COMPANY**
**CONSOLIDATED INCOME STATEMENT**
For the year ended December 31, Year 6

| | |
|---|---|
| Miscellaneous revenues (200,000 + 150,000) | $350,000 |
| Miscellaneous expenses (130,000 + 90,000) | 220,000 |
| Equipment depreciation (0 + 20,000 + 2,500) | 22,500 |
| Goodwill impairment loss (0 + 0 + 6,000) | 6,000 |
| | 248,500 |
| Net income | $101,500 |
| Attributable to: | |
| Shareholders of Par Company | $ 95,515 |
| Non-controlling interest [19% × (40,000 − 8,500)] | 5,985 |

---

*The non-controlling interest is charged with its share of the amortization of the acquisition differential.*

---

At December 31, Year 6, Par's investment in Star account under the equity method would have a balance of $300,915 calculated as follows:

| | |
|---|---|
| Balance, January 1, Year 6 | $319,500 |
| Sold to non-controlling interest | (31,950) |
| Share of Star's income for Year 6 | 32,400 |
| Dividends from Star for Year 6 | (12,150) |
| Share of amortization of acquisition differential for Year 6 | (6,885) |
| Balance, December 31, Year 6 | $300,915 |

Now assume that on January 1, Year 7, Par sold 4,000 shares in Star to an unrelated party for $156,000 or $39 per share. Par would still own 4,100 shares, which represents a 41% (4,100 ÷ 10,000) ownership percentage. Par would no longer have control of Star and would no longer prepare consolidated financial statements. It would likely have significant influence and would report its investment in Star using the equity method. This transaction is not treated as a transaction between shareholders of the consolidated entity because non-controlling interest would no longer appear on Par's financial statements.

Therefore, any gain or loss on this transaction is reported in net income. Par would make the following entry to record the sale of 4,000 shares under the equity method:

| | | |
|---|---|---|
| Cash | 156,000 | |
|     Investment in Star (4,000 / 8,100 × 300,915) | | 148,600 |
|     Gain on sale of investment in subsidiary | | 7,400 |

In addition to the gain from the sale of the investment, any investment retained in the former subsidiary must be remeasured at fair value when there is a loss of control.[4] The retained interest of 4,100 shares has a fair value of $159,900 (4,100 × $39) and a carrying amount of $152,315 (4,100/8,100 × $300,915). Par would make the following entry to remeasure the retained 4,100 shares under the equity method:

| | | |
|---|---|---|
| Investment in Star (159,900 − 152,315) | 7,585 | |
|     Remeasurement gain on investment in former subsidiary | | 7,585 |

---

*When an investor loses control of an investee, it recognizes any gain or loss through net income.*

---

Over the past few pages, we have accounted for a series of acquisitions and dispositions of shares in an investee. Exhibit 8.1 summarizes the key decisions made in each step of the process.

**EXHIBIT 8.1**

## Overview of Step-by-Step Acquisitions

| | Step Number | | | | | | |
|---|---|---|---|---|---|---|---|
| | 1 | 2 | 3 | 4 | 5 | 6 | 7 |
| Percentage acquired | 10 | 20 | 10 | 30 | 20 | (9) | (40) |
| Percentage owned | 10 | 30 | 40 | 70 | 90 | 81 | 41 |
| Reporting method | FVTPL | Equity | Equity | Cons | Cons | Cons | Equity |
| Previous investment revalued to fair value? | N.A. | Yes | No | Yes | No | No | Yes |
| New allocation of acquisition differential required? | No | Yes | Yes | Yes | No | No | Yes |
| Acquisition differential for what percentage? | N.A. | 30 | 10 | 100 | N.A. | N.A. | 41 |

---

*Any time there is a change to or from having significant influence or control, the investment is remeasured at fair value.*

---

See Self-Study Problem 1 for a comprehensive problem involving changes in ownership. It includes most of the issues we have covered so far this chapter.

# SUBSIDIARY ISSUES ADDITIONAL SHARES TO PUBLIC

Let us assume that Par did not sell 900 shares on January 1, Year 6, or 4,000 shares on January 1, Year 7, and that, instead, Star Company issued an additional 2,500 shares for $95,000 on January 1, Year 6. Star would record this transaction as follows:

| Cash | 95,000 | |
| Common shares | | 95,000 |
| To record the issuance of 2,500 shares | | |

> *The parent's percentage interest decreases when the subsidiary issues additional shares and the parent does not purchase any of the additional shares.*

Star now has 12,500 common shares issued. Because Par did not buy any of the new issue, its holdings have remained constant (9,000 shares) but its ownership interest has declined to 72% (9,000 ÷ 12,500). This represents a 20% reduction in its investment, calculated as follows:

| | |
|---|---:|
| Ownership before share issue | 90% |
| Ownership after share issue | 72% |
| Change | 18% |
| Percentage of investment reduced: 18 ÷ 90 = 20% | |

The effect of this reduction on the unamortized acquisition differential is the same as if the parent had sold a portion of its holding in the subsidiary to the non-controlling interest. In this case, 20% of the parent's share of the unamortized acquisition differential has been "disposed of" as a result of the share issue. However, at this point, the only entry to record the transaction is made by Star. Parent must also adjust its investment account to record the effect of this transaction on its investment. The following analysis indicates the amount of the adjustment:

| | |
|---|---:|
| Loss due to reduction of investment account—20% × 319,500 | $63,900 |
| Gain due to ownership of new assets resulting from subsidiary share issue—72% × 95,000 | 68,400 |
| Net benefit to parent due to share issue | $ 4,500 |

> *The parent gave up 20% of its old investment and received 72% of the increase in the subsidiary's equity.*

In our previous example, we explained the reasoning for removing 20% from the investment account. The unamortized acquisition differential is included in the $319,500 amount, and if this differential has been reduced by 20%, a logical extension is to remove 20% from the total investment balance. If the subsidiary had issued the 2,500 shares for no consideration, the investment account would have to be reduced by $63,900 (20% × $319,500), and a loss equal to that amount would be recorded by Par as a direct charge to owner's equity. But Star received $95,000 for its new share issue, and Par now owns 72% of the net assets of its subsidiary, including the additional cash received as a result of the new share issue. Par has gained by the 72% ownership interest in the assets received by Star. It should be obvious that the net charge or credit to owners' equity resulting from the transaction depends on the amount that the subsidiary received from its new share issue. This gain is not reported in net income, since this transaction between owners has not resulted in a change in control. The gain will be recognized as a direct increase to consolidated contributed surplus and to the parent's separate-entity contributed surplus under the equity method. Given the facts of this particular example, Par would make the following journal entry under the equity method on January 1, Year 6:

| | | |
|---|---|---|
| Investment in Star | 4,500 | |
|     Contributed surplus | | 4,500 |
| To record the effect of subsidiary's issue of 2,500 shares on parent's investment | | |

---

*Gains (losses) on transactions with shareholders are not reported in net income.*

---

As in our previous example, we assume that in Year 6, Star reported a net income of $40,000 and paid $15,000 in dividends. Par's equity method journal entries for Year 6 would be as follows:

| | | |
|---|---|---|
| Investment in Star | 28,800 | |
|     Investment income | | 28,800 |
| To record 72% of Star's net income for Year 6 (40,000 × 72%) | | |
| Cash | 10,800 | |
|     Investment in Star | | 10,800 |
| To record dividends received from Star in Year 6 (15,000 × 72%) | | |
| Investment income | 6,120 | |
|     Investment in Star | | 6,120 |
| To record Par's share of the amortization of the acquisition differential for Year 6 (8,500 × 72%) | | |

---

*The parent absorbs 72% of the amortization of the acquisition differential.*

---

The elimination of the parent's interest in the subsidiary's shareholders' equity against the parent's investment account leaves a balance equal to the unamortized acquisition differential. This will now be illustrated.

| | | |
|---|---|---|
| Investment in Star: | | |
|     Balance, December 31, Year 5 | | $319,500 |
|     Increase due to subsidiary share issue | | 4,500 |
|     Star net income (40,000 × 72%) | | 28,800 |
|     Star dividends (15,000 × 72%) | | (10,800) |
|     Acquisition differential amortization | | (6,120) |
|       Balance, December 31, Year 6 | | 335,880 |
| Shareholders' equity of Star: | | |
|     Common shares—December 31, Year 5 | 100,000 | |
|     Share issue—Year 6 | 95,000 | |
|     Common shares, December 31, Year 6 | 195,000 | |
|     Retained earnings, December 31, Year 6 (180,000 + 40,000 − 15,000) | 205,000 | |
|       Total, December 31, Year 6 | 400,000 | |
| Par's ownership interest | 72% | 288,000 |
| Balance—unamortized acquisition differential | | $ 47,880 |

---

*The investment account comprises the parent's share of the subsidiary's equity plus the unamortized acquisition differential.*

---

The $47,880 represents Par's 72% of the total acquisition differential of $66,500, as per the earlier discussion under "Income Statement Analysis." Non-controlling interest at December 31, Year 6, is $130,620 (28% × [$400,000 + $66,500]).

> *The unamortized acquisition differential is not revalued when the parent's percentage ownership changes as long as the parent still has control.*

The Year 6 income statements of Par and Star are shown below, followed by the consolidated income statement.

| | Par | Star |
|---|---|---|
| Miscellaneous revenue | $200,000 | $150,000 |
| Investment income | 22,680 | — |
| | 222,680 | 150,000 |
| Miscellaneous expenses | 130,000 | 90,000 |
| Equipment depreciation expense | — | 20,000 |
| | 130,000 | 110,000 |
| Net income | $ 92,680 | $ 40,000 |

**PAR COMPANY**
**CONSOLIDATED INCOME STATEMENT**
For the year ended December 31, Year 6

| | |
|---|---|
| Miscellaneous revenues (200,000 + 150,000) | $350,000 |
| Miscellaneous expenses (130,000 + 90,000) | 220,000 |
| Equipment depreciation (0 + 20,000 + 2,500) | 22,500 |
| Goodwill impairment loss (0 + 0 + 6,000) | 6,000 |
| | 248,500 |
| Net income | $101,500 |
| Attributable to: | |
| Shareholders of Par Company | $ 92,680 |
| Non-controlling interest [28% × (40,000 − 8,500)] | 8,820 |

**CONSOLIDATED CASH FLOW ANALYSIS**   To recap, the issue of 2,500 shares on January 1, Year 6, was recorded by Star Company with the following journal entry:

| | | |
|---|---|---|
| Cash | 95,000 | |
| Common shares | | 95,000 |

Also, in order to record the effect of the reduction on its investment, Par made the following journal entry on this date:

| | | |
|---|---|---|
| Investment in Star | 4,500 | |
| Contributed surplus | | 4,500 |

As a result of this share issue, the non-controlling interest increased by $90,500 calculated as follows:

NCI after subsidiary share issue:

| | | |
|---|---|---|
| Shareholders' equity before issue | $280,000 | |
| New share issue | 95,000 | |
| Shareholders' equity after issue | 375,000 | |
| Unamortized acquisition differential | 75,000 | |
| | 450,000 | |
| NCI's share | 28% | |
| | | 126,000 |
| NCI before subsidiary share issue | | 35,500 |
| Increase in non-controlling interest | | $90,500 |

---

*Non-controlling interest can be reconciled to the subsidiary's shareholders' equity and the unamortized acquisition differential at any point in time.*

---

The effect of this transaction on the consolidated financial statements can be depicted as follows:

| | | |
|---|---|---|
| Cash | 95,000 | |
| Non-controlling interest | | 90,500 |
| Contributed surplus | | 4,500 |

---

*The consolidated entity received cash from the non-controlling interest.*

---

This transaction increased the equity of both the controlling and the non-controlling interests. The $95,000 cash inflow should appear in the financing activities section of the cash flow statement and would be described as "Issuance of shares by subsidiary to non-controlling interest."

**DISCLOSURE REQUIREMENTS** The disclosure requirements for a business combination were listed near the end of Chapter 3. Exhibit 8.2 is an extract from Onex Corporation's 2014 consolidated financial statements. It provides an example of disclosure when a parent sells a partial interest in a subsidiary. Onex Corporation and its subsidiaries have operations in a range of industries including electronics manufacturing services, healthcare imaging, health and human services, customer care services, building products, insurance services, credit strategies, aerospace automation, tooling and components, aircraft leasing and management, business services/trade shows, plastics processing equipment, business services/packaging, and gaming. In 2014, Onex reported a direct credit of $102 million to retained earnings pertaining to partial sales of operating companies under continuing control.[5] In our previous examples, we recorded the gain from these transfers of equity in contributed surplus. In both cases, the gain went directly to shareholders' equity without being recognized in net income. Both methods are acceptable under IFRS.

---

*The excess of proceeds over the value of the transfer of equity to the non-controlling interests was recorded directly to retained earnings or contributed surplus.*

---

EXHIBIT 8.2

**EXTRACTS FROM ONEX'S 2014 FINANCIAL STATEMENTS**

*26. Sale of Interests in Operating Company Under Continuing Control*

In March 2014, under a secondary public offering of Spirit AeroSystems, Onex, Onex Partners I, Onex management and certain limited partners sold 6.0 million shares of Spirit AeroSystems, of which Onex' portion was approximately 1.6 million shares. The offering was completed at a price of $28.52 per share. Onex' cash cost for these shares was $3.33 per share. Since this transaction did not result in a loss of control by the Company at the time of the transaction, it has been recorded as a transfer of equity to non-controlling interests.

Total cash proceeds received from the sale were $171, resulting in a transfer of the historical accounting carrying value of $69 to the non-controlling interests in the consolidated statements of equity. The net cash proceeds in excess of the historical accounting carrying value of $102 were recorded directly to retained earnings. Onex' share of the net proceeds was $52, including carried interest and after the reduction for distributions paid on account of the MIP.

Amounts received on account of the carried interest related to this transaction totalled $16. In accordance with the terms of Onex Partners, Onex is allocated 40% of the carried interest with 60% allocated to management. Onex' share of the carried interest received was $6 and is included in the net proceeds to Onex. Management's share of the carried interest was $10. Amounts paid on account of the MIP totalled $4 for this transaction and have been deducted from the net proceeds to Onex.

As a result of this transaction, Onex, Onex Partners I, Onex management and certain limited partners' economic interest in Spirit AeroSystems was reduced to 11% from 16%. Onex' economic ownership was reduced to 3% from 5%. Onex continued to control and consolidate Spirit AeroSystems until the June 2014 secondary offering and share repurchase, as described in note 6(b). In August 2014, under a secondary public offering of Spirit AeroSystems, Onex, Onex Partners I, Onex management and certain limited partners sold their remaining shares of Spirit AeroSystems, as described in note 23(f).[6]

*Source: ONEX, Management's Discussion and Analysis and Financial Statements, December 31, 2014,*

*Pages 93, 96, 114. Reproduced with permission from ONEX.*

> *Even though Onex only had an economic interest in Spirit AeroSystems of 3%, it still had control of Spirit.*

LO4 # SUBSIDIARY WITH PREFERRED SHARES OUTSTANDING

All of the consolidation examples that we have used up to this point have assumed that the subsidiary companies have only one class of shares, common shares, in their capital structures. We now examine situations where the subsidiary also has preferred shares. The basic concepts of consolidation do not change, but when there is more than one class of shares outstanding, there is an additional problem involved in determining the amount of non-controlling interest in the net assets and net income of the subsidiary. The following example will illustrate the approach that is used.

## Illustration—Preferred Shareholdings

On December 31, Year 1, the shareholders' equity of Sonco Inc. was as follows:

Preferred shares, $10 dividend, cumulative, redeemable at $105 per share:

| | |
|---|---:|
| Issued and outstanding 1,000 shares | $100,000 |
| Common shares: | |
| Issued and outstanding 30,000 shares | 360,000 |
| Total share capital | 460,000 |
| Retained earnings (Note 1) | 140,000 |
| | $600,000 |

*Note 1:* On December 31, Year 1, dividends on preferred shares were one year in arrears.

---

*If the subsidiary were wound up today, how much of its equity would go to the preferred shareholders?*

---

On January 1, Year 2, Parco Ltd. purchased 27,000 common shares of Sonco for $450,000. The acquisition differential was allocated entirely to franchise agreements, to be amortized over a 10-year period.

Because the parent company acquired control by purchasing 90% of the voting common shares, the non-controlling interest consists of the shareholdings represented by 10% of the common shares and 100% of the preferred shares. In order to calculate any acquisition differential associated with the common share purchase, and the amount of the non-controlling interest in both classes of shares, it is necessary to split the shareholders' equity of Sonco into its preferred and common share capital components in the following manner:

| | Total | Preferred | Common |
|---|---:|---:|---:|
| Preferred shares | $100,000 | $100,000 | $    — |
| Redemption premium on preferred | — | 5,000 | (5,000) |
| Common shares | 360,000 | — | 360,000 |
| Total share capital | 460,000 | 105,000 | 355,000 |
| Retained earnings | 140,000 | 10,000 | 130,000 |
| | $600,000 | $115,000 | $485,000 |

---

*The preferred shareholders would get the first $115,000, and the common shareholders would get the rest.*

---

The $115,000 allocated to preferred share capital represents the total amount that the company would have to pay to the preferred shareholders if the preferred shares were redeemed on this date. It is made up of the redemption price on 1,000 shares ($105,000) and the one year's dividends in arrears ($10,000) on these shares.

By using the two components of shareholders' equity, both the acquisition differential and the non-controlling interest on the date of acquisition can be calculated, as follows:

| | |
|---|---:|
| Cost of 90% of common shares | $450,000 |
| Implied value of 100% of Sonco's common shares | $500,000 |
| Carrying amount of common shares of Sonco | 485,000 |
| Acquisition differential | 15,000 |
| Allocated: Franchise agreement | 15,000 |
| Balance | $    —0— |
| Non-controlling interest, January 1, Year 2: | |
| Preferred shares (115,000 × 100%) | $115,000 |
| Common shares (500,000 × 10%) | 50,000 |
| | $165,000 |

---

*The acquisition differential on the common shares is calculated in the same way as before.*

---

The preparation of the consolidated balance sheet on January 1, Year 2, will not be illustrated, but it should be obvious that the only difference from previous examples lies in how the non-controlling interest is calculated on this date.

The financial statements of Parco and Sonco on December 31, Year 2, are shown in Exhibit 8.3. Parco uses the cost method to account for its investment.

**EXHIBIT 8.3**

### YEAR 2 INCOME STATEMENTS

|  | Parco | Sonco |
|---|---|---|
| Revenues—miscellaneous | $750,000 | $420,000 |
| Dividends from Sonco | 27,000 | — |
|  | 777,000 | 420,000 |
| Expenses—miscellaneous | 688,000 | 360,000 |
| Net income | $ 89,000 | $ 60,000 |

*The parent received 90% of the dividends paid to common shareholders.*

### YEAR 2 RETAINED EARNINGS STATEMENTS

|  | Parco | Sonco |
|---|---|---|
| Balance, January 1 | $381,000 | $140,000 |
| Net income | 89,000 | 60,000 |
|  | 470,000 | 200,000 |
| Dividends | 90,000 | 50,000 |
| Balance, December 31 | $380,000 | $150,000 |

### BALANCE SHEETS
At December 31, Year 2

|  | Parco | Sonco |
|---|---|---|
| Assets—miscellaneous | $510,000 | $810,000 |
| Investment in Sonco—at cost | 450,000 | — |
|  | $960,000 | $810,000 |
| Liabilities | $180,000 | $200,000 |
| Preferred shares | — | 100,000 |
| Common shares | 400,000 | 360,000 |
| Retained earnings | 380,000 | 150,000 |
|  | $960,000 | $810,000 |

*The parent has an investment in the common shares of the subsidiary but no investment in the preferred shares.*

In order to prepare the Year 2 consolidated financial statements, it is again necessary to split the shareholders' equity of Sonco into its preferred and common share components. Because there has been no change in total share capital, the allocation of this component is identical to the one made as at

January 1 (see above). But retained earnings *has* changed, so we will allocate the retained earnings statement in the following manner:

|  | Total | Preferred | Common |
|---|---|---|---|
| Balance, January 1, Year 2 | $140,000 | $10,000 | $130,000 |
| Net income (see point 2) | 60,000 | 10,000 | 50,000 |
|  | 200,000 | 20,000 | 180,000 |
| Dividends (see point 1) | 50,000 | 20,000 | 30,000 |
| Balance, December 31, Year 2 | $150,000 | $ –0– | $150,000 |

---

*Any calculations involving the subsidiary's equity must be split between common and preferred shareholders.*

---

It is important to note the following regarding the allocation process:

1. All dividends in arrears plus the current year's dividends must be paid to preferred shareholders before any dividends are paid to common shareholders. In this situation, the dividends paid by Sonco were as follows:

| | |
|---|---|
| Preferred ($10 × 1,000 × 2 years) | $20,000 |
| Common | 30,000 |
| | $50,000 |

2. When preferred shares are cumulative, the preferred shareholders are entitled to income equal to the yearly dividend, even when the company has no income or has suffered a loss for the year. This means that the net income (or loss) for a particular year must be allocated to its preferred and common shareholders. In the situation we are examining, the Year 2 net income is allocated as follows:

| | |
|---|---|
| To preferred shareholders | $ 10,000 |
| To common shareholders | 50,000 |
| Total net income | $ 60,000 |

---

*For cumulative shares, the preferred shareholders' claim on income is one year's worth of dividends in any given year, whether or not dividends are declared in that year.*

---

The allocation of Sonco's total shareholders' equity as at December 31, Year 2, can now be prepared as shown below:

|  | Total | Preferred | Common |
|---|---|---|---|
| Share capital | $460,000 | $105,000 | $355,000 |
| Retained earnings | 150,000 | –0– | 150,000 |
|  | $610,000 | $105,000 | $505,000 |

Because Parco has used the cost method to account for its investment, we must make the two calculations shown in Exhibit 8.4 before preparing the Year 2 consolidated financial statements.

The Year 2 consolidated financial statements are shown in Exhibit 8.5.

**EXHIBIT 8.4**

### CALCULATION OF CONSOLIDATED NET INCOME
Year 2

| | | |
|---|---:|---:|
| Net income, Parco | | $ 89,000 |
| Less: Common dividends from Sonco (90% × 30,000) | | 27,000 |
| | | 62,000 |
| | | |
| Net income, Sonco | 60,000 | |
| Less: Allocated to preferred shares | 10,000 | |
| Net income, common shares | 50,000 | |
|    Less: Acquisition-differential amortization (15,000 ÷ 10) | 1,500 **(a)** | |
|    Adjusted income for common shares | | 48,500 **(b)** |
|    Income for preferred shares | | 10,000 |
|    Consolidated net income | | $120,500 |
| Attributable to: | | |
|    Shareholders of Parent (62,000 + 90% × 48,500) | | $105,650 **(c)** |
|    Non-controlling interest | | |
|      Preferred net income (100% × 10,000) | 10,000 | |
|      Common net income (10% × 48,500) | 4,850 | |
| | | 14,850 **(d)** |

> *The preferred shareholders' claim on income is one year's worth of dividends.*

### CALCULATION OF NON-CONTROLLING INTEREST
at December 31, Year 2

| | |
|---|---:|
| Non-controlling interest: | |
|    Date of acquisition (see text just prior to Exhibit 8.3) | $165,000 |
|    Share of income from subsidiary **(d)** | 14,850 |
|    Share of dividends (100% × 20,000 + 10% × 30,000) | (23,000) |
|    At December 31, Year 2 | $156,850 **(e)** |

> *The non-controlling interest owns all of the preferred shares and 10% of the common shares of the subsidiary.*

**EXHIBIT 8.5**

**YEAR 2 CONSOLIDATED STATEMENTS**
(when subsidiary has preferred shares)

**PARCO LTD.**
**CONSOLIDATED INCOME STATEMENT**
For the year ended December 31, Year 2

| | |
|---|---:|
| Revenues (750,000 + 420,000) | $1,170,000 |
| Expenses (688,000 + 360,000 + **[4a] 1,500**) | 1,049,500 |
| Net income | $ 120,500 |
| Attributable to: | |
| Shareholders of Parent **(4c)** | $ 105,650 |
| Non-controlling interest **(4d)** | 14,850 |

> *The non-controlling interest includes all of the income pertaining to the preferred shares and 10% of the income pertaining to the common shares.*

**PARCO LTD.**
**CONSOLIDATED RETAINED EARNINGS STATEMENT**
for the year ended December 31, Year 2

| | |
|---|---:|
| Balance, January 1 | $ 381,000 |
| Net income | 105,650 |
| | 486,650 |
| Dividends | 90,000 |
| Balance, December 31 | $ 396,650 |

**PARCO LTD.**
**CONSOLIDATED BALANCE SHEET**
At December 31, Year 2

| | |
|---|---:|
| Assets—miscellaneous (510,000 + 810,000) | $1,320,000 |
| Franchise agreements (15,000 − **[4a] 1,500**) | 13,500 |
| | $1,333,500 |
| | |
| Liabilities (180,000 + 200,000) | $380,000 |
| Common shares | 400,000 |
| Retained earnings | 396,650 |
| Non-controlling interest **(4e)** | 156,850 |
| | $1,333,500 |

> *The subsidiary's common and preferred shares do not appear on the consolidated balance sheet.*

## Other Types of Preferred Shares

In the example above, the preferred shares are cumulative. If the shares were non-cumulative, net income would be allocated to the preferred shares only if preferred dividends were declared during the year, since dividends are never in arrears with this type of preferred share. If dividends are not declared in a particular year, no income would be allocated to the preferred shares because the preferred shareholders would never get a dividend for that year. If the preferred shares are participating, the allocation of net income will follow the participation provisions.

> *The amount of income, dividends, and equity belonging to the preferred shareholders depends on the rights of the preferred shareholders.*

## Subsidiary Preferred Shares Owned by Parent

A parent company may own all or a portion of its subsidiary's preferred shares in addition to its common share investment. When the cost of the investment in preferred shares is different from the carrying amount of the shares acquired, a problem arises as to how to treat the preferred share acquisition differential in the consolidated financial statements. Since preferred shares do not typically share in earnings beyond the amount of the specified dividend rate (the exception is fully participating shares), the value of the preferred shares is usually based on the present value of future dividends and not any goodwill or fair value excess for identifiable net assets. Therefore, it would not be appropriate to allocate any acquisition differential to identifiable net assets or goodwill.

Since the dividend rate is usually specified when the preferred shares are issued, there is a fair amount of certainty as to the amount of future dividends. Interest rates have the biggest impact on the value of preferred shares because they affect the discount rate used in determining the present value of future dividends; the higher the discount rate, the lower the value of the preferred shares, and vice versa. The acquisition of the subsidiary's preferred shares by the parent is viewed as a retirement of the preferred shares. Any acquisition differential should be charged to consolidated retained earnings or credited to contributed surplus. This practice is consistent with the accounting treatment when a company repurchases its own shares from the market.

> *Any acquisition differential related to the acquisition of the subsidiary's preferred shares should be treated similarly to a retirement of the preferred shares by the subsidiary itself.*

Let us now assume that in addition to Parco's 90% investment in Sonco's common shares, it also purchased 30% of Sonco's cumulative preferred shares for $40,000. The purchase price would be allocated as follows:

| | | |
|---|---|---|
| Cost of 30% of preferred shares | | $40,000 |
| Carrying amount of Sonco's preferred shares | 115,000 | |
| Portion acquired by Parco (30%) | | 34,500 |
| Acquisition differential | | 5,500 |
| Allocated to consolidated retained earnings | | 5,500 |
| Balance | | $    –0– |

The non-controlling interest's share of the preferred shares at January 1, Year 2, would be $80,500 ($115,000 × 70%).

> *The portion of the subsidiary's preferred shares that was not purchased by the parent is included in non-controlling interest at its carrying amount.*

If Parco used the equity method to account for both investments, the journal entry to record its investment in Sonco's preferred shares would be as follows:

| | | |
|---|---:|---:|
| Investment in Sonco's preferred shares | 34,500 | |
| Retained earnings | 5,500 | |
| Cash | | 40,000 |

Consolidated retained earnings at the date of acquisition would be $375,500 (Parco's separate-entity retained earnings of $381,000 minus premium paid to retire Sonco's preferred shares of $5,500).

See Self-Study Problem 2 for a comprehensive consolidation problem where the parent has an investment in both the common shares and preferred shares of its subsidiary.

## LO5 INDIRECT SHAREHOLDINGS

When one company has control over another company, financial reporting by means of consolidated financial statements is required. In all the examples that we have used up to this point, the parent has had a direct ownership of over 50% of the common shares of the subsidiary. We continue to assume that over 50% ownership of the voting shares is necessary for control, but we now modify the assumption to allow this percentage to be achieved by both direct and indirect ownership. The following diagrams illustrate both direct and indirect holdings. In this first diagram, B and C are subsidiaries of A through direct control:

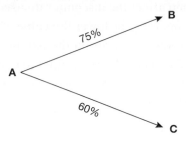

The second example below illustrates indirect control. G is a subsidiary of F, but F, in turn, is a subsidiary of E. Because E can control the voting shares of G through its control of F, G is also a subsidiary of E.

*Both F and G are considered to be subsidiaries of E and therefore should be consolidated with E.*

In the third example, K is a subsidiary of J through direct control. L is also a subsidiary of J through indirect control, because 55% of its voting shares are controlled directly or indirectly by J, even though only 43% [25% + (60% × 30%)] of L's net income will flow to J under the equity method of accounting.

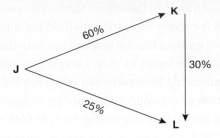

---

*J can control L because it has control of 55% of the votes at L's shareholders' meetings.*

---

While many Canadian companies have intercorporate structures that are far more complex than those illustrated, the consolidation procedures for indirect holdings are not as complicated as the diagrams might indicate. Remember that if a parent company has 50 subsidiaries, the amount of cash appearing on the consolidated balance sheet is the sum of the cash from 51 separate balance sheets. This basic concept applies to most items appearing in the consolidated statements. In addition, we emphasized in past chapters the following statements that describe the fundamental relationships resulting from the parent's use of the equity method to account for its investment:

1.  The parent's net income equals consolidated net income attributable to the parent.

2.  The parent's retained earnings equal consolidated retained earnings.

3.  The elimination of the parent's share of the shareholders' equity of the subsidiary against the investment account leaves a balance consisting of the parent's share of the unamortized acquisition differential. This balance is used to revalue the net assets of the subsidiary when the consolidated balance sheet is prepared.

4.  The portion of the shareholders' equity of the subsidiary that is not eliminated, and the non-controlling interest's share of the unamortized acquisition differential appear on the consolidated balance sheet as non-controlling interest.

---

*The parent's separate-entity net income under the equity method should be equal to consolidated net income attributable to the parent's shareholders.*

---

Since these fundamental relationships also apply when we have indirect holdings, the key to the preparation of consolidated statements when control is achieved by a mixture of direct and indirect investments is the use of the equity method of accounting for each investment for internal record-keeping purposes. (If the cost method has been used, adjustments to the equity method must be made.) The following example will illustrate these concepts.

---

*The principles applied when consolidating directly controlled subsidiaries apply equally well when consolidating indirectly controlled subsidiaries.*

---

Parent Inc. owns 80% of the common shares of Subone Ltd. (which is sufficient for control) and 45% of the common shares of Subtwo Ltd. (which we assume is not sufficient for control). However, Subone owns 25% of the common shares of Subtwo. This investment combined with the parent's 45% investment gives the parent control of 70% of the voting shares; therefore, Subtwo is considered a subsidiary of Parent.

Each investment is accounted for using the equity method for internal record-keeping purposes. In order to simplify the illustration, we assume that on acquisition date the fair values of the identifiable net assets of the investee corporations were equal to their carrying amounts, with the acquisition differentials from each investment being allocated to unrecorded computer databases.

We will illustrate the preparation of consolidated financial statements for Year 6, during which Parent had a net income from its own operations amounting to $135,000. Subone had a net income from its own operations amounting to $75,000, while the net income of Subtwo was $40,000. Exhibit 8.6, which shows the calculation of the Year 6 consolidated net income, is useful because it illustrates the use of the equity method of accounting by both Subone and Parent.

> *The amortization of the acquisition differential is allocated to the subsidiary to which it pertains.*

Regarding the preparation and interpretation of Exhibit 8.6, the following should be noted:

1. Acquisition-differential amortizations are recorded by each company owned by another company in the group. This is the first adjustment shown. The amounts have been assumed. Any adjustments required for intercompany gains and losses are also made here (as would the deduction for intercompany dividends if the cost method had been used by Parent and Subone).

**EXHIBIT 8.6**

### CALCULATION OF CONSOLIDATED NET INCOME
Year 6

| | Parent | Subone | Subtwo | Total | |
|---|---|---|---|---|---|
| Net income before equity method income | $135,000 | $75,000 | $40,000 | $250,000 | |
| Less: Database amortization—Subtwo | | | (300) | (300) | **(a)** |
| | | | 39,700 | | |
| Allocate Subtwo: | | | | | |
|    25% to Subone | | 9,925 | (9,925) | | |
|    45% to Parent | 17,865 | | (17,865) | | |
| Less: Database amortization—Subone | | (200) | | (200) | **(b)** |
| Consolidated net income | 152,865 | 84,725 | 11,910 | 249,500 | |
| Allocate Subone 80% to Parent | 67,780 | (67,780) | | | |
| Non-controlling interest | | $16,945 | $11,910 | 28,855 | **(c)** |
| Parent net income—equity method | $220,645 | | | | |
|   Consolidated net income attributable to parent | | | | $220,645 | **(d)** |

> *Subone accrues its share of Subtwo's income before Parent accrues its share of Subone's income.*

2. Because Parent cannot record its 80% share of Subone's net income until Subone has recorded its 25% share of Subtwo's net income, Subtwo's net income is allocated first.

3. Subone's net income using the equity method can now be determined.

> *The allocation of income to investors must start at the lowest level of the corporate hierarchy and work its way up.*

4. After Subone's net income has been allocated, Parent's net income using the equity method is determined. This amount, of course, equals consolidated net income attributable to Parent.

5. The portion of the net income of Subtwo and Subone that was not allocated to the parent is the non-controlling interest in that net income.

6. The "Total" column shows amounts that appear in the consolidated income statement. Consolidated net income attributable to the parent is $220,645, while non-controlling interest is $28,855.

Exhibit 8.7 shows the Year 6 financial statements of the three companies.

## EXHIBIT 8.7

### INCOME STATEMENTS
### Year 6

|  | Parent | Subone | Subtwo |
|---|---|---|---|
| Miscellaneous revenues | $475,000 | $285,000 | $90,000 |
| Investment income—Subone | 67,780 | — | — |
| Investment income—Subtwo | 17,865 | 9,925 | — |
|  | 560,645 | 294,925 | 90,000 |
| Miscellaneous expenses | 340,000 | 210,000 | 50,000 |
| Net income | $220,645 | $ 84,925 | $40,000 |

> *For these separate-entity statements, the investor has used the equity method to account for its investment.*

### RETAINED EARNINGS STATEMENTS
### Year 6

|  | Parent | Subone | Subtwo |
|---|---|---|---|
| Balance, January 1 | $279,120 | $116,400 | $ 80,000 |
| Net income | 220,645 | 84,925 | 40,000 |
|  | 499,765 | 201,325 | 120,000 |
| Dividends | 45,000 | 30,000 | 10,000 |
| Balance, December 31 | $454,765 | $171,325 | $110,000 |

### BALANCE SHEETS
### At December 31, Year 6

|  | Parent | Subone | Subtwo |
|---|---|---|---|
| Other assets | $608,500 | $402,925 | $460,000 |
| Investment in Subone | 281,900 | — | — |
| Investment in Subtwo | 104,365 | 53,400 | — |
|  | $994,765 | $456,325 | $460,000 |
| Liabilities | $300,000 | $110,000 | $250,000 |
| Common shares | 240,000 | 175,000 | 100,000 |
| Retained earnings | 454,765 | 171,325 | 110,000 |
|  | $994,765 | $456,325 | $460,000 |

In preparing the Year 6 consolidated income statement, we eliminate the three equity method income accounts and replace them with the revenues and expenses of the two subsidiaries, the database amortization expense, and the non-controlling interest in the net incomes of the subsidiaries. The consolidated retained earnings statement is identical to that of Parent and requires no preparation.

In preparing the consolidated balance sheet, we eliminate the investors' portion of the shareholders' equity of the investee companies against the investment accounts; this leaves a balance consisting of the unamortized acquisition differentials. The amount of shareholders' equity not eliminated represents non-controlling interest. The following calculations illustrate this:

*Parent:*

| | | |
|---|---:|---:|
| Investment in Subone | | $281,900 |
| Shareholders' equity, Subone: | | |
|    Common shares | 175,000 | |
|    Retained earnings | 171,325 | |
| | 346,325 | |
| Parent's ownership | 80% | 277,060 |
|   Balance—Parent's share of unamortized databases | | 4,840 |
|   Non-controlling interest's share of unamortized databases (assumed) | | 1,210 |
|   Total unamortized databases from Subone | | $6,050 |
| Investment in Subtwo | | $104,365 |
| Shareholders' equity, Subtwo: | | |
|    Common shares | 100,000 | |
|    Retained earnings | 110,000 | |
| | 210,000 | |
| Parent's ownership | 45% | 94,500 |
|   Balance—Parent's share of unamortized databases | | 9,865 |

---

*The unamortized acquisition differential can be derived by backing out the parent's share of the subsidiary's equity from the investment account.*

---

*Subone:*

| | | |
|---|---:|---:|
| Investment in Subtwo | | 53,400 |
| Shareholders' equity, Subtwo (above) | 210,000 | |
| Subone's ownership | 25% | 52,500 |
|   Balance—Subone's share of unamortized databases | | 900 |
| Parent's and Subone's total share of unamortized databases (9,865 + 900) | | 10,765 |
| Non-controlling interest's share of unamortized databases (assumed) | | 4,615 |
|   Total unamortized databases from Subtwo | | $15,380 |

---

*The unamortized acquisition differential relating to the non-controlling interest is an assumed figure, which must be incorporated in the consolidated financial statements.*

---

### CALCULATION OF NON-CONTROLLING INTERESTS
#### at December 31, Year 6

| | |
|---|---:|
| Shareholders' equity, Subone (346,325 × 20% + 1,210) | $ 70,475 |
| Shareholders' equity, Subtwo (210,000 × 30% + 4,615) | 67,615 |
| | $138,090 |

Exhibit 8.8 shows the preparation of the Year 6 consolidated financial statements using the direct approach.

**EXHIBIT 8.8**

### PARENT INC.
### CONSOLIDATED FINANCIAL STATEMENTS
For Year 6

### CONSOLIDATED INCOME STATEMENT

| | |
|---|---:|
| Miscellaneous revenues (475,000 + 285,000 + 90,000) | $ 850,000 |
| Miscellaneous expense (340,000 + 210,000 + 50,000) | 600,000 |
| Database amortization (**[6a] 300** + **[6b] 200**) | 500 |
| | 600,500 |
| Net income | $ 249,500 |
| Attributable to: | |
| Shareholders of Parent **(6d)** | $ 220,645 |
| Non-controlling interests **(6c)** | 28,855 |

*The consolidated income statement includes the amortization of the acquisition differential for a period of time for the directly controlled and indirectly controlled subsidiaries.*

### CONSOLIDATED RETAINED EARNINGS STATEMENT

| | |
|---|---:|
| Balance, January 1 | $ 279,120 |
| Net income | 220,645 |
| | 499,765 |
| Dividends | 45,000 |
| Balance, December 31 | $ 454,765 |

### CONSOLIDATED BALANCE SHEET

| | |
|---|---:|
| Other assets (608,500 + 402,925 + 460,000) | $1,471,425 |
| Databases (0 + 0 + 6,050 + 15,380) | 21,430 |
| | $1,492,855 |
| Liabilities (300,000 + 110,000 + 250,000) | $ 660,000 |
| Common shares | 240,000 |
| Retained earnings | 454,765 |
| Non-controlling interest | 138,090 |
| | $1,492,855 |

*The consolidated balance sheet includes the unamortized acquisition differential at a point in time for the directly controlled and indirectly controlled subsidiaries.*

## LO6 ANALYSIS AND INTERPRETATION OF FINANCIAL STATEMENTS

In this chapter, we prepared consolidated financial statements where the subsidiary had preferred shares in its capital structure. We will now compare how the financial statements would look if the parent had used the cost method or equity method.

Exhibit 8.9 presents the Year 2 income statements and balance sheets for Parco's separate-entity statements under two scenarios: (1) when Parco uses the cost method and (2) when Parco uses the equity method. The last column presents the consolidated financial statements taken from Exhibit 8.5. The values for the cost method are taken directly from Exhibit 8.3. The values for the equity method are the same as the cost method except for the equity method income, retained earnings, and investment in Sonco. The equity method income replaces the dividend income and is the amount required to make net income under the equity method equal to consolidated net income attributable to the shareholders of Parco. Retained earnings under the equity method are equal to consolidated retained earnings. The investment account under the equity method changes by the same amount as the change in retained earnings. The exhibit also indicates the debt-to-equity ratio and return-on-equity ratio for each set of financial statements.

**EXHIBIT 8.9**

## Impact of Presentation Method on Debt-to-Equity and Return-on-Equity Ratios

**INCOME STATEMENTS**
For the year ended December 31, Year 2

|  | Parco—Separate Entity | | Cons. |
|---|---|---|---|
|  | Cost | Equity |  |
| Revenues—miscellaneous | $750,000 | $750,000 | $1,170,000 |
| Dividends income from Sonco | 27,000 | | |
| Equity method income from Sonco | | 43,650 | |
|  | 777,000 | 793,650 | 1,170,000 |
| Expenses—miscellaneous | 688,000 | 688,000 | 1,049,500 |
| Net income | $ 89,000 | $105,650 | $ 120,500 |
| Attributable to: | | | |
| Shareholders of Parco | | | $ 105,650 |
| Non-controlling interest | | | 14,850 |

> *The net income for the parent's separate-entity income statement under the equity method is equal to consolidated net income attributable to the shareholders of the parent.*

**BALANCE SHEETS**
At December 31, Year 2

|  | Cost | Equity | Cons. |
|---|---|---|---|
| Assets—miscellaneous | $510,000 | $510,000 | $1,320,000 |
| Investment in Sonco | 450,000 | 466,650 | |
| Franchise agreements | | | 13,500 |
|  | $960,000 | $976,650 | $1,333,500 |
| Liabilities | $180,000 | $180,000 | $380,000 |
| Common shares | 400,000 | 400,000 | 400,000 |
| Retained earnings | 380,000 | 396,650 | 396,650 |
| Non-controlling interest | | | 156,850 |
|  | $960,000 | $976,650 | $1,333,500 |
| Debt to equity | 0.23 | 0.23 | 0.40 |
| Return on equity: | | | |
| For all shareholders | n/a | n/a | 12.6% |
| For shareholders of Parco | 11.4% | 13.3% | 13.3% |

Note the following from Exhibit 8.9:

- The separate-entity net income and return-on-equity ratio under the cost and equity methods are different.

- The separate-entity net income and retained earnings under the equity method are equal to consolidated net income attributable to the shareholders of Parco and consolidated retained earnings, respectively.

- The separate-entity return on equity under the equity method is equal to the consolidated return on equity for the shareholders of Parco.

- The solvency position looks worst on the consolidated financial statements because the subsidiary's debt is included on the consolidated financial statements. This increases the debt-to-equity ratio.

> *Retained earnings for the parent's separate-entity balance sheet under the equity method are equal to consolidated retained earnings.*
>
> *The return on equity for the separate-entity statements under the equity method is equal to the consolidated return on equity for the shareholders of Parent.*

## ASPE Differences

- As mentioned in Chapter 3, private companies can either consolidate their subsidiaries or report their investments in subsidiaries under the cost or equity method.

- When consolidated statements are not prepared, any investment in preferred shares that are quoted in an active market should be reported at fair value, with any adjustments to fair value reported in net income. These are the requirements normally applied to equity instruments traded in an active market. Investments in preferred shares that are not quoted in an active market should be reported at cost less accumulated impairment losses with the impairment losses reported in net income, unless the entity has made an irrevocable election to measure at fair value.

## SUMMARY

While the consolidated balance sheet and income statement are prepared by combining the statements of the parent and its subsidiaries, the consolidated cash flow statement is best prepared by analyzing the changes in successive consolidated balance sheets. **(LO1)**

The investor's percentage ownership can change when the investor buys or sells shares of the investee or when the investee issues new shares or buys back some shares. When an investor increases its percentage ownership in stages and obtains either significant influence or control, it should remeasure its previously held equity interest in the investee at fair value and recognize the resulting gain or loss, if any, in net income. The sum of the fair value of the previously held equity interest and the cost of the new investment represent the total consideration, which is used to determine and allocate the acquisition differential. **(LO2)** When an investor decreases its percentage ownership in the investee and loses either control or significant influence, it should recognize any gains or losses, if any, in net income including the remeasurement of any retained interest in the investee at fair value. **(LO3)** When a parent's percentage ownership changes without losing control, the controlling and non-controlling interests should be adjusted to reflect the changes in their relative interests in the subsidiary without adjusting the total carrying amount. The entity shall recognize directly in equity any difference between the amount by which the non-controlling interest is adjusted and the fair value of the consideration paid or received, and attribute it to the owners of the parent.

Preferred shares in the capital structure of subsidiary companies present unique problems in calculating non-controlling interest if the parent's ownership of the preferred shares is not the same as its ownership of the common shares. The problem is solved by allocating shareholders' equity and any changes therein to preferred and common share components. **(LO4)**

Control by a parent company can be achieved through direct ownership of the subsidiary's voting shares or through indirect ownership through other subsidiaries or investees. The consolidation has to be undertaken in steps starting at the lowest tier of the intercorporate hierarchy. For each tier, the investee's net income and shareholders' equity is allocated between the controlling and non-controlling interests based on their relative interests in the investee. The equity method is used to capture the investor's share of the investee's net income and changes in equity. **(LO5)** Even though the consolidated net income attributable to the parent and consolidated retained earnings are equal to the parent's net income and retained earnings, respectively, under the equity method, the account balances for individual lines on the two set of financial statements will be very different and will produce significantly different financial ratios. **(LO6)**

## Self-Study Problem 1

LO2, 3

On January 1, Year 11, Mio Company acquired 1,000 ordinary shares of Aaron Company for $12,000 when the shareholders' equity of Aaron was as follows:

| | |
|---|---|
| Ordinary shares (10,000 no par value shares issued and outstanding) | $50,000 |
| Retained earnings | 40,000 |
| | $90,000 |

In addition, Mio had the following investments and divestments in Aaron:

| Date | Action | # of Shares | Price |
|---|---|---|---|
| Jan. 1, Year 12 | Bought | 2,000 | 26,000 |
| Jan. 1, Year 13 | Bought | 2,500 | 35,000 |
| Jan. 1, Year 14 | Bought | 3,000 | 45,000 |
| Jan. 1, Year 15 | Sold | 1,500 | 24,000 |

The following are the statements of retained earnings for Mio from Year 11 to Year 15:

| | Year 11 | Year 12 | Year 13 | Year 14 | Year 15 |
|---|---|---|---|---|---|
| Retained earnings, beginning of year | $70,000 | $78,000 | $87,000 | $ 96,000 | $105,000 |
| Profit | 17,000 | 18,000 | 19,000 | 20,000 | 21,000 |
| Dividends | (9,000) | (9,000) | (10,000) | (11,000) | (12,000) |
| Retained earnings, end of year | $78,000 | $87,000 | $96,000 | $105,000 | $114,000 |

The following are the statements of retained earnings for Aaron from Year 11 to Year 15:

|  | Year 11 | Year 12 | Year 13 | Year 14 | Year 15 |
|---|---|---|---|---|---|
| Retained earnings, beginning of year | $40,000 | $44,000 | $48,000 | $52,000 | $57,000 |
| Profit | 10,000 | 11,000 | 12,000 | 13,000 | 14,000 |
| Dividends | (6,000) | (7,000) | (8,000) | (8,000) | (10,000) |
| Retained earnings, end of year | $44,000 | $48,000 | $52,000 | $57,000 | $61,000 |

## Additional Information

- For internal record-keeping purposes, Mio uses the cost method to account for its investment in Aaron.

- Aaron's ordinary shares are publicly traded. The market value of the shares at the close on December 31 of one year was the same as the market value on January 1 of the next year.

- Any acquisition differential is allocated to patents with a life expectancy until December 31, Year 18. Neither company has any patents recorded on their separate-entity records.

- There were no unrealized profits from intercompany transactions since the date of acquisition.

## Required

A.  For each of Years 11 to 15, determine and prepare the following items for Mio's general-purpose financial statements prepared in accordance with IFRS:
   (a)  Method to be used to report the investment in Aaron and the balance in the investment account under the relevant reporting method at the end of each year
   (b)  Net income attributable to the shareholders of Mio
   (c)  Patents
   (d)  Non-controlling interest on the balance sheet
   (e)  Statement of retained earnings
B.  Prepare a schedule to show that the difference in the investment account between the cost and equity methods is equal to the difference in the sum of retained earnings (RE) and contributed surplus between the cost and equity methods for each of Years 11 through 15.

## Solution to Self-Study Problem 1

|  |  | Jan. 1, Year 12 |  | Jan. 1, Year 13 |
|---|---|---|---|---|
| Cost of purchase |  | 26,000 |  | 35,000 |
| Previous equity interest remeasured at fair value |  |  |  |  |
| 1,000 shares @ $13 per share |  | 13,000 |  |  |
| 3,000 shares @ $14 per share |  | ——— |  | 42,000 |
| Acquisition cost of 30% |  | 39,000 |  |  |
| Acquisition cost of 55% |  |  |  | 77,000 |
| Implied value of 100% |  |  |  | 140,000 |
| Carrying amount of Aaron's net assets: |  |  |  |  |
| Common shares | 50,000 |  | 50,000 |  |
| Retained earnings | 44,000 |  | 48,000 |  |
|  | 94,000 |  | 98,000 |  |
|  | 30% | 28,200 | 100% | 98,000 |
| Acquisition differential |  | 10,800 |  | 42,000 |
| Allocated to: |  |  |  |  |
| Patents |  | 10,800 |  | 42,000 |
| Patent amortization, Year 12 (over 7 years) |  | 1,543 |  | **(a)** |

### ALLOCATION AND AMORTIZATION OF ACQUISITION DIFFERENTIAL ALLOCATED TO PATENTS

| | Total | Parent | NCI | |
|---|---|---|---|---|
| Purchase on Jan. 1, Year 13 | 42,000 | 23,100 | 18,900 | |
| Amortization for Year 13 (over 6 years) | (7,000) | (3,850) | (3,150) | **(b)** |
| Dec. 31, Year 13 | 35,000 | 19,250 | 15,750 | **(c)** |
| NCI sold 3,000/4,500 × 15,750 | | 10,500 | (10,500) | |
| | 35,000 | 29,750 | 5,250 | |
| Amortization for Year 14 (over 5 years) | (7,000) | (5,950) | (1,050) | **(d)** |
| Dec. 31, Year 14 | 28,000 | 23,800 | 4,200 | **(e)** |
| Mio sold 1,500/8,500 × 23,800 | | (4,200) | 4,200 | |
| | 28,000 | 19,600 | 8,400 | |
| Amortization for Year 15 (over 4 years) | (7,000) | (4,900) | (2,100) | **(f)** |
| Dec. 31, Year 15 | 21,000 | 14,700 | 6,300 | **(g)** |

(a) Investment in Aaron:

| | Year 11 | Year 12 | Year 13 | Year 14 | Year 15 |
|---|---|---|---|---|---|
| Percentage owned, end of year | 10 | 30 | 55 | 85 | 70 |
| Reporting method | FVTPL | Equity | Consol[1] | Consol[1] | Consol[1] |
| Balance, beginning of year | 0 | 13,000 | 38,657 | 75,350 | 114,750 |
| Cost of purchase | 12,000 | 26,000 | 35,000 | 45,000 | |
| Adjustment to fair value on Jan 1 | | | 3,343[5] | | |
| Loss on equity transaction | | | | (3,900)[8] | |
| Average cost of investment sold | | | | | (20,250)[11] |
| Equity income | | 3,300[3] | 6,600[6] | 11,050[9] | 9,800[13] |
| Dividends received | | (2,100)[4] | (4,400)[7] | (6,800)[10] | (7,000)[14] |
| Amortization of patent | | (1,543)[a] | (3,850)[b] | (5,950)[d] | (4,900)[f] |
| Adjustment to fair value on Dec 31 | 1,000[2] | | | | |
| Balance, end of year | 13,000 | 38,657 | 75,350 | 114,750 | 92,400 |

**Notes:**

1. Consolidated statements are required. Investment account does not appear on consolidated statements. However, equity method will provide all relevant information required for consolidated statements.
2. 26,000/2,000 shares × 1,000 shares − 12,000 = 1,000 through net income
3. 30% × 11,000 = 3,300
4. 30% × 7,000 = 2,100
5. 35,000/2,500 × 3,000 − 38,657 = 3,343
6. 55% × 12,000 = 6,600
7. 55% × 8,000 = 4,400
8. 45,000 − 61,650 (from (d) below) × 3,000/4,500 = 3,900
9. 85% × 13,000 = 11,050
10. 85% × 8,000 = 6,800
11. 114,750 × 1,500/8,500 = 20,250
12. 24,000 − 20,250 = 3,750 through contributed surplus
13. 70% × 14,000 = 9,800
14. 70% × 10,000 = 7,000
15. 24,000 − (12,000 + 26,000 + 35,000 + 45,000) × 1,500/8,500 = 3,176

(b) Net income attributable to shareholders of Mio:

| | Year 11 | Year 12 | Year 13 | Year 14 | Year 15 |
|---|---|---|---|---|---|
| Mio's net income under cost method | 17,000 | 18,000 | 19,000 | 20,000 | 21,000 |
| Dividends from Aaron | | (2,100)[4] | (4,400)[7] | (6,800)[10] | (7,000)[14] |
| Reverse gain on sale under cost method | | | | | (3,176)[15] |
| Equity income | | 3,300[3] | 6,600[6] | 11,050[9] | 9,800[13] |
| Amortization of patent | | (1,543)[a] | (3,850)[b] | (5,950)[d] | (4,900)[f] |
| Adjustment to fair value | 1,000[2] | | 3,343[5] | | |
| Mio's net income under FVTPL | 18,000 | | | | |
| Mio's net income under equity method | | 17,657 | 20,693 | 18,300 | 15,724 |

| | Year 11 | Year 12 | Year 13 | Year 14 | Year 15 |
|---|---|---|---|---|---|
| (c) Patents on consolidated balance sheet: | n/a | n/a | 35,000 | 28,000 | 21,000 |

(d) NCI on balance sheet:

| | | | | | |
|---|---|---|---|---|---|
| Aaron's ordinary shares | | | 50,000 | 50,000 | 50,000 |
| Aaron's retained earnings | | | 52,000 | 57,000 | 61,000 |
| | | | 102,000 | 107,000 | 111,000 |
| NCI's share | | | 45% | 15% | 30% |
| | | | 45,900 | 16,050 | 33,300 |
| NCI's share of patent | | | 15,750$^c$ | 4,200$^e$ | 6,300$^g$ |
| Total NCI | | | 61,650 | 20,250 | 39,600 |

(e) Statement of Retained Earnings

| | Year 11 | Year 12 | Year 13 | Year 14 | Year 15 |
|---|---|---|---|---|---|
| Retained earnings, beginning of year | $70,000 | $79,000 | $87,657 | $ 98,350 | $101,750 |
| Profit | 18,000 | 17,657 | 20,693 | 18,300 | 15,724 |
| Loss on equity transaction | | | | (3,900)$^8$ | |
| Dividends | (9,000) | (9,000) | (10,000) | (11,000) | (12,000) |
| Retained earnings, end of year | $79,000 | $87,657 | $98,350 | $101,750 | $105,474 |
| (f) Retained earnings—cost method | $78,000 | $87,000 | $96,000 | $105,000 | $114,000 |
| RE & contributed surplus—equity method | 79,000 | 87,657 | 98,350 | 101,750 | 109,224 |
| Difference | $ (1,000) | $(657) | $ (2,350) | $3,250 | $ 4,776 |
| Investment—cost method | $12,000 | $38,000 | $73,000 | $118,000 | $ 97,176* |
| Investment—equity method | 13,000 | 38,657 | 75,350 | 114,750 | 92,400 |
| Difference | $ (1,000) | $ (657) | $ (2,350) | $3,250 | $ 4,776 |

*$118,000 × 7,000 shares/8,500 shares.

# Self-Study Problem 2

**LO4**

On January 1, Year 4, X Company acquired 800 common shares of Y Company for $24,000 and 180 $5 cumulative, nonparticipating preferred shares for $19,800. On this date, the shareholders' equity accounts of Y Company were as follows:

| | |
|---|---|
| Common shares (1,000 no par value shares issued) | $10,000 |
| Preferred shares (200 no par value shares issued) | 20,000 |
| Retained earnings (note 1) | 12,000 |

**Note 1**: Preferred dividends were two years in arrears on January 1, Year 4.

The income statements for the two companies for the year ended December 31, Year 8, are presented on the next page.

## Additional Information

- Any acquisition differential is allocated to patents, to be amortized over 10 years.
- In Year 8, Y paid dividends totalling $9,000. Preferred dividends were two years in arrears on December 31, Year 7.
- X uses the cost method to account for its investment in Y.

- Y purchases merchandise for resale from X. In Year 8, Y purchased $33,000 in merchandise from X and had items in inventory on December 31, Year 8, on which X had made a profit of $2,500. The January 1, Year 8, inventory contained an intercompany profit of $1,400.

- X rents equipment from Y, and in Year 8 paid a rental charge of $3,000 and recorded an account payable to Y of $2,000 for the balance of the rentals.

- On July 1, Year 6, Y sold a building to X at a profit of $13,000. X is depreciating this building on a straight-line basis over a 10-year useful life.

- Depreciation and rent of tangible capital assets are included in distribution expense, whereas amortization of intangible assets is included in selling and administrative expense.

- Y paid $20,000 to X for management fees in Year 8.

- Assume a corporate tax rate of 40%.

**INCOME STATEMENTS**
For year ended December 31, Year 8

|  | X Company | Y Company |
|---|---|---|
| Sales | $600,000 | $400,000 |
| Dividend and management fees | 27,500 | — |
| Rental revenue | — | 11,200 |
|  | 627,500 | 411,200 |
| Cost of sales | 343,900 | 234,700 |
| Distribution expense | 25,000 | 70,000 |
| Selling and administrative expense | 207,000 | 74,000 |
| Interest expense | 1,700 | 6,000 |
| Income tax expense | 20,000 | 9,000 |
|  | 597,600 | 393,700 |
| Profit | $ 29,900 | $ 17,500 |

### Required

Prepare a consolidated income statement for Year 8.

## Solution to Self-Study Problem 2

**Calculation of acquisition differential**

| | | |
|---|---|---|
| Cost of 90% of preferred shares (180/200) | | $19,800 |
| Carrying amount of preferred: | | |
| Preferred shares | $20,000 | |
| Dividends in arrears (200 × 5 × 2) | 2,000 | |
| | 22,000 | |
| | 90% | 19,800 |
| Acquisition differential | | $ –0– |
| Cost of 80% of common shares (800/1,000) | | $24,000 |
| Implied value of 100% of common shares | | $30,000 |
| Carrying amount of common: | | |
| Common shares | 10,000 | |
| Retained earnings | 12,000 | |
| Less: Preferred dividend arrears | (2,000) | |
| | | 20,000 |
| Acquisition differential—patents | | $10,000 |

**Intercompany revenues and expenses:**

| | | |
|---|---|---|
| Dividends—preferred (90% × 1,000 × 3) | $ 2,700 | |
| Dividends—common (80% × [9,000 − 3,000]) | 4,800 | |
| | $ 7,500 | **(a)** |
| Management fees | $20,000 | **(b)** |
| Rent (3,000 + 2,000) | $5,000 | **(c)** |
| Sales | $33,000 | **(d)** |

| *Intercompany Profits* | *Before Tax* | *Tax 40%* | *After Tax* | |
|---|---|---|---|---|
| Opening inventory—X selling | $1,400 | $ 560 | $ 840 | **(e)** |
| Closing inventory—X selling | $2,500 | $1,000 | $ 1,500 | **(f)** |
| Building realized—Y selling | $1,300 | $ 520 | $ 780 | **(g)** |

**Calculation of Consolidated Net Income—Year 8**

| | | | |
|---|---|---|---|
| X net income | | | $29,900 |
| Less: Dividends from Y **(a)** | | 7,500 | |
| Closing inventory profit[7] **(f)** | | 1,500 | 9,000 |
| | | | 20,900 |
| Add: Opening inventory profit **(e)** | | | 840 |
| | | | 21,740 |

| | *Total* | *Preferred* | *Common* | |
|---|---|---|---|---|
| Y net income | 17,500 | 1,000 | 16,500 | |
| Less: Patent amortization (10,000 ÷ 10) | | | (1,000) | **(h)** |
| Add: Building profit **(g)** | | | 780 | |
| | | 1,000 | 16,280 | 17,280 | **(i)** |
| Consolidated net income | | | | $39,020 |
| Attributable to: | | | | |
| Shareholders of Parent (21,740 + 90% × 1,000 + 80% × 16,280) | | | | $35,664 | **(j)** |
| Non-controlling interest (10% × 1,000 + 20% × 16,280) | | | | 3,356 | **(k)** |

### CONSOLIDATED INCOME STATEMENT
#### For Year 8

| | |
|---|---|
| Sales (600,000 + 400,000 − **[d] 33,000**) | $967,000 |
| Dividend and management fees (27,500 + 0 − **[a] 7,500** − **[b] 20,000**) | 0 |
| Rental revenue (0 + 11,200 − **[c] 5,000**) | 6,200 |
| | 973,200 |
| Cost of sales (343,900 + 234,700 − **[d] 33,000** − **[e] 1,400** + **[f] 2,500**) | 546,700 |
| Distribution (25,000 + 70,000 − **[c] 5,000** − **[g] 1,300**) | 88,700 |
| Selling and administrative (207,000 + 74,000 − **[b] 20,000**) + **[h] 1,000**) | 262,000 |
| Interest (1,700 + 6,000) | 7,700 |
| Income tax (20,000 + 9,000 + **[e]** 560 + **[g] 520** − **[f] 1,000**) | 29,080 |
| | 934,180 |
| Net income | $ 39,020 |
| Attributable to: | |
| Shareholders of Parent **(j)** | $ 35,664 |
| Non-controlling interest **(k)** | 3,356 |

## Review Questions

LO1    **1.**  Is the consolidated cash flow statement prepared in the same manner as the consolidated balance sheet and income statement? Explain.

LO1    **2.**  A parent company acquired a 75% interest in a subsidiary company in Year 4. The acquisition price was $1,000,000, made up of cash of $700,000 and the parent's common shares with a current market value of $300,000. Explain how this acquisition should be reflected in the Year 4 consolidated cash flow statement.

LO1    **3.**  Why is the amortization of the acquisition differential added back to consolidated net income to compute net cash flow from operating activities in the consolidated cash flow statement?

LO1    **4.**  Why are dividend payments to non-controlling shareholders treated as an outflow of cash in the consolidated cash flow statement but not included as dividends paid in the consolidated retained earnings statement?

LO2    **5.**  When should the change in accounting for a long-term investment from the cost method to the equity method be accounted for retroactively, and when should it be accounted for prospectively?

LO2    **6.**  When a parent increases its investment in a subsidiary from 60 to 75%, should the acquisition differential from the 60% purchase be remeasured at fair value? Explain.

LO3    **7.**  When a parent decreases its investment in a subsidiary from 76 to 60%, should the non-controlling interest be remeasured at fair value? Explain.

LO3    **8.**  A parent company will realize a loss or a gain when its subsidiary issues common shares at a price per share that differs from the carrying amount per share of the parent's investment, and the parent's ownership percentage declines. Explain why this is so. Also explain how the gain or loss is recognized in the financial statements.

LO3    **9.**  If a gain or a loss is realized by a parent company as a result of the sale of a portion of the investment in a subsidiary, should the gain or loss be eliminated in the preparation of the consolidated income statement? Explain.

LO4    **10.**  The shareholders' equity of a subsidiary company contains preferred and common shares. The parent company owns 100% of the subsidiary's common shares. Will the consolidated financial statements show non-controlling interest? Explain.

LO4    **11.**  A company's net income for the year was $17,000. During the year, the company paid dividends on its non-cumulative preferred shares amounting to $12,000. Calculate the amount of the year's net income that "belongs to" the common shares.

LO4    **12.**  Explain how an acquisition differential from an investment in preferred shares should be reflected in the consolidated financial statements.

LO4    **13.**  Explain how the non-controlling interest in the net assets and net income of a subsidiary is calculated and reported when the parent owns 90% of the subsidiary's common shares and 30% of the subsidiary's cumulative preferred shares.

LO4    **14.**  Explain the difference in the calculation of consolidated net income attributable to shareholders of parent and consolidated retained earnings depending on whether the preferred shares of a subsidiary are cumulative or non-cumulative.

LO5    **15.**  What is the major consolidation problem associated with indirect shareholdings?

# CASES

## Case 8-1

LO3

On December 31, Year 7, Pepper Company, a public company, agreed to a business combination with Salt Limited, an unrelated private company. Pepper issued 72 of its common shares for all (50) of the outstanding common shares of Salt. This transaction increased the number of outstanding Pepper shares from 100 to 172. Pepper's shares were trading at around $20 per share in days leading up to the business combination. The condensed balance sheets for the two companies on this date were as follows:

|  | **Pepper** | | **Salt** | |
|---|---|---|---|---|
|  | Carrying Amount | Fair Value | Carrying Amount | Fair Value |
| Tangible assets | $1,000 | $1,200 | $200 | $240 |
| Intangible assets (excluding goodwill) | 400 | 1,000 | 500 | 700 |
|  | $1,400 | | $700 | |
| Liabilities | $800 | 820 | $340 | 400 |
| Shareholders' equity | 600 | | 360 | |
|  | $1,400 | | $700 | |

On January 1, Year 8, Pepper sold 40% of its investment in Salt to an unrelated third party for $900 in cash. The CFO at Pepper stated that Salt must have been worth $2,250 if the unrelated third party was willing to pay $900 for a 40% interest in Salt. If so, Pepper saved $810 by buying Salt for only $1,440. Accordingly, the CFO wants to recognize a gain of $810 in the Year 7 income statement to reflect the true value of the Salt shares.

You have been asked by the CFO to prepare a presentation to senior management on the accounting implications for the business combination and subsequent sale of 40% of the investment. She would like you to consider two alternative methods of valuing Salt on the consolidated balance at the date of acquisition—one based on cost of purchase and one based on the implied value of the subsidiary based on the sales price on January 1, Year 8.

### Required

Prepare this presentation, answering the following questions:

(a) How would Pepper's consolidated balance sheet differ at the date of acquisition under the two different valuation alternatives? Which method best reflects economic reality? Which method is required by GAAP?

(b) How would Pepper's consolidated balance sheet look after the sale of the 40% interest in Salt to the unrelated third party under the two alternatives?

## Case 8-2

LO2

For the past 10 years, Prince Company (Prince) has owned 75,000 or 75% of the common shares of Stiff Inc. (Stiff). Elizabeth Winer owns another 20% and the other 5% are widely held. Although Prince has the controlling interest, you would never know it during the annual shareholders' meetings. Winer keeps the board of directors on its toes by asking a lot of tough questions and continually threatening legal action if her rights as a minority shareholder are not protected.

Rick Impatient owns 100% of the shares of Prince. After Prince's latest shareholders' meeting, he decided that Prince would offer to purchase Winer's shares in Stiff or Prince would sell its interest in Stiff as Impatient was tired of all of the heckling from Winer. The shares of Stiff were recently trading for $50 per share.

On November 13, Year 13, Prince offered to pay $54 per share to Winer for her 20% interest in Stiff. To Impatient's surprise, Winer accepted the offer and the transaction was consummated on December 31, Year 13. At December 31, Year 13, the unamortized acquisition differential relating to prior purchases by Prince was $250,000, which pertained solely to goodwill. On the closing date, the shares of Stiff had a carrying amount of $35 per share and all identifiable net assets had a fair value equal to carrying amount except for unrecognized patents, which had a fair value of $0.65 million and an estimated useful life of four years.

The CFO of Prince wants to recognize the entire acquisition differential related to the new purchase from Winer as goodwill in order to minimize the impact on earnings for Years 13 and 14. The controller, on the other hand, believes that some of the acquisition differential should be charged to income in Year 13 as a loss because of the excessive price paid for the shares.

**Required**

How would you resolve the dispute? Provide the arguments to support your position, and indicate the impact of your decision on consolidated profit attributable to Prince's shareholders for Years 13 and 14. State your assumptions.

## Case 8-3

........

### LO3

Traveller Bus Lines Inc. (TBL) is a wholly owned subsidiary of Canada Transport Enterprises Inc. (CTE), a publicly traded transportation and communications conglomerate. TBL is primarily in the business of operating buses over short- and long-distance routes in central and western Canada and the United States. TBL also has a school bus division operating in eastern Canada. CTE and its subsidiaries are audited by DeBoy Shoot, which issued an unqualified audit opinion on CTE's June 30, year-end consolidated financial statements. This was the only audit opinion issued on the CTE group of companies. TBL has a July 31 year-end. It is now September 8, Year 7. CTE has been reporting operating losses for several years and has put TBL up for sale as part of a strategy to change its focus. This is the first of several planned divestitures, designed to restore CTE's lacklustre share price.

Currently, the only interested party is an employee group led by TBL's president, Dan Williams. Williams's management buyout team consists of the vice-president of operations and the CFO. Handling the negotiations at CTE's corporate office is Eva Joel, vice-president of strategic divestitures.

The buyout team has submitted the first draft agreement of purchase and sale for review. Exhibit I contains extracts from the draft agreement; a note made by CTE's lawyer is shown in italics. You, a CPA at Heatley Dan LLP, have gathered some additional background information (shown in Exhibit II).

Andrew wants to maximize the total selling price. He asked the partner in charge of the advisory services at Heatley Dan LLP to review the information given and provide recommendations on how CTE can maximize the total selling price and how the agreement should be changed to minimize possible disputes in the future. In addition, he would like a summary of the accounting issues of significance to CTE that will arise on the sale of TBL. The partner has asked you to prepare the draft report to Joel.

## EXHIBIT I

## Extracts of Draft Purchase and Sale Agreement

Agreement of purchase and sale between the employee group (hereinafter the Purchaser) and Canada Transport Enterprises Inc. (hereinafter CTE) for the assets and liabilities of the business known as Traveller Bus Lines Inc. (TBL).

1. The assets and liabilities of TBL are those included in its draft July 31, Year 7, financial statements.
2. Excluded from the liabilities to be assumed by the purchaser are all environmental liabilities, including, but not limited to, gasoline and diesel fuel spills and tank leakage, pesticide residues, and all other chemical contamination.
3. The purchase price is determined by the sum of (A) the carrying amount of the net assets at July 31, Year 7, which is twelve million dollars ($12 million), plus (B) 55% of the net reported income after taxes, for the 12-month period ending July 31, Year 8 (the contingent consideration). *Lawyer's Note: The contingent consideration should be worth at least $3.6 million, since the division's earnings computed on this basis have averaged more than $6.6 million for the last four years before deducting head office charges.*
4. This agreement is conditional on the Purchaser obtaining adequate financing and, after inspection, finding TBL's records satisfactory.
5. CTE agrees not to compete with the Purchaser for 10 years.
6. CTE will provide a loan guarantee for up to 25% of the purchase price for the Purchaser.
7. The Purchaser agrees to provide full maintenance services to the truck and trailer fleet of one of CTE's other subsidiaries for five years. Charges will be based on cost plus 10%.
8. The central bus station will be restored by CTE to its original condition by December 31, Year 7.
9. CTE will provide free advertising to the Purchaser, on request, for one year following the closing date. The Purchaser will create all the advertising material, including TV commercials.
10. All bus route rights will be assigned to the Purchaser.
11. The purchase price will be allocated based on carrying amounts.
12. The sale will close on October 1, Year 7, at 12:01 a.m., and the entire consideration with the exception of the contingent consideration will be due and payable one (1) month after closing. The contingent consideration is due one (1) month after the July 31, Year 8, financial statements are finalized.
13. Overdue amounts will be charged interest at a rate of 11% per annum.
14. CTE will act in a consulting capacity to advise the Purchaser for a fee of $25,000 per annum.

## EXHIBIT II

## Information Gathered

1. Exclusive rights to most bus routes were obtained almost 40 years ago when the provincial governments were handing out the routes at no cost to the local bus lines. They had no competition at that time. Other similar bus routes were subsequently purchased for significant amounts.
2. TBL's summary draft financial statements for July 31, Year 7, are as follows (in thousands of dollars):

| | |
|---|---:|
| Revenue | $48,123 |
| Expenses (including $2,403 of head office charges) | 40,239 |
| Income before income taxes | 7,884 |
| Current taxes | 2,995 |
| Deferred taxes | 567 |
| Net income | $ 4,322 |
| Current assets | $14,133 |
| Long-term assets | 25,131 |
| Liabilities | (21,264) |
| Deferred taxes | (6,000) |
| Equity | $12,000 |

*(continued)*

**EXHIBIT II**  *(continued)*

3. The TBL maintenance department has recently completed a study that demonstrated that the school buses would last 15 years, rather than the 10 years on which the straight-line depreciation rates have always been based.

4. All school boards pay a non-refundable deposit, three months before the beginning of the school year in September, to guarantee bus service for the coming school year.

5. TBL ran a "Travel the Country" promotion in June Year 7. Sales of the three-month passes for unlimited travel, costing $400, were brisk. The driver punches the pass each time the holder takes a trip. To compensate travellers who use their passes fewer than 10 times in the three-month period, TBL permits them to trade in their passes for either a pair of skis or a pair of in-line skates or the cash value of these items ($150).

6. CTE's consolidation entries for Year 7 related to TBL include a fair value increment of $432,300 for property, plant, and equipment and $2,332,000 for goodwill, which is checked for impairment on an annual basis.

7. Included in TBL's long-term assets is a note receivable for $3.1 million, secured by the real property of a chain of four gas stations. Because of fierce competition from stations owned by the large oil companies, the value of the properties has declined from $4.2 million, the amount stated in the May Year 6 appraisal, to $2.4 million, according to the May Year 7 appraisal released on July 22, Year 7. The payments on the note are being made on schedule.

8. On August 18, Year 7, the Panamee School District announced the cancellation of all school bus services previously contracted for Year 7/8 in the school district.

9. The management buyout team plans to spend $500,000 on TV advertisements that promote bus travel in a national advertising campaign starting in early Year 8. The team also plans to retrofit all long-distance buses at substantial cost.

10. TBL moved all maintenance operations to a new facility in June Year 7. The building was purchased for $3.4 million, and the company had to vacate a leased facility 18 months before the end of the lease. The prospects of subletting the facility do not look good.

*(CPA Canada adapted)*[8]

# Case 8-4

LO2

Dry Quick (DQ) is a medium-sized, private manufacturing company located near Timmins, Ontario. DQ has a June 30 year-end. Your firm, Poivre & Sel (P&S), has recently been appointed as auditors for DQ.

It is now August 2, Year 10. You, CPA, have been asked to take on the senior role on the audit. The following information has been provided to help you familiarize yourself with the client: information on DQ (Exhibit III), a draft income statement prepared by management in accordance with ASPE (Exhibit IV), notes from your firm's meetings with management and the Board Chair (Exhibit V), and excerpts from the current-year audit file (Exhibit VI).

The following week, the audit partner on the file calls you into his office and says, "Now that you've had the file for a week, can you let me know what accounting issues you've identified and your recommendations for resolution of these issues."

## EXHIBIT III

## Information on Dry Quick

DQ manufactures portable heating and drying units. The units include heat exchangers that heat and circulate dry air, making them useful on construction sites. The technology was invented by Yuda Mann, the current Chief Executive Officer (CEO). DQ holds a number of patents and is protective of its proprietary technology. Seed capital was provided from the sale of shares to Yuda's friends, family members, and employees, as well as through bank financing.

As the company grew, Yuda recognized the need for a CFO, particularly since he is more involved with research and development and manufacturing operations. Since it was difficult to recruit someone to come to Timmins, Yuda decided to recruit someone with the right skill set, regardless of location. Two years ago, DQ hired Randy Wall, a CPA located in Toronto. Randy works out of Toronto and spends about one week per month in Timmins. The bookkeeper, Melanie Beech, works in Timmins but reports to Randy. Despite the fact that Randy was hired as the CFO, he really enjoys sales and marketing. Randy has been instrumental in DQ's rapid sales growth because he is willing to travel extensively throughout North America to meet potential customers. With Randy involved in sales, Yuda says he thinks of himself as more of a Chief Operating Officer (COO) than a CEO. Yuda says that he completely trusts Randy, and defers most decisions other than those related to manufacturing to him.

A venture capital firm, VC Ventures (VC), obtained a 20% interest in DQ about three years ago. Yuda owns 40% of the outstanding common shares of the company, while Randy holds 15%. The remaining shares are held by Yuda's friends, family members, and DQ employees. Two directors of VC sit on DQ's Board, along with Yuda, Randy, and one other member of DQ's management.

VC and DQ's management have been actively pursuing a buyer for the company. In the past year, DQ engaged in negotiations with one company; however, the deal was not completed and is no longer being pursued. A second potential buyer has now been identified and has started some preliminary due diligence. The current year's earnings are expected to be a key part of the determination of the purchase price.

## EXHIBIT IV

## Draft Income Statement Prepared by Management

**DRY QUICK**
**INCOME STATEMENT**
For the year ended June 30, Year 10
(unaudited)

| | |
|---|---:|
| Sales | $16,973,450 |
| Cost of sales | 7,012,495 |
| Gross profit | 9,960,955 |
| Administrative expenses | 6,123,560 |
| Selling and marketing expenses | 487,988 |
| Interest on long-term debt | 624,333 |
| Amortization of fixed assets | 369,421 |
| Amortization of intangibles | 48,709 |
| Earnings before income taxes | 2,306,944 |
| Income taxes | 647,065 |
| Net earnings | $ 1,659,879 |

EXHIBIT V

## Notes from Meetings with Management and Board Chair

**Bookkeeper: Melanie Beech**—Melanie has been cooperative. She provided us with a schedule supporting the sales commission expense accrual of $150,000 prior to Randy's review, which showed a commission rate of 5%. This was higher than the rate accrued in the general ledger of 3%, which was supported by a schedule prepared by Randy. Melanie didn't know which percentage was correct, because she can't seem to find a written agreement with the salespeople.

**Board Chair: Nathan Cole of VC**—The Board has not met regularly as a group for most of the past year because Randy has been unavailable. Nathan has also not received the monthly reports promised to him by management. Nathan finds Randy difficult to contact and has given up trying to obtain information from him.

**CEO: Yuda Mann**—Yuda is proud of the products DQ produces and the business he has built up; however, he prefers dealing with product development and is grateful that, except for manufacturing, Randy has taken over almost everything, including sales. Not only is DQ selling more products, but its gross margin which was around 50% has increased. With these results, Yuda is happy to continue to focus on the products and to let Randy deal with everything else.

**CFO: Randy Wall**—Randy has indicated that he has achieved increased sales due in part to the new Early Order Program, which provides a 15% discount to buyers committing to purchases in advance. Any purchase orders that were placed by June 15 and accompanied by a 10% deposit were eligible for the program, with delivery of the units to occur within four months. The program was highly successful, resulting in total sales of $1.5 million being recognized related to these bill and hold arrangements.

In addition, DQ sends demonstration units to customers (demos) which they have the option to return within six months if they are not satisfied with performance. Demos with a total sales value of $400,000 were delivered to customers fairly evenly throughout the year. Based on his estimate of returns over the past two years, Randy has recognized 80% of the items as sales.

EXHIBIT VI

## Excerpts from the Current-Year Audit File

Preliminary audit work included the following:

**Accounts receivable confirmations**—Sample size was calculated based on a preliminary materiality of $80,000, which represents 5% of net earnings. A number of confirmations received were initially returned with discrepancies. One customer indicated that a total of four of the units confirmed, worth approximately $25,000 each, were demos and would be returned. For other outstanding confirmations, Randy followed up with those customers, and the confirmations were received by him shortly thereafter. He also dealt with confirmation discrepancies related to the Early Order Program, as customers seemed unsure whether or not to include these purchases in the amounts confirmed. Accounts receivable includes approximately $1,350,000 related to the Early Order Program.

**Inventory count**—A junior audit team member attended the inventory count in Timmins on June 30, Year 10. A few discrepancies were noted. In some instances, the junior noted that there were more items on the floor than were reported on the inventory listing. This finding may be due to the Early Order Program because those units remain on site with the rest of the inventory. During the count, the staff noted some returned demos that were included as part of the new inventory. Randy recorded the returned units at the same value as new units.

**Inventory overhead testing**—We still need to test the overhead allocated to inventory. Per Randy, other than some of the specific percentages noted below, he generally allocates 60% of administrative costs to inventory because most of DQ's operations are ultimately about production. Some items in overhead include:

- 100% of the depreciation related to manufacturing
- 60% of the depreciation related to the head office building
- 60% of the advertising costs
- Partial allocation of several employees' salaries, including 75% of each of the following salaries: CEO, CFO, and administrative staff

*(continued)*

**Merger & acquisition costs**—DQ has capitalized $350,000 of costs related to legal and other expenses for the first offer to purchase. While the first offer is no longer active, much of the work done on the first offer can be leveraged for future offers. Most of the costs incurred related to preparing the company for purchase, thus greatly improving its marketability.

**Subsequent disbursements**—The disbursements subsequent to year-end that were selected for testing include commissions to a salesperson of approximately $37,500 (related to $750,000 in sales during the last quarter of the Year 10 fiscal year) and $26,420 for one of Randy's expense reports. The expense report had not been approved by anyone other than Randy. It appeared to be for expenses incurred subsequent to year-end, and therefore was appropriately not accrued.

*(CPA Canada adapted)*[9]

# Case 8-5

LO2

You, a CPA, have recently accepted a job at the accounting firm of Cat, Scan & Partners, as a manager, and have been assigned the audit of Vision Clothing Inc. (VCI). The partner in charge had been at VCI the previous week and had met with the controller to discuss the year-end audit. The partner has requested that you review his notes and prepare a detailed report for the client regarding accounting and other issues (excluding tax and assurance).

He handed you his notes and extracts from the current year's preliminary financial statements (Exhibit VII), from which you learn the following about the company.

**EXHIBIT VII**

**VISION CLOTHING COMPANY**
**EXTRACTS FROM CONSOLIDATED INCOME STATEMENT**
For the years ended January 31
(in thousands of dollars)

| | Year 3 (Preliminary) | Year 2 (Audited) |
|---|---|---|
| Sales | $1,305,125 | $1,244,102 |
| Cost of goods sold | 848,332 | 721,579 |
| Gross margin | 456,793 | 522,523 |
| Selling expenses | 272,453 | 315,333 |
| Head office expenses | 138,938 | 150,186 |
| Earnings before the following: | 45,402 | 57,004 |
| Amortization | 52,600 | 42,380 |
| Interest | 37,484 | 31,381 |
| Earnings before taxes | (44,682) | (16,757) |
| Income taxes | 17,873 | 6,660 |
| | (26,809) | (10,097) |
| Earnings (loss) from investment in affiliated companies | 4,700 | (850) |
| Net earnings | $ (22,109) | $ (10,947) |
| Attributable to: | | |
| Shareholders of VCI | $ (19,684) | $ (7,523) |
| Non-controlling interest | (2,425) | (3,424) |
| | $ (22,109) | $ (10,947) |

*(continued)*

EXHIBIT VII (continued)

| | Year 3 (Preliminary) | Year 2 (Audited) |
|---|---|---|
| **Assets** | | |
| Current: | | |
| Cash and short-term investment | $ 42,420 | $145,400 |
| Inventory | 250,713 | 250,209 |
| Other current assets | 61,962 | 57,432 |
| Income taxes recoverable | 0 | 2,660 |
| Deferred taxes | 17,873 | 0 |
| | 372,968 | 455,701 |
| Investment in affiliated companies | 27,825 | 23,125 |
| Property, plant, and equipment—net | 353,420 | 312,800 |
| Goodwill | 127,472 | 123,842 |
| | $881,685 | $915,468 |
| **Liabilities and Shareholders' Equity** | | |
| Accounts payable | $212,790 | $257,135 |
| Current portion of long-term debt and financing lease obligations | 55,412 | 22,160 |
| Other current liabilities | 34,800 | 4,200 |
| | 303,002 | 283,495 |
| Long term: | | |
| Long-term debt | 93,000 | 133,000 |
| Finance lease obligations | 58,208 | 48,889 |
| Debentures payable | 100,000 | 150,000 |
| | 251,208 | 331,889 |
| Shareholders' equity: | | |
| Ordinary shares | 195,500 | 146,000 |
| Retained earnings | 75,566 | 95,250 |
| Non-controlling interest | 56,409 | 58,834 |
| | 327,475 | 300,084 |
| | $881,685 | $915,468 |

## General background:

VCI was incorporated 15 years ago under the *Canada Business Corporations Act* and operates stores across Canada and the United States. Its principal business is the operation of women's and men's clothing stores. These chains operate through different divisions and subsidiaries. The retail clothing industry has been hit hard by the recession in recent years, and many large companies and familiar names have been forced out of business.

Each VCI chain functions as an autonomous unit to which VCI provides capital and central services. This decentralized organization permits the chains to remain sensitive to the needs of their markets.

The corporation's year-end is January 31. It is now February Year 3.

## Notes from the meeting with the client:

1. In February Year 2, VCI successfully completed a public share offering of 6 million Class A non-voting shares at an offering price of $8.25 per share. Underwriter's fees amounted to $5 million. In November Year 2, VCI considered another public offering; however, the price per share had fallen to $4 and the directors decided to defer the issue to a later date. To date, fees of $1 million related to this deferred offering have been incurred and capitalized to current assets.

   The share issue was used to redeem debentures of $50 million in March Year 2. Under the provisions of the debenture agreement, one third of the original $150 million debenture can be redeemed each March at the discretion of the debenture holders. At any time, debenture holders have the option to convert the debentures at their face value for voting shares at their market value.

2. The company recorded a gain of $3.7 million from an increase in its ownership interest of an affiliated company, XYZ Ltd. The increase occurred as a result of a share redemption by XYZ Ltd. Following the redemption, VCI's ownership rose from 25% to 29%. The gain represents 4% of the fair market value of XYZ Ltd.

3. Two years ago, VCI decided to diversify and purchased the assets of a chain of children's shoe stores, Tiny Tot Togs (TTT). They have operated TTT as a division of VCI. The assets of TTT will be sold in the near future for an estimated $5 million. TTT has lost $18 million to date. VCI believes that $5 million is the fair market value for the company, even though it has invested over $30 million in TTT.

4. During the year, VCR invested in a new management reporting and consolidation software package, which the finance department has just implemented and tested. VCI's management information systems department produced the package internally. Total costs to develop, implement, and test the software package have been estimated at about $2 million. This amount has been allocated to property, plant, and equipment. It includes about $800,000 to $1 million in salaries and benefits for those employees who devoted most of their time to this project. The amount also includes $700,000 to $1 million spent on new hardware, including monitors, enhanced keyboards, computer chips, and extended memory upgrades necessary to run the new software package.

5. On October 31, Year 2, VCI amalgamated with a subsidiary, Style Co. The amalgamation occurred because VCI had large loss carry-forwards due to expire soon, and future losses were anticipated. Style Co. had been profitable for several years and was forecasting further profits of $9 million for the year ending January Year 3.

   Because of Style Co.'s size, inventory was counted at year-end only. The quarterly inventory valuations were estimated using prior-year gross margins less a provision for shrinkage. During Year 2, Style Co. began installing a state-of-the-art inventory system that was far superior to its old system. The new system was installed prior to the year-end inventory count at January 31, Year 3.

   When the count was taken, inventory was found to be overstated by $20 million, turning Style Co.'s original $9 million profit for the year into an $11 million loss. The problem was explained as being possibly a combination of a shrinkage problem, gross margin miscalculations (on which original budgets were based), and/or system conversion problems (e.g., incorrectly inputted data). Inventory averages approximately $100 million at cost and $150 million at retail.

   VCI's controller suggested that the inventory shortage must have occurred throughout the year and that Style Co.'s third-quarter profit should be restated.

6. VCI has strong representation in many shopping malls, so it has been able to negotiate favourable leases. In many cases, landlords have provided funds to cover all, or a significant portion of, the leasehold improvements as a result of the economic pressures to attract and keep good tenants. VCI received approximately $20 million in September Year 2, to remodel new and existing locations. Leases are generally signed for seven years, at the end of which time the stores are usually remodelled. VCI has recorded these transactions as a credit against divisional expenses on the preliminary January 31, Year 3, statements.

*(CPA Canada adapted)*[10]

## PROBLEMS

## Problem 8-1

........

LO1

The following Year 5 consolidated cash flow statement was prepared for Standard Manufacturing Corp. and its 60%-owned subsidiary, Pritchard Windows Inc.:

**STANDARD MANUFACTURING CORP.**
**CONSOLIDATED CASH FLOW STATEMENT**
for the year ended December 31, Year 5

| | | |
|---|---:|---:|
| Cash flows from operating activities: | | |
| Consolidated net income* | $129,800 | |
| Non-cash items included in income: | | |
| Depreciation | 45,200 | |
| Goodwill impairment loss | 1,000 | |
| Bond premium amortization | (2,000) | |
| Loss on sale of equipment | 23,000 | |
| Decrease in inventory | 20,000 | |
| Increase in accounts receivable | (12,000) | |
| Net cash provided by operating activities | | $205,000 |
| Cash flows from investing activities: | | |
| Purchase of buildings | (150,000) | |
| Sale of equipment | 60,000 | |
| Net cash used in investing activities | | (90,000) |
| Cash flows from financing activities: | | |
| Dividends paid: | | |
| To Standard's shareholders | (50,000) | |
| To non-controlling shareholders | (6,000) | |
| Bond issue | 100,000 | |
| Preferred share redemption | (120,000) | |
| Net cash used in financing activities | | (76,000) |
| Net increase in cash | | 39,000 |
| Cash balance, January 1 | | 50,000 |
| Cash balance, December 31 | | $ 89,000 |

*Consolidated net income was $120,000 attributable to Standard's shareholders and $9,800 attributable to non-controlling interest.

### Required

(a) Did the loss on the sale of equipment shown above result from a sale to an affiliate or a non-affiliate? Explain.

(b) Explain why the amortization of bond premium is treated as a deduction from net income in arriving at net cash flow from operations.

(c) Determine the net income of Pritchard Windows for Year 5. (Assume no intercompany transactions or unrealized profits and that the only change in the unamortized acquisition differential during the year was the goodwill impairment loss.)

(d) Explain why dividends to non-controlling shareholders are not shown as a dividend in the consolidated retained earnings statement but are shown as a distribution of cash in the consolidated cash flow statement.

(e) Determine the amount of dividends paid by Pritchard Windows in Year 5.

# Problem 8-2

## LO3, 4, 6

Financial statements of Par Corp. and its subsidiary Star Inc. on December 31, Year 12, are shown below:

### BALANCE SHEETS
At December 31, Year 12

|  | Par | Star |
|---|---|---|
| Cash | $ 57,000 | $ 2,700 |
| Accounts receivable | 117,000 | 102,000 |
| Inventories | 84,360 | 65,000 |
| Land | 47,000 | 87,000 |
| Plant and equipment | 520,000 | 870,000 |
| Accumulated depreciation | (197,000) | (317,000) |
| Investment in Star common shares | 232,400 | — |
|  | $860,760 | $809,700 |
|  |  |  |
| Accounts payable | $ 98,800 | $197,000 |
| Accrued liabilities | 9,700 | 13,400 |
| Preferred shares | — | 67,000 |
| Common shares | 450,000 | 180,000 |
| Retained earnings | 302,260 | 352,300 |
|  | $860,760 | $809,700 |

### RETAINED EARNINGS STATEMENTS
for the year ended December 31, Year 12

|  | Par | Star |
|---|---|---|
| Balance, January 1 | $297,260 | $417,300 |
| Net income (loss) | 31,000 | (28,000) |
|  | 328,260 | 389,300 |
| Dividends | 26,000 | 37,000 |
| Balance, December 31 | $302,260 | $352,300 |

## Other Information

- On January 1, Year 5, the balance sheet of Star showed the following shareholders' equity:

| | |
|---|---|
| $8 cumulative preferred shares, 500 shares issued | $ 67,000 |
| Common shares, 2,000 shares issued | 180,000 |
| Deficit (Note 1) | (97,000) |
| | $150,000 |

*Note 1:* Dividends on preferred shares are two years in arrears.

On this date, Par acquired 1,400 common shares of Star for a cash payment of $232,400.

The fair values of Star's identifiable net assets differed from carrying amounts only with respect to the following:

|  | Carrying Amount | Fair Value |
|---|---|---|
| Accounts receivable | $51,000 | $49,000 |
| Inventory | 61,000 | 68,000 |
| Plant | 580,000 | 630,000 |
| Long-term liabilities | 332,000 | 352,000 |

The plant had an estimated remaining useful life of five years on this date, and the long-term liabilities had a maturity date of December 30, Year 12. Any goodwill is to be tested annually for impairment.

- Both Par and Star make substantial sales to each other at an intercompany selling price that yields the same gross profit as the sales they make to unrelated customers. Intercompany sales in Year 12 were as follows:

| | |
|---|---|
| Par to Star | $360,000 |
| Star to Par | 381,000 |

- During Year 12, Par billed Star $2,000 per month in management fees. At year-end, Star had paid for all months except for December.

- The January 1, Year 12, inventories of the two companies contained unrealized intercompany profits as follows:

| | |
|---|---|
| Inventory of Par | $31,000 |
| Inventory of Star | 30,000 |

- The December 31, Year 12, inventories of the two companies contained unrealized intercompany profits as follows:

| | |
|---|---|
| Inventory of Par | $52,000 |
| Inventory of Star | 54,000 |

- On July 1, Year 7, Star sold equipment to Par for $76,000. The equipment had a carrying amount in the records of Star of $56,000 on this date and an estimated remaining useful life of five years.

- Goodwill impairment losses were recorded as follows: Year 7, $83,000; Year 9, $51,570; and Year 12, $20,560.

- Assume a 40% corporate tax rate.

- Par has accounted for its investment in Star by the cost method.

- All dividends in arrears were paid by December 31, Year 11.

### Required

(a) Prepare, with all necessary calculations, the following:
- (i) Year 12 consolidated retained earnings statement
- (ii) Consolidated balance sheet as at December 31, Year 12

(b) How would the return on equity attributable to Par's shareholders for Year 12 change if Star's preferred shares were non-cumulative instead of cumulative?

(c) On January 1, Year 13, Star issued common shares for $100,000 in cash. Because Par did not purchase any of these shares, Par's ownership percentage declined from 70 to 56%. Calculate the gain or loss that would be charged or credited to consolidated shareholders' equity as a result of this transaction.

## Problem 8-3

LO2

On January 1, Year 4, Hidden Company acquired 25,000 ordinary shares of Jovano Company for $142,400 when the shareholders' equity of Jovano was as follows:

| | |
|---|---|
| Ordinary shares (100,000 no par value shares issued and outstanding) | $200,000 |
| Retained earnings | 300,000 |
| | $500,000 |

In addition, Hidden purchased 20,000 shares in Jovano for $121,600 on January 1, Year 5, and 10,000 shares in Jovano for $63,000 on January 1, Year 6.

The following are the statements of retained earnings for Jovano from Year 4 to Year 6:

|  | Year 4 | Year 5 | Year 6 |
|---|---|---|---|
| Retained earnings, beginning of year | $300,000 | $330,000 | $361,000 |
| Profit | 50,000 | 52,000 | 56,000 |
| Dividends | (20,000) | (21,000) | (22,000) |
| Retained earnings, end of year | $330,000 | $361,000 | $395,000 |

## Additional Information

- Jovano's ordinary shares are publicly traded. The market value of the shares at the close on December 31 of one year was the same as the market value on January 1 of the next year.

- Any acquisition differential is allocated to customer lists with a useful life of three years on each of the three acquisition dates. Neither company has any customer lists recorded on their separate-entity records.

- There were no unrealized profits from intercompany transactions since the date of acquisition.

## Required

(a) For each of Years 4 to 6, prepare the journal entries that Hidden would use to account for its investment in Jovano under the
  (i) cost method
  (ii) equity method

(b) Calculate the balance in Hidden's investment in Jovano account at the end of Year 4, 5, and 6 under the
  (i) cost method
  (ii) equity method

(c) At the end of Year 6, reconcile the balance in the investment account under the equity method to Jovano's shareholders' equity and the unamortized acquisition differential.

(d) Calculate the following account balances for the Year 6 consolidated financial statements:
  (i) Customer lists
  (ii) Non-controlling interest on the statement of financial position
  (iii) Consolidated net income attributable to the non-controlling interest

## Problem 8-4

LO1, 3

The comparative consolidated statement of financial position at December 31, Year 2, and the consolidated income statement for Year 2, of Parent Ltd. and its 70%-owned subsidiary are shown below.

|  | Year 2 | Year 1 |
|---|---|---|
| Plant and equipment | $6,850,000 | $6,600,000 |
| Accumulated depreciation | (2,800,000) | (2,430,000) |
| Goodwill | 560,500 | 610,000 |
| Inventory | 1,040,500 | 505,000 |
| Accounts receivable | 645,000 | 734,600 |
| Cash | 710,900 | 350,000 |
|  | $7,006,900 | $6,369,600 |

| | Year 2 | Year 1 |
|---|---|---|
| Ordinary shares | $ 800,000 | $ 800,000 |
| Retained earnings | 1,091,000 | 535,000 |
| Non-controlling interest | 534,500 | — |
| Long-term liabilities | 4,180,000 | 3,884,600 |
| Current liabilities | 401,400 | 1,150,000 |
| | $7,006,900 | $6,369,600 |
| Revenues | $8,650,000 | |
| Cost of purchases and other expenses | 8,182,100 | |
| Change in inventory | (535,500) | |
| Depreciation | 370,000 | |
| Goodwill impairment loss | 49,500 | |
| | 8,066,100 | |
| Profit | $ 583,900 | |
| Attributable to: | | |
| Shareholders of Parent | $ 544,000 | |
| Non-controlling interest | 39,900 | |

## Additional Information

- On December 31, Year 1, Parent owned 100% of Sub. On this date, the shareholders' equity of Sub amounted to $1,135,000, and the parent's unamortized acquisition differential of $610,000 was allocated entirely to the goodwill of Sub.

- On January 1, Year 2, Parent sold 30% of its shares of Sub for $644,000 cash and recorded an increase to retained earnings of $12,500 on the transaction. Parent uses the equity method to account for its investment.

- Parent paid $108,500 in dividends during Year 2.

## Required

Prepare, in good form, a consolidated cash flow statement for Year 2 in accordance with the requirements of IAS 7.

## Problem 8-5

LO5

On April 1, Year 7, Princeton Corp. purchased 70% of the ordinary shares of Simon Ltd. for $910,000. On this same date, Simon purchased 60% of the ordinary shares of Fraser Inc. for $600,000. On April 1, Year 7, the acquisition differentials from the two investments were allocated entirely to broadcast rights to be amortized over 10 years. The cost method is being used to account for both investments.

During Year 7, the three companies sold merchandise to each other. On December 31, Year 7, the inventory of Princeton contained merchandise on which Simon recorded a gross margin of $32,000. On the same date, the inventory of Fraser contained merchandise on which Princeton recorded a gross margin of $18,000. Assume a 40% tax rate.

The following information is available:

| | Princeton | Simon | Fraser |
|---|---|---|---|
| Ordinary shares | $600,000 | $550,000 | $300,000 |
| Retained earnings—Jan. 1, Year 7 | 650,000 | 400,000 | 300,000 |
| Profit—Year 7* | 100,000 | 200,000 | 150,000 |
| Dividends declared—Dec. 31 | 25,000 | 30,000 | 70,000 |

*Earned evenly throughout the year.

**Required**

Calculate the following:

(a) Consolidated profit attributable to Princeton's shareholders for Year 7

(b) Non-controlling interest as at December 31, Year 7

(c) Consolidated broadcast rights as at December 31, Year 7

(d) Profit on Princeton's separate-entity income statement, assuming that Princeton was a private company, uses ASPE, and uses the equity method to report its investments in subsidiaries

# Problem 8-6

**LO4**

On January 1, Year 5, PET Company acquired 900 ordinary shares of SET Company for $63,000. On this date, the shareholders' equity accounts of SET Company were as follows:

| | |
|---|---|
| Ordinary shares (1,000 no par value shares issued) | $20,000 |
| Preferred shares (4,000 no par value shares issued) (Note 1) | 40,000 |
| Retained earnings | 30,000 |
| | $90,000 |

*Note 1:* The preferred shares are $1, cumulative, nonparticipating with a liquidation value of 1.05. They were two years in arrears on January 1, Year 5.

The following are the statements of retained earnings for the two companies for Year 5:

| | PET | SET |
|---|---|---|
| Retained earnings, beginning of year | $50,000 | $30,000 |
| Profit | 30,000 | 22,000 |
| Dividends | (25,000) | (15,000) |
| Retained earnings, end of year | $55,000 | $37,000 |

**Additional Information**

- PET uses the cost method to account for its investment in SET.

- Any acquisition differential is allocated to patents with an estimated useful life of six years as at January 1, Year 5. Neither company has any patents recorded on their separate-entity records.

**Required**

(a) Prepare a consolidated statement of retained earnings for Year 5.

(b) Prepare an independent calculation of consolidated retained earnings at the end of Year 5.

(c) Calculate non-controlling interest for the consolidated income statement for Year 5 and non-controlling interest for the consolidated statement of financial position at the end of Year 5.

# Problem 8-7

**LO3**

On January 1, Year 8, Summer Company's shareholders' equity was as follows:

| | |
|---|---|
| Common shares | $20,000 |
| Retained earnings | 70,000 |
| | $90,000 |

Plumber Company held 90% of the 4,000 outstanding shares of Summer on January 1, Year 8, and its investment in Summer Company account had a balance of $126,000 on that date. Plumber accounts for its investment by the equity method. Any acquisition differential was allocated to unrecorded trademarks with a remaining useful life on January 1, Year 8, of 10 years.

The following events took place subsequent to January 1, Year 8:

- On July 1, Year 8, Plumber sold 720 of the Summer Company shares it held at a price of $30 per share.

- During Year 8, Summer reported a net income of $20,000 (earned equally throughout the year) and declared dividends of $5,000 on December 31.

- During Year 9, Summer reported a net income of $28,000 and paid dividends of $8,000 on November 15.

- On December 29, Year 9, Summer issued an additional 500 shares to third parties at a price of $46 per share.

**Required**

(a) Calculate the gain or loss in Year 8 and Year 9 as a result of the ownership change that took place each year.
(b) Would the gain or loss appear on the consolidated income statement each year? Explain.
(c) Calculate the consolidated trademarks as at December 31, Year 9.
(d) Does the value for the trademarks on the consolidated balance sheet as calculated in part (c) comply with the historical cost principle? Explain.

## Problem 8-8

LO3

At December 31, Year 4, Hein Company owned 90,000 ordinary shares of Jensen Company when the shareholders' equity of Jensen was as follows:

| | |
|---|---|
| Ordinary shares (100,000 no par value shares issued and outstanding) | $400,000 |
| Retained earnings | 500,000 |
| | $900,000 |

The unamortized acquisition differential at December 31, Year 4, was as follows:

| | |
|---|---|
| Equipment—net (remaining useful life of 9 years) | $ 90,000 |
| Goodwill | 120,000 |
| | $210,000 |

On January 1, Year 5, Hein sold 20,000 ordinary shares of Jensen to an unrelated party for $250,000. Jensen's statement of retained earnings for Year 5 was as follows:

| | |
|---|---|
| Retained earnings, beginning of year | $500,000 |
| Profit | 105,000 |
| Dividends | (50,000) |
| Retained earnings, end of year | $555,000 |

On January 1, Year 6, Hein sold 25,000 ordinary shares of Jensen to an unrelated party for their fair value of $13 per share.

**Additional Information**

- Hein Company uses the equity method to account for its investment in Jensen for its separate entity financial statements.

- The unamortized acquisition differential at December 31, Year 4, was split between the controlling and non-controlling interests in direct proportion to their respective percentage ownership. There was no impairment of goodwill in Year 5.

- There were no unrealized profits from intercompany transactions since the date of acquisition.

**Required**

(a) Calculate the balance in the investment account at December 31, Year 4, and non-controlling interest on the consolidated balance sheet at December 31, Year 4.

(b) Prepare the journal entries relating to Hein investment in Jensen for Year 5.

(c) Calculate the balance in the investment account at December 31, Year 5, and non-controlling interest on the consolidated balance sheet at December 31, Year 5.

(d) Prepare the journal entry to record the sale of 30,000 ordinary shares by Hein on January 1, Year 6.

## Problem 8-9

LO1, 3

Parent Co. owns 9,500 shares of Sub Co. and accounts for its investment by the equity method. On December 31, Year 5, the shareholders' equity of Sub was as follows:

| | |
|---|---|
| Common shares (10,000 shares issued) | $100,000 |
| Retained earnings | 170,000 |

On January 1, Year 6, Parent sold 1,900 shares from its holdings in Sub for $66,500. On this date and prior to the sale, the balance in the investment in Sub account was $320,000, and the unamortized acquisition differential was allocated in the following manner:

45% to land

30% to equipment (remaining useful life, 4 years)

25% to patents (remaining useful life, 10 years)

During Year 6, Sub reported a net income of $150,000 and paid dividends totalling $70,000.

**Required**

(a) (i) Prepare the journal entry that Parent would make on January 1, Year 6, to record the sale of the 1,900 shares.

(ii) Calculate the amount of the unamortized acquisition differential that would be allocated to land, equipment, and patents on December 31, Year 6.

(iii) Prepare an independent proof of the unamortized acquisition differential on December 31, Year 6.

(b) The accountant of Parent must prepare a consolidated cash flow statement for Year 6 by analyzing the changes in the consolidated balance sheets from December 31, Year 5, to December 31, Year 6. She needs some assistance in determining what effect Parent's sale of 1,900 shares had on the consolidated financial statements.

Prepare a journal entry to record the effect that the January 1, Year 6, sale of shares had on the consolidated entity.

## Problem 8-10

LO2

On January 1, Year 5, Pic Company acquired 7,500 ordinary shares of Sic Company for $600,000. On January 1, Year 6, Pic Company acquired an additional 2,000 ordinary shares of Sic Company for $166,000. On January 1, Year 5, the shareholders' equity of Sic was as follows:

| | |
|---|---:|
| Ordinary shares (10,000 no par value shares issued) | $200,000 |
| Retained earnings | 300,000 |
| | $500,000 |

The following are the statements of retained earnings for the two companies for Years 5 and 6:

| | Pic | | Sic | |
|---|---|---|---|---|
| | Year 5 | Year 6 | Year 5 | Year 6 |
| Retained earnings, beginning of year | $500,000 | $530,000 | $300,000 | $310,000 |
| Profit | 130,000 | 140,000 | 100,000 | 110,000 |
| Dividends | (100,000) | (120,000) | (90,000) | (90,000) |
| Retained earnings, end of year | $530,000 | $550,000 | $310,000 | $330,000 |

### Additional Information

- Pic uses the cost method to account for its investment in Sic.

- Any acquisition differential is allocated to customer contracts, which are expected to provide future benefits until December 31, Year 7. Neither company has any customer contracts recorded on their separate-entity records.

- There were no unrealized profits from intercompany transactions since the date of acquisition.

### Required

(a) Calculate consolidated profit attributable to Pic's shareholders for Year 6.
(b) Calculate the following account balances for the consolidated statement of financial position at December 31, Year 6:
    (i) Customer contracts
    (ii) Non-controlling interest
    (iii) Retained earnings

## Problem 8-11

LO5

Intercompany shareholdings of an affiliated group during the year ended December 31, Year 2, were as follows:

| York Ltd. | Queen's Company | McGill Company |
|---|---|---|
| 90% of Queen's Company | 70% of Carleton Ltd. | 60% of Trent Ltd. |
| 80% of McGill Company | 10% of McGill Company | |

The equity method is being used for intercompany investments, but no entries have been made in Year 2. The profits before equity method earnings for Year 2 were as follows:

|  | *Profit* |
|---|---|
| York Ltd. | $54,000 |
| Queen's Company | 22,000 |
| McGill Company | 26,700 |
| Carleton Ltd. | 15,400 |
| Trent Ltd. | 11,600 |

Intercompany profits before taxes in the December 31, Year 2, inventories and the selling companies were as follows:

| *Selling Corporation* | *Profit Made by Selling Corporation* |
|---|---|
| York Ltd. | $10,000 |
| McGill Company | 1,000 |
| Carleton Ltd. | 2,400 |

Use income tax allocation at a 40% rate. Assume that there is no acquisition differential for any of the intercompany shareholdings.

**Required**

(a) Calculate consolidated profit attributable to York's shareholders for Year 2.

(b) Calculate the amount of consolidated profit attributable to non-controlling interest that would appear on the Year 2 consolidated income statement.

(c) Will the consolidation adjustment for unrealized profits be any different if McGill Company sells inventory to Carleton Ltd. or York Ltd.? Use the revenue recognition principle to explain your answer.

## Problem 8-12

LO3, 6

Craft Ltd. held 80% of the outstanding ordinary shares of Delta Corp. as at December 31, Year 12. In order to establish a closer relationship with Nonaffiliated Corporation, a major supplier to both Craft and Delta, all three companies agreed that Nonaffiliated would take an equity position in Delta. Accordingly, for a cash payment of $15 per share, Delta issued 12,250 additional ordinary shares to Nonaffiliated on December 31, Year 12. This was the last transaction that occurred on this date. Statements of financial position for the two companies just prior to this transaction were as follows:

**CRAFT LTD.**
**STATEMENT OF FINANCIAL POSITION**
at December 31, Year 12

| | |
|---|---|
| Buildings and equipment (net) | $ 600,000 |
| Investment in Delta | 490,000 |
| Inventory | 180,000 |
| Accounts receivable | 90,000 |
| Cash | 50,000 |
| | $1,410,000 |
| Ordinary shares | $ 480,000 |
| Retained earnings | 610,000 |
| Mortgage payable | 250,000 |
| Accounts payable | 70,000 |
| | $1,410,000 |

**DELTA CORP.**
**STATEMENT OF FINANCIAL POSITION**
At December 31, Year 12

| | |
|---|---|
| Buildings and equipment (net) | $400,000 |
| Inventory | 200,000 |
| Accounts receivable | 120,000 |
| Cash | 65,000 |
| | $785,000 |
| Ordinary shares (Note) | $250,000 |
| Retained earnings | 350,000 |
| Accrued liabilities | 85,000 |
| Accounts payable | 100,000 |
| | $785,000 |

*Note:* 49,000 ordinary shares outstanding on December 31, Year 12.

### Additional Information

- Craft has used the equity method of accounting for its investment in Delta since it acquired its 80% interest in Delta in Year 2. At that time, the acquisition differential was entirely allocated to inventory and patent, which still exists but is not recorded on Delta's separate-entity books.

- There were no unrealized intercompany asset profits as at December 31, Year 12.

### Required

(a) Prepare a consolidated statement of financial position as at December 31, Year 12 (show calculations for all items on the balance sheet).

(b) If Craft had used parent company extension theory rather than entity theory, how would this affect the return-on-equity ratio for Year 12?

## Problem 8-13

LO5

A Company owns 75% of B Company and 40% of C Company. B Company owns 40% of C Company. The following information was assembled at December 31, Year 7.

| | A Company | B Company | C Company |
|---|---|---|---|
| Cash | $ 119,100 | $ 50,600 | $ 21,300 |
| Accounts receivable | 226,000 | 126,000 | 57,000 |
| Inventory | 303,000 | 232,000 | 71,000 |
| Investment in C | 69,570 | 99,320 | — |
| Investment in B | 1,068,990 | — | — |
| Property, plant, and equipment | 3,000,000 | 2,300,000 | 240,000 |
| Accumulated depreciation | (990,000) | (580,000) | (101,000) |
| | $3,796,660 | $2,227,920 | $288,300 |
| Accounts payable | $ 120,000 | $ 101,000 | $ 7,000 |
| Bonds payable | 800,000 | 700,000 | — |
| Preferred shares | — | 50,000 | — |
| Common shares | 1,200,000 | 400,000 | 200,000 |
| Retained earnings, January 1 | 1,601,860 | 908,920 | 48,300 |
| Net income | 131,800 | 68,000 | 33,000 |
| Dividends | (57,000) | — | — |
| | $3,796,660 | $2,227,920 | $288,300 |

**Additional Information**

- A Company purchased its 40% interest in C Company on January 1, Year 4. On that date, the negative acquisition differential of $42,500 on the 40% investment was allocated to equipment with an estimated useful life of 10 years.

- A Company purchased its 75% of B Company's common shares on January 1, Year 6. On that date, the 100% implied acquisition differential was allocated $40,000 to buildings with an estimated useful life of 20 years, and $89,600 to patents to be amortized over eight years. The preferred shares of B Company are non-cumulative.

- On January 1, Year 6, B Company's accumulated depreciation was $450,000.

- On January 1, Year 7, B Company purchased its 40% interest in C Company for $99,320. The carrying amount of C Company's identifiable net assets approximated fair value on this date and C Company's accumulated depreciation was $52,700.

- The inventory of B Company contains a profit of $7,600 on merchandise purchased from A Company. The inventory of A Company contains a profit of $6,900 on merchandise purchased from C Company.

- On December 31, Year 7, A Company owes $33,000 to C Company and B Company owes $4,000 to A Company.

- Both A Company and B Company use the equity method to account for their investments but have made no equity method adjustments in Year 7.

- An income tax rate of 40% is used for consolidation purposes.

**Required**

(a) Calculate non-controlling interest's share of consolidated net income for Year 7.

(b) Prepare a consolidated statement of retained earnings for Year 7.

(c) Prepare a consolidated balance sheet as at December 31, Year 7. Show all calculations.

# Problem 8-14

LO1

Parento Inc. owns 80% of Santana Corp. The consolidated financial statements of Parento follow:

**PARENTO INC.**

**CONSOLIDATED BALANCE SHEET**

At December 31, Year 4

| | Year 4 | Year 3 |
|---|---|---|
| Cash | $121,100 | $ 49,800 |
| Accounts receivable | 115,000 | 136,000 |
| Inventory | 230,000 | 192,000 |
| Land | 86,000 | 114,000 |
| Buildings and equipment | 598,000 | 500,000 |
| Accumulated depreciation | (205,500) | (168,000) |
| Databases | 16,800 | 19,200 |
| | $961,400 | $843,000 |
| | | |
| Accounts payable | $55,400 | $31,200 |
| Accrued liabilities | 27,200 | 27,000 |
| Bonds payable | 300,000 | 240,000 |
| Bond premium | 9,600 | 10,800 |
| Common shares | 180,000 | 180,000 |
| Retained earnings | 362,480 | 330,000 |
| Non-controlling interest | 26,720 | 24,000 |
| | $961,400 | $843,000 |

**PARENTO INC.**
**CONSOLIDATED INCOME STATEMENT**
For the year ended December 31, Year 4

| | | |
|---|---:|---:|
| Sales | | $962,000 |
| Cost of sales | $535,000 | |
| Selling expense | 144,600 | |
| Administrative expense | 159,800 | |
| Interest expense | 31,400 | |
| Income tax | 37,000 | 907,800 |
| Net income | | $ 54,200 |
| Attributable to: | | |
| Parento's shareholders | | $ 49,480 |
| Non-controlling interest | | 4,720 |

Parento Inc. purchased its 80% interest in Santana Corp. on January 1, Year 2, for $114,000 when Santana had net assets of $90,000. The acquisition differential was allocated $24,000 to databases (10-year life), with the balance allocated to equipment (20-year life). Parento issued $60,000 in bonds on December 31, Year 4. Santana reported a net income of $26,000 for Year 4 and paid dividends of $10,000.

Selling and administrative expense includes the following:

| | |
|---|---:|
| Depreciation of buildings and equipment | $37,500 |
| Database amortization | 2,400 |
| Loss on land sale | 2,500 |

Parento reported a Year 4 equity method income of $49,480 and paid dividends of $17,000.

**Required**

(a) Prepare a consolidated cash flow statement for Year 4.
(b) Why are 100% of the dividends paid by Santana not shown as a cash outflow on the cash flow statement?

# Problem 8-15

LO3

On January 1, Year 5, Wellington Inc. owned 90% of the outstanding common shares of Sussex Corp. Wellington accounts for its investment using the equity method. The balance in the investment account on January 1, Year 5, amounted to $244,800. The unamortized acquisition differential on this date was allocated entirely to vacant land held by Sussex.

The shareholders' equity of Sussex on January 1, Year 5, was as follows:

| | |
|---|---:|
| Common shares (7,200 shares outstanding) | $ 28,000 |
| Retained earnings | 124,000 |
| | $152,000 |

The following events occurred in Year 5:

• The net income of Sussex for Year 5 amounted to $48,000, earned equally throughout the year.

• On April 1, Year 5, Sussex issued 1,800 shares at a price of $35 per share. Wellington did not acquire any of these shares.

- On June 30, Year 5, Sussex paid dividends amounting to $24,000.

- On September 15, Year 5, Sussex sold 40% of its vacant land at its carrying amount.

- On December 31, Year 5, Wellington sold 648 shares of its investment in Sussex for $23,000.

**Required**

Calculate the following as at December 31, Year 5:

(a) The acquisition differential allocated to vacant land and the split in value between the parent and the non-controlling interest.

(b) The balance in the investment account, assuming that Wellington is a private company, uses ASPE, and chooses to use the equity method to report its investment in Sussex.

(c) The amount of non-controlling interest on the consolidated balance sheet.

## Problem 8-16

LO2, 4, 6

On January 1, Year 8, Panet Company acquired 40,000 common shares of Saffer Corporation, a public company, for $500,000. This purchase represented 8% of the outstanding shares of Saffer. It was the intention of Panet to acquire more shares in the future in order to eventually gain control of Saffer.

On January 1, Year 10, Panet purchased an additional 135,000 common shares of Saffer for $1,890,000. Saffer's shareholders' equity section was as follows:

| | |
|---|---|
| 10% non-cumulative preferred shares | $ 500,000 |
| Common shares, no par value, 500,000 shares outstanding | 3,000,000 |
| Retained earnings | 2,700,000 |

On this date, the fair values of Saffer's assets were equal to carrying amounts, except for inventory, which was undervalued by $120,000, and land, which was undervalued by $1,000,000.

On January 1, Year 11, Panet purchased an additional 225,000 common shares of Saffer for $3,600,000. Saffer's shares were trading on the open market for $15 per share on the date of acquisition. The shareholders' equity section for Saffer was as follows:

| | |
|---|---|
| 10% non-cumulative preferred shares | $ 500,000 |
| Common shares, no par value, 500,000 shares outstanding | 3,000,000 |
| Retained earnings | 3,200,000 |

On January 1, Year 11, the fair values of Saffer's assets were equal to carrying amounts except for the following:

| | Carrying Amount | Fair Value |
|---|---|---|
| Accounts receivable | $ 310,000 | $ 246,400 |
| Plant and equipment (net) | 10,110,000 | 11,010,000 |
| Long-term liabilities | 2,110,000 | 2,310,000 |

The plant and equipment had a remaining useful life of 20 years. The long-term liabilities mature on December 31, Year 20.

The balance sheets as at December 31, Year 12, and the income statements for the year ending December 31, Year 12, for the two companies are as follows:

### BALANCE SHEET

| | Panet | Saffer |
|---|---|---|
| Assets: | | |
| Cash | $   522,000 | $   178,000 |
| Accounts receivable | 2,455,000 | 333,000 |
| Inventories | 500,000 | 400,000 |
| Plant and equipment (net) | 10,720,000 | 9,110,000 |
| Investment in Saffer | 7,411,380 | — |
| Land | 5,390,000 | 1,000,000 |
| Total assets | $26,998,380 | $11,021,000 |
| Liabilities: | | |
| Current liabilities | $ 3,055,000 | $   555,000 |
| Long-term liabilities | 4,055,000 | 2,055,000 |
| Total liabilities | 7,110,000 | 2,610,000 |
| Shareholders' equity: | | |
| 10% non-cumulative preferred shares | — | 500,000 |
| Common shares | 9,000,000 | 3,000,000 |
| Retained earnings | 10,888,380 | 4,911,000 |
| | 19,888,380 | 8,411,000 |
| Total liabilities and shareholders' equity | $26,998,380 | $11,021,000 |

### INCOME STATEMENT

| | Panet | Saffer |
|---|---|---|
| Sales | $16,100,000 | $10,100,000 |
| Investment income from Saffer | 1,627,660 | — |
| | 17,727,660 | 10,100,000 |
| Cost of goods sold | 9,660,000 | 6,060,000 |
| Selling and administrative expense | 2,522,000 | 552,000 |
| Income tax | 1,054,000 | 752,000 |
| Other expenses | 479,000 | 451,000 |
| | 13,715,000 | 7,815,000 |
| Net income | $ 4,012,660 | $ 2,285,000 |

## Additional Information

- Dividends declared and paid during Year 12:

| | |
|---|---|
| Panet | $500,000 |
| Saffer | 250,000 |

- On January 1, Year 12, the inventory of Panet contained a $107,000 intercompany profit, and the inventory of Saffer contained an intercompany profit amounting to $157,000.

- During Year 12, Saffer sold inventory to Panet for $3,200,000 at a gross profit margin of 35%. Sales of $400,000 remained in Panet's inventory at December 31, Year 12.

- During Year 12, Panet sold inventory to Saffer for $2,800,000 at a gross profit margin of 45%. Sales of $250,000 remained in Saffer's inventory at December 31, Year 12.

- Saffer sold a piece of equipment to Panet on July 1, Year 12, for $560,000. At that time, the carrying amount of the equipment in Saffer's books was $350,000, and it had a remaining useful life of 10.5 years. Panet still owes Saffer for 30% of the purchase price of the equipment. The gain on sale has been netted against other expenses in Saffer's Year 12 income statement.

- Panet uses the equity method to account for its investment in Saffer. Both companies follow the straight-line method for depreciating plant and equipment, and for premiums or discounts on long-term liabilities.

- A goodwill impairment loss of $103,000 was recorded in Year 11, and a further loss of $69,000 occurred in Year 12. The impairment losses are to be applied at 80% to Panet's shareholders and 20% to non-controlling interest.

- Depreciation expense is included with selling and administrative expenses, whereas goodwill impairment losses are included in other expenses.

- Assume a 40% tax rate.

**Required**

(a) Prepare the following Year 12 consolidated financial statements:
    (i)  Income statement
    (ii) Balance sheet

(b) Calculate goodwill impairment loss and non-controlling interest on the consolidated income statement for the year ended December 31, Year 12, under parent company extension theory.

(c) If Panet had used parent company extension theory rather than entity theory, how would this affect the debt-to-equity ratio at the end of Year 12?

    (d) Prepare the consolidated financial statements using the worksheet approach.

## Problem 8-17

LO4

On December 31, Year 6, Ultra Software Limited purchased 70,000 common shares (70%) of a major competitor, Personal Program Corporation (PPC), at $30 per share. Several shareholders who were unwilling to sell at that time owned the remaining common shares and the preferred shares.

The preferred shares, which are non-cumulative, are entitled to a $12 dividend. Each is convertible into two common shares. Immediate conversion of these preferred shares has been, and will continue to be, highly unlikely due to the current market conditions for the shares. Management is concerned, however, about the effect that any future conversion would have.

At December 31, Year 6, PPC's net assets had a carrying amount of $1,525,000. The identifiable assets and liabilities had carrying amounts equal to fair values, with the following exceptions:

- Software patents and copyrights had a total market value estimated as $300,000 above carrying amount. These were expected to have a five-year useful life.

- Inventories of packaged software had a cost to PPC of $20,000 and an estimated selling price of $140,000. Estimated future selling expenses for these items were $15,000.

- An unrecorded brand name had an estimated fair value of $2,375,000. This will be amortized over 40 years.

- In determining the purchase price, the management of Ultra noted that PPC has two years remaining on a long-term contract to supply seats to a major car manufacturer. Given the rapid rise in input costs, PPC earns a negative gross margin on this contract. An independent appraiser indicated that the fair value of this unfavourable supply contract is a negative $500,000.

The trial balances at December 31, Year 8, for these two companies are provided as Exhibit VIII.

**EXHIBIT VIII**

**TRIAL BALANCES**

At December 31, Year 8, in thousands of dollars

| | Ultra | | PPC | |
|---|---|---|---|---|
| Cash | $ 320 | | $ 150 | |
| Accounts receivable | 300 | | 280 | |
| Inventory | 350 | | 380 | |
| Patents and copyrights | 350 | | 450 | |
| Furniture and equipment (net) | 540 | | 675 | |
| Building (net) | 800 | | 925 | |
| Land | 450 | | 200 | |
| Investment in PPC | 2,100 | | | |
| Accounts payable | | $ 340 | | $ 138 |
| Mortgage payable | | 350 | | |
| Bank loan payable | | | | 320 |
| Preferred shares (12,500 outstanding) | | | | 1,400 |
| Common shares (300,000 outstanding) | | 3,000 | | |
| Common shares (100,000 outstanding) | | | | 100 |
| Retained earnings | | 1,300 | | 117 |
| Sales | | 6,200 | | 4,530 |
| Other income | | 120 | | 7 |
| Gain on sale of patent | | | | 50 |
| Loss on sale of computer | 1,080 | | | |
| Cost of purchases | 4,035 | | 2,590 | |
| Change in inventory | 15 | | 10 | |
| Other expenses (including tax) | 850 | | 675 | |
| Depreciation | 75 | | 142 | |
| Interest | 45 | | 35 | |
| Dividends | | | 150 | |
| | $11,310 | $11,310 | $6,662 | $6,662 |

In Year 7, PPC sold packaged software costing $30,000 to Ultra at a price of $45,000. Of this software, 60% was still in Ultra's inventory at December 31, Year 7. During Year 8, packaged software costing $42,000 was sold by PPC to Ultra for $60,000. Ultra's inventory at December 31, Year 8, included $22,000 of goods purchased in this sale. Neither of these packaged software inventories sold to Ultra had a fair value difference at acquisition.

Goodwill is tested for impairment on an annual basis. Each year, it was determined that goodwill was not impaired.

Included in the Year 8 income of PPC was a gain of $50,000 on the sale of patents to another company. This sale took place on June 30, Year 8. These patents had a fair value difference of $20,000 at acquisition.

On September 30, Year 8, Ultra sold surplus computer hardware to PPC. This equipment had a cost of $6,000,000, was one-half depreciated, and was sold for its fair value of $2,000,000. Disassembly and shipping costs of $80,000 were paid by Ultra. There was estimated to be a nine-year remaining useful life in its new use.

Preferred dividends were paid in all years, and no new shares have been issued since the acquisition date.

Assume a 40% tax rate.

**Required**

(a) In accordance with GAAP, prepare the following:

(i) Consolidated income statement for the year ended December 31, Year 8.

(ii) Consolidated statement of retained earnings for the year ended December 31, Year 8.

(iii) Schedule showing the values of the following consolidated balance sheet accounts as at December 31, Year 8:

(1) Software patents and copyrights

(2) Packaged software inventory

(3) Non-controlling interest

(b) Write a brief note to the management of Ultra outlining the financial reporting implications in the event that the preferred shareholders of PPC exercise their conversion privilege.

(c) Prepare the consolidated financial statements using the worksheet approach.

*(Adapted from problem prepared by Peter Secord, St. Mary's University)*

## Problem 8-18

..........

LO2

The summarized trial balances of Phase Limited and Step Limited as of December 31, Year 5, are as follows (amounts in thousands):

|  | Phase | Step |
|---|---|---|
| Property, plant, and equipment | $ 540 | $298 |
| Investment in Step | 257 | — |
| Current assets | 173 | 89 |
| Dividends declared | 80 | 40 |
| Cost of goods sold | 610 | 260 |
| Other expenses | 190 | 55 |
|  | $1,850 | $742 |
| Ordinary shares | $ 400 | $200 |
| Retained earnings, beginning | 360 | 104 |
| Liabilities | 88 | 38 |
| Sales, gains, and other revenue | 1,002 | 400 |
|  | $1,850 | $742 |

Phase had acquired the investment in Step in three stages:

| Date | Shares | Cost | Step's Retained Earnings |
|---|---|---|---|
| Jan. 1/Year 2 | 4,000 | $ 50,700 | $ 28,000 |
| Jan. 1/Year 4 | 6,000 | 98,300 | 69,000 |
| Jan. 1/Year 5 | 6,000 | 108,000 | 104,000 |

The January 1, Year 2, acquisition enabled Phase to elect 3 members to the 10-member board of directors of Step. The January 1, Year 4, acquisition did not give Phase control over Step. Any difference between cost and the underlying carrying amount for each acquisition is attributable equally to land and to patents, which are expected to produce benefits until December 31, Year 11. Step had issued 20,000 shares on July 1, Year 1, the date of incorporation, and has neither issued nor retired shares since that date.

Other information follows:

- Sale of depreciable assets (six-year remaining useful life), from Phase to Step, on June 30, Year 5, at a gain of $60,000.

- Intercompany sales:

| Year 4 | Phase to Step | $50,000 |
|--------|---------------|---------|
|        | Step to Phase | 20,000  |
| Year 5 | Phase to Step | 80,000  |
|        | Step to Phase | 10,000  |

- Opening inventory of Phase contained merchandise purchased from Step for $10,000. Company policy was for a 20% gross margin on intercompany sales. Ending inventory of Phase contained merchandise purchased from Step for $5,000. One-half of the goods sold intercompany during Year 5 had not been paid for by year-end.

- Assume a 40% tax rate.

### Required

Compute the following consolidated amounts as of December 31, Year 5:

(a) Patents

(b) Property, plant, and equipment

(c) Current assets (ignore deferred income taxes)

(d) Non-controlling interest on statement of financial position

(e) Retained earnings, beginning

(f) Cost of goods sold

(g) Profit attributable to Phase's shareholder's (statement not required)

*(Adapted from problem prepared by Peter Secord, St. Mary's University)*

## Endnotes

1   ONEX, *Management's Discussion and Analysis and Financial Statements, December 31, 2014*, Pages 93, 96, 144. Reproduced with permission from ONEX.

2   IAS 7, paragraphs 39 and 40.

3   See the section near the end of Chapter 2 for a further discussion of changes to and from the equity method.

4   IFRS 10, paragraph B98.

5   ONEX, *Management's Discussion and Analysis and Financial Statements, December 31, 2014*, Pages 93, 96, 144. Reproduced with permission from ONEX.

6   ONEX, *Management's Discussion and Analysis and Financial Statements, December 31, 2014*, Pages 93, 96, 144. Reproduced with permission from ONEX.

7   In Chapter 7, we used the following description for this line in various calculations: "Unrealized closing inventory profit." From now on, we will not specify "unrealized" or "realized" in the description. If you need clarification for the missing word, review Chapters 6 and 7.

8   Adapted from *CICA UFE Report,* 1997-II-4, with permission. Chartered Professional Accountants of Canada, Toronto, Canada. Any changes to the original material are the sole responsibility of the author (and/or publisher) and have not been reviewed or endorsed by the Chartered Professional Accountants of Canada.

9   Adapted from *CICA UFE Report,* 2010-III-3, with permission. Chartered Professional Accountants of Canada, Toronto, Canada. Any changes to the original material are the sole responsibility of the author (and/or publisher) and have not been reviewed or endorsed by the Chartered Professional Accountants of Canada.

10  Adapted from *CICA UFE Report,* 1992-III-4, with permission. Chartered Professional Accountants of Canada, Toronto, Canada. Any changes to the original material are the sole responsibility of the author (and/or publisher) and have not been reviewed or endorsed by the Chartered Professional Accountants of Canada.

# Other Consolidation Reporting Issues

## LEARNING OBJECTIVES

**After studying this chapter, you should be able to do the following:**

**LO1** Identify when a special-purpose entity should be consolidated and prepare consolidated statements for a sponsor and its controlled special-purpose entities.

**LO2** Describe and apply the current accounting standards that govern the reporting of interests in joint arrangements.

**LO3** Understand the deferred tax implications of the accounting for a business combination.

**LO4** Describe the requirements for segment disclosures and apply the quantitative thresholds to determine reportable segments.

**LO5** Analyze and interpret financial statements involving other consolidation reporting issues.

## Introduction

In the previous chapters, the parent controlled the subsidiary through voting rights. However, there are other means of controlling the operating and financial policies of the subsidiary. Shoppers Drug Mart, the leading player in Canada's retail drugstore marketplace and the number one provider of pharmacy products and services, controls associate-owned stores through franchise and operating agreements.[1] As we will see in this chapter, the entities that are controlled by contracts and operating agreements must be consolidated in a fashion similar to that used in previous chapters.

> *An entity can be controlled without holding the majority of the voting shares.*

Many Canadian companies participate in arrangements whereby they jointly control the operations of another entity. For example, West Fraser Timber Co. Ltd., a British Columbia-based integrated wood products company, has a 50% ownership interest in a newsprint company and a pulp and paper company, which are jointly controlled with other entities.[2] Later in this chapter, we will consider various types of joint arrangements. After that, we look at how deferred income taxes affect the accounting for a business combination. This chapter concludes with the disclosure requirements associated with a company's operating segments.

# LO1 SPECIAL-PURPOSE ENTITIES

Special-purpose entities (SPEs) have long been used by businesses as a vehicle to carry out specific activities. Until the beginning of this century, the only financial reporting involvement for a company establishing an SPE was the disclosure requirements regarding related-party transactions. Now GAAP require that some types of SPEs be subject to consolidation in the same manner as is a subsidiary.

An SPE is a proprietorship, partnership, corporation, or trust set up to accomplish a very specific and limited business activity. Over the past decade, SPEs have been used to lease manufacturing assets, hedge financial instruments, borrow against high-quality receivables, conduct research and development activities, and carry out a variety of other specified functions.

> *An SPE is an entity created to accomplish a very specific business activity.*

Low-cost financing of asset purchases is often a major benefit of establishing an SPE. Rather than engaging in the business transaction directly, the sponsoring business sets up an SPE to purchase and finance the asset acquisition. The SPE then leases the asset to the sponsor. This strategy saves the sponsor money because the SPE is often eligible for a lower interest rate. This advantage is achieved for several reasons. First, the SPE typically operates with a very limited set of assets—in many cases, just one. By isolating an asset in an SPE, the risk of the asset is isolated from the overall risk of the sponsoring firm. Thus, the SPE's creditors remain protected by the specific collateral in the asset. Second, the business activities of an SPE can be strictly limited by its governing documents. These limits further protect lenders by preventing the SPE from engaging in any activities not specified in its agreements.

> *SPEs are often able to obtain debt financing at very favourable interest rates.*

Another apparent reason for establishing an SPE was to avoid the consolidation of the SPE with the sponsoring enterprise and to thereby avoid having to show additional debt on the consolidated balance sheet. Because governing agreements limited the activities and decision making in most SPEs, the sponsoring enterprise was able to control the activities of the SPEs through the governing agreements. They did not have to own a majority of the voting shares to maintain control. In fact, a sponsoring enterprise usually owned very little, if any, of the voting shares of the SPE. Therefore, the sponsoring enterprise did not control the SPE through a voting interest and did not, until the late 1990s, have to consolidate the SPE. Like all business entities, SPEs generally have assets, liabilities, and investors with equity interests. Unlike most businesses, the role of the equity investors can be fairly minor. They may serve simply as a technical requirement to allow the SPE to function as a legal entity. Because they bear relatively low economic risk, equity investors are typically provided only a small rate of return.

> *Before GAAP were changed, many companies used SPEs as a vehicle for "off-balance-sheet financing."*

Small equity investments are normally insufficient to induce lenders to provide a low-risk interest rate for an SPE. As a result, another party (often the sponsoring firm that benefits from the SPE's activities) must be prepared to contribute substantial resources to enable the SPE to secure the additional financing needed to accomplish its purpose. For example, the sponsoring firm may guarantee the debt of the SPE. In exchange, it receives the bulk of the returns earned by the SPE and is thereby referred to as the primary beneficiary of the SPE. Other contractual arrangements may limit returns to equity holders, while participation rights provide increased profit potential and risks to the sponsoring firm. Risks and rewards such as these cause the sponsor's economic interest to vary depending on the success of the created entity. In contrast to a traditional entity, an SPE's risks and rewards may not be distributed according to share ownership but according to other variable interests. Exhibit 9.1 provides several examples of variable interests in SPEs.

> *The risks and rewards may not be distributed in accordance with equity ownership but rather with some other variable interest attaching to a sponsoring firm as a result of contractual arrangements.*

### EXHIBIT 9.1

## Variable Interests in SPEs

The following are some examples of variable interests in SPEs and the related potential for losses or returns accruing to the sponsor:

| Variable Interests | Potential Losses or Returns |
|---|---|
| • Guarantees of debt | • If an SPE cannot repay liabilities, sponsor will pay and incur a loss. |
| • Subordinated debt instruments | • If an SPE cannot repay its senior debt, the sponsor as subordinated debt holder may be required to absorb the loss. |
| • Variable-rate liability | • Sponsor as holder of debt may participate in returns of SPE. |
| • Lease residual guarantee | • If the value of a leased asset declines below the residual value guarantee, the sponsor, as lessee, will make up the shortfall. |
| • Non-voting equity instruments | • Sponsor as holder of debt or equity may participate in residual profits. |
| • Services | • Sponsor, as the service provider, receives a portion of residual profits. |

A firm with variable interests in an SPE increases its risk with the level (or potential level in the case of a guarantee) of resources provided. With increased risks come increased incentives to exert greater influence over the decision making of the SPE. In fact, the primary sponsor of the SPE will regularly limit the decision-making power of the equity investors through the governance documents that establish the SPE. Although, technically, the equity investors are the owners of the SPE, in reality they may retain little of the traditional responsibilities, risks, and benefits of ownership. In fact, the equity investors often cede financial control of the SPE to the primary sponsor in exchange for a guaranteed rate of return.

> *The equity investors of an SPE typically receive a guaranteed rate of return as a reward for ceding control to the SPE's sponsor.*

Under IFRS 10 *Consolidated Financial Statements*, an entity must consolidate the entities that it controls regardless of the means of obtaining control. As we learned in Chapter 3, when assessing control, it is necessary to identify how returns from the entity's activities are shared and how decisions, if any, are made about the activities that affect those returns. A reporting entity must consider all relevant facts and circumstances, including the items discussed below, in making the judgment as to whether it has control.

Understanding the purpose and design of a structured entity helps us assess how the activities of that entity are directed and how returns are shared among its participants. For example, a reporting entity is likely to control a structured entity that has been created to undertake activities that are part of the reporting entity's ongoing activities (e.g., the entity might have been created to hold legal title to an asset that the reporting entity uses in its own activities, providing a source of financing for the reporting entity).

> *Many SPEs are created to conduct activities that are part of the reporting entity's ongoing activities.*

Generally, the more a reporting entity is exposed to the variability of returns from its involvement with an entity, the more power the reporting entity likely has to direct the activities of that entity which cause the returns to vary. A reporting entity likely has the power to direct the activities of a structured entity if it is exposed to a variability of returns that is potentially significant to the structured entity, and if the reporting entity's exposure is more than that of any other party.

> *The more risks taken on by the sponsor, the greater the returns received by the sponsor.*

Control of an entity that has a limited range of activities, such as an entity that manages an asset securitization, is determined on the basis of how that limited range of activities is directed and how the returns it receives from its involvement with the entity are shared. A reporting entity identifies what activities cause the returns to vary and assesses whether it has the power to direct those activities. A reporting entity's ability to act when circumstances arise constitutes power if that ability relates to the activities that cause the reporting entity's returns to vary. A reporting entity does not have to exercise its power in order to have power to direct the activities of a structured entity.

For example, if the only assets of an entity are receivables, then managing any defaulting receivables is the only activity that causes the returns to vary and, thus, affects the returns of the structured entity's participants. In this example, the party with the power to direct how defaulting receivables are managed and can affect its returns from its involvement through this power, controls that entity.

> *Control of an SPE is usually based on who directs the key activities of the SPE.*

A reporting entity can control a structured entity by means of related arrangements. For example, a reporting entity could establish a structured entity whose founding documents restrict its activities to purchasing fixed-rate receivables of the reporting entity for cash, collecting payments from those receivables, and passing those payments to the investors in the structured entity. Receivables that are overdue by more than a specified period are sold back to the reporting entity.

A reporting entity can have the power to direct the activities of a structured entity if it can change the restrictions or predetermined strategic operating and financing policies by which the structured entity operates. For example, a reporting entity can have the power to direct the activities of a structured entity by having the right to dissolve the entity or to change (or veto any changes to) the entity's charter or by-laws. Or it can have the right to dissolve an entity by holding liquidation, redemption, or other rights.

Since the primary beneficiary controls the resources of the SPE and will obtain the future returns from these resources, these resources meet the definition of an asset and should be included on the consolidated balance sheet of the primary beneficiary. Similarly, since the primary beneficiary usually bears the risk of absorbing the bulk of any expected loss of the SPE, it is effectively assuming responsibility for the liabilities of the SPE. Accordingly, these liabilities should be included on the consolidated balance sheet of the primary beneficiary. The fact that the primary beneficiary may own no voting shares whatsoever becomes inconsequential because such shares do not effectively allow the equity investors to exercise control. Thus, in assessing control, a careful examination of the SPE's governing documents and the contractual arrangements among the parties involved is necessary, to determine who bears the majority of the risks and has the greatest participation in the potential upside in the value of the net assets of the SPE. The following scenario provides an example of a structured entity and its primary beneficiary.

> *The definitions of assets and liabilities can be used to support the inclusion of the SPE's assets and liabilities on the consolidated balance sheet.*

**EXAMPLE 1** Fleur Co. is a Quebec-based utility company. It is negotiating to acquire a power-generating plant from Rouyn Inc. for $105 million. If Fleur purchased the plant directly, it would finance the acquisition with a 5% bank loan for $100 million and $5 million in cash. Alternatively, it could set up a separate legal entity whose sole purpose would be to own the power-generating plant and lease it to Fleur. Because the separate entity would isolate the plant from Fleur's other risky assets and liabilities and provide specific collateral, the interest rate of the financing would be 4%, which would save the company $1 million per year. To obtain the lower interest rate, Fleur must guarantee the separate entity's debt and must also maintain certain predefined debt-to-equity ratios on its own balance sheet.

To take advantage of the lower interest rate, on January 1, Year 1, Fleur establishes Energy Co. for the sole purpose of owning and leasing the power plant to Fleur. An outside investor will provide $5 million in cash in exchange for 100% of the common shares of Energy Co. Fleur and Energy sign an agreement with the following terms:

- Energy's sole purpose is to purchase and own a power-generating plant. The purchase price will be financed by a $100 million loan and a $5 million equity investment.

- Fleur has veto power on all key operating, investing, and financing decisions.

- Fleur will lease the power plant for five years for annual payments of $4.5 million to cover the cost of the interest and provide a 10% return on the $5 million investment by the outside investor.

- At the end of five years (or any extension), Fleur can renew the lease for a further five years, purchase the power plant for $105 million, or pay $5 million to buy the common shares from the outside investor.

> *The equity investors will earn a 10% return and bear very little risk.*

It appears that Energy is a structured entity controlled by Fleur for the following three reasons:

1. Energy was established to provide power solely to Fleur, and the power is essential to Fleur's ongoing activities.

2. The outside investor will earn a 10% return and has very little risk. Fleur bears most of the risk of a change in utility rates and will receive any profit from the sale of power or the sale of the plant at the end of the lease term after the investor has received the guaranteed return.

3. The activities of Energy are restricted to owning and operating a power-generating plant. Fleur has the power to direct these activities through its veto power on all key operating, investing, and financing decisions.

Fleur is the primary beneficiary. It has control over Energy, receives most of the benefits, and is exposed to the major risks, even though it has invested no assets in Energy. Accordingly, Energy should be consolidated with Fleur.

> *The primary beneficiary bears most of the risks and receives the residual returns.*

An implied value of the SPE has to be determined in order to perform the initial consolidation.

**INITIAL MEASUREMENT ISSUES** The financial reporting principles for consolidating SPEs are basically the same as for consolidating a parent and its subsidiary. The total consideration given is identified, and this determines the total implied value of the SPE. When the primary beneficiary gets control of the net assets of an existing business by purchasing these net assets from the existing owners, the total consideration given is the sum of the following:

- Fair value of consideration paid by the primary beneficiary to the owners of the business (plus the fair value of any previously held interests)
- Fair value of the NCI of the SPE

When the primary beneficiary contributes its own assets to an existing business and gets control of the net assets of this business, these assets are measured at the carrying amount of these assets prior to the transfer. Since the primary beneficiary had control of these assets both before and after this transfer, there is no change in the benefits and risks associated with them. Accordingly, these assets are measured at carrying amount rather than fair value. Any profit recognized by the primary beneficiary will be eliminated when determining the carrying amount for the SPE. This treatment is consistent with the entries made in Chapters 6 and 7 to eliminate unrealized profits from intercompany transactions.

Once the total implied value is determined, this value is allocated first to the identifiable assets received and the liabilities assumed in this business combination. In general, the identifiable assets and liabilities are measured at fair value. However, the assets contributed by the primary beneficiary are measured at carrying amount. In addition, IFRS 3 identifies some instances where the SPE's assets and liabilities are not reported at fair value at the date of acquisition.

If the implied value of consideration given is greater than the value attributed to the identifiable net assets, the difference is reported as goodwill when the SPE is a business or as a loss on purchase when the SPE is not a business. The definition of a business was discussed in Chapter 3. If the implied value of consideration given is less than the value attributed to the identifiable net assets received, then there is negative goodwill. All fair values used for NCI and assets and liabilities of the structured entity must be carefully reviewed to ensure that they are accurate. Once the values are confirmed, the excess of the value attributed to the net assets received over the implied value of the consideration given is reported as a gain on purchase if the SPE is a business. If the SPE is not a business, then the total consideration given is allocated to the identifiable assets on a proportionate basis such that there is no negative goodwill.

> *With a few exceptions, the initial consolidation records the assets and liabilities of a SPE at fair values.*
>
> *The amounts of the implied value and the consideration received are compared to determine the amount of any goodwill or negative goodwill.*

The following example will illustrate the consolidation process for a SPE.

**EXAMPLE 2** XYZ Co. contributes a patent to VAR Inc. on January 1, Year 3. VAR is a business and is deemed to be a SPE. XYZ is the primary beneficiary. The patent had a carrying amount of $5 million on XYZ's separate-entity balance sheet and a fair value of $15 million. VAR owned property, plant, and equipment with a carrying amount of $60 million and a fair value of $80 million. The balance sheet of VAR at the date of acquisition after XYZ's investment is as follows (in millions):

|  | Carrying Amount | Fair Value |
|---|---|---|
| Patent | $ 5 | $15 |
| Property, plant, and equipment | 60 | 80 |
| Total assets | $65 | |
| Liabilities | 40 | 40 |
| Owners' equity: | | |
| XYZ | 5 | 15 |
| NCI | 20 | ?? |
| Total liabilities and equity | $65 | |

The allocations to be used in the consolidation of XYZ and VAR depend on the value assigned to NCI. We will demonstrate these valuation principles using the following fair values for NCI:

| Situation | Fair Value of NCI |
|---|---|
| A | $40 |
| B | 37 |
| C | 44 |

---

*In this example, the fair value of NCI is varied for illustrative purposes.*

---

|  | A | B | C |
|---|---|---|---|
| Implied value of consideration given: | | | |
| Carrying amount of amount contributed by XYZ | 5 | 5 | 5 |
| Fair value of NCI in VAR | 40 | 37 | 44 |
| Total implied value | 45 | 42 | 49 |
| Value of VAR's identifiable net assets received: | | | |
| Carrying amount of patents contributed by XYZ | 5 | 5 | 5 |
| Fair value of VAR's own assets | 80 | 80 | 80 |
| Less: Fair value of VAR's liabilities | (40) | (40) | (40) |
| Total value allocated to net assets received | 45 | 45 | 45 |
| Difference between consideration given and received | 0 | (3) | 4 |
| Assigned on consolidation to: | | | |
| Goodwill | | | 4 |
| Gain on purchase | | (3) | |
| Balance to assign | 0 | 0 | 0 |

---

*A gain on purchase is reported if the implied value of consideration given is less than the fair value of identifiable net assets.*

---

Note that the fair value assigned to the NCI is used to determine the total value of consideration given for VAR Inc. as a whole. This amount becomes the equivalent of the acquisition cost. In situation A, the total consideration given equals the sum of the values attributed to VAR's identifiable assets and liabilities. In situation B, the consideration given is less than the sum of VAR's identifiable net assets, resulting in a "negative goodwill" situation, which is accounted for as prescribed in IFRS 3. In situation C, the consideration given is greater than the sum of the values attributed to VAR's identifiable net assets and the difference is reflected as goodwill. The following journal entries summarize the investment elimination entry to be used by XYZ when it is consolidating VAR under the three different scenarios:

|  | A | B | C |
|---|---|---|---|
| Goodwill |  |  | 4 |
| Patent | 5 | 5 | 5 |
| Property, plant, and equipment | 80 | 80 | 80 |
| Liabilities | (40) | (40) | (40) |
| NCI | (40) | (37) | (44) |
| Gain on purchase |  | (3) |  |
| Investment in VAR | (5) | (5) | (5) |

> *If VAR meets the definition of a business, positive goodwill can be reported on the consolidated balance sheet.*

The credit to owners' equity of $5 million will be eliminated against the debit balance for the investment in VAR on XYZ's books when preparing the consolidated balance sheet.

**CONSOLIDATION ISSUES SUBSEQUENT TO INITIAL MEASUREMENT**   After the initial measurement, consolidations of SPEs with their primary beneficiary should follow the same process as if the entity were consolidated based on voting interests. The implied acquisition differential must be amortized. All intercompany transactions must be eliminated. The income of the SPE must be allocated among the parties involved (i.e., equity holders and the primary beneficiary). For a SPE, contractual arrangements, as opposed to ownership percentages, typically specify the distribution of its income.

> *In subsequent years, the normal consolidation procedures are followed.*

**DISCLOSURE REQUIREMENTS**   IFRS 12 requires an entity to disclose information that enables users of its consolidated financial statements to understand the nature of, and changes in, the risks associated with its interests in consolidated structured entities. In particular, an entity shall disclose the terms of any contractual arrangements that could require the parent or its subsidiaries to provide financial support to a consolidated structured entity, including events or circumstances that could expose the reporting entity to a loss.

> *The primary beneficiary must disclose its basis of control and the nature and extent of risks resulting from its involvement with the SPE.*

Horizon North Logistics Inc. provides camp and catering services and ground matting services to oil and gas exploration and production companies, oilfield service companies and mining companies working on oil sands, mineral exploration and development, and conventional oil and gas projects primarily in western Canada. Horizon consolidates a number of SPEs, which it controls. Relevant excerpts from Horizon North Logistics Inc.'s 2014 financial statements are presented in Exhibit 9.2.[3]

**EXHIBIT 9.2**

# Extracts from Horizon North Logistics Inc.'s 2014 Financial Statements

3.  Significant Accounting Policies
    (a) Basis of consolidation
        (ii) Special purpose entities
        The Corporation has established a number of special purpose entities ("SPE") for operating purposes. An SPE is consolidated when, based on an evaluation of the substance of its relationship with the Corporation and the SPE's risks and rewards, the Corporation concludes that it controls the SPE. SPE's controlled by the Corporation were established under terms that impose strict limitations on the decision-making powers of the SPE's management and that result in the Corporation receiving the majority of the benefits related to the SPE's operations and net assets, being exposed to the majority of risks incident to the SPE's activities, and retaining the majority of the residual or ownership risks related to the SPEs or their assets.

27. Significant Subsidiaries
    (a) Special purpose entities
        The Corporation has a 49% interest in the ownership and voting rights of Kitikmeot, Acho, and Secwepemc and maintains two out of four board of director seats in these special purpose entities ("SPE"). These SPE's are consolidated when, based on an evaluation of the substance of its relationship with the Corporation and the SPE's risks and rewards, the Corporation concludes that it controls the SPE. The SPE's do not generate profit but rather have limited assets and the only non-flow through expenses are management fees paid to the partners. An aboriginal billing vehicle or partnership is required to achieve aboriginal participation and secure projects in specific regions of Canada. The Corporations control is established under terms that impose strict limitations on the decision-making powers of the SPE's management. The control results in the Corporation receiving the majority of the benefits related to the SPE's operations and net assets, being exposed to the majority of risks incident to the SPE's activities, and retaining the majority of the residual or ownership risks related to the SPEs or their assets.

        The summarized aggregate financial information of the special purpose entities is provided below.

| (000s) | Total Assets | Total Liabilities | Revenue | Profit or (Loss) |
|---|---|---|---|---|
| Kitikmeot Caterers Ltd | $1,590 | $1,590 | $ 2,178 | $— |
| Acho Horizon North Camp Services Limited Partnership | 2,594 | 2,594 | 17,890 | — |
| Secwepemc Camps & Catering Limited Partnership | 2,481 | 2,481 | 12,529 | — |
| December 31, 2014 | $6,665 | $6,665 | $32,597 | $— |

Source: HORIZON NORTH Logistics Inc., Consolidated Financial Statements of Horizon North Logistics Inc. For the years ended December 31, 2014 and 2013. Pages 2, 31. Reproduced with permission from Horizon North Logistics Inc.

*Horizon controls a number of SPEs even though it does not own the majority of the voting shares of these SPEs.*

Some examples of SPEs in Canada are described below.

1.  Air Canada has aircraft and engine leasing transactions with a number of structured entities. As at December 31, 2014, Air Canada controlled leasing entities covering 22 aircraft.[4]

*Air Canada uses SPEs for leasing aircraft and engines.*

2.  Empire Company Limited, which owns 100% of Sobeys, consolidates certain enterprises considered structured entities ("SEs"), where control is achieved on a basis other than through ownership of a majority of voting rights.[5]

*Empire consolidates structured entities, even though it does not own a majority interest in these entities.*

## LO2 JOINT ARRANGEMENTS

A joint arrangement is a contractual arrangement whereby two or more parties undertake an activity together and jointly control that activity. Joint arrangements are established for a variety of purposes (e.g., as a way for parties to share costs and risks, or as a way to provide the parties with access to new technology or new markets) and can be established using different structures and legal forms. IFRS 11 *Joint Arrangements* requires that parties to a joint arrangement assess their rights and obligations to determine the type of joint arrangement in which they are involved. A common example of a joint arrangement is where one party provides the technical expertise, and the other party provides marketing and/or financial expertise. Joint arrangements are often formed for expensive and risky projects. They are fairly common in the oil-and-gas exploration sector and in large real estate developments. Also, a Canadian company will often form a joint arrangement with a foreign company or the government of a foreign country as a means of expanding into international markets. For example, Bombardier produces trains for China by operating under a joint agreement with a Chinese car manufacturer.

> *In a joint arrangement, participants contribute resources to carry out a specific undertaking.*

Joint arrangements are classified into two types: joint operations and joint ventures. The type of joint arrangement an entity is a party to depends on the rights and obligations that arise from the arrangement. An entity assesses its rights and obligations by considering the structure and legal form of the arrangement, the contractual terms agreed to by the parties to the arrangement, and, when relevant, other facts and circumstances. A joint arrangement that is structured without a separate vehicle is a joint operation. A joint arrangement in which the assets and liabilities relating to the arrangement are held in a separate vehicle can be either a joint venture or a joint operation.

A joint operation is a joint arrangement whereby the parties (i.e., joint operators) that have joint control of the arrangement have rights to the assets and obligations for the liabilities relating to the arrangement. Each operator contributes the use of assets or resources to the activity. An example would be a case in which one operator manufactures part of a product, a second operator completes the manufacturing process, and a third operator handles the marketing of the product with each operator using its own assets to perform its work. Revenue and expenses are shared in accordance with the joint operations agreement. Some joint operations involve the establishment of a corporation, partnership, or other entity, or a financial structure that is separate from the operators themselves. However, the agreement amongst the operators would indicate that each operator retains rights to certain or all assets with the separate vehicle and has responsibility for a portion of the liabilities of the separate vehicle. An example of this type of arrangement is setting up a separate vehicle to operate an oil pipeline. The operators may contribute assets to a separate legal entity for the construction of the pipeline. Once the pipeline is completed, it is jointly owned and used by the operators, who share the costs in accordance with an agreement.

> *In many joint operations, the venturers contribute the use of assets but retain title to the assets.*

A joint venture is an arrangement whereby the parties (i.e., joint venturers) that have joint control of the arrangement have rights to the net assets of the arrangement. An entity is a party to a joint venture when the separate vehicle has the rights to the assets and responsibility for the liabilities. The venturers do not have any specific rights to the assets or responsibility for the liabilities. They have rights only to a share of the outcome generated by the separate entity—that is, its share of the profits of the entity or its share of the excess of assets over liabilities at the time of winding up the entity.

> *In joint ventures, the venturers contribute assets to a separate legal entity, which has title to the assets.*

It would be very unusual for a joint operation to be established through an incorporated company because in an incorporated company the owners typically do not have any responsibility for the liabilities of the company. However, if the terms of the joint venture agreement require the owners to guarantee some or a portion of the liabilities of the company, the joint arrangement could be considered to be a joint operation.

It is possible for a joint operation to be established through a partnership because in a partnership the partners typically do have responsibility for the liabilities of the partnership.

The accounting principles involved with reporting a joint arrangement are contained in IFRS 11. It deals with the financial reporting of an interest in a joint arrangement. Appendix A in IFRS 11 presents the following definitions relevant to our discussions:

> **Joint control** is the contractually agreed sharing of control of an arrangement, which exists only when decisions about the relevant activities require the unanimous consent of the parties sharing control.
>
> **Joint operator** is a party to a joint operation that has joint control of that joint operation.
>
> **Joint venturer** is a party to a joint venture that has joint control of that joint venture.

A distinctive feature of these descriptions is the concept of *joint control,* which must be present for a joint arrangement to exist. Joint control is established by an agreement between the parties (usually in writing) whereby no one party can unilaterally control the joint arrangement regardless of the number of assets it contributes. For example, a single entity (Company L) could own more than 50% of the voting shares of Company M. This would normally indicate that Company M is a subsidiary; however, if there was an agreement establishing joint control, Company M would be a joint arrangement and not a subsidiary, and Company L would be a joint operator or joint venturer and not a parent.

> *Joint control is the key feature in a joint arrangement. This means that no one venturer can unilaterally control the venture regardless of the size of its equity contribution.*

We will now illustrate the accounting for both types of joint arrangements.

## Accounting for Joint Operations

According to IFRS 11.20, a joint operator must recognize, in relation to its interest in a joint operation,

    (a) its assets, including its share of any assets held jointly;

    (b) its liabilities, including its share of any liabilities incurred jointly;

    (c) its revenue from the sale of its share of the output arising from the joint operation;

    (d) its share of the revenue from the sale of the output by the joint operation; and

    (e) its expenses, including its share of any expenses incurred jointly.

**EXAMPLE 3**  APP Inc., BIB Ltd., and COT Inc. sign an agreement to produce fridges for sale to wholesalers. APP will produce the motors and condensers for use in the fridges. BIB will receive the motors and condensers from APP, purchase all other parts, and assemble the fridges. COT will market, sell, and distribute the fridges to wholesalers. The three companies must agree to all major operating and financing decisions. The proceeds from sale of the fridges will be distributed 25% to APP, 45% to BIB, and 30% to COT.

APP will account for the assets, liabilities, and expenses involved with producing the motors and condensers for the joint operations in the same manner as it would if it were producing these items for its own operations. The cost of the motors and condensers would be included in inventory. When the inventory is shipped to BIB, it is similar to inventory on consignment. No revenue is recognized until the inventory is eventually sold by COT. At that time, APP would recognize its 25% share of the sales revenue related to the sale of the fridges. In this example, each of the three companies used their own assets to fulfill their contribution to the joint arrangement. They shared in the revenues only from the sale of the fridges.

> *APP reports the assets contributed to the joint operations on its own books until the final product is sold to the end customer.*

When the joint operators jointly own certain assets, the accounting becomes a bit more complicated. In addition to accounting for their own assets and liabilities used in the joint operation, they would have to account for their share of the costs and expenses involved with the jointly owned assets. This is a form of proportionate consolidation but on a very limited basis.

**EXAMPLE 4**  DOC Inc., EGG Ltd., and FRY Inc. sign an agreement to collectively purchase an oil pipeline and to hire a company to manage and operate the pipeline on their behalf. The costs involved in running the pipeline and the revenue earned from the pipeline are shared by the three parties based on their ownership percentage. All major operating and financing decisions related to the pipeline must be agreed to by the three companies. The cost of purchasing the pipeline was $10,000,000. The pipeline has an estimated 20-year useful life with no residual value. The management fee for operating the pipeline for Year 1 was $2,000,000. Revenue earned from the pipeline in Year 1 was $3,300,000. DOC invested $3,000,000 for a 30% interest.

DOC would prepare the following entries for Year 1 to capture its share of the activities related to the pipeline:

| | | |
|---|---|---|
| Pipeline (30% × 10,000,000) | 3,000,000 | |
|     Cash | | 3,000,000 |
| Pipeline operating expenses (30% × 2,000,000) | 600,000 | |
|     Cash | | 600,000 |
| Cash (30% × 3,300,000) | 990,000 | |
|     Revenue from pipeline | | 990,000 |
| Amortization expense—pipeline (3,000,000/20 years) | 150,000 | |
|     Accumulated amortization—pipeline | | 150,000 |

> *DOC reports its proportionate share of the assets, liabilities, revenues, and expenses of the joint operation.*

**EXAMPLE 5**  Instead of contributing cash for a 30% interest in the pipeline, DOC contributed steel pipes to be used by the company constructing the pipeline. DOC had manufactured the pipes at a cost of $2,200,000. All parties to the contract agreed that the fair value of these pipes was $3,000,000 and the fair value of the pipeline once it was completed was $10,000,000. All other facts are the same as in Example 4.

IFRS 11.B34 and B35 indicate the following:

When an entity enters into a transaction with a joint operation in which it is a joint operator, such as a sale or contribution of assets, it is conducting the transaction with the other parties to the joint operation and, as such, the joint operator shall recognize gains and losses resulting from such a transaction only to the extent of the other parties' interests in the joint operation.

When such transactions provide evidence of a reduction in the net realizable value of the assets to be sold or contributed to the joint operation, or of an impairment loss of those assets, those losses shall be recognized fully by the joint operator.

> *A portion of the gain can be recognized on the contribution of assets to a joint operation.*

In our illustration, the other venturers have a 70% interest in the joint operation. DOC should recognize a gain of $560,000 (70% × [$3,000,000 − $2,200,000]).

The following journal entries would be recorded:

| | | |
|---|---|---|
| Pipeline | 3,000,000 | |
|   Steel pipes | | 2,200,000 |
|   Gain on steel pipes (70% of gain) | | 560,000 |
|   Unrealized gain—contra account (30% of gain) | | 240,000 |
| Amortization expense (3,000,000/20) | 150,000 | |
|   Accumulated amortization | | 150,000 |
| Unrealized gain—contra account (240,000/20) | 12,000 | |
|   Amortization expense | | 12,000 |

> *A gain can be recognized when the significant risks and rewards have been transferred.*

The unrealized gain is a contra account to the pipeline account; it should not be reported as a deferred gain on the liability side of the balance sheet. When DOC prepares a balance sheet, the unrealized gain will be offset against the pipeline such that the pipeline's net cost is $2,760,000 ($3,000,000 − $240,000). As the net cost of the pipeline is being amortized, the unrealized gain account is also being amortized. In effect, the unrealized gain is being brought into income over the life of the pipeline. As the pipeline is being used to generate revenue on transactions with outsiders, the venturer's own share of the unrealized gain is being recognized in income. This is similar to what happened in Chapter 7, when the unrealized profits from an intercompany sale of a depreciable asset were realized over the life of the depreciable asset.

> *The joint operator's own interest in the gain is recognized over the life of the asset.*

When a separate entity is established or purchased and this entity is jointly controlled by two or more parties, then, this separate entity is a joint arrangement. It would be classified as a joint operation if the parties have rights to use the assets of this separate entity and have some responsibility for paying the obligations of this separate entity.

The joint operator must use a form of proportionate consolidation to account for its interest in a joint operation carried out through a separate entity. Proportionate consolidation[6] is a method of accounting whereby a joint operator's share of each of the assets, liabilities, income, and expenses of a jointly controlled entity is combined line by line with similar items in the operator's own financial statements or reported as separate line items in the operator's financial statements. Under IFRS 11, the operator's share of the joint operation is recognized in the operator's separate entity financial statements; consolidated financial statements are not prepared. Furthermore, the operator recognizes its share of assets, liabilities, income, and expenses for which it has rights and responsibilities. It may not have rights and responsibilities for all assets, liabilities, income and expenses of the joint operation. In addition, the operator needs to make adjustments for its share of the following items, which are illustrated below:

- Acquisition differentials
- Unrealized profits from intercompany transactions
- Contributions to the joint operation

> *A form of proportionate consolidation is required for reporting joint operations conducted through a separate vehicle.*

**ACQUISITION DIFFERENTIALS** The formation of a joint operation by its joint operators cannot result in acquisition differentials. However, if an operator purchased an interest in an existing entity, it could pay an amount different from its interest in the carrying amount of the joint operation's net assets. The joint operator would record its share of the fair value of the assets including goodwill and liabilities directly on its separate entity financial statements.

**INTERCOMPANY TRANSACTIONS** You will recall from our discussions in past chapters that intercompany profits in assets are fully eliminated from the consolidated statements of a parent and its subsidiaries. If the subsidiary was the selling company, 100% of the profit, net of income tax, is eliminated and allocated to both the NCI and the controlling interest. If the parent was the selling company, the entire net-of-tax profit is eliminated and allocated to the shareholders of the parent.

For intercompany transactions between an operator and the joint operation, only the operator's share of the unrealized profit is eliminated. The other operators' share of the profit from the intercompany transaction is considered realized if the other operators are not related to each other. Since none of the operators can individually control the entity, any transaction carried out by the joint operation should be viewed as an arm's-length transaction to the extent of the other operators' interest in the joint venture. The operator's own interest in the profit from the intercompany transaction is not realized because the operator cannot make a profit by selling to or buying from itself.

> *For a joint operation, the operator's share of any intercompany asset profits is eliminated regardless of whether the sale was upstream or downstream.*

The same treatment is prescribed for the sale of assets at a loss except in situations where the transaction provides evidence of a reduction in the net realizable value of the asset, in which case the full amount of the loss is immediately recognized.

Example 6 below illustrates the reporting by a joint operator of an interest in a joint operation operated through a separate vehicle.

**EXAMPLE 6** Explor is a Calgary-based oil exploration partnership, jointly owned by A Company and B Company. Under the partnership agreement, both A Company and B Company have joint control over Explor and have rights to the assets, responsibility for the liabilities and share in the revenues and expenses of Explor according to their ownership percentages, which is 45% for A Company and 55% for B Company. Explor maintains separate accounting records for its operations and provides financial statements prepared in accordance with IFRS for use by the partners in preparing their IFRS-based separate entity financial statements, which will be referred to below as proportionately adjusted financial statements.

As a partnership, Explor does not pay income tax. Instead, the income earned by Explor is flowed through to the owners of Explor for tax purposes. In effect, the partners must report their share of the income earned by the partnership on their own tax returns and pay the related income tax. Therefore, when accruing the before tax income earned by the partnership, the partners should also accrue the income tax to be paid on their share of the partnership income.

A Company, an original founder of Explor, uses the equity method to account for its investment for internal purposes but has made no entries to its investment account for Year 4. At year end, it prepares working papers to incorporate the yearly activity for Explor in its proportionately adjusted financial statements for external users and updates the investment account for its internal records.

The following are the preliminary financial statements of the two entities on December 31, Year 4 based on internal record keeping:

### PRELIMINARY INCOME STATEMENTS
#### For Year 4

|  | A Company | Explor |
|---|---|---|
| Sales | $900,000 | $370,000 |
| Cost of sales | 500,000 | 180,000 |
| Miscellaneous expenses | 100,000 | 40,000 |
|  | 600,000 | 220,000 |
| Income before taxes | 300,000 | 150,000 |
| Income tax expense | 120,000 | 0,000 |
| Net income | $180,000 | $150,000 |

### PRELIMINARY BALANCE SHEETS
#### At December 31, Year 4

|  | A Company | Explor |
|---|---|---|
| Miscellaneous assets | $654,500 | $337,000 |
| Inventory | 110,000 | 90,000 |
| Investment in Explor | 85,500 | — |
|  | $850,000 | $427,000 |
| Liabilities | $130,000 | $ 87,000 |
| Contributed capital | 300,000 | 100,000 |
| Accumulated earnings | 420,000 | 240,000 |
|  | $850,000 | $427,000 |

*These statements are the preliminary financial statements of a joint operator and a joint operation.*

During Year 4, neither company declared any dividends. During Year 4, A Company sold merchandise totalling $110,000 to Explor and recorded a gross profit of 30% on these sales. On December 31, Year 4, the inventory of Explor contained items purchased from A Company for $22,000, and Explor had a payable of $5,000 to A Company on this date. A Company will use a form of proportionate consolidation to incorporate Explor's activities in its proportionately adjusted financial statements. Following are the calculations of the amounts that are used in the elimination of intercompany transactions in the preparation of the proportionately adjusted financial statements:

| | | |
|---|---:|---|
| Intercompany sales and purchases: | | |
| Total for the year | $110,000 | |
| A Company's contractual interest | 45% | |
| Amount eliminated | $ 49,500 | (a) |
| Intercompany receivables and payables: | | |
| Total at end of year | $ 5,000 | |
| A Company's contractual interest | 45% | |
| Amount eliminated | $ 2,250 | (b) |
| Intercompany profits in inventory: | | |
| Total at end of year (22,000 × 30%) | $ 6,600 | |
| Profit considered realized—55% | 3,630 | |
| Unrealized—45% | 2,970 | (c) |
| Tax on profit (40%) | 1,188 | (d) |
| After-tax unrealized profit | $ 1,782 | |

> *The other operator's share of the intercompany transactions is considered realized for the proportionately adjusted financial statements.*

The following explanations will clarify the calculations made:

1. Because the proportionate consolidation method will add only 45% of Explor's financial statement items, we eliminate only 45% of the intercompany revenues, expenses, receivables, and payables. If we eliminated 100% of these items, we would be eliminating more than we are adding in the summation process.

> *Only the operator's share of intercompany transactions is eliminated when the combined statements are prepared.*

2. The inventory of Explor contains an intercompany profit of $6,600 recorded by A Company. Because there is joint control, A Company has realized $3,630 of this profit by selling to the other unaffiliated operators, and therefore only A Company's 45% interest is considered unrealized.

> *Unrealized profit is always eliminated from the selling company's income.*

3. Income tax allocation is required when timing differences occur. Using A Company income tax rate of 40%, the tax effect of the inventory profit elimination is $1,188.

The combined net income for Year 4 is $218,718 calculated as follows:

| | | |
|---|---:|---:|
| Income of A Company | | $180,000 |
| Less unrealized in closing inventory **(d)** | | 1,782 |
| Adjusted net income | | 178,218 |
| Income of Explor | $150,000 | |
| A's ownership interest | 45% | |
| A's share of Explor's before tax income | 67,500 | |
| Less accrued income tax on Explor's share of partnership income (40%) | (27,000) | **(e)** |
| A's share of Explor's income, net of taxes | | 40,500 |
| Combined net income | | $218,718 |

The preparation of the Year 4 combined statements is illustrated next using the direct approach.

**A COMPANY**
**PROPORTIONATELY ADJUSTED INCOME STATEMENT**
For the year ended December 31, Year 4

| | |
|---|---:|
| Sales (900,000 + [45% × 370,000] − **[a] 49,500**) | $1,017,000 |
| Cost of sales (500,000 + [45% × 180,000] − **[a] 49, 500 + [c] 2,970**) | 534,470 |
| Miscellaneous expenses (100,000 + [45% × 40,000]) | 118,000 |
| | 652,470 |
| Income before taxes | 364,530 |
| Income taxes (120,000 + 45% × 0 − **[d] 1,188 + [e] 27,000**) | 145,812 |
| Net income | $ 218,718 |

**A COMPANY**
**PROPORTIONATELY ADJUSTED BALANCE SHEET**
At December 31, Year 4

| | | |
|---|---:|---:|
| Miscellaneous assets (654,500 + [45% × 337,000] − **[b] 2,250**) | | $803,900 |
| Inventory (110,000 + [45% × 90,000] − **[c] 2,970**) | | 147,530 |
| Deferred income taxes **(d)** | | 1,188 |
| Total assets | | $952,618 |
| Liabilities (130,000 + [45% × 87,000] − **[b] 2,250 + [e] 27,000**) | | $193,900 |
| Shareholders' equity: | | |
| Common shares | 300,000 | |
| Retained earnings | 458,718 | 758,718 |
| Total liabilities and shareholders' equity | | $952,618 |

> *Intercompany revenues and expenses, receivables and payables, and unrealized profits in assets are eliminated in the preparation of the proportionately adjusted financial statements.*

The amounts used in the preparation of these statements are explained as follows:

1. With the exception of shareholders' equity and deferred income tax, the first two amounts used come from the preliminary financial statements and consist of 100% of A Company plus 45% of Explor.

> *Under the adjustment process, only the operator's contractual share of the joint operation's financial statement items is used.*

2. The adjustments labelled **(a)** through **(d)** eliminate the intercompany revenues and expenses, receivables and payables, unrealized inventory profit, and income tax on the unrealized inventory profit. Adjustment **(e)** accrues the income tax expense on A Company's share of Explor's income.

3. Shareholders' equity consists of the common shares of A Company plus proportionately adjusted retained earnings since date of acquisition.

After the IFRS-based financial statements have been prepared, A Company would make the following journal entries to incorporate the above results in the Investment in Explor account for its internal records:

| | | |
|---|---|---|
| Investment in Explor (45% × 150,000) | 67,500 | |
|     Equity method income (45% × 150,000) | | 67,500 |
| To recognize contractual interest in income from joint operation | | |
| Income tax expense (40% × 67,500) | 27,000 | |
|     Income tax payable | | 27,000 |
| To accrue income tax on share of income from joint operation | | |
| Equity method income | 1,782 | |
|     Investment in Explor | | 1,782 |
| To eliminate unrealized profit in ending inventory | | |

## Accounting for an Interest in a Joint Venture

Let's now assume that Explor is not a partnership but is an incorporated company, jointly owned by A Company and B Company. When the parties established the joint arrangement, they only had rights to the net assets of the separate vehicle. Therefore, the separate vehicle would be called a joint venture.

Under IFRS 11, the venturer must use the equity method to report its investment in a joint venture. The equity method is described in IAS 28. Under this method, the venturer recognizes its share of the income earned by the joint venture through one line on the income statement, income from joint venture, and through one line on the balance sheet, investment account.

As a corporation, Explor would pay income tax on its own income and would report income tax expense on its own income statement. Accordingly, the following additional entry would have been made by Explor in Year 4:

| | | |
|---|---|---|
| Income tax expense | 60,000 | |
|     Cash | | 60,000 |

We will now the same data as in the previous situation and add the journal entry above. Assuming that A Company has not yet made any entries pertaining to its investment in Explor for Year 4, the preliminary financial statements of the two entities on December 31, Year 4 would appear as follows:

### PRELIMINARY INCOME STATEMENTS
#### Year 4

| | A Company | Explor |
|---|---|---|
| Sales | $900,000 | $370,000 |
| Cost of sales | 500,000 | 180,000 |
| Miscellaneous expenses | 100,000 | 40,000 |
| | 600,000 | 220,000 |
| Income before taxes | 300,000 | 150,000 |
| Income tax expense | 120,000 | **60,000** |
|     Net income | $180,000 | $ 90,000 |

### PRELIMINARY BALANCE SHEETS
#### At December 31, Year 4

| | A Company | Explor |
|---|---|---|
| Miscellaneous assets | $654,500 | **$277,000** |
| Inventory | 110,000 | 90,000 |
| Investment in Explor | 85,500 | — |
| | $850,000 | **$367,000** |
| Liabilities | $130,000 | $ 87,000 |
| Common shares | 300,000 | 100,000 |
| Retained earnings | 420,000 | **180,000** |
| | $850,000 | **$367,000** |

The changes from the previous set of statements are shown in bold.

> *These statements are the preliminary financial statements of a joint venturer and a joint venture.*

All of the previous calculations pertaining to intercompany profits and combined net income would apply in this situation. The only difference is the treatment of the $60,000 of income tax expense. In the previous example, the $60,000 for income tax was accrued and reported as income tax expense by A Company. In the current example where Explor is a corporation, the $60,000 for income tax was paid and reported as income tax expense by Explor.

The following entries would be made at the end of Year 4 by A Company to report its investment in Explor under the equity method:

| | | |
|---|---|---|
| Investment in Explor (45% × 90,000) | 40,500 | |
|     Equity method income (45% × 90,000) | | 40,500 |
| To recognize contractual interest in after-tax income from joint operation | | |
| Equity method income | 1,782 | |
|     Investment in Explor | | 1,782 |
| To eliminate unrealized profit in ending inventory | | |

These entries will increase Company A's net income to $218,718 as shown above. The equity method income will have a balance of $38,718 and will be reported as a separate line on A Company's income statement. Now, net income on A's separate entity income statement, which uses the equity method to report the joint venture, will be the same amount as net income on A's combined income statement when it used proportionately adjusted financial statements to report the joint operation.

> *The equity method is required for reporting joint ventures under IFRS 11.*

## Contributions to the Joint Venture

Suppose that on the date of formation of a joint venture, instead of contributing cash, a venturer contributes non-monetary assets and receives an interest in the joint venture and that the assets contributed have a fair value that is greater than their carrying amount in the records of the venturer. Would it be appropriate for the venturer to record a gain from investing these non-monetary assets in the joint venture? If so, how much, and when should it be recognized? The requirements set out in IAS 28 regarding this matter are as follows:[7]

1. The investment should be recorded at the fair value of the non-monetary assets transferred to the joint venture.

2. Only the gain represented by interests of the other nonrelated venturers should be recognized on the date of the contribution and only if the transaction has commercial substance as the term is described in IAS 16. A transaction has commercial substance if the amount, timing and uncertainty of future cash flows have changed as a result of the transaction. This principle was applied in Example 5 when the joint operator transferred steel to the joint operator. This transaction had commercial substance because DOC's prospects for future cash flows changed significantly when it went from owning steel to owning 30% of a pipeline.

3. If the transaction does not have commercial substance, then the entire gain is considered to be unrealized unless the venture receives assets in addition to an interest in the joint venture. If so, the assets received can be considered the proceeds from the partial sale of the assets to the other unrelated venturers and a gain can be recognized for the portion of the asset deemed to be sold. The unrealized gain shall be accounted for in the same manner as the venturer's share of the gain, which is described in the next paragraph.

4. The portion of the gain represented by the venturer's own interest should be unrealized until the asset has been sold to unrelated outsiders by the joint venture. Alternatively, the unrealized gain can be recognized over the life of the asset if the asset is being used to generate a positive gross profit for the joint venture. In effect, the product or service being sold by the joint venture to an outsider is allowing the venturer to recognize a portion of the unrealized gain. It is similar to selling a portion of the asset to outsiders. The unrealized gains are contra accounts to the investment in joint venture account. They will be offset against the investment account on the balance sheet.

> *The unrealized gain is recognized in income as the asset is used to generate a profit on transactions with outsiders.*

5. If a loss results from the recording of the investment, the portion of the loss represented by the interest of the other unrelated venturers is recognized immediately into income. When it is evident that the asset contributed to the joint venture is impaired, the entire loss is immediately recognized.

The following examples will illustrate these concepts.

**EXAMPLE 7** A Co. and B Inc. formed JV Ltd., a joint venture, on January 1, Year 1. A Co. invested equipment with a carrying amount of $200,000 and a fair value of $700,000 for a 40% interest in JV Ltd., while B Inc. contributed equipment, which was similar to the equipment contributed by A Co., with a total fair value of $1,050,000, for a 60% interest in JV Ltd. We will concern ourselves only with the recording by A Co. of its 40% interest in JV Ltd., and we will assume that the equipment has an estimated useful life of 10 years. On December 31, Year 1, JV Ltd. reported a net income of $204,000.

We will assume that the transaction does not have commercial substance in this situation because A Co. owned a similar portion of the same type of equipment both before and after the contribution to the joint venture. The gains are calculated as follows:

| | |
|---|---:|
| Fair value of equipment transferred to JV Ltd. | $700,000 |
| Carrying amount of equipment on A Co.'s books | 200,000 |
| Unrealized gain on transfer to JV Ltd. | $500,000 |

A Co.'s journal entry to record the initial investment on January 1, Year 1, is as follows:

| | | |
|---|---:|---:|
| Investment in JV Ltd. | 700,000 | |
| Equipment | | 200,000 |
| Unrealized gain—contra account | | 500,000 |

> *A Co.'s $500,000 gain from investing equipment is unrealized because the transaction does not meet the commercial substance test.*

Using the equity method of accounting, A Co. will record its 40% share of the yearly net incomes or losses reported by JV Ltd.; in addition, it will recognize the unrealized gains in income over the life of the equipment.

The December 31, Year 1, entries are as follows:

| | | |
|---|---:|---:|
| Investment in JV Ltd. | 81,600 | |
| Equity method income from JV Ltd. (40% × 204,000) | | 81,600 |
| Unrealized gain–contra account (500,000/10) | 50,000 | |
| Gain on transfer of equipment to JV Ltd. | | 50,000 |

This method of recognizing the gain from the initial investment will be repeated over the next nine years, unless JV Ltd. sells this equipment before that period expires. If it does, A Co. will immediately take the balance in the unrealized gains account into income.

**EXAMPLE 8**   The facts from this example are identical in all respects to those from Example 7, except that we assume that B Co. contributes technology (rather than equipment) with a fair value of $1,050,000. We will assume that the transaction does have commercial substance in this situation because A Co. owned equipment before its contribution to the joint venture but indirectly owned a portion of equipment and technology after the contribution. Of the $500,000 difference between the fair value and carrying amount of the equipment, the percentage ownership of the other venturers, 60%, can be recognized as a gain. A Co.'s 40% portion is an unrealized gain and is presented as a contra account to the investment account.

A Co.'s journal entry to record the initial investment on January 1, Year 1, is as follows:

| | | |
|---|---|---|
| Investment in JV Ltd. | 700,000 | |
| Equipment | | 200,000 |
| Gain on sale of equipment (60% × 500,000) | | 300,000 |
| Unrealized gain—contra account (40% × 500,000) | | 200,000 |

*A Co. recognizes a gain of $300,000, which is the portion of the gain deemed sold to outsiders.*

Using the equity method of accounting, A Co. will record its 40% share of the yearly net incomes or losses reported by JV Ltd.; in addition, it will recognize the unrealized gains in income over the life of the equipment.

The December 31, Year 1, entries are as follows:

| | | |
|---|---|---|
| Investment in JV Ltd. | 81,600 | |
| Equity method income from JV Ltd. (40% × 204,000) | | 81,600 |
| Unrealized gain—contra account (200,000/10) | 20,000 | |
| Gain on transfer of equipment to JV Ltd. | | 20,000 |

*A portion of the unrealized gain is taken into income each year.*

This method of recognizing the gain from the initial investment will be repeated over the next nine years, unless JV Ltd. sells this equipment before that period expires. If it does, A Co. will immediately take the balance in the unrealized gains account into income.

**EXAMPLE 9**   The facts from this example are identical in all respects to those from Example 7, except that we assume that A Co. receives a 40% interest in JV Ltd., plus $130,000 in cash in return for investing equipment with a fair value of $700,000.

The original gain on the transfer ($500,000) is the same as in Example 7. However, since A Co. received $130,000 in cash in addition to its 40% in the joint venture, it is considered to be the sale proceeds of the portion of the equipment deemed to have been sold. In other words, A Co. is considered to have sold a portion of the equipment to JV Ltd. and will immediately record a gain from selling, computed as follows:

| | |
|---|---|
| Sale proceeds | $130,000 |
| Carrying amount of equipment sold (130 ÷ 700 × 200,000) | 37,143 |
| Immediate gain from selling equipment to JV Ltd. | $ 92,857 |

*A gain is recognized for the portion (130/700) of the equipment deemed to be sold.*

A Co.'s January 1, Year 1, journal entry to record the investment of equipment and the receipt of cash would be as follows:

| | | |
|---|---:|---:|
| Cash | 130,000 | |
| Investment in JV Ltd. | 570,000 | |
|     Equipment | | 200,000 |
|     Gain on sale of equipment to JV Ltd. | | 92,857 |
|     Unrealized gain—contra account | | 407,143 |

The December 31, Year 1, entries are as follows:

| | | |
|---|---:|---:|
| Investment in JV Ltd. | 81,600 | |
|     Equity method income from JV Ltd. (40% × 204,000) | | 81,600 |
| Unrealized gain–contra account (407,143/10) | 40,714 | |
|     Gain on sale of equipment to JV Ltd. | | 40,714 |

Assuming a December 31 year-end, the $133,571 ($92,857 + $40,714) gain on transfer of equipment to JV Ltd. will appear in A Co.'s Year 1 income statement. The unamortized balance of the A's share of the unrealized gain of $366,429 ($407,143 − $40,714) will be offset against the investment account.

**INVESTOR IN JOINT ARRANGEMENT**  An investor in a joint arrangement is a party to a joint arrangement but does not have joint control over that joint arrangement. For example, a joint venture could have some owners who have joint control over the key decisions and other investors who are passive investors and do not participate in the key decisions for the joint venture. The investor receives a return on investment without being actively involved in the operating and financing decisions of the joint arrangement. The investor must account for the investment in accordance with IRFS 9 or by using the equity method if it has significant influence in the joint arrangement.

---

*We need to differentiate between venturers who have joint control and investors who do not have joint control.*

---

**DISCLOSURE REQUIREMENTS**  IFRS 12 requires an entity to disclose information that enables users of its financial statements to evaluate the following:

(a) The nature, extent, and financial effects of its interests in joint arrangements, including the nature and effects of its contractual relationship with the other investors with joint control of joint arrangements

(b) The nature of, and changes in, the risks associated with its interests in joint ventures. To meet these objectives, the more substantial items required to be disclosed are as follows:

- The nature of the entity's relationship with the joint arrangement and the proportion of ownership interest held.

- The venturer's interest in each of current assets, noncurrent assets, current liabilities, noncurrent liabilities, revenues, and profit or loss from joint ventures.

- The nature and extent of any significant restrictions on the ability of the joint ventures to transfer funds to the venture.

- Information about significant judgments and assumptions it has made

---

*An entity must disclose the nature and extent of its operations conducted through joint arrangements.*

---

Exhibit 9.3 is an extract from Torstar Corporation's 2014 consolidated financial statements. It provides an example of disclosure for joint arrangements. Torstar Corporation is a broadly based, progressive media company with a long history in daily and community newspapers, book publishing and digital businesses.[8]

**EXHIBIT 9.3**

## Extracts from Torstar's 2014 Financial Statements

2. Significant Accounting Policies

(e) Investments in Joint Ventures and Associated Businesses

A joint venture is a type of joint arrangement in which the parties that have joint control of the arrangement have rights to the net assets of the joint venture. Joint control is the contractually agreed sharing of control of an arrangement, which exists only when decisions about the relevant activities require unanimous consent of the parties sharing control.

An associate is an entity in which the Company has significant influence. Significant influence is the power to participate in the financial and operating policy decisions of the investee but does not represent control or joint control over those decisions.

The considerations made in determining joint control or significant influences are similar to those necessary to determine control over subsidiaries.

Investments in joint ventures and associates are accounted for using the equity method, whereby the investment is carried in the consolidated statement of financial position at cost plus post-acquisition changes in the Company's share of the net assets of the investment. Goodwill relating to the joint venture or associate is included in the carrying amount of the investment and is neither amortized nor individually tested for impairment. When the Company's share of losses of a joint venture or associate exceeds the Company's carrying value of the investment, the Company discontinues recognizing its share of further losses. Additional losses are recognized only to the extent that the Company has incurred legal or constructive obligations or made payments on behalf of the joint venture or associate.

The consolidated statement of income reflects the Company's share of the results of operations of the joint venture or associate. Where there has been a change recognized directly in the OCI of the joint venture or associate, the Company recognizes its share of any changes and discloses this, when applicable, in OCI.

When there has been a change recognized directly in the equity of the joint venture or associate, the Company recognizes, when applicable, its share of any changes in the statement of changes in equity. The financial statements of the joint venture or associate are prepared for the same reporting period as the Company except when the joint venture or associate does not have coterminous year-end and quarter-ends with the Company, in which case the most recent period-end available in a quarter is used. When necessary, adjustments are made to bring the accounting policies of the joint venture or associate in line with those of the Company.

After the initial application of the equity method, the Company determines at each reporting date whether there is any objective evidence that the investment in the joint venture or associate is impaired and consequently whether it is necessary to recognize an impairment loss with respect to the Company's investment. If this is the case, the Company calculates the amount of impairment as the difference between the recoverable amount of the investment and its carrying value and recognizes the impairment in the consolidated statement of income.

Upon loss of significant influence over an associate, the Company measures and recognizes any retained investment at its fair value. Upon loss of joint control over a joint venture, the Company considers whether it has significant influence, in which case the retained investment is accounted for as an associate using the equity method, otherwise the Company measures and recognizes any retained investment as a portfolio investment at its fair value. Any difference between the carrying amount of the investment and the fair of the retained investment or proceeds from disposal of the investment is recognized in profit or loss.

> *Torstar's accounting policies provide a nice summary of what has been discussed in this chapter pertaining to joint ventures.*

*(continued)*

**EXHIBIT 9.3** (continued)

7. Investments in Joint Ventures

The Company's joint ventures are primarily in the SMG Segment and include investments in Workopolis (50%) and Sing Tao Daily (approximately 50%). Effective April 1, 2014, pursuant to the Company entering into an agreement for the sale of Harlequin, the amounts related to the Book Publishing Segment joint venture operations were reclassified to Assets held for sale. The sale transaction closed on August 1, 2014 as indicated in Note 24.

The table below provides a continuity of Investments in joint ventures:

|  | Year Ended December 31, | |
| --- | ---: | ---: |
|  | 2014 | 2013 |
| Balance, beginning of year | $80,901 | $91,258 |
| Reclassified to Assets held for sale | (7,968) | |
|  | 72,933 | 91,258 |
| Loss from joint ventures | (9,152) | (3,733) |
| Distribution from joint ventures | (9,250) | (5,735) |
| Investment and other | | 87 |
| Net change related to Investments in joint ventures of discontinued operations | | (976) |
| Balance, end of year | $54,531 | $80,901 |

(i) Statement of Financial Position

|  | AS AT DECEMBER 31, 2014 | | AS AT DECEMBER 31, 2013 | |
| --- | ---: | ---: | ---: | ---: |
|  | SMG Segment | SMG Segment | Book Publishing Segment | Total Segments |
| Cash and cash equivalents | $ 8,331 | $ 6,825 | $ 4,606 | $11,431 |
| Other current assets | 8,153 | 12,811 | 4,475 | 17,286 |
| Total current assets | 16,484 | 19,636 | 9,081 | 28,717 |
| Property, plant, and equipment | 6,244 | 6,351 | 149 | 6,500 |
| Goodwill on joint ventures | 23,419 | 38,419 | 4,739 | 43,158 |
| Intangible assets | 18,950 | 19,478 | 277 | 19,755 |
| Other noncurrent assets | | | 74 | 74 |
| Total assets | $65,097 | $83,884 | $14,320 | $98,204 |
| Bank overdraft | | | $4 | $4 |
| Other current liabilities | $9,333 | $10,432 | 5,851 | 16,283 |
| Total current liabilities | 9,333 | 10,432 | 5,855 | 16,287 |
| Other noncurrent liabilities | 1,233 | 519 | 497 | 1,016 |
| Total equity | 54,531 | 72,933 | 7,968 | 80,901 |
| Total liabilities and equity | $65,097 | $83,884 | $14,320 | $98,204 |

> *Torstar disclosed the details of the financial position of its joint ventures. The equity of the joint ventures reconciles to the ending balance in the investment account under the equity method.*

(ii) Statement of Income and Comprehensive Income

|  | Year Ended December 31, | |
| --- | ---: | ---: |
|  | 2014 | 2013 |
| Operating revenue | $46,740 | $48,510 |
| Salaries and benefits | (18,627) | (20,056) |
| Other operating costs | (18,511) | (19,069) |
| Amortization and depreciation | (2,727) | (2,736) |
| Restructuring and other charges | (60) | (659) |
| Impairment of assets (note 12) | (15,000) | (9,000) |
| Operating loss | (8,185) | (3,010) |

**EXHIBIT 9.3** *(continued)*

|  | Year Ended December 31, | |
|---|---|---|
|  | *2014* | *2013* |
| Interest and financing costs | 2 | 2 |
| Foreign exchange | 24 | (8) |
| Other income | 207 | 197 |
|  | (7,952) | (2,819) |
| Income and other taxes | (1,200) | (914) |
| Net loss and comprehensive loss from continuing operations | ($9,152) | ($ 3,733) |

> *Torstar disclosed the details of the net loss from its joint ventures. The net income from the joint ventures reconciles to the equity method income.*

Source: TORSTAR CORPORATION, TORSTAR CORPORATION 2014 ANNUAL REPORT, Pages 54–55, 71–72. COPYRIGHT © 2014 TORSTAR CORPORATION. Reproduced with permission from TORSTAR CORPORATION.

See Self-Study Problem 1 for a comprehensive problem involving joint ventures. It includes most of the issues we have covered in this chapter pertaining to joint ventures.

# LO3 DEFERRED INCOME TAXES AND BUSINESS COMBINATIONS

Up to this point, we have ignored the income tax implications associated with business combinations. Corporate tax law in this area is quite complex and can be fully understood only by readers who have been exposed to the topic through in-depth tax courses. There is always the danger that essential accounting concepts associated with business combinations and consolidated financial statements could be overshadowed if an attempt is made to combine basic accounting issues with complex tax allocation procedures. Attentive readers will now have achieved a reasonable understanding of the broad accounting concepts behind consolidated statements. To complete our coverage of this financial reporting process, we now turn our attention to the additional effects that income tax allocation can have on the accounting for a business combination. But before we do this, we provide the following useful background material.

## Deferred Income Tax Concepts

IAS 12 *Income Taxes* uses the balance sheet (or liability) approach. This approach requires that the differences between the carrying amount of an asset or a liability in the balance sheet and its tax base be accounted for. These differences are called *temporary differences*. The tax base of an asset is the amount that will be deductible for tax purposes against any taxable economic benefits that will flow to an entity when it recovers the carrying amount of the asset. If those economic benefits will not be taxable, the tax base of the asset is equal to its carrying amount. The tax base of a liability is its carrying amount, less any amount that will be deductible for tax purposes in respect of that liability in future periods. In the case of revenue received in advance, the tax base of the resulting liability is its carrying amount, less any amount of the revenue that will not be taxable in future periods.

> *A temporary difference occurs when the carrying amount of an asset or a liability does not equal its tax base.*

Under IAS 12, there are two basic types of temporary differences: deductible and taxable. A *deductible temporary difference* is one that can be deducted in determining taxable income in the future when the asset or liability is recovered or settled for its carrying amount. These differences exist when (a) the carrying amount of an asset is less than its tax base, or (b) an amount related to a liability can be deducted for tax purposes. Accounting for these differences results in *deferred income tax assets*.

A *taxable temporary difference* is one that will result in future taxable amounts when the carrying amount of the asset or the liability is recovered or settled. Such differences, which result in *deferred income tax liabilities*, occur mainly when the carrying amount of an asset is greater than its tax base.

> *When the carrying amount of an asset is greater than its tax base, the result is a deferred tax liability.*

A few examples will illustrate some of these concepts. We assume a 40% tax rate in each case.

**EXAMPLE 10**   A company has an account payable of $3,000 on its balance sheet at the end of Year 1 for unpaid expenses that were deducted for tax purposes during Year 1. The carrying amount is $3,000. The tax base of the liability is as follows:

| | |
|---|---:|
| Carrying amount | $3,000 |
| Less: Amount deductible for tax in future periods | –0– |
| Tax base | $3,000 |

Because the carrying amount and the tax base are equal, a temporary difference does not exist.

**EXAMPLE 11**   At the end of Year 1, a company has an account receivable of $1,000 from sales made during the year. This receivable is expected to be collected through a series of instalments during Years 2 and 3. For tax purposes, the revenue is taxable in the year of collection. The carrying amount at the end of Year 1 is $1,000, while the tax base is zero. This creates a taxable temporary difference of $1,000, requiring a deferred tax liability of $400.

**EXAMPLE 12**   At the end of Year 1, a company has a warranty liability of $1,500. Warranty costs are deductible for tax purposes only when they have been paid. The carrying amount is $1,500, while the tax base is zero. We have a deductible temporary difference of $1,500, requiring a deferred tax asset of $600.

> *A deductible temporary difference gives rise to a deferred tax asset.*

**EXAMPLE 13**   An asset is purchased at a cost of $2,000. For financial statement purposes, it will be depreciated using the straight-line method over a five-year life, with no estimated residual value. For tax purposes, capital cost allowance (CCA) will be taken at a 30% rate, subject to the half-year rule in the first year. The following illustrates the yearly depreciation and CCA over the first three years:

|  |  | Carrying Amount | Tax Base |
|---|---|---|---|
| Year 1 cost |  | $2,000 | $2,000 |
| Year 1: | Depreciation | 400 | — |
|  | CCA | — | 300 |
| Balance, end of Year 1 |  | 1,600 | 1,700 |
| Year 2: | Depreciation | 400 | — |
|  | CCA | — | 510 |
| Balance, end of Year 2 |  | 1,200 | 1,190 |
| Year 3: | Depreciation | 400 | — |
|  | CCA | — | 357 |
| Balance, end of Year 3 |  | $ 800 | $ 833 |

Note that at the end of Year 1, there is a deductible temporary difference of $100 ($1,600 – $1,700), requiring a deferred tax asset of $40. At the end of Year 2, we have a taxable temporary difference of $10 ($1,200 – $1,190), requiring a deferred tax liability of $4. By the end of Year 3, we are back to a deductible temporary difference of $33, requiring a deferred tax asset of approximately $13. Note also that while the carrying amount of this asset becomes zero at the end of Year 5, it will have a positive tax base for an infinite number of future years. In other words, the reversing that inevitably must occur is often a very long time happening.

> *When the carrying amount of the asset is higher than the tax base, the result is a deferred tax liability.*

These examples have focused on some of the basics behind the liability method and will be useful in understanding some of the business combination illustrations that follow. However, before we examine the deferred income tax effects associated with a business combination, one other interesting provision of IAS 12 needs to be examined.

**THE ACQUISITION OF AN ASSET AT A PRICE DIFFERENT FROM THE TAX BASE (OTHER THAN IN A BUSINESS COMBINATION)** Because the liability method requires the recording of a deferred tax asset or liability whenever the carrying amount of an asset or liability differs from its tax base, a unique situation exists when a single asset is purchased and its tax base is different from its cost on the date that it was acquired. IAS 12 states that when an asset is acquired other than in a business combination, and the transaction does not affect accounting profit or taxable profit, the entity does not recognize any deferred tax liability or asset either on initial recognition or subsequently. For example, an entity purchases an asset for $1,000 with an estimated useful life of five years and an estimated residual value of zero. However, the tax base is zero because the cost of this particular asset will never be deductible for tax purposes. On disposal, any capital gain would not be taxable and any capital loss would not be deductible. Although there is a taxable temporary difference on the date the asset was acquired, IAS 12 states that a deferred tax liability should not be recognized in this situation. If the liability were recorded, the carrying amount of the asset would have to be increased by this amount. Then, the reported amount would be different than the amount paid, which may be confusing or less transparent to the users of the financial statements.

> *Deferred taxes are not recorded when acquiring a single asset for which there is a temporary difference.*

## Business Combination Examples

IAS 12 not only requires application of the liability method, but also requires that deferred income taxes associated with the acquisition differential be accounted for. We use the following simple illustrations to convey the basic concepts involved and the reasoning behind them.

**EXAMPLE 14**   Sub Co. has a single productive asset. The balance sheet of this company is shown below:

**SUB CO.—BALANCE SHEET**
At December 31, Year 3

| | |
|---|---:|
| Asset | $800 |
| Deferred tax asset | 12 |
| | $812 |
| Liabilities | $300 |
| Shareholders' equity | 512 |
| | $812 |

*There is a deferred tax asset on the separate-entity books of the subsidiary.*

The tax bases of the single asset and the liabilities are as follows:

| | |
|---|---:|
| Asset | $830 |
| Liabilities | 300 |
| Net | $530 |

Using a 40% tax rate, Sub Co. has correctly applied the provisions of IAS 12 by setting up in its separate-entity statements a deferred tax asset of $12 for the deductible temporary difference of $30.

On January 1, Year 4, Parent Inc. purchased 100% of Sub Co. for $1,000 cash. Parent determines that the fair value of Sub's single asset is $950 and that the fair value of its liabilities is $300. The calculation of the acquisition differential is made in the following manner:

| | | |
|---|---:|---:|
| Cost of 100% of Sub Co. | | $1,000 |
| Carrying amount of net assets of Sub Co. | | 512 |
| Acquisition differential | | 488 |
| Allocated: | | |
| Asset (950 − 800) | 150 | |
| Deferred income tax asset (liability) (see calculation below) | (60) | 90 |
| Balance, goodwill | | $  398 |

*When a business combination occurs, the acquirer records the net assets acquired at fair values, and when the tax base of these net assets are a different amount, a deferred tax asset or liability becomes part of the allocation of the acquisition cost.*

The calculation of the deferred tax liability to be used for consolidation purposes is as follows:

| | |
|---|---:|
| Asset fair value used in consolidation | $950 |
| Tax base of the asset | 830 |
| Taxable temporary difference | 120 |
| Tax rate of Sub Co. | 40% |
| Deferred tax liability—as recalculated for consolidation | 48 |
| Deferred tax asset—as previously stated by Sub | 12 |
| Adjustment required on consolidation | $  60 |

> *A subsidiary's deferred tax asset is replaced by a deferred tax liability upon consolidation.*

Because the fair value and the tax base of Sub's liabilities are both $300, no deferred income tax implications are associated with these liabilities. Note that in applying these concepts, we are replacing a $12 deferred tax asset on the balance sheet of Sub Co. with a deferred tax liability of $48 on the consolidated balance sheet, with respect to the same asset. Note also that no deferred taxes are recorded in relation to the goodwill of $398. Goodwill is measured as a residual. Therefore, it would be inappropriate to recognize a deferred tax liability on the temporary difference related to the goodwill because it would increase the carrying amount of goodwill and it would no longer be a residual amount. Also, goodwill is usually not deductible for tax purposes. Any difference between the carrying amount for goodwill and the tax base would be a permanent difference.

> *No deferred taxes are recognized for the difference between the tax base and carrying amount for goodwill.*

Let us assume that Parent Inc. was formed on December 31, Year 3, by the issuance of common shares for $1,000 in cash. The non-consolidated balance sheet of Parent is shown below, followed by the consolidated balance sheet (with bracketed amounts indicating its preparation using the direct approach):

**PARENT INC.—BALANCE SHEET**
At January 1, Year 4

| | |
|---|---|
| Investment in Sub Co. | $1,000 |
| Common shares | $1,000 |

**PARENT INC.—CONSOLIDATED BALANCE SHEET**
At January 1, Year 4

| | |
|---|---|
| Assets (800 + 150) | $ 950 |
| Goodwill | 398 |
| | $1,348 |
| Liabilities | $ 300 |
| Deferred tax liability | 48 |
| Common shares | 1,000 |
| | $1,348 |

The deferred tax liability that appears on the consolidated balance sheet can be verified as follows:

| | |
|---|---|
| Carrying amount of assets above (excluding goodwill) | $950 |
| Tax base of assets | 830 |
| Taxable temporary difference | 120 |
| Tax rate | 40% |
| Deferred tax liability | $ 48 |

The treatment of the acquisition differential at the date of acquisition is fairly complicated in situations involving deferred income taxes. In subsequent periods, we must compare the carrying amount of an asset or liability with its tax base on each date that a balance sheet is prepared, and make an adjustment to the previously recorded deferred tax balances. When we prepare a consolidated balance sheet subsequent to acquisition, we will amortize the acquisition differential for all items, including deferred income taxes. See Self-Study Problem 2 for a comprehensive problem involving deferred income taxes pertaining to the acquisition differential. It illustrates the calculation of deferred income taxes at the date of acquisition and the amortization of the acquisition differential pertaining to deferred income taxes subsequent to the date of acquisition.

> *In preparing consolidated financial statements in subsequent periods, the values used for each subsidiary's net assets have to be compared with their tax base in order to determine new values for deferred tax assets and liabilities.*

## Operating Loss Carry-Forwards

Under IAS 12, accounting recognition can be given to the carry-forward of unused tax losses, to the extent it is probable that there will be a taxable profit which the deductible temporary difference can be utilized against. If the acquired company has already recognized a deferred tax asset due to the potential carry-forward of unused tax losses, this deferred tax asset will be allowed to stand on the date of the business combination. The combining of the two companies does not ordinarily change this status. However, if the acquired company was not able to recognize unused tax losses, the fact that it is combining with the acquiring company may provide the additional impetus to satisfy the "probability" criterion. This could be the result of the combined companies doing business with each other or because they will be able to reduce future costs, both of which could result in greater possibilities of having future taxable incomes higher than they were before the combination. The deferred income tax asset would be identified as part of the acquisition differential and recognized on the consolidated financial statements. Note that recognizing such a deferred tax asset as part of the acquisition differential reduces the amount that otherwise would have been allocated to goodwill. This concept must also be taken into account in situations where a deferred tax asset was *not* recognized as an asset on the acquisition date, but subsequently becomes recognizable. An entity shall recognize acquired deferred tax benefits that it realizes after the business combination as follows:

(a) Acquired deferred tax benefits recognized within the measurement period (maximum of one year from acquisition date) that result from new information about facts and circumstances that existed at the acquisition date must be applied to reduce the carrying amount of any goodwill related to that acquisition. If the carrying amount of that goodwill is zero, any remaining deferred tax benefits must be recognized in profit or loss.

(b) All other acquired deferred tax benefits realized must be recognized in profit or loss.

> *The tax benefits of operating loss carry-forwards, which were not previously recognizable by either party to the business combination, may be recognized as an asset.*

The acquiring company could also benefit from a business combination in that the probability of realizing a pre-acquisition deferred tax asset of the acquirer could change. An acquirer may consider it probable that it will recover its own deferred tax asset that was not recognized before the business combination. For example, the acquirer may be able to utilize the benefit of its unused tax losses against the future taxable profit of the acquiree. In such cases, the acquirer recognizes a change in the deferred tax asset in the period of the business combination but does not include it as part of the accounting for the business combination. Therefore, the acquirer does not take it into account in measuring the goodwill or bargain purchase gain it recognizes in the business combination.

**DISCLOSURE REQUIREMENTS** The following summarizes the more substantial items required to be disclosed pertaining to deferred income tax arising from a business combination:

- The amount of the change, if it is a business combination in which the acquirer causes a change in the amount recognized for its pre-acquisition deferred tax asset.

- A description of the event or change in circumstances that caused the deferred tax benefits to be recognized, if the deferred tax benefits acquired in a business combination are not recognized at the acquisition date but then are recognized after.

> *The entity must disclose the amount and reason for changes in deferred tax assets pertaining to a business combination.*

## LO4 SEGMENT DISCLOSURES

For simplicity, most of the examples used in previous chapters were unrealistic, in that they consisted of a parent company and a single subsidiary. When you consider all companies that trade on the Toronto Stock Exchange, very few are made up of only two companies, and many of the larger ones consist of the parent and a substantial number of subsidiaries. The consolidation process treats these separate legal entities as a single economic entity by aggregating the components of their financial statements. In past years, all companies making up a given consolidated group were often in a single line of business and located in Canada, so this aggregation of statements provided useful information to the users of the consolidated statements. However, the tremendous corporate expansion that started in the 1970s created companies engaged in many diversified activities and in many parts of the world, and it became obvious that the basic consolidated financial statements were not providing adequate information. Financial statement users needed information about a company that would allow them to assess all of its different components, which have different growth potentials, profitability characteristics, and inherent risks, which all vary with the products and services being provided and the markets being entered. Consolidated financial statements do not provide this information.

> *Corporate expansion has created multifaceted companies engaged in diversified activities.*

### IFRS 8: Operating Segments

IFRS 8 *Operating Segments* must be applied for the separate and consolidated financial statements of an entity whose debt or equity instruments are traded in a public market, or of an entity that files, or is in the process of filing, the financial statements with a securities commission or other regulatory organization for the purpose of issuing any class of instruments in a public market. The entity must disclose information about its operating segments in addition to information about its products and services, the countries in which it operates, and its major customers. It is expected that such information will provide users with a better understanding of a company's performance and its prospects for future cash flows.

> *Public companies are required to disclose information about their lines of business, products and services, countries where they operate, and major customers.*

Operating segments are identified based on how a company's management organizes its components internally for assessing performance and making strategic decisions. This identification focuses on the financial information that the company's decision makers use for that purpose. Each component is called an *operating segment* and is defined as follows:

(a) It engages in business activities from which it may earn revenues[9] and incur expenses (including those relating to transactions with other components of the same enterprise);

(b) its operating results are regularly reviewed by the entity's chief operating decision maker to allocate resources to the segment and assess its performance; and

(c) discrete financial information is available for it.[10]

## Identification of Reportable Operating Segments

IFRS 8.13 requires information to be disclosed about all operating segments that meet certain *quantitative thresholds*. The requirement description follows.

An enterprise should disclose separately information about an operating segment that meets *any* of the following quantitative thresholds:

(a) Its reported revenue, including both sales to external customers and intersegment sales or transfers, is 10% or more of the combined revenue, internal and external, of all operating segments.

(b) The absolute amount of its reported profit or loss is 10% or more of the greater, in absolute amount, of
  (i) the combined reported profit of all operating segments that did not report a loss, and
  (ii) the combined reported loss of all operating segments that did report a loss.

(c) Its assets are 10% or more of the combined assets of all operating segments.

> *Three tests (revenue, profit, and assets) are used to determine whether or not a particular operating segment is reportable. Each test applies a 10% rule.*

These quantitative thresholds establish which operating segments require separate disclosures. Any segments falling outside these guidelines may be combined under the category "Other," provided that at least 75% of a company's total external revenue is included in reportable segments. If it is not, additional operating segments must be disclosed. IFRS 8 also suggests that from a practical point of view, the total number of operating segments reported will probably not exceed 10.

> *At least 75% of a company's total external revenue must be reported in a segment other than the "Other" segment.*

**EXAMPLE 15**  The following illustrates an application of quantitative thresholds. For internal evaluation purposes, JK Enterprises Inc. generates information from its six divisions. In terms of IFRS 8, these divisions are operating segments. The following amounts (stated in millions) have been assembled to determine which of these operating segments are reportable in accordance with the standard's quantitative thresholds.

| Operating Segments | Revenues | Operating Profit (Loss) | Assets |
|---|---|---|---|
| Auto parts | $53.9 | $18.1 | $10.9 |
| Office furnishings | 8.6 | 1.3 | 1.2 |
| Publishing | 6.5 | (2.1) | 1.4 |
| Retail | 5.0 | (2.8) | 3.2 |
| Finance | 11.8 | 3.7 | 14.0 |
| Software | 7.9 | 3.9 | 0.9 |
| | $93.7 | $22.1 | $31.6 |

**REVENUE TEST**   $10\% \times \$93.7 = \$9.37$

From this test, auto parts and finance are identified as reportable segments.

**OPERATING PROFIT (LOSS) TEST**   To apply this test, first compute separate totals for all profits and all losses. Then choose the largest of the absolute amount of the two totals, as follows:

| | |
|---|---:|
| Total of all operating profits | $27.0 |
| Total of all operating losses | 4.9 |
| $10\% \times \$27.0 = \$2.7$ | |

Auto parts, retail, finance, and software are identified as reportable segments.

> *The operating profit test considers the larger of the absolute amount of total profits and total losses.*

**ASSET TEST**   $10\% \times \$31.6 = \$3.16$

Auto parts, retail, and finance are identified as reportable segments.

Following is a summary of all three quantitative tests for JK Enterprises:

| Operating Segments | Revenues | Operating Profit (Loss) | Assets |
|---|:---:|:---:|:---:|
| Auto parts | X | X | X |
| Office furnishings | | | |
| Publishing | | | |
| Retail | | X | X |
| Finance | X | X | X |
| Software | | X | |

> *Separate disclosure is required if a segment satisfies any one test.*

Thus, separate disclosures are required for auto parts, retail, finance, and software, as each satisfies at least one of the tests. The cumulative revenue for these four segments is 83.9%, which satisfies the requirement of having at least 75% of total revenue being reported in segments other than the "Other" segment. Office furnishings and publishing can be combined and reported as "Other."

> *IFRS 8 outlines extensive disclosures required for each reportable segment.*

**DISCLOSURE REQUIREMENTS**   The following disclosures are required under IFRS 8 for each reportable segment that has been identified by the quantitative thresholds:

1. Factors used by management to identify segments
2. The types of products and services that generate revenues
3. A measure of profit (loss)
4. Total assets
5. Liabilities for each reportable segment if such amounts are regularly provided to the chief operating decision maker
6. Each of the following, *if* the specific amounts are included in the measure of profit (loss) regularly reviewed by the chief operating decision maker:
   (a) Revenues from external customers
   (b) Intersegment revenues

(c) Interest revenue and expense (This may be netted for a particular segment only if that segment receives a majority of its revenues from interest *and* if the chief operating decision maker uses the net number to assess performance.)

(d) Depreciation and amortization

(e) Material income and expense items

(f) Equity method income from associates and joint ventures

(g) Income taxes

(h) Significant non-cash items other than depreciation and amortization

7. The amount of investment in associates and joint ventures accounted for by the equity method

8. The amounts of additions to noncurrent assets other than financial instruments, deferred tax assets, and post-employment benefits assets

9. Explanations of how a segment's profit (loss) and assets have been measured, how common costs and jointly used assets have been allocated, and of the accounting policies that have been used

10. Reconciliations of the following:

(a) The total of the reportable segments' revenues to the entity's revenue

---

*Reconciliations of the segments' total revenues, profits, assets, and liabilities to the entity's overall revenues, profits, assets, and liabilities must be provided.*

---

(b) The total of the reportable segments' measures of profit or loss to the entity's profit or loss

(c) The total of the reportable segments' assets to the entity's assets

(d) The total of the reportable segments' liabilities to the entity's liabilities if segment liabilities are reported separately

(e) The total of the reportable segments' amounts for every other material item of information disclosed to the corresponding amount for the entity

The following information must also be disclosed, unless such information has already been clearly provided as part of the segment disclosures. This additional information is also required in situations where the company has only a single reportable segment:

1. The revenue from external customers for each product or service, or for each group of similar products and services, whenever practical.

2. The revenue from external customers broken down between those from the company's country of domicile (e.g., Canada) and those from all foreign countries. Where revenue from an individual country is material, it must be separately disclosed.

---

*Revenue must be segregated by product or service and by geographical area.*

---

3. Goodwill; property, plant, and equipment; and intangible assets broken down between those located in Canada and those in foreign countries. Where assets located in an individual country are material, they must be separately disclosed.

4. When a company's sales to a single external customer are 10% or more of total revenues, the company must disclose this fact, as well as the total amount of revenues from each customer and which operating segment reported such revenues. The identity of the customer does not have to be disclosed.

As with all financial reporting, comparative amounts for at least the last fiscal year must also be presented.

The disclosures required by IFRS 8 provide external users with the information that top management uses to assess performance. The presentation of a measure of profit, revenue, and assets for each reportable segment allows a statement user to calculate a measure of return on assets, margin, and turnover and the risks associated with each segment, so that the relative contribution of each segment to the overall profitability of the company can be assessed and compared with that of the previous year.

---

*The entity must disclose a measure of profit, revenue, and assets for each reportable segment.*

---

BCE is Canada's largest telecommunication company. Relevant excerpts from its 2014 financial statements pertaining to its different operating segments are presented in Exhibit 9.4.[11]

**EXHIBIT 9.4**

## Extracts from BCE's 2014 Financial Statements

**NOTE 5 SEGMENTED INFORMATION**

The accounting policies used in our segment reporting are the same as those we describe in Note 2, Significant accounting policies. Our earnings are reported in four segments: Bell Wireless, Bell Wireline, Bell Media and Bell Aliant. Our segments reflect how we manage our business and how we classify our operations for planning and measuring performance. Accordingly, we operate and manage our segments as strategic business units organized by products and services. Segments negotiate sales with each other as if they were unrelated parties.

We measure the performance of each segment based on segment profit, which is equal to operating revenues less operating costs for the segment. We report severance, acquisition and other costs and depreciation and amortization by segment for external reporting purposes. Substantially all of our finance costs and other income (expense) are managed on a corporate basis and, accordingly, are not reflected in segment results.

Our operations and virtually all of our assets are located in Canada. Below is a description of our segments at December 31, 2014:

Our Bell Wireless segment provides wireless voice and data communication products and services to Bell's residential, small and medium-sized business and large enterprise customers across Canada.

Our Bell Wireline segment provides data, including Internet access and TV, local telephone, long distance, as well as other communications services and products to Bell's residential, small and medium-sized business and large enterprise customers, primarily in the urban areas of Ontario and Québec. In addition, this segment includes our wholesale business, which buys and sells local telephone, long distance, data and other services from or to resellers and other carriers.

Our Bell Media segment provides conventional, specialty and pay TV, digital media, and radio broadcasting services to customers across Canada and out-of-home advertising services. On July 5, 2013, BCE acquired 100% of the issued and outstanding shares of Astral. The results of Astral are included in our Bell Media segment from the date of acquisition.

Our Bell Aliant segment provides Internet, data, TV, local telephone, long distance, wireless, home security and value-added business solutions to residential and business customers in the Atlantic Provinces and in rural and regional areas of Ontario and Quebec.

---

*BCE breaks down its operations into four different segments, based on how it manages its business.*

*Certain costs are managed on a total company basis and are not segregated by segment.*

---

*(continued)*

**EXHIBIT 9.4** *(continued)*

| For the year ended December 31, 2014 | Note | Bell Wireless | Bell Wireline | Bell Media | Inter-segment Eliminations | Bell | Bell Aliant | Inter-segment Eliminations | BCE |
|---|---|---|---|---|---|---|---|---|---|
| Operating revenues: | | 6,188 | 9,687 | 2,642 | 0 | 18,517 | 2,525 | 0 | 21,042 |
| External customers | | 53 | 353 | 295 | (484) | 217 | 232 | (449) | 0 |
| Intersegment | | | | | | | | | |
| **Total operating revenues** | | **6,241** | **10,040** | **2,937** | **(484)** | **18,734** | **2,757** | **(449)** | **21,042** |
| Operating costs | 6 | (3,677) | (6,272) | (2,203) | 484 | (11,668) | (1,520) | 449 | (12,739) |
| **Segment profit**[1] | | **2,564** | **3,768** | **734** | **0** | **7,066** | **1,237** | **0** | **8,303** |
| Severance, acquisition and other costs | 7 | (5) | (78) | (46) | 0 | (129) | (87) | 0 | (216) |
| Depreciation and amortization | 14,15 | (545) | (2,254) | (126) | 0 | (2,925) | (527) | 0 | (3,452) |
| Finance costs: | | | | | | | | | |
| Interest expense | 8 | | | | | | | | (929) |
| Interest on post-employment benefit obligations | 22 | | | | | | | | (101) |
| Other income | 9 | | | | | | | | 42 |
| Income taxes | 10 | | | | | | | | (929) |
| **Net earnings** | | | | | | | | | **2,718** |
| Goodwill | 18 | 2,302 | 2,521 | 2,592 | 0 | 7,415 | 970 | 0 | 8,385 |
| Indefinite-life intangible assets | 15 | 3,063 | 1,315 | 2,680 | 0 | 7,058 | 340 | 0 | 7,398 |
| Capital expenditures | | 671 | 2,334 | 137 | 0 | 3,142 | 575 | 0 | 3,717 |

[1] *The chief operating decision maker uses primarily one measure of profit to make decisions and assess performance, being operating revenues less operating costs.*

## REVENUES BY PRODUCT

| For the year ended December 31, | 2014 | 2013 |
|---|---|---|
| Revenues | | |
| Wireless | **5,705** | 5,362 |
| Data | **5,991** | 5,828 |
| Local and access | **2,364** | 2,497 |
| Long distance | **668** | 722 |
| Media | **2,642** | 2,342 |
| Equipment and other | **1,147** | 1,139 |
| **Total external revenues** | **18,517** | 17,890 |
| Intersegment revenues | **217** | 219 |
| Bell | **18,734** | 18,109 |
| Bell Aliant | **2,757** | 2,759 |
| Intersegment eliminations | **(449)** | (468) |
| BCE | **21,042** | 20,400 |

*Source: BCE Inc., BCE Inc. 2014 ANNUAL REPORT, Pages 128–130. Reproduced with permission from BCE Inc.*

> *Data is the largest product line in terms of sales.*
>
> *Intersegment transactions are eliminated.*

## LO5 ANALYSIS AND INTERPRETATION OF FINANCIAL STATEMENTS

Under IFRS, the equity method must be used to report an investment in a joint venture, whereas a form of proportionate consolidation is used to report an investment in a joint operation. Exhibit 9.5 presents the income statements and balance sheets for Example 6 under two scenarios: equity method for a joint venture and proportionately adjusted financial statements for a joint operation. The exhibit also indicates the return-on-equity ratio and debt-to-equity ratio for each reporting method.

**EXHIBIT 9.5**

## Impact of Presentation Method on Return-on-Equity and Debt-to-Equity Ratios

### INCOME STATEMENTS
### Year 4

|  | Joint Venture Equity Method | Joint Operation Proportionately Adjusted |
|---|---|---|
| Sales | $900,000 | $1,017,000 |
| Income from joint venture | 38,718 | |
|  | 938,718 | 1,017,000 |
| Cost of sales | 500,000 | 534,470 |
| Miscellaneous expenses | 100,000 | 118,000 |
|  | 600,000 | 652,470 |
| Income before taxes | 338,718 | 364,530 |
| Income tax expense | 120,000 | 145,812 |
| Net income | $218,718 | $ 218,718 |

> *The equity method reports income from the joint venture on one line, whereas the income from a joint operation is reported on a line-by-line basis.*

### BALANCE SHEETS
### At December 31, Year 4

|  | | |
|---|---|---|
| Miscellaneous assets | $654,500 | $ 776,900 |
| Inventory | 110,000 | 147,530 |
| Deferred charge—income taxes | | 1,188 |
| Investment in Explor (85,500 + 40,500 − 1,782) | 124,218 | — |
|  | $888,718 | $ 925,618 |
| Liabilities | $130,000 | $ 166,900 |
| Common shares | 300,000 | 300,000 |
| Retained earnings | 458,718 | 458,718 |
|  | $888,718 | $ 925,618 |
| Return on equity (net income/shareholders' equity) | 28.8% | 28.8% |
| Debt to equity (liabilities/shareholders' equity) | 0.17 | 0.22 |

> *Net income and retained earnings under the equity method are equal to proportionately adjusted net income and retained earnings for the joint operation.*

Note the following from Exhibit 9.5:

- Net income and retained earnings under the equity method are equal to proportionately adjusted net income and retained earnings for the joint operation.

- The return on equity under the equity method is equal to the proportionately adjusted return on equity.

- The debt-to-equity ratio is higher on the proportionately adjusted statements because the operator's share of the joint operations debt is included on the proportionately adjusted financial statements but not included on the venturer's balance sheet under the equity method.

- The solvency position looks worst on the proportionately adjusted financial statements due to the higher debt-to-equity ratio.

---

*The debt-to-equity ratio is higher under proportionately adjusted financial statements.*

---

## ASPE Differences

- May report association with subsidiaries that are controlled through contractual arrangements using either consolidated financial statements or according to the nature of contractual arrangements in accordance with the applicable *Handbook* section.

- May report interests in jointly controlled enterprises using the cost method or the equity method.

- May use the taxes payable method or the future income tax payable method, which is similar to the liability method under IFRS, to account for income tax.

- Not required to disclose any information about operating segments.

For the third point above, deferred income taxes need not be recognized; however, the entity must prepare and disclose a reconciliation between the statutory rate and the effective tax rate.

## SUMMARY

In this chapter, we have examined four different topics, which almost wind up our study of business combinations and the preparation of consolidated financial statements. Consolidation is required for a special-purpose entity (SPE) that is controlled by the sponsor on a basis other than through ownership of a voting interest. The non-controlling interest could be substantially higher than the sponsor's interest in the SPE. **(LO1)** For an interest in a joint operation, proportionately adjusted financial statements are used to report the joint operator's proportionate share of the joint operation's assets, liabilities, revenues, and expenses. The equity method should be used to report a venturer's investment in a joint venture. For intercompany transactions between a party with joint control and a joint venture/operation, only the venturer's percentage interest in the intercompany gains/losses are considered to be unrealized. **(LO2)**

Deferred tax assets and liabilities should be recognized on the consolidated financial statements for the differences between the carrying amounts and the tax bases of subsidiary's net assets arising from the acquisition differential pertaining to identifiable assets and liabilities. **(LO3)**

Consolidated financial statements provide information at an aggregate level. Segment reporting is required disclosure to provide disaggregated information by industry, geographical area and/or major customers. This segmented information will aid users in assessing the profitability and risks of the different operating segments. **(LO4)**

The key financial ratios for a reporting entity could be substantially different depending on whether the reporting entity uses the equity method for an interest in a joint venture or uses a form of proportionate consolidation to report an interest in a joint operation. Users of financial statements should always be mindful of the different accounting policies being used by a reporting entity. **(LO5)**

## Self-Study Problem 1

The following are the Year 5 draft financial statements of MAR Corporation and OTT Inc., a joint arrangement in which MAR has a 35% contractual interest:

### INCOME STATEMENTS
For Year 5

| | MAR | OTT |
|---|---|---|
| Sales | $906,750 | $250,000 |
| Management fees | 25,000 | — |
| Interest | — | 3,600 |
| Gain on land sale | — | 20,000 |
| Dividends | 5,250 | = |
| | 937,000 | 273,600 |
| Cost of sales | 540,000 | 162,000 |
| Interest expense | 3,600 | — |
| Other expenses | 196,400 | 71,600 |
| Income tax expense | 80,000 | 16,000 |
| | 820,000 | 249,600 |
| Profit | $117,000 | $ 24,000 |

### RETAINED EARNINGS STATEMENTS
For Year 5

| | MAR | OTT |
|---|---|---|
| Balance, January 1 | $153,000 | $ 72,000 |
| Profit | 117,000 | 24,000 |
| | 270,000 | 96,000 |
| Dividends | 50,000 | 15,000 |
| Balance, December 31 | $220,000 | $ 81,000 |

### BALANCE SHEETS
At December 31, Year 5

| | MAR | OTT |
|---|---|---|
| Cash | $ 12,000 | $ 15,000 |
| Accounts and notes receivable | 70,000 | 63,000 |
| Inventory | 32,000 | 27,000 |
| Property, plant, and equipment (net) | 448,000 | 66,000 |
| Investment in OTT Company | 30,000 | — |
| | $592,000 | $171,000 |
| Notes payable | $ 60,000 | $ — |
| Other liabilities | 212,000 | 40,000 |
| Common shares | 100,000 | 50,000 |
| Retained earnings | 220,000 | 81,000 |
| | $592,000 | $171,000 |

### Additional Information

- On January 1, Year 3, MAR purchased a 35% interest in OTT for $30,000 and signed an agreement to establish joint control of OTT with the other two parties. On that date, OTT had retained earnings of $10,000, and the carrying amounts of its identifiable net assets were equal to fair values.

- The companies sell merchandise to each other. MAR sells to OTT at a gross profit rate of 38%; OTT earns a gross profit of 40% from its sales to MAR.

- The December 31, Year 4, inventory of MAR contained purchases made from OTT amounting to $7,000. There were no intercompany purchases in the inventory of OTT on this date.

- During Year 5 the following intercompany transactions took place:
  - (a)   OTT made a $25,000 payment to MAR for management fees, which was recorded as "other expenses."
  - (b)   OTT made sales of $75,000 to MAR. The December 31, Year 5, inventory of MAR contained merchandise purchased from OTT amounting to $16,500.
  - (c)   MAR made sales of $100,000 to OTT. The December 31, Year 5, inventory of OTT contained merchandise purchased from MAR amounting to $15,000.
  - (d)   On July 1, Year 5, MAR borrowed $60,000 from OTT and signed a note bearing interest at 12% per annum. Interest on this note was paid on December 31, Year 5.
  - (e)   In Year 5, OTT sold land to MAR, recording a gain of $20,000. This land is being held by MAR on December 31, Year 5.

- Goodwill impairment tests have been conducted yearly by MAR since the date of acquisition. MAR's 35% share of the losses due to impairment was as follows: Year 3, $1,040; Year 4, $320; Year 5, $680.

- MAR has accounted for its investment using the cost method for internal record keeping.

- Both companies pay income tax at a rate of 40%. Ignore income tax on the acquisition differential.

### Required

Part A: Assume that OTT Inc. is classified as a joint venture because MAR only has rights to the net assets of OTT.

(a)  Calculate the following account balances to be reported by MAR under the equity method:
   - (i) Retained earnings as at January 1, Year 5.
   - (ii) Net income for Year 5.
   - (iii) Investment in OTT as at December 31, Year 5.

(b)  Prepare MAR's journal entries under the equity method for Year 5.

Part B: Assume that OTT Inc. is classified as a joint operation because the contractual agreement gives MAR rights to OTT's assets and responsibilities for OTT's liabilities.

(a)  Prepare proportionately adjusted financial statements for MAR for Year 5.

## Solution to Self-Study Problem 1

### CALCULATION AND AMORTIZATION OF THE ACQUISITION DIFFERENTIAL

| | | |
|---|---:|---:|
| Cost of 35% of OTT, Jan. 1, Year 3 | | $30,000 |
| Carrying amount of OTT, Jan. 1, Year 3: | | |
|   Common shares | 50,000 | |
|   Retained earnings | 10,000 | |
| | 60,000 | |
|   MAR's share (35%) | | 21,000 |
| Acquisition differential | | 9,000 |
| Allocated to revalue the net assets of OTT | | –0– |
| Goodwill, Jan. 1, Year 3 | | 9,000 |
| Amortized (impairment losses): | | |
|   Year 3–Year 4 | 1,360 **(a)** | |
|   Year 5 | 680 **(b)** | 2,040 |
| Goodwill, Dec. 31, Year 5 | | $ 6,960 **(c)** |

### INTERCOMPANY ITEMS

| | | |
|---|---:|---:|
| Notes receivable and payable (35% × 60,000) | | $21,000 **(d)** |
| Management fee revenue and expense (35% × 25,000) | | 8,750 **(e)** |
| Sales and purchases (35% × [75,000 + 100,000]) | | 61,250 **(f)** |
| Interest revenue and expense (35% × [12% × 60,000 × 1/2 yr.]) | | 1,260 **(g)** |
| Dividend from OTT (35% × 15,000) | | 5,250 **(h)** |

### UNREALIZED PROFITS

| | Before Tax | 40% Tax | After Tax | |
|---|---:|---:|---:|---|
| Inventory | | | | |
| Opening (7,000 × 40% × 35%)—OTT selling | $ 980 | $ 392 | $ 588 | **(i)** |
| Ending: | | | | |
|   OTT selling (16,500 × 40% × 35%) | $2,310 | $ 924 | $1,386 | **(j)** |
|   MAR selling (15,000 × 38% × 35%) | 1,995 | 798 | 1,197 | **(k)** |
| | $4,305 | $1,722 | $2,583 | **(l)** |
| Land—OTT selling (20,000 × 35%) | $7,000 | $2,800 | $4,200 | **(m)** |

## Part A:

(a) (i)
### CALCULATION OF RETAINED EARNINGS
#### at January 1, Year 5

| | | |
|---|---:|---:|
| Retained earnings, Jan. 1, Year 5—MAR under cost method | | $153,000 |
| Less: Amortization of acquisition differential **(a)** | | 1,360 |
| | | 151,640 |
| Retained earnings, Jan. 1, Year 5—OTT | 72,000 | |
| Acquisition retained earnings | 10,000 | |
| Increase | 62,000 | |
| MAR's interest (35%) | 21,700 | |
| Less: Unrealized opening inventory profit **(i)** | 588 | |
| Adjusted increase | | 21,112 **(n)** |
| Retained earnings, Jan. 1, Year 5 under equity method | | $172,752 **(o)** |

(ii)
## CALCULATION OF NET INCOME
### Year 5

| | | |
|---|---:|---:|
| Income of MAR under cost method | | $117,000 |
| Less: Dividends from OTT **(h)** | 5,250 | |
| Unrealized ending inventory profit **(k)** | 1,197 | |
| Amortization of acquisition differential **(b)** | 680 | 7,127 |
| Adjusted net income | | 109,873 |
| Income of OTT | 24,000 | |
| MAR's interest (35%) | 8,400 | |
| Less: Unrealized ending inventory profit **(j)** | 1,386 | |
| Unrealized land gain **(m)** | 4,200 | 5,586 |
| | | 2,814 |
| Add: Realized opening inventory profit **(i)** | | 588 |
| Adjusted net income | | 3,402 **(p)** |
| Net income under equity method | | $113,275 **(q)** |

(iii)
## BALANCE IN INVESTMENT ACCOUNT
### At December 31, Year 5

| | | |
|---|---:|---:|
| Balance in investment account under cost method | | $ 30,000 |
| Less: Unrealized ending inventory profit **(k)** | 1,197 | |
| Amortization of acquisition differential **(a + b)** | 2,040 | 3,237 |
| Adjusted | | 26,763 |
| Retained earnings, Dec. 31, Year 5—OTT | 81,000 | |
| Acquisition retained earnings | 10,000 | |
| Increase | 71,000 | |
| MAR's interest (35%) | 24,850 | |
| Less: Unrealized ending inventory profit **(j)** | 1,386 | |
| Unrealized land gain **(m)** | 4,200 | 5,586 |
| Adjusted increase | | 19,264 |
| Balance in investment account under equity method | | $46,027 |

(b)
## YEAR 5 EQUITY METHOD JOURNAL ENTRIES
### (see calculation of net income)

| | | |
|---|---:|---:|
| Investment in OTT **(p)** | 3,402 | |
| Equity method income **(p)** | | 3,402 |
| Adjusted net income of OTT | | |
| Cash | 5,250 | |
| Investment in OTT **(h)** | | 5,250 |
| Dividends from OTT | | |
| Equity method income | 1,197 | |
| Investment in OTT **(k)** | | 1,197 |
| Unrealized ending inventory profit—MAR selling | | |
| Equity method income **(b)** | 680 | |
| Investment in OTT | | 680 |
| Amortization of acquisition differential | | |

Part B:

(a)
## MAR CORPORATION
## PROPORTIONATELY ADJUSTED INCOME STATEMENT

| | |
|---|---:|
| Sales (906,750 + 35% × 250,000 − **[f] 61,250**) | $933,000 |
| Management fees (25,000 + 35% × 0 − **[e] 8,750**) | 16,250 |
| Interest (0 + 35% × 3,600 − **[g] 1,260**) | 0 |

*(continued)*

| | |
|---|---|
| Gain on land sale (0 + 35% × 20,000 − **[m] 7,000**) | 0 |
| Dividends (5,250 + 35% × 0 − **[h] 5,250**) | 0 |
| | 949,250 |
| | |
| Cost of sales (540,000 + 35% × 162,000 − **[f] 61,250** − **[i] 980** + **[j] 2,310** + **[k] 1,995**) | 538,775 |
| Interest expense (3,600 + 35% × 0 − **[g] 1,260**) | 2,340 |
| Other expenses (196,400 + 35% × 71,600 − **[e] 8,750**) | 212,710 |
| Goodwill impairment loss (0 + 35% × 0 + **[b] 680**) | 680 |
| Income tax expense (80,000 + 35% × 16,000 + **[i] 392** − **[j] 924** − **[k] 798** − **[m] 2,800**) | 81,470 |
| | 835,975 |
| Profit | $113,275 |

### PROPORTIONATELY ADJUSTED RETAINED EARNINGS STATEMENT

| | |
|---|---|
| Balance, January 1 **(o)** | $172,752 |
| Profit | 113,275 |
| | 286,027 |
| Dividends | 50,000 |
| Balance, December 31 | $236,027 |

### PROPORTIONATELY ADJUSTED BALANCE SHEET

| | |
|---|---|
| Cash (12,000 + 35% × 15,000) | $ 17,250 |
| Accounts and notes receivable (70,000 + 35% × 63,000 − **[d] 21,000**) | 71,050 |
| Inventory (32,000 + 35% × 27,000 − **[j] 2,310** − **[k] 1,995**) | 37,145 |
| Property, plant, and equipment (net) (448,000 + 35% × 66,000 − **[m] 7,000**) | 464,100 |
| Deferred income taxes (0 + 35% × 0 + **[j] 924** + **[k] 798** + **[m] 2,800**) | 4,522 |
| Goodwill **(c)** | 6,960 |
| | $601,027 |
| | |
| Notes payable (60,000 + 35% × 0 − **[d] 21,000**) | $ 39,000 |
| Other liabilities (212,000 + 35% × 40,000) | 226,000 |
| Common shares | 100,000 |
| Retained earnings | 236,027 |
| | $601,027 |

## Self-Study Problem 2

On December 31, Year 2, Pat Inc. purchased 80% of the outstanding ordinary shares of Sam Company for $620,000. At that date, Sam had ordinary shares of $400,000 and retained earnings of $125,000. In negotiating the purchase price, it was agreed that the assets on Sam's balance sheet were fairly valued except for plant assets, which had an $80,000 excess of fair value over carrying amount. It was also agreed that Sam had unrecognized intangible assets consisting of trademarks that had an estimated value of $50,000. The plant assets had a remaining useful life of eight years at the acquisition date, and the trademarks would be amortized over a 10-year period. Any goodwill arising from this business combination would be tested periodically for impairment. Pat accounts for its investment using the cost method and prepares consolidated statements using the parent company extension theory.

### Additional Information

- Impairment tests performed at the end of Year 6 indicated that Sam's portion of the goodwill had a recoverable amount of $85,000 and the trademarks had a recoverable amount of $29,000. The impairment loss on these assets occurred entirely in Year 6.

- On December 26, Year 6, Pat declared dividends of $72,000, while Sam declared dividends of $40,000.

- Depreciation and amortization expense is reported in selling expenses, while impairment losses are reported in other expenses.

- Both companies pay income tax at the rate of 40%.

Condensed financial statements for Pat and Sam for the year ended December 31, Year 6, were as follows:

### STATEMENTS OF FINANCIAL POSITION
#### At December 31, Year 6

| Assets | Pat | Sam |
|---|---|---|
| Plant assets—net | $ 460,000 | $ 320,000 |
| Investment in Sam Company | 620,000 | — |
| Other assets | 580,000 | 804,000 |
| | $1,660,000 | $1,124,000 |

| Shareholders' Equity and Liabilities | | |
|---|---|---|
| Ordinary shares | $1,000,000 | $ 400,000 |
| Retained earnings | 220,000 | 300,000 |
| Deferred tax liability | 40,000 | 30,000 |
| Other liabilities | 400,000 | 394,000 |
| | $1,660,000 | $1,124,000 |

### INCOME STATEMENTS
#### For the year ended December 31, Year 6

| | Pat | Sam |
|---|---|---|
| Sales | $1,740,000 | $1,030,000 |
| Interest and dividend income | 68,000 | 4,000 |
| | 1,808,000 | 1,034,000 |
| Cost of goods sold | 1,276,000 | 720,000 |
| Selling expenses | 44,000 | 70,000 |
| Other expenses | 166,000 | 74,000 |
| Income tax expense | 130,000 | 70,000 |
| | 1,616,000 | 934,000 |
| Profit | $ 192,000 | $ 100,000 |

## Required

(a) Prepare a schedule to allocate the acquisition differential at the date of acquisition and a schedule to amortize the acquisition differential from the date of acquisition to the end of Year 6. Deferred income taxes should be recognized on the acquisition differential at the date of acquisition.

(b) Prepare the journal entries for Pat's separate-entity books to account for the investment in Sam for Year 6 and determine the investment income from Sam for Year 6 under
  (i) the equity method, and
  (ii) the cost method.

 (c) Prepare consolidated financial statements for Year 6.

## Solution to Self-Study Problem 2

(a) Cost of 80% of Sam 620,000

Implied value of 100% 775,000

Carrying amount of Sam's net assets

= Carrying amount of Sam's shareholders' equity:

| | | | |
|---|---|---|---|
| Ordinary shares | | 400,000 | |
| Retained earnings | | 125,000 | 525,000 (a) |
| Acquisition differential | | | 250,000 |
| Allocated: | | FV − CA | |
| Plant assets | | 80,000 | |
| Trademarks | | 50,000 | |
| | | 130,000 | |
| Deferred income tax liability (130,000 × 40%) | | (52,000) | |
| Subtotal | | | 78,000 (b) |
| Goodwill for 100% | | | 172,000 |
| Less: NCI's share at 20% (not recognized on consolidated SFP) | | | 34,400 |
| Goodwill for Pat's 80% (recognized on consolidated SFP) | | | 137,600 |
| NCI at date of acquisition (20% × [(a) 525,000 + (b) 78,000]) | | | 120,600 (c) |

| | Bal. Dec. 31, Year 2 | Amortization To Dec. 31, Year 5 | Year 6 | Loss Year 6 | Bal. Dec. 31, Year 6 | |
|---|---|---|---|---|---|---|
| Plant assets (8 years) | 80,000 | 30,000 | 10,000 | | 40,000 | (d) |
| Trademarks (10 years) | 50,000 | 15,000 | 5,000 | 1,000 | 29,000 | (e) |
| | 130,000 | 45,000 | 15,000 | 1,000 | 69,000 | (f) |
| Deferred tax liability (@ 40%) | 52,000 | 18,000 | 6,000 | 400 | 27,600 | (g) |
| Subtotal | 78,000 | 27,000 | 9,000 | 600 | 41,400 | (h) |
| Goodwill for Pat's 80% | 137,600 | — | — | 52,600 | 85,000 | (i) |
| Total | 215,600 | 27,000 | 9,000 | 53,200 | 126,400 | (j) |
| NCI's share [20% × (h)] | 15,600 | 5,400 | 1,800 | 120 | 8,280 | (k) |
| Pat's share [(j) − (k)] | 200,000 | 21,600 | 7,200 | 53,080 | 118,120 | (l) |

(b)

| | Equity Method | | Cost Method |
|---|---|---|---|
| Investment in Sam (80% × 100,000) | 80,000 | | |
| Equity method income | | 80,000 | |
| To record Pat's share of Sam's income | | | |
| | | | |
| Cash (80% × 40,000) | 32,000 | | 32,000 |
| Investment in Sam | | 32,000 | |
| Dividend income | | | 32,000 (m) |
| To record Pat's share of Sam's dividend | | | |
| Equity method income [(l) (7,200 + (l) 53,080) | 60,280 | | |
| Investment in Sam | | 60,280 | |
| To record Pat's share of amortization and impairment of acquisition differential | | | |

Investment income for Year 6 under the equity method is $19,720 ($80,000 − $60,280) and $32,000 under the cost method. Total income under equity method is $179,720 ($192,000 − $32,000 + $19,720).

(c)
## CALCULATION OF CONSOLIDATED PROFIT ATTRIBUTABLE TO NCI

| | | |
|---|---|---|
| Sam's profit | 100,000 | |
| NCI's share @ 20% | 20,000 | |
| Acquisition differential amortization [**(k) 1,800** + **(k) 120**] | (1,920) | |
| | 18,080 | **(n)** |

## CALCULATION OF CONSOLIDATED RETAINED EARNINGS
### at December 31, Year 6

| | | | |
|---|---|---|---|
| Pat's retained earnings, Dec. 31, Year 6 (under cost method) | | 220,000 | |
| Sam's retained earnings Dec. 31, Year 6 | 300,000 | | |
| Acquisition retained earnings | 125,000 | | |
| Increase | 175,000 | | |
| Pat's share | × 80% | 140,000 | |
| Less: Acquisition differential amortization and impairment | | | |
| [**(l) 21,600** + **(l) 7,200** + **(l) 53,080**] | | (81,880) | |
| | | 278,120 | **(o)** |

## CALCULATION OF NCI
### at December 31, Year 6

| | | | |
|---|---|---|---|
| NCI at acquisition **(c)** | | 120,600 | |
| Sam's retained earnings Dec. 31, Year 6 | 300,000 | | |
| Acquisition retained earnings | 125,000 | | |
| Increase | 175,000 | | |
| NCI's share | × 20% | 35,000 | |
| Less: Acquisition differential amortization  [**(k) 5,400** + **(k)** **1,800** + **(k) 120**] | | (7,320) | |
| | | 148,280 | **(p)** |

## PAT INC.
## CONSOLIDATED INCOME STATEMENT
### For the year ended December 31, Year 6

| | |
|---|---|
| Sales (1,740,000 + 1,030,000) | $2,770,000 |
| Interest and investment income (68,000 + 4,000 − [**m**] **32,000**) | 40,000 |
| | 2,810,000 |
| Cost of sales (1,276,000 + 720,000) | 1,996,000 |
| Selling expenses (44,000 + 70,000 + [**f**] **15,000**) | 129,000 |
| Other expenses (166,000 + 74,000 + [**f**] **1,000** + [**i**] **52,600**) | 293,600 |
| Income tax expense (130,000 + 70,000 − [**g**] **6,000** − [**g**] **400**) | 193,600 |
| | 2,612,200 |
| Profit | $ 197,800 |
| Attributable to: | |
| Pat's shareholders (= income under equity method) | $ 179,720 |
| Non-controlling interest **(n)** | 18,080 |
| | $ 197,800 |

## PAT INC.
## CONSOLIDATED BALANCE SHEET
### At December 31, Year 6

| | |
|---|---|
| Plant assets (460,000 + 320,000 + [**d**] **40,000**) | $ 820,000 |
| Trademarks (0 + 0 + [**e**] **29,000**) | 29,000 |
| Goodwill (0 + 0 + [**i**] **85,000**) | 85,000 |
| Other assets (580,000 + 804,000) | 1,384,000 |
| | $2,318,000 |
| Ordinary shares | $1,000,000 |
| Retained earnings **(o)** | 278,120 |
| Non-controlling interest **(p)** | 148,280 |
| Deferred income tax liability (40,000 + 30,000 + [**g**] **27,600**) | 97,600 |
| Other liabilities (400,000 + 394,000) | 794,000 |
| | $2,318,000 |

## Review Questions

LO1  **1.** Explain the similarities and differences between a subsidiary and a controlled special-purpose entity and between a majority shareholder for a subsidiary and a sponsor for a controlled special-purpose entity.

LO1  **2.** Explain how the definitions of assets and liabilities can be used to support the consolidation of special-purpose entities.

LO2  **3.** Explain how to account for an interest in a joint operation.

LO2  **4.** Y Company has a 62% interest in Z Company. Are there circumstances where this would not result in Z Company being a subsidiary of Y Company? Explain.

LO2  **5.** The treatment of an unrealized intercompany inventory profit differs between a parent–subsidiary affiliation and a venturer–joint venture affiliation. Explain where the differences lie.

LO2  **6.** A venturer invested non-monetary assets in the formation of a new joint venture and did not receive any monetary consideration. The fair value of the assets invested was greater than the carrying amount in the accounting records of the venturer. Explain how the venturer should account for the investment.

LO2  **7.** Explain how the revenue recognition principle supports the recognition of a portion of gains occurring on transactions between the venturer and the joint venture.

LO3  **8.** X Company recently acquired control over Y Company. On the date of acquisition, the fair values of Y Company's assets exceeded their tax bases. How does this difference affect the consolidated balance sheet?

LO3  **9.** A parent company has recently acquired a subsidiary. On the date of acquisition, both the parent and the subsidiary had unused income tax losses that were unrecognized in their financial statements. How would this affect the consolidation figures on the date of acquisition?

LO3  **10.** What is the difference between a *deductible* temporary difference and a *taxable* temporary difference?

LO3  **11.** Explain how it is possible to have a deferred tax liability with regard to the presentation of a subsidiary's assets in a consolidated balance sheet, whereas on the subsidiary's balance sheet the same assets produce a deferred tax asset.

LO3  **12.** Explain how the definition of a liability supports the recognition of a deferred income tax liability when the fair value of an asset acquired in a business combination is greater than the tax base of this asset.

LO4  **13.** Describe the three tests for identifying reportable operating segments.

LO4  **14.** For each of its operating segments that require separate disclosure, what information must an enterprise disclose?

LO4  **15.** In accordance with IFRS 8 *Operating Segments,* answer the following:
  (a)  What information must be disclosed about business carried out in other countries?
  (b)  What information must be disclosed about a company's products or services?
  (c)  What information must be provided about a company's customers?

LO4  **16.** What sort of reconciliations are required for segmented reporting?

LO4  **17.** Explain how the use of the information provided in segment disclosures can aid in the assessment of the overall profitability of a company.

# CASES

## Case 9-1

LO1, 2, 6

Mr. Landman has spent the last 10 years developing small commercial strip malls and has been very successful. He buys a residential property in a high-traffic area, rezones the property, and then sells it to a contractor who builds the plaza and sells it to investors. Mr. Landman has often been hired to manage the commercial plazas for a fee. Now Mr. Landman wants to become a real estate baron. Rather than just developing the plazas for resale, he wants to form partnerships with builders and/or investors to build commercial properties and keep them as long-term investments.

He has found two properties suitable for development and made offers to the current owners to purchase these properties on January 1, Year 2. The offers are conditional upon arranging suitable financing for the acquisition.

Mr. Landman intends to set up two separate companies to buy, develop, and hold the properties. Elgin Company will purchase the property on Elgin Street for $1,200,000 and build a small office building at an expected cost of $2,800,000. Mr. Landman's holding company, Holdco, will invest $1,200,000 in Elgin for 30% of its common shares. Ms. Richer, a private investor, will invest $2,800,000 for a 70% interest in Elgin. According to the terms of the shareholders' agreement, Mr. Landman and Ms. Richer must agree on all major operating and financing decisions. Otherwise, the property will be sold in the open market and the company will be wound up.

The second company, Metcalfe Inc., will buy a recently developed strip mall on Metcalfe Street for $2,000,000. The purchase will be financed with a first mortgage of $1,500,000 and $500,000 of equity. Mr. Landman's holding company will invest $200,000 in Metcalfe for 40% of its common shares and will manage the property. Ms. Richer will invest $300,000 for a 60% interest in Metcalfe. The shareholders' agreement contains the following terms:

- Ms. Richer is guaranteed a return of her investment of $300,000 plus cumulative dividends of $24,000 a year.

- Mr. Landman is responsible for making all key operating, investing, and financing decisions.

- Mr. Landman's holding company guarantees the payment of dividends to Ms. Richer on an annual basis. After both shareholders have received cumulative dividends equal to 8% of their initial investments, Ms. Richer will receive 10% and Mr. Landman's holding company will receive 90% of the undistributed profits.

Holdco intends to use the cost method for internal purposes to account for these two investments. Holdco typically finances its acquisitions with 75% debt and 25% equity. The debt financing has a maximum debt-to-equity ratio of 3:1.

**Required**

(a) How should these two investments be reported on the financial statements of Holdco? Provide arguments to support your recommendations.

(b) What impact will the adoption of the reporting methods suggested in part (a) have on Holdco's debt-to-equity ratio? Briefly explain.

## Case 9-2

LO1, 6

P Co. is looking for some additional financing in order to renovate one of the company's manufacturing plants. It is having difficulty getting new debt financing because its debt-to-equity ratio is higher than the 3:1 limit stated in its bank covenant. It is unable to attract an equity partner because the sole owner of P Co. has set equity partner conditions that make it practically impossible to find a new equity investor.

Part of the problem results from the use of historical cost accounting. If the company's assets were recorded at fair value, the debt-to-equity ratio would be much lower. In order to get around the requirements for historical cost accounting, the CFO for P Co. came up with the following plan.

On September 2, Year 5, P Co. will sell its manufacturing facility to SPE for $1,350,000 in the form of a non-interest-bearing note receivable. SPE will be set up for the sole purpose of renovating the manufacturing facility. No other activities may be carried out by SPE without the approval of P Co. Mr. Renovator, an unrelated party, will invest $900,000 in cash to cover the estimated cost of the renovation and will be the sole owner of SPE. On January 1, Year 6, after the renovation is complete and one day after P Co.'s year-end, SPE will sell the manufacturing facility back to P Co. at $2,340,000 and will be wound up. P will finance the repurchase with a $990,000 bank loan and by offsetting the remaining $1,350,000 against the note receivable from SPE from the original sale of the manufacturing facility to SPE. By selling the unrenovated facility and repurchasing the renovated facility, P Co. hopes to reflect the facility at its fair value, borrow the money to finance the renovation, and improve its debt-to-equity position.

The existing and pro forma balance sheets (in 000s) and debt-to-equity ratios for P Co. and SPE are presented below in condensed form:

|  | P Co. Sep. 1/5 | P Co. Dec. 31/5 | P Co. Jan. 1/6 | SPE Dec. 31/5 |
|---|---|---|---|---|
| Note receivable from SPE |  | $ 1,350 |  |  |
| Manufacturing facility | $ 225 |  | $2,340 | $2,250 |
| Other assets | 2,025 | 2,025 | 2,025 | 0 |
|  | $ 2,250 | $ 3,375 | $4,365 | $2,250 |
| Note payable to P Co. |  |  |  | $1,350 |
| Other liabilities | $ 1,800 | $ 1,800 | $2,790 |  |
| Common shares | 30 | 30 | 30 | 900 |
| Retained earnings | 420 | 1,545 | 1,545 | 0 |
|  | $ 2,250 | $ 3,375 | $4,365 | $2,250 |
| Debt-to-equity ratio | 4:1 | 1.14:1 | 1.77:1 | 1.5:1 |

The CFO would like you to prepare a memo in which you discuss the accounting issues related to these proposed transactions.

**Required**

Prepare the memo requested by the CFO. Ignore income taxes.

## Case 9-3

LO2, 6

Tropical Juices Limited (Tropical) was incorporated under Canadian federal legislation two years ago as a 50:50 joint venture of Citrus Growers Cooperative (Citrus) of the United States and Bottle Juices Corporation (Bottle) of Canada to sell Citrus's juices in Canada. Excerpts from the joint venture agreement are provided in Exhibit I. Both Citrus and Bottle produce and sell juices separately as well as through Tropical.

One year ago the owners of Bottle sold all their shares in Bottle to Douglas Investments Limited (DIL). The contract of sale between DIL and the former shareholders of Bottle included representations and warranties with respect to Tropical. Excerpts from the sale contract are provided in Exhibit II.

DIL required that representations and warranties about Tropical be written into the sale contract because Citrus and Bottle were still negotiating the accounting policies to be used by Tropical. The selection of accounting policies is still not resolved, and the two parties cannot come to an agreement.

Draft financial statements for Tropical for the years ended June 30, Year 1, and June 30, Year 2, were prepared based on the accounting policies selected by Bottle's controller. For the second year, the results were as follows:

| | |
|---|---|
| Revenue | $2,959,000 |
| Operating expenses, excluding depreciation, interest, and imputed charges | 2,128,500 |
| Depreciation, interest, and imputed charges | 643,500 |

The joint venture agreement between Citrus and Bottle permits the appointment of an arbitrator to resolve disputes over accounting policies. Your firm has been appointed arbitrator and has been asked by all three parties (owners of Citrus and present and previous owners of Bottle) to submit a report containing binding decisions on all matters of contention. Each decision in this arbitration report must be supported by sound reasoning so that each party can fully understand the decisions.

You interview each of the parties and are told the following.

## Comments of Citrus

1. "We disagree with Bottle's charge for the cost of returnable bottles. It charged the entire cost of the bottles (which it owns) to Tropical in the first year even though the bottles have a life of 20 to 25 months."

2. "Bottle had to purchase new machinery for bottling Tropical juices because a different shape of bottle is used. It borrowed the necessary funds and charged the interest to Tropical. We reject this charge."

3. "Bottle spent $360,800 training its employees to manufacture and sell Tropical juices. We disagree with this sum being expensed and charged to Tropical in the first year."

4. "Bottle charged Tropical 16% on the capital investment being used to produce Tropical juices. We agree with the 16%, but we do not agree with the 16% being applied from the date that the first Tropical juices were produced."

5. "Bottle charged Tropical fair value for the computer services it provided. We believe that Bottle should have charged Tropical for these services at cost."

6. "Bottle had a three-week strike. When the strike was over, Bottle produced its own juices to replenish its own inventory, and did not produce Tropical juices for almost one month. We believe that Tropical should be credited in the first year for imputed gross profits lost during the months after the strike."

### Comments of Previous Owners of Bottle

7.  "Tropical has benefited from Citrus's advertising of the Citrus brand names in the United States. Citrus has charged Tropical for this advertising using the ratio of the Canadian population reached by the U.S. television-advertising signal to the combined Canadian and U.S. populations reached by the signal. In our opinion, this does not make sense."

8.  "We understand that Citrus is complaining that we were charging proportionate repair costs for the machinery and equipment being used to produce Tropical juices and our own juices. We consider this to be an appropriate charge."

9.  "We charged Tropical on the basis of our costs of producing Tropical juices. Citrus objects to our use of full absorption costing even though this was the method we used for our financial statements."

### Comments of DIL

10. "After completing the purchase of Bottle, we discovered that Bottle's management had been manipulating the profits between years."

11. "Tropical sells large quantities of juices to distributors who pay Tropical only when the juices are resold. However, Tropical has recorded revenue when the juices are shipped to the distributors. We disagree with this practice."

12. "Citrus bought a new refrigerated tanker truck in the second year to deliver bulk concentrates to Tropical. It is charging the cost to Tropical at one-third per year, commencing in the second year. We disagree with this approach."

13. "Citrus charges interest to Tropical on the account receivable from Tropical. We disagree." You, the CPA, have been asked to prepare the arbitration report.

**EXHIBIT I**

## Tropical Juices Limited—Excerpts from the Joint Venture Agreement

Citrus shall provide the following to Tropical:

- Blending formula and drink recipes
- Brand names
- Ongoing supply of juice concentrates
- Advertising in Canada

Bottle shall provide the following to Tropical on an ongoing basis:

- Capital equipment and personnel needed to process the juice at their existing premises
- Returnable bottles supply
- Processing and distribution of the juice

Citrus and Bottle shall share equally in the net income of Tropical, after specific charges are made to Tropical for services provided by Citrus and Bottle. The specific charges are as follows:

1. Bottle is allowed to charge Tropical 16% per year on the capital investment in assets needed to process, bottle, and distribute the juices.
2. Both Bottle and Citrus are permitted to charge Tropical for
   a. Disbursements they make on behalf of Tropical, and
   b. Reasonable charges for administrative and other allocations of joint costs incurred on behalf of Tropical juices and their own juices.
3. Citrus is permitted to charge fair value for all juice concentrates provided to Tropical.

Citrus and Bottle shall help market Tropical juices, although Tropical shall have primary responsibility for selling its own juices. Citrus and Bottle shall allocate to Tropical its proportionate share of any revenue from sales that consist of both Tropical juices and their own juices.

---

**EXHIBIT II**

## Bottle Juices Corporation Excerpts from the Sale Contract

The following terms, representations, and warranties are made with respect to Tropical:

1. DIL is entitled to one-half of the net income of Tropical commencing with the second year of operations, which ends on June 30, Year 2. One-half of the net income of Tropical for the first year of operations shall be paid to the former shareholders of Bottle.
2. Bottle warrants that the total revenue will not be less than $3.3 million for each of the years ended June 30, Years 2 and 3.
3. Bottle warrants that operating expenses excluding depreciation, interest, and imputed charges shall not exceed $1.76 million for each of the years ended June 30, Years 2 and 3.
4. Bottle warrants that depreciation, interest, and imputed charges shall not exceed, for each of the years ended June 30, the following amounts:

| | |
|---|---|
| Year 2 | $605,000 |
| Year 3 | 550,000 |

5. All computations are to be in accordance with generally accepted accounting principles for private enterprises.
6. If the representations and warranties are not fulfilled, then DIL shall be fully compensated for its portion of the amount of the deficiency.

*(CPA Canada adapted)*[12]

## Case 9-4

LO4

Segment reporting can provide useful information for investors and competitors. Segment disclosures can result in competitive harm for the company making the disclosures. By analyzing segment information, potential competitors can identify and concentrate on the more successful areas of a disclosing company's business. Indeed, the IASB recognizes that competitive harm is an issue of concern for companies disclosing segment information. In developing IFRS 8, the IASB considered giving, but ultimately decided not to give, companies an exemption from providing segment information if they believed that doing so would result in competitive harm. The IASB believed that such an exemption would be inappropriate because it would provide a means for broad non-compliance with the new standard.

IFRS 8 requires disclosures to be provided by country when revenues or long-lived assets in an individual country are material. However, IFRS 8 does not specify what is material for this purpose but leaves this to management judgment. Some commentators have expressed a concern that firms might use high materiality thresholds to avoid making individual country disclosures, perhaps to avoid potential competitive harm.

**Required**

What factors might a company consider in determining whether an individual foreign country is material to its operations? Should the IASB establish a percentage test to determine when an individual country is material?

## Case 9-5

LO2, 6

Pluto Technology Venture (PTV) is an unincorporated joint operation with three current joint operators. A few other prospective investors are awaiting an opportunity to invest in PTV. PTV was organized three months ago to combine the knowledge, assets, and finances of a group of organizations that specialize in computer graphics and animation. One of the operators, Flash Limited (FL), required a considerable infusion of cash to survive. FL transferred the assets and liabilities of one of its major operating divisions to PTV in exchange for PTV ownership units and cash. The second operator, Bulge Capital Corporation (BCC), invested in PTV mainly by way of a cash contribution. The third operator, Everest Properties Limited (EPL), contributed a building to house PTV's main operations and also provided some office and administrative personnel. The three current operators have agreed that an unincorporated joint operation is the appropriate form of organization for the next several years.

The directors of PTV would like your firm to prepare a report that discusses all of the important accounting issues. They would like specific recommendations as to how PTV should account for its transactions, and explanations as to why the recommended accounting is appropriate.

In your meetings with various interested parties, you have learned the following:

1. Profits of PTV are to be divided in proportion to the number of ownership units that are held by each operator. According to the Agreement Among Operators:

   "Profits" are to be "all inclusive" for all activities of PTV. All inclusive is defined as profits from operations and from all changes in the valuation of assets and liabilities. In arriving at the profit, deductions are allowed for individual payments to the operators for various services that they provide over and above the initial contribution to PTV.

2. Financial statements have to be provided each quarter to PTV's banker. The banker and PTV have arranged a lending formula that is closely linked to two PTV measurements: quarterly and annual cash flow, and the fair market value of PTV's assets less liabilities.

3. The financial statements are to be used in part to set the prices that are to be paid to PTV for any new joint operation units.

4. PTV develops software for specific clients and develops software products that it sells to the general educational market. Software that is developed for specific clients tends to be on a cost-plus basis, whereby PTV is paid 60–120 days after successful completion of each phase of the software. Different clients specify different definitions of cost. PTV carries the costs on its books as work in progress until clients are invoiced.

   FL has been granted non-exclusive marketing rights to some of PTV's educational products. FL may sell the products in specified regions at prices that it deems appropriate. FL is entitled to a 20% discount from the price that other distributors have to pay.

5. The identifiable assets and liabilities of FL initially contributed to PTV were (in thousands of dollars):

| | Carrying Amount | Fair Value |
|---|---|---|
| Receivables | $ 340 | $ 310 |
| Inventory | 915 | 735 |
| Prepaid expenses | 60 | 60 |
| Equipment | 6,410 | 6,100 |
| Accumulated amortization | (3,830) | |
| Software under development | 100 | 1,500 |
| Liabilities | (605) | (605) |
| | $3,390 | $8,100 |

The assets and liabilities were assigned a value of $8.8 million. In exchange, FL was given a 30% interest in PTV and $2.2 million in cash.

6. BCC invested $8.8 million in cash, in exchange for a 40% interest in PTV. In addition, BCC loaned $2 million to PTV at 5% interest. The market rate of interest is currently 8%.

7. EPL received a 30% interest in PTV in exchange for a building that was recorded on its books at $4.9 million (cost $6 million and accumulated depreciation of $1.1 million). EPL also rents space in another building to PTV at an amount below fair market value.

8. EPL has signed a "management agreement" with PTV to perform management services until PTV grows to the point where it needs its own management team. EPL is allowed under the agreement to charge for its services at cost plus 25%. The agreement also covers the use of equipment by PTV. PTV can either rent the equipment or rent with an option to purchase, at specified rates and amounts.

9. One prospective joint operator has loaned PTV $1 million at the market rate of interest for a period of one year. After one year, the prospective venturer is permitted to acquire a 10% interest in PTV at its fair market value. At that time, the prospective operator must pay the balance of the purchase price or forgo the $1 million.

10. PTV is in the process of renovating the building. The value of the building is expected to rise because of the renovations and because of general economic conditions.

11. PTV leases computers and equipment under a three-year contract. Since PTV signed the lease, prices have dropped by 30%, and a further drop is possible.

12. Competition in the industry has been very aggressive in recent months and is expected to persist. Costs of inputs can fluctuate significantly. The selling prices of finished goods can also fluctuate significantly.

13. PTV has invested some of the cash that was received from the current and prospective joint operators in short-term, high-yielding bonds.

14. PTV has begun to conduct joint projects with other organizations and has contributed about $320,000 to date to developing specialized computer graphics packages.

15. Last week PTV signed a two-year contract with a film company to develop animation materials. The contract should generate revenue of $10 million to $14 million.

*(CPA Canada adapted)*[13]

## Case 9-6

.........

LO2

You, CPA, have been working for Plener and Partners, Chartered Professional Accountants (P&P), a mid-size CPA firm, for three years. You have been assigned a new project for a long-term client of your firm, Oxford Developments Inc. (ODI). Information on ODI's operations and the property development industry can be found in Exhibit III.

It is now September 5, Year 11. You and Wendy Yan, the engagement partner, just sat down with Mike D'Silva, Chief Executive Officer of ODI. Mike came in to discuss a new business opportunity that ODI has recently undertaken.

"At ODI, we are always searching for new opportunities related to property development. ODI's focus is on providing a superior return on investment for its shareholders. ODI leverages existing equity with an appropriate amount of debt to acquire and develop properties for resale. As I've mentioned to you before, we have been thinking of getting into the hotel market for a couple of years now, but we were unsure how to get started. A little while ago, I had a chance meeting with

Linda Kim, the general manager of Hospitality Management Inc. (HMI). After many meetings and much research, we decided that ODI and HMI are a good fit, and we have started working together on the development and operation of a boutique hotel. Our hotel will have a special feature—the hotel rooms will be sold to individual investors.

"We have established a separate company, Genuine Investments Inc. (GI), for this unique project. HMI agreed to contribute cash and ODI contributed the land and the building. To be successful and profitable, the hotel will require excellent marketing and management. HMI has a good track record in these areas, and I'm confident they will be able to achieve similar results for this property. HMI will operate the hotel under a management contract. I've provided some excerpts from the finalized agreement between ODI and HMI (Exhibit IV)."

After Mike leaves, Wendy says to you, "It is likely that we will also be asked to perform the annual audit engagement of GI's financial statements in accordance with IFRS, so I would appreciate your analysis of the accounting implications for the initial transactions and ongoing operations of GI. I had a chance to meet with ODI's Chief Financial Officer, Amber Wolfe. My notes from that conversation are attached (Exhibit V).

### EXHIBIT III

## Information on Oxford Developments Inc. and the Property Development Industry

Oxford Developments Inc. (ODI) is a mid-size real estate development and sales company. It was founded by a small group of individuals who felt there was a significant amount of money to be made in real estate, and it has been in business for 10 years. As the company grew, it brought in additional investors, and it is now owned by 25 individual shareholders. The investors have never been involved in the day-to-day management of the company; rather, it is professionally managed.

Over the past several years, ODI has acquired over 100 commercial and industrial properties all over Canada, which showed significant potential. ODI has renovated these properties and resold them, usually for a substantial gain. The average time between acquisition and sale of the properties has been 12 months, and the average profit margin has been over 12%.

Between Year 2 and Year 10, the Canadian real estate industry has been strong. The average annual increase in the value of commercial real estate has been 8.2% over this time period, compared with the historical annual rate of 4.6% in the previous 20 years. ODI has been able to achieve a profit margin of over 12% due to its strategic acquisitions and its strong control of the renovation costs associated with these properties.

The hotel industry in Canada is fragmented, and significant differences exist between the various geographical areas of the country as well as the quality of hotel properties. Overall, the industry has achieved an occupancy rate of 76% over the past decade. This percentage has been steadily increasing over the past 10 years, with the occupancy rate going from 72% in Year 1 to 79% in Year 10.

More recently, the Canadian economy has slowed. The difficulties in the U.S. housing market, as well as the uncertainties surrounding the financial industry in the U.S., have precipitated a worldwide economic slowdown. Canada is not immune to these events.

ODI believes it is well situated to take advantage of the opportunities that a declining real estate market may present. ODI's strategy is to maintain a strong balance sheet, purchase strategic properties at distressed prices, renovate these properties at low costs using well-priced labour and construction materials, and resell the properties as the real estate market starts to recover.

## Excerpts from Genuine Investments Inc. Agreement

### Incorporation
Genuine Investments Inc. (GI) was incorporated on December 1, Year 10, to develop and operate a boutique hotel known as "The Genuine Hotel." The financial year-end for GI will be November 30.

### Authorized Share Capital of GI
There are two classes of shares, as follows:
- Class A voting common shares—20,000 shares authorized
- Class B non-voting shares—an unlimited number of shares authorized

### Contributions
Oxford Developments Inc. (ODI) will contribute the land and building and $1,000 in cash to GI in exchange for 1,000 Class A shares and 100,000 Class B shares. The building is expected to have a useful life of 40 years. Hospitality Management Inc. (HMI) will contribute cash equal to the fair value of the land and building contributed by ODI plus $1,000 in exchange for 1,000 Class A shares and 100,000 Class B shares.

### Restriction on Share Sale
Shares in GI cannot be sold or traded without the approval of both ODI and HMI. Both companies agree to hold the shares for five years. After that period, if either party wants to sell, the other party will have the right to purchase the shares at 90% of the market value at the time of sale.

### Loans
ODI and HMI may periodically loan funds to GI. If funds need to be advanced to GI, both investors will provide an equal amount. Any funds advanced will bear interest at the prevailing market rate, and will be repayable on demand at the request of either ODI or HMI.

### Board of Directors
ODI and HMI will each appoint two individuals to the board of directors of GI. A fifth member, who will act as board chair, will be jointly appointed by ODI and HMI.

### Profit Distribution
GI will distribute 90% of its net earnings on an annual basis provided there is cash available. The distributions will be performed on a tax-effective basis in the form of either dividends or management fees. If the company is wound up or dissolved for any reason, the final distribution of any amounts remaining shall be made in proportion to the Class B shareholdings of each investor.

### Transactions between GI and ODI
All sales (and subsequent resales) of rooms will be done through the real estate division of ODI. ODI will receive a commission on initial sales from GI of 2.5% and on subsequent resales by room owners of 5%. These rates are based on existing market rates.

### Operation
Operation of The Genuine Hotel will be contracted to HMI at a fee approximating the current market rate for management fees. HMI will be responsible for reservations, guest services, housekeeping, regular ongoing maintenance of the hotel, and security. GI will be responsible for general administration. The contract will be renegotiated every five years. The management fee for the first five years is set at $75 per night per occupied hotel room.

## Notes from Conversation with Amber Wolfe, Chief Financial Officer of Oxford Developments Inc.

"Thanks so much for meeting with me. Ever since this project began, I've had more work than I can handle. GI has minimal staff right now, including a manager looking after the construction and some secretarial and administrative support, so I've been helping out. As a result, I have questions about both ODI and GI.

"I'm hoping that P&P can take over the day-to-day bookkeeping for the next several months until GI can hire an experienced controller. On the bright side, a marketing person was recently hired, and we are actively hiring additional staff as required.

"Extensive renovations were required on the building, and they are now complete. Most of the furnishings, fixtures, and equipment have been installed, and we are busy planning for the grand opening. Since we wanted to get the project started quickly, ODI and HMI provided all of the initial financing. However, in the future, we would like GI to obtain its own bank financing. If GI does obtain financing, it would like to repay the amounts owing to ODI and HMI and repurchase 50% of the Class B shares held by each company at carrying amount. I have brought along some financial information related to GI (Exhibits VI and VII).

"Given that this investment is new and unique for ODI, it could become a model for future investments. Our shareholders are therefore very interested in how the accounting for our investment in GI will affect ODI's financial statements for the November 30, Year 11, year-end and in the future. I expect the gain on the sale of the land and building transferred to GI to improve ODI's overall financial position and increase its net income. I think it should also increase ODI's net assets, which is a key financial indicator reported to ODI's shareholders and ODI's bank.

"I think that's it for now. Again, thanks for your help with all of this, as my time seems to be at a premium these days."

---

**EXHIBIT VI**

# Trial Balance for Genuine Investments Inc.

**GENUINE INVESTMENTS INC.**
**TRIAL BALANCE**
For the nine months ended August 31, Year 11
(in thousands of dollars)
Generated for Internal Purposes Only

| Account Description | Note | Debits | Credits |
|---|---|---|---|
| Cash (overdraft) | A | | $    24 |
| Construction in progress | A | $10,034 | |
| Land | A | 1,890 | |
| Building | A | 4,560 | |
| Furnishings and equipment—rooms | A | 5,082 | |
| Furnishings and equipment—common areas | A | 2,100 | |
| Furnishings and equipment—restaurant/retail space | A | 0 | |
| Accounts payable and accruals | L | | 1,425 |
| Loan—ODI | L | | 2,922 |
| Loan—HMI | L | | 2,922 |
| Class A shares | E | | 2 |
| Class B shares | E | | 12,900 |
| Room sales | R | | 4,000 |
| Other income | R | | 348 |
| Cost of room sales | X | 0 | |
| Operating expenses | X | 243 | |
| Architect and project management fees | X | 137 | |
| Landscaping fees | X | 87 | |
| Financing arrangement fees | X | 63 | |
| Incorporation costs | X | 54 | |
| Property taxes | X | 41 | |
| Building permits | X | 50 | |
| Insurance | X | 27 | |
| Interest expense related to construction | X | 175 | |
| | | $24,543 | $24,543 |

Notes:
A—Asset
L—Liability
E—Equity (net asset)
R—Revenue/Income
X—Expense

---

**EXHIBIT VII**

## Financial Information about Genuine Investments Inc.

1. Details of the land and building transferred from ODI to GI are as follows (in thousands):

| Asset Transferred | Carrying Amount | Market Value |
|---|---|---|
| Land | $ 480 | $1,890 |
| Building | 4,000 | 4,560 |
| Total | $4,480 | $6,450 |

2. Twenty-five hotel rooms have been sold to date at the listed price. Deposits of 5% of the sales price have been received for an additional 40 rooms. Investors interested in seven of these 40 rooms have recently backed out. The deposits are non-refundable and are included in other income. GI expects that all hotel rooms will be sold to investors within the next three months.

3. All of the owners of the hotel rooms that have been sold to date (25 owners) have also entered into management contracts with GI to rent out their hotel rooms on their behalf. We anticipate that the buyers of the remaining 75 rooms will enter into management contracts as well. This is consistent with what similar projects have experienced: a very high percentage of owners have entered into management contracts to rent out their rooms.

4. GI retains 100% of the gross room rental revenue related to unsold rooms.

5. Room owners will be charged $2,000 per year to fund renovations and major furniture and equipment purchases (the "Reserve Fund Contribution"). The monies collected will be paid to GI and put into a reserve fund to be drawn upon as needed. The fund will not be used for ongoing maintenance, which will be done by HMI as part of its management responsibility. The $2,000 amount charged to each owner may be adjusted in future years to ensure the reserve fund is adequate to cover the costs associated with renovations and major furniture and equipment purchases.

   Industry data indicates that annual major renovations typically amount to approximately 1% of the original cost of the building in the first five years of a building's life, and increase to 5% after five years.

6. Annual operating and administrative expenses are estimated at $360,000 and $300,000, respectively. These estimated expenses include property taxes, insurance, interest charges on shareholder and bank loans, accounting fees, and salaries associated with the overall administrative and financial areas of GI.

7. The hotel will include retail space and a restaurant. Agreements are in place with two retailers, and GI is in the process of sorting out the details of an agreement with Gizmos, a great restaurant chain. We anticipate that all the commercial operators will be in place by November 30, Year 11. Budgeted sales revenue (annual) for each of these establishments is as follows:

| | |
|---|---|
| Restaurant | $ 2,500,000 |
| Convenience store | 700,000 |
| Art gallery | 1,500,000 |

   GI will receive a percentage of the operators' gross revenue. That percentage is 3% for the restaurant, 5% for the convenience store, and 3% for the art gallery.

8. GI intends to capitalize all the costs associated with the building renovations for accounting purposes. Many of the soft costs, such as interest and landscaping fees, will be expensed for tax purposes, if possible.

*(CPA Canada adapted)*[14]

# PROBLEMS

## Problem 9-1

LO1

Pharma Company (Pharma) is a pharmaceutical company operating in Winnipeg. It is developing a new drug for treating multiple sclerosis (MS). On January 1, Year 3, Benefit Ltd. (Benefit) signed an agreement to guarantee the debt of Pharma and guarantee a specified rate of return to the common shareholders. In return, Benefit will obtain the residual profits of Pharma. After extensive analysis, it has been determined that Pharma is a controlled special-purpose entity and Benefit is its sponsor. The balance sheets (in millions) of Benefit and Pharma on January 1, Year 3, were as follows:

|  | Benefit | Pharma | |
| --- | --- | --- | --- |
|  | Carrying Amount | Carrying Amount | Fair Value |
| Current assets | $ 400 | $150 | $150 |
| Property, plant, and equipment | 600 | 180 | 190 |
| Intangible assets | 100 | 70 | 120 |
|  | $1,100 | $400 | $460 |
| Current liabilities | $ 245 | $160 | $160 |
| Long-term debt | 525 | 250 | 255 |
| Common shares | 60 | 1 | |
| Retained earnings | 270 | (11) | |
|  | $1,100 | $400 | |

An independent appraiser determined the fair values of Pharma's noncurrent assets. The appraiser was quite confident with the appraised value for the property, plant, and equipment but had some reservations in putting a specific value on the intangible assets.

**Required**

Prepare a consolidated balance sheet at January 1, Year 3, assuming that the agreement between Benefit and Pharma established the following fair values for the common shares of Pharma:

(a) $45 million

(b) $40 million

(c) $55 million

## Problem 9-2

LO3

On January 1, Year 5, AB Company (AB) purchased 80% of the outstanding common shares of Dandy Limited (Dandy) for $8,000. On that date, Dandy's shareholders' equity consisted of common shares of $1,000 and retained earnings of $6,000.

In negotiating the purchase price at the date of acquisition, it was agreed that the fair values of all of Dandy's assets and liabilities were equal to their carrying amounts and tax base except for the following:

|  | Fair Value | Carrying Amount | Tax Base |
| --- | --- | --- | --- |
| Equipment | $950 | $700 | $600 |

Dandy has recorded deferred income taxes on its separate-entity balance sheet on all temporary differences. Dandy had a loss carry-forward of $800 as at December 31, Year 4. This carry-forward can be applied against taxable income in the future. Dandy did not previously recognize the benefit of the carry-forward because it was not sure whether it would earn $800 in taxable income in the future. Now that AB controls Dandy, AB is sure that Dandy will be able to utilize the loss carry-forwards because AB will transfer income-earning assets to Dandy if necessary to generate taxable income in Dandy. AB plans to utilize these loss carry-forwards as soon as possible.

Both companies use the straight-line method for amortizing their property, plant, and equipment and pay taxes at a rate of 40%. Dandy's equipment had a remaining useful life of 10 years at the date of acquisition.

Dandy reported income before application of any loss carry-forwards as follows for the first three years after being acquired by AB:

| Year | Income before Tax |
|------|-------------------|
| Year 5 | $0 |
| Year 6 | 100 |
| Year 7 | 200 |

## Required

(a) Calculate goodwill at the date of acquisition. Be sure to consider the deferred tax implications on the acquisition differential.

(b) Calculate non-controlling interest at the date of acquisition.

(c) Prepare a schedule to show the amortization of the acquisition differential for the three-year period ending December 31, Year 7. Assume that the goodwill impairment loss was $300 in Year 6, the deferred income tax liability is amortized at the same rate as the equipment, and the loss carry-forwards are applied against income as the income is earned.

(d) Explain why the acquisition differential related to the equipment gives rise to a deferred income tax liability.

## Problem 9-3

LO3

On January 1, Year 5, Green Inc. purchased 100% of the common shares of Mansford Corp. for $353,000. Green's balance sheet data on this date just prior to this acquisition were as follows:

|  | Carrying Amount | Tax Base |
|--|-----------------|----------|
| Cash | $  355,300 | $  355,300 |
| Accounts receivable | 168,100 | –0– |
| Inventory | 275,920 | 275,920 |
| Land | 327,700 | 327,700 |
| Buildings (net) | 252,700 | 150,000 |
| Equipment (net) | 79,900 | 46,200 |
|  | $1,459,620 | $1,155,120 |
|  |  |  |
| Current liabilities | $  137,500 | $  137,500 |
| Deferred tax liability | 106,575 | — |
| Noncurrent liabilities | — |  |
| Common shares | 387,200 |  |
| Retained earnings | 828,345 |  |
|  | $1,459,620 |  |

The balance sheet and other related data for Mansford are as follows:

**MANSFORD CORP.—BALANCE SHEET**
At January 1, Year 5

| | Carrying Amount | Fair Value | Tax Base |
|---|---|---|---|
| Cash | $ 54,300 | $ 54,300 | $ 54,300 |
| Accounts receivable | 64,150 | 64,150 | 64,150 |
| Inventory | 128,000 | 135,800 | 128,000 |
| Land | 93,000 | 228,000 | 93,000 |
| Buildings (net) | 39,000 | 42,000 | 16,800 |
| Equipment (net) | 27,800 | 26,800 | 15,600 |
| | $406,250 | $551,050 | $371,850 |
| Current liabilities | $ 43,815 | $ 43,815 | $ 43,815 |
| Noncurrent liabilities | 153,600 | 155,000 | 153,600 |
| Deferred tax liability | 12,040 | | — |
| Common shares | 105,400 | | |
| Retained earnings | 91,395 | | |
| | $406,250 | | |

### Additional Information

- As at January 1, Year 5, the estimated useful lives of the building and equipment were 15 years and 4 years, respectively, and the term to maturity was 10 years for the noncurrent liabilities.
- There has been no goodwill impairment since the date of acquisition.
- For both companies, the income tax rate is 35%. Deferred income taxes are recognized on the consolidated financial statement pertaining to the temporary differences arising from the acquisition differential.

### Required

(a) Prepare a consolidated balance sheet at January 1, Year 5.
(b) Prepare a schedule of amortization/impairment of the acquisition differential for the period from January 1, Year 5, to December 31, Year 8.
(c) Prepare the consolidated balance sheet using the worksheet approach.

## Problem 9-4

LO3

Assume that all of the facts in Problem 3 remain unchanged except that Green paid $211,800 for 60% of the voting shares of Mansford.

### Required

(a) Prepare a consolidated balance sheet at January 1, Year 5.
(b) Calculate goodwill and non-controlling interest under parent company extension theory.
(c) Explain how the definition of a liability supports the recognition of a deferred income tax liability when a parent purchases shares in a subsidiary and the fair values of the subsidiary's identifiable net assets are greater than their carrying amounts.

# Problem 9-5

LO1

The statements of financial position of Hui Inc. and Kozikowski Ltd. on December 31, Year 11, were as follows:

|  | **Hui** | **Kozikowski Ltd.** |  |
|---|---|---|---|
|  | *Carrying Amount* | *Carrying Amount* | *Fair Value* |
| Land | $   400,000 | $   80,000 | $200,000 |
| Manufacturing facility | 1,050,000 | 520,000 | 300,000 |
| Accumulated depreciation | (300,000) | (200,000) |  |
| Accounts receivable | 250,000 | 50,000 | 50,000 |
| Cash | 200,000 |  |  |
|  | $1,600,000 | $450,000 | $550,000 |
| Ordinary shares | $     50,000 | $   10,000 |  |
| Retained earnings | 750,000 | 90,000 |  |
| Long-term debt | 525,000 | 290,000 | $280,000 |
| Current liabilities | 275,000 | 60,000 | 60,000 |
|  | $1,600,000 | $450,000 |  |

Kozikowski's manufacturing facility is old and very costly to operate. For the year ended December 31, Year 11, the company lost money for the first time in its history. Kozikowski does not have the financial ability to refurbish the plant. It must either cease operations or find a partner to carry on operations.

On January 1, Year 12, Hui agreed to provide an interest-free loan of $200,000 to Kozikowski on the following terms and conditions:

- Hui Inc. would be hired by Kozikowski to refurbish the manufacturing facility at a fixed cost of $200,000 and would be retained to manage the business.
- Hui Inc. would have full authority to make all major operating, investing, and financing decisions related to Kozikowski.
- The ordinary shares of Kozikowski were valued at $208,000 as at January 1, Year 12. Hui has the option to buy the shares of Kozikowski at any time after January 1, Year 17, at $208,000 plus any dividends in arrears.
- The existing shareholders of Kozikowski would be guaranteed a cumulative dividend of 8% a year on the value of their shares. Hui would receive the residual profits after the dividends were paid to the ordinary shareholders.

Kozikowski earned income of $200,000 and paid dividends of $50,000 over the five-year period ended December 31, Year 16. The statements of financial position of Hui Inc. and Kozikowski Ltd. on December 31, Year 16 were as follows:

|  | Hui | Kozikowski |
|---|---|---|
| Land | $   400,000 | $   80,000 |
| Manufacturing facility | 650,000 | 260,000 |
| Accounts receivable | 275,000 | 70,000 |
| Cash | 20,000 | 180,000 |
|  | $1,345,000 | $590,000 |
| Ordinary shares | $     50,000 | $   10,000 |
| Retained earnings | 660,000 | 240,000 |
| Long-term debt | 450,000 | 290,000 |
| Current liabilities | 185,000 | 50,000 |
|  | $1,345,000 | $590,000 |

Assume that Kozikowski is a controlled special-purpose entity and Hui is the sponsor. The manufacturing facility had an estimated remaining useful life of 10 years as at January 1, Year 12. The long-term debt matures on December 31, Year 21. Prior to Year 12, Hui had no business relations with Kozikowski.

**Required**

(a) Calculate consolidated retained earnings at December 31, Year 16.

(b) Prepare a consolidated statement of financial position for Hui at December 31, Year 16.

(c) Use the definition of a liability to explain the rationale for including the liabilities of the special-purpose entity on the consolidated statement of financial position for the sponsor.

# Problem 9-6

LO2

On January 1, Year 6, HD Ltd., a building supply company, JC Ltd., a construction company, and Mr. Saeid, a private investor, signed an agreement to carry out a joint operation under the following terms and conditions:

- JC would buy and renovate homes on behalf of the three parties to the joint operation in addition to its other construction activities. It would arrange a first mortgage on the property when purchasing the home.
- HD would supply all of the construction materials at a reduced markup from its regular sales.
- Mr. Saeid would guarantee the payment of the mortgage and would lend money to JC for the down payment on the purchase of the property and to finance the cost of materials and labour during the renovation. The loans would be interest free with no monthly payments and would be repayable out of the proceeds on sale of the property.
- All three parties would have a one-third interest in the properties under renovation and cash for joint properties, would be responsible for one-third of the mortgage payable and loan payable to Mr. Saeid and would receive one-third of the profit from sale of the renovated properties.
- JD would pay the other two joint operators their share of the profit on each property within 30 days of the closing date for the sale of the property.
- All three parties must agree on major operating and financing decisions with respect to joint operations of the renovated houses.

Condensed financial statements for HD Ltd. and JC Ltd. for the year ended December 31, Year 6, were as follows:

### STATEMENTS OF FINANCIAL POSITION
At December 31, Year 6

**Assets**

| | HD Ltd. | JC Ltd. |
|---|---|---|
| Joint properties under renovation | $ — | $ 360,000 |
| Inventory | 460,000 | — |
| Cash for joint properties | | 36,000 |
| Other assets | 1,200,000 | 728,000 |
| | $1,660,000 | $1,124,000 |

*(continued)*

*(continued)*

|  | *HD Ltd.* | *JC Ltd.* |
|---|---|---|
| **Shareholders' Equity and Liabilities** | | |
| Ordinary shares | $  500,000 | $  200,000 |
| Retained earnings | 220,000 | 300,000 |
| Mortgage payable | | 270,000 |
| Loan payable to Mr. Saeid | | 126,000 |
| Other liabilities | 940,000 | 228,000 |
| | $1,660,000 | $1,124,000 |

### INCOME STATEMENTS
For the year ended December 31, Year 6

|  | *HD Ltd.* | *JC Ltd.* |
|---|---|---|
| Sales—joint operations | $ | $  621,000 |
| Sales—other | 1,700,000 | 1,529,000 |
| Income from joint operations | 40,000 | |
| | 1,740,000 | 2,150,000 |
| Cost of goods sold—joint operations | | 474,000 |
| Cost of goods sold—other | 1,176,000 | 1,244,000 |
| Selling expenses—joint operations | | 27,000 |
| Payment to other venturers | | 80,000 |
| Other expenses | 360,000 | 169,000 |
| Income tax expense | 80,000 | 60,000 |
| | 1,616,000 | 2,054,000 |
| Profit | $  124,000 | $  96,000 |

### Additional information:

- During Year 6, HD had sales of $102,000 to JC at a markup of 20 percent of selling price. On December 31, Year 6, the property under renovation included supplies purchased from JC of $30,000.
- HD reports its share of income from the joint operations when it is received from JC.
- Both companies pay income tax at a rate of 40% on taxable income.

### Required

Prepare corrected Year 6 financial statements for HD in accordance with IFRS 11.

## Problem 9-7

LO4

The following information has been assembled about Casbar Corp. as at December 31, Year 5 (amounts are in thousands):

| Operating Segment | Revenues | Profit | Assets |
|---|---|---|---|
| A | $12,000 | $3,100 | $24,000 |
| B | 9,600 | 2,680 | 21,000 |
| C | 7,200 | (1,440) | 15,000 |
| D | 3,600 | 660 | 9,000 |
| E | 5,100 | 810 | 8,400 |
| F | 1,800 | (270) | 3,600 |

**Required**

Determine which operating segments require separate disclosures.

# Problem 9-8

LO4, 5

Access the 2014 consolidated financial statements for Rogers Communications Inc. by going to the investor relations section of the company's website. Answer the questions below. For each question, indicate where in the financial statements you found the answer, and/or provide a brief explanation.

(a) Are the company's operating segments based on product lines, geographical areas, or some other factor?

(b) Does the company provide disclosures about major customers? If so, what is the nature of the disclosure?

(c) Which of the operating segments is the biggest in terms of revenues?

(d) Which of the operating segments reported the highest percentage of growth in revenues from the previous year and what was that percentage? Based on this growth rate, approximately how many years will it take for the sales of this segment to double?

(e) Which of the operating segments is the biggest in terms of profit?

(f) Which of the operating segments reported the highest percentage of growth in profit margin from the previous year?

(g) Which of the operating segments is the biggest in terms of assets?

(h) Which of the operating segments reported the biggest change in return on assets from the previous year?

# Problem 9-9

LO2, 5

The following are the December 31, Year 9, balance sheets of three related companies:

|  | Pro Ltd. | Forma Corp. | Apex LLP |
|---|---|---|---|
| Cash | $ 70,000 | $ 1,500 | $200,000 |
| Accounts receivable | 210,000 | 90,000 | 110,000 |
| Inventory | 100,000 | 62,500 | 70,000 |
| Investment in Forma Corp.—at cost | 416,000 | — | — |
| Investment in Apex LLP—at cost | 150,000 | — | — |
| Land | 100,000 | 110,000 | 60,000 |
| Plant and equipment | 636,000 | 550,000 | 290,000 |
| Accumulated depreciation | (185,000) | (329,000) | (60,000) |
|  | $1,497,000 | $485,000 | $670,000 |
| Accounts payable | $ 175,000 | $ 90,000 | $130,000 |
| Bonds payable | 312,000 | — | — |
| Common shares/capital contributed | 800,000 | 100,000 | 500,000 |
| $12 preferred shares | — | 200,000 | — |
| Retained/accumulated earnings | 210,000 | 95,000 | 40,000 |
|  | $1,497,000 | $485,000 | $670,000 |

**Additional Information**

- On January 1, Year 5, Pro purchased 40% of Forma for $116,000. On that date, Forma's shareholders' equity was as follows:

| | |
|---|---|
| Common shares | $100,000 |
| Retained earnings | 80,000 |
| | $180,000 |

All of the identifiable net assets of Forma had fair values equal to carrying amounts except for the following, for which fair values exceeded carrying amounts as follows:

| | |
|---|---|
| Inventory | $20,000 |
| Plant and equipment | 50,000 |

- One of Forma's products, the Epod, was unique in the market place and was a hot seller. Forma could not produce this product fast enough to meet the customer demand. The order backlog would take more than six months to complete. An independent appraiser valued the order backlog at $40,000 at the date of acquisition.

- On September 30, Year 7, Pro purchased the remaining 60% of Forma for $300,000. On that date, Forma's shareholders' equity was as follows:

| | |
|---|---|
| Common shares | $100,000 |
| Retained earnings | 110,000 |
| | $210,000 |

On this date, the following net assets of Forma were undervalued by the amounts shown:

| | |
|---|---|
| Inventory | $10,000 |
| Land | 60,000 |
| Plant and equipment | 70,000 |

- For consolidation purposes, any acquisition differential allocated to plant and equipment is amortized over 20 years from each date of acquisition. A goodwill impairment loss amounting to $2,025 was recorded in Year 8.

- During Year 8, Forma issued 2,000 cumulative, $12, no-par-value preferred shares. Pro did not acquire any of these shares.

- The inventories of Pro contained intercompany profits from items purchased from Forma in the following amounts:

| | |
|---|---|
| December 31, Year 8 | $40,000 |
| December 31, Year 9 | 45,000 |

- During Year 9, Pro and two other unrelated companies formed Apex, which is a joint arrangement. Pro invested $150,000 cash for its 30% interest in Apex.

- The year-end inventories of Apex contained a $12,000 intercompany profit from items purchased from Pro since its formation in Year 9.

- Forma paid dividends in all years prior to Year 9.

- On December 31, Year 9, the accounts receivable of Pro contained the following:

| | |
|---|---|
| Receivable from Forma | $13,000 |
| Receivable from Apex | 40,000 |

- Use income tax allocation at a 40% rate as it applies to unrealized profits only. Ignore deferred income taxes on the acquisition differential.

**Required**

(a) Prepare the Year 9 consolidated balance sheet assuming that

   (i) Apex is a joint venture and Pro reports its investment in Apex using the equity method; and

   (ii) Apex is a joint operation and Pro reports its investment in Apex using proportionately adjusted financial statements. Pro has proportionate rights to all of Apex's assets and proportionate responsibilities for all of Apex's liabilities.

(b) Calculate the current ratio for each of the balance sheets in part (a). Which reporting method presents the strongest liquidity position? Briefly explain.

## Problem 9-10

LO2, 6

The following are the Year 9 income statements of Kent Corp. and Laurier Enterprises.

**INCOME STATEMENTS**

For the year ended December 31, Year 9

| | Kent | Laurier |
|---|---|---|
| Sales | $3,180,000 | $1,380,000 |
| Other income | 218,000 | 88,000 |
| Gain on sale of land | — | 118,000 |
| | 3,398,000 | 1,586,000 |
| Cost of sales | 1,445,000 | 605,000 |
| Selling and administrative expenses | 518,000 | 318,000 |
| Other expenses | 109,000 | 139,000 |
| Income tax | 418,000 | 168,000 |
| | 2,490,000 | 1,230,000 |
| Net income | $ 908,000 | $ 356,000 |

**Additional Information**

- Kent acquired its 40% interest in the common shares of Laurier in Year 3 at a cost of $843,000 and uses the cost method to account for its investment for internal record keeping.

- The acquisition-differential amortization schedule pertaining to Kent's 40% interest showed the following write-off for Year 9:

| | |
|---|---|
| Buildings | $18,000 |
| Goodwill impairment loss | 22,000 |
| | 40,000 |
| Long-term liabilities | 21,500 |
| Acquisition-differential amortization and impairment—Year 9 | $18,500 |

- Depreciation expense and goodwill impairment loss are included with selling and administrative expenses.

- In Year 9, rent amounting to $30,000 was paid by Laurier to Kent. Kent has recorded this as other income.

- In Year 6, Kent sold land to Laurier and recorded a profit of $93,000 on the transaction. During Year 9, Laurier sold 30% of the land to an unrelated land development company.

- During Year 9, Laurier paid dividends totalling $107,000.

- It has been established that Kent's 40% interest would *not* be considered control in accordance with IFRS.

- Assume a 40% tax rate.

**Required**

(a) Assume that Laurier is a joint venture that is owned by Kent and two other unrelated venturers. Also assume that Kent acquired its interest after Laurier's initial formation, and that the acquisition differentials are therefore valid. Prepare the income statement of Kent for Year 9 using the equity method. (Show all calculations.)

(b) Assume that Laurier is a joint operation. Prepare Kent's income statement for Year 9 using proportionately adjusted financial statements. (Show all calculations.)

# Problem 9-11

LO2

Albert Company has an investment in the voting shares of Prince Ltd. On December 31, Year 5, Prince reported a net income of $860,000 and declared dividends of $200,000.

During Year 5, Albert had sales to Prince of $915,000, and Prince had sales to Albert of $500,000. On December 31, Year 5, the inventory of Albert contained an after-tax intercompany profit of $40,000, and the inventory of Prince contained an after-tax intercompany profit of $72,000.

On January 1, Year 4, Albert sold equipment to Prince and recorded an after-tax profit of $120,000 on the transaction. The equipment had a remaining useful life of five years on this date. Albert uses the equity method to account for its investment in Prince.

**Required**

Prepare Albert's Year 5 equity method journal entries under each of the following two assumptions:

(a) Albert owns 64% of Prince, and Prince is a subsidiary.

(b) Albert owns 30% of Prince, and Prince is a joint venture.

# Problem 9-12

LO2

On January 1, Year 1, Amco Ltd. and Newstar Inc. formed Bearcat Resources, a joint venture. Newstar contributed miscellaneous assets with a fair value of $844,000 for a 65% interest in the venture. Amco contributed plant and equipment with a carrying amount of $319,000 and a fair value of $1,380,000 and received a 35% interest in the venture plus $469,000 in cash. On December 31, Year 1, Bearcat reported a profit of $199,000 and declared a dividend of $94,000. Amco has a December 31 year-end and will account for its 35% interest using the equity method. (Assume a 20-year useful life for the plant and equipment.)

**Required**

(a) Assume that the miscellaneous assets contributed by Newstar included cash of $469,000. Also, assume that the transaction had commercial substance when Amco transferred the plant and equipment to the joint venture. Prepare Amco's Year 1 journal entries.

(b) Assume that there was no cash in the assets contributed by Newstar and that the cash received by Amco had been borrowed by Bearcat. Also, assume that the transaction did not have commercial substance when Amco transferred the plant and equipment to the joint venture. Prepare Amco's Year 1 journal entries.

## Problem 9-13

........

LO2

The following are the Year 9 income statements of Poker Inc. and Joker Company:

### INCOME STATEMENTS
For the year ended December 31, Year 9

| | Poker | Joker |
|---|---|---|
| Sales | $1,000,000 | $800,000 |
| Other income | 200,000 | 110,000 |
| Gain on sale of trademark | = | 40,000 |
| | 1,200,000 | 950,000 |
| | | |
| Cost of goods sold | 600,000 | 550,000 |
| Selling and administrative expenses | 200,000 | 150,000 |
| Other expenses | 50,000 | 40,000 |
| | 850,000 | 740,000 |
| Income before income taxes | 350,000 | 210,000 |
| Income taxes | 105,000 | 63,000 |
| Profit | $ 245,000 | $147,000 |

### Additional Information

- Poker acquired a 60% interest in the common shares of Joker on January 1, Year 4, at a cost of $420,000 and uses the cost method to account for its investment. At that time, Joker's carrying amount of shareholders' equity was $600,000 and the fair value of each of its assets and liabilities equalled carrying amount except for equipment, which had a fair value of $100,000 in excess of carrying amount and an estimated remaining useful life of 10 years.
- In Year 9, Joker paid a management fee of $50,000 to Poker. Poker recorded this as other income.
- In Year 5, Poker sold two trademarks with an indefinite life to Joker and recorded a total gain on sale of $70,000 ($35,000 for each trademark). During Year 9, Joker sold one of these trademarks to an unrelated company for a gain of $40,000.
- Depreciation expense is included with selling and administrative expenses.
- During Year 9, Joker declared and paid dividends totalling $200,000.
- The income tax rate is 30% for both companies.

### Required

(a) Assume that Joker is a joint venture that is jointly owned by Poker and several unrelated venturers, and that Poker uses the equity method to report its investment. Prepare Poker's income statement for the year ended December 31, Year 9.

(b) Assume that Joker is not a joint venture and, furthermore, that Poker's long-term investment provides it with control over Joker. Prepare Poker's consolidated income statement for the year ended December 31, Year 9.

(c) Explain why consolidated net income attributable to Poker's shareholders in part (b) is substantially higher than Poker's net income under the equity method in part (a).

## Problem 9-14

........

LO2

Jager Ltd., a joint venture, was formed on January 1, Year 3. Clifford Corp., one of the three founding venturers, invested equipment for a 40% interest in the joint venture. The other two venturers invested land and cash for their 60% equity. All of the venturers agreed that the equipment had a fair value of $2,000,000, and a remaining useful life of approximately eight years. Clifford had acquired this equipment two years ago, and the carrying amount on Clifford's records on January 1, Year 3, was $1,700,000. Clifford recorded its investment in the joint venture at $2,000,000. On December 31, Year 3, Jager recorded a net income of $200,000. Clifford uses the equity method to record its investment.

**Required**

(a) Assume that the transaction did not have commercial substance when Clifford transferred the equipment to the joint venture. Prepare Clifford's Year 3 journal entries.

(b) Assume Clifford had received a 40% interest and $900,000 in cash in return for investing this equipment in the venture. Also assume that the other venturers contributed cash in excess of $900,000 for their ownership interests, and that the transaction did not have commercial substance when Clifford transferred the equipment to the joint venture. Prepare Clifford's Year 3 journal entries.

# Problem 9-15

LO2, 5

The following balance sheets have been prepared as at December 31, Year 6, for Kay Corp. and Adams Ventures:

|  | Kay | Adams |
|---|---|---|
| Cash | $ 74,000 | $ 37,000 |
| Accounts receivable | 108,000 | 191,000 |
| Inventory | 635,000 | 421,000 |
| Property and plant | 1,428,000 | 921,000 |
| Investment in Adams | 374,000 | — |
|  | $2,619,000 | $1,570,000 |
| Current liabilities | $ 414,000 | $ 164,000 |
| Bonds payable | 517,500 | 614,000 |
| Common shares | 956,000 | 478,000 |
| Retained earnings | 731,500 | 314,000 |
|  | $2,619,000 | $1,570,000 |

**Additional Information**

- Kay acquired its 40% interest in Adams for $374,000 in Year 2, when Adams's retained earnings amounted to $184,000. The acquisition differential on that date was fully amortized by the end of Year 6.

- In Year 5, Kay sold land to Adams and recorded a gain of $74,000 on the transaction. Adams is still using this land.

- The December 31, Year 6, inventory of Kay contained a profit recorded by Adams amounting to $49,000.

- On December 31, Year 6, Adams owes Kay $43,000.

- Kay has used the cost method to account for its investment in Adams.

- Use income tax allocation at a rate of 40%, but ignore income tax on the acquisition differential.

**Required**

(a) Prepare *three* separate balance sheets for Kay as at December 31, Year 6, assuming that the investment in Adams is a

    (i) control investment;

    (ii) joint operation and is reported using proportionately adjusted financial statements, and

    (iii) significant influence investment.

(b) Calculate the debt-to-equity ratio for each of the balance sheets in part (a). Which reporting method presents the strongest position from a solvency point of view? Briefly explain.

(c) Prepare the financial statements required for part (a) using the worksheet approach.

# Endnotes

1   "Loblaw 2014 Annual Report," www.loblaw.ca/files/doc_financials/2014/2014-FS_SEDAR_25-Feb-15.pdf.

2   "Consolidated Financial Statements," West Fraser Timber Co. Ltd., www.westfraser.com/sites/default/files/WFT_CFS_2014.pdf.

3   "Consolidated Financial Statements of West Fraser Timber Co. Ltd.," www.horizonnorth.ca/Portals/0/docs/Quarter_Reports/Financial%20Statements%20-%20December%202014%20FINAL.pdf.

4   "Annual Report 2014," www.aircanada.com/en/about/investor/documents/2014_ar.pdf.

5   "Consolidated Financial Statements," www.empireco.ca/site/media/Empireco/EmpireAR14_SEDAR%20financial%20statements.pdf.

6   Proportionate consolidation is an application of the proprietary theory, which was illustrated in Chapter 4. IFRS 11 does not use the term "proportionate consolidation." However, the IASB staff notes indicate that in most cases, proportionate consolidation would result in the same presentation required by IFRS 11.

7   The same requirements apply for an investment in an associate.

8   "2014 Annual Report," www.torstar.com/images/file/2014/Annual%20Report/2014%20TORSTAR%20AR%20Online%203%20(2).pdf.

9   Start-up operations may also be operating segments before earning revenues and incurring expenses.

10  IFRS 8 Appendix A.

11  "BCE Inc. 2014 Annual Report," www.bce.ca/assets/investors/AR_2014/BCE_2014_Annual_Report.pdf.

12  Adapted from *CICA UFE Report*, 1990-IV-1, with permission. Chartered Professional Accountants of Canada, Toronto, Canada. Any changes to the original material are the sole responsibility of the author (and/or publisher) and have not been reviewed or endorsed by the Chartered Professional Accountants of Canada.

13  Adapted from *CICA UFE Report*, 1997-III-3, with permission. Chartered Professional Accountants of Canada, Toronto, Canada. Any changes to the original material are the sole responsibility of the author (and/or publisher) and have not been reviewed or endorsed by the Chartered Professional Accountants of Canada.

14  Adapted from *CICA UFE Report*, 2009-I, with permission. Chartered Professional Accountants of Canada, Toronto, Canada. Any changes to the original material are the sole responsibility of the author (and/or publisher) and have not been reviewed or endorsed by the Chartered Professional Accountants of Canada.

# CHAPTER 10

# Foreign Currency Transactions

## LEARNING OBJECTIVES

**After studying this chapter, you should be able to do the following:**

**LO1**  Translate foreign currency transactions and balances into the functional currency.

**LO2**  Prepare journal entries and subsequent financial statement presentation for forward exchange contracts that are entered into for speculative purposes.

**LO3**  Describe the concept of hedging and ways to hedge against foreign currency risk.

**LO4**  Prepare journal entries and subsequent financial statement presentation for forward exchange contracts that hedge existing monetary positions.

**LO5**  Prepare journal entries and subsequent financial statement presentation for

forward exchange contracts that hedge firm commitments.

**LO6**  Prepare journal entries and subsequent financial statement presentation for forward contracts that hedge highly probable future transactions.

**LO7**  Analyze and interpret financial statements involving foreign currency transactions and forward contracts.

**LO8**  (Appendix 10A) Incorporate the time value of money when determining the fair value of a forward contract.

## Introduction

Many Canadian companies conduct business in foreign countries as well as in Canada. For some companies, foreign business simply means purchasing products and services from foreign suppliers or selling products and services to foreign customers. Other companies go far beyond importing and exporting; they borrow and lend money in foreign markets and conduct business in foreign countries through sales offices, branches, subsidiaries, and joint ventures. Bombardier Inc., a Canadian transportation company, in its 2014 annual report, reported export revenues of $8.086 billion, representing 40.2% of total revenues.[1]

*Many Canadian companies enter into foreign-currency-denominated transactions.*

No specific accounting issues arise when the parties involved in an import or export transaction agree that the settlement will be in Canadian dollars. Because it is a *Canadian-dollar-denominated transaction,* the company will record the foreign purchase or sale in exactly the same manner as any domestic purchase or sale. In many situations, however, the agreement calls for the transaction to be settled in a foreign currency. This means one of two things: (1) the Canadian company will have to acquire foreign currency in order to discharge the obligations resulting from its imports or (2) the Canadian company will receive foreign currency as a result of its exports and will have to sell it in order to receive Canadian dollars. Transactions such as these are called *foreign-currency-denominated transactions.*

As the foreign currency exchange rate fluctuates, so does the Canadian-dollar value of these foreign transactions. Companies often find it necessary to engage in some form of hedging activity to reduce potential losses arising from fluctuating exchange rates. The Bank of Nova Scotia uses derivative financial instruments to accommodate the risk management needs of its customers, for proprietary trading and asset/liability management purposes. Derivative instruments designated as "asset/liability management" are those used to manage the bank's interest rate, foreign currency, and other exposures, which include instruments designated as hedges. At the end of fiscal year 2014, the Bank of Nova Scotia, Canada's third-largest bank, had derivative financial instruments with a notional value of $4,970 billion.[2]

> *Many tools and techniques are available to hedge against different kinds of risks.*

This chapter covers accounting issues related to foreign currency transactions and foreign currency hedging activities. Chapter 11 deals with the translation of the financial statements of a foreign operation. To provide background for subsequent discussions, this chapter begins with a brief look at exchange rates.

# CURRENCY EXCHANGE RATES

Both the recording of foreign-currency-denominated transactions and the translation of foreign currency financial statements require the use of currency exchange rates. An exchange rate is simply the price of one currency in terms of another currency. Exchange rates fluctuate on a continuous basis. Historically, governments have tried to stabilize rates between their currencies. Shortly after World War II, a group of the world's major trading nations agreed to "peg" the rates at which their currencies would be exchanged in terms of U.S. dollars. Since these pegged rates stayed reasonably steady, the accounting for foreign transactions was fairly simple. Differences in inflation rates and major changes in the balance of payments among the participating nations were contributing factors to the eventual demise of this agreement in the early 1970s.

> *An exchange rate is the price to change one currency into another currency.*

The end of pegged rates led to the present system, in which market forces determine exchange rates. This system of floating exchange rates is not totally market-driven in the short term because governments often intervene in the market place to lessen the swings in the value of their currencies. It is not uncommon to hear that the Canadian dollar has weakened in relation to the U.S. dollar and the

Bank of Canada has made massive purchases of Canadian dollars in order to soften the decline or that the U.S. Federal Reserve Bank and the central banks of other countries have intervened in the foreign currency markets by purchasing U.S. dollars because the U.S. dollar was declining in relation to other major currencies. Sometimes, interventions of this nature are fruitless, as was the case in 1994, when Mexico's central bank abandoned its attempt to prop up the peso and allowed a substantial devaluation to take place.

**REASONS FOR FLUCTUATING EXCHANGE RATES**  Currencies trade in markets in such major cities as New York, London, Paris, and Tokyo, and transfers of enormous amounts of currency between countries can take place in a matter of seconds. The price of a currency will fluctuate in much the same manner as the price of any other commodity. There are many reasons why a country's currency price changes, of which the major ones are the following:

- *Inflation rates.* As a general rule, if country A has a higher rate of inflation than country B, the price of A's currency will weaken relative to B's. In a period of inflation, the purchasing power of a country's currency declines. If this currency will not buy as much in goods as it did before, then neither will it buy as much currency of another country as it did before.

- *Interest rates.* Higher interest rates attract foreign investment and in so doing drive up the price of the currency of the country with the higher interest rates.

- *Trade surpluses and deficits.* As a country exports more than it imports, its currency strengthens and becomes worth more.

> *Exchange rates fluctuate over time due primarily to differences in inflation rates, interest rates, and trading practices between the two countries.*

**EXCHANGE RATE QUOTATIONS**  Exchange rates showing the value of the Canadian dollar in terms of other foreign currencies are quoted daily on the Internet and in many Canadian business newspapers. The amounts that usually appear are called *direct quotations*, which mean that the amounts represent the cost in Canadian dollars to purchase one unit of foreign currency. For example, a quotation of EUR1.00 = CDN1.3825 means that it costs 1.3825 Canadian dollars to purchase one euro. An *indirect quotation* would state the cost in a foreign currency to purchase one Canadian dollar. For example, a quotation of CDN1.00 = EUR0.7233 indicates that it costs 0.7233 euros to purchase one Canadian dollar. An indirect quotation can be obtained by computing the reciprocal of the *direct* quotation. Conversely, a direct quotation can be obtained by computing the reciprocal of the *indirect* quotation (1 ÷ 1.3825 = 0.7233, and 1 ÷ 0.7233 = 1.3825).

> *Exchange rates can be quoted directly or indirectly.*
> *The direct method is the reciprocal of the indirect method.*

Direct quotations are the most useful ones for recording transactions denominated in foreign currencies. Using the exchange rates quoted above, a Canadian company would record the purchase of €10,000 of inventory from a European supplier as $13,825.

Examples of foreign exchange quotations on particular days in 2015 and 2012 for five countries' currencies are shown in Exhibit 10.1. These rates represent the amount in Canadian dollars that a commercial bank would charge if it sold one unit of foreign currency to a major customer. The rate quoted is called the *spot rate*, which is a rate for exchanges currency at that moment in time. If a customer wanted to purchase 1,000 euros on the date in 2015 that these rates were quoted, the cost would be $1,403 (€1,000 × 1.4032). Note that if the bank were to purchase euros from the customer, the amount that it would pay the customer would be slightly less than the amount quoted per euro. The bank's selling rate has to be greater than its purchasing rate in order to cover costs and make a little profit dealing in foreign currencies.

---

*The spot rate is the rate to exchange currency today.*

---

**EXHIBIT 10.1**

### FOREIGN EXCHANGE DIRECT QUOTATIONS

| Country | Currency | 2012 CDN$ per Unit | 2015 CDN$ per Unit |
|---|---|---|---|
| United States | U.S. Dollar | 1.0418 | 1.2436 |
| European Union | Euro | 1.3825 | 1.4032 |
| China | Renminbi | 0.1637 | 0.2007 |
| India | Rupee | 0.01872 | 0.2007 |
| Japan | Yen | 0.01331 | 0.01002 |

*Source: Bank of Canada, "Exchange Rates," www.bankofcanada.ca/rates/exchange, accessed June 4, 2015.*

---

*The Canadian dollar has declined relative to all of these currencies except for the yen from 2012 to 2015.*

---

A *forward exchange contract* is an agreement between a bank and a customer to exchange currencies on a specified future date at a specified rate. For example, when a bank enters into a forward exchange contract in 2015 with a customer to purchase 5,000 euros six months forward, the bank is committing itself to take delivery of this quantity of euros six months from this date. If the six-month forward rate was 1.2960, the bank would pay the customer $6,480 (€5,000 × 1.2960) at that time. Of course, there is also a commitment on the part of the customer to sell 5,000 euros to the bank in six months' time. The use of forward exchange contracts in hedging transactions will be illustrated later in this chapter.

---

*The forward rate is the rate agreed to today for exchanging currency at a future date.*

---

## LO1 ACCOUNTING FOR FOREIGN CURRENCY TRANSACTIONS

Before we deal with the detailed accounting requirements for foreign currency transactions, it is important to note that currency issues can be discussed and analyzed from many different perspectives. For Chapters 10 and 11, we need to differentiate among the following perspectives:

- Currency in which the transaction is denominated (denominated currency)

- Currency in which the transaction is recorded in the internal accounting records (recording currency or internal record-keeping currency)

- Currency of the primary economic environment in which the entity operates (functional currency)

- Currency in which the financial statements are presented by the reporting entity (presentation currency, which is commonly referred to as reporting currency)

> *We need to differentiate among the denominated, recording, functional, and presentation currencies.*

Exhibit 10.2 shows examples of how these different currency perspectives could exist for individual companies. The last line indicates the method used to translate from one currency to another in the order in which the currencies are translated. Company E will need to translate three different times.

**EXHIBIT 10.2**

### EXAMPLES OF CURRENCY PERSPECTIVES

| Company Type | Chapters 1–9 Company A | Chapter 10 Company B | Chapter 11 Company C | Chapter 11 Company D | Chapter 11 Company E |
|---|---|---|---|---|---|
| Incorporated in | Canada | Canada | Germany | Japan | Argentina |
| Transactions denominated in | Canadian $ | Various currencies | Various currencies | Various currencies | Various currencies |
| Transactions recorded in | Canadian $ | Canadian $ (1) | Euro (1) | Yen (1) | Peso (1) |
| Functional currency | Canadian $ | Canadian $ | Canadian $ (2) | Yen | Canadian $ (2) |
| Presentation currency | Canadian $ | Canadian $ | Canadian $ | Canadian $ (2) | U.S. $ (3) |
| Method used for translation | n/a | (1) FCT | (1) FCT (2) FCT | (1) FCT (2) PCT | (1) FCT (2) FCT (3) PCT |

> *Company E must translate from one currency to another currency three different times.*

Up until now in this book, we have been dealing with Company A, where the Canadian dollar was the currency used for the four perspectives listed above. The transactions were denominated in Canadian dollars—that is, the invoices, agreements, cheques, and so on were written in Canadian dollars; the general ledger was maintained in Canadian dollars; the company operated in Canada; and the financial statements were presented in Canadian dollars. In this chapter, we deal with Company B–type situations where transactions are denominated in different currencies, the general ledger will be maintained in Canadian dollars, and the financial statements will be presented in Canadian dollars. We are then faced with deciding which currency should be used to record the transaction and which currency should be used when presenting the financial statements to external users. In Chapter 11, we will deal with Companies C, D, and E, for which the recording currency is different from the functional and/or presentation currency.

> *A Canadian company would typically use the Canadian dollar as its recording and presentation currency.*

IAS 21 requires that individual transactions be *translated into* the *functional currency* of the reporting entity. In turn, IAS 21 states that an entity can *present* or *report* its financial statements in any currency it wants to use. Presumably, the entity will present its financial statements in the currency most useful to its users. Most Canadian companies will present their financial statements in Canadian dollars. However, some Canadian companies may present their financial statements in U.S. dollars, because many of the users of the financial statements will be American investors or creditors, or will be international investors or creditors who understand and monitor the U.S. dollar more easily and readily than the Canadian dollar.

> *All transactions must be translated to the functional currency of the reporting entity.*

IAS 21 defines *functional currency* as the currency of the primary economic environment in which the entity operates and *foreign currency* as any currency other than the functional currency of the entity. The primary economic environment is normally the one in which the entity primarily generates and expends cash. Exhibit 10.3 lists the indicators that should be considered when determining the functional currency and gives an example of a condition that would indicate that the Canadian dollar is or is not the functional currency.

**EXHIBIT 10.3**

### INDICATORS FOR CHOOSING FUNCTIONAL CURRENCY

#### Functional Currency

| Indicator | Canadian Dollar | Not Canadian Dollar |
|---|---|---|
| 1. Sales prices | Sales occur in Canada and are denominated in Canadian dollars. | Sales occur in foreign countries and are not denominated in Canadian dollars. |
| 2. Operating costs | Labour and materials are obtained in Canada and denominated in Canadian dollars. | Labour and materials are obtained from foreign countries and are not denominated in Canadian dollars. |
| 3. Competition and regulation | Competitors are Canadian, or company is listed on a Canadian exchange. | Competition comes from foreign entities or companies listed on a foreign exchange. |
| 4. Financing | Debt and equity instruments are issued in Canadian dollars. | Debt and equity instruments are issued in foreign currencies. |
| 5. Operating surpluses | Excess cash is retained in Canadian dollars. | Excess cash is retained in foreign currencies. |

> *The functional currency is the currency of the primary economic environment in which the entity operates.*

When the above indicators are mixed and the functional currency is not obvious, management uses its judgment to determine the functional currency that most faithfully represents the economic effects of the underlying transactions, events, and conditions. As part of this approach, management gives priority to indicators 1 and 2 before considering the others, which are designed to provide additional supporting evidence to determine an entity's functional currency.

Professional judgment must be exercised in identifying the functional currency. In this chapter, we will assume, unless otherwise noted, that we are dealing with a Company B-type entity, where the Canadian dollar is the recording currency, the functional currency, and the presentation currency.

> *In this chapter, the Canadian dollar is the recording, functional, and presentation currency.*

We will now focus on the issues associated with import/export transactions and foreign-currency-denominated debt. Accounting problems arise when there are exchange rate changes between the date of a transaction and the eventual settlement in foreign currency. During this period, the company holds foreign-currency-denominated monetary assets and liabilities, and questions arise as to how to measure these items if financial statements need to be prepared in the intervening period and what to do with any gains or losses that may result from such measurements. Monetary items are units of currency held and assets and liabilities to be received or paid in a fixed or determinable number of units of currency. Accounts receivable and investments in bonds are some obvious examples of monetary assets; accounts payable and bond liabilities are monetary liabilities. A foreign-currency-denominated monetary position is a net asset position if monetary assets exceed monetary liabilities or a net liability position if monetary liabilities exceed monetary assets.

> *A monetary item is converted into cash at a fixed and predetermined amount of currency.*

Some not-so-obvious examples of monetary items are pensions and other employee benefits to be paid in cash, provisions that are to be settled in cash, and cash dividends that are recognized as a liability. Similarly, a contract to receive (or deliver) a variable number of the entity's own equity instruments, or a variable amount of assets in which the fair value to be received (or delivered) equals a fixed or determinable number of units of currency, is a monetary item. Conversely, the essential feature of a non-monetary item is the absence of a right to receive (or an obligation to deliver) a fixed or determinable number of units of currency. Examples are amounts prepaid for goods and services (e.g., prepaid rent); goodwill; intangible assets; inventories; property, plant, and equipment; deferred income taxes; and provisions that are to be settled by the delivery of a non-monetary asset.[3]

For accounting purposes, there are basically three rates used in translating foreign currency into the reporting currency: the closing rate, the historical rate, and the forward rate. The spot rate at the end of the reporting period of the financial statements is called the *closing rate*. The spot rate on the date of a transaction is called the *historical rate* for that transaction. The agreed rate for exchange of currencies at a future date is called the *forward rate*. To illustrate the use of these terms, consider the following example.

> *The historical rate is the rate on the date of the transaction, and the closing rate is the rate at the end of the reporting period.*

**EXAMPLE 1**   ABC Co. has a year-end of December 31. On November 13, Year 1, ABC purchased inventory from a French supplier when the spot rate for one euro (€) was €1 = CDN$1.38. On November 14, Year 1, ABC entered into a contract with a bank to purchase euros in 60 days at a rate of €1 = CDN $1.36. The spot rate on December 31, Year 1, was €1 = CDN $1.37. The financial statements for Year 1 were finalized on March 14, Year 2, and released to users on March 15, Year 2. In this example, the closing rate is $1.37, the historical rate for the purchase of the inventory is $1.38, and the forward rate for the planned purchase of euros is $1.36.

If inventory was purchased every day throughout the year, the historical rate for each purchase should technically be used to translate the purchase for each day. This procedure is very costly and usually not worth the cost-benefit tradeoff. From a practical point of view, it is usually sufficient to use an average rate to approximate the actual rates for the period. The average rate represents the weighted average of the historical rates throughout the period. However, if exchange rates fluctuate significantly, the use of the average rate for a period is inappropriate.

> *The average rate is the weighted average of the historical rates for the period.*

According to IAS 21, a foreign currency transaction must be recorded, on initial recognition, in the functional currency by applying to the foreign currency amount the spot exchange rate between the functional currency and the foreign currency at the date of the transaction. At the end of each reporting period,

(a) foreign currency monetary items must be translated using the closing rate,

(b) non-monetary items that are measured in terms of historical cost in a foreign currency must be translated using the historical rate, and

(c) non-monetary items that are measured at fair value in a foreign currency must be translated using the spot exchange rates at the date when the fair value was determined.

For ease of identification, we will refer to this method of translation as the *functional currency translation (FCT) method.*

> *Individual transactions must be translated into the functional currency at the historical rate.*

Any exchange adjustments arising on the settlement of monetary items or on the translation of them at rates different from those at which they were translated on initial recognition or in previous financial statements must be recognized in profit or loss in the period in which they arise, with one exception. When a gain or loss on a non-monetary item is recognized in other comprehensive income, any exchange adjustment pertaining to that item must also be recognized in other comprehensive income. For example, IAS 16 requires some gains and losses arising on a revaluation of property, plant, and equipment to be recognized in other comprehensive income. When such an asset is measured in a foreign currency, any exchange difference resulting from the translation of the remeasured amount into the functional currency should also be recognized in other comprehensive income. This translation process should produce results consistent with the valuation practices for domestic operations. For a financial statement item to be reported at historical cost, the historical cost of the item in foreign currency multiplied by the historical rate will derive the historical cost in Canadian dollars. For a financial statement item to be reported at fair value at the end of the year, the fair value of the item in foreign currency multiplied by the spot rate on the date when fair value was determined will derive the fair value in Canadian dollars. If historical cost in foreign currency is multiplied by the closing rate or if the fair value in foreign currency is multiplied by the historical rate, the Canadian dollar figure is neither historical cost nor fair value.

> *The translation method should, ideally, produce either historical cost in dollars or fair value in dollars consistent with normal measurement requirements for the financial statement items.*

When an item is reported at fair value, the fair value is usually determined at the end of the reporting period. If so, the exchange rate at the end of the period (i.e., the closing rate) is used to translate this item into Canadian dollars. Unless otherwise specified, the examples in the text always assume that fair values were determined at the end of the reporting period.

According to IFRS, monetary assets and monetary liabilities are typically measured at fair value, non-monetary assets are usually measured at the lower of historical cost and recoverable amount, and non-monetary liabilities and shareholders' equity are usually measured at historical amounts. Revenues and expenses are usually measured at historical amounts. As we study the different translation methods in this and the next chapter, we should evaluate whether the translation methods preserve the normal measurement requirements under IFRS.

## Import/Export Transactions Denominated in Foreign Currency

When a Canadian company purchases goods from a foreign supplier, it is usually billed in the currency of the foreign country. However, the transaction is recorded in the company's accounting records in the functional currency, which is assumed to be the Canadian dollar. The following example illustrates the accounting for an import transaction.

---

*Unless otherwise noted, all examples in this chapter assume that the Canadian dollar is the functional currency.*

---

**EXAMPLE 2: AN IMPORT EXAMPLE** On June 1, Year 1, Maritime Importers Inc. purchased merchandise from a supplier in Australia at a cost of 10,000 Australian dollars (A$), with payment in full to be made in 60 days. The exchange rate on the date of purchase was A$1 = CDN$0.941 and A$1 = CDN$0.949 on June 30, Year 1, the company's year-end. Maritime paid its supplier on July 30, Year 1, when the exchange rate was A$1 = CDN$0.953. The following journal entries, recorded in Canadian dollars, illustrate the company's purchase of merchandise, year-end adjustments, and subsequent payment.

*June 1, Year 1*

| | | |
|---|---|---|
| Inventory | 9,410 | |
|     Accounts payable (10,000 × 0.941) | | 9,410 |

The purchase of the inventory at a cost of A$10,000 and the related liability are translated at the spot rate on the date of purchase. The value of the inventory has been fixed at its historical cost and is not exposed to exchange fluctuations except in the situation where the selling price declines and the lower of cost and net realizable value requirement is applied. In such a case, the lower of cost and net realizable value requirement would be applied by comparing the Canadian dollar historical cost of the inventory with the net realizable value in Canadian dollars.[4]

---

*The cost of the purchase is finalized when the item is purchased.*

---

On the other hand, Maritime now has a monetary position that is exposed to exchange fluctuations. The Canadian dollar amount required to pay A$10,000 will change as the exchange rate changes. To better reflect the cost of settling this obligation, this monetary liability should be remeasured to current value at each reporting date.

On the company's year-end, the account payable of A$10,000 must be translated at the closing rate. The previously recorded amount ($9,410) is increased by $80 to reflect a translated liability of $9,490 (A$10,000 × 0.949).

*June 30, Year 1*

| | | |
|---|---|---|
| Exchange loss | 80 | |
|     Accounts payable | | 80 |
| To adjust the account payable to the closing rate | | |

The resulting foreign exchange loss would be reported in net income for the year ended June 30, Year 1.

On the settlement date, the exchange rate has increased from CDN$0.949 to CDN$0.953. The A$10,000 account payable is increased by $40 to reflect its translation at the spot rate at this date (A$10,000 × 0.953 = CDN$9,530). The company purchases 10,000 Australian dollars from its bank at a cost of $9,530 and remits Australian dollars to its Australian supplier. The foreign exchange loss of $40 will appear on the income statement for the year ended June 30, Year 2. The following journal entries record the transactions:

*June 30, Year 1*

| | | |
|---|---|---|
| Exchange loss | 40 | |
|     Accounts payable | | 40 |
| To adjust the account payable to the spot rate | | |
| Accounts payable | 9,530 | |
|     Cash (10,000 × 0.953) | | 9,530 |
| Payment to supplier | | |

---

*Foreign exchange adjustments are included in profit in the period in which they occur.*

---

## EXAMPLE 3: AN EXPORT EXAMPLE

We will now consider an example of the export of goods by a Canadian company.

On November 15, Year 1, Regina Malt Producers Ltd. shipped a carload of malt to a brewery in the United States, with full payment to be received on January 31, Year 2. The selling price of the malt was US$26,000. Regina Malt has a December 31 year-end. The following exchange rates existed on the dates significant for accounting purposes:

| | |
|---|---|
| *Transaction date* | Nov. 15, Year 1 |
| Exchange rate | US$1 = CDN$1.125 |
| *Year-end* | Dec. 31, Year 1 |
| Exchange rate | US$1 = CDN$1.129 |
| *Settlement date* | Jan. 31, Year 2 |
| Exchange rate | US$1 = CDN$1.119 |

The journal entries required on the dates noted above are as follows:

*Nov. 15, Year 1*

| | | |
|---|---|---|
| Accounts receivable | 29,250 | |
|     Sales | | 29,250 |

The accounts receivable and the sales are recorded at the November 15 spot rate (US$26,000 × 1.125 = CDN$29,250). The sales amount has been established at historical value and is unaffected by future exchange rate fluctuations. The accounts receivable (a monetary item) is at risk to exchange rate fluctuations. Note that while accounts receivable has been recorded at CDN$29,250, it is, in fact, a receivable of US$26,000.

> *The sale is translated at the historical rate to produce a historical price in Canadian dollars. This is consistent with normal measurement requirements to record sales at historical values.*

At the company's year-end, the exchange rate has changed to US$1 = CDN$1.129, and the receivable must appear in the financial statements at $29,354 (US$26,000 × 1.129). The following journal entry adjusts the accounts receivable to the closing rate:

*Dec. 31, Year 1*

| | | |
|---|---|---|
| Accounts receivable | 104 | |
| Exchange gain | | 104 |

This exchange gain will appear in the company's Year 1 income statement.

> *The accounts receivable is translated at the closing rate to produce a current value in Canadian dollars. This is consistent with normal measurement requirements to record monetary items at current values.*

By January 31, Year 2, which is the settlement date, the value of the U.S. dollar has declined relative to the Canadian dollar. When Regina Malt collects US$26,000 from its customer and delivers the U.S. dollars to its bank, it receives only CDN$29,094 (US$26,000 × 1.119). The journal entry to record the receipt of US$26,000, its conversion to Canadian dollars and the resultant loss is as follows:

*Jan. 31, Year 2*

| | | |
|---|---|---|
| Cash | 29,094 | |
| Exchange loss | 260 | |
| Accounts receivable | | 29,354 |

The exchange loss of $260 will appear in the Year 2 income statement. Note that the actual exchange loss between the transaction date and the settlement date was $156 ($29,250 − $29,094). Because the company's year-end occurred between these two dates, the exchange loss will appear in the two income statements in the following manner:

**YEAR 1 INCOME STATEMENT**

| | |
|---|---|
| Exchange gain (loss) | $ 104 |

**YEAR 2 INCOME STATEMENT**

| | |
|---|---|
| Exchange gain (loss) | (260) |
| Total exchange gain (loss) on the accounts receivable | $(156) |

The previous examples have illustrated the concept that exchange gains and losses resulting from the translation of a *monetary position* (i.e., a receivable or payable) are reflected in income in the year in which they occur. Note that these exchange gains and losses are actually unrealized in the sense that they result from the translation of a liability or a receivable. The exchange gain or loss is realized when the liability is paid or the receivable is collected.

> *Exchange gains/losses are reported in profit, even though they may be unrealized.*

## Transaction Gains and Losses from Noncurrent Monetary Items

Many Canadian companies borrow money in foreign markets, mainly because the capital markets in Canada are relatively small. The following example illustrates the accounting for foreign-currency-denominated debt.

**EXAMPLE 4**   Sable Company has a calendar year-end. On January 1, Year 1, the company borrowed 2,000,000 Swiss francs from a Swiss bank. The loan is to be repaid on December 31, Year 4, and requires interest at 8% to be paid each December 31. Both the annual interest payments and the loan repayment are to be made in Swiss francs (SF).

During the term of the loan, the following exchange rates necessary for our analysis were in effect:

| | |
|---|---|
| Jan. 1, Year 1 | SF1 = $1.076 |
| Average, Year 1 | SF1 = $1.073 |
| Dec. 31, Year 1 | SF1 = $1.069 |
| Dec. 31, Year 2 | SF1 = $1.070 |
| Dec. 31, Year 3 | SF1 = $1.071 |
| Dec. 31, Year 4 | SF1 = $1.067 |

Sable Company would record the transactions as follows:

*Jan. 1, Year 1*

| | | |
|---|---|---|
| Cash | 2,152,000 | |
| Loan payable (2,000,000 × 1.076) | | 2,152,000 |

This entry records the incurrence of a four-year loan of SF2,000,000 translated at the spot rate. On December 31, the company purchases 160,000 Swiss francs (SF2,000,000 × 8%) from its bank to make the interest payment, at a cost of $171,040 (SF160,000 × 1.069). A question arises as to whether the amount paid should be reflected as the interest expense for the past year. Remember that interest expense was SF160,000, which accrued throughout the year. It seems logical, therefore, to translate the interest expense using the average of the Year 1 exchange rates, or better still, to translate the monthly interest at the average rate for each month. In either case, when the interest is actually paid at the end of the year, an exchange gain or loss will have to be recorded. Using the average exchange rate for Year 1, the journal entry to record the interest expense and payment is as follows:

*Dec. 31, Year 1*

| | | |
|---|---|---|
| Interest expense | 171,680 | |
| Exchange gain | | 640 |
| Cash | | 171,040 |

To record interest expense at the average Year 1 rate of SF1 = $1.073, and the payment of interest at the year-end rate of SF1 = $1.069

> *Interest expense is translated at the average of the historical rates to produce a historical price in Canadian dollars. This is consistent with normal measurement requirements to record interest expense at historical values.*

On December 31, the loan is translated for financial statement purposes at $2,138,000 (SF2,000,000 × 1.069). The next entry adjusts the loan payable to the amount required on that date:

*Dec. 31, Year 1*

| | | |
|---|---|---|
| Loan payable | 14,000 | |
| Exchange gain | | 14,000 |

> *The loan payable is translated at the closing rate to produce a current value in Canadian dollars. This is consistent with normal measurement requirements to record monetary items at current values.*

The $14,640 total exchange gain resulting from the interest payment and the translation of the loan payable will appear in the Year 1 income statement.

Journal entries for Years 2 through 4 will not be illustrated; however, the following summarizes the yearly exchange gains and losses from translating the principal amount of the loan liability. The exchange gains and losses on the interest are not included.

| | Total | Year 1 | Year 2 | Year 3 | Year 4 |
|---|---|---|---|---|---|
| Exchange gain (loss) | $18,000 | $14,000 | $(2,000) | $(2,000) | $8,000 |

> *Exchange gains and losses occur on items translated at the closing rate but not on items translated at historical rates.*

## LO2 SPECULATIVE FORWARD EXCHANGE CONTRACTS

A forward exchange contract is one in which an exchange broker (usually a bank) and its customer agree to exchange currencies at a set price on a future date. Forward contracts can be either fixed dated or option dated. A fixed-dated contract specifies a fixed date such as June 18. An option-dated contract specifies a certain period, such as the month of June. A company may enter into a forward exchange contract purely to speculate on future exchange movements. For example, a company might enter into a contract to purchase foreign currency at a 60-day forward rate in anticipation that the spot rate in 60 days' time will be greater than the original forward rate. If its projection turns out to be accurate, it will purchase the foreign currency from the bank at the contracted price and immediately sell the currency to the bank at the higher spot rate. The following example deals with a speculative forward exchange contract.

> *In a forward exchange contract, two parties agree today to exchange currencies at a future date at a specified exchange rate.*

**EXAMPLE 5** On December 1, Year 1, Raven Company enters into a forward contract to sell one million Philippines pesos (PP) to its bank in exchange for Canadian dollars on March 1, Year 2, at the market rate for a 90-day forward contract of PP1 = $0.0227. On December 31, Year 1, Raven's year-end, the 60-day forward rate to sell Philippines pesos on March 1 is quoted at PP1 = $0.0222. On March 1, Year 2, the currencies are exchanged when the spot rate is PP1 = $0.0220.

According to IFRS 9, this forward contract is considered a financial instrument. It must be recorded at fair value on the date the contract is entered into and be remeasured at fair value throughout its life, with any gains or losses reflected in net income as they occur. There are two methods of recording this forward contract: the gross method and the net method. Under the gross method, the receivable from the bank and the payable to the bank are recorded separately at fair value. Under the net method, the receivable and payable are netted against each other and only the net receivable or net payable is recorded. The entries for this contract under the gross and net methods are shown in Exhibit 10.4. Either method is acceptable for internal recording-keeping purposes. However, when the financial statements are prepared, the receivable from the bank and the payable to the bank will be netted against each other

### EXHIBIT 10.4

**JOURNAL ENTRIES FOR SPECULATIVE FORWARD CONTRACT**

|  | Gross Method | Net Method |
|---|---|---|
| **December 1, Year 1** | | |
| Receivable from bank ($) | 22,700 | |
| Payable to bank (PP) | | 22,700 |
| Record forward contract at forward rate    (PP1,000,000 × 0.0227) | | |

**MEMORANDUM ENTRY UNDER NET METHOD**

Company entered into forward contract to pay PP1,000,000 to the bank in exchange for $22,700 to be received from the bank on March 1, Year 2.

|  | Gross Method | Net Method |
|---|---|---|
| **December 31, Year 1** | | |
| Forward contract | | 500 |
| Payable to bank (PP) | 500 | |
| Exchange gain | 500 | 500 |
| Revalue forward contract at fair value [PP1,000,000 × (0.0227 − 0.0222)] | | |
| **March 1, Year 2** | | |
| Forward contract | | 200 |
| Payable to bank (PP) | 200 | |
| Exchange gain | 200 | 200 |
| Revalue forward contract at fair value [PP1,000,000 × (0.0222 − 0.0220)] | | |
| Payable to bank (PP) | 22,000 | |
| Cash (PP) | | 22,000 |
| Deliver PP1,000,000 to bank to pay off liability (PP1,000,000 × 0.0220) | | |
| Cash ($) | 22,700 | |
| Receivable from bank ($) | | 22,700 |
| Receive $22,700 from bank | | |
| Cash ($) | | 700 |
| Forward contract | | 700 |
| Settle forward contract on net basis by receiving (22,700 − 22,000) | | |

> *A forward contract is a financial instrument that must be measured at fair value throughout its life. When the forward rate changes, the fair value of the forward contract changes.*

and only the net amount shown as either an asset or a liability on the balance sheet. We will use the net method for all subsequent illustrations in this chapter.

> *Under the net method, no journal entry is required when the forward contract is signed. Thereafter, the forward contract is measured at its fair value at each reporting date.*

The "$" symbol behind receivable from bank in the first entry indicates that the account receivable is denominated in Canadian dollars, whereas the "PP" behind the payable to bank indicates that the accounts payable is denominated in Philippines pesos. In other words, Raven will receive Canadian dollars and will pay Philippines pesos to settle this forward contract. Every time the exchange rate changes, the payable to bank, which is denominated in peso, will be worth a different amount of Canadian dollars. However, the receivable from the bank will not change because it is already denominated in Canadian dollars. In other words, the receivable is fixed in Canadian dollars, whereas the payable is fixed in pesos but worth a variable amount of Canadian dollars.

The fair value of the forward contract on December 1, Year 1, is zero because the two parties have just entered into a contract at the market rate for forward contracts. Under the gross method, the receivable and payable are both recorded at the future rate. Since the receivable and payable are equal and offsetting, there is no entry under the net method.

Some accountants may object to using the gross method for recording the forward contract on December 1 because forward exchange contracts are "executory" in nature. An *executory contract* is one in which neither party has performed its obligation to the other. Most contracts trigger accounting recognition only when one of the parties fulfills the obligation as agreed. For example, when a company places an order with a manufacturer for the purchase of machinery, neither party makes an accounting entry. The delivery of the machinery, or a down payment prior to delivery, results in accounting recognition by both parties because of the performance by one.

While forward exchange contracts are certainly executory, they are also firm commitments and once entered cannot be unilaterally cancelled. Under the net method, the forward contract is noted with a memorandum entry on the date of signing. Under the gross method, a journal entry is recorded on the date of signing. However, the two accounts would be netted against each other for reporting purposes and would have a nil value at the date of signing the contract.

> *Forward contracts must be reported at fair value according to IFRS.*

On December 31, the forward contract is remeasured at fair value in accordance with IFRS 9. We use the market rate for forward contracts maturing on March 1 to determine the fair value of Raven's contract. On this date, the 60-day forward rate to sell Philippines pesos on March 1 is PP1 = $0.0222, whereas Raven's contract is locked in at PP1 = $0.0227. Raven's contract will generate $22,700 on March 1, whereas contracts executed on December 31 would generate only $22,200 on March 1 for 1 million Philippines pesos. Therefore, Raven's contract is worth an extra $500 as of March 1. Theoretically, we should discount this $500 for two months. Practically speaking, the amount would usually not be discounted because the difference between the nominal amount of $500 and the present value of $500 for two months is not material and is not worth the effort to calculate.

> *This forward contract is worth more when the Philippines peso declines in value; that is, the Canadian dollar increases in value.*

In the appendix to this chapter, we illustrate how this forward contract would be accounted for with discounting. Unless otherwise noted, no examples in the text will use discounting. The forward contract will simply be measured at the forward rate for the term to maturity.

Note that the gain of $500 is recorded under both the gross and net methods. When financial statements are prepared at December 31 under the gross method, the "due from bank" of $22,700 and the "due to bank" of $22,200 will be offset against each other and only the net receivable of $500 will be presented on the balance sheet, and will likely be called forward contract. Therefore, the financial statement presentation will be the same under both the gross and net methods, even though the underlying accounts have different balances.

On March 1, Year 2, the forward contract is once again remeasured to fair value. Since the contract is being settled on this date, the market value of this forward contract is based on the spot rate for this date; that is, PP1 = $0.0220. The contract is worth $700 because Raven will get $22,700 from the bank, whereas PP1,000,000 is worth only $22,000 in the market on March 1. Therefore, Raven has gained $700 on this contract in total, and $200 since December 31. The first entry on March 1 records this $200 gain. The other entries record the exchange of pesos for dollars.

If we combine all of the journal entries under either the gross and net methods, we end up with the following entry:

| | | |
|---|---:|---:|
| Cash ($) | 700 | |
| Exchange gain—Year 1 | | 500 |
| Exchange gain—Year 2 | | 200 |

*The gross and net methods produce the same overall result in the end.*

In the end, Raven gained $700 by speculating on rate changes. If the exchange rates had changed in the other direction—that is, if the Canadian dollar had decreased rather than increased in value—Raven would have lost money on this speculative contract.

In the next few sections, we will illustrate how forward contracts can be used to hedge existing and anticipated exposure to foreign currency risk. Throughout the remainder of this chapter and in the end-of-chapter material, we will use the net method of accounting for forward contracts. This method involves fewer entries and better reflects what is presented on the financial statements.

## LO3 HEDGES

The previous examples illustrated the accounting for the foreign exchange gains and losses that result from holding a foreign-currency-denominated monetary position during a period of exchange rate changes. There are many possible ways for an enterprise to protect itself from the economic (and accounting) effects that result from such a position. This type of protection is generally referred to as "hedging," which can be defined as a means of transferring risk arising from foreign exchange (or interest rate, or price) fluctuations from those who wish to avoid it to those who are willing to assume it.[5] In order to hedge the risk of exchange rate fluctuations, a company takes a foreign currency position opposite to the position that it wishes to protect. The item with the risk exposure that the entity wishes to hedge and has taken steps to hedge is called the *hedged item.* The item used to offset the risk is called the *hedging instrument.* In the ideal case, the hedged item is perfectly hedged by the hedging instrument and there is no longer any overall exposure to currency fluctuations.

The entity has eliminated the overall risk of further exchange losses but also loses any possibility of gains from currency fluctuations.

> *A hedging instrument is the item used to offset the risk exposure. The hedged item is the item with the risk exposure that the entity has taken steps to mitigate.*

When accounting for the hedge, we want to properly reflect whether the hedge has been effective. If the hedge is truly effective, there should be no overall exchange gain or loss reported on the income statement, other than the cost of establishing the hedge. The exchange gains or losses on the hedged item will be offset by exchange losses or gains on the hedging instrument. But what happens when the hedging instrument is purchased in advance of the hedged item? For example, a forward contract may be purchased in Year 1 to hedge a transaction expected to occur in Year 2. How can the Year 1 gains or losses on the forward contract be offset against the Year 2 losses or gains on the anticipated transaction when the anticipated transaction has not yet occurred?

> *A foreign exchange hedge is a means of reducing or eliminating exchange losses on an overall basis by entering into a position to offset the risk exposure.*

The solution is hedge accounting as defined and described in IFRS 9. Under hedge accounting, the exchange gains or losses on the hedging instrument will be recognized in profit in the same period as the exchange gains or losses on the hedged item when they would otherwise be recognized in different periods.

It is important at this stage to differentiate between the terms "hedge" and "hedge accounting." While they may sound similar, they are very dissimilar. A hedge is an item that attempts to minimize or eliminate the risk of suffering a loss. Foreign currency risk can be reduced or eliminated through the use of forward exchange contracts, foreign currency options, not engaging in foreign transactions and creating natural hedges by having both assets and liabilities in the same foreign currency. Hedge accounting, on the other hand, is a means of accounting for the hedging instrument—that is, the forward contract—in order to properly show that it is effective in minimizing or eliminating the potential loss. Hedge accounting involves special accounting requirements that allow the entity to defer or accelerate income recognition in order to show that a gain or loss on the hedged item is being offset by a loss or gain on the hedging instrument.

> *Under hedge accounting, the exchange gains or losses on the hedging instrument will be reported in income in the same period as the exchange gains or losses on the hedged item.*

It is also important to note that hedge accounting is optional. The entity can choose to apply hedge accounting and thereby ensure that gains and losses on the hedging instrument are reported in the same period as the gains and losses on the hedged item. Alternatively, it might choose to not apply hedge accounting and account for the hedged item and the hedging instrument in isolation of each other.

Prior to 2013, the requirements for hedge accounting were solely contained in IAS 39. These requirements were developed when hedging activities were relatively new and not as widely understood as they are today. In general, the hedging item had to be a derivative such as a forward contract or an option. A derivative is a financial instrument or other contract with all three of the following characteristics:

(a) Its value changes in response to the change in a specified interest rate, financial instrument price, commodity price, foreign exchange rate, index of prices or rates, credit rating or credit index, or other variable (sometimes called the "underlying" variable).

(b) It requires either no initial net investment or an initial net investment that is smaller than would be required for other types of contracts with a similar expected response to changes in market factors.

(c) It is settled at a future date.

> *A derivative is a financial instrument or other contract whose value changes in response to the change in some underlying variable, which requires no initial investment, and which will be settled at a future date.*

Over the years, managers have developed a better understanding of risks and ways to mitigate risk. Many new financial instruments and other management strategies have been invented to deal with risk. As such, the requirements in IAS 39 now appear to be too restrictive and may make it impossible to apply hedge accounting to faithfully represent the effectiveness of the companies hedging activities. With these restrictions, investors may not be able to understand the risks an entity faces, what management is doing to manage those risks, and how effective those risk management strategies are.

In 2013, new requirements for hedge accounting were adopted by the IASB and are now contained in IFRS 9. These requirements are effective January 1, 2018, but can be adopted earlier. Some of the major changes and how they differ from IAS 39 are as follows:

1. IAS 39 has been criticized as being too rules-based and often viewed as being too restrictive. This led to more volatility in profit or loss from risk management activities. The requirements for hedge accounting under IFRS 9 are less restrictive and are more closely aligned with risk management activities undertaken by companies when hedging their financial and nonfinancial risk exposures.

> *The new hedge accounting requirements in IFRS 9 are less restrictive and more closely aligned with the entity's risk management activities.*

2. IFRS 9 allows derivatives, any other financial assets and most financial liabilities measured at fair value through profit or loss to be designated as a hedging instrument. An entity may view in combination, and jointly designate as the hedging instrument, any combination of the following: (a) derivatives or a proportion of them and (b) non-derivatives or a proportion of them.

3. Under IAS 39, components (parts) of financial items can be hedged, but not components of nonfinancial items. IFRS 9 allows any financial or nonfinancial item that has a risk component that can be separately identified and reliably measured to be a hedged item.

4. IAS 39 does not allow net positions to be hedged. However, companies often hedge net positions; for example, they may hedge a net foreign exchange position of 20 that is made up of an asset of 100 and a liability of 80. This creates an inconsistency between hedge accounting and risk management activity. IFRS 9 extends the use of hedge accounting to net positions for a group of items and to components of a group, and thereby improves the link to risk management.

5. IFRS 9 introduces a new way to account for the time value of an option contract and the premium or discount on a forward contract. This reduces the volatility in net income.

6. IAS 39 sets a high hurdle before hedge accounting is available. It also sets a high hurdle for hedge accounting to continue. These hurdles result from a strict quantitative test. The accounting consequences of failing this test are drastic. This is widely criticized as being arbitrary and for causing hedge accounting not to be available or to stop when a hedge is a good one economically. Under IFRS 9, there must be an economic relationship between the hedged item and hedging instrument; but, there is no quantitative threshold. It allows hedging relationships to be adjusted without necessarily stopping and potentially restarting hedge accounting. This enables hedge accounting to better reflect risk management activity, which often requires adjustments to hedges to accommodate changes in market conditions.

7. Disclosure requirements are more comprehensive and focus on the risks that entities are managing, how they are managing those risks, and the outcomes of that risk management activity, including the effect on the financial statements. This is to help investors to understand better the extent and effect of companies' hedging activities and to assist them in forecasting future cash flows.

> *The new hedge accounting requirements in IFRS 9 will help investors to better understand the extent and effect of an entity's hedging activities and to assist them in forecasting future cash flows.*

We will now discuss and illustrate the requirements for hedge accounting as per IFRS 9 in more detail. We will use forward contracts as the hedging instrument.

A hedged item can be a recognized asset or liability, an unrecognized firm commitment, a highly probable forecast transaction, or a net investment in a foreign operation. The hedged item can be a single item, a group of items, or a component of these items. The hedged item must be reliably measurable. If a hedged item is a forecast transaction (or a component thereof), that transaction must be highly probable.

To qualify for hedge accounting, the following three conditions must be met:

1. The hedging relationship consists only of eligible hedging instruments and eligible hedged items.

2. At the inception of the hedge, there is formal designation and documentation of the hedging relationship and the entity's risk management objective and strategy for undertaking the hedge. That documentation includes identification of the hedging instrument, the hedged item, and the nature of the risk being hedged and how the entity will assess whether the hedging relationship meets the hedge effectiveness requirements.

3. The hedging relationship meets the hedge effectiveness requirements.

> *To qualify for hedge accounting, the entity must expect that the hedge will be effective and must document how the hedging relationship will meet the hedge effectiveness requirements.*

Hedge effectiveness is the extent to which changes in the fair value or cash flows of the hedging instrument offset changes in the fair value or cash flows of the hedged item. Hedge ineffectiveness is the extent to which there is no such offset or the changes in the fair value or cash flows of the hedging instrument more than offset those on the hedged item. An entity considers the relationship between the quantity of the hedging instrument and quantity of the hedged item (the hedge ratio) when assessing whether the hedging relationship will minimize the expected ineffectiveness. For example, an entity wants to hedge a forecast purchase of 100 tonnes of a commodity of a particular grade in Location A, and that commodity usually trades at about 90% of the price for the exchange-traded benchmark grade of the same commodity in Location B. If the entity wants to hedge the forecast purchase of 100 tonnes with exchange-traded forward contracts, then a forward contract volume to purchase 90 tonnes of the benchmark grade of the commodity in Location B would be expected to offset best the entity's exposure to changes in the cash flows for the hedged purchase. Hence, a hedge ratio of 0.9:1 would minimize expected hedge ineffectiveness.

At the inception of the hedging relationship and on an ongoing basis, an entity must assess whether a hedging relationship meets the hedge effectiveness requirements. At a minimum, an entity must perform the ongoing assessment at each reporting date or at the time of a significant change in the circumstances affecting the hedge effectiveness requirements, whichever comes first. The assessment relates to expectations about hedge ineffectiveness and offsetting and therefore is only forward-looking.

*Hedge effectiveness must be assessed at the inception of the hedging relationship and on an ongoing basis.*

Hedges can be designated for accounting purposes as fair value hedges, cash flow hedges, or hedges of a net investment in a foreign operation.[6] In a fair value hedge, the entity uses a hedging instrument to hedge against the fluctuation in the fair value of the hedged item. This method will be used when the hedged item (such as a long-term receivable) will be measured at fair value. The gain or loss in the fair values of the hedging instrument and hedged items are both recognized in profit or loss in the period of the change in values, with one exception. If the hedging instrument hedges an equity instrument for which an entity has elected to present changes in fair value in other comprehensive income, then the gain or loss on the hedging instrument is also presented in other comprehensive income.

In a cash flow hedge, the entity uses a hedging instrument (such as a derivative) to hedge against the fluctuation in the Canadian-dollar value of future cash flows (such as future sales). The gain or loss on the hedging instrument is initially reported in other comprehensive income and subsequently reclassified to profit when the hedged item affects profit.

*A hedge is designated as a fair value hedge or a cash flow hedge based on the exposure hedged.*

IFRS 11 paragraph 6.5 states the following:

- A fair value hedge can be used as a hedge of a recognized asset or liability or an unrecognized firm commitment.
- A cash flow hedge can be used as a hedge of a recognized asset or liability or a highly probable forecast transaction.
- A hedge of the foreign currency risk of a firm commitment may be accounted for as a fair value hedge or a cash flow hedge.

## LO4 Hedging a Recognized Monetary Item

Vulcan Corporation, of Toronto, has a December 31 year-end. On November 1, Year 1, when the Bulgarian lev (BL) was worth $0.870, Vulcan sold merchandise to a Bulgarian customer for BL200,000. The terms of the sale required payment in full on February 15, Year 2. On November 15, Year 1, the spot rate was BL1 = $0.865 and the three-month forward rate was BL1 = $0.842. In order to protect the account receivable from further exchange losses, Vulcan entered into a contract with its bank on this date to deliver BL200,000 in three months' time. At year-end, the spot rate was BL1 = $0.869 and the 45-day forward rate was $0.852. On February 15, Year 2, Vulcan received BL200,000 from the customer and settled the forward contract with the bank when the spot and forward rates were $0.860.

Before preparing the journal entries, try to understand the rationale for entering into the hedge and the expected results. From November 1 to November 15, the Canadian-dollar value of the receivable declined from $174,000 (BL200,000 × 0.870) to $173,000 (BL200,000 × 0.865) because of the strengthening of the Canadian dollar relative to the Bulgarian lev. Vulcan was concerned about a further slide in the value of the lev and further erosion in the value of the receivable. To minimize the loss from a further decline, Vulcan entered into a forward exchange contract to fix the amount it will receive in Canadian dollars when the receivable is collected, and that is $168,400 (BL200,000 × 0.842). In effect, Vulcan was prepared to lose $4,600 ($173,000 − $168,400) in order to avoid bigger losses. This differential of $4,600 is called a *discount on the forward contract*. It will be expensed as part of the foreign exchange loss over the term of the forward exchange contract.

> *The forward contract is used to offset the risk of decline in value of the accounts receivable from the customer.*

Although the forward contract is a hedge of the accounts receivable, we will not apply hedge accounting in this situation. Both the accounts receivable and the forward contract are measured at fair value at each reporting date, with the exchange adjustments reported in profit. Since the exchange adjustments on both items are already being reported in profit in the same period, it is not necessary to use hedge accounting. We will account for each item separately as we did for the previous examples in this chapter. If the company wanted to use hedge accounting and designated the forward contract as a fair value hedge, the accounting would look exactly the same as accounting for each item separately. So there is no point in using hedge accounting in this particular situation. Hedge accounting is necessary only when the exchange adjustments on the hedged item and the hedging instrument would otherwise be reported in profit in different periods.

> *Hedge accounting is optional and will not be applied in this situation.*

A timeline for the transactions follows:

| *Nov. 1* | *Nov. 15* | *Dec. 31* | *Feb. 15* |
|---|---|---|---|
| Sell goods on account | Hedge receivable | Year-end | Collect receivable and settle forward exchange contract |

Vulcan will record the sale and the receivable at the spot rate on the transaction date with the following journal entry:

*Nov. 1, Year 1*

| | | |
|---|---|---|
| Accounts receivable (BL200,000) | 174,000 | |
|     Sales ($) | | 174,000 |
| BL200,000 × 0.870 = $174,000 | | |

> *The "BL" indicates that the accounts receivable is denominated in Bulgarian levs. The "$" indicates that the sale is being measured in dollars and will not be adjusted for future exchange rate changes.*

On November 15, the receivable is hedged when the spot rate is BL1 = $0.865. The exchange loss that occurred during the period when the account receivable was *not* hedged is recorded next, followed by the memorandum entry to note the signing of the forward contract.

*Nov. 15, Year 1*

| | | |
|---|---|---|
| Exchange gains and losses | 1,000 | |
|    Accounts receivable (BL) | | 1,000 |
| Exchange loss prior to the date of hedge, BL200,000 × (0.870 − 0.865) | | |

**Memorandum Entry**

Company entered into a forward contract to pay BL200,000 to the bank in exchange for $168,400 to be received from the bank on February 15, Year 2. The payable to the bank will offset the receivable from the customer.

With the signing of the forward contract Vulcan has locked in the receipt of $168,400 when it delivers BL200,000 to the bank on February 15, Year 2. It has also created a hedge by having a BL200,000 obligation to the bank offset by the BL200,000 receivable from the customer. If it had reversed the forward contract and agreed to receive BL200,000 from the bank and deliver $168,400 to the bank it would have doubled its currency risk rather than eliminate the risk. To ensure that the appropriate forward contract is signed, always ensure that there is an offsetting payable and receivable in the foreign currency.

When exchange rates change, the amount to be received from the bank will not change. However, the Canadian dollar equivalent of the BL200,000 receivable from the customer and payable to the bank will change. Therefore, the receivable and forward contract must be remeasured to fair value at each reporting date throughout the term of the contract. The fair value of the forward contract is determined by multiplying BL200,000 by the forward rate for the remaining term of the contract. At year-end, the accounts receivable and forward contract with the bank are adjusted to fair value as follows:

*Dec. 31, Year 1*

| | | |
|---|---|---|
| Accounts receivable (BL) | 800 | |
|    Exchange gains and losses | | 800 |
| To adjust the account receivable to the December 31 spot rate—BL200,000 × (0.869 − 0.865) | | |
| Exchange gains and losses | 2,000 | |
|    Forward contract | | 2,000 |
| To adjust the forward contract to the December 31 forward rate—BL200,000 × (0.852 − 0.842) | | |

---

*The closing rate is used when the item can be settled at any time, whereas the forward rate is used when the item must be settled at a future date.*

---

The $2,000 adjustment on the forward contract can be broken down as follows:

- An $800 loss on the forward contract, the hedging instrument, to offset the $800 gain on the accounts receivable, the hedged item.
- The other $1,200 is the portion of the $4,600 discount on the forward contract being expensed in this period.

---

*The discount on the forward contract is, in effect, expensed over the term of the forward contract.*

---

Financial statements are prepared as at December 31. The following partial trial balance is presented to show only the accounts used to record these particular transactions.

**PARTIAL TRIAL BALANCE**

At December 31, Year 1

| | Dr. | Cr. |
|---|---|---|
| Accounts receivable | $173,800 | |
| Exchange gains and losses | 2,200 | |
| Sales | | $174,000 |
| Forward contract | | 2,000 |
| | $176,000 | $176,000 |

The presentation of how the items shown on the trial balance will be presented in the year-end financial statements is shown next.

**VULCAN CORP.**

Partial Balance Sheet

At December 31, Year 1

**Assets**

| | |
|---|---|
| Accounts receivable | $173,800 |
| Other items | XXX |
| | $   XXX |

**Liabilities and Shareholders' Equity**

| | |
|---|---|
| Forward contract | $   2,000 |
| Other items | XXX |
| | $   XXX |

**VULCAN CORP.**

Partial Income Statement

For the year ended December 31, Year 1

| | | |
|---|---|---|
| Sales | | $174,000 |
| Expenses: | | |
| Foreign exchange loss | $   2,200 | |
| Other | XXX | XXX |
| Profit | | $   XXX |

The $2,200 foreign exchange loss consists of the $1,000 loss before the hedge was put in place and $1,200 expense pertaining to the $4,600 discount on the forward contract.

On the February 15 settlement date, the receivable from the Bulgarian customer and the payable to bank are adjusted to current value as follows:

*Feb. 15, Year 2*

| | | |
|---|---|---|
| Exchange gains and losses | 1,800 | |
| Accounts receivable (BL) | | 1,800 |
| To adjust the account receivable to the spot rate—BL200,000 × (0.869 − 0.860) | | |
| Exchange gains and losses | 1,600 | |
| Forward contract | | 1,600 |
| To adjust the forward contract to the forward rate—BL200,000 × (0.860 − 0.852) | | |

*The foreign-denominated receivable and forward contract must be remeasured.*

The total of the exchange losses recognized in Year 2 is $3,400, which is the remaining amount of the discount on the forward contract. This brings the total exchange loss on the forward contract to $4,600 ($1,200 from Year 1 and $3,400 for Year 2), which is equal to the discount on the forward contract.

The Bulgarian customer sends BL200,000 to Vulcan, which is deposited in a Bulgarian lev cash account. Vulcan delivers the BL200,000 to the bank to discharge its forward contract obligation and receives $168,400 as agreed. The following journal entries record these events:

*Feb. 15, Year 2*

| | | |
|---|---|---|
| Cash (BL) | 172,000 | |
|     Accounts receivable (BL) | | 172,000 |
| Collection from Bulgarian customer | | |

| | | |
|---|---|---|
| Forward contract | 3,600 | |
| Cash ($) | 168,400 | |
|     Cash (BL) | | 172,000 |
| Settle forward contract with bank | | |

You might be overwhelmed with the number of entries above and not appreciate the overall effect. To see the big picture, all the above entries for Year 1 and Year 2 can be condensed into one overall entry as follows:

| | | |
|---|---|---|
| Cash ($) | 168,400 | |
| Foreign exchange loss before hedge | 1,000 | |
| Foreign exchange loss (= discount on forward contract) | 4,600 | |
|     Sales | | 174,000 |

The net impact on profit is equal to the amount of cash received. This is a typical result in accounting. Sales were recorded at the historical rate, which is consistent with our measurement model. The exchange losses occurred for two reasons. First, the company lost $1,000 in the value of the accounts receivable due to the increase in value of the Canadian dollar relative to the Bulgarian lev before the hedge was put into place. Then, the company incurred a loss of $4,600 to put the hedge into place. In the end, the accounting for the hedge reflects the objective of the hedge in the first place.

> *Accrual accounting is more complicated than cash accounting, but in total and over time, it presents the same overall effect on profit as cash accounting.*

You may wonder why there is a foreign exchange loss when a perfect hedge was put into place. There was a BL200,000 payable to offset a BL200,000 for the exact same term. The reason for the loss is that the forward rate in the contract was less than the spot rate when the forward contract was signed. In effect, Vulcan agreed to a discount of $4,600 to avoid the risk of losing more in the event of a decline in the value of the Bulgarian lev.

IFRS 9 paragraph 6.5.16 allows another option for recording the discount on the forward contract. The forward contract can be segregated in two components: the intrinsic portion to hedge the receivable ("the spot element") and the portion to buy protection ("the forward element"). Under this approach, the hedge portion would be translated at the spot rate, which is the same rate as used to translate the receivable from the customer. There would be no exchange gains/losses because there would be a perfect hedge. The protection portion would be accrued as a hedge expense over the term of the hedge. The condensed summarized entry would be as follows:

| | | |
|---|---:|---:|
| Cash ($) | 168,400 | |
| Foreign exchange loss before hedge | 1,000 | |
| Hedge expense | 4,600 | |
|     Sales | | 174,000 |

See Self-Study Problem 1 for an illustration of a hedge of accounts payable arising from a purchase of merchandise.

## LO5 Hedging an Unrecognized Firm Commitment

On June 2, Year 2, when the spot rate was US$1 = CDN$1.26, Manning Inc. of Vancouver ordered merchandise from an American supplier for US$350,000. Delivery was scheduled for August 1 with payment to be made in full on delivery. Upon placing the order, Manning immediately entered into a 60-day forward contract with its bank to purchase US$350,000 on August 1 at the forward rate of US$1 = CDN$1.28. Manning's year-end is June 30. On August 1, the merchandise was received, and Manning purchased the U.S. dollars from the bank at the previously agreed rate and paid its supplier.

> *The forward contract is used to offset the risk of an increase in the cost of the inventory.*

In this example, the purpose of the forward contract is to fix the amount to be paid for the inventory at $448,000 (US$350,000 × 1.280). The hedged item is the commitment to pay for the inventory and the hedging instrument is the forward contract. The commitment to purchase the inventory is normally not recognized for accounting purposes because there is no asset or liability at the time of the commitment. The inventory and related accounts payable will be recorded only when the inventory is actually received. Since we must report the forward contract once the contract is signed, we will have a mismatch in the current year because the hedging instrument is recognized but the hedged item is not. Without hedge accounting, the exchange gains or losses on the forward contract would be reported in the current year, whereas no exchange gain or losses would be reported on the accounts payable because it does not legally exist in the current year. Therefore, hedge accounting is necessary to report the exchange gains or losses on the hedged item and the hedging instrument in the same period.

We can designate the forward contract as a cash flow hedge and defer the recognition in net income by recognizing the exchange gains or losses on the forward contract in other comprehensive income (OCI) and not recording anything with respect to the commitment to purchase goods. Alternatively, we could designate the forward contract as a fair value hedge and advance the recognition in profit of the exchange gains or losses on the commitment to purchase goods so that they match against the exchange gains or losses being recorded in profit on the forward contract.

The premium on the forward contract is $7,000 [US$350,000 × (1.28 − 1.26)]. It is the amount that Manning is prepared to pay to fix the amount of the cash flows required to purchase the inventory. Since the forward contract was intended to fix the cost of the inventory, the $7,000 will be reported as a cost of the inventory and will be reflected in income when the inventory is sold.

> *The premium on the forward contract is a cost of fixing the purchase price of the inventory.*

The relevant exchange rates for this example are as follows:

| Date | Spot Rate | Forward Rate* |
|---|---|---|
| June 2 | US$1 = CDN$1.260 | US$1 = CDN$1.280 |
| June 30 | US$1 = CDN$1.268 | US$1 = CDN$1.275 |
| August 1 | US$1 = CDN$1.272 | US$1 = CDN$1.272 |

*For contracts expiring on August 1, Year 2.

A timeline for the transactions follows:

| June 2 | June 30 | August 1 |
|---|---|---|
| Order goods and hedge order | Year-end | Receive goods, settle forward contract, and pay supplier |

Manning's journal entries under the net method to record the forward contract and the purchase of inventory are presented in Exhibit 10.5 under three different accounting methods: (1) the forward contract is designated as a cash flow hedge, (2) the forward contract is designated as a fair value hedge, and (3) hedge accounting is not applied. The rationale for each entry is explained below.

**CASH FLOW HEDGE**   The memorandum entries note that Manning ordered supplies from an American supplier, will receive U.S. dollars from the bank, and will deliver Canadian dollars to the bank. In effect, it has a US$350,000 receivable from the bank to offset the US$350,000 payable to the supplier. Therefore, it has created a hedge as intended. It will pay CDN$448,000 to the bank in exchange for the U.S. dollars. In effect, it has locked in the amount of Canadian dollars required to pay out the supplier.

> The net method is used to account for the forward contract.

At year-end, the second journal entry is made to value the forward contract at fair value. The forward rate for contracts expiring on August 1, Year 2 has changed from 1.280 to 1.275. Therefore, the amount required to buy forward US$350,000 has changed from $448,000 (US$350,000 × 1.280) to $446,250 (US$350,000 × 1.275). With hindsight, Manning would have been better off waiting until June 30 to sign the forward contract. In effect, its existing forward contract is now worth a negative amount of $1,750, because the US$350,000 receivable portion of the forward contract has declined in value from $448,000 to $446,250.

Note that the exchange adjustment on the forward contract is reported in other comprehensive income, which is a component of comprehensive income. In turn, the balance at the end of the year for accumulated OCI for cash flow hedges is reported as a separate component of shareholders' equity. On the June 30, Year 2, balance sheet, the forward contract would be reported under current liabilities.

> The exchange gains or losses on the hedging instrument for the cash flow hedge are reported in other comprehensive income for now and will be reported in profit when the exchange gains or losses on the hedged items are reported in profit.

On August 1, the forward contract is adjusted to its fair value in the fourth journal entry and uses the same logic as the second journal entry. Journal entry six reports the settlement of the forward contract with the bank. Manning delivers $448,000 to the bank in exchange for US$350,000 as agreed under the terms of the forward contract. Then, journal entry seven records the payment of US$350,000 to the supplier upon delivery of the inventory.

**EXHIBIT 10.5**

**JOURNAL ENTRIES FOR HEDGING A FIRM COMMITMENT**

June 2, Year 2

Journal
Entry
No.

1. **Memorandum Entries**

   Company ordered merchandise from an American supplier for payment of US$350,000 on delivery on August 1, Year 2.

   Company entered into a forward contract to receive US$350,000 from the bank in exchange for a payment of CDN$448,000 to the bank on August 1, Year 2. The receipt of US$350,000 from the bank will offset the payable to the supplier.

| Journal Entries | Cash Flow Hedge | Fair Value Hedge | No Hedge Accounting |
|---|---|---|---|
| June 30, Year 2 | | | |
| 2. OCI—Exchange gains and losses | 1,750 | | |
| Exchange gains and losses | | 1,750 | 1,750 |
| Forward contract | 1,750 | 1,750 | 1,750 |
| To adjust forward contract to June 30 forward rate—350,000 × (1.280 − 1.275) | | | |
| 3. Commitment asset | | 1,750 | |
| Exchange gains and losses | | 1,750 | |
| To adjust value of upcoming accounts payable to June 30 forward rate—350,000 × (1.280 − 1.275) | | | |

> *The forward rate is used to revalue the forward contract and commitment asset at each reporting date.*

| | Cash Flow Hedge | Fair Value Hedge | No Hedge Accounting |
|---|---|---|---|
| August 1, Year 2 | | | |
| 4. OCI—Exchange gains and losses | 1,050 | | |
| Exchange gains and losses | | 1,050 | 1,050 |
| Forward contract | 1,050 | 1,050 | 1,050 |
| To adjust forward contract to August 1 forward rate—350,000 × (1.275 − 1.272) | | | |
| 5. Commitment asset | | 1,050 | |
| Exchange gains and losses | | 1,050 | |
| To adjust value of upcoming accounts payable to August 1 forward rate—350,000 × (1.275 − 1.272) | | | |

> *The exchange loss on the forward contract is reported in profit for the fair value hedge to match against the exchange gain on the commitment asset.*

| | Cash Flow Hedge | Fair Value Hedge | No Hedge Accounting |
|---|---|---|---|
| 6. Cash (US$) | 445,200 | 445,200 | 445,200 |
| Forward contract | 2,800 | 2,800 | 2,800 |
| Cash (CDN$) | 448,000 | 448,000 | 448,000 |
| Settle forward contract with bank | | | |
| 7. Inventory | 445,200 | 445,200 | 445,200 |
| Cash (US$) | 445,200 | 445,200 | 445,200 |
| To record the inventory purchase and pay cash at the August 1 spot rate—350,000 × 1.272 | | | |
| 8. Inventory | 2,800 | 2,800 | |
| OCI—reclassification of exchange gains and losses | 2,800 | | |
| Commitment asset | | 2,800 | |
| To reclassify OCI and commitment asset to cost of inventory | | | |

> *The commitment asset is closed out to inventory when the inventory is purchased.*

There are two options for removing the accumulated exchange adjustment of $2,800 from accumulated other comprehensive income. Option one is to remove the $2,800 when the inventory is delivered and report it as an adjustment of the inventory. In turn, this amount will affect the amount reported as cost of goods sold when the inventory is sold. The second option is to remove the $2,800 when the inventory is sold and show it as other income or net against cost of goods sold on the income statement. In both cases, the $2,800 will be reflected in the income statement when the inventory is sold. Since the objective of the hedge was to fix the price of the inventory, the first option will be used and is accounted for in journal entry 8.

Under the cash flow hedge, the exchange losses on the hedging instrument (i.e., the forward contract) were put into OCI until the hedged item (i.e., the inventory) was recognized. There was no mismatching of gains and losses going through net income during the period of the forward contract.

> *The exchange losses incurred on the hedging instrument increase the cost of the inventory and will be reported in net income when the inventory is sold.*

**FAIR VALUE HEDGE**   Most of the journal entries for the fair value hedge are the same as a cash flow hedge. The entries that are different are explained below.

The exchange gains and losses on the hedging instrument (i.e., the forward contract) are reported in net income as they occur as per journal entries 2 and 4. The exchange gains and losses on the hedged item (i.e., the firm commitment to purchase inventory) should also be reported in net income. The problem is that the obligation to pay for the inventory does not legally exist until the inventory is delivered. However, the forward contract hedges this upcoming liability as if it already exists. Special rules are required under hedge accounting to allow the recognition of the exchange gains/losses on the hedged item to be recognized in net income even before the hedged item legally exists. We will refer to this upcoming liability as *notional accounts payable*. In our example, the notional accounts payable is US$350,000 and is due on August 1. The forward rate is used to measure this notional liability because the forward contract signed with the bank determines the amount expected to be paid to settle this liability. Also, it has features similar to those of the forward contract, which also uses the forward rate. The notional liability was $448,000 (US$350,000 × 1.280) when the goods were ordered from the supplier on June 2.

On June 30, the notional accounts payable is revalued to its fair value of $446,250 (US$350,000 × 1.275). The decline in the notional liability is reported as an exchange gain as per journal entry 3. The offsetting account is a commitment asset, which will be reported as a current asset on Manning's balance sheet. As is evidenced by entries 2 and 3, the exchange loss on the forward contract will be offset by the exchange gain on the firm commitment. A similar entry is made on August 1 as per journal entry 5.

When the inventory is actually purchased on August 1, the commitment asset is reduced to zero. The options for the offsetting entry are the same as those discussed earlier for the cash flow hedge. Since the objective of the hedge was to fix the price of the inventory, the amount cleared out of the commitment asset will be added to the cost of the inventory as per journal entry 8.

> *The change in value of the commitment is recognized in profit to match the change in value of the forward contract.*

**NO HEDGE ACCOUNTING**   The third column of Exhibit 10.5 shows the journal entries when hedge accounting was not used. The forward contract was still used to hedge the commitment to purchase the inventory. However, the company elected to not use the special rules under hedge accounting. The forward contract is treated as if it was a speculative forward contract and the inventory is recognized only when it is delivered. There is no attempt to match the forward contract with the purchase of the inventory. As a result, the exchange losses on the forward contract are reported in net income as they occur.

> *The exchange losses incurred on the hedging instrument are reported in net income as they occur when the special rules under hedge accounting are not applied.*

The summarized entries for the combined effect of all of entries in Exhibit 10.5 are as follows:

|  | Cash Flow Hedge | Fair Value Hedge | No Hedge Accounting |
|---|---|---|---|
| Inventory | 448,000 | 448,000 | 445,200 |
| Exchange gains and losses |  |  | 2,800 |
| Cash (CDN$) | 448,000 | 448,000 | 448,000 |

Under all three methods, the net cash outflow is $448,000. This amount was fixed when the forward contract was signed. Under hedge accounting, the inventory is recorded at $448,000, the amount fixed by the forward contract. When hedge accounting is not used, the inventory and forward contract are reported separately as if they were not related. The inventory is reported at $445,200, which is the value of US$350,000 paid to the supplier using the spot rate on the date the inventory is purchased and, in this case, also paid. The $2,800 exchange loss on the forward contract is reported in net income in the same manner as a speculative forward contract.

> *Under hedge accounting, the forward contract fixed the purchase price of the inventory at the forward rate on the date of the hedge.*

Under all three reporting methods, $448,000 will eventually be expensed. However, the timing and line description on the income statement are different. Under hedge accounting, the $448,000 will be expensed as cost of goods sold when the inventory is sold. When hedge accounting is not applied, the $448,000 is expensed through a combination of $2,800 in exchange losses over a two-year period, and $445,200 as cost of goods sold when the inventory is sold. This is a typical result in accounting. The amount expensed on a cumulative basis is equal to the cash paid on a cumulative basis.

At the beginning of this problem, we determined that the company was willing to pay a premium of $7,000 to fix the amount of the inventory. When hedge accounting was applied, the premium ended up being reported as part of the cost of the inventory. Furthermore, no exchange gains or losses were reported in profit because the commitment to purchase inventory was effectively hedged by the forward contract. When hedge accounting was not applied, there was no relationship between the forward contract and the amount recorded for the cost of the inventory.

> *When hedge accounting is not applied, the forward contract is accounted for as if it were a speculative contract.*

In the above example, the forward contract was treated as a whole—that is, the premium was blended into the forward rate and was not accounted for separately. As previously mentioned, IFRS 9 paragraph 6.5.16 allows another option for recording the premium or discount on the forward contract. The forward contract can be segregated in two components: the intrinsic portion to hedge the notional payable (the "spot element") and the portion to buy protection or lock in the cost (the "forward element"). Under this approach, the intrinsic portion and the notional liability would be translated at the spot rate. There would be no exchange gains/losses, because there would be a perfect hedge. The protection portion would be added to the cost of the inventory similar to other ancillary costs such as freight and taxes. Although some of the individual journal entries may have been different, the overall result would have been the same.

IFRS 9 paragraph 6.5.4 states that a hedge of the foreign currency risk of a firm commitment may be accounted for as a fair value hedge or a cash flow hedge. However, only a fair value hedge may be used to hedge other risks related to an unrecognized firm commitment. According to a brief survey conducted by the author, Canadian companies typically used the cash flow hedge for the foreign currency risk of a firm commitment.

In the above example, the inventory was paid for on delivery. If Manning had purchased the inventory on credit, it would have also been exposed to foreign currency risk on the accounts payable. It could have entered into a forward contract to hedge both the commitment to buy inventory and the amount required to settle the account payable. In this case, the $7,000 premium would have to be split between the two objectives. The part of the $7,000 that had been incurred up to the date of delivery of the inventory would be reported as a cost of the inventory and reflected in net income when the inventory is sold. The other part would be recognized in net income over the period of time between the origination and settlement of the accounts payable.

For further analysis and discussion of the impact of the three reporting methods on key financial ratios, see the section "Analysis and Interpretation of Financial Statements" below. Also, see Self-Study Problem 2 for another illustration of a cash flow hedge of a firm commitment to sell equipment.

## LO6 Hedging a Highly Probable Forecasted Transaction

The following example illustrates the accounting when long-term debt is used as a hedge of a future revenue stream. The hedge will be accounted for as a cash flow hedge because it is hedging the variability of future cash flows.

Alana Enterprises, a Canadian company that has carried out business activities in Singapore for a number of years, has decided to protect itself against foreign currency fluctuations over the next three years, during which it expects a revenue stream of at least 200,000 Singapore dollars (SD) per year. On January 1, Year 1, the company borrows SD600,000, payable in full at the end of three years, and designates the loan as a hedge against the future three-year revenue stream. In order to simplify the illustration, we will omit the payment of yearly interest and assume that there is no difference between the exchange rate at the end of each year and the average exchange rate for that year. Furthermore, we will assume that the cash received in Singapore dollars will be immediately used to pay operating expenses.

> *The loan payable is the hedging instrument, and the future revenue stream is the hedged item.*

Relevant exchange rates for the Singapore dollar are as follows:

| | |
|---|---|
| Jan. 1, Year 1 | SD1 = $0.852 |
| Dec. 31, Year 1 | SD1 = $0.849 |
| Dec. 31, Year 2 | SD1 = $0.835 |
| Dec. 31, Year 3 | SD1 = $0.840 |

Applying the concepts of hedge accounting, Alana will make the following journal entries:

*Jan. 1, Year 1*

| | | |
|---|---|---|
| Cash | 511,200 | |
|     Loan payable (SD) (600,000 × 0.852) | | 511,200 |

During Year 1, the revenue stream is recorded at the average exchange rate for the year. Thus, the following entry is recorded:

| | | |
|---|---|---|
| Cash | 169,800 | |
|     Sales revenue (200,000 × 0.849) | | 169,800 |

On December 31, Year 1, the loan payable has to be reflected in the financial statements at fair value using the closing rate. The entry to record the exchange gain on the loan payable resulting from a decrease in the exchange rate from $0.852 to $0.849 is as follows:

*Dec. 31, Year 1*

| | | |
|---|---|---|
| Loan payable (SD) | 1,800 | |
|     OCI—cash flow hedge (Year 1) (600,000 × [0.852 − 0.849]) | | 1,800 |

> *In Year 1, the entire loan is needed to hedge three years of forecasted revenues, and the entire exchange gain on the loan should be reported in other comprehensive income to be eventually offset against the future revenue stream.*

One-third of the hedged revenue stream has been received, and so the following adjusting entry is made to match one-third of the gain from the hedge against the revenue received:

*Dec. 31, Year 1*

| | | |
|---|---|---|
| OCI—cash flow hedge (Year 1) | 600 | |
|     Sales revenue (200/600 × 1,800) | | 600 |

> *Since one-third of the revenue stream has been realized, one-third of the other comprehensive income should be brought into income.*

Two-thirds of the exchange gain is deferred in other comprehensive income to be matched against the foreign currency revenues when they are received in the following two years. The company has *lost* because it has received less revenue in Canadian dollars than would be the case if the exchange rate had not changed, but it has also *gained* due to the fact that its liability (measured in Canadian dollars) has decreased. The liability hedges the revenue stream; consequently, the gain in one offsets the loss in the other. The total revenue for the year is $170,400, which is made up of the translated revenue of $169,800 plus the recognized exchange gain on the hedge of $600. Note that this is the same amount as would have been received in translated revenue if the exchange rates had not changed since January 1, Year 1, that is, $170,400 ($200,000 × 0.852). If the exchange rates do not change over the next two years, the total translated revenue *plus* the recognized revenue from the hedge will be $170,400 each year.

Note also that while the loan is still SD600,000, one-third of the foreign revenue stream has been received; therefore, one-third of this loan balance no longer qualifies as a hedge and is exposed to foreign currency risk. Because of this, any future exchange gains and losses on this portion must be reflected immediately in income.

During Year 2, revenue in Singapore dollars is received and translated at the average rate. This results in the following entry:

| | | |
|---|---|---|
| Cash | 167,000 | |
| Sales revenue (200,000 × 0.835) | | 167,000 |

On December 31, Year 2, the loan payable is reduced by $8,400 (SD600,000 × [0.849 − 0.835]) to reflect its translation at the closing rate; also, the gain on the one-third portion that no longer qualifies as a hedge is immediately reflected in profit, and the balance of the gain from the hedge portion is initially deferred with the following entry:

*Dec. 31, Year 2*

| | | |
|---|---|---|
| Loan payable | 8,400 | |
| Exchange gain (⅓ × 8,400) | | 2,800 |
| OCI—cash flow hedge (Year 2) (2/3 × 8,400) | | 5,600 |

> *In Year 2, only two-thirds of the loan is a hedging instrument. The other one-third of the loan is exposed to foreign currency risk; the related exchange gain is reported in profit.*

The other comprehensive income hedges the foreign currency revenues of Years 2 and 3. Year 2 revenue has been received and translated at the average exchange rate for the year. Therefore, the Year 2 portion (one-half) of the deferred gain is matched against this revenue with the following entry:

*Dec. 31, Year 2*

| | | |
|---|---|---|
| OCI—cash flow hedge (Year 2) | 2,800 | |
| Sales revenue (½ × 5,600) | | 2,800 |

In addition, the portion of the deferred Year 1 exchange gain must be matched against Year 2 revenues with the following entry:

*Dec. 31, Year 2*

| | | |
|---|---|---|
| OCI—cash flow hedge (Year 1) | 600 | |
| Sales revenue | | 600 |

Remember that the purpose of the hedge was to ensure that the foreign currency revenue in Year 2 was at least $170,400 (SD200,000 × 0.852). The actual foreign revenue adjusted for the hedge gains was equal to this amount, as the following calculation indicates:

| | |
|---|---|
| Foreign currency revenue (200,000 × 0.835) | $167,000 |
| Exchange gain on Year 1 hedge | 600 |
| Exchange gain on Year 2 hedge | 2,800 |
| | $170,400 |

> *The final revenue figure of $170,400 is the equivalent Canadian dollar value of the anticipated sale when the hedge was first put into place.*

In addition, the Year 2 income statement will reflect the additional exchange gain ($2,800) that came from the portion of the loan that no longer qualifies as a hedge.

The balance of the accumulated other comprehensive income (AOCI) that will appear on the December 31, Year 2, balance sheet is calculated as follows:

| | | | |
|---|---|---|---|
| OCI, Year 1 | | 1,800 | |
| Less reflected in income: | | | |
| Year 1 | 600 | | |
| Year 2 | 600 | 1,200 | $ 600 |
| OCI, Year 2 | | 5,600 | |
| Less reflected in income Year 2 | | 2,800 | 2,800 |
| AOCI, December 31, Year 2 | | | $3,400 |

Because SD400,000 from the total revenue of SD600,000 has been received at the end of Year 2, the loan balance that still qualifies as a hedge is only SD200,000.

The Year 3 entries to record the foreign currency revenues and to adjust the loan to the current rate are as follows:

| | | |
|---|---|---|
| Cash | 168,000 | |
| Sales revenue (200,000 × 0.840) | | 168,000 |
| | | |
| *Dec. 31, Year 3* | | |
| OCI—cash flow hedge (Year 3) (1/3 × 3,000) | 1,000 | |
| Exchange loss (2/3 × 3,000) | 2,000 | |
| Loan payable (SD600,000 × [0.840 − 0.835]) | | 3,000 |

During Year 3, only one-third of the loan was being used as a hedge of the revenue stream. The exchange loss on this portion is initially reported in OCI. The remaining loss from the portion of the loan that is not a hedge ($2,000) is reported in profit in the year.

> *In Year 3, only one-third of the loan is a hedging instrument. The other two-thirds of the loan is exposed to foreign currency risk; the related exchange gain is reported in profit.*

A final entry is made to match the balance of the other comprehensive income from prior and current years against the Year 3 foreign currency revenue:

| | | |
|---|---|---|
| OCI—cash flow hedge (Year 1) | 600 | |
| OCI—cash flow hedge (Year 2) | 2,800 | |
| OCI—cash flow hedge (Year 3) | | 1,000 |
| Sales revenue | | 2,400 |

> *By the end of Year 3, all of the other comprehensive income has been transferred to profit to match the timing of the income recognition on the hedged item, being the revenue stream.*

An entry would also be made to pay off the loan that is due on this date. The following calculation summarizes the amount reflected in profit in Year 3 from the foreign currency revenue, the hedge gains and losses, and the exchange loss from the non-hedge portion of the loan:

| | | |
|---|---|---|
| Foreign currency revenue (200,000 × 0.840) | | $168,000 |
| Year 1 and 2 exchange gains on hedge | 3,400 | |
| Year 3 exchange loss on hedge | 1,000 | 2,400 |
| Hedged foreign currency revenue | | 170,400 |
| Remainder of Year 3 loan exchange loss | | 2,000 |
| Effect on Year 3 profit | | $168,400 |

> *The hedging instrument was used to fix the final revenue figure at $170,400, the equivalent Canadian dollar value of the anticipated sale when the hedge was first put into place.*

This simplified example has illustrated a possible use of hedge accounting. In a more realistic situation, differences would occur because the average rates used to translate the revenue stream are different from the year-end rates used to translate the foreign currency loan, and the actual revenues would probably turn out to be different from those expected when the hedge was designated. However, the broad concepts illustrated would still apply.

**DISCLOSURE REQUIREMENTS**   The following summarize the main disclosures required in IAS 21 for the effects of changes in foreign exchange rates:

(a) The amount of exchange differences recognized in profit or loss

(b) Net exchange differences recognized in other comprehensive income

   The following summarize the main disclosures required in IFRS 7 paragraph 21A related to hedges:

(a) An entity's risk management strategy and how it is applied to manage risk

(b) How the entity's hedging activities may affect the amount, timing, and uncertainty of its future cash flows

(c) The effect that hedge accounting has had on the entity's primary financial statements

> *The entity must disclose the type of hedge and the risks being hedged.*

Some of the specific disclosure requirements are as follows:

(a) The carrying amount of the hedging instruments (financial assets separately from financial liabilities)

(b) The notional amounts or other quantity (e.g., tonnes or cubic metres) related to the hedging instruments

   For fair value hedges:

(i) The carrying amount of the accumulated gains or losses on the hedged item presented in a separate line item in the statement of financial position, separating assets from liabilities

   For cash flow hedges:

(i) The balance in the cash flow hedge reserve for continuing hedges that will be reclassified when the hedged item affects profit or loss

(ii) For hedges of net positions, the hedging gains or losses recognized in a separate line item in the income statement

(iii) The amount reclassified from the cash flow hedge reserve into profit or loss as a reclassification adjustment

   For fair value and cash flow hedges:

(i) Changes in the value of the hedging instrument recognized in other comprehensive income

(ii) Hedge ineffectiveness recognized in profit or loss

> *The disclosure requirements pertaining to hedges and hedge accounting are quite extensive.*

Bombardier Inc., a Canadian company, is a manufacturer of transportation equipment, including business and commercial aircraft and rail transportation equipment and systems. It is the world's only manufacturer of both planes and trains. Exhibit 10.6 contains excerpts from Bombardier's 2014 financial statements pertaining to foreign currency transactions and hedges. In 2014, Bombardier had not yet adopted IFRS 9 and, therefore, did not provide the extensive disclosure required by this IFRS.

## EXHIBIT 10.6

### EXTRACTS FROM BOMBARDIER'S 2014 FINANCIAL STATEMENTS

2. Summary of Significant Accounting Policies

*Foreign currency transactions*—Transactions denominated in foreign currencies are initially recorded in the functional currency of the related entity using the exchange rates in effect at the date of the transaction. Monetary assets and liabilities denominated in foreign currencies are translated using the closing exchange rates. Any resulting exchange difference is recognized in income except for exchange differences related to retirement benefits asset and liability, as well as financial liabilities designated as hedges of the Corporation's net investments in foreign operations, which are recognized in OCI. Non-monetary assets and liabilities denominated in foreign currencies and measured at historical cost are translated using historical exchange rates, and those measured at fair value are translated using the exchange rate in effect at the date the fair value is determined. Revenues and expenses are translated using the average exchange rates for the period or the exchange rate at the date of the transaction for significant items.

> *Some revenues and expenses are translated at the exchange rate at the date of the transaction rather than the average rate for the period.*

### Financial instruments

a) Financial instruments classified as HFT

*Derivative financial instruments*—Derivative financial instruments are mainly used to manage the Corporation's exposure to foreign exchange and interest-rate market risks, generally through forward foreign exchange contracts, interest rate swap agreements and cross-currency interest-rate swap agreements. Derivative financial instruments include derivatives that are embedded in financial or nonfinancial contracts that are not closely related to the host contracts.

Derivative financial instruments are classified as HFT, unless they are designated as hedging instruments for which hedge accounting is applied (see below). Changes in the fair value of derivative financial instruments not designated in a hedging relationship, excluding embedded derivatives, are recognized in cost of sales or financing expense or financing income, based on the nature of the exposure.

Embedded derivatives of the Corporation include financing rate commitments related to the sale of aircraft, call options on long-term debt and foreign exchange instruments included in sale or purchase agreements. Upon initial recognition, the fair value of financing rate commitments linked to the sale of products is recognized as deferred charge in other assets. The deferred charge is recorded as an adjustment of the sale price of the related products. Call options on long-term debt that are not closely related to the host contract are measured at fair value, with the initial value recognized as an increase of the related long-term debt and amortized to net income using the effective interest method. Upon initial recognition, the fair value of the foreign exchange instruments not designated in a hedge relationship is recognized in cost of sales. Subsequent changes in fair value of embedded derivatives are recorded in cost of sales, other expense (income) or financing expense or financing income, based on the nature of the exposure.

### Hedge accounting

Designation as a hedge is only allowed if, both at the inception of the hedge and throughout the hedge period, the changes in the fair value of the derivative and non-derivative hedging financial instruments are expected to substantially

*(continued)*

offset the changes in the fair value of the hedged item attributable to the underlying risk exposure. The Corporation formally documents all relationships between the hedging instruments and hedged items, as well as its risk management objectives and strategy for undertaking various hedge transactions. This process includes linking all derivatives to forecasted cash flows or to a specific asset or liability. The Corporation also formally documents and assesses, both at the hedge's inception and on an ongoing basis, whether the hedging instruments are highly effective in offsetting the changes in the fair value or cash flows of the hedged items. There are three permitted hedging strategies.

---

*The company formally documents and assesses whether the hedging instruments are highly effective.*

---

*Fair value hedges*—The Corporation generally applies fair value hedge accounting to certain interest-rate derivatives and forward foreign exchange contracts hedging the exposures to changes in the fair value of recognised financial assets and financial liabilities. In a fair value hedge relationship, gains or losses from the measurement of derivative hedging instruments at fair value are recorded in net income, while gains or losses on hedged items attributable to the hedged risks are accounted for as an adjustment to the carrying amount of hedged items and are recorded in net income.

---

*The company applies both fair value and cash flow hedge accounting.*

---

*Cash flow hedges*—The Corporation generally applies cash flow hedge accounting to forward foreign exchange contracts and interest-rate derivatives entered into to hedge foreign exchange risks on forecasted transactions and recognized assets and liabilities. In a cash flow hedge relationship, the portion of gains or losses on the hedging item that is determined to be an effective hedge is recognized in OCI, while the ineffective portion is recorded in net income. The amounts recognized in OCI are reclassified in net income as a reclassification adjustment when the hedged item affects net income. However, when an anticipated transaction is subsequently recorded as a non-financial asset, the amounts recognized in OCI are reclassified in the initial carrying amount of the related asset.

*Hedge of net investments in foreign operations*—The Corporation generally designates certain long-term debt as hedges of its net investments in foreign operations. The portion of gains or losses on the hedging instrument that is determined to be an effective hedge is recognized in OCI, while the ineffective portion is recorded in net income. The amounts recognized in OCI are reclassified in net income when corresponding exchange gains or losses arising from the translation of the foreign operations are recorded in net income.

The portion of gains or losses on the hedging instrument that is determined to be an effective hedge is recorded as an adjustment of the cost or revenue of the related hedged item. Gains and losses on derivatives not designated in a hedge relationship and gains and losses on the ineffective portion of effective hedges are recorded in cost of sales or financing expense or financing income for the interest component of the derivatives or when the derivatives were entered into for interest rate management purposes.

Hedge accounting is discontinued prospectively when it is determined that the hedging instrument is no longer effective as a hedge, the hedging instrument is terminated or sold, or upon the sale or early termination of the hedged item.

## 13. Financial Instruments

### Derivatives and hedging activities

The carrying amounts of all derivative and non-derivative financial instruments in a hedge relationship were as follows, as at:

| | December 31, 2014 | | December 31, 2013 | | January 1, 2013 | |
|---|---|---|---|---|---|---|
| | *Assets* | *Liabilities* | *Assets* | *Liabilities* | *Assets* | *Liabilities* |
| **Derivative financial instruments designated as fair value hedges** | | | | | | |
| Cross-currency interest-rate swaps | $ — | $ — | $ 36 | $ — | $ 17 | $ 6 |
| Interest-rate swaps | 226 | — | 296 | 67 | 394 | — |
| | 226 | — | 332 | 67 | 411 | 6 |

*(continued)*

**EXHIBIT 10.6** *(continued)*

| | December 31, 2014 | | December 31, 2013 | | January 1, 2013 | |
|---|---|---|---|---|---|---|
| | *Assets* | *Liabilities* | *Assets* | *Liabilities* | *Assets* | *Liabilities* |
| **Derivative financial instruments designated as cash flow hedges**[1] | | | | | | |
| Forward foreign exchange contracts | **259** | **592** | 331 | 319 | 232 | 120 |
| **Derivative financial instruments classified as HFT**[2] | | | | | | |
| Forward foreign exchange contracts | **29** | **72** | 27 | 22 | 13 | 12 |
| Interest-rate swaps | | | | | | |
| Embedded derivative financial instruments | | **1** | | 2 | | 2 |
| Foreign exchange | **—** | **—** | 1 | 1 | 3 | 1 |
| Call options on long-term debt | **14** | **—** | 101 | — | 76 | — |
| | **43** | **73** | 129 | 25 | 92 | 15 |
| **Total derivative financial instruments** | **$528** | **$665** | $792 | $411 | $735 | $ 141 |
| **Non-derivative financial instruments designated as hedges of net investment** | | | | | | |
| Long-term debt | **$ —** | **$ 23** | $ — | $517 | $ — | $1,042 |

[1] *The maximum length of time of derivative financial instruments hedging the Corporation's exposure to the variability in future cash flows for anticipated transactions is 35 months as at December 31, 2014.*
[2] *Held as economic hedges, except for embedded derivative financial instruments.*

> *Forward foreign exchange contracts were designated as cash flow hedges.*
> *Long-term debt was designated as hedges of net investment.*

 The net gains on hedging instruments designated in fair value hedge relationships and net losses on the related hedged items attributable to the hedged risk recognized in financing expense, amounted to $173 million and $168 million respectively for fiscal year 2014 (net losses of $205 million and net gains of $213 million respectively for fiscal year 2013).

> *The net gains on the hedging instruments designated in fair value hedge relationships were reported in financing expense.*

 The methods and assumptions used to measure the fair value of financial instruments are described in note 33—Fair value of financial instruments.

## 32. Financial Risk Management

### Market risk

*Foreign exchange risk*

The Corporation is exposed to significant foreign exchange risks in the ordinary course of business through its international operations, in particular to the Canadian dollar, pound sterling, Swiss franc and euro. The Corporation employs various strategies, including the use of derivative financial instruments and by matching asset and liability positions, to mitigate these exposures.

 The Corporation's main exposures to foreign currencies are managed by the segments and covered by a central treasury function. Foreign currency exposures are managed in accordance with the Corporation's Foreign Exchange Risk

*(continued)*

Management Policy (the "FX Policy"). The objective of the FX Policy is to mitigate the impact of foreign exchange movements on the Corporation's consolidated financial statements. Under the FX Policy, potential losses from adverse movements in foreign exchange rates should not exceed pre-set limits. Potential loss is defined as the maximum expected loss that could occur if an unhedged foreign currency exposure was exposed to an adverse change of foreign exchange rates over a one-quarter period. The FX Policy also strictly prohibits any speculative foreign exchange transactions that would result in the creation of an exposure in excess of the maximum potential loss approved by the Board of Directors of the Corporation.

Under the FX Policy, it is the responsibility of the segments' management to identify all actual and potential foreign exchange exposures arising from their operations. This information is communicated to the central treasury group, which has the responsibility to execute the hedge transactions in accordance with the FX Policy.

In order to properly manage their exposures, each segment maintains long-term cash flow forecasts in each currency. BA has adopted a progressive hedging strategy while BT hedges all its identified foreign currency exposures to limit the effect of currency movements on their results. The segments also mitigate foreign currency risks by maximizing transactions in their functional currency for their operations such as material procurement, sale contracts and financing activities.

In addition, the central treasury function manages balance sheet exposures to foreign currency movements by matching asset and liability positions. This program consists mainly in matching the long-term debt in foreign currency with long-term assets denominated in the same currency.

---

*The company tries to mitigate foreign currency risk by matching asset and liability positions.*

---

The Corporation mainly uses forward foreign exchange contracts to manage the Corporation's exposure from transactions in foreign currencies and to synthetically modify the currency of exposure of certain balance sheet items. The Corporation applies hedge accounting for a significant portion of anticipated transactions and firm commitments denominated in foreign currencies, designated as cash flow hedges. Notably, the Corporation enters into forward foreign exchange contracts to reduce the risk of variability of future cash flows resulting from forecasted sales and purchases and firm commitments.

The Corporation's foreign currency hedging programs are typically unaffected by changes in market conditions, as related derivative financial instruments are generally held to maturity, consistent with the objective to lock in currency rates on the hedged item.

*Sensitivity analysis*

Foreign exchange risk arises on financial instruments that are denominated in foreign currencies. The foreign exchange rate sensitivity is calculated by aggregation of the net foreign exchange rate exposure of the Corporation's financial instruments recorded in its statement of financial position. The following impact on EBT for fiscal year 2014 is before giving effect to cash flow hedge relationships.

### Effect on EBT

|  | Variation | CAD/USD | GBP/USD | EUR/USD | EUR/CHF | Other |
|---|---|---|---|---|---|---|
| Gain (loss) | +10% | $20 | $13 | $5 | $1 | $(67) |

The following impact on OCI for fiscal year 2014 is for derivatives designated in a cash flow hedge relationship. For these derivatives, any change in fair value is mostly offset by the re-measurement of the underlying exposure.

### Effect on OCI before Income Taxes

|  | Variation | CAD/USD | GBP/USD | EUR/USD | EUR/CHF | Other |
|---|---|---|---|---|---|---|
| Gain (loss) | +10% | $235 | $77 | $35 | $88 | $24 |

*Source:* Bombardier Inc., *Bombardier Inc. Financial Report—Fiscal Year Ended December 31, 2014*, Pages 115, 117–118, 139, 168–169. Reproduced with permission from Bombardier Inc.

# LO7 ANALYSIS AND INTERPRETATION OF FINANCIAL STATEMENTS

Earlier in this chapter, we prepared journal entries to account for the hedge of a firm commitment by Manning Inc. to purchase inventory from a foreign supplier under three reporting methods. Exhibit 10.7 shows the net impact of the aforementioned journal entries on selected items on Manning's Year 2 income statement and balance sheet and on three key financial ratios. The first column shows assumed amounts for the numerator and denominator for three key ratios before Manning signed the purchase order and entered into the forward contract. The last three columns show the cumulative effect of the journal entries on the Year 2 financial statements and on the key ratios. We assume that there were no transactions other than the purchase order and the forward contract.

## EXHIBIT 10.7

### IMPACT OF HEDGE ACCOUNTING METHODS ON KEY RATIOS FOR YEAR 2

| | Before Transactions | Cash Flow Hedge | Fair Value Hedge | No Hedge Accounting |
|---|---|---|---|---|
| **Impact on income statement:** | | | | |
| Net income | | | | (1,750) |
| OCI | | (1,750) | | |
| Comprehensive income | | (1,750) | | (1,750) |
| **Impact on balance sheet:** | | | | |
| Current assets | | | 1,750 | |
| Current liabilities | | 1,750 | 1,750 | 1,750 |
| Shareholders' equity | | (1,750) | | (1,750) |
| **Impact on key ratios:** | | | | |
| **Current ratio** | | | | |
| Current assets | 2,000,000 | 2,000,000 | 2,001,750 | 2,000,000 |
| Current liabilities | 1,000,000 | 1,001,750 | 1,001,750 | 1,001,750 |
| | = 2.000 | = 1.997 | = 1.998 | = 1.997 |
| **Debt-to-equity ratio** | | | | |
| Total debt | 3,300,000 | 3,301,750 | 3,301,750 | 3,301,750 |
| Shareholders' equity | 1,100,000 | 1,098,250 | 1,100,000 | 1,098,250 |
| | = 3.000 | = 3.006 | = 3.002 | = 3.006 |
| **Return on equity** | | | | |
| Net income | 165,000 | 165,000 | 165,000 | 163,250 |
| Shareholders' equity | 1,100,000 | 1,098,250 | 1,100,000 | 1,098,250 |
| | = 15.00% | = 15.02% | = 15.00% | = 14.86% |

*The fair value hedge method shows the best liquidity position (i.e., highest current ratio) because the commitment asset is included in current assets.*

*The cash flow hedge method shows the best performance (i.e., highest return on equity) because exchange losses are reported in OCI and do not negatively affect net income.*

Note the following from Exhibit 10.7:

- There is no impact on net income or comprehensive income under the fair value hedge, because the exchange loss on the forward contract is offset by an exchange gain on the commitment asset.

- There is a negative impact of $1,750 on comprehensive income for the other two methods, but the cash flow hedge shows the loss in OCI, whereas the loss is reported in net income when hedge accounting is not used. The loss through OCI ends up in accumulated OCI, which is a separate component of shareholders' equity, whereas the negative net income ends up in retained earnings.

- All methods report a current liability of $1,750 but only the fair value hedge shows a current asset, which is the commitment asset of $1,750.

- Manning's liquidity looks the best under the fair value hedge because the current ratio is highest. The commitment asset was included in current assets under this method but not in the other methods.

- Manning's solvency looked the best under the fair value hedge because the debt-to-equity ratio was lowest. Shareholders' equity was not negatively affected by any exchange losses under the fair value hedge, whereas it was negatively affected for the other two methods.

- The return on equity uses net income rather than comprehensive income as the numerator. The cash flow method shows the best return on equity because of the higher net income and lower shareholders' equity. The no hedge accounting method shows the worst return on equity because the exchange loss is reported in net income.

> *The fair value hedge method shows the best solvency position (i.e., lowest debt-to-equity ratio) because shareholders' equity is not negatively affected by exchange losses.*

## ASPE Differences

- Hedge accounting is permitted only when the critical terms of the hedging instrument match those of the hedged item. Enterprises are not required to assess hedge effectiveness. An enterprise is required to determine only that the critical terms of the two components of the hedging arrangement continue to match.

- An entity may designate only the following hedging relationships pertaining to foreign currency exposure:

  - An anticipated purchase or sale of a commodity hedged with a forward contract to mitigate the effect of future price changes of the commodity

  - An anticipated transaction denominated in a foreign currency hedged with a forward contract to mitigate the effect of changes in future foreign currency exchange rates

  - A foreign-currency-denominated interest-bearing asset or liability hedged with a cross-currency interest rate swap to mitigate the effect of changes in interest rates and foreign currency exchange rates

  - The net investment in a self-sustaining foreign operation hedged with a derivative or a non-derivative financial instrument to mitigate the effect of changes in foreign currency exchange rates

- Hedge accounting for private companies follows an accrual-based model and is much simpler than hedge accounting for public companies. For example, an entity accounts for a qualifying hedge of an anticipated transaction as follows:

  - When the anticipated transaction occurs, it is recognized initially at the amount of consideration paid or received.

  - When the hedging item matures before the hedged item is recognized, the gain or loss on the hedging item is recognized as a separate component of equity until the hedged item is recognized. When the hedged item is recognized, the gain or loss on the hedging item is transferred from the separate component of equity to the carrying amount of the hedged item or to net income.

  - When the forward contract matures, the gain or loss on the contract is recorded as an adjustment of the carrying amount of the hedged item. When the hedged item is recognized directly in net income, the gain or loss on the forward contract is included in the same category of net income.

- Disclosure is minimal compared to the disclosure required for public companies.

*Hedge accounting is more restrictive and much simpler for private enterprises.*

## SUMMARY

Transactions denominated in foreign currency are recorded in Canadian dollars at the spot rate in effect on the date of the transaction. At the date of the balance sheet, foreign currency assets and liabilities are translated into Canadian dollars to preserve the normal measurement at either historical cost or fair value. Any gains or losses arising from changes in exchange rates on the exposed items are reflected in profit for the period. **(LO1)**

Forward contracts and other derivatives should be reported at fair value at each reporting date. In a speculative forward exchange contract, exchange gains and losses are recognized in profit as exchange rates change. **(LO2)**

Hedging is a means of eliminating exposure to risk. Foreign currency risk can be reduced or eliminated through the use of forward exchange contracts, foreign currency options, not engaging in foreign transactions and creating natural hedges by having both assets and liabilities in the same foreign currency. **(LO3)**

Monetary assets and liabilities and forward exchange contracts used to hedge these monetary assets and liabilities are reported at fair value at each reporting date. Hedge accounting is not necessary for these items because the gains and losses for the hedged items and hedging instruments are naturally reported in net income in the same period. **(LO4)**

Either a fair value hedge or cash flow hedge can be used to account for a forward contract as a hedge of an unrecognized firm commitment. In a fair value hedge, exchange gains and losses are recognized in profit in the period of the change in exchange rates. In a cash flow hedge, the exchange gains and losses on the hedging instrument are initially reported in other comprehensive income and subsequently reclassified to profit when the hedged item affects profit. **(LO5)** Only a cash flow hedge can be used to account for a hedge of a highly probable future transaction. **(LO6)**

The different methods for hedge accounting will produce different results on the balance sheet and income statement. When analyzing financial statements, it is important to note what method of hedge accounting has been used and how it will impact the amounts reported in the financial statements. **(LO7)**

## Self-Study Problem 1

**LO1, 4**

### Hedging an Existing Monetary Position

On November 15, Year 1, Domco Ltd. of Montreal bought merchandise from a supplier located in Brunei for 100,000 Brunei dollars (BD). The Brunei dollar was trading at $0.81 on that date, and the terms of the purchase required Domco to pay the account on January 30, Year 2. On December 1, when the spot rate was BD1 = $0.813, Domco entered into a forward contract with its bank to receive BD100,000 at the 60-day forward rate of BD1 = $0.82. On December 31, Year 1, Domco's year-end, the spot rate was BD1 = $0.825 and the 30-day forward rate was BD1 = $0.831. On January 30, Year 2, when the spot rate was BD1 = $0.838, Domco settled the forward contract with its bank and paid BD100,000 to the Swiss supplier.

### Required

(a) Prepare the journal entries required in Year 1 and Year 2, assuming that hedge accounting is not applied.

(b) Prepare a partial statement of financial position as at December 31, Year 1, which shows accounts payable and the forward contract.

(c) Prepare one journal entry to summarize the combined effect of all entries in Part (a).

## Solution to Self-Study Problem 1

(a) *Nov. 15, Year 1*

| | | |
|---|---|---|
| Inventory ($) | 81,000 | |
| Accounts payable (BD) (BD100,000 × 0.81) | | 81,000 |

*Dec. 1, Year 1*

| | | |
|---|---|---|
| Exchange gains/losses | 300 | |
| Accounts payable (BD) | | 300 |

To adjust the accounts payable to the Dec. 1 spot rate (BD100,000 × [0.813 − 0.810])

**Memorandum Entry**

Company entered into forward contract to receive BD100,000 from the bank in exchange for a payment of $82,000 to the bank on January 30, Year 2. The receivable from the bank will offset the payable to the supplier.

*Dec. 31, Year 1*

| | | |
|---|---|---|
| Exchange gains/losses | 1,200 | |
| Accounts payable (BD) | | 1,200 |

To adjust the accounts payable to the Dec. 31 spot rate (BD100,000 × [0.825 − 0.813])

| | | |
|---|---|---|
| Forward contract | 1,100 | |
|     Exchange gains/losses | | 1,100 |

To adjust the forward contract to the Dec. 31 forward rate (BD100,000 × [0.831 − 0.820])

*Jan. 30, Year 2*

| | | |
|---|---|---|
| Exchange gains/losses | 1,300 | |
|     Accounts payable (BD) | | 1,300 |

To adjust the accounts payable to the Jan. 30 spot rate (BD100,000 × [0.838 − 0.825])

| | | |
|---|---|---|
| Forward contract | 700 | |
|     Exchange gains/losses | | 700 |

To adjust the forward contract to the Jan. 30 forward rate (BD100,000 × [0.838 − 0.831])

| | | |
|---|---|---|
| Cash (BD) | 83,800 | |
|     Forward contract | | 1,800 |
|     Cash ($) | | 82,000 |

Settle forward contract with bank

| | | |
|---|---|---|
| Accounts payable (BD) | 83,800 | |
|     Cash (BD) | | 83,800 |

Pay BD100,000 to supplier (BD100,000 × 0.838)

(b)

**DOMCO LTD.**
**STATEMENT OF FINANCIAL POSITION**
At December 31, Year 1

| | |
|---|---|
| Assets | |
|     Forward contract | $ 1,100 |
| Liabilities | |
|     Accounts payable | $82,500 |

| | | |
|---|---|---|
| (c)  Inventory | 81,000 | |
|     Exchange loss (before hedge) | 300 | |
|     Exchange loss (= premium on contract) | 700 | |
|       Cash | | 82,000 |

# Self-Study Problem 2

LO1, 5

### Hedging an Unrecognized Firm Commitment

On October 15, Year 2, Sellcompany Ltd., located in Canada, signed a contract to sell equipment to Buycompany, which is located in a country whose currency is the foreign currency unit (FC). The selling price of the equipment was FC200,000 and the terms of the sale called for delivery to be made on January 30, Year 3, with payment in full due on delivery.

Having signed the sales order, Sellcompany immediately entered into a forward contract with its bank to sell FC200,000 on January 30, Year 3, at the forward rate of FC1 = $1.22. The spot rate on October 15 was FC1 = $1.20. On December 31, the year-end of Sellcompany, the spot rate was

FC1 = \$1.222 and the 30-day forward rate was FC1 = \$1.231. On January 30, Year 3, when the spot rate was FC1 = \$1.24, Sellcompany delivered the equipment, received FC200,000 from Buycompany, and settled the forward contract with the bank.

## Required

(a) Prepare the journal entries required in Year 2 and Year 3 for Sellcompany, assuming that the forward contract is designated as a cash flow hedge.

(b) Prepare a partial statement of financial position as at December 31, Year 2, which shows the presentation of the hedge accounts.

(c) Prepare one journal entry to summarize the combined effect of all entries in part (a).

## Solution to Self-Study Problem 2

(a) *Oct. 15, Year 2*

### Memorandum Entries

Company signed a contract to sell equipment for FC200,000 for delivery on January 30, Year 3.

Company entered into forward contract to pay FC200,000 to the bank in exchange for \$244,000 to be received from the bank on January 30, Year 3. The payable to the bank will offset the receivable from the customer.

To make note of sales contract and forward contract.

*Dec. 31, Year 2*

| | | |
|---|---|---|
| OCI—cash flow hedge | 2,200 | |
| Forward contract | | 2,200 |

To adjust the forward contract to the forward rate [FC200,000 × (1.231 − 1.220)]

*Jan. 30, Year 3*

| | | |
|---|---|---|
| OCI—cash flow hedge | 1,800 | |
| Forward contract | | 1,800 |

To adjust the forward contract to the Jan. 30 forward rate [FC200,000 × (1.240 − 1.231)]

| | | |
|---|---|---|
| Cash (FC) | 248,000 | |
| Sales | | 248,000 |

To record equipment sale at FC200,000 × 1.24

| | | |
|---|---|---|
| Cash (\$) | 244,000 | |
| Forward contract | 4,000 | |
| Cash (FC) | | 248,000 |

Settle forward contract with the bank

| | | |
|---|---|---|
| Sales | 4,000 | |
| OCI—cash flow hedge | | 4,000 |

To reclassify other comprehensive income as an adjustment of sales

(b)

**SELLCOMPANY LTD.**
**STATEMENT OF FINANCIAL POSITION**
At December 31, Year 2
**Liabilities**

| | |
|---|---|
| Forward contract | <u>\$ 2,200</u> |

| (c) | Cash | 244,000 | |
| | Sales | | 244,000 |

In the end, the sales were recorded at $244,000, the amount fixed by the forward contract. Furthermore, no exchange gains or losses were reported in income because the commitment to sell the equipment was effectively hedged by the forward contract.

# APPENDIX 10A

## Determining the Fair Value of Forward Exchange Contracts

**LO8**

The fair value of a forward exchange contract is based on the relative merits of the contract compared with other contracts in the market and the time value of money. If the contract states that the company must sell foreign currency at a rate that is better than what is currently available in the market, the contract has a positive value. On the other hand, if the contract states that the company must sell foreign currency at a rate that is worse than what is currently offered in the market, the contract has a negative value. Therefore, the following factors are usually considered to determine the fair value of a forward contract at any point in time:

1. The forward rate when the forward contract was entered into

2. The current forward rate for a contract that matures on the same date as the forward contract entered into

3. A discount rate, typically the company's incremental borrowing rate

> *The fair value of a forward contract is based on its relative merits compared with other contracts in the market and the time value of money.*

In Exhibit 10.4, we considered the first two factors above when we measured the forward contract at $500 at December 31, Year 1. Since the $500 value will be realized only on March 1, Year 2, it should be discounted to derive its present value at December 31, Year 1. Assuming that Raven's incremental borrowing rate is 12% per annum or 1% per month, the fair value of the forward contract at December 31 is $490.15 ($500 × 0.9803).[7]

The journal entries to record the fair value of the forward contract in Exhibit 10.4 under the gross and net methods when discounting is applied are shown in Exhibit 10A.1. Only the first three entries are shown here because the remaining entries would be the same as in Exhibit 10.4.

## Summary of Appendix 10A

Theoretically speaking, present value techniques should be used when determining the fair value of a forward contract. The time value of money is usually immaterial and can be ignored when the term of the contract is less than year. **(LO8)**

---

**EXHIBIT 10A.1**

### JOURNAL ENTRIES FOR SPECULATIVE FORWARD CONTRACT

|  | Gross Method | Net Method |
|---|---|---|

*December 1, Year 1*

**Memorandum Entry under Net Method**

Company entered into forward contract to deliver PP1,000,000 to the bank
in exchange for $22,700 to be received from the bank on March 1, Year 2.
To make note of forward contract.

*December 31, Year 1*

| | Gross Method | Net Method |
|---|---|---|
| Forward contract | | 490 |
| Payable to bank (PP) | 490 | |
|     Exchange gain | 490 | 490 |

Revalue forward contract at fair value (PP1,000,000 × [0.0227 − 0.0222] × 0.9803)

*March 1, Year 2*

| | Gross Method | Net Method |
|---|---|---|
| Forward contract | | 210 |
| Payable to bank (PP) | 210 | |
|     Exchange gain | 210 | 210 |

Revalue forward contract at fair value ([22,700 − 490] − PP1,000,000 × 0.0220)

> *The value of a forward contract should be recorded in present value terms.*

---

## Review Questions

LO1  **1.** Briefly summarize the accounting issues arising from foreign-currency-denominated transactions.

LO1  **2.** What is the difference between pegged and floating exchange rates?

LO1  **3.** You read in the newspaper, "One U.S. dollar can be exchanged for 1.15 Canadian dollars." Is this a direct or an indirect quotation? If your answer is *indirect*, what is the direct quotation? If your answer is *direct*, what is the indirect quotation?

LO1  **4.** Differentiate between a spot rate and a forward rate.

LO1  **5.** How are foreign-currency-denominated assets and liabilities measured on the transaction date? How are they measured on a subsequent balance sheet date?

LO1  **6.** Describe when to use the closing rate and when to use the historical rate when translating assets and liabilities denominated in a foreign currency. Explain whether this practice is consistent with the way we normally measure assets and liabilities.

LO1  **7.** Differentiate between a spot rate and a closing rate.

LO3, 5  **8.** Differentiate between the accounting for a fair value hedge and a cash flow hedge.

LO3  9. List some ways that a Canadian company could hedge against foreign currency exchange rate fluctuations.

LO3  10. What are some typical reasons for acquiring a forward exchange contract?

LO4  11. If a foreign-currency-denominated payable has been hedged, why is it necessary to adjust the liability for balance sheet purposes?

LO1  12. Explain the application of lower of cost and net realizable value to inventory that was purchased from a foreign supplier.

LO5  13. How does the accounting for a fair value hedge differ from the accounting for a cash flow hedge of an unrecognized firm commitment?

LO2  14. What is the suggested financial statement presentation of hedge accounts recorded under the gross method? Why?

LO5  15. What is meant by *hedge accounting*?

LO2, 16. Would hedge accounting be used in a situation in which the hedged item and the hedging
3  instrument were both monetary items on a company's statement of financial position? Explain.

LO6  17. When long-term debt hedges a revenue stream, a portion of the long-term debt becomes exposed to the risk of changes in exchange rates. Why is this?

LO5  18. When will the premium paid on a forward contract to hedge a firm commitment to purchase inventory be reported in income under a cash flow hedge? Explain.

# CASES

## Case 10-1

LO3, 4

Interfast Corporation, a fastener manufacturer, has recently been expanding its sales through exports to foreign markets. Earlier this year, the company negotiated the sale of several thousand cases of fasteners to a wholesaler in the country of Loznia. The customer is unwilling to assume the risk of having to make payment in Canadian dollars. Desperate to enter the Loznian market, the vice-president for international sales agrees to denominate the sale in lrubles (LR), the national currency of Loznia. The current exchange rate for the lruble is LR1 = $4. In addition, the customer indicates that he cannot make payment until all of the fasteners have been sold. Payment of LR400,000 is scheduled for six months from the date of sale.

Fearful that the lruble might depreciate in value over the next six months, the head of the risk management department at Interfast enters into a forward contract to sell lrubles in six months at a forward rate of LR1 = $3.60. The forward contract is designated as a fair value hedge of the lruble receivable. Six months later, when payment is received from the Loznian customer, the exchange rate for the lruble is LR1 = $3.40. The corporate treasurer calls the head of the risk management department into her office.

| Treasurer: | I see that your decision to hedge our foreign currency position on that sale to Loznia was a bad one. |
| --- | --- |
| Department Head: | What do you mean? We have a gain on that forward contract. We're $80,000 better off from having entered into that hedge. |
| Treasurer: | That's not what the books say. The accountants have recorded a net loss of $160,000 on that particular deal. I'm afraid I'm not going to be able to pay you a bonus this year. Another bad deal like this one and I'm going to have to demote you back to the interest rate swap department. |
| Department Head: | Those bean counters have messed up again. I told those guys in international sales that selling to customers in Loznia was risky, but at least by hedging our exposure, we managed to receive a reasonable amount of cash on that deal. In fact, we ended up with a gain of $80,000 on the hedge. Tell the accountants to check their debits and credits again. I'm sure they just put a debit in the wrong place or some accounting thing like that. |

## Required

Have the accountants made a mistake? Does the company have a loss, a gain, or both from this forward contract? Explain.

# Case 10-2

LO3

Long Life Enterprises was a well-established Toronto-based company engaged in the importation and wholesale marketing of specialty grocery items originating in various countries of the western Pacific Rim. They had recently also entered the high-risk business of exportation, to several of these same countries, of fresh Atlantic lobster and crab.

Although Canada has extensive trading relationships with several countries in the Pacific Rim, these transactions were not normally priced or settled in terms of the Canadian dollar. Both the U.S. dollar and the Japanese yen were somewhat more common in these transactions. Further, various local currencies were involved, especially for small transactions involving specialty items, and a wide variety of credit terms were in use for both imports and exports. The entire situation was complicated by the perishable nature of some of the imports and the high mortality risk for both lobster and crab. Both situations led to uncertainty as to the face amount of the associated receivable or payable and hindered the ability of the firm to adopt the policy of specific hedging of each of the receivable or payable contracts.

Most recently, the Canadian dollar had risen against other major currencies, leading to major losses on the large receivables outstanding because of the seasonal lobster harvest. More generally, management was concerned about losses that might arise from both export and import transactions. For the most recent fiscal year, foreign currency losses had exceeded gains by some $40,000—an amount the company could not afford during the present stage of rapid growth.

## Required

What steps would you propose to the management of Long Life Enterprises to reduce the foreign exchange costs associated with their receivables and payables? As a part of this process, suggest a way of structuring transactions or affairs that would reduce the impact of fluctuations in the relative values of currencies.

*(Case prepared by Peter Secord, St. Mary's University)*

## Case 10-3

LO1

Canada Cola Inc. (CCI) is a public company engaged in the manufacture and distribution of soft drinks across Canada. Its primary product is Canada Cola ("Fresh as a Canadian stream"), which is a top seller in Canada and generates large export sales.

You met with Jane MacNamara, the partner in charge of the CCI audit engagement, to commence planning for the upcoming audit of CCI. During this meeting, MacNamara informed you that early this year CCI entered into an agreement with the government of Russia and has commenced the manufacture and sale of Canada Cola in Russia. A short summary of this agreement is contained in Exhibit I. MacNamara would like you to prepare a detailed report that discusses the accounting implications of this new division of CCI for this engagement.

### EXHIBIT I

**SUMMARY OF AGREEMENT**

1. The Russian government will provide the land and the building for the plant. It will make no further investment.

2. CCI will install bottling machinery costing $5 million in the Russian plant. Once installed, this machinery may not be removed from Russia. No other plants may be established in Russia without the consent of the Russian government.

3. CCI will be required to provide the funds for the initial working capital. CCI will sell U.S. dollars to the Russian government in exchange for local currency (rubles).

4. CCI will be wholly responsible for the management and daily operations of the plant. Canadian managers will be transferred to Russia.

5. CCI will be permitted to export its cola syrup to Russia at CCI's Canadian cost.

6. Only Canada Cola may be bottled at the Russian plant and the entire output from the plant can only be sold in Russia. CCI and the Russian government will share equally in the profits from the sale of Canada Cola in Russia.

7. Although foreign currency can be converted into rubles, rubles cannot be converted back into any foreign currency. Therefore, the Russian government will sell vodka to CCI (at the prevailing export market price in Russia) in exchange for the rubles CCI earns in profits. CCI will be permitted to export this vodka to Canada, where it may be sold in the Canadian domestic market only.

*(CPA Canada adapted)*[8]

## Case 10-4

LO1, 7

The United Football League (UFL), a North American professional football league, has been in work stoppage since July 1, Year 9, immediately after the six-week training camp ended. Faced with stalled negotiations, the players' union representing the league's 28 teams, the UFL Players' Association (UFLPA), called a general strike. It led to the cancellation of games scheduled for the beginning of the regular season, which was to start on July 5 and end with playoffs in mid-December.

The main disputed issue is player compensation. According to the team owners, the current compensation system has created an excessive increase in players' salaries (more than 300% in 10 years), which has most teams incurring net losses and several facing extinction. Currently, players are contracted by the teams for fixed periods. Owners are free to negotiate personalized compensation terms with each player. The UFLPA likes the current system and wants it maintained for the duration of the next collective bargaining agreement.

The team owners are proposing a new compensation system. Under this new system, owners and players would still be free to negotiate, but the annual amount each team could spend on payroll could not be outside a predetermined range. The lower limit of this range would be based on a percentage of the annual "gross football revenues" generated by the team. The owners' last proposal suggested this percentage should be 55%. The upper limit of this range, also known as the salary cap, was proposed at US$30 million. Therefore, the annual amount each team could spend on payroll would be no less than 55% of the team's gross football revenues, but no more than US$30 million.

The UFLPA objects to this system for two reasons. First, the players are against the salary cap because they see it as a way for owners to pay players less than market value. They contend that owners wouldn't enter into these contracts if they didn't receive sufficient value for the high salaries they pay. Second, since the players' compensation would be based on the teams' gross revenues, the players are not convinced that the owners will properly account for revenues.

The dispute is dragging on: more than half of the current season games have already been cancelled, and some players and owners are growing impatient with the slow progress at the negotiating table. Faced with these pressures, the UFLPA's executive committee has decided to take a closer look at the owners' proposal, but wants to consult with public accountants to get a clearer picture. The team owners have, for the first time, agreed to show the UFLPA their financial statements. The Calgary Cowboys (the Cowboys), one of the teams that has incurred major losses in the last few seasons and claims that it is going under, has already handed over its unaudited GAAP financial statements to the UFLPA.

You, CPA, are employed by McMaster & Caisse, Chartered Professional Accountants (M&C). Your boss, Marie Caisse, calls you into a meeting with Billy Baker, star quarterback for the Regina Rebels and chair of the UFLPA executive committee. Billy is asking M&C to analyze the financial statements submitted by the Cowboys so that he can formulate sound arguments to bring to the negotiating table. Given the financial statements provided were unaudited, Billy wants M&C to evaluate the financial viability of the team and determine whether the Cowboys have a net loss in accordance with ASPE. Marie asks you to draft a report that will address Billy's requests.

Following the meeting, you receive the unaudited financial statements of the Cowboys for the year ended December 31, Year 8 (Exhibit II), and meet with the team's financial controller to obtain additional information (Exhibit III).

**EXHIBIT II**

**CALGARY COWBOYS LIMITED**
**STATEMENT OF LOSS AND DEFICIT**
For the year ended December 31
(in thousands of Canadian dollars)

| | Year 8 (unaudited) | Year 7 (unaudited) |
|---|---|---|
| Revenues: | | |
| National TV broadcast rights | $ 19,500 | $19,500 |
| Local TV broadcast rights | 1,500 | 1,250 |
| Ticket sales | 21,154 | 18,653 |
| Corporate boxes | 3,546 | 2,436 |
| Advertising revenue | 2,100 | 1,876 |
| | 47,800 | 43,715 |

*(continued)*

EXHIBIT II (continued)

| | Year 8 (unaudited) | Year 7 (unaudited) |
|---|---|---|
| Expenses: | | |
| Signing bonuses | 5,000 | 4,000 |
| Salaries and benefits (players) | 38,540 | 34,767 |
| Other salaries and benefits | 661 | 547 |
| Stadium rental | 375 | 375 |
| Business taxes | 90 | 89 |
| Miscellaneous supplies | 91 | 76 |
| Administration | 1,099 | 1,548 |
| Interest on advance from parent company | 344 | 551 |
| Travel | 2,610 | 3,267 |
| Amortization—capital assets | 15 | 19 |
| Amortization—non-competition clause | 5,000 | 5,000 |
| | 53,825 | 50,239 |
| Loss before income taxes | (6,025) | (6,524) |
| Income taxes | — | — |
| Net loss | (6,025) | (6,524) |
| Deficit, beginning of year | (6,524) | — |
| Deficit, end of year | $(12,549) | $ (6,524) |

### CALGARY COWBOYS LIMITED
### BALANCE SHEET
As at December 31
(in thousands of Canadian dollars)

| | Year 8 (unaudited) | Year 7 (unaudited) |
|---|---|---|
| **Assets** | | |
| Current assets: | | |
| Cash | $ — | $ 55 |
| Accounts receivable | 380 | 320 |
| Prepaid expenses | 177 | 170 |
| | 557 | 545 |
| Capital assets: | | |
| Furniture and equipment (net) | 96 | 91 |
| Other asset: | | |
| Non-competition clause (net) | 90,000 | 95,000 |
| | $90,653 | $95,636 |

(continued)

| | Year 8 (unaudited) | Year 7 (unaudited) |
|---|---|---|
| **Liabilities** | | |
| Current liabilities: | | |
| Bank overdraft | $ 110 | $ — |
| Accounts payable | 36 | 28 |
| GST and withholding taxes payable | 13 | 12 |
| Accrued liabilities | 3,343 | 657 |
| | 3,502 | 697 |
| Advance from parent company | 1,567 | 3,772 |
| Deferred exchange gains | 566 | 124 |
| **Shareholders' Equity** | | |
| Share capital | 567 | 567 |
| Deficit | (12,549) | (6,524) |
| Revaluation adjustment | 97,000 | 97,000 |
| | 85,018 | 91,043 |
| | $90,653 | $95,636 |

EXHIBIT III

### NOTES FROM DISCUSSION WITH THE FINANCIAL CONTROLLER OF CALGARY COWBOYS LIMITED

1. Calgary Cowboys Limited (CCL) was created 20 years ago by Crystal Roberts, a wealthy businesswoman from Calgary, when the company acquired the UFL franchise. On January 1, Year 7, Crystal sold all her shares in CCL to Crystal Roberts Management Inc. (CRM). She is the sole shareholder of CRM. Following the sale, a comprehensive fair value revaluation of CCL's assets and liabilities was undertaken. On January 1, Year 7, the fair values of CCL's assets and liabilities approximated their carrying amount, except for the non competi tion clause, which had a fair value of $100 million and a carrying amount of $3 million. This clause, included in the Cowboys' contract, states that no other UFL team can be established within a 200 kilometre radius of the Cowboys stadium until Year 27. As a result of the revaluation, push-down accounting was used to increase the intangible asset related to the non-compete clause by $97 million, with a corresponding amount disclosed as a separate equity item. The balance of retained earnings was reduced to zero and a corresponding amount was transferred to share capital. Before the revaluation, the non-compete clause was being amortized at a rate of $150,000 a year.
2. CRM is a financial holding company that owns several other subsidiaries, including the Calgary Sports Channel, which broadcasts all of the Cowboys games in the Calgary area. The amount billed by CCL was recorded under "Local TV broadcast rights" in the statement of income. Calgary Sports Channel's main competitor made an offer of $8 million per year to broadcast Cowboys games locally, but Crystal felt it would be more profitable to have the Calgary Sports Channel benefit from the team's popularity.
3. CRM leases the huge parking lot adjacent to the stadium from the city for one dollar per year and charges $10 per car. The parking lot can hold over 15,000 cars and is always full for Cowboys games. CRM owns the company that operates all the food concessions in the stadium where the Cowboys play.
4. Players who sign long-term contracts often ask for a signing bonus in addition to their annual salary. A typical contract is for two to four years with an additional one-year renewal option. When a player signs a contract, CCL expenses the bonus. Bonuses are disclosed separately in the statement of income to facilitate financial analysis. These bonuses are refundable if the player leaves within the first year of the contract.
5. UFL players are all paid in U.S. dollars, since most of the teams are American. The spectacular volatility of the Canadian dollar against the US dollar in Year 8 triggered a number of exchange gains and losses in the salaries payable. The net gains were shown separately as deferred exchange gains on the balance sheet.

*(continued)*

---

**EXHIBIT III** *(continued)*

6. Travel expenses include all costs related to the private jet owned by Crystal, which she graciously allows CCL to use during the football season. The team uses it for all out-of-province trips. The plane's operating costs are approximately $2 million per year. Without the plane, players would fly business class at an average return fare of $2,000 per trip.

7. The advance from the parent company bears interest at the annual rate of 20% due to the significant risk of operating a football team.

8. Accrued liabilities include C$3 million in salary for defensive tackle Jimmy Swagger for the Year 9 and Year 10 seasons ($1.5 million per season). Swagger, one of the best tackles in the UFL, was paid a signing bonus of $1 million at the start of the Year 8 season. However, he has formally asked to be traded to another team because of a run-in with the Cowboys' head coach during the last game of Year 8. The UFL has declared a trade moratorium until the strike is settled. Since Swagger will probably not provide any future benefit to the Cowboys, CCL has expensed the salary remaining in his contract. Once Swagger is traded to another team, CCL will no longer have an obligation to him.

9. The Cowboys' stadium seats 40,000 spectators and is almost always full. The team plays 10 home games per season and as many on the road. Spectators pay approximately $53 per ticket and around $25 for food and beverages per game. The team has 40 players, as well as 10 coaches and trainers who travel with the team.

*(CPA Canada adapted)*[9]

# Case 10-5

**LO1, 2, 3**

ZIM Inc. (ZIM) is a high-technology company that develops, designs, and manufactures telecommunications equipment. ZIM was founded in Year 5 by Dr. Alex Zimmer, the former assistant head of research and development at a major telephone company. He and the director of marketing left the company to found ZIM. ZIM has been very successful. Sales reached $8.3 million in its first year and have grown by 80% annually since then. The key to ZIM's success has been the sophisticated software contained in the equipment it sells.

ZIM's board of directors recently decided to issue shares to raise funds for strategic objectives through an initial public offering of common shares. The shares will be listed on a major Canadian stock exchange. ZIM's underwriter, Mitchell Securities, believes that an offering price of 18 to 20 times the most recent fiscal year's earnings per share can be achieved. This opinion is based on selected industry comparisons.

ZIM has announced its intention to go public, and work has begun on the preparation of a preliminary prospectus. It should be filed with the relevant securities commissions in 40 days. The offering is expected to close in about 75 days. The company has a July 31 year-end. It is now September 8, Year 8.

You, a CPA, work for Chesther Chathan, Chartered Professional Accountants, the auditors of ZIM since its inception. You have just been put in charge of ZIM's audit, due to the sudden illness of the senior. ZIM's year-end audit has just commenced. At the same time, ZIM's staff and the underwriters are working 15-hour days trying to write the prospectus, complete the required legal work, and prepare for the public offering. The client says that the audit must be completed so that the financial statements can go to the printer in 22 days. ZIM plans to hire a qualified chief financial officer as soon as possible.

An extract from ZIM's accounting records is found in Exhibit IV. You have gathered the information in Exhibit V from the client. You have been asked by the audit partner to prepare a memo dealing with the key accounting issues.

**EXHIBIT IV**

### EXTRACT FROM ACCOUNTING RECORDS (IN THOUSANDS OF DOLLARS)

| | Revenue | | Deferred |
| Product | Month of July | Total Fiscal Year 8 | Development Costs[1] |
|---|---|---|---|
| Zibor | $ 815 | $ 8,802 | $ 9,463 |
| Resale components | 540 | 4,715 | — |
| Webstar | 700 | 4,241 | 359 |
| IDSL 600 | — | 2,104 | 1,431 |
| Transact training | 2,077 | 2,077 | — |
| Firewall Plus | 402 | 1,640 | 1,500 |
| Transact | 670 | 1,350 | 2,159 |
| 700J | — | 400 | 725 |
| ATM 4000 | — | 394 | 1,825 |
| Photon phasing project | — | — | 691 |
| | $5,204 | $25,723 | $18,153 |

[1] Cumulative costs for each product that have been deferred and recorded on the balance sheet.

**EXHIBIT V**

### INFORMATION GATHERED FROM THE CLIENT

1. The job market for top software and hardware engineering talent is very tight. As a result, ZIM has turned to information technology "head hunters" to attract key personnel from other high-technology companies. During the year, ZIM paid $178,000 in placement fees, and the company is amortizing the payments over five years. The search firm offers a one-year money-back guarantee if any of the people hired leaves the company or proves to be unsatisfactory.

2. On July 29, Year 8, the company made a payment of $100,000 to a computer hacker. The hacker had given the company 10 days to pay her the funds. Otherwise, she said she would post on the Internet a security flaw she had detected in the ZIM's Firewall Plus software.

3. Ale Zimmer had been working on a photon-phasing project when he left the telephone company. He has moved this technology ahead significantly at ZIM, and a prototype has been built at a cost of $691,000. The project has been delayed pending a decision on the direction that the project will take.

4. ZIM defers and amortizes software and other development costs according to the following formula:

$$\text{Annual amortization rate} = \frac{\text{Sales in units for the year}}{\text{Total expected sales in units during product life}}$$

5. In line with normal software company practice, ZIM releases, via the Internet, software upgrades that correct certain bugs in previously released software.

6. During a routine visit to the AC&C Advanced Telecommunications laboratory in southern California, a ZIM engineer discovered that nearly 600 lines of code in an AC&C program were identical to those of some ZIM software written in Year 6—right down to two spelling mistakes and a programming error.

7. The ATM 4000 has been the company's only product flop. High rates of field failures and customer dissatisfaction led ZIM to issue an offer, dated July 30, Year 8, to buy back all units currently in service for a total of $467,500. Southwestern Utah Telephone is suing ZIM for $4 million for damages related to two ATM 4000 devices that it had purchased through a distributor. The devices broke down, affecting telephone traffic for two weeks before they were replaced.

8. ZIM also resells components manufactured by a Japanese telecommunications company. The effort required to make these sales to existing customers is minimal, but the gross margin is only 12% versus an average of 60% for the company's other products, excluding the Transact and 700J lines.

*(continued)*

**EXHIBIT V** *(continued)*

9. During the first two years of operation, ZIM expensed all desktop computers (PCs) when purchased, on the grounds that they become obsolete so fast that their value after one year is almost negligible. In the current year, ZIM bought $429,000 worth of PCs and plans to write them off over two years.

10. Revenue is recognized on shipment for all equipment sold. Terms are FOB ZIM's shipping location.

11. ZIM's director of marketing, Albert Buzzer, has come up with a novel method of maximizing profits on the Transact product line. Transact is one of the few ZIM products that has direct competition. Transact routes telephone calls 20% faster than competing products but sells for 30% less. ZIM actually sells the product at a loss. However, without a special training course offered by ZIM, field efficiency cannot be maximized. Customers usually realize that they need the special training a couple of months after purchase. Buzzer estimates that the average telephone company will spend three dollars on training for every dollar spent on the product. Because of the way telephone companies budget and account for capital and training expenditures, most will not realize that they are spending three times as much on training as on the product.

12. In May Year 2, ZIM paid back a U.S. denominated, $25 million long-term debt prematurely to take advantage of a favourable interest rate. The US$25 million loan was subject to a cross-currency swap. The agreement with the third party was to pay CAN$33 million and receive US$25 million from the third party in May Year 4. This represented the exchange rate at the time the transactions were entered into. Although the swap was used to hedge the currency risk on the long-term debt, it was not formally designated as a hedge for reporting purposes. The U.S. dollars exchange rate at the time of the payout was CAN$1.20. ZIM recognized the $3 million gain on the repayment of the U.S. loan. ZIM negotiated a CAN$30 million one-year loan with Beemow Bank to repay the US$25 million loan. The spot exchange rate as at January 31, Year 3, was CAN$1.27, whereas the forward exchange rate for contracts expiring in May Year 4 was CAN$1.25.

13. The IDSL equipment was sold to customers in May Year 8. In September Year, ZIM provided the custom software required to operate the IDSL 600 equipment. The software was "shipped" via the Internet.

*(CPA Canada adapted)*[10]

# PROBLEMS

*Note:* Some problems use direct exchange rate quotations; others use indirect quotations.

## Problem 10-1

LO1, 2, 4, 8

Manitoba Exporters Inc. (MEI) sells Inuit carvings to countries throughout the world. On December 1, Year 5, MEI sold 10,000 carvings to a wholesaler in a foreign country at a total cost of 600,000 foreign currency units (FCs) when the spot rate was FC1 = $0.741. The invoice required the foreign wholesaler to remit by April 1, Year 6. On December 3, Year 5, MEI entered into a forward contract with the Royal Bank at the 120-day forward rate of FC1 = $0.781 and the spot rate was still FC1 = $0.741. Hedge accounting is not applied.

The fiscal year-end of MEI is December 31, and on this date the spot rate was FC1 = $0.757 and the forward rate was FC1 = $0.791. The payment from the foreign customer was received on April 1, Year 6, when the spot rate was FC1 = $0.802.

**Required**

(a) Prepare the journal entries to record

(i) the sale and the forward contract,

(ii) any adjustments required on December 31, and

(iii) the cash received in Year 6.

(b) Prepare a partial balance sheet of MEI on December 31, Year 5, which shows the presentation of the receivable and the accounts associated with the forward contract.

*(c) Now assume that a discount rate of 6% per annum, or 0.5% per month, is applied when determining the fair value of the forward contract at December 31, Year 5. Prepare the journal entries to record

(i) the sale and the forward contract,

(ii) any adjustments required on December 31, and

(iii) the cash received in Year 6.

## Problem 10-2

LO1, 4

Assume that all of the facts in Problem 1 remain unchanged except that MEI uses hedge accounting. Also, assume that the forward element and spot elements on the forward contract are accounted for separately.

**Required**

(a) Prepare the journal entries for the same items as in part (a) of Problem 1 assuming that MEI designates the forward contract as a cash flow hedge.

(b) Prepare the journal entries for the same items as in part (a) of Problem 1 assuming that MEI designates the forward contract as a fair value hedge.

(c) Explain the similarities and differences in the journal entries between the cash flow hedge and the fair value hedge.

## Problem 10-3

LO1

Moose Utilities Ltd. (MUL) borrowed $40,000,000 in U.S. funds on January 1, Year 1, at an annual interest rate of 12%. The loan is due on December 31, Year 4, and interest is paid annually on December 31. The Canadian exchange rates for U.S. dollars over the life of the loan were as follows:

| | |
|---|---|
| January 1, Year 1 | CDN$1.159 |
| December 31, Year 1 | CDN$1.168 |
| December 31, Year 2 | CDN$1.160 |
| December 31, Year 3 | CDN$1.152 |
| December 31, Year 4 | CDN$1.155 |

Exchange rates changed evenly throughout the year.

**Required**

(a) Prepare journal entries for MUL for Year 1.

(b) Calculate the exchange gains or losses that would be reported in the profit of the company each year over the life of the loan.

## Problem 10-4

**LO1, 6**

Lamont Company is a Canadian company that produces electronic switches for the telecommunications industry. Lamont regularly imports component parts from Sousa Ltd., a supplier located in Mexico, and makes payments in Mexican pesos (MP). Based on past experience, Lamont Company expects to purchase raw materials from Sousa at a cost of MP10,000,000 on March 1, Year 2. To hedge this forecasted transaction, Lamont enters into a three-month forward contract on October 31, Year 1 to purchase 10 million pesos on March 1, Year 2. It appropriately designates the forward contract as a cash flow hedge of the Mexican peso liability exposure. On March 1, Year 2, the forward contract is settled with the bank and Sousa is paid for delivering the goods to Lamont.

The following spot and forward exchange rates exist during the period October to March:

|  | Spot Rates | Forward Rates[*] |
|---|---|---|
| October 31, Year 1 | MP1 = $0.072 | MP1 = $0.075 |
| December 31, Year 1 | MP1 = $0.074 | MP1 = $0.076 |
| March 1, Year 2 | MP1 = $0.078 | MP1 = $0.078 |

[*]For contracts expiring on March 1, Year 2.

**Required**

(a) Prepare all journal entries required to record the transactions described above.

(b) Prepare a December 31, Year 1, partial trial balance of the accounts used in part (a), and indicate how each account would appear in the year-end financial statements.

## Problem 10-5

**LO1**

On January 1, Year 5, Ornate Company Ltd. purchased US$2,200,000 of the bonds of the Gem Corporation. The bonds were trading at par on this date, pay interest at 12% each December 31, and mature on December 31, Year 7. The following Canadian exchange rates were quoted during Year 5:

| January 1, Year 5 | US$1 = CDN$1.392 |
|---|---|
| December 31, Year 5 | US$1 = CDN$1.341 |

Exchange rates changed evenly throughout the year. These bonds were trading at 102 at December 31, Year 5.

**Required**

Prepare the journal entries for Year 5 assuming that the investment in bonds is

(a) held to maturity,

(b) held for trading, and

(c) available for sale.

## Problem 10-6

LO1, 2, 5, 7

On October 1, Year 6, Versatile Company contracted to sell merchandise to a customer in Switzerland at a selling price of SF400,000. The contract called for the merchandise to be delivered to the customer on January 31, Year 7, with payment due on delivery. On October 1, Year 6, Versatile arranged a forward contract to deliver SF400,000 on January 31, Year 7, at a rate of SF1 = $1.20. Versatile's year-end is December 31.

The merchandise was delivered on January 31, Year 7, and SF400,000 were received and delivered to the bank.

Exchange rates were as follows:

|  | Spot Rates | Forward Rates[*] |
|---|---|---|
| October 1, Year 6 | SF1 = $1.18 | SF1 = $1.20 |
| December 31, Year 6 | SF1 = $1.21 | SF1 = $1.22 |
| January 31, Year 7 | SF1 = $1.19 | SF1 = $1.19 |

[*]For contracts expiring on January 31, Year 7.

**Required**

(a) Prepare the journal entries that Versatile should make to record the events described assuming that the forward contract is designated as a cash flow hedge.

(b) Prepare a partial trial balance of the accounts used as at December 31, Year 6, and indicate how each would appear on the company's financial statements.

(c) Prepare the journal entries that Versatile should make to record the events described, assuming that the forward contract is designated as a fair value hedge.

(d) Prepare a partial trial balance of the accounts used as at December 31, Year 6, and indicate how each would appear on the company's financial statements.

(e) Describe how the accounting for the hedge affects the current ratio, and indicate which accounting treatment for the hedge would show the strongest liquidity position.

## Problem 10-7

LO1, 2, 4, 8

Hamilton Importing Corp. (HIC) imports goods from countries around the world for sale in Canada. On December 1, Year 3, HIC purchased 11,300 watches from a foreign wholesaler for DM613,000 when the spot rate was DM1 = $0.754. The invoice called for payment to be made on April 1, Year 4. On December 3, Year 3, HIC entered into a forward contract with the Royal Bank at the 120-day forward rate of DM1 = $0.794. Hedge accounting is not applied.

The fiscal year-end of HIC is December 31. On this date, the spot rate was DM1 = $0.770 and the 90-day forward rate was DM1 = $0.799. The payment to the foreign supplier was made on April 1, Year 4, when the spot rate was DM1 = $0.815.

**Required**

(a) Prepare the journal entries to record
    (i) the purchase and the forward contract,
    (ii) any adjustments required on December 31, and
    (iii) the payment in Year 4.

(b) Prepare a partial statement of financial position for HIC on December 31, Year 3, which presents the liability to the foreign supplier and the accounts associated with the forward contract.

*(c) Now assume that a discount rate of 9% per annum or 0.750% per month is applied when determining the fair value of the forward contract at December 31, Year 3. Prepare the journal entries to record

   (i) the purchase and the forward contract,
   (ii) any adjustments required on December 31, and
   (iii) the payment in Year 4.

## Problem 10-8

..................

LO1, 5, 7

On August 1, Year 3, Carleton Ltd. ordered machinery from a supplier in Hong Kong for HK$500,000. The machinery was delivered on October 1, Year 3, with terms requiring payment in full by December 31, Year 3. On August 2, Year 3, Carleton entered a forward contract to purchase HK$500,000 on December 31, Year 3, at a rate of $0.165. On December 31, Year 3, Carleton settled the forward contract and paid the supplier.

Exchange rates were as follows:

|  | Spot Rates | Forward Rates* |
|---|---|---|
| August 1 and 2, Year 3 | HK$1 = C$0.160 | HK$1 = C$0.165 |
| October 1, Year 3 | HK$1 = C$0.164 | HK$1 = C$0.168 |
| December 31, Year 3 | HK$1 = C$0.169 | HK$1 = C$0.169 |

*For contracts expiring on December 31, Year 3.

**Required**

(a) Assume that the forward contract was designated as a cash flow hedge of the firm commitment to purchase the machinery and that the balance in accumulated other comprehensive income on October 1 was transferred to the machinery account when the machinery was delivered. Prepare the journal entries for Year 3 to record all the activity described above and prepare a summary journal entry for the combined effect of all entries.

(b) Assume that the forward contract was designated as a fair value hedge of the firm commitment to purchase the machinery and that the balance in the commitment asset/liability account on October 1 was transferred to the machinery account when the machinery was delivered. Prepare the journal entries for Year 3 to record all the activity described above and prepare a summary journal entry for the combined effect of all entries.

(c) Assume that hedge accounting was not applied. Prepare the journal entries for Year 3 to record all the activity described above and prepare a summary journal entry for the combined effect of all entries.

(d) Explain the similarities and differences between the account balances under the three scenarios above.

## Problem 10-9

..................

LO1, 2, 5, 7

EnDur Corp (EDC) is a Canadian company that exports computer software. On February 1, Year 2, EDC contracted to sell software to a customer in Denmark at a selling price of 600,000 Danish krona (DK) with payment due 60 days after installation was complete. On February 2, Year 2, EDC entered into a forward contract with the Royal Bank at the five-month forward rate of CDN$1 = DK5.20. The installation was completed on April 30, Year 2. On June 30, Year 2, the payment from the Danish customer was received and the forward contract was settled.

Exchange rates were as follows:

| | Spot Rates | Forward Rates[*] |
|---|---|---|
| February 1 and 2, Year 2 | $1 = DK5.06 | $1 = DK5.20 |
| April 30, Year 2 | $1 = DK5.09 | $1 = DK5.18 |
| June 30, Year 2 | $1 = DK5.14 | $1 = DK5.14 |

[*]For contracts expiring on June 30, Year 2.

**Required**

(a) Assume that the forward contract was designated as a cash flow hedge of the firm commitment for the sale and that the entire balance in accumulated other comprehensive income (AOCI) on April 30 was transferred to sales when the installation was completed. Calculate the following amounts for the financial statements for the year ended June 30, Year 2:

(i) Sales

(ii) Exchange gains/losses

(iii) Cash flows for the period

(b) Assume that the forward contract was designated as a fair value hedge of the firm commitment for the sale and that the entire balance in the commitment asset/liability on April 30 was transferred to sales when the installation was completed. Calculate the following amounts for the financial statements for the year ended June 30, Year 2:

(i) Sales

(ii) Exchange gains/losses

(iii) Cash flows for the period

(c) Assume that hedge accounting was not applied. Calculate the following amounts for the financial statements for the year ended June 30, Year 2:

(i) Sales

(ii) Exchange gains/losses

(iii) Cash flows for the period

(d) Explain the similarities and differences between the account balances under the three scenarios above.

## Problem 10-10

LO1

Gemella Ltd. manufactures construction equipment for sale throughout eastern Canada and north-eastern United States. Its year-end is June 30. The following foreign currency transactions occurred during the Year 11 calendar year:

1. On January 10, Gemella agreed to sell equipment to an American customer for US100,000 for delivery on or before March 31 and received a deposit of US$10,000. The balance is payable on July 31.

2. On March 17, the equipment was delivered to the American customer.

3. On May 1, Gemella purchased 100 acres of land in Syracuse, New York, for US$200,000 as a long-term investment. Fifty percent of the purchase price was paid on May 1. The balance is due on May 1, Year 2 along with interest at the rate of 6%.

4. On June 30, the 100 acres of land had a market value of US$210,000. Gemella reports its long-term investments in land at historical cost and discloses the market value of the land in the notes to its financial statements.

5. On July 31, the balance owing was received from the American customer.

The following spot rates exist during the period January to July, Year 1:

|  | Spot Rates | Forward Rates[*] |
| --- | --- | --- |
| January 10, Year 1 | US$1 = C$1.16 | US$1 = C$1.20 |
| March 17, Year 1 | US$1 = C$1.17 | US$1 = C$1.21 |
| May 1, Year 1 | US$1 = C$1.19 | US$1 = C$1.22 |
| June 30, Year 1 | US$1 = C$1.23 | US$1 = C$1.24 |
| July 31, Year 1 | US$1 = C$1.25 | US$1 = C$1.25 |

[*]For contracts expiring on July 31, Year.

Exchange rates changed evenly between the dates indicated above.

**Required**

(a) Prepare the journal entries for the transactions stated above including year-end adjusting entries.

(b) What value will be disclosed in the notes to the year-end financial statements pertaining to the land purchased in Syracuse?

## Problem 10-11

LO1, 5

On May 1, Year 1, JDH orders equipment from a supplier in Germany for €100,000 with delivery scheduled for October 1, Year 1. Payment is due on December 31, Year 1. On May 2, Year 1 JDH enters into an 8-month forward contract with its bank at a rate of €1 = $1.38 to purchase €100,000 on December 31, Year 1, the date the accounts payable is due. The equipment is delivered on October 1, Year 1, and immediately put into use. The forward contract and the payable to the supplier are settled on December 31, Year 1.

Exchange rates for one euro for Year 1 were as follows:

|  | Spot Rate | Forward Rate[*] |
| --- | --- | --- |
| May 1 and 2, Year 1 | $1.35 | $1.38 |
| October 1, Year 1 | $1.37 | $1.39 |
| December 31, Year 1 | $1.36 | $1.36 |

[*]For contract expiring on December 31, Year 1.

**Required**

Prepare journal entries to reflect the above transactions from May 1 to December 31, Year 1, excluding adjusting entry for depreciation expense. Assume that JDH designates the forward contract as a cash-flow hedge and clears the cumulative other comprehensive income account when the equipment is delivered on October 1, Year 1.

## Problem 10-12

LO1, 5, 7

On June 1, Year 3, Forever Young Corp. (FYC) ordered merchandise from a supplier in Turkey for Turkish lira (TL) 217,000. The goods were delivered on September 30, with terms requiring cash on delivery. On June 2, Year 3, FYC entered a forward contract as a cash flow hedge to purchase TL217,000 on September 30, Year 3, at a rate of $0.90. FYC's year-end is June 30.

On September 30, Year 3, FYC paid the foreign supplier in full and settled the forward contract. Exchange rates were as follows:

| | Spot Rates | Forward Rates* |
|---|---|---|
| June 1 and 2, Year 3 | TL1 = $0.870 | TL1 = $0.900 |
| June 30, Year 3 | TL1 = $0.860 | TL1 = $0.895 |
| September 30, Year 3 | TL1 = $0.910 | TL1 = $0.910 |

*For contracts expiring on September 30, Year 3.

**Required**

(a) (i) Prepare all journal entries required to record the transactions described above.

    (ii) Prepare a June 30, Year 3, partial trial balance of the accounts used in part (i), and indicate how each account would appear in the year-end financial statements.

(b) Prepare all necessary journal entries under the assumption that no forward contract was entered.

(c) Prepare all necessary journal entries to record the transactions described above, assuming that the forward contract was designated as a fair value hedge.

(d) Assume that FYC is a private company and uses ASPE for reporting purposes. Prepare all necessary journal entries to record the transactions described in the body of the question above.

(e) Which of the above reporting methods would present the highest current ratio at September 30, Year 3? Briefly explain.

## Problem 10-13

LO1, 2, 4

Hull Manufacturing Corp. (HMC), a Canadian company, manufactures instruments used to measure the moisture content of barley and wheat. The company sells primarily to the domestic market, but in Year 3, it developed a small market in Argentina. In Year 4, HMC began purchasing semi-finished components from a supplier in Romania. The management of HMC is concerned about the possible adverse effects of foreign exchange fluctuations. To deal with this matter, all of HMC's foreign-currency-denominated receivables and payables are hedged with contracts with the company's bank. The year-end of HMC is December 31.

The following transactions occurred late in Year 4:

- On October 15, Year 4, HMC purchased components from its Romanian supplier for 820,000 Romanian leus (RL). On the same day, HMC entered into a forward contract for RL820,000 at the 60-day forward rate of RL1 = $0.428. The Romanian supplier was paid in full on December 15, Year 4.

- On December 1, Year 4, HMC made a shipment to a customer in Argentina. The selling price was 2,520,000 Argentinean pesos (AP), with payment to be received on January 31, Year 5. HMC immediately entered into a forward contract for AP2,520,000 at the two-month forward rate of AP1 = $0.246.

During this period, the exchange rates were as follows:

|  | Spot Rates | Forward Rates |
|---|---|---|
| October 15, Year 4 | RL1 = $0.415 | |
| December 1, Year 4 | AP1 = $0.269 | |
| December 15, Year 4 | RL1 = $0.407 | |
| December 31, Year 4 | AP1 = $0.253 | AP1 = $0.242 |

Hedge accounting is not adopted.

**Required**

(a) Prepare the Year 4 journal entries to record the transactions described above and any adjusting entries necessary.

(b) Prepare the December 31, Year 4, balance sheet presentation of the receivable from the Argentinean customer, and the accounts associated with the forward contract.

# Problem 10-14

### LO1, 6

As a result of its export sales to customers in Switzerland, the Lenox Company has had Swiss-franc-denominated revenues over the past number of years. In order to gain protection from future exchange rate fluctuations, the company decides to borrow its current financing requirements in Swiss francs. Accordingly, on January 1, Year 1, it borrows SF1,400,000 at 12% interest, to be repaid in full on December 31, Year 3. Interest is paid annually on December 31. The management designates this loan as a cash flow hedge of future SF revenues, which are expected to be received as follows:

| Year 1 | SF | 560,000 |
|---|---|---|
| Year 2 | | 490,000 |
| Year 3 | | 350,000 |
| | SF | 1,400,000 |

Actual revenues turned out to be exactly as expected each year and were received in cash. Exchange rates for the Swiss franc during the period were as follows:

| January 1, Year 1 | $1.05 |
|---|---|
| Average, Year 1 | $1.10 |
| December 31, Year 1 | $1.15 |
| Average, Year 2 | $1.20 |
| December 31, Year 2 | $1.25 |
| Average, Year 3 | $1.27 |
| December 31, Year 3 | $1.30 |

**Required**

Prepare the journal entries required each year.

## Problem 10-15

### LO1

On January 1, Year 4, a Canadian firm, Canuck Enterprises Ltd., borrowed US$208,000 from a bank in Seattle, Washington. Interest of 7.5% per annum is to be paid on December 31 of each year during the four-year term of the loan. Principal is to be repaid on the maturity date of December 31, Year 7. The foreign exchange rates for the first two years were as follows:

| | |
|---|---|
| January 1, Year 4 | US$1.00 = CDN$1.46 |
| December 31, Year 4 | US$1.00 = CDN$1.49 |
| December 31, Year 5 | US$1.00 = CDN$1.43 |

Exchange rates changed evenly throughout the year.

### Required

Determine the exchange gain (loss) on the loan to be reported in the financial statements of Canuck Enterprises for the years ended December 31, Year 4 and Year 5.

*(CGA Canada adapted)*[11]

## Endnotes

1  http://ir.bombardier.com/modules/misc/documents/43/08/ 16/34/14/Bombardier-Financial-Report-2014-en2.pdf, accessed June 2, 2015.

2  http://media.scotiabank.com/AR/2014/files/9314/1774/ 5846/Consolidated_Financial_Statements.PDF, accessed June 2, 2015.

3  See IAS 21, paragraph 16.

4  For example, if the goods are sold to customers in Australia and the selling price of the inventory is A$9,950 on June 30 (assuming that none of the inventory purchased had been sold by year-end), the selling price in Canadian dollars would be $9,443 (A$9,950 × 0.949). Because the translated selling price is greater than the previously translated historical cost of $9,410, a write-down would not be required.

5  See John E. Stewart, "The Challenges of Hedge Accounting," *Journal of Accountancy*, November 1989, pp. 48–56.

6  Accounting for a net investment in a foreign operation will be discussed in Chapter 11.

7  The present value factor for two months at 1% per month is calculated as $1/1.01^2$ or 0.9803.

8  Adapted from *CICA UFE Report, 1990-II-3*, with permission. Chartered Professional Accountants of Canada, Toronto,

Canada. Any changes to the original material are the sole responsibility of the author (and/or publisher) and have not been reviewed or endorsed by the Chartered Professional Accountants of Canada.

9  Adapted from *CICA UFE Report, 2009-III-3*, with permission. Chartered Professional Accountants of Canada, Toronto, Canada. Any changes to the original material are the sole responsibility of the author (and/or publisher) and have not been reviewed or endorsed by the Chartered Professional Accountants of Canada.

10  Adapted from *CICA UFE Report, 1998-III-1*, with permission. Chartered Professional Accountants of Canada, Toronto, Canada. Any changes to the original material are the sole responsibility of the author (and/or publisher) and have not been reviewed or endorsed by the Chartered Professional Accountants of Canada.

11  Adapted from CGA Canada's FA4 Exam, September 1997, Q1, with permission. Chartered Professional Accountants of Canada, Toronto, Canada. Any changes to the original material are the sole responsibility of the author (and/or publisher) and have not been reviewed or endorsed by the Chartered Professional Accountants of Canada.

# CHAPTER 11

# Translation and Consolidation of Foreign Operations

## LEARNING OBJECTIVES

**After studying this chapter, you should be able to do the following:**

**LO1**  Contrast an enterprise's foreign currency accounting exposure with its economic exposure and evaluate how effectively the translation methods capture the economic effects of exchange rate changes.

**LO2**  Differentiate between the functional currency and the presentation currency for a foreign operation, and describe the translation method that is used in the translation to each type.

**LO3**  Prepare translated financial statements for foreign operations using the functional currency translation method.

**LO4**  Prepare translated financial statements for foreign operations using the presentation currency translation method.

**LO5**  Use translated financial statements to prepare consolidated financial statements.

**LO6**  Analyze and interpret financial statements involving foreign operations.

**LO7**  (Appendix 11A) Prepare translated financial statements for foreign operations in a highly inflationary environment.

## Introduction

Consolidated financial statements are required when one entity has control over another entity. With the ever-expanding global economy, it is now very common for a subsidiary to be in a foreign country, as is indicated by the following:

- Manulife Financial Corporation, a leading Canadian-based financial services company, operating worldwide, offering a diverse range of financial protection products and services, directly or indirectly owned 47 or more foreign subsidiaries in 14 countries at December 31, 2014.[1]
- Power Corporation of Canada, a diversified international management and holding company, directly or indirectly owned eight or more foreign subsidiaries in six countries at December 31, 2014.[2]
- Royal Bank of Canada, Canada's largest bank and one of the world's most highly rated financial institutions, directly or indirectly owned 22 foreign subsidiaries in 10 countries at October 31, 2014.[3]

676

> *Most Canadian public companies have subsidiaries in foreign countries.*

Companies establish operations in foreign countries for a variety of reasons, including developing new markets for their products, taking advantage of lower production costs, or gaining access to raw materials. Some multinational companies have reached a stage in their development in which domestic operations are no longer considered to be of higher priority than international operations.

Prior to preparing consolidated financial statements or accounting for an investment under the equity method, the financial statements of the foreign subsidiary or investee company must be translated into the investor company's presentation currency. IFRS 10 requires that consolidated financial statements be prepared using uniform accounting policies for like transactions and other events in similar circumstances. This means that the financial statements of the foreign operations should be adjusted to reflect the accounting policies of the parent company. Unless otherwise noted, we will assume the reporting entity is a Canadian company and its functional currency is the Canadian dollar. This chapter deals with the issue of translating the foreign entity's financial statements into the parent's presentation currency prior to consolidation.

> *Foreign-currency-denominated financial statements must be translated to the presentation currency of the reporting entity.*

Three major issues are related to the translation process: (1) what the functional currency of the foreign operation is, (2) what the presentation currency (also known as the reporting currency) of the parent company is, and (3) where the resulting translation adjustment should be reported in the consolidated financial statements. These issues are examined first from a conceptual perspective and second by the manner in which they have been resolved by the IASB. We will start by discussing the difference between accounting exposure and economic exposure.

# LO1 ACCOUNTING EXPOSURE VERSUS ECONOMIC EXPOSURE

Exposure is the risk that something could go wrong. Foreign currency exposure is the risk that a loss could occur if foreign exchange rates changed. Foreign currency risk can be viewed from three different perspectives: translation exposure (accounting exposure), transaction exposure, and economic exposure. Readers must keep these in mind as they interpret financial statements that contain foreign currency gains and losses.

**TRANSLATION (ACCOUNTING) EXPOSURE**  This exposure results from the translation of foreign-currency-denominated financial statements into Canadian dollars. Only those financial statement items translated at the closing rate or the forward rate create an accounting exposure. If an item is translated at the historical rate, the Canadian-dollar amount is fixed at historical cost and will not be affected by rate changes. However, if an item is translated at the closing rate or the forward rate, the Canadian-dollar amount will change every time the exchange rate changes. Each item translated at the closing rate is exposed to translation adjustment. A separate translation adjustment exists for each of the exposed items. Positive translation adjustments increase shareholders' equity, whereas negative translation adjustments decrease shareholders' equity. Positive translation adjustments on assets can be offset by negative translation adjustments on liabilities. If total exposed assets are equal to total exposed liabilities throughout the year, the translation adjustments (although perhaps significant on an individual basis) net to a zero balance. The net translation adjustment needed to keep the consolidated balance sheet in balance is based solely on the net asset or net liability exposure.

---

*Accounting exposure exists when financial statement items are translated at the closing rate or the forward rate.*

---

A foreign operation has a net asset exposure when assets translated at the closing or forward exchange rate are larger in amount than liabilities translated at the closing or forward exchange rate. A net liability exposure exists when liabilities translated at the closing or forward exchange rate are larger than assets translated at the closing or forward exchange rate. The relationship among exposure, exchange rate fluctuations, and effect on shareholders' equity (S/E) is summarized as follows:

| Balance Sheet Exposure | Foreign Currency | |
|---|---|---|
| | Appreciates | Depreciates |
| Net asset | Increases S/E | Decreases S/E |
| Net liability | Decreases S/E | Increases S/E |

---

*Net asset exposure means that more assets than liabilities are exposed.*

---

The gains and losses that result from the translation are usually unrealized in the sense that they do not represent actual cash flows. Because these accounting gains and losses are reflected in the financial statements, they may have an impact on the enterprise's dividend policies, share prices, and so on. It is important to assess the extent to which they represent transaction and/or economic exposure.

**TRANSACTION EXPOSURE**  This exposure exists between the time of entering a transaction involving a receivable or payable and the time of settling the receivable or payable with cash. It affects the current cash flows of the enterprise. The resulting cash gains and losses are realized and affect the enterprise's working capital and earnings. The concept of transaction exposure was discussed in Chapter 10.

---

*Transaction exposure exists when there is a lapse in time between the origination of a receivable or payable and the settlement of the receivable or payable.*

---

**ECONOMIC EXPOSURE**  Economic exposure is the risk that the economic value of the entity could decrease due to the occurrence of a future event such as a change in foreign exchange rates. Economic value, theoretically speaking, is the present value of future cash flows. Practically speaking, it is difficult to measure the impact on economic value because it is affected by so many variables. When exchange rates change, it could affect the cost of purchases, the selling price of sales, the volume of sales, interest rates, inflation rates, and so on. The economic impact could vary from company to company or from year to year depending on the nature of operations of the company.

> *Economic exposure exists when the present value of future cash flows would change as a result of changes in exchange rates.*

For example, a Canadian assembly plant that purchases components from a company in Japan will suffer economically if the dollar weakens in relation to the Japanese yen. It will cost the Canadian importer more dollars to purchase the product, and the Canadian competition may be such that the cost increase cannot be passed on to the customers. On the other hand, a Canadian company selling to customers in Japan may be economically better off when the dollar weakens relative to the Japanese yen. The Japanese customer's cost to buy the goods would go down and that could increase the volume of purchases.

What is the impact for a Canadian parent when it has a subsidiary in Japan and the Canadian dollar weakens relative to the yen? It depends on the nature of operations of the subsidiary and whether it is highly integrated with the Canadian parent or fairly independent. If the subsidiary manufactures locally and sells locally, its own income in yen may not be affected. However, the Canadian-dollar equivalent will increase because each yen of income translates in to more dollars. If it buys from and sells to the Canadian market, its income may go down because the volume of sales may decrease with the higher cost to Canadian customers. But, the Canadian-dollar equivalent of the reduced net income may be similar to before. Therefore, the economic exposure is dependent on whether the foreign subsidiary is closely linked to the activities of the parent or operating independently of the parent. IAS 21 tries to capture the economic effects by establishing a situational approach to determining the translation method to be used for certain foreign operations.

> *Economic exposure is not easy to measure.*

Even though it is difficult to measure the net impact of exchange rate changes on the present value of future cash flows, it is desirable to capture as much of the impact as possible in the financial statements. We do report assets and liabilities at fair values for certain situations. In so doing, we are capturing the economic value of these assets and liabilities.

To illustrate the difference between accounting exposure and economic exposure, let us consider a basic example with simplified assumptions. Distant Ltd. is a wholly owned subsidiary of Parent Co. Distant was incorporated on January 1, Year 1, with Parent Co. being its sole shareholder. It is located in Foreign Land, whose currency is foreign currency (FC). Throughout Year 1, the exchange rate was FC1 = $2, and there was no inflation in Foreign Land. Its condensed balance sheet as at December 31, Year 1, is presented below both in FC and Canadian dollars:

| | | |
|---|---|---|
| Monetary assets | FC 300 | $ 600 |
| Inventory | 800 | 1,600 |
| Property, plant, and equipment | 1,900 | 3,800 |
| | FC3,000 | $6,000 |
| | | |
| Monetary liabilities | FC2,100 | $4,200 |
| Shareholders' equity | 900 | 1,800 |
| | FC3,000 | $6,000 |

The fair value was equal to carrying amount for all assets and liabilities at December 31, Year 1. General price levels increased by 10% and the exchange rate changed to FC1 = $1.81818 on January 1, Year 2.

> *Generally, there is an inverse relationship between inflation rates and exchanges rates; that is, when inflation goes up, the value of the currency goes down.*

Distant's balance sheet as at January 1, Year 2, is presented below under two different scenarios: (1) using traditional GAAP and (2) where all assets and liabilities are revalued to their true economic value, which is represented by fair value. The 10% general price level increase will usually cause the non-monetary assets to increase in value. We will assume that the inventory did increase in value by 10% to FC880. However, the property, plant and equipment increased by 12% to FC2,128. The monetary items remain at their previous values because these values were set by contract and the values do not change when economic conditions change. Under traditional GAAP, the balance sheet does not change to reflect the change in purchasing power of the foreign currency units and the non-monetary assets are retained at their historical cost. Under the second scenario, the non-monetary assets are revalued to fair value to reflect their true economic value on that date.

|  | GAAP | Economic Value |
|---|---|---|
| Monetary assets | FC 300 | FC 300 |
| Inventory | 800 | 880 |
| Property, plant, and equipment | 1,900 | 2,128 |
|  | FC3,000 | FC3,308 |
| Monetary liabilities | FC2,100 | FC2,100 |
| Shareholders' equity | 900 | 1,208 |
|  | FC3,000 | FC3,308 |

*Fair values may be a good proxy for economic values.*

There are two methods for translating financial statements of foreign operations: the functional currency translation (FCT) method and the presentation currency translation (PCT) method. We will discuss these methods in detail throughout this chapter. These methods would be applied to the GAAP-based balance sheet above. To present the true economic value of Distant to the Canadian shareholders, the economic value balance sheet should be translated into Canadian dollars. The three balances sheets would appear as follows:

|  | FCT | PCT | Economic Value |
|---|---|---|---|
| Monetary assets | $ 545 | $ 545 | $ 545 |
| Inventory | 1,600 | 1,455 | 1,600 |
| Property, plant, and equipment | 3,800 | 3,455 | 3,869 |
|  | $5,945 | $5,455 | $6,014 |
| Monetary liabilities | $3,818 | $3,818 | $3,818 |
| Shareholders' equity, as previously reported | 1,800 | 1,800 | 1,800 |
| Gain (loss) due to change in value of assets in FC (3,308 − 3,000) × 2 |  |  | 616 |
| Gain (loss) due to change in exchange rate (3,308 − 2,100) × (1.81818 − 2) | 327 | (163) | (220) |
|  | $5,945 | $5,455 | $6,014 |

As we will see later in this chapter, the FCT method translates certain items at the historic rate and certain items at the closing rate, whereas the PCT method translates all assets and liabilities at the closing rate. For the economic value column, all assets and liabilities are translated at the closing rate.

> *The FCT and PCT methods use the GAAP-based balance sheet where some items are measured at current value and some items are measured at historical cost.*

Note the following from the above balance sheets:

- Neither the FCT method nor the PCT method truly reflects economic reality. In order to accurately reflect economic reality, all assets and liabilities should be reported at fair value. At present, GAAP requires some, but not all, assets and liabilities to be reported at fair value.

- The FCT method shows a gain from translating at the new exchange rate, whereas the PCT method reports a loss. Which one is right? We will now direct our attention to the two translation methods.

> *Neither translation method captures the true economic value of the reporting entity.*

## LO2 TRANSLATION OF FOREIGN OPERATIONS

IAS 21 defines a *foreign operation* as an entity that is a subsidiary, associate, joint arrangement or branch of a reporting entity, the activities of which are based or conducted in a country or currency other than those of the reporting entity. The financial statements of the foreign operation will usually need to be translated to the reporting currency of the reporting entity in order to consolidate the foreign subsidiary or to use the equity method to report investments in associates and joint ventures. There are two methods used under IAS 21 to translate the financial statements of a foreign operation. In this text, we will refer to the two methods as the functional currency translation (FCT) method and the presentation currency translation (PCT) method. The FCT method was used in Chapter 10 to translate and account for foreign transactions. The same method will be used in this chapter to translate the financial statements of a foreign operation from its recording currency to its functional currency. The PCT method will be used to translate the financial statements of a foreign operation from its functional currency to a different presentation currency.

As discussed in Chapter 10, the functional currency is the currency of the primary economic environment in which the entity operates. Exhibit 11.1 lists the indicators that should be considered when determining the functional currency for a foreign operation and gives an example of a condition that would indicate whether the Canadian dollar is the functional currency. The first five indicators were explained in Chapter 10; they apply to domestic and foreign operations.

When the functional currency of the foreign operation is the same currency as the parent's functional currency, the foreign operation would be highly integrated with the Canadian parent. When the above indicators are mixed and the functional currency is not obvious, management uses its professional judgment to determine the functional currency that most faithfully represents the economic effects of the underlying transactions, events, and conditions. As part of this approach, management gives priority to the first three indicators before considering the others, which are designed to provide additional supporting evidence in determining an entity's functional currency.

Once we have determined the functional currency of the foreign operation, we can use the appropriate method to translate the financial statements of the foreign operation into the desired presentation currency. We will discuss these methods from the perspective of a Canadian-based multinational company that is translating financial statements of a foreign subsidiary into Canadian dollars, which we assume is the presentation currency for the Canadian company.

**EXHIBIT 11.1**

## Indicators for Evaluating a Foreign Operation

| Indicator | Functional Currency | |
|---|---|---|
| | Canadian Dollar | Not Canadian Dollar |
| 1. to 5. | See Exhibit 10.3. | See Exhibit 10.3. |
| 6. Extension of parent | Only goods imported from the parent are sold. | The foreign operation generates income, incurs expenses, and accumulates cash in its local currency. |
| 7. Autonomy | The parent dictates the operating procedures. | The foreign entity has a significant degree of autonomy. |
| 8. Intercompany transactions | Intercompany transactions are a high proportion of overall activities. | Intercompany transactions are a low proportion of overall activities. |
| 9. Cash flows | Cash flows of the foreign operation directly affect cash flows of the parent. | Cash flows of the foreign operation have little effect on cash flows of the parent. |
| 10. Financing cash flows | The parent provides cash to pay obligations. | Cash from local operations is sufficient to pay obligations. |

> In effect, the indicators determine whether the foreign operation is highly integrated with the Canadian operations.

## LO3 The Functional Currency Translation Method

The *functional currency translation (FCT)* method is used to translate foreign operations into its functional currency. We will assume, to start with, that the foreign operation's functional currency is the Canadian dollar. The basic objective underlying this FCT method is to produce a set of translated financial statements as if the transactions had occurred in the functional currency in the first place; in other words, use the same process we used in Chapter 10 to translate individual transactions and account balances into Canadian dollars. For example, assume a subsidiary in Germany had sales of €100,000 when the exchange rate was €1 = $1.25. These sales would be reported on its own income statement in euros. When the subsidiary's income statement is translated to Canadian dollars, the Canadian-dollar amount would be $125,000 (€100,000 × 1.25). Similarly, if a Canadian company had sales of €100,000 to a customer in Germany on the same date, it would report this sale at $125,000 in its Canadian-dollar general ledger. In both cases, the FCT method was used to report sales at $125,000 being the Canadian-dollar equivalent on the date of the sale. In effect, the FCT method preserves the Canadian dollar as the unit of measure and measures financial statement items according to the normal measurement practices for the financial statement items. Under normal measurement practices, certain financial statement items are reported at historical cost, whereas other items are reported at fair value. The FCT method is designed to maintain this reporting practice when translating the foreign currency statements into Canadian dollars.

> The FCT method gives the same results as if the transactions had occurred in Canadian dollars in the first place.

If the financial statement item is supposed to be reported at fair value, when translating the item into Canadian dollars we need to take the fair value of the item in foreign currency and apply the spot rate on the date that the fair value was determined.

To obtain historical values, revenues and expenses should be translated in a manner that produces substantially the same reporting currency amounts that would have resulted had the underlying transactions been translated on the dates they occurred. To translate revenues of a foreign subsidiary, use the exchange rate on the date that the transaction giving rise to the revenue occurred. The following examples illustrate this concept. In all of these examples, assume the following exchange rates:

| | |
|---|---|
| January 1 | FC1 = $1.50 |
| January 31 | FC1 = $1.60 |
| Average for January | FC1 = $1.56 |

> *Use historical exchange rates to translate revenues and expenses.*

**EXAMPLE 1**  On January 1, Subco sold goods for cash of FC100. The revenue is earned and determined on this date. The revenue of FC100 would be translated into $150, its historical value.

**EXAMPLE 2**  On January 1, Subco sold goods for FC100 with payment due within 30 days. On January 31, FC100 was received from the customer. The revenue is earned and determined on January 1. The revenue of FC100 would be translated into $150. Receiving the cash on January 31 does not change the historical value of the sale. It does result in an exchange gain on the accounts receivable of $10 [FC100 × (1.60 − 1.50)].

**EXAMPLE 3**  On January 1, Subco received FC100 as a prepayment for goods to be delivered within 30 days. The deferred revenue should be translated into $150. On January 31, Subco delivered the goods and completed the sale. Although the revenue was earned on January 31, the amount of the revenue in Canadian dollars was determined by the amount of deferred revenue recognized on January 1 when the cash was received. Therefore, the revenue of FC100 would be reported at $150.

**EXAMPLE 4**  On each day in January, Subco sold goods for cash of FC100. Rather than using 31 different exchange rates for the 31 days of the month, the average rate for the month, $1.56, can be applied to the total revenue for the month, FC100 × 31 × 1.56 = $4,836.

> *Use average rates to approximate historical exchange rates throughout the period.*

The same concept can be applied in translating expenses. Use the exchange rate on the date that the transaction giving rise to the expense occurred. Since depreciation expense is directly related to the purchase of a depreciable asset, depreciation expense should be translated using the exchange rate on the date that the depreciable asset was purchased. Similarly, cost of goods sold is based on the cost of the inventory. Therefore, use the exchange rate on the date when the inventory was purchased when translating the cost of goods sold.

> *Use historical rates to measure expenses based on the historical cost of the related balance sheet items.*

Exhibit 11.2 specifies the rates to be used for various financial statements items under the FCT method and PCT method. We will now apply the FCT method to an entire set of financial statements of a foreign operation.

**EXHIBIT 11.2**

## Exchange Rates

| Financial Statement Items | Functional Currency Translation Method | Presentation Currency Translation Method |
|---|---|---|
| Monetary | Closing | Closing |
| Non-monetary—at cost or amortized cost | Historical | Closing |
| Non-monetary—at fair values | (Note 1) | (Note 1) |
| Goodwill | Historical | Closing |
| Deferred revenues | Historical | Closing |
| Common shares | Historical | Historical |
| Dividends | Historical | Historical |
| Revenues | Historical | Historical |
| Depreciation and amortization | Historical | Historical |
| Cost of sales: | | Historical |
|   Opening inventory | Historical | — |
|   Purchases | Historical | — |
|   Ending inventory | Historical | — |

Note 1: The rate of the date that fair value was determined should be used. If fair value was determined on the last day of the period, then the closing rate should be used.

> *For depreciation, historical rate for FCT method is the rate when the asset was acquired, whereas it is the rate when expense was incurred for PCT method.*

**EXAMPLE 5** On December 31, Year 1, Starmont Inc., a Canadian company, acquired 100% of the common shares of Controlada S.A., located in Estonia, at a cost of 2,000,000 kroons (K). The exchange rate was K1 = $0.128 on this date. The Canadian dollar is the recording, functional and presentation currency for Starmont. The journal entry (in Canadian dollars) to record the share acquisition would be as follows:

| | | |
|---|---|---|
| *Dec. 31, Year 1* | | |
| Investment in Controlada | 256,000 | |
|   Cash | | 256,000 |
| (K2,000,000 × 0.128) | | |

Controlada's financial statements must be translated into Canadian dollars for inclusion in Starmont's consolidated financial statements. Even though Controlada purchased its assets and assumed its liabilities prior to being taken over by Starmont, the consolidated statements are presented as if the parent purchased the net assets on the date of acquisition. Therefore, the exchange rate on the date of acquisition is used to translate all accounts of the subsidiary on acquisition date and becomes the historical rate to be used in subsequent years, where appropriate. The translation of the balance sheet of Controlada from kroons into Canadian dollars at December 31, Year 1, is shown in Exhibit 11.3.

> *When the parent acquires the subsidiary, the parent indirectly buys all of the net assets of the subsidiary.*
>
> *For consolidation purposes, we never use an exchange rate older than the rate at the date of acquisition.*

**EXHIBIT 11.3**

**CONTROLADA S.A.**
**TRANSLATION OF BALANCE SHEET TO CANADIAN DOLLARS**
At December 31, Year 1

| | Estonian Kroons | Exchange Rate | Canadian Dollars | |
|---|---|---|---|---|
| Cash | K    40,000 | 0.128 | $    5,120 | |
| Accounts receivable | 360,000 | 0.128 | 46,080 | |
| Inventories | 1,200,000 | 0.128 | 153,600 | (a) |
| Plant and equipment (net) | 900,000 | 0.128 | 115,200 | |
| | K2,500,000 | | $320,000 | (b) |
| | | | | |
| Current liabilities | K    50,000 | 0.128 | $    6,400 | |
| Bonds payable | 450,000 | 0.128 | 57,600 | |
| | 500,000 | | 64,000 | (c) |
| Common shares | 1,500,000 | 0.128 | 192,000 | |
| Retained earnings | 500,000 | 0.128 | 64,000 | |
| | K2,500,000 | | $320,000 | |

*Controlada has to be translated into dollars in order to consolidate with Starmont's Canadian-dollar financial statements.*

On December 31, Year 2, Controlada forwarded the financial statements shown in Exhibit 11.4 to the Canadian parent. The statements were prepared in kroons, which is the currency of the country where Controlada is located. Since the Canadian dollar is Controlada's functional currency, the statements must be translated to Canadian dollars for reporting purposes using the FCT method.

**EXHIBIT 11.4**

**CONTROLADA S.A.**
**FINANCIAL STATEMENTS**
At December 31, Year 2 (in kroons)
**INCOME STATEMENT**

| | | |
|---|---|---|
| Sales | K9,000,000 | (a) |
| Cost of goods purchased | 7,400,000 | (b) |
| Change in inventory | (400,000) | |
| Depreciation expense | 100,000 | |
| Bond interest expense | 45,000 | (c) |
| Other expenses | 1,555,000 | (d) |
| | 8,700,000 | |
| Net income | K    300,000 | |

*(continued)*

**EXHIBIT 11.4** *(continued)*

### STATEMENT OF RETAINED EARNINGS

| | | |
|---|---:|---|
| Balance, beginning of year | K 500,000 | |
| Net income | 300,000 | |
| | 800,000 | |
| Dividends | 100,000 | **(e)** |
| Balance, end of year | K 700,000 | |

### BALANCE SHEET

| | | |
|---|---:|---|
| Cash | K 100,000 | |
| Accounts receivable | 400,000 | |
| Inventory | 1,600,000 | **(f)** |
| Plant and equipment (net) | 800,000 | |
| | K2,900,000 | |
| | | |
| Current liabilities | K 250,000 | |
| Bonds payable | 450,000 | |
| Common shares | 1,500,000 | |
| Retained earnings | 700,000 | |
| | K2,900,000 | |

> *The subsidiary uses its local currency, kroon, in its own financial records and for reporting in its own country.*

Sales, purchases, bond interest, and other expenses occurred evenly throughout the year. Translation of the numerous revenues, expenses, gains, and losses at the historical rates is generally impractical. A weighted-average exchange rate for the period would normally be used to translate such items. The exchange rates for the year were as follows:

| | |
|---|---|
| Dec. 31, Year 1 | K1 = $0.128 |
| Dec. 31, Year 2 | K1 = $0.104 |
| Average for Year 2 | K1 = $0.115 |
| Date of purchase for inventory on hand at end of Year 2 | K1 = $0.110 |
| Date dividends declared and paid | K1 = $0.106 |

> *The Canadian dollar strengthened during Year 2.*

Controlada's statements are translated into Canadian dollars using the FCT method in Exhibit 11.5. The following discussion regarding the exchange rates used and the disposition of the translation gain should be noted:

- Monetary items are translated at the closing rate, while non-monetary items are translated at appropriate historical rates, unless the non-monetary item is to be reported at fair value.

- Common shares and beginning-of-year retained earnings are translated at the historical rate on the date of acquisition. In future years, the translated amount for retained earnings will have to be calculated.

> *Shareholders' equity accounts are translated at historical rates.*

**EXHIBIT 11.5**

## CONTROLADA S.A.
### TRANSLATION OF FINANCIAL STATEMENTS TO CANADIAN DOLLARS
At December 31, Year 2
(functional currency translation method)

#### INCOME STATEMENT

|  | Kroons (from Ex. 11.4) | Exchange Rate | Canadian Dollars |
|---|---|---|---|
| Sales | K9,000,000 | 0.115 | $1,035,000 |
| Cost of goods purchased | 7,400,000 | 0.115 | 851,000 |
| Change in inventory | (400,000) | Calculated | (22,400) |
| Depreciation expense | 100,000 | 0.128 | 12,800 |
| Bond interest expense | 45,000 | 0.115 | 5,175 |
| Other expenses | 1,555,000 | 0.115 | 178,825 |
| Foreign exchange gain **(6a)** |  |  | (2,600) |
| Total expenses | 8,700,000 |  | 1,022,800 |
| Net income | K   300,000 |  | $      12,200   **(a)** |

> *Cost of goods sold and depreciation expense are translated using the historical rates of the related balance sheet accounts.*

#### RETAINED EARNINGS

|  | Kroons | Exchange Rate | Canadian Dollars |
|---|---|---|---|
| Balance—beginning | K  500,000 | 0.128 | $  64,000 |
| Net income **(a)** | 300,000 |  | 12,200 |
|  | 800,000 |  | 76,200 |
| Dividends | 100,000 | 0.106 | 10,600   **(b)** |
| Balance—end | K  700,000 |  | $  65,600 |

#### BALANCE SHEET

|  | Kroons | Exchange Rate | Canadian Dollars |
|---|---|---|---|
| Cash | K  100,000 | 0.104 | $  10,400 |
| Accounts receivable | 400,000 | 0.104 | 41,600 |
| Inventory | 1,600,000 | 0.110 | 176,000 |
| Plant and equipment (net) | 800,000 | 0.128 | 102,400 |
|  | K2,900,000 |  | $330,400 |
| Current liabilities | K  250,000 | 0.104 | $  26,000 |
| Bonds payable | 450,000 | 0.104 | 46,800 |
| Common shares | 1,500,000 | 0.128 | 192,000 |
| Retained earnings | 700,000 |  | 65,600 |
|  | K2,900,000 |  | $330,400 |

> *Assets to be reported at fair value are translated at the closing rate and assets to be reported at cost are translated at the historical rates.*

- Revenue and expenses, with the exception of depreciation and cost of goods sold, are translated at the average rate for the year. Depreciation is translated at the historical rates used to translate the related assets. The three components of cost of goods sold are translated at the historical rates when these goods were purchased.

Because the components of cost of goods sold are translated using different rates, the translated amount for this item is calculated as follows:

| | Kroons | | Rate | Canadian Dollars |
|---|---|---|---|---|
| Beginning inventory (3a) | K1,200,000 | × | 0.128 | $153,600 |
| Less: Ending inventory (4f) | 1,600,000 | × | 0.110 | 176,000 |
| Change in inventory | (400,000) | | | (22,400) |
| Purchases (4b) | 7,400,000 | × | 0.115 | 851,000 |
| Cost of goods sold | K7,000,000 | | | $828,600 |

> *The three components of cost of goods sold are each translated at the rate when these goods were purchased.*
>
> *Purchases are translated at the average rate for the year. Inventories are translated at historical rates.*

The foreign exchange gain is calculated in Exhibit 11.6. It represents the change in values due to accounting exposure, which was defined at the outset of this chapter. Accounting exposure exists only on items translated at the closing rate. In most cases, under the FCT method, the exposed items are the

**EXHIBIT 11.6**

### CALCULATION OF YEAR 2 TRANSLATION ADJUSTMENT
(functional currency translation method)

| | Kroons | Exchange Rates | Canadian Dollars |
|---|---|---|---|
| Net monetary position, Dec. 31, Year 1* below | K (100,000) | 0.128 | $ (12,800) |
| Changes during Year 2: | | | |
| Sales | 9,000,000 | 0.115 | 1,035,000 |
| Purchases | (7,400,000) | 0.115 | (851,000) |
| Bond interest expense | (45,000) | 0.115 | (5,175) |
| Other expenses | (1,555,000) | 0.115 | (178,825) |
| Dividends | (100,000) | 0.106 | (10,600) |
| Net changes | (100,000) | | (10,600) |
| Calculated net monetary position, Dec. 31, Year 2 | | | (23,400) |
| Actual net monetary position, Dec. 31, Year 2* below | K (200,000) | 0.104 | (20,800) |
| Exchange gain, Year 2 | | | $   2,600   (a) |

> *This schedule reconciles the change in accounting exposure during the year and calculates the gains or losses due to the change in exchange rates.*

*(continued)*

**EXHIBIT 11.6**

## *NET MONETARY POSITION, KROONS

### December 31

| | Year 2 (from Ex. 11.4) | Year 1 (from Ex. 11.3) |
|---|---|---|
| Cash | K 100,000 | K 40,000 |
| Accounts receivable | 400,000 | 360,000 |
| Current liabilities | (250,000) | (50,000) |
| Bonds payable | (450,000) | (450,000) |
| Net monetary position | K (200,000) | K (100,000) |

*Only monetary items are exposed to exchange rate changes in this illustration.*

monetary items. However, when non-monetary items are measured at fair value, these non-monetary items will be translated at the closing rate and will be included in the exposed position. When the rate changes, items translated at the closing rate will be measured at a different amount in Canadian dollars. At the start of Year 2, the net exposed position was a net liability position of K100,000. These items were translated at the closing rate of 0.128 at the end of Year 1. If there were no new transactions during Year 2, there would still be a net exposed liability position of K100,000 at the end of year. These exposed items would be translated at 0.104 to equal $(10,400). The translated amounts would have changed from $(12,800) to $(10,400) for an exchange gain of $2,400. However, there were new transactions that changed the net monetary position during the year. These new transactions were initially translated at the rate on the date of the transaction. These new transactions changed the net exposed position to a net liability position of K200,000 at the end of Year 2. The items making up the exposed position at the end of Year 2 are translated at the closing rate at the end of that year. This results in an overall exchange gain of $2,600 for the year for all items.

*Exchange gains or losses only occur on items translated at the closing rate.*

To determine the items that changed the exposed position during the year, we need to follow a process similar to that used when we prepare a cash flow statement, looking at all non-cash items on the balance sheet and determining whether cash was involved. For the exposed position, we look at all non-exposed items on the balance sheet and determine whether an exposed item was involved. For example, when sales occurred during the year, cash or accounts receivable would have increased. However, when depreciation was recorded, the other side of the entry was accumulated depreciation, which is not part of the exposed items. Therefore, sales do change the exposed position but depreciation does not.

The exchange gain is reported in net income under the FCT method. This is consistent with the reporting of exchange gains or loss on individual foreign currency transactions, which were covered in Chapter 10.

*The exchange gain or loss is reported in net income under the FCT method.*

After the translation adjustment is reflected in Controlada's income statement, the translated statements are ready for the consolidation process. They also become the basis for the following equity method journal entries by Starmont on December 31, Year 2:

| | | |
|---|---|---|
| Investment in Controlada | 12,200 | |
|     Equity method earnings **(5a)** | | 12,200 |
| To record 100% of the Year 2 net income of Controlada Company | | |
| Cash **(5b)** | 10,600 | |
|     Investment in Controlada | | 10,600 |
| Dividend received from Controlada Company | | |

See Self-Study Problem 1, part (a), for another example of the translation of a subsidiary using the FCT method.

## LO4 The Presentation Currency Translation Method

The *presentation currency translation (PCT) method* is used for translating a foreign operation from its functional currency to a different presentation currency. All assets and liabilities should be translated at the closing rate. This method is much simpler than the FCT method because it uses the same rate for all assets and liabilities. This maintains the relationship between assets and liabilities when switching from the functional currency to the presentation currency.

> *The PCT method should be used to translate a foreign operation from the functional currency to the presentation currency.*
>
> *The PCT method preserves the relationship of balance sheet items.*

Under the PCT method, share capital is translated at historical rates. All revenues and expenses are translated using the exchange rate in effect on the dates on which such items are recognized in income during the period. If the revenues or expenses were recognized in income evenly throughout the period, the average rate for the period is used to translate these items.

A peculiarity resulting from the PCT method is that a property carried at historical cost in the foreign entity's statements will be translated into differing Canadian dollar values if exchange rates fluctuate over some time frame. The following example will illustrate this.

**EXAMPLE 6** A German entity has land on its balance sheet with a historical cost of €100,000 euros. On five successive balance sheets, denominated in euros, the land appears as €100,000. If the value of the euro changes with respect to the Canadian dollar each year during the five-year period and the PCT method of translation is used, the translated amount will be different each year. A reader of the German financial statements would observe the same amount reflected each year, while a reader of the translated financial statements would see a different amount each year and may improperly conclude that land sales or purchases have taken place. Despite this particular shortcoming, this method is one of the two currently sanctioned under IFRS. The IASB recognizes that the exchange adjustments under the PCT method have little or no direct effect on the present and future cash flows from operations.

Accordingly, the exchange adjustments are not recognized in profit or loss; they are included in other comprehensive income.

> *Translating historical cost in foreign currency by using the closing rate does not provide historical cost or fair value in Canadian dollars.*

We now return to the Controlada example and will translate Controlada's financial statements using the PCT method.

**EXAMPLE 7**   The translation of the balance sheet of Controlada from kroons into Canadian dollars at December 31, Year 1, was shown in Exhibit 11.3. The same translated balance sheet is used under the PCT method because this balance sheet establishes the amount paid for the assets and assumed for the liabilities at the date of acquisition.

The translation of Controlada's Year 2 financial statements is shown in Exhibit 11.7.

**EXHIBIT 11.7**

**CONTROLADA S.A.**
**TRANSLATION OF FINANCIAL STATEMENTS TO CANADIAN DOLLARS**
At December 31, Year 2
(presentation currency translation method)

**INCOME STATEMENT**

|  | Kroons (from Ex. 11.4) | Exchange Rate | Canadian Dollars |
|---|---|---|---|
| Sales | K9,000,000 | 0.115 | $1,035,000 |
| Cost of goods purchased | 7,400,000 | 0.115 | 851,000 |
| Change in inventory | (400,000) | 0.115 | (46,000) |
| Depreciation expense | 100,000 | 0.115 | 11,500 |
| Bond interest expense | 45,000 | 0.115 | 5,175 |
| Other expenses | 1,555,000 | 0.115 | 178,825 |
|  | 8,700,000 |  | 1,000,500 |
| Net income | K  300,000 | 0.115 | $    34,500   **(a)** |

> *All revenues and expenses are assumed to have occurred evenly throughout the year.*

**STATEMENT OF COMPREHENSIVE INCOME**

|  | Kroons | Exchange Rate | Canadian Dollars |
|---|---|---|---|
| Net income | K300,000 | 0.115 | $ 34,500 |
| Other comprehensive income |  |  |  |
| Currency translation adjustments **(8a)** |  |  | (51,100)   **(b)** |
| Comprehensive income | K300,000 |  | $(16,600) |

*(continued)*

**EXHIBIT 11.7** (continued)

### STATEMENT OF RETAINED EARNINGS

| | Kroons | Exchange Rate | Canadian Dollars | |
|---|---|---|---|---|
| Balance, beginning of year | K500,000 | 0.128 | $64,000 | |
| Net income | 300,000 | 0.115 | 34,500 | |
| | 800,000 | | 98,500 | |
| Dividends | 100,000 | 0.106 | 10,600 | **(c)** |
| Balance, end of year | K700,000 | | $87,900 | |

> Only the net income from the income statement is carried forward to the statement of retained earnings.

### BALANCE SHEET

| | Kroons | Exchange Rate | Canadian Dollars | |
|---|---|---|---|---|
| Cash | K 100,000 | 0.104 | $ 10,400 | |
| Accounts receivable | 400,000 | 0.104 | 41,600 | |
| Inventory | 1,600,000 | 0.104 | 166,400 | |
| Plant and equipment (net) | 800,000 | 0.104 | 83,200 | |
| | K2,900,000 | | $301,600 | |
| Current liabilities | K 250,000 | 0.104 | $ 26,000 | |
| Bonds payable | 450,000 | 0.104 | 46,800 | |
| Common shares | 1,500,000 | 0.128 | 192,000 | **(d)** |
| Retained earnings | 700,000 | | 87,900 | **(e)** |
| Accumulated translation adjustments **(b)** | | | (51,100) | **(f)** |
| | K2,900,000 | | $301,600 | |

> All assets and liabilities are translated at the closing rate.
>
> Other comprehensive income is carried forward to accumulated other comprehensive income, which, in this case, is accumulated translation adjustments.

The procedure used in Exhibit 11.7 was to translate the income statement first, then the retained earnings statement, and then the balance sheet. The following features of the PCT method are emphasized:

- The average rate for Year 2 is used for all revenues and expenses in the income statement.

> *The average rate is used when the revenues and expenses occur evenly throughout the year.*

- All assets and liabilities are translated at the closing rate.
- Common shares and beginning retained earnings are translated at the acquisition date historical rate, thus establishing the translated amount on that date. In future periods, the amount for the translated beginning retained earnings will have to be calculated. In practice, the accountant will look at last year's translated financial statements for this amount. Dividends are translated at the historical rate on the date of declaration. In situations where the dividends were not paid by year-end, the dividends payable will be translated at the closing rate, and an exchange gain or loss will result from the translation of these items. (In this example, the dividends were declared and paid on December 31.)

> *All items within shareholders' equity are translated using the historical rate applicable for each item.*

- The amount required to balance the balance sheet is the unrealized exchange loss from the translation of the subsidiary's financial statements using the PCT method. The unrealized exchange losses for the year must be presented in other comprehensive income on the statement of comprehensive income. The accumulated exchange gains and losses for all years to date are presented as a separate component of shareholders' equity. Since Year 2 is the first year in which Controlada is reporting unrealized exchange losses, the cumulative losses on the balance sheet are equal to the loss reported in comprehensive income for the year. In this example, comprehensive income is presented as a separate statement. It includes net income from the income statement and other comprehensive income.

> *Differentiate between other comprehensive income for the year that is reported in comprehensive income and accumulated other comprehensive income that is reported in shareholders' equity.*

In this illustration, the financial statements were translated sequentially, with the foreign exchange loss being the last item needed to balance the balance sheet. In reality, the gain or loss can be calculated before attempting the translation process. Exhibit 11.8 illustrates this process. When the PCT method is used, it is the net assets (assets less liabilities) that are at risk and exposed to currency fluctuations. Net assets equal shareholders' equity, and if the common shares remain unchanged, the only changes that usually occur are changes to retained earnings, which are net income and dividends. The process involves translating the opening position, using the closing rates at that time, and translating the changes to the exposed items at the rates at which they occurred. The result is a calculated position. The actual end-of-year net asset position is translated at closing rates, with the difference between the two numbers representing the exchange gain or loss from translation. Notice that if the exchange rate had remained constant throughout Year 2, all items in Exhibit 11.8 would have been translated at $0.128 with no exchange gain or loss occurring.

> *Exchange gains and losses occur only on those items translated at the closing rate and only if the rates change during the period.*

**EXHIBIT 11.8**

## Independent Calculation of Exchange Adjustment for Year 2

| | **TRANSLATION LOSS** (presentation currency translation method) | | |
|---|---|---|---|
| | *Kroons* | *Exchange Rate* | *Canadian Dollars* |
| Net assets, Dec. 31, Year 1 | K2,000,000 | 0.128 | $256,000 |
| Changes in net assets, Year 2: | | | |
| Net income | 300,000 | 0.115 | 34,500 |
| Dividends | (100,000) | 0.106 | (10,600) |
| Calculated net assets | | | 279,900 |
| Actual net assets | K2,200,000 | 0.104 | 228,800 |
| Exchange loss from translation | | | $ 51,100    **(a)** |

> *Assets minus liabilities are called net assets and are equal in amount to shareholders' equity.*

Starmont uses the equity method for internal record keeping purposes. It would make the following journal entries on December 31, Year 2:

| | | |
|---|---|---|
| Investment in Controlada **(7a)** | 34,500 | |
|     Equity method income | | 34,500 |
| 100% of translated net income | | |
| | | |
| Cash **(7c)** | 10,600 | |
|     Investment in Controlada | | 10,600 |
| Dividends received | | |
| | | |
| Other comprehensive income **(7b)** | 51,100 | |
|     Investment in Controlada | | 51,100 |
| To record 100% of the change in the unrealized exchange loss from translation for Year 2 | | |

> *Starmont's journal entries are recorded in Canadian dollars in Stormont's separate-entity records.*

See Self-Study Problem 1, part (b), for another example of the translation of a foreign operation using the PCT method.

## Comparative Observations of the Two Translation Methods

Under the PCT method, the net assets position of the foreign entity is at risk from currency fluctuations, while under the FCT method it is typically the net monetary position that is at risk. For most companies, monetary liabilities are greater than monetary assets, so they are usually in a net monetary liability position. This is the case with Controlada S.A. If the foreign currency weakens with respect to the Canadian dollar, the PCT method will show a foreign exchange loss while the FCT method will show a foreign exchange gain. This can be seen in Exhibit 11.6, where the FCT method produced a gain of $2,600 and in Exhibit 11.8, whereas the PCT method produced a loss of $51,100. If the Canadian dollar weakens with respect to the foreign currency (i.e., the foreign currency strengthens) the PCT method will reflect an exchange gain and the FCT method will reflect an exchange loss. These observations are only true when monetary liabilities are greater than monetary assets and when there is not a major change in exposed position from beginning to the end of the period.

> *A company usually has more monetary liabilities than monetary assets but has more overall assets than overall liabilities.*

## LO5 CONSOLIDATION OF FOREIGN OPERATIONS

We will now illustrate the preparation of consolidated financial statements for Starmont and its wholly owned subsidiary, Controlada. The preparation of the acquisition-date consolidated balance sheet appears in Exhibit 11.9. The figures in the Starmont column come from Starmont's separate-entity financial statements. Note that the translated shareholders' equity of the subsidiary is equal to the parent's investment account, so the consolidating procedure is simply to eliminate one against the other. Also, note that there was no acquisition differential at the date of acquisition.

**EXHIBIT 11.9**

## Preparation of Consolidated Balance Sheet

At December 31, Year 1

| | Starmont | Controlada (from Ex. 11.3) | Starmont Consolidated |
|---|---|---|---|
| Cash | $ 70,000 | $ 5,120 | $ 75,120 |
| Accounts receivable | 90,000 | 46,080 | 136,080 |
| Inventories | 200,000 | 153,600 | 353,600 |
| Plant and equipment | 300,000 | 115,200 | 415,200 |
| Investment in Controlada | 256,000 | — | — |
| | $916,000 | $320,000 | $980,000 |
| Current liabilities | $ 80,000 | $ 6,400 | $ 86,400 |
| Bonds payable | 300,000 | 57,600 | 357,600 |
| Common shares | 200,000 | 192,000 | 200,000 |
| Retained earnings | 336,000 | 64,000 | 336,000 |
| | $916,000 | $320,000 | $980,000 |

*With no acquisition differential and the subsidiary wholly owned, the investment account is equal to the subsidiary's shareholders' equity.*

## Consolidation of Functional Currency Translated Statements

Exhibit 11.10 shows the Year 2 financial statements of Starmont (which would be taken from Starmont's separate-entity financial statements), the translated statements of Controlada using the FCT method, and the consolidated financial statements. Note that the investment account equals the shareholders' equity of the subsidiary, and that there is no non-controlling interest or acquisition differential. The investment account is replaced with the assets and the liabilities of Controlada, and equity method income is replaced with revenues and expenses.

*The exchange gains or losses are based on the accounting exposure, which is based on the translation method.*

## Consolidation of Presentation Currency Translated Statements

The preparation of the acquisition-date consolidated balance sheet appeared in Exhibit 11.9. The consolidated balance sheet is exactly the same under the two translation methods at the date of acquisition.

Exhibit 11.11 illustrates the preparation of the consolidated financial statements at the end of Year 2 using Controlada's statements translated under the PCT method. Starmont uses the equity method for internal record keeping. Note that equity method income is equal to the subsidiary's net income ($34,500) and is therefore eliminated and replaced with the subsidiary's revenue and expenses. The

*Equity method income should be equal to the subsidiary's net income when there is no acquisition differential or non-controlling interest.*

**EXHIBIT 11.10**

## Preparation of Consolidated Financial Statements, Year 2

**CONSOLIDATED FINANCIAL STATEMENTS**
Year 2
(FCT method translated statements)
**INCOME STATEMENT**

| | Starmont | Controlada (from Ex. 11.5) | Starmont Consolidated |
|---|---|---|---|
| Sales | $3,000,000 | $1,035,000 | $4,035,000 |
| Equity method income | 12,200 | — | — |
| | 3,012,200 | 1,035,000 | 4,035,000 |
| Cost of goods purchased | 2,520,000 | 851,000 | 3,371,000 |
| Change in inventory | (20,000) | (22,400) | (42,400) |
| Depreciation | 20,000 | 12,800 | 32,800 |
| Bond interest | 30,000 | 5,175 | 35,175 |
| Other expenses | 200,000 | 178,825 | 378,825 |
| Foreign exchange gain (6a) | — | (2,600) | (2,600) |
| | 2,750,000 | 1,022,800 | 3,772,800 |
| Net income | $ 262,200 | $ 12,200 | $ 262,200 |

> The foreign exchange gain is reported in net income.

**RETAINED EARNINGS**

| | Starmont | Controlada | Starmont Consolidated |
|---|---|---|---|
| Balance—beginning | $336,000 | $64,000 | $336,000 |
| Net income | 262,200 | 12,200 | 262,200 |
| | 598,200 | 76,200 | 598,200 |
| Dividends | 50,000 | 10,600 | 50,000 |
| Balance—end | $548,200 | $65,600 | $548,200 |

> The parent's income under the equity method is equal to consolidated net income attributable to the parent's shareholders.

**BALANCE SHEETS**

| | Starmont | Controlada | Starmont Consolidated |
|---|---|---|---|
| Cash | $ 100,200 | $ 10,400 | $ 110,600 |
| Accounts receivable | 290,400 | 41,600 | 332,000 |
| Inventories | 220,000 | 176,000 | 396,000 |
| Plant and equipment (net) | 280,000 | 102,400 | 382,400 |
| Investment in Controlada (equity) | 257,600 | — | — |
| | $1,148,200 | $330,400 | $1,221,000 |
| Current liabilities | $ 100,000 | $ 26,000 | $ 126,000 |
| Bonds payable | 300,000 | 46,800 | 346,800 |
| Common shares | 200,000 | 192,000 | 200,000 |
| Retained earnings | 548,200 | 65,600 | 548,200 |
| | $1,148,200 | $330,400 | $1,221,000 |

> The subsidiary's assets and liabilities replace the investment account when preparing the consolidated balance sheet.

**EXHIBIT 11.11**

# Preparation of Consolidated Financial Statements, Year 2

**CONSOLIDATED FINANCIAL STATEMENTS**
Year 2
(PCT method translated statements)

### STATEMENT OF NET INCOME AND COMPREHENSIVE INCOME

|  | Starmont | Controlada (from Ex. 11.7) | Starmont Consolidated |  |
|---|---|---|---|---|
| Sales | $3,000,000 | $1,035,000 | $ 4,035,000 | |
| Equity method income | 34,500 | — | — | |
|  | 3,034,500 | 1,035,000 | 4,035,000 | |
| Cost of goods purchased | 2,520,000 | 851,000 | 3,371,000 | |
| Change in inventory | (20,000) | (46,000) | (66,000) | |
| Depreciation | 20,000 | 11,500 | 31,500 | |
| Bond interest | 30,000 | 5,175 | 35,175 | |
| Other expenses | 200,000 | 178,825 | 378,825 | |
|  | 2,750,000 | 1,000,500 | 3,750,500 | |
| Net income | 284,500 | 34,500 | 284,500 | **(a)** |
| Other comprehensive income: |  |  |  | |
| Foreign currency translation adjustments **(8a)** | (51,100) | (51,100) | (51,100) | **(b)** |
| Comprehensive income | $ 233,400 | $ (16,600) | $ 233,400 | |

> *Other comprehensive income is reported separately from net income.*

### RETAINED EARNINGS

|  | | | | |
|---|---|---|---|---|
| Balance—beginning | $ 336,000 | $ 64,000 | $ 336,000 | |
| Net income | 284,500 | 34,500 | 284,500 | |
|  | 620,500 | 98,500 | 620,500 | |
| Dividends | 50,000 | 10,600 | 50,000 | **(c)** |
| Balance—end | $ 570,500 | $ 87,900 | $ 570,500 | |

> *Consolidated retained earnings are the same as the parent's retained earnings under the equity method.*

### BALANCE SHEETS

|  | | | | |
|---|---|---|---|---|
| Cash | $ 100,200 | $ 10,400 | $ 110,600 | |
| Accounts receivable | 290,400 | 41,600 | 332,000 | |
| Inventories | 220,000 | 166,400 | 386,400 | |
| Plant and equipment (net) | 280,000 | 83,200 | 363,200 | |
| Investment in Controlada (equity method) | 228,800 | — | — | **(d)** |
|  | $1,119,400 | $ 301,600 | $ 1,192,200 | |
| Current liabilities | $ 100,000 | $ 26,000 | $ 126,000 | |
| Bonds payable | 300,000 | 46,800 | 346,800 | |
| Common shares | 200,000 | 192,000 | 200,000 | **(e)** |
| Retained earnings | 570,500 | 87,900 | 570,500 | **(f)** |
| Accumulated translation adjustments | (51,100) | (51,100) | (51,100) | **(g)** |
|  | $1,119,400 | $ 301,600 | $ 1,192,200 | |

> *Accumulated translation adjustments are reported separately from retained earnings.*

parent's investment account is eliminated against the shareholders' equity of the subsidiary in the following manner:

| | | |
|---|---:|---:|
| Investment in Controlada (11d) | | $228,800 |
| Shareholders' equity—Controlada: | | |
| Common shares (11e) | 192,000 | |
| Retained earnings (11f) | 87,900 | |
| Accumulated translation adjustments (11g) | (51,100) | 228,800 |
| Acquisition differential | | $    –0– |

With no acquisition differential or non-controlling interest, the investment account is replaced with the assets and the liabilities of the subsidiary. Note that the parent's share (in this case, 100%) of the subsidiary's accumulated translation adjustments appears as a separate component of consolidated shareholders' equity. The parent's equity method journal entries made the consolidation process straightforward.

> *The investment account under the equity method should be equal to the subsidiary's shareholders' equity when there is no acquisition differential or non-controlling interest.*

The consolidated statement of changes in equity for the year ended December 31, Year 2, is presented in Exhibit 11.12. Note that net income is added to retained earnings, whereas other comprehensive income is added to accumulated translation adjustments.

**EXHIBIT 11.12**

**CONSOLIDATED STATEMENT OF CHANGES IN EQUITY**
(PCT method translated statements)

| | Common Shares | Retained Earnings | ATA* | Total |
|---|---:|---:|---:|---:|
| Balance—beginning | $200,000 | $336,000 | $    0 | $536,000 |
| Net income (11a) | | 284,500 | | 284,500 |
| Other comprehensive income (11b) | | | (51,100) | (51,100) |
| Dividends (11c) | | (50,000) | | (50,000) |
| Balance—end | $200,000 | $570,500 | $(51,100) | $719,400 |

*ATA = Accumulated translation adjustments.

## Complications with an Acquisition Differential

The previous example assumed a 100% controlled subsidiary and no acquisition differential. The existence of an acquisition differential adds complexity to the consolidation process. As shown in Exhibit 11.3, the exchange rate at the date of acquisition is applied to all of the subsidiary's assets and liabilities at the date of acquisition. The same rate would be applied to any acquisition differential at the date of acquisition. Subsequent to acquisition, the historical rate or the closing rate would be applied to assets and liabilities under the FCT method in order to present the financial statement items at historical cost or fair value, respectively. Subsequent to acquisition under the PCT method, the closing rate is applied to all unamortized assets and liabilities making up the acquisition differential. We will change some of the facts from the previous example in order to illustrate this.

**EXAMPLE 8** Assume that Starmont purchased 90% of Controlada on December 31, Year 1, at a cost of K2,340,000. The carrying amounts of Controlada's net assets were equal to fair values on this date except for a patent, which had a fair value of K600,000 in excess of carrying amount. The patent had a remaining useful life of 10 years and no residual value at the date of acquisition. The same exchange rates are assumed; thus, the financial statements of Controlada and their translation will not change from the previous example. However, the change in the acquisition cost and the percentage purchased creates an acquisition differential and a non-controlling interest. Starmont's journal entry to record the acquisition on December 31, Year 1, is as follows:

| | | |
|---|---|---|
| Investment in Controlada | 299,520 | |
| Cash | | 299,520 |

To record the acquisition of 90% of Controlada for $299,520 (K2,340,000 × 0.128)

The calculation in Exhibit 11.13 of the acquisition differential in kroons and Canadian dollars on December 31, Year 1, is made to prepare the acquisition-date consolidated balance sheet. Exhibit 11.14 shows the balance sheets of the parent and the subsidiary and the consolidated balance sheet at December 31, Year 1, the date of acquisition. The consolidated balance sheet at the date of acquisition would be exactly the same under the two translation methods.

> *The subsidiary's separate-entity financial statements are the same regardless of the parent's percentage ownership in the subsidiary.*

**EXHIBIT 11.13**

## Calculation of Acquisition Differential

| | | | | | | |
|---|---|---|---|---|---|---|
| Cost of 90% investment | K2,340,000 | × | 0.128 | = | $299,520 | |
| Implied value of 100% | K2,600,000 | × | 0.128 | = | $332,800 | **(a)** |
| Carrying amount of subsidiary's net assets | | | | | | |
| Assets | 2,500,000 | × | 0.128 | = | 320,000 | |
| Liabilities | (500,000) | × | 0.128 | = | (64,000) | |
| Net assets | 2,000,000 | | | | 256,000 | |
| Acquisition differential | 600,000 | × | 0.128 | = | 76,800 | |
| Patent | 600,000 | × | 0.128 | = | 76,800 | **(b)** |
| Balance—goodwill | K     –0– | | | | $     –0– | |
| Non-controlling interest (10% × **[a]** 332,800) | | | | | 33,280 | **(c)** |

> *The acquisition differential is translated at the exchange rate on the date of acquisition.*

**EXHIBIT 11.14**

## Preparation of Consolidated Balance Sheet

### At December 31, Year 1

| | Starmont | Controlada (from Ex. 11.9) | Starmont Consolidated |
|---|---|---|---|
| Cash | $ 26,480 | $ 5,120 | $ 31,600 |
| Accounts receivable | 90,000 | 46,080 | 136,080 |
| Inventories | 200,000 | 153,600 | 353,600 |
| Plant and equipment | 300,000 | 115,200 | 415,200 |
| Investment in Controlada | 299,520 | — | — |
| Patent (13b) | — | — | 76,800 |
| | $916,000 | $320,000 | $1,013,280 |
| Current liabilities | $ 80,000 | $ 6,400 | $ 86,400 |
| Bonds payable | 300,000 | 57,600 | 357,600 |
| Common shares | 200,000 | 192,000 | 200,000 |
| Retained earnings | 336,000 | 64,000 | 336,000 |
| Non-controlling interest (13c) | — | — | 33,280 |
| | $916,000 | $320,000 | $1,013,280 |

> *Patent and non-controlling interest appear on the consolidated balance sheet.*

**CONSOLIDATION OF FCT METHOD TRANSLATED STATEMENTS** We assume that 90%-owned Controlada was translated into Canadian dollars using the FCT method. The existence of an acquisition differential and a non-controlling interest pose no particular consolidation problems because there is no goodwill. The acquisition differential amortization schedule for Year 2 is shown in Exhibit 11.15.

**EXHIBIT 11.15**

### ACQUISITION DIFFERENTIAL AMORTIZATION SCHEDULE
(FCT method translated statements)

| | | | | | | |
|---|---|---|---|---|---|---|
| Patent—Dec. 31, Year 1 (13b) | K600,000 | × | 0.128 | = | $76,800 | |
| Amortization—Year 2 | 60,000 | × | 0.128 | = | 7,680 | (a) |
| Patent—Dec. 31, Year 2 | K540,000 | × | 0.128 | = | $69,120 | (b) |

> *There is no exchange adjustment because patent is translated at the historical rate under the FCT method.*

Exhibit 11.16 shows the preparation of the Year 2 consolidated financial statements.

The following points are worth noting in regard to the preparation of the consolidated statements:

1. Consolidated income statement:

   (a) Equity method income is eliminated and replaced with the revenues and the expenses of the subsidiary, patent amortization, and the non-controlling interest as follows:

   | | |
   |---|---|
   | Net income, Controlada (5a) | $12,200 |
   | Patent amortization (15a) | (7,680) |
   | | 4,520 |
   | Non-controlling interest @ 10% | (452) |
   | Equity method income | $ 4,068 |

   (b) Non-controlling interest is 10% of the subsidiary's net income less 10% of the patent amortization.

> *Patent amortization and non-controlling interest are consolidation adjustments.*

**EXHIBIT 11.16**

# Preparation of Consolidated Financial Statements, Year 2

## CONSOLIDATED FINANCIAL STATEMENTS
### Year 2
### (FCT method translated statements)
### INCOME STATEMENT

| | Starmont | Controlada (from Ex. 11.5) | Starmont Consolidated | |
|---|---|---|---|---|
| Sales | $3,000,000 | $1,035,000 | $4,035,000 | |
| Equity method income | 4,068 | — | — | |
| | 3,004,068 | 1,035,000 | 4,035,000 | |
| Cost of goods purchased | 2,520,000 | 851,000 | 3,371,000 | |
| Change in inventory | (20,000) | (22,400) | (42,400) | |
| Depreciation | 20,000 | 12,800 | 32,800 | |
| Bond interest | 30,000 | 5,175 | 35,175 | |
| Other expenses | 200,000 | 178,825 | 378,825 | |
| Patent amortization **(15a)** | — | — | 7,680 | |
| Foreign exchange gain **(6a)** | — | (2,600) | (2,600) | |
| | 2,750,000 | 1,022,800 | 3,780,480 | |
| Net income | $ 254,068 | $ 12,200 | $ 254,520 | **(a)** |
| Attributable to: | | | | |
| Shareholders of Starmont (**[a]** 254,520 − **[b]** 452) | | | $254,068 | |
| Non-controlling interest | | | 452 | **(b)** |

### RETAINED EARNINGS

| | Starmont | Controlada | Starmont Consolidated |
|---|---|---|---|
| Balance—beginning | $ 336,000 | $ 64,000 | $ 336,000 |
| Net income | 254,068 | 12,200 | 254,068 |
| | 590,068 | 76,200 | 590,068 |
| Dividends | 50,000 | 10,600 | 50,000 |
| Balance—end | $ 540,068 | $ 65,600 | $ 540,068 |

> *The parent's retained earnings under the equity method are equal to consolidated retained earnings.*

### BALANCE SHEETS

| | Starmont | Controlada | Starmont Consolidated | |
|---|---|---|---|---|
| Cash | $ 55,620 | $ 10,400 | $ 66,020 | |
| Accounts receivable | 290,400 | 41,600 | 332,000 | |
| Inventories | 220,000 | 176,000 | 396,000 | |
| Plant and equipment (net) | 280,000 | 102,400 | 382,400 | |
| Investment in Controlada (equity) | 294,048 | — | — | **(c)** |
| Patent **(15b)** | — | — | 69,120 | **(d)** |
| | $1,140,068 | $ 330,400 | $1,245,540 | |
| Current liabilities | $ 100,000 | $ 26,000 | $ 126,000 | |
| Bonds payable | 300,000 | 46,800 | 346,800 | |
| Common shares | 200,000 | 192,000 | 200,000 | **(e)** |
| Retained earnings | 540,068 | 65,600 | 540,068 | **(f)** |
| Non-controlling interest | — | — | 32,672 | |
| | $1,140,068 | $ 330,400 | $1,245,540 | |

> *There is no accumulated translation adjustment for exchange gains or losses under the FCT method.*

2. Consolidated retained earnings:

   Because the parent has used the equity method, consolidated retained earnings are identical to the parent's retained earnings.

3. Consolidated balance sheet:

   (a) The investment account is eliminated and replaced with the assets and the liabilities of the subsidiary, the unamortized acquisition differential, and the non-controlling interest.

   (b) The non-controlling interest is calculated as follows:

   | | |
   |---|---:|
   | Common shares **(16e)** | $192,000 |
   | Retained earnings **(16f)** | 65,600 |
   | Patent **(16d)** | 69,120 |
   | | 326,720 |
   | | 10% |
   | | $ 32,672 |

> *Non-controlling interest on the balance sheet is based on the subsidiary's shareholders' equity plus the unamortized patent at the end of the year.*

The unamortized acquisition differential can be verified by the following calculation:

| | | |
|---|---:|---:|
| Investment in Controlada **(16c)** | | $294,048 |
| Shareholders' equity of Controlada (**[16e]** 192,000 + **[16f]** 65,600) | 257,600 | |
| | 90% | 231,840 |
| Unamortized acquisition differential (patent)—parent's share | | 62,208 |
| Non-controlling interest's share (10% × **[16d]** 69,120) | | 6,912 |
| Total unamortized acquisition differential (patent) | | $ 69,120 |

When goodwill forms part of the acquisition differential, it must be checked for impairment at each reporting date. When goodwill is impaired, it is not measured at fair value as it is at the date of acquisition. It is written down by an amount equal to the excess of the carrying amount of the net assets over the recoverable amount for the cash-generating unit. The impairment loss is more like amortization than it is a revaluation to fair value. Therefore, the value of goodwill after the write-down is similar to an amortized cost amount. Accordingly, goodwill should be translated at the historical rate under the FCT method.

Using the Year 2 acquisition differential amortization schedule and Controlada's translated financial statements (Exhibit 11.16), Starmont would make the following equity method journal entries on December 31, Year 2:

| | | |
|---|---:|---:|
| Cash (90% × [5b] 10,600) | 9,540 | |
| Investment in Controlada | 1,440 | |
|    Equity method income (90% × **[5a]** 12,200) | | 10,980 |
| To record parent's share of dividends and net income | | |
| Equity method earnings (90% × **[15a]** 7,680) | 6,912 | |
|    Investment in Controlada | | 6,912 |
| Amortization of acquisition differential | | |

**CONSOLIDATION OF PCT METHOD TRANSLATED STATEMENTS**    Assuming that Controlada used the PCT method, we will now illustrate the preparation of the Year 2 consolidated financial statements. Controlada's statements have already been translated into Canadian dollars as per Exhibit 11.11. The next step is to translate the acquisition differential. Assuming that the amortization expense related to the patent occurred evenly throughout the year, the acquisition differential amortization schedule is translated as shown in Exhibit 11.17.

**EXHIBIT 11.17**

### TRANSLATION OF ACQUISITION DIFFERENTIAL AMORTIZATION SCHEDULE
(PCT method translated statements)

| | | | | | | |
|---|---|---|---|---|---|---|
| Patent—Dec. 31, Year 1 **(13b)** | K600,000 | × | 0.128 | = | $76,800 | |
| Patent amortization—Year 2 | 60,000 | × | 0.115 | = | 6,900 | **(a)** |
| Calculated patent—Dec. 31, Year 2 | | | | | 69,900 | |
| Actual patent—Dec. 31, Year 2 | K540,000 | × | 0.104 | = | 56,160 | **(b)** |
| Exchange loss—unrealized | | | | | $13,740 | **(c)** |

### DISPOSITION OF ACCUMULATED UNREALIZED LOSSES

| | Total | 90% Control | 10% Non-control | |
|---|---|---|---|---|
| Accumulated unrealized loss—subsidiary statements **(7b)** | $51,100 | $45,990 | $5,110 | **(d)** |
| Accumulated unrealized loss—acquisition differential **(c)** | 13,740 | 12,366 | 1,374 | **(e)** |
| | $64,840 | $58,356 | $6,484 | |

*A patent owned by a subsidiary is translated at the closing rate under the PCT method.*

The following points should be noted regarding Exhibit 11.17:

- The acquisition differential (in this case, patent) on December 31, Year 1, is translated at the historical rate on that date.

- The Year 2 amortization expense is translated at the average rate for Year 2 because the expense was incurred evenly throughout the year.

> *Amortization expense is translated at the average rate.*

- The unamortized balance on December 31, Year 2, is translated at the closing rate.

When different exchange rates are used to translate the schedule, an exchange gain or loss will always result. In this case, there is a loss of $13,740, which appears as part of the accumulated translation adjustments in the shareholders' equity of the parent company. The allocation of the two exchange losses resulting from the translation of the financial statements and the acquisition differential to controlling and non-controlling interest was illustrated above.

> *An exchange adjustment occurs because the patent is restated when it is translated at the closing rate at the end of the year.*

The preparation of the Year 2 consolidated financial statements is illustrated in Exhibit 11.18.

**EXHIBIT 11.18**

## Preparation of Consolidated Financial Statements, Year 2

**CONSOLIDATED FINANCIAL STATEMENTS**
Year 2
(PCT method translated statements)
**STATEMENT OF NET INCOME AND COMPREHENSIVE INCOME**

| | Starmont | Controlada (from Ex. 11.7) | Starmont Consolidated | |
|---|---|---|---|---|
| Sales | $3,000,000 | $1,035,000 | $4,035,000 | |
| Equity method income | 24,840 | — | — | |
| | 3,024,840 | 1,035,000 | 4,035,000 | |
| Cost of goods purchased | 2,520,000 | 851,000 | 3,371,000 | |
| Change in inventory | (20,000) | (46,000) | (66,000) | |
| Depreciation | 20,000 | 11,500 | 31,500 | |
| Bond interest | 30,000 | 5,175 | 35,175 | |
| Other | 200,000 | 178,825 | 378,825 | |
| Patent amortization **(17a)** | — | — | 6,900 | |
| | 2,750,000 | 1,000,500 | 3,757,400 | |
| Individual net incomes | 274,840 | 34,500 | | **(a)** |
| Net income | | | 277,600 | **(b)** |
| Other comprehensive income | | | | |
| Foreign currency translation adjustments | (58,356) | (51,100) | (64,840) | |
| Comprehensive income | $ 216,484 | $ (16,600) | $ 212,760 | **(c)** |

> *The parent accrues its share of the subsidiary's income after it has been translated into Canadian dollars.*

| | Starmont | Controlada (from Ex. 11.9) | Starmont Consolidated | |
|---|---|---|---|---|
| Net income attributable to: | | | | |
| Shareholders of Starmont (**[b]** 277,600 − **[d]** 2,760) | | | $ 274,840 | |
| Non-controlling interest | | | 2,760 | **(d)** |
| (10% × [**(a)** 34,500 − **(17a)** 6,900]) | | | | |
| | | | $ 277,600 | |
| Comprehensive income attributable to: | | | | |
| Shareholders of Starmont (**[c]** 212,760 − **[e]** (3,724)) | | | $ 216,484 | |
| Non-controlling interest (10% × [**(c)** (16,600) − **(17a)** 6,900 − **(17e)** 13,740]) | | | (3,724) | **(e)** |
| | | | $ 212,760 | |

> *Consolidated other comprehensive income includes $51,100 from translating the subsidiary's separate-entity statements plus $13,740 from translating the acquisition differential on consolidation.*

**EXHIBIT 11.18**

### RETAINED EARNINGS

| | | | |
|---|---:|---:|---:|
| Balance—beginning | $ 336,000 | $ 64,000 | $ 336,000 |
| Net income | 274,840 | 34,500 | 274,840 |
| | 610,840 | 98,500 | 610,840 |
| Dividends | 50,000 | 10,600 | 50,000 |
| Balance—end | $ 560,840 | $ 87,900 | $ 560,840 |

### BALANCE SHEETS

| | | | | |
|---|---:|---:|---:|---|
| Cash | $ 55,620 | $ 10,400 | $ 66,020 | |
| Accounts receivable | 290,400 | 41,600 | 332,000 | |
| Inventories | 220,000 | 166,400 | 386,400 | |
| Plant and equipment | 280,000 | 83,200 | 363,200 | |
| Investment in Controlada (equity) | 256,464 | — | — | **(f)** |
| Patent **(17b)** | — | — | 56,160 | **(g)** |
| | $1,102,484 | $ 301,600 | $ 1,203,780 | |
| Current liabilities | $ 100,000 | $ 26,000 | $ 126,000 | |
| Bonds payable | 300,000 | 46,800 | 346,800 | |
| Common shares | 200,000 | 192,000 | 200,000 | **(h)** |
| Retained earnings | 560,840 | 87,900 | 560,840 | **(i)** |
| Accumulated translation adjustments | (58,356) | (51,100) | (58,356) | **(j)** |
| Non-controlling interest | — | — | 28,496 | |
| | $1,102,484 | $ 301,600 | $ 1,203,780 | |

*Accumulated translation adjustments are only the parent's share. The non-controlling interest's share of accumulated translation adjustments is included in the $28,496 for non-controlling interest.*

The following explanations regarding the preparation of the consolidated statements should be noted:

1. Consolidated statement of comprehensive income:
   (a) Equity method income is eliminated and replaced with the revenues and expenses of the subsidiary, the patent amortization expense, and the non-controlling interest.

*Non-controlling interest on the consolidated statement of comprehensive income is based on the income recorded by the subsidiary, plus the consolidation adjustments for patent amortization loss and exchange loss.*

   (b) Non-controlling interest in net income is 10% of subsidiary net income less 10% of the patent amortization expense.
   (c) This statement takes the net income and deducts the unrealized foreign exchange loss to determine comprehensive income.
   (d) Non-controlling interest absorbs 10% of the unrealized exchange loss reported in other comprehensive income.

2. Consolidated retained earnings:
   Because the parent has used the equity method, all items are identical to the parent's retained earnings.

3. Consolidated balance sheet:

   (a) The investment account is eliminated and replaced with the assets and the liabilities of the subsidiary, the unamortized acquisition differential, and the non-controlling interest.

   (b) The non-controlling interest is calculated as follows:

   | | |
   |---|---:|
   | Common shares **(18h)** | $192,000 |
   | Retained earnings **(18i)** | 87,900 |
   | Accumulated translation adjustments **(18j)** | (51,100) |
   | Patent **(18g)** | 56,160 |
   | | 284,960 |
   | | 10% |
   | | $ 28,496 |

---

*Non-controlling interest on the balance sheet is based on the subsidiary's shareholders' equity plus the unamortized patent at the end of the year.*

---

4. Consolidated accumulated translation adjustments:

   This account shows the parent's share of the accumulated translation adjustments at the end of the year. Since Year 2 is the first year after acquisition, the accumulated losses are equal to the losses reported in other comprehensive income for the year.

   The unamortized acquisition differential can be verified by the following calculation:

   | | | |
   |---|---:|---:|
   | Investment in Controlada **(18f)** | | $256,464 |
   | Shareholders' equity of Controlada **(18h + 18i + 18j)** | 228,800 | |
   | | 90% | 205,920 |
   | Unamortized acquisition differential (patent)—parent's share | | 50,544 |
   | Non-controlling interest's share (10% × **[18g]** 56,160) | | 5,616 |
   | Total unamortized acquisition differential (patent) | | $ 56,160 |

   Using the translated financial statements of Controlada (see Exhibit 11.18) and the translated acquisition differential amortization schedule, Starmont would make the following equity method journal entries on December 31, Year 2:

   | | | |
   |---|---:|---:|
   | Cash (90% × **[7c]** 10,600) | 9,540 | |
   | Other comprehensive income (90% × **[7b]** 51,100) | 45,990 | |
   |    Equity method income (90% × **[7a]** 34,500) | | 31,050 |
   |    Investment in Controlada | | 24,480 |
   | To record the parent's share of dividends, net income, and loss on translation of statement | | |
   | | | |
   | Equity method income (90% × **[17a]** 6,900) | 6,210 | |
   | Other comprehensive income (90% × **[17c]** 13,740) | 12,366 | |
   |    Investment in Controlada | | 18,576 |
   | To record the amortization and exchange adjustment on the acquisition differential | | |

   Note that Year 2 equity method income is $24,840 ($31,050 − $6,210) when the PCT method was used. In the previous example, when the FCT method was used, the equity method income was $4,068. The difference is due to (a) the use of different exchange rates in the translation, and (b) the fact that there is no exchange loss on the translation of the acquisition differential amortization schedule under the FCT method.

---

*The equity method income is quite different under the FCT method than under the PCT method.*

---

# Other Considerations

The previous examples have illustrated the translation of a foreign operation's financial statements and the consolidation of these statements with those of the reporting enterprise. We will now look at some other items that must be considered when a foreign subsidiary is being consolidated.

**LOWER OF COST AND NET REALIZABLE VALUE (LCNRV)** Certain items, such as inventory, will be measured at the LCNRV.

Under the FCT method, assets carried at cost are translated at historical rates, while assets carried at net realizable value are translated at the closing rate. Remember that the FCT method remeasures, in Canadian dollars, transactions that have been incurred by the foreign operation. Therefore, the translated financial statements should reflect the LCNRV in Canadian dollars as if the parent itself had carried out the inventory acquisitions of its foreign subsidiary. When assets are measured at the LCNRV, a write-down to net realizable value may be required in the translated financial statements, even though no write-down is required in the foreign currency financial statements. For example, if the net realizable value (denominated in foreign currency) is greater than historical cost (denominated in foreign currency), no write-down will have occurred in the foreign operation's statements. But if the foreign currency weakens, it is quite possible that the net realizable value translated at the closing rate will be less than historical cost translated at the historical rate. In this situation, translated net realizable value will be used in the translated financial statements.

> *Under the FCT method, the LCNRV principle must be applied using historical cost in Canadian dollars and net realizable value in Canadian dollars.*

On the other hand, it may be necessary to reverse a write-down in the foreign currency financial statements prior to translation, if the net realizable value amount translated at the closing rate exceeds historical cost translated at the historical rates. For example, if the net realizable value (denominated in foreign currency) is less than historical cost (denominated in foreign currency), a write-down would have taken place in the foreign operation's statements. If the foreign currency has strengthened so that the net realizable value translated at the closing rate is greater than historical cost translated at the historical rate, this write-down will have to be reversed prior to translation. The inventory (now carried at cost) will be translated at the historical rate.

Under the PCT method, the method of valuation used is of no consequence in the translation because all of the assets are translated at the closing rate, regardless of whether they are carried at cost or net realizable value.

> *Inventory is translated at the closing rate under the PCT method and the LCNRV principle need not be applied.*

**INTERCOMPANY PROFITS** In the preparation of consolidated financial statements, intercompany profits in assets are eliminated. If the profits are contained in the assets of the Canadian parent, there is no particular problem eliminating them. The asset acquired was recorded by the parent at the foreign-currency-denominated price, translated at the exchange rate on the date of the transaction. The profit rate can be applied for the items still on hand to determine the amount of profit to be eliminated. If the profits are contained in the assets of the subsidiary and the FCT method is used, the amount of unrealized profit can still be determined in foreign currency. Because the asset itself is translated at the historical rate, using the historical rate to translate and eliminate the profit will result in a translated asset at historical cost to the consolidated entity.

> *The historical rate should be used in determining the intercompany profit to be eliminated. This eliminates the same profit that was recorded in the first place.*

When the profit is contained in the assets of the subsidiary and the PCT method is used, the asset has been translated at the closing rate. The historical exchange rate should be used to calculate the amount of the profit. This eliminates the same profit that was recorded in the first place. However, the translated assets will not be reported at historical cost to the consolidated entity. This is one of the anomalies of the PCT method.

**CASH FLOW STATEMENT**    To prepare a cash flow statement for a foreign subsidiary, we ignore the cash flow statement of the foreign subsidiary; that is, we do not translate each item on the foreign currency cash flow statement into Canadian dollars by applying a translation rate to each item. Rather, we use the translated balance sheet and translated income statement to determine the cash flows during the year. We analyze the changes in the translated balance sheet accounts from last year to this year using either a worksheet approach or T-account approach and then prepare the cash flow statement based on this analysis. This is a similar approach to what we used in Chapter 8 when we prepared a consolidated cash flow statement by analyzing the changes in the consolidated balance sheet from last year to this year.

> *A cash flow statement is prepared by analyzing the change in non-cash items on the balance sheet after they have been translated into Canadian dollars.*

**TAX EFFECTS OF EXCHANGE ADJUSTMENTS**    Exchange differences arising from translating the financial statements of a foreign operation into Canadian dollars are usually not taxable or deductible until the gains or losses are realized. Since these differences were recognized for accounting purposes but not for tax purposes, a temporary difference occurs, and deferred income taxes should be recognized in the financial statements of the reporting entity.

Also, as we learned in Chapter 9, a temporary difference arises on the consolidated financial statements when an acquisition differential is allocated to an asset other than goodwill. We ignored the tax impact on the acquisition differential and for the foreign exchange adjustments in the illustrations in this chapter to avoid complicating the illustrations.

**DISCLOSURE REQUIREMENTS**    The following summarizes the main disclosures required in IAS 21 for the effects of changes in foreign exchange rates related to foreign operations:

(a) The amount of exchange differences recognized in profit or loss.

> *An entity must disclose the exchange adjustments reported in profit and other comprehensive income.*

(b) Net exchange differences recognized in other comprehensive income.

(c) When the presentation currency is different from the functional currency, that fact must be stated with disclosure of the functional currency and the reason for using a different presentation currency.

(d) When there is a change in the functional currency, that fact and the reason for the change in functional currency must be disclosed.

In addition, IFRS 7.40 requires an entity to disclose:

(a) a sensitivity analysis for each type of market risk to which the entity is exposed at the end of the reporting period, showing how profit or loss and equity would have been affected by changes in the relevant risk variable that were reasonably possible at that date;

(b) the methods and assumptions used in preparing the sensitivity analysis; and

(c) changes from the previous period in the methods and assumptions used, and the reasons for such changes.

TransAlta Corporation is Canada's largest publicly traded power generator and marketer of electricity and renewable energy. Exhibit 11.19 contains excerpts from TransAlta's 2014 financial statements pertaining to foreign currency operations.

**EXHIBIT 11.19**

# Extracts from TransAlta's 2014 Financial Statements

## 2. Accounting Policies

### B. Foreign Currency Translation

The Corporation, its subsidiary companies, and joint arrangements each determine their functional currency based on the currency of the primary economic environment in which they operate. The Corporation's functional currency is the Canadian dollar while the functional currencies of the subsidiary companies and joint arrangements are either the Canadian, U.S., or Australian dollar. Transactions denominated in a currency other than the functional currency of an entity are translated at the exchange rate in effect on the transaction date. The resulting exchange gains and losses are included in each entity's net earnings in the period in which they arise.

The Corporation's foreign operations are translated to the Corporation's presentation currency, which is the Canadian dollar, for inclusion in the consolidated financial statements. Foreign-denominated monetary and non-monetary assets and liabilities of foreign operations are translated at exchange rates in effect at the end of the reporting period and revenue and expenses are translated at exchange rates in effect on the transaction date. The resulting translation gains and losses are included in Other Comprehensive Income (Loss) ("OCI") with the cumulative gain or loss reported in Accumulated Other Comprehensive Income (Loss) ("AOCI"). Amounts previously recognized in AOCI are recognized in net earnings when there is a reduction in a foreign net investment as a result of a disposal, partial disposal, or loss of control.

> *The Canadian dollar is both the functional currency and the presentation currency for TransAlta.*
>
> *The PCT method is used when the functional currency differs from the presentation currency.*

### C. Financial Instruments and Hedges

    II. Hedges

        c. Hedges of Foreign Currency Exposures of a Net Investment in a Foreign Operation

In hedging a foreign currency exposure of a net investment in a foreign operation, the effective portion of foreign exchange gains and losses on the hedging instrument is recognized in OCI and the ineffective portion is recognized in net earnings. The related fair values are recorded in risk management assets or liabilities, as appropriate. The amounts previously recognized in AOCI are recognized in net earnings when there is a reduction in the hedged net investment as a result of a disposal, partial disposal, or loss of control. The Corporation primarily uses foreign currency forward contracts and foreign-denominated debt to hedge exposure to changes in the carrying values of the Corporation's net investments in foreign operations that result from changes in foreign exchange rates.

14. Risk Management Activities

    II. Hedges

        a. Net Investment Hedges

            i. Hedges of Foreign Operations           *(continued)*

**EXHIBIT 11.19** *(continued)*

The Corporation's hedges of its net investment in foreign operations are comprised of U.S.-dollar-denominated long-term debt with a face value of U.S. $580 million (2013—U.S. $850 million) and the following foreign currency forward contracts:

| | 2014 | | | | 2013 | | | |
|---|---|---|---|---|---|---|---|---|
| As at Dec. 31 | Notional Amount Sold | Notional Amount Purchased | Fair Value Asset | Maturity | Notional Amount Sold | Notional Amount Purchased | Fair Value Asset | Maturity |
| Foreign currency forward contracts | **AUD 235** | **CAD 221** | **0** | **2015** | AUD 200 | CAD 188 | 1 | 2014 |
| | 0 | 0 | 0 | | USD 10 | CAD 11 | 0 | 2014 |

> *U.S.-dollar-denominated long-term debt has been designated as a part hedge of the net investment in foreign operations.*

## B. Nature and Extent of Risks Arising from Financial Instruments

The following discussion is limited to the nature and extent of risks arising from financial instruments.
  I. Market Risk
    c. Currency Rate Risk

The Corporation has exposure to various currencies, such as the euro, the U.S. dollar, the Japanese yen, and the Australian dollar, as a result of investments and operations in foreign jurisdictions, the net earnings from those operations, and the acquisition of equipment and services from foreign suppliers.

The foreign currency risk sensitivities outlined below are limited to the risks that arise on financial instruments denominated in currencies other than the functional currency.

The possible effect on net earnings and OCI, due to changes in foreign exchange rates associated with financial instruments denominated in currencies other than the Corporation's functional currency, is outlined below. The sensitivity analysis has been prepared using management's assessment that an average four cent (2013—five cent, 2012—five cent) increase or decrease in these currencies relative to the Canadian dollar is a reasonable potential change over the next quarter.

| Year Ended Dec. 31 | 2014 | | 2013 | | 2012 | |
|---|---|---|---|---|---|---|
| Currency | Net Earnings Increase (Decrease)[1] | OCI Gain[1,2] | Net Earnings Increase | OCI Gain[1,2] | Net Earnings Decrease[1] | OCI Gain[1,2] |
| USD | 4 | 5 | 2 | 8 | (2) | 11 |
| EUR | — | — | — | — | — | 1 |
| AUD | (2) | — | — | — | — | — |
| Total | 2 | 5 | 2 | 8 | (2) | 12 |

[1] These calculations assume an increase in the value of these currencies relative to the Canadian dollar. A decrease would have the opposite effect.

[2] The foreign exchange impact related to financial instruments designated as hedging instruments in net investment hedges has been excluded.

> *TransAlta discloses the effect on net earnings of a four-cent increase in the exchange rate.*

*Source: TRANSALTA, TransAlta Corporation Consolidated Financial Statements—December 31, 2014, Pages 11, 12, 13, 41, 46–47. Reproduced with permission from TransAlta Corporation.*

# LO6 ANALYSIS AND INTERPRETATION OF FINANCIAL STATEMENTS

A company must use the FCT method when translating to its functional currency and the PCT method when translating from its functional currency to a different presentation currency. Exhibit 11.20 presents the statements of comprehensive income and balance sheets for Controlada after they have been translated into Canadian dollars under these two translation methods. The exhibit also indicates the return on equity, debt-to-equity ratio, and current ratio for each translation method.

**EXHIBIT 11.20**

## Impact of Translation Methods on Key Ratios

### CONTROLADA'S STATEMENTS OF COMPREHENSIVE INCOME

| | FCT Method<br>(from Ex. 11.5) | PCT Method<br>(from Ex. 11.7) |
|---|---|---|
| Sales | $1,035,000 | $1,035,000 |
| Foreign exchange gain | 2,600 | |
| | 1,037,600 | 1,035,000 |
| Cost of goods purchased | 851,000 | 851,000 |
| Change in inventory | (22,400) | (46,000) |
| Depreciation | 12,800 | 11,500 |
| Bond interest | 5,175 | 5,175 |
| Other expenses | 178,825 | 178,825 |
| | 1,025,400 | 1,000,500 |
| Net income | 12,200 | 34,500 |
| OCI—translation adjustment | | (51,100) |
| Comprehensive income | $    12,200 | $   (16,600) |

> *Exchange gains and losses are reported in net income under the FCT method and in other comprehensive income under the PCT method.*
>
> *The FCT method reports an exchange gain, whereas the PCT method reports an exchange loss.*

### CONTROLADA'S BALANCE SHEETS

| | FCT Method | PCT Method |
|---|---|---|
| Cash | $    10,400 | $    10,400 |
| Accounts receivable | 41,600 | 41,600 |
| Inventories | 176,000 | 166,400 |
| Current assets | 228,000 | 218,400 |
| Plant and equipment (net) | 102,400 | 83,200 |
| | $  330,400 | $  301,600 |
| Current liabilities | $    26,000 | $    26,000 |
| Bonds payable | 46,800 | 46,800 |
| Common shares | 192,000 | 192,000 |
| Retained earnings | 65,600 | 87,900 |
| Accumulated translation adjustment | | (51,100) |
| | $  330,400 | $  301,600 |

*(continued)*

**EXHIBIT 11.20** *(continued)*

| | | |
|---|---|---|
| Return on equity (net income / shareholders' equity) | 4.7% | 15.1% |
| Debt to equity (liabilities / shareholders' equity) | 0.28 | 0.32 |
| Current ratio (current assets / current liabilities) | 8.8 | 8.4 |

> *Exchange gains and losses end up in retained earnings under the FCT method and in accumulated other comprehensive income under the PCT method.*

Note the following from Exhibit 11.20:

- The FCT method reports a gain from foreign currency, whereas the PCT method shows a loss; the gain is reported in net income under the FCT method, and the loss is reported in OCI under the PCT method.

- The FCT method reports a positive comprehensive income, whereas the PCT method reports a negative comprehensive income.

- The main profitability ratio, being return on equity, is better under the PCT method because it uses net income rather than comprehensive income as the numerator.

> *Profitability ratios look better under the PCT method, whereas liquidity and solvency ratios look better under the FCT method.*

- The debt-to-equity ratio is lower under the FCT method because shareholders' equity is higher due to the foreign exchange gain as compared with a negative translation adjustment under the PCT method.

- The solvency position looks worse under the PCT method due to the higher debt-to-equity ratio because of the lower equity.

- The current ratio is higher under the FCT method due to the higher amount for inventory.

- The liquidity position looks better under the FCT method due to the higher current ratio.

These ratios refer to one company for the same year. Which set of ratios more faithfully represents the true economic position of the company? That question needs to be answered to determine which accounting method should be used to better reflect the true financial position of the company.

## ASPE Differences

- As mentioned in Chapter 3, private companies can either consolidate their subsidiaries or report their investments in subsidiaries under the cost method or the equity method or at fair value if the securities are traded in an active market. Under the cost method or the fair value method, the financial statements of a foreign subsidiary do not have to be translated.

- The exchange rate at the end of the reporting period is called the current rate, not the closing rate.

- The functional currency is not used to determine the translation method. Instead, the foreign operation is classified as either integrated or self-sustaining using similar, but not exactly the same, factors to those used under IFRS to determine the functional currency.

- The functional currency translation method under IFRS is known as the temporal method under ASPE. The presentation currency translation method under IFRS is known as the current rate method under ASPE.

- The translation gains and losses from translating self-sustaining foreign subsidiaries do not go through OCI but are reported as a separate component of shareholders' equity because OCI does not exist under ASPE.

> *OCI does not exist under ASPE.*

- When the foreign operations are located in a highly inflationary environment, the temporal method is used regardless of whether the operation is integrated or self-sustaining. No adjustments are made for inflation prior to translation.

# SUMMARY

Accounting exposure to exchange rate changes arises for assets and liabilities translated at the closing rate. Economic exposure exists when the present value of future cash flows changes as a result of changes in exchange rates. **(LO1)**

The functional currency is the primary currency of the entity's operating environment, whereas the presentation currency is the currency used on the reporting entity's financial statements. **(LO2)** The financial statements of a foreign operation must be translated into its functional currency using the functional currency translation method. This method produces the same results as if the transactions had been denominated in the functional currency in the first place. Exchange gains or losses are included in net income. **(LO3)**

The foreign operation's financial statements must be translated again using the presentation currency translation method if the foreign operation's functional currency is not the same as the presentation currency used in the parent's consolidated financial statements. This method translates all assets and liabilities at the closing rate, which results in some assets being reported in the presentation currency at values other than historical cost or fair value. Exchange gains and losses are reported in other comprehensive income. **(LO4)**

When the foreign operation is consolidated with the parent, the acquisition differential must be translated to the reporting currency of the parent. This will give rise to further exchange gains/losses for assets and liabilities translated at the closing rate. Intercompany transactions and unrealized profits will need to be eliminated after they have been translated to the presentation currency. **(LO5)**

The two methods for translating foreign operations will produce different results on the balance sheet and income statement. When analyzing financial statements, it is important to note what method has been used and how it will impact the amounts reported in the financial statements. **(LO6)**

## Self-Study Problem 1

LO3, 4

Barros Corp. is located in Brazil. The company was incorporated on January 1, Year 1, and issued its no-par common shares for 3.0 million Brazilian reals (R). The Canadian parent acquired 90% of these shares on January 1, Year 4. The financial statements for Barros on December 31, Year 5, are shown below:

### STATEMENT OF FINANCIAL POSITION
#### at December 31, Year 5

|  | Year 5 | Year 4 |
|---|---|---|
| Property, plant, and equipment | R5,000,000 | R5,000,000 |
| Accumulated depreciation | (2,500,000) | (2,000,000) |
| Inventory | 1,050,000 | 1,155,000 |
| Accounts receivable | 2,710,000 | 2,550,000 |
| Cash | 1,000,000 | 500,000 |
|  | R7,260,000 | R7,205,000 |
| Ordinary shares | R3,000,000 | R3,000,000 |
| Retained earnings | 1,660,000 | 1,505,000 |
| Bonds payable—due Jan. 3, Year 11 | 2,500,000 | 2,500,000 |
| Accounts payable | 100,000 | 200,000 |
|  | R7,260,000 | R7,205,000 |

### INCOME STATEMENT
#### For the year ended December 31, Year 5

| | |
|---|---|
| Sales | R35,000,000 |
| Cost of sales | 28,150,000 |
| Selling and administrative | 2,440,000 |
| Miscellaneous expenses | 2,000,000 |
| Income tax | 1,045,000 |
| | 33,635,000 |
| Profit | R 1,365,000 |

### STATEMENT OF RETAINED EARNINGS
#### For the year ended December 31, Year 5

| | |
|---|---|
| Balance, January 1 | R 1,505,000 |
| Profit | 1,365,000 |
| | 2,870,000 |
| Dividends | 1,210,000 |
| Balance, December 31 | R 1,660,000 |

### Additional Information

- On January 1, Year 1, Barros issued bonds at par for R2.5 million.
- Barros acquired the plant assets on January 1, Year 1, for R5.0 million. The plant assets are being depreciated on a straight-line basis over a 10-year life.
- Barros uses the FIFO basis to value inventory. The December 31, Year 4, inventory was acquired on October 1, Year 4. The inventory on hand on December 31, Year 5, was acquired on December 15, Year 5.
- Selling and administrative expense includes depreciation expense of R500,000.
- Barros declared and paid dividends on December 31, Year 5.

- Under the FCT method, Barros's December 31, Year 4, retained earnings were translated as $778,607. Under the PCT method, Barros's December 31, Year 4, retained earnings were translated as $684,091 and accumulated other comprehensive income were translated as $174,547.
- Exchange rate information:

| Jan. 1, Year 1 | CDN$1 = R2.50 |
| Jan. 1, Year 4 | CDN$1 = R2.00 |
| Oct. 1, Year 4 | CDN$1 = R1.94 |
| Average, Year 4 | CDN$1 = R1.95 |
| Dec. 31, Year 4 | CDN$1 = R1.91 |
| Dec. 15, Year 5 | CDN$1 = R1.80 |
| Average, Year 5 | CDN$1 = R1.86 |
| Dec. 31, Year 5 | CDN$1 = R1.82 |

**Required**

(a) Translate Barros's Year 5 financial statements into dollars, assuming that Barros's functional currency is the Canadian dollar.

(b) Assume that Barros's functional currency is the Brazilian real:
  (i) Translate the Year 5 financial statements.
  (ii) Prepare the Year 5 equity method journal entries that would be made by the Canadian parent.

## Solution to Self-Study Problem 1

(a) Canadian dollar is functional currency

| | Reals | Rate | Dollars | |
|---|---|---|---|---|
| *Year 5* | | | | |
| Inventory Jan. 1 | 1,155,000 | / 1.94 | 595,361 | |
| Purchases | 28,045,000 | / 1.86 | 15,077,956 | |
| | 29,200,000 | | 15,673,317 | |
| Inventory Dec. 31 | 1,050,000 | / 1.80 | 583,333 | |
| Cost of sales | 28,150,000 | | 15,089,984 | **(a)** |
| Depreciation expense | 500,000 | / 2.00 | 250,000 | |
| Other selling and administrative | 1,940,000 | / 1.86 | 1,043,011 | |
| Total selling and administrative | 2,440,000 | | 1,293,011 | **(b)** |
| *Net monetary position* | | | | |
| Dec. 31, Year 4* | 350,000 | / 1.91 | 183,246 | |
| Changes Year 5 | | | | |
| Sales | 35,000,000 | / 1.86 | 18,817,204 | |
| Purchases | (28,045,000) | / 1.86 | (15,077,956) | |
| Selling and administrative | (1,940,000)** | / 1.86 | (1,043,011) | |
| Miscellaneous expenses | (2,000,000) | / 1.86 | (1,075,269) | |
| Income tax | (1,045,000) | / 1.86 | (561,828) | |
| Dividends | (1,210,000) | / 1.82 | (664,835) | |
| | 760,000 | | 394,305 | |
| Calculated Dec. 31, Year 5 | | | 577,551 | |
| Actual Dec. 31, Year 5*** | 1,110,000 | / 1.82 | 609,890 | |
| Exchange gain Year 5 | | | 32,339 | **(c)** |

\*2,550 + 500 − 2,500 − 200 = 350.
\*\*Excluding R500,000 of depreciation expense.
\*\*\*2,710 + 1,000 − 2,500 − 100 = 1,110.

*Translation of Year 5 income statement*

| | | | |
|---|---:|---:|---:|
| Sales | 35,000,000 | / 1.86 | 18,817,204 |
| Cost of sales | 28,150,000 | **(a)** | 15,089,984 |
| Selling and administrative | 2,440,000 | **(b)** | 1,293,011 |
| Miscellaneous expenses | 2,000,000 | / 1.86 | 1,075,269 |
| Income tax | 1,045,000 | / 1.86 | 561,828 |
| | 33,635,000 | | 18,020,092 |
| Net income before exchange gain | 1,365,000 | | 797,112 |
| Exchange gain | | **(c)** | 32,339 |
| Profit | 1,365,000 | | 829,451 **(d)** |

*Translation of Year 5 retained earnings*

| | | | |
|---|---:|---:|---:|
| Balance Jan. 1 | 1,505,000 | Given | 778,607 |
| Profit | 1,365,000 | **(d)** | 829,451 |
| | 2,870,000 | | 1,608,058 |
| Dividends | 1,210,000 | / 1.82 | 664,835 |
| Balance Dec. 31 | 1,660,000 | | 943,223 |

*Translation of Year 5 balance sheet*

| | | | |
|---|---:|---:|---:|
| Property, plant, and equipment | 5,000,000 | / 2.00 | 2,500,000 |
| Accumulated depreciation | (2,500,000) | / 2.00 | (1,250,000) |
| Inventory | 1,050,000 | / 1.80 | 583,333 |
| Accounts receivable | 2,710,000 | / 1.82 | 1,489,011 |
| Cash | 1,000,000 | / 1.82 | 549,451 |
| | 7,260,000 | | 3,871,795 |
| | | | |
| Ordinary shares | 3,000,000 | / 2.00 | 1,500,000 |
| Retained earnings | 1,660,000 | Above | 943,223 |
| Bonds payable | 2,500,000 | / 1.82 | 1,373,627 |
| Accounts payable | 100,000 | / 1.82 | 54,945 |
| | 7,260,000 | | 3,871,795 |

## (b) (i) Brazilian real is functional currency

*Year 5*

| | | | |
|---|---:|---:|---:|
| Net assets Jan. 1, Year 5 | 4,505,000 | / 1.91 | 2,358,639 |
| Profit—Year 5 | 1,365,000 | / 1.86 | 733,871 |
| | 5,870,000 | | 3,092,510 |
| Dividends | 1,210,000 | / 1.82 | 664,835 |
| Calculated Dec. 31, Year 5 | | | 2,427,675 |
| Actual net assets Dec. 31, Year 5 | 4,660,000 | / 1.82 | 2,560,440 |
| Exchange gain Year 5 (to be reported in other comprehensive income) | | | 132,765 **(e)** |

*Accumulated OCI—Translation adjustment*

| | |
|---|---:|
| Balance Dec. 31, Year 4 | 174,547 |
| Exchange gain—Year 5 | 132,765 |
| Balance Dec. 31, Year 5 | 307,312 **(f)** |

*Translation of Year 5 income statement*

| | | | |
|---|---:|---:|---:|
| Sales | 35,000,000 | / 1.86 | 18,817,204 |
| Cost of sales | 28,150,000 | / 1.86 | 15,134,408 |
| Selling and administrative | 2,440,000 | / 1.86 | 1,311,828 |
| Miscellaneous expenses | 2,000,000 | / 1.86 | 1,075,269 |
| Income tax | 1,045,000 | / 1.86 | 561,828 |
| | 33,635,000 | | 18,083,333 |
| Profit | 1,365,000 | | 733,871 |
| Other comprehensive income—unrealized exchange gains | | **(e)** | 132,765 |
| Comprehensive income | | | 866,636 |

*Translation of Year 5 retained earnings*

| | | | |
|---|---|---|---|
| Balance Jan. 1 | 1,505,000 | Given | 684,091 |
| Profit | 1,365,000 | / 1.86 | 733,871 |
| | 2,870,000 | | 1,417,962 |
| Dividends | 1,210,000 | / 1.82 | 664,835 |
| Balance Dec. 31 | 1,660,000 | | 753,127 |

*Translation of Year 5 balance sheet*

| | | | |
|---|---|---|---|
| Property, plant, and equipment | 5,000,000 | / 1.82 | 2,747,252 |
| Accumulated depreciation | (2,500,000) | / 1.82 | (1,373,626) |
| Inventory | 1,050,000 | / 1.82 | 576,923 |
| Accounts receivable | 2,710,000 | / 1.82 | 1,489,011 |
| Cash | 1,000,000 | / 1.82 | 549,451 |
| | 7,260,000 | | 3,989,011 |
| | | | |
| Ordinary shares | 3,000,000 | / 2.00 | 1,500,000 |
| Retained earnings | 1,660,000 | Above | 753,127 |
| Accumulated OCI—translation adjustment | | **(f)** | 307,312 |
| Bonds payable | 2,500,000 | / 1.82 | 1,373,627 |
| Accounts payable | 100,000 | / 1.82 | 54,945 |
| | 7,260,000 | | 3,989,011 |

### (ii) Equity method journal entries of Canadian parent—Year 5

| | | |
|---|---|---|
| Investment in Barros Corp. | 660,484 | |
|    Equity method income | | 660,484 |
| 90% of Year 5 translated net income (90% × 733,871) | | |
| Cash | 598,352 | |
|    Investment in Barros Corp. | | 598,352 |
| 90% of Year 5 dividends (90% × 664,835) | | |
| Investment in Barros Corp. | 119,489 | |
|    Other comprehensive income | | 119,489 |
| 90% of Year 5 exchange gain (90% × 132,765) | | |

## Self-Study Problem 2

On January 1, Year 4, Parento Ltd. purchased 90% of the shares of Barros Limited for 5.4 million Brazilian reals (R). The exchange rate at that time was CDN$1 = R2. Financial statements of Parento are presented below. Financial statements of Barros were presented and translated in Self-Study Problem 1.

**PARENTO LTD.**
**STATEMENT OF FINANCIAL POSITION**
At December 31, Year 5

| | |
|---|---|
| Property, plant, and equipment | $ 8,000,000 |
| Accumulated depreciation | (3,000,000) |
| Investment in Barros—at cost | 2,700,000 |
| Inventory | 1,400,000 |
| Accounts receivable | 1,960,000 |
| Cash | 800,000 |
| | $11,860,000 |

| Ordinary shares | $ 5,000,000 |
|---|---|
| Retained earnings | 1,500,000 |
| Bonds payable | 2,000,000 |
| Accounts payable | 3,360,000 |
| | $11,860,000 |

## STATEMENT OF PROFIT AND RETAINED EARNINGS
For the year ended December 31, Year 5

| Sales | $15,000,000 |
|---|---|
| Dividend income | 598,352 |
| | 15,598,352 |
| Cost of sales | 11,509,352 |
| Selling and administrative expense (including depreciation and impairment losses) | 2,100,000 |
| Miscellaneous expense | 889,000 |
| Income taxes | 440,000 |
| | 14,938,352 |
| Profit | 660,000 |
| Retained earnings, Jan. 1 | 1,240,000 |
| Dividends paid | (400,000) |
| Retained earnings, Dec. 31 | $ 1,500,000 |

## Additional Information

- On January 1, Year 4, Barros's shareholders' equity consisted of common shares of R3,000,000 and retained earnings of R1,350,000. The fair values of all identifiable net assets were equal to carrying amounts except for the following:

| | Carrying Amount | Fair Value |
|---|---|---|
| Inventory | R850,000 | R970,000 |
| Patent | –0– | 400,000 |

- The patent of Barros had a remaining legal life of eight years on January 1, Year 4. Any goodwill was tested annually for impairment. There was a goodwill impairment loss of R100,000 in Year 5 and no impairment loss in Year 4.

- On January 1, Year 5, the inventories of Parento contained items purchased from Barros on October 1, Year 4, on which Barros had made a profit of R90,000. During Year 5, Barros sold goods to Parento for R920,000, of which R210,000 remained unpaid at the end of the year. Barros made a profit of R330,000 on goods remaining in Parento's inventory at December 31, Year 5. These goods had been purchased from Barros on December 15, Year 2.

- Assume a corporate tax rate of 40%. Ignore income taxes on the acquisition differential.

- Parento's functional currency and presentation currency are the Canadian dollar.

- Exchange rates were provided in Self-Study Problem 1.

## Required

eXcel
(a) Prepare Parento's consolidated statement of financial position and consolidated statement of profit for Year 5, assuming that Barros' functional currency is the Canadian dollar. *Hint:* Use Barros' translated financial statements from part (a) of Self-Study Problem 1.

eXcel
(b) Prepare Parento's consolidated statement of financial position and consolidated statement of comprehensive income for Year 5, assuming that Barros's functional currency is the Brazilian real. *Hint:* Use Barros' translated financial statements from part (b) of Self-Study Problem 1.

## Solution to Self-Study Problem 2

### CALCULATION, ALLOCATION, AND AMORTIZATION OF ACQUISITION DIFFERENTIAL

| | | |
|---|---:|---:|
| Cost of 90% investment in Barros | | R5,400,000 |
| Implied value of 100% investment in Barros (5,400,000 / 0.9) | | R6,000,000 |
| Carrying amounts of Barros's net assets: | | |
| Ordinary shares | R3,000,000 | |
| Retained earnings | 1,350,000 | |
| Total shareholders' equity | | 4,350,000 |
| Acquisition differential, Jan. 1, Year 4 | | 1,650,000 |
| Allocation: | FV – CA | |
| Inventory | R 120,000 | |
| Patent | 400,000 | 520,000 |
| Balance—Goodwill | | R1,130,000 |
| | | |
| NCI at date of acquisition (10% × 6,000,000) | | R 600,000 |

| | Balance Jan. 1/4 | Amortization Year 4 | Balance Year 4 | Amortization Year 5 | Balance Dec. 31/5 |
|---|---:|---:|---:|---:|---:|
| Inventory | R 120,000 | R120,000 | R — | R — | R — |
| Patent | 400,000 | 50,000 | 350,000 | 50,000 | 300,000 |
| Goodwill | 1,130,000 | — | 1,130,000 | 100,000 | 1,030,000 |
| | R1,650,000 | R170,000 | R1,480,000 | R150,000 | R1,330,000 |

### INTERCOMPANY PROFITS AND TRANSACTIONS

| | Reals | Rate | CDN$ | Tax | After Tax | |
|---|---:|---:|---:|---:|---:|---|
| Opening inventory—Barros selling | 90,000 | 1.94 | 46,392 | 18,557 | 27,835 | (a) |
| Closing inventory—Barros selling | 330,000 | 1.80 | 183,333 | 73,333 | 110,000 | (b) |
| Sales and purchases | 920,000 | 1.86 | 494,624 | | | (c) |
| Receivables and payables | 210,000 | 1.82 | 115,385 | | | (d) |
| Dividend income (1,210,000 × 90%) | 1,089,000 | 1.82 | 598,352 | | | (e) |
| Deferred income taxes (Dec. 31, Year 5): | | | | | | |
| Closing inventory **(b)** | | | | 73,333 | | (f) |

(a) FCT method:

Use rate of CDN$1 = R2.00 for all items in acquisition differential because all items are measured at historical cost.

| | Balance Jan. 1/4 | Amortization Year 4 | Balance Year 4 | Amortization Year 5 | Balance Dec. 31/5 | |
|---|---:|---:|---:|---:|---:|---|
| Inventory | $ 60,000 | $60,000 | $ — | $ — | $ — | (g) |
| Patent | 200,000 | 25,000 | 175,000 | 25,000 | 150,000 | (h) |
| Goodwill | 565,000 | — | 565,000 | 50,000 | 515,000 | (i) |
| | $825,000 | $85,000 | $740,000 | $75,000 | $665,000 | (j) |

## CALCULATION OF CONSOLIDATED PROFIT
### Year 5

| | | |
|---|---:|---|
| Profit of Parento | | $660,000 |
| Less: Dividends from Barros **(e)** | | 598,352 |
| Adjusted profit | | 61,648 **(k)** |
| Profit of Barros | 829,451 | |
| Add: Realized opening inventory profit **(a)** | 27,835 | |
| Less: Unrealized closing inventory profit **(b)** | (110,000) | |
| Less: Amortization of acquisition differential **(j)** | (75,000) | 672,286 **(l)** |
| Profit | | $733,934 |
| Attributable to: | | |
| Shareholders of Parento (61,648 + 90% × **[l] 672,286**) | | $666,705 **(m)** |
| NCI (10% × **[l] 672,286**) | | 67,229 **(n)** |
| | | $733,934 |

## CALCULATION OF CONSOLIDATED RETAINED EARNINGS
### End of Year 5

| | | |
|---|---:|---|
| Parento's retained earnings, end of Year 5 | | $1,500,000 |
| Barros' retained earnings, end of Year 5 | 943,223 | |
| Barros' retained earnings, date of acquisition (1,350,000 / 2.00) | 675,000 | |
| Change since acquisition | 268,223 | |
| Unrealized closing inventory profit **(b)** | (110,000) | |
| Amortization of acquisition differential **(j)** (85,000 + 75,000) | (160,000) | |
| Adjusted change since acquisition | (1,777) | **(o)** |
| Parento's share @ 90% | | (1,599) |
| Consolidated retained earnings, end of Year 5 | | $1,498,401 **(p)** |

## CALCULATION OF NON-CONTROLLING INTEREST
### End of Year 5

| | | |
|---|---:|---|
| NCI, date of acquisition (R600,000 / 2.00) | | $300,000 |
| Change in Barros' retained earnings since acquisition **(o)** | (1,777) | |
| NCI's share @10% | | (178) |
| | | $299,822 **(q)** |

## CONSOLIDATED STATEMENT OF FINANCIAL POSITION
### At December 31, Year 5
### (FCT method)

| | |
|---|---:|
| Property, plant, and equipment (8,000,000 + 2,500,000) | $10,500,000 |
| Accumulated depreciation (3,000,000 + 1,250,000) | (4,250,000) |
| Patents (0 + 0 + **[h] 150,000**) | 150,000 |
| Goodwill (0 + 0 + **[i] 515,000**) | 515,000 |
| Deferred income tax (0 + 0 + **[f] 73,333**) | 73,333 |
| Inventories (1,400,000 + 583,333 − **[b] 183,333**) | 1,800,000 |
| Accounts receivable (1,960,000 + 1,489,011 − **[d] 115,385**) | 3,333,626 |
| Cash (800,000 + 549,451) | 1,349,451 |
| | $13,471,410 |

## CONSOLIDATED STATEMENT OF FINANCIAL POSITION
At December 31, Year 5
(FCT method)

| | |
|---|---:|
| Ordinary shares | $ 5,000,000 |
| Retained earnings **(p)** | 1,498,401 |
| Non-controlling interest **(q)** | 299,822 |
| Bonds payable (2,000,000 + 1,373,627) | 3,373,627 |
| Accounts payable (3,360,000 + 54,945 − **[d] 115,385**) | 3,299,560 |
| | $13,471,410 |

## CONSOLIDATED STATEMENT OF PROFIT
For the year ended December 31, Year 5
(FCT method)

| | | |
|---|---:|---:|
| Sales (15,000,000 + 18,817,204 − **[c] 494,624**) | | $33,322,580 |
| Dividend income (598,352 − **[e] 598,352**) | | 0 |
| | | 33,322,580 |
| Cost of sales (11,509,352 + 15,089,984 − **[c] 494,624** + **[b] 183,333** − **[a] 46,392**) | | 26,241,653 |
| Selling and administrative expense (2,100,000 + 1,293,011 + **[h] 25,000** + **[i] 50,000**) | | 3,468,011 |
| Miscellaneous expense (889,000 + 1,075,269) | | 1,964,269 |
| Exchange gain (0 + 32,339) | | (32,339) |
| Income taxes (440,000 + 561,828 − **[b] 73,333** + **[a] 18,557**) | | 947,052 |
| | | 32,588,646 |
| Profit | | $ 733,934 |
| Attributable to: | | |
| Shareholders of Parento **(m)** | | $ 666,705 |
| NCI **(n)** | | 67,229 |

(b) PCT method:

Translate to Canadian dollars. Use average rate for amortization. Then, adjust to amount using closing rate at end of year.

| | Balance Jan. 1/4 | Amort. Year 4 | Adjust. Year 4 | Balance Dec. 31/4 | Amort. Year 5 | Adjust. Year 5 | Balance Dec. 31/5 | |
|---|---|---|---|---|---|---|---|---|
| Inventory | 60,000[1] | 61,538[2] | 1,538[3] | — | — | — | | **(ba)** |
| Patent | 200,000[4] | 25,641[5] | 8,887[3] | 183,246[6] | 26,882[7] | 8,471[8] | 164,835[9] | **(bb)** |
| Goodwill | 565,000[10] | — | 26,623[3] | 591,623[11] | 53,763[12] | 28,074[8] | 565,934[13] | **(bc)** |
| | 825,000 | 87,179 | 37,048 | 774,869 | 80,645 | 36,545 | 730,769 | **(bd)** |

**Notes:**
1. 120,000 / 2.00
2. 120,000 / 1.95
3. Exchange adjustment to get to desired amount at end of Year 4 as per next column
4. 400,000 / 2.00
5. 50,000 / 1.95
6. 350,000 / 1.91
7. 50,000 / 1.86
8. Exchange adjustment to get to desired amount at end of Year 5 as per next column
9. 300,000 / 1.82
10. 1,130,000 / 2.00
11. 1,130,000 / 1.91
12. 100,000 / 1.86
13. 1,030,000 / 1.82

## CALCULATION OF CONSOLIDATED PROFIT
### Year 5

| | | | |
|---|---:|---:|---|
| Profit of Parento | | $ 660,000 | |
| Less: Dividends from Barros **(e)** | | 598,352 | |
| Adjusted profit | | 61,648 | **(be)** |
| Profit of Barros | 733,871 | | |
| Add: Realized opening inventory profit **(a)** | 27,835 | | |
| Less: Unrealized closing inventory profit **(b)** | (110,000) | | |
| Less: Amortization of acquisition differential **(bd)** | (80,645) | 571,061 | **(bf)** |
| Profit | | $ 632,709 | |
| Attributable to: | | | |
| Shareholders of Parento (**61,648 + 90% × [bf] 571,061**) | | $ 575,603 | **(bg)** |
| NCI (**10% × [bf] 571,061**) | | 57,106 | **(bh)** |
| | | $ 632,709 | |

## CALCULATION OF CONSOLIDATED RETAINED EARNINGS
### End of Year 5

| | | | |
|---|---:|---:|---|
| Parento's retained earnings, end of Year 5 | | $1,500,000 | |
| Barros' retained earnings, end of Year 5 | 753,127 | | |
| Barros' retained earnings, date of acquisition (1,350,000/2.00) | 675,000 | | |
| Change since acquisition | 78,127 | | |
| Unrealized closing inventory profit **(b)** | (110,000) | | |
| Amortization of acquisition differential **(bd)** | (167,824) | | |
| | (199,697) | | **(bi)** |
| Parento's share @ 90% | | (179,727) | |
| Consolidated retained earnings, end of Year 5 | | $1,320,273 | **(bj)** |

## CALCULATION OF ACCUMULATED TRANSLATION ADJUSTMENT
### End of Year 5

| | | | |
|---|---:|---:|---|
| On Barros' separate-entity statement of financial position | | $ 307,312 | |
| Adjustments on consolidation (**[bd] 37,048 + [bd] 36,545**) | | 73,593 | |
| | | $ 380,905 | |
| Attributable to: | | | |
| Shareholders of Parento (90%) | | $ 342,814 | **(bk)** |
| NCI (10%) | | 38,091 | **(bl)** |
| | | $ 380,905 | |

## CALCULATION OF NON-CONTROLLING INTEREST
### End of Year 5

| | | | |
|---|---:|---:|---|
| NCI, date of acquisition (R600,000/2.00) | | $ 300,000 | |
| Change in Barros' retained earnings since acquisition **(bi)** | (199,697) | | |
| NCI's share @10% | | (19,970) | |
| Share of accumulated translation adjustment **(bl)** | | 38,091 | |
| | | $ 318,121 | **(bm)** |

## CONSOLIDATED STATEMENT OF FINANCIAL POSITION
At December 31, Year 5
(PCT method)

| | |
|---|---:|
| Property, plant, and equipment (8,000,000 + 2,747,252) | $10,747,252 |
| Accumulated depreciation (3,000,000 + 1,373,626) | (4,373,626) |
| Patents (0 + 0 + **[bb] 164,835**) | 164,835 |
| Goodwill (0 + 0 + **[bc] 565,934**) | 565,934 |
| Deferred income tax (0 + 0 + **[f] 73,333**) | 73,333 |
| Inventories (1,400,000 + 576,923 − **[b] 183,333**) | 1,793,590 |
| Accounts receivable (1,960,000 + 1,489,011 − **[d] 115,385**) | 3,333,626 |
| Cash (800,000 + 549,451) | 1,349,451 |
| | $13,654,395 |
| | |
| Ordinary shares | $ 5,000,000 |
| Retained earnings **(bj)** | 1,320,273 |
| Accumulated translation adjustment **(bk)** | 342,814 |
| Non-controlling interest **(bm)** | 318,121 |
| Bonds payable (2,000,000 + 1,373,627) | 3,373,627 |
| Accounts payable (3,360,000 + 54,945 − **[d] 115,385**) | 3,299,560 |
| | $13,654,395 |

## CONSOLIDATED STATEMENT OF COMPREHENSIVE INCOME
For the year ended December 31, Year 5

| | | |
|---|---:|---|
| Sales (15,000,000 + 18,817,204 − **[c] 494,624**) | $33,322,580 | |
| Dividend income (598,352 − **[e] 598,352**) | 0 | |
| | 33,322,580 | |
| Cost of sales (11,509,352 + 15,134,408 − | 26,286,077 | |
|   **[c] 494,624** + **[b] 183,333** − **[a] 46,392**) | | |
| Selling and administrative expense (2,100,000 + 1,311,828 + **[bb] 26,882** | 3,492,473 | |
|   + **[bc] 53,763**) | | |
| Miscellaneous expense (889,000 + 1,075,269) | 1,964,269 | |
| Income taxes (440,000 + 561,828 − **[b] 73,333** + **[a] 18,557**) | 947,052 | |
| | 32,689,871 | |
| Profit | 632,709 | |
| Other comprehensive income: | | |
|   Exchange adjustments (0 + 132,765 + **[bd] 36,545**) | 169,310 | **(bo)** |
| Comprehensive income | $ 802,019 | |
| Profit attributable to: | | |
|   Shareholders of Parento **(bg)** | $ 575,603 | |
|   NCI **(bh)** | 57,106 | |
| | $ 632,709 | |
| | | |
| Comprehensive income attributable to: | | |
|   Shareholders of Parento (**[bg] 575,603** + 90% × **[bo] 169,310**) | $ 727,982 | |
|   NCI (**[bh] 57,106** + 10% × **[bo] 169,310**) | 74,037 | |
| | $ 802,019 | |

# APPENDIX 11A

## Translation in Highly Inflationary Economies

**LO7**

While Canada has had fairly low rates of inflation in the past 25 years, this has not been the case in other parts of the world. Argentina, Brazil, Chile, Mexico, Turkey, and Israel have all had inflation rates higher than Canada's during this period. Between 1985 and 1993, Argentina experienced yearly rates of between 120% and 3,000%.

When a company operates in a hyperinflationary economy (i.e., its functional currency is the currency of a hyperinflationary economy), IAS 29 requires that the company's functional currency financial statements be restated by adjusting for inflation. Hyperinflation is indicated by characteristics of the economic environment of a country that include, but are not limited to, the following:

(a) The general population prefers to keep its wealth in non-monetary assets or in a relatively stable foreign currency.

(b) The general population regards monetary amounts not in terms of the local currency but in terms of a relatively stable foreign currency. Prices may be quoted in that currency.

(c) Sales and purchases on credit take place at prices that compensate for the expected loss of purchasing power during the credit period, even if the period is short.

(d) Interest rates, wages, and prices are linked to a price index.

(e) The cumulative inflation rate over three years is approaching, or exceeds, 100%.

> *Hyperinflation may cause the population to measure wealth and value using a currency of a more stable country.*

When IAS 29 is applied, both the current year's figures and last year's comparatives must be stated in terms of the measuring unit current at the end of the reporting period. Non-monetary items that were carried at historical costs are restated by applying a general price index. Monetary and non-monetary items that were carried at fair value or recoverable amount are not restated because they are already expressed in terms of the monetary unit current at the end of the reporting period. After the restatement, all assets and liabilities are stated at fair value or at a price-level-adjusted value, which may approximate fair value.

> *Price-level-adjusted financial statements are useful for countries experiencing high inflation.*

If the Canadian economy is subject to hyperinflation, Canadian companies reporting in Canadian dollars would have to apply IAS 29. In the ensuing discussion, we will assume that the Canadian dollar is not subject to hyperinflation and the foreign operation is located in a country with hyperinflation.

When the foreign operation's functional currency is the Canadian dollar, the foreign operations will be translated into Canadian dollars using the FCT method as usual. No adjustments will have to be made for inflation because the Canadian dollar is not subject to inflation. When the foreign operation's functional currency is not the Canadian dollar, the foreign operation's financial statements will have to be adjusted for inflation prior to translation. Otherwise, there will be distortions in the financial statements as shown in the following example.

**EXAMPLE A1**   On January 1, Year 3, a Canadian company purchased a subsidiary located in Chile. The exchange rate at this time was 1 peso (Ps) = \$1, and it remained constant during the year. The subsidiary has land carried at a historical cost of Ps1,000,000. On December 31, Year 3, the land is translated into dollars for consolidation purposes under the PCT method as follows:

$$Ps1,000,000 \times 1.00 = \$1,000,000$$

During Year 4, Chile experienced an inflation rate of 500%. Because the inflation rate in Canada was minuscule during this period, this large inflation differential is fully reflected in the foreign exchange market. The result is a weakening of the peso relative to the Canadian dollar. On December 31, Year 4, the exchange rate is Ps1 = \$0.20. If the land were translated at the closing rate on this date, the result would be as follows:

$$Ps1,000,000 \times 0.20 = \$200,000$$

> *There is usually an inverse relationship between the strength of a country's currency and the level of inflation in that country.*

While it is easy to see in this example that the \$800,000 difference is due to the exchange rate change, large differences such as this are difficult to interpret without all the facts.

If the Chilean subsidiary prepared price-level-adjusted historical cost statements, the land would appear on the subsidiary's balance sheet at Ps5,000,000. Translation using the closing rate on December 31, Year 4, would *not* produce distorted results, as the following illustrates:

$$Ps5,000,000 \times 0.20 = \$1,000,000$$

After restating for inflation under IAS 29, the company's restated statements must be translated into Canadian dollars using the following procedures:

(a) All amounts (i.e., assets, liabilities, equity items, income, and expenses for the current year) must be translated at the closing rate.

(b) Comparative amounts must be those that were presented as current-year amounts in the relevant prior-year financial statements (i.e., they are not adjusted for subsequent changes in exchange rates).

This is slightly different than the normal PCT method where assets and liabilities are translated at the closing rate and revenues and expenses are translated at the average rate. The combination of restating for inflation under IAS 29 and applying the closing rate under IAS 21 produces a value in Canadian dollars that approximates the fair value for the foreign operation's assets and liabilities.

When the economy ceases to be hyper-inflationary and the entity no longer restates its financial statements in accordance with IAS 29, it must use as the historical costs for translation the amounts restated to the price level at the date the entity ceased restating its financial statements.

## Summary

When a company's functional currency is the currency of a country experiencing hyperinflation, the company's functional currency financial statements must be restated by adjusting for inflation. These adjustments must be made prior to translating the financial statements to a different presentation currency. **(LO7)**

## Review Questions

*Questions, cases, and problems that deal with the appendix material are denoted with an asterisk.*

LO1 **1.** The FCT and PCT methods each produce different amounts for translation gains and losses due to the items at risk. Explain.

LO2 **2.** What are the three major issues related to the translation of foreign currency financial statements?

LO1 **3.** Why might a company want to hedge its balance sheet exposure? What is the paradox associated with hedging balance sheet exposure?

LO4 **4.** How are gains and losses on financial instruments used to hedge the net investment in a foreign operation reported in the consolidated financial statements when the PCT method is used to translate the foreign operation?

LO2 **5.** Define a foreign operation as per IAS 21.

LO2 **6.** What should happen if a foreign subsidiary's financial statements have been prepared using accounting principles different from those used in Canada?

LO2 **7.** What difference does it make whether the foreign operation's functional currency is the same or different than the parent's presentation currency? What method of translation should be used for each?

LO4 **\*8.** What translation method should be used for a subsidiary that operates in a highly inflationary environment? Why?

LO2 **9.** How are translation exchange gains and losses reflected in financial statements if the foreign operation's functional currency is the Canadian dollar? Would the treatment be different if the foreign operation's functional currency were not the Canadian dollar? Explain.

LO3, 4 **10.** Does the FCT method use the same unit of measure as the PCT method? Explain.

LO5 **11.** The amount of the accumulated foreign exchange adjustments appearing in the translated financial statements of a subsidiary could be different from the amount appearing in the consolidated financial statements. Explain how.

LO3, 4 **12.** "If the translation of a foreign operation produced a gain under the FCT method, the translation of the same company could produce a loss if the operation were translated under the PCT method." Do you agree with this statement? Explain.

LO3 **13.** Explain how the FCT method produces results that are consistent with the normal measurement and valuation of assets and liabilities for domestic transactions and operations.

LO5 **14.** When translating the financial statements of the subsidiary at the date of acquisition by the parent, the exchange rate on the date of acquisition is used to translate plant assets rather than the exchange rate on the date when the subsidiary acquired the plant assets. Explain the rationale for this practice.

LO3, 4 **15.** If the sales of a foreign subsidiary all occurred on one day during the year, would the sales be translated at the average rate for the year or the rate on the date of the sales? Explain.

# CASES

## Case 11-1

LO1, 3, 4

The Rider Corporation operates throughout Canada buying and selling widgets. In hopes of expanding into more profitable markets, the company recently decided to open a small subsidiary in California. On October 1, Year 2, Rider invested CDN$1,000,000 in Riderville USA Ltd. Its investment was immediately converted into US$900,000. One-half of this money was used to purchase land to be held for the possible construction of a plant, and one-half was invested in held-for-trading equity securities. Nothing further happened at Riderville throughout the remainder of Year 2. However, the U.S. dollar weakened relative to the Canadian dollar and the exchange rate at December 31, Year 2, was US$1 = CDN$1.08. Fortunately, the value of the land purchased by Riderville increased to US$500,000 and the securities were worth US$490,000 at the end of the year.

The accountant for Rider realized that the investments of the U.S. subsidiary had increased in value but did not plan to report this unrealized gain in the consolidated financial statements. However, the CEO wants to report the true economic value of these investments.

**Required**

(a) What is the true economic value of the assets owned by Riderville USA at the end of Year 2?

(b) Can Rider report the economic value of these assets in the consolidated balance sheet under IFRS? If not, how should Rider report each of these assets on its consolidated balance sheet and how should the related gains be reported? Assume that the securities are classified as fair value through profit or loss.

## *Case 11-2

LO2, 4, 7

Nova Mine Engineering is a junior Canadian company with a variety of operating subsidiaries and other undertakings that provide mine engineering and management services in Canada and in several less-developed countries. One of these subsidiaries is active in Zimbabwe, which is rich in mineral resources and has an active mining industry. This company, Zimbabwe Platinum Management (ZPM), is under review prior to year-end translation and consolidation. The staff of ZPM consists primarily of junior and intermediate Nova staff who have been seconded to the operation on one-to-three-year terms. Between the companies there is information flow but no product movement.

Capital investment in Zimbabwe is restricted to movable equipment and working capital with a value of about CDN$3,000,000.

Management of Nova has long been concerned about its inability to hedge against fluctuations in the Zimbabwean dollar. All payments to ZPM from the state Mineral Marketing Corporation have recently been made in this currency, rather than in U.S. dollars as specified in earlier contracts. It is this inability to hedge that has increased Nova's concern about the long-run fit of ZPM within the portfolio of Nova companies, as well as the current financial statement presentation. The currency has declined in value by 65% during the year. Other concerns include Zimbabwe's persistent high inflation, recently about 35%, which is expected to increase even further. Political uncertainty is also a concern, as a result of recent nationalizations in the agricultural sector and growing unrest among the poor.

### Required

In a briefing note, advise senior management of Nova how the investment in the subsidiary ZPM should be measured and reported, and what disclosures should be made with respect to this investment in the annual report of the parent company.

*(Case prepared by Peter Secord, St. Mary's University)*

## *Case 11-3

LO2, 3, 4, 7

Vulcan Manufacturing Limited (VML) is a Canadian-based multinational plastics firm, with subsidiaries in several foreign countries and worldwide consolidated total assets of $500 million. VML's shares are listed on a Canadian stock exchange. VML is attracted to developing countries by their growing demand for its products. In recognition of trade barriers designed to encourage domestic production in those countries, and in order to service local demand, VML incorporated a foreign subsidiary in a South American country on September 1, Year 4. The subsidiary, South American Plastics Inc. (SAPI), manufactures patented sheet plastic and sells virtually all of its output locally. Also, almost all labour and raw materials are provided locally. SAPI finances its day-to-day activities from its own operations and local borrowing.

During Year 4 and Year 5, the South American country suffered an inflation rate of more than 100%, accompanied by substantial devaluation of the local currency and a drastic increase in interest rates. The government is expected to impose wage and price controls in Year 6. The inflation rate is expected to stabilize at more moderate levels sometime in Year 6 or Year 7.

The CFO of VML has recently received SAPI's draft balance sheet as at August 31, Year 5 (Exhibit I), together with some comments prepared by SAPI's controller (Exhibit II). He is somewhat surprised by the return on investment of nearly 12%. This figure is well above the target rate agreed upon for bonus purposes, which was set at 3% in recognition of start-up costs associated with the first year of operations. The apparently favourable performance will result in large bonuses for SAPI's management.

Increases in SAPI's domestic selling price have kept pace with the general rate of inflation and increases in input prices and borrowing costs in the South American country. The CFO is satisfied that the inflation and devaluation the country has experienced has not seriously affected SAPI's cash flows from operations.

In the annual report to Canadian shareholders for the year ended August 31, Year 5, the CFO wants to communicate to shareholders the economic impact that inflation and devaluation in the South American country have had on VML's investment in SAPI. He is concerned that gains or losses arising from translation of the statements in accordance with IAS 21 will mislead shareholders. The

CFO believes that the exchange gains and losses will obscure the true impact of foreign inflation and devaluation on SAPI's economic value in Canadian-dollar terms. He has called the audit partner and you, the Senior, into his office. The following conversation ensues:

**CFO:** We have to issue our financial statements soon, and we have to apply IAS 21 to our South American subsidiary. I must confess that I don't know IAS 21 as well as you two do. My staff tells me that we must use a special method this year, due to the local hyperinflation, although I confess that I don't see why. Apparently we will have a choice between the FCT method and the PCT method once the inflation rate stabilizes, which I expect to happen in Year 6 or Year 7. I am very reluctant to use a special method on this year's statements. It forces me to include fictitious gains and losses in our consolidated income statement.

**Partner:** Your staff is correct in stating that IAS 21 requires the use of a special method for the year just ended. However, shareholders should not be misled by exchange gains or losses in comprehensive income provided that they are fully disclosed as such.

**CFO:** I guess I just do not understand IAS 21. For example, how might the adoption of the PCT method in Year 6 or Year 7 improve matters? It seems to me that an overall exchange loss will arise if the rate keeps on going down. What does the loss mean? As long as our subsidiary's cash flows keep pace with local inflation, it will be able to maintain its expected rate of profitability and therefore its ability to pay dividends to us. Yet shareholders will see an exchange loss!

**Partner:** I will have Senior prepare a report that explains to you how the exchange gains or losses under either translation method tie in with the notion of risk underlying IAS 21. We will also explain how this notion alleviates your concern about communicating the true economic risk to shareholders. Senior will recommend ways to tell the whole story to shareholders.

**CFO:** Sounds great. I would also like Senior to provide advice on any other important issues related to SAPI. For starters, I have some concerns about the way our bonus plan for SAPI's management is working. One possibility I am considering is to evaluate SAPI's performance in Canadian-dollar terms.

---

**EXHIBIT I**

### SOUTH AMERICAN PLASTICS INC.
### EXTRACTS FROM DRAFT BALANCE SHEET AS AT AUGUST 31, YEAR 5 (IN THOUSANDS)
**Assets**

| | |
|---|---:|
| Cash | FC 10,020* |
| Held-to-maturity investments | 3,120 |
| Accounts receivable | 93,000 |
| Inventory (at cost) | 67,200 |
| Prepaid expenses | 8,040 |
| | 181,380 |
| Plant assets | 143,111 |
| Less accumulated depreciation | 14,311 |
| | 128,800 |
| | FC 310,180 |

*(continued)*

**EXHIBIT I** (continued)

**Liabilities and Shareholders' Equity**

| | |
|---|---|
| Current monetary liabilities | FC 65,140 |
| Long-term debt | 157,200 |
| | 222,340 |
| Common shares | 51,000 |
| Retained earnings | 36,840 |
| | 87,840 |
| | FC310,180 |

*An FC is a unit of the currency used in the South American country in which SAPI is located.

**EXHIBIT II**

## South American Plastics Inc.—Controller's Comments on Financial Statements

1. Opening Balances:

   SAPI's balance sheet on September 1, Year 4, consisted of cash of FC208,200,000; long-term debt of FC157,200,000; and common shares of FC51,000,000.

2. Held-to-maturity Investments:

   The held-to-maturity investments were purchased when 1FC = $0.31. The aggregate market value for the investments at August 31, Year 5, was FC3,000,000 due to an increase in interest rates in the market.

3. Inventories:

   Inventories were purchased when 1FC = $0.30. VML values inventory at the lower of cost and net realizable value. The aggregate net realizable value of the inventory was FC100,000,000 at August 31, Year 5.

4. Prepaid Expenses:

   The amounts, representing prepaid rent and property taxes, were paid when 1FC = $0.26.

5. Plant Assets:

   Plant assets were purchased shortly after the date of SAPI's formation at a time when 1FC = $0.40. The recoverable amount of the fixed assets (in their current condition) was FC200,000,000 at August 31, Year 5.

6. Current Liabilities:

   All current liabilities were incurred at a time when 1FC = $0.25.

7. Long-Term Debt:

   The debt represents a floating interest rate loan, which will be repaid in foreign currency units on August 31, Year 8.

8. Retained Earnings:

   No dividends were paid during the Year 5 fiscal year.

9. Exchange Rates:

   | | |
   |---|---|
   | Sep. 1, Year 4 | 1 FCU = $0.40 |
   | Aug. 31, Year 5 | 1 FCU = $0.20 |
   | Average rate for year | 1 FCU = $0.30 |

*(CPA Canada adapted)*[4]

# Case 11-4

LO5

RAD Communications Ltd. (RAD), a Canadian public company, recently purchased the shares of TOP Systems Inc. (TOP), a Canadian-controlled private corporation. Both companies are in the communications industry and own television, radio, and magazine and newspaper businesses. Both companies have subsidiaries operating worldwide.

After it purchased TOP, RAD decided to divest itself of some of the TOP subsidiaries (the Group). BritCo is a private British company that is in the process of acquiring the shares of the Group from TOP. The purchase price for the Group being sold has been determined, in general terms, to be a fixed price adjusted for the working capital balance of the Group at RAD's year-end date of March 31, Year 9. March 31, Year 9, was also the closing date of the purchase-and-sale transaction. The parties have 90 days after the closing date of the transaction to agree on the calculation of the working capital balance.

Janis Marczynski, the chief negotiator for BritCo, has approached Paul Bouchard, a partner at Bouchard and Beatrix, Chartered Professional Accountants (B&B), to provide her with advice on the purchase transaction. Specifically, Marczynski wants B&B to review the agreement and relevant facts to determine whether RAD has appropriately determined the amount of the closing working capital. Furthermore, if any matters come to B&B's attention that suggest the financial statements of the Group may have misled BritCo, then B&B should bring these items to her attention.

Marczynski has stated that BritCo now thinks that the purchase price for the Group may be too high and is looking for ways to reduce the price. Thus, she wants to be made aware of any possible points that she can use in her final negotiations.

BritCo has provided B&B with a copy of the purchase-and-sale agreement, excerpts of which are presented in Exhibit III.

It is now May 15, Year 9, and BritCo has received the unaudited consolidated working capital statement of the Group prepared by RAD (Exhibit IV). Marczynski is concerned about the dramatic increase in the working capital compared with that reflected in previous financial statements.

RAD has arranged for Jeanette Riley, Chartered Professional Accountant (JR), the auditor of TOP's financial statements for the year in question, to supply the necessary working papers to assist B&B in its review. JR will provide B&B with her working papers once they have completed their audit for Year 9. RAD has already provided B&B with excerpts of JR's working papers for Year 8, reproduced in Exhibit V, copies of which TOP had obtained informally from the audit staff during the course of the audit.

You, a CPA, work for B&B. Bouchard asks you to draft a memo addressing the concerns and requirements of Marczynski.

---

**EXHIBIT III**

## Top Systems Inc. (Vendor) and Britco (Purchaser)—Excerpts from Purchase-and-Sale Agreement

5.1. The share purchase price shall be adjusted by an amount equal to the "consolidated working capital." This amount is hereafter referred to as the "price adjustment," as defined in clause 5.2.

5.2. The price adjustment shall be determined as follows:

　　a. Combine the working capital of the Group (aggregated current assets of the Group less aggregated current liabilities of the Group), less the non-controlling interest as at March 31, Year 9, adjusted for any sums payable to or receivable from other members of the Group.

*(continued)*

**EXHIBIT III** *(continued)*

b. Include accounts for each of the companies of the Group and, in the case of those companies with subsidiaries, on a consolidated basis, in accordance with IFRS.

5.3. The vendor shall prepare a draft consolidated working capital statement as soon as practicable after the agreement date.

5.4. For the purpose of review, the vendor agrees to instruct JR to permit the purchaser to examine all final working papers, schedules, and other documents used or prepared by JR.

5.5. If the purchaser objects to the calculation of the price adjustment, the purchaser shall give notice in writing to the vendor. The purchaser shall set out in reasonable detail the nature of any such objections and the amount by which the purchase price will be reduced if the purchaser's objections are accepted. The vendor shall have the right to recover from the purchaser any costs associated with reviewing and analyzing objections of the purchaser that are of a frivolous and unsupportable nature.

**EXHIBIT IV**

**CONSOLIDATED WORKING CAPITAL STATEMENT OF THE GROUP (NOTE 1)**
At March 31, Year 9
(in millions of Canadian dollars)

| | |
|---|---:|
| Current assets: | |
| Cash | $ 215 |
| Receivables | 19,763 |
| Inventory | 4,225 |
| Prepaids | 7,655 |
| Other | 2,917 |
| | 34,775 |
| Current liabilities: | |
| Bank indebtedness | 7,000 |
| Accounts payable | 1,191 |
| Deferred revenue | 6,332 |
| Other | 1,345 |
| | 15,868 |
| Consolidated working capital (price adjustment) | $18,907 |

Note 1: Comprises the accounts of the companies being sold, i.e., GermanyCo., FranceCo., U.K.Co., SwitzerlandCo., and a Canadian subsidiary, CanadaCo.

**EXHIBIT V**

## Excerpts from the Working Papers of JR Relating to the Audit of Top Systems Inc. and Its Subsidiaries for the Year 8 Fiscal Period

1. Only selected subsidiaries of TOP were audited. Those companies were audited on a limited basis only, owing to the consolidated materiality level.

2. Included in the "Receivables" balance of FranceCo. is an intercompany note receivable from a Canadian company that is not part of the Group. The note bears interest at the prime rate in Canada plus 3%. The rate charged on the note was generally about 4% below interest rates on French notes of similar terms and risks at the time that the note was issued. The Canadian company has recorded the note as a long-term obligation.

*(continued)*

3. "Other current assets" include an amount reflecting the refundable dividend tax on hand (RDTOH). The amount of the RDTOH was immaterial; thus, no audit work in this area was warranted.

4. Included in the "Receivables" balance are certain income tax refunds that GermanyCo. will receive when dividends are paid to its shareholders. No accruals are made for foreign withholding taxes that may be payable when dividends are paid by GermanyCo.

5. "Other current assets" include an amount for goodwill. This goodwill relates to the acquisition of a subsidiary by CanadaCo.

6. "Deferred revenues" include payments made by advertisers for long-term contracts. Some of these contracts can be for up to five years. Some advertisers pay up-front signing fees, which are taken into income when received. Some advertisers who sign up for long-term contracts may receive one additional year of free advertising. Advertisers can elect to take this free year at the beginning or at the end of the contract term.

7. "Prepaids" include costs for various broadcasting licences. The accounts include the initial costs of obtaining the licences, such as various regulatory fees, legal and accounting fees, other consulting fees, etc., and various fees for limited-term licences, ranging from one- to ten-year periods.

8. Certain printing presses of SwitzerlandCo. were leased instead of being purchased. The future lease payments were not disclosed in the consolidated financial statements. The lease was immaterial and thus did not warrant any further audit work.

9. A Belgian company that is not being acquired effectively hedged certain current debts payable by CanadaCo. The financial statements did not record any gain or loss because of the fluctuations in the value of the Canadian dollar.

10. Foreign exchange losses on transactions were included as part of "Deferred revenue," while gains were taken into income in the current period.

*(CPA Canada adapted)*[5]

# Case 11-5

LO4

Mega Communications Inc. (MCI) is a Canadian-owned public company operating throughout North America. Its core business is communications media, including newspapers, radio, television, and cable. The company's year-end is December 31.

You, a CPA, have recently joined MCI's corporate office as a finance director, reporting to the chief financial officer, Robert Allen. It is October Year 3.

MCI's growth in Year 3 was achieved through expansion into the United States by acquiring a controlling interest in a number of newspapers, television, and cable companies. Since the U.S. side of MCI's operations is now significant, management has decided to change the reporting currency from the Canadian dollar to the U.S. dollar for MCI's consolidated financial statements.

MCI uses the Canadian dollar for its internal record keeping and to account for its Canadian operations. All of MCI's foreign subsidiaries, which are all wholly owned, use the local currency for internal record keeping and for reporting purposes. MCI's shareholders' equity at the beginning of the period was $220 million, including a separately disclosed cumulative foreign exchange gain of $45 million primarily relating to its U.S. subsidiaries. Management merged this balance with retained earnings because "the operations it relates to are no longer considered foreign for accounting purposes, and as a result, no foreign currency exposure will arise."

With recent trends to international free trade, MCI decided to position itself for future expansion into the South American market. Therefore, in Year 3, MCI bought a company that owns a radio network in a country in South America, which has high inflation. MCI was willing to incur losses in the start-up, since it was confident that in the long run it would be profitable. The South American country has had a democratic government for the last two years. Its government's objectives are to open the country's borders to trade and lower its inflation rate. The government was rather reluctant to let a foreign company purchase such a powerful communication tool. In exchange for the right to buy the network, MCI agreed, among other conditions, not to promote any political party, to broadcast only pre-approved public messages, and to let the government examine its books at the government's convenience. Management has recorded this investment on the books using the cost method.

In Year 3, MCI acquired a conglomerate, Cyril's Holdings (CH), which held substantial assets in the communications business. Over the past three months, MCI has sold off 80% of CH's non-communications-related businesses. In the current month, MCI sold CH's hotel and recreational property business for $175 million, realizing a gain of $22 million ($14.5 million after tax). The assets related to the non-communications businesses were scattered throughout the U.S. and MCI lacked the industry expertise to value them accurately. Management therefore found it difficult to determine the net realizable value of each of these assets at the time CH was acquired.

Newspaper readership has peaked leaving no room for expansion. In Year 2, to increase its share of the market, MCI bought all the assets of a competing newspaper for $10 million. In Year 3, MCI ceased publication of the competing newspaper and liquidated the assets for $4.5 million.

In Year 3, MCI decided to rationalize its television operations. Many of CH's acquisitions in the television business included stations in areas already being served by other stations operated by MCI. MCI systematically identified stations that are duplicating services and do not fit with MCI's long-range objectives. These assets have been segregated on the balance sheet and classified as current. The company anticipates generating a gain on the disposal of the entire pool of assets, although losses are expected on some of the individual stations. Operating results are capitalized in the pool. Once a particular station is sold, the resulting gain or loss is reflected in income.

Nine stations are in the pool at the present time. In Year 3, three were sold, resulting in gains of $6.5 million after tax. Losses are expected to occur on several of the remaining stations. Although serious negotiations with prospective buyers are not underway at present, the company hopes to have disposed of them in early Year 4. In order to facilitate the sale of these assets, MCI is considering taking back mortgages.

In Year 3, MCI estimated the fair market value of its intangible assets at $250 million. Included, as intangibles, are newspaper and magazine circulation lists, cable subscriber lists, and broadcast licences. Some of these assets have been acquired through the purchase of existing businesses; others have been generated internally by operations that have been part of MCI for decades.

Amounts paid for acquired intangibles are not difficult to determine; however, it has taken MCI staff some time to determine the costs of internally generated intangibles. In order to increase subscriptions for print and electronic media, MCI spends heavily on subscription drives by way of advertisements, cold calls, and free products. For the non-acquired intangibles, MCI staff has examined the accounting records for the past 10 years and have identified expenditures totalling $35 million that were expensed in prior years. These costs relate to efforts to expand customer bases. In addition, independent appraisers have determined the fair market value of these internally generated intangibles to be in the range of $60 million to $80 million. In order to be conservative, management has decided to reflect these intangibles on the December 31, Year 3, balance sheet at $60 million.

The market value of companies in the communications industry has been escalating in the past few years, indicating that the value of the underlying assets (largely intangibles) is increasing over time. MCI management would prefer not to amortize broadcasting licences, arguing that these licences do not lose any value and, in this industry, actually increase in value over time.

One of the items included in the intangible category is MCI's patented converter, which was an unplanned by-product of work being done on satellite communications devices a few years ago.

MCI has sold $25 million of its accounts receivables to a medium-sized financial intermediary, PayLater Corp. The receivables are being resold to a numbered company whose common shares are owned by PayLater Corp. MCI receives one half of the consideration in cash and one half in subordinate non-voting, redeemable shares of the numbered company, bearing a dividend rate of 9%. The dividend payments and share redemption are based on the collectibility of the receivables. The purchase price is net of a 4% provision for doubtful accounts. MCI has recorded a loss of $1 million on this transaction. PayLater has an option to return the receivables to MCI at any time for 94% of their face value.

The arrival of direct broadcast satellite that transmits multiple TV signals to digital boxes will revolutionize the television industry. The technology is expected to provide the choice of over 150 channels. In response to this new development, which is seen as a threat, the communication industry is developing its own interactive communication services at a cost of over $6 billion. This service will allow viewers to interact with banks, shops, and other viewers through the television. MCI hopes this will allow it to maintain its market share of viewers.

MCI has invested in the installation of fibre optic cable, which can transmit far more, far faster than conventional cable. The cost of the cable itself is negligible. MCI will be using it for transmission between its stations in two major Canadian cities. MCI needed only six cables to link all its television and radio stations between the two cities, but decided that it might as well put in 36 cables, since it was doing the digging anyway. To date, MCI has sold six cables and charges a monthly fee to new owners to cover their share of all maintenance expenses. MCI is leasing 10 other cables for 15 year periods.

MCI's CFO, Mr. Allen, has asked you to prepare a report that discusses the accounting issues that might arise with the auditors during their visit in November.

*(CPA Canada adapted)*[6]

## Case 11-6

LO3

Foreign Infants Adoption Inc. (FIA) is a consulting company wholly owned by Roger Tremblay, a wealthy, recently retired lawyer. FIA helps Canadian families adopt infants from other countries. Typically, these infants have been abandoned or have lost their parents to disease or war, and are being sheltered in government-sponsored orphanages. Further information on the activities of FIA can be found in Exhibit VI.

FIA is a full-service coordinator, helping parents with all aspects of the international adoption process (Exhibit VII). The company charges a fee to cover the costs associated with the adoption process and its consulting service. FIA is required to be registered as an international adoption coordinator with the Canadian government, and as such must follow certain criteria set out by Citizenship and Immigration Canada (CIC).

Effective July 1, Year 7, CIC now requires all registered coordinators to submit audited financial statements in accordance with IFRS, and to hold fees collected in trust on behalf of the parents. The fees requirement also applies to all adoptions already in process. Throughout the adoption process, FIA can only withdraw funds from the trust to pay for adoption-related expenses. Once an adoption has been finalized, FIA can withdraw the remaining funds.

FIA's financial statements have never been audited or reviewed. The company relies on the services of a full-time bookkeeper to complete its internal financial statements. The financial statements for the most recently completed year are presented in Exhibit VIII, and additional information is presented in Exhibit IX.

It is August 15, Year 8, and you are a CPA with the firm of Mitton Horne McKnight Chartered Professional Accountants (MHM). The partner on the engagement, Kate Horne, has asked you to address the accounting issues for the FIA engagement.

## EXHIBIT VI

## Further Information on the Operations of FIA

The international adoption process can be daunting. FIA managers assist potential adoptive parents with every step of the process, from the initial application through to the post-adoption report. Managers also travel with parents to the countries where the adoptions take place, usually in groups of 10 families or fewer. Adoptive parents must cover their own travel expenses.

Upon signing a contract, FIA charges a flat fee of $25,000, regardless of which country the parents adopt from. This fee pays all costs related to the adoption (averaging $20,000), and must also cover FIA's administrative and overhead costs.

The following are the countries FIA supports through its international adoption assistance programs, and the number of adoptive families currently awaiting child proposals from each country:

| Country | Pending Child Proposals |
|---|---|
| China | 68 |
| India | 58 |
| Pakistan | 47 |
| Ethiopia | 40 |
| Sudan | 38 |
| Haiti | 10 |
| Philippines | 8 |
| | 269 |

Due to local hostilities and the deteriorating relationship between the Sudanese and Canadian governments, Sudan recently announced that they will not permit adoptions by Canadian residents after October 1, Year 8.

To replace the number of adoptions FIA will lose as a result of the decision made by the Sudanese government, the company is considering expanding its list to include countries like Vietnam, Cambodia, and Afghanistan. However, FIA does not have experience with these countries, or any formal criteria for determining whether a country should be added, so the managers are not sure how they should proceed.

## EXHIBIT VII

## International Adoption Process

Several steps must be completed in order to adopt a child from a foreign country. While the steps vary slightly between countries, the adoption process is similar.

1. *Adoption application.* The adoptive parents complete an application in the format prescribed by the foreign authorities. A social worker performs a home assessment to ensure the applicants would be suitable parents for international adoption. The social worker prepares a report and forwards it to the foreign authorities. There is a long waiting period (anywhere from 6 to 24 months) before the adoptive parents receive a proposal from the foreign country.

*(continued)*

2. *Child proposal/acceptance.* The foreign authorities propose a child for adoption. The adoptive parents must indicate within 48 hours whether they accept the proposed child.
3. *Adoption finalization.* About four weeks after the Child Proposal is accepted, the parents travel to the country to finalize the adoption. This includes paying legal fees, a mandatory orphanage donation, a medical examination fee, and other government fees. Typically this step takes between 10 and 12 days.
4. *Post-adoption reports.* Foreign countries require a progress report six months after adoption in order to ensure the child's well-being. The one-page report must be prepared by a social worker.

**Direct Adoption-Related Costs**

Although the costs can vary significantly between countries, the estimated average adoption-related costs are as follows:

| | |
|---|---:|
| Adoption application (includes home assessment report) | $ 4,100 |
| Accommodation, airfare, and other travel costs for FIA staff only | 3,500 |
| Legal and court costs in foreign country | 3,200 |
| Mandatory donation to orphanage | 4,000 |
| Medical examination in foreign country | 900 |
| Other foreign government fees | 4,300 |
| | $20,000 |

**EXHIBIT VIII**

## FOREIGN INFANTS ADOPTION INC.
### BALANCE SHEET
As at June 30
(unaudited)

| | Year 8 | Year 7 |
|---|---:|---:|
| **Assets** | | |
| Current assets: | | |
| Cash | $2,097,474 | $2,002,308 |
| Accounts receivable | 125,657 | 76,904 |
| Prepaid insurance | 35,500 | 26,575 |
| | 2,258,631 | 2,105,787 |
| Capital assets | 127,768 | 123,459 |
| | $2,386,399 | $2,229,246 |
| **Liabilities** | | |
| Current liabilities: | | |
| Accounts payable and accrued liabilities | $ 391,062 | $ 358,131 |
| Wages payable | 43,567 | 35,678 |
| Other current liabilities | 170,968 | 164,298 |
| | 605,597 | 558,107 |
| Shareholder loan | 400,000 | 400,000 |
| **Shareholder's Equity** | | |
| Common shares | 100 | 100 |
| Retained earnings | 1,380,702 | 1,271,039 |
| | 1,380,802 | 1,271,139 |
| | $2,386,399 | $2,229,246 |

*(continued)*

**EXHIBIT VIII** *(continued)*

**FOREIGN INFANTS ADOPTION INC.**
**INCOME STATEMENT**
For the years ended June 30
(unaudited)

| | Year 8 | Year 7 |
|---|---|---|
| Revenue: | | |
| Adoption fees | $5,912,500 | $5,467,500 |
| Interest and other | 20,542 | 18,674 |
| | 5,933,042 | 5,486,174 |
| Expenses: | | |
| Adoption application fee | 1,027,915 | 965,830 |
| Travel costs | 765,745 | 726,706 |
| Legal and court costs | 675,420 | 660,398 |
| Mandatory orphanage donations | 827,600 | 796,500 |
| Medical examinations | 189,675 | 175,678 |
| Miscellaneous foreign government fees | 965,405 | 1,005,345 |
| Administrative wages and benefits | 485,672 | 421,876 |
| Foreign country assistants' wages | 250,224 | 345,698 |
| China subsidiary operations (Exhibit X) | 267,985 | — |
| Rent | 145,985 | 154,325 |
| Other expenses | 182,320 | 170,986 |
| | 5,783,946 | 5,423,342 |
| Income before tax | 149,096 | 62,832 |
| Income tax | 39,433 | 16,789 |
| Net income | $ 109,663 | $ 46,043 |

**EXHIBIT IX**

## Additional Information on the Financial Statements

At June 30, Year 7, 242 adoptive families were awaiting a Child Proposal. FIA completed 203 adoptions during the fiscal year. At June 30, Year 8, 269 adoptive families were in the adoption process, and all of them were awaiting a Child Proposal.

FIA records revenue when payments are due from adoptive parents. Half of the total payment is due up front (with the adoption application) and the remaining half is due one month prior to travel. Accounts receivable at June 30, Year 8, represent fees not yet received for a trip to China in late July Year 8. All amounts were eventually collected.

FIA records an expense when it receives the invoice. In the absence of an invoice, the expense is recorded when paid. Certain countries require cash payments, for miscellaneous costs such as orphanage donations, so FIA maintains bank accounts or similar facilities in all the countries to which it travels so staff can quickly obtain cash in local currencies. Most cash payments are provided on the same day that the adoptive parents take charge of the infant. Payments are usually due in local currencies or US dollars.

None of the parents awaiting an adoption from Sudan have asked for a refund yet, and FIA hopes they will try to adopt from another country. These parents will need to go through the adoption process again, potentially all the way back to the initial application.

The $25,000 fee has been sufficient to cover FIA's minimal costs and allow the operations to continue. Roger has not focused on the detailed financial information, and really only monitors the financial affairs to ensure there is enough money available to pay the bills. He does not know the detailed costs for each country.

## EXHIBIT X

## China Subsidiary Operations

During fiscal Year 8, FIA incorporated a wholly owned subsidiary in Beijing, China, to deal with administration issues in China. The company maintains an office in Beijing that employs one full-time person. It holds a bank account, and receives funds from FIA for expenditures made in China. A summary of the expenditures made in fiscal Year 8 is as follows (amounts are in Chinese yuan):

| | |
|---|---:|
| Accommodation, airfare, and other travel costs for FIA staff only | ¥ 763,125 |
| Legal and court costs | 331,210 |
| Required donations to orphanages | 436,534 |
| Medical examinations | 101,567 |
| Miscellaneous government fees | 142,908 |
| Wages and benefits | 135,596 |
| Rent | 35,768 |
| Furniture, fixtures, and computers | 156,784 |
| Total expenditures in Chinese yuan | ¥2,103,492 |
| Exchange rate at June 30, Year 8 | 0.1274 |
| Total expenditures in Canadian dollars | $ 267,985 |

*(CPA Canada)*[7]

# PROBLEMS

*Note:* Some problems use direct exchange rate quotations, while others use indirect quotations. For direct quotations, the foreign currency is multiplied by the exchange rate to arrive at Canadian dollars; for indirect quotations, division is used.

## Problem 11-1

LO3, 4, 6

On December 31, Year 1, Precision Manufacturing Inc. (PMI) of Edmonton purchased 100% of the outstanding ordinary shares of Sandora Corp. of Flint, Michigan.

Sandora's comparative statement of financial position and Year 2 income statement are as follows:

### STATEMENT OF FINANCIAL POSITION
At December 31

| | Year 2 | Year 1 |
|---|---:|---:|
| Plant and equipment (net) | US$ 6,600,000 | US$ 7,300,000 |
| Inventory | 5,700,000 | 6,300,000 |
| Accounts receivable | 6,100,000 | 4,700,000 |
| Cash | 780,000 | 900,000 |
| | US$19,180,000 | US$19,200,000 |
| Ordinary shares | US$ 5,000,000 | US$ 5,000,000 |
| Retained earnings | 7,480,000 | 7,000,000 |
| Bonds payable—due Dec. 31, Year 6 | 4,800,000 | 4,800,000 |
| Current liabilities | 1,900,000 | 2,400,000 |
| | US$19,180,000 | US$19,200,000 |

**INCOME STATEMENT**

For the year ended December 31, Year 2

| | |
|---|---:|
| Sales | US$30,000,000 |
| Cost of purchases | 23,400,000 |
| Change in inventory | 600,000 |
| Depreciation expense | 700,000 |
| Other expenses | 3,800,000 |
| | 28,500,000 |
| Profit | US$ 1,500,000 |

### Additional Information

- Exchange rates

| | |
|---|---|
| Dec. 31, Year 1 | US$1 = CDN$1.10 |
| Sep. 30, Year 2 | US$1 = CDN$1.07 |
| Dec. 31, Year 2 | US$1 = CDN$1.05 |
| Average for Year 2 | US$1 = CDN$1.08 |

- Sandora declared and paid dividends on September 30, Year 2.

- The inventories on hand on December 31, Year 2, were purchased when the exchange rate was US$1 = CDN$1.06.

### Required

(a) Assume that Sandora's functional currency is the Canadian dollar:
   (i) Calculate the Year 2 exchange gain (loss) that would result from the translation of Sandora's financial statements.
   (ii) Translate the Year 2 financial statements into Canadian dollars.

(b) Assume that Sandora's functional currency is the U.S. dollar:
   (i) Calculate the Year 2 exchange gain (loss) that would result from the translation of Sandora's financial statements and would be reported in other comprehensive income.
   (ii) Translate the Year 2 financial statements into Canadian dollars.

(c) Which functional currency would Sandora prefer to use if it wants to show the following?
   (i) The strongest solvency position for the company
   (ii) The best return on shareholders' equity

   Briefly explain your answers.

## Problem 11-2

LO3, 4

Refer to Problem 11-1. All of the facts and data given in the problem are the same except that PMI only purchased 40% of the outstanding ordinary shares of Sandora for US$6,400,000.

### Additional Information

- PMI's 40% in Sandora gave it significant influence over Sandora's key operating and financial policies.

- PMI uses the equity method to account for its investment in Sandora.

- The carrying amounts of Sandora's net assets were equal to fair values on December 31, Year 1, except for the manufacturing plant which had a fair value in excess of carrying amount of US$600,000 and a remaining useful life of 15 years. A goodwill impairment loss of US$500,000 on PMI's 40% share of Sandora's goodwill occurred evenly throughout Year 12.

**Required**

(a) Assume that Sandora's functional currency is the Canadian dollar. Using the translated financial statements prepared in Problem 11-1 part (a), prepare PMI's journal entries pertaining to its investment in Sandora account for Years 1 and 2.

(a) Assume that Sandora's functional currency is the US dollar. Using the translated financial statements prepared in Problem 11-1 part (b), prepare PMI's journal entries pertaining to its investment in Sandora account for Years 1 and 2.

## Problem 11-3

LO3, 4, 6

On December 31, Year 1, Kelly Corporation of Toronto paid 13.7 million Libyan dinars (LD) for 100% of the outstanding common shares of Arkenu Company of Libya. On this date, the fair values of Arkenu's identifiable assets and liabilities were equal to their carrying amounts. Arkenu's comparative balance sheets and Year 2 income statement are as follows:

### BALANCE SHEET
At December 31

|  | Year 2 | Year 1 |
|---|---|---|
| Current monetary assets | LD11,361,000 | LD 9,670,000 |
| Inventory | 1,898,000 | 2,421,000 |
| Plant and equipment (net) | 6,957,000 | 7,363,000 |
|  | LD20,216,000 | LD19,454,000 |
| Current monetary liabilities | LD 2,005,000 | LD 2,433,000 |
| Bonds payable, due Dec. 31, Year 6 | 4,870,000 | 4,870,000 |
| Common shares | 5,070,000 | 5,070,000 |
| Retained earnings | 8,271,000 | 7,081,000 |
|  | LD20,216,000 | LD19,454,000 |

### INCOME STATEMENT
For the year ended December 31, Year 2

| | |
|---|---|
| Sales | LD16,206,000 |
| Inventory, Jan. 1 | 2,421,000 |
| Purchases | 10,938,000 |
| Inventory, Dec. 31 | (1,898,000) |
| Depreciation expense | 406,000 |
| Other expenses | 1,598,000 |
|  | 13,465,000 |
| Net income | LD 2,741,000 |

## Additional Information

- Exchange rates

| | |
|---|---|
| Dec. 31, Year 1 | LD1 = $0.52 |
| Sep. 30, Year 2 | LD1 = $0.62 |
| Dec. 31, Year 2 | LD1 = $0.65 |
| Average for Year 2 | LD1 = $0.58 |

- Arkenu Company declared and paid dividends on September 30, Year 2.

- The inventories on hand on December 31, Year 2, were purchased when the exchange rate was LD1 = $0.63.

## Required

(a) Assume that Arkenu's functional currency is the Canadian dollar:

   (i) Calculate the Year 2 exchange gain or loss that would result from the translation of Arkenu's financial statements.

   (ii) Prepare translated financial statements for Year 2.

(b) Assume that Arkenu's functional currency is the Libyan dinar:

   (i) Calculate the Year 2 exchange gain or loss that would result from the translation of Arkenu's financial statements.

   (ii) Prepare translated financial statements for Year 2.

   (iii) Calculate the amount of goodwill that would appear on the December 31, Year 2, consolidated balance sheet if there was an impairment loss of LD50,000 during the year.

   (iv) Calculate the amount, description, and location of the exchange gain or loss that would appear in Kelly's Year 2 consolidated financial statements.

(c) Which functional currency would Arkenu prefer to use if it wants to show the following?

   (i) The strongest solvency position for the company

   (ii) The best return on shareholders' equity

   Briefly explain your answers.

# Problem 11-4

LO3, 4, 5

Refer to Problem 11-3. All of the facts and data given in the problem are the same. Your answer to Problem 11-3 will be incorporated in the answer to this problem.

   Kelly Corporation's comparative balance sheets and Year 2 income statement are as follows:

**BALANCE SHEET**
At December 31

| | Year 2 | Year 1 |
|---|---|---|
| Current monetary assets | C$27,472,000 | C$26,780,000 |
| Inventory | 2,909,000 | 3,532,000 |
| Investment in Arkenu—at cost | 7,124,000 | 7,124,000 |
| Plant and equipment (net) | 13,644,000 | 13,939,000 |
| | C$51,149,000 | C$51,375,000 |

## BALANCE SHEET
### At December 31

| | Year 2 | Year 1 |
|---|---|---|
| Current monetary liabilities | C$12,006,000 | C$12,582,000 |
| Bonds payable, due Dec. 31, Year 7 | 15,980,000 | 15,980,000 |
| Common shares | 10,000,000 | 10,000,000 |
| Retained earnings | 13,163,000 | 12,813,000 |
| | C$51,149,000 | C$51,375,000 |

## INCOME STATEMENT
### For the year ended December 31, Year 2

| | |
|---|---|
| Sales | C$ 46,317,000 |
| Dividend income from Arkenu | 961,620 |
| | 47,278,620 |
| Inventory, Jan. 1 | 3,532,000 |
| Purchases | 30,817,000 |
| Inventory, Dec. 31 | (2,909,000) |
| Depreciation expense | 717,000 |
| Other expenses | 12,887,000 |
| | 45,044,000 |
| Net income | C$ 2,234,620 |

## Additional Information

- Exchange rates

| | |
|---|---|
| Dec. 31, Year 1 | C$1 = US$0.84 |
| Sep. 30, Year 2 | C$1 = US$0.82 |
| Dec. 31, Year 2 | C$1 = US$0.80 |
| Average for Year 2 | C$1 = US$0.83 |

- Kelly Corporation declared and paid dividends on September 30, Year 2.

- The inventories on hand on December 31, Year 2, were purchased when the exchange rate was C$1 = US$0.81.

- The recoverable amount of Arkenu's goodwill increased during Year 2.

- The Canadian dollar is the functional currency for both Kelly Corporation and Arkenu Company.

## Required

(a) Prepare Kelly Corporation's consolidated financial statements for Year 2 using the Canadian dollar as the presentation currency.

(b) Prepare Kelly Corporation's consolidated financial statements for Year 2 using the US dollar as the presentation currency. (*Hints:* Start with your answer to part (a). Then, use the PCT method to convert to the US dollar. When eliminating the investment account, part of the entry should go to OCI.)

 (c) Prepare the consolidated financial statements using the worksheet approach for the two presentation currencies above.

## Problem 11-5

LO2, 3

EVA Company was incorporated on January 2, Year 5, and commenced active operations immediately. Ordinary shares were issued on the date of incorporation and no new ordinary shares have been issued since then. On December 31, Year 9, PAL Company purchased 70% of the outstanding ordinary shares of the EVA for 1.5 million euros (€).

EVA's main operations are located in Germany. It manufactures and sells German equipment throughout Europe. PAL acquired control over EVA so that it could utilize EVA's extensive distribution network. EVA continued to manufacture and sell German equipment. However, it also purchases and sells equipment manufactured by PAL in Canada. EVA has 90 days to pay for its purchases from PAL. During this time, EVA is usually able to resell the equipment in Europe and collect the receivables. EVA did not have to hire additional sales people to sell the product. It built a new distribution centre in Frankfurt. This facility was financed with retained earnings from EVA Company.

For the year ending December 31, Year 13, the condensed income statement for EVA was as follows:

**EVA COMPANY**
**CONDENSED INCOME STATEMENT**
Year ended December 31, Year 13

| | |
|---|---:|
| Sales and other revenue | €4,250,000 |
| Cost of goods sold | 2,000,000 |
| Depreciation expense | 150,000 |
| Loss on decline in value of inventory | 25,000 |
| Other expenses | 1,825,000 |
| Total expenses | 4,000,000 |
| Net income | € 250,000 |

The condensed balance sheet for EVA was as follows:

**EVA COMPANY**
**BALANCE SHEET**
At December 31, Year 13

| | |
|---|---:|
| Inventory (Note 1) | € 300,000 |
| Property, plant, and equipment—net (Note 2) | 1,800,000 |
| Other assets | 2,500,000 |
| Total assets | €4,600,000 |
| Unearned revenue (Note 3) | € 295,000 |
| Other monetary liabilities | 2,500,000 |
| Ordinary shares | 100,000 |
| Retained earnings | 1,705,000 |
| Total | €4,600,000 |

### Additional Information:

1.  At December 31, Year 12, inventory was €280,000. The inventory at the end of Year 12 and Year 13 was purchased evenly throughout the last month of each year. The inventory at December 31, Year 13, had cost EVA €325,000 but had been written down to its net realizable value of €300,000. Purchases and sales of inventory occurred evenly throughout the year.

2.  EVA purchased its property, plant and equipment on March 17, Year 9. There were no purchases or sales of property, plant, and equipment since March 17, Year 9.

3. The unearned revenue represents non-refundable deposits received from customers evenly throughout the last quarter of the year.

4. Foreign exchange rates were as follows:

| | |
|---|---|
| January 2, Year 5 | €1 = $1.50 |
| March 17, Year 9 | €1 = $1.45 |
| December 31, Year 9 | €1 = $1.44 |
| Average for Year 12 | €1 = $1.35 |
| Average for quarter 4 for Year 12 | €1 = $1.34 |
| Average for December Year 12 | €1 = $1.32 |
| December 31, Year 12 | €1 = $1.30 |
| Average for Year 13 | €1 = $1.28 |
| Average for quarter 4 for Year 13 | €1 = $1.27 |
| Average for December Year 13 | €1 = $1.26 |
| December 31, Year 13 | €1 = $1.25 |

## Required

(a) Provide two facts from EVA's situation that would indicate that EVA's functional currency is the Canadian dollar and two facts from EVA's situation that would indicate that EVA's functional currency is the euro.

(b) Assuming that EVA's functional currency is the Canadian dollar, calculate the Canadian dollar amount for the following items on EVA's translated financial statements:
   (i)   Cost of goods sold for the year ended December 31, Year 13
   (ii)  Depreciation expense for the year ended December 31, Year 13
   (iii) Inventory at end of year Year 13
   (iv)  Unearned revenue at end of year Year 13
   (v)   Ordinary shares at end of year Year 13

(c) Assume that foreign exchange gains (losses) for Year 13 would be $125,000 of gains under the FCT method and $85,000 in losses under the PCT method. Explain the main reason that would cause the difference in the foreign exchange gains/losses between the two methods. Explain how one method could report a gain, whereas the other method would report a loss for the same situation.

*(CGA Canada adapted)*[8]

# Problem 11-6

......................

LO3, 4, 5

On January 1, Year 4, P Company (a Canadian company) purchased 90% of S Company (located in a foreign country) at a cost of 15,580 foreign currency units (FC).

The carrying amounts of S Company's net assets were equal to fair values on this date except for plant and equipment, which had a fair value of FC22,000, with a remaining useful life of 10 years. A goodwill impairment loss of FC100 occurred evenly throughout Year 4.

The following exchange rates were in effect during Year 4:

| | |
|---|---|
| Jan. 1 | FC1 = $1.10 |
| Average for year | FC1 = $1.16 |
| When ending inventory purchased | FC1 = $1.19 |
| Dec. 31 | FC1 = $1.22 |

The statement of financial position of S Company on January 1, Year 4, is as follows:

|  | S Company (FC) |
|---|---|
| Plant and equipment (net) | 20,000 |
| Inventory | 9,100 |
| Monetary assets (current) | 11,100 |
|  | 40,200 |
| Ordinary shares | 10,000 |
| Retained earnings | 3,650 |
| Bonds payable (mature in eight years) | 16,000 |
| Current liabilities | 10,550 |
|  | 40,200 |

The December 31, Year 4, financial statements of P Company (in $) and S Company (in FC) are shown below:

**STATEMENT OF FINANCIAL POSITION**

|  | P Company ($) | S Company (FC) |
|---|---|---|
| Plant and equipment (net) | 68,800 | 18,000 |
| Investment in S Company (at cost) | 17,138 | — |
| Inventory | 34,400 | 12,100 |
| Monetary assets (current) | 31,552 | 19,200 |
|  | 151,890 | 49,300 |
| Ordinary shares | 34,400 | 10,000 |
| Retained earnings | 47,900 | 9,750 |
| Bonds payable | 46,500 | 16,000 |
| Current monetary liabilities | 23,090 | 13,550 |
|  | 151,890 | 49,300 |

**INCOME STATEMENT**

|  | P Company ($) | S Company (FC) |
|---|---|---|
| Sales | 411,800 | 210,000 |
| Dividend income | 4,502 | — |
| Cost of sales | (206,400) | (132,600) |
| Other expenses (including depreciation) | (178,100) | (67,200) |
| Profit | 31,802 | 10,200 |

Dividends were declared on December 31, Year 4, in the amount of $23,200 by P Company and FC4,100 by S Company.

**Required**

(a) Prepare the December 31, Year 4, consolidated financial statements, assuming that S Company's functional currency is each of the following:
   (i)  The Canadian dollar
   (ii) The foreign currency unit

(b) Now assume that P Company is a private company. It uses ASPE and has chosen to use the equity method to report its investment in S Company. Calculate the balance in the investment account at December 31, Year 4, assuming that S Company's functional currency is the Canadian dollar.

 (c) Prepare the consolidated financial statements using the worksheet approach for the two scenarios for functional currency.

# Problem 11-7

LO3, 4, 5

Athena Ltd. is a subsidiary located in Greece. It uses the euro for internal reporting purposes. At December 31, Year 11, the company's inventory on hand had a cost of €20,000 and a net realizable value of €21,000. The inventory had been purchased evenly over the last quarter of Year 11. The parent company's inventory on hand at December 31, Year 11, had a cost of $45,000 and a net realizable value of $44,000.

Foreign exchange rates were as follows:

| | |
|---|---|
| Average for Year 11 | €1 = $1.28 |
| Average for quarter 4 for Year 11 | €1 = $1.27 |
| December 31, Year 13 | €1 = $1.20 |

**Required**

(a) At what amount should the inventory be shown on Athena's balance sheet before translation?

(b) At what amount should the inventory be shown on Athena's balance sheet after translation assuming that Athena's functional currency is the
  (i) euro?
  (ii) Canadian dollar?

(c) At what amount should the inventory be shown on the consolidated balance sheet assuming that Athena's functional currency is the
  (i) euro?
  (ii) Canadian dollar?

# Problem 11-8

LO3, 4

Maple Limited (Maple) was incorporated on January 2, Year 1, and commenced active operations immediately in Greece. Common shares were issued on the date of incorporation for 100,000 euros (€), and no more common shares have been issued since then.

On December 31, Year 4, the Oak Company (Oak) purchased 100% of the outstanding common shares of Maple. The balance sheet for Maple at December 31, Year 10, was as follows:

| | |
|---|---|
| Cash | €  100,000 |
| Accounts receivable (Note 1) | 200,000 |
| Inventory (Note 2) | 300,000 |
| Equipment—net (Note 3) | 1,100,000 |
| | €1,700,000 |
| | |
| Accounts payable | €  250,000 |
| Bonds payable (Note 4) | 700,000 |
| Common shares | 100,000 |
| Retained earnings | 650,000 |
| | €1,700,000 |

### Additional Information

- The accounts receivable relate to sales occurring evenly throughout the month of December, Year 10.

- Maple uses the FIFO method to account for its inventory. The inventory available for sale during the year was purchased as follows:

| Date of Purchase | Cost of Purchase | Exchange Rate |
|---|---|---|
| December 31, Year 9 | €100,000 | €1 = $1.56 |
| March 1, Year 10 | 1,000,000 | €1 = $1.60 |
| November 1, Year 10 | 180,000 | €1 = $1.63 |

- The equipment was purchased on May 26, Year 4.

- The bonds were issued on May 26, Year 4, to finance the purchase of the equipment.

- Maple reported net income of €200,000, which was earned evenly throughout the year, and paid dividends of €160,000 on July 1, Year 10.

- Foreign exchange rates were as follows:

| | |
|---|---|
| January 2, Year 1 | €1 = $1.30 |
| May 26, Year 4 | €1 = $1.40 |
| December 31, Year 4 | €1 = $1.42 |
| December 31, Year 9 | €1 = $1.56 |
| July 1, Year 10 | €1 = $1.61 |
| Average for Year 10 | €1 = $1.59 |
| Average for December Year 10 | €1 = $1.64 |
| December 31, Year 10 | €1 = $1.66 |

### Required

(a) Translate the balance sheet of Maple at December 31, Year 10, into Canadian dollars assuming that Maple's functional currency is the Canadian dollar. Assume that the translated balance sheet will be consolidated with Oak's balance sheet. For retained earnings, simply use the amount required to balance your balance sheet.

(b) Calculate the foreign exchange gain or loss on the bonds payable for the year ended December 31, Year 10, and state how it would be reported on the year-end financial statements.

(c) Prepare an independent calculation of the unrealized exchange gains or losses that would be reported in other comprehensive income for Year 10, assuming that Maple's functional currency is the euro.

(d) Since the PCT method uses the closing rate to translate equipment, the translated amount should represent the fair value of the equipment in Canadian dollars. Do you agree or disagree? Briefly explain.

*(CGA Canada adapted)*[9]

## Problem 11-9

LO3, 4, 6

On December 31, Year 2, PAT Inc. of Halifax acquired 90% of the voting shares of Gioco Limited of Italy, for 690,000 euros (€). On the acquisition date, the fair values equalled the carrying amounts for all of Gioco's identifiable assets and liabilities. Selected account balances from Gioco's general ledger on December 31, Year 2, were as follows:

| | |
|---|---:|
| Equipment | € 150,000 |
| Building | 1,350,000 |
| Accumulated amortization | 195,000 |
| Common shares | 600,000 |
| Retained earnings | 96,000 |

Gioco purchased the building and equipment on January 1, Year 1.

The condensed trial balance of Gioco for the year ending December 31, Year 5, was as follows:

| | |
|---|---:|
| Accounts receivable | € 197,000 |
| Inventory | 255,000 |
| Building | 1,350,000 |
| Equipment | 350,000 |
| Cost of goods purchased | 1,080,000 |
| Change in inventory | 120,000 |
| Amortization expense | 130,000 |
| Other expenses | 470,000 |
| Dividends paid | 300,000 |
| Total debits | €4,252,000 |
| Current monetary liabilities | € 682,000 |
| Common shares | 600,000 |
| Retained earnings, beginning | 300,000 |
| Sales | 2,250,000 |
| Accumulated amortization | 420,000 |
| Total credits | €4,252,000 |

## Additional Information

- Gioco's sales, inventory purchases, and other expenses occurred uniformly over the year.

- Gioco's inventory on hand at the end of each year was purchased uniformly over the last quarter. On December 31, Year 4, the inventories totalled €375,000, and on December 31, Year 5, they totalled €255,000.

- On January 1, Year 5, Gioco purchased equipment for €200,000. The equipment has an estimated useful life of eight years and a residual value of €5,000. Gioco uses the double-declining-balance method to calculate amortization expense. There were no other purchases of property, plant, and equipment between Year 2 and Year 5.

- The dividends were declared and paid on January 1, Year 5.

- The exchange rates for the euro and the Canadian dollar were as follows:

| | |
|---|---|
| Jan. 1, Year 1 | $1 = €0.50 |
| Dec. 31, Year 2 | $1 = €0.60 |
| Average for the Year 4 fourth quarter | $1 = €0.68 |
| Dec. 31, Year 4/Jan. 1, Year 5 | $1 = €0.70 |
| Dec. 31, Year 5 | $1 = €0.80 |
| Average for Year 5 | $1 = €0.76 |
| Average for the Year 5 fourth quarter | $1 = €0.79 |

**Required**

(a) Translate into Canadian dollars the following items on Gioco's financial statements for the year ended December 31, Year 5, assuming that Gioco's functional currency is the Canadian dollar:
  - (i) Accounts receivable
  - (ii) Inventory
  - (iii) Equipment
  - (iv) Accumulated amortization
  - (v) Common shares

(b) Translate into Canadian dollars the following items on Gioco's financial statements for the year ended December 31, Year 5, assuming that Gioco's functional currency is the euro:
  - (i) Cost of goods purchased
  - (ii) Amortization expense
  - (iii) Inventory
  - (iv) Common shares

(c) For Gioco, which functional currency would show the strongest current ratio for the company's translated financial statements? Briefly explain.

(d) Prepare an independent calculation of the unrealized exchange gains or losses to be included in other comprehensive income for Year 5, assuming that Gioco's functional currency is the euro.

*(CGA Canada adapted)*[10]

## Problem 11-10

LO2, 3, 4

In Year 1, Victoria Textiles Limited decided that its Asian operations had expanded such that an Asian office should be established. The office would be involved in selling Victoria's current product lines; it was also expected to establish supplier contacts. In the Asian market, there were a number of small manufacturers of top-quality fabrics, particularly silk and lace, but from Victoria's home office in Ontario it was difficult to find and maintain these suppliers. To assist in doing so, a wholly owned company, Victoria Textiles (India) Limited, was created, and a facility was established in India in January Year 2. The new company, VTIL, was given the mandate from head office to buy and sell with other Victoria divisions and offices across Canada, as if it were an autonomous, independent unit. To establish the company, an investment of 10,000,000 Indian rupees (IR) was made on January 1, Year 2.

VTIL proved to be quite successful, as shown in the following financial statements at December 31, Year 4. After one year of operations, VTIL had borrowed funds and expanded facilities substantially, as the initial market estimates had turned out to be quite conservative. However, during this time the rupee had fallen in value relative to the Canadian dollar. As a result, Victoria's management was somewhat confused about how to evaluate VTIL's success, given the changing currency values.

## FINANCIAL STATEMENTS
(in thousands of Indian rupees)
### BALANCE SHEET

|  | Year 4 | Year 3 |
|---|---|---|
| Cash | 4,100 | 3,900 |
| Accounts receivable | 2,900 | 2,100 |
| Inventories | 4,800 | 3,500 |
| Prepaid expenses | 1,900 | 1,700 |
| Plant assets (net) | 7,900 | 8,900 |
|  | 21,600 | 20,100 |
| Current monetary liabilities | 2,400 | 900 |
| Unearned revenue | 800 | 500 |
| Long-term debt | 6,000 | 6,000 |
|  | 9,200 | 7,400 |
| Common shares | 10,000 | 10,000 |
| Retained earnings | 2,400 | 2,700 |
|  | 21,600 | 20,100 |

### INCOME STATEMENT

|  | Year 4 | Year 3 |
|---|---|---|
| Sales | 20,200 | 12,000 |
| Cost of sales | 11,300 | 6,300 |
| Gross profit | 8,900 | 5,700 |
| Operating expenses | 4,400 | 2,800 |
| Interest | 700 | 400 |
| Taxes | 600 | 400 |
| Net income | 3,200 | 2,100 |

## Additional Information

- The exchange rate at January 1, Year 2, when VTIL was originally established, was $0.075 per rupee.

- Of the original investment of IR10 million, IR4 million was used to acquire plant and equipment, which is being depreciated on a straight-line basis over 10 years.

- At June 30, Year 3, an expansion was completed at a cost of IR6 million, which was financed entirely by a six-year note obtained from an Indian bank. Interest is to be paid semiannually. The exchange rate at July 1, Year 3, was $0.062 per rupee. The new expansion is also to be depreciated on a straight-line basis over 10 years. (A half-year's depreciation was recorded in Year 3.) Depreciation expense of IR1,000 in Year 4 and IR700 in Year 3 is included in operating expenses.

- Inventory is accounted for on the FIFO basis. The inventory at the end of Year 3 and Year 4 was acquired when the exchange rates were $0.045 and $0.027 per rupee, respectively.

- Sales, purchases, and operating expenses were incurred evenly throughout the year, and the average exchange rate for the year was $0.031.

- The prepaid expenses and unearned revenue at December 31, Year 4, arose when the exchange rates were $0.03 and $0.028 per rupee, respectively.

- Income taxes were paid in equal monthly instalments throughout the year.

- Dividends of 3,500 in Year 4 and 500 in Year 3 were declared and paid each year on December 31.

- The foreign exchange rates per rupee at each of the following dates were as follows:

| | |
|---|---|
| Dec. 31, Year 3 | $0.041 |
| June 30, Year 4 | $0.036 |
| Dec. 31, Year 4 | $0.025 |

**Required**

(a) Prepare a Canadian-dollar balance sheet at December 31, Year 4, and an income statement for the year then ended, assuming that VTIL's functional currency is as follows:
   (i)  The Canadian dollar
   (ii) The Indian rupee
   (*Note:* There is insufficient information to translate retained earnings and accumulated foreign exchange adjustments. Plug these two items with the amount required to balance the balance sheet.)

(b) Which method should Victoria Textiles Limited apply to its investment in this subsidiary? Explain.

*(Adapted from a problem prepared by Peter Secord, St. Mary's University)*

# Problem 11-11

LO1, 3, 4

The financial statements of Malkin Inc., of Russia, as at December 31, Year 11, follow:

**FINANCIAL STATEMENTS**
**BALANCE SHEET**
At December 31, Year 11

| | | |
|---|---:|---:|
| Cash | | RR 105,000 |
| Accounts receivable | | 168,000 |
| Inventories—at cost | | 357,000 |
| Land | | 430,000 |
| Buildings | 1,460,000 | |
| Accumulated depreciation | 420,000 | 1,040,000 |
| Equipment | 483,000 | |
| Accumulated depreciation | 168,000 | 315,000 |
| | | RR2,415,000 |
| Accounts payable | | RR 210,000 |
| Miscellaneous payables | | 105,000 |
| Bonds payable | | 600,000 |
| Common shares | | 850,000 |
| Retained earnings | | 650,000 |
| | | RR2,415,000 |

*(continued)*

## RETAINED EARNINGS STATEMENT

| | |
|---|---|
| Balance, January 1 | RR 470,000 |
| Net income | 630,000 |
| | 1,100,000 |
| Dividends | 450,000 |
| Balance, December 31 | RR 650,000 |

## INCOME STATEMENT

| | |
|---|---|
| Sales | RR3,150,000 |
| Cost of sales | 1,680,000 |
| Other expenses | 840,000 |
| | 2,520,000 |
| Net Income | RR 630,000 |

## Additional Information

- On January 1, Year 11, Crichton Corporation of Toronto acquired 40% of Malkin's common shares for RR800,000.

- Relevant exchange rates for the Russian ruble (RR) were as follows:

  | | |
  |---|---|
  | Jan. 1, Year 11 | $1 = RR28.00 |
  | Dec. 31, Year 11 | $1 = RR28.20 |
  | Average for Year 11 | $1 = RR28.09 |

- The land and buildings were purchased in Year 5 when the exchange rate was RR26.50.

- During Year 11, equipment costing RR125,000 was purchased for cash. Depreciation totalling RR25,000 has been recorded on this equipment. The exchange rate on the date of the equipment purchase was RR28.18.
  The remaining equipment was purchased on the date the subsidiary was acquired, and no other changes have taken place since that date. Depreciation on the buildings of RR105,00 and depreciation of RR63,000 on all the equipment are included in other expenses.

- The December 31, Year 11, inventory was acquired during the last quarter of the year, when the average exchange rate was RR28.04.

- On January 1, Year 11, the inventory was RR525,000 and was acquired when the average exchange rate was RR28.27.

- The bonds mature on December 31, Year 16.

- Other operating expenses were incurred equally throughout the year.

- Dividends were declared and paid on December 31, Year 11.

- On January 1, Year 11, liabilities were greater than monetary assets by the amount of RR1,033,000.

- The common shares were issued in Year 1 when the exchange rate was RR25.00.

**Required**

(a) Assume that Malkin's functional currency is the Canadian dollar. Translate the financial statements into Canadian dollars for purposes of using the equity method to account for the associate.

(b) Assume that Malkin's functional currency is the Russian ruble. Translate the balance sheet only into Canadian dollars for equity-method purposes.

(c) Explain whether the PCT method produces results that are consistent with the normal measurement and valuation of assets and liabilities for domestic transactions and operations.

*(CGA Canada adapted)*[11]

# Problem 11-12

LO2, 3, 4

SPEC Co. is a Canadian investment company. It acquires real estate properties in foreign countries for speculative purposes. On January 1, Year 5, SPEC incorporated a wholly owned subsidiary, CHIN Limited. CHIN immediately purchased a property in Shanghai, China, for 70 million Chinese yuan (Y). At that time, the land and building were valued at Y30 million and Y40 million, respectively. The previous owner had purchased the property in Year 1 for Y36 million when the exchange rate was $1 = Y5.13. The building had an estimated useful life of 20 years with no residual value on January 1, Year 5.

The draft financial statements for CHIN as at and for the year ended December 31, Year 5, follow:

**CHIN LIMITED**
**STATEMENT OF FINANCIAL POSITION**
At December 31, Year 5

| | |
|---|---:|
| Land | Y30,000,000 |
| Building | 40,000,000 |
| Accumulated amortization | (2,000,000) |
| | Y68,000,000 |
| | |
| Common shares | Y20,000,000 |
| Retained earnings (deficit) | (2,000,000) |
| Mortgage payable | 50,000,000 |
| | Y68,000,000 |

**CHIN LIMITED**
**INCOME STATEMENT**
For the year ended December 31, Year 5

| | |
|---|---:|
| Rent revenue | Y 6,000,000 |
| Interest expense | (5,000,000) |
| Amortization expense | (2,000,000) |
| Other expenses | (1,000,000) |
| Profit (loss) | Y (2,000,000) |

**Additional Information**

- The purchase of the property was financed with Y20 million of equity provided by SPEC and a Y50 million mortgage from a Chinese investor. The mortgage payable has a term of 10 years and requires interest-only payments of Y5 million on December 31 each year, and a final payment of

Y50 million on December 31, Year 14. The market rate of interest on the mortgage was equal to the stated rate throughout Year 5.

- The property is rented for Y0.5 million per month, which is consistent with rent being charged by other property owners in the area. The rent is due on the last day of each month. CHIN hires local workers and buys all of its materials and supplies from local suppliers. CHIN incurred the other expenses evenly throughout the year.

- The exchange rates were as follows:

| | |
|---|---|
| Jan. 1, Year 5 | $1 = Y6.92 |
| Average for Year 5 | $1 = Y7.20 |
| Average for 12 days when rent payments were received | $1 = Y7.25 |
| Dec. 31, Year 5 | $1 = Y7.50 |

## Required

(a) Is CHIN's functional currency the Chinese yuan or Canadian dollar? Explain.

(b) Ignore your answer to part (a). Calculate the foreign exchange adjustment for Year 5, assuming that CHIN's functional currency is the Chinese yuan, and indicate how this adjustment will be reported in CHIN's Canadian-dollar financial statements. Show supporting calculations.

(c) Ignore your answers to parts (a) and (b). Translate CHIN's Year 5 income statement into Canadian dollars, assuming that CHIN's functional currency is the Canadian dollar. Ignore foreign exchange gains and losses.

(d) Assume that SPEC does not own any shares of CHIN. Instead, SPEC acquired the property in Shanghai directly. SPEC financed the acquisition with Y20 million of its own funds and a Y50 million mortgage. If SPEC argued that the mortgage payable is a hedge of the anticipated sale of the land, what difference would it make for reporting purposes whether the mortgage payable is deemed to be an effective hedge of the anticipated sale of the land? Briefly explain.

# Problem 11-13

## LO3, 4

White Company was incorporated on January 2, Year 1, and commenced active operations immediately. Common shares were issued on the date of incorporation and no new common shares have been issued since then. On December 31, Year 5, Black Company purchased 70% of the outstanding common shares of White for 1.33 million foreign pesos (FP). On this date, the fair values of White's identifiable net assets were equal to their carrying amounts except for a building, which had a fair value of FP99,000 in excess of carrying amount. The remaining useful life of the building was 10 years at the date of acquisition.

The following information was extracted from the financial records of the two companies for the year ended December 31, Year 6:

| | Black | White |
|---|---|---|
| Building—net | $2,999,000 | FP2,699,000 |
| Common shares | 99,000 | 199,000 |
| Retained earnings, beginning of year | 799,000 | 899,000 |
| Depreciation expense—buildings | 199,000 | 299,000 |
| Income before foreign exchange | 149,000 | 159,000 |
| Dividends paid | 79,000 | 99,000 |

### Additional Information

- Black uses the cost method to account for its investment in White.

- White purchased its building on December 31, Year 3.

- The recoverable amount for goodwill at the end of Year 6 was FP719,000.

- Dividends were declared and paid on July 1.

- Foreign exchange rates were as follows:

| | |
|---|---|
| Jan. 2, Year 1 | FP1 = $0.30 |
| Dec. 31, Year 3 | FP1 = $0.24 |
| Dec. 31, Year 5 | FP1 = $0.20 |
| Average for Year 6 | FP1 = $0.18 |
| July 1, Year 6 | FP1 = $0.17 |
| Dec. 31, Year 6 | FP1 = $0.15 |

### Required

(a) Compute the balances that would appear in the Year 6 consolidated financial statements for the following items, assuming that White's functional currency is the Canadian dollar. White's income before foreign exchange gains is $29,000, and the exchange gains from translating White's separate-entity financial statements to Canadian dollars are $49,000.

   (i)   Building—net

   (ii)  Goodwill

   (iii) Depreciation expense—building

   (iv) Net income (excluding other comprehensive income)

   (v)  Other comprehensive income

   (vi) Non-controlling interest on the income statement

   (vii) Non-controlling interest on the balance sheet

(b) Compute the balances that would appear in the Year 6 consolidated financial statements for the same accounts as in part (a), assuming that White's functional currency is the foreign peso.

## Problem 11-14

LO3, 4, 5

On January 1, Year 4, Par Company purchased all the outstanding common shares of Bayshore Company, located in California, for US$260,000. The carrying amount of Bayshore's shareholders' equity on January 1, Year 4, was US$202,000. The fair value of Bayshore's plant and equipment was US$24,000 more than carrying amount, and the plant and equipment are being depreciated over 10 years, with no salvage value. The remainder of the acquisition differential is attributable to a trademark, which will be amortized over 10 years.

    During Year 4, Bayshore earned US$48,000 in income and declared and paid US$22,000 in dividends on December 1, Year 4. Par uses the equity method to account for its investment in Bayshore. Management has determined that the Canadian dollar is the recording, functional and presentation currency for Par Company.

The exchange rates were as follows throughout the year:

| | |
|---|---|
| Jan. 1, Year 4 | US$1 = CDN$0.99 |
| Dec. 1, Year 4 | US$1 = CDN$0.96 |
| Dec. 31, Year 4 | US$1 = CDN$0.95 |
| Average for year | US$1 = CDN$0.97 |

**Required**

(a) Assume that the Canadian dollar is the functional currency for Bayshore Company.
   (i) Prepare a schedule showing the differential allocation and amortization for Year 4. The schedule should present both Canadian dollars and U.S. dollars.
   (ii) Prepare Par Company's journal entry for adjustments pertaining to the amortization of the acquisition differential for Year 4.

(b) Assume that the U.S. dollar is the functional currency for Bayshore Company.
   (i) Prepare a schedule showing the differential allocation and amortization for Year 4. The schedule should present both Canadian dollars and U.S. dollars.
   (ii) Prepare Par Company's journal entry for adjustments pertaining to the amortization of the acquisition differential for Year 4.

# Endnotes

1  SEDAR Filings, http://sedar.com/GetFile. do?lang=EN&docClass=5&issuerNo-00024480&fileName=/ csfsprod/data150/filings/02309771/00000001/h%3A% 5CSEDAR%5C2015%5C19Feb2015%5CE-MFC-FS2014.pdf, accessed June 5, 2015.

2  "Annual Report 2014," www.powercorporation.com/media/ upload/reports/annual/PCC_AR_2014_ENG.pdf, accessed June 5, 2015.

3  "Annual Report 2014," www.rbc.com/investorrelations/pdf/ ar_2014_e.pdf, accessed June 5, 2015.

4  Adapted from *CICA UFE Report,* 1990-II-3, with permission. Chartered Professional Accountants of Canada, Toronto, Canada. Any changes to the original material are the sole responsibility of the author (and/or publisher) and have not been reviewed or endorsed by the Chartered Professional Accountants of Canada.

5  Adapted from *CICA UFE Report,* 199-IV-2, with permission. Chartered Professional Accountants of Canada, Toronto, Canada. Any changes to the original material are the sole responsibility of the author (and/or publisher) and have not been reviewed or endorsed by the Chartered Professional Accountants of Canada.

6  Adapted from *CICA UFE Report,* 1993-IV-3, with permission. Chartered Professional Accountants of Canada, Toronto, Canada. Any changes to the original material are the sole responsibility of the author (and/or publisher) and have not been reviewed or endorsed by the Chartered Professional Accountants of Canada.

7  Adapted from *CICA UFE Report,* 2008-II-3, with permission. Chartered Professional Accountants of Canada, Toronto,

Canada. Any changes to the original material are the sole responsibility of the author (and/or publisher) and have not been reviewed or endorsed by the Chartered Professional Accountants of Canada.

8  Adapted from CGA Canada's FA4 Exam, September 2014, Q4, with permission. Chartered Professional Accountants of Canada, Toronto, Canada. Any changes to the original material are the sole responsibility of the author (and/or publisher) and have not been reviewed or endorsed by the Chartered Professional Accountants of Canada.

9  Adapted from CGA Canada's FA4 Exam, September 2003, Q4, with permission. Chartered Professional Accountants of Canada, Toronto, Canada. Any changes to the original material are the sole responsibility of the author (and/or publisher) and have not been reviewed or endorsed by the Chartered Professional Accountants of Canada.

10  Adapted from CGA Canada's FA4 Exam, December 2001, Q3,with permission Chartered Professional Accountants of Canada, Toronto, Canada. Any changes to the original material are the sole responsibility of the author (and/or publisher) and have not been reviewed or endorsed by the Chartered Professional Accountants of Canada.

11  Adapted from CGA Canada's FA4 Exam, December 2006, Q4,with permission Chartered Professional Accountants of Canada, Toronto, Canada. Any changes to the original material are the sole responsibility of the author (and/or publisher) and have not been reviewed or endorsed by the Chartered Professional Accountants of Canada.

# CHAPTER 12

# Accounting for Not-for-Profit and Public Sector Organizations

## LEARNING OBJECTIVES

**After studying this chapter, you should be able to do the following:**

**LO1** Define not-for-profit organizations (NFPOs) and describe how they differ from profit-oriented organizations.

**LO2** Describe and apply the not-for-profit accounting and reporting practices currently mandated in the *CPA Canada Handbook*.

**LO3** Explain the objectives of fund accounting, and prepare financial statements using fund accounting.

**LO4** Prepare journal entries and financial statements under the restricted fund method.

**LO5** Prepare journal entries and financial statements under the deferral method.

**LO6** Analyze and interpret the financial statements of NFPOs.

**LO7** (Appendix 12A) Identify similarities and differences in financial statement accounts for a not-for-profit organization and a profit-oriented organization.

**LO8** (Appendix 12B) Account for net assets invested in capital assets.

**LO9** (Appendix 12C) Outline the basics of public sector financial reporting.

## Introduction

A substantial portion of Canada's economic activity is conducted by organizations whose purpose is to provide services (or products) on a non-profit basis. The size of the portion becomes clear when one considers that included in this *non-business area* is the *government sector,* encompassing the federal, provincial, and local governments, as well as the *not-for-profit sector.* This latter sector encompasses a wide variety of organizations such as charities, hospitals, universities, professional and fraternal organizations, and community clubs. A charity is a type of NFPO that is established and operated for charitable purposes and must devote its resources to charitable activities. It cannot use its income for the personal benefit of its members or governing officials.

**LO1**  Not-for-profit organizations are defined in Part III of the *CPA Canada Handbook* as

> . . . entities, normally without transferable ownership interests, organized and operated exclusively for social, educational, professional, religious, health, charitable or any other not-for-profit purpose. A not-for-profit organization's members, contributors and other resource providers do not, in such capacity, receive any financial return directly from the organization. [4400.02]

NFPOs differ from profit-oriented organizations in the following ways:

- They typically provide services or goods to identifiable segments of society without the expectation of profit. They accomplish this by raising resources and subsequently spending or distributing these resources in a manner that fulfills the organization's objectives.
- The resources are provided by contributors without the expectation of gain or repayment. Most of these resources consist of donations from the general public and grants from governments and other NFPOs. Often, a portion of the resources received has restrictions attached that govern the manner in which they can be spent.
- As the definition cited above indicates, there is no readily defined ownership interest that can be sold, transferred, or redeemed in any way by the organization.
- While many NFPOs have paid employees, they are governed by volunteers who receive little or no remuneration or gain for the time and effort they provide. In some small organizations, there are no paid employees and all effort is provided entirely by volunteers.

---

*There are a number of ways in which NFPOs differ from profit-oriented organizations.*

---

While financial reporting for NFPOs in Canada is well defined today, this has been the case only since April 1997, when seven very detailed *Handbook* sections became operational. Prior to this date, accounting in this area was in a state of flux, moving from a situation where there were no real authoritative pronouncements at all, to one where there was just a single *Handbook* section that gave only broad guidance for some issues and left many other important ones unresolved. A few large organizations, such as hospitals and universities, published detailed manuals in an attempt to establish consistent reporting practices for all members of a given association. Unfortunately, the practices set out for hospitals were different from those recommended for universities, and in both situations, members did not have to follow their organization's recommendations. Smaller NFPOs followed a wide range of diverse practices, such as using the cash basis only, or a mixture of cash and accrual accounting. Many did not capitalize capital asset acquisitions, and of the few that did capitalize, many did not provide for subsequent periodic amortization. A wide range of practices was also followed for donated materials, services, and capital assets, ranging from no recording to a full recording of all items. A large number of NFPOs used fund accounting in their end-of-year financial statement presentations, and many organizations still do. Later in this chapter we fully explore the concepts involved in fund accounting and fund presentations in accordance with current *Handbook* requirements. First, though, it is useful to examine the main accounting and reporting requirements for NFPOs today.

---

*Well-defined GAAP for NFPOs have existed in Canada only since 1997.*

---

## LO2 NOT-FOR-PROFIT REPORTING TODAY

In December 2010, the *Handbook* was restructured into five parts to implement the strategy of the Accounting Standards Board (AcSB) of adopting different sets of standards for different categories of entities. As part of this restructuring, the not-for-profit (NFP) sector was classified into two sectors: the public NFP sector and the private NFP sector. The public NFP sector includes NFPOs (such as hospitals) that are controlled by the government. These NFPOs have a choice to follow the *CPA Canada Public Sector Accounting (PSA) Handbook* including the 4200 series or the *PSA Handbook* without the 4200 series. Appendix 12C of this chapter discusses accounting standards applicable to the public sector.

The private NFP sector includes NFPOs that are not controlled by the government. They have a choice to follow either Part I (IFRS) or Part III (Accounting Standards for Not-for-Profit Organizations) of the *CPA Canada Handbook*. In choosing between the two options, the organization would consider the needs of the users of their financial statements and the comparability of their financial reporting with counterparts in industry. It is expected that most private sector NFPOs will adopt Part III of the *CPA Canada Handbook,* because it is less costly and burdensome than IFRS. Furthermore, IFRS does not have any special rules for NFPOs and therefore is not as useful as Part III for most NFPOs. The remainder of this chapter will describe accounting standards for the private sector NFPOs, and will refer to the private NFPOs simply as NFPOs. Furthermore, any references to Part II or Part III will be references to these parts of the *CPA Canada Handbook.*

An NFPO applying Part III of the *Handbook* also applies Part II (ASPE) to the extent that the Part II standards address topics not addressed in Part III. Some of the standards in Part II are of limited or no applicability to NFPOs either, because the topics are specifically addressed in Part III or the standards in Part II relate to transactions or circumstances that do not pertain to NFPOs.

> *Private sector NFPOs can either follow IFRS or Part III of the* CPA Canada Handbook *combined with relevant sections from ASPE.*

In the material that follows, the pronouncements of each section of Part III will be discussed and in some instances illustrated. For the first five sections presented below, the standards in Part III are very similar to the standards in Part II. The main differences between the two sections will be described.[1]

> *Part III of the* Handbook *now contains the accounting standards that deal with issues that are unique to NFPOs.*

> **Cautionary Note:** *Unless otherwise noted, all of the illustrations in the body of the chapter and end-of-chapter material will use Part III of the* CPA Canada Handbook *in combination with Part II.*

### SECTION 1001 *FINANCIAL STATEMENT CONCEPTS FOR NOT-FOR-PROFIT ORGANIZATIONS*

This section describes the objectives of financial statements, qualitative characteristics of financial information, elements of financial statements, and recognition and measurement in financial statements. The mains users of the NFPOs' financial statements are the members, contributors, and creditors. They are interested, for the purpose of making resource allocation decisions, in the entity's cost of service and how that cost was funded and in predicting the ability of the entity to meet its obligations and achieve its service delivery objectives. The excess or deficiency of revenues and gains over expenses and losses can be an important indicator of the entity's ability to obtain resources to cover the cost of its services.

> *The cost of service and how that cost was funded are key information needs for the users of an NFPO.*

Members and contributors also require information about how the management of an entity has discharged its stewardship responsibility to those that have provided resources to the entity. Information regarding discharge of stewardship responsibilities is especially important as resources are often contributed for specific purposes, and management is accountable for the appropriate utilization of such resources.

## SECTION 1101 *GENERALLY ACCEPTED ACCOUNTING PRINCIPLES FOR NOT-FOR-PROFIT ORGANIZATIONS*

This section describes the primary and other sources of GAAP for NFPOs. The primary sources of GAAP, in descending order of authority, follow:

(i)   Sections 1470–4470 of Part III of the *Handbook*, including appendices

(ii)  Sections 1505–3870 in Part II, to the extent that the topics in those sections are not specifically discussed in Part III, including appendices

(iii) "Accounting Guidelines" in Part II, including appendices

> *Part II of the* Handbook *provides a substantial portion of GAAP for NFPOs.*

An NFPO should present only one set of general-purpose financial statements prepared under Part III of the *Handbook* in any particular period. If it prepares additional sets of financial statements under Part III for different purposes, these are special-purpose financial statements and should refer to the general-purpose financial statements.

## SECTION 1401 *GENERAL STANDARDS OF FINANCIAL STATEMENT PRESENTATION FOR NOT-FOR-PROFIT ORGANIZATIONS*

This section describes fair presentation in accordance with GAAP, going concern, financial statements required for NFPOs, and comparative information. The standards in this section are similar to the standards in Section 1400 in Part II. The general-purpose financial statements consist of the statement of financial position, statement of operations, statement of changes in net assets, and statement of cash flows. Notes to financial statements, and supporting schedules to which the financial statements are cross-referenced, are an integral part of such statements. When financial statements are not prepared on a going-concern basis, that fact shall be disclosed, together with the basis on which the financial statements are prepared and the reason why the organization is not regarded as a going concern. Financial statements shall be prepared on a comparative basis, unless the comparative information is not meaningful or the standards set out in Part III permit otherwise.

> *The financial statements for an NFPO are similar to the financial statements required under ASPE.*

**SECTION 1501** *FIRST-TIME ADOPTION BY NOT-FOR-PROFIT ORGANIZATIONS*   This section applies when an NFPO is adopting Part III for the first time. Most NFPOs will have used this section when they converted from the old *Handbook* to Part III of the *Handbook* in 2012. For the NFPOs that adopted Part I rather than Part III in 2012 or earlier and later decide to change to Part III, they would follow Section 1501 of Part III at that time.

When converting to Part III for the first time, changes in accounting policies must be applied retrospectively, unless there are exemptions or restrictions as outlined and defined in Section 1501. The entity's first set of financial statements must show comparative numbers for the previous year as if Part III had always been applied. In addition, the entity must present a statement of financial position on the transition date, which is the beginning of the earliest period for which an organization presents full comparative information. For example, if the first set of financial statements is presented for the year ended December 31, 2016, comparative numbers would be presented for 2015 and an opening statement of financial position would be presented as at January 1, 2015. The entity has an option to not retrospectively adjust when it changes its accounting policies in its first set of financial statements under Part III for certain standards in the following areas: business combinations; fair value for property, plant, and equipment; employee future benefits; cumulative translation differences for self-sustaining foreign operations; financial instruments; and asset retirement obligations. These same elective exemptions are available for private entities transitioning to Part II.

> *Changes in policies would normally be applied retrospectively when first adopting Part III of the* Handbook.

On the other hand, retrospective application is prohibited for some aspects of the standards. The prohibitions include derecognition of financial assets and financial liabilities, hedge accounting, estimates, and non-controlling interests.

**SECTION 3032** *INVENTORIES HELD BY NOT-FOR-PROFIT ORGANIZATIONS*   Except as otherwise provided for in this section, an NFPO applies the section on inventories in Part II. When an NFPO recognizes donations of materials and services, the inventories should initially be recorded at fair value, which is its deemed cost from that point forward. Without this requirement, the inventory would not be recognized because it had no cost to the NFPO.

An NFPO may hold inventories whose future economic benefits or service potential are not directly related to their ability to generate net cash flows. These types of inventories may arise when an NFPO distributes certain goods at no charge or for a nominal charge. For example, a food bank would buy food, not to resell it, but to distribute it for free to the homeless. In this case, the future economic benefits or service potential of the inventory for financial reporting purposes is the amount the organization would need to pay to acquire the economic benefits or service potential, if this was necessary to achieve the objectives of the organization. Therefore, an NFPO measures inventories at the lower of cost and current replacement cost (instead of net realizable value), when they are held for distribution at no charge or for a nominal charge or for consumption in the production process of goods to be distributed at no charge or for a nominal charge.

> *An NFPO may receive inventory without any cost and may have no intention of ever selling the inventory.*

**SECTION 3463** *REPORTING EMPLOYEE FUTURE BENEFITS BY NOT-FOR-PROFIT ORGANIZATIONS* This section provides guidance for defined benefit plans on the recognition and presentation of remeasurements and other items that differs from the guidance in Section 3462 *Employee Future Benefits* in Part II of the *Handbook*. The requirements in Section 3462 apply in all other respects.

The main features of Section 3463 are as follows:

- Remeasurements and other items are:
  - recognized directly in net assets in the statement of financial position rather than in the statement of operations; and
  - presented as a separately identified line item in the statement of changes in net assets.
- Remeasurements and other items are not reclassified to the statement of operations in a subsequent period.

**SECTION 4400** *FINANCIAL STATEMENT PRESENTATION BY NOT-FOR-PROFIT ORGANIZATIONS* An NFPO must present the following financial statements for external reporting purposes:

- Statement of operations
- Statement of financial position
- Statement of changes in net assets
- Statement of cash flows

> *An NFPO must present four financial statements.*

The names provided here are for descriptive purposes only; an organization can choose the titles it wishes to use. For example, the statement of operations is sometimes called the *statement of revenues and expenses*, the statement of financial position is a *balance sheet*, and net assets are *fund balances* or *accumulated surplus*. The statement of operations can be combined with the statement of changes in net assets.

The primary purpose of a statement of operations is to communicate information about changes in the organization's economic resources and obligations for the period. Specifically, this statement provides information about the cost of the organization's service delivery activities for the period and the extent to which these expenses were financed or funded by contributions and other revenue. The information provided in the statement of operations is useful in evaluating the organization's performance during the period, including its ability to continue to provide services, and in assessing how the organization's management has discharged its stewardship responsibilities.

The statement of financial position should show classifications for current assets, non-current assets, current liabilities, and non-current liabilities. Net assets (total assets less total liabilities) must be broken down into the following categories (if applicable):

- Net assets maintained permanently in endowments
- Internally restricted and other externally restricted net assets
- Unrestricted net assets

> *The equity section of the statement of financial position is called "net assets" and must be broken down into three categories (if applicable).*

Prior to 2009, net assets invested in capital assets had to be shown as a separate component of net assets. Starting in 2009, a reporting entity has three options for reporting this item:

- Continue to show it as a separate component of net assets
- Disclose it in the notes to the statements
- Do not present or disclose it separately

Many organizations still present or disclose this item separately because it indicates that this portion of net assets is not available for current use. However, some organizations will not present or disclose the item separately because their users may not fully understand its nature. The accounting for this item is illustrated in Appendix 12B.

Information about total gross revenues and expenses is necessary for users to fully understand the organization's operations. The statement of operations will show the revenues and the expenses for the period. Expenses may be classified by object (salaries, rent, utilities), by function (administrative, research, ancillary operations), or by program. An organization should use the method that results in the most meaningful presentation under the circumstances. When an organization has expenses and revenues from the provision of goods or services and acted as a principal in the transactions involved, it recognizes the expenses and the revenues on a gross basis. When it is not acting as a principal in the transactions, it earns the equivalent of a commission or fee or receives the equivalent of a contribution and recognizes revenue for only the net amount received. The following two examples provide guidance in determining whether to recognize revenues and expenses on the gross basis or the net basis.

**EXAMPLE 1** An NFPO engages in a number of fundraising activities, which include a fundraising telethon, a telephone campaign, a direct mail campaign, special events, and a lottery. The organization uses an outside fundraising consultant to conduct the telethon but uses the NFPO's own staff and volunteers in the telethon and the telephone campaign. Funds solicited in each of the activities are raised in the name of the organization.

The NFPO is the principal when it receives most of the benefits and/or incurs most of the risks. Even though the organization uses an outside fundraising consultant to conduct the telethon, the organization is the principal in the relationship with the donors as the funds are raised in its name and using its staff and volunteers. The organization has discretion in selecting the outside fundraiser, in establishing the fees to be paid, and in determining the specifications of the telethon. It also has the credit risk if donors to the telethon do not pay according to their pledge. Thus, the organization recognizes the gross fundraising amounts raised in each of the activities as revenue of the organization and the total expenses of each activity, including the fees charged by any outside party, as expenses of the organization.

> *Revenues and expenses should be reported on a gross basis when the entity acts as a principal in the transactions.*

**EXAMPLE 2** An NFPO is given the net proceeds from an event held by others to benefit the organization, but without having any control over, or responsibility for, the gross amounts of revenues or expenses involved. In this situation, the organization is not the principal in the fundraising event as it was not involved in organizing the event and did not bear any risks in connection with it. The amount received by the organization is a donation from the organizers. Neither the gross revenues nor the gross expenses of the event are recognized in the organization's financial statements. The net proceeds received are recognized as a contribution. Disclosure of gross revenues and expenses is not required.

The statement of operations does not have a section for other comprehensive income. Similar to a private for-profit entity, foreign exchange adjustments for a self-sustaining foreign operation and the exchange adjustments for a cash flow hedge are given special treatment. These adjustments are recognized directly and accumulated separately in the net assets section of the statement of financial position.

---

*Other comprehensive income does not exist as a separate category on the statement of operations.*

---

The statement of changes in net assets must show changes in each of the three net asset categories required on the statement of financial position. The cash flow statement must segregate changes in cash between operating, investing, and financing activities. Cash flows from operations can be presented using either the direct method or the indirect method.

Section 4400 also provides guidance on the use of fund accounting, which is discussed and illustrated later in this chapter.

The 2015 financial statements (excluding footnotes) of the United Way of Ottawa-Carleton presented in Appendix 12A provide an example of an NFPO's financial statements.

**SECTION 4410** *CONTRIBUTIONS—REVENUE RECOGNITION*   An NFPO can have two basic types of revenues:

- Contributions (in cash or in kind)
- Other types (investments, the sale of goods and services)

A contribution is a type of revenue unique to NFPOs. It is defined as "a non-reciprocal transfer to a not-for-profit organization of cash or other assets or a non-reciprocal settlement or cancellation of its liabilities" (paragraph 4420.02). Non-reciprocal means that the contributor does not directly receive anything for the contribution. Included here are donations of cash, property or services, government grants, pledges, and bequests.

---

*Contribution revenue is a type of revenue that is unique to NFPOs, because it is non-reciprocal.*

---

Besides receiving contribution revenue, NFPOs may also receive other types of revenue, such as from investments or from the sale of goods and services. These other types of revenue are accounted for in accordance with Part II Section 3400 *Revenue*. Government funding to an NFPO is typically classified as a contribution, because the government itself does not receive anything from the contribution. When the government is the direct recipient of the good or the service, the receipt from the government is recognized as revenue earned rather than contribution revenue. In the same fashion, payments received from members of an NFPO are classified as either revenues earned or contributions, depending on whether the member does or does not receive goods or services for the amount paid.

The *Handbook* defines three different types of contributions:

- Restricted contributions
- Endowment contributions
- Unrestricted contributions

---

*NFPOs receive three different types of contributions: restricted, endowment, and unrestricted.*

---

*Restricted contributions* are subject to *externally imposed* stipulations as to how the funds are to be spent or used. The organization must use the resources in the manner specified by the donor. There may be times when the directors of an organization decide to use certain contributions for certain purposes, but these are considered to be *internally imposed* restrictions and are often referred to as reserves or appropriations. They are reported differently than the restrictions imposed by external parties, mainly because future boards could reverse the designation.

*Endowment contributions* are a special type of restricted contribution. The donor has specified that the contribution cannot be spent, but must be maintained permanently. Endowment contributions are often invested in high-grade securities. There are many examples of endowments. University scholarships are often funded by the investment income earned on endowment contributions made by donors in prior years. Some well-known private universities, such as Harvard and Stanford, have hundreds of millions of dollars in endowment funds, and use the earnings as their major source of revenue since they do not receive government funding. The Toronto Symphony Orchestra has established an endowment fund as a device to help fund its daily operations. And finally, the Winnipeg Foundation operates with substantial endowment funds. Quite often, restrictions are also placed on how the endowment income can be spent. In other words, investment income can be restricted or unrestricted.

---

*Many NFPOs receive a major source of their revenues from endowment earnings.*

---

*Unrestricted contributions* are those that are not restricted or endowment contributions. They can be used for any purposes that are consistent with the goals and objectives of the organization.

There are two methods for accounting for contributions: deferral method and restricted fund method. These methods will be explained and illustrated later in this chapter.

**SECTION 4420 *CONTRIBUTIONS RECEIVABLE*** Section 4420 provides guidance on how to apply accrual accounting concepts to contributions. It states the following:

A contribution receivable should be recognized as an asset when it meets the following criteria:

(a) The amount to be received can be reasonably estimated

(b) Ultimate collection is reasonably assured [4420.03]

Normally a contribution receivable represents a future inflow of cash, but it could also represent the future receipt of other assets or services valued at fair value. The credit side of the journal entry could be to revenue, using the restricted fund method, or if the deferral method of recording is being used, to deferred revenue for a restricted contribution, or to increase net assets of endowments for an endowment contribution. The section provides additional guidelines for the recording of receivables associated with pledges and bequests.

Because pledges cannot be legally enforced, collectibility is out of the control of the organization. If the organization has the ability to estimate the collectibility based on historical results, it should recognize the pledged amounts as a receivable offset with an allowance for estimated uncollectible amounts. Otherwise, the recognition of pledges should be delayed until the time cash is received. When an allowance for pledges is established, the debit is typically made to contribution revenue rather than to bad debt expense. Since the pledge is not legally binding, it is inappropriate to call the non-payment of a pledge a bad debt expense.

*Pledges are promises to donate cash or other assets to an NFPO, but they are legally unenforceable.*

Bequests also pose a problem of uncertainty relating both to the timing of receipt and to the amount to be collected. Wills must be probated and at times are subject to legal challenges. Because of this extreme uncertainty, bequests are generally not accrued until probation has been completed and the time for appeal has passed.

*Bequests are normally not recorded until a will has been probated.*

## SECTION 4431 *TANGIBLE CAPITAL ASSETS HELD BY NOT-FOR-PROFIT ORGANIZATIONS*

In December 2010 when Part III of the *Handbook* was introduced, accounting for capital assets was split into two sections, 4431 and 4432. Prior to the introduction of NFPO standards into the *Handbook* in 1997, NFPOs followed a variety of practices with regard to the financial reporting of their capital assets. Some organizations capitalized all acquisitions and amortized them over their estimated useful lives in the operating statement. Others capitalized them but did not provide amortization. A fairly large number wrote them off in their operating statements in the year of acquisition. In this latter situation, the operating statement showed revenues and expenditures, and from a user perspective reflected the inflow and outflow of spendable resources.

When the AcSB proposed the requirement of capitalization and amortization of all acquisitions, respondents to the exposure drafts voiced strong opposition. The arguments against capitalization were as follows:

- It would change the nature of the operating statement from one that reflects resources spent to one that reflects the cost of resources used.
- Users would not understand the new accounting, having become used to seeing capital asset acquisitions as expenditures.
- As most other assets appearing in a statement of financial position represent spendable resources, the addition of non-spendable resources such as unamortized capital assets would confuse readers.
- Capitalization and amortization would be costly to apply, especially on a retroactive basis.
- Small NFPO financial statement users are interested in seeing only what money has been spent and what money is left over.

> *There was strong opposition to the proposal that all NFPOs be required to capitalize and amortize acquisitions of capital assets.*

The counterarguments, in favour of capitalization, were as follows:

- Readers of the financial statements of profit-oriented entities are quite used to seeing capital assets in the statement of financial position and amortization in the operating statement. They are confused when they do not see these items in the financial statements of an NFPO.

- The cash flow statement adequately shows resources spent. The operating statement should reflect resources used.

Section 4431 requires an NFPO to capitalize all tangible capital assets in the statement of financial position and to amortize them as appropriate in the statement of operations. The cost of a purchased capital asset includes all costs incurred to make the asset ready for use. When a capital asset is donated, it is recorded at fair value (if known), and the resultant credit is recorded based on the requirements for contributions, which will be discussed later in this chapter. If the entity paid less than fair value, the asset is recorded at fair value and the difference between fair value and cost is recorded as a contribution. Capital assets of limited useful life are to be amortized on a rational basis over their estimated useful lives. No maximum period of amortization is specified. When an NFPO enters into a lease agreement that would be treated as a capital lease in accordance with Part II Section 3065, the asset is capitalized in accordance with the provisions of that section. When an asset no longer contributes to the organization's ability to provide services, it should be written down to estimated residual value, with the resulting loss reported as an expense in the statement of operations. Note that this is not the same impairment test as prescribed in Part II Section 3063.

> *GAAP require large NFPOs to capitalize and amortize their capital assets.*

**SMALL NFPOs**    Section 4431 contains a compromise provision applicable to NFPOs whose average of annual revenues recognized in the statement of operations for the current and preceding period is less than $500,000. Organizations such as these are encouraged to follow the section's recommendations but are exempted from doing so if they disclose the following:

- Accounting policy for capital assets

- Information about capital assets not shown in the statement of financial position

- Amount expensed in the current period if their policy is to expense capital assets when acquired

> *An exemption from the requirement to capitalize is granted to small NFPOs (those whose two-year average of annual revenues is less than $500,000).*

Under the exemption, the small NFPO has the following choices:

- Expensing when acquired

- Capitalizing but not amortizing

- Capitalizing and amortizing

If an NFPO has revenues above $500,000, it is required to capitalize and amortize. If its revenues subsequently fall below $500,000, it is not allowed to change its policy.

If an NFPO has revenues below $500,000, chooses not to capitalize and amortize, and subsequently has revenues above $500,000, then it ceases to be a small NFPO and must capitalize and amortize. The change should be accounted for prospectively because the application of the new policy is being driven by a change in circumstance.

> *When an NFPO no longer meets the exemption test, it must capitalize and amortize its capital assets and apply the new policy on a prospective basis.*

**SECTION 4432** *INTANGIBLE ASSETS HELD BY NOT-FOR-PROFIT ORGANIZATIONS* This section was introduced to clarify that Part II Section 3064 *Goodwill and Intangible Assets* applies to an NFPO's intangible assets. The same requirements as discussed above for tangible capital assets also apply for intangible assets.

**SECTION 4440** *COLLECTIONS HELD BY NOT-FOR-PROFIT ORGANIZATIONS* Collections are works of art and historical treasures that have been excluded from the definition of capital assets because they meet all of the following criteria:

- Held for public exhibition, education, or research
- Protected, cared for, and preserved
- Subject to organizational policies that require any proceeds from their sale to be used to acquire other items for the collection, or for the direct care of the existing collection

The requirements of Section 4440 allow an NFPO to choose an accounting policy from the following:

- Expense when acquired
- Capitalize but do not amortize
- Capitalize and amortize

> *Collections have been excluded from the definition of capital assets, and NFPOs are allowed three alternative reporting options.*

Although collections are usually held by museums or galleries, other organizations may also have items that meet the definition of a collection. For example, an organization's library may include rare books that would be considered to be a collection for purposes of this section. The regular library materials, however, would not usually meet the definition of a collection.

Organizations holding collections act as custodians for the public interest. They undertake to protect and preserve the collection for public exhibition, education, or research. The existence of a policy requiring that any proceeds on the sale of collection items be used to acquire additional items or for the direct care of the collection provides evidence of the organization's commitment to act as custodian of the collection.

NFPOs that have collections are required to include in their disclosures a description of the accounting policies followed with regard to collections, a description of the collection, any significant changes made to the collection during the period, the amount spent on the collection during the period, the proceeds from any sales of collection items, and a statement of how the proceeds were used.

## SECTION 4450 *REPORTING CONTROLLED AND RELATED ENTITIES BY NOT-FOR-PROFIT ORGANIZATIONS*  This section outlines the financial statement presentation and disclosures required when an NFPO has a control, significant influence, joint venture, or economic interest type of relationship with both profit-oriented and NFPOs. The breakdown used is quite similar to that for profit-oriented organizations, but the required financial reporting has some differences.

### CONTROL INVESTMENTS  An NFPO can have an investment or relationship that gives it the continuing power to determine the strategic operating, investing, and financing policies of another entity without the cooperation of others. The other entity can be profit-oriented or an NFPO. Control of a profit-oriented organization is normally evidenced by the right to appoint the majority of the board of directors because of ownership of voting shares. Because an NFPO does not issue shares, control of such an entity is normally evidenced by the right to appoint the majority of the board of directors as allowed by that entity's by-laws or articles of incorporation.

> *A control investment is one that gives an NFPO control over either profit-oriented organizations or other NFPOs.*

### CONTROL OVER NFPOs  An example of a not-for-profit control situation is a national organization with local chapters. A large portion of funds raised by the local chapters goes to the national body, and any projects carried out by the local bodies must be approved (and perhaps funded) by the national organization.

The *Handbook*'s reporting requirements are described below.

An organization should report each controlled NFPO in one of the following ways:

(a) Consolidating the controlled organization in its financial statements.
(b) Providing the disclosure set out in paragraph 4450.22.
(c) If the controlled organization is one of a large number of individually immaterial organizations, providing the disclosure set out in Paragraph 4450.26. [4450.14]

> *Consolidation of an NFPO is one of three alternatives allowed. The alternatives apply to each controlled NFPO.*

Because there is no investment account in the statement of financial position and no shareholders' equity in the others, consolidation is achieved by simply combining the financial statements on a line-by-line basis, and at the same time eliminating any transactions that occurred between the organizations. Accordingly, in the NFP sector, consolidated financial statements have often been referred to as combined financial statements

Since three alternatives are allowed, the management of the organization has to determine the accounting policy to be used. Note that the alternatives listed above are for each controlled entity.

This means that if an organization has control over three NFPOs, all of which are material, it could choose to consolidate only one, and provide the required disclosure for the other two, provided that it reports consistently on a year-to-year basis. Later paragraphs further clarify the overall meaning by suggesting that if an NFPO has control over a large number of NFPOs, the decision to consolidate or not should be applied on a group basis. For example, it could establish a policy to consolidate all organizations in Groups A and B and not consolidate the organizations in Group C.

Paragraph 4450.22 requires the disclosure of the totals of all of the assets, liabilities, net assets, revenues, expenses, and cash flows of any controlled NFPOs that are not consolidated. Paragraph 4450.26 requires the disclosure of the reasons that the controlled organizations have been neither consolidated nor included in the disclosure set out in paragraph 4450.22. Possible reasons could include cost–benefit considerations and the decision not to exercise financial control.

**CONTROL OVER PROFIT-ORIENTED COMPANIES** Section 4450 states an NFPO should report each controlled profit-oriented enterprise in either of the following ways:

(a) Consolidating the controlled enterprise in its financial statements

(b) Accounting for its investment in the controlled enterprise using the equity method and disclosing total assets, liabilities, and shareholders' equity at the reporting date and revenues, expenses, net income and cash flows for the period

It should be noted that the requirements here are also applicable to each controlled entity, which could result in some subsidiaries being reported under the equity method and others being consolidated.

> *A controlled profit-oriented organization can either be consolidated or reported using the equity method.*

**JOINT CONTROL** This is the contractual right to jointly control an organization with at least one other entity. An interest in a joint venture would be reported by either of the following methods:

- Proportionately consolidating the joint venture.
- Reporting the interest using the equity method.

> *A jointly controlled organization can be either proportionately consolidated or reported using the equity method.*

Consistent with the requirements for controlled entities, the alternatives here apply to each joint venture, so that some may be proportionately consolidated and others may not, depending on the accounting policy determined by management. The section also states that if the NFPO's proportionate interest in the joint venture cannot be determined, it should not be considered to be a joint venture in accordance with this section, but might be either a significant influence or a control type of relationship. This seems to indicate that the joint venture would have to be one that issued shares, and thus probably a profit-oriented organization. However, if two or three NFPOs created another NFPO as a joint venture to carry out certain activities, and agreed to the percentage owned by each of the non-profit venturers, then the reporting alternatives outlined here would apply.

**SIGNIFICANT INFLUENCE**   When control is not present, the NFPO may still be able to exercise significant influence over the strategic operating, investing, and financing activities of the other entity. Factors suggesting the presence of significant influence include the ability to place members on the board of directors, the ability to participate in policy-making, substantial transactions between the entities, and the sharing of senior personnel. If the significant-influence investment is in a profit-oriented enterprise, it must be accounted for using the equity method. If the significant-influence relationship is with another NFPO, the equity method is not used; instead, full disclosure of the relationship is required. This provision makes sense when one considers that applying the equity method requires using a percentage based on the number of shares held. Because an NFPO does not issue shares, it would be virtually impossible to determine the percentage needed to apply the method.

> *A significant-influence investment in a profit-oriented organization is reported using the equity method. A significant-influence investment in another NFPO requires only full disclosure of the relationship.*

**ECONOMIC INTEREST**   An economic interest in another NFPO exists if that organization holds resources for the reporting organization or if the reporting organization is responsible for the other organization's debts. There are varying degrees of economic interest, ranging from control or significant influence to neither of the two. When an organization has an economic interest in another NFPO over which it does not have control or significant influence, the nature and extent of this interest should be disclosed.

> *When an organization has an economic interest in another NFPO, the nature and extent of this interest should be disclosed.*

An investment in a profit-oriented organization that is not subject to control, significant influence, or joint control, is reported at fair value or using the cost method as per the requirements in Part II, Section 3856 *Financial Instruments*.

This concludes the discussion of Section 4450. A summary of the various types of investment that an NFPO can have and the reporting requirements for each follows:

| *Investment* | *Required Reporting* |
|---|---|
| Control of NFPO | Consolidate or disclose |
| Control of profit entity | Consolidate or equity method |
| Joint venture | Proportionately consolidate or equity method |
| Significant influence: | |
| NFPO | Full disclosure |
| Profit entity | Equity method |
| Economic interest | Full disclosure |
| Other investment: | |
| Profit entity | Fair value method or cost method or amortized cost method |

**SECTION 4460** *DISCLOSURE OF RELATED-PARTY TRANSACTIONS BY NOT-FOR-PROFIT ORGANIZATIONS*   Related parties exist where one party is able to exercise control, joint control, or significant influence over another party. The other party may be either another NFPO or a profit-oriented enterprise. If one NFPO has an economic interest in another NFPO, the two parties are related. A related-party transaction has occurred when there has been a transfer of economic resources or obligations or services between the parties. Unlike Part II Section 3840, which prescribes both measurement and disclosure, this standard prescribes only disclosure for related-party transactions and does not state any requirements related to measurement. The disclosures required here are virtually identical to those required in Part II Section 3840. This section requires that the NFPO should disclose the following information about its transactions with related parties:

(a) A description of the relationship between the transacting parties

(b) A description of the transaction(s), including those for which no amount has been recorded

(c) The recorded amount of the transactions classified by financial statement category

(d) The measurement basis used for recognizing the transaction in the financial statements

(e) Amounts due to or from related parties and the terms and conditions relating thereto

(f) Contractual obligations with related parties, separate from other contractual obligations

(g) Contingencies involving related parties, separate from other contingencies

> *An NFPO must disclose all related-party transactions with another NFPO or a profit-oriented entity.*

### SECTION 4470 *DISCLOSURE OF ALLOCATED EXPENSES BY NOT-FOR-PROFIT ORGANIZATIONS*

When an organization classifies its expenses by function on the statement of operations, it may need or want to allocate certain expenses to a number of functions to which the expenses relate. For example, fundraising expenses and general support expenses usually contribute to or produce the output of more than one function and are often considered to be directly related to the output of each of those functions. Since aggregate amounts reported for fundraising and general support functions are often of particular significance to financial statement users, this standard requires that the following be disclosed when these two types of expenses are allocated to other functions:

- The accounting policy for the allocation of expenses among functions, the nature of the expenses being allocated, and the basis on which such allocations have been made.

- The amounts allocated from functions, and the amounts and the functions to which they have been allocated.

However, this section does not require organizations to classify their expenses by function or to undertake any allocations. Only if it does so is the above disclosure necessary.

> *An NFPO must disclose details related to any allocation of fundraising and general support costs to different functions.*

## LO3 THE BASICS OF FUND ACCOUNTING

Fund accounting can be and has been used very successfully to keep track of restricted resources and/or programs, and to convey information through the financial statements about the restrictions placed on the organization's resources. The concepts involved can be summarized as follows:

Fund accounting comprises the collective accounting procedures resulting in a self-balancing set of accounts for each fund established by legal, contractual or voluntary actions of an organization. Elements of a fund can include assets, liabilities, net assets, revenues and expenses (and gains and losses where appropriate). Fund accounting involves an accounting segregation, although not necessarily a physical segregation, of resources. [4400.02]

The following simple example illustrates the use of fund accounting as a means of reporting this form of stewardship.

**EXAMPLE 3**   The financial statements of the Helpful Society (HS) at the end of Year 1 are presented in Exhibit 12.1. HS presents two funds in its year-end financial statements. The resources in the *general*

**EXHIBIT 12.1**

**HELPFUL SOCIETY**
**STATEMENT OF FINANCIAL POSITION**
December 31, Year 1

|  | General Fund | Building Fund | Total |
|---|---|---|---|
| *Assets* |  |  |  |
| Cash | $17,500 | $ 6,000 | $ 23,500 |
| Pledges receivable | 50,000 |  | 50,000 |
| Investments in debt securities | 25,000 | 88,635 | 113,635 |
| Total | $92,500 | $94,635 | $187,135 |
| *Liabilities and Fund Balance* |  |  |  |
| Accounts payable and accrued liabilities | $60,300 |  | $ 60,300 |
| Fund balance | 32,200 | $94,635 | 126,835 |
| Total | $92,500 | $94,635 | $187,135 |

**STATEMENT OF REVENUE AND EXPENSES**
**AND CHANGES IN FUND BALANCES**
For the year ended December 31, Year 1

|  | General Fund | Building Fund | Total |
|---|---|---|---|
| *Revenues* |  |  |  |
| Contributions | $923,000 | $102,000 | $1,025,000 |
| Interest | 2,700 |  | 2,700 |
| Total | 925,700 | 102,000 | 1,027,700 |
| *Expenses* |  |  |  |
| Program A | 625,000 |  | 625,000 |
| Program B | 190,000 |  | 190,000 |
| Program C | 100,000 |  | 100,000 |
| Fundraising | 3,600 | 6,410 | 10,010 |
| Miscellaneous |  | 955 | 955 |
| **Total** | 918,600 | 7,365 | 925,965 |
| Excess of revenue over expenses | 7,100 | 94,635 | 101,735 |
| Fund balance, January 1 | 25,100 | 0 | 25,100 |
| Fund balance, December 31 | $ 32,200 | $ 94,635 | $ 126,835 |

*This exhibit illustrates fund accounting. When combined with a policy of non-capitalization of capital assets it becomes a resources-in-and-out form of stewardship reporting.*

fund can be used to carry out the normal activities of the organization, while the resources in the *building* fund, which was established during the current year, are restricted. Each year, the organization raises money through donations and spends the funds raised on programs A, B, and C. During the current year, the general fund's revenues were $7,100 greater than its expenses; as a result, its equity (described as fund balance) increased by that amount. Note that revenues and expenses are measured under the accrual method, so the statement does not show cash inflows and outflows. The assets on hand at the end of the year can be viewed as resources that are spendable. The liabilities at this date are a claim against these resources; therefore, the fund balance at the end of the current year represents net resources amounting to $32,200 that is available for spending in future years.

> *Fund accounting is often used to convey information about restricted resources.*

During the current year, a special fundraising campaign was initiated to raise the money necessary to purchase and furnish a building. The building fund's resources on hand at the end of the year, amounting to $94,635, were the result of $102,000 collected during the year, less the fundraising costs and miscellaneous expenses incurred, which amounted to $7,365. The campaign will continue until its goal is reached. At that time, the purchase of the building and furnishings will be recorded as an asset of this fund.

> *Helpful Society presents funds in separate columns for both the statement of financial position and the statement of revenues and expenses, and for changes in fund balances.*

This example was presented to illustrate the basic idea behind financial reporting on a fund basis. In our example, the columnar approach is used to present the two funds. An alternative that gained some prior acceptance was the layered approach, which presented funds one after another, so that the first page would show the operating fund statements, the second page would show the building fund, and so on. The columnar approach is preferred because of a requirement to show totals for each financial statement item for all funds presented.

A fund basis can be used, but it is not necessary to prepare all statements using this method. For example, the operating statement could be presented on a fund basis while the rest of the statements could be presented on a non-fund basis. An organization that uses fund accounting in its financial statements should provide a brief description of the purpose of each fund reported in the notes to the financial statements.

# ACCOUNTING FOR CONTRIBUTIONS

Part III has defined two methods of accounting for contributions: the *deferral* method and the *restricted fund* method. The deferral method can be used with or without fund accounting. The restricted fund method has to be used in combination with fund accounting.

> *An NFPO can choose either the deferral method or the restricted fund method to account for contributions.*

If the organization wants to present an overall picture of the organization—that is, a set of statements with only one column for each year—it must use the deferral method. If it wants to report on a fund accounting basis—separate columns for different funds—it can choose the deferral method for all funds or the restricted fund method.

With fund accounting, it is easier to present and report on the different restrictions placed on contributions. However, as we will see, the deferral method does a better job of matching revenues to expenses, which makes it easier to see what portion of expenses is financed by contributions and what portion is financed by other sources.

## LO4 The Restricted Fund Method

This method requires an NFPO to report a general fund, at least one restricted fund, and, if it has endowments or receives endowment contributions, an endowment fund. The general fund reports all unrestricted revenue and restricted contributions for which no corresponding restricted fund is presented. The fund balance represents net assets that are not subject to externally imposed restrictions. Separate accounts for each fund will be used in the general ledger to record externally restricted revenue. In turn, separate columns will be used in the financial statements to report the restricted funds. Specific requirements are outlined as follows:

- Endowment contributions will be reported as revenue in the endowment fund, and because there are no related expenses associated with endowment contributions, no expenses will appear in the statement of operations for the endowment fund.

- The general fund records all unrestricted contributions and investment income, including unrestricted income from endowment fund investments.

- If some of the endowment fund income is restricted, it is reflected as revenue in the particular restricted fund involved.

- If some of the endowment fund income is permanently restricted, because the purchasing power of the endowment is required to be maintained, it is recorded as revenue of the endowment fund.

- Externally restricted contributions for which there is a corresponding restricted fund are recorded as revenue of the restricted fund when received or receivable.

- If an externally restricted contribution or externally restricted investment income is received for which there is no corresponding restricted fund, the amounts are recorded in the general fund in accordance with the deferral method. In other words, they are recorded as deferred revenue in the general fund and matched with the related expenses in that fund when these expenses are incurred.

- If management decides to impose internal restrictions on general fund unrestricted contributions, the contributions are initially reported as revenue in the general fund. The transfers are reported in the statement of changes in fund balances below the line "excess of revenue over expenses." Note disclosure should clearly indicate the amount of resources shown in restricted funds that have been designated as such by management, because these amounts do not satisfy the *Handbook*'s definition of a contribution.

> *Contributions are reported as revenue when received/receivable if a separate restricted or endowment fund has been established for these contributions.*
>
> *The provisions of the deferral method might have to be applied when the restricted fund method is used.*

The excess of revenues over expenses in the general fund represents the increase in unrestricted resources during the period. The fund balance in the general fund shows the unrestricted net assets at the end of the period. A restricted fund shows no deferred revenue. The fund balance of a restricted fund represents the amount of net assets that are restricted for that particular fund's purpose. The fund balance in the endowment fund represents the net assets that have permanent restrictions on them.

> *Fund balances for the restricted and endowment funds represent the amount of net assets restricted for that fund's purpose.*

Under the restricted fund method, instead of presenting a statement of changes in net assets (as is required under the deferral method of recording contributions), a statement of changes in fund balances is prepared. Because of the requirement to capitalize long-lived assets, capital assets must appear on the statement of financial position of either the general fund or one of the restricted funds (excluding the endowment fund).

The following example on Blue Shield Agency (with 000s omitted) will be used to illustrate the journal entries made for various funds and the annual general-purpose financial statements prepared using the restricted fund method of accounting for contributions.

The Blue Shield Agency is a charitable organization located in a mid-sized Canadian city. The major goal of the organization is to provide food and shelter for the homeless. It operates out of its own premises, and while it has some permanent employees, it also relies heavily on volunteers.

The agency's funds have four sources:

- Government grants are received annually to fund the regular food and shelter operating activities. When the need arises, special government grants are solicited to fund capital asset additions and major renovations.

- Donations are received as a result of public campaigns held each March to raise funds for the current year's operating costs.

- A United Way grant is received each November to help fund the next year's operations.

- Investment income is received from an endowment fund and other investments.

The agency maintains its records in accordance with the restricted fund method of accounting for contributions, and prepares its annual financial statements on this basis. The three funds being used are described below.

**GENERAL FUND**  This fund is used to record the agency's operating activities. Revenues consist of government operating grants, the proceeds from the annual fundraising campaign, the United Way grant, investment income from the endowment fund, and term deposit interest. Each year, the grant from the United Way is recorded as deferred revenue to be matched against the operating expenses of the year following. Expenses are for the food and shelter programs and for administration costs. While some donated materials and services are received each year, no record of these donations is made in the ledger accounts. Small-equipment purchases made from this fund are capitalized in the capital fund.

> *The general fund captures the agency's operating activities.*

**CAPITAL FUND** This fund is used to account for restricted funds raised for building and equipment acquisitions. The capital fund also records the capitalization of buildings and equipment and the amortization taken. Equipment acquisitions made from the general fund are also capitalized in this fund.

Approximately 20 years ago the city donated a building to the agency. While the city retained title to the land on which the building is situated, the agency will not be required to move, and the building will not be torn down, as long as the agency continues with its programs. The value of the donated building was *not* recorded at the time of the donation because it was the organization's policy not to capitalize buildings and equipment.

When the *Handbook*'s current NFPO sections became operative several years ago, the organization spent considerable time and money searching past records to determine the cost of capital assets purchased from both restricted and non-restricted contributions, as well as the fair values of capital assets donated. Because the new *Handbook* had to be applied retrospectively, the following journal entries were made at that time to accomplish this:

| | | |
|---|---|---|
| Equipment and furniture | 1,100 | |
| Accumulated amortization | | 300 |
| Fund balance—unrestricted | | 800 |

This entry recognized the cost of equipment acquired in past years using unrestricted contributions and the accumulated amortization taken to the date when the new *Handbook* sections were applied.

| | | |
|---|---|---|
| Buildings | 2,000 | |
| Accumulated amortization | | 900 |
| Fund balance—restricted | | 1,100 |

This entry recorded the fair value of the building donated by the city and the accumulated amortization taken to the date when the new *Handbook* sections were applied.

> *The previously unreported capital assets were recorded in the capital fund with an accompanying increase in net assets.*

**ENDOWMENT FUND** The $500 in this fund was bequeathed to the agency by its founder five years ago. Investment income earned is to be used for operating purposes and is recorded in the general fund.

The statements of financial position of the funds of Blue Shield as at January 1, Year 6, are presented in Exhibit 12.2. The net assets of the capital fund consists of $1,712 pertaining to capital assets that had been donated or purchased with funds restricted for the purchase of capital assets and $360 pertaining to capital assets that had been purchased with unrestricted funds.

This form of presentation of fund financial statements is called the *multicolumn approach* because each of the fund's financial statements is presented in its own separate column. If fund accounting is used, the *Handbook* requires that totals be shown for each item presented in the statement of financial position and statement of changes in fund balances, so that the "big picture" for the entire organization can be seen. This approach can become very cumbersome if an organization has a large number of funds that need to be presented separately because of all of the restrictions involved. An alternative is to combine the funds into a single set of statements, use the deferral method of accounting for contributions, and provide extensive footnote disclosure of resource restrictions. For the statement of operations, a total column must be presented for general funds, endowment funds, and restricted funds. Although it is desirable to show a total for all funds, it is not necessary under the restricted fund method.

**EXHIBIT 12.2**

**BLUE SHIELD AGENCY**
**STATEMENT OF FINANCIAL POSITION**
January 1, Year 6
(in thousands of dollars)

| | General Fund | Capital Fund | Endowment Fund | Total |
|---|---|---|---|---|
| **Current Assets** | | | | |
| Cash and term deposits | $417 | $ 62 | | $ 479 |
| Pledges receivable | 490 | | | 490 |
| | 907 | 62 | | 969 |
| Investments | | | $500 | 500 |
| Capital assets: | | | | |
| Equipment and furniture | | 1,482 | | 1,482 |
| Buildings | | 2,095 | | 2,095 |
| Accumulated amortization | | (1,517) | | (1,517) |
| | | 2,060 | | 2,060 |
| Total assets | $907 | $2,122 | $500 | $3,529 |
| **Current Liabilities** | | | | |
| Accounts payable | $613 | $ 50 | | $ 663 |
| Wages payable | 70 | | | 70 |
| Accrued liabilities | 82 | | | 82 |
| Deferred revenue | 40 | | | 40 |
| | 805 | 50 | | 855 |
| **Fund Balances** | | | | |
| Externally restricted | | 1,712 | $500 | 2,212 |
| Unrestricted | 102 | 360 | | 462 |
| | 102 | 2,072 | 500 | 2,674 |
| Total liabilities and fund balances | $907 | $2,122 | $500 | $3,529 |

> *When reporting on a fund basis, the total for each statement of financial position item must be shown.*
>
> *Instead of a section for owner's equity, an NFPO's statement of financial position has a section called "fund balances" or "surplus."*

**YEAR 6 EVENTS**  The year's events are summarized below (all dollar amounts are in thousands unless stated otherwise). Journal entries to account for each of the events are presented at the end of the list of events.

(a) The accounts and wages payable and the accrued liabilities at the beginning of the year were paid.

(b) The deferred revenue from Year 5 consisted of the grant from the United Way. An entry was made to recognize this as revenue in Year 6.

(c) The pledges receivable at the beginning of the year were collected in full.

(d) The fundraising campaign was held in March to collect funds for Year 6 operations. Cash of $1,187 was collected, and an additional $800 was pledged and is expected to be received in the early part of Year 7. Total fundraising costs were $516, of which $453 was paid in cash, $50 is owed to suppliers, and $13 has been accrued.

(e) During Year 6, the agency announced a plan to construct an addition to its building at an estimated cost of $1,500. The budget includes equipment acquisitions. The addition will be built in two phases, with completion expected in Year 8. At the end of Year 6, the first phase was out for tender, with construction to commence early in Year 7.

   The government announced a grant of $600 in Year 6 to cover the first phase and has remitted $450 of this, with the balance promised in Year 7. The agency spent $103 on equipment near the end of Year 6, of which $91 has been paid and $12 is owed. A public campaign will be conducted next year to raise the balance of the funds needed to complete the project.

(f) Government grants for operating purposes totalled $1,200 in Year 6, of which $910 was received during the year, with the balance expected in January, Year 7.

(g) Invoices totalling $1,866 were received on purchase orders originally recorded at an estimated cost of $1,870. Suppliers were paid $1,446 on account for these invoices, and the balance owing is still outstanding. The costs were allocated as follows:

| | |
|---|---:|
| Shelter program | $650 |
| Food program | 960 |
| Administration | 256 |

(h) The total wage costs, of which $357 was paid and $183 is payable at year-end, were as follows:

| | |
|---|---:|
| Shelter program | $ 90 |
| Food program | 150 |
| Administration | 300 |

(i) The United Way grant amounting to $65 was received in December.

(j) Late in the year a prominent supporter donated $50 to be held in endowment, with the income earned to be unrestricted.

(k) The investments in the endowment fund earned interest of $40; a further $14 in interest was received from the term deposits held in the general fund.

(l) Refrigeration equipment costing $3 was purchased with general fund cash (and transferred to the capital account).

(m) The Year 6 amortization charges amounted to $150 of which $90 pertains to capital assets that had been donated or purchased with funds restricted for the purchase of capital assets and of which $60 pertains to capital assets that had been purchased with unrestricted funds.

   The journal entries required to record these events in each of the three funds are presented next in the order listed:

| | | | |
|---|---|---:|---:|
| (a) | *General fund* | | |
| | Accounts payable | 613 | |
| | Wages payable | 70 | |
| | Accrued liabilities | 82 | |
| |    Cash | | 765 |
| | *Capital fund* | | |
| | Accounts payable | 50 | |
| |    Cash | | 50 |

---

*Accounting records are maintained for each individual fund. Journal entries show the fund being adjusted.*

---

(b)  *General fund*

| | | |
|---|---:|---:|
| Deferred revenue | 40 | |
|     Revenue—United Way grant | | 40 |

(c)  *General fund*

| | | |
|---|---:|---:|
| Cash | 490 | |
|     Pledges receivable | | 490 |

(d)  *General fund*

| | | |
|---|---:|---:|
| Cash | 1,187 | |
| Pledges receivable | 800 | |
|     Revenue—donations | | 1,987 |
| Expenses—fundraising | 516 | |
|     Cash | | 453 |
|     Accounts payable | | 50 |
|     Accrued liabilities | | 13 |

---

*Contributions and pledges for the current year are reported as revenue in the current year.*

---

(e)  *Capital fund*

| | | |
|---|---:|---:|
| Cash | 450 | |
| Government grant receivable | 150 | |
|     Revenue—government grant | | 600 |
| Equipment | 103 | |
|     Cash | | 91 |
|     Accounts payable | | 12 |

(f)  *General fund*

| | | |
|---|---:|---:|
| Cash | 910 | |
| Government grant receivable | 290 | |
|     Revenue—government grant | | 1,200 |

---

*Contributions and pledges for a restricted fund are reported as revenue when received/receivable.*

---

(g)  *General fund*

| | | |
|---|---:|---:|
| Expenses—shelter program | 650 | |
| Expenses—food program | 960 | |
| Expenses—administration | 256 | |
|     Cash | | 1,446 |
|     Accounts payable | | 420 |

(h) *General fund*

| | | |
|---|---|---|
| Expenses—shelter program | 90 | |
| Expenses—food program | 150 | |
| Expenses—administration | 300 | |
|     Cash | | 357 |
|     Wages payable | | 183 |

(i) *General fund*

| | | |
|---|---|---|
| Cash | 65 | |
|     Deferred revenue—United Way | | 65 |

> *Contributions for next year's activities are deferred when a separate restricted fund is not established for the contributions.*

(j) *Endowment fund*

| | | |
|---|---|---|
| Cash | 50 | |
|     Revenue—contribution | | 50 |

(k) *General fund*

| | | |
|---|---|---|
| Cash | 54 | |
|     Revenue—investment income | | 54 |

(l) *General fund*

| | | |
|---|---|---|
| Transfer to capital fund | 3 | |
|     Cash | | 3 |
| *Capital fund* | | |
| Equipment | 3 | |
|     Transfer from general fund | | 3 |

(m) *Capital fund*

| | | |
|---|---|---|
| Expenses—amortization | 150 | |
|     Accumulated amortization | | 150 |

After these journal entries are posted, financial statements as at December 31, Year 6, can be prepared as shown in Exhibit 12.3. Note that while a fund type of cash flow statement could be prepared, the one in this illustration has been prepared on a non-fund basis, which is in accordance with the *Handbook*'s pronouncements. Letters shown in parentheses represent the journal entries affecting the cash account.

The net assets of the capital fund can be reconciled as follows:

| | Restricted | Unrestricted | Total |
|---|---|---|---|
| Balance, beginning of year | $1,712 | $ 360 | $2,072 |
| Revenue | 600 | | 600 |
| Amortization expense | (90) | (60) | (150) |
| Transfer in of unrestricted funds | 0 | 3 | 3 |
| Balance, end of year | $2,222 | $ 303 | $2,525 |

**EXHIBIT 12.3**

**BLUE SHIELD AGENCY**
**STATEMENT OF FINANCIAL POSITION**
December 31, Year 6
(in thousands of dollars)

| | General Fund | Capital Fund | Endowment Fund | Total |
|---|---|---|---|---|
| *Current Assets* | | | | |
| Cash and term deposits | $    99 | $   371 | $  50 | $   520 |
| Pledges receivable | 800 | | | 800 |
| Government grants receivable | 290 | 150 | | 440 |
| | 1,189 | 521 | 50 | 1,760 |
| *Investments* | | | 500 | 500 |
| Capital assets: | | | | |
| Equipment and furniture | | 1,588 | | 1,588 |
| Buildings | | 2,095 | | 2,095 |
| Accumulated depreciation | | (1,667) | | (1,667) |
| | | 2,016 | | 2,016 |
| Total assets | $1,189 | $2,537 | $550 | $4,276 |
| *Current Liabilities* | | | | |
| Accounts payable | $   470 | $    12 | | $   482 |
| Wages payable | 183 | | | 183 |
| Accrued liabilities | 13 | | | 13 |
| Deferred revenue | 65 | | | 65 |
| | 731 | 12 | | 743 |
| *Fund Balances* | | | | |
| Externally restricted funds | | 2,222 | $550 | 2,772 |
| Unrestricted funds | 458 | 303 | | 761 |
| | 458 | 2,525 | 550 | 3,533 |
| Total liabilities and fund balances | $1,189 | $2,537 | $550 | $4,276 |

The deferral method is used to account for contributions reported in the general fund.

**BLUE SHIELD AGENCY**
**STATEMENT OF REVENUES, EXPENSES, AND**
**CHANGES IN FUND BALANCES**
For the year ended December 31, Year 6
(in thousands of dollars)

| | General Fund | Capital Fund | Endowment Fund | Total |
|---|---|---|---|---|
| *Revenues* | | | | |
| Government grants | $1,200 | $600 | | $1,800 |
| United Way grant | 40 | | | 40 |
| Contributions | 1,987 | | $50 | 2,037 |
| Investment income | 54 | | | 54 |
| | 3,281 | 600 | 50 | 3,931 |

(continued)

**EXHIBIT 12.3** *(continued)*

| | General Fund | Capital Fund | Endowment Fund | Total |
|---|---|---|---|---|
| *Expenses* | | | | |
| Shelter program | 740 | | | 740 |
| Food program | 1,110 | | | 1,110 |
| Administration | 556 | | | 556 |
| Fundraising | 516 | | | 516 |
| Amortization | | 150 | | 150 |
| | 2,922 | 150 | | 3,072 |
| Excess of revenue over expenses | 359 | 450 | 50 | 859 |
| Interfund transfers | (3) | 3 | | |
| Fund balances, January 1 | 102 | 2,072 | 500 | 2,674 |
| Fund balances, December 31 | $ 458 | $2,525 | $550 | $3,533 |

> *Fund balances show the restrictions on the net assets of the organization.*
>
> *Expenses are classified by function.*

## BLUE SHIELD AGENCY
## CASH FLOW STATEMENT
For the year ended December 31, Year 6
(in thousands of dollars)

| | |
|---|---|
| *Cash Flows from Operating Activities* | |
| Cash received from government operating grants **(f)** | $ 910 |
| Cash received from United Way grant **(i)** | 65 |
| Cash received from general contributions **(c)**, **(d)** | 1,677 |
| Cash received from investment income **(k)** | 54 |
| Cash paid to suppliers **(a)**, **(g)** | (2,141) |
| Cash paid to employees **(a)**, **(h)** | (427) |
| Cash paid for fundraising **(d)** | (453) |
| Net cash used in operating activities | (315) |
| *Cash Flows from Investing Activities* | |
| Cash paid for capital asset acquisitions **(a)**, **(e)**, **(l)** | (144) |
| Net cash used in investing activities | (144) |
| *Cash Flows from Financing Activities* | |
| Contributions of cash for endowment **(j)** | 50 |
| Cash received from government grant **(e)** | 450 |
| Net cash generated through financing activities | 500 |
| Net increase in cash and term deposits | 41 |
| Cash and term deposits—January 1 | 479 |
| Cash and term deposits—December 31 | $ 520 |

> *It is not required to present a cash flow statement on a fund basis.*

The closing entries for each fund are prepared as follows:

*General fund*

| | | |
|---|---|---|
| Revenue—government grant | 1,200 | |
| Revenue—United Way grant | 40 | |
| Revenue—contributions | 1,987 | |
| Revenue—investment income | 54 | |
| Expenses—shelter program | | 740 |
| Expenses—food program | | 1,110 |
| Expenses—administration | | 556 |
| Expenses—fundraising | | 516 |
| Fund balance | | 359 |
| Fund balance | 3 | |
| Transfer to capital fund | | 3 |

*Capital fund*

| | | |
|---|---|---|
| Revenue—government grant | 600 | |
| Expenses—amortization | | 150 |
| Fund balance | | 450 |
| Transfer from general fund | 3 | |
| Fund balance | | 3 |

*Endowment fund*

| | | |
|---|---|---|
| Revenue contributions | 50 | |
| Fund balance | | 50 |

> *Revenues, expenses, and fund transfers are closed to fund balances.*

This comprehensive example has illustrated the accounts used and the resulting financial statements under the restricted fund method. The extensive footnote disclosures required by the *Handbook* have not been illustrated.

## LO5 The Deferral Method

The deferral method matches contribution revenues with related expenses. Unrestricted contributions are reported as revenue in the period received or receivable, because there are no particular related expenses associated with them.

> *The deferral method requires that contribution revenue be matched to expenses.*

Endowment contributions are not shown in the operating statement; rather, they are reflected in the statement of changes in net assets. This is because endowment contributions, by definition, will never have related expenses.

Restricted contributions must be matched against related expenses. This matching principle has different implications for different kinds of restricted contributions, as follows:

- Restricted contributions for expenses of future periods are deferred and recognized as revenue in the same periods as the related expenses are incurred.

- The handling of restricted contributions for the acquisition of capital assets depends on whether related expenses are associated with them. If the capital asset is subject to amortization, the related expense is the yearly amortization. The restricted contribution is deferred and recognized as revenue on the same basis as the asset is being amortized. If the capital asset is not subject to amortization (e.g., land), there will be no expenses to match against. In the same manner as for endowment contributions, the restricted capital asset contributions of this type are reflected in the statement of changes in net assets.

- Restricted contributions for expenses of the current period are recognized as revenue in the current period. Matching is achieved, and there is no need for deferral.

> *Contributions for a depreciable asset are recognized as revenue as the asset is being amortized.*

Investment income can be either unrestricted or restricted. Unrestricted investment income is recognized as revenue when it is earned. Restricted investment income has to be recognized in the same manner as restricted contributions. For example, if an endowment contribution states that the purchasing power of the contribution must be preserved, some portion of the income earned must be used to increase the endowment. This portion is treated in exactly the same manner as an endowment contribution, and is reflected in the statement of changes in net assets. Other types of restricted investment income must be deferred and matched against expense in the manner previously discussed. If all investment income is restricted, it is quite possible that all investment income earned in a period will be deferred.

The matching of revenue and expense for an NFPO is the exact opposite to that for a profit-oriented enterprise. With the latter, revenues are recognized and then expenses are matched with those revenues. With an NFPO, restricted revenues are matched to expenses. This means that if contributions have been collected to fund certain expenses and those expenses have yet to be incurred, the contributions are recognized as deferred revenue until a later period, when they can be matched with the expenses.

To illustrate the journal entries made and the annual general-purpose financial statements prepared using the deferral method of accounting for contributions, we will return to the Blue Shield example and use the same basic information as previously provided (with 000s omitted).

When the *Handbook*'s current NFPO sections became operative several years ago, Blue Shield would have made the following entry under the deferral method:

| | | |
|---|---|---|
| Equipment and furniture | 1,100 | |
| Accumulated amortization | | 300 |
| Unrestricted net assets | | 800 |

This entry recognized the cost of equipment acquired in past years using unrestricted contributions and the accumulated amortization taken to the date when the new *Handbook* sections were applied.

| | | |
|---|---|---|
| Buildings | 2,000 | |
| Accumulated amortization | | 900 |
| Deferred contributions related to capital assets | | 1,100 |

> *Deferred contributions represent the unamortized amount of capital assets either donated or acquired with restricted contributions.*

This entry recorded the fair value of the building donated by the city and the accumulated amortization taken to date. A capital asset donation is treated in the same manner as a contribution restricted for the purchase of a capital asset. As the asset is amortized, a portion of the deferred contribution is recognized as a match against this expense.

The statement of financial position of Blue Shield as at January 1, Year 6, is presented in Exhibit 12.4.

When this statement of financial position is compared to the statement of financial position under the restricted fund method (see Exhibit 12.2), the amounts used on the asset side are fairly obvious. The liability side needs further clarification. The amount in deferred revenue is the United Way grant. The deferred building campaign contributions balance is the externally restricted fund balance from the capital fund, and represents restricted funds received but not spent on capital assets. When this money

**EXHIBIT 12.4**

**BLUE SHIELD AGENCY**
**STATEMENT OF FINANCIAL POSITION**
January 1, Year 6
(in thousands of dollars)

| | |
|---|---:|
| *Current Assets* | |
| Cash and term deposits | $ 479 |
| Pledges receivable | 490 |
| | 969 |
| *Investments* | 500 |
| Capital assets: | |
| Equipment and furniture | 1,482 |
| Buildings | 2,095 |
| Accumulated amortization | (1,517) |
| | 2,060 |
| Total assets | $3,529 |
| *Current Liabilities* | |
| Accounts payable | $ 663 |
| Wages payable | 70 |
| Accrued liabilities | 82 |
| Deferred revenue | 40 |
| | 855 |
| *Long-Term Liabilities* | |
| Deferred contributions related to capital assets | 920 |
| Deferred building campaign contributions | 12 |
| | 932 |
| Total liabilities | 1,787 |
| *Net Assets* | |
| Net assets restricted for endowment purposes | 500 |
| Unrestricted net assets | 1,242 |
| | 1,742 |
| Total liabilities and net assets | $3,529 |

*It is quite common to not present separate funds when the entity uses the deferral method.*

is spent, an amount will be transferred from this deferred contribution account to the deferred contributions related to capital assets account. The deferred contributions related to capital assets balance represents that portion of the unamortized balance of capital assets that was either donated or purchased from contributions restricted for capital asset purchases. This will be transferred to revenue in future periods as these assets are amortized.

> *The deferred contributions distinguish between unspent contributions and the unamortized portion of contributions being matched to amortization expense.*

The differences in presentation are as follows:

| | |
|---|---:|
| Restricted fund method: | |
|    Fund balances—unrestricted | $462 |
|    Fund balances—externally restricted | 2,212 |
| | $2,674 |
| Deferral method: | |
|    Liability—deferred contributions related to capital assets | $920 |
|    Liability—deferred building campaign contributions | 12 |
| | 932 |
|    Net assets restricted for endowment purposes | 500 |
|    Net assets—unrestricted | 1,242 |
| | 1,742 |
| | $2,674 |

> *The financial statement presentation for contributions is substantially different under the two different reporting methods.*

**YEAR 6 EVENTS**  The year's events for all transactions are the same as were used in the previous example. The journal entries required to record these events are presented next in the order listed.

| | | | |
|---|---|---:|---:|
| (a) | Accounts payable | 663 | |
| | Wages payable | 70 | |
| | Accrued liabilities | 82 | |
| |    Cash | | 815 |

> *Fund accounting is not applied and journal entries are not segregated by fund.*

| | | | |
|---|---|---:|---:|
| (b) | Deferred revenue | 40 | |
| |    Revenue—United Way grant | | 40 |
| (c) | Cash | 490 | |
| |    Pledges receivable | | 490 |
| (d) | Cash | 1,187 | |
| | Pledges receivable | 800 | |
| |    Revenue—donations | | 1,987 |
| | Expenses—fundraising | 516 | |
| |    Cash | | 453 |
| |    Accounts payable | | 50 |
| |    Accrued liabilities | | 13 |

*(continued)*

> *Contributions and pledges for the current year are reported as revenue in the current year.*

| | | | |
|---|---|---|---|
| (e) | Cash | 450 | |
| | Government grant receivable | 150 | |
| |     Deferred building campaign contributions | | 600 |
| | Equipment | 103 | |
| |     Cash | | 91 |
| |     Accounts payable | | 12 |
| | Deferred building campaign contributions | 103 | |
| |     Deferred contributions—capital assets | | 103 |

> *Contributions restricted for depreciable capital assets are reported as deferred contributions.*

| | | | |
|---|---|---|---|
| (f) | Cash | 910 | |
| | Government grant receivable | 290 | |
| |     Revenue—government grant | | 1,200 |
| (g) | Expenses—shelter program | 650 | |
| | Expenses—food program | 960 | |
| | Expenses—administration | 256 | |
| |     Cash | | 1,446 |
| |     Accounts payable | | 420 |
| (h) | Expenses—shelter program | 90 | |
| | Expenses—food program | 150 | |
| | Expenses—administration | 300 | |
| |     Cash | | 357 |
| |     Wages payable | | 183 |
| (i) | Cash | 65 | |
| |     Deferred revenue—United Way | | 65 |

> *Contributions for next year's activities are deferred until related expenses are recognized.*

| | | | |
|---|---|---|---|
| (j) | Cash | 50 | |
| |     Net assets—endowment | | 50 |

> *Endowment contributions are reported directly in net assets.*

| | | | |
|---|---|---|---|
| (k) | Cash | 54 | |
| |     Revenue—investment income | | 54 |
| (l) | Equipment | 3 | |
| |     Cash | | 3 |
| (m) | Expenses—amortization | 150 | |
| |     Accumulated amortization | | 150 |
| | Deferred contributions—capital assets | 90 | |
| |     Amortization of deferred contributions | | 90 |

> *Deferred contributions are brought into income as the capital assets are amortized over their useful lives.*

After these journal entries are posted, financial statements as at December 31, Year 6, can be prepared as shown in Exhibit 12.5. The statement of revenue and expenses shows not only unrestricted revenues and expenses but also the restricted revenues recognized during the year as a match to the expenses associated with them (amortization in this case).

The endowment contribution received during the year does not appear on the operating statement, because no expenses will ever appear for the required matching process to occur. Instead, this special restricted resource is shown on the statement of changes in "net assets" as an increase in net assets restricted for endowment. Extensive footnote disclosure is required when statements are prepared using the deferral method, in order to clearly define the amount and nature of restricted and unrestricted resources.

## EXHIBIT 12.5

**BLUE SHIELD AGENCY**
**STATEMENT OF FINANCIAL POSITION**
December 31, Year 6
(in thousands of dollars)

| | |
|---|---:|
| *Current Assets* | |
| Cash and term deposits | $ 520 |
| Pledges receivable | 800 |
| Government grants receivable | 440 |
| | 1,760 |
| *Investments* | 500 |
| *Capital Assets* | |
| Equipment and furniture | 1,588 |
| Buildings | 2,095 |
| Accumulated amortization | (1,667) |
| | 2,016 |
| Total assets | $4,276 |
| *Current Liabilities* | |
| Accounts payable | $ 482 |
| Wages payable | 183 |
| Accrued liabilities | 13 |
| Deferred revenue | 65 |
| | 743 |
| *Long-Term Liabilities* | |
| Deferred contributions related to capital assets | 933 |
| Deferred building campaign contributions | 509 |
| | 1,442 |
| Total liabilities | 2,185 |
| *Net Assets* | |
| Net assets restricted for endowment purposes | 550 |
| Unrestricted net assets | 1,541 |
| | 2,091 |
| Total liabilities and net assets | $4,276 |

*The unamortized portion of spent restricted contributions is segregated from the unspent restricted contributions.*

*(continued)*

| Revenues | |
|---|---:|
| Government grants | $1,200 |
| United Way grant | 40 |
| Contributions | 1,987 |
| Investment income | 54 |
| Amortization of deferred contributions | 90 |
| | 3,371 |
| | |
| Expenses | |
| Shelter program | 740 |
| Food program | 1,110 |
| Administration | 556 |
| Fundraising | 516 |
| Amortization of capital assets | 150 |
| | 3,072 |
| Excess of revenues over expenses | $ 299 |

**BLUE SHIELD AGENCY**
**STATEMENT OF CHANGES IN NET ASSETS**
For the year ended December 31, Year 6
(in thousands of dollars)

| | Restricted for Endowment Purposes | Unrestricted | Total |
|---|:---:|:---:|:---:|
| Balance, Jan. 1 | $500 | $1,242 | $1,742 |
| Excess of revenues over expenses | | 299 | 299 |
| Endowment contributions | 50 | | 50 |
| Balance, Dec. 31 | $550 | $1,541 | $2,091 |

**BLUE SHIELD AGENCY**
**CASH FLOW STATEMENT**
For the year ended December 31, Year 6
(in thousands of dollars)

| *Cash Flows from Operating Activities* | |
|---|---:|
| Cash received from government operating grants **(f)** | $ 910 |
| Cash received from United Way grant **(i)** | 65 |
| Cash received from general contributions **(c)**, **(d)** | 1,677 |
| Cash received from investment income **(k)** | 54 |
| Cash paid to suppliers **(a)**, **(g)** | (2,141) |
| Cash paid to employees **(a)**, **(h)** | (427) |
| Cash paid for fundraising **(d)** | (453) |
| Net cash used in operating activities | (315) |
| *Cash Flows from Investing Activities* | |
| Cash paid for capital asset acquisitions **(a)**, **(e)**, **(l)** | (144) |
| Net cash used in investing activities | (144) |

*(continued)*

**EXHIBIT 12.5**  *(continued)*

*Cash Flows from Financing Activities*

| | |
|---|---:|
| Contributions of cash for endowment **(j)** | 50 |
| Cash received from government grant **(e)** | 450 |
| Net cash generated through financing activities | 500 |
| Net increase in cash and term deposits | 41 |
| Cash and term deposits, Jan. 1 | 479 |
| Cash and term deposits, Dec. 31 | $520 |

> *The cash flow statement segregates cash flows by operating, investing, and financing activities.*

Closing entries as at December 31, Year 6, are presented next.

| | | |
|---|---:|---:|
| Revenue—government grant | 1,200 | |
| Revenue—United Way grant | 40 | |
| Revenue—contributions | 1,987 | |
| Revenue—investment income | 54 | |
| Revenue—amortization of deferred contributions | 90 | |
| Expenses—shelter program | | 740 |
| Expenses—food program | | 1,110 |
| Expenses—administration | | 556 |
| Expenses—fundraising | | 516 |
| Expenses—amortization | | 150 |
| Unrestricted net assets | | 299 |
| To close the unrestricted revenues and expenses | | |

> *Revenues and expenses are closed to fund balances.*

# DONATED CAPITAL ASSETS, MATERIALS, AND SERVICES

**DONATED CAPITAL ASSETS**  An NFPO is required to record the donation of capital assets at fair value. If fair value cannot be determined, a nominal value will be used. A nominal value could be in the range of $1 to $100 for small NFPOs, and $1,000 and higher for large NFPOs. If an organization receives an unsolicited donation of a capital asset that it has no intention of using, it should be reflected in its financial statements as "other assets" instead of as a capital asset, and a loss or gain should be reflected in the statement of operations when disposal of the asset occurs. The following illustrates the recording of donated capital assets.

> *Donated capital assets must be recorded at fair value or, if fair value cannot be determined, at a nominal value.*

**EXAMPLE 4**   A capital asset with a fair value of $10,000 is donated to an NFPO. The initial treatment depends on which of the two methods of recording contributions is being used. If the deferral method is used and the capital asset is subject to amortization (e.g., equipment), the contribution should be deferred and revenue should be recognized later to match to the amortization expense. The journal entry would be as follows:

| | | |
|---|---|---|
| Equipment | 10,000 | |
|     Deferred contributions—capital assets | | 10,000 |

> *A donated depreciable asset is reported as deferred contributions under the deferral method.*

Assuming a five-year useful life, in each succeeding year the following entries will be made as the equipment is amortized:

| | | |
|---|---|---|
| Amortization expense | 2,000 | |
|     Accumulated amortization | | 2,000 |
| Deferred contributions—capital assets | 2,000 | |
|     Contribution revenue | | 2,000 |

If the deferral method is being used and the asset is not subject to amortization (e.g., land), the following entry is made:

| | | |
|---|---|---|
| Land | 10,000 | |
|     Net assets—contribution of land | | 10,000 |

Because no future expense will be associated with the asset, deferral is not required and the donation of land is reflected in the statement of net assets.

If the restricted fund method is being used, the fair value of the donated capital asset is recorded as revenue in the capital fund as follows:

| | | |
|---|---|---|
| *Capital fund* | | |
| Equipment | 10,000 | |
|     Contribution revenue—donated equipment | | 10,000 |

> *A donated depreciable asset is reported as contribution revenue under the restricted fund method.*

Donated land will be treated in the same manner, except that the debit will be to land instead of equipment. Small NFPOs that have adopted a policy of non-capitalization of acquisitions of capital assets will still be required to record donated capital assets at fair value. For example, the donation of equipment with a fair value of $10,000 is recorded in the following manner:

| | | |
|---|---|---|
| Equipment expense | 10,000 | |
| Contribution revenue—donated equipment | | 10,000 |

Regardless of whether the organization uses the deferral method or the restricted fund method, the entry is the same because the required matching automatically occurs with the entry.

**DONATED MATERIALS AND SERVICES** The requirements for the reporting of donated materials and services are different from those for donated capital assets. An NFPO has the option of reporting or not reporting donated material and services; however, it can only report these donations if fair value can be determined, if the materials and services would normally be used in the organization's operations and if the NFPO would have purchased these material and services if they had not been donated.

> *Donated materials and services can be reported if they are needed by the organization.*

Section 4410 also makes it clear that the fair value of the services of volunteers is normally not recognized due to the difficulty in determining such values. Furthermore, an organization would probably not record donated materials if it acts as an intermediary for immediate distribution. For example, due to the difficulty of determining fair values and the large number of transactions, a food bank would not normally record the donation of food that it distributes to its clients.

**EXAMPLE 5** A radio station donated free airtime to help a charity publicize its fundraising campaign. The fair value of the airtime is $5,200, and the policy of the organization is to record the value of donated materials and services. The journal entry is as follows:

| | | |
|---|---|---|
| Advertising expense | 5,200 | |
| Revenue—donated airtime | | 5,200 |

If the restricted fund method was being used, this entry would be made in the general fund. If the donation consisted of office supplies rather than airtime, the entry to record the donation under the deferral method would be as follows:

| | | |
|---|---|---|
| Office supplies (asset) | 5,200 | |
| Deferred contribution | | 5,200 |

If half of the supplies were used, the entries would be as follows:

| | | |
|---|---|---|
| Supplies expense | 2,600 | |
| Office supplies (asset) | | 2,600 |
| Deferred contribution | 2,600 | |
| Contribution revenue | | 2,600 |

> *Under the deferral method, donated materials and services should be reported as contribution revenue when the materials and services are expensed.*

The same entries would likely be used under the restricted fund method. Due to the nature of the items donated, the transaction would normally be recorded in the general fund. Under the restricted fund method, the deferral method must be used for the general fund.

See Self-Study Problem 1 for a comprehensive problem involving an NFPO. It includes many of the issues we have covered in this chapter.

## LO6 ANALYSIS AND INTERPRETATION OF FINANCIAL STATEMENTS

Now that you have prepared journal entries and financial statements for NFPOs, you are now ready to analyze and interpret the financial statements of an NFPO. Let's use the Blue Shield financial statements to calculate and interpret key financial ratios for an NFPO.

Blue Shield operates a 50-bed homeless shelter. It is open 365 days a year but is not necessarily fully occupied every night. For Year 6, the number of person days that the facility was used was 15,000. The following three ratios would typically be used by donors and other users to assess the efficiency and effectiveness of the organization:

| Name of Ratio | Numerator/Denominator | What It Tells |
|---|---|---|
| Cost per person day | Total expenses/Total person days | Efficiency of operations |
| Debt-to-equity ratio | Total liabilities/Total net assets | Ability to meet obligations |
| Stewardship ratio | Total revenues/Total expenses | How the entity discharged its stewardship responsibility |

> *The cost per person day or cost per unit of output is a key ratio for many NFPOs.*

The following table presents these three ratios under the two different methods of reporting contributions. The first two columns are taken from Exhibit 12.3 for the restricted fund method and the last column is from Exhibit 12.4 for the deferral method.

| | Restricted Fund Method | | Deferral Method |
|---|---|---|---|
| Name of Ratio | General Fund | All Funds | |
| Cost per person day | $195 | $205 | $205 |
| Debt-to-equity ratio | 1.60 | 0.21 | 1.04 |
| Stewardship ratio | 1.12 | 1.28 | 1.10 |

Notice the following from the table above:

- The ratios are significantly different between the two reporting methods. Which method best reflects reality for this organization? Which method would be most useful to the user?

- The ratios are significantly different between the general fund and the total of all funds under the restricted fund method. Which column would the user use in calculating the ratios? Is it useful to have all the columns under the restricted fund method?

- The organization looks most efficient using only the general fund under the restricted fund method. Should one use only the general fund, all funds, or any combination of funds under the restricted fund method?

- The solvency of the entity looks much better using all funds under the restricted fund method. Why is there such a big difference between the restricted fund method and the deferral method? Under the restricted fund method, the restricted funds are shown as revenue when received and end up as an addition to net assets. Under the deferral method, many of the contributions are deferred as a long-term liability.

> *The debt-to-equity ratio is usually higher under the deferral method because some contributions are reported as deferred contributions, which appears in the liability section of the statement of financial position.*

- The stewardship ratio compares revenues to expenses. Some donors would not want to see a high ratio because it implies that the funds were not used as expected. The deferral method matches the contribution revenues to expenses on an accrual basis. Therefore, it is expected that the ratio would be lower under the deferral method.

See Self-Study Problem 2 for a comprehensive problem involving the preparation of a balance sheet under the two methods of reporting contributions. The NFPO uses fund accounting under both methods of reporting contributions.

It is important to note how the NFPO has accounted for donated goods and services. By recording donated goods or services, the bottom line on the statement of operations is usually not affected. However, both revenues and expenses would likely increase. This could have a significant impact on the cost per person day and stewardship ratio.

**DISCLOSURE REQUIREMENTS**   The disclosure requirements for NFPOs are quite extensive. Some of those requirements were briefly described throughout the chapter. The following summarizes the main disclosures required in Section 4410 related to revenue from contributions:

- Contributions by major sources, including the nature and amount of contributed materials and services recognized in the financial statements.

- The policies followed in accounting for endowment contributions, restricted contributions, and contributed materials and services.

- The nature and amount of changes in deferred contribution balances for the period.

- How and where net investment income earned on resources held for endowment is recognized in the financial statements.

> *The major sources of and accounting policies for contributions must be disclosed.*

United Way/Centraide Ottawa is a non-profit Ontario corporation and a registered charity. Excerpts from United Way/Centraide Ottawa's 2015 financial statements are provided in Exhibit 12.6.

**EXHIBIT 12.6**

# Extracts from United Way/Centraide Ottawa's 2015 Financial Statements

## 1. Significant accounting policies:

The financial statements have been prepared in accordance with Canadian accounting standards for not-for-profit organizations and include the following significant accounting policies:

(a) Revenue recognition:

The organization follows the deferral method of accounting for contributions.

> *United Way/Centraide Ottawa used the deferral method to account for contributions.*

### UW Campaign Revenue

Campaign pledges and donations that are undesignated or are directed to a focus area or priority goal by the donor are recognized as revenue in the year that they are received or pledged at the amount committed less a provision for uncollectible pledges. Funds raised during a campaign, net of related campaign expenses and provisions are used to provide funds for operations in the current year and fund partner programs and services in the following fiscal year.

### Funds Received from Other United Ways

National or regional workplace campaigns that are coordinated by one United Way on behalf of other United Ways are known as Centrally Coordinated Campaigns. The pledges and donations received by other United Ways on behalf of the organization are reported separately and included in pledges receivable until the revenue is received.

### Targeted Community Investments (TCI)

TCI are an investment in a focus area, priority goal, program or project, achieved through highly customized cultivation, solicitation, and stewardship of a donor and in consultation with priority goal partners. Each investment is monitored and measured for results. Investments that have not been spent at the end of the year are recorded as deferred revenue. Revenue is recognized in the year in which the related expenses are incurred.

### Designated Campaign Revenue

Campaign pledges and donations that are designated by the donor to other Canadian registered charities and other United Ways are considered to be restricted by purpose, and are recognized as revenue in the year they are distributed to the designated charity.

### Grants

Grant revenue represents funds received from federal, provincial and municipal governments, foundations and from corporations, for specific programs or Community Wide Initiatives administered by the organization. Grants are recognized as revenue when costs are incurred or disbursed to other agencies. Grants that have not been spent at the end of the year are reported as deferred revenue.

### Investment Income

Restricted investment income and unrealized gains/losses are recognized as revenue when the related expense is incurred. Restricted endowment investment income is recorded in the statement of changes in net assets when earned. Unrestricted investment income is recognized when earned in the statement of operations.

### Endowment Contributions

Contributions to the endowment fund are recorded as direct increases to the endowment net asset balance.

(b) Expense recognition:

The organization recognizes expenses in the year they are incurred and donor directed designations when they are distributed. Expenses are reported within the following three categories:

### Fundraising

The cost of fundraising is recognized in the year it is incurred, and includes an allocation of the associated general and administration costs. A designation fee is charged to designated charities to recover the cost of fundraising and

*(continued)*

**EXHIBIT 12.6** *(continued)*

processing. The fee is reported as a reduction of the fundraising expenses and is recognized when it is deducted from the designations paid out to other charities.

The organization also incurs Government of Canada Workplace Charitable Campaign (GCWCC) fundraising costs on behalf of participants of the GCWCC campaign (i.e. HealthPartners and other United Ways) and recovers their portion of the costs based on a pro-rata share of the revenue. GCWCC recoveries are reported as a reduction of the fundraising costs and recognized when deducted or received from recipients.

*Directed Program Expenses*

Program expenses that are externally directed or mandated are reported as directed program expenses and are recognized when distributed.

*Priority Goal Investments*

*Partner programs and services*—are investments made to agencies and community organizations through a call for proposal process to deliver front-line programs and services that align to priority goals. Also included are one-time investments funded from the internally restricted for community services fund. These expenses are recognized in the year when distributed or distributable to the recipient agencies.

*Community Wide Initiatives (CWI)*—are investments made to mobilize multiple stakeholders in order to address community wide challenges and create a collective response to affect systemic change. They are developed as a complement to existing community programs, initiatives, networks and coalitions. There are currently four CWI: Employment Accessibility Resource Network (EARN), Hire Immigrants Ottawa (HIO), Ottawa Child and Youth Initiative and project step. These initiatives are primarily funded through grants and supplemented by in-kind contributions from the organization. Expenses are recognized when incurred.

*Targeted Community Programs*—see note 2(a) above. These expenses are recognized when distributed to the service delivery program.

*Grant distributions*—investments from private corporations, foundations or other funders that are directed towards a specific community need are stewarded by the organization and delivered by another agency. These expenses are recognized when paid.

*UW community development strategies*—the organization's operations in support of priority goal community development strategies, including research, convening and advocacy. These expenses are recognized when incurred and include an allocation of associated general and administrative costs.

*UW investment stewardship*—the organization's operations in support of best practice research, evaluation and management of the investment in partner programs and services. These expenses are recognized when incurred and include an allocation of associated general and administrative costs.

(j) Donated services:

No amounts have been reflected in the financial statements for donated services, since no objective basis is available to measure the value of such services. Nevertheless, a substantial number of volunteers have donated significant amounts of their time to the organization's programs, services and fundraising campaigns.

*Source:* UNITED WAY/CENTRAIDE OTTAWA, *Financial Statements of United Way/Centraide Ottawa for the year ended March 31, 2015*, Pages 11–12, 14. Reproduced with permission from United Way Ottawa.

> *The United Way does not recognize donated services in its financial statements.*

## ASPE Differences

- Part II does not contain any standards specifically tailored for NFPOs. However, if the NFPO chooses to follow Part III of the *Handbook*, it must follow the relevant standards in Part II.

- IFRS do not contain any standards specifically tailored for NFPOs. If the NFPO chooses to follow IFRS, it does not apply Part III or Part II of the *Handbook*.

# SUMMARY

Not-for-profit organizations are entities, normally without transferable ownership interests, organized and operated exclusively for social, educational, professional, religious, health, charitable, or any other not-for-profit purpose. A not-for-profit organization's members, contributors and other resource providers do not, in such capacity, receive any financial return directly from the organization. **(LO1)** Fifteen sections in Part III of the *Handbook* are specifically dedicated to NFPOs. In addition, NFPOs must follow relevant sections of Part II of the *Handbook*. **(LO2)** Fund accounting comprises the collective accounting procedures resulting in a self-balancing set of accounts for each fund. Elements of a fund can include assets, liabilities, net assets, revenues, and expenses. Fund accounting can be and has been used very successfully to keep track of restricted resources and/or programs, and to convey information through the financial statements about the restrictions placed on the organization's resources. **(LO3)**

The restricted fund method can only be used in conjunction with fund accounting. Under this method, contribution revenue is recognized in each restricted fund when the funds are received or receivable. **(LO4)** The deferral method can be used with or without fund accounting. Under this method, contribution revenue is recognized in the same period as the expense emanating from the use of the funds contributed. When the funds are permanently invested in an asset that is not being expensed (such as land or investment in bonds as part of an endowment contribution), then the contribution is credited directly to net assets. **(LO5)** An NFPO's financial statements will differ depending on the method used to report contributions. This will affect the ratios typically used when analyzing financial statements. **(LO6)**

## Self-Study Problem 1

LO2, 3, 5

Watrous Housing Corporation (WHC) is a community-sponsored not-for-profit housing organization that was incorporated on September 1, Year 5. Its purpose is to provide residential accommodation for physically disabled adults in the town of Watrous. The nature of WHC's operations and its source of funding are described in Exhibit A. The executive director of WHC has asked for your assistance in establishing accounting policies for WHC for its general-purpose, year-end financial statements. The accounting policies should be consistent with Part III combined with relevant sections of Part II of the *CPA Canada Handbook*.

**Required**

Identify the major accounting issues, and provide recommendations on the accounting treatment of these issues in WHC's financial statements for the year ended August 31, Year 6. Assume that WHC wants to use fund accounting with two funds, a general fund and a capital fund, and wants to use the deferral method to account for contributions. Also assume that annual revenues exceed $700,000.

## NATURE OF OPERATIONS

- In October Year 5, WHC purchased a 15-unit apartment building in downtown Watrous for $750,000. It then spent $250,000 in renovations to upgrade the building to make it accessible for physically disabled adults.

- WHC offers 24-hour non-medical attendant care. Support care services are provided through a combination of staff members and volunteers. The staff members receive a monthly salary. As an inducement to recruit and retain qualified support care workers, each staff member is allowed 15 sick days per year. The employee can bank the sick days not used in any one year. Upon termination or retirement, the employee is paid for banked sick days at the wage rate in effect at that time.

- Rental payments are due the first day of each month and are geared to each tenant's income. Most of the tenants are very good about making their rent payments on time. Some rental payments are received late. On August 31, Year 6, there was $13,000 of unpaid rent.

- WHC plans to install central air conditioning in the building in April Year 7 at an expected cost of $50,000. This expenditure is being financed by a special fundraising drive. By August 31, Year 6, this fundraising drive had raised $20,000 in cash and $15,000 in pledges from citizens in the local community.

## SOURCES OF FUNDING

- The cost of acquiring and renovating the apartment building was financed by a $1,000,000 cash donation received from the estate of Mr. Smith who had stipulated that the funds be used for the purchase of a building.

- The provincial government funds approximately 70% of non-medical care and support costs. Claims are made monthly for the previous month's eligible costs.

- WHC depends on outside fundraising efforts, primarily door-to-door canvassing and sponsored bingos, to cover the remaining non-medical care and support costs.

## Solution to Self-Study Problem 1

WHC should adopt the following recommendations for the related accounting issues for its year-end financial statements:

- The accrual basis of accounting should be used in order to properly match revenues to expenses.

- The cost of acquiring and renovating the apartment building should be capitalized as an asset in the capital fund.

- The building should be amortized over its useful life. Amortization expense should be reported as an expense of the capital fund.

- The $1,000,000 cash donation from Mr. Smith and the cash received for the planned expenditures on air conditioning equipment should be recorded as deferred contributions in the capital fund. The deferred contributions should be amortized into revenue over the life of the related assets to match to the amortization expense on these assets.

- Salary costs should be expensed as incurred in the general fund.

- The estimated costs of unpaid sick leave should be set up as a liability and as an expense of the general fund on an annual basis.

- The value of the volunteers' time provided for support care services can be set up as revenue and an expense of the general fund, if the amount is measurable and such services would be purchased had the volunteers not provided them.

- The contributions from the provincial government should be accrued as a receivable and revenue of the general fund at the end of each month, based on actual costs incurred during the month.

- The rent from the tenants should be recognized as revenue of the general fund in the month in which it is due. At the end of the year, an allowance should be set up for any doubtful accounts.

- Donations from door-to-door canvassing and proceeds received from bingos should be recognized as revenue of the general fund as the cash is received.

- The pledges received for the planned expenditure on air conditioning equipment should be recorded as pledges receivable and deferred contributions of the capital fund to the extent that the amount to be received can be reasonably estimated and the ultimate collection is reasonably assured. Since this is the first year of operation for WHC, it may not be possible to reasonably estimate the collectibility of the pledges as there is no history for collection of pledges.

## Self-Study Problem 2

**LO2, 3, 4, 5**

Morina Homes is a not-for-profit organization established over 40 years ago. It provides care services to seniors in the local community. Fifteen years ago, it raised $2,800,000 of restricted funds to fully fund the purchase of land and to construct and equip a new residence. In Year 4, it undertook a new public campaign to raise funds to replace some of its equipment and expand the home.

Prior to Year 4, the home had only one fund, the general fund. In Year 4, the home set up a separate fund, the capital fund, to account for any new funds restricted for the replacement and expansion of the home. It used the deferral method to account for both funds.

The following are the unclassified statements of financial position for the 2 funds of the Home at December 31, Year 4:

|  | General Fund | Capital Fund |
|---|---|---|
| Cash | $ 20,000 | $216,000 |
| Accounts receivable | 137,000 | |
| Allowance for doubtful accounts | (17,000) | |
| Inventory of supplies | 14,000 | |
| Investments in marketable securities | | 284,000 |
| Land | 370,000 | |
| Building | 1,760,000 | |
| Accumulated amortization of building | (528,000) | |
| Equipment | 675,000 | |
| Accumulated amortization of equipment | (540,000) | |
| Totals | $1,891,000 | $500,000 |
|  |  |  |
| Accounts payable | $ 32,000 | |
| Deferred contributions—building and equipment | 1,367,000 | |
| Deferred contributions—future expansion | | $500,000 |
| Net assets contributed for land | 370,000 | |
| Unrestricted net assets | 122,000 | |
| Totals | $1,891,000 | $500,000 |

## Additional Information for Year 5

a.  Every month, the home bills the provincial government and its residents for home services. The accounts are due in 30 days. Total billings for the year were $1,101,000.

b.  Collections of accounts receivable totalled $1,087,000. Accounts receivable written off as uncollectible amounted to $11,000.

c.  The estimate of doubtful accounts was 10% of accounts receivable outstanding at December 31, Year 5.

d.  The home received $500,000 from the estate of one of its founders. The donor requested that the principal not be spent but invested in government bonds. The interest income from the bonds is restricted for recreational activities, which are accounted for in the general fund.

e.  The home received unrestricted donations of $50,000 and interest revenue of $30,000 from the bonds in the endowment fund. The cash received for interest was spent on recreational projects and is included in operating expenses.

f.  The home paid the following amounts during the year:

| | |
|---|---:|
| Operating expenses | $1,125,000 |
| Inventory of supplies | 60,000 |
| Total | $1,185,000 |

g.  Equipment costing $100,000 was acquired using funds from the capital fund.

h.  The accounts payable at the end of Year 4 and Year 5 consisted of the following:

| | Year 4 | Year 5 |
|---|---:|---:|
| Operating expenses | $20,000 | $25,000 |
| Inventory of supplies | 12,000 | 15,000 |
| | $32,000 | $40,000 |

No entries affecting accounts payable were made during the year.

i.  Supplies on hand at the end of the year were $16,000.

j.  Amortization was $44,000 for the building and $51,000 for the equipment, of which $6,000 pertained to equipment purchased by the capital fund. The cost of these capital assets was fully funded by contributions restricted for the purchase of these assets.

k.  On December 31, Year 5, the fair value of the marketable securities in the capital fund was $300,000. These securities are being held until the funds are needed for future expansion of the home. The future expansion will not likely occur until Year 8, at the earliest. Any income on these funds is restricted for use in the capital fund. The investment is classified at FVTPL for reporting purposes.

## Required

Prepare a classified statement of financial position for the three funds at December 31, Year 5, assuming that Morina Homes uses the following:

(a) Deferral method combined with fund accounting

(b) Restricted fund method (assume that the change from the deferral method to the restricted fund method is a change in accounting policy and should be applied retrospectively)

# Solution to Self-Study Problem 2

(a)

**MORINA HOMES**
**STATEMENT OF FINANCIAL POSITION**
At December 31, Year 5

| | General Fund | Capital Fund | Endowment Fund | Total |
|---|---|---|---|---|
| **Current assets:** | | | | |
| Cash (1) | $ 2,000 | $116,000 | | $ 118,000 |
| Accounts receivable (2) | 140,000 | | | 140,000 |
| Allowance for doubtful accounts (3) | (14,000) | | | (14,000) |
| Inventory of supplies (4) | 16,000 | | | 16,000 |
| | 144,000 | 116,000 | | 260,000 |
| **Property, plant, and equipment:** | | | | |
| Land | 370,000 | | | 370,000 |
| Building | 1,760,000 | | | 1,760,000 |
| Accumulated amortization of building (6) | (572,000) | | | (572,000) |
| Equipment (7) | 675,000 | 100,000 | | 775,000 |
| Accumulated amortization of equipment (8) | (585,000) | (6,000) | | (591,000) |
| | 1,648,000 | 94,000 | | 1,742,000 |
| Long-term investments (5 & 9) | | 300,000 | $500,000 | 800,000 |
| | $1,792,000 | $510,000 | $500,000 | $2,802,000 |
| Accounts payable (10) | $ 40,000 | | | $ 40,000 |
| Deferred contributions—building and equipment (11) | 1,278,000 | $ 94,000 | | 1,372,000 |
| Deferred contributions—future expansion (12) | | 416,000 | | 416,000 |
| Net assets contributed for land (13) | 370,000 | | | 370,000 |
| Net assets for endowment (14) | | | $500,000 | 500,000 |
| Unrestricted net assets (15) | 104,000 | | | 104,000 |
| | $1,792,000 | $510,000 | $500,000 | $2,802,000 |

**Notes (values in 000s)** The first number is the account balance at December 31, Year 4 (letters refer to letters in the Additional Information in the original question):

1. 20 + (b) 1087 + (e) 50 + (e) 30 − (f) 1185; 216 − (g) 100
2. 137 + (a) 1101 − (b) 1087 − (b) 11
3. 17 − (b) 11 + (c) 8
4. 14 + (f) 60 + (h) 3 − (i) 61
5. 284 + (k) 16
6. 528 + (j) 44
7. 675; 0 + (g) 100
8. 540 + (j) 45; 0 + (j) 6
9. 0 + (d) 500
10. 32 + (h) 8
11. 1,367 − (j) 44 − (j) 51 + (j) 6; (g) 100 − (j) 6
12. 500 − (g) 100 + (k) 16
13. 370
14. 500
15. 122 + (a) 1101 − (c) 8 + (e) 50 + (e) 30 − (f) 1125 − (h) 5 − (i) 61 − (j) (44 + 45) + (j) (44 + 45)

(b)

**MORINA HOMES**
**STATEMENT OF FINANCIAL POSITION**
At December 31, Year 5
(Note 1)

| | General Fund | Capital Fund | Endowment Fund |
|---|---|---|---|
| Current assets: | | | |
| Cash | $ 2,000 | $ 116,000 | |
| Accounts receivable | 140,000 | | |
| Allowance for doubtful accounts | (14,000) | | |
| Inventory of supplies | 16,000 | | |
| Investments in marketable securities | | 300,000 | |
| | 144,000 | 416,000 | |
| Property, plant, and equipment: | | | |
| Land | | 370,000 | |
| Building | | 1,760,000 | |
| Accumulated amortization of building | | (572,000) | |
| Equipment (2) | | 775,000 | |
| Accumulated amortization of equipment (3) | | (591,000) | |
| | | 1,742,000 | |
| Long-term investment in bonds | | | $500,000 |
| | $144,000 | $2,158,000 | $500,000 |
| Accounts payable | $ 40,000 | | |
| Fund balance (4) | 104,000 | $2,158,000 | $500,000 |
| | $144,000 | $2,158,000 | $500,000 |

**Notes:**

1. All of the account names and account balances are the same as in part (a), except for the following:
2. 675 + (g) 100
3. 540 + (j) 45 + (j) 6
4. All of the contributions to the capital and endowment funds would have been reported as revenue when received and would end up in fund balances. The revenues and expenses for the current year also end up in fund balances. There are no deferred contributions in the capital and endowment funds.

# APPENDIX 12A

## Sample Financial Statements for Not-for-Profit Organizations

LO7

This appendix contains the 2015 statement of financial position, statement of operations, statement of changes in net assets, and statement of cash flows for United Way/Centraide Ottawa.[2] This organization brings people together from all parts of its community to identify, develop, and provide solutions for community needs, helping to ensure that the donations received will go where they are needed most and where they will have the greatest impact. The deferral method of accounting has been used for contributions, and expenses have been recorded using the accrual basis.

**UNITED WAY/CENTRAIDE**
**STATEMENT OF FINANCIAL POSITION**
As at March 31, 2015
(with comparative figures for 2014)

| | 2015 | 2014 |
|---|---|---|
| **Assets** | | |
| Current assets: | | |
| Cash | $ 3,369,280 | $ 7,541,920 |
| Pledges receivable | 15,348,539 | 17,771,067 |
| Accounts receivable | 913,497 | 1,059,705 |
| Prepaid expenses | 126,428 | 56,614 |
| | 19,757,744 | 26,429,306 |
| Long-term assets: | | |
| Investments | 5,699,524 | 3,519,757 |
| Tangible capital assets | 291,033 | 315,652 |
| | 5,990,557 | 3,835,409 |
| | **$25,748,301** | **$30,264,715** |
| **Liabilities and Net Assets** | | |
| Current liabilities: | | |
| Accounts payable and accrued liabilities | $ 1,972,939 | $ 4,626,654 |
| Deferred revenue | 1,651,339 | 1,343,879 |
| Deferred designated campaign revenue | 8,534,297 | 9,689,234 |
| | 12,158,575 | 15,659,767 |
| Long-term liabilities: | | |
| Deferred lease inducement | 36,852 | 45,869 |
| Other long-term liabilities | — | 750,000 |
| | 36,852 | 795,869 |
| Total liabilities | 12,195,427 | 16,455,636 |
| Net assets: | | |
| Unrestricted | 1,833,518 | 1,301,358 |
| Invested in tangible capital assets | 291,033 | 315,652 |
| Internally restricted | 10,985,740 | 11,725,286 |
| Endowment | 442,583 | 466,783 |
| | 13,552,874 | 13,809,079 |
| | **$25,748,301** | **$30,264,715** |

Commitments
Contingency and guarantee

Most of the items on United Way's statement of financial position are typically seen on the balance sheet for a profit-oriented organization. Some of the unique items for the United Way are

- Deferred designated campaign revenue
- Net assets
  - Unrestricted
  - Invested in tangible capital assets
  - Internally restricted
  - Endowment

**UNITED WAY/CENTRAIDE OTTAWA**
**STATEMENT OF OPERATIONS**
Year ended March 31

| | 2015 | 2014 |
|---|---|---|
| **Revenue** | | |
| UW campaign revenue | $13,427,794 | $14,813,015 |
| Funds transferred from other United Ways | 1,656,737 | 1,620,838 |
| Targeted community investments | 482,878 | 695,833 |
| Designated campaign revenue | 12,752,792 | 13,180,957 |
| Total donations | 28,320,201 | 30,310,643 |
| Less: provision for uncollectible pledges | (673,786) | (824,834) |
| Recovery of provisioned pledges from prior-year campaigns | 380,104 | 534,214 |
| Net fundraising revenue | 28,026,519 | 30,020,023 |
| Grants | 849,146 | 847,697 |
| Investment income | 498,755 | 105,362 |
| Other revenue | 392,544 | 254,730 |
| Total revenue | **29,766,964** | **31,227,812** |
| **Expenses** | | |
| Fundraising expenses: | | |
| Community campaign | 3,050,225 | 2,913,633 |
| GCWCC | 1,472,065 | 1,649,683 |
| Strategic giving | 1,679,363 | 1,249,813 |
| Recovery of fundraising costs from designated charities | (1,513,492) | (1,588,589) |
| Total fundraising expenses | **4,688,161** | **4,224,540** |
| Directed program expenses: | | |
| Donor directed designations | 12,692,028 | 13,200,518 |
| **Total directed program expenses** | **17,380,189** | **17,425,058** |
| **Available for priority goal investments** | **12,386,775** | **13,802,754** |
| Priority goal investments: | | |
| Partner programs and services | 8,169,085 | 8,689,234 |
| Community-Wide Initiatives | 865,313 | 679,830 |
| Targeted Community Programs | 438,874 | 668,793 |
| Grant distributions | 254,221 | 301,825 |
| UW community development strategies | 1,510,645 | 1,344,483 |
| UW investment stewardship | 1,380,642 | 1,621,575 |
| **Total priority goal investments** | **12,618,780** | **13,305,740** |
| **(Deficiency) excess of revenue over expenses** | **$ (232,005)** | **$ 497,014** |

The items on the statement of operations for the United Way look quite different from those on an income statement for a profit-oriented organization. The United Way's expenses are classified by function and program rather than by nature. The bottom line is called *(deficiency) excess of revenue over expenses* rather than *net income*.

**UNITED WAY/ CENTRAIDE OTTAWA**
**STATEMENT OF CHANGES IN NET ASSETS**
Year ended March 31, 2015
(with comparative figures for 2014)

| | Unrestricted | Invested In Tangible Capital Assets | Internally Restricted | Endowment | 2015 Total | 2014 Total |
|---|---|---|---|---|---|---|
| Balance, beginning of year | $1,301,358 | $315,652 | $11,725,286 | $466,783 | $13,809,079 | $13,329,454 |
| Excess of revenue over expenses | (232,005) | — | — | — | (232,005) | 497,014 |
| Invested in tangible capital assets | 24,619 | (24,619) | — | — | — | — |
| Internal restrictions | 739,546 | — | (739,546) | — | — | — |
| Contributions | — | — | — | 800 | 800 | 19,187 |
| Transfer of named fund to agency | — | — | — | (25,000) | (25,000) | (37,341) |
| Net change in fair value | — | — | — | — | — | 765 |
| **Balance, end of year** | **$1,833,518** | **$291,033** | **$10,985,740** | **$442,583** | **$13,552,874** | **$13,809,079** |

The statement of changes in net assets has separate columns for each of the net asset items from the statement of financial position. All of these items are somewhat unique to an NFPO.

**UNITED WAY/CENTRAIDE OTTAWA**
**STATEMENT OF CASH FLOWS**
Year Ended March 31

| | 2015 | 2014 |
|---|---|---|
| Cash flows from operating activities: | | |
| Cash receipts from donors and funders | $31,031,563 | $30,816,044 |
| Cash paid to suppliers, employees, agencies and stakeholders | (33,386,519) | (28,455,585) |
| | (2,354,956) | 2,360,459 |
| Cash flows from investing activities: | | |
| Acquisition of tangible capital assets | (70,377) | (42,856) |
| Acquisition of investments | (2,780,842) | (2,685,699) |
| Proceeds from sale of investments | 1,057,735 | 2,855,570 |
| Change in endowment (net) | (24,200) | (18,154) |
| | (1,817,684) | 108,861 |
| Net increase (decrease) in cash | (4,172,640) | 2,469,320 |
| Cash, beginning of the year | 7,541,920 | 5,072,600 |
| **Cash, end of the year** | **$ 3,369,280** | **$ 7,541,920** |

*Source: Reproduced with permission from United Way/Centraide Ottawa. www.unitedwayottawa.ca/wp-content/uploads/2015/03/ 2014-15-full-financial-statements.pdf, accessed June 25, 2015.*

The United Way has used the direct method for the statement of cash flows. Most profit-oriented organizations use the indirect method. The United Way does not have a section for cash flows from financing activities. It has not borrowed any money from lenders and has not raised any funds from shareholders. Its activities are being funded primarily through donations and grants.

# SUMMARY

The financial statements for an NFPO have lots of similarities to those of a profit-oriented organization, especially the statement of financial position and the statement of cash flows. The main differences between the two types of organization is the source of revenues and the source of financing.

An NFPO receives most of its revenues from donations and grants. It may borrow funds but does not have financing through owners/shareholders. **(LO7)**

# APPENDIX 12B

........

**LO8**

## Net Assets Invested in Capital Assets

The *Handbook* provides an option to report "net assets invested in capital assets" as a separate component of net assets. This amount represents resources spent on and tied up in capital assets and therefore not available for future spending. The amount shown depends on the method used to account for contributions. If the restricted fund method is used, the amount represents the unamortized portion of *all* capital assets less associated debt, regardless of whether they were purchased from restricted or unrestricted resources. If the deferral method is used, the amount presented represents the unamortized portion of capital assets (net of associated debt) that were purchased with *unrestricted* resources. The following example will illustrate the differences.

**EXAMPLE B1** At the beginning of the current period, an NFPO purchases equipment costing $5,000 with a useful life of two years. We will assume first that the equipment is acquired from restricted resources, and then from unrestricted resources. We will focus on the equipment transaction only, and the effect of the transaction on the financial statements of the NFPO. In order to do this, we also assume that the organization was formed at the beginning of the period and that the equipment acquisition is the only transaction that has occurred.

## The Restricted Fund Method

**PURCHASE FROM RESTRICTED RESOURCES** Assume that the equipment is purchased from a restricted fund contribution of $5,100. The capital fund records contributions of this nature, as well as the acquisition of capital assets and their subsequent amortization. The journal entries are as follows:

| | | |
|---|---|---|
| *Capital fund* | | |
| Cash | 5,100 | |
|   Contribution revenue | | 5,100 |
| Equipment | 5,000 | |
|   Cash | | 5,000 |
| Amortization expense | 2,500 | |
|   Accumulated amortization | | 2,500 |

Because the capital fund did not exist before the start of the period, the financial statements at the end of the period appear as follows:

**CAPITAL FUND**
**OPERATING STATEMENT AND CHANGES IN FUND BALANCE**

| | |
|---|---|
| Contribution revenue | $5,100 |
| Amortization expense | 2,500 |
| Excess of revenue over expense | 2,600 |
| Fund balance—start of period | 0 |
| Fund balance—end of period | $2,600 |

*The restricted contribution is reported as revenue when received.*

**STATEMENT OF FINANCIAL POSITION**

| | | |
|---|---:|---:|
| Cash | | $100 |
| Equipment | $5,000 | |
| Accumulated amortization | 2,500 | 2,500 |
| Total assets | | $2,600 |
| Fund balance | | |
| Invested in capital assets | | $2,500 |
| Externally restricted funds | | 100 |
| Total fund balance | | $2,600 |

---

*An NFPO can report "net assets invested in capital assets" as a separate component of net assets.*

---

Note that the fund balance section shows two classifications:

- The $2,500 invested in capital assets represents the unamortized balance of spent resources that have not yet been reflected in the statement of operations as an expense.

- Externally restricted funds of $100 represent resources that can be spent only to acquire capital assets.

---

*The unamortized balance of equipment purchased with restricted resources is reflected in the amount of fund balance invested in capital assets.*

---

As the equipment is amortized on the operating statement, the fund balance itself is reduced, and it is the statement of financial position category "invested in capital assets" that reflects the reduction.

**PURCHASE FROM UNRESTRICTED RESOURCES**   Now assume that the equipment is purchased from unrestricted resources. The general fund receives an unrestricted contribution of $5,100 and uses it to acquire equipment.

The journal entries in the general fund and the capital fund are as follows:

| | | |
|---|---:|---:|
| *General fund* | | |
| Cash | 5,100 | |
|    Contribution revenue | | 5,100 |
| Transfer to capital fund | 5,000 | |
|    Cash | | 5,000 |

The general fund's operating statement after the transaction shows the following:

**GENERAL FUND**
**STATEMENT OF OPERATIONS AND CHANGES IN FUND BALANCE**

| | |
|---|---:|
| Revenues | $5,100 |
| Expenses | 0 |
| Excess of revenue over expense | 5,100 |
| Fund balance—start of period | 0 |
| Transfer to capital fund | (5,000) |
| Fund balance—end of period | $  100 |

---

*Transfers between funds are reported in changes in fund balances, not as revenues and expenses.*

---

**STATEMENT OF FINANCIAL POSITION**

| | |
|---|---|
| Cash | $100 |
| Total assets | $100 |
| Fund balance | |
| Unrestricted funds | $100 |
| Total fund balance | $100 |

The capital fund records the acquisition of the equipment and its amortization with the following entries:

*Capital fund*

| | | |
|---|---|---|
| Equipment | 5,000 | |
| Transfer from general fund | | 5,000 |
| Amortization expense | 2,500 | |
| Accumulated amortization | | 2,500 |

The end-of-period financial statements show the following:

**CAPITAL FUND**
**STATEMENT OF OPERATIONS AND CHANGES IN FUND BALANCE**

| | |
|---|---|
| Amortization expense | $2,500 |
| Excess of revenue over expense | (2,500) |
| Fund balance—start of period | 0 |
| Transfer from general fund | 5,000 |
| Fund balance—end of period | $2,500 |

**STATEMENT OF FINANCIAL POSITION**

| | |
|---|---|
| Equipment | $5,000 |
| Accumulated amortization | 2,500 |
| Total assets | $2,500 |
| Fund balance | |
| Invested in capital assets | $2,500 |
| Total fund balance | $2,500 |

Note that regardless of the source of resources used to acquire the equipment (restricted or unrestricted), the unamortized balance appears as an asset on the statement of financial position of the capital fund, and the fund balance shows a classification "invested in capital assets" in an amount equal to the asset balance. This is not the case when the deferral method with no fund accounting is used.

---

*The unamortized balance of equipment purchased with unrestricted resources is also reflected in the amount of fund balance invested in capital assets.*

---

## The Deferral Method

**PURCHASE FROM RESTRICTED RESOURCES**  Assume that the equipment is purchased from a restricted fund contribution of $5,100. The journal entries to record the contribution, acquisition, and first year's amortization are as follows:

| | | |
|---|---|---|
| Cash | 5,100 | |
| Deferred contribution revenue—capital assets | | 5,100 |
| Equipment | 5,000 | |
| Cash | | 5,000 |
| Amortization expense | 2,500 | |
| Accumulated amortization | | 2,500 |
| Deferred contribution revenue—capital assets | 2,500 | |
| Contribution revenue | | 2,500 |

---

*Deferred contribution revenue includes contributions that have not yet been matched to related expenses.*

---

Financial statements that reflect these transactions are as follows:

### STATEMENT OF OPERATIONS AND CHANGES IN NET ASSETS

| | |
|---|---:|
| Contribution revenue | $2,500 |
| Amortization expense | 2,500 |
| Excess of revenue over expenses | 0 |
| Net assets—start of period | 0 |
| Net assets—end of period | $  0 |

### STATEMENT OF FINANCIAL POSITION

| | | |
|---|---:|---:|
| Cash | | $100 |
| Equipment | $5,000 | |
| Accumulated amortization | 2,500 | 2,500 |
| Total assets | | $2,600 |
| Deferred contribution revenue—capital assets | | $2,600 |
| *Net Assets* | | |
| Unrestricted | | 0 |
| Total | | $2,600 |

---

*Deferred contribution revenue includes restricted resources that have been spent to acquire capital assets but have not yet been matched to amortization expense.*

---

Deferred contribution revenue of $2,600 includes two components: $100 in unspent resources restricted to future spending on capital assets and $2,500 in restricted resources that has been spent acquiring capital assets, but has not yet been reflected as revenue on the operating statement because there has yet to be an expense to match it against. When amortization occurs, an equal amount is recognized as revenue. Because there is no effect on the "excess of revenue over expense" amount, there is no effect on the equity section "net assets." As the equipment decreases on the asset side due to amortization, the amount "deferred contributions" decreases by the same amount on the liability side. Because this equipment was purchased from restricted resources, there can be no amount shown under "invested in capital assets" in the net assets section.

**PURCHASE FROM UNRESTRICTED RESOURCES**   Assume now that the equipment was purchased from an unrestricted contribution of $5,100. The journal entries to record the events are as follows:

| | | |
|---|---:|---:|
| Cash | 5,100 | |
|    Contribution revenue | | 5,100 |
| Equipment | 5,000 | |
|    Cash | | 5,000 |
| Amortization expense | 2,500 | |
|    Accumulated amortization | | 2,500 |

---

*Unrestricted contributions are reported as revenue when received.*

---

The financial statements that reflect these transactions are as follows:

### STATEMENT OF OPERATIONS

| | |
|---|---:|
| Contribution revenue | $5,100 |
| Amortization expense | 2,500 |
| Excess of revenue over expenses | $2,600 |

### STATEMENT OF FINANCIAL POSITION

| | |
|---|---:|
| Cash | $ 100 |
| Equipment | 5,000 |
| Accumulated amortization | 2,500 |
| | 2,500 |
| Total assets | $2,600 |
| *Net Assets* | |
| Invested in capital assets | $2,500 |
| Unrestricted | 100 |
| Total | $2,600 |

> *Net assets invested in capital assets represents the unamortized balance of equipment purchased with unrestricted resources.*

Note that the statement of operations does not include a reconciliation of opening and ending net assets. A separate statement is usually presented. Because net assets represents total equity, the changes in the classifications of this equity must be shown in the statement as follows:

### STATEMENT OF CHANGES IN NET ASSETS

| | Invested in Capital Assets | Unrestricted | Total |
|---|---:|---:|---:|
| Balance—start of period | $ 0 | $ 0 | $ 0 |
| Excess of revenue over expenses | ($ 2,500) | 5,100 | 2,600 |
| Investment in capital assets | 5,000 | (5,000) | 0 |
| Balance—end of period | $ 2,500 | $ 100 | $2,600 |

> *Under the deferral method, a statement of changes in net assets is prepared.*

The "unrestricted" column represents resources that can be spent for any purpose. The organization received an unrestricted contribution of $5,100 and spent $5,000 on equipment. At the end of the period, it has $100 left to spend. The transfer of $5,000 to the category "invested in capital assets" depicts the acquisition of capital assets from unrestricted resources. The operating statement shows an excess of revenue over expenses of $2,600. A $2,500 deduction for the amortization of assets purchased with unrestricted resources was used to arrive at the excess of revenue over expenses. Note that this does not represent resources spent, but rather the cost of services provided by the equipment. By transferring this deduction to "invested in capital assets," the amount of the operating results allocated to unrestricted resources becomes $5,100, which represents the actual inflow of spendable resources, and the amount shown for "invested in capital assets" is equal to the unamortized balance of the equipment purchased from unrestricted resources.

# SUMMARY

The net assets invested in capital assets account is reported as a separate component of net assets. This amount represents resources spent on and tied up in capital assets and therefore not available for future spending. If the restricted fund method is used, the amount represents the unamortized portion of *all* capital assets less associated debt, regardless of whether they were purchased from restricted or unrestricted resources. If the deferral method is used, the amount presented represents the unamortized portion of capital assets (net of associated debt) that were purchased with *unrestricted* resources. **(LO8)**

# APPENDIX 12C

## Accounting for Public Sector Organizations

### LO9

The public sector consists of governments, government organizations, and not-for-profit organizations controlled by governments. Governments differ from business organizations in many ways, some of which can be summarized as follows:

- Governments exist not to make a profit, but rather to provide services.

- While the major source of business revenue comes from the sale of goods or services or both, most of a government's revenue comes from taxation.

- Businesses have to compete, while governments operate in essentially a non-competitive environment.

- Often a major goal of government is the redistribution of wealth. A major goal of a business is the maximization of the wealth of its owners.

- The federal and provincial governments have virtually an unlimited capacity to borrow, constrained only by their ability to raise taxes in order to repay. A business's earning capacity is a major constraining factor in its ability to issue debt.

- While a business purchases capital assets in order to earn a return, a government's capital asset acquisitions are made to provide services.

- A government's budget plan, approved by a legislative process at the start of a fiscal period, attracts considerable attention in the press, as does the eventual comparison of actual results with those budgeted for originally. Businesses do not normally report their budgets, and their annual results are usually compared with results of prior periods with no mention of the year's budget.

> *Governments exist not to make a profit, but rather to provide services for the common good of all people.*

With such differences, it is not surprising that government-reporting models have been quite different from those used by businesses. This was certainly the case 10 or 15 years ago, but lately, changes have been made that have brought government accounting requirements much closer to those required for business, although many differences still exist. This will be more evident when government accounting standards are summarized later in this appendix.

Prior to the 1980s, a comprehensive body of accounting principles for governments did not exist. The CICA was involved only with setting the financial reporting standards for business organizations; no other body had established authoritative standards for governments. The desperate financial condition of some large American cities, which, it was argued, was not adequately reported in their financial statements, became the focus of attention of standard-setting bodies in the United States, soon followed by the CICA in Canada. Before plunging into this area, the CICA created a committee with a mandate to determine what practices were being followed by the federal, provincial, and territorial governments[3] and to recommend needed changes. As a result of the findings and recommendations of this committee, the CICA established the Public Sector Accounting and Auditing Committee (PSAAC) in 1981 and charged it with the development of accounting principles for governments. Before proceeding, the PSAAC created a second study group, with a mandate similar to that of the first, to report on the financial reporting practices of cities, municipalities, towns, and villages.[4] This study group made reference to a previous research study commissioned by the Certified General Accountants Association of Canada[5] and concluded that it would use the CGA study's findings and recommendations as a starting point for its own study. All three research studies came to similar conclusions about government financial reporting practices in general. These conclusions can be summarized by saying that (1) there was such a diversity of terminology, measurements, and reporting practices being used that comparability among similar government organizations[6] was virtually impossible and (2) the situation should not be allowed to continue.

> *Prior to 1980, there was much diversity in reporting by government organizations.*

At first the standard-setting process proceeded slowly and only a few statements on accounting and auditing were issued by PSAAC. Then in 1998, the CICA formed the Public Sector Accounting Board (PSAB) and proceeded with the reorganization of the *CPA Canada Handbook* by transferring the auditing recommendations to the assurance section of the *Handbook,* and the creation of a new *Public Sector Accounting Handbook (PSA Handbook).* Previously issued accounting statements were revised and amended as *PSA Handbook* sections.

> *CPA Canada has created a* new Public Sector Accounting Handbook, *which contains the GAAP applicable to federal, provincial, territorial, and local governments.*

## Compliance with PSAB Reporting Standards

If a business organization does not follow the *CPA Canada Handbook* in its financial reporting it can suffer substantial penalties, because legislation and security regulations require the *CPA Canada Handbook* to be used. When a new accounting standard is issued, businesses (especially public companies) tend to adopt the new standard immediately. NFPOs also tend to follow the *Handbook* in their financial reporting. Failure to do so could result in a reduction of support, especially in the area of grants from governments and from other NFPOs. Governments, though, are different. They often exhibit tardiness in adopting new standards, and sometimes refuse to adopt certain standards. The reasons for this are as follows:

- The federal government and each of the provincial and territorial governments prepare their financial reports in accordance with the legislation enacted by each body. The adoption of a new reporting standard often requires an amendment to an act.

- Local governments are created by an act of the legislature of the province or territory in which they are located. Changes in local government reporting often require changes in legislation.

- Legislative changes necessary to adopt new accounting standards do not rank high in the priorities of many governments.

- When auditors report that a government is not following proper accounting practices in its financial statements (an event that often occurs), the press notes the outrage of the opposition parties and the government's denial of any impropriety, and then the matter is forgotten. The general public, which by and large does not understand accounting at all, does not seem to be particularly interested.

- The adoption of certain new standards may be perceived by a government as having the potential to make its financial condition look worse than the government is currently reporting. If so, a change in reporting would not be a high priority.

> *Some governments in Canada have failed to adopt new government accounting standards for a number of reasons.*

## GAAP for Governments

Prior to February 2007, the *PSA Handbook* contained four sections that applied only to federal, provincial, and territorial governments; two sections that applied only to local governments; and a number of specific-item sections that applied to all governments. In 2005, a new model for senior governments was introduced that involved some drastic changes from previous practices. While the old model focused mainly on government spending (the operating statement showed revenues and expenditures), the new model presents a government-cost approach, although it still contains the reporting of government spending. One major change that took place was the requirement that senior governments capitalize their tangible asset acquisitions and amortize them in the statement of operations. In February 2007, an amendment withdrew both the local government sections and any references to federal, provincial, and territorial governments.

Appendix A of "Introduction to Public Sector Accounting Standards" in the *PSA Handbook* contains the flowchart[7] on the top of the next page. The flowchart indicates the reporting requirements for the various types of public sector entities.

As indicated in the flowchart, all levels of government must follow the *PSA Handbook*. Government business enterprises must follow Part I of the *CPA Canada Handbook*. Other government organizations can either follow Part I of the *CPA Canada Handbook* or the *PSA Handbook*. A public sector NFPO can elect to use or not use the 4200 series of the *PSA Handbook*.

The *PSA Handbook* presently contains 56 sections, including eight sections for NFPOs and seven accounting guidelines. The sections for NFPOs apply only to public sector NFPOs. These sections deal with matters unique to not-for-profit organizations or issues in which the needs of financial statement users indicate that different requirements from those that apply to governments, other government organizations, or government business enterprises are appropriate.

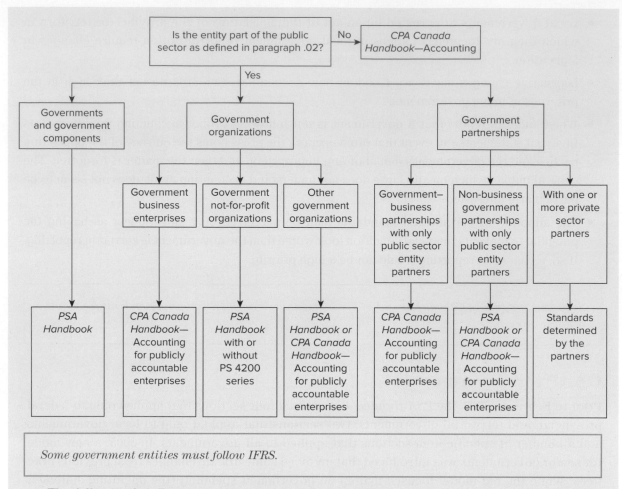

| | | | |
|---|---|---|---|
| | Is the entity part of the public sector as defined in paragraph .02? | No → | *CPA Canada Handbook—Accounting* |

Yes

| Governments and government components | Government organizations | | | Government partnerships | | |
|---|---|---|---|---|---|---|
| | Government business enterprises | Government not-for-profit organizations | Other government organizations | Government– business partnerships with only public sector entity partners | Non-business government partnerships with only public sector entity partners | With one or more private sector partners |
| *PSA Handbook* | *CPA Canada Handbook— Accounting for publicly accountable enterprises* | *PSA Handbook* with or without PS 4200 series | *PSA Handbook or CPA Canada Handbook— Accounting for publicly accountable enterprises* | *CPA Canada Handbook— Accounting for publicly accountable enterprises* | *PSA Handbook or CPA Canada Handbook— Accounting for publicly accountable enterprises* | Standards determined by the partners |

*Some government entities must follow IFRS.*

The following briefly summarizes some of the reporting requirement of the standards in the *PSA Handbook.*

**PS 1000 FINANCIAL STATEMENT CONCEPTS**   The two main groups of users of the government financial statements are the elected representatives of the public and investors and enterprises providing financial resources to the government. They want to gain an understanding of and assess:

- a government's ability to meet its financial obligations, both short- and long-term;

- a government's ability to maintain the level and quality of its services and to finance new programs;

- future tax and other revenue requirements;

- the performance of government in managing the economic resources for which it is responsible. [para. 20]

*Users want to assess the government's ability to pay its obligations and provide current services and its potential for providing new programs.*

**PS 1201 FINANCIAL STATEMENT PRESENTATION**   Five financial statements are required: a statement of financial position, a statement of operations, a statement of remeasurement gains and losses, a statement of change in net debt, and a statement of cash flow. The appendices to PS 1201 contain illustrative financial statements for different levels of government.

> *Governments are required to present five financial statements.*

**STATEMENT OF FINANCIAL POSITION** This statement presents financial assets and then deducts liabilities, with the resultant difference presented as "net debt." Then nonfinancial assets are added or subtracted to arrive at a final line called "accumulated surplus/deficit."

> *The statement of financial position must show financial assets, liabilities, net debt, nonfinancial assets, and accumulated surplus/deficit.*

Financial assets include cash and equivalents, receivables, inventories for resale, loans to other governments, available-for-sale investments, and investments in government enterprises. Liabilities include accounts payable and accrued liabilities, pension and employee future-benefit liabilities, deferred revenue, borrowings, and loans from other governments. The net debt position indicates the extent to which the government will have to raise revenues in the future to cover its past spending.

Nonfinancial assets are tangible capital assets, inventories held for consumption or use, and pre-paid expenses. Tangible capital assets are assets used by the government to provide services and include land, buildings, equipment, roads, and so on. They *do not* include intangible assets, natural resources, and Crown lands. The accumulated surplus/deficit represents the net recognized economic resources (net assets) of the government, and provides an indicator of the government's ability to pro-vide future services at the end of a fiscal period. An accumulated deficit would indicate that future rev-enues would have to cover both the cost of future services and the unpaid amount from past services.

**STATEMENT OF OPERATIONS** This statement reports the government's revenues and expenses, other than remeasurement gains and losses for the period, with the difference described as the peri-od's surplus or deficit (rather than profit or loss, which would be used for a profit-oriented entity). This result is added to the accumulated surplus/deficit at the beginning of the period to arrive at the last line, which is called the accumulated surplus/deficit at the end of the period.

Revenues include taxes, non-tax sources (including gains), and transfers from other govern-ments. Revenue for the period should be accrued unless it is impractical to measure. If this is the case the cash basis should be used. Expenses are to be reported by function or major program. Note disclosure should report the breakdown between the major types of expenses such as salaries, debt-servicing costs, amortization of the costs of tangible capital assets, and transfer payments to other governments. A comparison must be made between the actual results for the period and results of the prior period and also with expectations (the budget) at the beginning of the period.

> *The operating statement must show revenues, expenses, and the period's surplus or deficit. Compar-ative amounts for the previous period are required to be shown as well as the current period's budget.*

**STATEMENT OF REMEASUREMENT GAINS AND LOSSES** This statement should report the remeasurement gains and losses during the period, distinguishing between amounts arising during the period and those reclassified to the statement of operations; any other comprehensive income that arises when a government includes the results of government business enterprises and government–business partnerships in its summary financial statements; and the accumulated remeasurement gains and losses at the beginning and end of the period. The remeasurement gains and losses should be segregated between exchange gains and losses on items in the amortized cost category denominated in a foreign currency, and changes in the fair value of (1) derivatives, (2) portfolio investments in equity instruments quoted in an active market, and (3) financial instruments designated to the fair value category. The accumulated remeasurement gains are reported as a separate category in the accumulated surplus section of the statement of financial position.

**STATEMENT OF CHANGE IN NET DEBT**   This statement reconciles the net surplus/deficit for the period with the change in net debt for the period by adding back period amortization expense (and other items) and deducting the cost of tangible capital assets and other nonfinancial assets acquired during the period. The change in net debt is then added to the net debt at the beginning of the period to arrive at the net debt at the end of the period.

This statement is designed to provide information about the extent to which expenditures for the period have been met by the period's revenues. An increase in net debt indicates that revenues of future periods will have to be raised to pay for this period's spending. This statement also has to be prepared in comparative form to the budget and the prior period's results.

> *A statement showing the period's changes in net debt is required in comparative form with both the budget and the previous period.*

**STATEMENT OF CASH FLOW**   This statement reconciles cash and cash equivalents at the beginning of the period with cash and cash equivalents at the end of the period by providing details of receipts and payments in the four categories of operating transactions, capital transactions, investing transactions, and financing transactions. Either the direct or the indirect method can be used to arrive at cash from operations, but the direct method is strongly encouraged because it provides details of cash receipts from a number of categories, and therefore is much more informative than the indirect method. This statement is similar to the statement used by business organizations, except that the latter would report capital asset acquisitions as an investing activity, while this one reports such acquisitions as a separate category.

> *The cash flow statement shows operating, capital, investing, and financing transactions.*

**PS 1300 *THE FINANCIAL REPORTING ENTITY***   PS 1300 states the following:

- The government reporting entity comprises all organizations controlled by the government. An organization is controlled if the government has power over its financial and operating policies and benefits from or is exposed to the results of its operating activities.

- The government statements are prepared by consolidating the statements of the organizations making up the government entity.

- An exception is that government business enterprises are not consolidated on a line-by-line basis but rather reported using the modified equity method. This will reflect the government's share of the business enterprise's profit or loss in the government's operating results on one line in the statement of operations and the government's share of the business enterprise's assets and liabilities on one line on the government's statement of financial position.

- The modified equity method is exactly the same as the equity method described in Chapter 2, except that the business enterprise's accounting principles are not adjusted to conform to the accounting principles used by the government.

> *PS 1300 requires the consolidation of the financial statements of all organizations controlled by the government except for controlled business organizations which are not consolidated but rather are reported using the modified equity method.*

# SUMMARY

The PSAB has exerted considerable effort on the establishment of a new financial reporting model covering federal, provincial, territorial, and local governments. The resultant standards exhibit significant differences from those required for businesses and NFPOs. Differences will always exist because the operations and user needs of governments, NFPOs, and business organizations are different. While separate standards previously existed for local governments, recent amendments have eliminated any differences so that one set of standards applies to all government organizations. **(LO9)**

## Review Questions

*Questions, cases, and problems that deal with the appendix material are denoted with an asterisk.*

LO1   **1.** Briefly outline how NFPOs differ from profit-oriented organizations.

LO2   **2.** The *Handbook* describes revenue that is unique to NFPOs. What is this revenue called, and what characteristic does it have that makes it unique?

LO2   **3.** Distinguish between unrestricted and restricted contributions of a charitable organization.

LO3   **4.** Briefly explain the concept of fund accounting.

LO2   **5.** When and why would an NFPO use replacement cost rather than net realizable value to determine whether inventory should be written down?

LO2   **6.** It is common for an NFPO to receive donated supplies, equipment, and services. Do current accounting standards require the recording of donations of this kind? Explain.

LO2   **7.** Outline the *Handbook*'s requirements for NFPOs with regard to accounting for the capital assets of NFPOs.

LO2   **8.** What guidelines does the *Handbook* provide for pledges received by an NFPO?

LO2   **9.** The net assets section of an NFPO's statement of financial position should be divided into three main sections. List the sections, and explain the reasons for each.

LO3 **10.** How should transfers of resources between funds be presented in fund financial statements? How should they be presented in a single set of non-fund financial statements?

LO2 **11.** Contrast the revenue recognition and matching concepts that apply to profit-oriented organizations with those that apply to NFPOs.

LO4, **12.** Name the two methods of accounting for contributions, and explain how the methods
5 differ from each other.

LO4 **13.** Is it possible that an organization would be required to use certain aspects of the deferral method even though it reports using the restricted fund method? Explain.

LO8 *\*14.* Explain the meaning of the account "net assets invested in capital assets" and describe how it is used under the two methods of accounting for contributions.

LO9 *\*15.* Governments are different from business organizations and NFPOs in many respects and yet in some respect they are similar. Explain.

LO9 *\*16.* Briefly outline how the presentation of assets and liabilities on the statement of financial position of a government differs from the presentation shown on the balance sheet of a typical business enterprise.

# CASES

## Case 12-1

LO2

Beaucoup Hospital is located near Montreal. A religious organization created the not-for-profit hospital more than 70 years ago to meet the needs of area residents who could not otherwise afford adequate health care. Although the hospital is open to the public in general, its primary mission has always been to provide medical services for the poor.

On December 23, Year 2, a gentleman told the hospital's chief administrative officer the following story: "My mother has been in your hospital since October 30. The doctors have just told me that she will soon be well and can go home. I cannot tell you how relieved I am. The doctors, the nurses, and your entire staff have been just wonderful; my mother could not have gotten better care. She owes her life to your hospital.

"I am from Alberta. Now that my mother is on the road to recovery, I must return immediately to my business. I am in the process of attempting to sell an enormous tract of land. When this acreage is sold, I will receive $15 million in cash. Because of the services that Beaucoup Hospital has provided for my mother, I want to donate $5 million of this money."

The gentleman proceeded to write this promise on a piece of paper that he dated and signed.

Obviously, all of the hospital's officials were overwhelmed by this individual's generosity. This $5 million gift was 50 times as large as any other gift ever received. However, the controller was concerned about preparing the financial statements for Year 2. "I have a lot of problems with recording this type of donation as an asset. At present, we are having serious cash flow problems; but if we show $5 million in this manner, our normal donors are going to think we have become rich and don't need their support."

### Required

What problems are involved in accounting for the $5 million pledge? How should Beaucoup Hospital report the amount?

## Case 12-2

##### LO2

You have just completed an interview with the newly formed audit committee of the Andrews Street Youth Centre (ASYC). This organization was created to keep neighbourhood youth off the streets by providing recreational facilities where they can meet, exercise, play indoor sports, and hold dances. Since its inception, the organization has managed to survive on the basis of user fees charged to parents whose children use the program. This year the centre received support from a new provincial government program, in the form of an operating grant along with subsidy fees for those parents whose income is considered insufficient to pay the user fee. A local foundation, with a long history in the community and a reputation for honouring its commitments, has also come to the aid of the centre. This outside financial support came with the provision that the centre now present audited financial statements annually.

Your firm is attempting to obtain the audit, as it is a November year-end, and the audit would be completed at a traditionally slow time of year. Many questions were posed during the interview, and the ASYC audit committee has requested a written response to the issues raised. Excerpts from the interview follow:

- "We are looking for financial statements that are understandable to the board. For example, we have heard that we might have to capitalize and depreciate leasehold improvements. We have just completed $20,000 in expenditures to set up a weight room. We don't understand this amortization idea. Will it make us look like we exceeded our operating budget since this budget is based on all expenditures, capital and operating? The government might consider reducing our next operating grant because of this accounting. If you were selected as our auditor, would you have any problem if we simply expensed capital assets as incurred?"

- "The Parent Advisory Group has organized several fundraising events. They raised $250,000 in cash donations. They hired a part-time manager and paid for advertising on a local radio station. The total costs for salaries and advertising were $65,000. The net receipts of $185,000 have been deposited in a separate 'Computer Fund' bank account to allow for the purchase of some PCs. Our financial statements do not reflect this fund. Is that okay with you?"

- "The manager of Sports Supplies Ltd. is a good friend of the centre. This year his company gave us a variety of items, such as exercise and bodybuilding apparatus and some basketball equipment. This is pretty neat stuff and must be worth at least $12,000 to $15,000. The audit committee does not want to record this because they are concerned that if it ends up in revenue our operating grants might be reduced."

- "Certain of the parents have donated goods or their time and would like to receive a tax receipt for the value of these donations. We are not certain whether we will have to reflect these in our financial statements this year. For example,

    1. Jane Barnes provided valuable advice on improved management efficiency. She is a professional consultant and although these consulting fees were not budgeted for, the

centre made several changes that resulted in a reduction of administrative costs. Ms. Barnes estimates that her full-rate fee would have been $7,500.

2. Rick James, who is a qualified Phys. Ed. instructor, has been substituting one day a week at no charge, which reduced our budgeted expenditures by $4,500 this year.

3. Parents have donated an awful lot of their time to operate fundraising activities (in addition to those involved with the Computer Fund). This time must be worth thousands of dollars."

- "Some of the staff have not been able to take their vacation this year due to scheduling problems. As a result, we will have to pay them vacation pay. These funds will be paid out after the year-end and will likely be covered by next year's operating grant. To keep revenues and expenses matched, we want to record the vacation pay on a cash basis. Would that be okay? Otherwise, we'll record a portion of next year's grant as receivable this year."

- "The local foundation has provided the centre with a $30,000 grant to cover the expenses of a volunteer coordinator for two years. We received an instalment of $12,000, but we haven't hired a coordinator yet. The coordinator will be paid on an hourly basis, and the number of hours each month will fluctuate over the next two years depending on the monthly activities."

- "The cost of the fundraising program for the year was $100,000, which includes the salary of one full-time employee and the costs of preparing and mailing brochures to past and prospective donors. The brochures provide a summary of the programs at ASYC and some tips and early warnings sign to help parents recognize when their children may be involved with drugs. We are wondering whether these fundraising costs can be classified as educational costs on the statement of operations."

**Required**

Prepare a draft of the response that will be sent to the audit committee.

## Case 12-3

LO2

Confidence Private is a high school in the historic city of Jeanville. It engages students in a dynamic learning environment and inspires them to become intellectually vibrant, compassionate, and responsible citizens. The private school has been run as an NFPO since its inception 20 years ago.

In an effort to attract sports-minded students from a variety of economic backgrounds, Confidence initiated a fundraising program in July Year 8, to raise $5 million to build a new gymnasium, swimming pool, and fitness centre, and to create an endowment fund for scholarships. The fundraising campaign was a huge success. By May 31, Year 9, the school had received the following contributions:

1. $2.0 million in cash contributions specifically designated for construction and maintenance of the facilities.
2. $3.1 million in cash contributions specifically designated for the scholarship fund.
3. Fitness equipment valued at $0.2 million.

On June 15, Year 9, at the graduation ceremony, the headmaster thanked the parents, students, alumni, and staff for all their support, and officially closed the capital campaign. He provided the following details of the campaign:

- The construction of the facility was nearing completion and would be ready for classes in September Year 9. The final cost for the facility would be approximately $1.9 million.

- The contribution of fitness equipment would more than adequately equip the fitness centre.

- $3.1 million in cash would be invested and managed by a professional investment advisor.

The income earned on the endowment fund would be used to provide scholarships to students. Five students would receive full or partial scholarships in the fall of Year 10. Each year thereafter, it was expected that 25 to 30 students would receive full or partial scholarships to offset the annual tuition fee of $15,000.

You are proud to be an alumnus of Confidence. You attended the graduation ceremony. At the garden reception after the ceremony, you accepted the headmaster's request to help out with the accounting for the capital campaign and related events. He was unsure of whether the school should use the restricted fund or deferral method of accounting for contributions. You agreed to provide a memo in which you would provide recommendations for accounting policies to be applied for the year ended June 30, Year 9, and for future years when the facilities are being used and the scholarships are disbursed.

### Required

Prepare a memo for the headmaster. Explain the rationale for your recommendations and state your assumptions.

*(CGA Canada adapted)*[8]

## Case 12-4

LO2

In the fall of Year 5, eight wealthy business people from the same ethnic background formed a committee (CKER committee) to obtain a radio licence from the Canadian Radio-television and Telecommunications Commission (CRTC). Their goal is to start a non-profit, ethnic community radio station for their area. They plan to call the station CKER-FM Ethnic Radio (CKER). It will broadcast music, news and sports from their country of origin, cultural information, ethnic cooking, and other such programs, seven days a week.

The station's capital requirements are to be financed by memberships, donations, and various types of loans. It is expected that ongoing operations will be supported by advertising paid for by business people from that ethnic community and by the larger business community targeting that ethnic audience, as well as by donations and memberships.

It is now March Year 6, and the CRTC has announced that hearings will start in one month on a number of broadcasting licence applications, including the CKER committee's application. The CKER committee members are fairly confident about the viability of their proposal; however, they have decided to seek the advice of a professional accounting firm to assist with the endeavour. The CKER committee has engaged Maria & Casano, Chartered Professional Accountants, for the assignment, as three of the five partners of the firm are from the same ethnic community. The partner in charge of the assignment has stated that the firm will donate half its fee for the work.

You, a CPA, work for Maria & Casano and have been put in charge of the assignment. You have met with the CKER committee and various volunteers associated with the project. Information gathered on station start-up is contained in Exhibit I. Exhibit II provides other information on the CKER committee's proposal. The partner has asked you to prepare a draft report to the committee members discussing the viability of the proposed radio station over the initial three-year period. Since the committee is fairly confident that they will receive the licence, the partner has also asked you to recommend accounting policies for the transactions that CKER is contemplating.

**EXHIBIT I**

*INFORMATION ON STATION START-UP*

1. Costs to date have totalled $50,000 and are mostly transportation and meeting costs, as well as postage. The CKER committee members have paid for these costs personally.

2. To approve the licence application, the CRTC must see written commitments to finance the station's start-up costs and operating losses in the first two years. Remaining costs to obtain the licence, excluding donated legal work, are expected to be about $8,000, and will be paid by CKER committee members.

3. If the CRTC approves the licence application, the CKER committee will immediately set up a non-profit organization and apply to Revenue Canada for charitable status, which it will likely receive.

4. Fairly exhaustive efforts to obtain commercial financing have failed. As a result, four wealthy individuals have volunteered to provide CKER with the financing for the start-up costs. They will each personally borrow $25,000 from financial institutions and give the funds to the station. These individuals expect the loans to be cost free to them as the station will make the interest and principal payments. (Assume that the loan principal is expected to be repaid over a 10-year period and that the rate of interest is 8% annually.)

5. A "Reverse Life-Time Contribution" program will also be instituted. Under this program, a donor will pay the station a capital sum of at least $50,000. The station can do whatever it wants with the funds, but it will repay the donor an equal annual amount calculated as the capital sum divided by 90 years less the individual's age at the time of contribution. Upon the death of the donor, the station will retain the balance of the funds. Currently, a 64-year-old station supporter has committed $78,000, and seven other individuals are considering this method of assisting the station.

6. Initially, the station is to broadcast with a 2,500 watt signal. It is hoped that within three to four years it will be possible to obtain commercial financing for a second transmitter that will boost the power of the signal and the broadcast range.

**EXHIBIT II**

*OTHER INFORMATION ABOUT PLANS FOR STATION*

1. The CKER committee has analyzed census and other data to determine the potential market for the station. Engineering studies have mapped out the area that will be covered by the broadcast signal. There are about 1.1 million people in the target listening area. The latest Canadian census shows that 14% of the population comes from the target ethnic group. A number of surveys have shown that, of a given population, nearly 80% listen regularly to the radio. By applying a conservative factor of 50% to these findings, the CKER committee has arrived at a listenership figure of 5.6% or about 62,000 people. The CKER committee has found that about one in five of the businesses in the area are run by

*(continued)*

members of the ethnic community, many of whom would like a medium for reaching their own people through direct advertising.

2. The amount of time expected to be devoted to commercials per hour is four minutes in Year 1, five minutes in Year 2, and six minutes in Year 3. Advertising cost per minute, discounted to 25% below the current market rate, will be:

| | |
|---|---|
| Prime time (6 hours a day) | $42 |
| Regular time (10 hours a day) | $32 |
| Off-peak (8 hours a day) | $27 |

Advertising time will be sold by salespeople whose remuneration will be a 15% commission.

3. Miscellaneous revenue from renting out the recording studio when not in use by CKER could approach $3,000 per month in Year 3 but will start out at about $2,200 per month and will be $2,500 per month in Year 2.

4. At least 120 people have committed to pay a $125 annual membership fee. Membership carries no special privileges other than to be identified as a supporter of the station. Membership is expected to grow by 20% per year.

5. Start-up capital expenditures are as follows: transmission equipment $61,000; broadcast studio equipment $62,000; and production studio equipment $40,000. Administration and other costs, including rent, are expected to total about $1,337,000 per year and will not increase when advertising sales increase.

6. About one-third of the person-hours needed to run the station are expected to come from volunteers.

*(CPA Canada adapted)*[9]

# Case 12-5

LO2, 4, 5

Today is September 16, Year 2. You, CPA, work for Garcia & Garcia LLP, a medium-sized firm located in Montreal. Jules Garcia calls you into his office. "CPA, I have a very special engagement for you. A friend of mine, Louise Martin, is starting a not-for-profit organization named MMB. MMB is going to be Quebec's first breast milk bank. Louise was unable to breastfeed her newborn and obtained donated breast milk for the first year of her daughter's life. She was lucky enough to live in British Columbia at the time, and had access to donated breast milk. She now lives in Montreal and hopes to give babies here the same access to breast milk that she and her daughter had." Jules provides you with information on breast milk banking that he received from Louise (Exhibit III).

"The Breast Milk Agency (the Agency) is a government body that regulates breast milk banks. The role of the Agency is to eliminate the risk that a disease or contaminant is transferred in milk by ensuring controls are established to preclude contamination."

Jules continues, "To receive grants, MMB is required to prepare financial statements that follow Canadian Accounting Standards for Not-for-Profit Organizations. Louise has limited accounting knowledge and is feeling overwhelmed with how to account for all the different types of donations. Please help her select appropriate accounting policies, where necessary, and draw her attention to accounting issues she might encounter."

Jules hands you notes from his meeting with Louise (Exhibit IV). "Please help her with any other issues that you identify."

**EXHIBIT III**

### BACKGROUND ON BREAST MILK BANKS

For mothers who are unable to meet their babies' nutritional needs with their own breast milk, pasteurized donor milk is a viable option. Donor breast milk is often used for babies who

- are born prematurely,
- have medical conditions that affect their ability to be breastfed (e.g., cleft palate),
- are born to mothers with medical conditions that affect their milk supply and quality (e.g., breast cancer), or
- are adopted.

Women considering donating breast milk should ensure they adhere to the following guidelines:

- Maintain a healthy diet
- Limit exposure to pesticides and other contaminants, such as lead and mercury
- Limit use of prescription drugs
- Avoid use of alcohol, tobacco, and illegal substances

**EXHIBIT IV**

### NOTES FROM JULES'S MEETING WITH LOUISE

The federal government has provided Louise with a one-time grant of $100,000. The grant is intended specifically for the purchase of tangible capital assets and for other start-up costs and must only be used for these purposes. A local pediatrician who is very supportive of Louise's efforts, Dr. Sandra Oldmen, has donated $75,000. These two amounts should help fund operations until MMB can provide breast milk to mothers in need and recoup its costs. Louise has received the donation from Dr. Oldmen but is still waiting on the grant. MMB will not be operating as a registered charity, so Louise is not expecting a significant amount of cash funding, and therefore MMB will not provide donation receipts.

Several public hospitals are interested in purchasing milk from MMB, and their budgets allow them to spend up to $8 per 120 millilitres. Many private clinics have indicated that they are prepared to pay up to $20 per 120 millilitres.

Louise notes that her email inbox is inundated with requests from women all across Canada who are willing to pay as much as $40 per 120 millilitres for donor milk to help their babies. Her goal in the first year is to provide donor milk to 20 babies for the first 12 months of their lives. She mentions that she is not exactly sure how she is going to decide which babies are most deserving, given her estimate that up to 500 babies in Canada each year require donor milk.

Louise expects that, after meeting her own baby's needs, each mother can donate approximately 15,000 millilitres of milk a year, and she expects them to donate for one year. Louise is uncertain about the number of donor mothers needed to fulfill her goal of providing donated milk to 20 babies in MMB's first year. She hopes to be able to double the number of recipients on an annual basis (in other words, 40 babies in the second year, 80 in the third, and so on). Considering this aggressive growth strategy, she wonders whether she will need to financially compensate the donor mothers for their milk, and if that is inconsistent with her not-for-profit objective. Louise has obtained the following guidelines on the quantity of breast milk a baby requires:

| Age | Quantity per Day |
|-----|------------------|
| 0–6 months | 720 ml |
| 6–12 months | 600 ml |

*(continued)*

Louise expects a significant number of volunteers to donate their time to help run MMB. If she does not get enough volunteers, she may need to hire and pay additional staff. In addition to the volunteers, MMB will employ a lab technician, an employee in charge of milk donors, an employee in charge of operations and quality control, a receptionist, and Louise, the chief executive officer, with a total expected salary cost for all employees of $275,000 per year. Louise expects to spend approximately $60,000 on the freezers, pasteurizer, office furniture, computers, and software. She has priced some off-the-shelf inventory management software and expects it will cost about $500 per year.

*(CPA Canada adapted)*[10]

## *Case 12-6

**LO2, 9**

The Sassawinni First Nation is located adjacent to a town in northern Saskatchewan. The Nation is under the jurisdiction of the federal government's Aboriginal Affairs and Northern Development Canada, and for years has received substantial funding from that department. The money has been used mainly to fund housing construction on the reserve and to provide maintenance payments to families that do not have a source of income. The houses are the property of the Sassawinni First Nation, and the band council allocates them to families on the basis of need. In addition to the housing, the band has been able to build a recreational centre, which also contains the band's council chamber and administrative offices.

A few years ago, some council members with an entrepreneurial flair persuaded the Nation's members to build a shopping centre containing a large grocery store and several small specialty stores. The shopping centre is located on reserve land, and the band provided approximately 20% of the financing, with the balance coming from a provincially guaranteed bank loan. The shopping centre operates under the name Great Northern Centre Inc., and the Sassawinni First Nation owns 100% of its outstanding common shares. The centre has been a financial success, drawing a large proportion of its business from the adjoining town and surrounding agricultural area. Not only has it been a source of employment for First Nation families, but it has also generated enough cash to keep its loan payments current and has recently been able to declare and pay a dividend.

Flushed with its success, the Sassawinni First Nation has submitted to the provincial government a business plan to construct a gambling casino on band property. It will be an incorporated entity and will be under the complete control of the Nation, subject only to provincial government gambling regulations.

Up to the present time, the band has provided stewardship reports to the Department of Indian Affairs and Northern Development that outline the funds received from the federal government and the manner in which they have been spent. Government auditors have verified these statements, but no formal audit reports have been considered necessary. Now, with all of this new business activity taking place, proper audited financial statements will be required for the next fiscal year. You are employed by Fox, Fox, and Jameson, the public accounting firm that is the auditor of Great Northern Centre Inc. Your firm has just been appointed auditor of Sassawinni First Nation, and this will be the firm's first audit of an organization of this nature. Jane Fox, the managing partner in charge of this audit, has asked you to provide her with a written report outlining the specific accounting principles that will be applicable in this case. "I am going to have to catch up quickly," she said. "I am aware that there have been some changes in GAAP recently, but because our firm has not been involved with audits of this nature I have not paid much attention to what has been going on. One of the benefits of hiring new university grads like yourself is that you provide us with up-to-date technical knowledge."

You have just returned from interviewing the band chief, Joe Sullivan. "I am absolutely certain that we are going to get this casino," he said. "The announcement will be made by the premier within two weeks, and I have received information from a knowledgeable insider that we will be on the list of First Nations to be granted casino licenses. It will be a financial godsend to our people, employing well over 100 band members and providing us with substantial profits, a portion of which will have to be devoted entirely to accommodations in accordance with the licensing agreement. This will allow us to build more housing for our members, but with all the jobs that we now have, we will probably start charging rent for housing provided to those with jobs. Not only that, we have three permanent employees who have been with us for a while, and council has instructed me to investigate the possibility of providing a pension plan for them as well as for the permanent employees in our business enterprises."

When asked about the band's accounting records, Sullivan responded, "We have a very good bookkeeper, and the government auditor has always complimented her on the accuracy of her records. She provides timely statements showing us how much we have to spend. Our records are all here and go back at least 20 years. I would just as soon carry on the way we have been doing things, but with this new casino we'll have to provide audited financial statements to the two governments—and, of course, to our members."

## *Case 12-7

### LO9

The provincial government (50%) and three private companies (16.67% each) own Access Records Limited (ARL), which commenced operations on April 1, Year 1. The provincial government currently maintains, on a manual basis, all descriptive information on land in the province, such as information on ownership, legal descriptions, etc. ARL's mandate is to computerize this information and to provide additional data not available from the manual system. The conversion of the manual system for several geographical regions of the province commenced on May 1, Year 1, with a targeted completion of all regions by September Year 3. The manual systems for each region will be maintained by ARL until each regional computerized system is operational.

The computer files are to be available to online users; others not online must obtain the information they need by going to designated government offices for hard copies. The prime users are market research firms, publishers of databases, real estate companies, and a variety of individuals and corporations. ARL charges the users a fee based on the information obtained. Computerization will permit additional descriptive information to be added to the database. As a result, user fees will increase as a region is computerized. No other organization provides this information.

In calculating the pre-tax income of ARL, the following items must be taken into account:

- In return for providing the original information, the provincial government receives a royalty for revenue generated from information that was previously available from the manual system. Two of the private companies receive a royalty for revenue generated from any new information that they gather and enter into the database. The computer system automatically identifies charges for previously available information and charges for the new information.

- The three private companies are to receive, for 10 years, a 20% rate of return on the original cost of the computer equipment and technology they were required to provide to ARL. At the end of 10 years, the computer equipment and technology will become the property of ARL.

- One of the three private companies entered into a 10-year agreement to provide the land and building from which ARL operates. It receives a 12% rate of return per year on its investment in the land and building. All operating costs, including repairs and maintenance, property taxes, and necessary improvements, are to be paid by ARL.

- The shareholders of ARL are to receive interest at the rate of prime plus 1% on any funds lent to ARL.

If the private owners, in operating ARL, do not meet certain specified performance standards, the provincial government can acquire their shares at cost.

It is now September Year 1. Your employer, Martin and Partners, Chartered Professional Accountants, has been engaged by ARL as consultant for the fiscal year ending March 31, Year 2. Martin and Partners has been asked to submit a detailed report addressing significant accounting matters.

You obtain the following information:

1. The cash contribution of the four owners totals $40 million. Another $30–50 million will be needed to complete the computerization. ARL will borrow the additional cash from a chartered bank, using ARL's assets as collateral.

2. Most of the total conversion cost of $70–90 million is for the costs of mapping, aerial photography, and computer graphics.

3. At the end of 10 years, the government is entitled to acquire, at fair value, the 50% of the shares that it does not own. The private companies are entitled to a reduced royalty if the provincial government acquires their shares.

4. The user-fee schedule is set by the provincial government.

5. Discounts are offered to volume users.

6. ARL intends to sell its technology to other provinces.

7. The province's auditor is permitted access to ARL's financial records.

*(CPA Canada adapted)*[11]

# PROBLEMS

## Problem 12-1

LO2, 5

The OPI Care Centre is an NFPO funded by government grants and private donations. It prepares its annual financial statements using the deferral method of accounting for contributions, and it uses only the operations fund to account for all activities.

The following summarizes some of the transactions made in Year 6:

1. The founding member of OPI contributed $100,000 on the conditions that the principal amount be invested in marketable securities and that only the income earned from the investment is spent on operations.

2. During the year, a public campaign was held to raise funds for daily operations for the current year. Cash of $800,000 was collected, and pledges for an additional $100,000 were received by the end of the year. It is estimated that approximately 95% of these pledges will be collected early in the new year.

3. The provincial government pledged $600,000 for the year to cover operating costs and an additional $1,000,000 to purchase equipment and furniture. All of the grant money was received by the end of the year, except for the last $50,000 to cover operating costs for December.

4. OPI used the $1,000,000 received from the provincial government to purchase equipment and furniture for the care facility. The amortization of these assets amounted to $100,000 for the year.

5. Invoices totalling $1,450,000 were received for goods and contracted services. Of these invoices, 90% were paid by the end of the fiscal year.

**Required**

In accordance with the requirements of the *CPA Canada Handbook*, prepare the journal entries necessary to reflect the transactions.

*(CGA Canada adapted)*[12]

# Problem 12-2

LO2, 3, 4

The Perch Falls Minor Hockey Association was established in Perch Falls in January Year 5. Its mandate is to promote recreational hockey in the small community of Perch Falls. With the support of the provincial government, local business people, and many individuals, the association raised sufficient funds to build an indoor hockey arena and it also established an endowment fund for paying travel costs to tournaments on an annual basis.

The following schedule summarizes the cash flows for the year ended December 31, Year 5.

### PERCH FALLS MINOR HOCKEY ASSOCIATION
($000s)

| | Operating Fund | Capital Fund | Endowment Fund |
|---|---|---|---|
| Cash inflows: | | | |
| Government grant for operating costs | $ 45 | | |
| Government grant for hockey arena | | $400 | |
| Corporate donations for hockey arena | | 200 | |
| Registration fees | 20 | | |
| Contribution for tournaments | | | $35.0 |
| Rental of hockey arena | 40 | | |
| Interest received | | | 2.1 |
| | 105 | 600 | 37.1 |
| Cash outflows: | | | |
| Operating expenses | 102 | | |
| Construction of hockey arena | | 600 | |
| Purchase of corporate bonds | | | 35.0 |
| Travel costs for tournament | | | 2.1 |
| | 102 | 600 | 37.1 |
| Cash, end of year | $ 3 | $ 0 | $ 0 |

**Additional Information**

- The new hockey arena was completed in late August Year 5. The official opening was held on August 30, with a game between the Perch Falls Old-Timers and the local firefighters. The arena is expected to have a 40-year useful life and no residual value.

- A long-time resident of Perch Falls donated the land on which the arena was built. The land was valued at $70,000. The association gave a donation receipt to the donor.

- A former resident of Perch Falls donated ice-making and ice-cleaning equipment to the association. A receipt for $60,000 was issued for the donation. The equipment has a useful life of 10 years and no residual value.

- The donation for tournaments was contributed on January 1, Year 5, with the condition that the principal amount of $35,000 be invested in 6% corporate bonds. The interest earned on the investment can be used only for travel costs for out-of-town tournaments. All investments in bonds will be held to their maturity date.

- The provincial government pledged $50,000 a year for operating costs. Ninety percent of the grant is advanced throughout the year. Upon receipt of the association's annual report, the government will issue the last 10% of the annual grant to the association.

- Registration fees and rental fees for the hockey arena are received at the beginning of the hockey season and cover the entire season, from September 1, Year 5, to April 30, Year 6.

- At the end of the year, the association owed $3,000 for services received in the month of December.

- The association wants to use the restricted fund method of accounting for contributions and to use three separate funds: operating fund, capital fund, and endowment fund. All capital assets are to be capitalized and amortized, as applicable, over their estimated useful lives.

**Required**

(a) Prepare a statement of financial position and statement of operations for each of the three funds as at and for the year ended December 31, Year 5.

(b) Assume that 500 children registered with the Association in Year 5. What was the average cost per registered child for Year 5 for running the Association? What costs did you include/exclude and why?

*(CGA Canada adapted)*[13]

## Problem 12-3

LO2, 3, 4

All facts about this NFPO are identical to those described in Problem 2, except that the association wants to use the deferral method of accounting for contributions. The centre will continue to use the three separate funds.

**Required**

Prepare a statement of financial position and statement of operations for each of the three funds as at and for the year ended December 31, Year 5.

## Problem 12-4

LO2, 5

Protect Purple Plants (PPP) uses the deferral method of accounting for contributions and has no separate fund for restricted contributions. On January 1, Year 6, PPP received its first restricted cash contribution—$120,000 for the purchase and maintenance of land and a greenhouse building for its rare purple plant collection.

On July 1, Year 6, PPP acquired land and a building for $22,000 and $80,000 cash, respectively. The building has an estimated useful life of 20 years and zero residual value. On December 31, Year 6, the remaining $18,000 cash was paid to KJ Maintenance Ltd. for a three-year maintenance contract that requires KJ personnel to provide maintenance services four days per month until December 31, Year 9.

**Required**

Prepare the journal entries for the following dates:

 (i) January 1, Year 6
 (ii) July 1, Year 6
 (iii) December 31, Year 6 including year-end adjusting entries

*(CGA Canada adapted)*[14]

## Problem 12-5

LO2, 5

The Fara Littlebear Society is an NFPO funded by government grants and private donations. It was established in Year 5 by the friends of Fara Littlebear to encourage and promote the work of Native Canadian artists. Fara achieved international recognition for her art depicting images of journey and exploration.

The society leased a small building in January Year 5. The building contains a small art gallery on the first floor and office space on the second floor. The society spent $83,850 for leasehold improvements. The art gallery opened for public viewing on April 1, Year 5.

The unadjusted trial balance for the year ended December 31, Year 5, was as follows:

| | Debit | Credit |
|---|---|---|
| Cash | $  5,000 | |
| Investment in bonds (Note 1) | 80,000 | |
| Artwork (Note 2) | 300,000 | |
| Leasehold improvements (Note 3) | 83,850 | |
| Government grant—operating costs (Note 6) | | $ 90,000 |
| Government grant—restricted for purchase of artwork | | 150,000 |
| Corporate donations—restricted for purchase of artwork | | 150,000 |
| Corporate donations—restricted for leasehold improvements | | 78,000 |
| Individual donations restricted for scholarships (Note 1) | | 80,000 |
| Interest income | | 4,000 |
| Revenue from admission fees to art gallery | | 67,000 |
| Rent expense (Note 3) | 26,000 | |
| Salaries expense (Note 4) | 66,000 | |
| Other expenses | 53,150 | |
| Scholarship awarded | 5,000 | |
| | $619,000 | $619,000 |

## Additional Information

- A wealthy individual donated $80,000 with the condition that the principal be invested in low-risk investments. The principal was invested in long-term bonds, which are expected to be held to maturity. The interest on the bonds is to be used to provide scholarships to aspiring Native artists who wish to study art at a Canadian university or college. The first scholarship of $5,000 was awarded in September Year 5.

- The artwork consists of 20 paintings from a number of Canadian artists. These paintings are expected to be held for at least 10 years. The paintings will likely appreciate in value over the time they are owned by the art gallery.

- The society signed a five-year lease on the building with an option to renew for one further term of five years. The term of the lease commenced on January 1, Year 5. The total rent paid for the year included a deposit of $2,000 for the last month's rent. The leasehold improvements were completed on March 31, Year 5. The office space was occupied by the staff of the society, and the art gallery was opened for business on April 1, Year 5.

- Salaries earned but not yet paid amounted to $5,000 at December 31, Year 5.

- The society received office equipment from a local business person on January 1, Year 5. A donation receipt for $20,000 was given for this contribution. The office equipment has a useful life of five years with no residual value.

- The provincial government provided an operating grant of $100,000 for Year 5, of which $90,000 was received by the end of the year. The remaining $10,000 will be received once the society provides financial statements prepared in accordance with GAAP.

- The society will follow Part III of the *CPA Canada Handbook* and wishes to use the deferral method of accounting for contributions.

## Required

(a) Explain how the matching principle is applied when the deferral method is used to account for restricted contributions.

(b) Prepare a statement of financial position for the society at December 31, Year 5. Show your supporting calculations and state your assumptions. (You can use an assumed number for excess of revenue over expenses to balance your statement of financial position.)

*(CGA Canada adapted)*[15]

## Problem 12-6

LO2, 3, 4

All facts about this NFPO are identical to those described in Problem 5, except for the following:

1. The Society will use the restricted fund method of accounting for contributions.

2. The Society will use three separate funds for reporting purposes—operating fund, collections and long-term capital assets fund, and scholarship fund. Long-term capital assets include depreciable assets with a useful life in excess of 5 years, for example leasehold improvements.

3. The cash balance of $5,000 consisted of $1,000 in the scholarship fund and $4,000 in the operating fund.

4. The interest income is retained in the scholarship fund until it is paid out for scholarships.

5. The operating fund loaned $5,850 to the long-term capital asset fund for the shortfall between the cost of leasehold improvements and the corporate donations for leasehold improvements.

**Required**

Prepare a statement of financial position for the society at December 31, Year 5. Show your supporting calculations and state your assumptions. (You can use an assumed number for excess of revenue over expenses to balance your statement of financial position.)

# *Problem 12-7

## LO2,5

The Brown Training Centre is a charitable organization dedicated to providing computer training to unemployed people. Individuals must apply to the centre and indicate why they would like to take the three-month training session. If their application is accepted, they must pay a $200 deposit. The deposit is refunded upon successful completion of the course or is forfeited as a processing fee if the individual does not complete the course.

During the first year of operations in Year 3, 90 individuals were accepted into the course. Of these 90 individuals, 50 completed the course, 10 dropped out, and 30 were still taking the course at the end of the fiscal year.

The centre receives most of its funding from the provincial government. During the year, the government advanced $1,000,000 to cover operating costs. Within two months of the year-end, the centre must provide financial statements prepared in accordance with GAAP. The government will cover all operating costs. The excess of amounts advanced over the amount expended must be carried over and applied to operating costs of the next year. Operating costs to be reimbursed are defined to exclude purchases of capital assets and are to be reduced by the amount of application fees forfeited.

A private company donated computers and office equipment with a fair value of $320,000. The centre was fortunate to receive this donation. Otherwise, it would have had to raise money through other means to purchase these items. The capital assets were put into use as of April 1, Year 3, and have an estimated useful life of three years. The centre uses the straight-line method to amortize its capital assets.

The part-time bookkeeper for the centre prepared the following cash flow statement for the year ended December 31, Year 3:

| | |
|---|---:|
| Cash receipts: | |
| Government grant | $1,000,000 |
| Deposits from course participants | 18,000 |
| Total cash receipts | 1,018,000 |
| | |
| Cash expenditures: | |
| Salaries and benefits | 620,000 |
| Administration and supplies | 220,000 |
| Rent and utilities | 160,000 |
| Refund of deposits | 10,000 |
| Total cash disbursements | 1,010,000 |
| Cash balance at end of year | $      8,000 |

At the end of the year, the following costs had been incurred but not yet paid:

| | |
|---|---|
| Salaries and benefits | $8,000 |
| Utilities | 6,000 |

The executive director of the centre has asked you for assistance in preparing the financial statements for the centre for the first year of operations. The deferral method should be used in accounting for the contributions.

**Required**

(a) Briefly explain how the accrual basis of accounting is applied when accounting for capital assets for an NFPO.

(b) Prepare the statement of revenues and expenses for the centre for the year ended December 31, Year 3.

(c) Compute the following liabilities on the statement of financial position for the centre at December 31, Year 3:
  (i) Accrued liabilities
  (ii) Deposits from course participants
  (iii) Deferred contributions

*(CGA Canada adapted)*[16]

## Problem 12-8

LO2, 3, 4

The Ford Historical Society is an NFPO funded by government grants and private donations. It uses both an operating fund and a capital fund. The capital fund accounts for moneys received and restricted for major capital asset acquisitions. The operating fund is used for all other activities.

The society uses the restricted fund method of accounting for contributions. Donated materials and services are recorded if such items would have been purchased had they not been received as donations.

The following are some selected activities that took place during the current year:

- Pledges totalling $350,000 were made to the society, of which $150,000 applies to the operations of the following year. It is estimated that 3% of all pledges will be uncollectible.

- Pledges of $310,000 were collected, and pledges totalling $5,000 were written off.

- A government grant of $500,000 for acquisition and renovation of an office building for the society was approved by the government. All of the grant money was received except for the last 10%, which is expected to be received in the first month of the next fiscal year.

- Purchases of goods and services during the year totalled $510,000, of which $480,000 was paid for by the end of the year.

- An old office building was acquired and renovated for a cost of $500,000. Amortization expense on the office building was $10,000.

- A local radio station donated free airtime to the society. The society saved the $5,000 it would normally have paid for this airtime.

**Required**

Prepare the journal entries required to record these activities, and indicate which fund each journal entry will be recorded in.

*(CGA Canada adapted)*[17]

## Problem 12-9

**LO2, 5**

Fairchild Centre is an NFPO funded by government grants and private donations. It was established on January 1, Year 5, to provide counselling services and a drop-in centre for single parents.

On January 1, Year 5, the centre leased an old warehouse in the central part of Smallville for $1,600 per month. It carried out minor renovations in the warehouse to create a large open area for use as a play area for children and three offices for use by the executive director and counsellors. The lease runs from January 1, Year 5, to June 30, Year 7. By that time, the centre hopes to move into new quarters that are more suitable for the activities carried out.

The following schedule summarizes the cash flows for the year ended December 31, Year 5:

| | |
|---|---:|
| Cash inflows: | |
| Government grant for operating costs (Note 1) | $ 48,000 |
| Donations from individuals with no restrictions | 59,000 |
| Donations from individuals for rent of warehouse for 2½ years | 48,000 |
| Donations from individuals for purchase of land (Note 3) | 55,680 |
| | 210,680 |
| Cash outflows: | |
| Renovations of warehouse | 54,000 |
| Salary of executive director (Note 4) | 26,400 |
| Fees paid to counsellors (Note 4) | 21,500 |
| Rent paid for 2½ years | 48,000 |
| Other operating expenses | 21,000 |
| | 170,900 |
| Cash, end of year | $ 39,780 |

## Additional Information

1. The provincial government agreed to provide an operating grant of $48,000 per year. In addition, the government has pledged to match contributions collected by the centre for the purchase of land for construction of a new complex for the centre. The maximum contribution by the government toward the purchase of land is $96,000.

2. The centre has signed an agreement to purchase a property in the downtown area of Smallville for $216,000. There is an old house on the property, which is currently used as a rooming house. The closing date is any time between July 1, Year 6, and December 31, Year 6. The centre plans to demolish the existing house and build a new complex.

3. The centre has recently commenced a fundraising program to raise funds to purchase the land and construct a new building. So far, $55,680 has been raised from individuals toward the purchase of the land. In the new year, the centre will focus its efforts to solicit donations from businesses in the area. The provincial government will advance the funds promised under its pledge on the closing date for the purchase of the property.

4. All the people working for the centre are volunteers except for the executive director and the counsellors. The executive director receives a salary of $28,800 a year, while the counsellors bill the centre for professional services rendered based on the number of hours they work at the centre. The director has not yet received her salary for the month of December. One of the counsellors received an advance of $1,150 in December Year 5, for work to be performed in January Year 6.

5. The centre wishes to use the deferral method of accounting for contributions and to segregate its net assets between restricted and unrestricted. It capitalizes the cost of capital assets and amortizes the capital assets over their useful lives.

**Required**

(a) State the assumptions necessary to recognize the pledge from the provincial government pertaining to the purchase of land, and prepare the journal entry to record the pledge, if applicable.

(b) Prepare a statement of operations for the Fairchild Centre for the year ended December 31, Year 5. Show your supporting calculations and state your assumptions.

(c) Prepare a statement of changes in net assets for the Fairchild Centre for the year ended December 31, Year 5.

*(CGA Canada adapted)*[18]

# Problem 12-10

LO2, 4

All facts about this NFPO are identical to those described in Problem 9, except that the Centre wants to use the restricted fund method of accounting for contributions. The Centre will use two separate funds—operating and capital. The capital fund will capture contributions pertaining to property, building and equipment.

**Required**

(a) Prepare the journal entry to record the pledge by the provincial government towards the purchase of land, if applicable and indicate the fund in which the journal entry would be recorded.

(b) Prepare a statement of operations for the Fairchild Centre for each of the two funds for the year ended December 31, Year 5. Show your supporting calculations and state your assumptions.

(c) Prepare a statement of changes in net assets for the Fairchild Centre for each of the two funds for the year ended December 31, Year 5.

# Problem 12-11

LO2, 3, 4

The Far North Centre (the Centre) is an anti-poverty organization funded by contributions from governments and the general public. For a number of years, it has been run by a small group of permanent employees with the help of part-timers and dedicated volunteers. It owns its premises, which are in the process of being renovated. The funds for this were obtained through a special capital fund campaign carried out last year. Its main program is the daily provision of meals to the needy. It also distributes clothing, most of which is donated. Operating funds come from government grants, interest earned from endowment investments, and a public campaign held in the latter part of each year to raise funds for the needs of the next fiscal year. The Centre maintains its records in accordance with the restricted fund method of accounting for contributions, and prepares its financial statements using an operating fund, a capital fund (for all activities related to capital assets), and an endowment fund.

The following are the fund trial balances as at January 1, Year 6:

| | Debit | Credit |
|---|---|---|
| *Operating Fund* | | |
| Cash | $ 488,000 | |
| Pledges receivable | 700,000 | |
| Allowance for uncollectible pledges | | $ 44,500 |
| Grants receivable | 288,000 | |
| Accounts payable | | 484,000 |
| Wages payable | | 137,500 |
| Accrued liabilities | | 16,100 |
| Deferred revenue | | 758,000 |
| Fund balance | | 35,900 |
| | $1,476,000 | $1,476,000 |
| *Capital Fund* | | |
| Cash | $ 312,500 | |
| Grants receivable | 128,500 | |
| Land and building | 908,100 | |
| Furniture and equipment | 500,000 | |
| Accumulated amortization | | $ 668,500 |
| Accounts payable | | 12,400 |
| Fund balance | | 1,168,100 |
| | $1,849,000 | $1,849,000 |
| *Endowment Fund* | | |
| Cash | $ 37,800 | |
| Investments | 378,000 | |
| Fund balance | | $ 415,800 |
| | $ 415,800 | $ 415,800 |

The following transactions took place in Year 6:

1. $35,900 from endowment fund cash was invested in marketable securities.

2. Office equipment costing $4,700 was purchased with operating fund cash.

3. Invoices totalling $1,805,000 were received for goods and services. These invoices were recorded as accounts payable and were allocated 55% to food program, 20% to clothing program, and 25% to administration.

4. The capital fund grants receivable were collected in full, and the $12,400 in accounts payable was paid. During Year 6, building renovations costing $304,000 and equipment purchases of $119,500 were made. Of this cost, 90% was paid, with the balance held back and still owing at year-end.

5. Operating fund accounts payable amounting to $1,830,000 and the wages payable and accrued liabilities at the beginning of the year were all paid.

6. All of the operating fund pledges and grants receivable at the beginning of the year were collected in full.

7. The deferred revenue from the Year 5 fundraising campaign was made up of the following:

| | |
|---|---|
| Contributions | $1,194,000 |
| Less: Campaign expense | 436,000 |
| | $ 758,000 |

The Centre runs the campaign with its own people and is fully responsible for all decisions made during the campaign.

8. Government grants for operating purposes totalled $1,229,500, of which $1,208,000 was received during the year, with the balance expected early in Year 7.

9. The total wage costs for the year amounted to $263,000, of which $168,000 was paid and $95,000 is payable at year-end. These costs are to be allocated 40% each to the food and clothing programs, with the balance to administration.

10. The campaign to raise funds for next year's operations was held in December. Cash of $540,000 was collected and pledges of $872,000 were received. It is expected that 5% of these pledges will be uncollectible. Total fundraising costs were $688,000, of which $109,500 is still owed to suppliers.

11. An endowment contribution of $15,400 cash was received. In addition, the investments in the endowment fund earned $29,100 in interest.

12. The annual depreciation on the buildings and equipment amounted to $102,000.

**Required**

(a) Prepare the journal entries necessary to reflect the Year 6 events.

(b) For each fund, prepare a Year 6 statement of financial position and statement of operations and changes in fund balance.

(c) Prepare closing entries.

(d) What percentage of Year 6 revenues of the operating fund were spent on program costs and what percentage was spent on administration and fundraising? How will users of these financial statements feel about these percentages?

# Problem 12-12

LO2, 5

All facts about this NFPO are identical to those described in Problem 11, except that the deferral method of recording contributions is used for accounting and for external financial reporting. Fund accounting is not used. The Year 6 transactions are also identical to those described in Problem 11.

The organization's statement of financial position on January 1, Year 6, is shown below.

**FAR NORTH CENTRE**
**STATEMENT OF FINANCIAL POSITION**
January 1, Year 6

| | |
|---|---:|
| *Current Assets* | |
| Cash | $ 838,300 |
| Pledges receivable | 700,000 |
| Allowance for uncollectible pledges | (44,500) |
| Grants receivable | 416,500 |
| | 1,910,300 |
| *Investments* | 378,000 |
| Capital assets: | |
| Land and buildings | 908,000 |
| Furniture and equipment | 500,000 |
| Accumulated depreciation | (668,500) |
| | 739,500 |
| | $3,027,800 |

*(continued)*

*(continued)*

|  |  |
|---|---|
| *Current Liabilities* | |
| Accounts payable | $  496,400 |
| Wages payable | 137,500 |
| Accrued liabilities | 16,100 |
| | 650,000 |
| *Deferred Revenue* | |
| Deferred revenues | 758,000 |
| Deferred contributions related to capital assets | 724,400 |
| | 1,482,400 |
| *Net Assets* | |
| Net assets restricted for endowment purposes | 415,800 |
| Unrestricted net assets | 479,600 |
| | 895,400 |
| | $3,027,800 |

### Required

(a) Prepare the journal entries necessary to reflect the Year 6 events.

(b) Prepare a Year 6 statement of financial position, a statement of revenues and expenses, and a statement of changes in net assets for the year.

(c) Prepare closing entries.

(d) What are fundraising costs as a percent of total revenues for Year 6? What do you think donors to the Centre will think of this percentage?

## Problem 12-13

LO2, 3, 4

The William Robertson Society is a charitable organization funded by government grants and private donations. It prepares its annual financial statements using the restricted fund method in accordance with the *CPA Canada Handbook*, and uses both an operating fund and a capital fund.

The operating fund records the regular operating activities of the society. It is the policy of the society to record donated materials and services received during the year, if such items would have been purchased had they not been received as donations.

The capital fund accounts for moneys received from special fundraising campaigns conducted when there is a need for major fixed assets acquisitions.

The following are *some* selected events that took place during the current year:

- Pledges for current year's operating costs amounting to $125,000 were received, of which $90,000 was collected in cash.

- A grant of $70,000 for this year's operations was announced by the government, of which $55,000 had been received by the society at year-end.

- Employee wages totalled $60,000 for the year. Wages amounting to $2,000 were unpaid at year-end.

- Invoices for all of the goods and services received during the year totalled $100,000 for goods and services. Of the invoiced amounts, 70% was paid.

- Office equipment was purchased for $15,300 and was paid in cash, using operating funds.

- A local radio station donated free airtime to the society. The station would normally bill a customer $3,000 for this airtime.

- A prominent citizen made a pledge of $35,000 to help fund the operating expenditures of the next fiscal year.

**Required**

Prepare the journal entries required to record these events, and indicate in which fund each journal entry will be recorded.

# Problem 12-14

## LO2

The Valleytown Senior's Residential Home (Valleytown) engages in palliative care, education, and fundraising programs. The costs of each program include the costs of personnel, premises, and other expenses that are directly related to providing the program. Valleytown also incurs a number of general support expenses that are common to the administration of the organization and each of its programs.

Financial and nonfinancial data for the three programs for the year ended December 31, Year 12, were as follows:

| | Palliative | Education | Fundraising |
|---|---|---|---|
| Direct costs | $5,100,000 | $1,200,000 | $1,400,000 |
| Number of employees | 45 | 8 | 12 |
| Number of computer hours | 2,000 | 400 | 100 |

Both the education and fundraising programs include the use of the same brochures to further the work of Valleytown. The brochures are designed and intended to achieve a specific educational objective. Included in the fundraising costs above is $200,000 for brochures. Some of the brochures included in direct mail fundraising campaigns are mailed to individuals who have been identified as potential beneficiaries of the educational component of the brochures. Accordingly, 20% of the cost of those brochures is allocated from the fundraising to the education program. The majority of the direct mail campaign expenses remain a cost of the fundraising program.

Valleytown presents its expenses by function on the statement of operations. It allocates certain of its general support expenses by identifying the appropriate basis of allocating each component expense, and applies that basis consistently each year. Corporate governance and general management expenses are not allocated; other general support expenses are allocated on the following bases:

- Human resources department costs—proportionately, on the number of employees working for each program

- Information technology department costs—proportionately, on the number of hours of computer time provided for each of the programs.

The following summarizes the general support costs for the year ended December 31, Year 12:

| | |
|---|---|
| Corporate governance | $ 300,000 |
| Human resources department | 800,000 |
| Information technology department | 1,250,000 |
| General management | 650,000 |
| | $3,000,000 |

**Required**

(a) Prepare a schedule to allocate an appropriate amount of general support costs and any other costs to the three programs. Then, indicate the percentage of total costs pertaining to the three programs and general support costs.

(b) Write the note to Valleytown's Year 12 financial statements required by Section 4470.08 on the amounts allocated from fundraising and general support functions, and the amounts and the functions to which they have been allocated.

# Endnotes

1 Hereinafter, all *Handbook* sections referred to will be found in either Part II or Part III unless otherwise noted. The five sections discussed below and the 4400 series appear in Part III, whereas the other sections appear in Part II.

2 For a complete copy of United Way/Centraide Ottawa's financial statements, go to www.unitedwayottawa.ca.

3 "Financial Reporting by Governments," research study (Toronto: CPA Canada, 1980).

4 "Local Government Financial Reporting," research study (Toronto: CICA, 1985).

5 A. Beedle, "Accounting for Local Government in Canada: The State of the Art" (Vancouver: Canadian Certified General Accountants' Research Foundation, 1981).

6 For example, the provinces of Manitoba and Nova Scotia, and the cities of Vancouver and Montreal.

7 "Introduction to Public Sector Accounting Standards," Appendix A, *CPA Canada Public Sector Accounting Handbook,* © 2015 Chartered Professional Accountants of Canada.

8 Adapted from CGA Canada's FA4 Exam, December 2004, Q3, with permission. Chartered Professional Accountants of Canada, Toronto, Canada. Any changes to the original material are the sole responsibility of the author (and/or publisher) and have not been reviewed or endorsed by the Chartered Professional Accountants of Canada.

9 Adapted from *CICA UFE Report,* 1996-II-2, with permission. Chartered Professional Accountants of Canada, Toronto, Canada. Any changes to the original material are the sole responsibility of the author (and/or publisher) and have not been reviewed or endorsed by the Chartered Professional Accountants of Canada.

10 Adapted from *CICA UFE Report,* 2012-II-2, with permission. Chartered Professional Accountants of Canada, Toronto, Canada. Any changes to the original material are the sole responsibility of the author (and/or publisher) and have not been reviewed or endorsed by the Chartered Professional Accountants of Canada.

11 Adapted from *CICA UFE Report,* 1991-IV-5, with permission. Chartered Professional Accountants of Canada, Toronto, Canada. Any changes to the original material are the sole responsibility of the author (and/or publisher) and have not been reviewed or endorsed by the Chartered Professional Accountants of Canada.

12 Adapted from CGA Canada's FA4 Exam, December 2004, Q3, with permission. Chartered Professional Accountants of Canada, Toronto, Canada. Any changes to the original material are the sole responsibility of the author (and/or publisher) and have not been reviewed or endorsed by the Chartered Professional Accountants of Canada.

13 Adapted from CGA Canada's FA4 Exam, March 2006, Q5, with permission. Chartered Professional Accountants of Canada, Toronto, Canada. Any changes to the original material are the sole responsibility of the author (and/or publisher) and have not been reviewed or endorsed by the Chartered Professional Accountants of Canada.

14 Adapted from CGA Canada's FA4 Exam, December 2004, with permission. Chartered Professional Accountants of Canada, Toronto, Canada. Any changes to the original material are the sole responsibility of the author (and/or publisher) and have not been reviewed or endorsed by the Chartered Professional Accountants of Canada.

15 Adapted from CGA Canada's FA4 Exam, September 2006, Q5, with permission. Chartered Professional Accountants of Canada, Toronto, Canada. Any changes to the original material are the sole responsibility of the author (and/or publisher) and have not been reviewed or endorsed by the Chartered Professional Accountants of Canada.

16 Adapted from CGA Canada's FA4 Exam, June 2004, Q6, with permission. Chartered Professional Accountants of Canada, Toronto, Canada. Any changes to the original material are the sole responsibility of the author (and/or publisher) and have not been reviewed or endorsed by the Chartered Professional Accountants of Canada.

17 Adapted from CGA Canada's FA4 Exam, December 2003, Q5, with permission. Chartered Professional Accountants of Canada, Toronto, Canada. Any changes to the original material are the sole responsibility of the author (and/or publisher) and have not been reviewed or endorsed by the Chartered Professional Accountants of Canada.

18 Adapted from CGA Canada FA4 Exam, December 2005, Q5, with permission. Chartered Professional Accountants of Canada, Toronto, Canada. Any changes to the original material are the sole responsibility of the author (and/or publisher) and have not been reviewed or endorsed by the Chartered Professional Accountants of Canada.

# Index